# COMPREHENSIVE HANDBOOK
## OF
# PSYCHOLOGICAL ASSESSMENT

# COMPREHENSIVE HANDBOOK OF PSYCHOLOGICAL ASSESSMENT

## VOLUME 4
### INDUSTRIAL AND ORGANIZATIONAL ASSESSMENT

Jay C. Thomas

*Volume Editor*

Michel Hersen

*Editor-in-Chief*

**WILEY**

John Wiley & Sons, Inc.

*Library of Congress Cataloging-in-Publication Data:*

Comprehensive handbook of psychological assessment / editor-in-chief, Michel Hersen.
    p. cm.
    Includes bibliographical references and index.
    Contents: v. 1 Intellectual and neuropsychological assessment / editors, Gerald Goldstein and Sue R. Beers — v. 2. Personality assessment / editors, Mark J. Hilsenroth and Daniel L. Segal — v. 3. Behavioral assessment / editors, Stephen N. Haynes and Elaine M. Heiby — v. 4. Industrial and organizational assessment / editor, Jay C. Thomas.
    ISBN 0-471-41610-X (set : hardcover : alk. paper) — ISBN 0-471-41611-8 (v. 1 : hardcover : alk. paper) — ISBN 0-471-41612-6 (v. 2 : hardcover : alk. paper) — ISBN 0-471-41613-4 (v. 3 : hardcover : alk. paper) — ISBN 0-471-41614-2 (v. 4 : hardcover : alk. paper)
    1. Psychological tests.  I. Hersen, Michel.

BF176 .C654 2003
150′.28′7—dc21

                             2002193381

Printed in the United States of America.

10 9 8 7 6 5 4 3 2 1

# Contents

### SECTION FOUR
## BIOGRAPHICAL, EXPERIENCE DATA, AND INTERVIEWS

### SECTION FIVE
## JOB-SPECIFIC KNOWLEDGE AND SKILLS, SIMULATIONS, AND ASSESSMENT CENTERS

### SECTION SIX
## ASSESSING JOB PERFORMANCE

## SECTION SEVEN
## ASSESSING TEAMS AND TEAMWORK

## SECTION EIGHT
## EMPLOYEE REACTIONS TO THE WORKPLACE

# Handbook Preface

Over the last century the scope of activity of clinical psychologists has increased exponentially. In earlier times psychologists had a much more restricted range of responsibilities. Today psychologists not only provide assessments but treat a wide variety of disorders in an equally wide variety of settings, consult, teach, conduct research, help to establish ethical policies, deal with human engineering factors, have a strong media presence, work with law enforcement in profiling criminals, and have had increasing influence in the business world and in the realm of advertising, to identify just a few of the major activities in which they are engaged. Nonetheless, the hallmark of psychologists has always been assessment and it continues to be a mainstay of their practices in the twenty-first century. Indeed, in each of the activities just described, psychologists and their assistants are performing assessments of some sort.

In the nineteenth century our predecessors in Germany began to study individual differences and abilities in what then was the most scientific way. In the more than 120 years that have elapsed since these early efforts were carried out, the field of psychological assessment has seen many developments and permutations, ranging from educational needs to identify individuals with subnormal intelligence to attempts to measure unconscious dynamics with unstructured stimuli, wide-range governmental efforts to measure intelligence and other capabilities to screen out undesirable military recruits during wartime, development of evaluative tools to ensure successful personnel selection, the advent of behavioral and physiological assessments, the increased reliance on computerized assessments, and, most recently, the spectacular innovation of virtual reality assessments using the latest electronic technologies.

Thousands of specific assessment strategies and tests that are carried out on both an individual and group basis have been devised for almost every conceivable type of human endeavor. Many of these strategies have been carefully developed, tested, and refined, with norms available for many populations and excellent reliability and validity data reported. To keep abreast of all new developments in the field of assessment is a near impossibility, although scores of journals, books, and yearly publications are available that catalog such developments.

In considering how the field of psychological assessment has evolved over the last century with the resulting explosion of new technologies and new assessment devices, it seemed to us imperative to create a resource (*Comprehensive Handbook of Psychological Assessment:* CHOPA) that distilled this vast reservoir of data in a more manageable format for researchers, clinicians, educators, and students alike. Therefore, Tracey Belmont, our editor at John Wiley & Sons, the volume editors (Gerald Goldstein, Sue R. Beers, Mark J. Hilsenroth, Daniel L. Segal, Stephen N. Haynes, Elaine M. Heiby, and Jay C. Thomas), and I as editor-in-chief developed this four-volume format. This decision was both conceptual, in order to best capture the scope of the field, and pragmatic, so that individuals wishing to purchase a single volume (as a consequence of their unique interest) would be able to do so.

CHOPA includes four volumes with a total of 121 chapters written by renowned experts in their respective areas of expertise. In order the volumes are: 1, Intellectual and Neuropsychological Assessment; 2, Personality Assessment; 3, Behavioral Assessment; and 4, Industrial and Organizational Assessment. Each volume has an introductory chapter by the editor. In the case of Volume 2, there is an introductory chapter for objective tests and an introductory chapter for projective tests. In general, introductory chapters are concerned with a historical review, range of tests, theoretical considerations, psychometric concerns, range of populations for which the tests are appropriate, cross-cultural factors, accommodation for persons with disabilities, legal and ethical issues, computerization, and future perspectives. Chapters on individual tests or approaches cover many of the same areas but in much more specific detail, in addition, of course, to the test description and development. Other chapters are more conceptual and theoretical in nature and articulate an approach to evaluation, such as the chapters on clinical interviewing and program evaluation in Volume 3.

In developing the CHOPA concept and selecting chapters and contributors, our objective has been to be comprehensive in a global sense but not encyclopedic (i.e., detailing every conceivable and extant assessment strategy or test). However, we believe that we are sufficiently comprehensive so that the interested reader can move to greater specificity, if needed, on the basis of the very current list of references for each chapter.

An endeavor as complicated as CHOPA has required the efforts of many people, and here we would like to acknowledge their various contributions. First, I personally would like to thank Tracey Belmont and her superb staff at John Wiley & Sons for recognizing the value of this project and for helping to bring the pieces together. Second, I thank the volume editors for their Herculean efforts in monitoring, reviewing, and reworking the contributions of their colleagues. Next, we owe a debt of gratitude to our eminent contributors, who so graciously have shared their high levels of expertise with us. And finally, I would like to thank all of our staff here at Pacific University who contributed technical assistance to bringing this four-volume set to publication: Carole Londeree, Kay Waldron, Angelina Marchand, and Alex Duncan.

Michel Hersen
Forest Grove, Oregon

# Contributors

**Ram N. Aditya, PhD**
Florida International University
Miami, FL

**Winifred Arthur Jr., PhD**
Texas A & M University
College Station, TX

**Ronald A. Ash, PhD**
University of Kansas
Lawrence, KS

**Talya N. Bauer, PhD**
Portland State University
Portland, OR

**William K. Balzer, PhD**
Bowling Green State University
Bowling Green, OH

**Suzanne T. Bell, PhD**
Texas A & M University
College Station, TX

**Walter C. Borman, PhD**
University of South Florida
Personnel Decisions Research Institutes
Tampa, FL

**Jennifer P. Bott, MA**
University of Akron
Akron, OH

**Kevin W. Brown, MS**
Florida International University
Miami, FL

**Valentina Bruk Lee, MA**
University of South Florida
Tampa, FL

**C. Shawn Burke, PhD**
Institute for Simulation and Training
University of Central Florida
Orlando, FL

**Alana B. Cober, PhD**
University of Akron
Akron, OH

**Richard T. Cober, PhD**
University of Akron
Akron, OH

**Patrick Connell, PhD**
University of South Florida
Tampa, FL

**Lisa A. Cooper, PhD**
Georgia Southwestern University
Americus, GA

**John M. Cornwell, PhD**
Loyola University New Orleans
New Orleans, LA

**Michael J. Cullen, PhD**
University of Minnesota
Minneapolis, MN

**Rene V. Dawis, PhD**
University of Minnesota
Minneapolis, MN

**Erika L. D'Egidio, PhD**
Jeanneret & Associates, Inc.
Houston, TX

**Bryan J. Dik, BA**
University of Minnesota
Minneapolis, MN

**Robert L. Dipboye, PhD**
Rice University
Houston, TX

**Lisa M. Donahue, MS**
George Mason University
Fairfax, VA

**Dennis Doverspike, PhD**
University of Akron
Akron, OH

**James L. Farr, PhD**
Pennsylvania State University
University Park, PA

**John W. Fleenor, PhD**
Center for Creative Leadership
Greensboro, NC

**Jennifer E. Fowlkes, PhD**
Institute for Simulation and Training
University of Central Florida
Orlando, FL

**Dean E. Frost, PhD**
Portland State University
Portland, OR

**Gary J. Greguras, PhD**
Louisiana State University
Baton Rouge, LA

**W. Lee Grubb III, PhD**
Virginia Commonwealth University
Richmond, VA

**Stefanie K. Halverson, MA**
Rice University
Houston, TX

**Jo-Ida C. Hansen, PhD**
University of Minnesota
Minneapolis, MN

**Mary Ann Hanson, PhD**
Independent Consultant
Houston, TX

**P. Richard Jeanneret, PhD**
Jeanneret & Associates, Inc.
Houston, TX

**Jennifer D. Kaufman, PhD**
Tulane University
Personnel Decisions Research Institutes
New Orleans, LA

**Ted Kinney, PhD**
Pennsylvania State University
University Park, PA

**K. Galen Kroeck, PhD**
Florida International University
Miami, FL

**Daniel Kuang, PhD**
Portland State University
Portland, OR

**Edward L. Levine, PhD**
University of South Florida
Tampa, FL

**Jonathan D. Levine, PhD**
Workforce Dynamics
Tampa, FL

**Paul E. Levy, PhD**
University of Akron
Akron, OH

**Michael A. McDaniel, PhD**
Virginia Commonwealth University
Richmond, VA

**Robert M. McIntyre, PhD**
Old Dominion University
Norfolk, VA

**Paul M. Muchinsky, PhD**
University of North Carolina
Greensboro, NC

**Daniel A. Newman, PhD**
The Pennsylvania State University
University Park, PA

**Christina Norris-Watts, MA**
University of Akron
Akron, OH

**Matthew E. Paronto, PhD**
Portland State University
Portland, OR

**Heather A. Priest, MS**
Institute for Simulation and Training
University of Central Florida
Orlando, FL

**Patrick H. Raymark, PhD**
Clemson University
Clemson, SC

**Deborah E. Rupp, PhD**
University of Illinois at Urbana-Champaign
Champaign, IL

**Paul R. Sackett, PhD**
University of Minnesota
Minneapolis, MN

**Eduardo Salas, PhD**
Institute for Simulation and Training
University of Central Florida
Orlando, FL

**Paul E. Spector, PhD**
University of South Florida
Tampa, FL

**Garnett S. Stokes, PhD**
University of Georgia
Athens, GA

**Daniel J. Svyantek, PhD**
University of Akron
Akron, OH

**Sylvester Taylor, BS**
Center for Creative Leadership
Greensboro, NC

**Lara Tedrow, PhD**
Old Dominion University
Norfolk, VA

**Jay C. Thomas, PhD**
Pacific University
Portland, OR

**George C. Thornton, III, PhD**
Colorado State University
Fort Collins, CO

**Donald M. Truxillo, PhD**
Portland State University
Portland, OR

**Deborah L. Whetzel, PhD**
Caliber Associates
Fairfax, VA

**Kevin Wooten, PhD**
University of Houston–Clear Lake
Houston, TX

# CHAPTER 1

# Overview

JAY C. THOMAS

This fourth volume of the *Comprehensive Handbook of Psychological Assessment* (CHOPA) is dedicated to assessment in organizations. Traditionally, assessment is typically thought of in terms of evaluating an individual's fitness for hire, promotion, or similar personnel action. Constructs, instruments, and methods used for such decisions make up the bulk of this book. These include tests, inventories, interviews, simulations, and performance appraisal techniques. Expanding the concept a little further, the book includes the assessment of work groups or teams rather than just individuals. Expanding still further, another facet of assessment is also important; the employee's reaction to the workplace and organization. Finally, there is psychological assessment for research purposes in which the object of decision is not an individual, group, or organization but, rather, is in regard to the status of an idea. Regardless of what purpose or purposes motivate performing an assessment, it is necessary to know the psychometric properties or development methods of a technique and, equally important, the theoretical basis of the assessment instrument or method.

The need for some means to select, evaluate, and promote the people who work in large and important organizations has been recognized for centuries. Over 2,000 years ago the Chinese government was using tests in the selection of civil service employees. This practice had grown to the point of a sophisticated, multiple-hurdle approach by the fourteenth century (Wiggins, 1973). Interest in the measurement of the attributes of everyday people was one of the first areas to develop as scientific psychology began to blossom late in the nineteenth century, and applications were being made in the workplace well before World War I (Guion, 1976). By the mid–twentieth century, psychological assessment was well established as an important component in personnel decision making, and the basic concepts underlying instrument development and validation were recognized.

Assessment of people for the purpose of making personnel decisions can have significant impact on the lives of those individuals as well as the organizations sponsoring the assessment. Frank Landy (cited in Guion, 1998) reported that as many as 80,000 people have been tested in a single day for civil service jobs in New York City, many of whom are bound to be disappointed in their job search. It is well established that scores on many psychological tests may differ across ethnic, racial, and cultural groups, as well as between genders, often leading to different proportions of various groups being hired or promoted. There may also be a correlation of score with age on some tests. The format of some assessment methods may make it difficult for people with disabilities to perform well, even when the disability itself is not a barrier to effective job performance. These data have led to legal constraints on use of assessments in decision making. The user must ensure that assessment techniques are job related and free from improper bias. Methods of validating assessment devices for personnel decisions are beyond the scope of this book (see Guion, 1998, for a comprehensive depiction of validation strategies), but each chapter includes a consideration of past results and current concerns about score differences and typical accommodations for the disabled. Beyond legal issues, organizations have found that a perception of unfairness in assessment techniques can be a public relations nightmare and can even drive away desirable applicants. The past few years have seen a new area of research examining the effects of applicant reactions to assessment procedures. This burgeoning area is of such importance that it has been included in this volume as a separate chapter, even though it does not represent an assessment technique.

Assessment is frequently performed utilizing psychological tests and inventories, but other methods are equally important and have the same legal status as tests with regard to employment and discrimination law. The applicant's personal history would seem to be relevant for predicting future behavior, but two difficulties present themselves. One is how to evaluate prior life and job experience. The other problem lies in ensuring that such assessments are not biased against those who have experienced a lack of opportunity or differential opportunities. Together, these problems have resulted in some interesting, creative, and important domains of research and practice, which are presented in Part Three. For example, reference checks and interviews are nearly universally used to evaluate job applicants. For many decades both have been known to have serious shortcomings as assessment devices unless carefully developed and implemented, in which case both can be quite useful.

Simulations and job samples are additional methods for assessing skill, knowledge, and, sometimes, potential. Wernimont and Campbell (1968) distinguished between "signs" of performance and "samples" of performance, making the assumption that samples would provide a more accurate appraisal with higher criterion-related validity. Simulations, including assessment centers, and job samples certainly fall into the sample category. Whether they are consistently more predictive of performance depends on many factors, but they do provide different information than most other methods of assessment. Because they are derived from everyday tasks or situations, simulations and job samples are sometimes seen by the public as not being methods of psychological assessment. They do, however, come with a host of psychometric issues. Fidelity is one controversial area. Is it more important to mirror real-life trappings of the job or to design the assessment procedure to focus on the underlying psychological factors involved in performance? Face validity and possible acceptance by examinees and client organizations favor one form of fidelity, whereas content and construct validity may be heightened by the other. Of course, the more one emphasizes psychological over physical fidelity, the more one shifts from a pure "sample" toward obtaining a "sign." Additional issues in the use of simulations and job samples include deciding what to measure, not as simple as it may first appear, and how to measure it reliably. Since these methods often employ observers or raters as the source of scores, rater training to minimize bias is critical.

The "criterion problem" has been with us for more than a century (Austin & Villanova, 1992) and has yet to be resolved. The ultimate question in the criterion problem is "What constitutes success?," and the most important secondary question is "How is success measured?" This volume does not attempt to provide an answer to the first question, although Kaufman and Borman (Chapter 22) review the concept and measures for Organizational Citizenship Behavior (OCB), a recent addition to the list of success factors. I once developed a detailed measure of performance for a client or-

ganization consisting of a checklist of all required job behaviors as well as behaviors considered poor practice. Although everyone agreed that the checklists covered job performance well, everyone also agreed that it failed to distinguish "good" from "poor" performers. That is, almost all employees would engage in the required job behaviors almost all of the time. Those who were considered top performers went beyond what was required and did whatever was necessary at the time to advance their unit's or the whole organization's interests. In some cases the employees considered most valuable actually exhibited a lower level of specific job skills than those who were less valuable performers. Clearly, in that case OCB was an important factor in performance.

How to measure success is a question that, at times, seems to have been answered, but it continually resurfaces. Landy and Farr (1980) concluded that the time was ripe for a moratorium on research into rating formats, ratings being the predominant method of gaining performance data. The moratorium has expired, however, as Newman, Kinney, and Farr (Chapter 20) establish in their chapter. Using performance ratings involves more than just choosing a format. It involves an examination of the conditions of rating, the mental processes of raters, and, of course, training. Who should make the ratings, and for what purpose, is also a critical question. Within the workplace people with different roles often observe different behaviors or, possibly, interpret the same behavior differently. Psychologists and human resource managers were quick to identify this difference as opening new facets in performance assessment and appraisal. Having people above, below, and to the side in the organization complete a performance assessment about a given individual is said to provide important insights into many aspects of work behavior. However, such systems are complicated to set up and operate, and the value of multisource ratings (sometimes known as 360 degree) depends on the purpose. Multisource ratings are covered in Chapter 21.

One of the most pervasive innovations in organizational theory and practice over the past several years has been organizing around teams. A team-based organization presents a different environment than an individually oriented organization. Although teams present many advantages and operating challenges to management, they also present some assessment challenges, presented in Part Six. One of the most notable challenges is measuring individuals' teamwork skills. Identifying who is likely to succeed in working in a team environment and who is not apt to succeed is important from both selection and development perspectives. A second challenge lies in measuring a team's performance. Since the basis for team organization is the team's contribution being supposedly greater than the sum of individual contributions, both individual and team performances may need to be assessed.

The subtleties in developing team assessment instruments are important for a psychologist working with teams or a team environment.

Employee reactions are an important aspect of assessment in modern organizations. Job satisfaction (see Dawis, Chapter 26) represents the original domain of interest, dating back to the earliest days of industrial psychology. Satisfaction seems a simple concept, but the theoretical variations and controversies over the past three quarters of a century signal that it is complex, and its place in relation to other critical work variables such as performance is not yet clear. Employees react to the organization in ways far exceeding the formation of attitudes or beliefs about the work environment. The stress response to organizational stressors can be a critically important influence on a person's health and happiness (Sutherland and Cooper, 2002). Connell, Bruk, and Spector (Chapter 25) present the primary methods of assessing stress within the organization. Appropriately for a book on psychological assessment, they concentrate on details regarding psychological measures, but they also briefly review some of the more common physiological measures of strain. The assessment of the social organization is the domain of climate and culture. Again, this is a vitally important arena for research and practice around which continual controversy swirls. Svyantek and Philips (Chapter 28) note that whereas climate is traditionally measured using quantitative survey measures and culture is typically assessed qualitatively, the assessment of either construct is necessarily method bound. Choice of method depends on purpose, as is the case throughout assessment.

From the perspective of the beginning years of the twenty-first century we can look back and see assessment ideas that have proven to be useful and others that represent false starts. In a few cases we can identify methods that were of value but have largely been dropped due to changes in the workplace and in society. This volume of CHOPA attempts to present the viable branches of assessment as of 2002. The overarching goal is to inform the reader of the major theoretical and practical issues attending each form of assessment and to describe the major, and many minor, instruments or methods employed within each type of assessment. It differs from the preceding three volumes in that assessments performed for organizational or business purposes do not commonly assume the presence of an underlying pathology in the person being assessed. In fact, in some cases there isn't even a person as the primary target of the assessment, but rather the person's reaction to the organizational environment or the organization itself. The term *assessment* is taken in its broadest possible meaning, the taking of standardized measurements in order to make decisions. The 27 substantive chapters cover individual attributes (cognitive abilities, personality, interests), personal history (biodata), simulations, job performance, and reactions to the workplace. Reflecting current trends in organizing work, team skills and the performance of teams are chapters that probably would not have appeared had this book been written a decade or so earlier. On the other hand, the book does not contain chapters about such areas as clerical aptitudes and sensory motor skills because there is little, if any, contemporary research or theory being published on those topics. In addition, the text does not cover such related topics as job analysis. The assessment of the work and workplace are important areas of theory, research, and, certainly, practice, but to attempt to detail all that that entails would make for an impossibly long book. Thus, the decision was made to limit the scope of the volume to the assessment of people, of teams of people, and their reactions to the workplace. This is consistent with the scope of the other three volumes in the series.

The success of a science has its foundation in how it solves the issue of measurement (Domotor, 1992). Success at measurement breeds a strong science, and a strong science leads to ever more success in assessment. The science of psychology has been successful in studying organizations and in generating fruitful applications, as the authors of each chapter demonstrate. We will continue to have a strong discipline as long as science, measurement, and application proceed together as a unified method for assessment.

## REFERENCES

Austin, J.T., & Villanova, P. (1992). The criterion problem: 1917–1992. *Journal of Applied Psychology, 77,* 836–874.

Domotor, Z. (1992). Measurement from empiricist and realist points of view. In C.W. Savage & P. Ehrlich (Eds.), *Philosophical and foundation issues in measurement theory* (pp. 195–221). Hillsdale, NJ: Erlbaum.

Guion, R.M. (1976). Recruiting, selection, and job placement. In M.D. Dunnette (Ed.), *Handbook of industrial and organizational psychology* (pp. 777–828). Chicago: Rand McNally.

Guion, R.M. (1998). *Assessment, measurement, and prediction for personnel decisions.* Mahwah, NJ: Erlbaum.

Landy, F.J., & Farr, J.L. (1980). Performance rating. *Psychological Bulletin, 87,* 72–107.

Sutherland, V.J., & Cooper, C. (2002). Models of job stress. In J.C. Thomas & M. Hersen (Eds.), *Handbook of mental health in the workplace* (pp. 33–60). Thousand Oaks, CA: Sage.

Wernimont, P.F., & Campbell, J.C. (1968). Signs, samples, and criteria. *Journal of Applied Psychology, 52,* 372–376.

Wiggins, J.S. (1973). *Personality and prediction: Principles of personality assessment.* Reading, MA: Addison-Wesley.

# SECTION ONE
# COGNITIVE ABILITY

CHAPTER 2

# General Mental Ability Tests in Industry

W. LEE GRUBB III, DEBORAH L. WHETZEL, AND MICHAEL A. MCDANIEL

Employee productivity is a critical element that helps determine the success or demise of organizations. To increase an organization's ability to augment its human capital, personnel psychologists have strived to create methods of selecting optimal employees from a pool of applicants. Thus, a stream of research has been dedicated to studying the relationship between general mental ability (GMA) and job performance.

Cognitive ability has been studied for more than 100 years (Galton, 1892). The U.S. military conducted the first large-scale ability testing during World War I. During this time, almost 2 million individuals were tested on GMA. This testing led to the postwar proliferation of intelligence testing in private sector organizations (Wigdor & Garner, 1982). As the use of intelligence testing in private industry increased, researchers began to place greater emphasis on procedures that were designed to test multiple, specific abilities as opposed to GMA. Specific abilities included mathematical, verbal, spatial, reasoning, perceptual speed, and mechanical skills. Interest in the measurement of specific abilities led to the development of multiaptitude test batteries such as the Differential Aptitude Test (DAT), the General Aptitude Test Battery (GATB), and the Armed Services Vocational Aptitude Battery (ASVAB). These tests, designed specifically to measure individual abilities and to make predictions about future job performance and trainability (Ree & Earles, 1991), could be weighted to include more or less of any particular specific ability. In this way, tests could be tailored to specific work environments according to the skills and abilities deemed to be most important. Although these tests were designed to measure specific abilities, the overwhelming majority of these tests revealed strong positive correlations with each other, making it possible to identify a general factor (GMA) that they shared.

Soon after World War II, however, researchers began to recognize that the results of studies used to predict employee performance and learning ability often revealed varying levels of validity even though they were conducted using the same assessment procedures for the same jobs. It was also observed that the correlation between a test and job performance, labeled the *validity coefficient,* was sometimes statistically significant and at other times not statistically significant even though the same test was being used with the same jobs. This apparent phenomenon became known as *situational specificity.* It was argued that one could not generalize the validity for a test from one setting to another because there were important subtle differences among what appeared to be the same jobs that caused the validity to vary from one situation to another. These differences were believed to be difficult if not impossible to discern.

The use of mental ability tests continued to thrive in private industry until the 1960s, when the nature of these tests and hiring practices in general were challenged by equal employment opportunity legislation and federal selection guidelines. Because these tests were the most salient, objective, and documented portion of the hiring process, and because they frequently resulted in lower rates of minority hiring, they were the focus of restrictive federal regulations. Many of these regulations required the validation of all tests used in the employment setting. Given the high cost of test validation, coupled with industry's fear of litigation, a trend emerged in which organizations decreased their use of objective testing in favor of alternative methods of employee selection. These methods included employment interviews and reviews of education and job-related credentials. Although these methods of selection are still popular, they are less valid and less objective than GMA tests (Schmidt & Hunter, 1998). However,

7

researchers continued to address the validity concerns regarding mental ability testing and the theory of situational specificity.

The theory of situational specificity prevailed until the late 1970s, when it was determined that differences in validity could be attributed to statistical and measurement error rather than to subtle differences among jobs (Schmidt & Hunter, 1977; Schmidt, Hunter, Pearlman, & Shane, 1979). Sampling error, due to the use of small numbers of individuals in each study, had the greatest effect. Quantitative research techniques (i.e., meta-analysis) were used to combine validity estimates of individual studies and correct them for statistical and measurement error. Meta-analytic techniques permit the quantitative cumulation of previously conducted studies to provide an accurate estimate of the relationship between GMA and employee productivity and trainability. Meta-analytic findings revealed that the validity of GMA varied only slightly across different types of jobs and even less for the same type of job (Hunter & Hunter, 1984; Pearlman, Schmidt, & Hunter, 1980). Through the use of meta-analytic techniques, researchers have demonstrated, repeatedly, that GMA tests are the most valid testing tool for all jobs. As the value of GMA tests was firmly established, more public and private sector industries started to use tests of GMA for selection.

As the applied research concerning GMA as a predictor of job performance began yielding clear conclusions, theories of the structure of intelligence also matured, yielding the three-stratum theory of intelligence. Carroll (1993) is credited with the three-stratum theory of cognitive abilities. This theory organizes the total domain of intellectual abilities into three separate levels. These levels are listed in descending order of predominance (Figure 2.1). The third-level stratum contains a single measure of general intelligence, or g. Thus, this stratum represents GMA. The second-level stratum contains eight specific ability factors. These specific ability factors include: (1) fluid intelligence (which includes reasoning ability and creativity), (2) crystallized intelligence (which includes verbal and learned intelligence), (3) general memory and learning, (4) broad visual perception, (5) broad auditory perception, (6) broad retrieval ability, (7) broad cognitive speediness, and (8) processing speed. Lines connect the second-level stratum to the third-level stratum to indicate that the observable characteristics of the second-level factors are correlated with the dominant third-level stratum, g. The degree of correlation is depicted by the length of the line that connects the second-stratum factor to g. As noted by their short lines, fluid and crystallized intelligence are the most highly correlated with g, and processing speed is least highly correlated with g. Finally, the first stratum contains a number of factors that are dominated by the second-stratum factors. Although the first-stratum factors are depicted with connecting lines as being correlated with specific second-stratum factors, it should not be assumed that they are not correlated with other second-stratum factors to which they are not attached. The three-stratum theory of intelligence is the most widely accepted categorization of factors pertaining to the aggregate factor g. Carroll (1996) noted that additional factor-analytic research would increase our ability to accurately explain the true nature and structure of cognitive ability.

With the demise of the theory of situational specificity, research was focused on a general measure of intelligence as a predictor of job performance. Hunter (1980) found that a general measure of intelligence could be used to predict employee performance for all types of jobs regardless of their nature or complexity. In a meta-analysis conducted for the U.S. Department of Labor (Hunter, 1980; Hunter & Hunter, 1984), performance on the job and trainability was measured for more than 32,000 employees in 515 different civilian jobs. The job categories ranged from unskilled and skilled blue-collar jobs to midlevel white-collar administrative jobs and professional managerial jobs. Although the validity for the tests varied from .28 for completely unskilled jobs to .58 for professional managerial jobs, the validity of .51 for the middle-complexity jobs, which equates to roughly 60% of the jobs in the U.S. economy, is a commonly used estimate.

GMA measures are currently the best available procedures for predicting job-related learning. Several studies indicate that GMA is clearly the most accurate predictor of employees' ability to acquire knowledge on the job (Schmidt & Hunter, 1992; Schmidt, Hunter, & Outerbridge, 1986) and employees' ability to perform in job training programs (Hunter, 1986; Hunter & Hunter, 1984; Ree & Earles, 1992). Finally, another benefit of GMA measures is that they have the lowest application cost of selection processes that are appropriate for all job categories. One can purchase professionally developed GMA tests, applicable to all jobs, for a few dollars per test administration.

Studies have been conducted to determine the incremental validity of specific ability tests above GMA for predicting job and training performance (Carey, 1994; Ree & Earles, 1991, 1992; Ree, Earles, & Teachout, 1994; Thorndike, 1985). The results overwhelmingly indicate that for both the prediction of job and training performance, little value is added when specific ability tests are added to GMA tests.

The potential economic gains an organization can realize through the use of GMA for selection are enormous. Schmidt and Hunter (1998) summarized methods for measuring employee performance either as a dollar value of output or as a

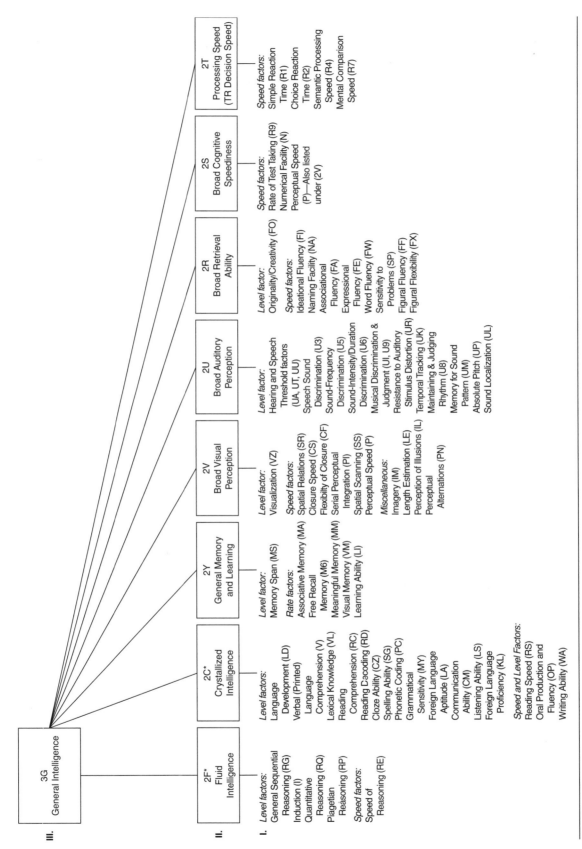

**Figure 2.1** The structure of cognitive abilities (from Carroll, 1993. Reprinted with permission of Cambridge University Press).

percentage of the mean output in a given job. The standard deviation across individuals of the dollar value output has been conservatively estimated as 40% (Schmidt & Hunter, 1983; Schmidt, Hunter, McKenzie, & Muldrow, 1979; Schmidt, Mack, & Hunter, 1984). For example, for a job with an annual salary of $30,000, a standard deviation would represent at least $12,000. If the performance of employees has a normal distribution, then employees at the 84th percentile (one standard deviation higher than the average employee at the 50th percentile) would produce $12,000 more per year than the average employee. The difference between high-performing individuals at the 84th percentile and poor-performing employees at the 16th percentile (two standard deviations lower than the high-performing employee at the 84th percentile) would be $24,000. Clearly, these differences represent considerable variance in both productivity and dollar value to organizations and contribute greatly to the success or failure of an organization.

The second method of measuring employee output is determined as a percentage of the mean output. In this method, each employee's output is divided by output of employees at the 50th percentile (representing average workers) and then multiplied by 100. Research shows that the standard deviation of output as a percentage of average output varies across job types (Hunter, Schmidt, & Judiesch, 1990). Unskilled and semiskilled jobs have an average standard deviation of 19%, skilled jobs have an average standard deviation of 32%, and managerial and professional jobs have an average standard deviation of 48%. Again, if the productivity of employees is normally distributed, more productive employees at the 84th percentile in unskilled jobs will produce 19% more work than average employees at the 50th percentile. The differences are even greater with skilled and professional jobs. These differences in employee productivity and trainability are quite significant and can be realized through the use of improved selection methods that include GMA tests. These benefits are multiplied by the number of individuals who are hired for each year that they remain employed by the organization. Using the previous example where the average annual income of employees hired is $30,000, if the company is able to hire 50 applicants using tests of GMA and their productivity is one standard deviation higher than the average employee (representing an increase in productivity of the new hires equal to $12,000 per person), the annual benefit for the organization is $600,000.

Racial and ethnic differences in GMA tests have been researched for more than 100 years, and this topic continues to be richly debated. Research indicates that there are significant mean differences on GMA tests between Blacks, Hispanics, and Whites (Dreger & Miller, 1960; Herrnstein & Murray,

1994; Hunter & Hunter, 1984; Jensen, 1973, 1985; Loehlin, Lindzey, & Spuhler, 1975; Neisser et al., 1996; Roth, Bevier, Bobko, Switzer, & Tyler, 2001; Williams & Ceci, 1997). Before proceeding, it is necessary to explain the terminology used in the research. The $d$ effect size summarizes the standardized mean differences between two groups. The $d$ effect size is calculated by taking the difference in group means and dividing that by the sample weighted average of the group standard deviations. For example, a $d$ of 1 indicates that averaged across the two groups, the mean of one group is one standard deviation higher than the other group. It is important to note that the use of the $d$ statistic is an indicator of the differences between groups, and it should not be taken to mean that there are not high-scoring individuals in each group.

Roth et al. (2001) conducted a comprehensive meta-analysis of ethnic group differences in GMA measures and found that moderating variables influence the often-cited $d$ of 1.0 between Blacks and Whites. For example, they found that job complexity (i.e., the extent to which a job requires information processing) moderates the effect size such that jobs higher in complexity have lower effect sizes (e.g., .86 for low-complexity jobs; .72 for medium-complexity jobs; and .62 for high-complexity jobs). The authors point out that using an effect size of 1.0 could seriously underestimate projected minority hiring. That is, for a given job, if the $d$ is really .9, minority hiring could be underestimated by as much as 19% and if the $d$ is .7, as found for medium-complexity jobs, minority hiring could be underestimated by 44%.

Another moderator of the magnitude of race differences is whether the participants in the studies are applicants or job incumbents. As one might imagine, given range restriction with incumbent samples, the effect size for applicant samples was .99 and for incumbent samples, the $d$ was .41 (with two large databases removed). For tests of quantitative ability, the $d$s were .74 for applicants and .54 for incumbents; for tests of verbal ability, the $d$s followed a similar pattern in which the applicant $d$ was .83 and the incumbent d was .63. Roth et al. (2001) pointed out that the implication of these results is that one must be cautious about using incumbent samples to make inferences about applicant samples because they are likely to result in underestimates of effect sizes.

The construct being measured by the test also moderates effect sizes. That is, tests assessing GMA are generally associated with larger differences between groups than verbal or mathematical abilities. For example, the Graduate Record Exam (GRE) total has an effect size of .72, whereas the verbal effect size is .60 and the math effect size is .51. Thus, one might expect lower levels of ethnic group differences if the tests assessing GMA focus on a more specific stratum of cognitive abilities (Pulakos & Schmitt, 1996). Although this may appear contradictory to the preceding discussion about the validity of specific abilities, a variety of issues should be considered when making decisions about which selection instruments to use.

The Hispanic–White differences are less than the Black–White differences—the Hispanic–White effect size is .72. As with the Black–White differences, specific abilities, such as verbal and math, had smaller group differences ($d = .28$ for math and $d = .40$ for verbal) than GMA. Applicant and incumbent samples showed the same patterns described earlier. The effect size on the Armed Forces Occupational Qualification Test (AFOQT) for applicants was 1.19 and for incumbents was .46. This difference again demonstrates the concern about using incumbent samples to estimate group differences in applicants.

Because of the current debate regarding racial group differences, it is important to recognize that efforts have been taken to study tests that could be used to reduce mean differences in scores on GMA tests. A comprehensive body of research indicates that although substantial mean differences exist, GMA tests do not underpredict the performance of minority group members (American Educational Research Association, American Psychological Association, & National Council of Measurement in Education, 1999; Neisser et al., 1996; O'Connor, 1989; Sackett & Wilk, 1994; Wilson, 1981). Therefore, it is very clear that tests of GMA are not biased against Blacks or Hispanics and that the score differences reflect true population differences in GMA.

Because organizations are typically interested in both maximizing productivity and striving to achieve a diverse workforce, several methods have been reviewed in an effort to help organizations achieve both goals (Sackett, Schmitt, Ellingson, & Kabin, 2001). The first strategy involved measuring additional abilities, such as personality or interpersonal skills. Measures of noncognitive predictors show smaller mean differences across race and ethnic groups and are also correlated with job performance (Bobko, Roth, & Potosky, 1999). Organizations could use noncognitive tests as part of their selection system to predict job performance and to satisfy their need for a diverse workforce. The second strategy involved identifying and removing items from tests that appear to be statistically culturally biased. Several studies have investigated the effect of items that appeared to be culturally biased (Berk, 1982; Freedle & Kostin, 1990, 1997; McCauley & Mendoza, 1985; Scheuneman & Gerritz, 1990; Whitney & Schmitt, 1997). The results showed that there was not a consistent, predictable pattern of test items that favored majority or minority test takers. Although differential item functioning for minority versus majority test takers may be detected in some items, the magnitude of the effect that these items intro-

duced was small. The third strategy advocated using computer-based tests or video-based technology to minimize the reading and writing requirements of a test. Sackett et al. (2001) reviewed three studies that compared video-based presentations of questions with written questions (Chan & Schmitt, 1997; Pulakos & Schmitt, 1996; Sackett, 1998). The results showed that a reduction in Black–White $d$ values was due to the reduction in the cognitive loading of the measure. The fourth strategy involved increasing test-takers' motivation to complete the test, as well as altering instructional sets to reduce the apprehension associated with terms like *intelligence test*. Studies of racial differences in test-taking motivation (Chan, Schmitt, DeShon, Clause, & Delbridge, 1997; O'Neil & Brown, 1997) and studies involving altered instructional sets (Steele & Aronson, 1995; Steele, 1997) have not produced large observed effects on subgroup differences. The fifth strategy was to use accomplishments and achievements contained in portfolios to assess knowledge, skills, and abilities. In addition, assessment centers may be used to help determine applicant's proficiency in completing work-related activities. There are several issues to consider when using these alternative methods. One issue involves the extent to which scoring of accomplishments is standardized. The last strategy involves the use of coaching or orientation programs to help prepare examinees for the test. Although the use of coaching and orientation programs has been shown to increase minority scores modestly on cognitively loaded tests, organizations may not wish to encounter the additional costs associated with coaching applicants to perform better on their selection assessment measures.

## MAJOR AND MINOR GMA TESTS USED IN ORGANIZATIONAL SETTINGS

In the following section we review several GMA tests used in organizational settings. The tests are primarily used in personnel screening for employment or promotion. Many of these tests were developed decades ago. In recent decades, test publishers focusing on organizational markets have developed multiaptitude test batteries so that end users can mix and match tests to build a battery that they perceive will meet their needs. Almost any reasonable mixture of these tests will yield a battery that assesses GMA. Since multiaptitude batteries are described in another chapter, they are not reviewed here.

The outline to be followed in these test reviews was delineated by the book editors. We offer some general remarks on a few of these categories. First, we were asked to comment on cross-cultural factors. If test bias existed in measures of

GMA, we would present an interesting discussion of the topic in this section. However, since there is no cultural bias in measures of GMA, we limit our cross-cultural comments to whether the tests have alternative language forms. We were also asked to address legal and ethical considerations. We are not aware of any ethical considerations in the professional use of GMA measures. Nor in most nations are there any legal considerations in the use of GMA tests. However, in the United States, tests that show mean test score differences across races may face legal scrutiny. As discussed earlier in this chapter, one can expect large differences in mean test scores between Whites and Blacks and between Whites and Hispanics. Although these score differences reflect true differences in GMA, various U.S. law and regulations are biased toward assuming that GMA tests and other tests showing true race differences are somehow unfair to lower scoring minorities. These false assumptions often force employers to expend substantial resources to show what is already well established (that the GMA tests are unbiased predictors of job performance). Third, we were to comment on the current research status. Many areas of GMA research are essentially dead because these research questions have been answered definitively. Thus, there is little current research on these measures because there is none needed. One will see the use of these measures in research studies, but typically the measures are being used as marker variables for GMA in studies that focus on other topics. Fourth, we were to address future developments on the use of these tests. As with our discussion concerning current research, the primary research questions concerning GMA tests in organizational applications have been answered.

We were also asked to divide the tests into major and minor tests. We considered various criteria for making the major-minor decision. Whereas all the tests are professionally developed measures of GMA, and thus would be highly correlated with each other, it would be difficult to say that one measure was better than another for assessing GMA. We chose to declare some tests as major tests when we judged that their frequency of use was relatively high. Those tests whose frequency of use was relatively low were deemed minor tests. The Association of Test Publishers reported that it did not tabulate statistics on the frequency of use of the various tests. A complicating issues is that many test publishers do not routinely release figures on tests sold and even if they did, there is no way for us to audit the veracity of the figures. Therefore, in designating tests as major or minor, we have used our experience to declare some tests to be highly used, and thus major tests, and other tests to be less frequently used, and therefore minor tests.

## Major Tests

### The Wonderlic Personnel Test

**Description.**    Our information concerning the Wonderlic Personnel Test (WPT) is primarily drawn from its current manual (Wonderlic, Inc., 2000) and from its web site (www.wonderlic.com). The WPT is a self-administered test in which applicants are directed to read the test instructions and to complete sample questions provided on the front page of the test booklet. The test itself is comprised of 50 questions and is administered for 12 minutes. Scoring the test is made convenient through the use of a scoring key. The scoring key is constructed so that the answers on the key line up with the answer blanks on the actual test. The test score is the total number of questions answered correctly.

The WPT is designed to measure GMA and is composed of three subsets that include vocabulary items, arithmetic reasoning, and spatial reasoning items. When combined, these subsets enable the WPT to establish a GMA score.

**Theoretical basis.**    The WPT was developed to be a measure of GMA.

**Test development.**    The WPT began in the 1930s as part of a doctoral thesis by Al Wonderlic. The test has been in use for more than 65 years and has been administered over 130 million times.

**Psychometric characteristics.**    The reliability of the WPT has been examined in many studies with alpha reliabilities ranging from .82 to .94. The alternate form reliabilities have ranged from .73 to .95. The test is an example of a spiral omnibus measure with items of various g-related content arranged in order of difficulty. The correlations of other tests support the construct validity of the WPT as a measure of GMA.

**Range of application and limitations.**    The WPT is used almost exclusively for applicant screening. Occasionally it is used as a marker test of GMA in research.

**Accommodations for people with disabilities.**    For visually impaired applicants, there are two different large-print versions of the test available as well as a Braille version. Audio versions are also available, and all of these special forms of the tests come with a supplemental user's manual.

**Cross-cultural factors.**    The WPT is currently offered in 11 alternate language forms: Chinese, French, German, Japanese, Korean, Portuguese, Russian, Spanish, Swedish, Tagalog, and

Vietnamese. Although these translations are offered, they are all considered experimental except for the Spanish language version.

**Legal and ethical considerations.**   As noted in the introduction to the test review section, any measure of GMA can be expected to show mean score differences by race. These race differences may require employers to expend effort to show that tests are unbiased and job related.

**Computer/Internet applications.**   The WPT is available in a computerized version called the WPT-PC. The PC version includes special diagnostic and reporting capabilities to support the testing programs. Independent researchers at the Air Force Institute of Technology (Hensley & Morris, 1992) have conducted studies and determined that the PC version and paper-and-pencil version offer comparable results.

**Current research status.**   The publishers of the Wonderlic support research using the Wonderlic. Whereas the major research questions concerning the use of GMA tests for organizational applications have long been resolved, much of the research involving the WPT is usually focused on some topic other than GMA.

**Use in organizational practice.**   The WPT has been used in more than 50,000 organizations worldwide ranging from the National Football League to MENSA. It has been administered on average over 2 million times annually for over 65 years (www.wonderlic.com).

**Future developments.**   As noted in the introduction to the test reviews, there is little need for additional research on any GMA tests used in organizational settings.

### Watson-Glaser Critical Thinking Appraisal

**Description.**   The information presented in this review of the Watson-Glaser Critical Thinking Appraisal (WGCTA) comes primarily from the technical manual (Watson & Glaser, 1994). The WGCTA is an 80-item, multiple-choice, paper-and-pencil test designed to measure applicants' critical thinking abilities.

The test measures five areas of critical thinking: inference, recognition of assumptions, deduction, interpretation, and the evaluation of arguments. Individuals taking the test evaluate and respond to sections of the test that include problems, statements, arguments, and the interpretation of information encountered on a daily basis. The test can be taken in less than an hour and requires a proctor. In addition, there is a short-form test, the WGCTA-S, that is made up of 40 questions and can be taken in about 45 minutes. The test can be hand scored with a key or machine scored.

**Theoretical basis.**   The original test was developed in 1942 by Goodwin Watson and Edward M. Glaser to measure five areas of critical thinking. Watson and Glaser defined critical thinking as a composite of skills, knowledge, and attitudes.

**Test development.**   The original test was first modified in the 1960s and included two versions, Ym and Zm. Each version consisted of 100 items. In 1980 the test was modified to update current word usage and eliminate racial and sexual stereotypes with the creation of Form A and B. More recently, a short form, Form S, was created to reduce the time and cost associated with administering the test. The short form is composed of questions taken from Form A. To support the use of Form S, scores from a sample of 3,727 adult participants were reviewed and correlated. First, a raw score was computed for Form A. Next, a raw score was calculated from the responses in Form A that appear in Form S. The overall correlation between the two sets of scores was .96.

**Psychometric characteristics.**   Test-retest reliability for Form S was calculated with a sample of 42 employees (92.9% nonminority, 54.8% female) over a two-week period. The test-retest correlation was .81. Internal consistency reliability of .81 was calculated using a sample of 1,608 applicants from a variety of occupations.

**Range of application and limitations.**   The WGCTA has been successfully used to assist in the selection of applicants for positions that specifically require analytical reasoning. This test is often used to screen individuals for jobs requiring a high level of cognitive ability.

**Accommodations for people with disabilities.**   The test can be administered untimed. An untimed or an extended administration of a test is a frequent accommodation for individuals with disabilities.

**Cross-cultural factors.**   We are aware of no forms of the test in languages other than English.

**Legal and ethical considerations.**   As noted in the introduction to the test review section, any measure of GMA can be expected to show mean score differences by race. These race differences may require employers to expend effort to show that tests are unbiased and job related.

**Computer/Internet applications.**   All three forms of the test (Form A, Form B, and Form S) are available as Internet-based tests; however, commensurability studies have not been conducted to determine the applicability of the original norms of the paper-and-pencil tests to the Internet-based tests.

**Current research status.**   Whereas the major research questions concerning the use of GMA tests for organizational applications have long been resolved, much of the research involving the WGCTA is usually focused on some topic other than GMA.

**Use in organizational practice.**   The WGCTA is primarily used in organizations as a personnel selection tool.

**Future developments.**   As noted in the introduction to the test reviews, there is little need for additional research on any GMA test used in organizational settings.

### Wesman Personnel Classification Test

**Description.**   The information in this review of the Wesman Personnel Classification Test (PCT) is based primarily on information presented in the test manual (Wesman, 1965). The PCT is a paper-and-pencil test designed to provide information regarding applicants' verbal and numeric reasoning skills as well as GMA. All of the tests are composed of two sections. Part I, the verbal section, contains 40 multiple-choice questions where applicants pick words to best complete a sentence. Part II, the numeric section, contains 20 mathematical problems for the applicants to solve. Time limits for the sections are 18 minutes and 10 minutes, respectively. Scores for the tests are calculated by summing the total number of questions answered correctly in each section. Whereas these subtests are not typically used individually and contribute to a global GMA score, we consider this test to be a measure of GMA and not a multiaptitude test battery.

**Theoretical basis.**   The PCT is designed specifically to measure verbal reasoning and numeric ability.

**Test development.**   The verbal reasoning questions draw on two skills, reasoning through analogy and an understanding of relationships. Respondents must choose two words to complete each question statement. Each question has two lists of words and one word must be chosen from each list to complete the question statement. This greatly reduces the chance of guessing the correct answer to 1 in 16 as opposed to 1 in 4 or 5 for most multiple-choice tests. The numeric ability section is designed to test the respondent's numeric and arithmetical skills. The questions are designed to measure one's ability to recognize relationships and inventive skill or

cleverness. It is important to note that pure figure-handling speed or numeric perception can be more correctly assessed with other tests. Three separate versions of the test are available, Form A, Form B, and Form C. Forms A and B are comparable; Form C, however, contains more challenging verbal skill questions.

**Psychometric characteristics.**   Test-retest reliabilities have been calculated by administering two different forms of the PCT to the same applicants. Applicants for plant and clerical jobs were tested using Forms B and C (test order was reversed for each group), resulting in a test-retest reliability of .91 and .89, respectively. Additionally, accounting and quality control personnel in a manufacturing company were tested using Forms B and C (test order was reversed for each group), resulting in a test-retest reliability of .89 and .87, respectively. The PCT has been correlated with the Wonderlic Personnel Test for several different types of employment situations: mechanical apprentice applicants ($N = 149$), $r = .76$; college seniors-sales understudy applicants ($N = 150$), $r = .70$; shop supervisors ($N = 210$), $r = .33$, and airline employees ($N = 100$), $r = .80$.

**Range of application and limitations.**   The PCT has been used successfully in industry with job types ranging from chain store clerks to executive-level candidates.

**Accommodations for people with disabilities.**   None.

**Cross-cultural factors.**   We are aware of no forms in languages other than English.

**Legal and ethical considerations.**   As noted in the introduction to the test review section, any measure of GMA can be expected to show mean score differences by race. These race differences may require employers to expend effort to show that tests are unbiased and job related.

**Computer/Internet applications.**   None.

**Current research status.**   Whereas the major research questions concerning the use of GMA tests for organizational applications have long been resolved, much of the research involving the PCT is usually focused on some topic other than GMA.

**Use in organizational practice.**   The PCT is primarily used in organizations as a personnel selection tool.

**Future developments.**   As noted in the introduction to the test reviews, there is little need for additional research on any GMA test used in organizational settings.

## Test of Learning Ability

**Description.**   The information we review concerning the Test of Learning Ability (TLA) is primarily drawn from the technical manual (ePredix, 2001) and a Test Critiques review (Rosenbach, 1994). In the literature, it is often referred to as the RBH Test of Learning Ability because, until recently, the test was primarily marketed by Richardson, Bellows, and Henry. The TLA is a 54-item multiple-choice test that tests verbal, spatial, and numerical skills. Each of the three skill sets are tested using 18 questions intermixed throughout the eight-page test booklet. Vocabulary questions include matching a word to another word with a similar definition; numerical questions involve simple arithmetic and some basic algebra, typically in the form of word problems. The spatial problems involve counting blocks or cubes in a picture. The questions are arranged in ascending order of difficulty. The test is administered for 12 minutes, and answers can be recorded on the actual test or on a scannable answer sheet.

**Theoretical basis.**   The test was developed as a GMA measure and drew items from the U.S. Army General Classification Test, which was a GMA measure used in World War II for applicant screening.

**Test development.**   The original version was published in 1947. The items in the test have received few changes over the years; however, in 1989 and in 2001, the questions were updated to contain more current content regarding the prices of items and other financial-related information contained in the arithmetic word problems.

**Psychometric characteristics.**   Test-retest reliabilities for both Black and White samples range from .87 to .95 and are more than sufficient to suggest that the test is reliable.

**Range of application and limitations.**   The test is used almost exclusively in applicant screening.

**Accommodations for people with disabilities.**   None.

**Cross-cultural factors.**   We know of no forms of the test in languages other than English.

**Legal and ethical considerations.**   As noted in the introduction to the test review section, any measure of GMA can be expected to show mean score differences by race. These race differences may require employers to expend effort to show that tests are unbiased and job related.

**Computer/Internet applications.**   There are no computer-based applications of the TLA available.

**Current research status.**   Whereas the major research questions concerning the use of GMA tests for organizational applications have long been resolved, much of the research involving the TLA is usually focused on some topic other than GMA.

**Use in organizational practice.**   The TLA is primarily used in organizations as a personnel selection tool.

**Future developments.**   As noted in the introduction to the test reviews, there is little need for additional research on any GMA test used in organizational settings.

## Thurstone Test of Mental Alertness

**Description.**   The information in our review of the Thurstone Test of Mental Alertness (TMA) is drawn primarily from the technical manual (Thurstone & Thurstone, 1998). The TMA is a paper-and-pencil test designed to measure one's ability to learn new information and skills as well as one's ability to understand relationships and remain flexible. The test has a time limit of 20 minutes, and each test takes about 10 minutes to grade. Three different scores are derived from the TMA: the L score of linguistic ability, the Q score of quantitative ability, and a Total score resulting from the summation of the previous two scores. Whereas applications of the tests primarily rely on the Total score, we consider the TMA to be a measure of GMA rather than a multiaptitude test battery.

**Theoretical basis.**   The test was developed to be a measure of GMA.

**Test development.**   The two forms of the TMA (Form A and Form B) contain 126 questions and have four main types of problems based on verbal and numerical skills. Verbal questions include understanding words (same and opposite) and verbal definitions. Numerical questions include number series and arithmetic reasoning.

**Psychometric characteristics.**   Using Forms A and B, over a time period of one month between versions, the test-retest reliability for the TMA was over .80. Test-retest scores of over .90 were reported when compiling test-retest statistics for each version of the test individually. For validity tests, the TMA was correlated with rank ratings and other measures of job-related performance reporting validity correlations between .30 and .60.

**Range of application and limitations.**   The TMA has been used to help successfully predict the future performance of a wide range of job categories, ranging from skilled and unskilled workers, retail and sales positions, and computer operators and programmers through all levels of management. Scoring norms are provided for a variety of positions and are offered as general guidelines.

**Accommodations for people with disabilities.**   None.

**Cross-cultural factors.**   We know of no forms of the test in languages other than English.

**Legal and ethical considerations.**   As noted in the introduction to the test review section, any measure of GMA can be expected to show mean score differences by race. These race differences may require employers to expend effort to show that tests are unbiased and job related.

**Computer/Internet applications.**   Computer-based versions of the TMA are available.

**Current research status.**   Whereas the major research questions concerning the use of GMA tests for organizational applications have long been resolved, much of the research involving the TMA is usually focused on some topic other than GMA.

**Use in organizational practice.**   The TMA is primarily used in organizations as a personnel selection tool.

**Future developments.**   As noted in the introduction to the test reviews, there is little need for additional research on any GMA test used in organizational settings.

**Minor Tests**

*Raven's Progressive Matrices*

**Description.**   The information in this review of the Raven's Progressive Matrices (RPM) is based primarily on information obtained from the manuals (Raven, Raven, & Court, 1998a, 1998b; Raven et al., 2000). The RPM is a general term used to encompass the family of matrices tests developed by Raven. The tests are designed to draw on respondents' observation and thinking skills and assess their ability to gain order from chaos. The RPM tests are divided into three main tests: Standard Progressive Matrices (SPM), Coloured Progressive Matrices (CPM), and Advanced Progressive Matrices (APM).

The SPM is an untimed test organized into five sets (A, B, C, D, and E) containing 12 problems each. The first set is designed to develop a theme that following sections build on;

these sections become progressively more difficult. The design allows the test to be used as a method of indexing respondents' ability to learn from previous sections.

The APM is organized into two sets of problems. The first set contains 12 problems designed to train the respondents in a method of completing the problems. The first section may be timed or simply given to respondents to take at their leisure and either is scored (in a timed administration) for a quick assessment of educative ability or, more often, is simply used to train the respondents in how to proceed with the second section. The second set, which may be timed or untimed, contains 36 problems arranged in ascending order of difficulty. The test is designed to enable the administrator to more accurately spread the scores of high achievers, that is, test applicants who are presumed to be at a higher level of cognitive ability, and to assess the speed of intellectual efficiency.

The CPM is typically used as an assessment tool for children, old people, and individuals who are intellectually impaired. Because the CPM is of little use in industry, this specific test is not reviewed.

**Theoretical basis.**   The RPM tests were developed for use in research concerning genetic and environmental influences on mental ability. Along with the Raven's Vocabulary Tests, the RPM tests were designed to measure two components of GMA identified by Spearman: educative ability and reproductive ability. Educative ability, seen as largely nonverbal, was viewed as the ability to determine meaning amid confusion. Reproductive ability concerned knowledge of the culture's store of verbal information. The RPM tests were developed as the measure of educative ability, and the Raven's Vocabulary Tests were the measure of reproductive ability.

**Test development.**   Raven's first series of progressive matrices was published in 1938. It was designed to measure educative ability, one of the two main components of Spearman's model of general intelligence. Educative ability involves one's ability to make sense out of confusion. The APM was developed in the early 1940s for use by the British War Office Selection Boards. A more complex matrices test was needed to provide better discrimination of upper level scores than the original SPM. All the tests have undergone subsequent revisions to shorten the tests.

In 1998, a special version of the SPM was developed to include more challenging problems. It is referred to as the Standard Progressive Matrices Plus, or SPM +. An additional parallel form of the SPM has been created as well, and it is referred to as the SPM Parallel Form, or SPM-P.

**Psychometric characteristics.**    Test-retest reliabilities for the APM were calculated using the 48-item version of the test that was used from 1947 to 1962 with 243 adult students. The test was administered for 40 minutes, and respondents took the test again six to eight weeks later. The test-retest reliability was highly reliable, $r = .91$.

**Range of application and limitations.**    The SPM is used to assess the majority of the population and can be used successfully to stratify applicants for most low- to midlevel-complexity positions. The SPM + is designed to increase the SPM's discriminant ability for higher scoring populations. Finally, the APM is designed to discriminate among individuals who score in the top 25% of respondents taking the SPM and may be suitable with more complex, executive-level job categories. In addition, the APM can be used to assess different components of educative ability. If the APM is administered as a timed test, it more closely measures intellectual efficiency. If the test is taken without time limits, it more closely measures perception and clear thinking.

**Accommodations for people with disabilities.**    None.

**Cross-cultural factors.**    RPM answer sheets, and in some cases, administrative procedures, manuals, and norms are available in many different languages. These languages include: Chinese (Taiwan), Croat, Czech, Finnish, French, French (Belgium), German, Hungarian, Italian, Japanese, Polish, Portuguese (Brazil), Slovak, Slovenian, Spanish, Spanish (Latin America), and Swedish.

**Legal and ethical considerations.**    As noted in the introduction to the test review section, any measure of GMA can be expected to show mean score differences by race. These race differences may require employers to expend effort to show that tests are unbiased and job related.

**Computer/Internet applications.**    Several versions of the SPM and APM have been developed for computer-based testing. Successful programs have been developed for Apple Macintosh computers, PC computers, and mainframes.

**Current research status.**    Much more so than other tests reviewed in this chapter, the RPM tests were developed as research tools. They have been used in more than 2,500 published studies. Their applied use in organizations for personnel selection represents a small segment of this research.

**Use in organizational practice.**    RPM tests have been successfully used to measure applicants' innovative thinking ability as a predictor of future success in managerial performance. In addition, they have been used to help select candidates for a broad range of employment categories, including clerical work, sales, protective professions, and simple industrial work.

**Future developments.**    The RPM tests are popular tools for research, although the amount of research examining the RPM in organizational settings is a minor segment of this research. A bibliography of research on the RPM is available from Catherine Raven. Contact information is available in the manual.

### Beta III

**Description.**    Information for the review of the Beta III was entirely drawn from the test manual (Kellogg & Morton, 1999). The Beta III is designed to assess various facets of nonverbal intelligence, including visual information processing, processing speed, spatial and nonverbal reasoning, and aspects of fluid intelligence. The Beta III consists of five tests:

1. *Coding.* Using a key, write the numbers that correspond to the hieroglyphic-like symbol.
2. *Picture Completion.* Draw what is missing to complete a picture.
3. *Clerical Checking.* Circle the equal ( $=$ ) or not equal ( $\neq$ ) sign depending on whether pairs of pictures, symbols, or numbers are the same or different.
4. *Picture Absurdities.* Place an X on the one picture out of four that illustrates something that is wrong or foolish.
5. *Matrix Reasoning.* Choose the missing symbol or picture that best completes a set of four symbols or pictures.

Whereas these subtests are not used individually and contribute to a global GMA score, we consider this test to be a measure of GMA and not a multiaptitude test battery. The test takes approximately 25–30 minutes to administer, including 10–15 minutes for instructions and practice and 14.5 minutes for actual testing.

**Theoretical basis.**    The test was developed to be a measure of GMA.

**Test development.**    The U.S. Army developed the Beta III during World War I to assess the intellectual ability of illiterate recruits. In 1934, Kellogg and Morton revised the content of the original edition to make it suitable for civilian use. The 1946 revision used procedures patterned after those of Wechsler.

**Psychometric characteristics.** Test-retest reliability (observed), $r = .87$; corrected for range restriction, $r = .91$. Correlation with WAIS-III ($N = 182$), (observed), $rs = .61$, .76, .73; corrected for variability of Beta III standardization sample, $rs = .67$, .80, .77. Factor analysis revealed two factors: Nonverbal Reasoning and Processing Speed. Correlations with other tests have low sample sizes. Beta III normative information is based on a nationally representative sample of the U.S. population aged from 16 to 89 years. The Beta III standardization sample was stratified by age, sex, race/ethnicity, education level, and geographic region of residence and consists of 1,260 adults.

**Range of application and limitations.** The Beta III is useful for individuals who are illiterate and for whom one needs a quick measure of GMA.

**Accommodations for people with disabilities.** Test has been administered to adults diagnosed as mentally retarded and those with attention-deficit hyperactivity disorder (ADHD).

**Cross-cultural factors.** Since the test is nonverbal, the test would be of use for individuals who do not read but can understand the language in which the instructions are spoken. The instructions are available in both English and Spanish.

**Legal and ethical considerations.** As noted in the introduction to the test review section, any measure of GMA can be expected to show mean score differences by race. These race differences may require employers to expend effort to show that tests are unbiased and job related.

**Computer/Internet applications.** None.

**Current research status.** The Beta III was last updated in 1999. Revisions included improving the quality of the testing materials, replacing outdated or potentially biased items, replacing the Paper Form Board with Matrix Reasoning, extending the age range from 64 years to 89 years, improving clinical utility and validity, improving the ceiling, and updating the norms.

**Use in organizational practice.** To the extent that this test is used in organizational settings, it is most applicable for assessing individuals who are illiterate. We have never encountered it being used in an organizational setting.

**Future developments.** Whereas the test recently underwent a revision and renorming in 1999, we doubt that there will be extensive need for additional research.

## REFERENCES

American Educational Research Association, American Psychological Association, & National Council of Measurement in Education. (1999). *Standards for educational and psychological testing.* Washington, DC: American Psychological Association.

Berk, R.A. (1982). *Handbook of methods for detecting test bias.* Baltimore: Johns Hopkins University Press.

Bobko, P., Roth, P.L., & Potosky, D. (1999). Derivation and implications of a meta-analytic matrix incorporating cognitive ability, alternative predictors, and job performance. *Personnel Psychology, 52,* 561–590.

Carey, N. (1994). Computer predictors of mechanical job performance: Marine Corps findings. *Military Psychology, 6,* 1–30.

Carroll, J.B. (1993). *Human cognitive abilities: A survey of factor-analytic studies.* New York: Cambridge University Press.

Carroll, J.B. (1996). A three-stratum theory of intelligence: Spearman's contribution. In I. Dennis & P. Tapsfield (Eds.), *Human abilities: Their nature and measurement* (pp. 1–17). Mahwah, NJ: Erlbaum.

Chan, D., & Schmitt, N. (1997). Video-based versus paper-and-pencil method of assessment in situational judgment tests: Subgroup differences in test performance and face validity perceptions. *Journal of Applied Psychology, 82,* 143–159.

Chan, D., Schmitt, N., DeShon, R.P., Clause, C.C., & Delbridge, K. (1997). Reactions to cognitive ability tests: The relationship between race, test performance, face validity perceptions, and test taking motivation. *Journal of Applied Psychology, 82,* 300–310.

Dreger, R.M., & Miller, K.S. (1960). Comparative psychological studies of Negros and Whites in the United States. *Psychological Bulletin, 57,* 361–402.

ePredix, Inc. (2001). Test of Learning Ability (Forms S01 and T01) Technical Manual. Minneapolis, MN: Author.

Freedle, T., & Kostin, I. (1990). Item difficulty of four verbal item types and an index of differential item functioning for Black and White examinees. *Journal of Educational Measurement, 27,* 329–343.

Freedle, T., & Kostin, I. (1997). Predicting Black and White differential item functioning in verbal analogy performance. *Intelligence, 24,* 417–444.

Galton, F. (1892). *Hereditary Genius.* London: Macmillan.

Hensley, A.C., & Morris, T.R. (1992). *A comparison of computer and paper media in psychological testing.* Unpublished thesis, Wright-Patterson Air Force Base, Ohio, Department of the Air Force, Air Force Institute of Technology.

Herrnstein, R.J., & Murray, C. (1994). *The bell curve: Intelligence and class structure in American life.* New York: Free Press.

Hunter, J.E. (1980). *Validity generalization for 12,000 jobs: An application of synthetic validity and validity generalization to the General Aptitude Test Battery (GATB).* Washington, DC: U.S. Department of Labor, Employment Service.

Hunter, J.E. (1986). Cognitive ability, cognitive aptitudes, job knowledge, and job performance. *Journal of Vocational Behavior, 29,* 340–362.

Hunter, J.E., & Hunter, R.F. (1984). Validity and utility of alternative predictors of job performance. *Psychological Bulletin, 96,* 72–98.

Hunter, J.E., Schmidt, F.L., & Judiesch, M.K. (1990). Individual differences in output variability as a function of job complexity. *Journal of Applied Psychology, 75,* 28–42.

Jensen, A.R. (1973). *Educability and group differences.* London: Metheun.

Jensen, A.R. (1985). The nature of Black-White differences on various psychometric tests. *Behavioral and Brain Sciences, 8,* 193–263.

Kellogg, C.E., & Morton, N.W. (1999). *Beta III manual.* San Antonio, TX: The Psychological Corporation.

Loehlin, J.C., Lindzey, G., & Spuhler, J.N. (1975). *Race differences in intelligence.* New York: Freeman.

McCauley, C.D., & Mendoza, J. (1985). A simulation study of item bias using a two-parameter item response model. *Applied Psychological Measurement, 9,* 389–400.

Neisser, U., Boodoo, G., Bouchard, T.J. Jr., Boykin, A.W., Brody, N., Ceci, S.J., Halpern, D.F., Loehlin, J.C., Perlof, R., Sternberg, R.J., & Urbina, S. (1996). Intelligence: Knowns and unknowns. *American Psychologist, 51,* 77–101.

O'Connor, M.C. (1989). Aspects of differential performance by minorities on standardized tests: Linguistic and sociocultural factors. In B.R. Gifford (Ed.), *Test policy and test performance: Education, language and culture* (pp. 129–181). Boston: Kluwer Academic.

O'Neil, H.F., & Brown, R.S. (1997). *Differential effects of question formats in math assessment on metacognition and effect.* (Tech. Rep. No. 449). Los Angeles: University of California, National Center for Research on Evaluation, Standards, and Student Testing.

Pearlman, K., Schmidt, F.L. & Hunter, J.E. (1980). Validity generalization results for tests used to predict job proficiency and training success in clerical occupations. *Journal of Applied Psychology, 65,* 373–406.

Pulakos, E.D., & Schmitt, N. (1996). An evaluation of two strategies for reducing adverse impact and their effects on criterion-related validity. *Human Performance, 9,* 241–258.

Raven, J. and others. (2000). *Raven manual research supplement 3. American norms. Neuropsychological applications. 2000 edition.* Oxford: Oxford Psychologists Press.

Raven, J., Raven, J.C., & Court, J.H. (1998a). *Raven manual: Section 1. General overview. 1998 edition.* Oxford: Oxford Psychologists Press.

Raven, J., Raven, J.C., & Court, J.H. (1998b). *Raven manual: Section 4. General overview. 1998 edition.* Oxford: Oxford Psychologists Press.

Ree, M.J., & Earles, J.A. (1991). Predicting training success: Not much more than g. *Personnel Psychology, 44,* 321–332.

Ree, M.J., & Earles, J.A. (1992). Intelligence is the best predictor of job performance. *Current Directions in Psychological Science, 1,* 86–89.

Ree, M.J., Earles, J.A., & Teachout, M.S. (1994). Predicting job performance: Not much more than g. *Journal of Applied Psychology, 79,* 518–524.

Rosenbach, J.H. (1994). The RBH test of Learning Ability. In D.J. Keyser & R.S. Sweetland (Eds.), *Test critiques. Volume 10.* Austin, TX: Pro-ed.

Roth, P.L., Bevier, C.A., Bobko, P., Switzer, F.S. III, & Tyler, P. (2001). Ethnic group differences in cognitive ability in employment and educational settings: A meta-analysis. *Personnel Psychology, 54,* 297–330.

Sackett, P.R. (1998). Performance assessment in education and professional certification: Lessons for personnel selection. In M.D. Hakel (Ed.), *Beyond multiple-choice: Evaluating alternatives to traditional testing for selection* (pp. 113–129). Mahwah, NJ: Erlbaum.

Sackett, P.R., Schmitt, N., Ellingson, J.E., & Kabin, M.B. (2001). High-stakes testing in employment, credentialing, and higher education: Prospects in a post-affirmative-action world. *American Psychologist, 54,* 302–318.

Sackett, P.R., & Wilk, S.L. (1994). Within-group norming and other forms of score adjusting in preemployment testing. *American Psychologist, 49,* 929–954.

Scheuneman, J., & Gerritz, K. (1990). Using differential item functioning procedures to explore sources of item difficulty and group performance characteristics. *Journal of Educational Measurement, 27,* 109–131.

Schmidt, F.L., & Hunter, J.E. (1977). Development of a general solution to the problem of validity generalization. *Journal of Applied Psychology, 62,* 529–540.

Schmidt, F.L., & Hunter, J.E. (1983). Individual differences in productivity: An empirical test of estimates derived from studies of selection procedure utility. *Journal of Applied Psychology, 68,* 407–415.

Schmidt, F.L., & Hunter, J.E. (1992). Development of causal models of processes determining job performance. *Current Directions in Psychological Science, 1,* 89–92.

Schmidt, F.L., & Hunter, J.E. (1998). The validity and utility of selection methods in personnel psychology: Practical and theoretical implications of 85 years of research findings. *Psychological Bulletin, 124,* 262–274.

Schmidt, F.L., Hunter, J.E., McKenzie, R.C., & Muldrow, T.W. (1979). The impact of valid selection procedures on work-force productivity. *Journal of Applied Psychology, 64,* 609–626.

Schmidt, F.L., Hunter, J.E., & Outerbridge, A.N. (1986). The impact of job experience and ability on job knowledge, work sample performance, and supervisory ratings of job performance. *Journal of Applied Psychology, 71,* 432–439.

Schmidt, F.L., Hunter, J.E., Pearlman, K., & Shane, G.S. (1979). Further tests of the Schmidt-Hunter Bayesian Validity Generalization Model. *Personnel Psychology, 32,* 257–281.

Schmidt, F.L., Mack, M.J., & Hunter, J.E. (1984). Selection utility in the occupation of U.S. Park Ranger for three modes of test use. *Journal of Applied Psychology, 69,* 490–497.

Steele, C.M. (1997). A threat in the air: How stereotypes shape intellectual identity and performance. *American Psychologist, 52,* 613–629.

Steele, C.M., & Aronson, J. (1995). Stereotype threat and the intellectual test performance of African Americans. *Journal of Personality and Social Psychology, 69,* 797–811.

Thorndike, R.L. (1985). The central role of general ability in prediction. *Multivariate Behavioral Research, 20,* 241–254.

Thurstone, L.L. & Thurstone, T.G. (1998). *Thurstone Test of Mental Alertness (TMA) examiner's manual.* Minneapolis: NCS Pearson.

Watson, G.B. & Glaser, E.M. (1994*). Watson-Glaser Critical Thinking Appraisal Form S manual.* San Antonio, TX: The Psychological Corporation.

Wesman, A.G. (1965). *Wesman Personnel Classification Test.* San Antonio, TX: The Psychological Corporation.

Whitney, D.J., & Schmitt, N. (1997). Relationship between culture and response to biodata employment items. *Journal of Applied Psychology, 82,* 113–129.

Wigdor, A.K., & Garner, W.R. (1982). *Ability testing: Uses, consequences and controversies. Part I: Report of the committee.* Washington, DC: National Academy Press.

Williams, W.M., & Ceci, S.J. (1997). Are Americans becoming more or less alike? Trends in race, class, and ability differences in intelligence. *American Psychologist, 52,* 1226–1235.

Wilson, K.M. (1981). Analyzing the long-term performance of minority and nonminority students: A tale of two studies. *Research in Higher Education, 15,* 351–375.

Wonderlic Personnel Test, Inc. (www.wonderlic.com).

Wonderlic, Inc. (2000). *Wonderlic Personnel Test and Scholastic Level Exam.* Libertyville, IL: Author.

CHAPTER 3

# Mechanical Aptitude and Spatial Ability Testing

PAUL M. MUCHINSKY

This chapter addresses the assessment of mechanical aptitude and spatial ability. The union of these two assessments is more a product of their similarity of use in personnel selection than the similarity of their conceptual origins or content. I believe they are often conjoined in an expository treatise because of an affinity in how the test items are presented. There may be some manifestations of spatial ability in selected items assessing mechanical aptitude, but in most cases the respective item domains are distinct.

Historically the emergence of spatial ability items occurred first, as relating to the construct of intelligence originally proposed over 100 years ago. The two classic theoretical bases of intelligence have contrasted mental ability as a single, general construct versus a constellation of specific mental abilities. Three of the classic specific mental abilities are quantitative, verbal, and spatial. Quantitative ability reflects fluency with numbers, verbal ability reflects fluency with words, and spatial ability reflects fluency with visualization and manipulation of objects in space. The space is invariably assessed two-dimensionally, as constrained by objects depicted in a printed medium. However, in theory (and ideally), the assessment would be conducted in three-dimensional space, being veridical with the external domain to which assessment inferences are drawn. Conversely, the most popular conception of mental ability is as a unitary or general construct. That is, mental ability is theorized to have a single, general basis, as opposed to a set of specific mental abilities. Assessments of a construct do (or should) follow from its theoretical spec-

ification. When items are selected or developed for a test of general mental ability (GMA), they most often consist of numerical and verbal abilities. That is, the "specific" mental abilities of numerical and verbal ability are conceptually reconstituted to measure "general" mental ability. Noticeably absent in tests of GMA are items assessing spatial ability. Thus, in the growing theoretical acceptance of the GMA construct, spatial ability has been relegated to the status of the conceptual "ugly stepchild" not invited to join its numerical and verbal siblings. An illustrative item from a test of spatial ability is shown in Figure 3.1.

Assessment of mechanical aptitude first appeared in the 1930s. Items measuring mechanical aptitude are characterized by their manner of presentation. Similar to items measuring spatial ability, mechanical aptitude tests often depict images of objects reflective of some mechanical functions or actions. The pictorial stimuli portray the application of the laws of physics or motion as represented in the use of household or conventional objects, such as a measuring cup, a child's swing, or an automobile. The underlying concepts being measured by these objects include sound and heat conductance, velocity, gravity, and force. Other types of items can include the identification and use of tools, measuring instruments, and machines. Other manifestations of items assessing mechanical ability can extend into reading industrial blueprints, knowledge of electricity, and machine maintenance. Technically it is a matter of debate whether electrical and mechanical knowledge are distinctive, or whether they

Consider the following figures:

Which of the following figures would be created by combining them?

(a)

(b)

(c)

(d)

Figure 3.1   Sample item from a typical test of spatial ability.

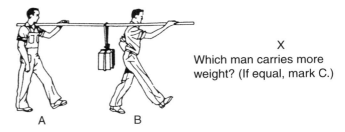

X
Which man carries more weight? (If equal, mark C.)

Figure 3.2   Sample item from the Bennett Mechanical Comprehension Test. Source: Copyright © 1976 by The Psychological Corporation.

both fall under the general rubric of "mechanical aptitude." For example, the engineering profession clearly differentiates electrical engineering from mechanical engineering, both in the design of engineering curricula offered in postsecondary education as well as the sections of a professional licensure examination. On the other hand, it would not be unusual for production workers, machine maintenance and repair workers, and technicians to be expected to have some proficiency in both mechanical and electrical domains of knowledge. In my experience, these bodies of knowledge begin to diverge in the respective job requirements only at the higher levels of aptitude required in industrial jobs. As such, one can reasonably conclude that, at least at lower levels of required aptitude, knowledge of electricity is a legitimate component of mechanical aptitude. As the aptitude level increases beyond a rudimentary level, the two domains of mechanical and electrical knowledge begin to have their own separate respective identities. An illustrative item from a test of mechanical aptitude is shown in Figure 3.2.

## JOBS/FUNCTIONS

A theme that unites mechanical aptitude and spatial ability tests is their common range of application. These two assessments are often used for personnel selection or advancement in jobs most typically associated with manufacturing or production. Such jobs have requisite requirements in matters pertaining to the operation, maintenance, and repair of in-

dustrial machinery or equipment, and related operations. The fundamental concepts involved in the conduct of this type of work most frequently embrace the application of the laws of physics and motion evidenced in machine operations. Knowledge of basic mechanical operations such as pulleys, gears, levers, and fulcrums are often associated with higher levels of job performance among people imbued with what is commonly referenced as "mechanical reasoning." At the core of mechanical reasoning is knowledge of how such concepts as mass, weight, density, velocity, and acceleration are represented in industrial work activities. Thus, mechanical aptitude and spatial ability assessments are often the hallmark of selection and advancement in traditional blue-collar jobs. They are not used for selection into managerial or supervisory jobs, nor are they typically used for selection into the functional areas of business such as accounting, finance, information systems, human resources, or sales.[1] I know of no traditional two-year junior colleges or four-year colleges that use assessments of mechanical aptitude and/or spatial ability to evaluate applicants. I am aware of selected programs in vocational/technical schools that do use assessments of mechanical aptitude to evaluate candidates. Finally, I know of no jobs in the health-related service sector that utilize assessments of mechanical aptitude and/or spatial ability.

## TEST VALIDITY

The past twenty years have witnessed the publication of several large meta-analytic reviews (e.g., Hunter & Hunter, 1984) of the literature on methods of personnel selection. The major focal point of such studies is on the respective criterion-related validity of the various types of assessment for personnel selection. A notable exemplar of this type of research study was written by Schmidt and Hunter (1998). The authors meta-analyzed the extant literature base on 19 types of assessments used for personnel selection, including tests of GMA, work sample tests, interviews, biographical data, and so on. Assessments of mechanical aptitude and spatial ability were not among the methods in their analysis. The authors concluded that GMA was the single most useful predictor of job performance and training across all jobs. The average validity coefficient for general mental ability was .51, and when used in combination with other selected assessment methods (as the interview), the level of predictive accuracy was enhanced to slightly above .60. The authors' major conclusion was stated: "Because of its special status, GMA can be considered the primary measure for hiring decisions, and one can consider the remaining 18 personnel measures as supplements to GMA measures" (p. 266). This conclusion is consistent with other statements that basically resolve that an assessment of GMA is about all one ever needs to make accurate and efficiently generated predictions of job performance. Hunter and Schmidt (1996) aptly presented the social, economic, and policy implications for such a conclusion. GMA (or as noted symbolically, $g$) has thus been touted as a "one-size-fits-all" solution for personnel selection assessment needs. As such, some authors have referred to this type of thinking as a "$g$-ocentric" solution to assessment.

Although assessments of mechanical aptitude were *not* included in the Schmidt and Hunter (1998) meta-analytic review, there is little doubt that GMA would emerge as a superior method of assessment compared with mechanical aptitude across all jobs. Indeed, it should be, since assessment of mechanical aptitude is not relevant for, nor intended for use in, "all jobs." In the full spectrum of jobs in society, GMA has very wide applicability. Conversely, in that same spectrum, assessments of mechanical aptitude would have very narrow applicability. It is the equivalent of shooting a shotgun versus a rifle. If it is one's intent to hit a broad target, a shotgun is the weapon of choice. However, if the target is very narrow, a rifle that fires a single bullet is the better weapon. Dunnette (1993) has used a different metaphor to describe assessment issues—that of a hammer. A hammer is a most apt metaphor for a discussion of mechanical aptitude. If a person were to have only one hammer in a tool chest, the conventional carpenter's claw hammer would be preferred. It has the widest applicability and, not surprisingly, is a staple of most workbenches. However, there are other occasions where the conventional hammer is not best suited for the job, be it gentle tapping (e.g., a tack hammer) or splitting wood (e.g., a sledge hammer). Jobs in the manufacturing sector requiring mechanical knowledge are more appropriately served by tests of mechanical aptitude than GMA.

I have no quarrel with the conclusion that GMA is the single best predictor across all jobs. However, in real life that conclusion is somewhat facile (if not specious). In practical reality a single organization is never populated with "all jobs." Although GMA may be the most broadly applicable predictor, other methods of selection are superior for certain types of jobs. These jobs are in the small minority given the full spectrum, but they belie the doctrine of the manifest destiny of the superiority of GMA over all other possible types of assessment. One such type of job would be a commercial artist or renderer. If an organization wanted the single best assessment of a candidate's ability to draw, paint, or sketch, a portfolio of past work (literally a work sample) would provide a more accurate inference about future job potential than the candidate's score on a test of GMA. Similarly, it is difficult to imagine that a test of GMA would be a better forecaster of performance for an on-air television job (e.g., news or weather anchor) than inspecting a videotape of past performance in a similar context. I would also unequivocally place tests of mechanical aptitude in such a favored status over tests of GMA in selecting employees for jobs in manufacturing or industrial maintenance. Proponents of the $g$-ocentric school of thinking would justifiably claim that artists, TV personalities, and machine operators are not "typical" jobs in society. Perhaps they are not, but they are legitimate jobs in our economy, even though they may be some of the exceptions to the eminent domain rule of GMA as the most widely applicable method of assessment.

What empirical evidence can be offered to corroborate the assertion that tests of mechanical aptitude are superior to tests of GMA with industrial employees? Very little research directly compares the two types of assessment with regard to predictive accuracy in such jobs. Part of the paucity of research stems from the rather "unfashionable" nature of studying industrial production workers. Such employee populations lack the panache of managers, scientists, engineers, and sales personnel as objects of scientific study. When industrial production workers are studied, it is rare to be able to directly compare the predictive accuracy of tests of mechanical aptitude and GMA. I conducted one such study several years ago (Muchinsky, 1993). The sample was approximately 200 industrial production workers who manufactured electromechanical components. The employees were administered the Bennett Mechanical Comprehension Test (Bennett, 1980) and the Thurstone Test of Mental Alertness (Thurstone & Thurstone, 1998). The Thurstone test has a quantitative component and a verbal component, and both of these dimensions can be combined into a total score. The current job performance of the employees was evaluated by their immediate supervisor using a 15-dimension performance appraisal instrument designed exclusively for the validation study. The sum of the evaluations on the 15 factors served as the overall criterion of job performance. The concurrent criterion-related validity coefficient for the Bennett Test of Mechanical Comprehension based on the total sample was

.38 (uncorrected). The validity coefficients for the quantitative, verbal, and total scores of the Thurstone Test of Mental Alertness were .22, .13, and .18, respectively. In summary, the validity of a test of mechanical aptitude was clearly superior to a test of GMA in this study of industrial production workers.

On conceptual grounds, what would be the logic of presuming that higher scores on assessments of GMA are associated with higher levels of job performance in manufacturing jobs? The logic would proceed as follows. If people are bright enough to exhibit fluency with words (e.g., vocabulary, analogies) and numbers (e.g., derivations, progressions), they would be bright enough to understand industrial material flow, machine operations, and diagnostic/repair functions. Thus, GMA would be predictive (to some degree) of performance in typical manufacturing jobs. I do not assert that tests of GMA are devoid of predictability for such jobs, but rather that they are less predictive than tests of mechanical aptitude. Why might this be so? I believe the answer (or at least an answer) lies in the subtle distinction between aptitude and ability. The conventional distinction between aptitude and ability is that "aptitude" represents an amalgam of ability and (vocational) interest. Although the terms "aptitude" and "ability" are often used interchangeably (and thus incorrectly) in assessment (while admitting that a fine line can, and often does, separate the two), I believe the format of the items in a mechanical aptitude test can have an engaging, invitational, if not curiously playful quality to it. People who have an *interest* in trying to deduce the "right answer" to a question about density, reflected in a diagram, for example, of two objects floating in water with different degrees of submersion are, in my opinion, intrigued by the very presentation of the question. I have administered tests of mechanical aptitude for more than 30 years. I have noted a pattern between the overt behaviors of test takers following my administration of a mechanical aptitude test and their score on the test. Among high scorers it is not at all uncommon to find two or three of them "debating" their respective answer to a particular question following the conclusion of the test. Likewise, among low scorers I have observed grim-faced people muttering comments such as "I just don't like tests like this. I'm not good at them." Such a comment succinctly combines their expressed interest level with their assessed ability level, both of which were low. I believe it is the individuals' inherent interest in tests of mechanical aptitude (coupled with their ability) that is related to their inherent interest (and performance) on the job. In summary, the range of jobs in the population for which tests of mechanical aptitude and spatial ability are relevant is small, especially compared with the broad relevance of GMA. However, these tests are highly relevant and useful for those jobs, and they deserve a small but legitimate role in the assessment repertoire. A small target needs to be hit with an accurate shot. Mechanical aptitude and spatial ability tests serve that function for manufacturing-related jobs.

## CONCERNS

The classic twin criteria for evaluating tests used for personnel selection are validity and adverse impact (Sackett, Schmitt, Ellingson, & Kabin, 2001; Sackett & Wilk, 1994). An evaluation of the validity of tests of mechanical aptitude and spatial ability is very positive (provided they are used in jobs for which they are appropriate). Unfortunately, the verdict on adverse impact is substantially negative. Although most evidence on adverse impact by race is not large, the degree of adverse impact by gender is large. Males consistently outperform females on tests of mechanical aptitude and spatial ability. The mean difference in test scores between males and females has exceeded the standard deviation on some tests of mechanical aptitude. In the study by Muchinsky (1993), for example, the average score for males on the Bennett Test of Mechanical Comprehension was 7.34 points higher than the average score for females. Less pronounced differences have occurred in assessments of spatial ability. Although gender differences in composite measures of GMA have generally not been found, males, on average, do score higher than females on the specific factor of spatial ability. The empirical evidence indicates males have somewhat greater fluency than females in rotating objects in space and other manifestations of spatial ability.

The male-female difference on scores of mechanical aptitude is seemingly more understandable than the (lesser) difference in spatial ability. The research literature reveals large gender differences in response to interest inventory items. There is a strong interest component to mechanical aptitude measurement. Traditionally, more boys than girls enroll in shop or "mechanical arts" classes in high school. Males are typically more involved than females in mechanically oriented activities such as the repair and maintenance of automobiles and other motorized vehicles. This is also a physical ability dimension to mechanical activities. Some mechanical activities involve moderate to heavy lifting. Males have more upper-body and arm strength than do females, which induces females away from mechanical pursuits. Some of the long-standing tests of mechanical aptitude continue to exhibit strong gender differences in average test scores.[2] One recently developed test of mechanical aptitude has attempted to reduce the gender-based difference in score by using as examples objects that women would have more exposure to, such as high-heeled shoes, kitchen utensils and appliances, and so on. Because these tests are relatively new, an insufficient norm base is present upon which to draw reliable conclusions regarding reduced gender impact by inclusion of the more "female-friendly" questions.

Although in theory the laws of physics and motion have timeless applicability, questions on some of the long-standing tests of mechanical aptitude suffer from problems of face validity. For example, some items involve the depiction of an automobile, but even the most recent editions of these tests (copyright in the 1980s) depict automobiles that appear to be of 1940s vintage. Though they are line drawings, and the model of the automobile is irrelevant to the mechanical issue in question (e.g., whether a car's horn sounds louder in a tunnel versus on the open road), it is possible that women are more dissuaded than men from attempting to answer questions with such dated depictions. Similar problems occur in line drawings depicting dated clothing styles worn by male and female figures in the questions. Whether the cause of the male-female difference in average score is due to differential life experiences, vocational interests, physical abilities, or responses to items with questionable face validity, the gender difference in performance on tests of mechanical aptitude is substantial. The Civil Rights Act of 1991 expressly forbids score adjustments by gender, precluding an option that some companies entertained in previous years.

The overall results of mechanical aptitude and spatial ability tests judged against the twin criteria of validity and fairness yields the classic dilemma: high validity coupled with high adverse impact (particularly by gender). As Sackett et al. (2001) noted, attempts to reduce adverse impact by deletion of selected items that produce the greatest gender effect could well reduce the criterion-related validity of the test. Attempts at reducing adverse impact (of all kinds of tests) by coaching and practice have met with limited success. It appears that prevalent societal differences between men and women in preferences for, and participation in, jobs involving mechanical activities are reflected in the gender-based difference in scores on tests of mechanical aptitude. As Sackett et al. described, the fact that many employers value both diversity and productivity must be addressed head-on. Perhaps organizational needs to diversify their workforce by gender at the production level are not as acute as in other levels of the organization, as in management, for example. Nevertheless, while production/maintenance work is rarely regarded as a "high-status" job, the job often pays more than other classifications (such as clerical), and employment can be steady. In conclusion, strict reliance on mechanical aptitude and spatial ability tests in making personnel decisions will undoubtedly serve to abet the gender differences already present in the proportional composition of industrial workers by gender. A discussion of additional issues follows the presentation of the tests of spatial ability and mechanical aptitude.

## TESTS

### Employee Aptitude Survey (2nd ed.)

The Employee Aptitude Survey (EAS; Ruch, Stang, McKillip, & Dye, 1994) is a battery of 10 ability tests, one of which is Space Visualization. The EAS was constructed using the guiding principle of maximum validity per minute of testing time. The hallmark of this test is its very brief (5 minutes) time of administration. The questions consist of depictions of variously shaped squares and rectangles, portrayed as boxes. Each question consists of a different configuration of boxes, both in number and juxtaposition. The questions pertain to identifying the number of boxes that are touching each other (i.e., boxes that share a common surface area). It is a classic test of spatial ability in that it requires the examinee to envision two-dimensionally portrayed images in three-dimensional space, and to answer questions pertaining to such a configuration. The total score on the test is the number of questions answered correctly. Since the test is timed, as are most tests of spatial ability, there is concern about questions answered incorrectly versus questions that were never attempted in the 5-minute time limit. The test is available in Spanish, Polish, German, and Indonesian. As a 5-minute test, there are legitimate questions about the social validity of the test. That is, to what degree is it acceptable to make decisions regarding suitability for employment based on a 5-minute sample of behavior? I believe this concern can be partially allayed by using the test in combination with other tests appropriate for relevant job classes, such as tests of reading ability, industrial math, and mechanical aptitude. I have used the Space Visualization test on several occasions in my career, and I have found it particularly useful in the selection of packers and shippers (such as the loading of a cargo truck that maximizes the usable space in the packing area).

As is the case with most tests of spatial ability and mechanical aptitude, there is a strong nonverbal component to the questions. The stimuli appear before examinees in the form of a sketch, diagram, or drawing. The examinees must have sufficient reading ability to understand the questions being asked, but the answer is derived from examination of an image, not words. Accordingly, I've experienced less of a decrement in scores with tests of spatial ability (versus reading ability) for applicants where English is not their first language. The Space Visualization test is now available electronically, a recent advancement in the administration of the EAS. I believe the Space Visualization test is one of the more pure measures of spatial ability commercially available. It can be purchased, administered, and interpreted independently of the other tests in the EAS battery. I hold a high opinion of this subtest of the EAS, as it is supported by extensive psychometric evidence as reported in the test manual. Although no single test should ever be the sole basis of an employment decision, I am particularly sensitized to this issue given its very brief administrative time. Nevertheless, I regard the EAS Space Visualization test as a valuable and useful member of an assessment portfolio.

## Revised Minnesota Paper Form Board Test (2nd ed.)

The Revised Minnesota Paper Form Board Test (RMPFBT) is the most venerable method of assessing spatial ability. First developed in the 1930s, it has stood the test of time as a means of assessment. The test has a 20-minute time limit and is available in two forms. It is also available in both machine-scorable and hand-scorable versions. The equivalence of the two forms has been established. The test is comprised of 64 items that have the examinee match a geometric object to one of five possible rearrangements. The items increase in difficulty throughout the test. The RMPFBT has recently undergone a cosmetic overhaul. The test booklet cover, answer sheets, and scoring keys have been redesigned, and the manual has been updated. The actual questions, however, have not been changed. The manual reports supportive validity data to justify use of the test for industrial application. It also states that more recent research indicates the gender gap in average test score is narrowing.

The RMPFBT is available in one foreign language edition (French). Given the growing influx of Hispanic workers in industrial jobs, I hope the test will one day be available in Spanish. I am not aware of any intent by the publisher to make this test available via electronic technology. The greater administration time of the RMPFBT (20 minutes) compared with the EAS Space Visualization test (5 minutes) tips the scale in favor of the former for greater social validity. However, the 20-minute time limit could serve to decrease its attractiveness if it were to be combined with other tests with longer times of administration culminating in an unwieldy battery. One of the traditional uses of this test is for assessing students in vocational/technical schools and retraining workers in vocational rehabilitation centers. The RMPFBT has norms based on larger samples than nearly all other tests of spatial ability and mechanical aptitude. Published reviews of the RMPFBT have generally included the caveat that use of this test is more supportable for training and guidance than

for personnel selection. Although I cannot disagree with this statement for tests of unknown psychometric quality, most certainly the RMPFBT is among the most heavily used tests for the selection of industrial workers, having been administered for 70 years to thousands of examinees. The classic standards for test interpretation and use apply to the RMPFBT (as to all tests), such as understanding the meaning of the standard error of measurement and not placing exclusive reliance on a single test score in making personnel decisions. However, if the extensive body of knowledge gleaned about this test from its many years of use does not inspire confidence regarding its value, it is difficult to imagine what other test of spatial ability would evoke a more confident appraisal by the administrator. In summary, my assessment of the RMPFBT is wholly positive, subject to the standard concerns about the interpretation and use of all tests. The RMPFBT is one of the classics in the field of psychological assessment.

## Bennett Mechanical Comprehension Test (2nd ed.)

The Bennett Mechanical Comprehension Test (BMCT; Bennett, 1980) is the most venerable assessment of mechanical aptitude. Coupled with the RMPFBT, this two-test battery comprises the most frequently used means of assessing mechanical aptitude and spatial ability. The BMCT was first published in 1940. The current version consists of 68 questions with a 30-minute time limit. Each question portrays a line drawing illustrating an object that reflects the concepts of force, energy, density, velocity, and so on. The examinee must choose from three possible answers. The test is published in two parallel forms (Forms S and T). Tape recordings of the test questions read aloud are available for use with examinees who have limited reading abilities. A version of the test is written in Spanish.

A very large amount of validational evidence supports use of the test. The norms are based on thousands of examinee scores, and compelling criterion-related validity evidence indicates that the test is predictive of success in training and job performance for jobs requiring mechanical aptitude. I consider the BMCT to be the premier method of assessing mechanical aptitude. However, the test is not without its problems, despite its legacy within the field of assessment. A pronounced gender effect is persistently evident for scores on the test. This may be due, in part, to two factors associated with the questions. Although most of the questions reflect mechanical concepts that appear to be "gender neutral" in substance (e.g., the differential rate at which snow would melt under a black versus a white cloth), some questions portray mechanical concepts involving objects that females may be less familiar with than males. Examples include depictions of gears, pulleys, and hand tools. An item analysis would reveal whether these items produce exaggerated gender differences in score. The second issue, as noted previously in this chapter, is that the line drawings of automobiles and clothing styles are extremely dated. No automobiles of today look like those depicted in the drawings. Perhaps their presentation produces a differential effect on females versus males with regard to face validity.

The total score on the test is the number of questions answered correctly. I have administered the BMCT very often in my career, and I would estimate less than 5% of all examinees attempt all 68 questions in the 30-minute time limit. I would be interested in psychometric evidence that examines the validity of the test as a function of the number of correct answers as related to the numbers of items attempted. Perhaps research could explore the effect of increasing the time limit, perhaps to 40 minutes. Though my concerns about the test are long-standing, the BMCT remains a classic in the field of assessment. There is room for improvement in the design of the test, which more recently developed tests of mechanical aptitude have tried to address. Nevertheless, the BMCT remains the standard against which all other tests of mechanical aptitude are judged.

## Maintest

Maintest (Ramsay, 1991) was developed to measure the mechanical and electrical knowledge and skills required for industrial machine maintenance jobs. If the distinction between ability and aptitude can be blurred, so too can the distinction between aptitude and achievement tests. In theory, achievement tests measure the mastery of a body of learned knowledge, while aptitude tests measure suitability to learn a body of knowledge. Maintest splits the elusive difference between these two assessment rationales. It consists of 153 multiple-choice items covering 21 knowledge areas: hydraulics, pneumatics, welding, power transmission, lubrication, pumps, piping, rigging, mechanical maintenance, shop machines, combustion, motors, digital electronics, schematics and print reading, control circuits, power supplies, AC/DC theory, power distribution, computers and PLC, test instruments, and electrical maintenance. The test is intended for use with applicants for jobs where mechanical and electrical knowledge are requisite for job performance. The test is untimed, but the publisher indicates the test should be completed in 2.5 hours.

Maintest is published by The Ramsay Corporation, the leading producer of tests specifically designed for assessing candidates for industrial jobs at the higher end of the distribution of mechanical/electrical knowledge. This test is *not* a

"basic aptitude test" in the sense of the BMCT. I have used Ramsay Corporation tests on several occasions in my own work. I have mixed reviews of their tests, but generally they are more positive than negative. On the negative side is the consistent scant information of a psychometric nature regarding the test's quality and usability. Norms are based on very small samples, which is true of many higher-end aptitude/achievement tests. I have had to rely on my own internal validation studies to establish validity and propose passing scores. The second limitation is that the content domain of these knowledge tests is far from universal. For example, I have submitted the prints and schematics test to companies as a prospective means of assessing applicants, only to be informed "the blueprints and schematics we work with in our company don't look anything like some of those depicted in the test." As such, the more technical and specific the test questions, the lower is their generalizability and applicability. On the positive side, I know of no other publisher of tests in the high-end areas of mechanical and electrical knowledge. The 21 subtests of the Maintest do cover the domain of knowledge needed for maintenance mechanics. It is some of the specific questions within the subtests that may be problematic. In short, The Ramsay Corporation has a niche market. Although there are legitimate concerns about some aspects of Maintest (and other tests they publish), few other alternatives are on the market. Furthermore, the sheer volume of people who would ever take such advanced tests as Maintest is limited, thereby automatically precluding the creation of large sample norms and other psychometric indicators of test quality as evidenced with the BMCT, for example. I consider Maintest to be a major test within this general area of assessment, although the demand for its use will undoubtedly be limited.

## MecTest

MecTest (Ramsay, 1998/2000) is primarily an abbreviated version of Maintest, published by The Ramsay Corporation. The MecTest consists of 60 multiple-choice questions covering 11 areas: hydraulics, pneumatics, welding, power transmission, lubrication, pumps, piping, rigging, mechanical maintenance, shop machine tools and equipment, and print reading. Although no time limit is mandated, the publisher states the test should be completed in 1 hour. The chief advantage of the MecTest (over the Maintest) is its reduced time of administration. The test is also available in Spanish.

My evaluation of the MecTest is more guarded than of the Maintest. Both tests have the same stated purpose, to measure the mechanical knowledge and skills required for maintenance jobs. It is not clear how the 11 areas assessed in this test were chosen out of the 21 areas assessed in the Maintest. One explanation could be that the electronically oriented areas were excluded from the Maintest, but so too were such areas as combustion and instruments. Nevertheless, my experience with maintenance jobs is they invariably have some electrical component to them. In my opinion, an assessment of a candidate's suitability for employment in a machine maintenance job is incomplete without some evaluation of electrical knowledge. Second, the number of items per content area is not uniform, and in some areas is so small as to be of questionable psychometric value. For example, the welding and piping subtests consist of three items each, while four other subtests have four items each. I would not place much confidence in any assessment of a content area based on three to four items. My preference for constructing the MecTest would be to develop a series of subtests, each consisting of perhaps 15 items. The user could then "mix and match" an assessment tailored to the requirements of a particular job. I have worked with machine maintenance jobs where rigging, for example, is not a relevant component, but as currently constructed rigging is part of the overall assessment.

The MecTest suffers from the same limitations as the Maintest with regard to thin psychometric evidence to support its use. I again attribute this result in part to the limited range of job applicants who would ever take this test. My general experience is that for about every 50 machine workers, perhaps 1 worker is assigned to maintaining the machines. As such I have tempered respect for the inherent difficulty of obtaining large sample norms for such tests. Nevertheless, I have some concerns about the MecTest that cannot be dismissed even given the unusual subject matter being assessed. The principal advantage of the MecTest over the Maintest is its briefer administration time, which at 1 hour is still twice as long as the BMCT.

### Wiesen Test of Mechanical Aptitude

The Wiesen Test (Wiesen, 1997, 1999) is one of the most recently created assessments of mechanical aptitude, developed in 1997. It consists of 60 multiple-choice items with the test having a 30-minute time limit. It is also available in Spanish. Each item consists of a line drawing reflecting the application or illustration of a mechanical concept. Unlike the BMCT, a conscious attempt was made to create items based on their representation in three specific domains: kitchen objects, household objects, and everyday objects. Furthermore, the items were written and are scored based on eight mechanical/physical concepts such as movement of objects, gravity, basic machines, and transfer of heat. The intent of having eight different concepts (each measured by seven or eight items) and three different areas of applications (each consisting of 20 items) was to try to make the test independent of specialized learning about mechanics. In contrast, The Ramsay Corporation tests (e.g., MecTest, Maintest) definitely reflect some degree of job-related or school-related learning. Preliminary validation research indicates that scores on the Wiesen Test correlate about .80 with scores on the BMCT.

Although the amount of psychometric data available on the Wiesen Test is much less than the BMCT, some findings appear promising. The level of adverse impact against females appears considerably less with the Wiesen compared with the BMCT. Unfortunately, there are larger degrees of adverse impact with the Wiesen for racial minorities than for females. The problems of face validity characterized in the BMCT are not evidenced in the Wiesen. None of the line drawings in the test appear to be dated or obsolete. I think the inclusion of kitchen-related objects may have also contributed to the reduction in adverse impact against females.

It is possible to obtain subscores on the test by area of application and by concept area, but I would discourage their separate identification and interpretation. The test should best be used based solely on the total score. Containing eight fewer questions than the BMCT, I surmise a higher proportion of the examinees will complete the test in the allotted time compared with the BMCT. This should serve to weaken criticisms by some examinees that they would have attained a higher score if they had been given enough time to complete the test. The test is not available on tape, as is the BMCT. As noted previously, psychometric evidence is noticeably slim on the Wiesen compared with the BMCT. However, such a result is understandable given its novelty. Nevertheless, the amount of psychometric data with the Wiesen is greater than is found with most tests from The Ramsay Corporation. A reviewer of the Wiesen has described the test as a "welcome attempt to measure mechanical aptitude." Though I have not yet used this test in my own work, I would fully concur with the reviewer's comment.

### Electrical Maintenance Trainee Test

The Electrical Maintenance Trainee Test (Ramsay, 1998) is a member of the family of assessments developed by The Ramsay Corporation. As its title suggests, the focus of this test is an electrical aptitude, rather than strictly mechanical. The test consists of 121 multiple-choice items. Items were written to cover the following content categories: Motors, Digital Electronics, Analog Electronics, Schematics and Electrical Point Reading, Control, Power Supplies, Basic AC/DC Theory, Power Distribution, Test Instruments, Mechanical, Computer and PLC, Hand and Power Tools, Electrical Maintenance, Construction and Installation, Equipment Operation, and Transducers. The test is designed to be completed in 3.5 hours, but the manual states most examinees complete the test in 2.5 hours.

I would describe the test as being more of the "achievement" rather than "aptitude" variety, although the technical distinction between these two types of assessments is not always clear in practice. The test was developed based on subject matter experts' (SMEs) judgments as to the appropriate domain of the test. The manual supports use of the test from a content validity perspective, but no criterion-related validity data are offered. There is also no information provided in the manual regarding adverse impact. I have some substantial concerns regarding the psychometric integrity of content areas measured by a very small number of items. I would have preferred more items devoted to the assessment of fewer content areas. The length of administration time is very long. I am aware of a shorter version of this test (Form UKE-IC), which contains 60 items. I regard this shorter version of the test of electrical aptitude to be comparable to what the MecTest is to the Maintest in the assessment of mechanical aptitude. However, the degree of psychometric evidence to support this shorter version is unknown. With half the number of items, presumably the administration time would also be half.

The longer version of this test represents a comprehensive assessment of electrical aptitude needed to learn the job of an electrical maintenance technician. One could not score well on this test unless the examinee had some prior experience with electrical concepts. For example, there are items pertaining to capacitors, transformers, oscillators, and shunts. Unlike the BMCT, which poses questions that can be understood at an intuitive level, the questions in these electrical tests reflect knowledge that can be acquired only through some formal training or experience in electricity. Such a rationale is most reasonable given the intent of the test is to select candidates either into advanced training programs in electricity or to assess current command of knowledge in electricity. The lack of supporting psychometric data behind these tests is obviously troublesome. Nevertheless, they are intended for use with a very small and narrowly defined population. I know of no other tests on the market that measure electrical aptitude as comprehensively as the Electrical Maintenance Trainee Test. I would not classify this test (in either form) as a job knowledge test, because the items are not specific to any job. Rather, they have applicability to a wide range of jobs requiring possession of electrical knowledge. I believe the test would be useful as part of the assessment process in evaluating candidates. However, such issues as a recommended passing score and the differential impor-

tance of the content areas covered in the test to a particular job or company would all have to be established by the user. The strength of this test is the content matter it assesses. The weaknesses of the test include its lengthy administration time and the lack of guidance as to what specific interpretations should be drawn from test scores after having attained them.

**Differential Aptitude Test**

The Differential Aptitude Test (DAT; Bennett, Seashore, & Wesman, 1984) is one of the classic multiaptitude test batteries in assessment. It assesses eight aptitudes, two of which are mechanical reasoning and space relations. The mechanical reasoning and spatial ability tests can be purchased, scored, and interpreted independently of the others. This test has three versions. First is the original version, now in its fifth edition. The original version is, in essence, the "long" version of the test. The complete eight-test assessment takes approximately 3.5 hours to complete. Each test also has two parallel forms. The second version of the test is the "short" version and is referenced as the "DAT for Personnel and Career Assessment." This version takes approximately 2 hours to complete. There is no parallel form for these tests. The third version is computerized and takes 90 minutes to complete.

I have used the traditional long version of this test, but neither the short version nor the computerized version. The mechanical reasoning test presents items that are highly similar in style and content to the BMCT. Indeed, George Bennett authored the items for the test. The BMCT contains 68 items, while the mechanical reasoning test (long version) contains 60 questions. The spatial relations test (long version) contains 50 questions. The format of both tests is multiple choice. Reviewers of the short version and computerized version have questioned their psychometric equivalence to the traditional long version. According to the test manuals, attempts were made in all versions of this test to reduce the frequency of items that produced gender bias. One approach taken to help achieve that outcome was balancing the number of male and female figures depicted in the items. Nevertheless, both the mechanical reasoning and spatial relations tests continue to yield higher average scores for males than for females. However, the magnitude of the difference has been reduced compared with previous editions of the test.

The current psychometric evidence supporting the use of the DAT is impressive. The size of the norm group is in excess of 100,000 (student) examinees. Norm groups for job-seeking adults are much smaller, but still far greater than for most tests of mechanical aptitude or spatial relations. The computerized version of the test has been criticized for its unavailability in some computer systems, but more recent advances in this form of the test may have resolved this issue. If one were interested in assessing (just) mechanical reasoning and spatial relations, I believe the long version of these tests would be preferable. The administration time is not excessive, and the norms and other supporting psychometric evidence are more substantial than for the short version of these tests. If it were deemed desirable to use a test of both mechanical reasoning and spatial relations from the same publisher (in this case, The Psychological Corporation), these two tests from the DAT would be an obvious choice. The DAT was first developed over 50 years ago and remains a staple in the field of assessment.

## OTHER ISSUES

A number of issues cut across these eight major tests of mechanical aptitude and spatial ability, as well as the tests cited in the appendix. These issues pertain to several factors endemic to psychological assessment in general.

First, use of any of these tests should be predicated on job analytic information that indicates the assessed constructs are indeed relevant for the job. As a general rule I believe that job analysis can be overemphasized as a precursor to assessment. It would be difficult to imagine that anyone could seriously argue that jobs in manufacturing facilities, for example, that involve the operation, maintenance, and/or repair of machines do not require mechanical aptitude or spatial ability. Thus, it might be tempting to conclude that since a job analysis will serve to confirm the obvious, it may not be needed. However, given the repeated scientific evidence supporting the adverse impact against females with these types of tests, failing to conduct a job analysis creates a level of legal exposure to potential discrimination charges. The alternative is to assume a judge or jury would "intuitively believe" that tests of mechanical aptitude and spatial ability are appropriate for manufacturing jobs. It is an assumption that is too risky to make.

Second, I believe that only a small number of tests that measure mechanical aptitude and spatial ability meet the conventional standards of rigor of assessment desired in all tests. I considered only four tests to have met rigorous standards of psychometric evaluation: EAS, RMPFBT, BMCT, and DAT. These tests were originally developed many years ago, have been modified or updated over the years, and have substantial psychometric evidence to support their use. But these tests are in the minority. Most tests of mechanical aptitude reviewed in venerable references such as the *Mental Measurements Yearbooks* often contain the following refrains: "this test should be used with caution," "insufficient psychometric evidence is presented to warrant use of this test," and/or "this test should be used for initial counseling of individuals but not for selection." The stated justifications for such comments are legitimate, as they often originate from the test(s) having been developed on small samples. Although what is a "small" sample size can and is debated among psychometricians, many of these tests are based on sample sizes in the range of 30–200 individuals. By any reasonable standard that is "small." If the temptation is therefore not to use these at all because of limited developmental work, such a decision could be premature. Test constructors, test reviewers, and test users would all have more confidence in tests if they were based on sample sizes found in the DAT. Unfortunately, the realities of assessment in industry are rarely so accommodating. I do not believe the "solution" to these problems is not to use the tests at all. Rather, one should exercise care and prudence in the interpretation of the test scores, however flawed their generation may be. In my work I implement the following procedures to minimize misuse or misinterpretation of these tests. First, I ask SMEs at each company to verify the appropriateness of each item on the test for use in that company. I have learned, for example, that all blueprints are not the same. Different industries and different companies in the same industry work with different types of prints and schematics. An off-the-shelf test that measures irrelevant technical knowledge for a particular company is useless, no matter how many thousands of examinees may have taken the test previously. As the test content moves from assessing more general concepts (as do the EAS and BMCT, for example) to more specific concepts (as do the MecTest and Maintest, for example), the more critical issue is the SME review. Second, I routinely conduct local validation studies with companies. I am fully aware of the scientific arguments (e.g., Hoffman, Holden, & Gale, 2000; Murphy, 2000) pertaining to why the precepts of validity generalization are more scientifically defensible than a supposedly flawed local validation study based on a finite sample size. I have three reasons for conducting my own validation studies. First, the companies invariably ask me about the legal defensibility of whatever actions we discuss. The literature on validity generalization reveals that while, in theory, it should be legally sound, in practice, it may not be. Hoffman and McPhail (1998) stated, "Depending on the stringency with which the job analysis and investigation of fairness are enforced, the area of validity generalization arguments in support of test use in a particular setting may or may not be acceptable. . . . (S)ole reliance on validity generalization to support test use is probably premature" (p. 990). Although companies are respectfully mindful of the scientific basis of psychological assessment and personnel selection, they are often more mindful of practical and legal reality (Guion, 1998).

Second, though it is knowledge of validity that generalizes in validity generalization, such a paradigm has nothing to offer on the matter of where to set the passing score on a test. Test norms can be helpful, but only when based on a reliable and representative sample. Companies often have concerns and questions as to the degree to which their employees and applicants compare with a norm group, particularly a norm group established many years previously in an unknown labor market. Economic conditions can affect the motivation of candidates who apply for jobs in industry, and in turn, the selectivity of the hiring organization. I have never in my career read a set of norms that describes the economic conditions in effect at the time the normed tests were administered. Whereas regional or industry-specific economic conditions may be of no interest to psychometricians, they are of great practical interest to hiring organizations. Cascio, Alexander, and Barrett (1988) have addressed the multitude of issues affecting selection of a passing score. Individual companies want to be as certain as possible that they are not competitively disadvantaged by the choice of the passing score. Comfort with selection of the passing score can be facilitated by conducting a local validation study. Finally, in an industrial context, the activities and functions of the department unit within the company responsible for assessment and selection decisions do not operate in a vacuum. They are intimately tied to manufacturing and sales functions, operations that often possess the most clout and influence with the organization's decision-making system. A local validation study helps put the stamp of local ownership on the assessment (and subsequent selection) process. These matters can be critically important in getting organizations to adopt and implement the tests that have been painstakingly developed by psychologists. In short, I use the validity generalization paradigm to buttress the findings from a local validation study. Like it or not, psychology is often perceived to be arcane and detached from mainstream business functions. If one criterion of our success as a profession is to get our products and services utilized within our respective professional communities, we need to become more skilled in marketing ourselves in ways that result in adopting what we have to offer.

In short, despite legitimate concerns about insufficient knowledge bases to use some tests, I believe there are mechanisms to ameliorate some of the concerns. I also think there are more bad uses of good tests than there are bad tests. To categorically reject tests because of limited psychometric data supporting their use leaves us with no better alternatives. What better ways do we have to measure mechanical aptitude and spatial ability—an interview, resume evaluation, person-

ality test? Although I agree with reviewers that some tests should be buttressed with more supporting evidence, no other available tests on the market measure these constructs. I believe intelligent use of these tests, using the full body of knowledge available to the psychologist from both local and published sources, is often preferable to not using them at all. Mechanical aptitude and spatial ability tests are highly specialized in their focus of inquiry. Like all tests they should not be used indiscriminately. However, when their use is justified, I know of no better way to assess what they measure.

Third, the manufacturing sector of the economy is currently in the midst of a technological revolution. The predominant means of production today is, in one form or another, computer-based. While the average person tends to be more aware of the high-tech influence on communication than manufacturing, production processes of 20 years ago are as outdated as the rotary-dial telephone. Many of the tests of mechanical aptitude and spatial relations were developed decades ago. A fair question to ask is whether the jobs of today call for new aptitudes and abilities that these traditional tests do not measure. Perhaps mechanical aptitude and spatial ability are as timeless in their relevance as are tests of numerical and verbal abilities. And perhaps not. Although I believe such tests are valid predictors of job performance in manufacturing-related jobs, I question if they are as valid today as they were 20 years ago. Perhaps when averaged across a myriad of contexts in which they are used, the validity of such tests today is not much less than in years past. However, I believe in selected contexts they may be considerably less valid. The new technology of manufacturing places increased reliance on computer-related knowledge as analog, digital, PLC, and so on. It is the growing reliance of such concepts that prompted selected publishers (such as The Ramsay Corporation) to develop tests assessing them. Will tests of GMA be more predictive of this new-age technologically driven aptitude than traditional tests of mechanical aptitude? It is an open question, but I would surmise not. Tests of mechanical aptitude have been found to have greater validity than tests of GMA when used in selected organizations. I believe the next generation of mechanical aptitude tests might benefit from inclusion of items representative of the abilities manifested in modern manufacturing technology. What is certain is that the nature of manufacturing work has changed and continues to do so. Whether we as psychologists need to develop a new generation of tests to be predictive of job performance in this domain is unknown. This would be a propitious time to consider expanding the domain of items assessing mechanical aptitude and spatial ability.

Finally, it has been customary in our profession to differentiate among ability tests, aptitude tests, and achievement tests. Traditionally, achievement tests are geared toward specific knowledge or skills that are required over a precise time frame. Ability and aptitude tests generally refer to assessing broad attributes that are acquired over long periods of time. Thus, achievement tests tend to be *retrospective* in nature, while ability and aptitude tests tend to be *prospective* in nature. Furthermore, when we attempt to validate such test, different strategies are often taken. Achievement tests are evaluated with the content validity paradigm, while ability and aptitude tests are evaluated with the criterion-related validity paradigm. While these distinctions may have some merit on the surface, it is not clear whether the distinctions are all that useful in the long run. On theoretical grounds a unitarian doctrine of validity is preferred over the trinitarian doctrine. That is, there is only one kind or type of validity (construct), not three (content, criterion-related, and construct). Content and criterion-related are viewed as manifestations of the underlying unitary concept of construct validity. As such, it is theoretically inconsistent to establish the content validity of achievement tests and the criterion-related validity of ability and aptitude tests. On practical grounds the distinction between these types of tests blurs upon selected application. If individuals have taken a prescribed course on computer programming language (for example), it is highly plausible they would score higher on a(n) (achievement) test that assessed such knowledge. But if knowledge of computer programming language is necessary for job performance, and scores on such a test are predictive of job performance, this test would manifest criterion-related validity. As such it would be used as a(n) (aptitude) test. Perhaps in the context of educational assessment there is a meaningful distinction between ability, aptitude, and achievement tests. This distinction appears far less useful in industrial contexts. I consider tests that measure job-related concepts predictive of job performance to be of the same general family of assessment techniques irrespective of what they are called.

In conclusion, mechanical aptitude and spatial ability tests have long been used in the selection of employees for manufacturing jobs. On a conceptual level they represent an amalgam of assessment strategies along the ability/aptitude/achievement test continuum. On a practical level many of these tests have limited psychometric evidence to support their use. It has been my experience that when utilized in an intelligent and professionally responsible manner, better personnel decisions can be made with them than without them. While of limited applicability to the full spectrum of jobs in the economy, they have earned their place as a useful means of assessing individuals.

## APPENDIX: OTHER TESTS OF MECHANICAL APTITUDE AND SPATIAL ABILITY

1.  Mechanical Ability Test (Educational and Industrial Test Services Ltd.)
    A 35-item test of mechanical principles similar in style to the BMCT.
2.  Electrical and Electronics Test (The Test Agency Ltd.)
    30-item test of fundamental laws, symbols, and definitions related to electricity and electronics.
3.  ETSA—Mechanical Familiarity (Employers' Tests & Services Associates)
    50-item test involving identification of commonly used tools.
4.  ETSA—Mechanical Knowledge (Employers' Tests & Services Associates)
    121-item test of mechanical knowledge having a 90-minute administration time.
5.  Flanagan Aptitude Classification Tests (FACT) (Science Research Associates)
    A subtest of this battery measures the ability to understand mechanical principles and analyze mechanical measurements.
6.  Flanagan Industrial Tests (FIT) (Science Research Associates)
    A subtest of this battery measures the ability to understand mechanical principles (somewhat higher level than FACT).
7.  Shapes Test (The Test Agency Ltd.)
    60-item test involving the spatial manipulation of figures.
8.  Space Relations (London House Press)
    A brief (9-minute) test assesses the ability to visually select a combination of flat pieces that together cover a given two-dimensional space.
9.  ElecTest (The Ramsay Corporation)
    60-item test of electrical concepts and applications.
10. WeldTest (The Ramsay Corporation)
    60-item test for selecting journey-level welders.
11. BldgTest (The Ramsay Corporation)
    60-item test for selecting candidates for building maintenance jobs.
12. Maintenance Electrician Test (The Ramsay Corporation)
    60-item test for selecting candidates for process maintenance jobs.
13. Maintenance Mechanic Tests (The Ramsay Corporation)
    60-item tests (three versions with increasing levels of

difficulty) for selecting candidates for manufacturing maintenance jobs.

14. PipeTest (The Ramsay Corporation)
60-item test for selecting journey-level plumbers and pipefitters.

15. Millwright Test (The Ramsay Corporation)
60-item test for selecting millwright candidates.

16. Machinist Test (The Ramsay Corporation)
60-item test for selecting journey-level machinists.

17. PrinTest (The Ramsay Corporation)
60-item test for selecting entry-level production workers where reading of prints and drawings is required.

18. InstrumenTest (The Ramsay Corporation)
60-item test for use in selecting instrument technicians.

19. Electrical Repair Apprentice Battery (The Ramsay Corporation)
Five-test battery for selecting electrical repair apprentices; less demanding than the Electrical Maintenance Trainee Test.

The Ramsay Corporation tests contain sets of items that are common across different tests. No two tests are totally independent in content.

## NOTES

1. As an exception to this general practice of nonuse, I know of a company that sold (but did not manufacture) pumps and other products relating to fluid power transmission. The company wanted its sales force to be "mechanically inclined" at a level it could effectively respond to customer questions regarding the mechanical capacity of the products it sold. As such the company used a test of mechanical aptitude to assess (in part) candidates for sales jobs. Although it is beyond the scope of this chapter to discuss how personnel selection affects organizational culture, the overall importance of mechanical reasoning (as assessed by a test of mechanical aptitude) as a core competency in this company was a defining dimension of its culture. The linkage between personnel selection and organizational culture is cogently presented in Schneider's (1987) articled entitled "The People Make the Place."

2. Approximately 20 years ago I talked to a company about the male-female difference in the average score on a particular test of mechanical aptitude. The company was concerned about both the magnitude and perseverance of the difference over the years they had used the test. I speculated that with the growing acceptance of less gender segregated high school classes (i.e., more girls were taking shop classes than ever before in history) and less gender stereotyping in occupations (e.g., more women were selecting traditionally male-dominated academic majors in college as science,

business, and engineering), the male-female gap in average score on mechanical aptitude tests would dissipate, perhaps substantially. It appears my speculation was erroneous. I know of no reduction in the male-female difference in mechanical aptitude test scores among the same version of a test administered to men and women in 1980 versus 2000.

## REFERENCES

Bennett, G.K. (1980). *Test of mechanical comprehension.* New York: Psychological Corporation.

Bennett, G.K., Seashore, H.G., & Wesman, A.G. (1984). *Differential aptitude tests: Technical Supplement.* San Antonio, TX: Psychological Corporation.

Cascio, W.F., Alexander, R.A., & Barrett, G.V. (1988). Setting cutoff scores: Legal, psychometric, and professional issues and guidelines. *Personnel Psychology, 41,* 1–24.

Dunnette, M.D. (1993). My hammer or your hammer? *Human Resource Management, 32,* 373–384.

Guion, R.M. (1998). *Assessment, measurement, and prediction for personnel decisions.* Mahwah, NJ: Erlbaum.

Hoffman, C.C., Holden, L.M., & Gale, K. (2000). So many jobs, so little "N": Applying expanded validation methods to support generalization of cognitive test validity. *Personnel Psychology, 53,* 955–991.

Hoffman, C.C., & McPhail, S.M. (1998). Exploring options for supporting test use in situations precluding local validation. *Personnel Psychology, 51,* 987–1003.

Hunter, J.E., & Hunter, R.F. (1984). Validity and utility of alternative predictors of job performance. *Psychological Bulletin, 96,* 72–88.

Hunter, J.E., & Schmidt, F.L. (1996). Intelligence and job performance: Economic and social implications. *Psychology, Public Policy, and Law, 2,* 447–472.

Muchinsky, P.M. (1993). Validation of intelligence and mechanical aptitude tests in selecting employees for manufacturing jobs. *Journal of Business and Psychology, 7,* 373–382.

Murphy, K.R. (2000). Impact of assessments of validity generalization and situational specificity on the science and practice of personnel selection. *International Journal of Selection and Assessment, 8,* 194–206.

Ramsay, R.T. (1991). *Maintest: Form NL-1.* Pittsburgh, PA: Ramsay Corporation.

Ramsay, R.T. (1998/2000). *MecTest: Form AU-C.* Pittsburgh, PA: Ramsay Corporation.

Ramsay, R.T. (1998). *Electrical maintenance trainee test: Form UKE-1C.* Pittsburgh, PA: Ramsay Corporation.

Ruch, W.W., Stang, S.W., McKillip, R.H., & Dye, D.A. (1994). *Employee Aptitude Survey technical manual* (2nd ed.). Los Angeles, CA: Psychological Services.

Sackett, P.R., Schmitt, N., Ellingson, J.E., & Kabin, M.B. (2001). High-stakes testing in employment, credentialing, and higher education: Prospects in a post-affirmative-action world. *American Psychologist, 56,* 302–318.

Sackett, P.R., & Wilk, S.L. (1994). Within-group norming and other forms of score adjustment in preemployment testing. *American Psychologist, 49,* 929–954.

Schmidt, F.L., & Hunter, J.E. (1998). The validity and utility of selection methods in personnel psychology: Practical and theoretical implications of 85 years of research findings. *Psychological Bulletin, 124,* 262–274.

Schneider, B. (1987). The people make the place. *Personnel Psychology, 40,* 437–454.

Thurstone, L.L., & Thurstone, T.G. (1998). *Thurstone Test of Mental Alertness (TMA) examiner's manual.* Minneapolis, MN: NCS Pearson.

Wiesen, J.P. (1997). *WTMA; The Wiesen Test of Mechanical Aptitude (version 3.12).* Newton, MA: Applied Personnel Research.

Wiesen, J.P. (1999). *WTMA; Wiesen Test of Mechanical Aptitude (PAR edition).* Odessa, FL: Psychological Assessment Resources.

CHAPTER 4

# Multiaptitude Test Batteries

DENNIS DOVERSPIKE, ALANA B. COBER, AND WINFRED ARTHUR JR.

Psychology involves the understanding and prediction of human behavior. Of course, human behavior turns out to be quite complex and difficult to predict. One of the major reasons human performance is so difficult to predict is that there appears to be substantial variation across individuals in both performance and the intrinsic attributes that predict such performance. This variation in human performance is usually referred to as individual differences and the intrinsic attributes predicting performance are usually referred to as abilities.

This chapter deals with the measurement of individual differences in one type of ability—aptitudes. Specifically, it deals with attempts to develop tests of general aptitudes. Aptitudes are defined here as latent traits that correspond to a capacity, capability, or competency to perform a related set of behaviors (Ackerman & Humphreys, 1990; Anastasi & Urbina, 1997; Cronbach, 1990; Dunnette, 1976; Lubinski & Dawis, 1992). Multiaptitude test batteries are then defined here as a collection of instruments designed to measure a number of specific aptitudes in one, comprehensive battery. It should be noted that the dividing line between a multiaptitude test and a test of general intelligence, or learning ability, could sometimes be unclear; the closely related topic of general mental ability tests is covered in Chapter 2 of this volume.

In selection for occupational or employment purposes, perhaps the most famous example of a multiaptitude test is the General Aptitude Test Battery (a product of the United States Employment Services), or GATB. However, during the 1980s a controversy erupted over the GATB (Hartigan & Wigdor, 1989), and this debate helped to focus attention on other measures of general multiaptitudes.

In this chapter, we discuss the following topics:

- The basic history of and theory underlying multiaptitude tests.

- The prototypical multiaptitude test for occupational selection—the GATB, and the controversy over the GATB.

- Major alternatives for the measurement of general aptitudes. This includes a discussion of available information on the psychometric properties, and strengths and weaknesses, of selected tests.

- Limitations and problems in testing for multiaptitudes.

- Concluding comments including a discussion of the future of multiaptitude measures.

Somewhat surprisingly, there is a lack of available, published information on most multiaptitude tests. Therefore, to collect the information used in writing this chapter, a letter was sent to all major tests publishers requesting any information that they might have on available multiaptitude tests. Unfortunately, in most cases the information received was of limited use. (We thank all the publishers who did reply and especially those who took the time to send more detailed information. Due to space and editorial considerations it was not possible to include an entry for every test we received information on, especially those tests of more specialized aptitudes as opposed to multiaptitude batteries.) In addition, a literature search was performed using several different search engines. Finally, we relied on our own extensive backgrounds in the area and our professional libraries.

## HISTORY AND THEORY

In this section, we discuss the history and theory of multiaptitude measures. As might be expected, the history and theory of the development of measures of multiaptitudes are intermixed and also linked to the development of the statistical technique of factor analysis.

### History

Prior to the Binet-Simon scale in 1905 (Binet & Simon, 1905), most psychological measures dealt with simple specialized functions, such as reaction time or prowess in arithmetic. The success of the Binet-Simon scales and later measures, such as the Stanford-Binet (Terman, 1916), led the emerging testing industry to concentrate on measures of intelligence. Of course, many of these early measures of intelligence actually measured a number of different attributes or aptitudes.

In the late 1910s and early 1920s, group tests were developed, including the Army Alpha and Beta. The ability to administer tests to groups in a standardized fashion led to the widespread use of tests and also established the pattern for modern tests of multiaptitudes.

Although most individually administered intelligence tests measure a number of abilities, during the 1920s it soon became apparent that other important abilities were not being assessed by group tests of intelligence. Thus, the 1920s saw a switch from measures of general intelligence to the measurement of more specific aptitudes. It soon also became clear that more specific aptitudes could be combined into a single battery or a multiaptitude test.

The case for the existence of general multiaptitudes was greatly aided by the introduction during the 1920s and 1930s of a statistical technique known as factor analysis (Comrey & Lee, 1992; Tabachnick & Fidell, 2001). Through the use of factor analysis it was possible to demonstrate that many specific abilities were really the product of more general aptitudes. It was also possible to demonstrate that more general aptitudes were independent, or at least somewhat independent, of general intelligence.

Based on the work completed during the 1920s and 1930s, and follow-up efforts during World War II, general multiaptitude test batteries began to appear in the 1940s and 1950s. Based on factor analytic work, Thurstone published his Chicago Tests of Primary Mental Abilities in 1941 (Thurstone, 1938, 1941). In 1947, one of the most widely used multiple aptitude test batteries, the Differential Aptitude Test (Bennett, Seashore, & Wesman, 1951, 1984), was first published.

From 1942 to 1945, the U.S. Employment Service (USES) worked on a multiaptitude battery that was based on a number of existing tests for specific occupations but that could be used across occupational categories (Hartigan & Wigdor, 1989). This research effort culminated in the release in 1947 of the General Aptitude Test Battery, or GATB. The GATB became a very popular instrument and its use grew until the 1980s when a controversy erupted over its use. In response to the popularity of the GATB, a number of competing measures also appeared that did not require administration by the USES.

Although the controversy over the GATB is complicated and involves a number of subsidiary issues, the main issue was that the GATB resulted in substantial adverse impact against African Americans (Hartigan & Wigdor, 1989). In response to this adverse impact, within-group scoring was proposed as a solution (Hartigan & Wigdor, 1989). However, within-group scoring was itself a controversial procedure.

Based on the information contained in the report issued by Hartigan and Wigdor (1989), the USES suspended the use of the GATB pending further study. As a result, a situation was created where many organizations that had previously relied on the GATB for the prescreening of applicants had to search for alternatives.

### Theory

Multiaptitude test batteries grew out of both the success of and dissatisfaction with general intelligence testing. They also were a result of a specific statistical technique—factor analysis (Comrey & Lee, 1992; Tabachnick & Fidell, 2001).

As psychometricians began to analyze the results from both intelligence tests and tests of specific abilities, they found that the various items or subtests tended to cluster into more general factors.

Various theories began to emerge regarding the nature of these factors. For example, Spearman (1904, 1927) developed a two-factor theory consisting of a general, or *g*, factor and a list of specific factors. Both Kelley (1928) and Thurstone (1938) proposed multiple-factor theories of primary mental abilities. A matrix type model of intellect was developed by Guilford (1967, 1972, 1988).

A common list of so-called primary factors or general aptitudes would include:

- *General Intelligence.* General learning ability; can be considered a higher-level factor. General intelligence appears to be related to performance on almost all jobs (Hunter, 1982; Hunter & Hunter, 1984; Schmidt & Hunter, 1981, 1998). Group-administered general intelligence tests tend to include content corresponding to verbal ability and numerical ability.

- *Verbal Ability.* General verbal aptitude, such as the basic understanding of words, language and information, plus the ability to apply verbal aptitude in problem solving, including finding similarities and social judgments.

- *Numerical Ability.* General numerical aptitude, including the ability to perform simple and more complex arithmetic quickly and accurately, and the application of mathematical reasoning in problem solving.

- *Spatial Ability.* The ability to visualize and rotate objects in space and also the ability to apply spatial reasoning to problems involving figures and spatial domains.

- *Mechanical Comprehension.* General mechanical aptitude including information regarding the use of tools and machines and also the application of reasoning to mechanical problems. This factor is somewhat controversial as it can be argued that it is a knowledge domain rather than an aptitude. A variety of specialized tests of mechanical comprehension (Rechenberg, 2000; Rechenberg & Snell, 1997) have also been developed, including one of the best-known tests of a specialized aptitude—the Bennett Mechanical Comprehension Test (Bennett, 1994). Chapter 3 of this volume covers the topics of mechanical and spatial aptitude.

- *Memory.* The ability to recall or recognize after a brief exposure words, symbols, numbers, or pictures.

- *Perceptual Speed.* The ability to work quickly and accurately in scanning and perceiving similarities and differences in words, numbers, and pictures. This would also include many tests of clerical aptitude.

- *Psychomotor Ability.* The ability to move one's hands and fingers and coordinate their movement, so as to accomplish tasks requiring the manipulation of objects.

Of course, many aptitudes could be added to the preceding list. More recently, theorists such as Sternberg (1982, 1984, 1985) have argued for an expanded view of aptitudes and, more specifically, general intelligence that includes adaptation ability and social intelligence. Measures of situational judgment have also generated a great deal of research and applied attention (Clevenger, Pereira, Wiechmann, Schmitt, & Harvey, 2001; McDaniel, Morgeson, Finnegan, Campion, & Braverman, 2001; Schmitt, & Mills, 2001).

Perhaps the most infamous new aptitude is emotional intelligence (Goleman, 1995). Although the widespread recognition and popularity of the construct of emotional intelligence is a fairly recent phenomenon, its origins can be traced back to Gardner's (1983) theory of multiple intelligences, which includes interpersonal intelligence, defined as the ability to understand others' emotions and intentions, and intrapersonal intelligence, defined as the ability to know one's emotions. In an attempt to operationalize and measure emotional intelligence, researchers have created a number of scales and measures (Davies, Stankov, & Roberts, 1998; Dawda & Hart, 2000; Newsome, Day, & Catano, 2000; Schutte et al., 1998).

Tests of personality and vocational interest are also sometimes incorporated into multiaptitude batteries. On the other hand, tests of personality or attitudes have also started to incorporate aptitude measures. For example, National Computer Systems (NCS)–London House (1996) offers the option of including measures of math ability and also customer service aptitudes in its Personnel Selection Inventory, depending on the configuration of the inventory chosen for a particular job.

Regardless of the exact nature of the underlying theory, multiaptitude tests appear to be based on the following basic assumptions:

1. *The Measurement Assumption.* There are multiple aptitudes that can be measured in a reliable and valid fashion.
2. *The Single Battery Assumption.* The best and most efficient method of measuring multiaptitudes is using a single, wide-range test or battery. This single battery assumption can then be combined with the specific question asked or the domain (Doverspike, 1999) in which the testing is taking place, in order to create a series of more specific assumptions as follows:
   a. *The Vocational Behavior–Single Battery Assumption.* Differences within individuals in their scores on the different aptitudes provide useful information for vo-

cational counseling decisions. The best and most efficient method of measuring multiaptitudes in vocational counseling is using a single, wide-range test or battery.

b. *The Psychological Assessment–Single Battery Assumption.* Differences within an individual in aptitudes and the absolute level of those aptitudes in comparison to norms provides useful information in conducting psychological assessments for employment purposes. The best and most efficient method of measuring multiaptitudes in psychological assessment is using a single, wide-range test or battery.

c. *The Selection–Single Battery Assumption.* Differences among individuals in aptitudes can be used to predict success in a wide range of occupations and, thus, can be used to select individuals into jobs in organizations. The best and most efficient method of measuring multiaptitudes in making selection decisions is using a single, wide-range test or battery.

d. *The Classification–Single Battery Assumption.* Information on aptitudes is useful in making classification decisions (American Educational Research Association, 1999; Cascio, 1998). The best and most efficient method of measuring multiaptitudes in making classification decisions is using a single, wide-range test or battery.

By their very nature, multiaptitude batteries are usually seen as being valid for all jobs. The only question is one of what specific combination of aptitudes is valid for a job. In operational use, the method of validating a multiaptitude battery is generally a function of the user, domain, and specific situation. Most individual psychologists using a multiaptitude battery in a vocational, psychological assessment, or selection setting, will probably rely on a validity generalization argument; that is, meta-analytic studies suggest that multiaptitude batteries are valid for all jobs. Or the individual psychologist may rely on a validity transfer argument; that is, based on a job analysis, the current job is sufficiently similar to jobs for which documented validity evidence exists. Consulting firms or organizations conducting large-scale selection or classification studies are more likely to rely on the results of local, criterion-related validation studies.

## THE GENERAL APTITUDE TEST BATTERY

The GATB was developed by the USES for use by state employment offices (Anastasi & Urbina, 1997; Cronbach, 1990; Hartigan & Wigdor, 1989). Its original intended use was in matching applicants for jobs with potential employers in the private and public sectors to find employment for individual applicants. In most respects, the federal government appeared to succeed in its goal in that the GATB became a very popular instrument. Many private sector organizations found that they could use the combination of the state employment offices and the GATB to do a quick prescreen of large numbers of applicants for open positions. The success of the GATB also led to the Department of Labor proposing that the GATB could be used as a prescreen and referral instrument for almost all jobs in the United States (Hartigan & Wigdor, 1989).

The GATB uses 12 tests to generate nine factor scores. There is a mix of apparatus and paper-and-pencil tests, and speed and power tests. This results in a somewhat difficult, although still standardized, administration process.

Based on the 12 tests, a composite of factor scores is created. The nine factors (and corresponding tests) are as follows:

1. General Learning Ability (Vocabulary, Arithmetic Reasoning, Three Dimensional Space).
2. Verbal Aptitude (Vocabulary).
3. Numerical Aptitude (Computation, Arithmetic Reasoning).
4. Spatial Aptitude (Three-Dimensional Space).
5. Form Perception (Tool Matching, Form Matching).
6. Clerical Perception (Name Comparison).
7. Motor Coordination (Mark Making).
8. Finger Dexterity (Assemble, Disassemble).
9. Manual Dexterity (Place, Turn).

The factor scores are obtained through a conversion of the individual test scores. The factor or aptitude scores are then converted into a cognitive composite, a perceptual composite, and a psychomotor composite score. Based on an extensive database, the USES created aptitude batteries specifically tailored to various occupations and also identified various score patterns associated with success in different occupations. The test battery takes approximately 2.5 hours.

As might be expected, a wealth of psychometric data was available on the GATB (Hartigan & Wigdor, 1989). Overall, the results were stronger for the cognitive measures than for the psychomotor or perceptual measures. Both equivalent form and test-retest reliabilities were adequate (above .80). The factor and composite scores of the GATB appear to possess adequate convergent validity with other multiaptitude measures, and the mean uncorrected validities for the prediction of job performance fall within the .20–.30 range (Hartigan & Wigdor, 1989).

Versions of the GATB have been used all over the world (Murphy & Davidshofer, 1998). Nelson Thomson Learning offers a version of a test referred to as the GATB for use in

Canada. This test is not sold in the United States and was validated for Canadian samples.

**The Controversy**

The controversy over the GATB began in the 1980s when the U.S. Department of Labor suggested that states use the test as part of a new selection system with all jobs. This system had two features that created controversy. First, given the adverse impact inherent in test scores and decisions made using the GATB, job candidates were selected and their scores calculated based on the use of within-group norms, where the groups were based on race or ethnicity—Black, Hispanic, and Other.

Second, based on the then relatively new procedure of validity generalization (Hunter & Hunter, 1984; Schmidt & Hunter, 1981), the argument was made that the GATB was a valid instrument for all jobs (Hartigan & Wigdor, 1989; Hunter, 1982). This argument was based on research that suggested that the general ability measured by the GATB was a valid predictor for all jobs.

In 1986, the U.S. Department of Justice challenged the GATB program based on its use of within-group race norming. As a result, the National Academy of Sciences conducted a study of the GATB's role (Hartigan & Wigdor, 1989). The end result was the suspension of the GATB program by the USES (Baydoun & Neuman, 1992; National Research Council, 1995). Unfortunately, many organizations had relied on the GATB as an initial prescreen, and its elimination created a hole in many employee selection systems. Thus, employers began to look for alternative measures of multiaptitudes; in the next section we review some of the major multiaptitude test batteries.

## MULTIAPTITUDE TEST BATTERIES

In this section of the chapter, we present information on various measures of multiaptitudes. This list is not meant to be exhaustive, but it does attempt to provide short summaries for some of the major instruments; this list is also summarized in table form in the appendix. (*Note:* The appendix also includes additional measures of specific aptitudes that, although not listed here, are mentioned at other points in this chapter.) For simplicity, we list the batteries here in alphabetical order.

**ACT WorkKeys**

The ACT WorkKeys (American College Testing Program, 1994) was designed to assess competencies or aptitudes re-

lated to employability. The test is group administered and consists of eight timed paper-and-pencil aptitude measures. The test is intended for use in schools (e.g., high school and postsecondary), as well as by employers. The tests and accompanying job analysis system were developed based on a comprehensive study of a variety of occupations in a number of industries. The eight areas that are assessed include: locating information, applied mathematics, reading for information, applied technology, teamwork, observation, listening, and writing. It takes approximately 45 minutes to give the subtests corresponding to each area.

Based on the reports of Lee et al. (1995) and Lee and Nathan (1997), three of the basic assessments—Locating Information, Applied Mathematics, and Reading for Information—can be used to validly predict the success of workers in over 1,700 jobs. Content validity can be established based on the job analysis, which uses a job profiling system (Lee & Nathan, 1997). The assessments in the ACT WorkKeys are regarded as criterion referenced and performance based, as opposed to norm referenced. Thus, within a test, the content can be thought of as organized into levels, which correspond to performance levels in employment or training environments. Obviously, this has implications for training and education, as well as for job analysis and assessment. The ACT WorkKeys test battery is reported to have low adverse impact, since the assessments are based on a job analysis process that consists of task and skill analyses (Nathan, 1995). However, it is unclear as to why the ACT WorkKeys would be expected to have lower adverse impact than alternative measures of similar constructs.

The ACT WorkKeys was based on a carefully conducted program of research and it appears to have been developed specifically to meet the needs of employers and educators searching for a substitute for the GATB. ACT provides a mechanism for linking the assessments to the job, and, as with most other multiaptitude assessment batteries, one would expect it to predict performance in a wide range of jobs. In addition to ACT, WorkKeys is offered through a network of consultants and educational institutions licensed to provide their assessment services.

## APTICOM

APTICOM is a computer-assisted vocational evaluation system that was developed in 1982 by the Vocational Research Institute of the Philadelphia Jewish Employment and Vocational Services (Vocational Research Institute, 2001b). The test is a self-contained system that can be administered in 90 minutes or less, consisting of an 18-by-24-inch wedge-shaped control board. On the front of the control board are holes that correspond with answers to test items. To select an answer the test taker punches a hole by the corresponding answer with a special electronic probe (sensor). The system scores the test and then prints the following information: raw, standard, and percentile scores.

The three major job-related areas assessed by the APTI-COM are occupational interests, educational skills, and aptitudes. The system has three test batteries: an Aptitude Test, an Occupational Interest Inventory, and an Education Skills Development Battery. The aptitude areas identified include intelligence, verbal aptitude, numerical aptitude, spatial aptitude, form perception, clerical perception, motor coordination, finger dexterity, manual dexterity, and coordination. Interest areas include artistic, scientific, plants and animals, protective, mechanical, industrial, business detail, selling, accommodating, humanitarian, leading-influencing, and physical performance. The Education Skills Battery includes math and language tests.

The APTICOM should probably be considered to be an apparatus test rather than a computer-administered test. Although frequently described as a test for use in "rehabilitation," it is clearly used for a range of employment-related purposes, including selection.

Based on the results of Alston and Mngadi (1992) we would expect that the reliability and validity information for the battery and its subtests to be in the range of other multiaptitude batteries.

## Basic Skills Test (BST)

The BST is published by Psychological Services, Inc. (Ruch, Weiner, McKillip, & Dye, 1985). The BST was designed for use in business, industry, and government organizations. The test includes 16 paper-and-pencil tests that measure cognitive and perceptual abilities and skills, along with four additional tests of typing performance. The tests measure both speed and accuracy, since each test has strict time limits. The test battery can be tailored for different administration needs, since the individual tests are available separately.

The BST was designed to assess skills and abilities that are important for clerical work. Specifically, the different subtests are designed for use in selecting and placing clerical employees. The BST measures six general skills and abilities: reasoning, perceptual speed, verbal comprehension, numerical ability, memory, and typing. The Reasoning subtest is composed of five sections that take a total of 25 minutes. The five Perceptual Speed tests take approximately 19 minutes. Verbal Comprehension has three sections that take a total of 20 minutes. The Numerical Ability test is composed of two sections that take 15 minutes. The Memory subtest is com-

posed of one section and takes 10 minutes. Typing skills are assessed with four typing tests, one being a practice test, taking a total of 19 minutes.

A concurrent validation study comparing BST scores with supervisor-rated job performance yielded validity coefficients for the five dimensions (not including typing) ranging from .27 to .34 for individual tests (Ruch et al., 1985). A predictive validation study was also conducted that yielded validity coefficients ranging from .08 to .45 for the five dimensions excluding typing (Ruch et al., 1985). An investigation of the tests' fairness to Blacks, Hispanics, Whites, males, and females was also conducted. Through the use of regression equations, it was found that all the tests were fair for all of the different groups and none would significantly underpredict any group's performance (Ruch et al., 1985).

The BST can be optically scored or hand scored by using a scoring template. The test is also available in a computer-administered version. National norms are provided for more than 2,550 workers to assist in score interpretation (Ruch et al., 1985).

## CareerScope

The CareerScope test battery was created by the Vocational Research Institute (Vocational Research Institute, 2001a). CareerScope can be administered in groups or individually. CareerScope is a computerized battery; therefore, it is relatively easy to administer and should take about an hour to complete.

The abilities measured are similar to those assessed by the GATB and include general learning ability, verbal aptitude, numerical aptitude, spatial aptitude, form perception, and clerical perception. The test battery also measures an individual's interest in the different aptitudes. The administration of the battery can be modified to also incorporate physical performance subtests, including Motor Coordination, Finger Dexterity, and Manual Dexterity.

Reliability and validity information on this test was not readily available to the reviewers. However, based on the available literature (Lustig, Brown, & Lott, 1998), we would expect reliabilities and validities to be in the range reported for other multiaptitude batteries.

## Comprehensive Ability Battery (CAB)

The CAB was designed by Ralph Hakstian and Raymond Cattell and is published by the Institute for Personality and Ability Testing (IPAT, 2001; personal communication with IPAT staff, October 11, 2001). The CAB measures 20 abilities, which are important in predicting performance in a range of tasks for individuals of high school age and older. According to information provided to us by the IPAT, the CAB can be used in selection contexts as long as a local validation study has been conducted (personal communication, IPAT staff, October 11, 2001).

Norms for the CAB are available; however, they are based on high school students. Based on the available literature, we would expect reliabilities and validities to be in the range reported for other multiaptitude batteries.

IPAT, the publishers of the CAB, is currently in the process of developing a multiaptitude battery of ability tests, the Cognitive Ability Selection Tests (CAST), that can be used in a variety of selection contexts (personal communication from IPAT staff, October 11, 2001). The CAST will be designed so that test users can select the most appropriate set of subtests for their individual needs and situation. In addition to the development of the component subtests, IPAT staff will be involved in conducting or coordinating a number of studies to establish the psychometric properties and validity of the CAST. The expected completion date for the project to develop and validate the CAST is 2004.

### Differential Aptitude Test (DAT)

As indicated earlier, the DAT (Bennett et al., 1951, 1984) and the Chicago Tests of Primary Mental Abilities and the GATB were among the first recognized multiaptitude measures. The use of the DAT in organizations is somewhat limited, because it is intended primarily for educational purposes and the vocational counseling of high school students. However, obviously, this is a group that will be entering the labor force.

The DAT (5th edition) is composed of eight subtests: Verbal Reasoning, Numerical Ability, Abstract Reasoning, Perceptual Speed and Accuracy, Mechanical Reasoning, Space Relations, Spelling, and Language Usage. The DAT also yields a Total Scholastic Aptitude score. The full battery takes approximately 2 to 4 hours depending on the version given. Paper-and-pencil and computerized versions are available, as are versions that allow for the selection of particular tests corresponding to specific occupations.

Reliability and validity data are similar to that for other general aptitude batteries, although the data on the DAT, including norms, tends to be based on school-aged samples, as might be expected given its target market. The various composite scores or aptitude scores tend to be highly correlated (Anastasi & Urbina, 1997; Cronbach, 1990).

### Employee Aptitude Survey (EAS)

The EAS was developed by Psychological Services, Inc. (Ruch, Stang, McKillip, & Dye, 1994) and designed for two primary purposes, employee selection and vocational guidance. Ten different aptitudes are measured, including verbal comprehension, numerical ability, visual pursuit, visual speed/accuracy, space visualization, numerical reasoning, verbal reasoning, word fluency, manual speed/accuracy, and symbolic reasoning.

The subtests that are actually used from the battery can be chosen for administration depending on one's purpose or needs. The battery can be administered individually or in groups and takes approximately 5 to 10 minutes per subtest or 2 hours for the entire test. The tests are hand scored with a scoring stencil or are optically scanned. An individual's test scores can be compared with norms for a wide variety of occupational and educational classifications and then used either for ranking examinees or in conjunction with cutoff scores.

Test-retest reliability estimates range from .75 to .91 (Ruch et al., 1994). Criterion-related validity information and validity generalization evidence are provided in the manual for a broad classification of occupational families such as professional, managerial, and supervisory as well as clerical and mechanical. The validity generalization estimates ranged from .13 to .67 for job performance and .27. to .76 for training success for all occupational categories (Ruch et al., 1994). Kolz, McFarland, and Silverman (1998) found that the validity of the EAS Numerical Ability subtest increased as job experience increased.

### Educators'/Employers' Tests and Services Associates (ETSA)

The ETSA test was developed to measure aspects of intelligence, specific abilities, or aptitudes and certain personality characteristics to supplement other factors upon which hiring, placing, training, and promotion decisions are based. The battery consists of eight specific subtests, which range in administration time from 30 to 90 minutes. The subtests include: General Mental Ability, Office Arithmetic, General Clerical Ability, Stenographic Skills, Mechanical Familiarity, Mechanical Knowledge, Sales Aptitude, and a Personal Adjustment Index. Raw scores on each subtest are then classified into one of the following categories: poor, questionable, average, good, or excellent. The test battery is administered individually and is designed for individuals of working age.

The manual does not provide information on the establishment of the cutoffs for the different performance categories, and performance scores vary greatly across the different subtests. Reliability and validity information on this test was not readily available to the reviewers. Based on the data given by Good (1999), we would expect that it would be in the range of other multiaptitude batteries.

## Flanagan Tests

Two tests can be included here, the Flanagan Aptitude Classification Tests (FACT) and the Flanagan Industrial Tests (FIT). The FACT was originally published in 1953 in an effort to establish a classification system for aptitudes that were important for successfully performing various occupational tasks (Flanagan, 1953). The test was designed for use in both vocational counseling and employee selection and placement. The FACT contains 16 subtests, which range in administration time from 2 to 30 minutes. The FACT is composed of the following 16 subtests: Inspection, Coding, Memory, Precision, Assembly, Scales, Coordination, Judgment and Comprehension, Arithmetic, Patterns, Components, Tables, Mechanics, Expression, Reasoning, and Ingenuity. The test was designed to allow for versatility in administration so that all the subtests need not be administered for every occupational category. Depending on a comprehensive job analysis of the occupation, specific tests could then be selected. A typical test battery usually includes two to seven subtests. Reliability and validity information on this test was not readily available to the reviewers. However, we would expect that it would be in the range of other multiaptitude batteries.

The FIT (Flanagan, 1975) grew out of the FACT tests and consists of 18 brief tests intended for personnel selection. The individual tests are relatively short, taking 5 to 15 minutes each, and are basically self-administered. The 18 tests include Arithmetic, Assembly, Components, Coordination, Electronics, Expression, Ingenuity, Inspection, Judgment and Comprehension, Mathematics and Reasoning, Mechanics, Memory, Patterns, Planning, Precision, Scales, Tables, and Vocabulary. Reliability and validity information on this test was not readily available to the reviewers. However, we would expect that it would be in the range of other multiaptitude batteries.

## Job Effectiveness Prediction System (JEPS)

The JEPS was created by the Life Office Management Association (LOMA; Life Office Management Association, 2001). Although the JEPS is available only to insurance and financial services companies, we have included it here because of its specialized nature.

The JEPS is designed to be part of a selection system for applicants for entry-level jobs, including clerical positions and technical/professional positions. The JEPS assesses job applicants on basic skills such as math, reading, and filing. The actual battery takes approximately 45 minutes to complete. The tests can be administered in groups or individually and can be hand scored or optically scanned. This test battery is also available in a computerized version, the CJEPS.

In terms of validation, a 46-area job description questionnaire is available to customize the battery and demonstrate its job relatedness. Reliability and validity information on this test was not readily available to the reviewers. However, we would expect that it would be in the range of other multiaptitude batteries.

LOMA is currently in the process of replacing the JEPS with a computerized test battery known as the LOMA Employee Assessment Program for Non-management or LEAP (Life Office Management Association, 2001). The LEAP is described by LOMA as measuring adaptability to change, degree of conscientiousness, reading comprehension, quantitative reasoning, ability to learn, and proofing and checking.

## Kit of Factor Referenced Tests

The Kit of Factor Referenced Cognitive Tests (Ekstrom, French, & Harman, 1976, 1979; Educational Testing Service [ETS], 1976; French, Ekstrom, & Price, 1963) is unique among multiaptitude measures in that it is intended solely for research and is also based on a combination of factor analysis and information-processing theory. The 1976 version of the Kit consists of two to three measures each for 23 basic cognitive factors that include dimensions such as reasoning, verbal comprehension, number facility, spatial ability, perceptual speed, memory, and fluency. The Kit is supported by a large body of research dating back to the 1940s (Ekstrom et al., 1979), which supports its reliability and validity. More information on the Kit and on other tests of information processing is available in Chapter 5 of this volume.

## Military Multiaptitude Tests

The use of multiaptitude tests by the military, beginning with the Army Alpha and Beta during World War I, has had a great influence on parallel developments in the private sector. The Army Alpha Test was originally developed for use in assessing draftees and consisted of 212 multiple-choice questions covering vocabulary, sentence structure, arithmetic problems, number series, general knowledge, and "common-sense" questions. The Army Beta was developed for those draftees who could not read.

The Army General Classification Test was developed as a replacement for the Army Alpha and Beta and was used during World War II. The civilian version of the Army General Classification Test (Science Research Associates, 1956) was designed to classify individuals according to their ability levels. The test battery consisted of 150 items, covering language, quantitative, and spatial abilities, and took 50 minutes to administer. Reliability estimates were above .90, and criterion-related validity studies resulted in correlations ranging from .16 to .62. The time span is not reported.

The Armed Forces Qualification Test was an instrument developed by the Department of Defense as a replacement for the Army General Classification Test. This test was administered from the 1950s to the mid-1970s.

In the 1960s, the Department of Defense developed another standardized military selection and classification test, the Armed Services Vocational Aptitude Battery (ASVAB) and began administering it in 1968 in U.S. high schools. The ASVAB is administered in the schools through an arrangement where recruiters conduct the administration of the test and then use it to identify potential recruits. When used in the schools, the ASVAB generates expectancy charts for occupations in the services. In 1976, the military services began using the ASVAB as their standard test battery.

The battery takes approximately 180 minutes. It is composed of 10 separate subtests, including tests of Auto and Shop Knowledge. The scores from the tests are combined into three academic composite scores and four occupational composite scores. The academic composites are Academic Ability, Verbal Ability, and Math Ability. The occupational composites are Mechanical and Crafts, Business and Clerical, Electronics and Electrical, and Health and Technology (Murphy & Davidshofer, 1998).

The ASVAB is based on an impressive program of research; it was revalidated as part of a large research effort known as Project A. It is probably one of the few tests where the program of research has included studies on classification efficiency.

However, the ASVAB has been criticized for its lack of reliability as a counseling or a classification device (Cronbach, 1990; Murphy, 1984; Murphy & Davidshofer, 1998). This criticism rests on the use of composite scores and the redundancy in such composite scores; the average intercorrelation is reported to be .86 (Murphy & Davidshofer, 1998). This has led to the suggestion, which we will revisit for multiaptitude tests in general, that it could be easily replaced with a simple test of general intelligence (Murphy, 1984).

## The Morrisby Profile (MP)

The MP (The Morrisby Organisation, 1995) is a matched set of tests designed to give a complete statement in objective terms about the basic mental structure of a person. The Morrisby Profile is applicable for personnel selection, career counseling, and personal counseling. It measures 12 different mental functions. The 12 tests of the MP can be regarded as forming five subbatteries or groups of tests corresponding broadly with five operating areas of mental functioning:

1. The compound series: the understanding and integration of concepts and relationships underlying observations.
2. Three general ability tests: the manipulation and utilization of conceptual knowledge, using verbal, numerical, and perceptual symbols to represent various concepts.
3. Shapes and mechanical ability: mental organization and control of practical activities.
4. The speed tests 1 to 4: the characteristic mode or style of personal behavior.
5. The speed tests 5 and 6: manual dexterity.

The raw scores that are obtained are converted to give standard scale scores, which are then graphed to form a bar chart that exemplifies the individual's distinctive profile or pattern. The profile indicates three aspects of a person's mental structure:

1. The ability structure: a person's talents, aptitudes and potentialities; the preferred ways of learning, of thinking about things generally, of problem solving and of putting knowledge and understanding into practical use.
2. The modal structure: the characteristic pattern or style of behavior adopted by a person in various real-life situations.
3. Manual dexterity: the speed and skill with which a person's hands are used.

When interpreting a profile, it is important to look at the whole set of scores for all of the subtests and not to take any of the scores out of context. Test administrators need to take a recognized course on the MP and obtain proper accreditation. The whole MP usually takes 3 hours and 10 minutes to administer, which includes an 8-minute break halfway through administration. The test can be administered in a group or individually and can either be hand or optically scored. The test-retest reliability for all 12 subtests is $r = .95$, although the time span was not reported. Individual tests range from .92 (Shapes) to .72 (Speed Test 2). The manual also reported coefficient alphas ranging from .96 (Numerical) to .81 (Mechanical) (The Morrisby Organisation, 1995).

## Multidimensional Aptitude Battery II (MAB-II)

The MAB-II (Jackson, 1998) is published by Sigma Assessment Systems, Inc. The original MAB was restandardized and revised to increase its effectiveness and usefulness as a measure of general mental ability and is now the MAB-II.

The MAB-II is designed to assess the intellectual abilities of both adults and adolescents age 16 and older. This test is appropriate for use in educational and career counseling settings, business and industry, clinics and mental health facilities, and for basic research. This battery is also available in French and Spanish. An individual, audiotape, or computer can administer instructions. The test battery can also be given in a group or individually. The Verbal and Performance subtests each take approximately 50 minutes for complete administration. If the test battery is hand scored, it will take approximately 10 minutes; or the test can be computer scored, which would result in faster scoring.

There are five Verbal subtests and five Nonverbal or Performance subtests. The Verbal and Performance subtests can either be administered separately or together to get one composite score. In addition to the 10 subscale scores, the MAB-II yields a verbal IQ, performance IQ, and a full-scale IQ. Alternatively, standard scores may be used in place of verbal, performance, and full-scale IQs.

The available Verbal subscales are Information, Comprehension, Arithmetic, Similarities, and Vocabulary. Information reflects the degree to which an individual has accumulated a fund of knowledge about diverse topics. Comprehension assesses the ability to evaluate social situations to identify behavior that is more socially desirable and to give the reasons why certain laws and social customs are practiced. Arithmetic requires the solution of numerical problems and reflects reasoning and problem-solving abilities. Similarities requires an individual to conceptualize and rank likenesses and differences as properties of an object and to compare these abstract likenesses with those of another object, identifying the one that is most appropriate. Vocabulary is an indication of the number of words or verbal concepts that have been learned and stored. It also indicates the individual's openness to new information and concepts and reflects the capacity to store, categorize, and retrieve this information appropriately.

The Performance dimensions are Digit Symbol, Picture Completion, Spatial, Picture Alignment, and Object Assembly. Digit Symbol requires the learning of a new coding system and its use in a context in which visual-motor activity is important. Picture Completion requires the identification of important missing elements in a picture and requires knowledge of a variety of common objects and the rules used for simplified sketches. Spatial is the ability to visualize abstract objects in different positions in two-dimensional space and to be sensitive to critical differences among alternatives. Picture Alignment requires the respondent to identify a meaningful sequence from a random sequence where the meaningful sequence often has a humorous interpretation. Object Assembly requires that the respondent identify a meaningful object from a left-to-right sequence of disarranged segments.

All of the subtests are composed of multiple-choice items for ease in recording and scoring responses. This battery underwent strict item selection to have a fair level of generality across diverse groups, including those classified in terms of gender, nationality, age, and culture. Age norms are provided in the manual (Jackson, 1998). Reliabilities range from .94 to .97 for the Verbal scale, .95 to .98 for the Performance scale, and .96 to .98 for the Full scale (Jackson, 1998). The MAB is correlated .91 with the WAIS-R (Jackson, 1998).

**Personnel Test Battery (PTB)**

The PTB is published by Saville Holdsworth, Ltd (SHL) and is primarily available for administration outside of the United States (personal communication, SHL staff, October 2001). The test battery was designed for use with adults and, specifically, to select and place job applicants and incumbents, not as a counseling device. The test battery is geared toward fields such as office and sales groups, especially those requiring heavy use of words, numbers, and symbols (i.e., bookkeeping, restaurant work, proofreading). The test battery is composed of two levels. Level 1 is composed of three subtests that measure basic skills and comprehension and range from 10 to 15 minutes in length. They are: Verbal Usage, Numerical Comprehension, Checking, and the optional tests of Basic Checking and Audio Checking. Level 2 is composed of three subtests that measure higher-order reasoning skills and range from 12 to 15 minutes in length. They are: Classification, Verbal Meaning, and Numerical Reasoning. The Personnel Test Battery also provides two optional supplementary tests, Basic and Audio Checking. Reliability and validity information was not readily available to the reviewers. However, we would expect it to be in the range of other multiaptitude test batteries.

**Select Assessment**

An example of a newer approach to multiaptitude assessment is offered by the Select Assessments available from Select International. Separate batteries are offered for manufacturing and customer service.

Select Assessment™ for Manufacturing (SAM) is a computer-based interactive assessment created by Select International that was originally released in 1995 and updated in 1998. SAM was developed to measure a number of key competencies for predicting performance at entry-level manufacturing, assembly, and warehouse positions. The entire assessment process takes approximately 2 hours to complete and includes a self-guided introduction and mouse tutorial. SAM is written at the fourth-grade reading level.

SAM consists of four distinct groups of assessment tools: (1) personality scales, (2) situational judgment scales, (3) interactive simulations, and (4) a logical and numerical reasoning series. These four separate groups of assessments combine to provide ratings on eight key competency areas: attention to detail, conscientiousness, process monitoring, qualitative problem solving, quantitative problem solving, responsibility, teamwork, and work tempo. Ratings of these eight competencies are provided as well as one or more overall predictor composites. In addition, a ninth competency measuring potential aberrant behavior is also computed. The assessment is scored over the Web and links into an applicant tracking system, SelecTrack™. The unique weighting profile, recommended cutoff scores, and so on are set on a client-by-client basis by Select consultants.

A meta-analysis, based on 12 concurrent studies with a sample of approximately 1,191 individuals, indicated that the general unit-weighted composite of the eight competencies resulted in a validity of $r = .64$ (raw correlation of $r = .34$) (O'Connell, 2000). Normative data from a national sample of over 6,500 individuals are available (O'Connell & Smith, 1999). Across the 14 empirical studies, there was no evidence of differential prediction against Blacks, Hispanics, Asian/Pacific Islanders, Native Americans, or females, using a moderated regression approach (Stone & Hollenbeck, 1989).

Select Assessment™ for Customer Service (SACS) is a computer-based interactive assessment created by Select International that was originally released in 1999. SACS was developed to measure a number of key competencies for predicting performance at entry-level customer service and call center positions. The entire assessment process takes approximately 2 hours to complete and includes a self-guided introduction and mouse tutorial. SACS is written at the fifth-grade reading level.

SACS consists of five distinct groups of assessment sections: (1) personality scales; (2) interactive call center simulation; (3) data entry/typing simulation; (4) logical reasoning; and (5) data comparison—focusing on visual acuity. These five separate groups of assessments combine to provide ratings on 11 key competency areas: attention to detail, conscientiousness, process monitoring, qualitative problem solving, problem solving, processing speed, quality focus, sales focus, service orientation, working with others, and work ethic/responsibility. Ratings of these 11 competencies are provided as well as one or more overall predictor composites. In addition, a 12th competency measuring potential aberrant behavior is also computed. Concurrent validation studies with call center employees resulted in correlations with supervisor

ratings of performance ranging from .29 to .44 uncorrected, or .55 to .76 corrected (O'Connell, 2001). There was no evidence of differential prediction against Blacks, or females, using a moderated regression approach (Stone & Hollenbeck, 1989).

## Systems for Testing and Evaluation of Potential (STEP)

STEP, (Baehr, 1992; NCS, 2000) is published by NCS. The test is designed for use by organizations in placing applicants in appropriate positions. It can also be used to assist individuals in determining their own degree of fit with current or future positions. The STEP is specifically oriented to higher managerial or professional personnel (Dobbins & Steiner, 1988; Keyser & Sweetland, 1991; NCS, 2000) and can be used in selection, training, and promotion decisions.

The steps in the STEP begin with the completion of a job analysis form that describes functions performed in managerial and professional jobs. The Managerial and Professional Test Battery is then used to assess the individual's potential, in terms of his or her abilities, skills, and attributes. This battery consists of tests that assess an applicant's background and experience, mental abilities, creativity, personality characteristics, and personal and emotional adjustment (Dobbins & Steiner, 1988). The STEP can be administered in three different ways depending on the type of knowledge and use (e.g., selection, training, and counseling) that is desired. Accordingly, the STEP may take from 1.5 up to 4 hours, with the typical administration time being 2.5 hours (Keyser & Sweetland, 1991; NCS, 2000). The test is scored by mailing the results to the publisher.

Dobbins and Steiner (1988) reported acceptable reliabilities for some of the tests in STEP. For example, reliabilities were above .70 for cognitive measures. However, the reported reliabilities for subfactors for the creativity tests tend to run lower. Analyses using the Potential for Successful Performance composite score have resulted in an average validity coefficient of .62, but in general the research does not appear to address the validity of the individual predictors. Thompson (1994) concluded that STEP predictors and potential scores are related to management position level and salary; however, these results do not make clear the unique explanation of each predictor. Thompson (1994) did find that predictors and potential scores did not adversely affect African Americans or women.

## Technical Test Battery

The Technical Test Battery was developed and is published by SHL. The Technical Test Battery is intended for occupations that require specialized technical skills such as operators, supervisors, technicians, and technical sales positions. The test battery is composed of nine independent tests: Following Instructions, Numerical Computation, two Mechanical Comprehension tests, Numerical Estimation, Fault Finding, Diagrammatic Thinking, Spatial Reasoning, and Diagrammatic Reasoning. The subtests can be administered in any combination.

The test battery can be administered to individuals or in a group setting. It is distributed by SHL primarily outside of the United States (personal communication with SHL staff, October 2001). Reliability estimates range from .71 to .89.

## LIMITATIONS

Although a number of advantages are associated with multiaptitude batteries, they have limitations as well. As with measures of general cognitive ability, there will be substantial adverse impact against minority groups, specifically African Americans (Barrett, Carobine, & Doverspike, 1999; Bobko, Roth & Potoksy, 1999; Campbell, 1996; Gottfredson, 1988; Hunter & Hunter, 1984; McKay & Doverspike, 2001; McKay, Doverspike, Bowen-Hilton, & Martin, in press; Roth, Bevier, Bobko, Switzer, & Tyler, 2001; Sackett & Wilk, 1994). This is likely to lead to charges that such tests are unfair to minorities (Helms, 1992). Previous research has shown that minorities report negative attitudes toward cognitive ability tests (Chan, Schmitt, DeShon, Clause, & Delbridge, 1997; Chan & Schmitt, 1997; McKay et al., in press; Steele & Aronson, 1995), although whether this would generalize to multiaptitude batteries is somewhat unclear.

Multiaptitude batteries may also be inappropriate for administration to groups such as the disabled and speakers of foreign languages, unless acceptable accommodations are made or alternative versions are available. The psychomotor and apparatus tests, frequently found on multiaptitude batteries, present a particular administration challenge in regard to dealing with disabled test takers. Although many of the tests do offer alternative versions, or can be modified to handle unique testing situations, these accommodations raise concerns about the applicability of norms or cutoffs that were not generated or developed under these testing conditions.

One problem with many multiaptitude tests is their popularity, which results in many organizations offering the same tests for many different jobs. As a result, a job applicant may end up taking the same test over and over. This introduces three critical questions. First, what are the effects of repeated administrations? Second, if applicants know they will be taking a test, what happens to the test validity if they obtain coaching? Third, what are the effects of repeated test administration on security? Clearly, repeated opportunities to take a test and coaching would appear to have positive effects on test performance; however, the exact size of the effects and/or the effects on validity are generally unknown (Anastasi, 1981; Messick, 1981; Millman, Bishop, & Ebel, 1965). The security question is an important one for any company to consider when making a decision concerning the adoption of a particular test battery.

Obviously, another question that could be asked of any multiaptitude test is whether it would be more valid and more efficient to simply use a general intelligence or general ability test and supplement it with specialized tests relevant to that job. For example, in selecting for a machine operator, one might decide to use a general intelligence test supplemented by a test of mechanical comprehension (Bennett, 1994; Rechenberg, 2000; Rechenberg & Snell, 1997). However, the importance of this question seems to have diminished with the advent of computer administration. Many test publishers now allow for the customization of multiaptitude tests to match the specific job. Thus, the multiaptitude test now becomes a general ability test plus job-specific tests. Still, despite their established predictive validity, multiaptitude batteries when used as employment tests often contain material that is less than optimally linked with task performance requirements (Barrett, 1992). This limitation of multiaptitude tests may cause rejected job applicants to challenge cognitive tests as lacking job relevance (i.e., *Griggs v. Duke Power,* 1971), may reduce test-taking motivation, particularly among minorities (Arvey, Strickland, Drauden, & Martin, 1990; Chan et al., 1997), and may reduce face-validity perceptions of such tests (Chan & Schmitt, 1997). However, the typical multiaptitude test includes a mix of items, some of which may be seen as face valid and others that may be viewed as less than face valid. What effect this mix of items may have on the applicant is generally unclear.

A question that is somewhat unique to multiaptitude measures is the issue of whether they can actually predict success in different occupations. That is, can they be used for classification as well as selection? Unfortunately, little data are available on the usefulness of multiaptitude measures for classification as opposed to selection, since classification is a question that has generally received relatively little attention in the applied literature (Cascio, 1998).

A related question of importance to both classification and vocational counseling is whether the profile of scores has any meaning; that is, within an individual whether the pattern of high and low scores can be interpreted in any meaningful manner. The problem is that test publishers appear to be under increased pressure to measure more, in this case more aptitudes, in less and less time. Measuring 12 aptitudes in 60 minutes equates to tests that are 5 minutes in length. If 30 seconds are allowed per question, the result is a 10-item test. Generally, it takes 20 to 30 dichotomous questions to achieve a reliable aptitude test. In the absence of tailored testing, and even with tailored testing, it is difficult to achieve a reliable test score with only 10 items. As a result, as the time allotted to measuring aptitudes is reduced, the reliability of the measures also tends to be reduced. As we have seen, the reliabilities for subtest scores on multiaptitude batteries are within an acceptable range. However, difference scores tend to be much less reliable than the scores on which they are based (Crocker & Algina, 1986). This means that profile comparisons are unlikely to be very reliable for multiaptitude tests.

## CONCLUSIONS

Multiaptitude test batteries are designed to measure a number of specific aptitudes in one comprehensive battery. As evidenced by the popularity of multiaptitude test batteries, they appear on the surface to accomplish this goal. However, as demonstrated by the debate over the GATB, multiaptitude batteries do not accomplish this goal without also generating some degree of controversy. Perhaps unfairly, the major controversy concerning multiaptitude batteries surrounds the possibility that they may lead to adverse impact, although clearly many other tests result in similar degrees of adverse impact, and many valid predictors will result in adverse impact. Difficulties may also be encountered in adapting multiaptitude batteries for use with the disabled and other special populations.

As a group, multiaptitude batteries offer a number of positive features. They are easy to administer and score, and they tend to be carefully normed and standardized. In many cases, computerized versions of batteries are available that allow for further customization of the subtests, and we imagine that in the near future all multiaptitude batteries will be computerized.

Compared with general intelligence tests, multiaptitude batteries incorporate a diversity of tasks and measure a number of different aptitudes in one testing session. Thus, they provide for a more complete measurement of the whole person than would a simple intelligence or general learning ability test. In addition, the test content is structured to allow for the administration of the battery to a range of ages and ability levels.

Multiaptitude test batteries also possess favorable psychometric properties. As a group, multiaptitude tests tend to be highly reliable, with internal consistency reliabilities above .80 for almost all subtests. Many multiaptitude batteries offer as validity evidence their correlation with other batteries, especially the GATB or DAT, and such evidence does tend to support convergent and divergent validity.

Based on meta-analyses of cognitive abilities, the validity of multiaptitude batteries for predicting job performance is probably in the .20 to .30 range, uncorrected (Hunter & Hunter, 1984). Thus, multiaptitude test batteries tend to be valid for a wide range of jobs. Overall, the personnel research literature has consistently shown cognitive ability tests to be valid predictors of job performance (Hunter & Hunter, 1984; Ree, Earles, & Teachout, 1994; Schmidt & Hunter, 1998). In fact, general intelligence ($g$) has been identified as the most valid predictor of job performance for nearly all jobs (Hunter & Hunter, 1984). However, the measurement of aptitudes other than general ability is also critical. Recently, Farrell and McDaniel (2001) presented results showing that the relative predictive validities of cognitive ability, perceptual speed, and psychomotor ability were dependent on task quality. Across a wide range of employment positions (i.e., professional-managerial, clerical, sales, and machine trades), Farrell and McDaniel's (2001) findings demonstrated that general cognitive ability was highly predictive of performance in complex jobs, while psychomotor ability was more predictive of performance in simpler jobs. Thus, it may be erroneous to assume that cognitive ability is an equally high valid predictor of all job tasks. The predictive validity of mental ability appears to be relative and dependent upon the criterion with which validity is assessed (Hunter & Hunter, 1984). Thus, as compared with general ability tests, multiaptitude tests provide the advantage of offering data on additional aptitudes including psychomotor ability.

Although consulting firms and large organizations are likely to rely on local criterion-related studies to support the validity of decision making based on multiaptitude batteries, the features of multiaptitude tests make them particularly attractive to individual psychologists conducting vocational or psychological assessments, or to small companies searching for a simple method of prescreening employees. For individual psychologists and small companies, the validity evidence used to support decision making is most likely to be based on validity generalization or validity transfer. Fortunately, as already indicated, the meta-analytic evidence is fairly strong for the general validity of multiaptitude batteries, or at least the general learning ability component of multiaptitude tests (Hunter & Hunter, 1984; Ree et al., 1994). However, psychologists in such situations should make sure that the existing evidence does support their decisions, and they should be extremely cautious in relying on the generalized claims of validity so often found in promotional materials or test manuals.

In our discussion of theory at the beginning of this chapter, we listed two basic assumptions in the use of multiaptitude test batteries. We can now evaluate the validity of these assumptions based on what we currently know about multiaptitude test batteries.

The first assumption was a measurement assumption; that is, multiple aptitudes can be measured in a reliable and valid fashion. Overall, this assumption appears to be a valid one. Most published multiaptitude batteries are based on extensive programs of psychometric research. The individual subtests, or measures of individual aptitudes, appear to result in scores that are reliable, based on internal consistency and test-retest reliability over short time periods. The subtests appear to be measuring the factors they claim to measure, as demonstrated by adequate convergent validities among various multiattribute tests. Overall, most multiattribute tests possess more than adequate reliability and construct validity. The only question marks tend to surround measures of psychomotor abilities.

The second assumption was the single battery assumption: that is, the best and most efficient method of measuring multiaptitudes is the use of a single, wide-range test or battery. Different versions of this single battery assumption exist as a function of the specific question asked or the domain in which the testing is taking place. As a result, this assumption is made in vocational counseling, psychological assessments conducted for employment purposes, selection, and classification.

The use of multiaptitude tests, and thus the single battery assumption, is perhaps most questionable in vocational counseling, yet it is here where such batteries seem to be most needed and potentially useful. This problem is perhaps best exemplified by the ASVAB, where criticisms have been raised concerning the independence and utility of composite scores. Reliability concerns further complicate the issue of a lack of independence in the composite scores. Although total or overall composite scores may be reliable, difference scores or profile scores, and interpretations based upon such differences and profiles, may be much less valid. Clearly, multiaptitude tests can tell us that one person has higher aptitude than another and is thus more likely to achieve higher performance in a range of occupations. However, from a vocational standpoint, we would like to be able to say to an individual that "Yes, you are bright, but you would do better as an engineer than as an artist, or a doctor, or a manager."

Unfortunately, based on the existing research, it is unclear as to whether current multiaptitude batteries allow us to arrive at a valid answer to basic classification questions. Obviously, the comprehensive nature of most multiaptitude batteries would lead one to believe that they would be a valuable tool in any vocational assessment; yet the existing literature does not yet support that conclusion. Thus, although we cannot accept the single battery assumption for use in vocational counseling, it would appear that multiaptitude batteries have a place as a quick prescreen and when combined with other vocational information.

To be fair, most psychologists or vocational counselors are unlikely to rely solely on a multiaptitude test in making vocational recommendations. When combined with other information, multiaptitude tests may lead to valid decisions. In addition, when used for vocational decision making, multiaptitude tests may be more informative in terms of indicating what professions a person should *not* consider, or would be unsuited for, rather than what occupations to consider. In our earlier example, if the individual had achieved a very high score on general ability, but a low score on spatial aptitude, the vocational counselor might indicate that the client should reconsider the choice of a career in engineering.

Multiaptitude batteries have frequently been used in psychological assessments conducted for industry or employment purposes. The questions asked in psychological assessments appear to be a cross between those asked in vocational testing and selection. Usually the psychologist is asked to write a report summarizing the candidate's strengths and weaknesses for a specific job. Multiaptitude instruments clearly have a role in psychological assessments in that they provide a broad base of information on a number of aptitudes and usually provide a great deal of normative data. Given the nature and time constraints involved in psychological assessments, the single battery assumption would appear to be supported. That is, in assembling a battery of tests for administration in a psychological assessment, the use of a multiaptitudes instrument would appear to provide a great deal of information at minimal costs in terms of time and money. Thus, the use of a single, wide-range test or battery in such situations would appear to be highly efficient.

In selection contexts, multiaptitude batteries tend to be reliable, valid, and efficient. As indicated in the Limitations section in this chapter, the question is one of whether it would be more valid and more efficient to simply use a general intelligence or general ability test and supplement it with specialized tests relevant to that job. Of course, multiaptitude tests do provide the advantage of offering data on additional aptitudes including psychomotor ability. The answer then is probably "it depends." In situations where a single battery is desired that can predict for a range of jobs, some of which are likely to involve abilities outside of verbal and mathematical, then the use of a multiaptitude battery may be the best solution.

In selection, there is an opening in one job and a number of candidates for that job. In classification, a number of jobs are open and a number of candidates are available for the jobs, and the problem then becomes one of assigning people to tasks or jobs based on a number of criteria (Cascio, 1998). Classification has long been a problem for the military, which is faced with placing recruits into available job openings. Although the military has conducted classification research on the ASVAB, in general, relatively little published research exists on classification problems (Campbell, 1990a, 1990b; Cascio, 1998). However, given the problems mentioned regarding the use of multiaptitude batteries in vocational counseling, one might doubt the efficiency of multiattribute batteries in making accurate classification decisions.

Overall, in evaluating the single battery assumption, the question comes down to whether the use of a single, multiaptitude battery is better and more efficient than the use of a general intelligence test alone or a general intelligence test supplemented with specific aptitude tests. Given that many multiaptitude batteries can be given in roughly the same time as some of the longer intelligence tests, the measurement of the additional abilities provided by the multiaptitude battery would appear to be a real advantage. For the practicing psychologist, a multiaptitude test provides a great deal of reliable and valid information in one, comprehensive, standardized package.

## The Future

What does the future hold in terms of multiaptitude batteries? Clearly, the computerization of tests has changed the nature of multiaptitude tests. This has both positive aspects and negative aspects. One positive aspect is that computerization allows the user to customize many of the multiaptitude batteries. Of course, this further blurs the distinctions between multiaptitude tests and intelligence tests. A second positive aspect is that computerization should lead to improvements in reliability and validity. This can come about through the use of tailored-testing approaches and greater attention to item properties and information quality (Crocker & Algina, 1986).

One of the negative aspects is that multiaptitude tests are basically a one-size-fits-all approach. However, with computerization, there is little need for one-size-fits-all. One can use the Internet to order the exact sizes a person desires or even have a garment customized. In a similar fashion, a psychologist can use the computer or the Internet to customize a test battery. This feature has particular importance in the administration of tests in the domains of psychological assessment and selection. Multiaptitude tests are also analogous to warehouses in an age of just-in-time inventories. Multiaptitude batteries provide a psychologist with a lot of information they might need but probably do not need, but offer the comfort of knowing the information is there if you should eventually need it. The computerization of test batteries allows a psychologist to request or access exactly the data they need, when they want it. It makes obsolete the older warehousing provided by traditional paper-and-pencil measures of multiaptitudes.

A second negative aspect of computerization is the demand for more information in a shorter time. Today, many consumers of tests want to measure 10 competencies in 10 minutes, regardless of the feasibility. Thus, multiaptitude test developers will be pressured to make their batteries shorter and shorter. This should not affect the validity of composite scores, and thus selection decisions, but it will affect the reliability of individual factors and, thus, the reliability of profiles and difference scores. Given that the reliability of interpretations of differences on factors has already been questioned for tests such as the ASVAB, further reduction in reliability will lead to even more questions regarding the viability of multiaptitude batteries in making vocational and classification decisions.

## Summary

Multiaptitude batteries have many positive features, which no doubt contributes to their popularity and widespread use. They are easy to administer and score, have favorable psychometric properties, and provide a great deal of information in relatively little time. However, the question as to whether the administration of a single, wide-range battery is better and more efficient than the administration of a general intelligence test is one that is difficult to answer and depends on the domain and the specific situation. In terms of the future, the computerization of multiaptitude batteries will allow users to customize their batteries but will also place demands on test developers to create batteries that can provide maximum information in minimum time, while still achieving adequate psychometric properties.

## APPENDIX: SUMMARY OF SELECTED MULTIAPTITUDE TESTS

| Test | Type | Publisher/Address/Web site |
| --- | --- | --- |
| ACT WorkKeys | Multiaptitude | ACT, Inc.<br>FD2201 North Dodge Street<br>P.O. Box 168<br>Iowa City, IA 52243-0168<br>www.act.org/workkeys |
| APTICOM | Multiaptitude | Vocational Research Institute<br>1528 Walnut St., Suite 1502<br>Philadelphia, PA 19102<br>www.vri.org/apticom |
| Armed Services Vocational Aptitude Battery (ASVAB) | Multiaptitude | United States Military Entrance Processing Command<br>ATTN: Operations Directorate<br>2500 Green Bay Road<br>North Chicago, IL 60064-3094<br>www.dmdc.osd.mil/asvab |
| Basic Skills Test (BST) | Multiaptitude | Psychological Services, Inc.<br>100 West Broadway, Suite 1100<br>Glendale, CA 91210<br>www.PSIonline.com |
| Bennett Mechanical Comprehension Test (BMCT) | Mechanical aptitude | Psychological Corporation<br>555 Academic Court<br>San Antonio, TX 78204-2498<br>www.HBEM.com |
| CareerScope | Multiaptitude | Vocational Research Institute<br>1528 Walnut St., Suite 1502<br>Philadelphia, PA 19102<br>www.vri.org/careerscope |
| Cognitive Ability Selection Tests (CAST) (expected 2004) | Multiaptitude | Institute for Personality and Ability Testing, Inc.<br>P.O. Box 1188<br>Champaign, IL 61824-1188<br>www.ipat.com |
| Comprehensive Ability Battery (CAB) | Multiaptitude | Institute for Personality and Ability Testing, Inc.<br>P.O. Box 1188<br>Champaign, IL 61824-1188<br>www.ipat.com |
| Differential Aptitude Test (DAT) | Multiaptitude, primarily for educational use | The Psychological Corporation<br>555 Academic Court<br>San Antonio, TX 78204-2498<br>www.psychcorpcenter.com |
| Employee Aptitude Survey (EAS) | Multiaptitude | Psychological Services, Inc.<br>100 West Broadway, Suite 1100<br>Glendale, CA 91210<br>www.PSIonline.com |

| Test | Type | Publisher/Address/Web site |
| --- | --- | --- |
| Educators'-Employers' Tests and Services Associates (ETSA) | Multiaptitude | Educators'/Employers' Tests & Services Associates<br>P.O. Box 327<br>Saint Thomas, PA 17252<br>www.eetsa.com |
| Flanagan Aptitude Classification Tests (FACT) | Multiaptitude | NCS (London House)<br>9701 West Higgins Road<br>Rosemont, IL 60018-4720<br>www.assessments.ncs.com |
| Flanagan Industrial Tests (FIT) | Multiaptitude | NCS (London House)<br>9701 West Higgins Road<br>Rosemont, IL 60018-4720<br>www.psychcorpcenter.com |
| Job Effectiveness Prediction System (JEPS) | Multiaptitude, insurance and financial services companies | Life Office Management Association (LOMA)<br>2300 Windy Ridge Parkway, Suite 600<br>Atlanta, GA 30339-8443<br>www.loma.org/JEPS.HTM |
| Kit of Factor Referenced Cognitive Tests | Multiaptitude (for research purposes only) | Educational Testing Service<br>Princeton, NJ 08541<br>www.ets.org |
| LEAP | Multiaptitude, insurance and financial services companies | Life Office Management Association (LOMA)<br>2300 Windy Ridge Parkway, Suite 600<br>Atlanta, GA 30339-8443<br>www.loma.org/JEPS.HTM |
| Mechanical Experiences Background Questionnaire (MEBQ, Mechanical Ability Only) | Mechanical aptitude | Andrea Snell Center for Organizational Research<br>University of Akron<br>Akron, OH 44325-4301<br>www.uakron.edu/cor |
| Morrisby Profile (MP) | Multiaptitude | The Morrisby Organisation<br>83 High Street<br>Hemel Hempstead<br>Hertfordshire HP1 3AH<br>www.morrisby.co.uk |
| Multidimensional Aptitude Battery II (MAB-II) | Multiaptitude | Sigma Assessment Systems, Inc.<br>511 Fort Street, Suite 435<br>P.O. Box 610984<br>Port Huron, MI 48061-0984<br>www.sigmaassessmentsystems.com |
| Personnel Selection Inventory (PSI) | Attitude and interests, plus selected aptitudes | NCS (London House)<br>9701 West Higgins Road<br>Rosemont, IL 60018-4720<br>www.assessments.ncs.com |

*(continued)*

| Test | Type | Publisher/Address/Web site |
| --- | --- | --- |
| Personnel Test Battery (PTB) | Multiaptitude | Saville Holdsworth, Ltd (SHL) Flatiron Park West 2555 55th Street, Suite 201D Boulder, CO 80301 www.shlgroup.com |
| Select Assessment™ for Customer Service (SACS) | Multiaptitude, plus attitudes, interests, and personality. For customer service positions. | Select International, Inc. 5700 Corporate Drive, Suite 250 Pittsburgh, PA 15237 www.selectintl.com |
| Select Assessment™ for Manufacturing (SAM) | Multiaptitude, plus attitudes, interests and personality; for manufacturing positions | Select International, Inc. 5700 Corporate Drive, Suite 250 Pittsburgh, PA 15237 www.selectintl.com |
| Systems for Testing and Evaluation of Potential (STEP) | Multiaptitude | NCS 9701 West Higgins Road Rosemont, IL 60018-4720 www.assessments.ncs.com |
| Technical Test Battery | Multiaptitude | Saville Holdsworth, Ltd (SHL) Flatiron Park West 2555 55th Street, Suite 201D Boulder, CO 80301 www.shlgroup.com |

## REFERENCES

Ackerman, P.L., & Humphreys, L.G. (1990). Individual differences theory in Industrial and Organizational Psychology. In M.V. Dunnette & L.M. Hough (Eds.), *Handbook of industrial and organizational psychology: Vol. 1* (2nd ed., pp. 223–282). Palo Alto, CA: Consulting Psychologists Press.

Alston, R.J., & Mngadi, P.S. (1992). A study of the APTICOM's effectiveness in assessing level of physical functioning. *Journal of Rehabilitation, 58,* 35–39.

American College Testing Program. (1994). *Characteristics of the WorkKeys assessments.* [Brochure]. Iowa City, IA: ACT Publications.

American Educational Research Association, American Psychological Association, and National Council on Measurement in Education. (1999). *Standards for educational and psychological testing.* Washington, DC: Author.

Anastasi, A. (1981). Coaching, test sophistication, and developed abilities. *American Psychologist, 36,* 1086–1093.

Anastasi, A., & Urbina, S. (1997). *Psychological testing* (7th ed.). New York: Macmillan.

Arvey, R.D., Strickland, W., Drauden, G., & Martin, C. (1990). Motivational components of test taking. *Personnel Psychology, 43,* 695–716.

Baehr, M.E. (1992). *Predicting success in higher-level positions. A guide to the system for testing and evaluation of potential.* New York: Quorum Books.

Barrett, G.V. (1992). Clarifying construct validity: Definitions, processes, and models. *Human Performance, 5,* 13–58.

Barrett, G.V., Carobine, R.G., & Doverspike, D. (1999). The reduction of adverse impact in an employment setting using a short-term memory test. *Journal of Business and Psychology, 14,* 371–376.

Baydoun, R.B., & Neuman, G.A. (1992). The future of the general aptitude test battery (GATB) for use in public and private testing. *Journal of Business and Psychology, 7,* 81–91.

Bennett, G.K. (1994). *Manual: BMCT-Bennett Mechanical Comprehension Test* (2nd ed.). San Antonio, TX: Psychological Corporation.

Bennett, G.K., Seashore, H.G., & Wesman, A.G. (1951). *Counseling from profiles: A casebook for the differential aptitude tests.* New York: Psychological Corporation.

Bennett, G.K., Seashore, H.G., & Wesman, A.G. (1984). *Differential aptitude tests: Technical Supplement.* San Antonio, TX: Psychological Corporation.

Binet, A., & Simon, T. (1905). Methods nouvelles pour le diagnostic du niveau intellectual des anormaux. *Annee Psychologique, 11,* 191–244.

Bobko, P., Roth, P.L., & Potosky, D. (1999). Derivation and implications of a meta-analytic matrix incorporating cognitive ability, alternative predictors, and job performance. *Personnel Psychology, 52,* 561–589.

Campbell, J.P. (1990a). An overview of the Army Selection and Classification Project (Project A). *Personnel Psychology, 43,* 231–239.

Campbell, J.P. (1990b). Modeling the performance prediction problem in industrial and organizational psychology. In M.V. Dunnette & L.M. Hough (Eds.), *Handbook of industrial and organizational psychology: Vol. 1* (2nd ed., pp. 687–732). Palo Alto, CA: Consulting Psychologists Press.

Campbell, J.P. (1996). Group differences and personnel selection decisions: Validity, fairness, and affirmative action. *Journal of Vocational Behavior, 49,* 122–158.

Cascio, W.F. (1998). *Applied psychology in human resource management* (5th ed.). Upper Saddle River, NJ: Prentice Hall.

Chan, D., & Schmitt, N. (1997). Video-based versus paper-and-pencil method of assessment in situational judgment tests: Subgroup differences in test performance and face validity perceptions. *Journal of Applied Psychology, 82,* 143–159.

Chan, D., Schmitt, N., DeShon, R.P., Clause, C.S., & Delbridge, K. (1997). Reactions to cognitive ability tests: The relationships between race, test performance, face validity perceptions, and test-taking motivation. *Journal of Applied Psychology, 82,* 300–310.

Clevenger, J., Pereira, G.M., Wiechmann, D., Schmitt, N., & Harvey, V.S. (2001). Incremental validity of situational judgment tests. *Journal of Applied Psychology, 86,* 410–417.

Comrey, A.L., & Lee, H.B. (1992). *A first course in factor analysis* (2nd ed.). Hillsdale, NJ: Erlbaum.

Crocker, L.M., & Algina, J. (1986). *Introduction to classical and modern test theory.* New York: Holt, Rinehart & Winston.

Cronbach, L.J. (1990). *Essentials of psychological testing* (5th ed.). New York: Harper & Row.

Davies, M., Stankov, L., & Roberts, R.D. (1998). Emotional intelligence: In search of an elusive construct. *Journal of Personality and Social Psychology, 75,* 989–1015.

Dawda, D., & Hart, S.D. (2000). Assessing emotional intelligence: Reliability and validity of the Bar-On Emotional Quotient Inventory (EQ-I) in university students. *Personality and Individual Differences, 28,* 797–812.

Dobbins, G.H., & Steiner, D.D. (1988). System for testing and evaluation of potential. In D.J. Keyser & R.C. Sweetland (Eds.), *Test critiques* (Vol. 7, pp. 570–581). Austin, TX: Pro-Ed.

Doverspike, D.D. (1999). On organizational and individual abilities: A short, rambling essay on implications for testing and assessment. *IPMAAC Assessment Council News,* 17–18.

Dunnette, M.D. (1976). Aptitudes, abilities, and skills. In M.V. Dunnette (Ed.), *Handbook of industrial and organizational psychology* (pp. 473–520). Chicago, IL: Rand McNally College Publishing.

Ekstrom, R.B., French, J.W., Harman, H.H., & Dermen, D. (1976). *Kit of factor-referenced cognitive tests.* Princeton, NJ: Educational Testing Service.

Ekstrom, R.B., French, J.W., & Harman, H.H. (1979). Cognitive factors: Their identification and replication. *Multivariate Behavioral Research Monographs, 79–2,* 1–84.

Educational Testing Service. (1976). *ETS kit of factor-referenced cognitive tests.* Princeton, NJ: Author.

Farrell, J.N., & McDaniel, M.A. (2001). The stability of validity coefficients over time: Ackerman's (1988) model and the General Aptitude Test Battery. *Journal of Applied Psychology, 86,* 60–79.

Flanagan, J.C. (1975). *Flanagan Industrial Tests: Examiner's manual.* Chicago: Science Research Associates.

Flanagan, J.C. (1953). *Flanagan Aptitude Classification Tests: Examiner's manual.* Chicago: Science Research Associates.

French, J.W., Ekstrom, R.B., & Price, L.A. (1963). *Kit of Factor Referenced Tests for Cognitive Factors.* Princeton, NJ: Educational Testing Service.

Gardner, H. (1983). *Frames of mind: The theory of multiple intelligences.* New York: Bantam Books.

Goleman, D. (1995). *Emotional intelligence.* New York: Bantam Books.

Good, R.H. (1999). Review of the ETSA tests. *Mental measurements yearbook (Online)* [Electronic Reference Book and Database]. New Brunswick, NJ: Buros Institute of Mental Measurements [Producer and Distributor].

Gottfredson, L.S. (1988). Reconsidering fairness: A matter of social and ethical priorities. *Journal of Vocational Behavior, 33,* 293–319.

*Griggs v. Duke Power Co.* (1971). 401 U.S. 424, 3EPD p8137, 3FEP Cases 175.

Guilford, J.P. (1967). *The nature of human intelligence.* New York: McGraw-Hill.

Guilford, J.P. (1972). Thurstone's primary mental abilities and structure-of-intellect abilities. *Psychological Bulletin, 77,* 129–143.

Guilford, J.P. (1988). Some changes in the structure-of-intellect model. *Educational and Psychological Measurement, 48,* 1–4.

Hartigan, J.A., & Wigdor, A.K. (1989). *Fairness in employment testing. Validity generalization, minority issues, and the General Aptitude Test Battery.* Washington, DC: National Academy Press

Helms, J.E. (1992). Why is there no study of cultural equivalence in standardized cognitive ability testing? *American Psychologist, 47,* 1083–1101.

Hunter, J.E. (1982). *The dimensionality of the General Aptitude Test Battery and the dominance of general factors over specific factors in the prediction of job performance.* Washington, DC: U.S. Employment Service, U.S. Department of Labor.

Hunter, J.E., & Hunter, R.F. (1984). Validity and utility of alternative predictors of job performance. *Psychological Bulletin, 96,* 72–98.

IPAT. (2001). *Ability assessment.* Retrieved October 18, 2001, from http://www.ipat.com/abilass.com.

Jackson, D.N. (1998). *Multidimensional Aptitude Battery-II manual.* Port Huron, MI: Sigma Assessment Systems.

Keyser, D.J., & Sweetland, R.C. (Eds.). (1991). *Tests: A comprehensive reference for assessments in psychology, education, and business.* Austin, TX: Pro-Ed.

Kelley, T.L. (1928). *Crossroads in the mind of man: A study of differentiable mental abilities.* Stanford University, CA: Stanford University Press.

Kolz, A.R., McFarland, L.A., & Silverman, S.B. (1998). Cognitive ability and job experience as predictors of work performance. *The Journal of Psychology, 132,* 539–548.

Lee, S., McLarty, J.M., Robie, C., Reichert, M., Edwards, L., & Tozer, J. (1995). *A concurrent validation study of the WorkKeys locating information assessment at the Louisiana Department of Civil Service.* Paper presented at the annual meeting of the International Personnel Management Association Assessment Council, New Orleans, LA.

Lee, S., & Nathan, B.R. (June, 1997). *Obtaining reliable job analysis information: A progress report from the WorkKeys System: ACT's nationwide program for improving workplace skills.* Invited presentation to the International Personnel Management Association Assessment Council Annual Meeting, Newport Beach, CA.

Life Office Management Association. (2001). *JEPS: Job Effectiveness Prediction System.* Retrieved October 5, 2001, from http://www.loma.org/JEPS.HTM.

Lubinski, D., & Dawis, R.V. (1992). Aptitudes, skill, and proficiencies. In M.V. Dunnette & L.M. Hough (Eds.), *Handbook of industrial and organizational psychology: Vol. 3* (2nd ed., pp. 1–59). Palo Alto, CA: Consulting Psychologists Press.

Lustig, D.C., Brown, C.D., & Lott, A.C. (1998). Reliability of the CareerScope career assessment and reporting system. *Vocational Evaluation & Work Adjustment Bulletin, 31,* 19–21.

McDaniel, M.A., Morgeson, F.P., Finnegan, E.B., Campion, M.A., & Braverman, G.P. (2001).Use of situational judgment tests to predict job performance: A clarification of the literature. *Journal of Applied Psychology, 86,* 730–740.

McKay, P.F., & Doverspike D. (2001). African-Americans' testing taking attitudes and their effect on cognitive ability test performance: Implications for public personnel management selection practice. *Public Personnel Management, 30,* 67–75.

McKay, P.F., Doverspike, D., Bowen-Hilton, D., & Martin, Q.D. (in press). Stereotype threat effects on the Raven's scores of African-Americans. *Journal of Applied Social Psychology.*

Messick, S. (1981). The controversy over coaching: Issues of effectiveness and equity. In B.F. Green (Ed.), *Issues in testing: Coaching, disclosure, and ethnic bias* (pp. 21–53). San Francisco: Jossey-Bass.

Millman, J., Bishop, C.H., & Ebel, R. (1965). An analysis of test-wiseness. *Educational and Psychological Measurement, 25,* 70–726.

The Morrisby Organisation. (1995). *Morrisby profile manual.* Hemel Hempstead, Hertfordshire: The Morrisby Organisation.

Murphy, K.R. (1984). Review of Armed Services Vocational Aptitude Battery. In D. Keyser & R. Sweetland (Eds.), *Test critiques* (Vol. 1). Kansas City, MO: Test Corporation of America.

Murphy, K.R., & Davidshofer, C.O. (1998). *Psychological testing: Principles and applications* (4th ed.). Upper Saddle River, NJ: Prentice Hall.

Nathan, B.R. (June, 1995). "Tests great, less filling": Reducing adverse impact through job analysis. In the symposium, *Reports from the hiring line: Applications of the WorkKeys system for selection, training, and reducing adverse impact.* International Personnel Management Association Assessment Council annual meeting, New Orleans, LA

National Computer Systems (NCS). (2000). *2000 business and industry assessment.* Rosemont, IL: NCS.

National Computer Systems (NCS–London House). (1996). *Personnel selection inventory information guide.* Rosemont, IL: NCS.

National Research Council. (1995). *Evaluation of the U.S. Employment Service's workplan for the GATB improvement project.* Washington, DC: National Academy Press.

Newsome, S., Day, A.L., & Catano, V.M. (2000). Assessing the predictive validity of emotional intelligence. *Personality and Individual Differences, 29,* 1005–1016.

O'Connell, M.S. (2000). *Meta-analysis of the Select Assessment™ for manufacturing system.* Technical Report: Select International.

O'Connell, M.S. (2001). *Summary of validation results Select Assessment™ for customer service system.* Technical report, Select International.

O'Connell, M.S., & Smith, M. (1999). *Normative and validity results for entry-level assessment scales.* Technical Report, Select International.

Rechenberg, C. (2000). *Understanding gender differences in mechanical performance.* Unpublished doctoral dissertation, University of Akron, Akron, OH.

Rechenberg, C., & Snell, A.F. (1997). *Construct validity of mechanical aptitude measures: An examination of convergent validity evidence.* Unpublished master's thesis, University of Akron, Akron, OH.

Ree, M.J., Earles, J.A., & Teachout, M.S. (1994). Predicting job performance: Not much more than g. *Journal of Applied Psychology, 79,* 518–524.

Roth, P.L., Bevier, C.A., Bobko, P., Switzer, F.S. III, & Tyler, P. (2001). Ethnic group difference in cognitive ability in employment and educational settings: A meta-analysis. *Personnel Psychology, 54,* 297–330.

Ruch, W.W., Stang, S.W., McKillip, R.H., & Dye, D.A. (1994). *Technical manual for the Employee Aptitude Survey* (2nd ed.). Los Angeles, CA: Psychological Services.

Ruch, W.W., Weiner, J.A., McKillip, R.H., & Dye, D.A. (1985). *Technical manual for the PSI Basic Skills Tests for business, industry, and government.* Los Angeles, CA: Psychological Services.

Sackett, P.R., & Wilk, S.L. (1994) Within group norming and other forms of score adjustment in pre-employment testing. *American Psychologist, 49,* 929–954.

Schmidt, F.L., & Hunter, J.E. (1981). Employment testing: Old theories and new research findings. *American Psychologist, 36,* 1128–1137.

Schmidt, F.L., & Hunter, J.E. (1998). The validity of selection methods in personnel psychology: Practical and theoretical implications of 85 years of research findings. *Psychological Bulletin, 124,* 262–274.

Schmitt, N., & Mills, A.E. (2001). Traditional tests and job simulations: Minority and majority performance and test validities. *Journal of Applied Psychology, 86,* 451–458.

Schutte, N.S., Malouff, J.M., Hall, L.E., Haggerty, D.J., Cooper, J.T., Golden, C.J., & Dornheim, L. (1998). Development and validation of a measure of emotional intelligence. *Personality and Individual Differences, 25,* 167–177.

Spearman, C.S. (1904). General intelligence objectively determined and measured. *American Journal of Psychology, 15,* 201–209.

Spearman, C.S. (1927). *The abilities of man.* New York: Macmillan.

Science Research Associates. (1956). *Summary report for the selective service system college qualification tests.* Chicago, IL: Author.

Steele, C.M., & Aronson, J. (1995). Stereotype threat and the intellectual test performance of African Americans. *Journal of Personality & Social Psychology, 69(5),* 797–811.

Sternberg, R.J. (Ed.) (1982). *Handbook of human intelligence.* New York: Cambridge University Press.

Sternberg, R.J. (1984). Toward a triarchic theory of human intelligence. *Behavioral and Brain Sciences, 7,* 269–315.

Sternberg, R.J. (1985). *Beyond IQ: A triarchic theory of human intelligence.* New York: Cambridge University Press.

Stone, E.F., & Hollenbeck, J.R. (1989). Clarifying some controversial issues surrounding statistical procedures for detecting moderator variables: Empirical evidence and related matters. *Journal of Applied Psychology, 74,* 3–10.

Tabachnick, B.G., & Fidell, L.S. (2001). *Using multivariate statistics* (4th ed.). Boston, MA: Allyn & Bacon.

Terman, L.M. (1916). *The measurement of intelligence.* Boston: Houghton Mifflin.

Thompson, J.W. (1994). An internal validation of London House's STEP battery. *Journal of Business and Psychology, 9,* 81–99.

Thurstone, L.L. (1938). Primary mental abilities. *Psychometric Monographs, 1,* ix + 121.

Thurstone, L.L. (1941). Factorial studies of intelligence. *Psychometric Monographs, 2,* 94.

Vocational Research Institute. (2001a). *CareerScope 5.0: Career assessment and reporting system.* Retrieved October 5, 2001, from http://www.vri.org/careerscope.

Vocational Research Institute. (2001b). *Vocational and career assessment that work.* Retrieved October 5, 2001, from http://www.vri.org/apticom.

CHAPTER 5

# Information-Processing Tests

WINFRED ARTHUR JR., DENNIS DOVERSPIKE, AND SUZANNE T. BELL

Information-processing theories view the human mind as an information processor that codes, stores, and retrieves environmental inputs (Ackerman, 1988; Neisser, 1967; Newell & Simon, 1972; Sternberg, 1977). Since at least the 1970s information-processing-based theories and approaches have been dominant in many areas of psychology, including human factors, instructional, social, and cognitive psychology (Sternberg, 1977, 1979; Whitely, 1977). Logically, researchers and practitioners have attempted to develop tests based on information-processing theory and these tests are generically described as "information-processing tests."

Historically, the development of information-processing tests has been characterized as having unlimited promise; unfortunately, there has been very little practical success. Specifically, although they have been shown to predict performance on such complex real-world perceptual, psychomotor information-processing tasks like flying an aircraft (Carretta, Perry, & Ree, 1996; Carretta & Ree, 1996; Gopher, 1982; Gopher & Bareket, 1994; Gopher & Kahneman, 1971; North & Gopher, 1976), monitoring and maintenance tasks (e.g., Forbes & Barrett, 1978; Forbes, Barrett, Alexander, & Phillips, 1976; O'Connor, Barrett, & Alexander, 1977), driving (Arthur, Barrett, & Alexander, 1991; Arthur, Barrett, & Doverspike, 1990; Arthur & Doverspike, 1992; Arthur, Strong, & Williamson, 1994; Avolio, Kroeck, & Panek, 1985; Mihal & Barrett, 1976), and air traffic control (Ackerman & Kanfer, 1993), their use in mainstream industrial/organizational psychology and personnel selection and testing has been very limited. Indeed the most extensive use of these

tests is found in the U.S. Air Force (e.g., see Carretta, 2000 for a review of U.S. Air Force pilot selection and training methods; Carretta & Ree, 1994; Hunter, 1989; Ree & Carretta, 1998). Therefore, in this chapter we discuss not only the underlying theory and rationale for information-processing tests, but also the limitations. We hope this discussion of limitations will spur a renewed interest in information-processing test research.

There are relatively few published or commercially available information-processing tests. Thus, the approach we take in this chapter is first to discuss the basic rationale and theory underlying information-processing tests. We follow this with a discussion of the various approaches to developing information-processing tests, including a discussion of the method of testing. Various approaches to scoring information-processing tests are also discussed. Next, we discuss several different prototypical information-processing tests—this presentation is organized by the construct measured and includes (1) information-processing as multiple aptitudes; (2) short-term memory capacity; (3) processing speed; (4) selective attention; and (5) field dependence-independence. We then present a discussion of the limitations of information-processing tests and conclude with comments and a discussion of the future of information-processing tests.

Given the paucity of published information on information-processing tests, in order to collect the information used in writing this chapter, a letter was sent to all major tests publishers requesting any information they might have on available commercial information-processing tests. In addition, a literature search was conducted using several electronic (e.g., *Education Research Information Center* [*ERIC*], *Econ-Lit, Government Printing Office, PsycInfo, Social Science Citation Index, Wilson*) and nonelectronic (e.g., the *Mental Measurement Yearbooks, Tests in Print, Test Critiques, Test Critiques Compendium*) sources. Finally, we relied on our own extensive backgrounds in information-processing testing and our professional libraries. Two of us, Arthur and Doverspike, have a combined 40 years of personal experience with information-processing tests, including involvement with field and laboratory research with occupations as varied as secretarial, clerical, firefighter, police officer, petroleum transport driver, process control worker, maintenance mechanic, and pilot.

Based on the information collected, this chapter presents an overview or survey of some of the major information-processing-based approaches to testing. As such, our intent was not to provide a comprehensive list of every measure, but rather to give the reader some fundamental insight into this area of personnel selection research.

## THEORY AND RATIONALE

"Information processing" is an ambiguous term and can refer to many different perspectives in cognitive and social psy-

chology. However, as previously noted, in general, when we speak of an information-processing test, we are referring to a test that is based on an approach that views the human mind as an information processor that codes, stores, and retrieves environmental inputs (Neisser, 1967; Newell & Simon, 1972).

There are many different information-processing models (Card, Moran, & Newell, 1980; Kandra, 1991; Newell & Simon, 1972); however, most models include certain basic components. Figure 5.1 presents an illustration of the basic elements common to most information-processing models. Inspection of Figure 5.1 reveals that the components of the information-processing model include:

- *A Short-Term Sensory Store.* This serves as the initial input mechanism for external stimuli. Typically, the short-term sensory store only retains information for a very short time, less than 300 ms.

- *A Perceptual Mechanism.* This mechanism controls pattern detection, discrimination, identification, organization, and recognition. This is where some cues taken in during sensory store become more important than others. This processing takes place very rapidly, and again, the information is retained for a very short time.

- *A Mechanism for Decision Making or Response Selection.* This mechanism activates the appropriate action or re-

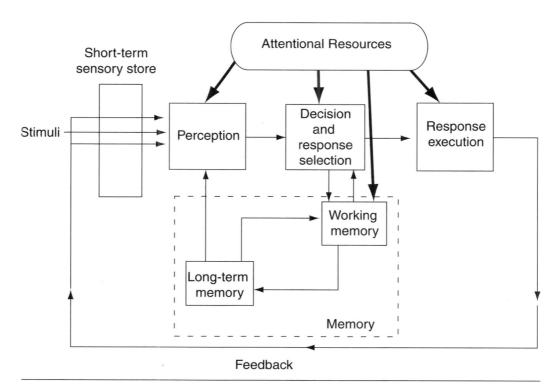

**Figure 5.1** A general information-processing model.

sponse, which includes retrieving information from memory, making comparisons, and a host of additional decision-making and thought processes.

- *Short-Term Memory.* Also often referred to as working memory. The size and speed of working memory serves as a major constraint or bottleneck for the information-processing system. Working memory stores information for a brief length of time while elements like order of presentation are preserved.

- *Long-Term Memory.* Used for the long-term storage of information. The contents of long-term memory are dependent on which information has passed through short-term memory. Although the capacity of long-term memory is virtually limitless, information tends to be stored in various kinds of knowledge structures (e.g., schemas, scripts, and prototypes).

- *Mechanisms for Response Execution.* Controls the selection and execution of a response.

- *An Attentional Pool.* A limited pool of attentional resources determines which aspects of the environment are allowed to filter through for conscious or controlled processing. Along with working memory, this is often considered to be a major bottleneck in the information-processing system.

In addition to structural components, most information-processing models share certain basic assumptions. In terms of the development of information-processing tests, the most critical assumptions include:

- *Nonimmediacy.* There is always a time interval between the presentation of a stimulus and the generation of a response. This time corresponds to time spent in mental processing and can be divided or added up to correspond to the amount of time required to accomplish various mental tasks or activities (Posner & Mitchell, 1967; for a critique of this view see McClelland, 1979).

- *Limited Capacity.* This is one of the most critical assumptions. Individuals are viewed as having limited attentional and structural capabilities or capacities (Broadbent, 1957; Fisher, 1982; Navon & Gopher, 1979). This limited capacity is a result of the necessity to share attentional resources and the cause of various bottlenecks in the system.

- *Individual Differences.* There are individual differences among normal adults in information-processing speed and capacity and these individual differences can be effectively measured to differentiate among individuals (Ackerman, 1987, 1988).

Given that there are individual differences in information-processing ability, it should be possible then to develop tests of information-processing ability. Thus, information-processing tests can be described as a class of paper-and-pencil, computerized, or performance/apparatus-based tests in which the test taker's recognition, retention, reaction time, capacity, or other responses are measured in response to verbal or perceptual stimuli.

Of course, one could argue that the measurement of information-processing abilities is nothing new and that the earliest approaches to psychological assessment involved the evaluation of fundamental processes such as reaction time. Were it not for Binet's success with his approach to intelligence testing, information-processing tests might have been developed much earlier. The controversy between the Binet tradition and the Galton−Spearman tradition is still present in testing today (Eysenck, 1998; Murphy & Davidshorfer, 1998).

Modern tests of information processing arose out of an experimental tradition that ignored individual differences but demonstrated the viability of the information-processing approach (Carroll, 1976). A number of researchers soon discovered that individual differences in information-processing ability, especially short-term memory, were related to differences in intelligence (Hunt, 1980; Hunt, Frost, & Lunneborg, 1973; Hunt, Lunneborg, Lewis, 1975; Lunneborg, 1977, 1978; Snow, 1978). Other early advances were offered by the Kit of Reference Tests for Cognitive Factors (Ekstrom, French, Harman, & Dermen, 1976; French, Ekstrom, & Price, 1963), which could be viewed as a paper-and-pencil-based attempt to measure information-processing abilities, and the Rod-and-Frame Test (Witkin, Lewis, Machover, Meissner, & Wapner, 1954; Witkin, Oltman, Raskin, & Karp, 1971), a very early attempt at an apparatus-based measure of cognitive or information-processing style.

## DEVELOPMENT

When developing information-processing tests, a number of approaches can be followed. Although information-processing tests appear to be particularly compatible with computerized testing, it is possible to develop paper-and-pencil or performance/apparatus-based tests. For paper-and-pencil testing, two basic developmental approaches have been used. The first is to convert a test from the experimental literature to a paper-and-pencil format (see Cory, 1977). The second is to build or construct a test using a construct/content strategy of test development (Doverspike, 1996).

Similarly, several options are also available for computerized and apparatus-based tests. One simple option is to convert a paper-and-pencil test into a computerized format (e.g., Carretta, 1987; Carretta et al., 1996; Carretta & Ree, 1993). A second option is to turn to the experimental psychology literature, look for successful measures, and turn these measures into computerized information-processing tests (e.g., Arthur & Doverspike, 1993; Carretta, 1987; Gopher & Kahneman, 1971; Mihal & Barrett, 1976; Ree & Carretta, 1998). A very good illustrative example of this approach is the U.S. Air Force Learning Abilities Measurement Program (LAMP), which was established in the early 1980s (Kyllonen, 1993; Kyllonen & Christal, 1986). The third option would be to build or construct a test based on a construct/content strategy (Doverspike, 1996).

Regardless of the approach followed, the first step in the development of information-processing tests as selection tools in organizations is to conduct a job analysis. The information-processing test construction process requires a much more detailed, intensive job analysis approach than might be normally required. Incumbents are asked to think and talk aloud about the performance of tasks and duties, a procedure similar to protocol analysis that has been described elsewhere as an information-processing job analysis (Arthur, Barrett, & Doverspike 1990; Barrett & Maurer, 1989). For instance, in their study of transport drivers, Arthur, Barrett, and Doverspike (1990) used a combination of semistructured interviews, observation, and the review of training materials to collect information similar to that obtained in a procedural or fault-tree analysis. Axton, Doverspike, Park, and Barrett (1997) also used a similar job analysis procedure in a study of mechanical troubleshooting. These analyses suggested that the following abilities and information-processing events were critical in troubleshooting:

1. Ability to detect differences between standard and comparative (other) figures.
2. Ability to search for discrepancy-cause relations.
3. Ability to remember behavior sequences.
4. Ability to process information while holding information in short-term memory.
5. Basic reaction time (Axton et al., 1997).

The job or task analysis can be performed at a macro or micro level. At the macro level, decision points and general cognitive operations are identified. Examples might be retrieving names from memory or a particular method of scanning a map. At the micro level, the analysis focuses on more detailed information-processing speed and capacity.

For example, the job analysis might determine how many bits of information have to be held in memory and for how long.

## METHOD OF TESTING

In the design and development of tests, the distinction between the content and method is an important one. *Content* refers to the constructs and variables (e.g., cognitive ability, finger dexterity, field dependence-independence, reaction time, and visual attention) that are being measured, and *method* refers to the techniques or procedures (e.g., paper-and-pencil tests, computer-administered tests, and performance tests) that we use to accomplish the measurement of the specified content (Campbell, 1990). The theoretical, conceptual, and informative value of the method/content distinction is highlighted by Arthur, Archuleta, Sheehan, and Villado's (2003) meta-analysis on predictors in personnel selection; Huffcutt, Conway, Roth, and Stone's (2001) meta-analysis of the constructs measured by employment interviews; and Arthur, Day, McNelly, and Edens's (in press) meta-analysis of assessment center dimensions. For instance, from a methodological perspective, specified comparisons of different test formats or constructs require that one (e.g., method) be held constant while the other (e.g., construct) is varied. Consequently, wherever it is pertinent in our discussion of information-processing constructs, we highlight the testing methods.

The test methods commonly used with information-processing testing are (1) paper-and-pencil tests, (2) performance/apparatus-based tests, and (3) computerized tests. The traditional method of assessment for information-processing tests has been via paper-and-pencil. Examples of paper-and-pencil information-processing tests reviewed in this chapter are the Kit of Reference Tests for Cognitive Factors (Ekstrom et al., 1976; French et al., 1963), and the Group Embedded Figures Test (Witkin & Goodenough, 1981; Witkin et al., 1971).

Performance or apparatus-based tests require a physical, behavioral action (response) from the test taker or the manipulation of an object or some aspect of the environment by the test taker in response to the test stimulus. Thus, the Auditory Selective Attention Test (Arthur & Doverspike, 1993; Mihal & Barrett, 1976), which is reviewed later in this chapter, requires test takers to verbally call out or repeat the relevant stimuli in the cued ear. The Portable Rod-and-Frame Test (Oltman, 1968), which is also reviewed later in this chapter, requires the test taker to move a rod to true vertical. Finally, reaction time tests may require a test taker to push a button as quickly as possible when a cued light is lit.

With the advent, pervasiveness, and ubiquity of computers, there has been an increase in the computerization of information-processing tests. In addition to their potential to facilitate adaptive testing (Lord, 1970; Wood, 1974), the increasing popularity of computerized information-processing tests may also be due to their ability to provide stimulus characteristics and formats that can be closer to those found in jobs than those provided by paper-and-pencil tests. Computerized tests can be designed to be self-administered in a standardized manner and also have advantages associated with administration and scoring. For instance, computers can immediately score the test and provide both accuracy and speed scores or some weighted composite of the two. The Computer-Administered Visual Attention Test (Arthur et al., 1995; Arthur, Strong, & Williamson, 1994) is an example of a computer-administered test that is reviewed in this chapter. Other examples of computerized tests include the Basic Attributes Test (BAT; Carretta, 1987; Carretta & Ree, 1993; Carretta, Zelenski, & Ree, 2000), the Graphic and Information Processing Tests (GRIP, Cory, 1977), and the CogScreen-AE (Callister, King, & Retzlaff, 1996; Kay, 1995; Taylor, O'Hara, Mumenthaler, & Yesavage, 2000). The reader may also refer to Ree and Carretta (1998), who present an informative review of computerized testing in the U.S. Air Force.

It is important to note that it is sometimes difficult, if not impossible, to draw a distinction between computerized tests and performance/apparatus-based tests. For instance, the Time Sharing II test (Fleishman, 1964), which is a BAT test and was also evaluated as part of the Aircrew Situational Awareness Technology Project (Arthur, 1995), appears to be a test that meets the definitions of *both* performance/apparatus-based and computerized tests. Specifically, the BAT hardware includes a 386-based computer, a monitor, a specialized keypad, a single-axis control stick for the left hand, and a dual-axis control stick for the right hand. Test takers respond to the tests by entering responses on the keypad and/or manipulating the control sticks. Time Sharing II is a test of attention, reaction time, and rate control (Fleishman, 1964). The first part of the test is a compensatory tracking task where the test taker maneuvers the right-hand control stick to keep a "gunsight" centered on an airplane on the monitor. The second part of the test is an attention task. Single digits appear, one at a time, in sequence (e.g., 0 1 2 3 4 5 6 7 8 9 0 1 2 3 . . .) on the lower part of the screen. Occasionally, a digit is omitted from the sequence (e.g., 0 1 2 3 5 6 7 . . . [4 is omitted here]). The test taker's task is to type the missing digit on the keypad. During the third and final part of the test, the test taker simultaneously performs the tracking and attention tasks.

Thus, Time Sharing II highlights the difficulty that can sometime be encountered in trying to draw a distinction between computerized and performance tests. Indeed, as a summary statement, although all computerized tests that require a physical/performance response—either via the keyboard, mouse, joystick, or some other peripheral—can be considered to be performance/apparatus-based tests, but not all performance/apparatus-based tests are computerized tests.

## SCORING OF INFORMATION-PROCESSING TESTS

Another decision in the design and development of information-processing tests is how they will be scored. Information-processing tests can be scored in one of three ways, either in terms of (1) correct responses (accuracy), (2) response time (speed—how quickly the test taker responds to items), or (3) some weighted composite of accuracy and speed using specified algorithms. The choice of scoring procedure is probably most important in the design and development of specific tests because scoring procedures should match the operational construct on the job. For instance, tests should be scored in terms of correct responses only if this is indeed the primary criterion in performance on the job. This information should be obtained from the job analysis. Examples of tests scored only in terms of correct responses are the Group Embedded Figures tests and the Rod-and-Frame tests. Although they are timed, these tests have generous time limits that allow most test takers to complete all items.

Some tests are also designed to specifically measure speed of information processing and, consequently, are scored in terms of response time. Standard simple and complex reaction time tests are examples of tests that are scored in this manner. Speed scores are typically associated with computerized testing and indicate how quickly individuals think, solve problems, make decisions, or more generally, how quickly individuals process information. It is also possible to score speed-of-information-processing tests in terms of the number of correct responses. Indeed, most of these measures (e.g., the Visual Search test described later in this chapter) can be scored in terms of *both* correct responses and response time. However, because they are designed to have very high rates of correct responding, the use of such tests in a correct response format is likely to lead to relatively low levels of reliability and generally poor psychometric properties.

Where appropriate, information-processing tests can be designed to be scored both in terms of accuracy and response time. This scoring approach requires some weighted composite of accuracy and speed using specified algorithms that are consistent with the operation of the construct on the job.

Again, the pertinent information should be obtained from the job analysis. Weighted speed/accuracy scoring approaches are easy to implement with computer-administered tests. For instance, the CA-VAT can be scored using the following algorithm:

$$Item\ score\ =\ (T_i\ -\ E_i)\ +\ \left[(T_i\ -\ E_i)\ \times\ \left(\frac{1}{RT_c}\right)\right]\quad (1)$$

where $T_i$ = total number of subitems (or stimuli; as described in the review of the CA-VAT later in this chapter; each CA-VAT item consists of 19 or 21 stimuli or subitems to which the test taker has to respond); $E_i$ = number of errors (includes incorrect responses and nonresponses), and $RT_c$ = response time for correct responses. Thus, the test taker's score is a function of both the number of correct responses and the response time for those correct responses. The number of correct responses is multiplied by the inverse of the response time to assign higher scores to those test takers who get a large number of items correct and who respond quickly. The test score is then the mean or sum of the item scores.

Another example of an information-processing test that is scored in terms of both speed and accuracy is the Encoding Speed Test from the Aircrew Situational Awareness Technology Project (Arthur, 1996). The Encoding Speed Test is a verbal test of processing speed (Posner & Mitchell, 1967) where two letters are simultaneously presented to the test taker. The test taker is then required to make a judgment about whether the letters are the same or different. The complexity of the decision rule used to make this judgment increases from the first to the third part of the test. Specifically, in the first part, the test taker has to determine whether the letters, as *figures,* are the same or different. In the second part, the test taker has to determine whether the letters have the same *name* or not. And in the third and last part, the decision is one of whether the letters are both *vowels or consonants.* In all three parts of the test, the letter pairs are presented as various combinations of lower and upper case letters. The Encoded Speed Test can subsequently be scored using the following algorithm:

$$Item\ score\ =\ (A\ \times\ B)\ +\ (B\ -\ D)\quad (2)$$

where $A$ = response (correct response = +1; incorrect response or no response = −1); $B$ = maximum allowable item response time, and $D$ = test taker's response time. This algorithm penalizes test takers for incorrect responses. Test takers who get an item correct and respond quickly receive higher scores. On the other hand, those who respond incorrectly and take longer to respond receive lower scores.

Although it is commonly accepted that correct responses will add to a test taker's score, the way to handle incorrect and nonresponses can vary according to whether the latter two response options are considered equally undesirable or whether one is considered less desirable than the other (e.g., it is worse to respond incorrectly than not to answer at all). Again, this information will be obtained through the job analysis. The algorithm presented in Equation 2 assumes that an incorrect response and a nonresponse are equally undesirable. However, if one wants to differentiate between an incorrect response and a nonresponse, and one also assumes that an incorrect response is less desirable than a nonresponse, then the algorithm could be modified to score responses as +1, 0, and −1 for correct responses, nonresponses, and incorrect responses, respectively. (It should be noted that if nonresponses are considered less desirable than incorrect responses, then incorrect responses should be assigned a value of 0 and nonresponses, a value of −1.)

## TYPES OF TESTS

In this section, major categories of information-processing tests are reviewed. This review is structured around the construct being measured or the general approach to measurement and thus focuses on the following: (1) information processing as consisting of multiple aptitudes; (2) short-term memory capacity; (3) processing time; (4) selective attention; and (5) field dependence-independence.

### Multiaptitude Approach to Information Processing

We use the term "multiaptitude approach" in the same way in which it is used to describe the standard approach to measuring multiple aptitudes using a battery of tests as epitomized by the General Aptitude Test Battery (GATB, Hartigan & Wigdor, 1989). Specifically, a multiaptitude test battery refers to a collection of instruments designed to measure a number of specific aptitudes in one comprehensive battery. So in this context, information processing is treated as an aptitude, capacity, or capability that can be measured in the same way as any other similar latent trait can be measured. Thus, a test can be formed by constructing or writing a series of problems corresponding to the information-processing aptitude and then a person's score on the latent trait can be calculated by counting the number of correct answers. As with many other aptitudes, the tests can be written to be very general or specific to various jobs, occupations, or tasks.

The following section discusses two basic categories of multiaptitude tests, specifically general (e.g., the Kit of Reference Tests for Cognitive Factors) and specific multiaptitude information-processing tests.

### *Kit of Reference Tests for Cognitive Factors*

One of the early, influential attempts to measure basic cognitive factors was provided by the Kit of Reference Tests for Cognitive Factors (Ekstrom, French, & Harman, 1979; Ekstrom et al., 1976; French et al., 1963). The Kit measures 23 basic, cognitive factors. More important, several of these factors can be seen as representing attempts to measure more basic information-processing components. The Kit is a paper-and-pencil battery, and most tests are scored in terms of correct responses. Multiple tests exist for each of the 23 basic cognitive factors. For most factors, there are three separate tests—this allows at least two different tests to be used to measure a factor. The 23 factors include measures of the major factors of reasoning, verbal comprehension, number facility, spatial ability, perceptual speed, memory, and fluency. These tests were purposely kept short because they are intended primarily for research.

The Kit of Reference Tests for Cognitive Factors serves as an example of the amount of work that can go into constructing and researching a multiaptitude test of cognitive factors. The Kit is based on an impressive body of research conducted on its psychometric properties over a number of years beginning in 1951, and in some cases dating back to the 1940s (Ekstrom et al., 1976). The Kit is supported by a large body of research on its factor structure and reliability (most subtests have internal consistency reliabilities above .70).

The tests in the Kit are described by the Educational Testing Service (ETS; www.ets.org) as intended for research use only, and not for use in selection, counseling, or operational purposes. For interested researchers, further information about the Kit is available from ETS.

### *Specific Information-Processing Aptitudes*

As described, the Kit involved an attempt to develop measures of more *general* information-processing aptitudes. It is also possible to develop measures of more *specific* information-processing events or aptitudes. When using a specific information-processing approach, a content valid information-processing test, specific to the demands of the particular situation, is developed. Thus, tests are tailored to a specific job or task and are consequently based on an intensive job or task analysis.

A number of studies have been completed at the University of Akron that employ this approach. The tests developed in this research program have been computerized tests and have been scored in terms of correct responses. For example,

in Axton et al.'s (1997) study of mechanical troubleshooting, a measure was developed that required test takers to determine whether a probe letter was the same or different from a standard letter; the differences could include small discrepancies in color or font. The test consisted of 60 trials and was scored in terms of correct responses. Another test required the test taker to learn a simple set of rules and then inspect a simple system of sensors to determine if there was a break in the rules. Again, this test was scored in terms of number of correct. Other studies have assessed the ability of task-specific information-processing measures to predict performance on resource-dependent and resource-independent clerical tasks (Gussett, 1992), legal tasks (Szmania, 1993), and process control tasks (Carr, 1992); the prediction of performance in maintenance positions (Park, 1991); and a position classification task (Roos, 1993).

Typically, measures of specific information processing have adequate internal consistency reliabilities, that is, .80 or higher (Axton et al., 1997; Kandra, 1991). They also tend to be valid predictors of task, job, and simulator performance with validities often in the .20 to .50 range. However, the validities for measures of general cognitive ability are often as high or higher (Axton et al., 1997; Kandra, 1991). Although measures of specific information processing do appear to add incremental validity to that offered by general cognitive ability tests, the additional variance explained tends to be small (Carretta & Ree, 1994, 1996; Ree & Earles, 1992; Ree, Earles, & Teachout, 1994).

### **Short-Term Memory Capacity**

A major class of standard, paper-and-pencil tests devoted to the measurement of information processing is short-term memory tests. As the name implies, short-term memory tests attempt to assess individual differences in short-term memory processing. Perhaps the most common format for paper-and-pencil short-term memory tests is the one used for the picture–number test. Another format, used with individually administered short-term memory tests is to have the test administrator read the stimuli aloud to the applicant. It is also possible to develop computerized measures of accuracy in the ability to remember a series of letters or numbers.

### *Picture–Number Tests*

As the name suggests, picture–number tests require the test taker to memorize and then recall a series of picture and number pairs. A sample item that might appear in a picture–number test is presented in Figure 5.2. It is relatively easy to manipulate the content of the picture–number pair for different purposes. For example, pictures of people might be

Study Page

Test Page

**Figure 5.2**   Example of three picture–number test items.

used for police officers, and pictures of buildings might be used for firefighters. In addition, the numbers can be replaced with letters.

A typical picture number test consists of a number of pages of picture–number combinations. The test taker is shown a page and given an opportunity to study the page (as illustrated in the top half of Figure 5.2). The page is then removed and a test page then appears that consists of the pictures without numbers (e.g., bottom half of Figure 5.2). The test taker's task is to recall and write down the numbers corresponding to the pictures. The short time interval between the presentation of the study and test items ensures that this information is being retrieved from short-term memory. The test taker's score is the number of letters/numbers correctly recalled.

Picture–number tests have more than adequate reliability and are also valid predictors of performance in jobs requiring this type of memory (Kandra, 1991; Verive & McDaniel, 1996). Paper-and-pencil versions of short-term memory tests have also been found to have fewer subgroup differences and less adverse impact than general cognitive ability tests (Barrett, Carobine, & Doverspike, 1999; Jensen, 1973; Jensen & Inouye, 1980; Verive & McDaniel, 1996).

### Short-Term Memory Sequence

A variety of tests that require the test taker to remember a series of letters or numbers in a particular order are available or easily constructed. In this type of task, the test taker is presented with a series of number or letters either orally or by computer. The test taker is then asked to recall the series in either a forward or backward direction.

Tests of the ability to recall a sequence in short-term memory tend to be highly reliable, with internal consistency re-

liabilities in excess of .90. Furthermore, Verive and McDaniel (1996) found short-term memory tests to have the highest predictive validity for occupations with medium cognitive demands ($\rho = .51$) compared with high ($\rho = .29$) and low ($\rho = .34$) cognitive demand occupations.

### Short-Term Memory Capacity

It is also relatively easy to develop measures of short-term memory capacity or of the ability to manipulate information in working memory. Many of these same instruments can also be used to measure processing speed if accuracy rates approach 100%. But if the tests are made more difficult, they can then be used to assess individual differences in the ability to store and manipulate information in memory.

For example, Kyllonen and Christal (1990) describe a measure of working memory. The participant is asked to memorize a series of letters and then told to add or subtract a number, which causes them to move forward or backward in the series. The task is to recall the letter that is removed by the target number of digits from the probe letter. With a sufficient number of trials, this test appears to have adequate internal consistency reliability and validities similar to those for other short-term memory tests (e.g., Axton et al., 1997; Verive & McDaniel, 1996).

### Information-Processing Speed

Although it is possible to measure accuracy in information processing, recently more attention has been paid to the speed of information processing. The speed of processing corresponds to the arrows between elements in Figure 5.1 and appears to be related to general intelligence (Hunt, 1980;

Lunneborg, 1977, 1978). As a result, a number of information-processing tests are designed to have accuracy rates approaching 100% but are then scored in terms of the average time to produce a response, where time is often measured in milliseconds. The introduction of personal computers with sensitive timing mechanisms has greatly eased the administrative burden associated with these measures, to the point that it would be difficult to imagine how many of the measures discussed in this section could be administered without personal computers.

The Choice Reaction Time Test, Sequential Memory Test, Simultaneous Memory Test, and Visual Search Test are four examples of frequently used measures that are based on the memory-scanning paradigm of Sternberg (1967, 1969, 1975), as also employed by Chiang and Atkinson (1976). In this paradigm, the time required to compare an immediate stimulus with a stimulus set in short-term memory consists of encoding, binary decision, and response production. As stimuli are added to the memory set, it is possible by regressing response time on memory set size to arrive at a slope measure that is interpreted as an index of speed of scanning short-term memory (Taylor, 1976) and an intercept measure that corresponds to choice reaction time.

The *Choice Reaction Time Test* is frequently used as a type of baseline measure, although individual differences on this task may predict job performance (the specific description presented here is based on its use in the research labs at the University of Akron; cf. Barrett, Alexander, Doverspike, Cellar, & Thomas, 1982). A standard version of the Choice Reaction Time Test involves the presentation of a warning signal (an asterisk) followed 1 to 5 s later (the interval is randomly determined) by the presentation of a letter or a number. The test taker then responds by pressing an appropriate button on a response panel according to whether a letter or a number had been presented. A series of trials is administered. The score consists of mean response time in milliseconds, with only correct responses being included in the calculation of the mean response time. This test serves as a baseline measure of reaction time, although it should be noted that this measure includes the physical reaction time plus the time required to make a choice.

In the *Sequential Memory Test,* one to five letters are presented sequentially; each letter is presented for a short time period (e.g., 800 ms), followed by a short delay (e.g., 200 ms). Following the presentation of the last letter, there is a delay, then a probe letter is presented. The test taker responds by pressing the appropriate button on a response panel, reflecting whether the probe letter was the same or different from any one of the memory set letters. Based on a regression

analysis, number of letters predicting response time, measures of slope, intercept, and number correct are computed.

The *Simultaneous Memory Test* consists of one to five letters presented simultaneously in a horizontal array for a short period of time (e.g., 3 s). These letters are then erased and after a short delay (e.g., 2 s), the probe letter is presented. The test taker responds by pressing the appropriate button on a response panel, reflecting whether the probe letter was the same or different from any one of the memory set letters. Based on a regression analysis, number of letters predicting response time, measures of slope, intercept, and number correct are computed.

The *Visual Search Test* consists of the presentation of a probe letter. After a short delay, the probe letter is erased and then one to five letters are presented simultaneously. Following the presentation of the string of letters, the test taker responds by pressing the appropriate button on a response panel, reflecting whether the probe letter was the same or different from any one of the letters displayed on the screen. Based on a regression analysis, number of letters predicting response time, measures of slope, intercept, and number correct are computed.

The four measures discussed in the preceding are among the most common, and many variations of them have been developed. The common feature underlying these measures is that they rely on a measure of response time and then decompose this reaction time, usually through the use of regression analysis, to arrive at a measure of processing time.

Large individual differences are found on these information-processing measures (Barrett et al., 1982). Split-half reliabilities tend to be better for the intercept measures, above .80, than the slope measures, .17–.68 (Barrett et al., 1982; Kandra, 1991). Test-retest and alternative form reliabilities are also more likely to be in a reasonable range for ability measures for intercept or mean reaction time than for slope (Barrett et al., 1982; Kandra, 1991). Although various measures do appear to possess convergent and divergent validity with other computerized measures, the correlations with paper-and-pencil measures are typically low to moderate, although it could be argued that the correlation with general cognitive ability is still higher than desirable, if it is that shared variance which explains the ability of these measures to predict task and job performance (Barrett et al., 1982; Kandra, 1991). Given the generally more positive psychometric properties of intercept measures (which correspond to choice reaction time), empirical research (Cellar et al., 1982) has supported the expectation that they are better predictors of job or task performance than slope measures.

In summary, measures of reaction or response time appear to predict task or job performance. However, because cognitive ability also predicts said performance, often with stronger effects, this inevitably raises the question of whether measures of speed of processing contribute incremental validity over and beyond measures of cognitive ability. Although research suggests that speed of processing contributes additional variance beyond the predictive power of cognitive ability, the gains are usually modest and fail to dispel questions about whether this additional variance has *practical* significance (Carr, 1992; Kandra, 1991).

The paradigm for developing the computerized speed of processing tests described in the preceding can be readily applied to the measurement of other general or specific information-processing abilities. Computerized measures of information processing can also be used with a range of ability and demographic (e.g., age, sex) subpopulations, as long as the basic assumption that the same processing strategies are being used is met. For instance Chiang and Atkinson (1976) have suggested that the processes used by men and women may reflect a fundamental difference in their approach to the processing of information. Specifically, they obtained a positive relationship between information-processing speed and cognitive ability for men, but a negative relationship for women. However, although this result can be explained by male-female differences in risk taking or decision criteria, a follow-up study by Doverspike, Cellar, Barrett, and Alexander (1984) failed to replicate Chiang and Atkinson's results.

Other sex differences have been noted. For instance, women have been found to obtain higher average scores than men on multiple speed tasks (Born, Bleichrodt, & van de Flier, 1987) and embedded-letters tests (Kimura & Hampson, 1994), which are both measures of perceptual speed. In contrast, men have been found to obtain higher average scores on tasks that require transformation in visual working memory, such as mental rotation (Halpern & Wright, 1996; Voyer, Voyer, & Bryden, 1995) and the Piaget Water Level Test (Robert & Ohlmann, 1994; Vasta, Knott, & Gaze, 1996). Finally, one can also readily see how speed of information-processing tests can adversely impact disabled populations. Thus, clearly, additional research is needed on the effects of strategy differences, including group differences, on information-processing test performance and the associated validity of such tests (see Phillips & Rabbitt, 1995).

From a legal and practical perspective, the primary problem with information-processing speed measures is their lack of face or content validity. However, although the typical general measure of information-processing speed may lack face validity, it is possible to develop measures of information-processing speed that contain more face valid, job relevant content.

Most computerized measures of information-processing speed, especially those involving the calculation of slope or decomposed times, also assume that prior learning is not necessary, that prior practice effects are stable, and that times required in subtask performance are relatively independent and performed sequentially (Dunlap, Kennedy, Harbeson, & Fowlkes, 1989; Larson, Merritt, & Williams, 1988; McClelland, 1979). Unfortunately, the assumption regarding the lack of influence of prior learning and practice effects may only be true when more extensive pretest practice periods are allowed. However, in many cases, allowing time for extensive pretest practice may not be practical. Finally, the calculation of slope measures has always been complicated, and such measures are unlikely to be reliable unless based on an extremely large number of trials (Barrett et al., 1982; Chiang & Atkinson, 1976; Dunlap et al., 1989; Larson et al., 1988).

## Selective Attention

A review of the experimental cognitive psychology literature identifies two critical issues that have been discussed regarding the operationalization of attention. The first is whether attention should be thought of as an undifferentiated or unitary construct or as a multimodal or multidimensional construct. The second and related question is whether attention should be conceptualized as an ability on which individual differences are task specific or measurable and generalizable.

The dichotomy of single-resource theories versus multiple-resource theories suggested by Wickens (1984a, 1984b) corresponds closely to the relevant psychometric question concerning the dimensionality of the attention construct. Wickens (1984b) defined single-resource theories as assuming "that only a single reservoir of undifferentiated resources, which is equally available to all stages of processing or mental operations, exists within the human processing system" (p. 75). Single-resource theories include those offered by Kahneman (1973), Knowles (1963), Moray (1967), Navon and Gopher (1979), and Norman and Bobrow (1975). In addition, Ackerman's integrative, aptitude-treatment approach to skill-acquisition theory is dependent on a partial acceptance of the single-resource view of attention (Ackerman, 1987; Kanfer & Ackerman, 1989).

The view that attention can be conceptualized as a single entity has not gone unchallenged. Multiple-resource theorists argue that several different pools of attention exist. This view, proposed by Navon and Gopher (1979) and Wickens (1984a), developed a structure for representing the dimensions required defining differences in resources.

The issue of whether attention can be conceptualized as a single entity is related to the question of whether attention can be thought of as an ability for which individual differences are measurable and generalizable to a variety of different tasks or whether attention is instead a task-specific skill. Although selective attention has often been measured in experimental investigations using a dichotic listening task and although a number of individual-difference measures of selective attention exist (Davies, Jones, & Taylor, 1984), most of the work on attention as a predictor of performance in applied settings has used a version of a dichotic listening task known as the Auditory Selective Attention Test (ASAT).

### Auditory Selective Attention Test

The ASAT (Arthur & Doverspike, 1993; Doverspike, Cellar, & Barrett, 1986; Gopher & Kahneman, 1971; Mihal & Barrett, 1976) was developed based on an extensive body of experimental and theoretical literature on human information processing—specifically, dichotic listening. The basic theory is that dichotic listening taps the ability to use the attentional pool or to manage and direct attentional resources with maximum efficiency (Gopher, 1992). It can also be interpreted as tapping the ability to selectively attend to relevant information while disregarding interfering or unimportant information. The dichotic listening task places demands on the attentional pool that the test taker must resolve; the better the performance on the test, the higher the individual's selective attention ability. The emphasis on the measurement of auditory selective attention can be traced to Broadbent (1958), who hypothesized that auditory selective attention is directly linked to a central attentional mechanism.

Based on dichotic listening tasks, Gopher and Kahneman (1971) first developed an ASAT in Israel. An English version of the ASAT was initially developed by Mihal and Barrett (1976) and then later revised by Arthur and Doverspike (1993). The ASAT involves 24 dichotic messages presented simultaneously to the test taker via stereo headphones. Each message is broken down into two parts, which consist of a series of pairs of numbers and letters. The initial portion of the tape informs the test taker of the nature of the test and his or her responsibilities. After completion of the instructions, there are four practice trials to help familiarize the test taker with the testing procedure. The practice and 24 test messages are based on the following framework:

1. A verbal announcement of the message number, which the test taker reports to the examiner.
2. A cue presented 2.5 s after the voice on the tape indicates the message number, specifies the relevant ear. The cue "RIGHT" indicates the test taker should attend to the right ear; "LEFT" indicates the left ear is relevant. (Earlier versions of the test used a 250-Hz and 2500-Hz tone to cue the left and right ears, respectively.)
3. Once the cue has been presented, there is a 1.5-s gap before 16 pairs of numbers and letters are presented. Each pair consists of either single English letters or digits ranging from 1 to 9. (To avoid being mistaken for 0 [zero], the letter "O" is not used in the test.) These are presented to both ears at a rate of two per second.
4. The test taker's task is to repeat aloud the numbers presented to the relevant ear immediately upon hearing them.
5. After these 16 pairs are presented, there is again a 1.5-s interval before the indicator cue for Part Two of the message. The second part of the message contains three pairs of numbers. These pairs are preceded by either none, one, or two additional pairs of letters. The test taker repeats the three numbers presented to the relevant ear.
6. In Part One of each message, there are either two, three, four, or six numbers on the relevant channel, while the irrelevant channel always has six numbers.
7. There is no occasion in Part One of the message where two numbers are presented simultaneously to both ears.
8. At the end of a message, there is a 5-s gap. This time interval allows the test taker to prepare for the next message.

The ASAT generates a number of scores. It can be scored in terms of correct responses or errors. Scores can be obtained on Part One or Part Two, left or right ear, omissions or intrusions, for switching from one ear to the other when going from Part One to Part Two, and various combinations of the preceding. However, the basic error scores from which several of the preceding may be derived are omission, intrusion, and switching errors.

An *omission error* is made when the test taker fails to report a number presented on the relevant channel. An *intrusion error* is made when a nonmessage number or letter is reported (or when a message number is reported out of sequence). *Switching errors* are errors on trials following a cue to switch channels (e.g., from left to right ear). So Part Two omission and intrusion errors made following a switch cue are scored as switching errors. Our experience and past research indicate that favorable results are obtained by simply using the total error score (i.e., the sum of omission and intrusion errors; Doverspike, Cellar, & Barrett, 1986).

The ASAT has been found to have adequate test-retest and internal consistency reliability. Doverspike, Szmania, Barrett, and Cellar (1986) reported two-week test-retest reliabilities of .81 for omissions, .39 for intrusions, and .71 for total errors. Avolio, Alexander, Barrett, and Sterns (1981) reported coefficient alphas of .87 for omissions, .61 for intrusions, and .88 for total errors. Total error alphas of .85 and .90 have also been reported by Strong (1992). Given that the ASAT is intended to measure a single construct, selective attention, correlations between various error indices should provide additional information on its internal consistency. Gopher and Kahneman (1971) found low (.20 to .43), but significant, correlations between various error scores for a highly select sample of 100 flight cadets with a restricted range of error scores. However, based on other studies, the correlation between various error indices would seem to be wider and more moderate, with intercorrelations typically falling within a range of .20 to .80 (Avolio et al., 1981; Avolio et al., 1985; Doverspike, Cellar, & Barrett, 1986).

The ASAT has been investigated as a predictor of tasks such as piloting an aircraft, driving a motor vehicle, and vigilance or monitoring tasks. Overall, low to moderate correlations have been found between the ASAT and skilled task performance (Arthur, Barrett, & Alexander, 1991; Forbes & Barrett, 1978; Gopher, 1982; Gopher & Kahneman, 1971; Kahneman, Ben-Ishai, & Lotan, 1973; Mihal & Barrett, 1976; Ranney & Pulling, 1989, 1990). In a meta-analysis in which several categories of predictors were compared, Arthur et al. (1991) found selective attention (operationalized as scores on the ASAT) to be one of the best predictors of driving accident involvement. Selective attention, as measured by Scheduling II of the BAT, has also been found to be predictive of situational awareness in F-15 pilots (Carretta et al., 1996). Interestingly, although the ASAT is an auditory task, many of the tasks that it predicts have a heavy visual component.

The ASAT has been found to be correlated with other measures of information processing, including choice reaction time (Barrett et al., 1982; Mihal & Barrett, 1976). The ASAT has also been found to be related to alternative measures of selective attention, including measures of visual selective attention (Arthur, Strong, & Williamson, 1994; Avolio et al., 1981; Avolio et al., 1985). Correlations with measures of field dependence-independence have also been low to moderate ($r = .04$ to .57; Arthur, Barrett, & Doverspike, 1990; Avolio et al., 1981; Barrett et al., 1982; Mihal & Barrett, 1976; Ranney & Pulling, 1989, 1990; Strong, 1992). The ASAT has also been found to be significantly correlated with a measure of preference for pace of presentation (Panek, Barrett, Alexander, & Sterns, 1979).

Sex differences on the ASAT appear to be small (Avolio, 1978; Strong, 1992). Based on a sample of 1191, Arthur and Doverspike's (1993) analysis for sex effects failed to obtain a significant relationship between ASAT total error scores and sex ($r = -.05$, $p > .06$). However, older adults show performance decrements on the ASAT (Barrett, Mihal, Panek, Sterns, & Alexander, 1977; Panek et al., 1979). For instance, Arthur, Fuentes, and Doverspike (1990) found a performance difference of $d = .64$, with younger petroleum transport drivers (less than 40 years old, $N = 35$) scoring higher than those 40 years and older ($N = 36$). However, using a much larger sample, Arthur and Doverspike (1993) obtained a smaller difference ($d = .18$, less than 40 years $N = 795$, 40 and older $N = 437$). Panek and McGowan (1981) found that increased cautiousness on the part of older adults could not adequately account for the age differences on the ASAT. The age difference results on the ASAT are consistent with experimental investigations of dichotic listening tasks (Layton, 1975).

A major limitation of the ASAT is that it must be individually administered and is thus a time- and labor-intensive test to administer. Although a group version was developed by Gopher (1982), individual administration appears to be the format of choice. It should be possible, however, to fully automate the ASAT so that both the administration and scoring are accomplished by computer, although this would require voice recognition capabilities.

### Visual Selective Attention Test

The Computer-Administered Visual Attention Test (CA-VAT; Arthur et al., 1994, 1995) is a PC-administered and -scored test of visual attention. In its general design, the test is constructed as an approximate visual counterpart to the ASAT (Gopher & Kahneman, 1971; Mihal & Barrett, 1976). Like the ASAT, the stimuli in the CA-VAT are pairs of numbers and letters that appear on a computer monitor. A given pair of characters consists of either two numbers, a number and a letter, or two letters. Cue words preceding each item signal the appropriate response sequence. There are 12 items, and a test taker's score is a function of the number of correct responses and overall response time (see Equation 1). Because it is computer-administered, the number of test takers who can be tested at the same time is only limited by the availability of computer stations, space, and proctors.

Arthur et al. (1994) report moderate convergent validity for the CA-VAT and ASAT ($r = .25$) and internal consistencies of .93 to .98. A test-retest reliability of .83 has also been reported for the CA-VAT (Strong, 1992). The CA-VAT has been found to display low correlations with computer attitudes (.05), computer familiarity (.07), and computer intimidation (.10) in a study sample. However, Arthur et al. (2001) found the CA-VAT to correlate more strongly with $g$ (as operationalized by the Raven Advanced Progressive Matrices, $r = .32-.59$) and .45 to .49 with the GEFT. Predictive validity for the CA-VAT has also been demonstrated by Arthur et al. (1994, 1995).

Like the ASAT, sex differences on the CA-VAT appear to be small—based on a sample of 157 men and 202 women, Arthur et al. (2001) obtained a sex difference of $d = .03$. However, again like the ASAT, Arthur et al. (2001) obtained large age effects with younger adults (39 years and younger, $N = 218$) scoring higher ($d = .91$) than older adults (40 years and older, $N = 141$). This larger difference may also be associated with the mode of testing (i.e., computer-based) because in this nonstudent, more general sample, computer use/familiarity was also related to both age ($r = -.33, p > .001$) and the CA-VAT ($r = -.48, p > .001$). Partialing out computer use/familiarity from age and CA-VAT scores did not eliminate the age effect ($r = -.42, p > .001$).

## Field Dependence-Independence

The construct of field dependence-independence refers to an individual's ability to extract relevant information from a complex visual scene. A person who can easily separate relevant information from the complex visual background is referred to as field independent, whereas an individual who has difficulty ignoring the context of the field is referred to as field dependent. Field dependence-independence, or perceptual style, is regarded as a cognitive style, and no a priori judgment is made regarding the superiority of one style over the other (cf. Arthur & Day, 1991). A large body of literature exists on this construct (Witkin & Goodenough, 1981), and the two major classes of methods used to measure field dependence-independence are the rod-and-frame tests and its variants, and various embedded figures tests.

### *Rod-and-Frame Tests*

The Rod-and-Frame Test (RFT) refers to a number of variations of an apparatus-based test that requires the test taker to adjust to the gravitational vertical of a tilted rod centered within a frame, while the frame remains in a tilted position. The standard RFT requires the dedication of an entire specially constructed room. The room is completely black and is kept darkened to remove external visual horizontal and vertical cues. The test taker is led into a room and seated in a chair. An illuminated rod and frame then appears. The task is to adjust the rod to true gravitational vertical while the frame remains tilted. A large number of variations of this task are available, including tilting the chair. The score is typically the total or average deviation from true vertical across trials, and a high score would indicate field dependence while a

low score would indicate field independence. (See Tinajero, Paramo, Quiroga, & Rodriguez-Gonzalez [2000] for a comparison of five different methods for scoring the RFT.)

A portable version of the RFT is also available (Oltman, 1968). The Portable Rod-and-Frame Test (PRFT) is also an apparatus-based test in which test takers place their head in a fixed position at the end of a small white translucent tube. At the other end of the tube is a rod and frame. Again, the test takers' task is to move the rod to true vertical while the frame remains in a tilted position. The score is the total, or average, deviation from true vertical across eight trials. A Spearman–Brown split-half reliability of .95 has been reported for the PRFT (Oltman, 1968).

The PRFT display moderate to strong convergent validity with GEFT ($r = .44-.64$, Arthur & Day, 1991; Arthur, Barrett, & Doverspike, 1990). As would be expected, smaller relationships have been found with the ASAT ($r = .29-.45$, Arthur & Day, 1991; Arthur et al., 1990), and $g$ ($r = .32-.34$, Arthur & Day, 1991; Arthur et al., 1990). And although Arthur et al. (1990) found the PRFT to be related to performance in a lab computer simulation, these results were not replicated in the field. Relatively little information is available on age, sex, or race differences on rod-and-frame tests within the personnel selection or testing context. However, Arthur and Day (1991) report an absence of sex differences on the PRFT ($r = .08, p < .05$). In addition, the PRFT and, more extensively, the RFT have been used to investigate a wide variety of relationships in other areas of psychology including educational (e.g., Amador-Campos & Kirchner-Nebot, 1999; Tinajero & Paramo, 1998) and sport/physiological (e.g., Apitzsch & Liu, 1997; Kitamura & Matsunaga, 1990) contexts. The wider use and variety of applications of rod-and-frame tests are encouraging for further exploration within the job performance and selection context.

### *Embedded Figures Tests*

As with the RFTs, the Embedded Figures Tests (EFTs) are considered a measure of cognitive style, or more specifically, field dependence (cf. Arthur & Day, 1991). Several versions of the EFT (Witkin & Goodenough, 1981) are available, including children, group, and colored versions. Another EFT alternative is the Hidden Figures Test (HFT, Ekstom et al., 1976). They are all paper-and-pencil tests. Because of their similarity in structure and format, we collectively refer to them as the Embedded Figures Tests (EFTs).

In the EFT, the test taker is required to find simple forms embedded in complex forms. Although they are timed, the time limits are liberal enough to permit the completion of all items by most test takers. Consequently, they are scored in terms of the number of figures correctly identified. The most commonly used EFT with adults in personnel-related contexts is the Group Embedded Figures Test (GEFT).

The GEFT (Witkin et al., 1971) is a paper-and-pencil measure of field dependence-independence and requires test takers to perceptually identify a simple geometric form embedded in complex geometric figure by tracing out its outline. The test is timed (two sets of nine items each, with 5 minutes to complete each set) and scored as the total number of figures correctly identified. A higher score denotes field independence and a lower score, field dependence. An average split-half reliability of .82 and a three-year test-retest reliability of .89 are reported in the test manual (Witkin et al., 1971).

The GEFT has been found to be significantly related to driving crash involvement in a number of studies (Avolio et al., 1985; Mihal & Barrett, 1976; Ranney & Pulling, 1989), with field dependence associated with elevated crash rates. Arthur, Fuentes, and Doverspike (1990) also found it to be related to the cost of spills and blends in a sample of petroleum transport drivers. Numerous studies have also used the GEFT to assess the relationship between field dependence-independence and organizational variables such as job performance rating accuracy (Cardy & Kehoe, 1984; Cellar, Durr, Halsell, & Doverspike, 1989), job satisfaction (Gruenfeld & Weissenberg, 1970) and perceptions of task characteristics (Stone, 1979). Other research has investigated changes in field dependence-independence over time in financial specialists (Mykytyn, 1989) and accountants (Bernardi, 1993; Mills, 1997) using the GEFT.

The GEFT has been found to be correlated with other measures of information processing, including the PRFT ($r = .44-.64$, Arthur & Day, 1991; Arthur, Fuentes, & Doverspike, 1990), the ASAT ($r = .29-.58$, Arthur & Day, 1991; Arthur, Fuentes, & Doverspike, 1990), and the CA-VAT ($r = .45$, Arthur et al., 2001). Fairly strong relationships with $g$, ranging from .58 to .62, have been reported (Arthur & Day, 1991, Arthur et al., 2001), lending some support to the argument that field dependence-independence as operationalized by the GEFT (in contrast to the PRFT) may be a cognitive ability and not cognitive style (see Arthur & Day, 1991).

Relatively little information is available on age, sex, or race differences on the GEFT. However, Arthur and Day (1991) report an absence of sex differences on the GEFT ($r = .09$, $p < .05$). Similar results were reported by Arthur et al. (2001, $r = .13$). In contrast, significant effects were obtained for age, with younger individuals being more field independent and older individuals, more field dependent ($r = .39$, $p > .001$, Arthur et al., 2001).

## LIMITATIONS

Given the wide variety of information-processing tests, our discussion of limitations is based on the fact that they share certain common assumptions. First, as indicated in our discussion of the theoretical foundations of information-processing tests, these tests are based on an assumption of nonimmediacy. This means that there is a latency between the stimulus and the response because time is needed to generate and articulate the response. Thus, the time spent responding is theorized to correspond to the time spent on mental processing. However, as we indicated in our discussion of measures of information-processing speed, newer models of information processing tend to be based on parallel processing and network theories. Thus, the assumption of nonimmediacy and the idea that information processing can be decomposed into independent stages is more questionable today than it was 20 years ago (Dunlap et al., 1989; Larson et al., 1988; McClelland, 1979; Posner & Mitchell, 1967).

A second, critical assumption is that of limited capacity. Individuals are viewed as having limited attentional and structural capabilities or capacities (Broadbent, 1957; Fisher, 1982; Navon & Gopher, 1979), which result in the necessity to share attentional resources. Although this view of attention as a single, unitary pool has been questioned, it nevertheless remains the most dominant since most information-processing models are based on single resource theories of attention (Ackerman, 1987; Kahneman et al, 1973; Kanfer & Ackerman, 1989; Knowles, 1963; Moray, 1967; Navon & Gopher, 1979).

An additional problem or limitation with most information-processing tests is that they assume that all individuals process information in a similar way or at least in the manner as envisioned by the test creators. Obviously, this is true of all tests; however, as highlighted in our discussion of specific information-processing measures, this issue appears to be more problematic for information-processing tests.

From a legal and practical standpoint, the primary problem with information-processing measures is their lack of face validity. However, although the typical general measure of information-processing speed lacks face validity, it is possible to develop measures of information-processing speed that contain more face valid, job relevant content. Another problem with information-processing tests is that when they are computerized or computer-administered, these tests may adversely impact disabled or older adults, not as a result of construct-related differences but as a result of the mode of testing. From a personnel testing and selection perspective, this is clearly an issue that must be addressed by information-processing test developers. However, it may be less of an issue if the mode of testing is representative of performance on the job.

Finally, perhaps the biggest limitation of information-processing tests is their practicality or lack thereof. Most information-processing tests require special equipment, apparatus, or computers, and many require individual administration. This can make them quite expensive and reduces their feasibility in large-scale personnel testing.

## CONCLUSION

In this chapter, we have discussed the history of and theory underlying information-processing tests. Because many of these tests are unpublished and primarily used as research instruments, we have also discussed techniques for their development and some of the major categories of information-processing tests. In our initial comments on information-processing tests, we noted that, unfortunately, the history of attempts to develop batteries of information-processing tests can probably be best described as one of unlimited promise and potential, accompanied by very little practical success. This, of course, has been the major problem with information-processing tests. Although psychology is currently dominated by theories of information processing, it is difficult to develop reliable and valid measures that are also practical. Although tests of information processing do predict performance, so do general ability tests. However, general ability tests have the advantages of being readily available, easy to administer, easy to score, and relatively cheap. Thus, although information-processing tests remain popular in research investigations, they have not proved to be popular or practical in testing for selection or employment purposes.

Nevertheless, the increased power and speed of personal computers does increase the possibility of developing information-processing tests that are much easier to administer and score than their apparatus-based predecessors. Thus, we predict that computer-based testing of basic information-processing abilities will continue to grow in importance as we move further into the new century; we must caution, however, that we have predicted the same thing in the past and been wrong. Although a number of problems still need to be solved, computerized information-processing tests are already a viable alternative to traditional tests. In addition, unlike measures of cognitive ability, information-processing-

based approaches can link testing and training and can serve as a foundation for both.

## REFERENCES

Ackerman, P.L. (1987). Individual differences in skill learning: An integration of psychometric and information processing perspectives. *Psychological Bulletin, 102,* 3–27.

Ackerman, P.L. (1988). Determinants of individual differences during skill acquisition: Cognitive abilities and information processing. *Journal of Experimental Psychology: General, 117,* 288–318.

Ackerman, P.L., & Kanfer, R. (1993). Integrating laboratory and field study for improving selection: Development of a battery for predicting air traffic controller success. *Journal of Applied Psychology, 78,* 413–432.

Amador-Campos, J.A., & Kirchner-Nebot, T. (1999). Correlations among scores on measures of field dependence-independence cognitive style, cognitive ability, and sustained attention. *Perceptual and Motor Skills, 88,* 236–239.

Apitzsch, E., & Liu, W.H. (1997). Correlation between dependence-independence and handball shooting by Swedish male handball players. *Perceptual and Motor Skills, 84,* 1395–1398.

Arthur, W. Jr. (1995). *Psychometric review and analysis of the Time Sharing II Test.* Brooks Air Force Base, TX: Aircrew Selection Research Branch, Manpower and Personnel Division, AL/HRMA, The Armstrong Laboratory Human Resources Directorate.

Arthur, W. Jr. (1996). *Psychometric review and analysis of the Encoding Speed Test.* Brooks Air Force Base, TX: Aircrew Selection Research Branch, Manpower and Personnel Division, AL/HRMA, The Armstrong Laboratory Human Resources Directorate.

Arthur, W. Jr., Barrett, G.V., & Alexander, R.A. (1991). Prediction of vehicular accident involvement: A meta-analysis. *Human Performance, 4,* 89–105. (See also Erratum [publisher's correction] to this article in *Human Performance, 4,* 231.)

Arthur, W. Jr., Barrett, G.V., & Doverspike, D. (1990). Validation of an information processing based test battery for the prediction of handling accidents among petroleum product transport drives. *Journal of Applied Psychology, 75,* 621–628.

Arthur, W. Jr., Bell, S.T., Edwards, B.D., Day, E.A., Tubré, T.C., & Tubré, A.H. (2001). A longitudinal investigation of three macro predictors of driving accident involvement (Tech. Rep. No. 11). College Station: Texas A&M University, Psychology Department.

Arthur, W. Jr., & Day, D.V. (1991). Examination of the construct validity of alternative measures of field dependence/independence. *Perceptual and Motor Skills, 72,* 851–859.

Arthur, W. Jr., Day, E.A., McNelly, T.L., & Edens, P. (in press). The criterion-related validity of assessment center dimensions: Distinguishing between methods and constructs. *Personnel Psychology.*

Arthur, W., Jr., & Doverspike, D. (1992). Locus of control and auditory selective attention as predictors of driving accident involvement: A comparative longitudinal investigation. *Journal of Safety Research, 23,* 73–80.

Arthur, W. Jr., & Doverspike, D. (1993). *ASAT: The Auditory Selective Attention Test manual.* Psychology Department, Texas A&M University.

Arthur W. Jr., Fuentes, R., & Doverspike, D. (1990). Relationships among personnel tests, age, and job performance. *Experimental Aging Research, 16,* 11–16.

Arthur, W. Jr., Archuleta, K.D., Sheehan, M.K., & Villado, A.J. (2003). *Distinguishing between method and construct: A comparative evaluation of predictors in personnel selection.* Manuscript in preparation.

Arthur, W. Jr., Strong, M.H., Jordan, J.A., Williamson, J.E., Shebilske, W.L., & Regian, W.J. (1995). Visual attention: Individual differences in training and predicting complex task performance. *Acta Psychologica, 88,* 3–23.

Arthur, W. Jr., Strong, M.H., & Williamson, J.E. (1994). Validation of a visual attention test as a predictor of driving accident involvement. *Journal of Occupational and Organizational Psychology, 67,* 173–182.

Avolio, B.J. (1978). *The relationship between measures of visual and auditory selective attention and differences in information-processing ability.* Unpublished master's thesis, University of Akron, Akron, OH.

Avolio, B.J., Alexander, R.A., Barrett, G.V., & Sterns, H.L., (1981). Designing a measure of visual selective attention to assess individual differences in information processing. *Applied Psychological Measurement, 5,* 29–41.

Avolio, B.J., Kroeck, K.G., & Panek, P.E. (1985). Individual differences in information processing ability as a predictor of motor vehicles accidents. *Human Factors, 27,* 577–588.

Axton, T.R., Doverspike, D., Park, S.R., & Barrett, G.V. (1997). A model of the information-processing and cognitive abilities requirements for mechanical troubleshooting. *International Journal of Cognitive Ergonomics, 1,* 245–266.

Barrett, G.V., Alexander, R.A., Doverspike, D., Cellar, D., & Thomas, J.C. (1982). The development and application of a computerized information processing test battery. *Applied Psychological Measurement, 6,* 13–29.

Barrett, G.V., Carobine, R.G., & Doverspike, D. (1999). The reduction of adverse impact in an employment setting using a short-term memory test. *Journal of Business and Psychology, 14,* 373–377.

Barrett, G.V., & Maurer, T.J. (1989). *The job analysis-predictor development process: Beyond g and generic constructs in employment aptitude testing.* Unpublished manuscript, The University of Akron, Department of Psychology.

Barrett, G.V., Mihal, W.L., Panek, P.E., Sterns, H.L., & Alexander, R.A. (1977). Information processing skills predictive of accident involvement for younger and older drivers. *Industrial Gerontology, 4,* 173–182.

Bernardi, R.A. (1993). Group Embedded Figures Test: Psychometric data documenting shifts from prior norms in field independence of accounts. *Perceptual and Motor Skills, 77,* 579–586.

Born, M.P., Bleichrodt, N., & van de Flier, H. (1987). Cross-cultural comparisons of sex-related differences on intelligence tests. *Journal of Cross-Cultural Psychology, 18,* 283–314.

Broadbent, D.E. (1957). A mechanical model for human attention and immediate memory. *Psychological Review, 64,* 205–215.

Broadbent, D.E. (1958). *Perception and communication.* London: Pergamon.

Callister, J.D., King, R.E., & Retzlaff, P.D. (1996). Cognitive assessment of USAF pilot training candidates. *Aviation, Space, and Environmental Medicine, 67,* 1124–1129.

Campbell, J.P. (1990). Modeling the performance prediction problem in industrial and organizational psychology. In M.D. Dunnette & L.M. Hough (Eds.), *Handbook of industrial and organizational psychology* (2nd ed., Vol. 1, pp. 687–732). Palo Alto, CA: Consulting Psychologists Press.

Card, S.K., Moran, T.P., Newell, A. (1980). Computer text-editing: An information-processing analysis of a routine cognitive skill. *Cognitive Psychology, 12,* 32–74.

Cardy, R.L., & Kehoe, J.F. (1984). Rater selective attention ability for appraisal effectiveness: The effect of cognitive style on the accuracy of differentiation among rates. *Journal of Applied Psychology, 69,* 589–594.

Carr, L.S. (1992). *The development of a task specific information processing battery and the detection of individual differences in resource dependent and resource independent process control tasks.* Unpublished doctoral dissertation, University of Akron, Akron, OH.

Carretta, T.R. (1987). *Basic Attributes Test (BAT) system: The development of an automated test battery for pilot selection* (Rep. No. AFHRL-TR-87-9). Brooks Air Force Base, TX: Air Force Human Resources Laboratory, Manpower and Personnel Division.

Carretta, T.R. (2000). U.S. Air Force pilot selection and training methods. *Aviation, Space, and Environmental Medicine, 71,* 950–956.

Carretta, T.R., Perry, D.C., & Ree, J.R. (1996). Prediction of situational awareness in F-15 pilots. *The International Journal on Aviation Psychology, 6,* 21–41.

Carretta, T.R., & Ree, J.R. (1993). Basic Attributes Test: Psychometric equating of a computer-based test. *International Journal of Aviation Psychology, 3,* 189–201.

Carretta, T.R., & Ree, J.R. (1994). Pilot-candidate selection method: Source of validity. *The International Journal of Aviation Psychology, 4,* 103–117.

Carretta, T.R., & Ree, J.R. (1996). U.S. Air Force pilot selection tests: What is measured and what is predictive? *Aviation, Space, and Environmental Medicine, 67,* 279–283.

Carretta, T.R., Zelenski, W.E., & Ree, J.R. (2000). Basic Attributes Test (BAT) retest performance. *Military Psychology, 12,* 221–232.

Carroll, J.B. (1976). Psychometric tests as cognitive tasks: A new "structure of intellect." In L. Resnick (Ed.), *The nature of intelligence* (pp. 27–57). Hillsdale, NJ: Erlbaum.

Cellar, D., Barrett, G.V., Alexander, R.A., Doverspike, D., Thomas, J.C., Binning, J.A., & Kroeck, G. (1982). Cognitive information processing measures as predictors of monitoring performance. *Perceptual and Motor Skills, 54,* 1299–1302.

Cellar, D.F., Durr, M.L., Halsell, S., & Doverspike, D. (1989). The effect of field independence, job analysis format, and sex of rater on the accuracy of job evaluation ratings. *Journal of Applied Social Psychology, 19,* 363–376.

Chiang, A., & Atkinson, R.C. (1976). Individual differences and interrelationships among a selection set of cognitive skills. *Memory and Cognition, 4,* 661–672.

Cory, C.H. (1977). Relative utility of computerized versus paper-and-pencil tests for predicting job performance. *Applied Psychological Measurement, 1,* 551–564.

Davies, D.R., Jones, D.M., & Taylor, A. (1984). Selective- and sustained-attention tasks: Individual and group differences. In R. Parasuraman & D.R. Davies (Eds.), *Varieties of attention* (pp. 395–447). San Diego, CA: Academic Press.

Doverspike, D. (December, 1996). Information processing approaches to test development and construction as evidence for test validity. *IPMA Assessment Council News,* 15–16.

Doverspike, D., Cellar, D., & Barrett, G.V. (1986). The auditory selective attention test: A review of field and laboratory studies. *Educational and Psychological Measurement, 46,* 1095–1104.

Doverspike, D., Cellar, D., Barrett, G.V., & Alexander, R.A. (1984). Sex differences in short-term memory processing. *Perceptual and Motor Skills, 58,* 135–139.

Doverspike, D., Szmania, J.M., Barrett, G.V., & Cellar, D.F. (1986). *The Auditory Selection Attention Test: Reliability and construct validity.* Unpublished manuscript, University of Akron.

Dunlap, W.P., Kennedy, R.S., Harbeson, M.M., & Fowlkes, J.E. (1989). Problems with individual difference measures based on some componential cognitive paradigms. *Applied Psychological Measurement, 13,* 9–17.

Ekstrom, R.B., French, J.W., & Harman, H.H. (1979). Cognitive factors: Their identification and replication. *Multivariate Behavioral Research Monographs, 79–2,* 1–84.

Ekstrom, R.B., French, J.W., Harman, H.H., & Dermen, D. (1976). *Kit of Factor-Referenced Cognitive Tests.* Princeton, NJ: Educational Testing Service.

Eysenck, H.J. (1998). *Intelligence: A new look.* New Brunswick, NJ: Traditions Publishers.

Fisher, D.L. (1982). Limited-channel models of automatic detection: Capacity and scanning in visual search. *Psychological Review, 89,* 662–692.

Fleishman, E.A. (1964). *The structure and measurement of physical fitness.* Englewood Cliffs, NJ: Prentice Hall.

Forbes, B.J., & Barrett, G.V. (1978). Individual abilities and task demands in relation to performance and satisfaction on two repetitive monitoring tasks. *Journal of Applied Psychology, 63,* 188–196.

Forbes, B.J., Barrett, G.V., Alexander, R.A., & Phillips, J.S. (1976). *Organizational policy decisions as a function of individual differences and task design: Monitoring tasks* (Tech. Rep. No. 9). University of Akron, Psychology Department, ONR contract N00014-75-C-0985, NR 151-377, Office of Naval Research.

French, J.W., Ekstrom, R.B., & Price, L.A. (1963). *Manual for Kit of Reference Tests for cognitive factors.* Princeton, NJ: Educational Testing Service.

Gopher, D. (1982). A selective attention test as a predictor of success in flight training. *Human Factors, 24,* 173–183.

Gopher, D. (1992). The skill of attention control: Acquisition and execution of attention strategies. In D. Meyer and S. Korenblum (Eds.), *Attention and Performance XIV: Synergies in experimental psychology, artificial intelligence, and cognitive neuroscience* (pp. 299–322). Cambridge, MA: MIT Press.

Gopher, D., & Bareket, T. (1994). The transfer of skill from a computer game trainer to actual flight. *Human Factors, 36,* 387–405.

Gopher, D., & Kahneman, D. (1971). Individual differences in attention and the prediction of flight criteria. *Perceptual and Motor Skills, 33,* 1335–1342.

Gussett, N.J. (1992). *The validity of task-specific information processing measures: Predicting performance on resource dependent and resource independent clerical tasks.* Unpublished doctoral dissertation, University of Akron, Akron, OH.

Gruenfeld, L.P., & Weissenberg, P. (1970). Field independence and articulation of sources of job satisfaction. *Journal of Applied Psychology, 54,* 424–426.

Halpern, D.F., & Wright, T. (1996). A process-oriented model of cognitive sex differences [Special issue]. *Learning and Individual Differences, 8,* 3–24.

Hartigan, J.A., & Wigdor, A.K. (1989). *Fairness in employment testing. Validity generalization, minority issues, and the General Aptitude Test Battery.* Washington, DC: National Academy Press.

Huffcutt, A.I., Conway, J.M., Roth, P.L., & Stone, N.J. (2001). Identification and meta-analytic assessment of psychological constructs measured in employment interviews. *Journal of Applied Psychology, 86,* 897–913.

Hunt, E. (1980). Intelligence as an information-processing concept. *British Journal of Psychology, 71,* 449–474.

Hunt, E., Frost, N., & Lunneborg, C. (1973). Individual differences in cognition: A new approach to intelligence. In G.H. Bower (Ed.), *Advances in learning and motivation* (Vol. 7). New York: Academic Press.

Hunt, E., Lunneborg, C., & Lewis, J. (1975). What does it mean to be highly verbal? *Cognitive Psychology, 7,* 194–227.

Hunter, D.R. (1989). Aviator selection. In M.F. Wiskoff, & G.M. Rampton (Eds.), *Military personnel measurement: Testing, assignment, and evaluation* (pp. 129–167). New York: Praeger.

Jensen, A.R. (1973). Personality and scholastic achievement in three ethnic groups. *British Journal of Educational Psychology, 43,* 115–125.

Jensen, A.R., & Inouye, A.R. (1980). The level I and level II abilities in Asian, White, and Black children. *Intelligence, 4,* 41–49.

Kahneman, D. (1973). *Attention and effort.* Englewood Cliffs, NJ: Prentice Hall.

Kahneman, D., Ben-Ishai, R., & Lotan, M. (1973). Relation of a test of attention to road accidents. *Journal of Applied Psychology, 58,* 113–115.

Kandra, J. (1991). *The development and validation of an information processing test battery.* Unpublished master's thesis, University of Akron, Akron, OH.

Kanfer, R., & Ackerman, P. (1989). Motivation and cognitive abilities: An integrative/aptitude treatment interaction approach to skill acquisition. *Journal of Applied Psychology, 74,* 657–690.

Kay, G.G. (1995). *CogScreen Aeromedical edition professional manual.* Odessa, FL: Psychological Assessment Resources.

Kimura, D., & Hampson, E. (1994). Cognitive pattern in men and women is influenced by fluctuations in sex hormones. *Current Directions in Psychological Science, 3,* 57–61.

Kitamura, F., & Matsunaga, K. (1990). Field dependence and body balance. *Perceptual and Motor Skills, 71,* 723–734.

Knowles, W.B. (1963). Operator loading tasks. *Human Factors, 5,* 151–161.

Kyllonen, P.C. (1993). Aptitude testing inspired by information processing: A test of the four-sources model. *The Journal of General Psychology, 120,* 375–405.

Kyllonen, P.C., & Christal, R.E. (1986). *Cognitive modeling of learning abilities: A status report of LAMP* (AFHRL-TP-87-86). Brooks, AFB, Air Force Human Resources Laboratory, Manpower and Personnel Division.

Kyllonen, P.C., & Christal, R.E. (1990). Reasoning ability is (little more than) working-memory capacity?! *Intelligence, 14,* 389–433.

Larson, G.E., Merritt, C.R., & Williams, S.E. (1988). Information processing and intelligence: Some implications of task complexity. *Intelligence, 12,* 131–147.

Layton, B. (1975). Perceptual noise and aging. *Psychological Bulletin, 82,* 875–883.

Lord, F.M. (1970). Some test theory for tailored testing. In W.H. Holtzman (Ed.), *Computer-assisted instruction, testing, and guidance* (pp. 139–183). New York: Harper & Row.

Lunneborg, C.E. (1977). Choice reaction time: What role in ability measurement? *Applied Psychological Measurement, 1,* 309–330.

Lunneborg, C.E. (1978). Some information processing correlated of measures of intelligence. *Multivariate Behavioral Research, 13,* 153–161.

McClelland, J.L. (1979). On the time relations of mental processes: An examination of systems of processes in cascade. *Psychological Review, 86,* 287–330.

Mihal, W.L., & Barrett, G.V. (1976). Individual differences in perceptual information processing and their relation to automobile accident involvement. *Journal of Applied Psychology, 61,* 229–233.

Mills, T.Y. (1997). An examination of the relationship between accountants' scores on field independence and use of and attitude toward computers. *Perceptual Motor Skills, 84,* 715–720.

Moray, N. (1967). Where is capacity limited? A survey and model. *Acta Psychologica, 27,* 84–92.

Murphy, K.R., & Davidshofer, L.O. (1998). *Psychological testing: Principles and applications* (4th ed.). Englewood Cliffs, NJ: Prentice Hall.

Mykytyn, P.P. (1989). Group Embedded Figures Test (GEFT): Individual differences, performance, and learning effects. *Educational and Psychological Measurement, 49,* 951–959.

Navon, D., & Gopher, D. (1979). On the economy of the human-processing system. *Psychological Review, 86,* 214–255.

Neisser, U. (1967). *Cognitive psychology.* New York: Appleton.

Newell, A., & Simon, H. (1972). *Human problem solving.* Englewood Cliffs, NJ: Prentice Hall.

Norman, D.A., & Bobrow, D.B. (1975). On data-limited and resource-limited processing. *Journal of Cognitive Psychology, 7,* 44–64.

North, R.A., & Gopher, D. (1976). Measures of attention as predictors of flight performance. *Human Factors, 18,* 1–14.

O'Connor, E.J., Barrett, G.V., & Alexander, R.A. (1977). *Organizational policy decisions as a function of individual differences and task design: Maintenance tasks* (Tech. Rep. No. 10). University of Akron, Psychology Department, Contract N0014-75-C-0985, NR 151-377, Office of Naval Research.

Oltman, P.K. (1968). A portable rod-and-frame apparatus. *Perceptual and Motor Skills, 26,* 503–506.

Panek, P.E., Barrett, G.V., Alexander, R.A., & Sterns, H.L. (1979). Age and self-selected performance pace on a visual monitoring inspection task. *Aging and Work, 2,* 183–191.

Panek, P.E., & McGown, W.P. (1981). Risk-taking across the life span as measured by an intrusion-omission ratio on a selective attention task. *Perceptual and Motor Skills, 52,* 733–734.

Park, S.R. (1991). *The development and validation of information processing measures for maintenance positions.* Unpublished doctoral dissertation, University of Akron, Akron, OH.

Phillips, L.H., & Rabbitt, P.M.A. (1995). Impulsivity and speed-accuracy strategies in intelligence test performance. *Intelligence, 21,* 13–29.

Posner, M.I., & Mitchell, R.F. (1967). Chronometric analyses of classification. *Psychological Review, 74,* 392–409.

Ranney, T.A., & Pulling, N.H. (1989). Relation of individual differences in information-processing ability to driving performance. *Proceedings of the Human Factors Society 33rd Annual Meeting,* pp. 965–969.

Ranney, T.A., & Pulling, N.H. (1990). *Performance differences on driving and laboratory tasks between drivers of different ages.* Paper presented at the 69th Annual Meeting of the Transportation Research Board, Washington, DC.

Ree, M.J., & Carretta, T.R. (1998). Computerized testing in the United States Air Force. *International Journal of Selection and Assessment, 6,* 82–106.

Ree, M.J., & Earles, J.A. (1992). Intelligence is the best predictor of job performance. *Current Directions in Psychological Science, 1,* 86–89.

Ree, M.J., Earles, J.A., & Teachout, M.S. (1994). Predicting job performance: Not much more than g. *Journal of Applied Psychology, 79,* 518–524.

Robert, M., & Ohlmann, T. (1994). Water-level representation by men and women as a function of rode-and-frame test proficiency as visual and postural information. *Perception, 23,* 1321–1333.

Roos, G.B. (1993). *Differences in the predictive validity of a specific information processing test, general cognitive ability test, and a selective attention ability test at different stages of practice on a position classification task.* Unpublished dissertation, University of Akron.

Snow, R.E. (1978). Theory and method for research on aptitude processes. *Intelligence, 2,* 225–278.

Sternberg, R.J. (1977). *Intelligence, information processing, and analogical reasoning: The componential analysis of human abilities.* Hillsdale, NJ: Erlbaum.

Sternberg, R.J. (1979). The nature of mental abilities. *American Psychologist, 34,* 214–230.

Sternberg, S. (1967). Retrieval of contextual information from memory. *Psychonomic Science, 8,* 55–56.

Sternberg, S. (1969). The discovery of processing stages: Extensions of Donders' method. *Acta Psychologica, 30,* 276–315.

Sternberg, S. (1975). Memory scanning: New findings and current controversies. *Quarterly Journal of Experimental Psychology, 27,* 1–32.

Stone, E.F. (1979). Field independence and perceptions of task characteristics: A laboratory investigation. *Journal of Applied Psychology, 64,* 305–310.

Strong, M.H. (1992). *An assessment of the criterion-related validity and improvements in the utility of the Computer Administered Visual Selective Attention Test.* Unpublished master's thesis, Texas A&M University, College Station, TX.

Szmania, J.M. (1993). *Development of an information processing test battery to predict performance on resource dependent and resource independent legal tasks.* Unpublished doctoral dissertation, University of Akron, Akron, OH.

Taylor, D.A. (1976). Stage analysis of reaction time. *Psychological Bulletin, 83,* 161–191.

Taylor, J.L., O'Hara, R., Mumenthaler, M.S., & Yesavage, J.A. (2000). Relationship of CogScreen-AE to flight simulator performance and pilot age. *Aviation, Space, and Environmental Medicine, 71,* 373–380.

Tinajero, C., & Paramo, F. (1998). Field dependence-independence in second-language acquisition: Some forgotten aspects. *Spanish Journal of Psychology, 1,* 32–38.

Tinajero, C., Paramo, M.F., Quiroga, M.A., & Rodriguez-Gonzalez, J. (2000). Comparative analysis of different correction methods for measuring Rod-and-Frame Test performance. *Perceptual and Motor Skills, 90,* 93–101.

Vasta, R., Knott, J.A., & Gaze, C.E. (1996). Can spatial training erase the gender differences on the water-level task? *Psychology of Women Quarterly, 20,* 549–568.

Verive, J.M., & McDaniel, M.A. (1996). Short-term memory tests in personnel selection: Low adverse impact and high validity. *Intelligence, 23,* 15–32.

Voyer, D., Voyer, S., & Bryden, M.P. (1995). Magnitude of sex differences in spatial abilities: A meta-analysis and consideration of critical variables. *Psychological Bulletin, 117,* 250–270.

Whitely, S.E. (1977). Information-processing of intelligence test items: Some response components. *Applied Psychological Measurement, 1,* 465–476.

Wickens, C.D. (1984a). *Engineering psychology and human performance.* Columbus, OH: Charles E. Merrill.

Wickens, C.D. (1984b). Processing resources in attention. In R. Parasuraman & D.P. Davies (Eds.), *Varieties of attention* (pp. 63–102). San Diego, CA: Academic Press.

Witkin, H.A., & Goodenough, D.R. (1981). *Cognitive styles: Essence and origins.* New York: International Universities Press.

Witkin, H.A., Lewis, H.B., Machover, K., Meissner, P.M., & Wapner, S. (1954). *Personality through perception.* New York: Haynes.

Witkin, H.A., Oltman, P.K., Raskin, E., & Karp, S.A. (1971). *Manual for the Embedded Figures Tests.* Palo Alto, CA: Consulting Psychologists Press.

Wood, R. (1974). Response-contingent testing. *Review of Educational Research, 48,* 529–544.

CHAPTER 6

# The Assessment of Creativity

JOHN W. FLEENOR AND SYLVESTER TAYLOR

## INTRODUCTION

In the 50 years since Guilford (1950) made his historic American Psychological Association presidential address on the scientific study of creativity, interest in creativity research has experienced both highs and lows. Currently, the scientific investigation of creativity appears to be experiencing an upswing in popularity, and, according to Plucker and Renzulli (1999), most of this resurgence is related to the psychometric assessment of creativity. Given the conventional wisdom that creativity is something that is not easily measured, the current dominance of psychometric methods in creativity research may seem surprising. A review of the creativity literature, however, indicates that, historically, many of the advances in this field have resulted from the psychometric study of creativity.

This chapter provides an overview of creativity assessment and addresses relationships between creativity and related constructs such as intelligence and personality. The emphasis is on the assessment of creativity in work organizations. Additionally, this chapter describes specific tools for assessing creativity and how these tools have been used to study creativity. An in-depth discussion of the theories of creativity is beyond the scope of this chapter; however, a review of these theories can be found in Runco and Albert (1990).

---

*Acknowledgments:* The authors thank Stan Gryskiewicz, Carl Bryant, and Cindy McCauley for their invaluable assistance and support in the preparation of this chapter.

## What Is Creativity?

Although creativity has been widely studied in a variety of contexts, it remains a somewhat elusive concept, according to King and Pope (1999). Though definitions differ, most researchers define creativity as the production of new and useful ideas or products by individuals or small groups. To be creative, the idea or product must be novel; that is, it must be different in some important way from what preceded it. It cannot simply be different, however; it also must be useful, valuable, or appropriate for the situation at hand. Most definitions of creativity, therefore, emphasize an individual's ability to produce products that are both novel and high in quality (Sternberg & Lubart, 1999).

Creativity may be best understood in terms of its relationship to intelligence. Carroll (1993) and others claim that creativity and intelligence are not distinct abilities, and there is no need for a separate concept of creativity. King and Pope (1999), however, believe that while creativity may be related to intelligence, it is not identical but, instead, represents a separate area of study in understanding human behavior. Sternberg (2001) argues that whereas intelligence largely is used to advance existing agendas, creativity is its antithesis, often questioning and opposing these societal agendas as well as proposing new ones.

According to Sternberg (2001), creativity goes beyond intelligence because products that intelligent people produce may be high in quality but may not necessarily be novel. Creativity refers to the potential to produce novel ideas that are not only high in quality but also task appropriate. Highly creative individuals, therefore, may create quality products that do not meet the expectations or desires of the intended audience. Sternberg's view implies that creativity is meaningful only in the context of the system that judges it, and what is creative in one context may not be in another (Amabile, 1983; Csikszentmihalyi, 1996). Consequently, creativity may be viewed as a property of an individual within a particular context. For example, artists who were considered to be highly creative in their time might be viewed as less creative today because their works are no longer seen as novel.

On the surface, the contextual view of creativity may seem to make the measurement of this construct more difficult. However, the key is to select a method of assessing creativity that is appropriate for the context in which it will be used. This idea is similar to the concept of test validity, which holds that validity is not a characteristic of a test itself, but rather how the results of the test are used to make decisions about individuals (American Psychological Association, 1999).

## Why Measure Creativity?

Creativity assessment is used in several different contexts, including industry, schools, government, and research organizations. In industry, it is employed to provide information about potential employees for selection purposes. Creativity assessment can be used to screen individuals for hiring, job assignments, promotions, and succession planning. Similarly, organizations can use creativity assessment to help identify high-potential employees. For example, creativity assessment is often employed for employee and leadership development; scores from these assessments are used to identify weaknesses and to develop strengths of individual employees. In employee development programs, the results of creativity assessments are provided to participants by a supervisor, coach, or mentor in a feedback session. The participant, with the assistance of his or her coach, explores the assessment results and creates a development plan to address areas in which improvement is needed.

Schools use creativity assessment to identify creative and gifted students for assignments to special programs where their creativity can be further developed. Creativity assessment also is employed by researchers to evaluate efforts to enhance creativity, to provide a common metric for discussing creativity, and for further scientific study of creativity.

## Methods for Assessing Creativity

Hocevar (1981) classifies creativity measurement into 10 categories: tests of divergent thinking, attitude and interest inventories, personality inventories, biographical inventories,

teacher nominations, peer nominations, supervisor ratings, judgments of products, eminence, and self-reported creative activities and achievements. These categories can be further grouped into three primary methods for assessing creativity: the psychometric method, the historiometric method, and the biographical approach (Plucker & Renzulli, 1999). The *psychometric approach* uses instrumentation to measure creativity. These instruments, often paper-and-pencil self-report measures, are developed using scientifically accepted statistical methods known as psychometrics. The psychometric method focuses on the personality, behavioral and cognitive correlates of creativity, the characteristics of creative products, and the attributes of creativity-enhancing environments.

The *historiometric approach,* unlike the psychometric approach, uses quantitative data drawn from historical documents to measure creativity. Rather than using self-report measures, the historiometric researcher employs empirical methods to assess creativity in historical figures who demonstrated high levels of creativity in music, science, art, and so on (e.g., Newton, da Vinci, Beethoven, etc.) (Simonton, 1999). The *biographical approach* involves investigations of famous creators using qualitative methodologies, such as case studies (Gruber & Wallace, 1999).

Plucker and Renzulli (1999) add a fourth method of assessing creativity, the *biometric approach.* The biometric method involves the monitoring of certain biological functions of individuals while performing creative or cognitive tasks. For example, recent studies have investigated the level of glucose metabolism in the brain during the performance of certain tasks. The purpose of this research is to pinpoint the areas of the brain in which activity occurs during creative thinking (Martindale, 1999).

The various approaches to assessing creativity involve the use of different measurement techniques. According to Cropley (2000), creativity assessment entails the measurement of specific cognitive processes such as thinking divergently, making remote associations, constructing and combining broad categories, and working on several ideas simultaneously. Creativity assessment also can take the form of biographical inventories, adjective checklists, and the identification of personal characteristics thought to be associated with creativity. Additionally, creativity assessment can involve the measurement of motivation and attitudes, such as curiosity, imagination, risk taking, preference for complexity, ability to produce unconventional ideas, and desire to reorganize and restructure problems.

The various techniques of creativity assessments typically show substantial levels of agreement, and the scores are usually internally stable. Creativity assessments also have been found to be correlated with various criteria of creativity, such as teacher ratings, and, in general, appear to be useful predictors of adult behavior (Cropley, 2000). However, according to Cropley, these assessments are best thought of as measures of creative potential, rather than creative achievement, because creative achievement depends on additional factors not typically measured by creativity assessments.

# THE PSYCHOMETRIC ASSESSMENT OF CREATIVITY

This chapter focuses on the psychometric approach to assessing creativity, which involves the use of instrumentation (e.g., surveys, questionnaires, tests, rating scales, etc.) to measure creativity. Several reviews of this approach to assessing creativity can be found in the literature (e.g., Cooper, 1991; Cropley, 2000; Hocevar, 1981; Kaltsounis & Honeywell, 1980; Torrance & Goff, 1989). In general, these reviews have been supportive of the psychometric measurement of creativity, although some instruments were criticized because of their technical deficiencies. As with any method of psychological assessment, certain basic psychometric requirements must be met to ensure that the construct of interest is being measured in a reliable and valid manner. Some of the essential requirements for creativity assessment are listed next.

## Psychometric Requirements for Creativity Assessment

The psychometric requirements for the valid assessment of creativity include the following aspects:

1. *Reliability.* The stability of the assessment over time, and the internal stability of the instrument.
2. *Construct Validity.* The ability of the assessment to measure a phenomenon that is hypothesized to exist (i.e., the construct of creativity).
3. *Predictive Validity.* The relationship between scores on an assessment and performance measured at a future time.
4. *Respondent Honesty.* Honest responses from the respondents. A weakness of self-assessment is that respondents may not provide accurate data but instead may distort their answers to place themselves in a more favorable light; also known as socially desirable responding.

## Two Approaches to Assessing Creativity

According to Torrance (1979), the psychometric measurement of creativity is conducted by two primary methods—the *personality approach* and the *cognitive approach*. Others (e.g., Cropley, 2000) refer to these two approaches as the measurement of the creative person and the creative process.

## The Personality Approach

The personality approach considers creativity to be a personality trait or characteristic that is developed at an early age and is fairly stable over time. This view of creativity as an individual difference variable allows measurement of the construct using well-known personality tests such as the California Psychological Inventory (CPI) (Gough, 1987) and the Myers-Briggs Type Indicator (MBTI) (Myers & McCaulley, 1985).

### Assessing Creativity Level Versus Creativity Style

Measures of creativity level attempt to describe how much of a personality trait an individual possesses, using a continuous scale ranging from a low level of creativity to a high level. Using items from the MBTI and the CPI, Gough (described in Myers & McCaulley, 1985) developed two experimental scales to measure the level of creativity in individuals—*the CPI Creativity Scale (CPI-CT)* and the *MBTI Creativity Index (MBTI-CI)*. (In 1992, Gough refined a special-purpose scale for the CPI, called the Creative Temperament Scale, as the successor to the CPI-CT).

The MBTI-CI, which is a linear combination of MBTI continuous scores, is an example of a *level measure*. According to Myers and McCaulley (1985), the MBTI-CI represents the level of creative potential that an individual possesses. The MBTI itself, however, is a *style measure*. Style measures typically are designed to place the respondent into one of several qualitatively different categories based on the preference for behaving in a certain manner. The MBTI classifies individuals as being introverted versus extraverted (IE), sensing versus intuitive (SN), thinking versus feeling (TF), and judging versus perceiving (JP), based on their preferences for these processes.

To measure the creativity style of individuals (as opposed to creativity level), Kirton (1976, 1987) designed an instrument known as the *Kirton Adaption-Innovation Inventory (KAI)*. According to Kirton, creativity style (adaptive or innovative) is independent of creativity level; that is, adaptors and innovators can demonstrate equal levels of creativity while presenting different creativity styles.

Fleenor and Taylor (1994) examined relationships among the two measures of creativity level (the CPI-CT and the MBTI-CI) and the measure of creativity style (the KAI). As expected, they found significant relationships between the CPI-CT and the MBTI-CI. Contrary to expectations, however, the researchers also found that KAI scores were related to creativity levels as measured by the CPI-CT and the MBTI-CI. Innovators were found to have scored significantly higher on the two level measures than adaptors, although according to Kirton (1989), there should be no relationship between creativity style as measured by the KAI and measures of creativity level. These results indicate that the KAI appears to be measuring the same construct as the CPI-CT and the MBTI-CI (i.e., level of creativity).

There is, however, some disagreement on how levels of creativity should be operationalized. Creativity is commonly defined as the production of a high volume of new products or ideas (i.e., Kirton's innovative style). For Kirton (1989), creativity also includes adapting, improving, advancing, or finding a new application for an existing process or product (i.e., Kirton's adaptive style). He argues that the level measures of creativity tap only the innovative style and ignore the adaptive style. According to Gough (1987), the CPI-CT measures the "level of creativity in research and scholarship" (p. 89), while Myers and McCaulley (1985) define creativity as "the creation of something entirely new" (p. 214). The CPI-CT and the MBTI-CI, therefore, may be only measuring creativity by innovation, but not creativity by adaption. Regardless of one's position on the definition of creativity or on the style versus level issue, however, the KAI, the CPI-CT, and the MBTI-CI all appear to be measuring similar constructs.

The results of the Fleenor and Taylor (1994) study offer some evidence of construct validity for the two creativity level measures by linking them to the same nomological network. However, more evidence of criterion-related validity is needed before the instruments can be fully accepted as valid measures of creativity. For example, the scales should be shown to exhibit the expected relationships with external criterion measures of creativity, such as observer ratings.

### Five-Factor Model of Personality

With the emergence of the five-factor model of personality (Digman, 1990), there has been a resurgence of interest in personality research. The five-factor model appears to represent a robust taxonomy of personality; its structure has been replicated numerous times using various measures of personality (Goldberg, 1993; McCrae & Costa, 1987). The five factors are commonly labeled Neuroticism, Extraversion, Openness to Experience, Agreeableness, and Conscientiousness.

To understand how two of the five factors, Openness to Experience and Conscientiousness, are related to creative behavior in the workplace, George and Zhou (2001) adopted an interactional approach. They theorized that Openness to Experience would result in high levels of creative behavior and Conscientiousness would result in low levels of creative behavior, when the situation allowed for the demonstration of these personality traits. With a sample of office workers, they found that Openness to Experience resulted in high levels of creativity when feedback was positive and employees were presented with a task that allowed them to be creative. They also found that Conscientiousness resulted in low levels of creative behavior when supervisors engaged in close monitoring and coworkers were unsupportive. These findings show some promise for the five-factor model of personality as a measure of creativity.

### Rorschach

The Rorschach Inkblot test has traditionally been used for psychological assessment and diagnosing mental illness. Answers typically are classified according to whether the subject sees a fixed form, movement, or color. Cannoni, Burla, and Lazzari (1999) examined score correlations between the Rorschach test and the Torrance Tests of Creative Thinking (Torrance, 1999) by administering the two tests to graduate students. They found that the figural form of the Torrance test was associated with the Developmental Quality-Synthesized Responses of the Rorschach test, with the exception of the Figural Elaboration scores. They also found that the verbal scores from the Torrance tests were correlated with the scores on Space and Unusual Form Quality Responses from the Rorschach. This research indicates that the Rorschach is a potentially useful instrument for assessing and studying creativity.

Gregory (2000) suggests that "reversing" the Rorschach—from assessing kinds of people to kinds of patterns—might show what stimulates creativity. This leads to the experimental question of which kinds of patterns evoke the richest variety of perceptions and ideas. Gregory proposes that this reversed Rorschach could reveal the creative nature of humans for generating perceptions and conceptions for art and perhaps also for science. The author notes that although its clinical validity may be dubious, the Rorschach might evoke creativity in controlled ways for both research and applied purposes.

King and Pope (1999) developed a preliminary creativity scale for the Rorschach that focuses on four areas: complexity, tone, novelty, and liveliness. Using this instrument, they examined creativity as it relates to healthy psychological functioning. According to the authors, when examining the construct of creativity, it is important to consider its implications for psychological health.

### Adjective Checklists

The Adjective Check List (ACL; Gough & Heilbrun, 1983) is an instrument that can be used to assess both self-awareness and others' perceptions of an individual's personality. Its scales include measures of psychological needs, intellect and creativity, and ego functioning. Gough (1992) developed the Creative Personality Scale (CPS) as a subscale of the ACL. This 30-item scale, which is scored as part of the ACL, has been found to differentiate between highly creative and less creative individuals. Its scores are correlated with Openness to Experience as well as Divergent Thinking (Cropley, 2000). Reportedly, the vendor of the ACL, Consulting Psychologists Press, is in the process of developing a revised version of the ACL for use in corporate settings.

In an application of an adjective checklist in creativity research, Soh (2000) developed a self-rating checklist as a measure of creativity to validate the Creativity Fostering Teacher Index, a 45-item self-rating scale based on nine creativity fostering behaviors. According to Soh, research on teachers' creativity fostering behavior has been neglected in spite of the important role teachers play in developing student creativity. A possible reason for this was the lack of a suitable measure of teachers' creativity-fostering behavior. Psychometric analyses conducted by Soh found adequate construct and concurrent validity for the Creativity Fostering Teacher Index.

## The Cognitive Approach to Assessing Creativity

With the cognitive approach, processes such as rational and logical thinking are considered to be important for creative behavior. The cognitive view regards creative thinking to be similar in nature to intelligence (Torrance, 1979). In this approach, creativity typically is assessed by cognitive tests, such as the Torrance Tests of Creative Thinking and the Remote Associates Test.

### Torrance Tests of Creative Thinking

The Torrance Tests of Creative Thinking (TTCT; Torrance, 1966, 1999) are among the most widely used measures of divergent thinking. The test yields three verbal subscores, which Torrance calls mental characteristics: Fluency, Flexibility, and Originality. There are also two figural (nonverbal) forms (A and B), each of which yield five subscores: Fluency, Originality, Abstractness of Titles, Elaboration, and Resistance to Premature Closure. The figural tests also provide subscores on 13 creative scales, such as Synthesis of Incomplete Figures.

The TTCT have been used extensively for both assessing and researching creativity. For example, Rubenstein (2000) examined the effects of print and television content on children's creativity and measures of possibility and curiosity.

She identified eight science-related television programs as having high or low creative content and developed illustrated booklets to mirror the programs' content. Fifth and sixth graders were randomly assigned to one of four conditions: high-content television, low-content television, high-content print or low-content print. The students then completed the TTCT, The Possibilities Index, and The Children's Science Curiosity Scale. Students in the low-content condition significantly outscored the high-content group on Visual Originality and the high-content group significantly outscored the low-content group on measures of possibility and curiosity. These results suggest that content has more effects on creativity and attitude than do media.

Numerous studies have been conducted to determine the psychometric characteristics of the TTCT. For example, an empirical comparison of the factor structures of the figural Forms A and B conducted by Clapham (1998) found that the forms have equivalent structure. Using advanced statistical techniques, Plucker (1999) reanalyzed 20 years of Torrance's TTCT validity data. He found that TTCT composite verbal creativity scores (the average of the scores on the three verbal subscales) accounted for about half of the variance in the relationship between the composite scores and criteria related to creative achievement, performing much better in this area than did the figural test of the TTCT or a cognitive ability test.

Although many of these studies have reported evidence of reliability and validity for the TTCT scores (e.g., Torrance, 1999), some researchers have expressed concern over their construct validity (Chase, 1985; Cooper, 1991). One of the concerns is the high intercorrelations among the creativity dimensions measured by the tests—several studies have reported that the divergent thinking dimensions (e.g., Fluency, Flexibility, and Originality) have poor discriminant validity. For example, Hocevar and Michael (1979) found that TTCT Originality and Flexibility subscores became unreliable when Fluency subscores were partialed out. This study suggests that Fluency is the primary dimension measured by the divergent thinking subscores of the TTCT, leading Hocevar and Michael to suggest that Fluency be used as the sole indicator of divergent thinking.

Factor analyses of divergent thinking subscores conducted by Plass, Michael, and Michael (1974) indicate that the dimensions lack independence—the resulting factors represented tasks (test content) rather than creativity dimensions. These studies have led researchers to question the construct validity of the divergent thinking subscores of the TTCT.

Heausler and Thompson (1988) examined the factor structure of subscores from figural Form A of the TTCT and concluded that the subscores primarily represent one general creativity factor. Clapham (1998) factor-analyzed the TTCT subscores from figural Forms A and B and found that one general creativity factor adequately represented the subscores of both forms. The results of these analyses confirmed that the five subscores of each form provide little unique variance.

### Test of Creative Thinking (Divergent Production)

A better measure of creative thinking may be the Test of Creative Thinking (Divergent Production) (TCT-DP; Urban & Jellen, 1996). The TCT-DP takes a different approach to assessing creativity than does the TTCT. It is based on a more general theory of creativity, a Gestalt theory the authors call *image production*. On the TCP-DP, respondents are presented with drawings of incomplete figures and asked to complete the drawings. The respondents' productions of the images are then rated on 13 dimensions, including Boundary Breaking, New Elements, and Humor and Affectivity. The instrument has two parallel forms, A and B.

Research conducted by the authors indicates acceptable reliabilities and validities for the instrument. Correlations with various criteria indicate that TCP-DP scores are able to distinguish individuals who follow creative pursuits from those who do not. According to Cropley (2000), the instrument is appropriate for administration to a wide range of respondents, is easy to administer, and is suitable for counseling purposes.

### Remote Associates Test

The Remote Associates Test (RAT; Mednick, 1962) is a 30-item creativity assessment on which respondents are asked to find a remote associate for three apparently unrelated words. The remote associate is a fourth word that links the three stimulus words. The RAT is based on the hypothesis that individuals who are better at finding remote associates are more creative. According to the author, the instrument demonstrates acceptable levels of reliability and validity. He reports a correlation of .70 between RAT scores and ratings of creativity. In a review of several studies of the RAT, however, Kasof (1997) reports that the instrument typically demonstrates less impressive correlations with creative behavior.

### Triarchic Abilities Test

The Triarchic Abilities Test (Sternberg, 1997) was developed in response to recent advances in the theory of creativity. Rickards (1994) has suggested that creative thinking not only involves divergent thinking, but also requires convergent thinking. Sternberg, therefore, designed the Triarchic Abili-

ties test to measure three facets of intellectual ability: Analytical Ability, Practical Ability, and Synthetic Ability. Synthetic Ability, the creative facet of intellectual ability, is assessed by multiple-choice items, novel numerical operations, and open-ended responses. The author reports that the Synthetic Ability scale is a reliable and valid measure of creativity. The three scales are not highly correlated, providing some evidence of discriminant validity. He also indicates that the scores on the Synthetic Ability scale have been found to be significantly related to creativity criteria.

## Using Observer Ratings to Assess Creativity

Rather than using the self-assessment methods described previously to measure creativity, some researchers advocate the use of the ratings of observers for this purpose. These ratings typically involve the judgments of coworkers, such as bosses, peers, and direct reports, but may also be extended to include friends, spouses, and other family members.

In one such study, Tierney, Farmer, and Graen (1999) measured creativity using supervisor ratings, invention disclosure forms, and research reports for research and development employees in a chemical company. The study tested a multi-domain, interactionist creativity model of the dynamics between personal and contextual factors responsible for creative performance in work settings. In particular, the authors were interested in identifying the role of leadership in creativity. Their findings indicate that creative performance is related to employee intrinsic motivation and cognitive style, and leader-employee relationships.

Another approach to assessing creativity is to determine what one must do to be creative and then, using the ratings of observers, measure the degree to which one successfully performs these activities. According to Kirschenbaum (1998), creativity assessments should provide information that is accurate and useful in facilitating creative functioning in the individuals being assessed. With this in mind, he developed the Creativity Classification System (CCS) as a taxonomy of creativity that consists of nine essential dimensions of creative activity. The CCS was used to develop the Creative Behavior Inventory, a behavioral rating scale that can be used to rate the creative behavior of individuals. According to the author, the Creative Behavior Inventory has demonstrated some utility in predicting creative productivity.

With the Creativity Checklist, developed by Johnson (1979), observers rate the creative behavior of individuals on eight dimensions including Fluency, Flexibility, Ingenuity, Resourcefulness, and Independence. According to Cropley (2000), interrater reliabilities for this instrument ranged from

.70 and .80, and the test correlated .51 with the RAT and .56 with the TTCT.

### Assessing Creative Products

According to MacKinnon (1978), the assessment of creative products is the foundation of all creativity research. Cropley (2000) lists creative products, along with the creative process and the creative person, as one of three major approaches to assessing creativity. This method involves an analysis of what makes creative products different from less creative products. Although this method possibly could help address some of the concerns about the poor psychometric qualities of certain creativity measures, limited research on creative products has been reported in the literature (Plucker & Renzulli, 1999).

The most common approach to assessing creative products is to use the ratings of expert judges. Research suggests that rating creativity on criteria such as effectiveness, usefulness, and complexity may not be as difficult as once assumed (Cropley, 2000). For example, Hennessey (1994) reported interrater agreement indexes as high as .93 for judgments of the creativity of various works of art.

A few rating scales have been developed for assessing creative products. The Creative Product Inventory (Taylor, 1975) provides measures on seven criteria of creativity: Generation, Reformulation, Originality, Relevancy, Hedonics, Complexity, and Condensation. The Creative Product Semantic Scale (Besemer & O'Quin, 1987) measures three dimensions of creativity: Novelty, Resolution, and Elaboration and Synthesis. Psychometric studies of this instrument indicate that it appears to be a reliable and valid measure of creative products (Cropley, 2000).

### Assessing Creativity With 360-Degree Feedback

Developed in Sweden by Ekvall and Arvonen (1994), Farax is a 360-degree assessment that collects ratings from the manager him- or herself as well as ratings from the manager's boss, peers, direct reports, and others. It is a leader development tool designed to help managers improve their creative leadership skills by providing behavioral and performance feedback on three dimensions: Change, Relationship, and Structure. Farax, therefore, is a combination of traditional measures of leadership effectiveness (relationship and structure) and a third dimension, change. The instrument provides feedback on leaders' creative contribution, both in terms of their individual creative behaviors and their nurturing of others' creativity. It also incorporates feedback on the extent to which behaviors on the three dimensions are viewed as appropriate for effective performance in the organization.

Farax maps the managers' observed leadership behavior as well as ideal leadership behavior. When managers' self-ratings are compared with those of bosses, colleagues, and employees, they can gain insight into and awareness of their role as leaders. When demands and expectations are clarified, managers gain a clear target as the objective of development. Farax also facilitates a dialogue related to leadership between managers and their employees. The instrument is often used in leadership development programs and for coaching individual managers.

Farax is designed to support assessment for development, but it is not intended to be used for performance appraisal or placement. Trainers using this survey need to be proficient in delivering 360-degree feedback. The instrument has been translated into English in a collaboration between the authors and the Center for Creative Leadership (CCL); however, the psychometric properties of this instrument are still under investigation.

### Assessing the Climate for Creativity

In addition to the assessment of individual creativity, some researchers have argued that it is also important to measure the context in which creativity occurs (Amabile, 1983; Csikszentmihalyi, 1988). In this vein, several attempts have been made to develop measures to quantitatively assess the environment for creativity in the workplace.

### The Siegel Scale of Support of Innovation

The Siegel Scale of Support of Innovation (Siegel & Kaemmerer, 1978) assesses perceptions of leadership, ownership, norms for diversity, continuous development, and consistency. However, the instrument was validated on school teachers and students; therefore, its utility for use in business organizations may be limited.

### Situational Outlook Questionnaire

Isaksen, Lauer, and Ekvall (1999) developed a multidimensional measure, called the Situational Outlook Questionnaire, designed to assess characteristics that influence creativity and change at the individual, group, and organizational levels. They investigated the psychometric properties of the assessment instrument with a sample of individuals from six different organizations. This study provided some support for the reliability and construct validity of the Situational Outlook Questionnaire.

## KEYS: Assessing the Climate for Creativity

KEYS (Amabile, Taylor, & Gryskiewicz, 1995) is an organizational survey designed to assess aspects of the work environment that relate to creativity. It assesses stimulants and obstacles to creativity, as well as two primary work outcomes: creativity and productivity. The theoretical foundation of KEYS is based on contextual theories, which integrate the creativity dimensions of work environments that have been identified by empirical research (e.g., Woodman, Sawyer, & Griffin, 1993).

The underlying theory of KEYS posits that three organizational components constitute the work environment that influences individual or team creativity (Amabile, 1988, 1996):

1. *Organizational Motivation to Innovate.* A basic orientation of the organization toward innovation, as well as supports for creativity and innovation throughout the organization.
2. *Resources.* Everything that the organization has available to aid work in the domain targeted for innovation (e.g., sufficient time for producing novel work in the domain, funding, materials, and information).
3. *Management Practices.* Allowance of freedom or autonomy in the conduct of work; provision of challenging, interesting work; specification of clear overall strategic goals; and formation of work teams by drawing together individuals with diverse skills and perspectives.

KEYS theory also proposes that individual creativity depends on three components within the individual:

1. *Expertise.* Knowledge and skill in the particular area where the individual is trying to do creative work.
2. *Creativity Skills.* Techniques for taking new perspectives on problems, for incubating and persevering on difficult problems, and for taking risks with solutions to problems.
3. *Task Motivation.* The desire to solve the problem or do the task because it is interesting, involving, or personally challenging.

According to the authors, the work environment affects all three individual components, but it appears to have its most immediate and salient impact on motivation. Creativity that results from the work of individuals or teams has a major role in determining the overall level of innovation within the organization.

In an early study leading to the development of KEYS, Amabile and Gryskiewicz (1987) interviewed more than 100 R&D scientists from several different companies, using a critical-incident technique. They asked the scientists to describe in detail two significant events from their work experience: one that exemplified low creativity and one that exemplified high creativity. The results of this study were used to develop the item content of KEYS. A full description of the development of KEYS and its psychometric properties can be found in Amabile, Conti, Coon, Lazenby, and Herron (1996).

### The Creative Climate Questionnaire

Developed in Swedish by Ekvall, Arvonen, and Waldenstrom-Lindblad (1983), the Creative Climate Questionnaire is similar to KEYS in several ways. However, its psychometric properties have not yet been documented in the literature as has KEYS, although a large amount of data has been collected with this instrument, according to the authors.

## SUMMARY

Although the literature cited in this chapter is generally supportive of the psychometric measurement of creativity, users of these instruments should exercise vigilance when selecting creativity assessments for use in applied settings. It is incumbent on users to investigate several potential measures before choosing the one that will best meet their needs. An instrument should be selected that is appropriate for the context in which it will be used. Users should be aware that some psychometric measures of creativity, which focus only on a specific area of creativity such as a task-specific process, may be too narrow in scope. As more comprehensive theories of creativity are developed, reliance on a single aspect of creativity measurement such as process, person, product, or context will become less defensible (Plucker & Renzulli, 1999). Additionally, much of the creativity research currently available was conducted years ago, and recent advances in statistical analysis will permit more rigorous evaluations of assessments of creativity. Before making a final decision on which instrument is most appropriate for their situation, users should ensure that they have access to the latest information available on the creativity assessments under consideration.

## REFERENCES

Amabile, T. (1983). *The social psychology of creativity.* New York: Springer-Verlag.

Amabile, T. (1988). A model of creativity and innovation in organizations. In B. Staw & L. Cummings (Eds.), *Research in organizational behavior,* Vol. 10. Greenwich, CT: JAI Press.

Amabile, T. (1996). *Creativity in context: Update to the social psychology of creativity.* Boulder, CO: Westview Press.

Amabile, T., Conti, R., Coon, H., Lazenby, J., & Herron, M. (1996). Assessing the work environment for creativity. *Academy of Management Journal, 39,* 1154–1184.

Amabile, T., & Gryskiewicz, S. (1987). *Creativity in the R&D laboratory.* Greensboro, NC: Center for Creative Leadership.

Amabile, T., Taylor, S., & Gryskiewicz, N. (1995). *Technical manual for KEYS: Assessing the climate for creativity.* Greensboro, NC: Center for Creative Leadership.

American Psychological Association. (1999). *Standards for educational and psychological testing.* Washington, DC: Author.

Besemer, S., & O'Quin, K. (1987). Creative product analysis: Testing a model by developing a judging instrument. In S. Isaksen (Ed.), *Frontiers of creativity research: Beyond the basics* (pp. 367–389). Buffalo, NY: Bearly.

Cannoni, E., Burla, F., & Lazzari, R. (1999). Correlations for the Rorschach with the Torrance Tests of Creative Thinking. *Perceptual & Motor Skills, 89,* 863–870.

Carroll, J. (1993). *Human cognitive abilities.* New York: Cambridge University Press.

Chase, C. (1985). Review of the Torrance Tests of Creative Thinking. In J.V. Mitchell Jr. (Ed.), *The ninth mental measurements yearbook* (pp. 1631–1632). Lincoln, NE: Buros Institute of Mental Measurement.

Clapham, M. (1998). Structure of figural forms A and B of the Torrance Tests of Creative Thinking, *Educational & Psychological Measurement, 58,* 275–283.

Cooper, E. (1991). A critique of six measures for assessing creativity. *Journal of Creative Behavior, 25,* 194–204.

Cropley, A. (2000). Defining and measuring creativity: Are creativity tests worth using? *Roeper Review, 23,* 72–79.

Csikszentmihalyi, M. (1996). *Creativity: Flow and the psychology of discovery and invention.* New York: HarperCollins.

Csikszentmihalyi, M. (1988). Society, culture and person: A systems view of creativity. In R. Sternberg (Ed.), *The nature of creativity: Contemporary psychological perspectives* (pp. 325–339). New York: Cambridge University Press.

Digman, J. (1990). Personality structure: Emergence of the five-factor model. *Annual Review of Psychology, 41,* 417–440.

Ekvall, G., & Arvonen, J. (1994). Leadership profiles, situation and effectiveness. *Creativity and Innovation Management, 3,* 139–161.

Ekvall, G., Arvonen, J., & Waldenstrom-Lindblad, I. (1983). *Creative organizational climate: Construction and validation of a measuring instrument.* Stockholm, Sweden: The Swedish Council for Management and Organizational Behavior.

Fleenor, J., & Taylor, S. (1994). The construct validity of three self-report measures of creativity. *Educational and Psychological Measurement, 54,* 462–468.

George, J., & Zhou, J. (2001). When openness to experience and conscientiousness are related to creative behavior: An interactional approach. *Journal of Applied Psychology, 86,* 513–524.

Goldberg, L. (1993). The structure of phenotypic personality traits. *American Psychologist, 48,* 26–34.

Gough, H. (1987). *California Psychological Inventory administrator's guide.* Palo Alto, CA: Consulting Psychologists Press.

Gough, H. (1992). Assessment of creative potential in psychology and the development of a creative potential scale for the CPI. In J. Rosen & P. McReynolds (Eds.), *Advances in psychological assessment* (Vol. 8, pp. 225–257). New York: Plenum.

Gough, H., & Heilbrun, A. (1983). *The Adjective Check List manual* (2nd ed.). Palto Alto, CA: Consulting Psychologists Press.

Gregory, R. (2000). Reversing Rorschach. *Nature, 404,* 19.

Gruber, H., & Wallace, D. (1999). The case study method and evolving systems approach for understanding unique creative people at work. In R. Sternberg (Ed.), *Handbook of creativity* (pp. 93–115). New York: Cambridge University Press.

Guilford, J.P. (1950). Creativity research: Past, present and future. *American Psychologist, 5,* 444–454.

Heausler, N., & Thompson, B. (1988). Structure of the Torrance Tests of Creative Thinking. *Educational and Psychological Measurement, 48,* 463–468.

Hennessey, B. (1994). The consensual assessment technique: An examination of the relationships between ratings of product and process creativity. *Creativity Research Journal, 7,* 193–208.

Hocevar, D. (1981). Measurement of creativity: Review and critique. *Journal of Personality Assessment, 45,* 450–464.

Hocevar, D., & Michael, W. (1979). The effects of scoring formulas on the discriminant validity of tests of divergent thinking. *Educational and Psychological Measurement, 39,* 917–921.

Isaksen, S., Lauer, K., & Ekvall, G. (1999). Situational Outlook Questionnaire: A measure of the climate for creativity and change. *Psychological Reports, 85,* 665–674.

Johnson, D. (1979). *The Creativity Checklist.* Wood Dale, IL: Stoelting.

Kaltsounis, B., & Honeywell, L. (1980). Instruments useful in studying creative behavior and creative talent. *Journal of Creativity Behavior, 14,* 56–67.

Kasof, J. (1997). Creativity and breadth of attention. *Creativity Research Journal, 10,* 303–315.

King, B., & Pope, B. (1999). Creativity as a factor in psychological assessment and healthy psychological functioning. *Journal of Personality Assessment, 72,* 200–207.

Kirschenbaum, R. (1998). The Creativity Classification System: An assessment theory. *Roeper Review, 21,* 20–26.

Kirton, M. (1976). Adaptors and innovators: A description and measure. *Journal of Applied Psychology, 61,* 622–629.

Kirton, M. (1987). *Kirton Adaption and Innovation Inventory (KAI) manual* (2nd ed.). Hatfield, UK: Occupational Research Center.

Kirton, M. (Ed.). (1989). *Adaptors and innovators: Styles of creativity and problem solving*. New York: Routledge.

MacKinnon, D. (1978). *In search of human effectiveness: Identifying and developing creativity*. Buffalo, NY: Creative Education Foundation.

Martindale, C. (1999). Biological bases of creativity. In R. Sternberg (Ed.), *Handbook of creativity* (pp. 137–152). New York: Cambridge University Press.

McCrae, R., & Costa, P.T. (1987). Validation of the five-factor model of personality across instruments and observers. *Journal of Personality and Social Psychology, 52,* 81–90.

Mednick, S. (1962). The associative basis of the creative process. *Psychological Review, 69,* 220–232.

Myers, I., & McCaulley, M. (1985). *Manual: A guide to the development and use of the Myers-Briggs Type Indicator*. Palo Alto, CA: Consulting Psychologists Press.

Plass, H., Michael, J., & Michael, W. (1974). The factorial validity of the Torrance Tests of Creative Thinking for a sample of 111 sixth-grade children. *Educational and Psychological Measurement, 34,* 413–414.

Plucker, J. (1999). Is the proof in the pudding? Reanalysis of Torrance's (1958 to present) longitudinal data. *Creativity Research Journal, 12,* 103–114.

Plucker, J., & Renzulli, J. (1999). Psychometric approaches to the study of human creativity. In R. Sternberg (Ed.), *Handbook of creativity* (pp. 35–61). New York: Cambridge University Press.

Rickards, T. (1994). Creativity from a business school perspective: Past, present and future. In S. Isaksen, M. Murdock, R. Firestein, & D. Treffinger (Eds.), *Nurturing and developing creativity: The emergence of a discipline* (pp. 155–176). Norwood, NJ: Ablex.

Rubenstein, D. (2000). Stimulating children's creativity and curiosity: Does content and medium matter? *Journal of Creative Behavior, 34,* 1–17.

Runco, M., & Albert R. (Eds.). (1990). *Theories of creativity*. Newbury Park, CA: Sage.

Siegel, S., & Kaemmerer, W. (1978). Measuring the perceived support for innovation in organizations. *Journal of Applied Psychology, 63,* 553–562.

Simonton, D. (1999). Creativity from a historiometric perspective. In R. Sternberg (Ed.), *Handbook of creativity* (pp. 116–136). New York: Cambridge University Press.

Sternberg, R. (1997). Intelligence and lifelong learning: What's new and how can we use it? *American Psychologist, 52,* 1132–1139.

Sternberg, R. (2001). What is the common thread of creativity? Its dialectical relation to intelligence and wisdom. *American Psychologist, 56,* 360–362.

Sternberg, R., & Lubart, T. (1999). The concept of creativity: Prospects and paradigms. In R. Sternberg (Ed.), *Handbook of creativity* (pp. 3–15). New York: Cambridge University Press.

Soh, K. (2000). Indexing creativity fostering teacher behavior: A preliminary validation study. *Journal of Creative Behavior, 34,* 118–134.

Taylor, I. (1975). An emerging view of creative actions. In I. Taylor & J. Getzels (Eds.), *Perspectives in creativity* (pp. 297–325). Chicago: Aldine.

Tierney, P., Farmer, S., & Graen, G. (1999). An examination of leadership and employee creativity: The relevance of traits and relationships. *Personnel Psychology, 52,* 591–620.

Torrance, E. (1966). *The Torrance Tests of Creative Thinking—Figural*. Bensenville, IL: Scholastic Testing Services.

Torrance, E. (1979). Unique needs of the creative child and adult. In A. Passow (Ed.), *The gifted and talented: Their education and development* (pp. 352–371). Chicago: National Society for the Study of Education.

Torrance, E. (1999). *Torrance Tests of Creative Thinking: Norms and technical manual*. Bensenville, IL: Scholastic Testing Services.

Torrance, E., & Goff, K. (1989). A quiet revolution. *Journal of Creative Behavior, 23,* 136–145.

Urban, K., & Jellen, H. (1996). *Test for Creative Thinking–Divergent Production (TCT-DP)*. Lisse, Netherlands: Swets and Zeitlinger.

Woodman, R.W., Sawyer, J.E., & Griffin, R.W. (1993). Toward a theory of organizational creativity. *Academy of Management Review, 18,* 293–321.

# BASIC SKILLS

# CHAPTER 7

# Basic Skills

JOHN M. CORNWELL

Writing a chapter on "basic skills" assessment for the field of industrial/organizational psychology seems, at first glance, to be a straightforward endeavor. However, the phrase "basic skills" is much more generic and widely used than other domain names usually found in personnel selection. In fact, tests and inventories found in the other major content areas covered in this volume (e.g., cognitive ability, personality, integrity, interests, biographical data, and job-specific tests) are often included or cross-listed under the heading of "basic skills" in the marketing materials and catalogs of various test publishers and consulting firms. First, I have defined the basic skills domain. The next section is an analysis of the need for basic skills assessment in employee selection. Finally, the chapter concludes with the review of associated assessments suitable for employee selection purposes.

## BASIC SKILLS DOMAIN DEFINED

A first attempt to define the basic skills domain was made using the phrase "basic skills" in a search of the *Mental Measurement Yearbook* (*MMY*) electronic database. The search generated 142 records and included published measures having a wide variety of formats, purposes, and skills. A self-assessment inventory for high school and college students, the Working-Assessing Skills Habits and Style (Miles, Grummon, & Maduschke, 1996), was among those listed. The inventory does not include basic academic skills, such as reading, math,

or language arts, but does assess other workplace basic skills specified in the Secretary's Commission on Achieving Necessary Skills (SCANS) framework (U.S. Department of Labor, 1992). Wasdyke, Freeberg, and Rock (1984) reported on the development of the Job Training Assessment Program (JOBTAP) measure to assess success of participants in job training programs under the Federal Job Training Partnership Act. The Diagnostic Employability Skills Inventory (Brigance, 1995) is a test of basic skills for individuals with special needs, such as disabilities or limited English proficiency. One can use Brigance's inventory to measure the basic skills compiled in the Comprehensive Adult Student Assessment System (CASAS, 1993) and SCANS (U.S. Department of Labor, 1992). Another example of a basic skills inventory listed in *MMY* is the Functional Skills Screening Inventory (Becker, Schur, Paoletti-Schelp, & Hammer, 1986), which focuses on the assessment of life and work-related skills in persons with moderate to severe handicaps. The search revealed that most of the 142 records are for academic basic skills tests used with students in Grades K–12 (e.g., Iowa Tests of Basic Skills [Hoover, Hieronymous, Frisbie, & Dunbar, 1996]). Thus, the use of a standard reference such as the *MMY* is not helpful in defining the basic skills domain for employee selection purposes.

The use of basic skills frameworks that were developed for the explicit purpose of identifying the skills required for employment is considered next. O'Neil, Allred, and Baker (1997) summarize five major taxonomies produced to define the essential skills required in the workplace: (1) SCANS (U.S. Department of Labor, 1992) (2) a compilation sponsored by the American Society for Training and Development (ASTD) (Carnevale, Gainer, & Meltzer, 1990), (3) a 1987 study conducted by the State of Michigan (Employability Skills Task Force, 1988), (4) a study conducted by the New York State Education Department (1990), and (5) an earlier study conducted under the auspices of the National Academy of Sciences (NAS) (1984).

Cornwell (2000) reviews these five taxonomies along with one from the National Institute for Literacy (Stein, 2000) to identify the common basic academic skills required in the workplace. Five basic academic skills are consistently mentioned: (1) reading, (2) writing, (3) arithmetic/mathematics, (4) listening, and (5) speaking. However, other skills are also mentioned as being needed across all jobs (Carnevale et al., 1990), necessary (Stein, 2000), or core (NAS, 1984) for the workforce of today and tomorrow.

Richens and McClain (2000) reported that, based on a recent survey of 400 employers, the SCANS taxonomy adequately identifies the skills that entry workers need. O'Neil et al. (1997) organized these additional skills and the academic skills into four general categories: (1) basic (academic) skills, (2) higher order thinking skills, (3) interpersonal and teamwork skills, and (4) personal characteristics and attitudes. These four categories contain the basic skills required to some extent in all jobs. The results from national and state-level job analyses of a broad range of jobs conducted over the last decade support this notion (e.g., Nash & Korte, 1997; National Academy of Sciences [NAS], 1984; New York State Education Department, 1990; and O'Neil et al., 1997). Table 7.1 is a compilation of these basic skills based on an adaptation of work by O'Neil et al. (1997). It also includes cross-references to the other chapters in this volume.

SCANS (U.S. Department of Labor, 1992) and other taxonomies (see O'Neil et al., 1997) also take into account competencies or the utilization of skills for specific functions (e.g., systems analysis, working with technologies, utilizing resources, managing ones career, fulfilling civic obligations). Equipped for the Future (EFF) (Stein, 2000) is a national initiative that has identified skills appropriate for all three roles within which an adult must function effectively: (1) citizen/community member, (2) parent/family member, and (3) worker or member of the economic community. Instead of maintaining that different skills are required for different aspects of one's life, the EFF methodology identifies the commonalities in skill requirements across all aspects of life. One can view those skills as basic to effective functioning in any arena of adult life. The four categories of EFF skills (i.e., communi-

**TABLE 7.1   Four Categories of Basic Employment/Work Skills and Associated Chapters**

Basic Academic Skills (Chapter 8)
   Arithmetic/mathematics
   Reading
   Writing
   Speaking
   Listening

Higher Order Thinking Skills
   Creative/divergent (Chapter 7)
   Decision making (Chapters 2, 4, 5)
   Problem solving (Chapters 2, 4, 5)
   Knowing how to learn (Chapters 2, 4, 5)

Interpersonal and Teamwork Skills
   Negotiates (Chapter 14)
   Teaches/mentors others (Chapter 15)
   Appreciates diversity (Chapter 14)
   Interpersonal (Chapter 14)
   Group process (Chapter 24)

Personal Characteristics
   Integrity (Chapter 11)
   Self-management (Chapters 9, 10)
   Responsibility (Chapters 9, 10)
   Self-esteem (Chapters 9, 10)

cation, decision making, interpersonal, and lifelong learning) easily fit into the schema presented in Table 7.1.

During the last decade the interest in skills essential to the workplace has continued to expand. The Canadian government, through its Center for Education Information (2001), has posted extensive information on web sites for youth and adults informing them of these essential skills. The Public Broadcasting System (PBS; 2001) of the United States has developed videos, workbooks, and web sites that support basic skills education. Entitled "Workplace Essential Skills," the PBS initiative supports adult students in mastering the basic academic skills listed in Table 7.1.

## BASIC SKILLS AND WORKFORCE DEVELOPMENT

Workforce development has become more important as both individual companies and countries vie to gain a competitive edge. Workforce development occurs in four distinct groups: the emerging workforce, the incumbent workforce, the underemployed workforce, and the chronically unemployed or never employed. This section defines and discusses issues relating to these four groups. The evidence for the need for basic skills employment selection testing is presented in the following section.

The "emerging workforce" consists of all youth in public and private, K–16+ education systems including graduate schools and proprietary schools. Whereas 50 years ago a high school diploma was a credential that was not achieved by the majority of the emerging workforce, today postsecondary credentials are necessary for one to have a chance at economic security (Berryman & Bailey, 1992).

The "incumbent workforce" refers to the majority of workers gainfully employed on a continuing basis in full-time or self-selected part-time employment. This population often has access to training and education with a strong emphasis on lifelong learning that is available through or paid for by their company. The relationship between these first two groups is clear. The emerging workforce develops into the incumbent workforce. The former is primarily engaged in education and makes little or no economic contribution. The latter primarily contributes to economic wealth and engages in little or no formal education.

The "underemployed workforce" has a substantial number of workers who are often called the "working poor" and often work more than one job in order to earn enough to cover expenses. Usually working for minimum wage or less than a "living wage," these workers almost never receive the benefits (e.g., health insurance, paid leave, retirement) that the incumbent workforce does. These workers provide services that are fundamental either to a business's mission (e.g., service and hospitality) or to its operations (e.g. custodians, security guards, laborers); yet, they are often the first to be laid off during economic downturns. Although those dropping out from the emerging workforce often end up in the underemployed workforce, recent immigrants who are non-English speakers as well as many of those who have moved from welfare to work over the last few years also fill this population of workers.

A criticism of the federal "welfare-to-work" programs of the last few years (i.e., Workforce Investment Act of 1998) is that they move people from the chronically unemployed or never-employed population into the underemployed category. That move, while decreasing welfare rolls, results in individuals losing important benefits once they begin working because they are then no longer eligible for entitlement programs. Specifically, subsidized rents, access to health care for one's spouse and children, food stamps, and not having an expense for child care are lost by moving from welfare to work. The low wages associated with being underemployed mean that they cannot afford to purchase goods and services to replace these lost benefits. Besides those living on welfare, the "never-employed" population includes those who are involved in illegal activities, incarcerated, or working without legal sanction (e.g., those without social security numbers, federal withholding, or unemployment or workers' compensation taxes, and those primarily working for and purchasing with cash or barter). They may reside with relatives or may be homeless. In many cases, these individuals have very low levels of basic skills. Additionally, programs to increase their skill levels are unavailable or ineffective.

## NEED FOR BASIC SKILLS EMPLOYMENT SELECTION TESTING

In the past two decades, numerous studies have documented the need for higher levels of basic workplace skills for incumbent workers (Hunt, 1995; Murnane & Levy, 1996; Osterman, 1995; U.S. Department of Labor, 1992). At the same time, researchers have identified a gap in the ability of the educational systems to produce students possessing these skills at the level required (e.g., emerging workforce) (Goldman, 1992; Hunt, 1995; Judy & D'Amico, 1997; Kelkar & Paranto, 1999; Murnane & Levy, 1996; Sticht, 1998). In fact, some have expressed concerns regarding the ability of colleges and professional schools to meet these needs (e.g., Bloom & Lafleur, 1999; Edge, 1985; Kimel & Monsees, 1979).

Two years into the Reagan administration, the U.S. Department of Education issued a report, entitled *A Nation at Risk,* that called attention to the fact that the emerging global economy required higher levels of basic skills than had been taught historically in the United States (U.S. Commission on Excellence in Education, 1983). This report had a profound effect on policies (e.g., increased state accountability, SCANS, Goals 2000) regarding K–12 education as related to the emerging workforce. The report also impacted federal workforce preparedness policy related to the chronically unemployed and finally resulted in the Workforce Investment Act of 1998. This act fundamentally revamped the federal welfare system, job training programs, and adult education and family literacy programs. A "work first" priority (i.e., moving people into jobs as quickly as possible) dominates all the traditional federal programs, and it is hoped that this emphasis will address the problem of the unemployed, underemployed, and incumbent workers not being able to meet the skill demands of a new, global economy. A federally mandated accountability system requires improvements over five years in core indicators such as mastery of basic skills at higher levels, higher high school certification rates (diplomas or GEDs), and increased rates in postsecondary education, training, or unsubsidized employment (Sticht, 1998). Unfortunately, it is not clear whether these federal programs whose primary purpose is to move people from welfare to work and assist the chronically unemployed in finding permanent jobs in the more demanding workforce can also develop the basic skills of those incumbent workers who have been reliably employed but trained under an older, less demanding standard. It is also not clear whether those federal programs can assist those underemployed who have very low skills in developing basic skills. The promise for incumbent workers may lie within those states that have begun to invest in skill development training for incumbent workers using their own funds in direct cooperation with their state employers (e.g., Louisiana Department of Labor, 2001).

To what extent are incumbent workers not prepared for the new economy? In Massachusetts it is estimated that one in three workers are not prepared (Comings, Sum, & Uvin, 2000). Roughly 58% of those not prepared are incumbent workers who possess at least a high school credential. Of the remaining, most of whom are underemployed, almost a quarter are high school dropouts, with the rest (17%) being recent immigrants with limited English language skills. Comings et al. (2000) identified three challenges that employers are facing today: the *language challenge* refers to immigrants with limited English language skills; the *education credential challenge* refers to adults who lack a high school diploma or GED; and the *new literacy challenge* refers to low-skilled workers who possess high school credentials and are not illiterate in the traditional sense but have limited reading, math, and analytical skills that restrict their ability to participate in the new economy.

The Department of Defense Voluntary Education Program Fact Sheet for 2000 (Defense Activity for Non-Traditional Education Support [DANTES], 2001) indicated that more than 39,400 Active Duty, Reserve, and National Guard members of the armed forces were enrolled in basic skills noncredit courses during that year. This number seems very large given that the military requires enlistees to have at least a GED or high school diploma (except under rare circumstances) and that the entrance test, the Armed Services Vocational Aptitude Battery (ASVAB), measures basic academic skills of reading and mathematics (as well as science, electronics, mechanical, and auto/shop knowledge). These statistics suggest that a high school education is not always sufficient to meet the basic skills required in today's military. It should also be noted that more than 580,000 members of the military were enrolled in for-credit postsecondary undergraduate courses and another 65,000 were taking graduate courses during the same time period.

The American Management Association (AMA) (2001) conducts annual surveys of human resources managers in AMA member companies. Member companies represent 25% of the U.S. workforce but underrepresent smaller companies, which are predominate in the national economy. The 2001 survey on workplace testing revealed that 41% of surveyed firms test job applicants in basic literacy and/or math skills.

Over the last three years, more than a third of tested applicants lacked sufficient math and/or literacy skills for the positions they sought. This is up from only 23% being deficient in 1997, which had not increased significantly from the deficiency rate in 1990 of 22% for job applicants (Greenberg, 1990). In spite of a relatively tight labor market in the first half of 2001, only 6.5% of companies were willing to hire such individuals and provide them with remedial training to elevate their skill level to job requirements. The AMA concludes that these figures possibly signify that the higher skill levels required in today's workplace are outpacing the ability of our school systems to meet these higher levels, especially in the manufacturing, wholesale, and retail segments where deficiency rates are the highest. It seems that new technologies continue to require higher levels of proficiency in reading, writing, and math.

While the AMA surveyed medium to large firms, the situation may be worse in smaller firms. A study of incumbent workers in small manufacturing firms located in rural areas found that 84% needed remedial training in one or more basic skill areas (Kuchinke, Brown, Anderson, & Hobson, 1998). The National Institute for Literacy estimates that American businesses lose more than $60 million in productivity each year due to employees' lack of basic skills (Tyler, 1999). The Conference Board reports that more than 40% of American workers have inadequate basic skills with more than 52% of recent high school graduates and 16% of college graduates having inadequate basic skills (Bloom & Lafleur, 1999).

Based on a review of the most recent International Adult Literacy Survey, the United States has a higher percentage of adults in the lowest level of literacy (20.7%) than Canada (16.6%), Australia (17.0%), New Zealand (18.4%), and most of Europe except for the United Kingdom (21.8%) and Ireland (22.6%) (Sticht, 1998). Atkinson and Spilsbury (1993) reported on an extensive survey of 24,000 firms with approximately 1.3 million employees covering England and Wales sponsored by the British government. They concluded that basic skills have become more important to employers since the late 1980s and will continue to become more important. In 1993, most employers still rated the basic skills possessed by their incumbent employees as fairly adequate. Of the 24,000 firms surveyed, 1 in 10 stated that their employees' basic skills were less than or just barely adequate for what their jobs required. A Canadian survey found that the number of firms in Manitoba that screen for basic skills has been increasing steadily since the early 1990s in response to a growing skill deficiency observed among applicants (Manitoba, 1996). Moy (1999) reported on the extensive work of conceptualizing key competencies required in the workplace and the development of relevant assessment and training methods that is occurring in Australia. She concluded that this effort is part of an international trend in which educators and industry representatives together consider the skills that are essential for work and life.

The shortage of skills is expected to grow worse according to studies released by the Employment Policy Foundation (EPF; 2001) and Educational Testing Service (ETS) (Barton, 2000). A high school diploma will provide the basic skill level necessary to compete for good-paying jobs, but postsecondary education is now required for jobs in the fastest growing occupations (e.g., management, professional services, technical support, and information technology) (EPF, 2001). Barton (2000), reviewing the last 60 years, documented a long-term trend, which is forecasted to continue into the future, of higher and higher literacy skill levels being required in the workplace. At the same time, the language challenge mentioned earlier (Comings et al., 2000) will continue to grow as more and more foreign residents enter the U.S. labor force. Since 1994 such workers have filled 47% of the new positions due to growth in U.S. jobs. Still, in the future even more foreign workers will enter the domestic workforce in order to meet domestic job growth. According to EPF, 12% of the total hours currently worked in a week within the United States are by foreign-born workers.

Individuals applying for jobs for which they are not qualified is also a problem. Sticht (1998) cited research showing that individuals at all basic skill levels greatly overestimate their proficiency in performing basic skills. Most functionally illiterate incumbent workers are unaware of or unwilling to acknowledge their low levels of proficiency and thus are reluctant to participate in basic skills training and apply for jobs for which they are not qualified.

## TESTS OF BASIC ACADEMIC SKILLS

Table 7.2 presents 11 tests specifically designed to measure one or more of the five basic academic skills listed in Table 7.1 (i.e., math, reading, writing, speaking, and listening). The 11 tests were included in this review based on their reported development for specific use in an employment setting (i.e., selection) versus use for placement and assessment purposes in K–12 or adult educational programs. Dozens of additional tests have been developed for these latter purposes. All these tests have been developed, renormed, or reissued in the past 15 years, with many developed in direct response to SCANS and other basic skills taxonomies.

Overall, these 11 tests have good psychometric qualities with demonstrated reliabilities and validities for their intended use and populations. Some have methods for establishing content validity evidence through a locally conducted job analysis but all have sufficient documentation so that a knowledgeable personnel specialist could review the test-job match for content validity support. The cost and time required in using these tests are consistent with most selection tests used by businesses today.

Basic academic skills selection tests are most appropriate for entry-level and low-skill-level jobs; however, the use of a screening assessment for higher skill jobs may also be warranted given the large numbers of applicants who are deficient in these skills and who may overestimate their own personal skill levels. Using these tests in such a manner could be useful in reducing the numbers to be assessed further.

### WorkKeys

#### Description

WorkKeys was developed during the 1990s by ACT in direct response to SCANS and other taxonomies of workplace basic skills (ACT, Inc., 1998b). This assessment includes eight tests, six of which correspond to basic academic skills (see Table 7.2) and are reviewed here and in Table 7.3. Two tests, Applied Technology and Teamwork, assess skills that SCANS and others taxonomies have identified as essential workplace skills; however, these are not academic in nature and therefore not included in this review. Each of the eight tests may be used individually or in combination with one another. WorkKeys includes a job profiling system of an employer's jobs to establish content validity for the use and the assignment of proficiency levels for the tests. In addition, the WorkKeys system can be used to develop training objectives for educational systems or in-house training efforts. ACT has committed resources and staff to develop new tests and to undertake ongoing psychometric research on the existing ones.

WorkKeys reports that all of the tests are performance based, meaning that they provide workplace scenarios to which the assessee must respond in multiple-choice format for Applied Mathematics, Reading for Information, Locating Information, and Observation, or in a constructed-response (essay) format for the Listening and Writing tests. Rather than norm referenced, scores are criterion referenced based on levels of proficiency.

#### Theoretical Basis and Test Development

ACT desired to satisfy the needs of both employers and educators with the WorkKey assessments. Initially, eight skills were selected based on a review of basic skills taxonomies such as SCANS for test development, but to date only eight have come to fruition. A panel of business, educators, and

**TABLE 7.2   Basic Skills Assessed by Reviewed Tests with Associated Scales or Subtests**

| Publisher | Test and Copyright Year[1] | Math | Reading | Writing | Speaking | Listening |
|---|---|---|---|---|---|---|
| ACT, Inc. | WorkKeys (1998a) | X<br>Applied Mathematics | X<br>Reading for Information, Locating Information | X<br>Listening and Writing: Writing | | X<br>Listening and Writing: Listening, Observation |
| The Australian Council for Educational Research, Ltd. | Work Potential Profile (1997) | X<br>Numeracy | X<br>Communication and Literacy | X<br>Communication and Literacy | X<br>Communication and Literacy | |
| The Australian Council for Educational Research, Ltd. | Work Readiness Profile (1995) | X<br>Literacy and Numeracy | X<br>Literacy and Numeracy | X<br>Communication Effectiveness | X<br>Communication Effectiveness | |
| G. Neil | SkillSeries (1998) | X<br>Math Skills | X<br>Analyzing Skills, Reading Comprehension Skills, Vocabulary Skills | X<br>Grammar Skills, Spelling Skills, Proofreading Skills | | |
| Institute for Personality and Ability Testing, Inc. | Comprehensive Ability Battery (CAB) (1982) | X<br>Numerical Ability | X<br>Verbal Ability | X<br>Spelling | | |
| Psychological Services, Inc. | Employee Aptitude Survey (1994) | X<br>Numerical Ability, Numerical Reasoning | X<br>Verbal Comprehension, Verbal Reasoning | | | |
| Psychological Services, Inc. | PSI Basic Skills Tests (1985) | X<br>Computation, Problem Solving | X<br>Reading Comprehension, Vocabulary, Following Written Directions, Forms Checking, Reasoning | X<br>Language Skills | | X<br>Following Oral Directions |
| National Computer Systems, Inc. | Reading and Arithmetic Indexes (2000) | X<br>Arithmetic Index | X<br>Reading Index | | | |
| Steck-Vaughn Company | Adult Measure of Essential Skills (AMES) (1999) | X<br>Computation Test, Applied Problem Solving Test | X<br>Reading Test | X<br>Communication Test | | |
| Wide Range, Inc. | Wide Range Achievement Test (WRAT3) (1993) | X<br>Arithmetic Test | X<br>Reading Test | X<br>Spelling Test | | |
| Wonderlic, Inc. | Wonderlic Basic Skills Test (1999) | X<br>Quantitative Test: Explicit, Applied, and Interpretive Subscales | X<br>Verbal Test: Word Knowledge and Information Retrieval Subscales | X<br>Verbal Test: Sentence Construction Subscale | | |

[1]The copyright year is the latest available associated with the test manual. In some cases it is equivalent to the edition or version of a test; in other cases, an older, original test has been renormed and/or the manual has been rewritten, resulting in a copyright year more recent than the edition of the actual test.

**TABLE 7.3  Assessment: WorkKeys**

*Applied Mathematics*
Time and Number of Items: 45 minutes, 33 problems.
Skill Measured: Applying mathematical reasoning to work-related problems.
Format: Multiple choice with workplace scenarios. Requires calculator and the use of a provided formula sheet, which includes all required formulas as well as distracter formulas.
Scores: Five proficiency levels (Levels 3–7) using a Guttman-like scale.
Psychometrics: Alpha = .86.

*Listening and Writing: Listening*
Time and Number of Items: 40 minutes, 6 messages.
Skill Measured: Listening and understanding work-related messages accurately and completely (writing skill is ignored).
Format: Writes down information (constructed response) heard from audiotaped messages to convey it to someone else. Writing test uses same stimulus.
Scores: Five proficiency levels (Levels 1–5) using a Guttman-like scale.
Psychometrics: Alpha = .85.

*Listening and Writing: Writing*
Time and Number of Items: 40 minutes, 6 messages.
Skill Measured: Writing work-related messages using standard writing mechanics and style (adequacy of content is ignored).
Format: Writes down information (constructed response) heard from audiotaped messages to convey it to someone else. Listening test uses same stimulus.
Scores: Five proficiency levels (Levels 1–5) using a Guttman-like scale.
Psychometrics: Alpha = .89.

*Observation*
Time and Number of Items: 60 minutes, 36 items.
Skill Measured: Paying attention to instructions and demonstrations and in noticing details.
Format: Multiple choice with video-based workplace scenarios as stimuli.
Scores: Four proficiency levels (Levels 3–6) using a Guttman-like scale.
Psychometrics: Alpha = .72.

*Locating Information*
Time and Number of Items: 45 minutes, 38 problems.
Skill Measured: Using information presented in workplace graphs, charts, gauges, etc.
Format: Multiple choice with workplace scenarios.
Scores: Four proficiency levels (Levels 3–6) using a Guttman-like scale.
Psychometrics: Alpha = .77.

*Reading for Information*
Time and Number of Items: 40 minutes, 30 problems.
Skill Measured: Reading and understanding work-related instructions and policies.
Format: Multiple choice with workplace scenarios.
Scores: Five proficiency levels (Levels 3–7) using a Guttman-like scale.
Psychometrics: Alpha = .80.

ACT staff reviewed the test specifications for each of the eight tests. Then, test specialists wrote items for the prototype test for each difficulty level specified. Because WorkKeys measures generic workplace skills, a balance was sought between too much specificity (which would have resulted in numerous individual tests) and too broad an assessment (which would have yielded individual tests too long and time-consuming to be administered). Each of these tests was de-

veloped to be criterion referenced, not norm referenced. The skill levels had to be able to:

> (a) be readily interpretable as a description of what the examinee can do, and the skills required by the job; (b) be appropriate for large-scale use, and for validation as part of a system for selecting qualified job applicants; and (c) provide information useful for an examinee wishing to improve skills in order to meet job requirements, an educator or trainer wishing to assist examinees in improving their job-related skills, and an employer wishing to select well-qualified employees. (ACT, 1998b, p. 45)

A common metric was forged between describing job skill proficiency and assessee skill proficiency such that a Level 4 requirement on the Reading for Information test for a particular job and an individual who scores at a Level 4 on the same test refer to identical skill proficiency. The levels are defined such that the lowest is approximately the level for lowest skill proficiency existing in entry-level jobs. The highest level assessed is beyond that for which specialized training would be required, that is, beyond basic skill level. (Note: Lower levels of proficiencies exist within educational settings, which is why most WorkKey tests start at Level 3 proficiency; the lowest level in which an employer would be interested. CASAS has worked with ACT to link their assessment system, which is geared to adults functioning at very low grade levels from elementary to GED, or a WorkKeys Level 1 or 2, though no such level exists within WorkKeys, to the WorkKeys assessment system [Comprehensive Adult Student Assessment System & ACT, 1997]. WorkKeys, though not linked by criterion to grade levels, would appear to measure proficiency levels starting at least in the early to mid high school grades.]

Test development followed a process to ensure "Guttman-like" scores for each of the eight tests. Four to five levels of proficiency could be reported with each higher level assuming and building on the skills assessed at the lower levels. Traditional techniques for developing Guttman scales were used as well as item response theory (IRT). Use of IRT resulted in the best Guttman-like and most reliable scales (internal consistency). ACT has produced extensive technical reports on the development of WorkKeys, which it provides at no cost to interested professionals (ACT, 1998b).

### Psychometric Characteristics

Table 7.3 presents the reliabilities and validities for each of the six tests reviewed here. The reported coefficient alphas ranged from .72 for the Observation test to .89 for the Writing test. The technical manual (ACT, 1998b) reports the results of a Generalizability Study for the Listening and Writing tests, with G calculated as .663 and .822, respectively, and provides a table of the total test score means by items correct, standard deviations, and standard errors of measurement for the multiple-choice tests.

Validity studies for WorkKeys have been demonstrated using a wide variety of approaches and types of evidence because of the use of WorkKeys in educational and employment settings. The technical manual (ACT, 1998b) contains information regarding the content validation effort, which analyzed more than 1,000 jobs to determine whether the various tests and their proficiency levels were appropriate. On average, across the six tests reviewed here, fewer than 1% of jobs analyzed either did not require the basic skill or required it at a proficiency lower than the lowest scale level reported. Thus, there seems to be strong support for the content validity of WorkKeys across large numbers of jobs. The WorkKeys job profiling (job analysis) system makes it relatively easy to document local content validity evidence. ACT is also conducting research on the construct validity of WorkKeys by comparing its tests with other ACT tests.

### Applicability, Accommodations, Fairness

WorkKeys development has produced assessments suitable for educational and employment purposes. Its job profiling system permits the user to conduct a job analysis to be assured of the appropriateness of a particular WorkKeys test and the cutoff score to be used. ACT has incorporated test fairness with respect to racial, ethnic, and gender groups in the development of WorkKeys. It has done so by using minority group reviewers during item development and conducting analysis for differential item functioning for gender and ethnicity. The *WorkKeys Administrator's Manual* (ACT, 1998a) provides an appendix devoted to test administration accommodations appropriate for each test, including using large print materials, providing a reader or signer, providing captioned audio or video, and permitting extended or unlimited time limits. In addition, accommodations are available for examinees for whom English is a second language or who may have difficulty marking responses.

### Other Information

WorkKeys assessments are cited as being developed in accordance with content validity standards described in the Equal Employment Opportunity Commission's Uniform Guidelines. Review by businesses was required in test development to ensure that the workplace scenarios were appropriate. Urban and suburban samples from across the country were used to develop the tests.

A major drawback of the use of WorkKeys for employment selection is the time requirements of the various tests. The six tests reviewed here would require more than 4 hours of testing time, and the answer sheets would have to be sent to ACT for scoring and processing.

### Work Potential Profile (WPP)

#### Description

The WPP (Rowe, 1997) was developed as a multidimensional tool for the initial descriptive assessment of older adolescents and adults seeking employment, particularly those who may be difficult to place in employment. Through its 19 subtests, the WPP measures a client's motivation to engage in employment, a client's self-image, his or her subjective well-being, and personal satisfaction. It also measures abilities and competencies relating to language and communication, technology use, numeracy, and problem-solving ability. For this basic academic skills review, only the Language and Communication subtest, and the Numeracy subtest are reviewed (see Table 7.4). The WPP can serve as a screening device for employers. Only the Numeracy items of the WPP contain verifiable test questions and require the respondent to write the correct answer. The Language and Communication items are presented in a self-report format on an agree/disagree scale.

---

**TABLE 7.4  Assessment: Work Potential Profile**

*Numeracy*
Time and Number of Items: Entire profile of 171 items requires 10–30 minutes; 12 items.
Skill Measured: Ability to use numbers and to make sense of numbers in counting and basic measurement; the ability to do basic arithmetical calculations.
Format: Correct answer must be written on answer sheet for each math problem.
Scores: Number correct converted to a Profile score ranging from 0 to 10; 4 to 6 average functioning, with lower scores indicating probability of difficulties in employment setting unless appropriate support is provided.
Psychometrics: Test-retest = .94.

*Communication and Literacy*
Time and Number of Items: Entire profile of 171 items requires 10–30 minutes; 10 items.
Skill Measured: Ability to receive and transmit messages between persons so that the meaning/information/emotion contained in the message can be understood. Ability to read and write.
Format: Agree/disagree with each statement.
Scores: Number endorsed converted to a Profile score ranging from 0 to 10; 4 to 6 average functioning, with lower scores indicating probability of difficulties in employment setting unless appropriate support is provided.
Psychometrics: Test-retest = .97.

### Theoretical Basis and Test Development

The items on which the descriptive assessment is based are criterion referenced. They measure six distinct areas that may facilitate or impede an individual's adaptation to coping in various work settings. The six areas are developed on theoretical grounds based on the literature and psychological experience: (1) coping, (2) freedom from major barriers, (3) social resources, (4) abilities (wherein the subtests for numeracy, and communication and literacy reside), (5) motivation, and (6) physical ability. Items for the WPP were identified by an expert panel of psychologists working in the field of employment and by identifying work-related characteristics through literature searches. Items measuring personality traits or items that applied to only subgroups of the adult population were eliminated.

### Psychometric Characteristics

Test-retest reliability estimates and standard errors of measurement are reported in the WPP manual (Numeracy, and Communication and Literacy reliabilities are .94 and .97, respectively). Of the 19 subtests of the WPP, 13 had test-retest reliabilities above .90, another 4 had over .80, and the lowest had a test-retest reliability of .68. Construct validity of the WPP was investigated by documenting the extent that the factor structure of the profile was invariant with regard to different samples (i.e., unemployed, employed, males, females, never employed). The author of the WPP states that the developmental process contributes to its content validity. Even though the WPP is recommended as an employment screening device, the purpose is "to describe and not to predict performance" (Rowe, 1997, p. 33) and thus no criterion-referenced validation studies are reported.

### Applicability, Accommodations, Fairness

Clients with reading and/or language problems can be assisted through having each item read and/or explained to them. An interpreter can administer the profile. For clients with disabilities who are seeking employment, it is recommended that the Work Readiness Profile (see next assessment) (Rowe, 1995) be used instead of the WPP.

### Other Information

Clients can complete the profile with very little supervision. It appears to have good face validity and is quick to administer. The WPP is recommended as a screening device to identify individuals who are likely to experience difficulty in an employment setting without appropriate support. This instrument was developed in Australia, and no information concerning its validity by gender or ethnic groups is provided. Users in the United States would need to closely monitor its use to determine if adverse impact occurs and would also need to conduct a criterion-referenced validation study as needed. Because this is a relatively new assessment, it is anticipated that additional research and development may occur in the future.

## Work Readiness Profile (WRP)

### Description

Developed by the same author as the WPP (Rowe, 1997), the WRP (Rowe, 1995) was developed first and is described as a criterion-referenced tool used to assist in the initial assessment of individuals with disabilities. It is designed for use with adults and older adolescents. Rowe believes that there should be a common set of indicators for disabled and non-disabled people. The WRP consists of 12 factors with one or more statements that are rated "True," "Not True," or "Does Not Know" as they apply to the client. The ratings can be obtained through self-administration of the inventory, through completion of the profile by an informant who knows the client very well, or through ratings obtained during an interview with the client or informant. The 12 factors are: Health, Hearing, Vision, Travel, Movement, Fine Motor Skills, Gross Motor Skills and Strength, Social and Interpersonal Skills, Work Adjustment, Abilities and Skills, Communication Effectiveness, and Literacy and Numeracy. These last two are reviewed here (see Table 7.5).

### Theoretical Basis and Test Development

The items assessing the 12 factors are criterion referenced; "this means that they permit the interpretation of the client's performance in relation to well-defined competencies or behaviours" (Rowe, 1995, p. 2). The instrument appears to have been developed using standard procedures to establish a content valid instrument. Literature reviews of behaviors and possible factors appropriate to work readiness were conducted along with consultation with various professionals and service providers to identify an appropriate content domain for the WRP. A multidisciplinary panel of experts in the field reviewed the identified factors and the items produced in order to make suggestions on appropriate scale and score reporting. Trials of prototypes of the WRP were conducted with educators and students who were representative of the intended population of users. Feedback from these reviews was used to arrive at the final version of the WRP. Research was

**TABLE 7.5   Assessment: Work Readiness Profile (WRP)**

*Communication Effectiveness*

Time and Number of Items: Entire profile requires 10–15 minutes; only a subset of items are used.

Skill Measured: Evidence of skill to comprehend and convey information with others (listening and speaking).

Format: Behavioral items are endorsed as being true, not true, or unknown for the client at each level (1 to 8). Rating is that level where all the items are endorsed as being true.

Scores: Ratings are from a high of 8 to a low of 1; ratings of 6 and above are generally regarded as indicators of strengths and 4 and below as indicators of areas where some intervention and/or appropriate support are essential.

Psychometrics: Interrater reliability low .90s; agreement rates low .70s.

*Literacy and Numeracy*

Time and Number of Items: Entire profile requires 10–15 minutes; only a subset of items are used.

Skill Measured: Evidence of skill to read and write and use arithemetic.

Format: Behavioral items are endorsed as being true, not true, or unknown for the client at each level (1 to 8). Rating is that level where the all the items are endorsed as being true.

Scores: Ratings are from a high of 8 to a low of 1; ratings of 6 and above are generally regarded as indicators of strengths and 4 and below as indicators of areas where some intervention and/or appropriate support are essential.

Psychometrics: Interrater reliability high .80s; agreement rates low .80s.

also conducted on the reliability and validity of the final instrument.

### Psychometric Characteristics

Rowe reports both test-retest reliability estimates and the agreement rate between raters on individual ratings. For a sample size of 79 college students, test-retest reliability estimates after approximately one week were .74 for Literacy and Numeracy and .78 for Communications with agreement rates of 84% and 71%, respectively. For Communication Effectiveness and Literacy and Numeracy the interrater reliability estimates averaged in the low .90s and high .80s, respectively, and the agreement rates were in the low .70s and the low .80s, respectively. The validity of the WRP was investigated by documenting the extent that the factor structure of the profile was invariant with regard to different samples (i.e., intellectual disabilities, persons with disabilities of different kinds, employed person with disabilities, university students without major disabilities). The author of the WRP states that the developmental process contributes to it content validity. Even though the WRP is recommended as an employment screening device, the purpose "is to describe and not to predict performance" (Rowe, 1995, p. 26) and thus no criterion-referenced validation studies are reported.

### Applicability, Accommodations, Fairness

Gender differences were not found in the scoring of the WRP.

### Other Information

The author calls for more research on the definition of low, medium, and high levels of support and how support needs might be assessed. It appears to have good face validity and is quick to administer. The WRP is recommended as a screening device to identify individuals with disabilities who are likely to experience difficulty in an employment setting without support. This instrument was developed in Australia and no information concerning its validity by gender or ethnic groups is provided. Users in the United States would need to closely monitor its use to determine if adverse impact occurs and to conduct a criterion-referenced validation study as needed. Additionally, since this instrument was developed for individuals with disabilities, it is unknown whether or how its use would be legal under ADA (American with Disabilities Act). Because this is a relatively new assessment, it is anticipated that additional research and development work may occur in the future.

## SkillSeries

### Description

SkillSeries is a battery of employment tests developed by J.M. Llobet (1998). The following seven are reviewed here: Analyzing Skills, Math Skills, Reading Comprehension Skills, Vocabulary Skills, Grammar Skills, Spelling Skills, and Proofreading Skills. The following five tests are not associated with basic academic skills: Assembly Skills, Attention to Detail Skills, Filing Skills, Inspection Skills, and Logic and Reasoning Skills. Each test takes between 2 and 8 minutes to administer and can be used alone or in combination with others. See Table 7.6 for a further description of each of the seven reviewed tests.

### Theoretical Basis and Test Development

The test manual does not provide information concerning how these tests were developed. The manual states that these tests "have been researched and developed by our own in-house staff of testing professionals, which includes industrial psychologists and attorneys" (Llobet, 1998, p. 1).

### Psychometric Characteristics

The manual presents no information regarding the reliability of these tests but does present the results of criterion-related

**TABLE 7.6   Assessment: SkillSeries**

*Analyzing Skills*
Time and Number of Items: 5 minutes, 20 questions.
Skill Measured: Reading and interpreting information presented in two
   simulated spreadsheets.
Format: Multiple choice with workplace scenarios.
Scores: Number correct and corresponding percentile score.
Psychometrics: No reliability information given. Validity $r = .19$ for
   overall job performance.[1]

*Grammar Skills*
Time and Number of Items: 5 minutes, 20 questions.
Skill Measured: Correct identification of grammatically correct
   statements.
Format: Multiple choice with workplace phrases.
Scores: Number correct and corresponding percentile score.
Psychometrics: No reliability information given. Validity $r = .23$ for
   overall job performance.[1]

*Math Skills*
Time and Number of Items: 4 minutes, 20 questions.
Skill Measured: Perform basic addition, subtraction, multiplication,
   division, and percentages.
Format: Multiple choice with simple math problems and some story
   problems in work setting.
Scores: Number correct and corresponding percentile score.
Psychometrics: No reliability information given. Validity $r = .22$ for on
   the job math skills.[1]

*Proofreading Skills*
Time and Number of Items: 3 minutes, one letter with 20 errors.
Skill Measured: Identifying errors related to spelling, grammar, and
   punctuation.
Format: Read the letter and circle as many errors as can be
   found.
Scores: Number correct and corresponding percentile score.
Psychometrics: No reliability information given. Validity $r = .18$ for
   overall job performance.[1]

*Reading Comprehension Skills*
Time and Number of Items: 4 minutes, 10 questions.
Skill Measured: Basic reading ability.
Format: Multiple choice based on two business memos.
Scores: Number correct and corresponding percentile score.
Psychometrics: No reliability information given. Validity $r = .21$ and .23
   for on the job reading and writing skill level, respectively.[1]

*Spelling Skills*
Time and Number of Items: 2 minutes, 25 words.
Skill Measured: Spelling of words common to business.
Format: Circle the words that are spelled incorrectly.
Scores: Number correct and corresponding percentile score.
Psychometrics: No reliability information given. Validity $r = .40$ for
   rating of cognitive skills.[1]

*Vocabulary Skills*
Time and Number of Items: 2 minutes, 20 vocabulary words.
Skill Measured: Choose word whose meaning most closely resembles the
   vocabulary word.
Format: Multiple choice with words common to business.
Scores: Number correct and corresponding percentile score.
Psychometrics: No reliability information given. Validity $r = .18$ for on
   the job vocabulary skills.[1]

[1]Author does not specify whether validity was estimated using a concurrent
or predictive strategy.

validation studies (see Table 7.6 for validity coefficients for each test). It is not clear from the manual whether these validation studies are predictive or concurrent in nature. Norms are provided for each test, but no description of the norming sample is given except for the sample sizes. These sizes range from 102 to 177 for spelling and grammar, respectively.

### Applicability, Accommodations, Fairness

One page in the manual presents individual paragraphs on selection (e.g., recommending that a thorough job analysis be performed first), monitoring (e.g., checking for evidence of adverse impact), validation (e.g., adverse impact requiring the test user to conduct a validation study), and scoring (e.g., conducting a concurrent validation study and using it to develop norms for setting cutoff scores) under the heading Test Selection and Follow-up Procedures. The facing page presents three paragraphs on "pinpointing skill competency for employment excellence" and "build[ing] your own employment testing program" (Llobet, 1998, p. 5). The manual states that the test user must be sure that the tests chosen are valid for the job in question, especially if adverse impact results from their use. Approximately two pages cover legal aspects of test use and administration, including sections devoted to Title VII, ADA, the Employee Polygraph Protection Act (EPPA), and state and local laws (i.e., consult with a qualified labor law attorney regarding your local laws). No mention is made anywhere about reasonable accommodations in the administration or use of the SkillSeries test for individuals with disabilities; still, the assurance is given that the testing products were reviewed "to avoid any conflict with the ADA guidelines" (Llobet, 1998, p. 3).

### Other Information

An organization choosing to use the SkillSeries tests would need to have a qualified selection specialist available to conduct a job analysis, to monitor the use of the test and any adverse impact that may occur, and to design and implement validation studies and norming studies in order to set cutoff scores on each of the tests. The tests are short, easy to administer, and the scoring is self-contained. However, there are no equivalent forms, and each test is consumed (i.e., the test and the answer sheet are not separate).

## Comprehensive Ability Battery (CAB)

### Description

Table 7.7 lists the various subtests of the CAB (Hakstian, Cattell, & IPAT staff, 1982). Of the 20 subtests that make up

**TABLE 7.7    Assessment: Comprehensive Ability Battery (CAB)**

*Verbal Ability*
Time and Number of Items: 3.5 minutes, 15 items for Part I; 3.25 minutes, 9 items for Part II.
Skill Measured: Comprehension of words and ideas, or a person's ability to understand written language.
Format: Multiple choice items on vocabulary (Part I) and on understanding proverbs (Part II).
Scores: No correction for guessing is applied. Total number correct with norms available.
Psychometrics: KR-20 internal consistency estimate of .77.

*Numerical Ability*
Time and Number of Items: 5.5 minutes and 20 items.
Skill Measured: Facility in manipulating numbers, quickly and accurately, in tasks involving addition, subtraction, multiplication, division, squaring, fractions, etc.
Format: Multiple choice, speeded test.
Scores: No correction for guessing is applied. Total number correct with norms available.
Psychometrics: Test-retest reliability estimate of approximately .80.

*Spelling*
Time and Number of Items: 5 minutes, 20 items.
Skill Measured: Recognize misspelled words. Spelling is not considered a primary mental ability but is included in the CAB because it is important for success in school and in many jobs.
Format: Multiple choice.
Scores: No correction for guessing is applied. Total number correct with norms available.
Psychometrics: KR-20 internal consistency estimate of .74.

the CAB, only 3 are reviewed here as being relevant to basic academic skills tests: Verbal Ability, Numerical Ability, and Spelling.

### Theoretical Basis and Test Development

Work began on the CAB in 1972, based on the theoretical foundations of Thurstone, Guilford, and Cattel on their multifactor view of intelligence. Twenty different subtests were conceptualized and developed based on a list of 20 primary mental abilities: verbal, numerical, spatial, speed of closure, perceptual speed and accuracy, inductive reasoning, flexibility of closure, associative (or rote) memory, mechanical, memory span, meaningful memory, spelling, auditory, esthetic judgment, spontaneous flexibility, ideational fluency, word fluency, originality, aiming, and representational drawing. According to the manual, the overall guiding principle was to provide a broad battery of short tests. Thus, items were written for each of the 20 tests such that each item was clearly identifiable with its ability and also independent of the other 19 abilities. The first 14 abilities are tested using a multiple-choice, machine-scorable format, whereas the final 6 require

hand scoring because they require the assessee to generate a written response.

### Psychometric Characteristics

Internal consistency reliabilities (KR-20) are provided for Verbal and Spelling; .77 and .74, respectively. Test-retest reliability is estimated to be around .80 for the speeded test of Numerical Ability. The manual cautions that the reliability studies were conducted using very homogeneous samples, suggesting that the reliability estimates are probably lower than would be obtained for a more representative sample. Standard errors of measurement are also provided for each test. Construct validity is demonstrated through studies showing the correlation of the various CAB subtests with relevant high school subject grades along with Otis and WAIS intelligence test scores. No criterion-related validities associated with work success are reported. Norms are reported for all high school students and subgroups of these students (i.e., males, females, Canadian, U.S.), for college freshmen, and for the prison population.

### Applicability, Accommodations, Fairness

The manual seems to suggest that the test was developed to measure primary abilities and skills necessary for success in education and work settings. The provided norms include only educational settings (i.e., high school and college) and a prison population. No mention is included of either reasonable accommodations for any of the tests or issues of test fairness addressed.

### Other Information

The three subtests, Verbal, Numerical, and Spelling, could be used to test for basic academic skills as part of an employer's selection system; however, norms and evidence of validity would need to be developed for the local site.

## Employee Aptitude Survey (EAS)

### Description

The EAS was originally published in 1963 (Ruch, Stang, McKillip, & Dye, 1994) and consists of 10 ability tests, 4 of which are reviewed here and are considered to be directly relevant to basic academic skills (i.e., Verbal Comprehension, Verbal Reasoning, Numerical Ability, Numerical Reasoning). The other six tests are: Visual Pursuit, Visual Speed and Accuracy, Space Visualization, Word Fluency, Manual Speed and Accuracy, and Symbolic Reasoning.

## Theoretical Basis and Test Development

The technical manual for the EAS states that the publisher hoped for a wise combination of factor analysis and practical validity studies in the development of the 10 tests that are included. EAS can trace its beginnings to the 1940s from an initial test developed to select employees for a factory producing plastic articles for the military. The technical manual describes the development of each of the 10 tests since that time. Contrary to other test batteries, the EAS tests were developed separately over a number of years and by a variety of authors. It appears that the tests chosen for development were based on a review of practical needs of industry and the literature that was accumulating regarding other aptitude tests' predictive validity. The authors searched the published literature looking for meritorious testing ideas applicable to the workplace. A conscious effort was maintained to ensure that the developed tests had ease of administration and short time limits, ease in scoring, alternative forms for repeated testing situations, and face validity to maintain motivation of the test taker and to ensure perceptions of fairness.

## Psychometric Characteristics

The manual provides equivalent form reliability estimates above .81 for all four of the tests (see Table 7.8) along with their standard error of measurement. Two equivalent forms of each test are available. Construct and criterion-referenced validity evidence is documented in the manual. A meta-analysis of 725 validity coefficients from 160 studies investigating the validity of EAS is presented in the appendix to the manual. To assist in interpretation, the validity studies are grouped by job family: professional, managerial, supervisory; clerical; production (skilled and semiskilled); and technical. Estimated true validities were highest for these four tests for job performance ratings among the first grouping (rhos = .53–.67) and lowest among the technical grouping (rhos = .15–53). Norms are reported in the EAS Examiner's Manual and in a separate EAS Norms Report for 82 different occupational and educational classifications based on over 210,000 test scores. The authors advise that whenever possible, local norms should be developed by testing samples of incumbent employees.

## Applicability, Accommodations, Fairness

These tests are intended to be applicable for a wide variety of jobs across industries. They are short and easy to administer, though no mention of reasonable accommodations regarding modifications for individuals with disabilities is made. Tests may be administered individually or in groups. Addi-

tionally, issues of fairness or the possibility of adverse impact are not mentioned within the technical manual.

## Other Information

The manual presents information on how to perform a utility analysis quantifying the dollar savings that a company can expect using EAS tests as part of their employee selection system.

---

**TABLE 7.8   Assessment: Employee Aptitude Survey (EAS)**

*Verbal Comprehension*
Time and Number of Items: 5 minutes, 30 items.
Skill Measured: Vocabulary.
Format: Multiple choice, select the synonym from among four possibilities.
Scores: Correction for guessing is applied. Total number correct with norms available.
Psychometrics: Alternate forms reliability estimated at .85. Estimated true validities for predicting job performance: .53, .38, .36, and .15 for managerial, clerical, production, and technical job families, respectively.

*Verbal Reasoning*
Time and Number of Items: 5 minutes, 30 items.
Skill Measured: Five conclusions are judged true, false, or uncertain after reviewing a series of facts.
Format: Multiple choice.
Scores: Correction for guessing is applied. Total number correct with norms available.
Psychometrics: Alternate forms reliability estimated at .82. Estimated true validities for predicting job performance: .67, .46, .13, and .33 for managerial, clerical, production, and technical job families, respectively.

*Numerical Ability (Parts 1, 2, and 3)*
Time and Number of Items: Part 1: 2 minutes; Part 2: 4 minutes; Part 3: 4 minutes.
Skill Measured: Part 1: Whole numbers; Part 2: Decimals; Part 3: Fractions.
Format: Multiple choice, select a response from the five alternatives provided: four numerical and one that states the correct answer is not given. Each part can be given independently of the others.
Scores: Correction for guessing is applied. Total number correct with norms available.
Psychometrics: Alternate forms reliability estimated at .87 for all three parts combined. Estimated true validities for predicting job performance: .55, .46, .38, and .53 for managerial, clerical, production, and technical job families, respectively.

*Numerical Reasoning*
Time and Number of Items: 5 minutes, 20 number series.
Skill Measured: Ability to analyze logical relationships and to discover underlying principles.
Format: Multiple choice, select the next number in the series from five alternatives.
Scores: Correction for guessing is applied. Total number correct with norms available.
Psychometrics: Alternate forms reliability estimated at .81. Estimated true validities for predicting job performance: .63, .29, n/a, and n/a for managerial, clerical, production, and technical job families, respectively.

**TABLE 7.9   Assessment: PSI Basic Skills Tests (BST)**

*Language Skills*
Time and Number of Items: 5 minutes, 25 items.
Skill Measured: Determine whether underlined portions of sentences contain writing errors.
Format: Multiple choice choosing among three options or a fourth that no change is needed.
Scores: Correction for guessing is applied. Total number correct with norms available.
Psychometrics: Communality estimates of alpha = .71.

*Reading Comprehension*
Time and Number of Items: 10 minutes, 23 items.
Skill Measured: Read a passage and answer questions that follow it.
Format: Four alternative multiple-choice format.
Scores: Correction for guessing is applied. Total number correct with norms available.
Psychometrics: Communality estimates of alpha = .71.

*Vocabulary*
Time and Number of Items: 5 minutes, 45 items.
Skill Measured: Identify synonym of word presented in a sentence.
Format: Multiple choice having four alternatives.
Scores: Correction for guessing is applied. Total number correct with norms available.
Psychometrics: Communality estimates of alpha = .81.

*Computation*
Time and Number of Items: 5 minutes, 40 items.
Skill Measured: Read an arithmetic expression.
Format: Multiple choice, select a response from the five alternatives provided: four numerical and one that states the correct answer is not given.
Scores: Correction for guessing is applied. Total number correct with norms available.
Psychometrics: Communality estimates of alpha = .83.

*Problem Solving*
Time and Number of Items: 10 minutes, 25 items.
Skill Measured: Read a word problem and apply the appropriate arithmetic operation.
Format: Multiple choice, select a response from the five alternatives provided: four numerical and one that states the correct answer is not given.
Scores: Correction for guessing is applied. Total number correct with norms available.
Psychometrics: Communality estimates of alpha = .83.

*Following Oral Directions*
Time and Number of Items: 5 Minutes (plus 6 1/2 minutes for listening to audiotape), 24 items.
Skill Measured: Listen, take notes, and select answers of fact based on audiotape recording of conversations occurring in an employment setting.
Format: Multiple choice with five alternatives based on questions on what the assessee heard during a 6.5 minute audio recording. Assessee may take notes.
Scores: Correction for guessing is applied. Total number correct with norms available.
Psychometrics: Communality estimates of alpha = .66.

*Following Written Directions*
Time and Number of Items: 5 minutes, 36 items.
Skill Measured: Read and apply rules to take action under various situations.
Format: Multiple choice, three or four alternatives.
Scores: Correction for guessing is applied. Total number correct with norms available.
Psychometrics: Communality estimates of alpha = .71.

*Forms Checking*
Time and Number of Items: 5 minutes, 42 items.
Skill Measured: Read a paragraph and checks to see if corresponding form has been completed correctly on the basis of information presented in the paragraph.
Format: Examinee indicates whether each form is correct or incorrect.
Scores: Correction for guessing is applied. Total number correct with norms available.
Psychometrics: Communality estimates of alpha = .68.

*Reasoning*
Time and Number of Items: 5 minutes, 30 items.
Skill Measured: Read a list of facts and a corresponding list of conclusions.
Format: Five conclusions are judged true, false, or uncertain after reviewing a series of facts.
Scores: Correction for guessing is applied. Total number correct with norms available.
Psychometrics: Communality estimates of alpha = .63.

## PSI Basic Skills Tests

### Description

The PSI Basic Skills Tests (BST) and the Employee Aptitude Survey tests are published by Psychological Services, Inc. (Ruch, Weiner, McKillip, & Dye, 1985) and have many similarities. The PSI BST consists of 20 tests, 9 of which are judged to be measures of basic academic skills (see Table 7.2 and 7.9). These nine are: Language Skills, Reading Comprehension, Vocabulary, Following Written Directions, Forms Checking, Reasoning, Following Oral Directions, Computation, and Problem Solving (of math problems). Of the remaining 11 tests, 4 are typing tests, 5 are perceptual speed tests, and the last 2 are tests of decision making and memory.

### Theoretical Basis and Test Development

The BST was designed to assess skills that are important for clerical work and are short, easy to administer, and are content valid based on a nationwide task analysis of 12,000 clerical positions.

### Psychometric Characteristics

Only communalities are reported as a lower bound estimate of internal consistency (alpha) for each of the tests from factor analytic studies. Three major criterion-related validity studies were conducted. Along with evidence of construct and content validity, these studies are reported in the technical manual. A validity generalization study is reported supporting the validity of these measures across jobs.

### Applicability, Accommodations, Fairness

The BST was specifically developed for clerical occupations. The technical manual states that special attention was given to ensure that questions did not contain material that might be offensive to any particular race or sex. Differential predictive validity by ethnicity or sex was not found in the validity studies.

### Other Information

The manual presents information on how to perform a utility analysis that quantifies the dollar savings that a company can expect if it uses the BST tests as part of its employee selection system. It also describes how to carry out a transportability study to support the use of these tests in a local setting by using validity evidence from another setting.

## Reading and Arithmetic Indexes (RAI)

### Description

Two separate basic skill tests are packaged together as the RAI (National Computer Systems, 2000; see Table 7.10). They were developed to estimate basic reading and arithmetic skills and are well suited for entry-level jobs and general training jobs. The Reading Index can assess reading levels (Levels 1–5) up to a level that is commonly achieved by ninth graders, and the Arithmetic Index is geared to levels (Levels 1–4) up to the eighth grade.

---

**TABLE 7.10  Assessment: Reading and Arithmetic Indexes (RAI)**

*Reading Index*
Time and Number of Items: Untimed, 60 items.
Skill Measured: Comprehension of words, phrases, sentences, and paragraphs.
Format: Multiple choice.
Scores: Total correct raw score can be converted to percentile through norms, or an examinee's proficiency at each developmental level can be determined. Grade equivalency can also be determined if necessary.
Psychometrics: Internal consistency estimate (KR-20) = .87. Criterion-related validities range from .14 to .32 depending on job.

*Arithmetic Index*
Time and Number of Items: Untimed, 54 items.
Skill Measured: Ability to add, subtract, multiply, and divide.
Format: Multiple choice.
Scores: Total correct raw score can be converted to percentile through norms, or an examinee's proficiency at each developmental level can be determined. Grade equivalency can also be determined if necessary.
Psychometrics: Internal consistency estimate (KR-20) = .91–.95.
Criterion-related validities range from .08 to .25 depending on job.

---

### Theoretical Basis and Test Development

Items for both tests were developed using a content validation approach that stressed item writing for each of the developmental levels (i.e., five for reading and four for arithmetic). Items were reviewed by subject matter experts and were administered to a large sample of adults in order to obtain item analysis information. Final items were selected to maximize homogeneity within levels, to minimize correlations between levels, and, for the Reading Index, to minimize correlation with a measure of general ability, the Pictorial Reasoning Test.

### Psychometric Characteristics

Internal consistency estimates (KR-20) were .87 and .91–.95, for Reading and Arithmetic Indexes, respectively. Because the final score for assessees is what proficiency level they are placed into, an analysis was conducted to determine the percentage who are rated "Not Proficient" at one level but "Proficient" at the next higher level. For Reading, 5% of participants and, for Arithmetic, 7% of participants fell into this situation. The manual presents evidence of convergent and divergent validity for each test for use in establishing construct validity. Approximately 25 criterion-related (job performance) validity studies are reported for jobs in office, technical, skilled, semiskilled, and unskilled positions. The manual concludes that the RAI tests can be effective screening tools for jobs requiring reading and arithmetic skills. The flexibility in scoring (i.e., percentile, proficiency level, grade equivalent scores) allows the user to use a scoring process most relevant to his or her needs.

### Applicability, Accommodations, Fairness

The RAI tests are designed for use in entry-level jobs requiring a level of reading or arithmetic that is attained typically by the end of middle school. Norms that cover jobs included in the criterion-related validation studies are included in the manual. The manual suggests that the development of localized norms may be best for an organization. Appropriate accommodations for individuals with disabilities during the administration of the RAI can be determined by calling a toll-free phone number maintained by the test publisher. During the development of the RAI tests, any items that were more likely to be interpreted differently by members of various cultures were eliminated.

### Other Information

The RAI assessments are available for computer-based administration and scoring and report generation. The manual states that the publisher encourages users of the RAI to carry out additional research and to share their findings with others.

## Adult Measure of Essential Skills (AMES)

### Description

The AMES tests is a recently developed battery of authentic assessments designed to measure the necessary workplace and educational basic skills of adults who may or may not have graduated from high school (Steck-Vaughn, 1999). It is a norm-referenced assessment reflecting the most current philosophies regarding which basic skills an adult will need to be successful in the "rapidly changing world of work" (p. 1). The battery consists of four tests (i.e., Reading, Communications, Computation, and Applied Problem Solving) (see Table 7.11). The last two tests can be combined into a total score for mathematics. There are actually four separate tests with progressive levels of difficulty (Levels B, C, D, and E) for each of the four skill areas. Further, there are two equiv-

---

**TABLE 7.11   Assessment: Adult Measure of Essential Skills (AMES)**

*Reading Test*
Time and Number of Items: 34 questions per each of the four level tests.
Skill Measured: Read and comprehend functional (work-related) and informational passages.
Format: Several passages with multiple-choice questions for each passage.
Scores: Raw score is number correct, which can be converted to percentiles using norms or grade equivalency.
Psychometrics: Reliability estimates range from .829 to .888.

*Communication Test*
Time and Number of Items: 32 or 36 questions per each of the four level tests.
Skill Measured: Basic written communication skills including grammar, spelling, mechanics, composition, etc.
Format: Several passages with multiple-choice questions for each passage.
Scores: Raw score is number correct, which can be converted to percentiles using norms or grade equivalency.
Psychometrics: Reliability estimates range from .777 to .881.

*Computation Test*
Time and Number of Items: 20 questions per each of the four level tests.
Skill Measured: Understand basic number operations, decimals, fractions, percents, algebraic operations.
Format: Multiple choice.
Scores: Raw score is number correct, which can be converted to percentiles using norms or grade equivalency.
Psychometrics: Reliability estimates range from .785 to .866.

*Applied Problem Solving Test*
Time and Number of Items: 33 questions per each of the four level tests.
Skill Measured: Apply mathematical reasoning to problems encountered daily.
Format: Multiple choice.
Scores: Raw score is number correct, which can be converted to percentiles using norms or grade equivalency.
Psychometrics: Reliability estimates range from .796 to .881. (Total Math range from .869 to .925)

---

alent forms for each of these. A locator test is first used to identify which of the four tests is at the appropriate level from which to begin testing an examinee. The Level A test is also available for those who cannot read English or for those with limited educational experience (i.e., one to two years of schooling). Grade equivalency corresponds to a test level (i.e., Level B—Grades 3–4; Level C—Grades 5–6; Level D—Grades 7–8; and Level E—Grades 9–12 +).

### Theoretical Basis and Test Development

Development of the AMES utilized the latest thinking and research in math and literacy currently necessary in the workplace and educational setting. The National Council of Teachers of Mathematics Standards was used along with the National Adult Literacy Survey (NALS) content domains funded by the U.S. Department of Education. Extensive literature reviews, SCANS documents, and consultation with subject matter experts all contributed to the publisher's efforts to develop these tests. Items were selected based on appropriate difficulty level for the level of the test. Two equivalent forms of all of the tests were developed. Norms were established using norming samples from adult education classes, prisons, and community and technical colleges. These samples were selected with regard to geographic, ethnic, age, and gender representativeness. Norms based on occupational groupings are not reported.

### Psychometric Characteristics

The manual reports that IRT was used to scale the AMES. Scaled scores were used to establish percentile ranks by norming group. The manual reports that grade equivalency can be determined based on the AMES scale score. Reliabilities and standard errors of measurement are reported for each form and for each level of the four tests. These reliabilities were calculated using the information from the Test Information Function from the Rasch Model of IRT. All the reliability estimates range between .77 and .925. No evidence is provided for content- or criterion-referenced validity. Construct validity is implied by the reporting of correlations between the tests of AMES and the Learning Progress Assessment test.

### Applicability, Accommodations, Fairness

The manual states that the AMES measures essential workplace skills needed in a wide variety of jobs. No research or evidence is cited confirming the validity of the AMES for predicting job success. Users would need to conduct their own validation study and develop localized norms for the four tests. The requirement of first administering a locator test would require that job applicants take two tests. First, they must take the locator, and, then, they must take the appropriate test for their level. No mention is made of any reasonable accommodations available for individuals with disabilities. The manual states that a panel of experts reviewed the final items for any racial, gender, ethnic, or regional bias.

### Other Information

The AMES tests were developed by a publisher devoted to curriculum products for adult education. Organizations using any of the AMES tests for employment selection would need to do considerable work to determine the validity of their use.

## Wide Range Achievement Test (WRAT3)

### Description

The WRAT3 was initially developed in the 1930s (Wilkinson, 1993). The 1993 edition consists of three subtests that measure reading, spelling, and arithmetic using two equivalent forms and is appropriate for individuals between the ages of 5 and 75. The Reading test must be administered individually, unlike the other tests reviewed in this chapter. However, this particular test can be administered in any convenient order. Though designed to be individually administered, the Spelling and Arithmetic tests could be given in large groups. All three tests should take between 15 and 30 minutes, total.

### Theoretical Basis and Test Development

The purpose and methods of the WRAT3 have been consistent since it was first published in the 1930s. The WRAT3 was developed using IRT Rasch analysis of all items to create a test that is omnifarious, capable of assessing skills over a "wide range" of abilities found in the general population across ages.

### Psychometric Characteristics

The WRAT3 raw scores can be converted to absolute scores, standard scores, grade scores, and percentiles. The two equivalent forms can be combined to increase the reliability and accuracy of the test scores if desired. Extensive norming efforts ($N = 4,433$) were begun for the 1993 version with attention to representativeness of ages, regional residence, gender, ethnicity, and socioeconomic level. Using the norm sample, the equivalent-form reliability estimates were found

**TABLE 7.12  Assessment: Wide Range Achievement Test (WRAT3)**

*Reading Test*
Time and Number of Items: Untimed, 57 points/items.
Skill Measured: Recognize and name letters and pronounce words out of context.
Format: Oral report to a test administrator who individually administers test.
Scores: Raw scores (number correct) can be converted to absolute scores, standard scores, grade scores, and percentiles.
Psychometrics: Equivalent-form reliability, $r = .984$; alphas $= .90–.95$.

*Spelling Test*
Time and Number of Items: Untimed, 55 items.
Skill Measured: Write names, letters, and words to dictation.
Format: Written response by examinee in response to oral instructions.
Scores: Raw scores (number correct) can be converted to absolute scores, standard scores, grade scores, and percentiles.
Psychometrics: Equivalent-form reliability, $r = .982$; alphas $= .89–.95$.

*Arithmetic Test*
Time and Number of Items: 15 minutes, 55 items.
Skill Measured: Count, read number symbols, solve oral problems, and perform written computations.
Format: Two subtests: One requiring oral report by examinee in response to oral instructions and stimuli and the other written response oral instructions and written stimuli. Can be modified for written format only for adults.
Scores: Raw scores (number correct) can be converted to absolute scores, standard scores, grade scores, and percentiles.
Psychometrics: Equivalent-form reliability, $r = .981$; alphas $= .85–.92$.

to be .984, .982, and .981, for Reading, Spelling, and Arithmetic, respectively. Coefficient alphas are reported in Table 7.12, and the median test coefficient alphas range from .85 to .95 over the tests. Test-retest reliability ranged from .91 to .98. Extensive evidence of the construct validity of the WRAT3 is provided in the manual, and a discussion of its content validity is also included. No mention of criterion-related validity is made; therefore, the correlation of the WRAT3 with actual academic or job success is unknown.

### Applicability, Accommodations, Fairness

The WRAT3 can be used with just about anyone. The norming sample included representatives from various occupational groups (i.e., managers/professionals, technical/sales/administrative, craft and repair, operators/laborers, service/farming/fishing), though no occupational group norms are included in the manual. Studies on item bias are not reported in the manual, but such references are available in monograph form from the publisher. Still, the manual states that bias is not expected by ethnicity or gender group. No mention of accommodations during administration of the WRAT3 for individuals with disabilities is made in the manual.

## Other Information

The WRAT3 has a long history and its development is well documented. Issues of its use as part of an employee selection system are not addressed in the manual (i.e., adverse impact, content validity typed to specific jobs, criterion-related validity evidence for predicting job success, and norms for occupational groups). Because the tests were developed to be norm referenced and to be used with a wide range of individuals, they have low face validity as employment tests. This low face validity could negatively impact applicants' motivation to do well.

## Wonderlic Basic Skills Test (WBST)

### Description

The WBST is a short form of two subtests of adult language (i.e., Test of Verbal Skills) and math (i.e., Test of Quantitative Skills) deemed necessary for job readiness. The WBST may be interpreted in terms of job requirements, occupational norms, or grade level achievement (Grades 4, 6, 8, and 10). There are two equivalent forms of each subtest. Each test is designed to be self-administered, has a 20-minute time limit, and requires about 5 minutes for instructions and practice questions. The Verbal test should be administered first, followed by the Quantitative test. The use of calculators is forbidden.

### Theoretical Basis and Test Development

According to the manual, Wonderlic conducted an extensive review of the literature and previously published skills tests. Additionally, Wonderlic worked directly with businesses and industries and used SCANS, DOT, and other similar resources to generate the content of these two skills tests. Specific job knowledge was avoided so that the tests could be used with any type of job. Items were written and field-tested in order to conduct both classical test theory analysis and item response theory. A three-parameter logistic model was used. Field testing also included the use of different time limits. The norming of the final test included a representative sample of more than 22,000 individuals.

### Psychometric Characteristics

The WBST can be interpreted in three ways: job requirements as specified in the *Dictionary of Occupational Titles,* percentile scores based on occupational norms, and grade level achievement. Test-retest and internal consistency reliability estimates along with their standard errors of measurement are

**TABLE 7.13   Assessment: Wonderlic Basic Skills Test**

*Test of Verbal Skills*
Time and Number of Items: 20 minutes, 50 questions.
Skill Measured: Locate, understand, and use information in various formats, recognize work meanings, identify proper grammar and sentence construction.
Format: Multiple-choice format.
Scores: Raw scores number correct, percentiles based on norms, grade equivalent, job requirement proficiency.
Psychometrics: Test-retest, $r = .91$; alpha $= .95$.

*Test of Quantitative Skills*
Time and Number of Items: 20 minutes, 45 questions.
Skill Measured: Job-related quantitative skills including basic math computation, algebra, and geometry.
Format: Multiple-choice format.
Scores: Raw scores number correct, percentiles based on norms, grade equivalent, job requirement proficiency.
Psychometrics: Test-retest, $r = .86$; alpha $= .93$.

presented in the manual (see Table 7.13). The WBST is a content-valid measure having been developed using subject matter experts and researching the basic skills required for jobs (e.g., SCANS).

### Applicability, Accommodations, Fairness

The WBST is for applicant selection for any job or occupational training program that requires basic language and math skills. Wonderlic Reporting Service is available from the publisher to assist organizations in developing their own norms and for monitoring their testing program for effectiveness, accuracy, and fairness. The manual discusses making accommodations during test administration for individuals with disabilities. An independent expert review for cultural sensitivity and for differential item functioning ensures that the test is equivalent and free of content bias across different cultural and gender groups.

### Other Information

A computer program can generate a report with all three of the score types reported. The tests results are also useful for career counseling purposes.

## REFERENCES

ACT, Inc. (1998a). *WorkKeys: Administrator's manual.* Iowa City, IA: Author.

ACT, Inc. (1998b). *WorkKeys: Preliminary technical handbook.* Iowa City, IA: Author.

American Management Association. (2001). *2001 AMA survey on workplace testing: Basic skills, job skills, and psychological measurement.* Retrieved September 29, 2001, from http://www .amanet.org/research/skillssurvey.htm and http://www.amanet.org /research/pdfs/bjp_2001.pdf.

Atkinson, J., & Spilsbury, M. (1993). *Basic skills and jobs. A report on the basic skills needed at work.* London, England: Adult Literacy and Basic Skills Unit. (ERIC Document Reproduction Service No. ED362705)

Barton, P.E. (2000). *What jobs require: Literacy, education, and training, 1940–2006. Policy Information Report.* Princeton, NJ: Educational Testing Service. (ERIC Document Reproduction Service No. ED439136)

Becker, H., Schur, S., Paoletti-Schelp, M., & Hammer, E. (1986). *Manual: Functional Skills Screening Inventory.* Austin, TX: Functional Resources Enterprises.

Berryman, S., & Bailey, T. (1992). *The double helix of education and the economy.* New York: Institute on Education and the Economy, Teachers College, Columbia University.

Bloom, M.R., & Lafleur, B. (1999). *Turning skills into profit: Economic benefits of workplace education programs* (Research Report 1247–99-RR). New York: The Conference Board.

Brigance, A.H. (1995). *Manual: Diagnostic Employability Skills Inventory.* North Billerica, MA: Curriculum Associates.

Carnevale, A.P., Gainer, L.J., & Meltzer, A.S. (1990). *Workplace basics.* San Francisco: Jossey-Bass.

Center for Education Information. (2001). *What works online.* Retrieved September 29, 2001, from http://www.whatworksonline .com.

Comings, J., Sum, A., & Uvin, J. (2000). *New skills for a new economy: Adult education's key role in sustaining economic growth and expanding opportunity.* Boston: The Massachusetts Institute for a New Commonwealth.

Comprehensive Adult Student Assessment System (CASAS). (1993). *CASAS technical manual.* San Diego, CA: Foundation for Educational Achievement.

Comprehensive Adult Student Assessment System (CASAS), & ACT, Inc. (1997). *Final report, Extending the ladder: From CASAS to WorkKeys assessments.* San Diego, CA: CASAS.

Cornwell, J.M. (2000, April). *Equipped for the future: What adults need to know and do in the 21st century.* Paper presented at the Year 2000 Conference of the Society for Industrial and Organizational Psychology, New Orleans, LA.

Defense Activity for Non-Traditional Education Support (DANTES). (2001). *DoD Voluntary Education Program fact sheet FY2000.* Retrieved September 18, 2001, from http://voled.doded.mil /dantes/slides/index.htm.

Edge, A.G. (1985). How personnel managers rank knowledge, skills, and attributes expected of business graduates. *Journal of Business Education, 60,* 230–233.

Employability Skills Task Force. (1988, April). *Jobs. A Michigan employability profile.* Lansing, MI: State of Michigan, Office of the Governor.

Employment Policy Foundation. (2001). *The American workplace 2001: Building America's workforce for the 21st century.* Washington, DC: Author.

Goldman, J.P. (1992). Satisfaction guaranteed or we'll take our graduates back! *School Administrator, 49*(3) 22–24, 41.

Greenberg, E.R. (1990). Workplace testing: *The 1990 AMA survey, Part 1. Personnel, 67*(6), 43–46, 48, 51.

Hakstian, A.R., Cattell, R.B., & IPAT Staff. (1982). *Manual for the Comprehensive Ability Battery (CAB).* Champaign, IL: Institute for Personality and Ability Testing.

Hoover, H.D., Hieronymous, A.N., Frisbie, D.A., & Dunbar, S.B. (1996). *Manual: Iowa Tests of Basic Skills.* Chicago: The Riverside Publishing Company.

Hunt, H.J. (1995). *Will we be smart enough? A cognitive analysis of the coming workforce.* New York: Russell Sage Foundation.

Judy, R., & D'Amico, C. (1997). *Workforce 2020: Work and workers in the 21st century.* Indianapolis, IN: Hudson Institute.

Kelkar, M., & Paranto, S.R. (1999). Employer satisfaction with job skills of business college graduates and its impact on hiring behavior. *Journal of Marketing for Higher Education, 9*(3), 73–89.

Kimel, W.R., & Monsees, M.E. (1979). Engineering graduates: How good are they? *Engineering Education, 70,* 210–212.

Kuchinke, K.P., Brown, J.M., Anderson, H., & Hobson, J. (1998). Assessing training needs of manufacturing employees in rural Minnesota: A model and results. *Journal of Industrial Teacher Education, 36,* 79–98.

Llobet, J.M. (1998). *SkillSeries administrator's manual.* Sunrise, FL: G. Neil Companies.

Long, E.R., Artese, V.S., Clonts, W.L. (1999). *The Wonderlic Basic Skills Test user's manual.* Libertyville, IL: Wonderlic.

Louisiana Department of Labor. (2001). *Incumbent worker training.* Retrieved September 30, 2001, from http://www.ldol.state.la.us /s3iwt.asp.

Manitoba. (1996). *Linkage: A Manitoba survey of basic skills awareness in the workplace.* (ERIC Document Reproduction Service No. ED399439)

Miles, C., Grummon, P., & Maduschke, K.M. (1996). *Manual: Working-assessing skills, habits, and style.* Clearwater, FL: H and H Publishing.

Moy, J. (1999). *The impact of generic competencies on workplace performance. Review of research.* Leabrook, Australia: National Center for Vocational Education Research. (ERIC Document Reproduction Service No. ED433422)

Murnane, R.J., & Levy, F. (1996). *Teaching the new basic skills: Principles for educating children to thrive in a changing economy.* New York: The Free Press.

Nash, B.E., & Korte, R.C. (1997). Validation of SCANS competencies by a national job analysis study. In H.F. O'Neil Jr. (Ed.), *Workforce readiness: Competencies and assessment* (pp. 77–102). Mahwah, NJ: Erlbaum.

National Academy of Sciences. (1984). *High schools and the changing workplace. The employers' view* (NTIS Report PB84–240191). Washington, DC: National Academy Press.

National Computer Systems, Inc. (2000). *Reading and Arithmetic Indexes (RAI) examiner's manual.* Minneapolis, MN: Author.

New York State Education Department. (1990, July). *Basic and expanded skills. Scales for validation study.* Albany, NY: Author.

O'Neil, H.F. Jr., Allred, K., & Baker, E.L. (1997). Review of workforce readiness theoretical frameworks. In H.F. O'Neil Jr. (Ed.), *Workforce readiness: Competencies and assessment* (pp. 3–25). Mahwah, NJ: Erlbaum.

Osterman, P. (1995). The youth labor market: Skill deficiencies and public policy. In A. Howard (Ed.), *The changing nature of work* (pp. 223–237). San Francisco: Jossey-Bass.

Public Broadcasting System. *Workplace essential skills.* Retrieved September 29, 2001, from http://www.pbs.org/literacy/wes/info_wes.html.

Richens, G.P., & McClain, C.R. (2000). Workplace basic skills for the new millennium. *Journal of Adult Education, 28,* 29–34.

Rowe, H.A.H. (1995). *Work readiness profile: Manual.* Melborne, Australia: The Australian Council for Educational Research Ltd.

Rowe, H.A.H. (1997). *Work Potential Profile: Manual.* Melborne, Australia: The Australian Council for Educational Research Ltd.

Ruch, W.W., Stang, S.W., McKillip, R.H., & Dye, D.A. (1994). *Employee Aptitude Survey technical manual* (2nd ed.). Los Angeles: Psychological Services.

Ruch, W.W., Weiner, J.A., McKillip, R.H., & Dye, D.A. (1985). *PSI Basic Skills Tests technical manual.* Los Angeles: Psychological Services.

Steck-Vaughn Company. (1999). *Adult Measure of Essential Skills (AMES) technical manual.* Austin, TX: Author.

Stein, S. (2000). *Equipped for the future content standards: What adults need to know and be able to do in the 21st century.* Washington, DC: National Institute for Literacy.

Sticht, T.G. (1998). *Beyond 2000: Future directions for adult education.* El Cajon, CA: Applied Behavioral & Cognitive Sciences.

Tyler, K. (October, 1999). Brushing up on the three R's. *HR Magazine, 44*(10), 82–88.

U.S. Commission on Excellence in Education. (1983). *A nation at risk.* Washington, DC: U.S. Government Printing Office.

U.S. Department of Labor. (1992). *Skills and tasks for jobs: A SCANS report for America 2000.* Washington, DC: U.S. Department of Labor, Secretary's Commission on Achieving Necessary Skills.

Wasdyke, R.G., Freeberg, N.E., Rock, D.A. (1984). *Manual: Job Training Assessment Program.* Princeton, NJ: Educational Testing Service.

Wilkinson, G.S. (1993). *The Wide Range Achievement Test administration manual.* Wilmington, DE: Wide Range.

# SECTION THREE

# PERSONALITY, INTEGRITY, AND INTERESTS

# CHAPTER 8

# Work Applications of the Big Five Model of Personality

K. GALEN KROECK AND KEVIN W. BROWN

## INTRODUCTION

The history of personality follows very closely the history of psychology itself. From its infancy, it has been a central topic of the field, and it has witnessed numerous theoretical incarnations and conceptualizations befitting nearly every major theory or school of thought posited over the previous century. Its relevance, while commonly understated, is typically thought to provide the foundation and stability of an individual's thoughts, actions, and behaviors. Its breadth, however, is perhaps its major limitation. That is, personality is defined in not one or even a few ways; it is defined in many. Therefore, the challenge of any discussion of personality is the need to proffer an appropriate definition. This chapter focuses on but one of the many conceptual models of personality—the Big Five theory of personality.

This chapter introduces and reviews the current state of the Big Five megataxonomy. Beginning with a discussion of its history and development, the chapter supplies a review of its validity, utility, and primary correlates in the context of individual workplace behavior. Further, controversies surrounding the Big Five, including faking, cultural considera-

tions, adverse impact, and the ongoing bandwidth-fidelity dilemma, are discussed. The chapter summarizes some of the instruments commonly used in measuring Big Five personality factors.

## HISTORY

The attempt to devise a taxonomy of personality traits was a mainstay of psychological research through most of the last century. In 1932, McDougall was the first to present a comprehensive theoretical framework of personality, stating that it could be best studied as five distinct and separate traits, which he labeled Intellect, Character, Temperament, Disposition, and Temper. Five years later, Allport and Odbert (1936) presented a rival taxonomy consisting of 4,500 personality traits that can be assigned to one of three levels of traits: cardinal traits, which are dominant traits that guide almost all behavior; central traits, which refer to general dispositions; and secondary traits, which refer to traits that guide behavior in some situations but not others. However, the most significant advance in the early development of a taxonomy

TABLE 8.1   The Big Five and Dimensions of Similar Breadths in Questionnaires and in Models of Personality and Interpersonal Behavior

| Theorist(s) | Surgency (I) | Agreeableness (II) | Conscientiousness (III) | Emotional Stability (IV) | Intellect/Openness to Experiences (V) |
|---|---|---|---|---|---|
| Bales (1970) | Dominant-Initiative | Social-Emotional Orientation | Task Orientation | | |
| Block (1961) | Low Ego Control | | High Ego Control | Ego Resiliency | Ego Resiliency |
| Buss & Plomin (1984) | Activity | | Impulsivity | Emotionality | |
| Cattell (1943) | Exvia (vs. Invia) | Pathemia (vs. Cortertia) | Super Ego Strength | Adjustment vs. Anxiety | Independence vs. Subduedness |
| Comrey Scales (Comrey 1970) | Extraversion and Activity | Femininity | Orderliness and Social Conformity | Emotional Stability | Rebelliousness |
| Costa & McCrae* (1992) | Extraversion | Agreeableness | Conscientiousness | Neuroticsm | Openness |
| Eysenck & Eysenck (1985) | Extraversion | Psychoticism | Psychoticism | Neuroticism | |
| Goldberg* (1992, 1993) | Extraversion | Agreeableness | Conscientiousness | Emotional Stability | Openness |
| Gough CPI Factors (Gough & Bradley, 1996) | Extraversion | Consensuality | Control | | Flexibility |
| Gough CPI Vectors (Gough & Bradley, 1996) | Externality | | Non-Favoring | Self-Realization | Self-Realization |
| Guilford (1975) | Social Activity | Paranoid Disposition | Thinking Introversion | Emotional Stability | |
| Hogan (1986) | Ambition and Sociability | Likability | Prudence | Adjustment | Intellectance |
| Jackson (1964, 1976) | Outgoing, Social Leadership | Self-Protective Orientation | Work Orientation | Dependence | Aesthetic-Intellectual |
| Myers-Briggs (Myers & McCaulley, 1985) | Extraversion vs. Introversion | Feeling vs. Thinking | Judging vs. Perception | | Intuition vs. Sensing |
| Tellegen (1985) | Positive Emotionality | Positive Emotionality | Constraint | Negative Emotionality | Absorption |
| Wiggins (1995) | Dominance | Love | | | |

*Indicates additions or derivatives from John's original table.
*Note.* Adapted from John (1990), Table 3.4.

of personality was made by Raymond Cattell in 1943. Using factor analysis, Cattell (1943) found that personality consisted of 16 primary factors and 8 second-order factors. This model was a significant step forward, as it was empirically driven and provided the basis for the development of Cattell's 16PF measure, one of the most widely used measures of personality to date.

In the 20 years that followed, several researchers attempted and failed to replicate Cattell's findings (e.g., Fiske, 1949; Norman, 1963; Tupes, 1957; Tupes & Christol, 1961), finding instead that a five-factor solution better fit the structure of personality than did any alternative. Of course, what exactly these five factors represented was not initially clear. Then in 1963, Norman made a significant contribution by providing the labels that remain, relatively intact, to this day. They are Extraversion, Agreeableness, Conscientiousness, Emotional Stability, and Culture (now referred to as Openness to Experience). This was the birth of the Big Five as we know it.

Despite the popularity of personality assessment in academic research, until the 1990s many selection specialists generally viewed it with disfavor (Hurtz & Donovan, 2000).

Since 1990 we have witnessed a proliferating investigation of the Big Five personality taxonomy regarding its utility and application within work settings, considerably bolstering its perceived legitimacy as a viable tool for personnel practice. Numerous interpretations and a plethora of instruments have been developed and designed to measure these traits. Despite general agreement on the five-factor model, however, disagreement exists as to exactly what aspects of personality those five factors envelop. According to Barrick and Mount (1991), most researchers agree on at least two of the factors—Extraversion and Emotional Stability. However, the remaining three evoke greater debate, with several researchers providing alternative labels. Table 8.1 illustrates the factor structure and labels proposed by engaged theorists and some of the instruments reflecting their definitional view. This schism in the literature brings attention to a much neglected concern for construct validity among Big Five taxonomies. The discrepancy may be at least partly attributable to different conceptual underpinnings that dominate the literature. That is, most Big Five taxonomies are derived from one of two traditions: (1) the lexical perspective or (2) several theoretical perspectives. The lexical perspective is derived from the analysis of

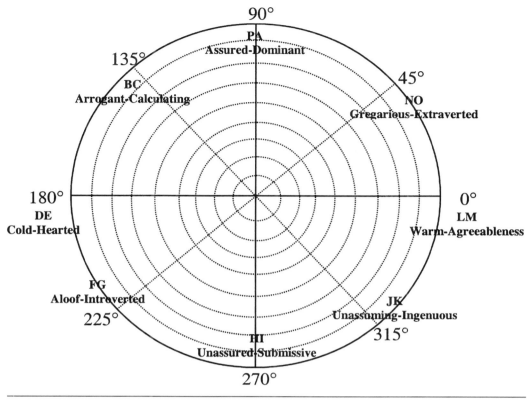

**Figure 8.1**   The interpersonal circumplex (Wiggins, 1995, p. 4).

language, with the assumption that all meaningful personality traits are represented in the lexical tradition of a society (Saucier & Goldberg, 1996). Therefore, by mapping the universe of personality adjectives, latent variables emerge to represent broad clusters or higher order factors. This perspective has been the basis of some of the most widely cited and regarded frameworks, including Cattell's and Goldberg's personality taxonomies.

In contrast, several frameworks are based more purely on theory than the lexical tradition. Prominent theories include Wiggins and Trapnell's (1996) dyadic-interactional perspective (which is based on the interpersonal circumplex shown in Figure 8.1), Hogan's (1986) socioanalytic perspective, and Buss's (1996) social adaptation perspective. Although the numerous Big Five theories share a common structure, the five factors require further conceptual refining and greater attention to issues of construct validity.

In this chapter, we focus on the most widely used and accepted labels mentioned previously: Extraversion, Agreeableness, Conscientiousness, Emotional Stability, and Openness to Experience. In the following section, we discuss in detail each of these five factors, including various conceptualizations, primary correlates, and general validity in predicting performance and other work behavior.

## THE BIG FIVE: AN OVERVIEW OF VALIDITY

In the previous decade, no fewer than five large-scale metaanalyses have been conducted on the relationship between Big Five personality factors and general work performance. Although the magnitude of some emergent correlations differs from one another, general patterns of relationships between the Big Five and performance seem rather consistent across the meta-analyses. Barrick and Mount (1991) and Tett, Jackson, and Rothstein (1991) contributed the first empirical reviews of the literature. The results of the rival reviews differed quite significantly in some cases, spawning a public controversy as the studies' authors challenged each other's methodologies and meta-analytical procedures. However, both reviews found that the Big Five, or at least some of the five, did show some validity and utility in predicting performance, thus effectively breathing new life into the use of personality assessment in employee selection.

The meta-analyses that followed by Mount and Barrick (1995) and Salgado (1997) further reinforced the strength of these findings. However, the four reviews share a potential threat to construct validity resulting from the common method used in deriving their meta-analytic coefficients (Hurtz & Donovan, 2000). That is, all four included coefficients yielded from studies that used measures other than those that measure the Big Five explicitly. Instead, results were classified into the Big Five dimensions in a post hoc manner, clearly casting doubt on the accuracy of the results. In the most recent meta-analysis by Hurtz and Donovan (2000), this criticism was addressed, and only studies using Big Five instruments (e.g., NEO-PI-R, PCI) were included. Despite the more stringent criteria for the inclusion of coefficients, the results were commensurate with the previous reviews.

The consensus is that the Big Five can be a useful tool in personnel selection, although some of the five are more useful than others (Barrick & Mount, 1991; Hurtz & Donovan, 2000; Mount & Barrick, 1995; Salgado, 1997), particularly when linked to specific performance criteria (Day & Silverman, 1989; Hough & Schneider, 1996). We next take a closer look at each of the five personality factors, considering basic issues of validity and utility, followed by an examination of important correlates.

## Conscientiousness

Conscientiousness refers to the "dependability" of the individual, typically characterized by one's thoroughness, responsibility, and reliability and frequently associated with volitional elements described as hardworking or persevering (Barrick & Mount, 1991). Conceptually, it seems appropriate that Conscientiousness should be related, at least to some extent, to work performance. In fact, some research has shown Conscientiousness to be related to performance by way of motivational variables (Gellatly, 1996; Martocchio & Judge, 1997). Thus, not surprisingly, Conscientiousness has emerged as the most robust of the five factors in its prediction of job performance. All five of the major meta-analyses have yielded moderate correlations (typically in the low .20s, though as high as .31 in Mount and Barrick's 1995 review) between Conscientiousness and performance across occupational groups. A comparison of the derived coefficients for four of the five reviews are presented in Table 8.2. As is apparent, there is some discrepancy in the reported magnitude of the relationship for the five meta-analyses. This is no doubt the result of

differing methodologies and procedures employed in the different analyses. However, with the most recent review by Hurtz and Donovan (2000), it is suspected that the results of Mount and Barrick (1995) and Salgado (1997) may be slight overestimates of the true correlations. Of course, such assertions only add to the long-standing debate over appropriate methods and procedures used in the respective reviews and quite possibly ensure that several more large meta-analyses of the relationship will follow before a consensus is reached.

Hurtz and Donovan (2000) address a key issue and frequent criticism of many, if not most, studies that include performance as a primary criterion in validity studies. That is, researchers take great liberty in operationalizing performance, frequently failing to distinguish between potential types of performance data or between the quality of different sources used in the measurement and capturing of performance. For instance, a primary distinction has been made between task performance, which is the performance of the basic functions and duties as required by the job, and contextual performance, which consists of extrarole and prosocial behaviors that go above and beyond the basic requirements of task performance (Borman & Motowidlo, 1993). Hurtz and Donovan (2000) took steps to address how the Big Five personality factors may differentially predict various performance dimensions, including both task and contextual. Their results indicate that Conscientiousness equally predicts different dimensions of performance.

In their meta-analysis of the validity and utility of various selection instruments, Schmidt and Hunter (1998) found that Conscientiousness offered some of the highest incremental validity over the use of cognitive ability tests alone. Specifically, they found that Conscientiousness enhanced overall validity by 12%, second only to integrity tests. This is important in that it illustrates that Conscientiousness, and personality as a whole perhaps, offers unique predictive utility above and beyond the use of more traditional cognitive ability assessments.

Despite consistent empirical evidence for the usefulness of Conscientiousness as a predictor of job performance, the nature of this relationship is not yet fully understood. That

**TABLE 8.2   Meta-analytic Results (True Validities)**

|  | Conscientiousness | Emotional Stability | Extraversion | Agreeableness | Openness to Experience |
|---|---|---|---|---|---|
| Barrick & Mount (1991) | .22 | .08 | .13 | .07 | .04 |
| Tett, Jackson, & Rothstein (1991) | .18 | .22 | .16 | .33 | .27 |
| Salgado (1997) | .25 | .19 | .12 | .02 | .09 |
| Hurtz & Donovan (2000) | .20 | .13 | .09 | .11 | .06 |

is, it is unknown whether this relationship operates differentially at various levels of the criterion. Few studies have described, for example, the nature of the linear function of the relationship: Although it is generally assumed that those with higher Conscientiousness scores tend to be better performers, the magnitude of the obtained covariance may be more profoundly precipitated by the poor performance of those scoring low on Conscientiousness, with less linearity at the upper ends of the distributions. The nature of the Conscientiousness-performance relationship may be moderated or differentially associated by a variety of organizational variables. For instance, Hochwarter, Witt, and Kacmar (2000) demonstrated that perception of organizational politics may moderate the Conscientiousness-performance relationship, such that when individuals perceived average to high levels of politics in the organization, Conscientiousness and performance were related, but when individuals perceived low levels of organizational politics, Conscientiousness and performance were found to be unrelated. In another study, Stewart (1999) investigated whether the relationship between Conscientiousness and performance would differ at various stages of employment. Results provided evidence that Conscientiousness does predict equally across the span of employment, though narrower, related subtraits predicted performance differentially for new hires and more seasoned employees. These studies mark an important direction in new research, exposing potential conceptual and empirical gaps in understanding how Conscientiousness, as well as other personality factors, may operate in the prediction of performance criteria. If Conscientiousness is to be our best personality variable predicting job performance, as it has been shown to be, we must understand the meaning of this relationship much more thoroughly, including the various items that make up the scales measuring this factor as well as more evidence as to how the scale predicts performance psychometrically.

## Extraversion

Extraversion refers to the extent to which an individual is described as sociable, gregarious, or assertive (Barrick & Mount, 1991). Next to Conscientiousness, it is thought to be the most useful predictor of the remaining four dimensions. Again, some discrepancy exists among the magnitudes cited in the various reviews. However, the findings agree that Extraversion is a valid predictor of performance for managers (e.g., Furnham, Crump, & Whelan, 1997) and sales personnel (e.g., Vinchur, Schippman, Switzer, & Roth, 1998), though the size of correlations are typically below .20. Mount and Barrick's (1995) review yielded significantly larger validities, ranging from .13 to .51. More recent studies have failed to

replicate these levels. A meta-analysis of predictors of job performance for sales positions conducted by Vinchur et al. (1998) found validities for Extraversion around .22, whereas recent reviews by Salgado (1997) and Hurtz and Donovan (2000) yielded respective coefficients of .12 and .09. Therefore, the predictive utility of Extraversion is still quite unknown, as large discrepancies remain as to the magnitude of its relationship with performance. Recent work by Witt (2000) has helped to shed light on this relationship by showing that Extraversion and sales performance might be moderated by Conscientiousness, such that performance is higher for individuals low in Conscientiousness and high in Extraversion. It follows then that if Conscientiousness is properly controlled for, then the observed discrepancies among studies may be reduced.

Although the magnitude of the relationship between Extraversion and performance is yet unresolved, some studies have suggested that Extraversion may be a valuable predictor of training proficiency (Barrick & Mount, 1991; Hurtz & Donovan, 2000). Barrick and Mount suggest that this may be due to the types of training frequently encountered on the job. That is, much of the training today is designed to be interactive, where a sociable, proactive individual may be more adept than more reserved, passive individuals.

## Emotional Stability

Emotional Stability, sometimes referred to as Neuroticism, is typified by anxiousness, depression, insecurity, and worry. Although most studies have found relatively stable but low correlations between Emotional Stability and criterion variables, most researchers are hesitant to make hasty conclusions as to the factor's worth in predicting employee performance. The literature is somewhat varied in its results, with some studies yielding encouraging findings that buoy the claims that Emotional Stability should be a valid predictor of job performance. For instance, a meta-analysis by Tett et al. (1991) yielded a true validity coefficient of .22, whereas Salgado's (1997) review yielded a corrected coefficient of .19, both quite larger than preceding and subsequent studies. It is also interesting that the results of both reviews place Emotional Stability as a stronger predictor of performance than even Extraversion, which has typically held the popular distinction of the number two spot, just behind Conscientiousness. This result was replicated in Hurtz and Donovan's (2000) later review. Although the latter study yielded a slightly smaller coefficient (.13), it exhibited greater ability to predict job performance than did Extraversion.

It is also interesting to note that some studies have found a negative correlation between Emotional Stability and performance in many professional occupations (Barrick & Mount, 1991). This suggests that for some jobs, heightened levels of anxiousness, worry, and nervousness are associated with higher levels of individual job performance. Of course, the nature of this relationship is not clear. Barrick and Mount (1991) suggested that certain jobs may have a high rate of pressure that could potentially result in displays of emotional strain that could translate into lower scores on measures of Emotional Stability. However, it could be too that certain jobs are better filled by individuals with heightened sensitivity to details, schedules, and general meticulousness that may be interpreted as elevated levels of Neuroticism.

Researchers have posed several reasons why Emotional Stability may not appear as strong and useful as many would expect. According to Barrick and Mount (1991), there are two primary potential causes for the low correlations. First, it may be that range restriction attenuates the size of the correlations. Unstable individuals may "self-select" themselves out of the labor force, thus leaving in tact a relatively stable pool of participants. Another explanation may be that the relationship between Emotional Stability and performance is not linear past a "critically unstable" range. That is, it may be that performance requires a certain level of Emotional Stability, but that any increments above that minimum required level are not matched with increments in performance.

### Agreeableness

Agreeableness is typically described using such terms as courteous, trusting, and polite (Barrick & Mount, 1991). For the most part, research indicates that Agreeableness is not a strong predictor of job performance. For instance, a meta-analysis conducted by Barrick and Mount (1991) yielded a coefficient of only .07 for the relationship between Agreeableness and performance. However, other results have provided a slightly different set of findings. Most notably, the review by Tett et al. (1991) yielded a true validity of .33 for Agreeableness, the highest of any of the five factors, including Conscientiousness. It should be noted that there does exist an ongoing controversy over the methodologies used in computing their meta-analytic coefficients. Furthermore, no review since has yielded anywhere near the magnitude of the reported coefficient, bringing into question whether the value may indeed be inflated.

More recent reviews have begun to spawn a more encouraging and realistic picture of the role of Agreeableness in predicting performance. Specifically, Hurtz and Donovan (2000) found some validity for Agreeableness in the prediction of interpersonal facilitation, a dimension of contextual performance as defined by the authors. This suggests that, although not predictive of general task performance, it may be predictive of prosocial behavior, extrarole behavior, or other forms of contextual performance, which has been shown to have incremental utility in personnel selection (Schmidt, Hunter, & Pearlman, 1983). Also, a more recent study conducted by Barrick and Mount (2002) proposed that Agreeableness may moderate the relationship between Conscientiousness and performance, such that conscientious individuals who are high on Agreeableness will likely perform at higher levels than those who are low on Agreeableness. Although the results were not clear-cut, the study did provide preliminary evidence in support of this hypothesis. Therefore, although the general belief holds that Agreeableness has very limited utility in personnel selection, evidence indicates that it may yet emerge as a useful predictor, at least for certain outcomes (Barrick & Mount, 1991; Hurtz & Donovan, 2000).

### Openness to Experience

Openness to Experience describes individuals who are creative, curious, and broad-minded. With the exception of a meta-analysis conducted by Tett et al. (1991), Openness to Experience has shown the lowest validities of the five factors. However, the relationship between Openness to Experience and performance may be masked by interactions with other personality traits. Specifically, Burke and Witt (2001) found that the relationship between Openness to Experience and performance was most strongly affected by Extraversion and Emotional Stability. That is, individuals high in Extraversion and low in Openness to Experience or low in both Emotional Stability and Openness to Experience were typically rated lower than their coworkers (Burke & Witt, 2001).

Although there is general agreement that Openness to Experience is not a constructive predictor of job performance (Barrick & Mount, 1991; Hurtz & Donovan, 2000; Salgado, 1997), evidence indicates that it may predict training proficiency (Barrick & Mount, 1991; Salgado, 1997). Measures of Openness to Experience may help pinpoint those individuals who are "training ready"; that is, it may help identify individuals who are willing to learn (Barrick & Mount, 1991). Barrick and Mount are also quick to point out that Openness to Experience exhibits the strongest relationship with measures of intelligence among the five factors. Therefore, it may be that the Openness to Experience factor is measuring not only willingness to learn, but also ability to learn. Whatever the case, the utility of Openness to Experience appears to lie in its prediction of training potential, rather than job performance.

## CORRELATES OF THE BIG FIVE

### Hard Versus Soft Performance Criteria

In reviewing the relationship between the Big Five personality factors and performance, it is important to consider the type of criteria used. That is, it is important to recognize how this relationship may change with the use of either hard or soft performance criteria. In a meta-analysis, Barrick and Mount (1991) addressed this distinction, finding that correlations between all Big Five factors and subjective, soft criteria exceed correlations of the factors with objective, hard criteria. Table 8.3 summarizes the corrected coefficients for each of the Big Five with both soft and hard criteria. Results demonstrate that Big Five measures are better predictors of subjective performance ratings than objective performance measures such as sales; of the several types of hard criteria included (e.g., productivity data, turnover, status change, salary), only status change yielded coefficients approaching those of subjective ratings. This may suggest that raters rely on personality when evaluating job performance, thereby bringing into question whether the relationship between personality and performance is the result of criterion contamination (i.e., rater bias) rather than actual performance. A corollary consideration of the criterion dilemma is further addressed in the next section, which investigates the distinction between task and contextual performance.

### Contextual Performance

Over the past decade, researchers have begun to expand the conceptualization of performance criteria, allowing for increased differentiation between distinct "types" of performance and their respective relationships with organizational outcomes. Borman and Motowidlo's (1993) notion of contextual performance is perhaps the most significant advancement to emerge from this new literature. Contextual performance consists of prosocial and extrarole behaviors that go above and beyond mere task performance. Although it could be argued that these behaviors may not contribute to actual task performance, they are nonetheless viewed as making positive contributions to the work environment and, therefore, may have utility in personnel selection.

Growing interest in contextual performance has given birth to a small body of literature that examines the role of personality in the prediction of contextual performance (Antonioni & Park, 2001; Hurtz & Donovan, 2000; LePine & Van Dyne, 2001; McManus & Kelly, 1999; Motowidlo & Van Scotter, 1994; Van Scotter & Motowidlo, 1996). Specifically, Motowidlo and Van Scotter (1994) found that Extraversion and Agreeableness showed the strongest relationship with measures of contextual performance. Hurtz and Donovan (2000) advanced these results, finding small but significant relationships between contextual performance and Conscientiousness, Emotional Stability, and Agreeableness; Table 8.4 summarizes Hurtz and Donovan's (2000) results, which were further substantiated by LePine and Van Dyne (2001) who found Conscientiousness, Extraversion, Emotional Stability, and Agreeableness to be useful predictors of specific forms of contextual performance. Continued research may advance the understanding of how personality impacts a variety of work behavior well beyond common, simplistic measures of job performance.

### Employee Absence and Turnover

Some authors have suggested that certain employees may be more prone to absences due to personality characteristics (Cooper & Payne, 1966; Judge, Martocchio, & Thoresen, 1997). That is, certain personality traits may predispose employees to miss work more or less frequently than other employees. The research to date has focused on two of the five factors—Extraversion and Conscientiousness. Although limited, research has provided evidence of a positive relationship between Extraversion and Absenteeism, such that individuals

---

**TABLE 8.3    Hard Versus Soft Performance Criteria and the Big Five**

| Trait | Hard Criteria Type | | | | | Soft Criteria (Subjective Ratings) |
| | Productivity Data | Turnover/ Tenure | Status Change | Salary | Mean Hard Criteria | |
|---|---|---|---|---|---|---|
| Conscientiousness | .17 | .12 | .15 | .17 | .14 | .26 |
| Extraversion | .10 | −.03 | .14 | .06 | .10 | .14 |
| Emotional Stability | −.04 | .02 | .11 | −.01 | .05 | .09 |
| Agreeableness | −.05 | .09 | .13 | −.02 | .05 | .09 |
| Openness to Experience | .01 | −.11 | .12 | .05 | .02 | .04 |

*Note.* From Barrick and Mount (1991).

**TABLE 8.4   Task Versus Contextual Performance and the Big Five**

|  | Conscientiousness | Emotional Stability | Extraversion | Agreeableness | Openness to Experience |
|---|---|---|---|---|---|
| Task Performance | .15 | .13 | .06 | .07 | − .01 |
| *Contextual Performance* |  |  |  |  |  |
| Job Dedication | .18 | .13 | .05 | .08 | .01 |
| Interpersonal Facilitation | .16 | .16 | .10 | .17 | .05 |

*Note.* From Hurtz and Donovan, 2000.

scoring high on measures of Extraversion were more likely to be absent more frequently than those with lower levels of the trait (Cooper & Payne, 1966; Judge et al., 1997). Judge et al. (1997) suggested that this may be due to the "carefree, excitement-seeking, hedonistic nature" of the extravert. It may be that extraverts are more prone and more willing to renege on their responsibilities when confronted with an opportunity that promises enjoyment or excitement.

The opposite has been found for individuals exhibiting high levels of Conscientiousness. Judge et al. (1997) found Conscientiousness to have a strong negative relationship with absence, such that individuals who score high on measures of Conscientiousness were more likely to be absent less often than those with lower levels of the trait. Since conscientious individuals are, by nature, "dutiful, rule-bound, and reliable," this finding makes sense and offers some utility in models of employee absenteeism.

In reviewing the literature, there is a conspicuous void in the study of personality and its relationship with turnover. Few studies have attempted to directly test the value of personality in predicting turnover within organizations. This is surprising noting the obvious interest and potential contributions that such research could impart upon the field of personnel selection. A dearth of studies has reported correlations between various personality variables and turnover or, more frequently, intention to quit. For example, George (1989) found negative affectivity to be positively correlated with intentions to quit, whereas positive affectivity was found to be unrelated. In a more recent study, Schaubroeck, Ganster, and Jones (1998) investigated the relationship between Extraversion and Neuroticism with intentions to quit, finding that neither exhibited significant associations with the withdrawal measure.

Although the literature is sparse, personality research has begun to make important advances in the prediction of expatriate performance. Most notably, Caligiuri (2000) investigated the relationship between the Big Five personality factors and expatriate performance. Results showed that Conscientiousness was positively related to expatriate performance, thus

identifying it as a potential predictor in selection. Furthermore, Extraversion, Agreeableness, and Emotional Stability were negatively related to an individual's desire to terminate his or her expatriate assignment. Taken together, the Big Five show promise in predicting expatriate performance.

## Group Composition and Performance

Despite the popularity of team research, studies of group composition are typically limited to standard demographic variables (Barrick, Stewart, Neubert, & Mount, 1998). That is, few studies have investigated the intricacies of group composition in terms of individual characteristics such as intelligence or personality. However, recent research has begun to delve into how individual personality can contribute to or hinder group performance. Though scant, recent studies have begun to elucidate the relationship between at least four of the five factors (Conscientiousness, Agreeableness, Emotional Stability, and Extraversion) and group performance.

The relationships between Conscientiousness, Emotional Stability, and Agreeableness with team performance are relatively straightforward. As demonstrated by Barrick et al. (1998), the three yielded respective correlations of .26, .24, and .34 with team performance, which are notably stronger than their corresponding coefficients at the individual level. Extraversion is a bit more complicated, however. Barry and Stewart (1997) found a curvilinear relationship between the number of extraverted group members and team performance. In other words, too many or too few extraverts can adversely hinder group outcomes; there should instead be enough variability in individual levels of extraversion to ensure that "complementary roles of leading and following are carried out" (Barrick et al., 1998, p. 381).

These findings are echoed by Neuman, Wagner, and Christiansen's (1999) more recent work that looked at average trait levels versus intragroup trait diversity of each of the five factors and their respective relationships to performance. Average trait levels of Conscientiousness, Agreeableness, and Openness to Experience were positively correlated with team performance, whereas diversity on Extraversion and Emotional Stability was strongly predictive of performance. These findings imply that for Conscientiousness, Agreeableness, and Openness to Experience, it is desirable to have individuals who exhibit high levels of each trait, whereas for Extraversion and Emotional Stability, it is desirable to have a collection of individuals with varying levels of each trait. Of course, the role of personality in group composition and performance has only begun to be explored, and much needs to be done before more concrete conclusions can be drawn.

## Leadership

Only recently has an attempt to link the Big Five to transformational leadership emerged. According to the conceptualization Bass (1985) put forth, transformational leaders possess three distinct traits: They are inspirational, they provide intellectual stimulation, and they exhibit individual consideration for their followers. Although it is asserted that transformational leadership is a behavioral theory and that leadership can be learned, there are consistent arguments expressing support for a trait component, which, by its very nature, is assumed to be a manifestation of stable personality traits. Therefore, investigation into the relationship between the Big Five and leadership seems only appropriate.

To date, only two studies have examined the relationship between the Big Five and transformational leadership. Judge and Bono (2000) found significant but modest correlations between three of the five factors and transformational leadership, with Agreeableness emerging as the strongest, followed by Extraversion and Openness to Experience. Conscientiousness and Emotional Stability were not found to related to transformational leadership. This provides some support for the argument that transformational leadership is, at least in part, contingent on stable traits of the individual, rather than wholly learned skills or behaviors.

In examining the relationship between the Big Five factors and typical versus maximum transformational leadership performance, Polyhart, Lim, and Chan (2001) found that Extraversion and Openness to Experience predicted maximum performance, whereas Extraversion and Emotional Stability predicted typical performance. Furthermore, Polyhart et al. noted that the strength of these relationships suggests that the Big Five may be most predictive of transformational leadership in challenging situations. These results are consistent with Judge and Bono's (1990) earlier work, thus providing a good beginning to a literature that will likely herald significant insight into the role of personality in the selection of leadership.

## Job Satisfaction

Research of the previous decade has begun to unravel the relationship between job satisfaction and the Big Five. Most notably, several studies have established a positive relationship between Emotional Stability and job satisfaction (Furnham & Zacherl, 1986; Judge, Higgins, Thoresen, & Barrick, 1999; Smith, Organ, & Near, 1983; Tokar & Subich, 1997), and others have begun to mount evidence in support of a positive association between Extraversion and satisfaction (Furnham & Zacherl, 1986; Tokar & Subich, 1997). However, empirical evidence in support of similar relationships among job satisfaction and the remaining three factors has been slow coming. Judge et al. (1999) revealed in a recent study a more complex relationship between the Big Five and job satisfaction. Specifically, they found that Emotional Stability, Openness to Experience, and Conscientiousness were significant predictors of satisfaction, but that when the variance accounted for by Conscientiousness was controlled for, the predictive power of the remaining two factors was negligent. Contrary to previous research, Judge et al. (1999) were not able to find evidence in support of a relationship between job satisfaction and Extraversion. Overall, the research is encouraging as to the potential utility of the Big Five in predicting job satisfaction; however, existing research is scant, and much still needs to be done toward understanding the nature of the relationship between personality and job satisfaction.

## Intelligence

It is frequently taken for granted that personality and intelligence are relatively unrelated constructs. In fact, this assumption has driven much of the renewed interest in personality over the previous decade or more. That is, the apparently nonredundant contribution to prediction that personality makes in combination with cognitive ability, as well as its reduced adverse impact, has made it the "supplementary instrument" of choice. However, when one reviews the literature, very little published research exists that explores the relationship between the two constructs. At best, some published studies may report correlations between the Big Five and cognitive ability as they relate to one another in whatever hypotheses a particular study may pursue. But in reviewing these studies, the relationship is not clearly evident. For instance, in a recent study, LePine and Van Dyne (2001) reported significant correlations between cognitive ability and Openness to Experience and Agreeableness (.18 and −.11, respectively). Though modest, the correlation between intelligence and Openness to Experience exceeds many of the correlations typically found between Big Five factors (with the exception of Conscientiousness) and performance. This suggests that some conceptual overlap may occur between certain personality traits and intelligence, a position evident in Cattell's inclusion of an intelligence factor on the 16PF inventory. Therefore, it seems that the relationship between personality and intelligence is not yet fully understood, and a wealth of understanding might be acquired through future research in this realm of cognition and personality.

### Rating Effects

Several researchers have investigated how the Big Five may contribute to rating effects and/or biases in the assessment of applicant qualifications and performance, particularly with respect to assessment centers (Antonioni & Park, 2001; Bernardin, Cooke, & Villanova, 2000; Dunn, Mount, Barrick, & Ones, 1995; Lievens, De Fruyt, & Van Dam, 2001). Most of these studies fall into one of two groups: those that explore the effects of the personality of raters, and those that explore the effects of the personality of ratees.

The first group of studies focuses on how personality characteristics of raters might contribute to the types of ratings they make in reviewing other individuals. Research has shown that certain personality traits are associated with certain outcomes. For instance, Bernardin et al. (2000) showed that individuals who are low on Conscientiousness and/or high on Agreeableness exhibit more leniency in their ratings. That is, those who exhibit low levels of Conscientiousness or high levels of Agreeableness tend to consistently rate applicants higher than do other raters. In another study, Antonioni and Park (2001) found that rater-ratee similarity on Conscientiousness was associated with higher peer ratings, even when partialing out interpersonal affect. Therefore, conscientious individuals frequently evaluate other conscientious individuals more positively than they do others.

The second group of studies focuses on how personality traits of the ratee might influence assessor evaluations. Lievens et al. (2001) showed that even when instructed to record only behavioral observations, nearly 20% of assessor notes contain descriptions of personality traits. Furthermore, they found that applicants thought to exhibit Extraversion, Conscientiousness, and Openness to Experience were more likely to be recommended for employment. This advances research conducted by Dunn et al. (1995) that found hiring managers perceived Conscientiousness to be a key factor in assessing an applicant's "hirability." More recently, Witt, Burke, Barrick, and Mount (in press) found that appraisals of individual performance were indeed correlated with Conscientiousness, but that this relationship is moderated by ratee levels of Agree-

ableness. That is, individuals who scored high on both traits received higher performance ratings than those who scored high on Conscientiousness but low on Agreeableness.

These findings are important in understanding how the Big Five contribute to evaluations of both applicants and employees. Although considerations of personality traits are frequently thought of as errors, there may be utility in allowing raters to consider personality traits in their assessment of an applicant or employee. Of course, far more needs to be done before we can truly begin to understand how personality impacts subjective evaluations in the workplace.

## SPECIAL ISSUES

With the burgeoning popularity of the Big Five in both research and application, a number of controversial issues have emerged that demand a share of the discussion. In the following sections, we focus on the most salient of these issues. We begin by exploring the effects of faking or response distortion on the validity of Big Five inventories. Then we address the practical issue of adverse impact and test bias in the uses of personality measures in personnel selection. Finally, we confront the bandwidth dilemma and attempt to evaluate whether the broad five-factor model is of greater usefulness than more narrowly defined trait frameworks.

### Faking and Response Distortion

With a growing presence of the Big Five in personnel selection, the susceptibility of personality measures to faking and response distortion has become a central topic of debate and discussion in the literature. Several researchers have attempted to address this issue, exploring multiple facets that may potentially invalidate personality measures in many settings. Questions regarding the extent to which personality measures are fakable and, perhaps more important, to what extent individuals distort their responses are questions with both legal and empirical importance.

Fakability of personality tests has been directly addressed by a handful of studies in the past decade. Hough, Eaton, Dunne, Kamp, & McCloy's (1990) study was one of the first to empirically examine the effects of response distortion on the validity of personality measures. They found that response distortion does not attenuate the validities of personality measures in their predictions of performance; they found that only careless responding seriously diminished the validities of the instruments used. Barrick and Mount (1996) reinforced this finding. In line with previous work, Barrick and Mount (1996) found that individuals can and do distort their responses, but they concluded that this distortion does not reduce the predictive validity of personality measures.

These findings were further substantiated by a recent meta-analysis that Viswesvaran and Ones (1999) conducted. Results showed that when instructed to do so, individuals *could* distort their responses by almost half a standard deviation on Big Five scales. However, measures were generally more susceptible to "faking bad" than "faking good." That is, studies in which individuals were instructed to "fake bad" yielded smaller effect sizes than studies in which individuals were instructed to "fake good." Also, it was found that all Big Five personality factors were equally fakable and, therefore, equally subject to the effects of response distortion.

More recently, Smith, Hanges, and Dickson (2001) investigated the controversy of socially desirable responding in personality research. In line with the previous findings, Smith et al. found no evidence to suggest that socially desirable responding significantly detracted from the usefulness of the Big Five in selection settings. Their findings further rebut critics who suggest that personality is best described by a less complex structure, with a primary loading on social desirability (Douglas, McDaniel, & Snell, 1996; Griffith, 1997).

Some research has focused on how faking or socially desirable responding impacts the validity of instruments, with limited concern for how to correct for it. The consensus is that individuals do indeed distort their responses on personality tests (Rosse, Stecher, Miller, & Levin, 1998), but the remedy remains a point of controversy. Those who argue that response distortion and social desirability do not detract from the validity of such tests (e.g., Barrick & Mount, 1996; Viswesvaran & Ones, 1999) would likely argue that no remedial steps are necessary. In contrast, those who take the position that correction is necessary may have difficulty in actually deriving accurate correction formulae. Ellingson, Sackett, and Hough (1999), for example, examined the usefulness of correcting scores for social desirability, finding that such procedures are ineffective and fail to "approximate" honest scores. Because of such lingering questions, skepticism remains toward conclusions that faking does not impact the validity of personality instruments. As such, continued research is needed before this issue is resolved.

## Adverse Impact

Since publication of the Equal Employment Opportunity (EEOC) guidelines in 1977 and 1978 adverse impact has emerged as a primary concern in personnel selection. The most pressing challenge of the 40 years prior to the EEOC guidelines had been finding a balance between pure utility and test fairness. Selection specialists are now charged with the additional task of using instruments that accurately predict the strongest performers while maintaining a fair and representative workplace in which minorities are not unfairly or disproportionately rejected.

Numerous studies have been conducted to evaluate the fairness of various types of selection measures, frequently producing results suggesting that utility and test fairness may be incompatible goals (Maxwell & Arvey, 1993). Measures of cognitive ability have been shown to provide the greatest utility among the variety of selection devices (Schmidt & Hunter, 1998). However, this utility may come at the expense of test fairness within some of its definitions (Bartlett, Bobko, Mosier, & Hannan, 1978). Hartigan and Wigdor (1989) showed that minorities consistently scored significantly lower than Whites on measures of cognitive ability, with African Americans and Hispanics typically scoring nearly a full standard deviation lower than the White majority. Therefore, major efforts have been undertaken to evaluate how alternative selection measures may improve test fairness without dramatically handicapping the ability of the organization to predict and select the best performers. Personality sits at the forefront of this research.

Much of the research to date has found no evidence of meaningful differences for either gender or ethnicity on personality tests (Hough, 1998; Ones, Viswesvaran, & Schmidt, 1993; Pulakos & Schmitt, 1996). Thus, personality is viewed as an attractive alternative to other selection procedures, as it should produce fair decisions with little if any adverse impact. However, as discussed, the Big Five, and personality measures in general, have relatively modest predictive validity as compared with cognitive ability. Therefore, using measures of personality alone would substantially reduce the utility of the selection process but would provide for fair decisions.

In an attempt to better balance the goals of utility and fairness, many researchers have proposed that the use of measures of personality in combination with other, more robust predictors may reduce adverse impact while retaining high utility. For instance, Ones et al. (1993) suggested that an optimally weighted composite of cognitive ability and integrity (which they hypothesized to be a manifestation of Conscientiousness) could better reconcile the disparate goals of utility and fairness than could either measure by itself. However, subsequent research on the matter has been mixed. Hattrup, Rock, and Scalia (1997) found that increasing weights on measures of personality in personnel selection can reduce adverse impact, but that improvement in fairness is accompanied by at least some decrement in predictive power. Ryan, Ployhart, and Friedel (1998) failed to replicate this finding. They found that increasing weights of personality measures in selection does not reduce adverse impact, and that the inclusion of personality tests should be based on improving prediction, not enhancing fairness. Of course, the literature is disparate and scant, and additional research must be conducted before a more conclusive determination may be asserted. Therefore, the potential role of personality in enhancing the fairness of selection decisions is far from clear; however, it remains the most promising candidate in creating a balance between the seemingly disjunctive goals of utility and fairness.

## The Bandwidth-Fidelity Dilemma

The growing dominance of the Big Five in personality measurement has spawned considerable controversy in and of itself. At the center of the controversy lies the ongoing debate regarding the comprehensiveness of the Big Five factors. That is, many dissenters (e.g., Ackerman, 1990; Hough, 1992; Levy, Cober, & Norris-Watts, Chapter 9 in this volume; Tett, Jackson, Rothstein, & Reddon, 1994) question whether five broad personality factors are robust enough to provide superior prediction over countless more narrowly defined and measured personality traits. This is most typically referred to as the "bandwidth-fidelity dilemma."

It has been argued that there is a necessary trade-off between precision of measurement of a single trait and the measurement of a large number of characteristics (Murphy, 1993). Cronbach and Gesler (1957) posited that the bandwidth-fidelity trade-off is marked by two primary hypotheses: (1) Broad constructs should predict broad criteria with moderate validity; and (2) narrow constructs should predict specific criteria with maximal validity. In actual practice, however, these intuitively apparent suppositions may not hold true. Currently, it is not clear that a loss in prediction occurs when broad measures rather than narrow measures of personality are used.

Ones and Viswesvaran (1996) addressed these concerns both empirically and conceptually. To begin, they noted that there is "nothing inherent in broad traits that precludes high fidelity assessment" (Ones & Viswesvaran, 1996, p. 610). Thus, from a conceptual standpoint, there is no reason why broad constructs should necessarily be less predictive or precise than narrow constructs.

When viewed from an empirical standpoint, the literature shows that using broad measures over narrow measures of personality has advantages. First, alpha reliabilities of narrow measures of personality are typically lower than those of the Big Five (Ones & Viswesvaran, 1996). In fact, Ones and Viswesvaran (1996) suggested that for specific personality trait measures to reach adequate reliability, scales would have to be lengthened by three to six times. Second, it has been shown that broad personality constructs are frequently more predictive of performance than are narrow traits. For instance, Barrick and Mount (1994) showed that a composite measure of Conscientiousness exhibited greater predictive power for performance criteria than did any individual component. When the general Conscientiousness factor was partialed out, the remaining relationships between the individual facets and performance were negligible. Similarly, Stewart (1999) examined the relationship of Conscientiousness and two related subtraits, Order and Achievement, with performance across different stages of employment and tenure. Results indicated that the broad measure of Conscientiousness predicted performance at all stages of employment, whereas its narrow subtraits exhibited differential relationships at different stages of employment with Order predicting for new hires while Achievement predicted for those with more career experience.

Paunonen, Rothstein, and Jackson (1999) and Paunonen and Jackson (2000) also challenged the assertion that broad traits are preferable. Using Ones and Viswesvaran's (1996) data, Paunonen et al. (1999) disputed the previous results, concluding that "Ones and Viswesvaran are wrong in declaring that a multi-dimensional predictor is necessary for accurately predicting a multidimensional criterion" (p. 393). The authors instead demonstrated that narrower variables can and often do afford predictive advantages over broader variables in employee selection in at least three ways: (1) Narrow variables can be more "purposefully" selected on the basis of conceptual similarity or relatedness to the criterion or its facets; (2) narrow variables may be combined to maximize the accuracy in predicting performance; and (3) narrow variables offer greater "psychological meaningfulness" in explaining behavior.

Taken as a whole, convincing arguments come from both sides of the debate, with equally impressive, and frequently contradicting, evidence to strengthen their positions. As such, the bandwidth-fidelity debate shows no end in sight. Although not directly addressed by any authors to date, the issue of naming scales with the implicit assumption that the name is an accurate representation of what the set of scaled items measures is also an argument for the broad trait preference in empirical research. For example, the 16PF scale "Openness to Change," if descriptively representing the items in it, would be presumed to be a component of or have convergence with the Big Five factor Openness to Experience. In fact, this scale is commonly included within the factor Extraversion rather than Openness to Experience (Byravan & Ramanaiah, 1995). The point is that the debate surrounding the probative and heuristic value of broad versus narrow traits seems to be a matter of construct validity. Through studies of convergent and divergent validity of both broad and narrow personality scales, our level of understanding and predictive prowess could be enhanced.

## Paralogical Assumptions About the Insular Nature of Personality Factors

Attendant to the bandwidth-fidelity issue, the Big Five concept of personality intuitively includes the notion that personality factors should be considered as a profile rather than as a set of isolated personality traits. Clearly, individual personality is ultimately unique and empirically elusive. The uniqueness of personality, however, may be partially identifiable as a set of traits viewed as a profile or at least in some combinatorial way. When humans are seen or studied as the embodiment of a unitary trait, however, understanding of personality distinctiveness is absent. Assuming that all extraverts or all emotionally stable individuals have common, predictable behavior requires a stretch of imagination that the field may find to be empirically convenient but heuristically vacant. An extraverted individual who is an agreeable person is quite different from a disagreeable extravert. An emotionally stable, conscientious individual is exceedingly different from an emotionally unstable, conscientious person. Much more of human distinctiveness is revealed by considering two traits in combination rather than grouping people within a single trait category. When the other three factors join the mix, the uniqueness of personality begins to emerge. However, virtually all research to date has focused on Big Five traits in isolation of one another, and the attempt to develop profiles for predictive purposes is notably absent in the literature.

Correlations between independent trait variables and some measure of work behavior, although sympathetic to limited sample size, is tantamount to dust bowl empiricism. The assumption that we can isolate traits of the whole person may be fallacious and detrimental to the development of our understanding and prediction of work behavior. The fission of personality traits for the purposes of measurement simplicity neglects the opportunity to enhance our understanding of personality in the workplace. It should be apparent that shared variance between a trait predictor and some measure of performance is, at best, about 7%, leaving a substantial amount of unexplained variance that might be explicated by profiles rather than insular trait measures. Our understanding of capacity for teamwork, leadership, or effort reinvigoration, for example, might require research on profiles or at least combinations of trait measures. Those who argue that we are better off with more narrow measures of personality than what is offered by eclectic Big Five factors certainly have a point, but narrowly defined traits tend to lack construct validity. Perhaps the greatest virtue of Big Five conceptualization is

the opportunity to study the more distinguishing facets of personality as combinations of Big Five traits. The Big Five model may offer the path to a clarity of understanding of personality in the workplace that 70 years of research has not revealed. However, as long as research continues to partake of what is readily available rather than what is needed, the science of industrial/organizational psychological inquiry will meander.

## PRIMARY TESTS OF THE BIG FIVE

### NEO-PI-R

| | |
|---|---|
| Authors: | Costa and McCrae (1992) |
| Item Format: | Self-report Likert scale (5-point) |
| Number of Items: | 240 |
| Reliability: | .72 to .87 (Egan, Deary, & Austin, 2000) |

### *Description*

The NEO-PI-R consists of 240 statements with which individuals are asked to rate their level of agreement on a five-point Likert scale. It divides each of the five personality domains into six facets, allowing for more precise measurement of the Big Five as conceptualized by Costa and McCrae (1992). A 60-item short version has been developed as well (called the NEO-FFI) that yields scores for only the five broad domains and not their underlying facets. The NEO-PI-R is the most widely used Big Five measure, with applications in varied settings. It has also benefited from quite extensive examinations of its reliability and validity, thus yielding strong empirical evidence in support of its measurement soundness.

### *Advantages*

The major advantages of the NEO-PI-R are its precision in tapping the Big Five domains, its utility in multiple settings, and the strength of empirical support for its validity and reliability (Widiger & Trull, 1997).

### *Disadvantages*

The primary limitation of the NEO-PI-R is the absence of validity and lie scales (Widiger & Trull, 1997); it makes no provision to identify careless or distorted responding, which is of obvious concern in personality assessment. Furthermore, some researchers remain critical of the selection of particular constructs as being representative of the five factor domains and/or their facets (Widiger & Trull, 1997). That is, there is ambiguity as to the Big Five structure and the proposed manifest variables of each that have been included in the instrument. In fact, Cellar, Doverspike, Miller, and Klawsky (1996) suggested that a six-factor solution better fits the structure of the NEO-PI-R than the five-factor model. There is also new concern over its use with culturally dissimilar groups. In a recent study, Caprara, Barbaranelli, Hahn, and Comrey (2001) administered the NEO-PI to both American and Italian samples, finding that the five-factor structure was supported in the American sample but not in the Italian sample. Only three of the five factors were well defined in the Italian sample.

### Sample Items

I often feel helpless and want someone to solve my problems.

I'm a superior person.

## 16PF

Authors:     Cattell, Eber, and Tatsuoka (1970)
Number of Items:   187

### Description

The 16PF is easily one of the most widely used tests of personality over the previous 30 years. Constructed from the landmark research of Raymond Cattell and colleagues, the 16PF yields 16 primary factors (hence, its name) and 8 second-order factors. However, recent research has begun to yield evidence that the 16PF may be useful in measuring the Big Five as well. Specifically, Byravan and Ramanaiah (1995) conducted a comprehensive examination of the factor structure of the 16PF in relation to the NEO-PI and Goldberg's Big Five Markers. The results of this study provided moderate to strong support for each of the five factors as measured by the 16PF. Factor structure is presented in Table 8.5. However, the study of the utility and precision of the 16PF in measuring the Big Five is in its infancy. Therefore, the use of the instrument as a measure of the Big Five should be approached with great caution.

### Advantages

The advantage of the 16PF lies primarily in its history and tradition. It is perhaps the first measure of personality as we know it, and it surely has one of the longest shelf lives of any personality measure still in use today. With this history comes a strong foundation of research and study, yielding a comprehensive literature of its usefulness in multiple domains.

**TABLE 8.5  Five-Factor Structure of the 16PF**

| Big Five Factor | 16PF Scale |
| --- | --- |
| Neuroticism | Privateness |
| | Perfectionism |
| | Emotional Stability |
| Extraversion | Social Boldness |
| | Warmth |
| | Liveliness |
| | Dominance |
| | Openness to Change |
| | Abstractness |
| Conscientiousness | Self-reliance |
| | Rule-consciousness |
| | Vigilance |
| Openness to Experience | Apprehension |
| | Vigilance |
| | Tension |
| Agreeableness | Dominance |

*Note.* From Byravan and Ramanaiah, 1995.

### Disadvantages

The primary disadvantage of the 16PF is its ambiguous relationship to the Big Five model. That is, although evidence has emerged that the 16 primary factors do indeed load on just five general factors, the 16PF lacks the precision of other measures developed specifically to assess the lexical foundations of the Big Five.

## Hogan Personality Inventory

Authors:       Hogan (1986); Hogan and Hogan
               (1992)
Item Format:   Self-report True/False
Number of Items:   206
Reliability:   .71 to .89

### Description

The Hogan Personality Inventory (HPI) consists of 206 true/false items that yield six scales: Adjustment, Prudence, Intellectance, Likeability, Sociability, and Ambition. The first four are comparable to Emotional Stability, Conscientiousness, Openness to Experience, and Agreeableness, respectively. The final two are considered facets of Extraversion. Perhaps more than most other alternatives, the HPI is very much oriented toward the domain of work and job performance and is not intended for use with clinical populations. It is based on a socioanalytic theory that makes a distinction between personality as viewed by the individual, termed his or her identity, and personality as viewed by an outside observer, termed his or her reputation. According to Hogan and

Hogan (1992), identity is difficult to measure reliably because individuals respond according to how they want to be seen, which may be dramatically different from how they are seen. Reputation, on the other hand, is simple to measure and "inherently valid," as reputation is based on past behavior, which is typically viewed as the best predictor of future performance (Hough & Oswald, 2000). Therefore, the HPI further differs from other measures in that it attempts to capture not how individuals view themselves, but how they are viewed by others who know them well. The HPI is one of the most extensively validated Big Five measures available and has yielded impressive correlations among the various dimensions and job performance.

### Advantages

The primary advantage of the HPI is its utility in work settings. The instrument is specifically designed to assess personality in the context of work. This, combined with evidence of good validity and reliability, makes it a strong candidate for use in personnel selection. Furthermore, the inclusion of scales to identify and correct for response distortion and carelessness is a clear advantage over most alternative measures (Widiger & Trull, 1997).

### Disadvantages

The primary limitation of the HPI is its deviation from the traditional five-factor model (Widiger & Trull, 1997). Though arguable, the failure of the HPI to faithfully and comprehensively measure the Big Five is at best an inconvenience, muddying the conceptual waters of the predominant personality paradigm. It is not clear that the Hogan conceptualization contributes much beyond the traditional model presented in this chapter.

## PSY-5

Authors:              Harkness (1992)

### Description

The PSY-5 consists of five subscales of the MMPI-2 that assess variations of the Big Five personality factors; Harkness has assigned the labels Aggressiveness, Psychoticism, Constraint, Negative Emotionality, and Positive Emotionality. Although most of the five scales included have a comparable scale in the traditional Big Five conceptualization, Harkness and McNully (1994) caution that some scales, such as Psychoticism, have virtually no relationship to the traditional

structure. Aside from differences in conceptualization, this measure differs from most other Big Five instruments in terms of its origins and intended use as well. Whereas most of the popular Big Five scales were developed for normal populations, the Psy-5 was designed to provide dimensional descriptions of personality disorders. As such, its intended use is in the clinical diagnosis and treatment of individuals who suffer from various personality disorders.

### Advantages

The primary advantage of the PSY-5 is its usefulness in clinical settings. Having been born out of the MMPI-2, the predominant measure in clinical assessment, the PSY-5 is a relatively robust measure of personality with strong links to both the lexical framework of the Big Five and the diagnostic properties of the *Diagnostic and Statistical Manual of Mental Disorders* (*DSM*).

### Disadvantages

The primary advantage of the Psy-5 is also its primary limitation. That is, some researchers fear the MMPI-2 may not have the versatility necessary to tap into the Big Five as well as any number of clinical disorders (Widiger & Trull, 1997). To illustrate, Widiger and Trull (1992) showed that individual self-descriptions of personality are frequently distorted during episodes of depression, anxiety, or psychosis. Therefore, it is questionable as to what the PSY-5 actually measures in clinical populations versus normal populations; as such, its application in nonclinical settings remains suspect.

## Interpersonal Adjective Scales-Big Five

Authors:              Trapnell and Wiggins (1990)
Item Format:          Self-report Likert scale (8-point)
Number of Items:      64

### Description

The Interpersonal Adjective Scales-Big Five (IAS-B5) is an adjective checklist not unlike Goldberg's Big Five Markers. It differs, however, in that it is based on the interpersonal circumplex (IPC) formulation of Extraversion and Agreeableness, which implies a circular structure of traits in which those traits that lie adjacent to one another are closely and positively related, and those that fall opposite of one another are negatively related. Traits that fall at 90-degree angles of one another are orthogonal and thus unrelated. Figure 8.1 (see earlier in the chapter) provides an illustration of the interpersonal circumplex proposed by Wiggins (1995). The scale consists of 64 adjectives that yield eight scales along two dimensions: control and affiliation. McCrae and Costa (1989) examined the structure of the IAS-B5 against their NEO-PI measure, finding that the interpersonal circumplex formulation does provide meaning conceptualizations of the Big Five that complement the more common dimensional models of personality.

### Advantages

The advantage of the IAS-B5 is that it is the first instrument to empirically demonstrate a circumplex structure of the measured personality variables (Wiggins, 1979). It has shown utility in describing personality at its lexical bases, rather than in theoretical derivations and dimensional interpretations. However, it has failed to become a dominant measure in applied business settings, though it is increasingly used in clinical settings to diagnose personality disorders.

### Disadvantages

Critics have long voiced skepticism about the circumplex structure put forth by Wiggins. Jackson and Helmes (1979) waged that the circular structure is likely an artifact of response bias. However, Gifford (1991) more recently provided evidence that the circular patterns of correlations were not the result of response bias and that the IPC is a valid representation of the interrelationships among the variables. Another criticism, as with Goldberg's measure, emerges out of the frequent ambiguity of certain terms being assigned to represent certain factors and not others.

### Sample Items

Crafty
Cheerful
Iron-hearted

## Goldberg Big Five Markers

Authors:              Goldberg (1990, 1992)
Item Format:          Self-report Likert scale (9-point)
Number of Items:      100 (Long Version) or 50 (Short Version)
Reliability           .88 to .97 (Goldberg, 1992)

### Description

Goldberg's Big Five Markers consists of adjective markers of the five personality factors. Although several formats exist,

the two most popular consist of either 100 unipolar adjectives or 50 bipolar adjectives, both of which are scored on a 9-point Likert scale. The adjectives may be delivered alphabetically, randomly, or clustered by trait. Goldberg's Big Five Markers are not intended for measuring individual differences to aid in decision making; instead, Goldberg (1992) maintained that the instrument is intended "solely as a means of locating other measures within a comprehensive structural representation" (p. 27). Therefore, its use in employment selection is suspect.

### Advantages

The advantages of Goldberg's adjective checklist are few but meaningful. First, the instrument is rather quick and easy to administer and score, taking only 10–15 minutes for an individual to complete. This makes it a practical instrument for use in applied settings. Furthermore, of all the available instruments, Goldberg's adheres most closely to the Big Five "lexical domains" (Widiger & Trull, 1997), contributing to its apparent construct validity.

### Disadvantages

The primary limitation of the Big Five Markers is that it is not intended to be used as a personality scale; as discussed briefly in the preceding Description section, it is meant as a tool to locate factor scales in other inventories. This being the case, it was not designed to identify individual differences or establish relationships between the Big Five and other constructs. Its use in such contexts is therefore arguably inappropriate. Another disadvantage of Goldberg's adjective checklist lies in his sampling of the lexical domain (Widiger & Trull, 1997). That is, ambiguity exists among terms, and Goldberg's decision to include a term in the domain of one factor and not another is a topic open to debate.

### Sample Items

Abrasive
Cold
Shy
Kind
Aggressive
Prompt

## SUMMARY

The five-factor model has brought about a new renaissance in personality research. It has returned personality to a place of high regard by academics and practitioners alike, particularly in its utility in personnel selection. Over the previous decade, the usefulness and robustness of the Big Five model has been more clearly evidenced, and the resulting proliferation of assessment instruments is nothing short of staggering. This chapter synthesized more than half a century of research into the Big Five framework, reviewing the major tests and their applications in the world of work. Research generally indicates that Conscientiousness, Extraversion, and

Emotional Stability are valuable and useful predictors of job performance for varying occupations. The implications of these findings have yet to be fully understood, but their impact has clearly fueled a previously stagnating literature. Though still far from a consensus, either on the structure of personality or the major criticisms that are frequently waged against its measurement, the Big Five has contributed tremendously to this renewed interest.

## APPENDIX: OTHER TESTS OF THE BIG FIVE

| Instrument | Description |
| --- | --- |
| Basic Personality Inventory | The Basic Personality Inventory is a multiphasic questionnaire consisting of 240 true/false items, yielding 12 scales. Designed for use with both clinical and normal populations, the publisher maintains that the scales load on five primary factors commensurate with the Big Five. |
| California Psychological Inventory (Gough & Bradley, 1996) | The CPI consists of 434 items, yielding 20 scales that load on three vectors: externality; non-favoring; self-realization. The CPI is extensively used in both work and clinical settings. |
| Comrey Personality Scales (Comrey, 1970) | The CPS consists of 180 items that yield eight personality scales and two validity scales. The CPS is designed for use with normal populations in work and educational settings. |
| Global Personality Inventory | Developed by Personnel Decisions International, the GPI was designed for use in business across the globe. With translations in more than 12 languages, the GPI was carefully developed with samples from around the world. |
| Guilford-Zimmerman Temperament Survey | The Guilford-Zimmerman Temperament Survey yields 10 personality scales designed for use with normal populations, particularly in the context of work. |
| Interpersonal Style Inventory | The ISI consists of 144 performance-based items that focus on the competencies required by international assignments. Developed to predict performance of individuals in foreign assignments. |
| Jackson Personality Inventory (Jackson, 1976) | The JPI consists of 320 true/false items, yielding 15 scales categorized along five higher-order clusters similar to the Big Five. |
| Minnesota Multiphasic Personality Inventory (Hathaway & McKinley, 1967) | The MMPI consists of 566 true/false items, yielding nine clinical scales and three validity scales. The PSY-5 (discussed previously) derives Big Five scales from the MMPI item pool. |
| Myers-Briggs Type Indicator (Myers & McCaulley, 1985) | The MBTI consists of 166 multiple-choice items that yield 16 personality types derived from four scales: introversion vs. extraversion; sensing vs. intuition; thinking vs. feeling; judging vs. perceptive. |
| Occupational Personality Questionnaire | The OPQ is designed for use with normal populations in work settings. It yields 32 dimensions that load on three higher-level factors: relationships with people, thinking style, and feelings and emotions. |
| Personal Characteristics Inventory | The PCI is a Big Five instrument developed for use in personnel selection. In addition to the Big Five, it also yields scales for four Occupational Success scales and three Employability indexes. |

*(continued)*

| Instrument | Description |
| --- | --- |
| Personality Research Form (Jackson, 1964) | The PRF consists of 352 true/false items, yielding 22 scales. Designed for use with normal populations, particularly in personnel settings. |
| Proactive Personality Scale (Crant, 1995) | The PPS is a 17-item instrument that focuses on proactive behaviors in the organizational setting. Research has shown that the scale is correlated with extraversion and conscientiousness, but not the remaining three Big Five factors (Taubert, 1999). |
| Five-Factor Personality Inventory (Hendriks, Hofstee, & De Raad, 1999) | The FFPI consists of 100 brief statements to which individuals are asked to rate the extent to which the statement is applicable to oneself. Designed as an alternative to the NEO-PI-R, the FFPI differs in that it is founded on the circumplex model rather than the lexical model. |

## REFERENCES

Ackerman, P.L. (1990). A correlational analysis of skill specificity: Learning, abilities, and individual differences. *Journal of Experimental Psychology: Learning, Memory, and Cognition, 16*, 883–901.

Allport, G.W., & Odbert, H.S. (1936). Trait names: a psycho-lexical study. *Psychological Monographs, 47*, 211.

Antonioni, D., & Park, H. (2001). The effects of personality similarity on peer ratings of contextual work behaviors. *Journal of Applied Psychology, 54*, 331–360.

Bales, R.F. (1970). *Personality and interpersonal behavior.* New York: Holt, Rinehart and Winston.

Barrick, M.R., & Mount, M.K. (1991). The big five personality dimensions and job performance: A meta-analysis. *Personnel Psychology, 44*, 1–26.

Barrick, M.R., & Mount, M.K. (1994, April). *Do specific components of conscientiousness predict better than the overall construct?* Paper presented at the symposium, Personality and Job Performance: Big Five versus Specific Traits, conducted at the meeting for the Society for Industrial and Organizational Psychology, Nashville, TN.

Barrick, M.R., & Mount, M.K. (1996). Effects of impression management and self-deception on the predictive validity of personality constructs. *Journal of Applied Psychology, 81*, 261–272.

Barrick, M.R., & Mount, M.K. (2002). The interactive effects of conscientiousness and agreeableness on job performance. *Journal of Applied Psychology, 87*, 164–169.

Barrick, M.R., Stewart, G.L., Neubert, M.J., & Mount, M.K. (1998). Relating member ability and personality to work-team processes and team effectiveness. *Journal of Applied Psychology, 83*, 377–391.

Barry, B., & Stewart, G.L. (1997). Composition, process, and performance in self-managed groups: The role of personality. *Journal of Applied Psychology, 82*, 62–78.

Bartlett, C.J., Bobko, P., Mosier, S.B., & Hannan, R. (1978). Testing for fairness with a moderated multiple regression strategy: An alternative to differential analysis. *Personnel Psychology, 31*, 233–241.

Bass, B.M. (1985). *Leadership and performance beyond expectations.* New York: Free Press.

Bernardin, H.J., Cooke, D.K., & Villanova, P. (2000). Conscientiousness and agreeableness as predictors of rating leniency. *Journal of Applied Psychology, 85*, 232–236.

Block, J. (1961). *The Q-Sort method in personality assessment and psychiatric research.* Palo Alto, CA: Consulting Psychologists Press.

Borman, W.C., & Motowidlo, S.J. (1993). Expanding the criterion domain to include elements of contextual performance. In N. Schmitt & W.C. Borman (Eds.), *Personnel selection in organizations* (pp. 71–98). San Francisco: Jossey-Bass.

Burke, L.A., & Witt, L.A. (2001). *Moderators of the openness to experience-job performance relationship.* Paper presented at the meeting of the Society for Industrial and Organizational Psychology, San Diego, CA.

Buss, A.H. (1997). Evolutionary perspectives on personality traits. In R. Hogan & J.A. Johnson (Eds.), *Handbook of personality psychology* (pp. 346–366). San Diego: Academic Press.

Buss, A.H. & Plomin, R. (1984). *A temperament theory personality development.* New York: Wiley.

Byravan, A., & Ramanaiah, N.V. (1995). Structure of the 16 PF fifth edition from the perspective of the five-factor model. *Psychological Reports, 76*, 555–560.

Caligiuri, P.M. (2000). The big five personality characteristics as predictors of expatriate's desire to terminate the assignment and supervisor-rated performance. *Personnel Psychology, 53*, 67–88.

Caprara, G.V., Barbaranelli, C., Hahn, R., & Comrey, A.L. (2001). Factor analyses of the NEO-PI-R Inventory and the Comrey Personality Scales in Italy and the United States. *Personality and Individual Differences, 30*, 217–228.

Cattell, R.B. (1943). The description of personality: Basic traits resolved into clusters. *Journal of Abnormal Social Psychology, 38*, 476–506.

Cattell, R.B., Eber, H.W., & Tatsuoka, M.M. (1970). *Handbook for the 16 Personality Factor Questionnaire.* Champaign, IL: Institute for Personality and Ability Testing.

Cellar, D.F., Doverspike, D.D., Miller, M.L., & Klawsky, J.D. (1996). Comparison and criterion-related validity coefficients for two measures of personality based on the five-factor model. *Journal of Applied Psychology, 81,* 694–704.

Cronbach, L.J., & Gesler, G.C. (1957). *Psychological tests and personnel decisions.* Urbana: University of Illinois Press.

Comrey, A.L. (1970). *Manual for the Comrey Personality Scales.* San Diego, CA: Education and Industrial Testing Services.

Cooper, R., & Payne, R. (1966). Extraversion and some aspects of work behavior. *Personnel Psychology, 29,* 45–57.

Costa, P.T. Jr., & McCrae, R.R. (1992). *NEO PI-R: Professional Manual.* Odessa, FL: Psychological Assessment Resources.

Crant, J.M. (1995). The Proactive Personality Scale and objective job performance among real estate agents. *Journal of Applied Psychology, 80,* 532–537.

Day, D.V., & Silverman, S.B. (1989). Personality and job performance: Evidence of incremental validity. *Personnel Psychology, 42,* 25–36.

Douglas, E.F., McDaniel, M.A., & Snell, A.F. (1996). The validity of non-cognitive measures decays when applicants fake. *Proceedings of Academy of Management, USA,* 127–131.

Dunn, W.S., Mount, M.K., Barrick, M.R., & Ones, D.S. (1995). Relative importance of personality and general mental ability in managers' judgments of applicant qualifications. *Journal of Applied Psychology, 80,* 500–509.

Egan, V., Deary, I., & Austin, E. (2000). The NEO-FFI: Emerging British norms and an item-level analysis suggests N, A, and C are more reliable than O and E. *Personality and Individual Differences, 29,* 907–920.

Ellingson, J.E., Sackett, P.R., & Hough, L.M. (1999). Social desirability in personality measurement: Issues of applicant comparison and construct validity. *Journal of Applied Psychology, 84,* 155–166.

Eysenck, H.J., & Eysenck, M.W. (1985). *Personality and individual differences: A natural science approach.* New York: Plenum.

Fiske, D.W. (1949). Consistency of the factorial structures of personality ratings from different sources. *Journal of Abnormal Social Psychology, 44,* 329–344.

Furnham, A., Crump, J., & Whelan, J. (1997). Validating the NEO Personality Inventory using assessor's ratings. *Personality and Individual Differences, 22,* 669–675.

Furnham, A., & Zacherl, M. (1986). Personality and job satisfaction. *Personality and Individual Differences, 7,* 453–459.

George, J.M. (1989). Mood and absence. *Journal of Applied Psychology, 74,* 317–324.

Gellatly, I.R. (1996). Conscientiousness and task performance: Test of a cognitive process model. *Journal of Applied Psychology, 81,* 474–482.

Gifford, R. (1991). Mapping nonverbal behavior on the interpersonal circle. *Journal of Personality and Social Psychology, 61,* 279–288.

Goldberg, L.R. (1990). An alternative "description of personality": The Big Five factor structure. *Journal of Personality and Social Psychology, 59,* 1216–1229.

Goldberg, L.R. (1992). The development of markers for the big-five factor structure. *Psychological Assessment, 4,* 26–42.

Goldberg, L.R. (1993). The structure of phenotypic personality traits. *American Psychologist, 48,* 26–34.

Gough, H.G., & Bradley, P. (1996). *CPI manual* (3rd ed.). Palo Alto, CA: Consulting Psychologists Press.

Griffith, R. (1997). *Faking of non-cognitive selection devices: Red herring is hard to swallow.* Unpublished doctoral dissertation, University of Akron, Akron, OH.

Guilford, J.P. (1975). Factors and factors of personality. *Psychological Bulletin, 81,* 820–814.

Harkness, A.R. (1992). Fundamental topics in the personality disorders: Candidate trait dimensions from lower regions of the hierarchy. *Psychological Assessment, 4,* 251–259.

Harkness, A.R., & McNully, J.L. (1994). The Personality Psychopathology Five (PSY-5): Issues from the pages of a diagnostic manual instead of a dictionary. In S. Strack & M. Lorr (Eds.), *Differentiating normal and abnormal personality* (pp. 291–315). New York: Springer.

Hartigan, J.A., & Wigdor, A.K. (Eds.). (1989). *Fairness in employment testing: Validity generalization, minority issues, and the General Aptitude Test Battery.* Washington, DC: National Academy Press.

Hathaway, S.R., & McKinley, J.C. (Rev. 1967). *Minnesota Multiphasic Personality Inventory manual.* New York: The Psychological Corporation.

Hattrup, K., Rock, J., & Scalia, C. (1997). The effects of varying conceptualizations of job performance on adverse impact, minority hiring, and predicted performance. *Journal of Applied Psychology, 82,* 656–664.

Hendriks, A.A.J., Hofstee, W.K.B., & De Raad, B. (1999). The Five-Factor Personality Inventory (FFPI). *Personality and Individual Differences, 27,* 307–325.

Hochwarter, W.A., Witt, L.A., & Kacmar, K.M. (2000). Perceptions of organizational politics as a moderator of the relationship between conscientiousness and job performance. *Journal of Applied Psychology, 85,* 472–478.

Hogan, R. (1986). *Hogan Personality Inventory manual.* Minneapolis: National Computer Systems.

Hogan, R., & Hogan, J. (1992). *Hogan Personality Inventory manual.* Tulsa, OK: Hogan Assessment Systems.

Hough, L.M. (1992). The "Big Five" personality variables-construct confusion: Description versus prediction. *Human Performance, 5,* 139–155.

Hough, L.M. (1998). Personality at work: Issues and evidence. In M. Hakel (Ed.), *Beyond multiple choice: Evaluating alternatives to traditional testing for selection* (pp. 131–166). Hillsdale, NJ: Erlbaum.

Hough, L.M., Eaton, N.K., Dunnette, M.D., Kamp, J.D., & McCloy, R.A. (1990). Criterion-related validities of personality constructs and the effects of response distortion on those validities. *Journal of Applied Psychology, 75,* 581–595.

Hough, L.M., & Oswald, F.L. (2000). Personnel selection: Looking toward the future—Remembering the past. *Annual Review of Psychology, 51,* 631–664.

Hough, L.M., & Schneider, R.J. (1996). Personality traits, taxonomies, and applications in organizations. In K.R. Murphy's (Ed.), *Individual differences and behavior in organizations* (pp. 31–88). San Francisco: Jossey-Bass.

Hurtz, G.M., & Donovan, J.J. (2000). Personality and job performance: The big five revisited. *Journal of Applied Psychology, 85,* 869–879.

Jackson, D.N. (1964). *Personality Research Form manual.* Port Huron, MI: Research Psychologists Press.

Jackson, D.N. (1976). *Manual for the Jackson Personality Inventory.* Goshen, NY: Research Psychologists Press.

Jackson, D.N., & Helmes, E. (1979). Basic structure content scaling. *Applied Psychological Measurement, 3,* 313–325.

John, O.P. (1990). The "Big Five" factor taxonomy: Dimensions of personality in the natural language and in questionnaires. In L.A. Pervin (Ed.), *Handbook of personality: Theory and research* (pp. 102–138). New York: Guilford.

Judge, T.A., & Bono, J.E. (2000). Five-factor model of personality and transformational leadership. *Journal of Applied Psychology, 85,* 751–765.

Judge, T.A., Higgins, C.A., Thoreson, C.J., & Barrick, M.R. (1999). The big five personality traits, general mental ability, and career success across the life span. *Personnel Psychology, 52,* 621–652.

Judge, T.A., Matocchio, J.J., & Thoresen, C.J. (1997). Five-factor model of personality and employee absence. *Journal of Applied Psychology, 82,* 745–755.

LePine, J.A., & Van Dyne, L. (2001). Voice and cooperative behavior as contrasting forms of contextual performance: Evidence of differential relationships with Big Five personality characteristics and cognitive ability. *Journal of Applied Psychology, 86,* 326–336.

Lievens, F., De Fruyt, F., & Van Dam, K. (2001). Assessors' use of personality traits in descriptions of assessment center candidates: A five-factor model perspective. *Journal of Occupational and Organizational Psychology, 74,* 623–636.

Martocchio, J.J., & Judge, T.A. (1997). Relationship between conscientiousness and learning in employee training: Mediating influences of self-deception and self-efficacy. *Journal of Applied Psychology, 82,* 764–773.

Maxwell, S.E., & Arvey, R.D. (1993). The search for predictors with high validity and low adverse impact: Compatible or incompatible goals? *Journal of Applied Psychology, 78,* 433–437.

McCrae, R.R., & Costa, P.T. Jr. (1989). Reinterpreting the Myers-Briggs Type Indicator from the perspective of the five-factor model of personality. *Journal of Personality, 57,* 17–40.

McDougall, W. (1932). Of the words character and personality. *Character Personality, 1,* 3–16.

McManus, M.A., & Kelly, M.L. (1999). Personality measures and biodata: Evidence regarding incremental value in the life insurance industry. *Personnel Psychology, 52,* 137–148.

Motowidlo, S.J., & Van Scotter, J.R. (1994). Evidence of task performance should be distinguished from contextual performance. *Journal of Applied Psychology, 79,* 475–480.

Mount, M.K., & Barrick, M.R. (1995). The Big Five personality dimensions: Implications for research and practice in human resources management. In K.M. Rowland & G. Ferris (Eds.), *Research in personnel and human resources management* (pp. 153–200). Greenwich, CT: JAI Press.

Murphy, K.R. (1993). *Honesty in the workplace.* Pacific Grove, CA: Brooks/Cole.

Myers, I.B., & McCaulley, M.H. (1985). *Manual: A guide to the development and use of the Myers-Briggs Type Indicator.* Palo Alto, CA: Consulting Psychologists Press.

Neuman, G.A., Wagner, S.H., & Christiansen, N.D. (1999). The relationship between work-team personality composition and the job performance of teams. *Group and Organization Management, 24,* 28–45.

Norman, W.T. (1963). Toward an adequate taxonomy of personality attributes: Replicated factor structure of peer nomination personality ratings. *Journal of Abnormal and Social Psychology, 66,* 574–583.

Ones, D.S., & Viswesvaran, C. (1996). Bandwidth-fidelity dilemma in personality measurement for personnel selection. *Journal of Organizational Behavior, 17,* 609–626.

Ones, D.S., Viswesvaran, C., & Schmidt, F.L. (1993). Comprehensive meta-analysis of integrity test validities: Findings and implications for personnel selection and theories of job performance. *Journal of Applied Psychology, 78,* 679–703.

Polyhart, R.E., Lim, B., & Chan, K. (2001). Exploring relations between typical and maximum performance ratings and the five-factor model of personality. *Personnel Psychology, 54,* 809–843.

Paunonen, S.V., & Jackson, D.N. (2000). What is beyond the Big Five? Plenty! *Journal of Personality, 68,* 821–835.

Paunonen, S.V., Rothstein, M.G., & Jackson, D.N. (1999). Narrow reasoning about the use of broad personality measures for personnel selection. *Journal of Organizational Behavior, 20,* 389–405.

Pulakos, E.D., & Schmitt, N. (1996). An evaluation of two strategies for reducing adverse impact and their effects on criterion-related validity. *Human Performance, 9,* 241–258.

Rosse, J.G., Stecher, M.D., Miller, J.L., & Levin, R.A. (1998). The impact of response distortion on preemployment personality testing and hiring decisions. *Journal of Applied Psychology, 83,* 634–644.

Ryan, A.M., Ployhart, R.E., & Friedel, L.A. (1998). Using personality testing to reduce adverse impact: A cautionary note. *Journal of Applied Psychology, 83,* 298–307.

Salgado, J.F. (1997). The five factor model of personality and job performance in the European community. *Journal of Applied Psychology, 82,* 30–43.

Saucier, G., & Goldberg, L.R. (1996). The language of personality: Lexical perspectives on the five-factor model. In J.S. Wiggins (Ed.), *The five-factor model of personality: Theoretical perspectives* (pp. 21–50). New York: Guilford Press.

Schaubroeck, J., Ganster, D.C., & Jones, J.R. (1998). Organization and occupation influences in the attraction-selection-attrition process. *Journal of Applied Psychology, 83,* 869–891.

Schmidt, F.L., & Hunter, J.E. (1998). The validity and utility of selection methods in personnel psychology: Practical and theoretical implications of 85 years of research findings. *Psychological Bulletin, 124,* 262–274.

Schmidt, F.L., Hunter, J.A., & Pearlman, K. (1983). Assessing the economic impact of personnel programs on workforce productivity. *Personnel Psychology, 35,* 333–347.

Smith, C.A., Organ, D.W., & Near, J.P. (1983). Organizational citizenship behavior: Its nature and antecedents. *Journal of Applied Psychology, 68,* 653–663.

Smith, D.B., Hanges, P.J., & Dickson, M.W. (2001). Personnel selection and the five-factor model: Reexamining the effects of applicant's frame of reference. *Journal of Applied Psychology, 86,* 304–315.

Stewart, G.L. (1999). Trait bandwidth and stages of job performance: Assessing differential effects for conscientiousness and its subtraits. *Journal Applied Psychology, 84,* 959–968.

Taubert, S. (1999). *Development and validation of a psychometric instrument for the assessment of proactive coping.* Unpublished master's thesis.

Tellegen, A. (1985). Structures of mood and personality in their relevance in assessing anxiety, with an emphasis on self-report. In A.H. Tuma & J.D. Maser (Eds.), *Anxiety and anxiety disorders* (pp. 681–706). Hillside, NJ: Erlbaum.

Tett, R.P., Jackson, D.N., & Rothstein, M. (1991). Personality measures as predictors of job performance: A meta-analytic review. *Personnel Psychology, 44,* 703–742.

Tett, R.P., Jackson, D.N., Rothstein, M., & Reddon, J.R. (1994). Meta analysis of personality job performance relations—A reply to Ones, Mount, Barrick, & Hunter (1994). *Personnel Psychology, 47,* 157–172.

Tokar, D.M., & Subich, L.M. (1997). Relative contributions of congruence and personality dimensions to job satisfaction. *Journal of Vocational Behavior, 50,* 482–491.

Trapnell, P.D., & Wiggins, J.S. (1990). Extension of the Interpersonal Adjective Scale to include Big Five dimensions of personality. *Journal of Personality and Social Psychology, 59,* 781–790.

Tupes, E.C. (1957). *Personality traits related to effectiveness of junior and senior Air Force officers* (USAF Personnel Training Research, No. 57–125). Lackland Air Force Base, TX: Aeronautical Systems Division, Personnel Laboratory.

Tupes, E.C., & Christol, R.E. (1961). *Recurrent personality factors based on trait ratings* (ASD-TR-61-97). Lackland Air Force Base, TX: Aeronautical Systems Division, Personnel Laboratory.

Van Scotter, J.R., & Motowidlo, S.J. (1996). Interpersonal facilitation and job dedication as separate facets of contextual performance. *Journal of Applied Psychology, 81,* 525–531.

Vinchur, A.J., Schippman, J.S., Switzer, F.S., & Roth, P.L. (1998). A meta-analytic review of predictors of job performance for salespeople. *Journal of Applied Psychology, 83,* 586–597.

Viswesvaran, C., & Ones, D.S. (1999). Meta-analysis of fakability estimates: Implications for personality measurement. *Educational and Psychological Measurement, 59,* 197–210.

Widiger, T.A., & Trull, T.J. (1997). Assessment of the five-factor model of personality. *Journal of Personality Assessment, 68,* 228–250.

Wiggins, J.S. (1979). A psychological taxonomy of trait-descriptive terms: The interpersonal domain. *Journal of Personality and Social Psychology, 37,* 395–412.

Wiggins, J.S. (1995). *Interpersonal Adjective Scales: Professional manual.* Odessa, FL: Psychological Assessment Resources.

Wiggins, J.S., & Trapnell, P.D. (1996). A dyadic-interactional perspective on the five-factor model. In J.S. Wiggins (Ed.), *The five-factor model of personality:Theoretical perspectives* (pp. 88–162). New York: Guilford Press.

Witt, L.A. (2000). Extroverts low in conscientiousness produce the greatest sales volume. Manuscript submitted for publication.

Witt, L.A., Burke, L.A., Barrick, M.R., Mount, M.K. (in press). The interaction effects of conscientiousness and agreeableness on job performance. *Journal of Applied Psychology.*

CHAPTER 9

# Specific Personality Measures

PAUL E. LEVY, RICHARD T. COBER, AND CHRISTINA NORRIS-WATTS

## INTRODUCTION

Perhaps more than any other predictor or assessment technique in industrial/organizational (I/O) psychology, personality scales have received a great deal of recent attention from the research community (Hurtz & Donovan, 2000; Mount, Witt, & Barrick, 2000). Personality assessment in organizations has a long history as well; personality tests were used even in the 1930s and 1940s to identify those individuals who were likely to become assertive union members or who were described back then as "thugs" or "agitators" (Zickar, in press). Personality refers to an individual's traits or predispositions to behave in a particular way across situations. Personality measurement includes any procedures that systematically assign numbers to characteristics of individuals based on a set of rules (Hogan, Hogan, & Roberts, 1996). Chapter 8 presented and discussed the "Big Five" model of personality (i.e., Openness to Experience, Conscientiousness, Extraversion, Agreeableness, and Neuroticism) and the various measures that are often used to tap into these constructs in an assessment context. This chapter reviews and discusses the assessment of more specific personality constructs that do not fall within the framework of the five-factor model.

Many personality researchers argue that it makes rational sense to use personality to predict performance because job analyses of incumbents usually result in statements reflective of personality, including "being a team player," "being responsive to client's needs," and "taking initiative," as char-

acteristic of excellent job performance (Hogan et al., 1996). In addition, there is a good deal of empirical research, much of which was reviewed in Chapter 8, suggesting that global personality measures are valid predictors of job performance (e.g. Barrick & Mount, 1991; Hough, 1998). Although estimating the size of the validity coefficient between personality and on-the-job performance is very difficult because so many personality dimensions have been examined in this light, one meta-analysis indexed the relationship between personality and managerial performance as being .24 (Tett, Jackson, & Rothstein, 1991). Barrick and Mount (1991) reported Conscientiousness (i.e., being dependable and hardworking) and Extraversion (i.e., being sociable and active) to be the best predictors of performance, and, thus, these two dimensions have received the most attention.

It seems clear that personality predicts performance on the job, but some personality researchers argue that our estimates (e.g., .24 noted in the last paragraph) are underestimates because in most studies specific personality dimensions are not linked to specific criteria. In fact, Hough (1998) argued that the five-factor model results in dimensions that are "too fat" and that prediction will be improved to the extent that specific personality dimensions are used to predict targeted performance criteria like effort and leadership, personal discipline, and counterproductive behavior. Project A data seem to support her arguments. In this very large data set, general cognitive ability, spatial ability, and psychomotor ability all predicted core job performance very well ($r$s = .63, .56, and

.53, respectively), but they did not predict personal discipline (i.e., the extent to which the individual follows army regulations and demonstrates responsibility) or effort/leadership (i.e., perseverance in adverse situations and leadership toward peers) nearly as well (coefficients ranged from .12 to .31). On the other hand, specific personality dimensions like achievement orientation and dependability predicted both personal discipline and effort/leadership better ($rs = .33$ and .32) than did any of the cognitive or psychomotor tests (McHenry, Hough, Toquam, Hanson, & Ashworth, 1990). These data support the potential benefits of specific personality predictors as assessment instruments in I/O psychology.

The debate over the potential importance of specific personality constructs separate from Big Five constructs has been called the "bandwidth-fidelity dilemma" and is defined by "whether broadly defined personality traits are better in predicting job performance as well as in explaining behaviors, than narrowly defined personality traits" (Ones & Viswesvaran, 1996; p. 610). Some researchers have argued that Big Five dimensions have great bandwidth, which limits their ability to predict specific criteria—too much data is lost when traits are categorized at such a general level (Ashton, 1998; Hough, 1998). Hough (1998) has argued that although specific personality constructs do not predict overall job performance so well, they do predict targeted performance criteria well and that matching the personality predictor to the criterion is the optimal way to improve prediction. Other investigators argue that broader personality measures are superior to more specific measures and that we will gain a better understanding of the personality determinants of performance through a focus on global personality measures (Ones & Viswesvaran, 1996).

The perspective taken here is that although measuring personality at the broad level such as is done within the framework of the Big Five is useful, a great deal can be gained from the assessment of specific personality traits. As suggested by Paunonen, Rothstein, and Jackson (1999), an emphasis on specific personality constructs can result in a better psychological understanding of the personality-work behavior relationships. Although practitioners in I/O psychology recognize that criteria are multidimensional, Paunonen et al. (1999) suggested that predicting these multidimensional criteria is better served by using specific, homogenous personality predictors (along with other types of predictors such as cognitive ability) than it is by combining these specific personality predictors into a less homogeneous composite or more general factor. Ashton (1998) said it very well, "It is likely that for some jobs, performance will be predicted optimally by broad measures, such as the Big Five factors. But the results of this study indicate that this is unlikely to be the

case for many other jobs, and that the use of narrow personality scales will be necessary to achieve maximum validity. Exclusive reliance upon broad personality measures is likely to limit validity in many employment contexts" (pp. 300–301).

Many of the leading figures in the area of I/O personality assessment suggest that predictors other than the Big Five are important and merit the attention of both researchers and practitioners. For instance, the breadth of Leaetta Hough's work is quite impressive, and she has consistently argued that the Big Five is inadequate and that it confuses the personality domain by specifying too few traits at too broad a level (Hough, 1992). Doug Jackson and his colleagues have done extensive work in the area of personality assessment within I/O contexts. He and Sampo Paunonen have been vocal in suggesting that the Big Five conceptualization is ineffective in furthering our understanding of personality at work. They have also provided empirical data that support the importance of more narrow measures of personality as providing incremental validity beyond that accounted for by more global dimensions (see Paunonen, 1998; Paunonen & Jackson, 2000; Paunonen et al., 1999). They conclude one of their papers by noting that much important variance in human behavior is not accounted for by the Big Five factors. If other more narrow, theoretically meaningful personality dimensions can be identified, they argue, and shown to predict some important criteria, then they are worthy of our interest and our exploration (Paunonen & Jackson, 2000). The bulk of this chapter is devoted to a survey of non-Big-Five personality predictors that seem to meet these criteria and/or have attracted considerable interest from practitioners and researchers. However, before we discuss the specific predictors, the next section of this chapter briefly outlines some issues of practical importance when considering organizational assessment in the twenty-first century.

## TWENTY-FIRST-CENTURY PRACTICAL ISSUES AND CONSIDERATIONS

When using any type of assessment measure in organizations, researchers and practitioners must consider three important questions: (1) Can the assessment instrument be used for all employees regardless of disabilities and other factors? (2) will the use of the assessment instrument present the potential for legal problems for the client/organization? and (3) can the instrument be administered in an efficient and unobtrusive manner? In light of these three issues, significant research attention has begun to focus on how information technology (IT) can facilitate organizational functioning (Dewett & Jones,

2001). Specifically, IT tools can be used to revolutionize the administration of self-report assessments.

In the twenty-first-century workplace, IT can positively affect the employee assessment process in a number of different ways. First, computer-based assessments can utilize voice-activation software and automatic manipulation of fonts/ screen sizes to facilitate data collection from all employees, regardless of disability. The organizational justice literature has proposed that organizational activities, like assessments, that employees perceive to be fair are less likely to lead to the filing of legal grievances (Dunford & Devine, 1998). One way to increase justice perceptions is to provide employees with information about the assessment process as well as immediate feedback regarding their responses (Colquitt, 2001). Therefore, a second way IT tools can be used in the assessment process is to facilitate assessment administration by providing more information about the processes involved and quickly delivering feedback to participants about their responses. Finally, IT enables organizations to effectively administer information-gathering assessments (Huber, 1990) and increase the accuracy of self-report responses. Assessments can be sent instantaneously to thousands of employees who can then automatically enter their responses into databases, accelerating the pace of information gathering. However, it is important that this acceleration not sacrifice the accuracy of assessment information.

One problem encountered with the use of self-report assessments is that responses can be intentionally faked or scales may not accurately reflect individual evaluations of item content because respondents' exert low effort in determining responses (Krosnick, 1991; Tourangeau & Rasinski, 1988). Schmit and Ryan (1992) found that individual attitudes toward taking a survey moderated the validity of a personality test used to predict performance. With computer-based assessments, scaling can be altered to capture more accurate responses to self-report items, and the relative ease with which a survey can be completed over the computer should have at least a minimally positive effect on response effort. Further, item presentation can be modified to more accurately measure a construct and increase the "interactivity" of a scale. For instance, Borman et al. (2001) have successfully used computer-adapted assessments to measure contextual performance in organizations.

## ASSESSMENT CONSTRUCTS

We now turn our attention to a description of important, non-Big-Five personality constructs often used in the I/O literature. Although the application of IT advancements are not directly discussed in the following sections, the issues discussed here are relevant to each assessment technique and should be kept in mind throughout the chapter.

### Proactive Personality Scale (PPS)

Proactive behavior has been mentioned and studied often in organizational research as a critical determinant of individual, group, and organizational success (Crant, 2000). Table 9.1 provides a summary of our review. Bateman and Crant (1993) developed the Proactive Personality Scale (PPS) to measure stable tendencies to engage in proactive behavior. Such behavior involves choosing courses of action to affect one's environment regardless of situational constraints. In other words, an individual with a highly proactive personality is one who aggressively acts to change his or her environment or to take control over life situations. The PPS is still a relatively new measure, but it has been prominently used in several recent high-quality publications (Crant, 1995; Crant & Bateman, 2000; Seibert, Crant, & Kraimer, 1999). The scale has demonstrated convergent validity with Locus of Control (Rotter, 1966), as well as both Need for Achievement and Dominance as assessed by the Personality Research Form (PRF). Scores on the PPS positively correlate with individual and team-level job performance (Crant, 1995; Kirkman & Rosen, 1999), organizational innovation (Parker, 1998), and perceptions of charismatic leadership (Crant & Bateman, 2000). There is a short-form, 10-item version that makes the PPS efficient to use. Because of the criterion relationships and nature of the measure, the PPS could prove a useful tool for personnel selection and employee development across many jobs. However, research is needed to determine whether scores on the PPS vary across gender, racial, or ethnic samples so that any potential legal issues pertaining to its use in employee assessment can be clarified and addressed.

### Sensation Seeking

When sensation seeking became a popular topic in psychological research, the focus of such research was certainly not on assessing this personality trait for organizational purposes. Rather, interest in this construct focused on understanding and predicting individual differences, and often on explaining why some individuals preferred more extreme situations. However, certain jobs (e.g., law enforcement, telephone line repair) require individuals who are more comfortable in more dangerous positions, and for these positions an assessment of the Sensation-Seeking construct may be very valuable. This scale is also applicable in other less dangerous occupations, especially when subscales of interest relevant for particular

**TABLE 9.1  Proactive Personality Scale (PPS)**

| | |
|---|---|
| Primary Researchers | • Bateman & Crant (1993); Crant (1995, 2000) |
| Description | • Self-report; scored on either a 5-point or 7-point Likert scale; 17-item full-version scale; 10-item short form. |
| Theoretical Basis | • Bateman & Crant (1993) define Proactive Personality as the relatively stable tendency to affect environmental change. People who have proactive personalities are unconstrained by situational factors when choosing courses of action. Such people identify opportunities and act on them until they bring about meaningful change (Seibert, Crant, & Kraimer, 1999). |
| Test Development | • Bateman & Crant (1993); Based on prior work regarding proactive behavior in organizations, a self-report scale was developed to measure the construct (originally 27 items). Construct validity was assessed by comparing it to Big Five factors, Locus of Control, Need for Achievement, and Need for Dominance. Criterion validity was assessed by examining relationships between the PPS and the nature of people's extracurricular and civic activities, personal achievements, and transformational leadership. They also outlined conceptual differences between the construct of Proactive Personality and the personality constructs used to validate the PPS. |
| Psychometric Characteristics | • Cronbach's alpha across 3 samples ranged from .87 to .89, test-retest reliability = .72 (at 3 months), and factor analysis suggested a unidimensional scale (Bateman & Crant, 1993). |
| | • 10-item short form correlated .96 with full version, $\alpha$ = .86 (Seibert et al., 1999). |
| | • 17 item scale $\alpha$ = .85 (Crant & Bateman, 2000). |
| Construct Validity | • Correlations with other constructs are as follows (Bateman & Crant, 1993): Locus of Control, $r$ = .18 (Rotter, 1966); Need for Achievement, $r$ = .45, and Need for Dominance, $r$ = .43 (Jackson PRF); Discriminant validity found between PPS and Big Five factors (Costa & McCrae, 1989) as well. |
| | • Criterion Validity (Bateman & Crant, 1993): Extracurricular Activities, $r$ = .26; Personal Achievements, $r$ = .18; Transformational Leadership, $r$ = .30. |
| Range of Application | • 10-item version facilitates assessment while maintaining factor structure and reliability. |
| Cross-cultural Research | • None |
| Current Research Status | • Crant and colleagues have used the PPS to explain a variety of organizational phenomenon (see below). |
| Use in Organizational Practice | • Relationships between Proactive Personality and the following factors have been established (Crant, 2000): Individual Job Performance, $r$ = .23 (Crant, 1995); Objective ($r$ = .15 for salary, $r$ = .17 for number of promotions) and Subjective ($r$ = .31) career outcomes (Siebert et al., 1999); Leadership, $r$ = .35 between manager PPS and perceptions of Charisma (Crant & Bateman, 2000); Role Breadth Self-Efficacy, $r$ = .44 (Parker, 1998); Team Performance, $r$ = .70 between team PPS and Team Productivity (Kirkman & Rosen, 1999); and Entrepreneurship, $r$ = .48 (Crant, 1996). |
| Future Developments | • Research has been limited to the study of main effects (Crant, 2000; Seibert et al., 1999). Future studies should examine variables that mediate or moderate the relationships between Proactive Personality and outcomes like career success and performance. |
| Limitations | • The PPS is still a new measure. Proactive Personality may operate differently across occupations (Seibert et al., 1999), which would affect its utility for selection and development purposes. Also, there has been no research with regard to how individuals from different backgrounds (race, culture, gender, and age) score on the PPS. |

jobs are examined. For example, an individual low on the Boredom Susceptibility scale may be a good fit for a more typical job low on danger, risk, and excitement. Similarly, knowing one's own level of sensation seeking may aid in career placement. Table 9.2 provides a summary of our review of sensation seeking.

Four factors make up the Sensation-Seeking Scale. The first, Thrill and Adventure Seeking (TAS) measures an individual's preference for engaging in activities that involve speed or danger (Zuckerman, Bone, Neary, Mangelsdorff, & Brustman, 1972). Experience Seeking (ES) measures a preference for nonconformity and an unconventional lifestyle in-

cluding an interest in the arts and travel. Disinhibition (DIS) measures an individual's extraverted preferences for inhibition and "wild" social gatherings. Boredom Susceptibility (BS) measures one's dislike of routine and monotonous activities (Zuckerman et al., 1972). Each of these facets of the Sensation-Seeking Scale can be used on its own, and some have been found to correlate with different outcome variables. For instance, alcohol experience was found to only significantly correlate with DIS and TAS in a male sample and was actually negatively related to BS (Zuckerman et al., 1972). Due to high intercorrelations among the facets, the scale is usually used as a whole.

**TABLE 9.2   Sensation-Seeking Scale**

| | |
|---|---|
| Primary Researchers | • Zuckerman and others (Form V—Zuckerman, Eysenck, & Eysenck, 1978) |
| Description | • Self-report; forced choice; four subscales: Thrill and Adventure Seeking (TAS), Experience Seeking (ES), Disinhibition (DIS), Boredom Susceptibility (BS). |
| Theoretical Basis | • Based on assumption that people differ in their optimal levels of stimulation/arousal, and that this difference is really a stable personality trait not measured by other instruments. |
| Test Development | • Zuckerman et al. (1964) created the Sensation-Seeking Scale (SSS). Construct validity was originally demonstrated via correlations with autonomy ( + ), change ( + ), exhibitionism ( + ), deference ( − ), nurturance ( − ), orderliness ( − ), affiliation ( − ). |
| | • The third form was written with new items added to tap the dimensional nature of the sensation-seeking construct. |
| | • The most recent form (Form V) contains 44 forced-choice items. |
| Psychometric Characteristics | • Male and female subscale scores differed for TAS, ES, and DIS. Four factors account for 20–23% of the variance (Rowland & Franken, 1986). |
| | • Reliabilities (Cronbach's alpha): TAS = .69 (.72M, .67F), ES = .54 (.57M, .53F), DIS = .65 (.71M, .54F), BS = .48 (.51M, .44F), Total Scale = .75 (.80M, .68F). Factors intercorrelated from .02 to .40 (Ridgeway & Russell, 1980) |
| Construct Validity | • A positive correlation was found between each subscale and the total scale score. A negative correlation was found between an achievement motivation scale and the DIS. The DIS correlated negatively with Sensing scores of the MBTI and positively with Intuition scores (Goldsmith, 1985). |
| Range of Application | • Some research has presented evidence that sensation-seeking behaviors may be present at time of test administration, and sensation seekers may require a more novel presentation of the test (Rogers, 1987). |
| Cross-cultural Research | • American and Canadian samples exhibited similar results. (Ridgeway & Russell, 1980). Not much research with non-Western cultures. |
| | • Test may have differential validity for males and females. |
| Current Research Status | • Correlating sensation seeking with other factors, such as Antisocial Behavior, Criminal Behavior, Impulsivity, Substance Abuse, Gambling, and Temperament. |
| Use in Organizational Practice | • Used with police (those on the force longer may have lower sensation-seeking rates) (Carlson & Lester, 1980). Sensation-seeking has been examined in relation to work stress (Rudestam, 1986). |
| Future Developments | • How sensation seeking is related to emotional regulation at work. How sensation seeking may be related to the acceptance of organizational norms. |
| Limitations | • Research has indicated that some items do not load on relevant dimensions, although there is conflicting evidence regarding this. Researchers should be cautioned when using this measure with samples composed of both genders. |

## Myers-Briggs Type Indicator (MBTI)

The MBTI was developed to measure personality by extending Jungian theory (Center for the Applications of Personality Type [CAPT], 2001). It is a typology that assesses the extent to which an individual has a dominant preference toward certain behaviors and modes of thinking (see Table 9.3). A common misconception about scores on the MBTI is that they indicate a totally dominant preference toward one of the types (e.g., Extraversion or Introversion). However, MBTI researchers have recognized the important information revealed by "shadow" scores, as nondominant preferences can still exert significant influence over individual behavior. The scoring of this instrument, though helpful for individual level diagnostic information, is not conducive to traditionally sound empirical research (Gardner & Martinko, 1996). Therefore, after more than 50 years of use in organizations, scholars still debate the reliability, validity, and factor structure of the MBTI (Gardner

& Martinko, 1996; Sipps, Alexander, & Friedt, 1985; Tzeng, Ware, & Chen, 1989).

Despite its psychometric shortcomings, the MBTI is the most administered personality test in history (CAPT, 2001). Approximately 2 million people take the MBTI every year, and it is currently available in more than 20 languages (Coe, 1992; Gardner & Martinko, 1996; CAPT, 2001). Practitioners find the MBTI to be helpful in organizational interventions and training involving teamwork, communication, and conflict management. One common misuse of the MBTI is to use it to "type out" individuals from certain kinds of jobs or work teams (Coe, 1992). Such a use is inconsistent with the intention of the measure and would be a legally questionable organizational practice. Alternate measures of the MBTI types using continuous variable scoring have been developed to test relationships between the preferences and different criteria in more psychometrically sound ways (Tzeng et al., 1989). Future research should use such scales to demonstrate more

**TABLE 9.3 Myers-Briggs Type Indicator (MBTI)**

| | |
|---|---|
| Primary Researchers | • Myers & McCaulley (1985); Nordvick (1994, 1996); Gardner & Martinko (1996); Center for the Applications of Personality Type (CAPT; 2001) |
| Description | • Self-report; forced choice; standard Form M contains 93 items; four "preference" scales include: Extraversion-Introversion (EI), Sensing-Intuiting (SN), Thinking-Feeling (TF), Judging-Perceiving (JP); According to the Center for Applied Psychological Type (CAPT), the MBTI is the most widely used personality inventory in history—taken by approximately 2 million people per year; available from Consulting Psychologists Press. |
| Theoretical Basis | • Originally developed by Isabel Briggs Myers and Katherine Cook Briggs in the 1940s based on Jungian theory of personality. Myers concluded from her experience with people and the study of Jung's writings that people differ from each other along four different preferences that influence they way they think and act toward others. Specific psychological types are the result of scores on the preference scales that sort individuals into 1 of 16 possible personality categories. |
| Test Development | • Test was developed conceptually by Myers and Briggs based on Myers study of Jungian personality theory. The test is based on a dichotomous scoring scheme meant to identify dominant personality preferences (CAPT, 2001). |
| | • Because of the scoring scheme, there have been legitimate concerns about the conceptual foundations and psychometric properties of the instrument, its use in applied settings, and its use in academic research (Gardner & Martinko, 1996). |
| Psychometric Characteristics | • Because the MBTI is designed to test personality based on dichotomies, the psychometric properties are unusual (CAPT, 2001). |
| | • Split-half reliabilities and alphas for continuous scales consistently exceed .75 across all scales. For dichotomous scales, split-half reliabilities usually exceed .60 (Gardner & Martinko, 1996). |
| | • Steckroth, Slocum, & Sims (1980)—used Form F and found alphas for EI = .78, SN = .74, TF = .73, JP = .72. |
| | • Nordvick (1994)—alphas for Norwegian translation of Form G ranged from .73 to .83. |
| | • Tzeng et al. (1989)—claimed that their factor analysis of items in Form G clearly yielded factors consistent with original conceptualization of the MBTI. |
| | • Sipps et al. (1985)—factor analysis of Form F yielded 6 factors that did not clearly match the traditional MBTI factors. |
| Construct Validity | • Validity evidence found in type distribution tables that indicates theoretical support based on the proportions of different types across occupations (Myers & McCaulley, 1985). |
| | • Difficulty establishing sound empirical relationships between types and organizational factors because of the forced-choice scoring of the scale and the lack of methodological rigor used in most published reports using the MBTI (Gardner & Martinko, 1996). |
| Range of Application | • Instrument has been used widely in organizations as a tool for self-exploration and employee development (CAPT, 2001; Coe, 1992; Gardner & Martinko, 1996). |
| | • Useful for identifying leadership styles, training employees in cooperation and conflict management, and forming work teams (Coe, 1992). |
| | • Must be careful that the MBTI does not result in stereotyping of individuals. Must be administered by trained and certified professionals to avoid misuse and misinterpretation of results (CAPT, 2001; Coe, 1992). |
| Cross-cultural Research | • The MBTI is available in approximately 20 foreign languages from Consulting Psychologists Press. |
| Computerization and Internet Usage | • The Center for Applications of Psychological Type (CAPT, 2001) founded by Myers and McCaulley has a web site extensively covering the MBTI (http://www.capt.org/). |
| | • A short form of the MBTI called the Keirsey Temperament Sorter can be found and taken on the Internet in 11 different languages (http://keirsey.com/). |
| Current Research Status | • Its predominant value is in practical use. Sound empirical investigations are rare. |
| Use in Organizational Practice | • Widely used in public and private organizations in the U.S. (Gardner & Martinko, 1996; Coe, 1992). |
| | • Nordvik (1996) found the MBTI types to correlate with dimensions of the Strong Interest Inventory. This analysis suggested that the Extraversion factor was especially important in predicting work interest. |
| Future Developments | • Work will continue to develop measures like Tzeng et al.'s (1989) that use a continuous scale to measure the types as opposed to the forced-choice format. |
| | • Rigor of future research needs to improve with regarding descriptive and inferential statistics. |
| | • Though originally considered equally important, it is clear that certain type preferences are superior in certain situations. Future research should provide empirical data supporting the utility of types in different situations. |

*(continued)*

**TABLE 9.3** *(Continued)*

| Limitations | • Scores on the MBTI should be confidential and respondents given feedback explaining their scores and what they mean. "It is unethical and in many cases illegal to require job applicants to take the Indicator if the results will be used to screen out applicants" (CAPT).<br>• One common misuse is to include the MBTI in a selection battery (Coe, 1992). The MBTI was never meant to be used as a selection instrument, so it should not be used as such. Further, its ubiquitous use in organizations has increased familiarity with the instrument, which contains many transparent items. Therefore, the test can be easily faked. |
|---|---|

psychometrically sound relationships between the MBTI preference types and organizationally relevant criteria.

## The Jackson Personality Research Inventory (JPI) and the Personality Research Form (PRF)

The JPI and PRF were developed by Douglas Jackson to assess specific personality characteristics relevant to organizational behavior. As indicated in Table 9.4, they have been used in research and practice for individual development. The scoring for both tests is calculated with scoring templates that can be obtained from Jackson. Raw scores are converted to standard scores based on this scoring key, and these standard scores are then examined with reference to normed scores. Scores should be interpreted in terms of norms that are based on gender. Norms for the JPI were created based on data from 2,000 males and 2,000 females from 43 colleges and universities within the United States and Canada.

In examining the differences and similarities between the PRF and the JPI it is important to remember that the PRF was published first, and the scale construction and scoring format of the JPI are based on research done with the PRF. Following from this, the JPI should be viewed as a revision and extension of the PRF, and it is argued to have more sound psychometric characteristics as a result (Jackson, 1976). However, both inventories assess different personality traits (see

**TABLE 9.4  The Jackson Personality Inventory (JPI) and Personality Research Form (PRF)**

| Primary Researchers | • D.N. Jackson and S.V. Paunonen |
|---|---|
| Description | • JPI: Self-report; 320 items; 15 substantive scales; 1 lie scale. Scales include: Anxiety, Breadth of Interest, Complexity, Conformity, Energy Level, Innovation, Interpersonal Affect, Organization, Responsibility, Risk Taking, Self-Esteem, Social Adroitness, Social Participation, Tolerance, Value Orthodoxy, Infrequency (lie scale).<br>• PRF: Six different formats ranging from 300 items to 440 items. The standard form contains 14 personality scales and one lie scale: Achievement, Affiliation, Aggression, Autonomy, Dominance, Endurance, Exhibition, Harmavoidance, Impulsivity, Nurturance, Order, Play, Social Recognition, Understanding, Infrequency (lie scale). Six additional scales appear on longer versions: Abasement, Change, Cognitive Structure, Defendence, Sentience, Succorance, Desirability.<br>• Both are measured with a bipolar true-false scale.<br>• The lie scale is designed to uncover careless or random responding.<br>• PRF Form G has eliminated the validity scale and is computer scored. These reports can be used to determine the relevancy of the different items for the context of interest as well as determining validity of the entire scale. |
| Theoretical Basis | • Designed to assess stable personality characteristics relevant to behaviors (and the prediction of behaviors) in a wide variety of situations. Characteristics include interpersonal cognitive and value orientations. |
| Test Development | • JPI: Scales constructed from large item pools based on the definitions of each scale title. Therefore, the interpretation of each scale rests on the operational definition of the scale name. The item pools were written to be bipolar.<br>• PRF: A study of the traits of interest was conducted, relevant research was analyzed; over 100 items were created for each scale; these were revised by experts, and then this revised list was administered to a large sample of respondents; items that correlated highly with the appropriate scale were retained, while low reliability and validity items were omitted. The remaining items were ranked based on their value in accounting for variance in their respective scales, and the final items were chosen dependent upon these rankings. |
| Psychometric Characteristics | • JPI: Median of all substantive scales coefficent alpha = .79–.82, coefficent theta = .90–.93 (Jackson, 1977).<br>• PRF: KR-20 internal consistency reliabilities for all substantive scales range from .57 to .86. Test-retest reliabilities range from .46 to .90. |

**TABLE 9.4** (Continued)

| | |
|---|---|
| Construct Validity | • Correlates with the Big Five but is said to account for variance the Big Five can't explain (Paunonen & Jackson, 1996). |
| | • PRF validation studies involving self-reported scores and peer-reported scores. Median correlation of self and peer ratings = .52 (Jackson, 1984). An analysis of 8 subscales revealed correlations between .35 and .71 for those individuals sharing living quarters. |
| | • The convergent validity of the PRF has been examined with respect to the CPI, The Strong Vocational Interest Blank, and the Allport Vernon Lidnzey Study of Values (see Jackson, 1984 for complete presentation of all scale correlates). |
| | • JPI: Self-ratings were compared with composite peer ratings and revealed convergent validities ranging from −.01 to .66. Correlations between the JPI and an adjective checklist measure of personality ranged from .15 to .79. Correlations between self-ratings of personality and JPI scores were all significant at the .01 level with the exception of the scales of Responsibility and Social Adroitness (Jackson, 1976). |
| Range of Application | • Designed for use in schools, colleges, universities as a counseling aid, and for personality research in business and industrial settings. |
| Cross-cultural Research | • Canadian, Finish, Polish, German, Russian, and Hong Kong samples all revealed a PRF factor structure similar to that of U.S. samples (Paunonen et al., 1996). |
| Current Research Status | • Compared with the Big Five factors of personality. Researchers argue that the JPI taps personality constructs too specific to be captured by the Big Five. More specifically, Risk Taking, Energy Level, and Value Orthodoxy of the JPI were found not to be measured by the NEO-PI (Paunonen & Jackson, 1996). Other researchers found Social Adroitness, Value Orthodoxy, and Risk Taking of the JPI as well as Harmavoidance and Energy Level of the PRF to load weakly on all factors of the Big Five and argue that these constructs as well are not well measured by the five-factor model (Ashton, Jackson, Helms, & Paunonen, 1998). |
| | • The JPI has been studied with respect to a migrane-prone personality type (Schmidt, Carney, & Fitzsimmons, 1986), the personality of female police officers (Manuel, Retzlaff, & Sheehan, 1993), one's tendency to fantasize, (Myers & Austrin, 1985) and intentions to immigrate (Winchie & Carment, 1988). |
| | • Achievement and dominance scales of the PRF are often used in leadership research (Mumford et al., 2000). |
| Use in Organizational Practice | • Scales used to determine leadership ability, and achievement and dominance scales of the PRF have been used to analyze and categorize successful types of leadership behavior (Mumford et al., 2000). |
| | • The PRF scales of Work Orientation and Interpersonal Orientation were found to positively correlate with job success, while Ascendancy negatively correlated with job success (Day & Silverman, 1989). |
| Future Developments | • How do the JPI and PRF overlap with other personality measures? What are their unique contributions? Are they useful in a cross-cultural setting? |
| Limitations | • Somewhat low reliabilities for different scales. More applied validity research is needed. |

Table 9.5), and for this reason more than any other, both are still currently used in research and practice.

## The Positive Affectivity Negative Affectivity Schedule (PANAS)

The past three decades have been characterized by extensive research into the effects of mood on behavior. Watson, Clark, and Tellegen (1988) developed the PANAS to measure both state and trait Positive and Negative Affect (see Table 9.6). Over the past decade, the PANAS has been widely used to measure individual differences in mood. It is important to note the conceptual distinction drawn between Positive and Negative Affect since it is more than just a difference between predominantly happy versus predominantly disgruntled individuals when measured with the PANAS. Positive

Affect (PA) reflects the extent to which a person feels enthusiastic, active, and alert. On the other hand, Negative Affect (NA) represents a dimension reflecting a general state of, or disposition toward, subjective distress and unpleasurable engagement (Watson, Clark, & Tellegen, 1988). PA and NA have been regarded to be conceptually similar to the Big Five factors of Extraversion and Neuroticism (Costa & McCrae, 1989). There is considerable empirical support for these relationships across diverse samples (Watson & Clark, 1992; Wilson & Gullone, 1999). On average, correlations between PA and Extroversion and NA and Neuroticism are around .40. Factor-analytic evidence for the similarity between constructs was demonstrated by Wilson and Gullone (1999), who found that items measuring PA and Extroversion loaded on one dimension and items measuring NA and Neuroticism loaded on another dimension.

**TABLE 9.5** **Defining Traits of Jackson's Scales**

| Personality Research Form | | Jackson Personality Inventory | |
|---|---|---|---|
| Scale Name | Defining Traits | Scale Name | Defining Traits |
| Abasement | Meek, self-accusing, obsequious | Anxiety | Worried, tense, nervous |
| Achievement | Striving, accomplishing, capable | Breadth of Interest | Curious, interested |
| Affiliation | Neighborly, loyal, warm | Complexity | Contemplative, clever, discerning |
| Aggression | Quarrelsome, irritable, argumentative | Conformity | Compliant, agreeing, acquiescent |
| Autonomy | Unmanageable, free, self-reliant | Energy Level | Lively, vigorous, active |
| Change | Inconsistent, fickle, flexible | Innovation | Ingenious, original, imaginative |
| Cognitive Structure | Precise, exacting, definite | Interpersonal Affect | Emotional, tender, kind |
| Defendence | Self-protective, justifying, denying | Organization | Orderly, disciplined, planful |
| Dominance | Governing, controlling, commanding | Responsibility | Honest, ethical, incorruptible |
| Endurance | Persistent, determined, steadfast | Risk Taking | Reckless, bold, impetuous |
| Exhibition | Colorful, entertaining, unusual | Self-esteem | Self-assured, composed, egotistical |
| Harmavoidance | Fearful, withdraws from danger, self-protecting | Social Adroitness | Shrewd, sophisticated, tactful |
| Impulsivity | Hasty, rash, uninhibited | Social Participation | Sociable, friendly, gregarious |
| Nurturance | Sympathetic, paternal, helpful | Tolerance | Impartial, open-minded, unprejudiced |
| Order | Neat, tidy, systematic | Value Orthodoxy | Moralistic, conventional, strict |
| Play | Jovial, jolly, pleasure-seeking | | |
| Sentience | Aesthetic, enjoys physical sensations, observant | | |
| Social Recognition | Approval seeking, proper, well-behaved | | |
| Succorance | Trusting, ingratiating, dependent | | |
| Understanding | Inquiring, curious, analytical | | |

**TABLE 9.6** **The Positive Affect and Negative Affect Schedule (PANAS)**

| | |
|---|---|
| Primary Researchers | • Watson, Clark, & Tellegen (1988); Bagozzi (1993); Burger & Caldwell (2000); Chan (2001) |
| Description | • Self-report; 20 items (adjective markers), 10 measuring Positive Affect and 10 for Negative Affect; can be given with seven different temporal instructions to measure State or Trait Affect; measured on a five-point scale ("very slightly or not at all" to "extremely"); 60-item PANAS-X available to measure more specific Affective factors. |
| Theoretical Basis | • Positive Affectivity (PA) reflects the extent to which a person feels enthusiastic, active, and alert. Negative Affectivity (NA) is a general dimension reflecting subjective distress and unpleasurable engagement (Watson et al., 1988). |
| | • PA ranges from active, content, and satisfied to lethargic or sad. NA ranges from nervousness, anger, and distress at one end to calmness and serenity at the other (Burger & Caldwell, 2000). |
| Test Development | • Watson et al. (1988) originally developed the 20-item scale with seven different temporal solutions. They wanted to measure PA and NA dimensions as simply and economically as possible, so they tried to use the most purely descriptive adjective markers for each construct. Based on factor analysis, they trimmed the scale from its original 60-item format to 20 items. |
| | • They used a variety of samples to test the PANAS with its different temporal instructions in order to comprehensively validate the instrument. |
| Psychometric Characteristics | • Watson et al. (1988) PA $\alpha$ = .86–.90, NA $\alpha$ = .84–.87. Test-retest (8 week intervals) PA = .47–.68, NA = .39–.71. A principal factor analysis of the mood descriptors in each of the data sets revealed two dominant factors that accounted for roughly 66% of the common variance in each solution (62.8% for moment ratings, 68.7% in general ratings). |
| | • Mackinnon et al. (1999) found PA $\alpha$ = .78, NA $\alpha$ = .87. |
| | • PANAS-X has an average $\alpha$ = .82 ($n$ = 261). |
| | • Roesch (1998) found PA $\alpha$ = .85, but also assessed the tenability of a three-factor PA model (Joviality, $\alpha$ = .90; Self-Assurnce, $\alpha$ = .79; Attentiveness, $\alpha$ = .63). Conducted a CFA and found support for a multifactor representation of PA. |
| | • PANAS-X measures of NA can be used to measure overall NA, but a lack of evidence with regard to discriminant validity calls into question how much they measure discrete effects (Bagozzi, 1993). |
| Construct Validity | • Watson et al. (1988) found that the PA descriptor scale was significantly related to Positive Affect scales used in the past and the NA descriptor scale was significantly related to existing Negative Affect scales. They also demonstrated excellent factorial validity. The correlation between PA and Beck Depression Inventory was significantly negative. |
| | • PA and NA have been associated with the Big Five personality factors of Extraversion and Neuroticism, respectively (Burger & Caldwell, 2000; Egloff, 1998; Wilson & Gullone, 1999). |

**TABLE 9.6** (*Continued*)

| | |
|---|---|
| Range of Application | • When used with long-term instructions, the PANAS has demonstrated appropriate stability over a two-month period. When used with short-term instructions, the PANAS has been shown to be sensitive to fluctuations in mood (Watson et al., 1988). |
| Cross-cultural Research | • PANAS factor structure and reliabilities have been found to be similar across juvenile (Melvin & Molloy, 2000), adolescent (Crocker, 1997), and adult (Watson et al., 1988) samples. |
| | • Across age groups, PA significantly correlates with Extraversion and NA with Neuroticism (Wilson & Gullone, 1999). |
| | • Using an Australian sample, Mackinnon et al. (1999) found that factor loadings on the PANAS and item functioning were invariant across the life span. They did find that females had higher scores on NA. The correlation between PA and NA does not change with age. |
| Current Research Status | • Mackinnon et al. (1999) found the 10-item PANAS to measure general PA and NA as effectively as the 20-item measure. |
| Use in Organizational Practice | • Burger and Caldwell (2000) found that PA accounted for significant variance in job search strategy, success in interviewing, and social activities. |
| | • Responses to PANAS items are important to control for in determining the influence of method effects when measuring work-related attitudes and behaviors with self-report surveys (Chan, 2001). |
| Future Developments | • Chan (2001) urges researchers to include PA and NA in future work attitude studies in order to examine method effects on substantive relations among work attitudes and constructs. |
| Limitations | • Some argue the PANAS is not sensitive to changes in mood or for assessing trait-based affect. An alternative, the Neutral Objects Questionnaire (Weitz, 1952) has been used in several studies by Judge (cf., Judge & Higgins, 1998) as an alternative to the PANAS. |
| | • PANAS has been criticized because it was empirically derived; therefore, it is difficult to use conceptual explanations of item content and relationships with other variables, like Extraversion and Neuroticism (Burger & Caldwell, 2000). |
| | • NA measures in PANAS-X should exhibit stronger discriminant validity (Bagozzi, 1993). |

A great deal of research has linked PA and NA to many important organizational behaviors (e.g., Burger & Caldwell, 2000; Mackinnon et al., 1999; Watson et al., 1988) as trait and state affect seem to act as a perceptual filter through which individuals interpret and respond to situations. Although the PANAS is the most widely used measure of PA and NA in current research, some other measures have been used and deserve notable attention. The Neutral Objects Satisfaction Questionnaire (NOSQ) was developed by Weitz (1952) and assesses affective disposition by asking individuals to rate their satisfaction with a list of 25 neutral objects common to everyday life (Judge & Higgins, 1998). Judge found that affect measured with this instrument significantly related to subjective well-being, job satisfaction (Judge & Hulin, 1993), and favorability of letters of reference (Judge & Higgins, 1998). Another valid and reliable measure of PA and NA that has been used in the literature was adapted from the Multidimensional Personality Index (Agho, Mueller, & Price, 1992; Iverson & Kuruvila, 1995; Iverson, Olekalns, & Erwin, 1998). Using this scale, Iverson et al. (1998) found Affectivity had a direct effect on job burnout. In a more recent study, PA accounted for variance in tardiness, early departure from an organization, and absenteeism while NA accounted for variance in early departure (Iverson & Deery, 2001). It seems that regardless of how trait and state Affect have been measured in organizational research, relationships have emerged that suggest Affect significantly influences individual behavior within an organizational context.

The measure of Affect has its own bandwidth-fidelity issues (Ones & Viswesvaran, 1996) with regard to effective measurement. There are multiple versions of the PANAS. The most commonly used versions are based on the original 20-item adjective checklist. However, the PANAS-X is a 60-item measure of Affect that was designed to measure more discrete factors of PA and NA. Support has been found for a multifactor representation of PA (Roesch, 1998), but support for discrete measurement of NA factors has been less convincing (Bagozzi, 1993). A short form of the PANAS (10 items) has also been used in research and has been found to reliably measure general PA and NA (Mackinnon et al., 1999). Despite disagreement about how best to measure Affect, there is considerable agreement and support regarding its important influence on organizational members and functioning. Recent literature has indicated that PA and NA may be especially important factors to consider when selecting individuals for highly demanding and stressful jobs (Iverson et al., 1998; Schaubroeck, Jones, & Xie, 2001). However, more work needs to be done to determine the sensitivity of the PANAS, especially its shorter versions, in assessing meaningful differences between individuals.

## Organization Based Self-Esteem (OBSE)

Pierce, Gardner, Cummings, and Dunham (1989) developed the OBSE scale to more directly measure self-esteem as it applies within an organizational context. Our review of this construct is provided in Table 9.7. They defined OBSE as the extent to which individuals believe they can fulfill esteem needs through their roles as organizational members (Pierce et al., 1989). Scale items were generated conceptually from past research and organizational experience. The OBSE construct has recently received considerable research attention. Pierce et al. (1989) found OBSE positively related to organizational outcomes like job satisfaction, job performance, and organizational citizenship behaviors. Findings from more recent studies suggest OBSE as an important moderating variable in the increasingly chaotic, demanding, and uncertain organizational environments found in modern companies (Hui & Lee, 2000; Jex & Elacqua, 1999; Pierce, Gardner, Dunham, & Cummings, 1993). Using behavioral plasticity theory (Brockner, 1988) as a framework, this construct will be of increasing concern to organizational scholars and practitioners as the trend of demanding and uncertain organizational life continues (Hui & Lee, 2000; Jex & Elacqua, 1999). The literature also suggests that this variable may be successfully used to diagnose the effectiveness of organizational interventions as effective interventions should positively influence employee OBSE (Madzar, 2001).

## Work Locus of Control (WLOC)

Work Locus of Control (WLOC) has been defined as the belief that rewards and outcomes relating to employment (e.g., salary, promotions) are controlled by an individual's own actions (Internal) or by other forces (External) outside of the individual's influence (Spector, 1988). Spector (1988) developed the WLOC Scale to directly apply Rotter's work (1966) on locus of control to organizational life (see Table 9.8). Items for the scale were derived from a conceptual analysis that benefited from an extensive literature stemming

**TABLE 9.7  Organization-Based Self-Esteem (OBSE)**

| | |
|---|---|
| Primary Researchers | • Pierce, Gardner, Cummings, & Dunham (1989); Hall, Matheson, Sterns, & Phillips (in press) |
| Description | • Self-report; typically scored on a 5-point Likert scale (strongly disagree–strongly agree); 10 items. |
| Theoretical Basis | • OBSE is the degree to which organizational members believe that they can satisfy their needs by participating in roles within the context of a given organization. Since it is supposed to measure self-esteem specifically within the context of employment, it is distinct from the more general concepts of self-efficacy and self-esteem. |
| Test Development | • Pierce et al. (1989) created the OBSE scale and published a paper defining, measuring, and validating the construct. Items for the scale were derived from comments heard in discussions with employees, managers, and organizational scientists. |
| Psychometric Characteristics | • Pierce et al. (1989) $\alpha = .86$ (across seven studies), test-retest reliability $= .75$ (controlled for perceived organizational change $= .87$). |
| | • $\alpha = .88$ (Hui & Lee, 2000). |
| | • $\alpha = .89$ (Brutus, Ruderman, Ohlott, & McCauley, 2000; Van Dyne, Vandewalle, Kostova, Latham, & Cummings, 2000). |
| | • $\alpha = .90$ (Pierce et al., 1993; Gardner & Pierce, 1998). |
| | • $\alpha = .91$ (Tang, Singer, & Roberts, 2000). |
| | • $\alpha = .93$ (Hall et al., in press). |
| | • $\alpha = .95$ (Jex & Elacqua, 1999; Madzar, 2001). |
| Construct Validity | • Pierce et al. (1989): OBSE positively relates to Global Self-Esteem (SE), Task and Job-Specific SE, Managerial Respect, Job Complexity. OBSE negatively relates to Membership in a Mechanistic Organization. OBSE is stable across time. Further, OBSE has a positive relationship to the following outcomes: Intrinsic Motivation, Job Performance, General Job Satisfaction, Organizational Citizenship, Organizational Commitment, and Organizational Satisfaction. |
| | • Hall et al. (in press): Used confirmatory factor analysis to show that OBSE is a distinct construct from Generalized Self-Esteem (GSE). Further, OBSE accounts for variance in Job Satisfaction, Organizational Satisfaction, Organizational Commitment (specifically the Affective and Continuance scales), and Turnover Intentions beyond the effect of GSE. |
| Range of Application | • OBSE appears to be a variable organizations can influence by providing more challenging and diverse assignments to employees (Brutus et al., 2000). |
| | • "Structural features of work environments can and do send strong messages that shape individuals' beliefs about their organizational value" (Pierce et al., 1993). The OBSE Scale can be used to diagnose organizational environments as well as identify people who can work well within them. |

**TABLE 9.7**   *(Continued)*

| | |
|---|---|
| Cross-cultural Research | • Tang, Singer, & Roberts (2000) reported similar means on OBSE Scale for males and females (Male = 40.94, *SD* = 6.56; Female = 39.70, *SD* = 6.87). They also found OBSE was an especially important factor for females with relation to organizational instrumentality. |
| Current Research Status | • Van Dyne et al. (2000) found that OBSE-mediated relationships between Collectivism and Organizational Citizenship behaviors (OCBs) and Trust and OCBs. |
| | • OBSE also moderated relationships between organizational variables (e.g., Role Ambiguity) and both attitudinal (Satisfaction) and behavioral (Performance) outcomes (Pierce et al., 1993). OBSE has been found to be an important moderating variable in studies testing behavioral plasticity theory (Pierce et al., 1993; Jex & Elacqua, 1999; Hui & Lee, 2000). |
| | • OBSE negatively related to Outcome-Related Feedback-Seeking Behavior and to Seeking Feedback from Transformational Leaders (Madzar, 2001). |
| Use in Organizational Practice | • OBSE is important because high-involvement organizations need personnel who are confident and self-directed. In the face of adversity, high OBSE employees should perform better (Pierce et al., 1993). |
| | • OBSE moderated relationships between Job Insecurity and Anticipated Change and both behavioral (Absenteeism) and attitudinal (Organizational Commitment) variables (Hui & Lee, 2000). |
| | • Has been used within the context of behavioral plasticity theory (Brockner, 1988) to examine how individuals are affected by external factors like social influence when performing their jobs (Pierce et al., 1993). |
| | • OBSE influenced how managers develop from job experiences (Brutus et al., 2000). |
| | • High-OBSE employees handle jobs with more ambiguous role requirements better than low-OBSE employees (Jex & Elacqua, 1999). |
| Future Developments | • Research using OBSE as an important individual difference moderator within a behavioral plasticity framework continues to be important (Jex & Elacqua, 1999; Hui & Lee, 2000). |
| | • As uncertainty increases in organizations, OBSE may become a more important individual difference variable to understand and assess as it has been shown to significantly influence employee behavior. |
| | • Studies focusing on the relationship between types of leadership and OBSE may be a future trend (c.f., Madzar, 2001). |
| | • Studies should examine the relationship between OBSE and GSE over time, and the possible motivating effect of individual perceptions of a discrepancy between their OBSE and GSE (Hall et al., in press). |
| Limitations | • Much of the research has been susceptible to problems with common method variance since the OBSE scale is self-report and often administered at the same time and in the same survey as other variables of interest. |

**TABLE 9.8   Work Locus of Control (WLOC)**

| | |
|---|---|
| Primary Researchers | • Spector (1988) |
| Description | • Self-report; 16 items; scored on either a 5-point, 6-point, or 7-point Likert scale (strongly disagree–strongly agree). |
| Theoretical Basis | • Work Locus of Control refers to the belief that rewards and outcomes associated with employment (e.g., salary increase, career advancement) are controlled by one's own actions (Internal Orientation) or by external forces (External Orientation). This construct and its scale was derived from Rotter's (1966) work on locus of control (Spector, 1988). |
| Test Development | • Initially, 49 items were generated from a conceptual analysis. Spector (1988) narrowed the Work Locus of Control Scale (WLCS) down to 16 items using six samples. Items were selected for inclusion in the scale based on their item–total correlations, a lack of correlation with Social Desirability, and a balance between Internal and External items. |
| Psychometric Characteristics | • Spector (1988) found that the mean item–total correlation of items in the scale was .25. Cronbach's alphas ranged from .75 to .85. |
| | • Spector (1992) reported validation evidence indicating the WLCS was unidimensional, but factor-analytic evidence suggested a two-factor WLCS structure (Internal and External). Claimed this discrepancy was due to range restricted responses that inflated the relationship between the two factors. |
| | • Macan et al. (1996) found alphas across three samples to be around .85. The two-factor structure of the WLCS was also supported with and exploratory factor analysis—8 items loaded on Internal and 8 items on External. |

*(continued)*

**TABLE 9.8**   *(Continued)*

| | |
|---|---|
| Construct Validity | • Spector (1988, 1992)—Work Locus of Control Scale (WLCS) negatively related to Job Satisfaction (Mean $r = -.54$), Organizational Commitment (Mean $r = -.24$), Work Influence (Mean $r = -.37$), Perceptions of Supervisor Consideration (Mean $r = -.31$), and Initiating Structure (Mean $r = .33$), meaning Internals report higher scores on scales associated with these constructs than Externals. WLCS positively related to Intention to Quit (Mean $r = .23$) and Role Stress (Mean $r = .32$), meaning Externals report higher scores on scales associated these constructs than Internals. WLCS also significantly related to the General Locus Scale (Mean $r = .54$) created by Rotter (1966), demonstrating convergent validity. |
| | • Macan et al. (1996)—Internal and External scales differentially related to constructs. The Internal scale was positively correlated with Job Satisfaction, Career Satisfaction, Organizational Commitment, and Intrinsic Motivation across two samples studied. The External scale was negatively correlated with Intrinsic Motivation across samples and with Job Satisfaction, Career Satisfaction, and Organizational Commitment only in one of their samples. |
| Range of Application | • This scale is used for the most part to explain motivational difficulties in incumbent employees (Spector, 1988). |
| | • The construct has been found to moderate the effects of stress in several studies (Cummins, 1989; Ganster & Fusilier, 1989; Roberts, Lapidus, & Chonko, 1997). |
| Cross-cultural Research | • Lu, Kao, Cooper, & Spector (2000)—Taiwanese sample $\alpha = .73$, UK sample $\alpha = .86$. UK workers score significantly higher on the scale than Taiwanese workers (Mean UK $= 64.91$, $SD = 8.21$; Mean Taiwan $= 62.33$, $SD = 5.77$). In UK, WLOC related to number of sources of stress, Externals reporting more sources, but no relationship found with Taiwanese sample. Internals in both samples reported higher job satisfaction. WLOC interacted with Stress to affect reports of mental health. |
| | • Leung, Siu, & Spector (2000)—In Hong Kong, Externals reported lower job satisfaction and higher levels of psychological distress ($\alpha = .76$). |
| Current Research Status | • Externals reported greater Negative Affect, Internals reported greater Positive Affect (Henson & Chang, 1998). |
| | • Used a good deal in mood and job stress research (Henson & Chang, 1998; Spector & O'Connell, 1994). |
| | • Spector & O'Connell (1994)—WLCS has been found to relate most strongly to Work Autonomy ($r = -31$), Work Anxiety ($r = .25$), NA ($r = .33$), and Role Conflict ($r = .25$) using a unidimensional scoring scheme. |
| Use in Organizational Practice | • WLCS relationships—Internals have reported greater satisfaction, more positive perceptions of supervisors, less role stress, more autonomy and control over their job, and enjoy longer job tenure. Externals have reported opposite levels of these variable scores (Spector, 1988). |
| | • Internals reported more autonomy, job satisfaction; Externals reported more role ambiguity, role conflict, and work anxiety (Spector & O'Connell, 1994). |
| Future Developments | • Scoring of the scale needs to be clarified; should be scored as a unidimensional scale or should be two scales based on the Internal and External factors. |
| | • Internal and External dimensions should be conceptualized as separate dimensions (Macan et al., 1996). |
| | • Establish the validity of the WLCS as a predictor within a selection context (Spector & O'Connell, 1994). |
| Limitations | • Gupchup and Wolfgang (1997) criticized the Spector (1988) scale on the basis of its items referring to "people in general." They developed a modified scale, following the suggestions of Ajzen and Fishbein (1977) for greater correspondence in scale measurement, containing self-referent items since the WLCS is usually used in correspondence with other self-referent measures (e.g., job satisfaction). They found $\alpha = .87$ for modified scale. |

from Rotter's work. The scale contains 16 items, 8 measuring Internal Locus and 8 measuring External Locus. In most studies using this scale, Internal Locus is indicated by lower scores on the scale and External Locus is indicated by higher scores. The scales have been found to differentially relate to criteria (Macan, Trust, & Trimble, 1996) indicating that the Internal WLOC dimension and the External WLOC dimension should not be considered as two ends of a continuum.

Gupchup and Wolfgang (1997) modified the items on Spector's scale to be directly self-relevant in order to more directly assess individual WLOC. In studies of mood and job stress, Internal Locus has been found to positively relate to Positive Affect and External Locus to relate to Negative Affect (Henson & Chang, 1998). Spector and O'Connell (1994) suggest that the more control employees perceive over job-related stressors, the better able they are to adapt to work-related demands.

Therefore, WLOC may be a useful individual difference variable to assess in people whose jobs require the ability to handle high degrees of stress and uncertainty.

## Teamwork Ability

Team functioning and performance have been examined extensively throughout many areas of psychological and organizational research. However, our interest here is on an individual's ability to perform well in teams and our summary of the work done in this area is presented in Table 9.9. Research in this area has examined personality constructs (such as intelligence, adjustment, introversion, dominance, masculinity, conservatism, interpersonal sensitivity) that predict team behavior (Mann, 1959). Situational variables such as group size, group history, group origin, and the gender of group members also affect group functioning (Mann, 1959). It is important to remember that team performance is affected by a host of explicit as well as implicit factors that need to be recognized in any assessment of team performance.

Despite the importance of teams to twenty-first-century organizations (Magjuka & Baldwin, 1991) and the projection that team-based processes will continue to be of great importance to cutting-edge organizations, there does not appear to be any well-established team-based personality measures useful in the assessment of teamwork ability. A couple of measures, however, seem to have some potential for this kind of assessment. To provide the reader with a glimpse of this potential we describe two measures that focus on different aspects of team-based processes. First, the Test of Teamwork

**TABLE 9.9   Constructs That Measure Team Performance Ability**

| | |
|---|---|
| Scale Titles | • Team Function Taxonomy (TFT) |
| | • Test of Teamwork KSAs (TKSA) |
| Primary Researchers | • TFT: Nivea, Fleishman, & Rieck (1978); Shiflett, Eisner, Price, & Schemmer (1982); Fleishman & Zaccaro (1992) |
| | • TKSA: Stevens & Campion (1994a), Stevens & Campion (1999) |
| Description | • TFT: Self-report; scales include: orientation functions, resource distribution functions, timing functions, response coordination functions, motivational functions, systems monitoring functions, procedure maintenance. Assesses an individual's ability to engage in the behaviors necessary for effective team performance. |
| | • TKSA: 35 item, self-report, multiple-choice test designed to assess an individual's ability to perform well in a team. Includes five scales assessing interpersonal KSAs including conflict resolution, collaborative problem solving, and communication skills as well as self-management KSAs including goal setting/performance management KSAs, and planning/task coordination KSAs. |
| Theoretical Basis | • TFT: Team performance is a function of individual task performance and coordinated team performance functioning. Member resources, team characteristics, and task demands all affect team performance. |
| | • TKSA: There are KSAs that are important for effective team functioning, and these should be assessed when creating teams and reviewed when attempting to improve team functioning. The measure here is designed to assess teamwork ability rather than task ability within a team using previous research on tasks that have been found to be predictive of effective teamwork. The goal of the creation of this measure was to be able to select people into a team position based on this assessment (Stevens & Campion, 1999) |
| Test Development | • TFT: Nivea et al. (1978) defined teams and team performance and created a Team Function Taxonomy including team orientation functions, team organizational functions, team adaptation functions and team motivational functions. Shiflett et al. (1982) revised this taxonomy and replaced organizational and adaptation functions with resource distribution functions, timing functions, and response coordination functions and created a 7-point rating scale for each individual team scale. Fleishman and Zaccaro (1992) made a second revision to this taxonomy and proposed a 7-point rating scale to accompany it. The current version consists of seven scales assessing orientation functions, resource distribution functions, timing functions, response coordination functions, motivational functions, systems monitoring functions, and procedure maintenance. |
| | • TKSA: 46 situational questions of hypothetical teamwork were created and pilot tested on 234 undergraduate students. Items were eliminated and revised based on reading level difficulty, discriminability, and item-total correlations—35 items remained. In subsequent analyses, two of the items were found to have negative item-total correlations and were therefore eliminated, and psychometric characteristic results, as well as validity results are reported for the remaining 33 items (Stevens & Campion, 1999). |
| Psychometric Characteristics | • No psychometric characteristics of the TFT currently available. |
| | • TKSA: In two studies the coefficient alphas ranged from .80 to .81, indicating acceptable reliability. |

*(continued)*

TABLE 9.9 *(Continued)*

| | |
|---|---|
| Construct Validity | • No validity results from the TKSA are currently available.<br>• TKSA: Four independent judges on the five scales then categorized the 35 items that remained after the pilot test; 28 items indicated 100% agreement and 6 items indicated 75% agreement. The TKSA was found to correlate significantly with employee aptitude tests measuring verbal, quantitative, perceptual and mechanical ability ($r = .81$ for TKSA and general ability composite score). Correlates with supervisor ratings of teamwork performance ($r = .44$), task performance ($r = .56$) and overall performance ($r = .52$). Hierarchical regression indicated that the TKSA explained significant variance in teamwork performance and overall job performance above and beyond the aptitude tests. However, these incremental effects were not replicated with a second sample (Stevens & Campion, 1999) |
| Range of Application | • TFT: Can be used to further research on group performance as it is affected by individual and interpersonal behavior. Can assess how well a team performs essential functions, as well as assessing how well an individual performs these functions.<br>• TKSA: Can be used in a selection or assessment setting to measure an individual's potential to perform well on a team. |
| Cross-cultural Research | • None. |
| Current Research Status | • TFT: Research is needed to apply this scale in a real-world setting in order to assess its practical implications.<br>• TKSA: Support has been found for assessing teamwork KSAs, which may increase team and possibly organizational effectiveness (Stevens & Campion, 1994b). Has been most often studied within a selection context (Stevens & Campion, 1999). |
| Use in Organizational Practice | • TFT: Can be used to assess team and individual functioning in organizations; however, no evidence of its use in an applied setting was found.<br>• TKSA: May be a useful tool in selection, assessment, and recruitment purposes within an organization to identify those individuals who would perform well in teams (Stevens & Campion, 1999). |
| Future Developments | • TFT: Making team members aware of the functions important for effective team performance may help improve this performance, and perhaps teamwork training could be designed to do this (Fleishman & Zaccaro, 1992)<br>• TKSA: Perhaps by training team members on important teamwork KSAs, overall team productivity can be increased. This test also has great potential in a selection context and could be used not only to select members of a team who perform teamwork functions well, but can also be used to design teams with members who perform different aspects of teamwork well (Stevens & Campion, 1999). |
| Limitations | • TKSA: The high correlation with preexisting measures of general aptitude. Perhaps the teamwork construct being measured here is really a measure of general ability.<br>• Much of the research here is cross-sectional in nature, relying on correlations and hence limiting our ability to make causal inferences. Thus, the relationship between team characteristics and effectiveness may not necessarily be in the direction hypothesized here.<br>• We should remember that teams will be continually affected by many other factors within the organization such as structure, culture, and climate. |

KSAs (Stevens & Campion, 1994a) presented here is the only measure designed for use before the team is formed. It was developed to aid in the selection of individuals into positions that emphasize teamwork ability, and it is similar to a situational judgment test, where all the situations are team situations (Stevens & Campion, 1999). The Team Function Taxonomy is designed to assess an individual's ability to perform well in an existing team (Fleishman & Zaccaro, 1992). While the origins and revisions of this taxonomy involve a better understanding of the tasks teams perform, the scale thus measures functions necessary for an effective team and can be used to assess how well an individual carries out, or would carry out, these functions. Neither of these instruments measures specific personality dimensions inherently related to teamwork ability, but each can be important in assessing an individual's likelihood of being an effective team player.

## REFERENCES

Agho, O.A., Mueller, C.W., & Price, J.L. (1992). Discriminant validity of measures of job satisfaction, positive affectivity, and negative affectivity. *Journal of Occupational and Organizational Psychology, 65,* 185–196.

Ajzen, I., & Fishbein, M. (1977). Attitude-behavior relations: A theoretical analysis and review of empirical research. *Psychological Bulletin, 84,* 888–918.

Ashton, M.C. (1998). Personality and job performance: The importance of narrow traits. *Journal of Organizational Behavior, 19,* 289–303.

Ashton, M.C., Jackson, D.N., Helmes, E., & Paunonen, S.V. (1998). Joint factor analysis of the Personality Research Form and the Jackson Personality Inventory: Comparisons with the Big Five. *Journal of Research in Personality, 32,* 243–250.

Bagozzi, R.P. (1993). An examination of the psychometric properties of measures of negative affect in the PANAS-X scales. *Journal of Personality and Social Psychology, 65,* 836–851.

Barrick, M.R., & Mount, M.K. (1991). The big five personality dimensions and job performance: A meta-analysis. *Personnel Psychology, 44,* 1–26.

Bateman, T.S., & Crant, J.M. (1993). The proactive component of organizational behavior. *Journal of Organizational Behavior, 14,* 103–118.

Borman, W.C., Buck, D.E., Hanson, M.A., Motowidlo, S.J., Stark, S., & Drasgow, F. (2001). An examination of the comparative reliability, validity, and accuracy of performance ratings made using computerized adaptive rating scales. *Journal of Applied Psychology, 86,* 965–973.

Brockner, J. (1988). *Self-esteem at work: Research, theory, and practice.* San Francisco: New Lexington Press.

Brutus, S., Ruderman, M.N., Ohlott, P.J., & McCauley, C.D. (2000). Developing from job experiences: The role of organization-based self-esteem. *Human Resource Development Quarterly, 11,* 367–380.

Burger, J.M., & Caldwell, D.F. (2000). Personality, social activities, job-search behavior and interview success: Distinguishing between PANAS trait positive affect and NEO extraversion. *Motivation and Emotion, 24,* 51–62.

Carlson, L.D., & Lester, D. (1980). Thrill seeking in police officers. *Psychological Reports* 47, 1102.

Center for the Applications of Personality Type (CAPT) (2001). *About the MBTI instrument.* Retrieved October 3, 2001, from http://www.capt.org.

Chan, D. (2001). Method effects of positive affectivity, negative affectivity, and impression management in self-reports of work attitudes. *Human Performance, 14,* 77–96.

Coe, C.K. (1992). The MBTI: Potential uses and misuses in personnel administration. *Public Personnel Management, 21,* 511–522.

Colquitt, J.A. (2001). On the dimensionality of organizational justice: A construct validation of a measure. *Journal of Applied Psychology, 86,* 386–400.

Costa, P.R., & McCrae, R. (1989). *The NEO-PI/FFI Manual Supplement.* Odessa, FL: Psychological Assessment Resources.

Crant, J.M. (1995). The proactive personality scale and objective job performance among real estate agents. *Journal of Applied Psychology, 80,* 532–537.

Crant, J.M. (1996). The proactivity personality scale as a predictor of entrepreneurial intentions. *Journal of Small Business Management, 34,* 42–49.

Crant, J.M. (2000). Proactive behavior in organizations. *Journal of Management, 26,* 435–462.

Crant, J.M., & Bateman, T.S. (2000). Charismatic leadership viewed from above: The impact of proactive personality. *Journal of Organizational Behavior, 21,* 63–75.

Crocker, P.R.E. (1997). A confirmatory factor analysis of the Positive and Negative Affect Schedule (PANAS) with a youth sport sample. *Journal of Sport and Exercise Psychology, 19,* 91–97.

Cummins, R. (1989). Locus of control and social support: Clarifiers of the relationship between job stress and job satisfaction. *Journal of Applied Social Psychology, 19,* 772–788.

Day, D.V., & Silverman, S.B. (1989). Personality and job performance: Evidence of incremental validity. *Personnel Psychology, 42,* 25–36.

Dewett, T., & Jones, G. (2001). The role of information technology in the organization: A review, model, and assessment. *Journal of Management, 27,* 313–346.

Dunford, B.B., & Devine, D.J. (1998). Employment at-will and employee discharge: A justice perspective on legal action following termination. *Personnel Psychology, 51,* 903–934.

Egloff, B. (1998). The independence of positive and negative affect depends on the affect measure. *Personality and Individual Differences, 25,* 1101–1109.

Fleishman, E.A., & Zaccaro, S.J. (1992). Toward a taxonomy of team performance functions. In R.N. Swezey & E. Salas (Eds.), *Teams: Their training and performance* (pp. 31–56). Stamford, CT: Ablex.

Ganster, D.C., & Fusilier, M.R. (1989). Control in the workplace. In C.L. Cooper & I.T. Robertson (Eds.), *International review of industrial/organizational psychology* (pp. 235–280). Chichester, UK: Wiley.

Gardner, D.G., & Pierce, J.L. (1998). Self-esteem and self-efficacy within the organizational context: An empirical examination. *Group & Organization Management, 23,* 48–70.

Gardner, W.L., & Martinko, M.J. (1996). Using the Myers-Briggs Type Indicator to study managers: A literature review and research agenda. *Journal of Management, 22,* 45–83.

Goldsmith, R.E. (1985). Sensation seeking and the sensing-intuition scale of the Myers-Briggs Type Indicator. *Psychological Reports, 56,* 581–582.

Gupchup, G.V., & Wolfgang, A.P. (1997). A modified work locus of control scale: Preliminary investigation of reliability and validity in a sample of pharmacists. *Psychological Reports, 81,* 640–642.

Hall, R.J., Matheson, N., Sterns, H., & Phillips, G.M. (in press). Construct clarity and incremental validity of organization-based self-esteem versus global self-esteem. *Academy of Management Journal.*

Henson, H.N., & Chang, E.C. (1998). Locus of control and the fundamental dimensions of moods. *Psychological Reports, 82,* 1335–1338.

Hogan, R., Hogan, J., & Roberts, B.W. (1996). Personality measurement and employment decisions: Questions and answers. *American Psychologist, 51,* 469–477.

Hough, L. (1992). The "big five" personality variables—construct confusion: Description versus prediction. *Human Performance, 5,* 139–155.

Hough, L. (1998). Personality at work: Issues and evidence. In M. Hakel (Ed.), *Beyond multiple choice: Evaluating alternatives to traditional testing for selection* (pp. 131–166). Hillsdale, NJ: Erlbaum.

Huber, G.P. (1990). A theory of the effects of advanced information technologies on organizational design, intelligence, and decision making. *Academy of Management Review, 15,* 47–71.

Hui, C., & Lee, C. (2000). Moderating effects of organization-based self-esteem on organizational uncertainty: Employee response relationships. *Journal of Management, 26,* 215–232.

Hurtz, G., & Donovan, J.J. (2000). Personality and job performance: The Big Five revisited. *Journal of Applied Psychology, 85,* 869–879.

Iverson, R.D., & Kuruvila, S. (1995). Antecedents of union loyalty: The influence of individual dispositions and organizational context. *Journal of Organizational Behavior, 16,* 557–582.

Iverson, R.D., Olekalns, M., & Erwin, P.J. (1998). Affectivity, organizational stressors, and absenteeism: A causal model of burnout and its consequences. *Journal of Vocational Behavior, 52,* 1–23.

Iverson, R.D., & Deery, S.J. (2001). Understanding the "Personological" basis of employee withdrawal: The influence of affective disposition on employee tardiness, early departure, and absenteeism. *Journal of Applied Psychology, 86,* 856–866.

Jackson, D.N. (1976). *Jackson Personality Inventory manual.* Port Huron, MI: Research Psychologists Press.

Jackson, D.N. (1977). Reliability of the Jackson Personality Inventory. *Psychological Reports, 40,* 613–614.

Jackson, D.N. (1984) *Personality Research Form manual* (3rd ed.). Port Huron, MI: Research Psychologists Press.

Jex, S.M., & Elacqua, T.C. (1999). Self-esteem as a moderator: A comparison of global and organization-based measures. *Journal of Occupational and Organizational Psychology, 72,* 71–81.

Judge, T.A., & Higgins, C.A. (1998). Affective disposition and the letter of reference. *Organizational Behavior and Human Decision Processes, 75,* 207–221.

Judge, T.A., & Hulin, C.L. (1993). Job satisfaction as a reflection of disposition: A multiple source causal analysis. *Organizational Behavior and Human Decision Processes, 56,* 388–421.

Kirkman, B.L., & Rosen, B. (1999). Beyond self-management: Antecedents and consequences of team empowerment. *Academy of Management Journal, 42,* 58–74.

Krosnick, J.A. (1991). Response strategies for coping with the cognitive demands of attitude measures in surveys. *Applied Cognitive Psychology, 5,* 213–236.

Leung, T., Siu, O., & Spector, P.E. (2000). Faculty stressors, job satisfaction, and psychological distress among university teachers in Hong Kong: The role of locus of control. *International Journal of Stress Management, 7,* 121–138.

Lu, L., Kao, S., Cooper, C.L., & Spector, P.E. (2000). Managerial stress, locus of control, and job strain in Taiwan and UK: A comparative study. *International Journal of Stress Management, 7,* 209–226.

Macan, T.H., Trust, M.L., & Trimble, S.K. (1996). Spector's Work Locus of Control Scale: Dimensionality and validity evidence. *Educational and Psychological Measurement, 56,* 349–357.

Mackinnon, A., Jorm, A.F., Chistensen, H., Korten, A.E., Jacomb, P.A., & Rodgers, B. (1999). A short form of the positive and negative affect schedule: evaluation of factorial validity and invariance across demographic variables in a community sample. *Personality and Individual Differences, 27,* 405–416.

Madzar, S. (2001). Subordinates' information inquiry: Exploring the effect of perceived leadership style and individual differences. *Journal of Occupational and Organizational Psychology, 74,* 221–232.

Magjuka, R.J., & Baldwin, T.T. (1991). Team-based employee involvement programs for continuous organizational improvement: Effect of design and administration. *Personnel Psychology, 44,* 793–812.

Mann, R.D. (1959). A review of the relationships between personality and performance in small groups. *Psychological Bulletin, 56*(4), 241–170.

Manuel, L.L., Retzlaff, P., & Sheehan, E. (1993). Policewomen personality. *Journal of Social Behavior and Personality, 8,* 149–153.

McHenry, J.J., Hough, L.M., Toquam, J.L., Hanson, M.A., & Ashworth, S. (1990). Project A validity results: The relationship between predictor and criterion domains. *Personnel Psychology, 43,* 335–354.

Melvin, G., & Molloy, G.N. (2000). Some psychometric properties of the Positive and Negative Affect Schedule among Australian youth. *Psychological Reports, 86,* 1209–1212.

Mount, M.K., Witt, L.A., & Barrick, M.R. (2000). Incremental validity of empirically keyed biodata scales over GMA and the five factor personality constructs. *Personnel Psychology, 53*(2), 299–354.

Mumford, M.D., Zaccaro, S.J., Johnson, J.F., Diana, M., Gilbert, J.A., & Threlfall, K.V. (2000). Patterns of leader characteristics: Implications for performance and development. *Leadership Quarterly, 11*(1), 115–133.

Myers, S.A., & Austrin, H.R. (1985). Distal eidetic technology: Further characteristics of the fantasy-prone personality. *Journal of Mental Imagery, 9,* 57–66.

Myers, I.B., & McCaulley, M.H. (1985). *Manual: A guide to the development and use of the Myers-Briggs Type Indicator.* Palo Alto, CA: Consulting Psychologists Press.

Nieva, V.F., Fleishman, E.A., & Rieck, A.M. (1978). *Team dimensions: Their identity, their measurement, and their relationships.* Washington, DC: ARRO.

Nordvik, H. (1994). Type, vocation, and self-report personality variables: A validity study of a Norwegian translation of the MBTI, Form G. *Journal of Psychological Type, 29,* 32–37.

Nordvik, H. (1996). Relationship between Holland's vocational typology, Schein's career anchors, and Myers-Briggs' types. *Journal of Occupational and Organizational Psychology, 69,* 263–275.

Ones, D.S., & Viswesvaran, C. (1996). Bandwidth-fidelity dilemma in personality measurement for personnel selection. *Journal of Organizational Behavior, 17,* 609–626.

Parker, S.K. (1998). Enhancing role breadth self-efficacy: The roles of job enrichment and other organizational interventions. *Journal of Applied Psychology, 83,* 835–852.

Paunonen, S.V. (1998). Hierarchical organization of personality and prediction of behavior. *Journal of Personality and Social Psychology, 74,* 538–556.

Paunonen, S.V., & Jackson, D.N. (1996). The Jackson Personality Inventory and the five-factor model of personality. *Journal of Research in Personality, 30,* 42–59.

Paunonen, S.V., & Jackson, D.N. (2000). What is beyond the Big Five? Plenty! *Journal of Personality, 68,* 821–835.

Paunonen, S.V., Keinonen, M., Trzebinski, J., Forsterling, F., Grishenko-Roze, N., Kouznetsova, L., Chan, D.W. (1996). The structure of personality in six cultures. *Journal of Cross-Cultural Psychology, 27,* 339–353.

Paunonen, S.V., Rothstein, M.G., & Jackson, D.N. (1999). Narrow reasoning about the use of broad personality measures for personnel selection. *Journal of Organizational Behavior, 20,* 389–405.

Pierce, J.L., Gardner, D.G., Cummings, L.L., & Dunham, R.B. (1989). Organization-based self-esteem: Construct definition, measurement, and validation. *Academy of Management Journal, 32,* 622–648.

Pierce, J.L., Gardner, D.G., Dunham, R.B., & Cummings, L.L. (1993). Moderation by organization-based self-esteem of role condition-employee response relationships. *Academy of Management Journal, 36,* 271–288.

Ridgeway, D., & Russell, J.A. (1980). Reliability and validity of the sensation-seeking scale: Psychometric problems in Form V. *Journal of Consulting and Clinical Psychology, 48,* 662–664.

Roberts, J.A., Lapidus, R.S., & Chonko, L.B. (1997). Salespeople and stress: The moderating role of locus of control on work stressors and felt stress. *Journal of Marketing Theory and Practice, 5,* 93–108.

Roesch, S. (1998). The factorial validity of trait positive affect scores: Confirmatory factor analyses of unidimensional and multidimensional models. *Educational and Psychological Measurement, 58,* 451–466.

Rogers, T.B. (1987). Evidence for sensation seeking behavior during assessment of the trait: A note on the construct validity of the measurement operation. *Personality & Individual Differences, 8(6),* 957–959.

Rotter, J.B. (1966). Generalized expectations for internalized versus externalized reinforcement. *Psychological Monographs, 80,* 609.

Rowland, G.L., & Franken, R.E. (1986). The four dimensions of sensation seeking: A confirmatory factor analysis. *Personality and Individual Differences, 7,* 237–240.

Rudestam, J.R. (1986). Sex differences in personality and social support resources for resisting the impact of work-related stress. *Dissertation Abstracts International 46(8-B),* 2873 (UMI, US)

Schaubroeck, J., Jones, J.R., & Xie, J.L. (2001). Individual differences in utilizing control to cope with job demands: Effects on susceptibility to infectious disease. *Journal of Applied Psychology, 86,* 265–278.

Schmidt, F.N., Carney, P., & Fitzsimmons, G. (1986). An empirical assessment of the migraine personality type. *Journal of Psychosomatic Research, 30,* 189–197.

Schmit, M.J., & Ryan, A.M. (1992). Test-taking dispositions: A missing link? *Journal of Applied Psychology, 77,* 629–637.

Seibert, S.E., Crant, J.M., & Kraimer, M.L. (1999). Proactive personality and career success. *Journal of Applied Psychology, 84,* 416–427.

Shiflett, S.C., Eisner, E.J., Price, S.J., & Schemmer, F.M. (1982). *The definition and measurement of team functions* (Final Report). Bethesda, MD: ARRO.

Sipps, G.J., Alexander, R.A., & Friedt, L. (1985). Item analysis of the Myers-Briggs Type Indicator. *Educational and Psychological Measurement, 25,* 1081–1095.

Spector, P.E. (1983). Locus of control and social influence susceptibility: Are externals normative or informational conformers? *Journal of Psychology, 115,* 199–201.

Spector, P.E. (1988). Development of the work locus of control scale. *Journal of Occupational & Organizational Psychology, 61,* 335–340.

Spector, P.E. (1992). *Summated rating scale construction: An introduction.* London, England: Sage Publications.

Spector, P.E., & O'Connell, B.J. (1994). The contribution of personality traits, negative affectivity, locus of control and type A to the subsequent reports of job stressors and job strains. *Journal of Occupational & Organizational Psychology, 67,* 1–12.

Steckroth, R.L., Slocum, J.W., & Sims, H.P. (1980). Organizational roles, cognitive roles, and problem-solving styles. *Educational and Psychological Measurement, 25,* 1081–1095.

Stevens, M.J., & Campion, M.A. (1994a). Staffing teams: Development and validation of the Teamwork-KSA test. Paper presented at the annual meeting of the Society of Industrial and Organizational Psychology, Nashville, TN.

Stevens, M.J., & Campion, M.A. (1994b). The knowledge, skill, and ability requirement for teamwork: Implications for human resource management. *Journal of Management, 20*(2), 503–530.

Stevens, M.J., & Campion, M.A. (1999). Staffing work teams: Development and validation of a selection test for teamwork settings. *Journal of Management, 25,* 207–228.

Tang, T.L., Singer, M.G., & Roberts, S. (2000). Employees' perceived organizational instrumentality: An examination of the gender differences. *Journal of Managerial Psychology, 15,* 378–406.

Tett, R.P., Jackson, D.N., & Rothstein, M. (1991). Personality measures as predictors of job performance: A meta-analytic review. *Personnel Psychology, 44,* 703–742.

Tourangeau, R., & Rasinski, K.A. (1988). Cognitive processes underlying context effects in attitude measurement. *Psychological Bulletin, 103,* 299–314.

Tzeng, O.C.S., Ware, R., & Chen, J. (1989). Measurement and utility of continuous unipolar ratings for the Myers-Briggs Type Indicator. *Journal of Personality Assessment, 53,* 727–768.

Van Dyne, L., Vandewalle, D., Kostova, T., Latham, M.E., & Cummings, L.L. (2000). Collectivism, propensity to trust and self-esteem as predictors of organizational citizenship in a non-work setting. *Journal of Organizational Behavior, 21,* 3–23.

Watson, D., Clark, L.A., & Tellegen, A. (1988). Development and validation of brief measures of positive and negative affect: The PANAS scales. *Journal of Personality and Social Psychology, 54,* 1063–1070.

Watson, D., & Clark, L.A. (1992). On traits and temperament: General and specific factors of emotional experience and their relations to the five factor model. *Journal of Personality, 60,* 441–476.

Weitz, J. (1952). A neglected concept in the study of job satisfaction. *Personnel Psychology, 5,* 201–205.

Wilson, K., & Gullone, E. (1999). The relationship between personality and affect over the lifespan. *Personality and Individual Differences, 27,* 1141–1156.

Winchie, D.B., & Carment, D.W. (1988). Intention to migrate: A psychological analysis. *Journal of Applied Social Psychology, 18,* 727–736.

Zickar, M.J. (in press). Using personality inventories to identify thugs and agitators: Applied psychology's contribution to the war against labor. *Journal of Vocational Behavior.*

Zuckerman, M., Eysenck, S., & Eysenck, H.J. (1978). Sensation seeking in England and America: Cross-cultural age, and sex comparisons. *Journal of Consulting and Clinical Psychology, 46,* 139–149.

Zuckerman, M., Bone, R.N., Neary, R., Mangelsdorff, D., & Brustman, B. (1972). What is the sensation seeker? Personality trait and experience correlates of the sensation-seeking scales. *Journal of Consulting and Clinical Psychology, 39,* 308–321.

Zuckerman, M., Kolin, A., Price, L., & Zoob, I. (1964). Development of a Sensation-Seeking Scale. *Journal of Consulting Psychology, 32,* 420–426.

CHAPTER 10

# Integrity Testing in the Workplace

MICHAEL J. CULLEN AND PAUL R. SACKETT

## OVERVIEW

The purpose of this chapter is twofold. First, we provide a review of the current state of theory and research in relation to integrity testing. Second, we provide a review of the major integrity tests currently being used. Our review of the current state of theory and research is organized around three key themes: (1) construct validity evidence, (2) recent criterion-related validity studies, and (3) legal issues related to the use of integrity tests.

An important emerging stream of research regarding integrity testing relates to the constructs integrity tests are measuring. Research in this area has taken many forms. Some studies have investigated the relationships between different types of integrity tests, whereas others have investigated the relationship between these tests and constructs in the personality and ability domain. Still more studies have attempted to identify the underlying dimensionality of the tests using factor-analytic and other techniques. We devote the first part of this chapter to this important new research stream.

Since the inception of integrity tests more than two decades ago a great deal of empirical research has been conducted on them. Much of this research has been validation research focused on the criterion-related validity of these tests in relation to various workplace criteria. Unfortunately, in the past many different criteria were used as part of these validation efforts. The use of different criteria often made it difficult to compare the results of studies. Some of these difficulties can be overcome by meta-analytic techniques. As part of this review, we discuss the results of the most important meta-analysis yet conducted regarding integrity tests, and we offer suggestions about where future validation research ought to be directed.

Over the years, a variety of legal developments have emerged regarding the use of integrity tests in work settings. These include (1) initiatives by individual states to ban the use of integrity tests, (2) debates concerning the potential adverse impact of these tests on minorities, (3) the passing of the Civil Rights Act of 1991, and (4) the passing of the Americans with Disabilities Act of 1990. These events are all covered in this chapter. In considering the legal issues pertaining to the use of integrity tests, we attempt to bring the reader up-to-date with the legal considerations that should be borne in mind prior to deciding to use these tests as part of a selection battery.

Other important issues that have arisen in connection with the use of integrity tests, and that we touch on in this chapter, include (1) debates concerning the impact of social desirability and faking on the criterion-related validity of integrity tests, (2) the relevance of base rates and misclassification rates to an evaluation of integrity tests, (3) an emerging research stream on test taker reactions to integrity tests, and (4) test publisher responses to the efforts of some states to ban the use of integrity tests.

Our second objective in this chapter is to provide a practical guide to the choice and use of integrity tests in the workplace. To this end, we present an overview of some of the major integrity tests currently in use.

Clearly, in providing this review of integrity tests, we cannot cover every integrity test in existence. Rather, we cover those integrity tests that have been reviewed the most in outlets such as the *Mental Measurement Yearbook and Test Critiques,* and those that have been utilized the most for the purposes of research in major academic journals. The integrity tests we review in this chapter include the following: Employee Attitude Inventory (London House), Employee Reliability Inventory, Personnel Decisions, Inc., Employment Inventory, Hogan Personnel Selection Series (Reliability Scale), Inwald Personality Inventory, Personal Outlook Inventory, Personnel Reaction Blank, Personnel Selection Inventory (London House), Phase II Profile, Reid Report, and Stanton Survey.

This review excludes paper-and-pencil tests intended to screen applicants for honesty in settings other than the workplace; also excluded are polygraphs, voice stress analyzers, and other devices used to predict or detect theft.

In recent years, a number of comprehensive reviews of integrity testing have appeared in the literature (e.g., Sackett, Burris, & Callahan, 1989; Sackett & Harris, 1984; Sackett & Wanek, 1996). In providing our review for this chapter, we rely heavily on these reviews.

## HISTORY OF INTEGRITY TESTING

Although it is difficult to obtain precise numbers regarding the prevalence of integrity testing in the workplace, there is no doubt it is a very popular industry by any standard. In an earlier review of integrity testing, Sackett and Harris (1984) estimated that as many as 5,000 companies may be using integrity tests to assess as many as 5,000,000 applicants annually. More recently, Ones and Viswesvaran (1998b) reported that survey research had indicated between 7% and 20% of companies in the United States may be using integrity tests.

The stated purpose of integrity tests is to provide a means of screening applicants for jobs in which honesty is important to the success of the job. They are commonly used in settings where employees have access to cash, and they are typically used for screening lower and higher level employees alike (Sackett & Harris, 1984).

Integrity tests were originally developed as an alternative to polygraph testing. Although popular many years ago, the use of polygraph testing in employment environments dwindled considerably with the passage of the Employee Polygraph Protection Act of 1988. This legislation by and large prohibited private employers from requiring or requesting preemployment polygraph exams (Sackett et al., 1989). This legislation left a gap in the ability of employers to screen applicants for honesty, and that gap was quickly filled by the burgeoning integrity testing industry.

## CATEGORIES OF INTEGRITY TESTS

Integrity tests can usefully be divided into two types: overt and personality-based integrity tests. "Overt" integrity tests inquire directly into (1) attitudes toward theft and (2) the prior dishonest and illegal acts of the test taker. The Employee Attitude Survey (EAS), Employee Reliability Inventory (ERI), Personnel Selection Inventory (PSI), Phase II Profile, and Reid Report are all overt integrity tests. "Personality-based" integrity tests, in contrast, do not make direct inquiries into attitudes toward theft or prior defalcations. Rather, they attempt to determine an individual's propensity for dishonesty on the basis of personality attributes thought to be predictors of dishonesty. Tests of this type include the Hogan Personnel Selection Series, Personnel Decisions, Inc., Employment Inventory (PDI-EI), Inwald Personality Inventory (IPI), Personal Outlook Inventory, and Personnel Reaction Blank (PRB).

Given their different orientations, it is not surprising that the content of these two types of tests should differ markedly. Overt tests typically have two sections. The first of these, dealing with attitudes toward theft, typically has questions inquiring into opinions concerning the frequency and extent of theft in society, attitudes toward punishment for theft, likelihood of detection, knowledge of employee theft, rationalizations about theft, and assessments of one's own honesty. The second section deals with admission of theft and other illegal activity, such as dollar amount stolen, drug use, or gambling (Sackett & Harris, 1984; Sackett et al., 1989). Personality tests do not have well-defined sections. Rather, they typically include questions aimed at determining an individual's standing with respect to personality traits—such as conscientiousness or emotional stability—hypothesized to be relevant to an individual's propensity to steal or engage in other counterproductive behavior.

Studies investigating the psychometric properties of the various overt and personality-based integrity tests covered in this chapter vary in the thoroughness with which they investigate these issues. For instance, some test manuals report internal consistency reliability estimates for their tests, whereas others report test-retest reliabilities. Moreover, the intervals presented for test-retest reliabilities often vary drastically, making direct comparisons difficult. Various reviews of integrity tests in recent versions of the *Mental Measurements Yearbook and Test Critiques* indicate that the reliabilities of all tests reviewed in this chapter are generally adequate.

The overt and personality-based tests covered in this chapter also differ in certain practical respects such as length, the number of scales employed, and the content of those scales and whether they include distortion scales. As these characteristics often vary from one edition of a test to the next, the interested reader is encouraged to contact test publishers directly for the most up-to-date information. The addresses and phone numbers of the test publishers for all tests reviewed in this chapter can be found in the Appendix.

Given the potentially invasive nature of the questions posed by integrity tests, one might expect test taker reactions to the tests to be somewhat negative. Two strategies have generally been employed to investigate this issue.

The first stream of research focuses on test taker reactions to integrity tests specifically. The second line of research compares test taker reactions to integrity tests with test taker reactions to a broad range of selection devices. In both research streams, researchers typically assess perceptions of job relatedness, invasion of privacy, fairness, and appropriateness.

In relation to the first stream of research, results have generally indicated positive reactions toward integrity tests. Jones and Joy (1989) found that 82% of retail job applicants reported no objections to taking the PSI, and Ryan and Sackett (1987) reported that, for a sample of 226 manager trainee applicants, 80% agreed the test was somewhat appropriate, 69% disagreed it was an invasion of privacy, and 82% disagreed that the test reflected negatively on the company's image. However, perceptions of integrity tests become somewhat more negative when they are used as a means to screen current employees, rather than job applicants, for dishonesty (Stone & Herringshaw, 1991).

Studies directly comparing overt and personality-based tests have yielded mixed results. In some cases, test taker reactions have been more favorable toward overt tests. In other cases, the opposite has been true. For instance, Jones (1991) found that the London House PSI, an overt integrity test, elicited a more favorable reaction than either the PDI-EI or PRB, both of which are personality-based instruments. In contrast, Stone and Jones (1992) reported more positive reactions to the PDI-EI than to the Reid Report, and Wanek (1991) and Henderson (1992) found more positive reactions to the PRB than to an overt instrument created by Ryan and Sackett.

Studies comparing test taker reactions to integrity tests vis-à-vis other selection instruments have placed integrity tests in the middle of the pack. These studies (e.g., Harris, Dworkin, & Park, 1990; Kravitz, Stinson, & Chavez, 1994) have typically compared reactions to integrity tests to a variety of selection devices, including work sample, personality tests, physical tests, interviews, cognitive ability tests, weighted application blanks, polygraph tests, references, accomplishment tests, drug tests, genetic tests, and medical exams. Results have indicated that integrity tests are perceived more negatively than interviews and work samples, but that they generally do not produce strong negative reactions.

In summary, integrity tests would not seem to elicit as strong a negative reaction as one would have anticipated, given their potentially invasive nature. However, it is probably not wise at this stage to draw any definitive conclusions on the issue, since a number of contextual variables, such as wages, other aspects of the job, and explanations concerning the purpose for using an integrity test, may influence those reactions (Sackett & Wanek, 1996).

In considering the two types of integrity tests, a natural question to ask is whether one type of test is a better predictor of dishonesty than the other type of test. In an earlier review of the integrity testing literature, Sackett et al. (1989) suggested that, from a theoretical standpoint, a narrower measure of dishonesty, such as an overt test, may be a better predictor of a narrow criterion, such as theft. In contrast, a personality-based measure of integrity, which is apt to measure broader dispositional levels of a trait such as conscientiousness and emotional stability, may be a better predictor of broader counterproductive behavior, such as an aggregate of counterproductive behaviors.

Unfortunately, answering this important question is not as straightforward as one would have hoped. The chief difficulty in comparing the results of the criterion-related validities of overt and personality-based tests, as well as comparing results for different tests within test type, is that researchers have used a variety of criteria. Those criteria include theft, absence, turnover, grievances, commendations, and supervisory ratings. When studies using similar criteria can be grouped together, meaningful comparisons between overt and personality-based studies can be made. As discussed in the validity section of this chapter, meta-analytic techniques, to some extent, allow us to compare studies using similar criteria and thus draw some tentative conclusions about the relative predictive superiority of the two types of test.

## WHAT CONSTRUCTS ARE INTEGRITY TESTS MEASURING?

In their 1984 review of integrity tests, Sackett and Harris noted that very little research had been done investigating

(1) the linkages between different types of integrity tests and (2) the linkages between integrity tests and other constructs in the personality and ability domain. Further, no research at that time had investigated the dimensionality of integrity tests.

Early studies attempted to address the issue of the similarity of different integrity tests by correlating those tests with different personality inventories and examining whether the pattern of correlations was similar. To the extent that the pattern of correlations between the different integrity tests and the same personality inventories was similar, this provided some indirect evidence that the different integrity tests were measuring the same thing.

The results of such studies were mixed. Some studies reported similar patterns of correlations; others did not. In addition, because overt and personality-based integrity tests were often correlated with different personality inventories, these studies yielded little information about the similarity of overt and personality-based tests.

For instance, for overt integrity tests, Jones and Terris (1982) found that the profile of correlations for the London House PSI and the Reid Report with the 16PF (Cattell, Eber, & Tatsouka, 1970) were very similar (.88). The profiles revealed that individuals who scored poorly on these tests tend to have low ego strength and weak superego strength, and they are suspicious, controlled, and tense. However, Logan, Koettel, and Moore (1986) found that the pattern of correlations for the 16PF and another overt instrument, the Phase II profile, were quite different from those obtained for the London House PSI and Reid Report (correlations between profiles of .28 and .30, respectively).

For personality-based integrity tests, Sackett et al. (1989) reported that the pattern of correlations for the Hogan Reliability Scale and the PRB with the 18 scales of the California Psychological Inventory (CPI; Gough, 1987) were similar. Based on a male sample of 146 and a female sample of 46, the correlations were .88 and .77 for the male and female samples, respectively. For both tests, the highest correlations were with the CPI Socialization, Self-control and Good Impression scales.

Another early strategy researchers used in their quest to understand the relationship between integrity tests was to correlate two different integrity tests with each other, or to correlate a given integrity test with a personality measure. In connection with the first approach, researchers correlated two personality-based measures, the PDI-EI and the PRB with each other. Correlations for the Performance and Tenure scales were .56 and .45, respectively (Personnel Decisions, Inc., 1985).

In connection with the second strategy, Hogan and Hogan (1986) reported positive correlations between the Hogan Re-

liability Scale and the Adjustment and Prudence scales of the Hogan Personality Inventory (HPI), and negative correlations with the Sociability scale of that inventory. Gough (1972) reported negative correlations between the PRB and the Mania and Paranoia scales of the MMPI, and positive correlations with the Personal Adjustment, Endurance, Nurturance, and Deference scales of the Adjective Check List. Other studies reported that the Dishonesty scale of the London House PSI was related to external locus of control (Wuebker, 1987), to child abuse as measured by the Child Abuse Potential Inventory (Jones & Fay, 1987), and to a number of adjustment factors of the Emo Questionnaire (Frost & Joy, 1987).

Early researchers also found low correlations between integrity tests and intelligence. When attitude and admissions scores of the London House PSI were correlated with the B scale, a brief measure of intelligence in the 16PF, nonsignificant correlations of $-.03$ and $-.02$ were obtained, respectively (Jones & Terris, 1983). Further, Hogan and Hogan (1989) found trivial correlations of $-.09$ and $.07$ between the Hogan Reliability Scale and the Verbal and Quantitative scales of the Armed Services Vocational Aptitude Battery, respectively.

In totality, these early studies yielded some preliminary insights into the relationships between different integrity tests of the same type (overt or personality-based) and the constructs these different type of tests were measuring. However, by this time, there were still no studies comparing overt and personality-based integrity tests directly. Thus, it was impossible to know whether overt and personality-based tests were measuring the same thing, or what the underlying dimensionality of the two tests might be.

## ONES AND COLLEAGUES' META-ANALYSIS OF 1993

Progress in investigating these issues was made when Ones, Viswesvaran, and Schmidt (1993a) conducted a meta-analysis of the criterion-related validities of integrity tests. The results of that study are discussed in detail in the validity section. Studies related to that meta-analysis are also relevant at this stage, however, because they provided a great deal of new information about the relationship between overt and personality-based integrity tests.

In two offshoot studies of their meta-analysis of integrity tests, and using unpublished data gathered from test publishers, Ones (1993) and Ones, Viswesvaran, and Schmidt (1993b) obtained 56 correlations among overt tests, 37 correlations among personality-based tests, and 117 correlations between overt and personality-based tests.

Meta-analytic estimates of the mean corrected correlations among these different types of test were .45 among overt tests, .70 among personality-based tests, and .39 between overt and personality-based tests.

Interestingly, these results suggested the underlying construct being assessed by integrity tests may be more similar in the case of personality-based tests than in the case of overt tests. These conclusions were qualified somewhat, however, by a follow-up study that Ones conducted. In that study, Ones (1993) administered various combinations of three overt tests (PSI, Reid Report, Stanton Survey) and four personality-based tests (PDI-EI, PRB, Hogan Personnel Selection Series, and IPI) to a sample of college students and job applicants. Correlations for the personality-based tests were similar to those found in the meta-analysis (.75). However, correlations between the overt tests were markedly higher in this study than in the meta-analysis (.85). Correlations between the overt and personality-based tests were also appreciably higher than the meta-analytic estimate (.52).

In their most recent review of the integrity testing literature, Sackett and Wanek (1996) pointed out that the differences obtained between this study and the earlier meta-analysis offer interesting insights into the differential correlations between different overt integrity tests. Since only 3 overt tests were used in the study, whereas 14 overt tests were used in the meta-analysis, it appears that there may be more commonality between the Reid, Stanton, and PSI in particular than there is between many other overt integrity tests. Unfortunately, the data as presented in Ones (1993; Ones et al., 1993b) do not permit us to examine which overt tests are responsible for lowering the overall correlations.

## INTEGRITY TESTS AND THE BIG FIVE PERSONALITY FACTORS

After concluding that there was a great deal of similarity between overt and personality-based integrity tests, a natural question to pursue was the manner in which these different types of tests were similar. If some similarity existed between overt integrity tests, on the one hand, and personality-based measures on the other hand, what were the similar constructs they were both measuring? One obvious possibility was that these tests were measuring personality variables. Earlier studies had suggested some links between overt and personality-based integrity measures and personality variables, but the links had never been investigated in a systematic, large-scale manner. Ones and colleagues used their large database to examine the issue within a meta-analytic framework.

Specifically, Ones and colleagues (Ones, 1993; Ones et al., 1993b) decided to investigate the relationship between overt and personality-based integrity tests and the Big Five personality dimensions.

The emergence of the Big Five theory of personality is traced in a number of recent reviews (Digman, 1990; Goldberg, 1993). Essentially, although some disagreement remains, most personality theorists agree that human personality can be distilled into five essential factors: Extraversion, Agreeableness, Conscientiousness, Emotional Stability, and Openness to Experience (Digman, 1990; Goldberg, 1993). These factors have been found to generalize across cultures (McCrae & Costa, 1997; Salgado, 1997) and to remain generally consistent across adulthood (Costa & McRae, 1988; Helson & Wink, 1992). Behavioral genetics research has demonstrated that all of the five factors are heritable, with estimated heritability rates of between 30% and 50% (Loehlin, 1992).

Ones et al. (1993b) commenced their analysis by classifying existing personality measures into the Big Five factors. Subsequently, they computed correlations between those measures and integrity tests. They corrected for unreliability and range restriction using correction factors obtained from studies reporting the data needed for these corrections.

As expected, both overt and personality-based integrity tests correlated substantially with the Conscientiousness factor. The corrected correlations obtained were .39 and .45, respectively. However, overt and personality-base integrity tests also correlated substantially with the Agreeableness and Emotional Stability factors. For the overt integrity tests, the corrected correlations were .34 and .28, respectively. The corrected correlations for the personality-based measures were .44 and .37, respectively.

Thus, as a result of this meta-analysis, Ones et al. (1993b) had determined that integrity tests were primarily tapping Conscientiousness-related traits, but also traits related to Agreeableness and Emotional Stability. However, due to the substantial correlations between these Big Five factors, it was still possible that the relationship between integrity tests, on the one hand, and Agreeableness and Emotional Stability, on the other hand, was simply due to the covariance of the three factors. By regressing integrity on the Big Five factors, Ones et al. eliminated this possibility by showing that Agreeableness and Emotional Stability both made an independent contribution to integrity test scores.

As many authors have noted, each Big Five factor of personality is a broad measure incorporating a number of narrower personality variables. For instance, although there is argument concerning which specific personality traits properly belong to the Conscientiousness factor (e.g. Hough & Schneider, 1996), most researchers agree that Conscientiousness measures a multifaceted array of more specific traits that include thoroughness, reliability, and perseverance, as well as their opposites, carelessness, negligence, and unreliability (Goldberg, 1993; Costa & McRae, 1985b). Similarly, neuroticism measures such traits as emotionality, nervousness, moodiness, and insecurity, as well as their opposites, calm, security, and equanimity (Goldberg, 1993; Costa & McRae, 1985b).

For this reason, it makes sense to explore the linkages between integrity tests and more specific facets of the Big Five factors. As mentioned earlier, some of this research was conducted by early researchers in their quest to understand the relationship between integrity tests and personality measures. However, that research was conducted outside of the Big Five framework. Now that we have an organizing framework for personality in terms of five factors, it is much more feasible to investigate the relationships between integrity tests and more specific personality traits related to those factors.

The attraction of this research is that it may better reveal the constructs that overt and personality-based tests are tapping. For instance, it may turn out that overt or personality-based integrity tests are related more closely to narrower, more specific personality traits than they are to any of the broader Big Five factors. If these results were obtained, they would significantly advance our understanding of the constructs that integrity tests are measuring. Thus, we encourage researchers to investigate the linkages between integrity tests and more specific facets of the Big Five factors.

Some advances have been made in this regard. For instance, in an effort to understand which specific personality facets are being measured by an overt measure, the Reid Report, Hogan and Brinkmeyer (1997) correlated scores on the Reid Report with the HPI. The Reid Report had correlations with the HPI Moralistic, Virtuous, Impulse Control, Avoid Trouble, No Guilt, Empathy, and Even-tempered scales of .42, .30, .32, .26, .39, .31, and .30, respectively, indicating that high scorers on the Reid Report will be reliable, conservative, and controlled. Perhaps not surprisingly, reliability is a facet of the Conscientiousness factor, whereas control is a facet of the Emotional Stability dimension.

## DIMENSIONALITY OF INTEGRITY TESTS

Ones and colleagues' examination of the relationship between overt and personality-based integrity measures and the Big Five factors provided a wealth of information concerning the constructs being measured by overt and personality-based integrity tests. It also yielded an interesting insight into the relationship between overt and integrity tests themselves. The fact that both overt and personality-based integrity tests had similar correlations with similar Big Five factors suggested, but did not prove, that the underlying dimensionality of the two types of tests might be similar. In an attempt to directly assess the underlying dimensionality of the two types of tests, researchers have utilized factor-analytic techniques.

Once again, work by Ones (1993) provided some initial insight into this issue. Using the seven tests (three overt and four personality-based) she had administered to college students and job applicants, she conducted confirmatory factor analysis to test the twin hypotheses that (1) all seven tests load on a single common factor, and (2) that the overt tests load on one factor, the personality-based tests load on another factor, and that the two factors are correlated. Results supported the second hypothesis. Both an overt and personality-based factor emerged, and both factors correlated .81 with an overarching general factor she labeled Conscientiousness.

Woolley and Hakstian (1992) challenged the finding that a Conscientiousness factor underlies both overt and personality-based tests. In that study, researchers administered two scales of an overt measure (the Honesty and Punitiveness scales of the Reid Report) and three personality-based measures to a sample of 289 undergraduates. Results yielded correlations from .11 to .39 for the Reid Honesty scale and the personality-based measures, but no significant correlations between the Reid Punitiveness scale and the personality-based measures. This result raised an important question. How can a general factor underlie the two types of integrity tests if a primary scale of an overt measure like the Reid Report does not correlate with a well-established personality-based test? Indeed, in contrast to Ones's finding of a single underlying factor of Conscientiousness, joint factor analysis of the two types of integrity measures in this study yielded distinct factors for each test type.

Reflecting on these results, Hogan and Brinkmeyer (1997) speculated that the different findings may be due to the fact that Ones and Woolley and Hakstian used different levels of measurement, and different populations in their studies.

In an attempt to clarify the issues, Hogan and Brinkmeyer (1997) administered an overt integrity measure (the Abbreviated Reid Report) and a personality-based measure (the Employee Reliability Index) to a sample of 2,168 applicants for driver, warehouse, and clerical jobs. The researchers then analyzed a correlation matrix of the items from both tests and found that the analysis yielded four factors, which they labeled Punitive Attitudes, Illegal Drug Use, Reliability, and Theft Admissions. The item loadings on the four factors revealed no overlap. Twenty Reid items loaded on the first factor, 7 Reid items loaded on the second factor, 18 ERI items loaded on the third factor, and 10 Reid items loaded on the fourth factor. Factor scores were computed for each person on these four components, and confirmatory factor analysis was used to test the hypothesis that a general factor underlay all four factors. The model provided a good fit, indicating, as Ones had found, that both kinds of integrity tests can be represented by a single underlying factor of Conscientiousness.

In another attempt to explore the dimensionality of integrity tests, Wanek, Sackett, and Ones (1998) judgmentally sorted items from three overt integrity tests (the London House PSI, the Reid Report, and the Stanton Survey) and four personality-based tests (ERI, PRB, PDI-EI, and IPI) into 21 distinct factors. A sample of between 330 and 562 individuals completed any one test, and between 71 and 279 individuals completed any two tests. The researchers then created factor scores for each participant for the 21 factors and correlated those factors with the different integrity test scale scores.

At the most general level, the researchers found that the overt tests correlated with factors related to an "honesty/theft" theme while the personality-based measures correlated with factors reflecting a "counterproductivity" theme.

More specifically, for the overt tests, the researchers found that two of their judgmentally sorted factors, the Honesty Image and Theft Thoughts/Temptations factors, correlated .79 or higher with all three overt instruments' integrity scores. Despite these commonalities among overt tests, however, there were some notable differences between them. Whereas the PSI correlated most highly with the Honesty Image factor (.89), the Stanton Survey correlated most highly with the Perception of Dishonesty Norms factor (.89), and the Reid Report correlated most highly with the Theft Thoughts/Temptations (.83) factor.

Substantial similarities were also found for personality-based instruments. For instance, all personality-based scales had low correlations with the Punitiveness factor (.20–.30), high correlations with the Impulse/Self-Control factor (.63–.72) and moderate correlations with the Home Life/Upbringing (.53–.77), Social Conformity (.54–.71), Risk Taking/Thrill Seeking (.50–.77), Association with Delinquents (.51–.71), Theft Thoughts/Temptations (.51–.63) and Perception of Dishonesty Norms (.49–.62) factors.

Important differences between the different personality-based tests were also observed. For instance, the IPI correlated most highly with the Emotional Stability factor (.81), whereas the PRB correlated most highly with the Home Life/Upbringing factor (.77). Consistent with past research indicating the PDI-EI does not correlate highly with the three personality-based tests used in the study, the researchers found that the PDI-EI correlated most highly with the Risk Taking/Thrill Seeking (.77) and Association with Delinquents (.71)

factors. High correlations with the Theft Admissions (.67) and Theft Thoughts/Temptations (.55) factors suggest this scale may resemble overt integrity tests more than personality-based tests.

Despite the specific differences in the focus of overt versus personality-based tests, generally, and within test-type differences for both tests, all integrity tests were found to be similar in that they all correlated at roughly similar levels with the Social Conformity, Impulse Control, Association with Delinquents, Theft Thoughts and Perception of Dishonesty Norms factors.

At this point, perhaps the most accurate statement that can be made regarding the dimensionality of overt and personality-based integrity tests is that they are broadly similar in that they each tap specific conscientiousness-related traits—such as social conformity and impulse control—but are dissimilar in their focus. Overt tests focus specifically on questions attempting to assess an applicant's honesty and proclivity to engage in theft specifically. In contrast, personality-based tests seem to focus more broadly on questions designed to ascertain whether an individual is likely to engage in a wide range of counterproductive behaviors on the job.

## CRITERION-RELATED VALIDITY OF INTEGRITY TESTS

By far the most important development in the investigation of the criterion-related validity of integrity tests was the meta-analysis conducted by Ones et al. (1993a). This meta-analysis provided a level of coherence to the analysis of the predictive validity of integrity tests that had not previously existed. The chief problem with examining and attempting to compare the results from individual studies prior to the meta-analysis was that the criteria used differed vastly. For instance, criteria used in the past as part of the validation process have included theft, absence, turnover, grievances, commendations, supervisory ratings, and the like. Clearly, results will differ depending on which of these criteria are used.

Results will also differ depending on whether the criteria used is an "admission" of wrongdoing or an externally verified instance of wrongdoing. In particular, due to the lack of variance in many externally verified criteria, correlations using these criteria are likely to be artificially low. In contrast, some of the earlier studies include admissions in both the predictor and criterion, thus leading to artificially inflated estimates of test validity. To some extent, meta-analytic techniques alleviate this problem by presenting an organizing framework in which to compare the results of different studies that use similar criteria.

In their meta-analysis of the integrity literature, Ones and colleagues utilized a database they collected containing 665 validity coefficients. Those validity coefficients were collected for 25 of the most commonly used integrity tests. All of the integrity tests covered in this chapter formed part of the database for this meta-analysis.

Generally, the researchers found that integrity tests were useful predictors of overall job performance and counterproductive behaviors alike. In relation to the criterion of overall job performance, they found that integrity tests had a mean operational validity of .34. For an overall counterproductivity criterion, they found that integrity tests had an operational validity of .47. These meta-analyses were conducted on 222 and 443 validity coefficients, respectively.

Although the results indicated that integrity tests as a whole had strong predictive validity in relation to performance and counterproductivity, the standard deviations of the true validities were high (.13 and .37, respectively), indicating that other variables may moderate those validities.

Ones and colleagues therefore conducted a moderator analysis. Two of the most important moderators studied were predictor type (overt vs. personality-based tests) and job complexity (low vs. medium vs. high complexity). Using overall job performance as the criterion, Ones et al. (1993a) found that the predictive validities of overt and personality-based tests were similar (.33 and .35, respectively) but that the operational validities differed depending on job complexity. The predictive validities of integrity tests in relation to overall job performance were higher for low and high complexity jobs (validities of .45 and .46, respectively) than for medium complexity jobs (validity of .32). In addition, the researchers found that validities were higher when a concurrent rather than a predictive strategy was employed.

In relation to the counterproductivity criterion, a number of important moderator effects were obtained. First, Ones et al. (1993a) found that prior to controlling for various studies' features such as the criterion measure (admissions versus externally verified counterproductivity), criterion breadth (theft versus broad counterproductivity), validation sample (applicants versus employees), validation strategy (concurrent versus predictive), or job complexity (high, medium, or low), overt personality tests had a higher mean operational validity (.55) than personality-based tests (.32).

As Sackett and Wanek (1996) have pointed out, the most compelling studies are those using a predictive validity strategy, an applicant sample, and external, non-self-report criteria. When the studies are broken down along these lines, the validities are reduced somewhat. In relation to the narrow criterion of external measures of theft and actual dismissals for theft, the mean operational validity of overt tests was a modest .13. It was not possible to compute an operational validity for personality-based measures in relation to theft due to the small number of such studies using a predictive validation strategy and applicant sample. In relation to a broader measure of counterproductivity, which included violence on the job, tardiness, absenteeism, and other disruptive behavior, the operational validity for overt measures was .39, and .29 for personality-based measures.

The results for the broad measure of counterproductivity suggest that overt tests may be superior to personality-based tests in relation to this criterion. However, such a conclusion may be premature for several reasons. First, the results for the overt integrity tests were based on only 10 studies, whereas the results for the personality-based measures were based on 62 studies. With such small sample sizes, the stability of the estimates is in question. In addition, the proportion of studies using similar criteria of counterproductivity was different for both types of tests. As a result, the coefficients obtained may have been very different if they were broken down by the individual counterproductive behaviors. Finally, although the criterion-related validity for overt measures is higher for an overall counterproductivity criterion than for the personality-based measures, the 90% credibility value is higher for the personality-based tests.

In sum, at this point, we do not believe the evidence is cogent enough to indicate one way or the other whether overt or personality-based measures are superior predictors of a broadly conceived counterproductivity criterion.

As mentioned, perhaps the greatest barrier to understanding the relationship between overt and personality-based tests and counterproductivity has been the fact that researchers have been forced to group counterproductive criteria together for the purposes of their meta-analysis. Given the fact that studies using overt and personality-based measures make differential use of each of these criteria, the validities of different types of integrity tests in relation to these different criteria still remains to be determined. As more validity studies using these criteria are conducted, it is hoped that more direct comparisons of the validities of overt and personality-based tests will be possible.

In considering the criterion-related validity of integrity tests, an important question is the incremental validity that integrity tests add over other potential selection tools. After all, integrity tests are not usually the only test administered in selection settings but may be combined with other selection tools, such as cognitive ability tests, interviews, biodata, and the like. If integrity tests do not add incremental validity over and above these other tools, the argument for using them becomes more tenuous.

Ones and Viswesvaran (1998b) recently investigated this important question in relation to cognitive ability. First, the researchers gathered meta-analytically established validities for several noncognitive predictors in relation to overall job performance. Next, they obtained estimates from the literature for the intercorrelations between cognitive ability and those noncognitive predictors. Finally, using an estimate of .51 for the criterion-related validity of cognitive ability tests for job performance, they computed the multiple correlation of cognitive ability and a number of individual noncognitive predictors for overall job performance. They found that integrity tests added more incremental validity to cognitive ability than any other noncognitive predictor. The operational multiple correlations for cognitive ability tests in addition to integrity tests, structured interviews, unstructured interviews, biodata, and assessment centers, respectively, were .65, .62, .58, .53, and .52.

Thus, at least in situations where cognitive ability is used as part of the selection system, integrity tests enhance the value of that system at least as much as any other noncognitive predictor.

## DOES PERSONALITY OR INTEGRITY PREDICT JOB PERFORMANCE AND COUNTERPRODUCTIVITY?

The revelation that integrity tests are in part measures of Conscientiousness, Agreeableness, and Emotional Stability invites consideration of a critical issue. Which constructs are responsible for the predictive validity of integrity tests in relation to performance and counterproductivity? Are these Big Five personality factors solely responsible for the predictive validity, or do integrity tests possess some construct over and above these factors that adds incremental validity to integrity tests?

An important question, for instance, is whether Conscientiousness explains the relationship between integrity and performance, and integrity and counterproductivity.

Murphy and Lee (1994) addressed the question of whether Conscientiousness explains the relationship between integrity and performance by partialing Conscientiousness from the integrity-performance relationship. They used meta-analytic estimates of the integrity-performance, Conscientiousness-performance and integrity-Conscientiousness relationships and found only slight decrements in the integrity-performance relationship after controlling for Conscientiousness. These results confirm that there is some construct in integrity tests other than Conscientiousness that explains their predictive power.

Ones (1993) reached a similar result using her own meta-analytic database. Interestingly, she also found that the Conscientiousness-performance relationship approached zero after controlling for integrity. In addition, Ones (1993) investigated the incremental validity of integrity tests over the Big Five factors by regressing performance on the Big Five factors, and then again on the Big Five factors and integrity. She reported an increase in the multiple $R$ from .22 to .46, thus establishing that integrity tests added something useful to the Big Five factors in predicting performance.

An important, though unresolved issue is whether integrity tests add incremental validity to personality variables in predicting performance when specific facets of the Big Five are used as predictors. Narrower measures of personality, for instance, have been shown to outpredict the Big Five factors in relation to a variety of performance-related criteria.

For instance, Ashton, Jackson, Paunonen, Helmes, and Rothstein (1995) found that affiliation and exhibition, which are facets of the broader Big Five factor Extraversion, are better at predicting fun-seeking behavior than overall extraversion itself. In addition, in this same study, dominance predicted surgent behavior, such as speaking out in class, better than general extraversion did. Similar results were reported by Ashton (1998) in relation to workplace delinquency. With respect to this criterion, Ashton found that the narrower constructs of risk-taking and responsibility were better predictors than more general factors.

Another important question is whether the integrity-counterproductivity relationship is explained by one of the Big Five factors. Ideally, to investigate this question, we should have a meta-analytic estimate of the relationship between the Big Five factors and counterproductivity. However, despite the intuitive appeal of investigating how personality is related to negative job outcomes, very little research has been conducted on this topic. Only one meta-analysis has investigated these relationships within the context of the Big Five theory of personality (Salgado, 2000), and only a small number of the extensive list of alternative criteria that fall under the umbrella "counterproductive behavior" have been investigated within the Big Five framework. Examples of counterproductive behaviors that have been investigated within the Big Five framework include absenteeism (Judge, Martocchio, & Thoresen, 1997), turnover (Barrick & Mount, 1996), and delinquency (Hough, 1992).

The question of the incremental validity of integrity tests vis-à-vis personality measures in predicting counterproductive criteria is an important one. After all, integrity tests were originally conceived as a means of predicting counterproductivity in the workplace. From a theoretical standpoint, then, integrity tests should add incremental validity to Big Five factors in predicting counterproductivity. Once again, this question awaits the results of further research. As was the case when the question was the incremental validity of integrity tests in relation to the Big Five factors and job performance, the answer may depend to some extent on the breadth chosen on the predictor and criterion sides of the equation.

## LEGAL ISSUES IN THE USE OF INTEGRITY TESTS

As mentioned earlier, the rapid growth in the use of integrity tests in the workplace was spawned in part by the Employee Polygraph Protection Act of 1988, which banned the use of polygraph tests pre- or postemployment in most circumstances. Originally, the bill that became the Employee Polygraph Protection Act included language that banned written and oral tests that purported to measure employee honesty, as well as physiological measures (Sackett et al., 1989). However, that language was later deleted, thus preserving the right of employers to administer integrity tests as part of the selection process.

Although no federal legislation currently bans or restricts the use of integrity tests, at least two states, Massachusetts and Rhode Island, have explicitly banned the use of integrity tests by statute. They accomplished this by amending definitions of the phrase "lie detector" in their state polygraph statutes to include any written instrument operated for the purpose of enabling an examiner to make determinations concerning deception. No other states have since made such amendments or enacted laws explicitly banning the use of integrity tests. Thus, it would appear that the use of integrity tests in employment settings is permissible in all but two states (Sackett et al., 1989).

Despite the fact that, to date, only two states have directly outlawed the use of integrity tests, test publishers remain concerned about the precedent that has been established by Rhode Island and Massachusetts. In an effort to stem any further restrictions on integrity testing, a group of integrity test publishers established a watchdog agency called the Association of Personnel Test Publishers in the late 1980s (Sackett & Wanek, 1996). In 1992, this group became the Association of Test Publishers. The stated purpose of this group is to lobby state and federal government concerning integrity testing, to monitor attempts to further restrict integrity testing, to raise public awareness about the benefits of integrity testing, and to create standards for the integrity-testing industry.

In states where integrity tests have not been banned outright by legislative fiat, the legality of integrity test use in employment settings is governed by three key pieces of federal legislation: the Civil Rights Act of 1964, the Civil Rights Act of 1991, and the Americans with Disabilities Act of 1990.

## THE CIVIL RIGHTS ACTS OF 1964 AND 1991

With the passage of the Civil Rights Act of 1964, it became unlawful for an employer to refuse to hire or discharge or in any way discriminate against any individual with respect to his or her compensation, terms, conditions, or privileges of employment on the basis of race, color, religion, sex, or national origin.

In considering whether the action of an employer was discriminatory under the 1964 Act, the chief consideration was whether that action had an *adverse impact* on a specified group. With respect to the hiring process, the Act and ensuing case law stipulated that a test administered as part of the selection process will demonstrate adverse impact if it results in one member of a protected group (e.g., males) being hired at a substantially higher rate than other members of that group (e.g., females).

As a rule of thumb, a selection device will be considered to have adverse impact if the selection rate for any race, sex, or ethnic group is less than four fifths of the rate for the group with the highest rate. This is the standard suggested by the *Uniform Guidelines on Employee Selection Procedures*, and it has been accepted by courts as the appropriate standard.

A finding of adverse impact does not automatically result in a declaration that a selection device can no longer be used for hiring purposes. Rather, once adverse impact has been demonstrated, the burden shifts to the employer to demonstrate that the selection device is job related. If the employer can satisfy the court that a given selection device is job related, it can continue to use that device for selection purposes irrespective of whether it demonstrates adverse impact against a protected group.

An employer can discharge the burden of establishing the job-relatedness of a test by demonstrating the content and/or criterion-related validity of the test in relation to a specific job. For instance, the criterion-related validity of an integrity test could be demonstrated through a criterion-related validity study of the integrity test in relation to key job performance criteria.

Given the legal considerations governing the use of integrity tests, the key issue is whether integrity tests demonstrate adverse impact against any protected group. Unfortunately, a determination of this issue is not as simple as examining whether individuals from minority and majority groups, or males and females, score differently on these tests.

The resolution to the question really depends on whether integrity tests are the sole instrument being used in the selection process, or whether, as is more often the case, they are being used as part of a selection battery. If the decision to hire is being made on the basis of the integrity test alone—which will rarely be the case—subgroup differences are the chief concern. In this case, given various selection ratios, we can examine the subgroup differences between females and males, for instance, and determine whether the four fifths rule is violated at each of those selection ratios.

On the other hand, as Sackett and Ellingson (1997) have pointed out, when multiple predictors are used in a selection system, calculating the potential for adverse impact requires consideration of subgroup differences on the integrity tests as well as many other factors. Those factors include (1) the composite effect size ($d$ value) for the predictors, (2) how the individual predictors are weighted, and (3) the selection ratio. Consideration of the technical aspects of using this information to make a determination about adverse impact is beyond the purview of this chapter, and the interested reader is referred to Sackett and Ellingson's article. It is essential to note, however, that in most situations, determining whether a selection system, of which an integrity test is a part, offends the four fifths rule will need to be conducted on a case-by-case basis by considering the preceding factors.

Bearing this proviso in mind, is there any evidence that individual integrity tests exhibit substantial subgroup differences? Fortunately, the weight of the evidence suggests there are no substantial race or sex subgroup differences on integrity tests.

In their 1984 review of integrity tests, Sackett and Harris reviewed the race and sex differences for nine overt integrity tests. The majority of the tests reported no differences. Two studies reported higher passing rates in favor of females, and one study reported slightly higher passing rates for Blacks. These results were confined to overt integrity tests, and by the time of their next review of the literature, Sackett et al. (1989) had obtained results for several personality-based integrity tests.

Regarding the PDI Employment Inventory, results indicated that females had slightly higher passing rates. Similar results for females were found for the Hogan Reliability Scale and the PRB. However, for gender and race, differences did not appear to be large enough to demonstrate adverse impact. For the PDI-EI, for instance, researchers investigated the issue of adverse impact using a pool of 30,000 individuals who had taken the test. Results indicated that, for cutoff scores at the 50th, 75th, and 96th percentiles, the ratios of Blacks who passed the test to Whites who passed the test was well over

the .80 guideline used to determine whether adverse impact exists (Sackett et al., 1989).

The question of the true difference in subgroup scores on integrity tests was raised again as a result of Ones et al.'s 1993 meta-analysis (1993a), which reported a minority-nonminority standardized mean difference of .72 for overt tests and .20 for personality tests, with the minority mean higher than the nonminority mean. With respect to gender differences, Ones et al. reported a standardized mean difference in favor of females of .82 and .39 for overt and personality-based tests, respectively. Because the results for minority-nonminority differences was at odds with much of the past research, Ones et al. decided to revisit the issue using a database of over 700,000 individuals who had completed the London House PSI, Reid Report, or Stanton Survey. Results were consistent with past research, indicating a negligible Black-White difference and slightly higher scores for females on both overt and personality-based tests.

A key issue in considering the potential adverse impact of integrity tests is the practice of making score adjustments within racial group to prevent adverse impact. Prior to 1991, the practice was permissible. In cases where adverse impact could be demonstrated, it also appeared to be a rational solution to the problem created by cutoff scores between minority and majority groups that were dissimilar. Since it had the effect of reducing differences in hiring rates between those two groups, such adjustments actually reduced the adverse impact of tests producing dissimilar cutoff scores for different groups.

However, with the passage of the Civil Rights Act of 1991, such a practice became unlawful. According to Title VII of the Act, it shall an be unlawful practice for an employer "in connection with the selection or referral of applicants or candidates for employment or promotion to adjust the scores of, use different cutoffs for, or otherwise alter the results of employment-related tests on the basis of race, color, religion, sex or national origin."

Since the pronouncement that score adjustments would no longer be permissible, it has become especially important to monitor research concerning subgroup differences on integrity tests. In light of the widespread use of integrity tests in employment settings, and the uncertainty surrounding the exact race and gender differences on these tests, more research should be conducted to clarify the scope of the subgroup differences.

## THE AMERICANS WITH DISABILITIES ACT

With the passage of the American with Disabilities Act (1990), it became illegal for employers to screen employees for medical conditions prior to making an offer for employment. The rationale for this prohibition is that it would prevent employers from discriminating against job applicants who were found to have a medical condition prior to making a job offer.

For those interested in administering integrity tests as part of the selection process, the relevant question therefore became which integrity tests, if any, could be considered "medical examinations" under the ADA. According to the ADA, those integrity tests that are considered medical examinations can only be administered after an offer of employment has been made.

In 1994, the Equal Employment Opportunity Commission (EEOC) issued an enforcement guideline document aimed at shedding light on this issue. The EEOC determined that the relevant factors to be borne in mind in considering whether a selection test should be considered a medical examination are (1) whether the test is administered and/or interpreted by a health care professional in a medical setting, (2) whether the test was designed to examine medical health, and (3) whether the employer's purpose is to determine the psychological health of the prospective employee (Sackett & Wanek, 1996).

In illustration of these principles, the EEOC offered a number of examples. One of these included a hypothetical integrity test. Primarily because the hypothetical test was designed to measure employee integrity in the workplace, and not employee health per se, the EEOC decided that such a test should not be considered a medical examination for the purposes of the ADA.

In determining whether any of the major integrity tests reviewed in this chapter might be considered a medical examination for the purposes of the ADA, it seems clear, to begin with, that none of the overt measures would offend the ADA. As mentioned earlier, overt integrity tests were formulated with the explicit purpose of measuring integrity, not any medical condition. Moreover, no overt integrity tests are used to diagnose a medical condition, and they will typically not be administered or interpreted by a health care professional in a medical setting. Considering these factors, no overt personality test is likely to be considered a medical examination for the purposes of the ADA.

In contrast, it is conceivable that some personality-based measures may fall within the purview of the ADA. The example that comes most readily to mind is the Minnesota Multiphasic Personality Inventory-2 (MMPI-2) (Butcher, Dahlstrom, Graham, Tellegen, & Kaemmer, 1989). The EEOC noted that a test that was originally designed to detect mental illness would come under the ADA even if it was subsequently used for a different purpose. Another test that probably falls within the act is the IPI (Inwald, 1992). Although the test was not originally conceived to determine mental disorders per se,

one of its explicit purposes is to assess the emotional stability of police officer applicants. For this reason, it is typically administered post job offer.

The ADA also prohibits inquiries into the extent of past drug use. As Sackett and Wanek noted in their 1996 review of integrity testing, most of the major integrity tests have been revised to comply with this proviso.

## FAKING

Notwithstanding the evidence that integrity tests are useful predictors of a variety of important performance-related criteria, some researchers remain skeptical of the validity of the empirical relationships found using integrity tests. The main concern relates to the effect of social desirability on integrity scores. One worry is that if response distortion takes place on integrity measures because people are trying to present themselves in a desirable manner, the criterion-related validities of integrity-performance relationships are in fact lower than they appear (Hough & Schneider, 1996).

In considering this issue, a preliminary concern is whether individuals can in fact increase their scores on integrity tests through faking. The weight of the evidence suggests that individuals can do so. Ones, Viswesvaran, and Korbin (1995) conducted a meta-analysis of fakability estimates in relation to the Big Five personality constructs and found that individuals asked to fake good could increase their scores by an average of .50 standard deviations. A host of earlier studies reached similar conclusions regarding personality measures and integrity tests (e.g., Cunningham, Wong, & Barbee, 1994; Moore, 1990; Ryan & Sackett, 1987).

However, as several commentators have pointed out, the fact that individuals can intentionally increase their integrity scores in an experimental setting does not mean that applicants routinely distort their responses (Hough, Eaton, Dunnette, Kamp, & McCloy, 1990; Ones et al., 1995).

If social desirability does influence criterion-related validities, it could do so in several ways. First, it could moderate those validities. In this case, different criterion-related validities would be observed for groups of individuals who do not fake on integrity tests and those who do fake on those tests. In the personality domain, this question has been addressed on a number of occasions. Generally, results indicate that social desirability does not appreciably moderate criterion-related validities (Barrick & Mount, 1996; Hough, 1998; Hough et al., 1990). In the integrity-testing domain, Ones et al. (1993a) found in their meta-analysis that, for studies using predictive strategies and applicant samples, the predictive validity of integrity tests was .41 in relation to job performance, and that there was no room for moderators to influence that relationship.

Social desirability could also act as a mediator or suppressor variable. If social desirability were a mediator of the integrity-performance relationship, then partialing social desirability would lead to a dramatic decrease in the validities of integrity tests. In contrast, if it were a suppressor variable, partialing social desirability would lead to an increase in the criterion-related validities of integrity tests. These effects can be investigated by partialing social desirability from integrity-performance relationships and observing whether validities change. When these social desirability corrections are made, results have generally yielded no change in criterion-related validities (Hough, 1998; Ones and Viswesvaran, 1998a). Thus, it would appear that social desirability is neither a mediator nor a suppressor variable.

If social desirability does not act as a moderator, mediator, or suppressor of integrity-performance relationships, the last remaining question is whether social desirability changes the rank ordering of applicants. Social desirability could change the rank order of applicants but not significantly affect overall criterion-related validities if it only changed the rank order of individuals at the higher end of the distribution of scores. If social desirability does effect such rank order changes, then it still has the potential to work unfairness into the hiring process. Since many selection systems employ a top-down selection strategy, social desirability could lead to the hiring of many individuals who have lower true scores than their integrity tests scores would lead one to believe.

Some studies have demonstrated that social desirability can indeed change the rank order of applicants (e.g., Zickar, Rosse, Levin, & Hulin, 1997). Assuming social desirability can affect the rank ordering of applicants, the important question is: what should be done about it? One option is to make social desirability corrections. The assumption in making these corrections is that we will be able to recover an individual's true score on the integrity instrument. If we can recover an individual's true score on the integrity test with these corrections, we will be able to make selection decisions based on this score alone. Such a result would increase the fairness of a selection system that uses integrity tests.

Unfortunately, recent research suggests that such corrections do not help researchers to recover an individual's "true" score on personality tests. Using a within-subjects design, Ellingson, Sackett, and Hough (1999) examined the proportion of correct selection decisions made (1) when social desirability corrections were made and (2) when they were not made to personality instruments completed by participants instructed to fake good on those inventories. Correct decisions were construed as selection decisions that would have

been made on the basis of the same personality instruments completed when those same participants were asked to do so honestly. Results indicated that at a variety of selection ratios, social desirability corrections unsystematically resulted in more correct decisions on some occasions and more incorrect decisions on an equal number of occasions.

In summary, although many of the original fears of the effect of social desirability on integrity test validities have been proven to be unfounded, there remains the important concern that social desirability may change the rank ordering of applicants, leading to nonoptimal selection decisions in many cases. It remains the task of creative researchers to devise a solution to this pressing problem.

## BASE RATES AND MISCLASSIFICATION RATES

An important issue that has surfaced repeatedly in debates concerning the merits of integrity testing is the relevance of (1) base rates of counterproductive behavior in the workplace and (2) false positives for the tests.

The chief concern raised in relation to base rates and false positive rates (e.g., see Ones, Schmidt, Viswesvaran, & Lykken, 1996) is that, to the extent that the true incidence of counterproductive behaviors in an organization is low, the false positive rate for integrity tests is also high for any given selection ratio. In a series of recent debates on the issue (Ones et al., 1996), one commentator asks the reader to consider the following scenario. Assuming (1) integrity tests have a predictive validity for job applicants of .39, (2) the true incidence of counterproductive behaviors is 50%, and (3) the cutting score is chosen to reject 50% of the applicants, then an integrity test used in a selection setting would yield 38% false positives. Further, in the situation where the incidence of counterproductive behaviors is only 25%, the false positive rate will be about 88%.

In light of the potential for substantial rates of false positives using integrity tests, this commentator suggests it may be time to rethink the use of integrity tests. The problem with this argument is that it ignores the fact that false positives are an inescapable result of using any selection device. More important, the argument fails to consider that the use of a valid predictor—such as integrity tests—will always result in a lower false positive rate relative to its nonuse. In other words, regardless of the base rate of counterproductivity, as long as a fixed number of applicants is to be selected from the applicant pool, the use of the most valid selection device minimizes false positive errors, false negative errors, and total errors (Martin & Terris, 1991). In our view, therefore, the issue of the base rate of counterproductive behaviors is in many respects a red herring and irrelevant to a decision about whether to use integrity tests in the workplace.

To date, a great deal of research has gone into establishing the actual base rate of counterproductivity in the workplace (e.g., Slora, 1991). This research has no doubt produced a wide body of interesting conclusions concerning the incidence of counterproductive behaviors in various organizations. However, we join with those who have argued that such research has little to add to the debate concerning the merits of integrity testing, and we would urge researchers to instead tackle the remaining construct and criterion-related validity research questions outlined earlier in this chapter.

## CONCLUSION

Over the past two decades, our accumulated knowledge base regarding integrity tests has grown considerably. In particular, we have made great strides in understanding the constructs that integrity tests are measuring. In this regard, we have learned that although overt and integrity tests are similar to the extent that they both employ questions tapping into the Big Five factors of Conscientiousness, Agreeableness, and Emotional Stability, they are very different in other respects. In particular, evidence is emerging that overt tests focus on questions related to the narrower themes of theft and honesty, while personality-based tests focus on questions related to a broadly conceived counterproductivity theme. To better understand the differences between overt and personality-based tests at the construct level, the time is ripe for research investigating how overt and personality-based tests are related to more specific facets of the Big Five factors of Conscientiousness, Agreeableness, and Emotional Stability.

Recent research has also revealed there are substantial within-test differences for the two types of integrity tests. For instance, with regard to overt integrity tests, Wanek et al. (1998) found that the PSI correlated most highly with the Honesty Image factor, the Stanton Survey correlated most highly with the Perception of Dishonesty Norms factor, and the Reid Report correlated most highly with the Theft Thoughts/Temptations factor. Similarly diverse results were found for the various personality-based instruments. This kind of research is invaluable for organizations trying to decide on the appropriate integrity test to be used as part of a selection battery, and its continuance is encouraged.

Ones and colleagues' comprehensive meta-analysis of integrity testing validities provided us with the best evidence yet that integrity tests are useful predictors of job performance and counterproductivity alike. Despite this meta-analysis, however, we are not yet in a position to conclude definitively whether overt tests have superior predictive ability vis-à-vis personality-based tests for the full range of counterproductive criteria. As mentioned earlier, the greatest hurdle to answering this question is the paucity of studies investigating the criterion-related validities of integrity tests in relation to specific counterproductive behaviors. As more validity studies using such criteria are conducted, more direct comparisons of the validities of overt and personality-based tests in relation to these criteria will become possible.

Research by Ones and others has also demonstrated that integrity tests do not derive their predictive capacity simply as a function of their relationship to personality variables. Rather, integrity tests make an independent contribution above and beyond Big Five measures in the prediction of job performance. In this vein, an important, though unresolved, issue is whether integrity tests add incremental validity to specific facets of the Big Five factors in predicting job performance. The question is ripe for investigation, and we encourage investigation of this issue. We also encourage researchers to explore the as yet unresolved question of whether integrity tests add incremental validity over personality variables in predicting counterproductive criteria. In light of the fact that integrity tests were conceived with the explicit purpose of predicting counterproductivity in the workplace, this remains a critical issue to explore.

For individuals reading this chapter who are convinced there may be some merit to the use of integrity tests in their organization, the critical issue is: Which test should be used? Unfortunately, there is no one "right" answer to this question. We do not believe the issue falls to be decided exclusively on the basis of the psychometric characteristics of the various instruments, for as we have indicated, the psychometric properties of the instruments are fairly similar. Nor does the choice rest on how test takers will react to the various tests, since the evidence is inconclusive as to whether one specific test or type of test yields more or less negative reactions than any other test. Rather, the choice of test must be determined on a case-by-case basis, considering a number of factors, including cost, whether social desirability scales are desired, the intended purpose of the test, and legal considerations relevant to the specific employment context where the test is to be introduced. We hope that, at the very least, we have provided the reader with a sound basis on which to make the decision.

## APPENDIX: PUBLISHERS OF INTEGRITY TESTS

### *Overt Integrity Tests*

Employee Attitude Survey—Reid London House, 9701 West Higgins Road, Rosemont, IL 60018. Tel: (800) 221–8378. Web site: www.reidlondonhouse.com.

Employee Reliability Inventory—Bay State Psychological Associates, Inc., 225 Friend Street, Boston, MA 02114. Tel: (800) 438–2772. Web site: www.eri.com.

Personnel Selection Inventory—Reid London House, 9701 West Higgins Road, Rosemont, IL 60018. Tel: (800) 221–8378. Web site: www.reidlondonhouse.com.

Phase II Profile—Lousig-Nont & Associates, Inc., 3740 South Royal Crest Street, Las Vegas, NV 89119. Tel: (800) 447–3211.

Reid Report—Reid London House, 9701 West Higgins Road, Rosemont, IL 60018. Tel: (800) 221–8378. Web site: www.reidlondonhouse.com.

Stanton Survey—Pinkerton Services Group, 13950 Ballantyne Corporate Place, Suite 300, Charlotte, NC 28277. Tel: (800) 528–5745. Web site: www.psg-pinkerton.com.

### Personality-Based Tests

Hogan Personnel Selection Series (now replaced by the Hogan Personality Inventory)—Hogan Assessment Systems, 2622 East 21st Street, Tulsa, OK 74114. Tel: (800) 756–0632. Web site: www.hoganassessments.com.

Inwald Personality Inventory—Hilson Research, Inc., P.O. Box 150239, Kew Gardens, NY 11415. Tel: (800) 926–2258. Web site: www.hilsonresearch.com.

Personal Outlook Inventory—Reid London House, 9701 West Higgins Road, Rosemont, IL 60018. Tel: (800) 221–8378. Web site: www.reidlondonhouse.com.

Personnel Decisions, Inc., Employment Inventory—Personnel Decisions, Inc., 2000 Plaza VII Tower, 45 South Seventh Street, Minneapolis, MN 55402. Tel: (800) 633–4410. Web site: www.pdi-corp.com.

Personnel Reaction Blank—Consulting Psychologists Press, Inc., 3803 East Bayshore Road, P.O. Box 10096, Palo Alto, CA 94303. Tel: (800) 624–1765. Web site: www.cpp-db.com.

## REFERENCES

Ashton, M.C. (1998). Personality and job performance: The importance of narrow traits. *Journal of Organizational Behavior, 19,* 289–303.

Ashton, M.C., Jackson, D.N., Paunonen, S.V., Helmes, E., & Rothstein, M.G. (1995). The criterion validity of broad factor scales versus specific factor scales. *Journal of Research in Personality, 29,* 432–442.

Barrick, M.R., & Mount, M.K. (1996). Effects of impression management and self-deception on the predictive validity of personality constructs. *Journal of Applied Psychology, 81,* 261–272.

Butcher, J.N., Dahlstrom, W.G., Graham, J.R., Tellegen, A.M., & Kaemmer, B. (1989). *Minnesota Multiphasic Personality Inventory-2 (MMPI-2): Manual for administration and scoring.* Minneapolis: University of Minnesota Press.

Cattell. R.B., Eber, H.W., & Tatsouka, M.M. (1970). *Handbook for the 16PF.* Champaign, IL: Institute for Personality and Ability Testing.

Costa, P.T. Jr., & McCrae, R.R. (1985b). *The NEO Personality Inventory Manual.* Odessa, FL: Psychological Assessment Resources.

Costa, P.T. Jr., & McRae, R.R. (1988). Personality in adulthood: A six-year longitudinal study of self-reports and self-ratings on the NEO Personality Inventory. *Journal of Personality and Social Psychology, 54,* 853–863.

Cunningham, M.R., Wong, D.T., & Barbee, A.P. (1994). Self-presentation dynamics on overt integrity tests: Experimental studies of the Reid Report. *Journal of Applied Psychology, 79*(5), 643–658.

Digman, J.M. (1990). Personality structure: Emergence of the five-factor model. *Annual Review of Psychology, 41,* 417–440.

Ellingson, J.E., Sackett, P.R., & Hough, L.M. (1999). Social desirability corrections in personality measurement: Issues of applicant comparison and construct validity. *Journal of Applied Psychology, 84,* 155–166.

Frost, A.G., & Joy, D.S. (1987). *The use of the Personnel Selection Inventory and the Emo Questionnaire in the selection of childcare workers* (Tech. Rep. No. 52). Park Ridge, IL: London House.

Goldberg, L.R. (1993). The structure of phenotypic personality types. *American Psychologist, 48,* 26–34.

Gough, H.G. (1972). *Manual for the Personnel Reaction Blank.* Palo Alto, CA: Consulting Psychologists Press.

Gough, H.G. (1987). *California Psychological Inventory administrator's guide.* Palo Alto, CA: Consulting Psychologists Press.

Harris, M.M., Dworkin, J.B., & Park, J. (1990). Pre-employment screening procedures: How human resource managers perceive them. *Journal of Business and Psychology, 4*(3), 279–292.

Helson, R., & Wink, P. (1992). Personality change in women from early 40s to early 50s. *Psychology and Aging, 7,* 46–55.

Henderson, M.W. (1992). *Job candidate's perceptions of pre-employment integrity testing.* Unpublished master's thesis, University of Minnesota.

Hogan, J., & Brinkmeyer, K. (1997). Bridging the gap between overt and personality-based integrity tests. *Personnel Psychology, 50,* 587–599.

Hogan, J., & Hogan, R. (1986). *Hogan Personnel Selection Series manual.* Tulsa, OK: Hogan Assessment Systems.

Hogan, J., & Hogan, R. (1989). How to measure employee reliability. *Journal of Applied Psychology, 74,* 273–279.

Hough, L.M. (1992). The "Big Five" personality variables—construct confusion: Description versus prediction. *Human Performance, 5,* 139–155.

Hough, L.M. (1998). Effects of intentional distortion in personality measurement and evaluation of suggested palliatives. *Human Performance, 11,* 209–244.

Hough, L.M., Eaton, N.K., Dunnette, M.D., Kamp, J.D., & McCloy, R.A. (1990). Criterion-related validities of personality constructs and the effect of response distortion on those validities. *Journal of Applied Psychology, 75,* 581–595.

Hough, L.M., & Schneider, R.J. (1996). Personality traits, taxonomies, and applications in organizations. In K.R. Murphy (Ed.), *Individual differences and behavior in organizations* (pp. 31–88). San Francisco: Jossey-Bass.

Inwald, R.E. (1992). *IPI Inwald personality inventory technical manual (revised).* Kew Gardens, NY: Hilson Research.

Jones, J.W. (1991, Summer). Assessing privacy invasiveness of psychological test items: Job relevant versus clinical measures of integrity. *Journal of Business and Psychology, 5*(4), 531–535.

Jones, J.W., & Fay, L. (1987). *Predicting child abuse potential with the Personnel Selection Inventory for childcare workers* (Tech. Rep. No. 54). Park Ridge, IL: London House.

Jones, J.W., & Joy, D.S. (1989, August). *Empirical investigation of job applicants' reactions to taking a preemployment honesty test.* Paper presented at the 98th Annual Conference of the American Psychological Association.

Jones, J.W., & Terris, W. (1982). Personality profiles of endorsers of nuclear crimes. *Personnel Selection and Training Bulletin, 3,* 31–41.

Jones, J.W., & Terris, W. (1983). Personality correlates of theft and drugs abuse among job applicants. *Proceedings of the Third International Conference on the 16PF Test,* 85–94.

Judge, T.A., Martocchio, J.J., & Thoreson, C.J. (1997). Five-Factor model of personality and employee absence. *Journal of Applied Psychology, 82,* 745–755.

Kravitz, D.A., Stinson, V., & Chavez, T.L. (1994, April). *Perceived fairness of tests used in making selection and promotion decisions.* Paper presented at the annual meeting of the Society for Industrial and Organizational Psychology, Nashville, TN.

Loehlin, J.C. (1992). *Genes and environment in personality development.* Newbury Park, CA: Sage.

Logan, T.G., Koettel, R.C., & Moore, R.W. (1986). Personality correlates of a test of honesty. *Psychological Reports, 59,* 1015–1018.

Martin, S.L., & Terris, W. (1991). Predicting infrequent behavior: Clarifying the impact on false-positive rates. *Journal of Applied Psychology, 76*(3), 484–487.

McCrae, R.R., & Costa, P.T. Jr. (1997). Personality trait structure as a human universal. *American Psychologist, 52,* 509–516.

Moore, R.W. (1990). Instructional effects on the Phase II Profile honesty test. *Psychological Reports, 67,* 291–294.

Murphy, K.R., & Lee, S.L. (1994). Does conscientiousness explain the relationship between integrity and job performance? *International Journal of Selection and Assessment, 2,* 226–233.

Ones, D.S. (1993, August). *The construct validity of integrity tests.* Unpublished doctoral dissertation, University of Iowa.

Ones, D.S., Schmidt, F.L., Viswesvaran, C., & Lykken, D.T. (1996). Controversies over integrity testing: two viewpoints. *Journal of Business and Psychology, 10,* 487–500.

Ones, D.S., & Viswesvaran, C. (1998a). The effects of social desirability and faking on personality and integrity assessment for personnel selection. *Human Performance, 11,* 245–271.

Ones, D.S., & Viswesvaran, C. (1998b). Integrity testing in organizations. In R.W. Griffin & A. O'Leary-Kelly (Eds.), *Dysfunctional behavior in organizations: Violent and deviant behavior. Monographs in organizational behavior and industrial relations, Vol. 23, Parts A & B* (pp. 243–276). Stamford, CT: Jai Press.

Ones, D.S., Viswesvaran, C., & Korbin, W. (1995, May). Meta-analyses of fakability estimates: Between-subjects versus within-subjects designs. In F.L. Schmidt (Chair), *Response distortion and social desirability in personnel testing and personnel selection.* Symposium conducted at the meeting of the Society for Industrial and Organizational Psychology, Orlando, FL.

Ones, D.S., Viswesvaran, C., & Schmidt, F. (1993a). Comprehensive meta-analysis of integrity test validities: Findings and implications for personnel selection and theories of job performance. *Journal of Applied Psychology Monograph, 78*(4), 679–703.

Ones, D.S., Viswesvaran, C., & Schmidt, F. (1993b, August). *Integrity tests predict substance abuse and aggressive behaviors at work.* Paper presented at the American Psychological Association Convention, Toronto, Canada.

Personnel Decisions, Inc. (1985). *Development and validation of the PDI Employment Inventory.* Minneapolis, MN: Personnel Decisions.

Ryan, A.M., & Sackett, P.R. (1987). Pre-employment honesty testing: Fakability, reactions of test takers, and company image. *Journal of Business and Psychology, 1,* 248–256.

Sackett, P.R., Burris, L.R., & Callahan, C. (1989). Integrity testing for personnel selection: an update. *Personnel Psychology, 42,* 491–529.

Sackett, P.R., & Ellingson, J.E. (1997). The effects of forming multipredictor composites on group differences and adverse impact. *Personnel Psychology, 50,* 707–721.

Sackett, P.R., & Harris, M.M. (1984). Honesty testing for personnel selection: A review and critique. *Personnel Psychology, 37,* 221–245.

Sackett, P.R., & Wanek, J.E. (1996). New developments in the use of measures of honesty, integrity, conscientiousness, dependability, trustworthiness, and reliability for personnel selection. *Personnel Psychology, 49,* 787–829.

Salgado, J.F. (1997). The five factor model of personality and job performance in the European Community. *Journal of Applied Psychology, 82,* 30–43.

Salgado, J.F. (2000, April 12–15). *The Big Five personality dimensions as predictors of alternative criteria.* Paper presented at the 15th Annual Conference of the Society for Industrial and Organizational Psychology, New Orleans, LA.

Slora, K.B. (1991). An empirical approach to determining employee deviance base rates. In J.W. Jones (Ed.), *Preemployment honesty testing: Current research and future directions* (pp. 21–38). Westport, CT: Quorum Books.

Stone, D.L., & Herringshaw, C. (1991, April). *Individuals' reactions to honesty testing.* Paper presented at the annual meeting of the Society for Industrial and Organizational Psychology, St. Louis, MO.

Stone, D.L., & Jones, G. (1992, April). *Effects of transparency and justification on reactions to honesty testing.* Paper presented at the annual meeting of the Society for Industrial and Organizational Psychology.

Wanek, J.E. (1991). *Testing the fakability of the Personnel Reaction Blank relative to the fakability of an overt integrity test.* Unpublished master's thesis, University of Minnesota.

Wanek, J.E., Sackett, P.R., & Ones, D.S. (1998, April). *Item-level analysis of integrity. A judgmental approach to defining subfactors.* Poster session presented at the annual meeting of the Society for Industrial and Organizational Psychology, Dallas, TX.

Wooley, R.M., & Hakstian, A.R. (1992). An examination of the construct validity of personality-based and overt measures of integrity. *Educational and Psychological Measurement, 52,* 475–489.

Wuebker, L.J. (1987, March). *The Safety Locus of Control Scale: A construct validation study.* Paper presented at the 8th Industrial and Organizational Psychology and Organizational Behavior Graduate Student Conference, Knoxville, TN.

Zickar, M.J., Rosee, J.G., Levin, R.A., & Hulin, C.L. (1997). *Modeling the effects of faking on personality instruments.* Manuscript submitted for publication.

CHAPTER 11

# Measures of Career Interests

JO-IDA C. HANSEN AND BRYAN J. DIK

Birds of a feather flock together. This is one of the premises that guides the use of assessment in industrial-organizational (I/O) psychology. In other words, people with similar interests, personalities, abilities, and values are drawn to similar jobs, occupations, types of people, work tasks, and employment settings. The matching that occurs between workers and their employment environments is known as person-environment fit (P-E fit). A number of models of P-E fit (e.g., Dawis & Lofquist, 1984; Holland, 1997; Schneider, 1987) have been developed in an effort to identify predictors (e.g., abilities, interests, values, needs) of vocational outcomes (e.g., occupational choice, work commitment, job satisfaction, productivity, occupational health, retention).

Research conducted at the University of Minnesota's Employment Stabilization Research Institute in the 1930s (Patterson & Darley, 1936) showed the usefulness of P-E fit models for developing a more effective and stable labor force. According to a recent review of over 100 studies testing P-E fit models, employee-work environment fit is positively related to work outcomes such as job involvement and work facet job satisfaction and is negatively related to unsatisfactory outcomes such as turnover and absenteeism (Tinsley, 2000). Another review of the literature ($N = 21$ studies) has reported median correlations of .30 between interests and job satisfaction (Hough, 1988).

The measurement of some P-E fit constructs, most notably interests, values, and personality, can be done reliably with self-report inventories. However, early attempts to assess interests were much less efficient than are today's self-report inventories. Thus, as is the case for much psychological assessment, interest inventories first were developed to provide an efficient means for determining a person's interests in preparation for addressing the practical problem of vocational choice and career decision making in educational, business, and industrial settings (Hansen, 1984).

In the early 1900s, educators realized that consideration of one's interests in selecting a career could lead to an improved quality of life (Parsons, 1909). By the 1920s, business and industry also recognized that employees who were interested in their work seemed to perform better (Ream, 1924) and experienced less turnover than did people with interests that did not match the requirements of their positions. Today interest assessment can contribute in several ways to work in the I/O setting. The uses can be divided roughly into those that benefit the organization and those that focus on the individual, although, of course, there often is mutual benefit to the organization as well as the individual.

From the organizational perspective, interests are assessed to make selection, classification, and placement decisions. Typically, an interest inventory is administered in conjunction with the assessment of personality, abilities, and the collection of biographical data and work histories. Although it is well documented (Gatewood, Perloff, & Perloff, 2000; Levine, Spector, Menon, Narayanan, & Cannon-Bowers, 1996) that abilities, especially general cognitive ability, contribute the most variance to selection outcomes such as training success, performance, and productivity (Ree & Earles, 1991; Roznowski & Hulin, 1992; Vinchur, Schippmann, Switzer, & Roth, 1998), studies also have shown that interests contribute additional variance above and beyond that of abilities (McHenry, Hough, Toquam, Hanson, & Ashworth, 1990; Wise, McHenry, & Campbell, 1990). Generally, people with the necessary ability to do a job, and an interest in the job they are doing, will do well. The result for someone who has the ability but not the interest is less certain; some individuals will do well, but many may not (Hansen, 1994). After initial selection, interest inventories often are used for placement purposes to help employees find the right position within an organization (Dunnette & Kirchner, 1965; Hansen, 1994).

As the study of vocational psychology has advanced, more attention has focused on the occupational health and adjustment of adults after they enter the workforce. In this context, interest inventories are used for several purposes to promote an individual's self-development. Although interest inventories provide some people with ideas for new career paths, a career change is not the only possible outcome of career exploration. For some people, interest inventory results help to identify ways in which they can modify their current occupation or career to maximize their satisfaction with their work lives. For still other individuals, the scores on their interest inventories serve to confirm that the career choice they have made is the right one for them (Hansen, 1992).

Life-span models of career development and occupational aspirations are particularly useful in working with employees who are (1) seeking more challenging positions (Dewhirst, 1991), (2) questioning initial career decisions (Korman, 1988), (3) experiencing plateaued careers (Hall & Rabinowitz, 1988), (4) facing layoffs and outplacement (Latack & Kaufman, 1988), or (5) preparing for retirement (Kim & Moen, 2001). In other words, career exploration and evaluation can be important to an individual's career development at all adult life stages (Greenhaus, 1988; Osipow, 1986). Ultimately, of course, employees must assume responsibility for managing their careers. However, organizations can provide support for the process through employee assistance (EAP), human resource (HR), or occupational health psychology (OHP) programs.

Career development programs within organizations can occur in a variety of formats, including group, self-directed, and support-oriented activities. Workshops typically have been the most popular group intervention. They can serve a large number of people at one time and also provide valuable networking opportunities with other employees and support from colleagues (Liebowitz, Farren, & Kaye, 1986). Self-directed career development exploration usually is accompanied by materials such as workbooks or computer-assisted programs that provide the employee with guidelines for completing the process. Support-oriented career exploration relies on career counselors or coaches who work one-on-one with the employee.

The career development intervention, regardless of its format, is designed to help employees become aware of their interests, values, and abilities and to understand how various work environments or jobs satisfy their interests and values and make use of their abilities. Often interventions are accompanied by follow-up activities that involve gaining more information about the work environment through discussions with other people (e.g., peers, acquaintances, managers) as well as reading about occupations and organizations.

## DEVELOPMENT OF INTEREST INVENTORIES

The earliest methods of estimating a person's interest in an activity involved try-out methods that included taking courses in the field, reading about the occupation, or actually seeking work experience. These techniques continue to be used in career exploration. However, they generally are procedures implemented after testing has provided an initial assessment of interests, and after occupational ideas have been generated and then reduced to a manageable few for more in-depth exploration. Administering a self-report interest inventory has numerous advantages over the try-out method, not the least of which is time efficiency.

Three basic tenets underlie the assumption that interest inventories can provide people with a measure of their interest for activities in which they never have engaged and for occupations about which they know little or nothing (Hansen, 1992). First, people can give informed responses about their degree of attraction (e.g., like, indifferent, dislike) to items that reflect familiar activities or occupations. Second, the interests that are reflected by these familiar activities and occupations have variance in common with unfamiliar activities. Third, responses to the familiar activities can be used to generalize to interest in unfamiliar occupations and activities.

One of the first interest inventories, the Strong Vocational Interest Blank®[1] (Strong, 1927) now called the Strong Interest Inventory™[2] (Harmon, Hansen, Borgen, & Hammer, 1994), continues to be widely used in business and educational settings. Another inventory, the Self-Directed Search (SDS;

Holland, 1971), also is popular in both educational and business settings. A relative newcomer to the field is the Campbell Interest and Skill Survey™ ³ (CISS® ³; Campbell, Hyne, & Nilsen, 1992). The CISS was developed for use in business and organizations but also is increasingly popular in college counseling settings. The CISS is part of a larger battery of inventories that includes the Campbell Leadership Index™ ⁴ (CLI® ⁴, Campbell, 1991), the Campbell Organizational Survey™ ⁵ (Campbell, 1990), and the Campbell-Hallam Team Development Survey™ ⁶ (Hallam & Campbell, 1994). In addition to these inventories, some personality measures, such as the 16PF (Cattell, Cattell, & Cattell, 1993), have been adapted to reflect occupational interests.

## STRONG INTEREST INVENTORY

The Strong Interest Inventory (SII; Harmon et al., 1994), the most recent inventory in the Strong tradition, enjoys the longest history of any vocational interest measure and continues to be one of the most widely used of all psychological inventories in both research and practice (Hansen & Campbell, 1985; Walsh & Betz, 1995). The SII has been under continuous research and revision since first published as the Strong Vocational Interest Blank (SVIB) by E.K. Strong Jr. in 1927. Strong's first SVIB consisted of 10 Occupational Scales, developed using the empirical method of contrast groups, in which the interests of the respondent were compared with the interests of men employed in particular occupations. The first form for women was published in 1933. Subsequent revisions of the inventory continued to use separate forms for men and women until, under fire for being insensitive to gender issues, a revision completed in 1974 (Campbell, 1974) produced the first combined-gender form. On each revision since then women and men have responded to the same items, though because of clear differences in response patterns between genders, separate norms for women and men continue to be used. The 1981 revision (Campbell & Hansen, 1981) began an effort to provide matched-gender Occupational Scales (i.e., female- and male-normed scales for each occupation), and the 1985 revision (Hansen & Campbell, 1985) added more nonprofessional and vocational/technical occupational scales to the profile.

### Item Booklet and Profile

The booklet for the 1994 revision of the SII contains 317 items, divided into eight categories: Part 1, Occupational Titles; Part 2, School Subjects; Part 3, Activities; Part 4, Leisure Activities; Part 5, Types of People; Part 6, Preference Between Two Activities; Part 7, Your Characteristics; and Part 8, Preference in the World of Work. The item format for the first five sections requires respondents to indicate the degree of their interest in each item by responding "Like," "Indifferent," or "Dislike." Parts 6 and 8 use a forced choice between two alternatives (and an "undecided" option), and Part 7 uses a yes/?/no response format.

The six-page profile presents scores on four sets of scales: six General Occupational Themes, 25 Basic Interest Scales, 211 Occupational Scales that represent a wide range of occupations (e.g., electrician, research and development manager, corporate trainer, elementary school teacher, human resources director, secretary), and four Personal Style Scales.

### Occupational Scales

The Occupational Scales provide the highest level of specificity among the scales on the SII. They represent the degree to which the likes and dislikes indicated by the respondent correspond to the patterns of likes and dislikes of workers in 109 different occupations. The Occupational Scales on the 1994 Strong were constructed using the empirical method of contrast groups, essentially the same procedure devised by Strong to construct his original 10 scales in the 1920s. This procedure compares item responses from satisfied members of a particular occupation to those of an in-general group of employed individuals from a wide variety of occupations. Items on which the two groups respond differently are retained for that occupation's scale.

For the construction of the 1994 scales, a set of occupations first was selected for possible inclusion. After this, occupational criterion samples were formed: Groups that represented each occupation were recruited and screened so that only those respondents who most characterized their respective occupation were retained. Contrast samples of people-in-general containing members of all occupations sampled for the SII were then formed for each gender; these consisted of 9,467 working women and 9,484 working men. Next, response percentages for each item were computed for the occupational criterion samples and the women-in-general and men-in-general samples. Comparisons were then made between percentages for a given criterion sample and its "in-general" sample to identify items that differentiate the two. Usually 40 to 50 items emerged as the interests ("Likes") or aversions ("Dislikes") of members in each occupation. Finally, raw scores for each occupational criterion sample on its own Occupational Scale were obtained. These were used to establish standard T-scores for that Occupational Scale, with the mean for samples of women- and men-in-general set equal to 50 and the standard deviation equal to 10.

The resulting 211 Occupational Scales include 102 matched-gender occupational scales (e.g., female and male engineers, female and male buyers) and seven more occupations represented by just one scale because the number of alternate-gender workers located in these occupations were too small to construct reliable scales. These include f Child Care Provider, f Dental Assistant, f Dental Hygienist, f Home Economics Teacher, f Secretary, m Agribusiness Manager, and m Plumber.

## Basic Interest Scales

The Basic Interest Scales (BIS), which first appeared on the 1968 revision of the Strong, were constructed using cluster analysis to identify highly correlated items (Campbell, Borgen, Eastes, Johansson, & Peterson, 1968). In contrast to the heterogeneous item content of the Occupational Scales, the BIS were developed to measure only one interest factor per scale. The resulting homogeneity makes the BIS easier to interpret than the Occupational Scales, which represent several interest factors and are based on dislikes as well as likes for each occupational group. The names of the 25 BIS on the 1994 Strong describe the homogeneous item content and the interest factor measured by each scale (e.g., Medical Science, Social Service, Public Speaking, Computer Activities).

## General Occupational Themes

The General Occupational Themes (GOT; Campbell & Holland, 1972; Hansen & Johansson, 1972), as their name suggests, provide the most general, global view of vocational interests on the Strong. Along with the BIS, they are an additional means to explain high and low scores on the Occupational Scales. They also provide the organizational structure evident in the SII profile. The introduction of the GOT on the 1974 Strong merged Strong's empiricism with John Holland's theory of vocational types, an event described as the greatest recent innovation in interest measurement (Donnay, 1997). The six homogeneous themes contain items selected to represent Holland's definition of each vocational type—Realistic, Investigative, Artistic, Social, Enterprising, and Conventional. Statistical evidence such as item intercorrelations, popularity of items among occupations of designated Holland types, and item-scale correlations aided the construction of the themes.

## Personal Style Scales

The four Personal Style Scales are modifications of scales that appeared on earlier versions of the Strong. They complement the other scales by measuring preferences for, and comfort with, more specific aspects of the work environment itself. These scales were developed using two different strategies. The Work Style and Learning Environment scales, in the same vein as the Occupational Scales, were developed using the empirical method of contrast groups. The Leadership Style and Risk Taking/Adventure scales were constructed as homogeneous scales using item intercorrelations, similar to the BIS.

The Work Style scale measures the degree to which people prefer to work with ideas, data, and things (low scores) or people (high scores). The Learning Environment scale indicates the extent to which people prefer practical, hands-on training (low scores) or traditional academic learning environments (high scores). The Leadership Style scale measures one's position on the dimension of leading quietly by example (low scores) versus taking charge of others (high scores). Finally, the Risk Taking/Adventure scale measures the degree to which one is comfortable taking risks.

## Profile Organization

Holland's theory, as represented by the GOT, provides the organizational framework for the SII profile. The GOT themselves are arranged on the profile in the hexagonal order hypothesized by Holland—Realistic, Investigative, Artistic, Social, Enterprising, and Conventional.

Each GOT score is reported in two ways. First, a standard score provides a comparison to people-in-general (i.e., the general reference sample) whose mean is 50 and standard deviation is 10. Second, a point is plotted on the profile, and interpretive bars provide a comparison of the individual's score to those of women- and men-in-general. For example, Figure 11.1 demonstrates that Client 1, a dental assistant employed at an oral surgery clinic, obtained a score of 60 on the Social theme. This score is 10 points above the mean for the general reference sample. Compared with women-in-general (upper bar against which her score is plotted), this score is about 8 points higher than the mean. Compared with men-in-general (lower gray bar), this score is about 12 points higher than the mean.

The BIS are clustered according to Holland types by identifying the theme with which each Basic Interest Scale has the highest correlation. This gives the BIS the appearance of representing subdivisions of the GOT. As shown in Figure 11.1, the BIS scores also are compared with people-in-general (standard scores) and to women- and men-in-general (interpretive bars). Perhaps serving as evidence that her career suits her well, the score on the Medical Service scale for Client 1

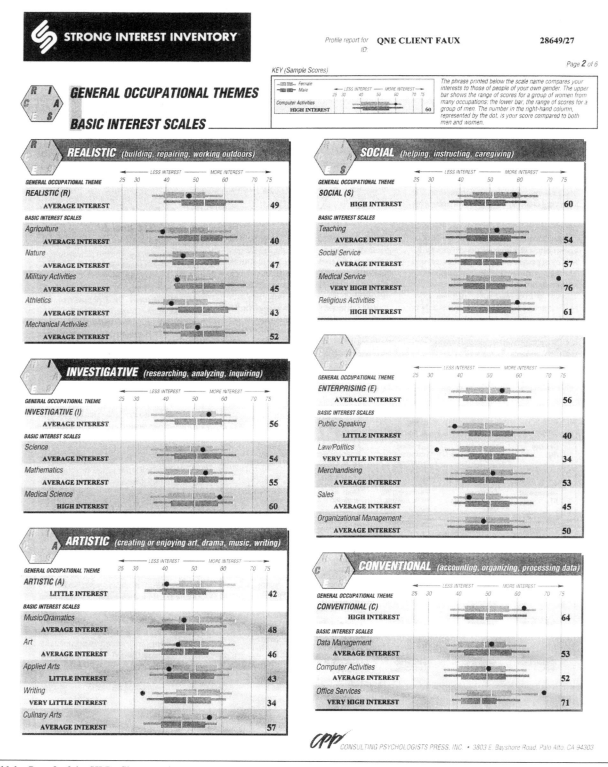

**Figure 11.1**   Page 2 of the SII Profile presenting scores on the General Occupational Themes and the Basic Interest Scales for Client 1. Modified and reproduced by special permission of the Publisher, Consulting Psychologists Press, Inc., Palo Alto, CA 94303 from Strong Interest Inventory Applications and Technical Guide of the Strong Interest Inventory of the Strong Vocational Interest Blanks® Form T317. By Lenore W. Harmon, Jo-Ida C. Hansen, Fred H. Borgen, Allen L. Hammer. Copyright © 1933, 1938, 1945, 1946, 1966, 1968, 1974, 1981, 1985, 1994 by the Board of Trustees of the Leland Stanford Junior University. All rights reserved. Printed under license from Stanford University Press, Stanford University Press, Stanford, CA 94305. Strong Vocational Interest Blanks is a registered trademark of Stanford University Press. Further reproduction is prohibited without the Publisher's written consent.

is 76, a full 25 points higher than the mean for women and 28 points higher than the mean for men.

The Occupational Scales are coded with one to three Holland types based on the criterion sample's highest scores on the GOT (e.g., female and male buyers are coded EC—Enterprising, Conventional; female and male English teachers are coded ASE—Artistic, Social, Enterprising). As shown in Figure 11.2, the Occupational Scales are clustered together and arranged on the profile according to their primary Holland type. A person receives a score on both the female- and male-normed scales. The scales are standardized so that the occupational sample's mean is 50 and standard deviation is 10. A point is plotted on the profile to represent the respondent's own gender score. For example, Figure 11.2 shows a plotted point representing the score of 60 that Client 1 obtained on the female Food Service Manager scale. Her score on the male Food Service Manager scale is 47. She also scored 60 on the female Dental Assistant scale; as mentioned earlier, there is no male Dental Assistant scale. Generally, scores of 40 or higher suggest that the similarity between the client's interests and those of members of that occupation may warrant further exploration and consideration of that occupation by the client.

Personal Style Scales were standardized using the combined-gender general reference sample and are presented on the profile, as shown in Figure 11.3, using interpretive bars that compare one's score to distributions based on women- and men-in-general samples. As Figure 11.3 indicates, scores for Client 1 suggest that (1) she may prefer to work alone in some situations while in others she may prefer to work with people (Work Style scale score of 55, close to the mean for women); (2) she probably has a strong preference for hands-on learning as opposed to traditional academic environments (Learning Environment scale score of 29); (3) she likely tends to prefer doing the job well and leading by example rather than seeking out leadership roles (Leadership Style scale score of 39); and (4) she probably prefers playing it safe as opposed to taking chances (Risk Taking/Adventure scale score of 32).

### Reliability and Validity

The test-retest reliability of scales on the Strong provides evidence of their stability over short and long periods of time. Median reliabilities over one- and three-month periods are .86 and .81, respectively, for the GOT; .85 and .80 for the BIS; and .87 and .85 for the Occupational Scales (Harmon et al., 1994).

Establishing evidence for criterion-related validity, particularly predictive validity, is important for interest inventories given their use in aiding decisions with long-term implications. No predictive validity data have been published for the 1994 Strong, though evidence supports its concurrent validity (Donnay & Borgen, 1996; Harmon et al., 1994; Lattimore & Borgen, 1999). Past research in interest measurement has demonstrated that participants aspiring to particular occupations usually share the interest patterns of people employed in those occupations, making it reasonable to expect concurrent validity to often lead to predictive validity (e.g., Borgen, 1972; Borgen & Helms, 1975; Campbell, 1971; Hansen, 1986; Harmon, 1969; Strong, 1955). The majority of validity studies on earlier revisions of the Strong focused on the Occupational Scales, which present the most specific level of prediction. These data repeatedly have indicated that respondents tend to enter occupations on which they earlier had obtained high Occupational Scale scores. Specifically, 54% to 74% of participants in predictive validity studies enter occupations predictable from earlier scores (Campbell, 1966; Dolliver, Irvin, & Bigley, 1972; Hansen, 1986; McArthur, 1954; Spokane, 1979).

## HOLLAND'S SELF-DIRECTED SEARCH

The Self-Directed Search (SDS; Holland, 1971, 1979, 1985a, 1994a) is a self-administered, self-scored, and (to a degree) self-interpreted instrument developed by Holland to measure his six vocational personality types. Holland's first inventory, developed using a series of theoretical and empirical reports, was the Vocational Preference Inventory (VPI). The evidence accumulated by the earliest VPI (1953) and its subsequent revisions played a primary role in refining the six typological definitions (Holland, 1959) and in identifying their hexagonal order (Holland, Whitney, Cole, & Richards, 1969). The first SDS was published shortly after Holland proposed the hexagonal order. In addition to incorporating Holland's theory and classification scheme, the SDS avoided the problems involved in separate answer sheets, elapsed time to accommodate scoring at a remote location, and the cost of machine scoring and mailing. The SDS quickly became popular with users and professionals (Holland, Powell, & Fritzsche, 1994). Although the VPI still is available (Holland, 1985b), the SDS is used more frequently and has become one of the most widely used interest inventories (Holland, Fritzsche, & Powell, 1994).

The assessment booklet for the most recent revision of the SDS Form R, 4th Edition (Holland, 1994a), includes 228 items divided into five sections: Occupational Daydreams, which does not include items but provides the respondent with an opportunity to list her or his "dream jobs"; Activities,

**STRONG INTEREST INVENTORY**

Profile report for   **QNE CLIENT FAUX**
ID:

28649/27

Page **5** of 6

**OCCUPATIONAL SCALES** (continued)

KEY (Sample Scores)

| THEME CODES | | OCCUPATION | YOUR SCORES | | DISSIMILAR INTERESTS | MID-RANGE | SIMILAR INTERESTS |
|---|---|---|---|---|---|---|---|
| FEMALE | MALE | | FEMALE | MALE | 15   32 | 30—MID-RANGE—40 | 50   55 |
| EA | (AE) | Interior Decorator | 46 | (AE) | | | ● |
| CSE | * | Dental Assistant | 15 | * | | | |

- The position of the dot shows how similar your interests are to those of individuals of your gender who say they are satisfied in their occupation.

( ) You can find your score compared to this gender under the Theme represented by the first letter of this code. For example, your score compared to male interior decorators is shown under the A or Artistic Theme.

* Not enough people of this gender who work in this occupation could be found to make a good comparison.

NOTES

**ENTERPRISING** (selling, managing, persuading)

| THEME CODES | | OCCUPATION | YOUR SCORES | | DISSIMILAR INTERESTS————SIMILAR INTERESTS |
|---|---|---|---|---|---|
| FEMALE | MALE | | FEMALE | MALE | 15   20   30—MID-RANGE—40   50   55 |
| * | ECR | Agribusiness Manager | * | 30 | |
| EC | EC | Buyer | 36 | 26 | |
| ERA | ER | Chef | 36 | 48 | |
| EIS | * | Dental Hygienist | 54 | * | |
| EAS | ESA | Elected Public Official | 14 | 12 | |
| EAS | EAS | Flight Attendant | 35 | 51 | |
| EAC | EAC | Florist | 31 | 32 | |
| EC | EA | Hair Stylist | 41 | 36 | |
| ECS | ECS | Housekeeping & Maintenance Supervisor | 49 | 51 | |
| EAS | ES | Human Resources Director | 26 | 30 | |
| EA | (AE) | Interior Decorator | 17 | (AE) | |
| EIR | ECI | Investments Manager | 17 | 12 | |
| E | E | Life Insurance Agent | 20 | 18 | |
| EA | EA | Marketing Executive | 8 | 14 | |
| ECR | ER | Optician | 52 | 45 | |
| ECR | ECR | Purchasing Agent | 34 | 27 | |
| E | E | Realtor | 14 | 26 | |
| ECR | ECR | Restaurant Manager | 39 | 39 | |
| ECA | ECS | Store Manager | 37 | 33 | |
| ECA | ECA | Travel Agent | 34 | 34 | |

**CONVENTIONAL** (accounting, organizing, processing data)

| THEME CODES | | OCCUPATION | YOUR SCORES | | DISSIMILAR INTERESTS————SIMILAR INTERESTS |
|---|---|---|---|---|---|
| FEMALE | MALE | | FEMALE | MALE | 15   20   30—MID-RANGE—40   50   55 |
| CE | CE | Accountant | 35 | 33 | |
| CI | CI | Actuary | 40 | 27 | |
| CE | CE | Banker | 47 | 43 | |
| C | C | Bookkeeper | 35 | 26 | |
| CES | CES | Business Education Teacher | 38 | 45 | |
| CE | CE | Credit Manager | 41 | 36 | |
| CSE | * | Dental Assistant | 60 | * | |
| CSE | (RC) | Farmer | 53 | (RC) | |
| CES | CES | Food Service Manager | 60 | 47 | |
| CIR | CIS | Mathematics Teacher | 45 | 37 | |
| C | C | Medical Records Technician | 51 | 54 | |
| CRE | (RCE) | Military Enlisted Personnel | 46 | (RCE) | |
| CES | CES | Nursing Home Administrator | 54 | 55 | |
| CE | CA | Paralegal | 22 | 20 | |
| CES | * | Secretary | 51 | * | |
| CE | (RE) | Small Business Owner | 46 | (RE) | |

*CPP* CONSULTING PSYCHOLOGISTS PRESS, INC. • 3803 E. Bayshore Road, Palo Alto, CA 94303

**Figure 11.2**   Page 5 of the SII Profile presenting scores on the Enterprising and Conventional Occupational Scales for Client 1. Modified and reproduced by special permission of the Publisher, Consulting Psychologists Press, Inc., Palo Alto, CA 94303 from Strong Interest Inventory Applications and Technical Guide of the Strong Interest Inventory of the Strong Vocational Interest Blanks® Form T317. By Lenore W. Harmon, Jo-Ida C. Hansen, Fred H. Borgen, Allen L. Hammer. Copyright © 1933, 1938, 1945, 1946, 1966, 1968, 1974, 1981, 1985, 1994 by the Board of Trustees of the Leland Stanford Junior University. All rights reserved. Printed under license from Stanford University Press, Stanford University Press, Stanford, CA 94305. Strong Vocational Interest Blanks is a registered trademark of Stanford University Press. Further reproduction is prohibited without the Publisher's written consent.

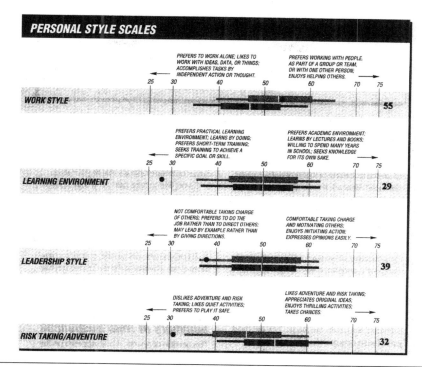

**Figure 11.3**   Portion of the SII Profile presenting scores on the Personal Style Scales for Client 1. Modified and reproduced by special permission of the Publisher, Consulting Psychologists Press, Inc., Palo Alto, CA 94303 from *Strong Interest Inventory Applications and Technical Guide* of the Strong Interest Inventory of the Strong Vocational Interest Blanks® Form T317. By Lenore W. Harmon, Jo-Ida C. Hansen, Fred H. Borgen, Allen L. Hammer. Copyright © 1933, 1938, 1945, 1946, 1966, 1968, 1974, 1981, 1985, 1994 by the Board of Trustees of the Leland Stanford Junior University. All rights reserved. Printed under license from Stanford University Press, Stanford University Press, Stanford, CA 94305. Strong Vocational Interest Blanks is a registered trademark of Stanford University Press. Further reproduction is prohibited without the Publisher's written consent.

for which the respondent indicates "Like" or "Dislike" for a variety of activities; Competencies, for which the respondent chooses "Yes" or "No" for a variety of activities according to her or his perceived proficiency in each; Occupations, which also uses a like/dislike response format; and Self-Estimates, for which the respondent rates her or his abilities in a variety of work-related areas on a 1–7 scale.

A briefer version of the SDS, Form CP (Holland, 1990), was designed for professionals and adults in career transition. In response to feedback from users in large organizations, the Daydreams and Self-Estimates sections were dropped from Form CP to reduce the time needed to complete it, and the remaining sections contain items more relevant for adult workers in organizations. Other versions of the SDS are available (e.g., Form E, developed for use with respondents of limited reading skill), but Form R and Form CP are used most commonly in organizational settings (Lenz, 1996). Computerized versions of the SDS also are available (Holland, 1995).

The key feature of the SDS profile is the Summary Code. The respondent uses the scoring key to compute a raw score for each of the six Holland types, and the three highest raw

scores represent her or his primary, secondary, and tertiary code assignment; this three-letter code is the Summary Code. The Summary Code then is used to identify occupational and educational alternatives with Holland Codes similar to that of the respondent. Several booklets are available to assist respondents with this task. *The Educational Opportunities Finder* (Rosen, Holmberg, & Holland, 1994), for example, provides three-letter Holland Codes for 750 programs of study, while *The Occupations Finder* (Holland, 1994b) provides codes for 1,335 occupations. The *Career Options Finder* (Holland, 2001), developed for use with SDS Form-CP, provides codes for 911 occupations, focusing primarily on careers from a wide range of industries and occupational groups that require at least a high school education. Since SDS Summary Codes should not be viewed as precise measures, but rather as approximations, Holland (1979) suggests flexibility in their use for career exploration.

Another helpful tool in linking SDS information to a respondent's work is the Position Classification Inventory (PCI; Gottfredson & Holland, 1991). The PCI provides a means for organizations and employees to assign scores on each of

Holland's six types to a current work position. SDS Summary Codes can be compared with PCI codes for specific positions, providing the respondent and the organization with a greater understanding of the degree of correspondence between the respondent's reported interests and the demands of her or his current occupation.

The self-scoring version of the SDS, shown in Figure 11.4, is more frequently used than the computerized version. As Figure 11.4 indicates, the scoring instructions are easy to follow. Client 2, an early-career electrical engineer who aspires to specialize in medical technology, obtained his highest scores on the Realistic, Investigative, and Conventional themes. (The Holland Code for electrical engineers is IRE.) After computing his Holland Code, Client 2 used the *Career Options Finder* (Holland, 2001) to generate the occupational alternatives shown in Figure 11.5. Since his Investigative and Conventional theme scores differed by only one point, occupations listed under the RIC and RCI codes are presented.

### Reliability and Validity

The test-retest reliability coefficients for the six SDS scales ranged from .76 to .89 for intervals ranging from 4 to 12 weeks. Scales on each section of Form CP correlate .80 or greater with Form R, while summary score correlations between the two forms were .94 or higher (Holland, Fritzsche, & Powell, 1994). Studies of predictive validity for the SDS have demonstrated that between 39.6% and 79.3% of participants obtained a high-point code that matched the first-letter code of their occupation or occupational aspiration one to seven years later, with considerable variability attributed to factors such as age and educational level (Gottfredson & Holland, 1975; O'Neil & Magoon, 1977; O'Neil, Magoon, & Tracey, 1978; Power, 1981; Touchton & Magoon, 1977). The range was 48.0% to 76.0% for concurrent validity studies, in which the criterion was current occupation or occupational aspiration (Holland, 1985a; Mount & Muchinsky, 1978).

### CAMPBELL DEVELOPMENT SURVEYS

The Campbell Interest and Skill Survey (CISS; Campbell et al., 1992) was developed by David Campbell, who oversaw work on the SII during the 1960s and1970s. The Campbell Leadership Index (CLI), which uses self and observer ratings to measure leadership characteristics, is another of his instruments (Campbell, 1991). These surveys were developed to measure the psychological aspects of the working environment and are intended for use in "developmental programs where well-established, quantifiable psychological measures are useful for providing assessment data" (Campbell et al., 1992, p. 1).

### Campbell Interest and Skill Survey

The distinctive innovation in the CISS, one of the most recently developed interest inventories, is that it is the first interest inventory to supplement respondents' interest scores with self-estimates of skills in a wide range of activities. The CISS profile reports two scores for each of its 98 scales—an interest score and a skill score. The interest scales of the CISS have much in common with the SII, reflecting Campbell's extensive experience with and respect for Strong's psychometric development of his inventory.

### *Item Booklet and Profile*

The booklet for the CISS includes 320 items; 200 items assess interests and 120 items assess self-reported skills. The interest items use a 6-point response format, ranging from "Strongly Like" to "Strongly Dislike." The skill items also use a 6-point scale that requires respondents to rate themselves as "Expert," "Good," "Slightly Above Average," "Slightly Below Average," "Poor," and "None" (have no skills in this area). The 11-page profile presents scores on four sets of scales: 7 Orientation Scales, 29 Basic Scales, 60 Occupational Scales, and two Special Scales.

### *Orientation Scales*

The Orientation Scales are the CISS's equivalent of the SII's General Occupational Themes in that they provide global-level information that aids the interpretation of score patterns on Occupational Scales. The Orientation Scales also are used to thematically structure the CISS profile. Instead of Holland's six types, however, there are seven Orientation Scales: Influencing (business and politics), Organizing (managing and attention to detail), Helping (service and teaching), Creating (the arts and design), Analyzing (science and math), Producing (hands-on and mechanical), and Adventuring (physical and competitive activities). These scales, constructed using a variety of statistical clustering procedures, have content that differs subtly from Holland's scales in ways that are intended to make them more appropriate for college-educated adults in organizational settings. For example, the CISS Influencing Orientation is focused slightly more on leadership and less on sales than is Holland's Enterprising theme (Campbell & Borgen, 1999.)

An individual's score on each Orientation Scale is reported in several ways on the CISS profile (see Figures 11.6 and

# Calculating Your Holland Code

To tie your interests to specific careers, you need to calculate your Holland code.
To calculate your Holland code, follow these steps:

1. ACTIVITIES
   Go to pages 4–5. Count the number of times
   you marked Y (YES) for the **R** Activities. Write
   that number in the box labeled Total Ys and
   copy the number above the **R** on the line to the
   right. Do the same for the **I, A, S, E,** and **C**
   Activities.

<u>9</u>  <u>7</u>  <u>3</u>  <u>3</u>  <u>8</u>  <u>7</u>
R   I   A   S   E   C

2. COMPETENCIES
   Go to pages 6–7. Count the number of times
   you marked Y (YES) for the **R** Competencies.
   Write that number in the box labeled Total Ys
   and copy the number above the **R** on the line to
   the right. Do the same for the **I, A, S, E,** and **C**
   Competencies.

<u>10</u>  <u>10</u>  <u>4</u>  <u>10</u>  <u>6</u>  <u>8</u>
R   I   A   S   E   C

3. CAREERS
   Go to pages 8–9. Count the number of times
   you marked Y (YES) for the **R** Careers. Write
   that number in the box labeled Total Ys and
   copy the number above the **R** on the line to the
   right. Do the same for the **I, A, S, E,** and **C**
   Careers.

<u>4</u>  <u>2</u>  <u>0</u>  <u>0</u>  <u>1</u>  <u>3</u>
R   I   A   S   E   C

4. TOTAL SCORES
   Add your three **R** scores and write that number
   above the **R** on the line to the right. Do the same
   for the **I, A, S, E,** and **C** scores.

<u>23</u>  <u>19</u>  <u>7</u>  <u>13</u>  <u>15</u>  <u>18</u>
R   I   A   S   E   C

5. HOLLAND CODE
   Enter the letter with the highest total score in
   the box marked Highest. Enter the letter with
   the next highest score in the box marked 2nd.
   Enter the letter with the third highest score in
   the box marked 3rd. If two letters are tied, put
   them in any order.

   These letters make up your code. For example,
   if your three highest letters are **E, I,** and **S,** your
   Holland code is **EIS.**

Highest   2nd   3rd

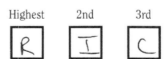

| Highest | 2nd | 3rd |
|---|---|---|
| R | I | C |

**Figure 11.4**   Profile for the Self-Directed Search Form CP, self-scored by Client 2. Adapted and reproduced by special permission of the publisher,
Psychological Assessment Resources, Inc., Odessa, FL 33556 from the Self-Directed Search Assessment Booklet Form CP by John L. Holland, Ph.D.,
Copyright 1970, 1973, 1977, 1985, 1990 by PAR, Inc. Further reproduction is prohibited without permission from PAR, Inc.

Code: RIC
Optical Engineer
Instrumentation Technician
Magnetic Resonance Imaging (MRI)
  Technologist
Quality Assurance Analyst (Tester)
Parking Analyst
Radio Station Operator
Solar-Energy-Systems Designer
Assembler and Tester, Electronics
Camera Operator, Animation
Civil Engineering Technician
Laboratory Tester

Code: RCI
Utilization Engineer (Utilities)
Audiovisual Technician
Automobile Mechanic
Computerized Environmental Control Installer
Custom Van Converter
Drafter, Architectural
Electrocardiograph Technician

**Figure 11.5**  List of occupations for the RIC and RCI Holland Codes as presented in the *Career Options Finder.*

11.7). In addition to Interest and Skill scale standard scores that compare the respondent with people-in-general (who have a mean score of 50 on each scale), a figure presents both scores visually along a continuum of interpretive comments, ranging from "Very Low" to "Very High." Measurement of both interests and self-perceived skills on the CISS provides interpretive information not available on other inventories. Based on a comparison of the magnitude of scores for each scale, the individual is advised to *Pursue* the area if both interest and skill scores are high, *Develop* the area if the interest score is high but the skill score is low, *Explore* the area if interest is low and skill is high, and *Avoid* if both interest and skill scores are low. (If interests and skills are both in the moderate range, no suggestion is printed.) Each page of the profile represents one of the Orientations (e.g., Influencing) and reports scores for all scales related to that Orientation. A short interpretive report, usually consisting of a few paragraphs, summarizes the individual's results for the Orientation, Basic, and Occupational scale scores presented on that page.

Figures 11.6 and 11.7 present 2 of the 13 pages of the CISS profile for Client 3, a founder and president of an international consulting firm, with a PhD in psychology. She scores high, for example, on both the Influencing Orientation Interest (62) and Skill (65) scales, which are scores consistent with the interpretive comment Pursue (see Figure 11.6). She also scores in the midrange on the Analyzing Orientation Interest (49) and Skill (46) scales (see Figure 11.7). Because these scores fall in the midrange, no interpretive comment is presented for them.

The Orientation Scales also serve on the CISS profile as the organizing framework by which the Basic Scales and Occupational Scales are presented. The Basic Scales (see Figures 11.6 and 11.7) are grouped under the Orientation with which they correlate most highly, while the Occupational Scales (see Figure 11.6 and 11.7) are clustered according to each occupational sample's highest Orientation Scale score. The computer programmer and systems analyst criterion samples, for instance, scored highest on the Analyzing Orientation and thus those scales are located under the Analyzing Orientation on the profile (see Figure 11.7).

### Basic Scales

The 29 Basic Scales were developed by identifying clusters of items that were highly intercorrelated in an effort to create homogeneous scales that measure interests and estimated skills in occupational areas such as Leadership, Public Speaking, Counseling, Mathematics, and Farming/Forestry. Similar to the SII's Basic Interest Scales, each Basic Scale on the CISS is intended to measure a single interest factor. The Basic Scales scores, illustrated in Figures 11.6 and 11.7, are presented on the CISS profile by Interest and Skill scale standard scores, a figure that plots both scores on the "Very Low" to "Very High" continuum, and a Pursue/Develop/Explore/Avoid interpretation. Client 3, for example, scores high on both the Leadership Interest scale (63) and Skill scale (65) compared with people-in-general (mean = 50) and is advised to Pursue this area. She scores relatively low on the Mathematics Basic Interest (40) and Skill (42) scales and is advised to Avoid this area.

### Occupational Scales

The Occupational Scales on the CISS index the degree of similarity between the expressed interests and skill estimates

# CAMPBELL™ INTEREST AND SKILL SURVEY INDIVIDUAL PROFILE REPORT

FAUX CLIENT 3

## Influencing Orientation

DATE SCORED: 8/06/2001

### Orientation Scale

| | Standard Scores | Very Low 30 35 | Low 40 45 | Mid-Range 50 55 | High 60 65 | Very High 70 | Interest/Skill Pattern |
|---|---|---|---|---|---|---|---|
| Influencing | I 62 / S 65 | | | | | | Pursue |

### Basic Interest and Skill Scales

| | Standard Scores | Very Low 30 35 | Low 40 45 | Mid-Range 50 55 | High 60 65 | Very High 70 | Interest/Skill Pattern |
|---|---|---|---|---|---|---|---|
| Leadership | I 63 / S 65 | | | | | | Pursue |
| Law/Politics | I 60 / S 57 | | | | | | Pursue |
| Public Speaking | I 58 / S 60 | | | | | | Pursue |
| Sales | I 48 / S 64 | | | | | | Explore |
| Advertising/Marketing | I 57 / S 53 | | | | | | Develop |

### Occupational Scales

| | Orientation Code | Standard Scores | Very Low 25 30 35 | Low 40 45 | Mid-Range 50 55 | High 60 65 | Very High 70 75 | Interest/Skill Pattern |
|---|---|---|---|---|---|---|---|---|
| Attorney | I | I 62 / S 60 | | | | | | Pursue |
| Financial Planner | IO | I 55 / S 66 | | | | | | Pursue |
| Hotel Manager | IO | I 65 / S 63 | | | | | | Pursue |
| Manufacturer's Representative | IO | I 57 / S 58 | | | | | | Pursue |
| Marketing Director | IO | I 63 / S 66 | | | | | | Pursue |
| Realtor | IO | I 63 / S 64 | | | | | | Pursue |
| CEO/President | IOA | I 59 / S 64 | | | | | | Pursue |
| Human Resources Director | IOH | I 53 / S 78 | | | | | | Explore |
| School Superintendent | IOH | I 69 / S 69 | | | | | | Pursue |
| Advertising Account Executive | IC | I 58 / S 59 | | | | | | Pursue |
| Media Executive | IC | I 65 / S 65 | | | | | | Pursue |
| Public Relations Director | IC | I 57 / S 61 | | | | | | Pursue |
| Corporate Trainer | ICH | I 59 / S 68 | | | | | | Pursue |

The Influencing Orientation focuses on influencing others through leadership, politics, public speaking, sales, and marketing. Influencers like to make things happen. They are often visible because they tend to take charge of activities that interest them. They typically work in organizations where they are responsible for directing activities, setting policies, and motivating people. Influencers are generally confident of their ability to persuade others and they usually enjoy the give-and-take of debating and negotiating. Typical high-scoring individuals include company presidents, corporate managers, school superintendents, sales representatives, and attorneys.

Your Influencing interest and skill scores are both very high. People who have scores as high as yours typically report very strong interest and very substantial confidence in leading, negotiating, marketing, selling, and public speaking.

Pursue some of these Influencing activities in your career.

Your scores on the Influencing Basic Scales, which provide more detail about your interests and skills in this area, are reported above on the left-hand side of the page. Your scores on the Influencing Occupational Scales, which show how your pattern of interests and skills compares with those of people employed in Influencing occupations, are reported above on the right-hand side of the page. Each occupation has a one-, two-, or three-letter code that indicates its highest Orientation score(s). The more similar the Orientation code is to your highest Orientation scores (which are reported on page 2), the more likely it is that you will find satisfaction working in that occupation.

* Standard Scores: I (♦) = Interests; S (◊) = Skills
** Interest/Skill Pattern: Pursue = High Interests, High Skills; Develop = High Interest, Lower Skills;
   Explore = High Skills, Lower Interests; Avoid = Low Interest, Low Skills
*** Orientation Code: I= Influencing; O= Organizing; H= Helping; C= Creating; N=aNalyzing; P= Producing;
   A= Adventuring
▬▬▬▬ Range of middle 50% of people in the occupation: Solid Bar = Interests; Hollow Bar = Skills

Page 4

**Figure 11.6**   Profile for the Influencing Orientation of the CISS®. Copyright © 1988, 1992 David P. Campbell, Ph.D. All rights reserved. Used here by permission.

## CAMPBELL™ INTEREST AND SKILL SURVEY INDIVIDUAL PROFILE REPORT

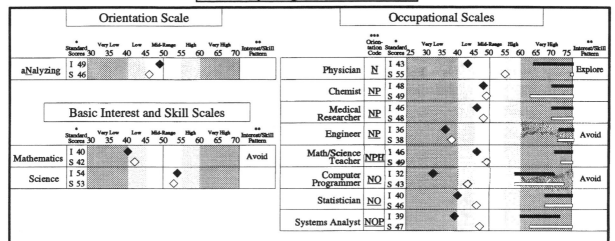

FAUX CLIENT 3                                                                                          DATE SCORED: 8/06/2001

(This Orientation is labelled with the letter "N" because the letter "A" is used for the Adventuring Orientation below.) The aNalyzing Orientation involves scientific, mathematical, statistical, and research activities. People who score high are comfortable with data and numbers and have a strong need to understand the world in a scientific sense. They usually prefer to work alone or in small groups in laboratory or academic settings, solving problems and designing experiments. ANalyzers are generally autonomous and like to work through problems for themselves. Typical high-scoring individuals include scientists, medical researchers, statisticians, computer programmers, and physicians.

Your aNalyzing interest and skill scores are both mid-range. People who have this pattern of scores typically report moderate interest and confidence in analyzing data, using mathematics, and conducting scientific research.

Your scores on the aNalyzing Basic Scales, which provide more detail about your interests and skills in this area, are reported above on the left-hand side of the page. Your scores on the aNalyzing Occupational Scales, which show how your pattern of interests and skills compares with those of people employed in aNalyzing occupations, are reported above on the right-hand side of the page. Each occupation has a one-, two-, or three-letter code that indicates its highest Orientation score(s). The more similar the Orientation code is to your highest Orientation scores (which are reported on page 2), the more likely it is that you will find satisfaction working in that occupation.

* Standard Scores: I (♦) = Interests; S (◊) = Skills
** Interest/Skill Pattern: Pursue = High Interests, High Skills; Develop = High Interest, Lower Skills;
    Explore = High Skills, Lower Interests; Avoid = Low Interest, Low Skills
*** Orientation Code: I= Influencing; O= Organizing; H= Helping; C= Creating; N=aNalyzing; P= Producing;
    A= Adventuring
▬▬▬▬  Range of middle 50% of people in the occupation: Solid Bar = Interests; Hollow Bar = Skills

**Figure 11.7**    Profile for the Analyzing Orientation of the CISS®. Copyright © 1988, 1992 David P. Campbell, Ph.D. All rights reserved. Used here by permission.

of the respondent to those of successful, satisfied workers in each of 60 occupations. Similar to their SII counterparts, the CISS Occupational Scales were developed using the empirical method of contrast groups, in which only items that differentiate an occupational criterion sample from the general reference sample were selected for that occupation's scale. In contrast to the SII, which includes separate scales for females and males, the CISS Occupational Scales were constructed using a combined-gender general reference sample that included 1,790 female and 3,435 male respondents. As the items were selected for each unisex Occupational Scale, the general reference sample statistics were weighted to reflect the ratio of females to males in the occupation being analyzed; this balanced the variability in female/male ratios across occupations. When scales were normed to produce standard T-scores (means set to 50, standard deviations to 10), the raw score means for males and females were averaged, giving each gender equal weighting in the raw-score-to-standard-score conversion. This method of creating norms also was used for the Basic Scales, Orientation Scales, and Special Scales on the CISS.

An individual's Interest and Skill score on each occupational scale is reported as a standard score that compares the respondent with people-in-general (who have a mean score of 50 on each scale). A figure also represents the scores on a continuum of interpretive comments that range from "Very Low" to "Very High." Interpretive bars representing the middle 50 percent of Interest and Skill scale scores for each occupational criterion sample on its own Occupational Scale provide points of reference for the respondent's scores.

Client 3 (see Figure 11.6), for example, scores 59 compared with people-in-general (who score 50) on the CEO/President Interest scale and 64 on the CEO/President Skill scale. The interpretive bars allow a comparison of the individual's score to those of the middle 50% of the occupational sample used to construct the scale. Client 3 is within a few points of the mean for the CEO/President criterion sample on both interests and skills, and the profile advice is to *Pursue* this interest area. However, on the Engineer scale (see Figure 11.7), Client 3 has low scores of 36 (Interest) and 38 (Skill), and she is advised to *Avoid* the occupation.

### Special Scales

The first of the two Special Scales on the CISS is the Academic Focus scale, which measures interests and self-estimated skills in academic pursuits, with particular emphasis on the arts and sciences. The Academic Focus scale was developed using the empirical method of contrast groups, with selected items discriminating between a sample of highly educated people from diverse occupations and the remaining CISS occupational samples. The second Special Scale is Extraversion, which measures interests and self-estimated skills in workplace activities that require high levels of social interaction. The Extraversion scale was developed by selecting CISS items that correlated highest with observer ratings of extraversion.

Interest and skill standard scores for the Academic Focus and Extraversion scales are presented on the CISS profile numerically and graphically, with accompanying interpretive reports. For example, Client 3, shown in Figure 11.8, scored in the midrange on the Academic Focus Interest (50) and Skill (52) scales, indicating an interest in pursuing educational and learning opportunities that are practical and action oriented. She scored high on the Extraversion Interest (61) and Skill (64) scales, indicating a very strong interest, and substantial confidence, in work situations that require interacting with others.

### Reliability and Validity

The median test-retest reliability coefficients over a 90-day period are .87, .83, and .87 for CISS Orientation Scales, Basic Scales, and Occupational Interest scales, respectively. The Skill scales are shorter in length and thus yield lower coefficients of .81, .79, and .79. This indicates that the Skill scales are slightly less stable than the Interest scales, though they are still safely within the range of acceptability. Substantial evidence of construct validity of all the CISS scales and concurrent validity of the Occupational Scales support their utility and are reported in the manual of the CISS (Campbell et al., 1992).

### Campbell Leadership Index

The Campbell Leadership Index (CLI; Campbell, 1991) is designed to assess personal characteristics relevant to the demands of leadership. Thus, although it is not a direct measure of interests per se, the CLI purports to measure a construct highly relevant to organizations that has an important relationship with interests. As such, it is particularly helpful when administered with an interest inventory. The CLI defines leadership as "actions which focus resources to create desirable opportunities" (Campbell, 1991, p. 3), an admittedly broad conceptualization that identifies seven global tasks as indicators of leadership. These tasks include provision of the following: organizational vision; effective management; empowerment of subordinates; deft politics (forging potentially beneficial coalitions); a listening ear and helpful feedback; entrepreneurship in creating future opportunities and desir-

## CAMPBELL™ INTEREST AND SKILL SURVEY INDIVIDUAL PROFILE REPORT

FAUX CLIENT 3

DATE SCORED: 8/06/2001

**Special Scales**

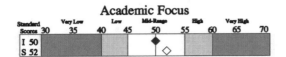

### Academic Focus

The Academic Focus Scales reflect your feelings toward the academic world. High scores do not necessarily lead to academic success, nor low scores to failure, but your pattern of scores reflects your degree of comfort in educational settings and can help you plan your educational strategy. High scorers are attracted to intellectual ideas, academic pursuits, and scientific research. Typical high-scoring individuals include university professors, research scientists, technical writers, and other scholars. People who score low usually see themselves as more action-oriented and practical. Business people, especially those in sales and marketing, tend to score low on the Academic Focus Scales.

Your Academic Focus interest and skill scores are both mid-range. People who have this pattern of scores typically report moderate interest and confidence in academic activities, such as studying, conducting research, and writing scientific papers.

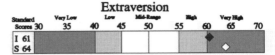

### Extraversion

The Extraversion Scales indicate level of interest and confidence working with all types of people in many different occupational settings. High scores reflect an attraction to a wide range of people-oriented activities. Lower scores may suggest a narrower focus, such as an interest in working with children but not adults, or confidence in counseling others but not selling. Low scores may indicate a preference for less contact with people on the job.

Occupational Extraverts (such as guidance counselors, hotel managers, corporate trainers, and realtors) are energized by frequent social contact and enjoy working closely with others. People who score low on the Extraversion Scales may prefer more independent work assignments and the opportunity for private time and space. Low-scoring individuals include scientists, skilled craftsworkers, and veterinarians.

Your Extraversion interest and skill scores are both very high. People who have scores as high as yours typically report very strong interest and very substantial confidence in work situations requiring a great deal of personal contact with others. Careers with an emphasis on people-oriented activities would probably be satisfying for you.

**Figure 11.8**　Special Scales of the CISS®. Used here by permission.

able change; and a personal example of competence, integrity, and optimism.

The CLI is an adjective checklist, with 100 adjectives (each presented along with its definition). The respondent is asked to indicate on a 6-point scale, ranging from "Always" to "Never," how well each adjective describes her or him. In addition to completing a self-assessment, the respondent is asked to select three to five observers familiar with her or his working style to rate the respondent on the same items, using the same 6-point scale. The CLI profile reports comparisons between self and observer ratings on 22 standardized scales representing specific leadership characteristics (e.g., ambitious, persuasive, optimistic) organized into five orientations. The orientations, conceptualized as major themes of leadership, include Leadership (taking charge, getting results); Energy (maintaining high levels of activity); Affability (valuing and empowering people); Dependability (competently managing resources); and Resilience (exhibiting mental dura-

bility and emotional balance). The selection of leadership characteristics and adjectives was guided by a combination of sources; informed discussions, case studies, and interviews were supplemented by a relatively limited body of relevant empirical research.

Scoring scales for the 22 characteristics were constructed by clustering items according to their intercorrelations, using common sense to ensure that the adjectives on each scale were sensibly related to one another. Once these scales were in place, factor analysis was used to select the five orientations. Scale norms were developed using 30 standardization samples containing 1,767 respondents rated by 7,414 observers. Statistical conversions were made to ensure that the resulting T-scores (mean equal to 50, standard deviation of 10) were reflective of scores in the population (see Campbell, 1991, for a thorough discussion of this process).

On the Standard Report, scores for the five orientations and 22 characteristics are presented numerically as well as graphically, with self and observer scores plotted alongside each other for purposes of comparison (see Figure 11.9). The Report also provides an interpretive summary and Self and Observer Response information for every item. An Enhanced Report also provides observer scores broken down by relationship level (i.e., subordinates, peers, and superiors). The 22 characteristics presented on the profile are assumed to be related to leadership effectiveness. However, good leaders do not necessarily exhibit all of the characteristics. Although high scores on more characteristics are assumed to relate to higher leadership effectiveness, the characteristics also are mutually interactive, so high scores can balance low scores. It also is assumed that knowing how others view the respondent can aid her or him in making future improvements in leadership.

Client 3, for example, appears to have a leadership style that creates a sense of excitement and energy for those around her. She is viewed as experienced, well informed, and able to deal skillfully with complex issues and unexpected challenges. She also is viewed as able to persuade and influence others and as willing and able to support others and help them succeed. Her scores are extremely positive compared with those of other leaders. However, even though her self-ratings are relatively high and consistent with the ratings of her observers, she still has not given herself enough credit for her strengths.

### Reliability and Validity

In two studies of test-retest reliability using the CLI over one- and two-month periods, coefficients range from .81 to .92 to for self ratings and .84 and .94 for observer ratings, respectively, on the Orientation Scales. For the shorter Characteristics scales, the coefficients range from .61 to .96 for self ratings and .71 to .94 for observer ratings, respectively. Interrater reliability of the observer ratings, measured with intraclass correlations, range from .68 to .82 for the Orientation Scales.

Data from the 30 standardization samples support the validity of the CLI in that samples of people in leadership positions generally obtained higher scores from self ratings and observer ratings than did other samples. Several studies of different categories of leaders within the same occupation or organizational setting demonstrate that although people who are perceived to be demonstrating different levels of leadership characteristics generally score in the hypothesized directions, score differences between categories are greater from the viewpoint of the observers than from that of the respondents themselves. For example, marketing managers, classified (based on their job performance) as "executive potential," "up-

and-coming," or "plateaued," rated themselves as having very similar (and high) leadership characteristics. Their observers, however, tended to rate the "executive-potential" managers high or very high on most characteristics, the "plateaued" managers in the midrange, and the "up-and-coming" somewhere in-between. Results are presented in more detail in the *Manual for the CLI* (Campbell, 1991). Nilsen, Hallam, and Campbell (1998) also report that CLI scales correlate highly with specific leadership skills, promotability as rated by senior managers, and with job performance.

## SIXTEEN PERSONALITY FACTOR QUESTIONNAIRE

The Sixteen Personality Factor Questionnaire (16PF; Cattell et al., 1993) is an example of an instrument developed to measure personality that has been enhanced with scales intended to predict interests. The fifth edition of the 16PF is the most recent revision of one of the oldest commercially available measures of normal adult personality. The questionnaire began with Raymond Cattell's early factor analyses of the entire domain of personality descriptors. Aiming to identify the basic structure of human personality, Cattell and his colleagues first developed self-report questions using a subset of trait adjectives taken from the 18,000 personality descriptors that Allport and Odbert (1936) had identified. Applying factor analyses of responses to these questions resulted in 16 elementary personality dimensions. These dimensions laid the foundation for the first 16PF, published in 1949. Half a century and four revisions of the questionnaire have produced an enormous amount of supporting research, and the 16PF is now widely used in a variety of settings.

### Item Booklet and Profile

The 16PF Fifth Edition is composed of 185 items, 170 of which utilize a forced-choice format in which the respondent chooses between two alternatives or "?" (i.e., a "Cannot Decide" option). The remaining 15 items are clustered at the end of the item booklet and assess reasoning ability (Factor B) according to correct or incorrect responses. In addition to a hand-scored scale profile, several options are available for computer-generated interpretive reports. The Basic Interpretive Report presents scores and narrative summaries for 16PF Primary Factors and Global Factors, as well as for criterion-based dimensions (e.g., self-esteem, leadership potential, creativity) and Holland's six vocational interest themes. The shorter Human Resource Development Report, which was developed to aid in hiring and promotion decisions, presents

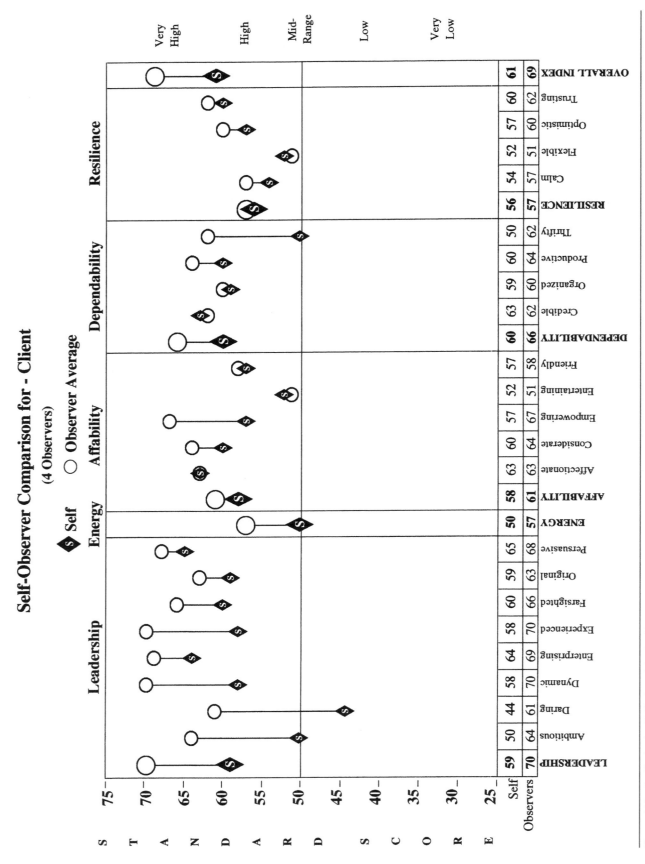

**Self-Observer Comparison for - Client**

(4 Observers)

◆ Self    ○ Observer Average

|  | | Self | Observers |
|---|---|---|---|
| **Leadership** | **LEADERSHIP** | 59 | 70 |
| | Ambitious | 50 | 64 |
| | Daring | 44 | 61 |
| | Dynamic | 58 | 70 |
| | Enterprising | 64 | 69 |
| | Experienced | 58 | 70 |
| | Farsighted | 60 | 66 |
| | Original | 59 | 63 |
| | Persuasive | 65 | 68 |
| **Energy** | **ENERGY** | 50 | 57 |
| **Affability** | **AFFABILITY** | 58 | 61 |
| | Affectionate | 63 | 63 |
| | Considerate | 60 | 64 |
| | Empowering | 57 | 67 |
| | Entertaining | 52 | 51 |
| | Friendly | 57 | 58 |
| **Dependability** | **DEPENDABILITY** | 60 | 66 |
| | Credible | 63 | 62 |
| | Organized | 59 | 60 |
| | Productive | 60 | 64 |
| | Thrifty | 50 | 62 |
| **Resilience** | **RESILIENCE** | 56 | 57 |
| | Calm | 54 | 57 |
| | Flexible | 52 | 51 |
| | Optimistic | 57 | 60 |
| | Trusting | 60 | 62 |
| | **OVERALL INDEX** | 61 | 69 |

Scale: 75 – 70 – 65 – 60 – 55 – 50 – 45 – 40 – 35 – 30 – 25

Very High / High / Mid-Range / Low / Very Low

**Figure 11.9** Profile for the CLI®. Copyright © 1988, 1990, 1998 David P. Campbell, Ph.D. All rights reserved. Published and distributed exclusively by NCS Pearson, One North Dearborn, Suite 1600, Chicago, IL 60602. Reproduced with permission by NCS Pearson, Inc.

scores and descriptions of the Primary Factors organized according to their relevance for five dimensions of effective management: leadership style, interacting with others, decision making, initiative, and personal adjustment. The Personal Career Development Profile presents the Primary and Global Factor scores as well as scores and narrative summaries in several career-related areas predicted from 16PF scores: broad patterns of work tendencies and preferences; leadership-subordinate role patterns; and career interest patterns.

## Primary Factor Scales

The 16PF Primary Factor scales are measures of Cattell's original 16 stable personality traits. For the Fifth Edition, the best items from earlier 16PF revisions were selected according to their empirical properties. After being updated to reduce ambiguity and bias, they were combined with new items and grouped into item parcels based on their intercorrelations. Ninety-five parcels (six per scale) of two to three items each were subjected to principal components factor analysis, which after a series of rotations yielded 16 interpretable factors. The standardization of the final experimental form allowed a final reduction in the number of items, leaving the 16 Primary Factor scales.

The Primary Factor scales historically have been labeled using letters (Factor A through Factor Q4); the 16PF Fifth Edition retains these and adds common vernacular names for each scale (e.g., Warmth, Emotional Stability, Sensitivity, Perfectionism). The scales are bipolar, with low and high scores indicating qualitative differences with respect to each factor (as opposed to low scores interpreted as "bad" and high scores as "good"). Scores on the Basic Interpretive Report are presented using sten scores, ranging from 1 to 10 with a mean of 5.5 and a standard deviation of 2. These are based on a normative sample of 1,245 males and 1,255 females stratified by race, age, and education. In keeping with 16PF precedent, the fifth edition refers to sten scores of 1–3, 4–7, and 8–10 as representative of the low range, average range, and high range, respectively. On the Basic Interpretive Report, the left and right poles of each factor are designated by verbal behavior descriptors. Sten scores are reported numerically and depicted graphically with a bar that begins between each set of poles and extends to the right or left, depending on the score.

Figure 11.10 shows the Primary Factor scales for Client 4, a pastor of a large Christian Reformed church. His scores of eight on Factor A (Warmth) and three on Factor E (Dominance), for example, indicate that he is probably personally responsive, valuing close relationships, and cooperative and in many cases likely to direct attention to others rather than making his own opinions or needs primary.

## Global Factor Scales

The five Global Factor scales, called "second-order" factors on earlier 16PF editions, are a result of factor analyses using the 16 Primary Factor scales. The Primary Factors are oblique factors and are allowed to correlate, reflecting Cattell's expectation that distinct personality traits would be related to each other. The intercorrelations allow the higher order factor structure to be identified. The five Global Factors parallel the popular Big Five personality traits and are labeled Extraversion, Anxiety, Tough-Mindedness, Independence, and Self-Control. (It should be noted that Primary Factor B [Reasoning] does not contribute directly to any of the Global Factors, because it uniquely measures ability, not personality.)

Like the Primary Factor scales, the Global Factor scales are measures of stable personality traits but reflect broader, more general dimensions. As Figure 11.10 demonstrates, they also are represented on the Basic Interpretive Report using sten scores presented numerically and depicted graphically with a bar that extends toward either of the poles, which are designated by verbal behavior descriptors.

## Response Style Indexes

Three indexes of response style serve as validity checks on the 16PF: Impression Management (IM), Acquiescence (ACQ), and Infrequency (INF). The 12-item bipolar Impression Management scale, constructed using a rational-intuitive approach, serves as a measure of social desirability. It was developed as a norm-referenced scale but can also be used as a criterion-referenced measure by setting cutoff scores for high and low Impression Management. The Acquiescence scale measures the respondent's tendency to agree with 16PF statements regardless of their item content. It was developed using an empirical approach based on endorsement frequencies in the normative sample of true responses to existing 16PF items. The Infrequency scale was developed using essentially the same empirical approach as the Acquiescence scale. It assesses the respondent's tendency to select options that have very low endorsement rates, as might be the case when a respondent replies randomly, is unable or unwilling to decide, or is in a starkly critical mood. These three scales are presented on the Basic Interpretive Report using only numerical descriptors and verbal descriptors. The scores on these scales for Client 4 indicate that his profile appears valid (see Figure 11.10).

Basic Interpretive Report                                    NAME: Client Faux Four
Profile                                                      DATE: November 1, 2001

                                                            Norms: Combined

```
┌──────────────────────────────────────────────────────────────────────┐
│                      Response Style Indices                            │
│                                                                        │
│   Index                        RS                                      │
│   Impression Management        13    within expected range             │
│   Infrequency                   1    within expected range             │
│   Acquiescence                 50    within expected range             │
│                                                                        │
│   All response style indices are within the normal range.              │
│                                                                        │
└──────────────────────────────────────────────────────────────────────┘
```

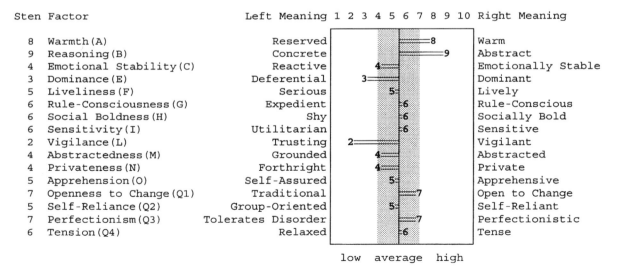

**Global Factors**

| Sten | Factor | Left Meaning | 1 2 3 4 5 6 7 8 9 10 | Right Meaning |
|---|---|---|---|---|
| 7 | Extraversion | Introverted | 7 | Extraverted |
| 5 | Anxiety | Low Anxiety | 5 | High Anxiety |
| 5 | Tough-Mindedness | Receptive | 5 | Tough-Minded |
| 4 | Independence | Accommodating | 4 | Independent |
| 7 | Self-Control | Unrestrained | 7 | Self-Controlled |

                                     low  average  high

**16PF Profile**

| Sten | Factor | Left Meaning | 1 2 3 4 5 6 7 8 9 10 | Right Meaning |
|---|---|---|---|---|
| 8 | Warmth(A) | Reserved | 8 | Warm |
| 9 | Reasoning(B) | Concrete | 9 | Abstract |
| 4 | Emotional Stability(C) | Reactive | 4 | Emotionally Stable |
| 3 | Dominance(E) | Deferential | 3 | Dominant |
| 5 | Liveliness(F) | Serious | 5 | Lively |
| 6 | Rule-Consciousness(G) | Expedient | 6 | Rule-Conscious |
| 6 | Social Boldness(H) | Shy | 6 | Socially Bold |
| 6 | Sensitivity(I) | Utilitarian | 6 | Sensitive |
| 2 | Vigilance(L) | Trusting | 2 | Vigilant |
| 4 | Abstractedness(M) | Grounded | 4 | Abstracted |
| 4 | Privateness(N) | Forthright | 4 | Private |
| 5 | Apprehension(O) | Self-Assured | 5 | Apprehensive |
| 7 | Openness to Change(Q1) | Traditional | 7 | Open to Change |
| 5 | Self-Reliance(Q2) | Group-Oriented | 5 | Self-Reliant |
| 7 | Perfectionism(Q3) | Tolerates Disorder | 7 | Perfectionistic |
| 6 | Tension(Q4) | Relaxed | 6 | Tense |

                                     low  average  high

**Figure 11.10** Page 2 for the 16PF Basic Interpretive Report presenting scores on the Response Style indexes, Global Factors, and Primary Factors for Client 4. Copyright © 1994, Institute for Personality and Ability Testing, Inc., Champaign, IL. Used by permission of IPAT.

## Interest Measurement Using the 16PF

The 16PF Basic Interpretive Report and the 16PF Personal Career Development Report Profile both report scores on scales measuring vocational interests. The Basic Interpretive Report devotes a page to scores on Holland's six types. These scores were generated using regression equations developed in a study examining the relationship between personality and interests (reported in Conn & Rieke, 1994). Intercorrelations between Holland's types as measured by the SDS-R (Holland, 1985a) and the 16PF Primary and Global Factors were first examined. Then, each Holland type was regressed on the 16PF Primary Factors to obtain a prediction equation for each type. Using these equations, the Basic Interpretive Report displays a respondent's predicted sten score for each of Holland's six types numerically and graphically, using a horizontal bar graph. The personality characteristics for Client 4 are associated with high scores on the Social, Conventional, and Artistic themes (see Figure 11.11). The Holland types on which the respondent scores highest, in this case Social and Conventional, are discussed in interpretive paragraphs on the following page of the report. The paragraphs describe the typical SDS item endorsement for types on which the respondent scored highly, the 16PF personality characteristics that are typical for those types, and a list of occupations relevant to the respondent's Holland type.

The Personal Career Development Profile uses Campbell's seven CISS Orientations to present interest scores predicted from 16PF scales. The Profile supplements scores on the seven orientations with scores for career field interests (a subset of the Basic Scales on the CISS and Basic Interest Scales on the SII) and occupational interests (a subset of the Occupational Scales on the CISS and SII). These predicted scale scores were developed from multiple regression studies using the CISS and SII (reported in Walter, 2000). First, equations were developed using 16PF Primary Factor scales to predict the seven CISS Orientation Scales; these are called Career Activity Interest scales on the Personal Career Development Profile. The Primary Factor scales also were found to predict 20 of the 29 CISS Basic Scales. These scales correlated with the Career Activity Interests in the expected directions, demonstrating high levels of correspondence and supporting the utility of the prediction equations. The Primary Factor scales also were used to predict Occupational Scales on the CISS, with 57 of the 60 CISS occupations chosen for inclusion on the Personal Career Development Profile.

A second multiple regression research project resulted in equations that used the 16PF Primary Factor scales to predict scores on several types of SII scales. Ten SII Basic Interest scores had multiple correlations high enough to warrant their

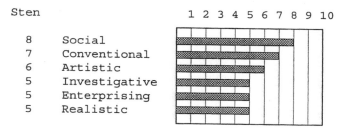

**Figure 11.11** Portion of 16PF Basic Interpretive Report presenting the predicted Holland theme scores for Client 4. Copyright © 1994, Institute for Personality and Ability Testing, Inc., Champaign, IL. Used by permission of IPAT.

inclusion in the Personal Career Development Profile. Of the SII Occupational Scales, 69 female-normed scales and 66 male-normed scales had predictive values that led to their selection for the Profile. Some of the SII scales represented occupations already included in the CISS scales that had been selected and thus were redundant. When this was the case, the scales with the higher predictive values were retained and the others were removed (e.g., the CISS Writing scale was dropped in favor of the SII Writing scale). Differences in norm groups also existed between the CISS Occupational Scales, which are combined-gender referenced, and the SII Occupational Scales, which have separate norms for females and males. This challenge was resolved by reporting three separate norms on the Personal Career Development Profile: Occupational Interest scales obtained from the CISS include scores based on combined-gender norms, while Occupational Interest scales selected from the SII include separate scores based on female and male norms. For Occupational Scales taken from both the CISS and SII, scores referenced on each of the three norms are reported. The Personal Career Development Profile currently presents seven Career Activity Interest scales, 27 Career Field Interest scales, and 98 Occupational Interest scales.

Figure 11.12 shows the Career Activity and Career Field Interest scales for Client 4. His scores predict that his strongest Career Activity Interests are in the areas of Helping (8.7), Creating (6.0), and Producing (6.0). These interests correspond to Holland's Social, Artistic, and Realistic types and thus are similar to, but do not entirely overlap with, Holland types predicted by the Basic Interpretive Report. The strongest Career Field Interests are predicted for Client 4 to be Counseling (9.0), Writing (7.8), Teaching (7.6), Music/Drama (7.3), Religious Activities (7.3), and Public Speaking (7.0). These accurately reflect many of the activities in which he engages as a pastor. Figure 11.13 presents some of the Occupational Interest scores for Client 4. Note his high scores

Personal Career Development Profile          NAME: Client Faux Four
Career Interest Scores          DATE: November 1, 2001

## CAREER INTEREST SCORES

The Career Interest Scores reported on this and the next three pages use 16PF Fifth Edition personality scores to predict these well-known and researched career activity, career field and occupational interest scores. As such, all predicted interest scores only reflect the similarity of one's personality patterns to persons who actually express interest for them. The research projects basic to these predicted Career Interest Scores are explained in the PCDP Manual.

Career Interest Scores should be reviewed for explorative counsel to help Mr. Faux Four learn whether he actually has interests related to his predicted scores. **These scores DO NOT PREDICT his ability, experience or suitability for making career choices. These scores are also inappropriate for making personnel selection decisions or for predicting performance on any job duties.**

### CAREER ACTIVITY and CAREER FIELD INTEREST SCORES

**Career Activity Interest Scores** reflect the broad areas of career/avocational interests found throughout the world of work. **Career Field Scores** reflect interests in broad categories of work fields which are subscales of the Career Activity Interests. Again, Mr. Faux Four's 16PF personality scores were used to predict his similarity to persons who express interest for them.

| Influencing Interest | 5.5 |
|---|---|
| Advertising/Marketing | 4.6 |
| Law/Politics | 4.5 |
| Management | 4.3 |
| Public Speaking | 7.0 |
| Sales | 5.2 |

| Helping Interest | 8.7 |
|---|---|
| Child Development | 6.9 |
| Counseling | 9.0 |
| Religious Activities | 7.3 |
| Social Service | 6.9 |
| Teaching | 7.6 |

| Organizing Interest | 3.8 |
|---|---|
| Office Practices | 4.3 |
| Supervision | 4.8 |

| Analyzing Interest | 4.5 |
|---|---|
| Data Management | 5.6 |
| Mathematics | 4.7 |
| Science | 4.1 |

| Creating Interest | 6.0 |
|---|---|
| Art | 6.7 |
| Arts/Design | 3.8 |
| Fashion | 3.5 |
| Music/Dramatics | 7.3 |
| Performing Arts | 6.2 |
| Writing | 7.8 |

| Producing Interest | 6.0 |
|---|---|
| Agriculture | 5.8 |
| Mechanical Activities | 3.5 |
| Mechanical Crafts | 4.6 |
| Woodworking | 5.9 |

| Venturing Interest | 3.9 |
|---|---|
| Athletics | 4.1 |
| Military/Law Enforcement | 4.0 |

**\*NOTE:** Scores range from 1 through 10. Scores of 8-10 are considered very high. Scores of 1-3 are considered very low. Scores of 4-7 are average.

**Figure 11.12** Page 4 of the 16PF Personal Career Development Profile Score Summary presenting the predicted Career Activity Interest Scores and Career Field Scores for Client 4. Copyright © 1995, 1998, 2000. Institute for Personality and Abilities Testing, Inc., Champaign, Illinois. Used by permission of IPAT.

Personal Career Development Profile
Career Interest Scores

NAME: Client Faux Four
DATE:  November 1, 2001

### OCCUPATIONAL INTEREST SCORES - Page 2 of 3

Mr. Faux Four's 16PF results were used to predict the **Occupational Interest Scores** presented on this page.  These occupational interest scores reflect only a similarity in personality to persons who express interest for these occupations.  **These scores are intended for personal career development purposes only and are inappropriate for making personnel selection decisions.**  Scores **DO NOT PREDICT** ability or suitability for performance of job duties.

CREATING INTEREST

| | Female | Male | Combined | 1 2 3 4 5 6 7 8 9 10 |
|---|---|---|---|---|
| Architect | **6.3** | 6.2 | 4.1 | |
| Art Teacher | **7.2** | 7.1 | * | |
| Artist, Commercial | 6.9 | **7.1** | 6.1 | |
| Artist, Fine | **6.6** | **6.6** | * | |
| Broadcaster | 7.5 | **7.6** | * | |
| English Teacher | **8.3** | 7.9 | * | |
| Fashion Designer | * | * | **3.1** | |
| Interior Decorator | **8.1** | 7.7 | * | |
| Liberal Arts Professor | * | * | **6.9** | |
| Librarian | 7.8 | **7.9** | 5.2 | |
| Medical Illustrator | 5.7 | **6.6** | * | |
| Musician | 6.9 | **7.1** | 5.8 | |
| Photographer | **6.7** | 6.2 | * | |
| Psychologist | 7.6 | **7.8** | 7.6 | |
| Reporter | 7.4 | **7.8** | * | |
| Sociologist | 7.6 | **7.7** | * | |
| Teacher, K-12 | * | * | **7.3** | |
| Technical Writer | **7.6** | 7.2 | * | |
| Translator/Interpreter | 7.1 | **7.3** | 7.2 | |
| Writer/Editor | * | * | **6.4** | |

low    average    high

HELPING INTEREST

| | Female | Male | Combined | 1 2 3 4 5 6 7 8 9 10 |
|---|---|---|---|---|
| Child Care Worker | 5.7 | * | **7.0** | |
| Community Service Director | 5.8 | **6.0** | * | |
| Elementary School Teacher | **5.5** | * | * | |
| Foreign Language Teacher | 7.3 | **7.5** | * | |
| Guidance Counselor | * | * | **8.9** | |
| High School Counselor | 8.1 | **8.2** | * | |
| Minister | **7.9** | 7.9 | * | |
| Nurse, LPN | 3.4 | **4.0** | * | |
| Occupational Therapist | 5.7 | **6.1** | * | |
| Religious Leader | * | * | **9.2** | |
| Social Science Teacher | **7.7** | 7.6 | * | |
| Social Worker | 7.4 | 7.1 | **8.5** | |
| Special Education Teacher | 6.1 | **6.6** | * | |
| Speech Pathologist | 6.5 | **7.1** | * | |

low    average    high

* Indicates no solid predictive data to predict meaningful scores.  The Female/Male and Combined-Sex labels refer to the gender on which the scores are computed.  Female/Male and Combined-Sex Score research is explained in the PCDP Manual.

---

**Figure 11.13**  Page 6 of the 16PF Personal Career Development Profile Score Summary presenting the predicted Occupational Interest Scores in the Creative and Helping orientation for Client 4. Copyright © 1995, 1998, 2000. Institute for Personality and Abilities Testing, Inc., Champaign, IL. Used by permission of IPAT.

for Religious Leader (9.2 on combined-gender norms) and minister (7.9 on both male and female norms).

**Reliability and Validity**

The mean test-retest reliability coefficients for the 16PF Primary Factor scales and Global Factor scales over a two-week period are .80 and .87, respectively. Over a two-month period, mean coefficients are .70 and .78. Cronbach alpha coefficients for Primary Factor scales range from .64 to .85, with a mean of .74 (Russell & Karol, 1994). Studies using the 16PF with the Personality Research Form-Form E (Jackson, 1989), the California Psychological Inventory (Gough, 1987), the NEO Personality Inventory-Revised (Costa & McCrae, 1992), and the Myers-Briggs Type Indicator (Myers & McCaulley, 1985) are described in the *16PF Fifth Edition Technical Manual* (Conn & Rieke, 1994) and provide evidence for the construct validity of the Primary Factor scales and Global Factor scales. A wealth of occupational research using the 16PF has been conducted, with most studies taking one of two broad approaches: (1) examining average 16PF profiles for particular occupations, and (2) examining correlations between 16PF scales and other measures or criteria. Schuerger (1995) provides a review of the extensive occupational research that supports the criterion-related validity of the 16PF in organizational contexts, including the ability of the instrument to predict scores in the domain of vocational interests.

**SUMMARY**

The Strong Interest Inventory, Self-Directed Search, Campbell Interest and Skill Survey and Leadership Index, and the 16PF all are widely used in organizational career development programs. Each of these inventories was created with substantial attention given to construction and development as well as generating evidence of reliability and validity. They all are accompanied by technical manuals and interpretive materials to assist career specialists who wish to include a measure of interests in employee career development interventions.

During the past decade there has been an increased focus on adult career development. As people move through careers, a large percentage of the workforce will experience career-related crises and transitions. Helping individuals to cope with change through career development programs can be mutually beneficial to the organization and the employee (Gutteridge, 1986). Ackerman and Heggestad (1997) have proposed that interests determine the motivation to attempt an activity and that abilities and personality are related more to the probability of successfully performing a task. In line with this proposition, virtually all career development programs incorporate some mechanism for evaluating the employee's interests. Other constructs typically assessed include abilities, values, and personality.

Research has shown that interests, personality, and abilities have some modest relationships but that the three constructs do not overlap completely (Ackerman & Heggestad, 1997; Tokar & Fisher, 1998). For example, Extraversion shows moderate correlations with Holland's Enterprising and Social types; the Conventional type is correlated moderately with Conscientiousness; and Agreeableness and Neuroticism show no appreciable correlations with any of the Holland types. Positive correlations also occur between Investigative and Realistic interest types and math, spatial, and mechanical ability scores and between Artistic interest types and verbal ability. The relationships among interests, personality, and abilities suggest that an integrative approach to assessment will provide employees with the data necessary to make informed career decisions.

**NOTES**

1. Strong Vocational Interest Blanks is a registered trademark of the Stanford University Press.
2. Strong Interest Inventory is a trademark of the Stanford University Press.
3. Campbell Interest and Skill Survey is a trademark and "CISS" is a registered trademark of David P. Campbell, Ph.D.
4. Campbell Leadership Index is a trademark and "CLI" is a registered trademark of David P. Campbell, Ph.D.
5. Campbell Organizational Survey is a trademark of David P. Campbell, Ph.D.
6. Campbell-Hallam Team Development Survey is a trademark of David P. Campbell, Ph.D.

**REFERENCES**

Ackerman, P.L., & Heggestad, E.D. (1997). Intelligence, personality and interests: Evidence for overlapping traits. *Psychological Bulletin, 121,* 219–245.

Allport, G.W., & Odbert, H.S. (1936). Trait-names: A psycho-lexical study. *Psychological Monographs, 47,* No. 211.

Borgen, F.H. (1972). Predicting career choice of able college men from occupational and basic interest scales of the Strong Vocational Interest Blank. *Journal of Counseling Psychology, 19,* 202–211.

Borgen, F.H., & Helms, J.F. (1975). Validity generalization of the men's form of the Strong Vocational Interest Blank with academically able women. *Journal of Counseling Psychology, 22,* 210–216.

Campbell, D.P. (1966). Occupations ten years later of high school seniors with high scores on the SVIB life insurance salesman scale. *Journal of Applied Psychology, 50,* 369–372.

Campbell, D.P. (1971). *Handbook for the Strong Vocational Interest Blank.* Stanford, CA: Stanford University Press.

Campbell, D.P. (1974). *Manual for the SVIB-SCII.* Stanford, CA: Stanford University Press.

Campbell, D.P. (1990). *Campbell Organizational Survey.* Minneapolis, MN: National Computer Systems.

Campbell, D.P. (1991). *Manual for the Campbell Leadership Index.* Minneapolis, MN: National Computer Systems.

Campbell, D.P., & Borgen, F.H. (1999). Holland's theory and development of interest inventories. *Journal of Vocational Behavior, 55,* 86–101.

Campbell, D.P., Borgen, F.J., Eastes, S.H., Johansson, C.B., & Peterson, R.A. (1968). A set of basic interest scales for the Strong Vocational interest Blank for Men. *Journal of Applied Psychology Monograph, 52,* 1–54.

Campbell, D.P., & Hansen, J.C. (1981). *Manual for the SVIB-SCII* (3rd edition). Stanford, CA: Stanford University Press.

Campbell, D.P., & Holland, J.L. (1972). Applying Holland's theory to Strong's data. *Journal of Vocational Behavior, 2,* 353–376.

Campbell, D.P., Hyne, S.A., & Nilsen, D.L. (1992). *Manual for the Campbell Interest and Skill Survey.* Minneapolis, MN: National Computer System.

Cattell, R.B., Cattell, A.K., & Cattell, H.E. (1993). *Sixteen Personality Factor Questionnaire, Fifth Edition.* Champaign, IL: Institute for Personality and Ability Testing.

Conn, S.R., & Rieke, M.L. (1994). *The 16PF Fifth Edition technical manual.* Champaign, IL: Institute for Personality and Ability Testing.

Costa, P., & McCrae, R.R. (1992). *NEO-PI-R professional manual.* Odessa, FL: Psychological Assessment Resources.

Dawis, R.V., & Lofquist, L.H. (1984). *A psychological theory of work adjustment.* Minneapolis, MN: University of Minnesota Press.

Dewhirst, D.H. (1991). Career patterns: Mobility, specialization, and related career issues. In R.F. Morrison & J. Adams (Eds.), *Contemporary career development issues* (pp. 73–107). Hillsdale, NJ: Erlbaum.

Dolliver, R.H., Irvin, J.A., & Bigley, S.E. (1972). Twelve-year follow-up of the Strong Vocational Interest Blank. *Journal of Counseling Psychology, 19,* 212–217.

Donnay, D.A.C. (1997). E.K. Strong's legacy and beyond: 70 years of the Strong Interest Inventory. *Career Development Quarterly, 46,* 2–22.

Donnay, D.A.C., & Borgen, F.H. (1996). Validity, structure, and content of the 1994 Strong Interest Inventory. *Journal of Counseling Psychology, 43,* 275–291.

Dunnette, M.D., & Kirchner, W.K. (1965). *Psychology applied to industry.* New York: Appleton-Century-Crofts.

Gatewood, R.D., Perloff, R., & Perloff, E. (2000). Testing and industrial application. In G. Goldstein & M. Hersen (Eds.), *Handbook of psychological assessment* (pp. 505–525). Oxford, UK: Elsevier Science, Ltd.

Gottfredson, G.D., & Holland, J.L. (1975). Vocational choices of men and women: A comparison of predictors from the Self-Directed Search. *Journal of Counseling Psychology, 22,* 28–34.

Gottfredson, G.D., & Holland, J.L. (1991). *Position Classification Inventory.* Odessa, FL: Psychological Assessment Resources.

Gough, H.G. (1987). *California Psychological Inventory administrator's guide.* Palo Alto, CA: Consulting Psychologists Press.

Greenhaus, J.H. (1988). Career exploration. In M. London & E.M. Mone (Eds.), *Career growth and human resource strategies: The role of the human resource professional in employee development* (pp. 17–30). New York: Quorum Books.

Gutteridge, T.G. (1986). Organizational career development systems: The state of the practice. In D.T. Hall (Ed.), *Career development in organizations* (pp. 50–94). San Francisco, CA: Jossey-Bass.

Hall, D.T., & Rabinowitz, S. (1988). Maintaining employee involvement in a plateaued career. In M. London & E.M. Mone (Eds.) *Career growth and human resource strategies: The role of the human resource professional in employee development* (pp. 67–80). New York: Quorum Books.

Hallam, G., & Campbell, D.P. (1994). *Manual for the Campbell-Hallam Team Development Survey.* Minneapolis, MN: National Computer Systems.

Hansen, J.C. (1984). The measurement of vocational interests: Issues and future directions. In S. Brown & R. Lent (Eds.), *Handbook of counseling psychology* (pp. 99–136). New York: Wiley.

Hansen, J.C. (1986, August). *12-Year longitudinal study of the predictive validity of the SVIB-SCII.* Paper presented at the meetings of the American Psychological Association, Washington, DC.

Hansen, J.C. (1992). *User's guide for the Strong Interest Inventory.* Palo Alto, CA: Consulting Psychologists Press.

Hansen, J.C. (1994). The measurement of vocational interests. In M. Rumsey, C. Walker, & J. Harris (Eds.), *Personnel and selection and classification* (pp. 293–316). Hillsdale, NJ: Erlbaum.

Hansen, J.C., & Campbell, D.P. (1985). *Manual for the SVIB-SCII* (4th ed.). Stanford, CA: Stanford University Press.

Hansen, J.C., & Johansson, C.B. (1972). The application of Holland's vocational model to the Strong Vocational Interest Blank. *Journal of Vocational Behavior, 2,* 479–493.

Harmon, L.W. (1969). Predictive power over ten years of measured social service and scientific interests among college women. *Journal of Applied Psychology, 53,* 193–198.

Harmon, L., Hansen, J.C., Borgen, F., & Hammer, A. (1994). *Strong interest Inventory applications and technical guide.* Stanford, CA: Stanford University Press.

Holland, J.L. (1959). A theory of vocational choice. *Journal of Counseling Psychology, 6,* 35–45.

Holland, J.L. (1971). *A counselor' guide to the Self-Directed Search.* Palo Alto, CA: Consulting Psychologists Press.

Holland, J.L. (1979). *The Self-Directed Search professional manual.* Palo Alto, CA: Consulting Psychologists Press.

Holland, J.L. (1985a). *Self-Directed Search professional manual.* Odessa, FL: Psychological Assessment Resources.

Holland, J.L. (1985b). *Vocational Preference Inventory (VPI) manual–1985 edition.* Odessa, FL: Psychological Assessment Resources.

Holland, J.L. (1990). *Self-Directed Search Form CP: Career Planning.* Odessa, FL: Psychological Assessment Resources.

Holland, J.L. (1994a) *Self-Directed Search Form R* (4th ed.). Odessa, FL: Psychological Assessment Resources.

Holland, J.L. (1994b). *The occupations finder.* Odessa, FL: Psychological Assessment Resources.

Holland, J.L. (1995). Self-Directed Search computer version [Computer software]. Odessa, FL: Psychological Assessment Resources.

Holland, J.L. (1997). *Making vocational choices* (3rd ed.). Odessa, FL: Psychological Assessment Resources, Inc.

Holland, J.L. (2001). *Career options finder.* Odessa, FL: Psychological Assessment Resources.

Holland, J.L., Fritzsche, B.A., & Powell, A.B. (1994). *Self-Directed Search technical manual.* Odessa, FL: Psychological Assessment Resources.

Holland, J.L., Powell, A. B., & Fritzsche, B.A. (1994). *Self-Directed Search professional users' guide.* Odessa, FL: Psychological Assessment Resources.

Holland, J.L., Whitney, D.R., Cole, N.S., & Richards, J.M. Jr. (1969). *An empirical occupational classification derived from a theory of personality and intended for practice and research.* (ACT Research Report No. 29). Iowa City, IA: American College Testing Program.

Hough, L.E. (Ed.). (1988). *Literature review: Utility of temperament, biodata, and interest assessment for predicting job performance* (ARI Research Note 88–02). Alexandria, VA: U.S. Army Research Institute.

Jackson, D.N. (1989). *Personality Research Form manual.* Port Huron, MI: Sigma Assessment Systems.

Kim, J.E., & Moen, P. (2001). Is retirement good or bad for subjective well-being? *Current Directions in Psychological Science, 10,* 83–86.

Korman, A.K. (1988). Career success and personal failure: Mid-to-late-career feelings and events. In M. London & E.M. Mone (Eds.), *Career growth and human resource strategies: The role of the human resource professional in employee development* (pp. 81–94). New York: Quorum Books.

Latack, J.C., & Kaufman, H.G. (1988). Termination and outplacement strategies. In M. London & E.M. Mone (Eds.), *Career*

*growth and human resource strategies: The role of the human resource professional in employee development* (pp. 289–313). New York: Quorum Books.

Lattimore, R.R., & Borgen, F.H. (1999). Validity of the 1994 Strong Interest Inventory with racial and ethnic groups in the United States. *Journal of Counseling Psychology, 46,* 185–195.

Lenz, J.G. (1996). Using Holland's theory and instruments in training and development. In M. Shahnasarian (Ed.), *The Self-Directed Search (SDS) in business and industry* (pp. 81–118). Odessa, FL: Psychological Assessment Resources.

Levine, E.L., Spector, P.E., Menon, S., Narayanan, L., & Cannon-Bowers, J. (1996). Validity generalization for cognitive psychomotor, and perceptual tests for craft jobs in the utility industry. *Human Performance, 9,* 1–22.

Liebowitz, Z.B., Kaye, B.L., & Farren, C. (1986). *Designing career development systems.* San Francisco: Jossey-Bass.

McArthur, C. (1954). Long term validity of the Strong Interest Test in two subcultures. *Journal of Applied Psychology, 38,* 346–354.

McHenry, J.J., Hough, L.M., Toquam, J.L., Hanson, M.A., & Ashworth, S. (1990). Project A validity results: The relationship between predictor and criterion domains. *Personnel Psychology, 43,* 335–354.

Mount, M.K., & Muchinsky, P.M. (1978). Concurrent validation of Holland's hexagonal model with occupational workers. *Journal of Vocational Behavior, 13,* 348–354.

Myers, I.B., & McCaulley, M.H. (1985). *Manual: A guide to the development and use of the Myers-Briggs Type Indicator.* Palo Alto, CA: Consulting Psychologists Press.

Nilsen, D., Hallum, G., & Campbell, D. (1998). *User's guide for the Campbell Leadership Index.* Minneapolis, MN: National Computer Systems.

O'Neil, J.M., & Magoon, T.M. (1977). The predictive power of Holland's Investigative Personality Type and consistency levels using the Self Directed Search. *Journal of Vocational Behavior, 10,* 39–46.

O'Neil, J.M., Magoon, T.M., & Tracey, T.J. (1978). Status of Holland's Investigative Personality Type and their consistency level seven years later. *Journal of Counseling Psychology, 25,* 530–535.

Osipow, S.H. (1986). Career issues through the life span. In M.S. Pallak & R.O. Perloff (Eds.), *Psychology and work: Productivity, change, and employment* (pp. 141–168). Washington, DC: American Psychological Association.

Parsons, F. (1909). *Choosing a vocation.* Boston: Houghton-Mifflin.

Patterson, D.G., & Darley, J.G. (1936). *Men, women, and jobs: A study in human engineering.* Minneapolis, MN: University of Minnesota Press.

Power, P.G. (1981). Aspects of the transition from education to beginning teacher. *Australian Journal of Education, 25,* 288–296.

Ream, M.J. (1924). *Ability to sell: Its relation to certain aspect of personality and experience.* Baltimore, MD: Williams & Wilkens.

Ree, M.J., & Earles, J.A. (1991). Predicting training success: Not much more than *g*. *Personnel Psychology, 44*, 321–332.

Rosen, D., Holmberg, K., & Holland, J.L. (1994). *The educational opportunities finder.* Odessa, FL: Psychological Assessment Resources.

Roznowski, M., & Hulin, C. (1992). The scientific merit of valid measures of general constructs with special reference to job satisfaction and job withdrawal. In C.J. Cranny, P.C. Smith, & E.F. Stone (Eds.), *Job satisfaction* (pp. 123–163). New York: Lexington Books.

Russell, M., & Karol, D. (1994). *16PF Fifth Edition administrator's manual.* Champaign, IL: Institute of Personality and Ability Testing.

Schneider, B. (1987). The people make the place. *Personnel Psychology, 40*, 437–453.

Schuerger, J.M. (1995). Career assessment and the Sixteen Personality Factor Questionnaire. *Journal of Career Assessment, 3*(2), 157–175.

Spokane, A.R. (1979). Occupational preference and the validity of the Strong-Campbell Interest Inventory for college women and men. *Journal of Counseling Psychology, 26*, 312–318.

Strong, E.K. Jr. (1927). *Vocational Interest Blank.* Palo Alto, CA: Stanford University Press.

Strong, E.K. Jr. (1955). *Vocational interests 18 years after college.* Minneapolis: University of Minnesota Press.

Tinsley, H.E.A. (2000). The congruence myth: An analysis of the efficacy of the person-environment fit model. *Journal of Vocational Behavior, 56*, 147–179.

Tokar, D.M., & Fisher, A.R. (1998). More on RIASEC and the five factor model of personality: Direct assessment of Prediger's (1982) and Hogan's (1983) dimensions. *Journal of Vocational Behavior, 52*, 246–259.

Touchton, J.B., & Magoon, T.M. (1977). Occupational daydreams as predictors of vocational plans for college women. *Journal for Vocational Behavior, 10*, 156–166.

Vinchur, A.J., Schippmann, J.S., Switzer, F.S., & Roth, P.L. (1998). A meta-analytic review of the predictors of job performance for salespeople. *Journal of Applied Psychology, 83*, 586–597.

Walsh, W.B., & Betz, N.E. (1995). *Tests and assessment* (3rd ed.). Upper Saddle River, NJ: Prentice-Hall.

Walter, V. (2000). *16PF Personal Career Development Profile: Technical and interpretive manual.* Champaign, IL: Institute for Personality and Ability Testing.

Wise, L.L., McHenry, J.J., & Campbell, J.P. (1990). Identifying optimal predictor composites and testing from generalizability across jobs and performance factors. *Personnel Psychology, 43*, 355–366.

CHAPTER 12

# Assessment and Development Opportunities Using the Occupational Information Network (O*NET)

P. RICHARD JEANNERET, ERIKA L. D'EGIDIO, AND MARY ANN HANSON

Assessment and development in the occupational world must be based first and foremost on information about work. The most recent advancement, both conceptually and theoretically, in the study of work is the *Occupational Information Network* (O*NET). This chapter links the O*NET to assessment and development in the workplace. It begins with a brief description of the development and content of the O*NET system, followed by an examination of possible workplace assessment and development applications, and concludes with a discussion of opportunities for future research and other potential applications.

The O*NET originated from a Department of Labor (DOL) endeavor initiated in the late 1980s in response to changes in the American economy and its workforce. The initiative was designed to update the job analytic methodology underlying the *Dictionary of Occupational Titles* (*DOT*) (U.S. Department of Labor, 1991) and to provide a framework for describing jobs or work (however it is constituted) in the twenty-first century. The DOL recognized the need to develop a new occupational information system that reflected the changing nature of work; these changes meant that many jobs are not defined as a specific set of tasks but rather as a broad range of duties that may shift in importance and likely change over time (Howard, 1995).

The change in philosophy regarding how to define and describe work provided the impetus for the development of a new approach to collecting, distributing, and analyzing occu-

pational information that resulted in the O*NET. The O*NET project officially began in 1990 when then Secretary of Labor Elizabeth Dole chartered the Advisory Panel for the Dictionary of Occupational Titles (APDOT). This panel was composed of representatives from government, vocational training, academia, and the private sector. Between 1990 and 1992, 50 experts and representatives of user groups addressed the panel, and the panel compiled numerous staff papers and technical reports on issues ranging from occupational classification options, reliability and validity of current *DOT* descriptors, alternative job analysis methodologies, automation issues and options, and the needs of special user groups, such as those associated with vocational counseling and rehabilitation. The project was "specifically commissioned with the goal of amassing all of the current knowledge on job analysis, both theoretically and methodologically, and then reflecting the sum of all of that knowledge in the design of the O*NET" (Campion, Morgeson, & Mayfield, 1999, p. 297).

The O*NET system consists of (1) the O*NET Content Model—the conceptual framework for the O*NET, (2) a relational electronic database of occupational information, and (3) data collection instruments for each component of the Content Model (i.e., surveys). The O*NET developers used a taxonomic approach to occupational classification to create a system that identifies, defines, and describes work according to a set of characteristics (i.e., subdomains) of work performance that is much more comprehensive than either a

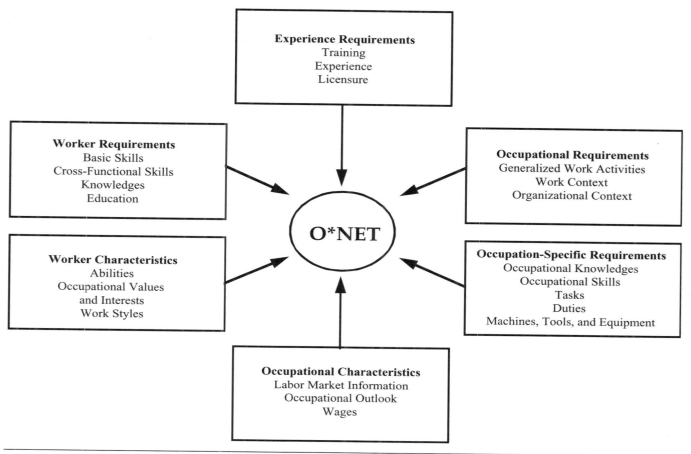

**Figure 12.1**    The O*NET content model. From Peterson et al., 1995, 1999, 2001.

detailed listing of task-level information or a summary of important duties and responsibilities (Peterson, Mumford, Borman, Jeanneret, & Fleishman, 1995, 1999).

The O*NET Content Model is a general descriptive framework within which more specific information is organized. Figure 12.1 presents the O*NET Content Model with its six major domains and the 21 categories (subdomains) within each domain. The individual O*NET content domains were based on over 50 years of cumulative knowledge on job analysis (Peterson et al., 2001). Each domain describes either the worker or the work performed. Together, the six domains are meant to provide a comprehensive description of any occupation from a variety of perspectives. The Worker Requirements, Worker Characteristics, and Experience Requirements domains include descriptors of the worker and "refer to developed attributes of the individual that might influence performance across a range of work activities" (Peterson et al., 1995, p. 9). The Occupational Requirements, Occupation-

Specific Requirements, and Occupational Characteristics domains include a variety of descriptors focused on the work itself (i.e., specific duties, tasks, etc.). Each major domain is divided into subdomains designed to represent "distinct, albeit interrelated, domains that might be used to answer different types of questions about jobs or about how people 'fit' to jobs" (Mumford & Peterson, 1999, p. 23).

Considerable research has been conducted to develop, measure, and analyze the content domains of work (Peterson et al., 1995, 1999, 2001), and it is now important to assess whether the O*NET will accomplish the objectives originally established by the DOL. It has been hypothesized that O*NET content domains can be used to identify job requirements, to estimate values for determining compensation, for job classification (e.g., to develop wage and salary grades), and to link job behaviors to knowledge, skills, and abilities (Peterson et al., 1999, 2001). Additionally, the O*NET can be used as the basis for career guidance systems (Hanson et al., 2000), and a database has been developed that can support training, education, and human resource management systems (Baughman, Dorsey, Cooke, & Rosse, 2000).

To meet today's human resource management challenges organizations need current and increasingly complex work and worker information on an ongoing basis. The information now available from the O*NET database can be used for a variety of assessment and development activities. Specifically, this chapter addresses several applications of O*NET related to assessing and developing workers, including job analysis, selection, job evaluation and classification, performance management, person-job matching, job bank development, vocational guidance/career exploration, and training.

## ASSESSMENT OPPORTUNITIES

For purposes of this chapter, assessment is viewed from a broad perspective. The evaluation of information about work is treated as equally important as the assessment of characteristics of individuals (workers or prospective workers). For most organizational purposes it is essential that assessment be completed for both work and workers. That is, an employer must have an accurate assessment of the work in order to recruit, select, train, and compensate workers; similarly that same employer must have an accurate assessment of individuals in order to select, train, appraise, promote, and compensate those who perform the work. The O*NET provides an excellent resource for satisfying both sides of the assessment equation.

### Job Analysis

Recent changes in the way work is accomplished have led industrial and organizational psychologists to acknowledge that changes must occur in how jobs are analyzed in order to meet the current needs of organizations. Cascio (1995) proposed that selection systems should continue to assess traditional constructs (e.g., cognitive ability) but also should be expanded to assess values, personality, and team-based constructs. "In today's (and tomorrow's) world of work, characteristics of the whole person—cognitive as well as personality—are required to improve continuously the business processes that satisfy the needs of internal and external customers" (Cascio, 1995, p. 933). Sanchez and Levine (1999) suggested replacing the term "job analysis" with "work analysis," reflecting the need to escape the boundaries of the job and move toward a description of work that includes the identification of general sets of knowledge, skills, and abilities

and other personal characteristics that are important across many jobs.

When job tasks are in flux and group level activities are more important than individual activities, a job analysis that focuses on general work activities and human attributes necessary for successful job performance may be more appropriate. Furthermore, greater diversity in the workforce and the globalization of the economy has increased the importance of identifying interpersonal behaviors and attributes that lead to successful job performance in team- and customer-oriented organizations.

The occupational information from the O*NET provides a broad range of job analysis information, including both what could be traditionally thought of as worker-oriented and task-oriented (or job-oriented) information (McCormick, 1979). In addition, the task/job information is presented at a fairly broad level in terms of Generalized Work Activities (GWAs) and within a broad Work Context, including the physical work setting and the social/organizational environment. Finally, the O*NET also includes information on definitive occupational requirements such as occupation-specific knowledge, skills, tasks, duties, and the use of machines, tools, and equipment.

One of the key considerations that led to the development of the O*NET system was the need to move away from task-specific descriptions of jobs to information that allowed for comparison and analysis across occupations. The descriptors for each of the domains of the O*NET (with the exception of the Occupation-Specific Characteristics) are designed at a level that allows for the analysis of widely divergent occupations from a common frame of reference. The O*NET Viewer, available from www.onetcenter.org, contains job information across each subdomain for 1,122 occupations that can be used as a foundation for any job analysis effort. In addition, the reports generated by the O*NET Viewer contain much of the information needed to develop job descriptions.

The current job information was collected by professional job analysts, but one goal of the O*NET project is to populate the job database with data collected from incumbents in each occupation. Questionnaires (i.e., surveys) are available for use in data collection for nine of the subdomains that are included within the Worker Requirements, Worker Characteristics, and Occupational Requirements domains. More specific uses of job analysis data derived from the O*NET database are discussed next.

### Creating Job Families

Several of the O*NET subdomains provide information appropriate for identifying job families. Specifically, the Basic and Cross-Functional Skills and GWAs have been successfully used to create job families in several studies (e.g., Baughman, Norris, Cooke, Peterson, & Mumford, 1999; Kubisiak, Borman, & Hanson, 1998). Two other subdomains that provide relevant information for developing job families are the Knowledges and Abilities subdomains. Any of these subdomains can be used as the basis for creating job families alone or in combination, depending on the reason for the development of the families. For example, if one were identifying job families in order to create preemployment tests, it might be useful to rely on the Skills and Abilities subdomains to identify clusters of jobs with common requirements. On the other hand, if one were creating job families in order to aggregate jobs for a validation study, the GWAs subdomain would be useful. Since each O*NET subdomain is designed to provide comparable information across occupations, these subdomains offer the perfect mechanism to collect information that can be used to create job families.

A more detailed discussion of one example involving both the use of O*NET information for job analysis and the creation of job families is provided here to highlight a real-world application of the ideas discussed in the preceding paragraph. Baughman, Cooke, Dorsey, and Threlfall (1999) used O*NET descriptors to conduct a skills-based job analysis for a federal agency. The goal of the project was to develop task statements for a number of jobs. However, because of the large number of job titles in the organization it was necessary to create job families. The researchers used ratings made by incumbents on the Skills and GWAs subdomains to create provisional job families. These provisional families were then used as sampling domains from and for which to derive more detailed, task-level information. The goal of the study was to provide evidence for the validity of the O*NET-based families as appropriate sampling domains for developing detailed job information. Job incumbents reviewed the list of 42 GWAs, identified 6 to 12 GWAs that best represented the type of work they performed, and then generated task statements related to these GWAs. The researchers calculated the number of tasks generated for each GWA and found that incumbents created more task statements for those GWAs identified as most characteristic of the job family. The results of the study suggest that this innovative method for conducting a task analysis can be very effective (Baughman et al., 1999).

### Support for Transporting Validity

The *Uniform Guidelines on Employee Selection Procedures* (1978) outline three requirements for transporting validity: job similarity, evidence of validity, and fairness. The most relevant component with regard to the O*NET is job simi-

larity. The *Uniform Guidelines* state that "the job or group of jobs on which the validity study was conducted perform substantially the same major work behaviors, as shown by appropriate job analyses both on the job or group of jobs on which the validity study was performed and on the job for which the selection procedure is to be used . . ." (Sec. 7B). Several O*NET domains provide information that could easily be used to establish job similarity in order to meet the requirements of the *Uniform Guidelines*. Specifically, the GWAs were designed to provide broad descriptions of work activities and facilitate comparisons of the work performed in different jobs. In addition, O*NET subdomains such as Abilities, Knowledges, Skills, and Work Context could be useful in establishing job similarity.

The process of establishing job similarity can be completed in several ways using O*NET information (see Baughman et al., 1999; Kubisiak, Hanson, & Buck, 1999). If a need to transport validity evidence is anticipated, collecting information using O*NET questionnaires for the original job analysis can provide a straightforward method for establishing job similarity when it is necessary to transport to new locations or situations.

### Development of Worker Safety and Health Guidelines

Research has shown that working conditions can contribute to occupational injuries and diseases (e.g., carpal tunnel syndrome, back injuries, etc.) and otherwise impact employee health (Cooper & Payne, 1979; Selye, 1980). Accordingly, worker safety and health guidelines are a crucial component of any organization's policies and procedures. The Work Context subdomain of the O*NET provides information relevant to the development of these guidelines. Numerous variables could be considered part of the work environment; however, the O*NET's Work Context subdomain focuses on those physical and social factors that would be expected to consistently differentiate between jobs (Strong, Jeanneret, McPhail, Blakley, & D'Egidio, 1999). Many of the O*NET Work Context descriptors are relevant for determining the types of body positions required to perform a job, as well as work conditions that require safety and health guidelines (e.g., climbing, lifting, environmental hazards, etc.).

### Selection

Selection is one of the most fundamental assessment functions. All organizations must select individuals to fill vacant or newly created positions, and the information provided by the O*NET establishes a foundation for the selection process. Not only does the O*NET provide information to potential employees about the characteristics and requirements of various occupations, but also it can serve as the basis for developing a job-relevant selection process. Two O*NET contributions to employment selection are discussed next.

### Job Component Validation

One assessment opportunity is related to the concept of job component validation. Job component validation is based on the concept of synthetic validation (Jeanneret, 1992; Lawshe, 1952; McCormick, Jeanneret, & Mecham, 1972). The GWAs subdomain was included in the O*NET in part to identify constructs that would support the synthetic validation of job performance predictors. Many of the GWAs are based on Position Analysis Questionnaire (PAQ) dimensions (Jeanneret & Borman, 1995). Additionally, the Skills and GWAs subdomains are complementary because they provide alternative, but related, perspectives of the job: Skills describe worker requirements (Mumford & Peterson, 1995), and GWAs describe occupational (work) requirements (Jeanneret & Borman, 1995).

A recent study (D'Egidio, 2001) examined the feasibility of a job component validation model using job data from the O*NET and a set of commercially available ability tests (i.e., Employment Aptitude Series published by Psychological Services, Inc.; Ruch, Stang, McKillip, & Dye, 1994, and Workplace Literacy Tests; Educational Testing Service, 1996) and personality inventories (i.e., Hogan Personality Inventory; Hogan & Hogan, 1992). Specifically, two subdomains of the O*NET were examined: GWAs and Skills. The results indicated generally positive support for using O*NET job data to predict mean test scores and validity coefficients, which provides some evidence regarding the usefulness of the O*NET for implementing a job component validity methodology. Although most of the prediction equations are based on relatively small sample sizes, the findings were nevertheless very encouraging. The magnitude of many of the multiple $R$ and adjusted $R^2$ values suggests the viability of both the Skills and GWAs subdomain databases for predicting both cognitive ability and personality test scores (D'Egidio, 2001).

Assuming the research findings are replicated in future research and statistical algorithms can be developed for a number of predictors, the process to be followed in using O*NET-based job component validity for developing a selection system would involve three basic steps: First, it would be necessary to obtain O*NET data for the job(s) of interest. Second, statistical predictions based on the O*NET profile (e.g., GWAs, Skills, or both) for the job(s) would be made regarding the types of selection instruments and levels of performance on the instruments needed to meet job require-

ments. Third, procedures would be set forth to guide hiring decisions including implementation of a specific selection test battery and establishing cutoff scores.

### Realistic Job Preview

Realistic job previews (RJPs) are commonly used for two reasons: (1) as an information resource to provide an accurate and complete picture of a job so some individuals self-select out of the preemployment process in hopes of reducing future turnover and (2) as a recruiting tool to increase an applicant's desire to become part of an organization (Wanous, 1973). The research on the effects of RJPs suggest that they generally have beneficial results. This is particularly true for complex jobs and work settings where the conditions are difficult or unpleasant. The O*NET provides a wealth of information that can be used in the design of RJPs. Not only does the O*NET provide information about the skills, abilities, and knowledge required to perform the job, but also it includes information about the work environment and organizational context (e.g., structure, culture, and the terms and conditions of employment). When combined, this information can provide almost a virtual reality description for any prospective applicant.

### Other Selection Applications

The developers of the O*NET have identified several other uses of specific O*NET subdomains in the selection process. For example, O*NET information encompassing education, training, experience, and licensure requirements can be used to establish minimum hiring standards. In addition, organizations can use labor market, occupational, and wage information in the development of recruitment strategies or for determining needs for industry-sponsored training programs.

## Job Evaluation and Classification for Compensation

Compensation is a key aspect of all human resource systems. Building fair, equitable, and competitive compensation systems is essential to maintaining a satisfied and motivated workforce. Job analysis data can play several key roles related to compensation, including establishing similarities and differences in the content of jobs and assisting in establishing an internally and externally equitable job structure (Milkovich & Newman, 1993). Philosophies on job evaluation are quite diverse, but all include making distinctions between the content and value of work, establishing links between job content and the external market, and establishing measurement and administration guidelines (Milkovich & Newman, 1993). Several subdomains of the O*NET provide information relevant to building compensation systems. Specifically, the Occupational Characteristics subdomain includes labor market and wage information. Other subdomains can be used to establish similarities and differences in job content, which in turn can be analyzed with respect to internal and external market equity. These subdomains include worker requirements such as Experience, Training, Licensure, Knowledges, and Skills. In addition, the GWAs and Work Context subdomains provide relevant job evaluation information. Data from these two subdomains should be useful in the same way that job dimension scores obtained when analyzing jobs with the PAQ have been found to determine job value and internal equity. These job evaluation results can be used to array jobs in a hierarchical compensation structure in order to assign them to labor grades or pay classifications. Research has documented that the PAQ job dimension scores are very predictive of the relative positions of jobs in terms of actual compensation (McCormick et al., 1972; McCormick & Jeanneret, 1988; Jeanneret, 1980).

## Employee Performance

Several O*NET subdomains have been identified as useful for either defining or measuring employee performance. Specifically, the Abilities subdomain can be used to link job task characteristics with the abilities required to effectively perform the tasks. Such a process would lead to the development of performance standards from the workers' perspective (see Fleishman, Costanza, & Marshall-Mies, 1999). From the occupational perspective, GWAs are in many respects equivalent to performance dimensions (see Jeanneret, Borman, Kubisiak, & Hanson, 1999). In addition, the Skills and Knowledges subdomains identify the required skills or knowledge needed to effectively perform a job. Thus, in combination, the relevant O*NET subdomains can be used as the basis for a comprehensive performance management system.

## DEVELOPMENT OPPORTUNITIES

Many of the current and potential uses of the O*NET are related to developmental opportunities for current and future employees. For example, initial efforts have been made to incorporate O*NET information into the many job banks provided by various entities for job seekers. This section of the chapter focuses on the use of O*NET information in a variety of development activities including matching people with occupations, developing vocational guidance/career exploration tools, and training.

## Matching People With Occupations

One primary purpose of the O*NET is to help people identify appropriate occupations. High school students, college students, displaced workers, vocational counselors, and many others can benefit from the O*NET's job description information. The extent to which this information can be used to match people with occupations is limited only by the amount of worker assessment data that can be gathered, and the creativity of the users and application developers. As mentioned previously, the O*NET contains job analysis data for more than 950 occupations and includes a wide variety of worker requirements and characteristics, grouped into several content subdomains: Knowledges, Skills, Abilities, Work Styles, and Occupational Values and Interests. The match between a person and an occupation can be assessed based on variables from one, several, or all of these subdomains. So, for example, if the main concern is to identify occupations for which an individual will be qualified, matching might focus on Abilities or Skills. If the desire also is to identify occupations that the individual would enjoy, Interest descriptors can be included in the matching.

The O*NET provides data concerning the worker requirements of occupations, but information is needed concerning workers' capabilities and preferences on these same descriptors in order to match people with occupations. The DOL has developed a set of career exploration tools designed to help users assess their own standing on some key O*NET descriptors. These worker assessment tools—the Interest Profiler, Work Importance Locator, and Ability Profiler—are available on the O*NET web site (www.onetcenter.org). These assessment tools are composed of self-directed career exploration and assessment measures designed to help workers consider and plan career options, and to help students who are moving into the workforce obtain needed information to ease the transition. These tools are designed to help individuals identify their work-related interests and abilities and determine what characteristics of a job are important to them, and then match this information with occupational data to identify jobs that relate most closely to their individual attributes.

The Interest Profiler is based on Holland's Realistic, Investigative, Artistic, Social, Enterprising, and Conventional (RIASEC) interest structure (Holland, 1985) and helps individuals identify the type of work activities and occupations they would find interesting and enjoyable. The Work Importance Locator assesses the importance individuals place on work values and characteristics of occupations (e.g., achievement, autonomy, and working conditions) and helps them identify occupations consistent with their most important values. The Ability Profiler measures nine job relevant abilities (i.e., verbal ability, arithmetic reasoning, computation, spatial ability, form perception, clerical perception, motor coordination, manual dexterity, and finger dexterity) and is designed to help individuals identify their strengths across these abilities. After taking these tests, job seekers are provided with profiles of scores from these measures, and they can use this "whole person" assessment to identify occupations in the O*NET that match their own profiles.

Information about a job seeker's standing on descriptors from other O*NET subdomains can be used to further enhance person-occupation matching based on O*NET. A wide variety of individual differences measures also have been developed in the past to target many of the O*NET variables, such as skills, abilities, personality traits, and so on. When existing measures are used to assess worker characteristics (e.g., ability tests, personality inventories, etc.), links will need to be established between the content of these measures and the ability requirements and other characteristics of occupations assessed by O*NET. This can be accomplished empirically, for example, by examining the ability test scores obtained by workers in various occupations for which O*NET job analysis ratings are available (Jeanneret & Strong, 1997) or examining validity data from the literature. Links also could be established rationally, using expert judges.

The efficiency and effectiveness of matching people with occupations based on O*NET can be further enhanced by identifying new or different ways to assess worker characteristics. For example, Vance and Day (1995) estimated military workers' knowledge, skills, and abilities based on their previous job titles. The O*NET is an excellent source of information concerning the skill, ability, and other worker requirements of any occupation in the U.S. economy and could be used for this type of "assessment." Self-assessments of abilities, skills, and other work-related characteristics are often used in career guidance. However, the literature on the accuracy of self-assessments is mixed (Mabe & West, 1982), so their usefulness for assessing worker characteristics will be limited. Finally, people develop and use a variety of work-related skills while participating in both leisure and volunteer activities (McDaniels, 1989), and it may be possible to identify additional work-related skills and other characteristics based on individuals' nonwork activities (see Horgen, Hanson, Borman, & Kubisiak, 2000 for an example).

Another important consideration in career guidance applications of the O*NET is the amount of information job seekers can process. The O*NET includes an overwhelming amount of information, probably much more than the typical job seeker would actually utilize. Although the O*NET Viewer is a good tool for accessing O*NET information, it was not intended to be the sole source of occupational information for job seekers. In the past, automated career information systems, developed and marketed by private vendors, were important vehicles for making occupational information more accessible. Sampson et al. (1996) provide a review of these systems and summarize the similarities and differences. Most of these career information systems help job seekers assess a wide variety of their own job-relevant characteristics; they then use this information to help job seekers identify occupations that might be appropriate. The DOT has been the primary source of the occupational information included in these systems, but as the O*NET approach replaces the DOT, similar systems will need to be developed to help job seekers take full advantage of the O*NET's job analysis information. One notable advantage of many of these systems is that they simplify the users' task by identifying appropriate occupations automatically; for example, by computing the percentage of the ability requirements for each occupation that corresponds to the job seekers' abilities.

Person-job matching applications based on DOT information have been constrained by the fact that the DOT only provided information concerning whether or not each ability is relevant for a given occupation. Matching has typically been based on a simple count of the number of "hits," that is, the number of characteristics relevant for the occupation that also are relevant for the person. The numerical rating scales used to collect O*NET information (e.g., importance ratings on a 1 to 7 scale) will allow computerized person-job matching applications to apply relatively powerful statistical matching algorithms, comparing the profile of worker requirement scores for an occupation with a profile of the client's standing on these same traits. A variety of statistical techniques could be used to compare these profiles, such as simply squaring and adding the differences between worker and occupation scores across descriptors, correlating the two profiles, or using both level and profile information to match workers to occupations (Kubisiak et al., 1999). A wide variety of different statistical algorithms could be used to match people with occupations, and the development of matching algorithms for career counseling applications will benefit from careful consideration of rational, in addition to statistical, issues. For example, identification of the lists of "matching" jobs presented to job seekers necessarily involves making some assumptions and setting priorities (e.g., deciding which subdomains to include and how to weight them). Allowing users to have some control over the process could improve these systems, by allowing users to explicitly include their own priorities in the career exploration process.

Rehabilitation counselors and other rehabilitation professionals encounter some unique problems in helping their clients focus on occupational alternatives and find jobs. The O*NET contains 9 physical ability descriptors (e.g., static strength, stamina), 10 perceptual ability descriptors (e.g., night vision, hearing sensitivity), and 10 psychomotor ability descriptors (e.g., manual dexterity, reaction time). These descriptors can be used to identify groups of occupations that require high levels of a particular ability or group of abilities. Such occupations are not likely to be appropriate for individuals with functional limitations in these particular areas. Conversely, these ability scales also can be used to identify those occupations with minimal physical and psychomotor ability requirements. Johnson, Dorsey, and Carter (2001) used the O*NET data to develop a variable that summarizes the overall strength requirements for each occupation, and this variable may be particularly useful for identifying occupations that are good and poor candidates for workers with physical disabilities. One critical linkage for rehabilitation professionals will be between the O*NET physical ability descriptors and the assessments of physical functioning used in rehabilitation; the standardized scaling of the O*NET constructs is well suited to the identification of these linkages.

Taken together, the O*NET descriptors provide a comprehensive, detailed picture of each occupation in the U.S. economy. Because this information is collected using a standardized set of descriptors, it is ideal for making systematic comparisons across occupations and for matching workers with appropriate occupations. Different worker characteristics are likely to be more useful for different career counseling purposes. For example, high school students might be more interested in finding occupations that match their abilities and interests, whereas workers who are in the middle of their careers might be more interested in occupations that take advantage of the skills and knowledge they have already developed.

### Training

The O*NET database provides information related to training not only for current employees but also to providers of training for new and/or displaced workers. Specifically, O*NET subdomains can be used for curriculum development for both internal and external training programs and for the development of educational and licensure programs, in order to align educational and training curricula with current workplace needs. Relevant O*NET subdomains that have application to the development of training initiatives include Knowledge, Skills, Education, and Abilities.

## CURRENT APPLICATIONS

The O*NET is still in a developmental phase with additional data collection activities occurring. Further, numerous states have participated or are participating in "demonstration" projects that involve applying the O*NET to workforce problems. Some example projects are described below. For a complete listing of completed or ongoing projects, see http://www.doleta.gov/programs/onet/synopses.asp.

A project in California is focused on integrating skills and occupational needs of the multimedia and entertainment industries. Two agencies, the California Employment Development Department and the SkillsNet Private Industry Skills council (a consortium of Los Angeles and San Francisco groups) are using O*NET information as a tool for developing training programs (curricula) and job matches in the two industries. In addition, they are forming an electronic clearinghouse for skills and training information through developed interfaces and linkages to the California Cooperative Occupational Information System.

The Minnesota Department of Economic Security is incorporating data on Skills to be delivered to employees through a variety of channels, including the World Wide Web, Career Information System, Occupational Information System, and the Work Force Information System. The New York Department of Labor, Research and Statistics Division is integrating O*NET information into the New York School-to-Work System. This integration includes developing O*NET Occupational Values and Interest Profilers as career/self-assessment guides, and the eventual goal is to have the O*NET serve as the cornerstone for career development systems in New York public schools.

In South Carolina, the Employment Security Commission is developing four O*NET applications as part of a system to register job applicants, register employer job orders, match job applicants and job openings, and identify training requirements and map them to the state's Technical Education System.

Finally, Texas is building an O*NET application for dislocated, experienced workers that explores the skill transferability process. The Occupational and Skill Computer-Assisted Researcher (OSCAR) allows individuals to compare their current occupations to new occupations for similar interests, abilities, and skills or to search for new occupations based on specific interest, abilities, and skills identified by the individuals. The system has five basic options. The *Assessment* option allows individuals to take an online self-assessment to identify occupations that are similar to their work values and/or interests. The *Search* option identifies potential occupations based on selected criteria such as Abilities, Interests, Knowledge, Skills, GWAs, and Work Values. The *Match* function determines other occupations that are the best relative match based on the same domains as the *Search* option. Users can *Compare* their current (or most recent) occupation to potential future occupations for similar Abilities, Interests, Knowledge, Skills, GWAs, or Work Values. Finally, the *Profile* option displays or prints a specific Occupational

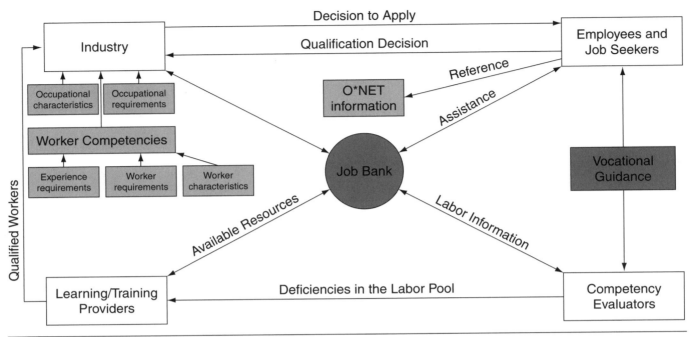

**Figure 12.2**  A model for building and implementing O\*NET-based assessment and development information.

Narrative Profile describing the preceding aspects of a selected occupation.

## SUMMARY

The O\*NET provides important occupational information to a variety of users including employers, job seekers, career explorers, vocational counselors, and researchers interested in jobs and work (Peterson et al., 1999, 2001). Figure 12.2 presents a potential model for utilizing O\*NET information within a system including input and output from industry, employees and job seekers, competency evaluators, and training providers. This model incorporates many of the uses of O\*NET information discussed in this chapter, using a job bank as the central depository for all of the information from the various sectors. Job banks are primarily designed to provide information to potential employees but also can be used by training providers, competency evaluators who provide assessment options to potential employees, and by organizations for information related to recruiting qualified workers. In the model, if one considers the axis between the Learning/Training Providers (lower left corner) and the Employees and Job Seekers (upper right corner) as dividing the information sources into two domains, then the information in the lower right side of the model is about individuals external to the work setting, and the information in the upper left side is about work and individuals in the work setting.

The O\*NET provides a means for populating the Job Bank with information about work—describing work in terms of activities, characteristics, and requirements. The O\*NET also provides a structure for how information about individuals (both internal and external to the work setting) should be incorporated in the Job Bank. If established and used with the opportunities described in this chapter, the O\*NET in combination with the Job Bank would clearly have a powerful influence on the design and implementation of tomorrow's assessment and development needs of the U.S. workforce.

In conclusion, the O\*NET provides a wealth of information for individuals and organizations related to a variety of human resource systems. The various domains of the O\*NET reflect a holistic view not only of the work, but also of the worker. There are endless opportunities to utilize O\*NET job information, especially with respect to assessment and developmental applications. Future research and additional data collection efforts will continue to highlight the usefulness of the Occupational Information Network.

## REFERENCES

Baughman, W.A., Cooke, A.E., Dorsey, D.W., & Threlfall, K.V. (1999, April). *Skills-based job analysis: Developing task sampling domains using O\*NET descriptors.* Poster session presented at the 14th Annual Conference of the Society for Industrial and Organizational Psychology, Atlanta, GA.

Baughman, W.A., Dorsey, D.W., Cooke, A.E., & Rosse, R.L. (2000, May). *Using the O\*NET Content Model as metadata for gathering and organizing work information.* Paper presented at the annual meeting of the Society for Industrial and Organizational Psychology, New Orleans, LA.

Baughman, W.A., Norris, D.G., Cooke, A.E., Peterson, N.G., & Mumford, M.D. (1999). In N.G. Peterson, M.D. Mumford, W.C. Borman, P.R. Jeanneret, & E.A. Fleishman (Eds.), *An occupational information system for the 21st century: The development of O\*NET* (pp. 259–272). Washington, DC: American Psychological Association.

Campion, M.C., Morgeson, F.P., & Mayfield, M.S. (1999). O\*NET's theoretical contributions to job analysis research. In N.G. Peterson, M.D. Mumford, W.C. Borman, P.R. Jeanneret, & E.A. Fleishman (Eds.), *An occupational information system for the 21st century: The development of the O\*NET* (pp. 297–304). Washington, DC: American Psychological Association.

Cascio, W.F. (1995). Whither industrial and organizational psychology in a changing world of work? *American Psychologist, 50,* 928–939.

Cooper, C.L., & Payne, R. (1979). *Stress at work.* New York: Wiley.

D'Egidio, E. (2001). *Building a job component validity model using job analysis data from the Occupational Information Network.* Unpublished doctoral dissertation, University of Houston.

Educational Testing Service. (1996). *Workplace literacy tests.* Princeton, NJ: Author.

Fleishman, E.A., Costanza, D.P., & Marshall-Mies, J. (1999). Abilities. In N.G. Peterson, M.D. Mumford, W.C. Borman, P.R. Jeanneret, & E.A. Fleishman (Eds.), *An occupational information system for the 21st century: The development of the O\*NET* (pp. 175–196). Washington, DC: American Psychological Association.

Hanson, M.A., Kubisiak, U.C., Horgen, K., Buck, D.E., Bunch, L., Foster, L.L., & Borman, W.C. (2000, May). *Basic research to support development of a career guidance system for displaced workers.* Paper presented at the annual meeting of the Society for Industrial and Organizational Psychology, New Orleans, LA.

Hogan, R., & Hogan, J. (1992). *Hogan Personality Inventory manual* (2nd ed.). Tulsa, OK: Hogan Assessment Systems.

Holland, J.L. (1985). *Making vocational choices. A theory of vocational personalities and work environments* (2nd ed.). Englewood Cliffs, NJ: Prentice-Hall.

Horgen, K.E., Hanson, M.A., Borman, W.C., & Kubisiak, U.C. (2000). *Leisure, volunteer, and social activities as sources of work-related skills.* Poster session presented at the 14th Annual Conference of the Society for Industrial and Organizational Psychology, New Orleans, LA.

Howard, A. (1995). Rethinking the psychology of work. In A. Howard (Ed.), *The changing nature of work* (pp. 513–555). San Francisco: Jossey-Bass.

Jeanneret, P.R. (1992). Applications of job component/synthetic validity to construct validity. *Human Performance, 5,* 81–96.

Jeanneret, P.R. (1980). Equitable job evaluation and classification with the Position Analysis Questionnaire. *Compensation Review, 12,* 32–42.

Jeanneret, P.R., & Borman, W.C. (1995). Generalized work activities. In N.G. Peterson, M.D. Mumford, W.C. Borman, P.R. Jeanneret, & E.A. Fleishman (Eds.), *Development of a prototype Occupational Information Network (O\*NET) content model* (pp. 6-1–6-99). Salt Lake City: Utah Department of Employment Security.

Jeanneret, P.R., Borman, W.C., Kubisiak, U.C., & Hanson, M.A. (1999). Generalized work activities. In N.G. Peterson, M.D. Mumford, W.C. Borman, P.R. Jeanneret, & E.A. Fleishman (Eds.), *An occupational information system for the 21st century: The development of the O\*NET* (pp. 105–125). Washington, DC: American Psychological Association.

Jeanneret, P.R., & Strong, M. (1997). Linking O\*NET job analysis information to the assessment of job requirements. In N.G. Peterson (Ed.), *Occupational Information Network (O\*NET) research and development.* Salt Lake City: Utah Department of Employment Security.

Johnson, J.W., Dorsey, D.W., & Carter, G.W. (2001). *Development of a composite "strength" measure from O\*NET descriptors* (Institute Report No. 385). Minneapolis: Personnel Decisions Research Institutes.

Kubisiak, U.C., Borman, W.C., & Hanson, M.A. (1998, April). *Job clustering using the O\*NET.* Paper presented at the 12th Annual Conference of the Society for Industrial and Organizational Psychology, Dallas, TX.

Kubisiak, U.C., Hanson, M.A., & Buck, D.E. (1999, April). *Person-job matching in the context of computerized career information delivery.* Poster session presented at the 14th Annual Conference of the Society for Industrial and Organizational Psychology, Atlanta, GA.

Lawshe, C.H. (1952). Employee selection. *Personnel Psychology, 5,* 31–34.

Mabe, P.A., & West, S.G. (1982). Validity of self-evaluation of ability: A review and meta-analysis. *Journal of Applied Psychology, 67(3),* 280–296.

McCormick, E.J. (1979). *Job analysis: Methods and applications.* New York: American Management Association.

McCormick, E.J., & Jeanneret, P.R. (1988). Position Analysis Questionnaire (PAQ). In S. Gael (Ed.), *The job analysis handbook for business and industry* (Vol. 2, pp. 825–842). New York: Wiley.

McCormick, E.J., Jeanneret, P.R., & Mecham, R.C. (1972). A study of job characteristics and job dimensions as based on the Position Analysis Questionnaire (PAQ) [Monograph]. *Journal of Applied Psychology, 56,* 347–368.

McDaniels, C. (1989). *The changing workplace: Career counseling strategies for the 1990s and beyond.* San Francisco: Jossey-Bass.

Milkovich, G.T., & Newman, J.M. (1993). *Compensation* (5th ed.). Chicago: Irwin.

Mumford, M., & Peterson, N. (1995). Skills. In N.G. Peterson, M.D. Mumford, W.C. Borman, P.R. Jeanneret, & E.A. Fleishman

(Eds.), *Development of a prototype Occupational Information Network (O\*NET) content model* (pp. 3-1–3-75). Salt Lake City: Utah Department of Employment Security.

Mumford, M., & Peterson, N. (1999). The O\*NET content model: Structural considerations in describing jobs. In N.G. Peterson, M.D. Mumford, W.C. Borman, P.R. Jeanneret, & E.A. Fleishman (Eds.), *An occupational information system for the 21st century: The development of the O\*NET* (pp. 21–30). Washington, DC: American Psychological Association.

Peterson, N.G., Mumford, M.D., Borman, W.C., Jeanneret, P.R., & Fleishman, E.A. (1995). *Development of a prototype Occupational Information Network (O\*NET) content model.* Salt Lake City: Utah Department of Employment Security.

Peterson, N.G., Mumford, M.D., Borman, W.C., Jeanneret, P.R., & Fleishman, E.A. (1999). *An occupational information system for the 21st century: The development of the O\*NET.* Washington, DC: American Psychological Association.

Peterson, N.G., Mumford, M.D., Borman, W.C., Jeanneret, P.R., Fleishman, E.A., Levin, K.Y., Campion, M.A., Mayfield, M.S., Morgeson, F.P., Pearlman, K., Gowing, M.K., Lancaster, A.R., Silver, M.B., & Dye, D.M. (2001). Understanding work using the Occupational Information Network (O\*NET): Implications for practice and research. *Personnel Psychology, 54*(2), 451–492.

Ruch, W.W., Stang, S.W., McKillip, R.H., & Dye, D.A. (1994). *Employee Aptitude Survey technical manual* (2nd ed.). Los Angeles: Psychological Services.

Sampson, J.P., Reardon, R.C., Norris, D.S., Greeno, B.P., Kolodinsky, R.W., & Rush, D. (1996). *A differential feature-cost analysis of seventeen computer-assisted career guidance systems.* Center for the Study of Technology in Counseling and Career Development: Tallahassee, FL.

Sanchez, J.I., & Levine, E.L. (1999). Is job analysis dead, misunderstood, or both? In A.I. Kraut & A.K. Korman (Eds.), *Evolving practices in human resource management* (pp. 43–68). San Francisco: Jossey-Bass.

Selye, H. (1980). *Selye's guide to stress research* (Vol. 1). New York: Van Nostrand Reinhold.

Strong, M.H., Jeanneret, P.R., McPhail, S.M., Blakley, B.R., & D'Egidio, E.L. (1999). Work context: Taxonomy and measurement of the work environment. In N.G. Peterson, M.D. Mumford, W.C. Borman, P.R. Jeanneret, & E.A. Fleishman (Eds.), *An occupational information system for the 21st century: The development of the O\*NET* (127–145). Washington DC: American Psychological Association.

U.S. Department of Labor (1991). *Dictionary of occupational titles.* Washington, DC: U.S. Government Printing Office.

*Uniform guidelines on employee selection procedures.* (1978). *Federal Register, 43*(166), 38290–39309.

Vance, R.J., & Day, D.V. (1995). Developing computerized outplacement counseling programs: The Philadelphia naval shipyard and base. In M. London (Series and Vol. Ed.), *Society for industrial and organizational psychology professional practice series: Employees, careers, and job creation* (pp. 258–286). San Francisco: Jossey-Bass.

Wanous, J.P. (1973). Effects of a realistic job preview on job acceptance, job attitude, and job survival. *Journal of Applied Psychology, 58*, 327–332.

# CHAPTER 13

# The Psychological Assessment of Emotional Intelligence

DEAN E. FROST

In this chapter, the popularity and social/historical context of the emotional intelligence construct are first described. Debates about the content of construct and its proper definition are next considered. Distinctions between the construct and related constructs in psychology are outlined, and a brief discussion of the jobs most suitable for the assessment of emotional intelligence is provided. Six approaches to the assessment of the emotional intelligence construct are presented: the Emotional Quotient Inventory; the Mayer, Salovey, and Caruso Emotional Intelligence Test; the Toronto Alexithymia Scale; the Psychological Mindedness Assessment Procedure; the Emotional Competence Inventory; and the NEO-PI-R Openness to Experience Scale. Finally, a brief comparison of the assessment choices is contained in a concluding comment.

## CURRENT POPULARITY

The concept of emotional intelligence achieved great public popularity in the 1990s. The topic served as a lead article in the newspaper *USA Today* in 1995, appeared on the cover of *Time* magazine that same year, and was the title of a best-selling popular book (Goleman, 1995b). Proof that it had passed into common language and discussion was evidenced by the phrase "emotional intelligence" being selected as the most useful new phrase of 1995 by the American Dialect Society.

Part of this popularity can be attributed to the historical and social context of its appearance. The year before, Herrnstein and Murray's (1994) book *The Bell Curve* initiated a debate about how intelligence, represented by the intelligence quotient, or IQ, was linked to social class standing and other measures of personal success. They described a fixed, or entity approach, to intelligence and argued that it was a fundamental difference possessed only by the elite and either acquired early or possessed from birth. Emotional intelligence became popular, in part, as a counterargument. In emotional intelligence many popular authors saw a psychological attribute that could be strengthened or acquired and, as a consequence, a person's goal achievement improved. Hence, it was an equalitarian answer to *The Bell Curve*'s argument of elitism.

Goleman (1995b) went so far as to say about emotional intelligence, "There is an old-fashioned word for the body of skills that emotional intelligence represents: character" (p. 285). Is then this construct a collection of human virtues? Scarr (1989) expressed concern about such sweeping statements, "There are many human virtues that are not sufficiently rewarded in our society, such as goodness in human relationships, and talents in music, dance, and painting. To call them intelligence does not do justice to either theories of intelligence or to the personality traits and special talents that lie beyond the consensual definition of intelligence" (p. 78).

A second, more scientific debate endures, however. Is emotional intelligence merely relabeling parts of personality as aspects of intelligence? Clearly, emotional intelligence has the image of a new field. However, the more emotional intelligence is seen as a restatement of personality research, the more the end result will be to lead psychologists away from relevant research and ultimately creating a theory of emotional intelligence that is disconnected from other theories. Since emotional intelligence does not refer exclusively to emotion or to intelligence, the scientific debate must focus on what emotional intelligence really does refer to. Empirical studies of the discriminant and convergent validity of emotional intelligence scales are only now beginning but will address whether these new measures are reinventions of earlier tests or whether they do actually measure something new.

## A DEFINITION OF EMOTIONAL INTELLIGENCE

Salovey and Mayer (1989/1990) provided an initial conceptual definition of emotional intelligence as "the ability to monitor one's own and others' feelings and emotions, to discriminate among them and use this information to guide one's thinking and actions" (p. 189). Generally, the psychological construct of intelligence is accepted as a group of mental abilities. Even more specifically, an ability of any type can be stated as a characteristic of an individual when that individual can "successfully complete (i.e., obtain a specific, desired, outcome on) a task of defined difficulty, when testing conditions are favorable" (Carroll, 1993, p. 4). Thus, most researchers see emotional intelligence as being composed of mental abilities or capacities. This chapter describes current attempts to create tasks and testing conditions whereby emotional intelligence is measured.

Mayer and Salovey (1997) revised their definition of emotional intelligence, and it currently appears to be the consensus definition. In this definition they identify four underlying components: emotional perception and identification, emotional facilitation, emotional understanding, and emotion management.

The emotional perception and identification component involves the ability to recognize and input information from the emotional system. It includes the capacities to perceive, appraise, and express emotions. The emotional facilitation component is described as the processing of emotional data with an emphasis on such data as being a complex of physiological, emotional-experiential, cognitive, and conscious events that require integration. Here, it is said, emotion enters into the cognitive system. The emotional understanding component entails the processing of emotional information to assist problem solving and improve cognitive processing. Finally, emotion management is the component constituted by self-management of the emotions and the management of emotions in other people. This final component involves consideration of various different emotional paths and the choice among them, both in reasoning directed toward the self and in interacting with others.

The concept of emotional management probably is the focus of most of the theoretical distinctions among authors' definitions of emotional management. For example, Taylor and Bagby (2000) state, "Noticeably absent from this revised formulation of the construct is any direct reference to interpersonal intelligence" (p. 45). They, and other authors, place a greater emphasis on the abilities individuals use in processing and reacting to others' emotional states.

## DISTINCTIONS FROM RELATED CONSTRUCTS

Emotional intelligence is related to a number of existing constructs in psychology. The following is a brief summary of these related constructs.

Social competence has been defined as "the possession and use of the ability to integrate thinking, feeling, and behavior to achieve social tasks and outcomes valued in the host context and culture" (Topping, Bremner, & Holmes, 2000). Assessment of social competence typically "represents a summary judgment of performance across a range of interpersonal situations" (Gersten, Weissberg, Amish, & Smith, 1987). Social skills are seen as more specific, purely behavioral components of effective social interactions; examples of social skills might include eye contact, smiling, and voice intonation.

Generally, social competence has been applied to studying the social interactions of school-age children in educational situations. An example would be a student who fails to successfully interact with peers and consequently is perceived as distractible or disruptive. The student then receives negative feedback based on the behavior, the student's learning performance suffers, and the student may seek out other social contexts in which he or she feels more socially competent (e.g., truancy, vandalism, drug use).

Social competence as a construct focuses on patterns of learned behaviors, which can be observed. There is little discussion of cognitive processing of emotional information, and discussion of emotional responses is usually represented by expressions of frustration or satisfaction. Additionally, this construct is applied most frequently to children, and the outcomes of interest are socialization failures or success in the classroom.

Emotional competence is another construct related to emotional intelligence and has been defined as "the demonstration of self-efficacy in emotion-eliciting social transactions" (Saarni, 2000). Although self-efficacy and even self-actualization are mentioned in the emotional intelligence literature, they are discussed as an outcome of emotional intelligence and its processes. Individuals with high self-efficacy believe themselves to have the capacity and skills to achieve a desired outcome or goal, and evidence of emotional intelligence may lead to such a belief. However, in emotional competence there is a focus on how the desired outcomes reflect a high degree of integration with the individual's moral commitments. The emotional intelligence literature contains references to ethical values and ego-identity, but the construct always is described as a set of mental aptitudes distinct from moral development.

E.L. Thorndike (1936) defined social intelligence as the abilities to understand others and to act or behave wisely in relations to others. He distinguished these abilities from abstract and mechanical forms of intelligence. More recent statements of the construct see goal-oriented behavior as central to the construct of social intelligence. In demonstrating a high level of social intelligence, individuals are seen as behaving in ways that are best understood in terms of how they actively seek to operate in their social environment, thereby pursuing the desired outcomes in the important domains of their life. This construct is most similar to emotional intelligence in that adaptability and functionality of an individual's cognitions are stressed in the current social environment.

The core assumptions of social intelligence are: (1) Behavior is purposive and strategic, definitely goal-oriented; (2) people are active in interpreting meanings of social context, opportunities, and risks faced; (3) behavior is inherently social and operates within a cultural frame as its context; (4) behavior is developmentally interpreted in terms of the current stage in an individual's life; and (5) there is a stress on cognition, creativity, and imagination (Zirkel, 2000). An example of social intelligence research would be the concept of possible selves (Markus & Nurius, 1986). A possible self is a concrete depiction of some anticipated outcome, or set of outcomes, that the individual refers to cognitively in choosing current actions. The link between cognition and action is represented by the approach or avoidance of particular goal-related interactions.

There is a greater emphasis on developmental stages and cultural relativity in social intelligence than there is in emotional intelligence. Much greater stress is placed on what individuals are trying to do, and more attention is given to specific goals and plans for action than on underlying mental capacities. But perhaps most important, little importance is given to the perception and integration of emotional information in the construct of social intelligence.

Gardner's theory of multiple intelligences (1983) includes two subtypes of personal intelligences: intrapersonal intelligence and interpersonal intelligence. He describes *intrapersonal intelligence* as the examination and knowledge of one's own feelings. *Interpersonal intelligence* is described as the ability to read moods, intentions, or desires in others and to consequently act on that information in interacting with others. Gardner describes this latter intelligence as empathy, or the awareness and appraisal of the subjective feelings evoked in oneself by others as well as the awareness and appraisal of nonverbal expressions of others with emotional content. The field of emotional intelligence could be viewed as a collective effort to develop more completely the theoretical constructs of intrapersonal and interpersonal intelligences and to provide systematic assessments for both subtypes.

## APPLICATIONS TO SELECTION, PLACEMENT, AND TRAINING

Not enough empirical studies have been conducted to date for a clear specification of what types of occupations or job titles for which emotional intelligence should be considered as a construct with substantial validity. At the conceptual level, clearly any job with supervisory responsibilities would benefit from the placement of individuals with high levels of emotional intelligence. Jobs with a high loading on client contact, whether internal or external, would also benefit. Also, individuals whose situations are characterized by frequent work in self-directed work teams would be appropriate for the assessment of emotional intelligence.

The value of typical cognitive ability tests to predict training proficiency or job performance in many positions is well accepted, but this assumes that the problems being solved or tasks performed in these jobs are relatively similar to academic problems; that is, they are well-defined problems or

**TABLE 13.1  A Comparison of Academic and Practical Problem Characteristics**

| Academic Problems Tend to Be | Practical, Everyday Problems Tend to Be |
| --- | --- |
| Formulated by others | Unformulated or in need of reformulation |
| Well defined | Poorly defined |
| Complete in the information they provide | Lacking in information necessary for solution |
| Characterized by having only one correct answer | Characterized by multiple "correct" solutions, each with liabilities as well as assets |
| Characterized by having only one method of obtaining the correct answer | Characterized by multiple methods for picking a problem solution |
| Disconnected from ordinary or everyday experience | Related to everyday experience |
| Of little or no intrinsic interest | Of personal interest |

Adapted from Hedlund and Steinberg (2000).

tasks. The greatest value for implementing assessments of emotional intelligence may be in the cases where significant problems are less well defined and are "fuzzier." This contrast can be seen in Table 13.1. To the degree that a functional job analysis indicates the presence of problems described in Table 13.1 as practical or everyday problems, then emotional intelligence may be an important construct to consider. The assessments described in the following pages may then assist in the selection, placement, or training of individuals in organizational settings.

## THE EMOTIONAL QUOTIENT INVENTORY (EQ-i)

The Emotional Quotient Inventory (EQ-i) was published in 1997 and reviewed in the Buros *Supplement to the Thirteenth Mental Measurements Yearbook* (Plake & Impara, 1999). The EQ-i was the first test of emotional intelligence to be published by a psychological test publisher.

### Test Description

The EQ-i includes 133 items and uses a Likert response scale ranging from "Very Seldom or Not True of Me" to "Very Often True of Me or True of Me." The reading level, based on the Flesch formula of readability (Flesch, 1948), is the North American sixth-grade level (Bar-On, 1997b). It is appropriate for ages 17 and older and requires 40 minutes to complete.

The EQ-i produces a total score and five composite scale scores (Bar-On, 2000). The first composite scale is the Intra-

personal EQ scale. It includes: Self-Regard, the ability to be aware of, understand, accept, and respect oneself; Emotional Self-Awareness, the ability to recognize and understand one's emotions; Assertiveness, the ability to express feelings, beliefs, and thoughts, and to defend one's rights in a nondestructive manner; Independence, the ability to be self-directed and self-controlled in one's thinking and actions and to be free of emotional dependency; and Self-Actualization, the ability to realize one's potential and to do what one wants to do, enjoys doing, and can do.

The second composite scale is the Interpersonal EQ scale. It includes: Empathy, the ability to be aware of, understand, and appreciate the feelings of others; Social Responsibility, the ability to demonstrate oneself as a cooperative, contributing, and constructive member of one's social group; and Interpersonal Relationship, the ability to establish and maintain mutually satisfying relationships that are characterized by emotional closeness, intimacy, and by giving and receiving affection.

The third composite scale is the Stress Management scale. It includes: Stress Tolerance, the ability to withstand adverse events, stressful situations, and strong emotions without "falling apart" by actively and positively coping with stress; and Impulse Control, the ability to resist or delay an impulse, drive, or temptation to act, and to control one's emotions.

The fourth composite scale is the Adaptability EQ scale. It includes: Reality Testing, the ability to assess the correspondence between what is internally and subjectively experienced and what externally and objectively exists; Flexibility, the ability to adjust one's feelings, thoughts, and behavior to changing situations and conditions; and Problem Solving, the ability to identify and define personal and social problems as well as to generate and implement potentially effective solutions.

The fifth composite scale is the General Mood EQ scale. It includes: Optimism, the ability "to look at the brighter side of life"; and Happiness, the ability to feel satisfied with one's life, to enjoy oneself and others, and to have fun and express positive emotions.

### Administration and Scoring

Administration of the EQ-i uses a self-report format, with a 30-minute time limit. Available manuals available include: a technical manual, a user's manual, an administrator's guide, and a facilitator's guide (for use in providing feedback to respondents). Online administration over the Internet is available through Multi-Health Systems, Inc. at www.mhs.com/assessments. A short version providing a total score and five subscale scores (Intrapersonal, Interpersonal, Adaptability, Stress Management, and General Mood) is available.

There are four validity indicators: Omission Rate, or the number of omitted responses; Inconsistency Index, or the degree of inconsistency between similar types of items; Positive Impression, or the tendency to give an exaggerated positive response; and Negative Impression, or the tendency to give an exaggerated negative response. The EQ-i has a built-in correction factor that automatically adjusts the scale scores based on the Positive Impression and Negative Impression scale scores.

The scores for the EQ-i are computer generated, and the results are displayed in numeric, verbal, and graphic fashion followed by a textual report. Raw scores are automatically tabulated and converted to standard scores based on a mean of 100 and a standard deviation of 15.

The published version of the EQ-i was normed on a large and representative sample of the North American population including 3,831 participants. No significant differences between males and females or by ethnic group are noted.

## Psychometric Characteristics

In terms of reliabilities, the average Cronbach alpha coefficients range from a low of .69 (Social Responsibility) to a high of .86 (Self-Regard) with an overall average internal reliability of .76. Test-retest reliability for a sample of 40 adults was .66 over three months in one study (Dayon, 2000) and was .73 over four months for a sample of 39 young adults in another (Bar-On, 1997b).

In factor-analytic studies, the average intercorrelation of the 15 subscales was .50. A principal components factor analysis was completed using 117 items from the total of 133 items. A 13-factor solution obtained with a varimax rotation afforded the most meaningful interpretation theoretically. Using the same sample of 3,831 respondents, a confirmatory factor analysis produced a 10-factor solution. This factor structure is different from the theoretically derived 15 factors listed in the EQ-i manual. The following 10 factors were obtained: Self-Regard (items 11, 24, 40, 56, 70, 85, 100, 114, 129; Interpersonal Relationship (items 31, 39, 62, 69, 99, 113, 128); Impulse Control (items 13, 73, 86, 117, 130); Problem Solving (items 1, 15, 29, 45, 60, 89); Emotional Self-Awareness (items 7, 9, 23, 35, 52, 116); Flexibility (items 14, 28, 43, 59, 74, 87, 103, 131); Reality Testing (items 8, 38, 53, 68, 83, 97); Stress Tolerance (items 4, 20, 33, 49, 64, 78, 108, 122); Assertiveness (items 37, 67, 82, 96, 111, 126); and Empathy (items 61, 72, 98, 119, 124). All items loaded at .35 or higher.

Both an exploratory and a confirmatory factor analysis have been reported for the factor structure of the normative sample. Given the use of the same sample for both factor analyses, the confirmatory factor analysis may be the best choice for a more conservative and empirically based factor structure. Otherwise, the use of the theoretically derived 15-factor structure given for the scale can be used until further empirical data are analyzed.

The convergent validity evidence is extensive for the EQ-i. Numerous studies of correlations between EQ-i factors and other scales' subscales have been conducted. For brevity's sake, results for the Interpersonal Relationship (IR) subscale of the EQ-i are surveyed here. The IR score correlated +.44 with the Emotional Stroop Task (Parker, 1999). The IR score correlated +.48 with the TMMS Clarity of Feelings scale (Henner, 1998). The correlation was −.48 with the TAS-20 DF scale (Dawda & Hart, 2000). The correlation was +.66 with Factor E on the NEO (Dawda & Hart, 2000). The IR subscale score correlated with a number of MMPI-2 interpersonal skills related subscales (SI −.77; CYN −.69; SOD −.79) (Dupertuis, 1996). Finally, it correlated with Factor H on the 16PF (+.56), the SCL-90 Interpersonal Sensitivity scale (−.85), and PAI Warmth scale (+.73) (Bar-On, 1997b).

Divergent validity evidence is less extensive on the EQ-i. The total EQ-i score correlated +.12 with the full IQ score on the Wechsler Adult Intelligence Scale (WAIS) in a study of 40 adults (Pallazza & Bar-On, 1995). The total EQ-i total score correlated +.01 with the Raven Progressive Matrices in one study (Hee-Woo, 1998) and +.01 in another study (Fund, 2000).

## Other Test Forms and Scoring Reports

The BarOn Emotional Quotient-interview is a one-hour structured interview protocol to be used following administration of the EQ-i and is structured according to its 15 subscales. Ratings are made on a 5-point scale from "Very Seldom True of Him/Her" to "Very Often True of Him/Her."

The EQ-i is available in the following languages: English, Chinese, Czech, Danish, Dutch, Finnish, French (Canadian), German, Hebrew, Korean, Norwegian, Russian, Spanish (U.S.) and Swedish.

Four scoring reports are available. The Individual Summary Report lists an overall EQ score, five composite scores, 15 subscale scores, and validity indicator results. The Development Report includes the preceding with an in-depth explanation of the meaning of the scores. The Resource Report presents EQ-i scores in a graphical format omitting numerical scores and using such verbal anchors as "Needs Improvement," "Effective Functioning," and "Enhanced Skills." The Group Report provides an anonymous summary of results for a group of respondents.

BarOn EQ-i Computer Program for Windows™ administers, scores, and reports the results for the BarOn Emotional Quotient Inventory. It can be administered online, or results of a paper-and-pencil administration can be entered for scoring and report generation. Like the EQ-i, an Individual Summary Report, a Development Report, and a Resource Report are provided.

The BarOn Emotional Quotient 360™ Assessment (or BarOn EQ-360™) provides a 360-degree perspective on an individual's EQ-i by obtaining ratings from a third person on a 46-item scale that is similar to the self-report EQ-i. Ratings are made on a 5-point scale from "Very Seldom True of Him/Her" to "Very Often True of Him/Her."

The Benchmarking Organizational Emotional Intelligence (BOEI) is an organizational survey consisting of 160 items rated on a 5-point response scale. Twenty subscale scores are provided on the following: Teamwork, Work Environment, Balancing Work/Life, Leveraging Diversity, Employee Empowerment, Pay, Job Satisfaction Attitude, Organizational Change, Supervisory Leadership, Positive Impression (validity scale), Coworker Relationships, Changes at Work, Diversity Climate, Workplace Tension, Training and Innovation, Benefits, Organizational Climate, Problem Solving/Decision Making, Change Management, and Senior Management Leadership. The BOEI is designed to measure the level of emotional intelligence in an entire organization or within individual departments or units.

## MAYER, SALOVEY, AND CARUSO EMOTIONAL INTELLIGENCE TEST (MSCEIT)

Unlike the EQ-i, which has similarities to a traditional personality test, the next assessment example has similar items to a traditional cognitive ability test.

### Test Description

Based on an earlier scale, the Multifactor Emotional Intelligence Scale (MEIS; see Mayer, Caruso, & Salovey, 1999), the MSCEIT is a measure of emotional intelligence that yields a total score as well as four subscale scores (i.e., called Branch scores). The four subscales are Perception of Emotion, Emotional Facilitation, Understanding Emotion, and Managing Emotion.

The Perception of Emotion subscale contains three subtests: Perception of Emotion in Faces, Perception of Emotion in Landscapes, and Perception of Emotion in Abstract Designs. For each stimulus the respondent rates the emotional content embedded in the stimulus. Thus, the respondent uses a 5-point response scale indicating how much happiness, fear, and sadness, and so on is perceived in the stimulus.

The Emotional Facilitation subscale contains a number of tasks, one of which is the Synesthesia subscale. The respondent is asked to judge the similarity between a specific emotional response, such as love, and other internal experience such as temperature and speed (e.g., hot or slow). The response is on a 5-point response scale (1 = "Not Alike" to 5 = "Very Much Alike").

For the Understanding Emotion subscale respondents choose from five multiple-choice alternatives that seek a match between a blend of two emotions with another single emotion. For example, the respondent chooses among (1) guilt, (2) challenge, (3) mania, (4) love, or (5) desire for the alternative that best combines "joy and acceptance."

For the Managing Emotion subscale, items ask the respondent to evaluate the best way to regulate emotions in one's self or others. Respondents are given items with such goals as maintaining a feeling, or feeling better. For example, given the goal of cheering up a sad person, the response alternatives involve "Talking to Some Friends," "Seeing a Violent Movie," "Eating a Big Meal," or "Taking a Walk Alone."

### Administration and Scoring

This assessment of emotional intelligence is available from Multi-Health Systems, Inc. The MSCEIT provides two validity scale scores, seven emotional IQ scores, and nine diagnostic scores. Forty-five to 60 minutes are needed to administer the paper-and-pencil self-report form, and an online version is in development.

### Psychometric Characteristics

Scale reliabilities for the MCSEIT were based on a sample of 277, and the coefficient alphas ranged from .59 to .87 (Mayer, Caruso, & Salovey, 2000a).

Two studies of divergent validity are available. The earlier version of the MCSEIT, the MEIS, is reported to have had a correlation of +.36 with a vocabulary test measure (Mayer, Caruso, & Salovey, 2000a). Ciarrochi, Chan, and Caputi (2000) reported a correlation of +.05 for the MEIS and the Raven Progressive Matrices.

In conducting a study of convergent validity, Ciarrochi et al. (2000) found the MEIS score correlated +.26 with a measure of Extroversion, +.24 with a measure of Openness to Feelings, and +.31 with a measure of Self-Esteem. Mayer, Caruso, Salovey, Formica, and Woolery (2000) looked at the correlation of the MEIS with the 16 PF subscales in a sample of 186 college students. They reported significant correlations of +.19 with Reasoning; +.22 with Sensitivity; −.17 with Vigilance; +.14 with Openness to Change; and −.21 with Self-Reliance. The MEIS did not correlated significantly with Warmth, Emotional Stability, Dominance, Liveliness, Rules-Consciousness, Social Boldness, Abstractness, Privateness, Apprehension, Perfectionism, and Tension. Mayer, Caruso, and Salovey (2000a) also report correlations between the FIRO-B and the MEIS. Here, the MEIS correlated significantly with Wanted Inclusion (+.22) and Wanted Affection (+.19) but did not correlate significantly with Expressed Affection or Expressed Control.

To assess concurrent validity Rice (1999) administered the MEIS to sample of 164 employees of an insurance company. The averaged MEIS score within a group of employees was then correlated with supervisors' rating of the group's performance on a customer service dimension ($r = +.46$). Team leaders' MEIS score correlated +.51 with their higher level manager's ranking of team leader overall effectiveness. However, team leader MEIS scores correlated negatively with the team's accuracy (−.35) and productivity in handling customer complaints (−.40). Team leader results should be viewed in light of the very small sample studied, an $N$ of 11.

## THE TORONTO ALEXITHYMIA SCALE (TAS-20)

### Test Description

Alexithymia is a clinical condition that might be typified as abnormally low emotional intelligence. Historical records show that patients suffering from so-called classical psychosomatic diseases showed an apparent inability to verbalize feelings (Ruesch, 1948). They tended to be unimaginative, used direct physical action or bodily channels for emotional expression, and responded poorly to insight-oriented psychotherapy. Thus, they showed a deficit in representing emotions symbolically. Their cognitive style was literal and externally oriented. In describing this condition, Sifneos (1973) coined the term *alexithymia* from the Greek: *a,* meaning a lack; *lexis,* meaning word; and *thymos* meaning emotion.

The salient features of alexithymia are: (1) difficulty identifying feelings and distinguishing between feelings and the bodily sensations of emotional arousal; (2) difficulty describing feelings to other people; (3) constricted imagination, a paucity of fantasy; and (4) a stimulus-bound, externally ori-

ented cognitive style. "They know little about their own feelings and, in most instances, are unable to link them with memories, fantasies, or specific situations" (Taylor, Bagby, & Parker, 1991, p. 155).

Alexithymia is not a categorical phenomenon, but a dimension on which the general population is assumed to be normally distributed.

LeDoux (1996) argued that emotional stimuli produce cognitive representations of the triggering stimuli along with affective states in working memory and thereby become integrated with representations of past experiences and representations of the self. The information that will be attended to at any given time thereby leads to heightened activity in the prefrontal cortex, the anterior cingulate cortex, and the orbitofrontal cortex (LeDoux, 1996). "Given current knowledge of cognitive and emotional processing in the brain, any theory that attempts to explain individual differences in alexithymia (or emotional intelligence) must consider variations in the level of complexity of representations of emotional states and in the neural organization associated with working memory" (Taylor & Bagby, 2000, p. 51). To further establish alexithymia as a construct relating to cognitive abilities, Taylor and Bagby (2000) state "an important aspect of linguistic processing is the ability to think about one's thoughts and other mental experiences (Rolls, 1995) some call metacognition and this appears related to aspects of emotional intelligence" (p. 51).

### Psychometric Characteristics

Bagby, Parker, and Taylor (1994) and Bagby, Taylor, and Parker (1994) reported the development of a 20-item, self-report measure of Alexithymia with good internal consistency and test-retest reliability. Exploratory factor analysis results yielded a three-factor structure identifying one factor describing difficulty in identifying feelings and distinguishing between feelings and bodily sensations of emotional arousal, a second factor involving difficulty in describing feelings to others, and a third factor involving externally oriented thinking.

In an attempt to empirically establish the relationship between alexithymia and emotional intelligence Parker, Taylor, and Bagby (forthcoming) in a large sample ($N = 734$) measured the 20-item Toronto Alexithymia Scale (TAS-20) and the BarOn Emotional Quotient Inventory (EQ-i) and obtained moderate to strong correlations between the two scales ranging from −.35 to −.72 (see Table 13.2).

To establish further evidence of convergent validity Taylor and Bagby (2000) provide empirical data based on correlations between the TAS and the Psychological Mindedness

**TABLE 13.2 Correlations Between the Toronto Alexithymia Scale (TAS-20) and the BarOn Emotional Quotient Inventory (EQ-i)**

| EQ-i score | DIF | DDF | EOT | TASTOT |
|---|---|---|---|---|
| EQ-i total | −.64 | −.61 | −.42 | −.72 |
| Intrapersonal factor | −.58 | −.62 | −.35 | −.66 |
| Interpersonal factor | −.38 | −.47 | −.41 | −.49 |
| Reality Testing subscale | −.60 | −.44 | −.25 | −.56 |
| Emotional Self-Awareness | −.46 | −.72 | −.41 | −.67 |
| Empathy subscale | −.29 | −.37 | −.41 | −.46 |

*Note.* DIF is Difficulty Identifying Feelings; DDF is Difficulty Describing Feelings; EOT is Externally Oriented Thinking; and TASTOT is Total Score on the TAS. All correlations are significant at $p < .05$.
Adapted from Taylor and Bagby (2000).

Scale (PMS) of Conte et al., (1990) using a sample of 85 university students. Psychological mindedness is "a person's ability to see relationships among thoughts, feelings, and actions, with the goal of learning the meanings and causes of his experiences and behavior" (Appelbaum, 1973, p. 36).

Correlations obtained between the PMS and Difficulty Identifying Feelings (DIF) was −.44, between the PMS and Difficulty Describing Feelings (DDF) was −.51, between the PMS and Externally Oriented Thinking (EOT) was −.54, and between the PMS and TAS total score was −.68.

Affective orientation is "the degree to which people are aware of their emotions, perceive them as important, and actively consider their affective responses in making judgments and interacting with others" (Booth-Butterfield & Booth-Butterfield, 1994, p. 332). The Affective Orientation Scale (AOS) is a 20-item self-report measure that assesses awareness of emotion, implementation of emotion, importance of emotion, and intensity of emotion (Booth-Butterfield & Booth-Butterfield, 1990). In an adult sample of 210, the correlation between the AOS and DIF was −.24; between the AOS and DDF, −.36; between the AOS and EOT, −.28; and between the AOS and the TAS total score, −.37.

Several studies have examined the relation between alexithymia and the five-factor model constructs. A consistent finding is that there is a moderately strong correlation between the Openness to Experience construct and measures of alexithymia like the TAS-20. For example, Bagby, Taylor, and Parker (1994) found in a sample of 85 college students correlations of Openness to Experience with DIF of −.28; with DDF it was −.30, with EOT it was −.61, and with the TAS total score it was −.49.

Mayer, DiPaolo, & Salovey (1990) placed alexithymia at the extreme lower pole of the emotional intelligence construct, describing it as a diagnostic category and stating their belief that it corresponds not just to Openness to Experience

or any of its lower order traits but that it is a reflection of a complex of narrow personality traits.

## THE PSYCHOLOGICAL MINDEDNESS ASSESSMENT PROCEDURE (PMAP)

The next assessment uses a videotaped social interaction as a stimulus. Thus, this example achieves high face validity.

### Theoretical Basis

McCallum and Piper (2000) argued that personal intelligence has been used interchangeably with psychological mindedness and emotional intelligence. From the "analyzability" literature of psychoanalytically oriented psychotherapy, they posited that self-awareness is fundamental to psychological insight and this is what psychotherapy strives to improve. "The patient's desire to learn the possible meanings and causes of his internal and external experiences . . . to potentially conceptualize the relationship between thoughts feelings and actions" (Silver, 1983, p. 516, as cited by McCallum & Piper, 2000) is their definition of psychological mindedness.

This is an interpretive approach to the focus on unconscious conflicts. Psychological mindedness in this perspective fosters insight into how patient's presenting problems reflect underlying psychic conflicts between unacceptable wishes, anxieties, and fears that give rise to defense mechanisms to cope with anxiety and maintain repression of the unacceptable wish. The psychological mindedness construct is a link between the current pattern of behavior, feelings, and cognitions with the unconscious process.

### Test Description

McCallum and Piper (1987) created an assessment instrument by scripting and videotaping two simulated patient-therapist interactions. Each interaction shows a patient describing a recent event to a therapist. After viewing the interaction, the person being assessed is asked, "What seems to be troubling this person?" The person's responses are scored according to how well they reflect basic assumptions of psychodynamic theory. Only commonly held assumptions are used in the scoring, and among the scoring keys are: Psychic Determinism, or all conscious experience is partially determined by intrapsychic processes; Intrapsychic Conflict, wherein tension/anxiety arises from conflictual unconscious forces of impermissible wishes/fears; and Defense Mechanisms, how a person minimizes, distorts, or avoids some part of his or her experience to alleviate fears and maintain the repression of threatening impulses.

## Administration and Scoring

The PMAP uses a videotape and scoring manual. It takes approximately 15 minutes and is individually administered. McCallum and Piper argue that use of a videotape avoids education and intelligence confounds and promotes reliability by using objective, clearly defined behavioral referents. They believe that high face validity and low evaluation apprehension perceptions among respondents are common.

## Psychometric Characteristics

The PMAP was found to be significantly and moderately related to other measures of psychological mindedness in five separate samples (McCallum, 1989; McCallum, Piper, & O'Kelly; Piper, Joyce, McCallum, & Azim, 1998; Piper, McCallum, & Azim, 1992; Piper, Rosie, Azim, & Joyce, 1993) (Ns vary from 39 to 190). Interrater reliabilities range from .88 to .96 (i.e., intraclass correlations). All of the preceding are based on clinical samples, but authors argue the assessment is free from biases due to psychopathology. "Our repeated finding that psychological mindedness, as assessed by the PMAP, is not significantly associated with (pretherapy) measures of psychiatric symptomatology or psychological distress supports the independence of psychological mindedness and mental health" (McCallum & Piper, 2000, p. 128).

# THE EMOTIONAL COMPETENCE INVENTORY (ECI)

The next assessment was developed specifically for predicting workplace behaviors. It was empirically derived from a self-report form of leadership competencies.

## Test Description

Boyatzis, Goleman, and Rhee (2000) describe the Emotional Competence Inventory (ECI) as an assessment of emotional intelligence based on theoretical expectations for clusters of behavioral groups of desired competencies in functioning within organizations. Derived from an earlier assessment called the Self-Assessment Questionnaire (Boyatzis, 1994), the ECI assesses the following dimensions: Emotional Self-Awareness, Accurate Self-Awareness, Self-Confidence, Self-Control, Trustworthiness, Conscientiousness, Adaptability, Achievement Orientation, Initiative, Empathy, Organizational Awareness, Developing Others, Service Orientation, Leadership, Influence, Communication, Change Catalyst, Conflict Management, Building Bonds, and finally, Teamwork and

Collaboration. The ECI asks the respondent to describe himself or herself on each item on a scale of 1 ("The Individual Behaves This Way Only Sporadically") to 7 ("The Individual Behaves This Way in Most or All Situations Where It Is Appropriate"). The ECI also exists in a form to be used by others as observers of the individual's behavior. Scores are reported for 20 subscales (see the preceding dimensions).

## Psychometric Characteristics

Internal reliabilities for each scale range from an alpha coefficient of .62 to .87 for the self-report format of the ECI.

On the basis of factor analysis and cluster analysis results for a sample of 596, the ECI subscales are grouped into three clusters: (1) Self-Awareness, which includes the Emotional Self-Awareness, Accurate Self-Assessment, and Conscientiousness subscales; (2) Self-Management, which includes the Self-Confidence, Adaptability, Achievement Orientation, Initiative, Change Catalyst, and Self-Control subscales; and (3) Social Skills, which includes the Empathy, Service Orientation, Developing Others, Communication, Organizational Awareness, Building Bonds, Collaboration, Trustworthiness, Leadership, Influence, and Team Capability subscales.

Criterion-related validity is reported in one study (Boyatzis, 1999) of experienced partners at a large consulting firm. In this study, those partners who were identified as superior performers (i.e., by generating more account revenues and incremental profit for the firm) demonstrated "a significant number of competencies" (p. 354) in the Self-Management and Social Skills clusters.

# THE NEO-PERSONALITY INVENTORY-REVISED OPENNESS TO EXPERIENCE SCALE

The very well-known NEO Personality Inventory-Revised has also been used in emotional intelligence research.

## Test Description

The NEO Personality Inventory-Revised (NEO-PI-R) is one of the most popular assessments of the so-called Big-Five or five-factor model of personality. Originally designed to assess Neuroticism, Extraversion, and Openness to Experience, the inventory now also includes measures of Agreeableness and Conscientiousness. All measures were developed primarily by the rational approach and further refined using factor-analytic studies to maximize the internal structure of the scales.

## Administration and Scoring

In the current version of the inventory (Costa & McCrae, 1992), each of the five domain scales (i.e., those described in the preceding section) is composed of six "facet" or subscales. Each facet is composed of eight items, and hence the entire inventory contains a total of 240 items. There is a Form S, which is a self-report form, and a Form R, which an observer rating form. All items are followed by a 5-point Likert response scale ranging from "Strongly Disagree" to "Strongly Agree." There is also a short version of the NEO-PI-R, which consists of 60 items, producing scores on only the five domains. The inventory is appropriate for adults and has no time limit. It can be administered by test booklet or by computer and can be scored by hand or by machine. Professional scoring and interpretation services are available from the publisher. All scores are reported as T-scores.

## Psychometric Characteristics

Internal reliability and test-retest reliability coefficients are reported to range from .85 to .93 for the domain scores. There are numerous studies in the literature on the content, construct, convergent and divergent, as well as criterion-related validity of the NEO-PI-R, including two major longitudinal studies of large samples (e.g., $N = 2,000$). In general, the results support the validity of the NEO-PI-R's domain scales.

McCrae (2000) conceptually compared the 15 factors listed in the EQ-i manual with the 30 facet scores of the NEO-PI-R and concluded that "these conceptualizations suggest that emotional intelligence should be associated with low scores on neuroticism and high scores on extraversion, openness to experience, agreeableness, and conscientiousness domain scores" (p. 266; see Table 13.3).

Focusing on the Openness to Experience factor, McCrae argued that it should be related to intelligence in ways not assessed by traditional IQ tests. In this mixed model of emotional intelligence, Openness to Experience predicts when individuals will chose to apply their capacities as cognitive abilities. Describing this as typical intellectual engagement, McCrae stated that it is related to the need for cognition construct, or the "tendency to engage in and enjoy effortful cognitive activity" (Cacioppo, Petty, Feinstein, & Jarvis, 1996, p. 197). Referring to the Baltimore Longitudinal Study of Aging (Shock et al., 1984), McCrae (2000) reported the correlations between NEO-PI-R domain scores and Openness facet scores with scores on a Need for Cognition measure and a WAIS-R vocabulary subtest. The Need for Cognition score correlated +.55 with Openness to Experience, and correlations with the six Openness facet scores ranged from +.13

**TABLE 13.3   Conceptual Correspondence Between NEO-PI-R Facets and EQ-i Factors**

| NEO-PI-R (Costa & McCrae, 1992) | EQ-i Factors (Bar-On, 1997a) |
|---|---|
| Neuroticism | |
| N1: Anxiety | |
| N2: Angry Hostility | |
| N3: Depression | Happiness [R] |
| N4: Self-Consciousness | Self-Regard [R] |
| N5: Impulsiveness | Impulse Control [R] |
| N6: Vulnerability | Stress Tolerance [R] |
| Extraversion | |
| E1: Warmth | |
| E2: Gregariousness | |
| E3: Assertiveness | Assertiveness |
| E4: Activity | |
| E5: Excitement Seeking | |
| E6: Positive Emotions | Optimism |
| Openness to Experience | |
| O1: Fantasy | |
| O2: Aesthetics | |
| O3: Feelings | Emotional Self-Awareness |
| O4: Actions | Flexibility |
| O5: Ideas | Reality Testing |
| O6: Values | Independence |
| Agreeableness | |
| A1: Trust | Interpersonal Relationships |
| A2: Straightforwardness | |
| A3: Altrusim | |
| A4: Compliance | |
| A5: Modesty | |
| A6: Tender-mindedness | Empathy |
| Conscientiousness | |
| C1: Competence | Problem Solving |
| C2: Order | |
| C3: Dutifulness | Social Responsibility |
| C4: Achievement | |
| C5: Self-Discipline | |
| C6: Deliberation | |

*Note.* [R] indicates the factor score is reversed coded.

to +.68. Similar correlations with the WAIS-R subtest were much weaker, ranging from −.04 to +.22. The correlations were strongest for the Openness to new ideas facet score and Need for Cognition ($r = +.68$) and WAIS-R Vocabulary ($r = +.22$), which appears to best support McCrae's point that emotional intelligence includes a disposition to engage intellectual abilities across a broad spectrum of contexts.

## CONCLUSIONS

Clearly, each of the assessments described in this chapter have different approaches to assessing emotional intelligence and potentially different applications as a result. The EQ-i measure is the most extensive paper-and-pencil measure available of the construct in a traditional inventory format. The MSCEIT is the assessment that best approaches emotional intelligence in an aptitude-test-style format. The TAS-20 is the assessment designed as a paper-and-pencil measure to identify individuals as abnormally low in emotional intelligence. The PMAP is a videotape assessment using an open-ended response format, which is unique among these assessment choices. The ECI is the only assessment designed explicitly for workplace applications and has the advantage of using common business-related terms. The NEO-PI-R inventory has appeal in that it has the longest history and prior empirical support, connects to the five-factor model, and exists in an observer-rating format. These represent a range of options for the practitioner. Although there is no explicit discussion in the literature of how the Americans with Disabilities Act (ADA) might apply here, it is apparent that all of the preceding assessments are untimed, and one option does not require any reading ability (i.e., the PMAP). There is an obvious need for extensive research on the criterion-related validities of these assessments. Users should keep in mind the need for future validity generalization efforts, and, therefore, users are urged to document the samples and job titles for which they collect any validity data.

In summarizing the theoretical issues that confront this exciting new area of assessment, the issues of construct validity, convergent and divergent validity, and psychometric adequacy of the measures stand out as areas for further research and discussion. As Hedlund and Steinberg (2000) stated:

> First, are the various factors that researchers have classified as social, emotional, or practical intelligence appropriately characterized as cognitive abilities? Second, can reliable and valid measures of these "nontraditional" intelligences be developed? Assuming these two questions are answered satisfactorily, uncertainty remains regarding the independence of these constructs. In other words, are social, emotional, and practical intelligence distinct or overlapping constructs? (p. 136).

The field of emotional intelligence has made an excellent start on addressing these issues and offers the hope for many new advances in research and practice.

## REFERENCES

American Dialect Society. (1995). American Dialect Society: Words of the year. (http://www.americandialect.org/woty). Cited in Mayer, J.D., Salovey, P., and Caruso, D.R. (2000). Emotional intelligence as zeitgeist, as personality, and as a mental ability. In R. Bar-On and J.D.A. Parker (Eds.), (2000). *The Handbook of Emotional Intelligence* (pp. 92–117). San Francisco: Jossey-Bass.

Appelbaum, S.A. (1973). Psychological-mindedness: Word, concept, and essence. *International Journal of Psychoanalysis, 54,* 34–45.

Bagby, R.M., Parker, J.D.A., & Taylor, G.J. (1994). The twenty-item Toronto alexithymia scale: Part I, item selection and cross-validation of the factor structure. *Journal of Psychosomatic Research, 38,* 23–32.

Bagby, R.M., Taylor, G.J., & Parker, J.D.A. (1994). The twenty-item Toronto alexithymia scale: Part II, convergent, discriminant, and concurrent validity. *Journal of Psychosomatic Research, 38,* 33–40.

Bar-On, R. (1997a). *BarOn Emotional Quotient Inventory (EQ-i): A test of emotional intelligence.* Toronto: Multi-Health Systems.

Bar-On, R. (1997b). *BarOn Emotional Quotient Inventory (EQ-i): Technical manual.* Toronto, Canada: Multi-Health Systems.

Bar-On, R. (2000). Emotional and social intelligence: Insights from the Emotional Quotient Inventory. In R. Bar-On & J.D.A. Parker (Eds.), *The handbook of emotional intelligence* (pp. 363–388). San Francisco: Jossey-Bass.

Booth-Butterfield, M., & Booth-Butterfield, S. (1994). The affective orientation to communication: Conceptual and empirical distinctions. *Communications Quarterly, 42,* 331–344.

Boyatzis, R.E. (1994). Stimulating self-directed change: A required MBA course called Managerial Assessment and Development. *Journal of Management Education, 18,* 304–323.

Boyatzis, R.E. (1999). *The financial impact of competencies in leadership and management of consulting firms* (Working Paper). Cleveland, OH: Case Western Reserve University, Department of Organizational Behavior.

Boyatzis, R.E., Goleman, D., & Rhee, K.S. (2000). Clustering competence in emotional intelligence: Insights from the Emotional Competence Inventory. In R. Bar-On & J.D.A. Parker (Eds.), *The handbook of emotional intelligence* (pp. 343–362). San Francisco: Jossey-Bass.

Cacioppo, J.T., Petty, R.E., Feinstein, J.A., & Jarvis, W.B.G. (1996). Dispositional differences in cognitive motivation: The life and times of individuals differing in the need for cognition. *Psychological Bulletin, 119,* 197–253.

Carroll, J.B. (1993). *Human cognitive abilities: A survey of factor-analytic studies.* New York: Cambridge University Press.

Ciarrochi, J.V., Chan, A.Y.C., & Caputi, P. (2000). A critical evaluation of the emotional intelligence construct. *Personality and Individual Differences, 28,* 539–561.

Conte, H.R., Plutchik, R., Jung, B.B., Picard, S., Karasu, T.B., & Lotterman, A. (1990). Psychological mindedness as a predictor of psychotherapy outcome: A preliminary report. *Comprehensive Psychiatry, 31,* 426–431.

Costa, P.T. Jr., & McCrae, R.R. (1992). *Revised NEO Personality Inventory (NEO-PI-R) and NEO Five-Factor Inventory (NEO-*

*FFI) professional manual.* Odessa, FL: Psychological Assessment Resources.

Dawda, R., & Hart, S.D. (2000). Assessing emotional intelligence: Reliability and validity of the BarOn Emotional Quotient Inventory (EQ-i) in university students. *Journal of Personality and Individual Differences, 28,* 797–812.

Dayon, Y. (2000). *Stability reliability of the EQ-i.* Unpublished manuscript. Cited in Bar-On, R. (2000). Emotional and social intelligence: Insights from the Emotional Quotient Inventory. In R. Bar-On & J.D.A. Parker (Eds.), *The handbook of emotional intelligence* (pp. 363–388). San Francisco: Jossey-Bass.

Dupertuis, D.G. (1996). *The EQ-i and MMPI-2 profiles of a clinical sample in Argentina.* Unpublished manuscript. Cited in Bar-On, R. (2000). Emotional and social intelligence: Insights from the Emotional Quotient Inventory. In R. Bar-On & J.D.A. Parker (Eds.), *The handbook of emotional intelligence* (pp. 363–388). San Francisco: Jossey-Bass.

Flesch, R. (1948). A new readability yardstick. *Journal of Applied Psychology, 32,* 221–233.

Fund, S. (2000). *Examining the contribution of emotional intelligence in occupational performance.* Unpublished manuscript. Cited in Bar-On, R. (2000). Emotional and social intelligence: Insights from the Emotional Quotient Inventory. In R. Bar-On & J.D.A. Parker (Eds.), *The handbook of emotional intelligence* (pp. 363–388). San Francisco: Jossey-Bass.

Gardner, H. (1983). *Frames of mind: The theory of multiple intelligences.* New York: Basic Books.

Gersten, E.L., Weissberg, R.P., Amish, P.L., & Smith, J.K. (1987). Social problem-solving training: A skills-based approach to prevention and treatment. In C.A. Maher & J.E. Zins (Eds.), *Psychoeducational interventions in the schools: Methods and procedures of enhancing student competence* (pp. 197–210). New York and Oxford: Pergamon.

Goleman, D. (1995). *Emotional intelligence.* New York: Bantam.

Hedlund, J., & Steinberg, R.J. (2000). Too many intelligences? Integrating social, emotional, and practical intelligence. In R. Bar-On & J.D.A. Parker (Eds.), *The handbook of emotional intelligence* (pp. 136–167). San Francisco: Jossey-Bass.

Hee-Woo, J. (1998). *Emotional intelligence and cognitive ability as predictors of job performance in the banking section.* Unpublished master's thesis, Ateneo de Manila University, Philippines. Cited in Bar-On, R. (2000). Emotional and social intelligence: Insights from the Emotional Quotient Inventory. In R. Bar-On & J.D.A. Parker (Eds.), *The handbook of emotional intelligence* (pp. 363–388). San Francisco: Jossey-Bass.

Henner, T. (1998). *Comparing EQ-i and TMMS scale scores.* Unpublished manuscript. Cited in Bar-On, R. (2000). Emotional and social intelligence: Insights from the Emotional Quotient Inventory. In R. Bar-On & J.D.A. Parker (Eds.), *The handbook of emotional intelligence* (pp. 363–388). San Francisco: Jossey-Bass.

Herrnstein, R.J., & Murray, C. (1994). *The bell curve: Intelligence and class in American life.* New York: Free Press.

LeDoux, J.E. (1996). *The emotional brain: The mysterious underpinnings of emotional life.* New York: Simon & Schuster.

Markus, H., & Nurius, P. (1986). Possible selves. *American Psychologist, 41,* 954–969.

Mayer, J.D., Caruso, D.R., & Salovey, P. (2000a). Selecting a measure of emotional intelligence: The case for ability scales. In R. Bar-On & J.D.A. Parker (Eds.), *The handbook of emotional intelligence* (pp. 320–342). San Francisco: Jossey-Bass.

Mayer, J.D., Caruso, D.R., & Salovey, P. (2000b). Emotional intelligence as zeitgeist, as personality, and as a mental ability. In R. Bar-On & J.D.A. Parker (Eds.), *The handbook of emotional intelligence* (pp. 92–117). San Francisco: Jossey-Bass.

Mayer, J.D., Caruso, D.R., Salovey, P., & Formica, S.A., & Woolery A. (2000). [A correlation of MEIS scores with data on the life space.] Unpublished raw data. Cited in Mayer, J.D., Caruso, D.R., & Salovey, P. (2000). Selecting a measure of emotional intelligence: The case for ability scales. In R. Bar-On & J.D.A. Parker (Eds.), *The handbook of emotional intelligence* (pp. 320–342). San Francisco: Jossey-Bass.

Mayer, J.D., DiPaolo, M., & Salovey, P. (1990). Perceiving affective content in ambiguous visual stimuli: A component of emotional intelligence. *Journal of Personality Assessment, 54,* 772–781.

Mayer, J.D., & Salovey, P. (1997). What is emotional intelligence? In P. Salovey & D.J. Sluyter (Eds.), *Emotional development and emotional intelligence: Educational implications* (pp. 3–34). New York: Basic Books.

Mayer, J.D., Salovey, P., & Caruso, D.R. (1999). *MSCEIT item booklet.* Toronto: Multi-Health Systems.

McCallum, M. (1989). *A controlled study of effectiveness and patient suitability for short-term group psychotherapy.* Unpublished doctoral dissertation, McGill University, Montreal, Canada.

McCallum, M., & Piper, W.E. (1987). *The Psychological Mindedness Assessment Procedure.* Unpublished manual and videotape.

McCallum, M., & Piper, W.E. (2000). Psychological mindedness and emotional intelligence. In R. Bar-On and J.D.A. Parker (Eds.), *The handbook of emotional intelligence* (pp. 118–135). San Francisco: Jossey-Bass.

McCallum, M., Piper, W.E., & O'Kelly, J. (1997). Predicting patient benefit from a group oriented, evening treatment program. *International Journal of Group Psychotherapy, 47,* 291–314.

McCrae, R.R. (2000). Emotional intelligence from the perspective of the five-factor model of personality. In R. Bar-On & J.D.A. Parker (Eds.), *The handbook of emotional intelligence* (pp. 263–276). San Francisco: Jossey-Bass.

Pallazza, R., & Bar-On, R. (1995). *A study of the emotional intelligence of convicted criminals.* Unpublished manuscript.

Parker, J.D.A. (1999). *An Emotional Stroop Task examination of the EQ-i.* Unpublished manuscript. Cited in Bar-On, R. (2000). Emotional and social intelligence: Insights from the Emotional Quotient Inventory. In R. Bar-On & J.D.A. Parker (Eds.), *The handbook of emotional intelligence* (pp. 363–388). San Francisco: Jossey-Bass.

Parker, J.D.A., Taylor, G.J., & Bagby, R.M. (forthcoming). The relationship between alexithymia and emotional intelligence. *Personality and Individual Differences.*

Piper, W.E., Joyce, A.S., McCallum, M., & Azim, H.F.A. (1998). Interpretive and supportive forms of psychotherapy and patient personality variables. *Journal of Consulting and Clinical Psychology, 66,* 558–567.

Piper, W.E., McCallum, M., & Azim, H.F.A. (1992). *Adaptation to loss through short-term group psychotherapy.* New York: Guilford Press.

Piper, W.E., Rosie, J.S., Azim, H.F.A., & Joyce, A.S. (1993). A randomized trial of psychiatric day treatment for patients with affective and personality disorders. *Hospital and Community Psychiatry, 44,* 757–763.

Plake, B.S., & Impara, J.G. (Eds.). (1999). *Supplement to the Thirteenth Mental Measurements Yearbook.* Lincoln, NE: Buros Institute for Mental Measurement.

Rice, C.L. (1999). *A quantitative study of emotional intelligence and its impact on team performance.* Unpublished master's thesis, Pepperdine University, Malibu, CA. Cited in Mayer, J.D., Caruso, D.R., & Salovey, P. (2000). Selecting a measure of emotional intelligence: The case for ability scales. In R. Bar-On & J.D.A. Parker (Eds.), *The handbook of emotional intelligence* (pp. 320–342). San Francisco: Jossey-Bass.

Rolls, E.T. (1995). A theory of emotion and consciousness, and its application to understanding the neural basis of emotion. In M.S. Gazzaniga (Ed.), *The cognitive neurosciences* (pp. 1091–1106). Cambridge, MA: MIT Press.

Ruesch, J. (1948). The infantile personality. *Psychosomatic Medicine, 10,* 134–144.

Saarni, C. (2000). Emotional competence: A developmental perspective. In R. Bar-On & J.D.A. Parker (Eds.), *The handbook of emotional intelligence* (pp. 68–91). San Francisco: Jossey-Bass.

Salovey, P., & Mayer, J.D. (1989/1990). Emotional intelligence. *Imagination, Cognition, and Personality, 9,* 185–211.

Scarr, S. (1989). Protecting general intelligence: Constructs and consequences for interventions. In R.L. Linn (Ed.), *Intelligence: Measurement, theory, and public policy.* Urbana: University of Illinois Press.

Shock, N.W., Greulich, R.C., Andres, R., Arenberg, D., Costa, P.T. Jr., Lakatta, E.G., & Tobin, J.D. (1984). *Normal human aging: The Baltimore Longitudinal Study of Aging* (NIH Publication No. 84-2450). Bethesda, MD: National Institutes of Health.

Sifneos, P.E. (1973). The prevalence of alexithymic characteristics in psychosomatic patients. *Psychotherapy and Psychosomatics, 22,* 255–262.

Silver, D. (1983). Psychotherapy of the characterologically difficult patient. *Canadian Journal of Psychiatry, 28,* 513–521.

Taylor, G.J., & Bagby, R.M. (2000). An overview of the alexithymia construct. In R. Bar-On & J.D.A. Parker (Eds.), *The handbook of emotional intelligence* (pp. 40–67). San Francisco: Jossey-Bass.

Taylor, G.J., Bagby, R.M., & Parker, J.D.A. (1991). The alexithymia construct: A potential paradigm for psychosomatic medicine. *Psychosomatics, 32,* 153–164.

Thorndike, R.L. (1936). Factor analysis of social and abstract intelligence. *Journal of Educational Psychology, 27,* 231–233.

Topping, K., Bremmer, W., & Holmes, E.A. (2000). Social competence: The social construction of the concept. In R. Bar-On & J.D.A. Parker (Eds.), *The handbook of emotional intelligence* (pp. 28–39). San Francisco: Jossey-Bass.

Zinkel, S. (2000). Social intelligence: The development and maintenance of purposive behavior. In R. Bar-On & J.D.A. Parker (Eds.), *The handbook of emotional intelligence* (pp. 3–27). San Francisco: Jossey-Bass.

# CHAPTER 14

# Leadership

RAM N. ADITYA

## INTRODUCTION

Through half a century of systematic investigation of leadership as a construct, its precise definition and measurement have proved elusive. Although the prediction of leadership effectiveness, or the identification of leadership potential, has motivated the academic study of leadership, spawning thousands of studies, the foremost obstacle has been the characterization of the construct. Everyone has a mental concept of "leader," but this concept is based on the individual's exposure to socially accepted leaders; his or her personal experience, view of the world, and human nature; and the historical context in which the individual exists. Through the years, the study of leadership has gone through a recursive evolutionary process that has turned the focus from personal traits to behaviors to situational factors to personal characteristics again (Aditya, House, & Kerr, 2000; House & Aditya, 1997). This time around, however, with more reliable and valid measures of personal traits and abilities, we have a greater appreciation

of several other contextual factors that come into play. In any case, the fact remains that the quintessence of leadership is to be found in not one but several perspectives or social phenomena: partly in the leader (e.g., Bass, 1985; Burns, 1978; House, 1977), partly in the perception of followers (e.g., Lord, Foti, & De Vader, 1984; Lord & Maher, 1991); partly in the context (e.g., Fiedler, 1964, 1995), and partly in the dynamics of the relationships between leader and followers (e.g., Graen & Cashman, 1975; Graen & Uhl-Bien, 1995). The need for a pluralistic and contextualist approach (Georgoudi & Rosnow, 1985; Rosnow, 1986) is perhaps nowhere more evident than in the understanding of leadership.

A distinction has been made in the literature between management and leadership (e.g., Zaleznik, 1977). Many scholars today subscribe to the view that (1) management is about maintenance of the status quo, whereas leadership is about progress; (2) management is about ensuring the accomplishment of organizational goals, whereas leadership is about vision, the creation of organizational goals, and the effective communication of the vision to the follower group; and (3) management is about stability, leadership about change. Although these distinctions help clarify some differences in priorities, the issues are more complex. Vision distinguishes

*Acknowledgments:* I am indebted to Robert House and Ralph Rosnow for their insightful comments on earlier drafts of this chapter.

leadership from management, yet the tasks of management are often those of leadership as well. Leadership appears to be a broader concept of which management is a part (Hersey & Blanchard, 1982).

Some scholars have noted that under certain environmental conditions, the distribution of leadership among two or more individuals may enhance organizational performance. Bales (1954) distinguished between task and social roles in coleadership and observed that the two roles are usually not compatible with each other. The task leader is rarely liked by the follower group, which accords the social role to a different individual. There are also situations in which several persons perform the same leadership roles, in what has been termed *peer leadership;* such cases have been documented by Bowers and Seashore (1966).

Leadership is also embedded in a larger context of organizational and national culture (Dickson, Aditya, & Chhokar, 2000; House, Wright, & Aditya, 1997). For instance, societal culture may determine what characteristics of a leader are valued by followers. Some characteristics may be universal (e.g., fairness, honesty); others may vary among societies (e.g., assertiveness, risk taking). Elements of organizational culture may also define what style of leadership would work best in a given situation.

Another way of understanding the various approaches to the study of leadership is to distinguish between rational and emotion-based models. Clover (1990), for instance, classified Hersey and Blanchard's (1982) behavioral model, Fiedler's (1964) contingency model, House's (1971) path-goal theory, Vroom and Yetton's (1973) decision tree model, and Hollander's (1978) social exchange model as belonging to the rational class of leadership theories. On the other hand, models addressing the role of emotions are exemplified in the works of House (1977), Zaleznik (1977), Burns (1978), and Bass (1985). As Clover (1990) noted, this classification runs parallel to the distinction between leadership and management. Leadership presumably has more emotional content than does management.

A veritable challenge in the preparation of this chapter has been deciding what measures to include here. In addition to the plethora of leadership measures used in leadership research over the years, numerous measures of leadership can be obtained directly from the Web. New measures appear on the Internet so often that a current listing may become dated in a few months. Therefore, I have attempted to delineate in this chapter primarily those measures that (1) are either widely used in current research or represent theories that define the state of the art in the field and have the potential for use in the future, (2) have demonstrated published psychometric properties, (3) involve a psychological approach to measure-

ment of the construct, and (4) are not dedicated measures addressing the requirements of a single organization. Consequently, a number of batteries to predict management potential, although developed through rigorous research, are not addressed in this chapter. Under the strict implementation of the criteria, only four measures have qualified to be part of the main list of leadership scales. Among the measures excluded on this account, for instance, are the Early Identification of Management Potential (EIMP; Sparks, 1990) and the tests involved in the Management Progress Study (MPS; Howard & Bray, 1990). The EIMP, developed in longitudinal research over 30 years, was designed to identify management potential for the Exxon Corporation. The MPS was a longitudinal investigation of managerial performance in six telephone companies starting in the mid-1950s. Typically, these studies used a battery of standardized tests and measures developed for the organization.

In keeping with the theme of this volume, this chapter focuses on organizational leadership, to the exclusion of other arenas (such as political leadership), although some of the theoretical developments have taken place in these other domains. However, briefly described in the appendix are a number of other measures that have not made it to the major list but that occupy a position of prominence in the theoretical exposition of leadership or that have been recently developed and, although not yet established with regard to psychometric properties, show potential for use in leadership practice or research.

## HISTORICAL OVERVIEW

Formal studies of leadership date back to the 1930s. Since then, although the number of empirical studies runs into thousands, as can be seen from Bass's (1990) extensive review, the pace of theoretical development has been much slower. The evolution of leadership theory and research has been summarized in House and Aditya (1997) and juxtaposed with a practical perspective in Aditya, House, and Kerr (2000); it is only briefly outlined here before the discussion of individual measures of leadership.

### Leader Characteristics

The initial conceptions of leadership focused on the personal characteristics of the leader, and several empirical studies were conducted through two decades starting in the 1930s. These studies examined physical characteristics such as height, appearance, gender, and energy level, as well as psychological attributes such as authoritarianism, the need for power and for achievement, and general intelligence for their contributions to follower performance. These studies turned up mixed results. Physical variables just did not correlate well with leader performance; history is replete with great leaders of all heights, both genders, and of all appearances. Psychological variables also did not produce encouraging results, for two reasons: (1) the nascent stage of development, and hence inadequate reliability, of psychological measures at the time; and (2) the fact that most of these studies used student and adolescent samples, or else supervisors rather than people who were leaders in the terms we recognize today. This last point is often characteristic of contemporary studies of leadership. At any rate, Stogdill's (1948) review of the literature on leadership traits is widely seen as sounding the death knell for traits in leadership. Stogdill, in fact, was pointing to the inadequacy of studying traits alone, calling attention to situational contingencies as playing a sizable role.

## Leader Behaviors

Following the premature abandonment of trait theories, the spotlight turned to behavioral variables. Three influential programs of research on leader behaviors emerged at Harvard, the University of Michigan, and Ohio State University to dominate the focus of leadership theory over the next three decades. Collectively known as the behavioral school, they shared the objective of finding observable universal behaviors in effective leadership. Two dimensions of leader behavior emerged in all three programs of research:[1] person-oriented behaviors and task-oriented behaviors (e.g., Bales, 1954; Kahn & Katz, 1953; Likert 1961; Mann, 1965; Stogdill & Coons, 1957). These two dimensions came to be known as *Consideration* and *Initiating Structure,* respectively, as labeled by the team at Ohio State University. Consideration referred to behaviors of the leader that were aimed at promoting close social relationships with subordinates. Initiating Structure referred to leader behaviors aimed at reducing role ambiguity and conflict in the subordinates' work environment. The Ohio State studies resulted in two leadership measures, the Leader Behavior Description Questionnaire (LBDQ; with a subsequent revised form, the LBDQ-XII) and the Supervisor Behavior Description Questionnaire.

## Contingency Theories

Leader behaviors, like personality factors, proved inadequate in explaining variance in the performance of follower groups, and the focus of academic inquiry then turned in the 1970s to environmental characteristics. Prominent in this new perspective were contingency theory (Fiedler, 1967, 1971), path-goal theory (House, 1971), the decision process model (Vroom

& Yetton, 1973), situational leadership theory (Hersey & Blanchard, 1982), cognitive resource theory (Fiedler, 1995; Fiedler & Garcia, 1987) and the revised path-goal theory (House, 1996).

Contingency theory (Fiedler, 1967, 1971) specified the relationship between leadership style and leader effectiveness (as measured by group performance) under varying degrees of "situational favorableness" (conceptualized in three dimensions). Leadership style was assessed by means of a scale that asked respondents (leaders) to rate their least-preferred coworker (LPC) on 16–24 attributes, with high scores connoting the positive side of each attribute in the final scoring. Broadly, a low LPC score was taken as indicative of task orientation, and a high LPC score as representing relationship orientation, in the leader. However, Fiedler (1971) cautioned that such interpretation was valid primarily in stressful situations. Although criticized on empirical as well as conceptual grounds (Ashour, 1973; Schriesheim & Kerr, 1977; for rejoinders to these, see Fiedler, 1973, 1977), meta-analytic reviews by Peters, Hartke, and Pohlman (1985) and Strube and Garcia (1981) yielded substantial support for parts of the contingency model. However, the LPC scale has seldom been used except in a few studies that examined the contingency model, and in a self-help manual for leadership training created by Fiedler, labeled "Leader-Match" (Fiedler & Chemers, 1984; Fiedler, Chemers & Mahar, 1976).

Path-goal theory (House, 1971; House & Mitchell, 1974) addresses the interaction of a number of situational factors (job autonomy, job scope, and role ambiguity, task structure, task interdependence), leader behaviors (initiating structure, participative behaviors, consideration, and achievement-oriented behaviors), follower traits (dependence, authoritarianism, ability, locus of control), and other variables such as follower expectancies, valences, and path instrumentalities in explaining leader effectiveness (measured as follower satisfaction and follower performance). Following a meta-analytic review of tests of this theory by Wofford and Liska (1993) and critiques by other scholars, House (1996) revised this theory to recognize a boundary assumption of rationality and the influence of uncertainty and stress as moderating variables.

The decision model (Vroom & Yetton, 1973) was designed as a heuristic model for use by organizational leaders to make effective decisions. The model takes the form of a decision tree with questions addressing situational variables at each node. The answers to these questions determine the choice of branches leading to a decision. Vroom and Yetton have specified seven decision-making styles ranging from autocratic to democratic decision processes that have different outcomes depending on the situation. A "feasible set" of decisions exists that will be effective for a given set of contingencies. Partial support has been found for the model (e.g.,

Field, 1982, Margerison & Glube, 1979). Vroom and Jago (1988) subsequently revised the Vroom-Yetton model. The decision tree is more easily seen as a rational model of decision making than a psychological assessment of leadership. However, it has been used in organizations for several years and is therefore included in the appendix.

Situational leadership theory (Hersey & Blanchard, 1982) specifies the appropriateness of one or another of four leadership styles—telling, selling, participating, and delegating—depending on the "maturity" level of the follower group. There appear to be few empirical tests of this theory, barring a study of high school teachers (Vecchio, 1987) and another of elementary school principals (Pascarella & Lunenburg, 1988). Vecchio (1987) argued that the theoretical predictions held primarily for recent employees who needed task structuring from their leaders. However, Hersey and Blanchard's theory forms the basis of a commercially available training program.

A formulation that has attracted much interest is cognitive resource theory, or CRT (Fiedler, 1995; Fiedler & Garcia, 1987). CRT addresses the moderating influence of stress on the relative strengths of relationships of intelligence and experience with performance. According to CRT, intelligence correlates better with performance than does experience in normal (low-stress) situations. Under high stress, however, the reverse is the case—that is, experience correlates better with performance. CRT has received support in a number of empirical investigations (Fiedler, 1995). Fiedler's theory is interesting in light of its counterintuitive findings regarding the role of intelligence, although other scholars also have noted the presumably moderating qualities of stress (e.g. Simon, 1987; Staw, Sandelands, & Dutton, 1981).

CRT has implications that reach beyond leadership. Some occupational fields, such as those of fighter pilots or firefighters, are inherently more stressful than others such as research and development. In stressful occupations, experience plays an important role, and "overlearning" strategies are recommended for performance in such professions. In fields such as research and development, on the other hand, intelligence plays a central role in performance.

The findings of extant research regarding the situational contingencies have been incorporated into the path-goal theory. The revised path-goal theory (House, 1996) specifies boundary conditions in terms of situational contingencies for eight classes of leader behaviors and their relation to unit performance.

## Revival of Trait Theories

In the late 1970s, in a development reminiscent of Rosnow's (1978) argument for cyclicality in the progress of social science, attention again turned to the role of traits in the prediction of leadership. Stogdill (1974) revised the conclusions from his 1948 review in light of the findings in the intervening period, observing that certain universal traits in leadership may have been missed in earlier research. House and Baetz (1979) pointed out that heterogeneity of the samples with regard to age may have obscured some patterns in the Stogdill (1948) review: When adolescent and juvenile samples were excluded from Stogdill's analysis, certain traits bore substantial correlations of up to .50 with follower perceptions and other indices of leadership. House and Baetz identified these traits as intelligence, prosocial assertiveness, task-relevant knowledge, self-confidence, and energy/activity level. Lord, DeVader, and Alliger (1986) also found, using a meta-analytic approach, that intelligence, assertiveness (dominance), masculinity, and adjustment were all important perceived characteristics of leadership.

Although critics of trait theories (e.g., Davis-Blake & Pfeffer, 1988) argue that traits are enduring characteristics of individuals, and must therefore be able to predict behavior over the long term, there is good reason to temper this perspective with considerations of the environment. Schneider (1983) pointed out that many traits become manifest in situations that provide arousal for these traits. To illustrate, an individual's ability and propensity to take risks may not be observed in actual behavior unless risky situations arise for that individual. Even otherwise, traits may be stable over extended periods of time but not necessarily for life (House, Shane, & Herold, 1996). However, Mischel (1973) argued that the influence of traits on behavior may be determined by the extent to which there are norms and incentives to guide behavior. Mischel called these *strong* situations. In contrast, *weak* situations are characterized by a lack of implicit or explicit guidelines to direct behavior. Mischel argued that traits have a relatively greater influence on behavior in relatively weak situations. Mischel's arguments have been upheld by Monson, Hesley, and Chernick (1982) in a laboratory study and in at least two field studies (viz., Barrick & Mount, 1993; Lee, Asford, & Bobko, 1990).

With the horizon looking brighter again for traits as explanatory variables in leadership, a number of theories were developed. Interestingly, a trait that became influential in the new wave of theories was one theoretically identified several decades earlier as achievement motivation (McClelland, 1961). Achievement motivation was posited as a predictor of effective entrepreneurial leadership (McClelland, 1985) and leadership of small, task-oriented groups (House, Spangler, & Woycke, 1991). However, this same trait appeared to be dysfunctional in large organizations (House, Delbecq, & Taris, 1997) because it interfered with effective delegation.

Issues of power are a ubiquitous fact of organizational functioning (e.g., Kipnis, 1976, 1984). McClelland (1975) and Winter (1973) were among the early scholars to postulate the need for power and need for affiliation (close relationships with others) as motivating forces in leadership. Specifically, effective leaders were theorized to have a high level of concern for the moral use of power, and a need for power that is higher than the need for affiliation. This theory found support in both field and laboratory studies using McClelland's (1975) Leader Motive Profile, or LMP (e.g., McClelland & Boyatzis, 1982; Miner & Dachler, 1973; Spangler & House, 1991; Winter, 1978, 1991; also see the review by House & Baetz, 1979).

It is noteworthy that LMP scores were theorized to be predictive of effective leadership primarily in medium to large organizations. In contrast, achievement motivation was presumably more relevant to small, entrepreneurial firms. However, House, Delbecq, and Taris (1997) found that LMP was most predictive of charismatic behaviors of CEOs of small entrepreneurial organizations.

Another formulation in the new era of leadership trait research was House's (1977) charismatic theory. Charismatic leaders were predicted to be self-confident, and to have a strong need for power, moral conviction in the correctness of their beliefs, willingness to take risks, and perseverance in the face of opposition. The theory received support in both field and laboratory studies (Yukl, 1993). Nevertheless, it has been broadened in scope and renamed as value-based leadership (House, Delbecq, & Taris, 1997).

### Leader Flexibility and Social Sensitivity

Kenny and Zaccaro (1983) reanalyzed data from a study by Barnlund (1962) that had examined the emergence of leaders supervising multiple groups over an extended period. Kenny and Zaccaro found that a substantial proportion of the variance associated with the emergence of leadership could be explained by (1) the leader's sensitivity to changes in the environment and in the follower group situations, which they labeled as *social sensitivity,* and (2) the leader's ability to adapt to a variety of situational parameters, or *behavioral flexibility.* Their finding of an association of leadership with social sensitivity and behavioral flexibility was supported in subsequent studies (e.g., Kenny & Hallmark, 1992; Simonton, 1987; Zaccaro, Foti, & Kenny, 1991).

### Leader-Member Exchange

Another perspective that originated in the early 1970s was reflected in leader-member exchange, or LMX, theory.

Originally termed the vertical dyadic linkage (VDL) model (Dansereau, Graen, & Haga, 1975; Graen & Cashman, 1975; Graen, Orris & Johnson, 1973), LMX theory addresses the role-making processes that transpire between leaders and followers. Several studies inspired by LMX have examined hypothesized associations between the quality of leader-follower relationships and follower satisfaction, turnover, and performance, all of which may be predicted intuitively. The more interesting contributions of LMX are expected from the directions for future research set out by Graen and Uhl-Bien (1995), namely, (1) examining the relational characteristics required for optimal outcomes and (2) the conditions and behaviors for the development of these characteristics. An important contribution of LMX theory is the idea that leader-follower relations may be individualized, with the eventual formation of in-groups and out-groups.

However, research using the LMX framework has been stymied by several loosely conducted studies, especially in the early stages, with reports of LMX and of leader effectiveness being obtained from the same respondents. As a result, correlations between these variables are likely to be inflated. Further, studies employing performance as an outcome variable often used subjective measures. Even so, correlations between LMX and performance have varied between .02 and .33. With only objective measures of performance, this range is narrowed to between .07 and .25 (Duarte, Goodson, & Klich, 1993; Vecchio & Gobdel, 1984). Studies of the association between LMX and employee turnover (Ferris, 1985; Graen, Liden & Hoel, 1982; Vecchio, 1985; Vecchio, Griffith, & Hom, 1986; Vecchio & Norris, 1996) have also yielded a wide range of results, with correlations ranging from .02 to − .44.

Another limitation of empirical research on LMX has been the variety of measures of LMX constructed by different researchers. Keller and Dansereau (2000) demonstrated that these LMX scales are not equivalent and can produce different results even in the same sample. Thus, findings across studies cannot be easily combined, making simplified meta-analysis of results from LMX studies questionable unless the studies used in the analyses involve the same instrument to measure LMX. More detailed reviews of theoretical advancements and empirical research in LMX theory are available in House and Aditya (1997) and Schriesheim, Castro, and Cogliser (1999).

### Implicit Leadership Theory

Implicit leadership theory, developed by Robert Lord and his associates (Lord, Binning, Rush, & Thomas, 1978; Lord, DeVader, & Alliger, 1986; Lord, Foti, & De Vader, 1984;

Lord & Maher, 1991; Rush, Thomas, & Lord, 1977), offers a cognitive approach to leadership by emphasizing the follower's perceptions of a leader. Lord and Maher (1991, p. 11) define leadership as the process of being perceived by others as a leader. These perceptions can occur through conscious inferences or through spontaneous recognition of leader prototypes. Empirical investigations support the notion that implicit theories of leadership can influence the enactment of leadership (e.g., Hanges et al., 1997; Sipe & Hanges, 1997). Results from the cross-cultural GLOBE study (House et al., 1999) also support the notion of implicitly endorsed theories of leadership.

## Neo-Charismatic Theories

The mid-1970s saw the beginning of another wave of leadership theories that centered on the concept of charisma. These formulations, integrated by House and Shamir (1993), included charismatic theory (House, 1977), transformational leadership (Bass, 1985; Burns, 1978), attributional theory of charismatic leadership (Conger & Kanungo, 1987), and visionary theories (Bennis & Nanus, 1985; Kouzes & Posner, 1987; Nanus, 1992; Sashkin, 1988). All of these theories focus on organizational leadership at the top level, addressing leader attributes and behaviors at a symbolic and emotional level (as opposed to the physical level in earlier theories). According to House and Shamir (1993), charismatic leadership involves visionary behaviors, including empowering, role modeling, image building, and risk taking. There is much support for the influence of these leader behaviors on organizational performance as well as in political administration (Curphy, 1990; Hater & Bass, 1988; Howell & Frost, 1989; Howell & Higgins, 1990; Howell et al., 1991; Koene, Pennings, & Schreuder, 1992; Koh, Terborg, & Steers, 1991; Pereira, 1987; Pillai & Meindl, 1991; Roberts, 1985; Simonton, 1987; Trice & Beyer, 1986; Waldman, Ramirez, House, & Puranam, 1996). In a meta-analysis of 32 studies using the Multifactor Leadership Questionnaire, Lowe, Kroek, and Sivasubramaniam (1996) obtained a mean uncorrected correlation of .30 between measures of leader charisma and independent ratings of leader effectiveness. A second analysis using subordinate rather than independent ratings of leader effectiveness yielded an uncorrected correlation of .71.[2] Howell and House (1992) distinguished between personalized and socialized charisma. Personalized charisma is self-aggrandizing and exploitative, whereas socialized charisma is altruistic, collectivist, and egalitarian.

In a recent extension of the 1976 theory of charismatic leadership, called value-based leadership, House, Delbecq, and Taris (1997) specified leader motive profile and leader self-confidence as predictors of charismatic behaviors. They also theorized that the emergence of value-based leadership will be facilitated by conditions of stress and uncertainty, the opportunity for moral considerations, lack of goal clarity, and unclear linkages between performance and reward. Although the moderating effect of uncertainty has been empirically demonstrated (Pillai & Meindl, 1991; Waldman, House, & Ramirez, 1996; Waldman, Ramirez, House, & Puranam, 1996), other effects merit testing.

Leadership at the top has also been referred to as strategic leadership (Finkelstein & Hambrick, 1996). Although the concept has been a substantive part of academic training for a long time (House & Aditya, 1997), strategic leadership has only recently come under empirical investigation.

## Cross-Cultural Leadership: The GLOBE Study

Many leadership theories have originated in the United States, and the question of whether they are applicable in other cultures has been debated (e.g., Bass, 1997; Hofstede, 1980). There is some evidence of universal leadership attributes (e.g., Bass, Burger, Doktor, & Barrett, 1979). In one of the largest cross-cultural studies of leadership undertaken to date, the cross-cultural endorsement of six implicit theories of leadership was examined. The Global Leadership and Organizational Behavior Effectiveness (GLOBE) research program was initiated by Robert J. House in 1993. Since its inception the GLOBE research program has grown into a cooperative network of over 170 researchers from 62 countries. The initial objectives of the project were (1) to identify effective universal and culture-specific leader behaviors and organizational practices, (2) to determine the influence of societal and organizational culture on effective and universally accepted leader behaviors, and (3) to assess the effect of violations of cultural norms relating to leader behaviors and organizational practices. The GLOBE database now contains information provided by approximately 17,000 individuals from 825 organizations in three industries. Coinvestigators from 38 nations first met in 1994 at the University of Calgary, Canada. At this conference, leadership was defined by consensus as "the ability of an individual to influence, motivate, and enable others to contribute toward the effectiveness and success of organizations of which they are members." (House et al., 1999, p. 184).

The first phase of the GLOBE project involved scale development and validation. The second phase involved the collection of data and testing for hypothesized relationships regarding culturally endorsed implicit theories of leadership. An interesting feature of this study was the use of triangulation of findings through qualitative data and unobtrusive measures of several of the constructs involved. The Country Co-Investigators (abbreviated CCIs) completed an inventory, called the Participant Observation Questionnaire (POQ) and the Unobtrusive Measures Questionnaire (UMQ). Additionally, interviews, content analyses of media reports, and focus groups were used to collect qualitative information. The qualitative information is being compiled in a set of anthologies soon to be published.

A primary objective of the program was to identify universally endorsed and culturally contingent leader attributes. Six distinct dimensions of culturally endorsed implicit leadership theories were extracted from the data: (1) charismatic/value-based leader behaviors, (2) team orientation, (3) participative leadership, (4) self-protective behaviors, (5) humane orientation, and (6) autonomous leadership. Of these, charismatic/value-based leadership and team-oriented leadership were universally endorsed as contributing to outstanding leadership. Participative leadership was nearly universally endorsed as a facilitator. The fourth dimension—self-protective behaviors—was universally endorsed in all cultures as *inhibiting* leadership effectiveness. Humane orientation and autonomous leadership were culturally contingent, being reported as either impeding or facilitating leadership effectiveness by the various cultures.

### Emerging Perspectives on Leadership: The Role of Multiple Intelligences

In recent years, there has been increasing interest in the contribution of multiple intelligences to effective leadership (Riggio, Murphy, & Pirozzolo, 2002). Proposed predictors of effective leadership in this new age of multiple intelligences include practical intelligence (Sternberg & Wagner, 1988), social intelligence (Zaccaro, 2002), sociopolitical intelligence (Hogan & Hogan, 2002), emotional intelligence (Caruso, Mayer, & Salovey, 2002), and interpersonal acumen (Aditya & House, 2002). The measures used in these investigations belong more appropriately to the domains of personality and cognitive ability, and they are also of recent origin. However, empirical explorations of multiple intelligences in leadership are gaining momentum. Consequently, measures that have gained some empirical support in the prediction of leadership effectiveness are briefly outlined in the appendix to this chapter.

### VALIDITY AND UTILITY OF MEASURES OF LEADERSHIP

The nature of leadership makes it difficult to define in terms that will allow for prediction of organizational outcomes.

The current state of the art has only succeeded in moving leadership from a definition in concrete physical terms to an abstract, emotional realm. Measures of leadership today typically attempt to profile an individual in terms of one or another leadership style. As the historical overview of theoretical developments in leadership reveals, the move from description to prediction has not been fully achieved at this time. Different leadership styles are known to be effective in certain situations, and the ability to switch from one to another style may itself be a characteristic of effective leadership.

To be sure, organizations have long used a variety of tests to identify individuals who will be effective leaders. These batteries are dedicated instruments that ostensibly work for the particular organization. What is effective in one organization and industry may not be suitable for another organization or industry.

Even on the question of descriptive instruments, a variety of theoretical perspectives have informed the development of measures, so that the use of a measure to sketch a leader's profile presumes subscription to that theoretical viewpoint. The one prominent instrument that claims a connection to performance is Vroom and Yetton's decision model. However, that is not a measure of leadership per se, but a decision-making tool. Two of the four measures of leadership described in this chapter—MLQ and LMX—are those that have been extensively tested in empirical research and qualify as major measures. A third set of leadership scales stems from the GLOBE study of leadership across 61 countries and measures various leadership styles that conform to culturally endorsed implicit theories of leadership. It is included here because of its extensive geographical and cultural coverage and its application in cross-cultural research. The fourth measure—ELQ—is included here because it represents recent theorizing and shows the most promise for future development.

### SPECIAL CONCERNS

This section addresses some concerns for the reader interested in the assessment of leadership potential or emergence, whether it is for research or for practical applications. Some of these considerations have to do with the nature of the construct; other issues have been noted in reviews as characteristic of research on leadership to date.

### Social Desirability Bias

In reviewing 11 measures of leadership, including six for children and youth, Oakland, Falkenberg, and Oakland (1996) argued that socially desirable responding may be a problem with self-report measures such as the Leadership Ability Evaluation (LAE; Cassel & Stancik, 1982), the Leadership Skills Inventory (LSI; Karnes & Chauvin, 1985), the Styles of Leadership Survey (SLS; Hall & Williams, 1986). and the Leadership Opinion Questionnaire (LOQ; Fleishman, 1989). Although Oakland et al.'s review included only a partial list of leadership scales, their argument may be applicable to other self-report measures as well, particularly if the respondent believes that the information revealed may not be treated as private disclosure (Esposito, Agard, & Rosnow, 1984).

### Diversity of Construct Definitions

As delineated in the historical overview of the topic, the construct of leadership has undergone many theoretical transformations and clarifications over the last several decades. Often, the terms *management* and *leadership* have been used interchangeably, and many measures of leadership in fact seem to focus more on management than leadership.

### Standardization of Scales

After thousands of studies on leadership, an all-encompassing, precise measure of leadership is still out of sight. At least part of the reason for this is the inherent nature of the construct, which precludes the kind of standardization achieved, say, in measures of cognitive ability or personality traits. Moreover, the major scales of leadership in use today are undergoing such frequent revisions that it would be pointless to describe only a particular version. Rather, an attempt has been made to briefly trace the development of these measures and to comment on the psychometric properties of the latest version available at the time of preparation of this chapter. In general, considerations of reliability and validity are the prime motivators for improvement of these measures, and therefore the psychometric properties noted here represent the best achieved within the particular theoretical framework.

### Confounding of Criterion Measures in Validation

Commonly found in the leadership literature are studies in which ratings on both independent variables (e.g., leader behavior or leadership style scores) and dependent variables (e.g., rating of leader effectiveness) are obtained from the same source, creating substantially inflated estimates of validity.

## MEASURES OF LEADERSHIP

This section sets out details of four major leadership scales that are sufficiently general to be useful in a variety of applications: the Multifactor Leadership Questionnaire (MLQ), Leader-Member Exchange (LMX), the GLOBE leadership scales, and the Empowering Leadership Questionnaire (ELQ).

### The Multifactor Leadership Questionnaire

#### Description

Bass's Multifactor Leadership Questionnaire (MLQ) is among the best-known and widely studied leadership scales. The MLQ-Form 5X (revised 36-item scale) is the latest version reported in the published literature, although the version in current use has nine additional items addressing outcome measures of leadership effectiveness (Antonakis, 2001). The 36 items of the MLQ-Form 5X address behaviors (except for the Charisma subscale) of a leader that followers rate on a frequency scale ranging from 0 ("Not at All") to 4 ("Frequently, If Not Always"). There are six factors (later identified as nine factors, see Current Research Status) that compose the theoretical platform for the MLQ: (1) Charisma/Inspirational, (2) Intellectual Stimulation, (3) Individualized Consideration, (4) Contingent Rewards, (5) Management by Exception, and (6) Passive/Avoidant. The Charisma scale contains impact items (e.g., "Has my respect"; "Proud of him/her") as well as behavioral items (e.g., "Talks of values"; "Expresses confidence") due to the nature of the construct. The Intellectual Stimulation scale contains such items as "Re-examines assumptions" and "Suggests different angles." The Individualized Consideration scale has items such as "Teaches and coaches" and "Focuses on your strengths." The Contingent Rewards scale is exemplified by items such as "Assists Based on Effort" and "Recognizes your achievement." The Management by Exception scale is illustrated by such items as "Puts out fires" and "Tracks your mistakes." Examples of Passive/Avoidant items are "Reacts to failure" and "Absent when needed."

#### Theoretical Basis

The conceptual foundations of the MLQ stem from Burns's (1978) description of transforming leadership. Burns viewed leadership as a continuum with transactional and transformational leadership anchoring the two ends. Empirical studies, however, suggested that these might be two conceptually distinct dimensions that could coexist. The best organizational leaders appeared to exhibit both forms of leadership (Bass & Avolio, 1993). Early work on this concept incorporated Bass's

(1985) model of transactional and transformational leadership, in which he conceptualized seven leadership dimensions. Subsequently, Bass (1988) reduced the number to six factors, combining Charisma and Inspirational Leadership on the argument that although conceptually distinct, they could not be distinguished empirically. The six-factor model formed the basis of the MLQ-Form 5X. Avolio, Bass, and Jung (1999) recently revised this form to improve the psychometric properties of the subscales while retaining the six-factor model. The revisions resulted in a 36-item scale. A more detailed report on the development of the MLQ-Form 5X is provided in Avolio, Bass, and Jung (1999).

### Test Development

The initial factor structure for the MLQ was obtained by asking executives to describe a leader who had made an impact on whatever they considered important in their leadership roles. They were also asked how, in their perception, the best leaders were able to get others to go beyond self-interest to achieve group objectives. Questionnaire items were constructed from the executives' responses and also from the literature on charisma. The 142 items thus generated were sorted by 11 judges into two categories—transformational and transactional (contingent reward) leadership. The 73 items that met an 80% agreement criterion (9 out of 11 judges) in the categorization task were then administered to U.S. Army colonels, who were asked to get ratings of their superiors. A principal components analysis of these data resulted in three transformational and two transactional leadership factors, and a sixth factor that was labeled by Bass (1985) as Passive/ Avoidant, or Laissez-Faire, Leadership. Following subsequent testing, critiques, and recommendations by a number of investigators (e.g., Bycio, Hackett, & Allen, 1995; Den Hartog, Van Muijen, & Koopman, 1997; House & Podsakoff, 1994; Yammarino & Bass, 1990), the MLQ has undergone a number of revisions and examinations of its factor structure. The present 36-item version of MLQ-Form 5X was derived from an original set of 80 items. These items came from several sources: a selection from MLQ 5R (Bass & Avolio, 1993); results from Howell and Avolio's (1993) analysis of an earlier version, the MLQ-Form 10; and new items written specifically for the MLQ-Form 5X based on recent literature distinguishing charismatic from transformational leadership. Reviews and recommendations from six academic experts in the field of leadership resulted in the modification or elimination of some items. Following suggestions from the research community, only behavioral items were retained for the scales. The only exception was the Charismatic/Inspirational Leadership scale, for which there existed specific arguments for

the inclusion of attributional, or "impact" items (e.g., Conger & Kanungo, 1987). The original MLQ-Form 5X had 80 items in all, with 18 items for Charisma (8 attributional and 10 behavioral); 10 items for Inspirational Leadership; 10 items for Intellectual Stimulation; 9 items for Individualized Consideration; 9 items for Contingent Rewards; 8 items for Management by Exception (active); and 16 items for Passive Management by Exception/Avoidant Leadership.

Avolio et al. (1999) combined data from 14 studies conducted over a period of several years using this version of the MLQ to revise the scale in order to obtain a better fit with the six-factor model. They split the studies into two groups. The first group of nine studies was used to run confirmatory factor analysis (CFA) on the six-factor model and used trimming procedures to improve the psychometric properties of the scales. The resulting 36-item measure was then tested on data from a second group of five studies.

### Psychometric Properties

The alpha coefficients for the six scales of the revised MLQ-Form 5X (36 items) ranged from .63 to .92 in the first sample (the group of nine studies) and from .64 to .92 in the second sample (group of five studies). All scales except Management by Exception had internal consistency reliability (alpha) coefficients greater than .70 in both samples. Factor loadings of individual items onto their respective scales ranged from .53 to .86 in the first sample and from .49 to .82 in the second sample. Fit indices for the six-factor model were also brought to acceptable levels through the trimming procedure. However, discriminant validity was low, with transformational leadership scales yielding sizable correlations with transactional leadership scales. The average interfactor correlations among the transformational scales were .81 and .80, respectively, in the two samples; the average correlations between transformational and contingent reward scales were .75 and .69 respectively. However, these correlations are consistent with the idea that transformational and transactional attributes may coexist in effective leadership.

### Range of Applicability and Limitations

Various versions of the MLQ have been used over the past 15 years in a variety of settings. Several studies have reported a positive correlation between MLQ transformational factors and objective as well as subjective measures of performance (see Lowe, Kroeck, & Sivasubramaniam, 1996, for a meta-analytic review). The MLQ has also been used in training and development. For instance, Avolio and Bass (1998) used the MLQ to identify training needs and monitor changes in individual factors of the MLQ framework.

### Accommodations for People With Disabilities

The questionnaire is completed by group members and not the leader. However, the instrument is in paper survey format and requires minimal accommodation for people with disabilities.

### Cross-Cultural Factors

No published report is available on the use of the MLQ-Form 5X (revised version) in a cross-cultural investigation. Although many of the items in the scale may seem sufficiently general in nature to foster an expectation of cross-cultural validity, evidence from the 61-nation GLOBE study (House et al., in press) implied possible differences stemming from dimensions of national culture, making some of the items less universal than others. For instance, "Emphasizes the collective mission" (Charismatic scale, Item 7) may emerge as a universally endorsed attribute because all cultures show some convergence toward collectivism; on the other hand, "Displays power and confidence" (Charismatic scale, Item 4) may not have as high a factor loading in some cultures as it does in American society.

### Legal and Ethical Considerations

Since the MLQ has been undergoing several modifications over the years, several criterion-related validation reports have become obsolete. At any given time, more than one form or version of MLQ is in use. Space constraints do not permit complete coverage of all versions in this chapter; however, a note of caution must be issued to potential users of the instrument to check that any validity or reliability characteristics reported on the MLQ pertain to the specific form that they are using. For instance, Lowe et al.'s (1996) meta-analytic findings of positive correlations between transformational leadership factors and performance do not apply to the MLQ-Form 5X (revised). Of course, the various versions have retained the basic six-factor structure, so that one may expect somewhat similar results with the revised form.

### Computerization and Internet Usage

The MLQ instrument in various formats is available on the Web at www.mindgarden.com.

### Current Research Status

The MLQ in its various versions remains one of the most widely studied instruments in leadership research. The MLQ-Form 5X (revised) is very recent but has the advantage of cumulative insights from the investigations of previous versions. At the time of this writing, there is a 45-item MLQ mentioned on the web site. The authors of the questionnaire are currently examining a nine-factor model that is supported by the dissertation work of Antonakis (2001). The nine factors identified are (1) Idealized Influence-Attributed, (2) Idealized Influence-Behavior, (3) Inspirational Motivation, (4) Intellectual Stimulation, (5) Individualized Consideration, (6) Contingent Reward, (7) Management-by-Exception-Active, (8) Management-by-Exception-Passive, and (9) Laissez-Faire Leadership. Internal reliabilities (alpha) range from .74 to 91, with most in the .80s and .90s; the composite scale reliabilities range from .81 to .89, except for Management-by-Exception (.76).

### Use in Organizational Practice

The MLQ has been used in studies in a number of organizations in several countries. It is now available for use by organizations as well as by researchers through www.mindgarden.com.

### Future Developments

Further research to validate the nine-factor model are under way. Avolio (personal communication, October 4, 2001) is currently working on triangulating the MLQ with qualitatively collected data to identify any other critical aspects of leadership that may not be addressed by the MLQ. He also notes that as the MLQ has been translated into several languages, the validity of the instrument across cultures and languages is being examined.

## The Leader-Member Exchange Questionnaire (LMX)

Several forms of the LMX scale, developed by various researchers, are in use. Two of the most recent forms, the LMX-6 (Schriesheim, Neider, Scandura, & Tepper, 1992) and the LMX-7 (Graen & Uhl-Bien, 1995; Scandura & Graen, 1984) are described in this section. The LMX-7 is not a revision of the LMX-6; rather, the two scales reflect rival perspectives on the leader-member exchange relationship. The LMX-7 precedes LMX-6 and has been in use before and after the development of LMX-6. Both measures are based on a three-dimensional model of LMX; the three dimensions, however, are not the same across the two measures. In the reader's best interests, both are described here.

### Description

**LMX-6.** The LMX-6 was developed and tested by Schriesheim et al. (1992) and is based on the three dimensions of the leader-member exchange process proposed by Dienesch and Liden (1986): Perceived Contribution, Loyalty, and Affect. Two items were used to measure each of these dimensions. Perceived Contribution measures the supervisor's estimation of the subordinate's professional worth. An example is "The way my supervisor sees me, he/she would probably say that my ability to do my job well is ____" (response categories: 5 = "Exceptional"; 4 = "Good to Very Good"; 3 = "Average"; 2 = "Below Average"; and 1 = "Poor"). Loyalty assesses the individual's support for the goals and personal character of the other person in the exchange relationship. An example is: "I feel that my work goals and those of my supervisor are ____" (response categories: 5 = "The Same"; 4 = "Similar"; 3 = "Unrelated"; 2 = "Different"; and 1 = "Opposite"). The third dimension, labeled Affect, measures the subordinate's satisfaction with the leader's (1) human relations and (2) technical ability in two separate items taken directly from the long-form Minnesota Satisfaction Questionnaire (Weiss, Dawis, England, & Lofquist, 1967; cited in Schriesheim et al., 1992). The two items are worded as, "On my present job, this is how I feel about the way my supervisor and I understand each other" and "My boss provides help on hard problems" (response categories: 5 = "Very Satisfied; 4 = "Satisfied"; 3 = "Undecided or Neutral"; 2 = "Dissatisfied"; and 1 = "Very Dissatisfied").

**LMX-7.** This measure was recommended by Graen and Uhl-Bien (1995) after a review of prior research conducted with various LMX measures. The scale, as the label suggests, has seven items—six items to assess the leader-member relationship on the three dimensions (respect, trust, and obligation), and one global item addressing the quality of the relationship. The global item is: "How would you characterize your working relationship with your leader?" (response categories: "Extremely Ineffective," "Worse Than Average," "Average," "Better Than Average," "Extremely Effective"). The same item, in the version completed by the leader, would have the phrase "member" substituted for "leader." Examples of other items are: "How well does your leader understand your job problems and needs?" (response categories: "Not a Bit," "A Little," "A Fair Amount," "Quite a Bit," "A Great Deal"); and "Do you know where you stand with your leader

. . . do you usually know how satisfied your leader is with what you do?" (response categories: "Rarely," "Occasionally," "Sometimes," "Fairly Often," "Very Often"). Item scores are unit-weighted and summed. The scale scores may be averaged to yield an average LMX for a unit (Graen, personal communication, October 10, 2001).

### Theoretical Basis

The LMX questionnaire is based on the leader-member exchange theory of leadership, originating from research on role-making processes in organizations (Dansereau, Graen & Haga, 1975; Graen & Cashman, 1975; Graen, Orris & Johnson, 1973; Graen & Schiemann, 1978; Haga, Graen, & Dansereau, 1974). LMX theory essentially addresses the role-making processes within organizations (Dansereau et al., 1975; Graen & Cashman, 1975) and the development of leader-follower relationships over time. Originally labeled the vertical dyad linkage (VDL) model (Dansereau et al., 1975), the theory addressed an aspect of leadership not represented in other theorizing on the topic, namely, the notion that a single leader may develop different types of relationships with different followers. In other words, LMX theory focuses on the individual relationship between a leader and a follower, and the way it evolves over a period of time into one of "hired hand" (out-group) or "cadre" (in-group). Graen and his associates proposed that the quality of the relationship had an important bearing on performance, job satisfaction, work commitment, and other organizational variables. The evolution of the LMX construct and future directions have been set out in Graen and Uhl-Bien (1995; see House & Aditya, 1997, for a detailed critique), and subsequently by Schriesheim et al. (1999). In a meta-analytic review of the LMX literature, Gerstner and Day (1997) concluded that the LMX-7 had the best psychometric properties of the various measures used.

### Test Development

There are a number of scales collectively referred to as LMX scales, inspired by the leader-member exchange theory. Over the years, these versions of the LMX were developed by various researchers presumably because the scale used by Graen and his associates originally was not publicly available (Graen & Uhl-Bien, 1995). The primary (and initially, the only) component of the scale was labeled as Negotiating Latitude and addressed the overall quality of a follower's relationship with a leader. From a 2-item measure (Dansereau et al., 1975), through a 4-item (e.g., Graen & Schiemann, 1978), a 5-item (e.g., Graen, Liden, & Hoel, 1982), 7-item (e.g., Graen, Novak, & Sommerkamp, 1982), 12-item (e.g.,

Wakabayashi & Graen, 1984), and 14-item (e.g., Wakabayashi, Graen & Uhl-Bien, 1990) scale, the LMX measure has seen the use of successively revised versions or independent creations by different researchers. The LMX-6 developed by Schriesheim et al. (1992) was contested by Graen and Uhl-Bien, who saw the dimensionality of the LMX construct in different terms. Arguing that only one dimension has come out consistently across studies, with Cronbach alphas in the .80–.90 range, Graen and Uhl-Bien (1995) nevertheless made the case for a three-dimensional measure (LMX-7). Instead of Perceived Contribution, Loyalty, and Affect, as proposed by Dienesch and Liden (1986), Graen and Uhl-Bien contended that Respect, Trust, and Obligation were the three dimensions that better captured the essence of the leader-member exchange relationship. The main conceptual difference in the domains postulated by Graen and Uhl-Bien (1995) is in the third dimension, Obligation, substituted for Affect.

### Psychometric Properties

**LMX-6.** Schriesheim et al. (1992) explored six different models using LISREL: a null model, a one-factor model, 3 two-factor models (combining two theorized factors in turn), and a three-factor model. Data were obtained from two different samples of working adults. The three-factor model yielded the best fit (chi-square = 11.17, $df$ = 6, GTL = .97, for the first sample; chi-square = 17.31, $df$ = 6, GTL = .92 for the second sample). Factor loadings of items onto their theorized scales for the three-factor model ranged from .47 to .93 in the first sample and .53 to .93 in the second sample. The authors used two additional samples of MBA students to assess test-retest reliability of the scales. The coefficients were .77 and .82, respectively, for the two samples, with disattenuated coefficients (Nunnally, 1978) of .96 and .99, respectively. Internal consistency reliability coefficients were .79 and .81 for the two administrations in the first sample, and .81 and .84, respectively, in the second sample. They also found convergence validity through a correlation of .82 with Scandura and Graen's (1984) LMX-7 scale, with a disattenuated correlation of .94.

**LMX-7.** The LMX-7 has an internal consistency reliability of .92 (Graen, personal communication, October 10, 2001). The measure yields an acceptable fit with a three-factor solution in confirmatory factor analysis (e.g., Graen & Uhl-Bien, 1995). However, Graen and Uhl-Bien (1995) and Graen (Personal communication, October 10, 2001) have reiterated that the construct is really unidimensional, since any three-factor model yields highly correlated factors. Gerstner and Day (1997) reported that the LMX-7 scale displayed higher average alphas than average reliability for all other measures; they also noted that the LMX-7 tended to yield higher correlations with outcomes than did other measures of LMX.

### Range of Applicability and Limitations

The LMX scale addresses a very practical aspect of the enactment of leadership, drawing attention to the individual relationships that followers have with their leader. The LMX measure can be used as a diagnostic tool to identify potential problems in a unit. In-groups and out-groups are a fact of organizational life, and effective leadership does not necessarily imply that all of the followers must have the same quality of relationship with the leader. From a performance perspective, therefore, the utility of the LMX measure is less clear. Theoretical and empirical investigations are still evolving with respect to Stages 3 and 4 of development of LMX theory proposed by Graen and Uhl-Bien (1995). Extant research on LMX with regard to outcome variables has been plagued by methodological biases introduced by correlated measures (House & Aditya, 1997), and future investigations need to take methodological considerations into account. Further, as Schriesheim et al. (1999) note, conceptual definitions of LMX have evolved in terms of subdomains, with little rationale to back the postulations. Operationalizations of the construct have also varied widely. Keller and Dansereau (2000) found that results varied depending on the measure of LMX used. Gerstner and Day (1997) inferred that the LMX is better assessed through member reports than through leader reports.

### Accommodation for People With Disabilities

The scale is a simple paper-and-pencil measure and presents no special problems for people with disabilities.

### Cross-Cultural Factors

Graen and Uhl-Bien (1995) have noted that a number of studies have found evidence for the theorized characteristics of mutual trust, respect, and obligation in differentiating among the relationships between leaders and followers in cross-cultural settings.

### Legal and Ethical Considerations

The LMX measures are useful in furthering our knowledge of leadership and in understanding the evolution of leader-follower relationships over time. The LMX measures may be useful as diagnostic aids in gauging the followers' levels of satisfaction with their leader, and in unearthing differences in perception of the relationship between leader and follower. In such applications, however, issues of confidentiality of responses and contractual restrictions on the use of information from responses may arise. The LMX is not suitable for use as a selection tool.

### Computerization and Internet Usage

Currently, the LMX measure is not available in computerized format on the Internet.

### Current Research Status

The LMX-7 has been used in several studies (Graen, personal communication, October 10, 2001). The three-factor model appears to be robust in factor-analytic studies. However, it is also noteworthy that these factors are highly correlated. Graen (personal communication, 2001) reiterates that the LMX construct is really unidimensional. Graen and Uhl-Bien (1995) have argued that the three dimensions they described emerge only in a confirmatory factor analysis that imposes a three-factor solution on the data and that these factors may well be represented by a single global factor.

### Use in Organizational Practice

The LMX scales have been used largely for academic research on leadership. However, several organizations and consultants in the United States and abroad have adopted the LMX model of leadership in the context of leader development.

### Future Developments

The LMX model started with a focus on the dyad. The ramifications of the model extend to work teams, which can be viewed as a collectivity of dyads (Graen & Uhl-Bien, 1995). Following the directions for future research set by Graen and Uhl-Bien (1995), research using LMX-7 is now under way to examine (1) how LMX develops in teams, and its relationship to team performance, and (2) the development of LMX in dyads as a function of leader and member effort, and its relationship to team motivation (e.g., McClane, 1991).

## GLOBE Leadership Scales

### Description

The items in the GLOBE leadership scales are designed to tap perceived attributes of leaders of organizations in each culture. Respondents were asked to indicate the extent to which each trait or behavior was perceived as impeding or facilitating outstanding leadership. Specific attributes were rated on a scale ranging from 1 ("This Behavior or Characteristic Greatly Inhibits a Person from Being an Outstanding Leader") to 7 ("This Behavior or Characteristic Contributes Greatly to a Person Being an Outstanding Leader"). The number of items in each scale varies. The Diplomacy scale, for instance, has five items (e.g., "Skilled in interpersonal relations, tactful"). It is important to recognize that the GLOBE leadership scales do not assess leadership behaviors or traits in individuals; rather, they profile leader prototypes in a social or cultural unit. This feature distinguishes the GLOBE scales from all other leadership scales described in this chapter.

### Theoretical Basis

The GLOBE project was undertaken to explore the implicit theories of leadership operative in different cultures, and to identify universal as well as culture-specific aspects of leadership. The various phases of the study are described in House et al. (1999). The GLOBE scales for leadership were developed from an initial pool of items addressing the various attributes of leadership found in the extant literature. The underlying model, however, addresses the implicit theories of leadership (Lord & Maher, 1991). Thus, the various scales are aimed at converging on the attributes characteristic of leader prototypes in a society.

### Test Development

The first stage of the project involved the construction and validation of measures addressing various dimensions of national culture and leadership based on current theory. Initially, several items were generated to cover the domain of leadership. The emphasis was on comprehensive coverage of leader behavior and traits, guided by the various dimensions identified in existing research. These items were then sorted by seven graduate psychology majors into the prespecified dimensions. Items were retained only if they met a set of three criteria, as detailed in Hanges and Dickson (in press). The short-listed items were subjected to a second round of sorting, this time by 36 coinvestigators. Items that met a 70 percent agreement criterion were retained. The items simply listed a behavior or trait, with the rating scale anchors described earlier. The final items in the survey were then translated and back-translated for administration in a number of countries where the use of English was not appropriate. The scale development and validation was carried out in two studies. In the first study, 433 middle-level managers from 28 countries provided data that were subjected to factor-analytic procedures and reliability tests. As the broad objective was to compare cultures on implicit theories of leadership, individual ratings were aggregated to the country level of analysis. On the basis of principal components analyses, 16 leadership scales were formed. These were: Diplomatic, Humane, Status-Seeking, Inspirational, Achievement, Autocratic, Bureaucratic, Collectivistic, Decisive, Face-Saving, Integrity, Self-absorbed, Equanimity, Procedural, Visionary, and Individualistic.

In the second study, the scales were cross-validated with data obtained from 346 middle-level managers from an additional group of 15 countries. Confirmatory factor analyses were conducted on these data at the individual level of analysis, for a number of reasons detailed in Hanges and Dickson (in press).

### Psychometric Properties

Two studies were conducted in the development and validation processes for the GLOBE leadership scales, the details of which are provided in Hanges and Dickson (in press). Cronbach's alpha for the 16 leadership scales in the first study ranged from .83 to .98. The reliability of scales aggregated to the societal level of analysis was tested through the multi-item scale estimate $r_{wg}$ (James, Demaree, & Wolf, 1984) and intraclass coefficients ICC(1). The average $r_{wg}$ ranged from .78 to .97, and the ICC(1) ranged from .07 to .35. These results compare favorably with standards articulated in the literature (Hanges and Dickson, in press). Intercorrelations between scales ranged from .00 to .86. On the basis of these results, a second-order factor analysis was performed with varimax rotation, yielding five second-order dimensions. These were labeled as (1) Charismatic and Action-Oriented, (2) Bureaucratic, (3) Considerate, (4) Individualistic, and (5) Autocratic Leadership Styles. In the second study, generalizability analyses were consistent with the results of the first. Confirmatory factor analyses could be performed for 8 of the 16 leadership scales (Achievement, Autocratic, Bureaucratic, Collectivistic, Decisive, Face-Saving, Integrity, and Self-Absorbed), and these showed acceptable levels of fit. The unidimensionality of four others was, however, established through other procedures as detailed in Hanges and Dickson (in press).

### Range of Applicability and Limitations

The GLOBE scales were developed expressly to examine the influence of cultural variables on implicit theories of leadership. As such, they do not profile an individual in terms of leadership attributes. Rather, they tap an individual's perception of an outstanding leader in terms of the leader's characteristics. Therefore, the scales are useful for examining implicit theories in various settings. The scales are comprehensive in their coverage of leader attributes. To the extent that leader prototypes in follower perceptions determine what is required of a leader, the GLOBE scales may be useful for constructing a measure of effective leadership for specific cultural settings. However, it must be noted that the scales were developed from an initial pool of items and not derived from open-ended items about what respondents in various cultures perceived as making for outstanding leadership.

### Accommodation for People with Disabilities

This is a paper-and-pencil questionnaire and does not call for special accommodations for people with disabilities.

### Cross-Cultural Factors

The GLOBE scales have been validated with data from 43 countries and is eminently suited to use in cross-cultural studies.

### Legal and Ethical Considerations

The GLOBE leadership scales are suitable primarily for use in surveys of leadership perceptions. Their development was not meant for use in selection or executive development applications, although the scales may facilitate the creation of other measures for such purposes. The association between ratings of managers on the GLOBE scales and the effectiveness of these individuals as leaders has not been established.

### Computerization and Internet Usage

The GLOBE measures are not available in computerized form; they are also not available online at this time.

### Current Research Status

The GLOBE research program is conceived in four phases, described in House et al. (1999). The first phase involved the development and validation of research instruments. Phase 2 involved the examination of relationships between cultural dimensions and implicit theories of leadership. Phase 3 addresses the impact of specific leader behaviors on subordinate performance and satisfaction, and on leader and organizational effectiveness. The final phase would involve laboratory studies to assess the causal nature of some of the relationships identified in the previous two phases. Of these, Phases 1 and 2 have been completed; Phase 3 is in progress.

### Use in Organizational Practice

As mentioned earlier, the GLOBE leadership scales in their current form are suited more for cross-cultural research purposes than for use in organizations.

### Future Developments

The scales developed in the GLOBE study address leadership from the perspective of follower perceptions. To the extent that these perceptions shape the requirements for effective leadership within a cultural setting, the scales may be adapted for organizational use. Further research may be gainfully directed toward this objective.

## The Empowering Leadership Questionnaire (ELQ)

### Description

The Empowering Leadership Questionnaire (ELQ; Arnold, Arad, Rhoades, & Drasgow, 2000) is based on evolving perspectives on leadership that address a changing environment. A number of researchers subscribe to the view that in the emerging era of flat organizational structures, effective leadership depends on the empowerment of followers (e.g., Bowen & Lawler, 1992; Burke, 1986; Conger, 1989; Conger & Kanungo, 1988; Liden & Arad, 1996; Liden & Tewksbury, 1995; Manz & Sims, 1987). Although this scale has been developed very recently, it shows at least as much potential as some of the other scales described in this section and is therefore included here.

The scale consists of five subscales addressing each of the following conceptual domains: (1) Leading by example (5 items), (2) participative decision making (6 items), (3) coaching (11 items), (4) informing (6 items), and (5) showing concern/interacting with the team (10 items). Each of these items describes a specific behavior of the leader, and others in the unit are asked to indicate on a scale of 1 to 5 (1 being "Never" and 5 being "Always") the frequency with which the leader exhibits each of the behaviors. The Leading by Example subscale has items such as: "Works as hard as anyone in my work group" and "Sets a good example by the way he/she behaves." Participative Decision Making has items such as "Listens to my work group's ideas and suggestions" and "Gives all work group members a chance to voice their opinions." Examples of items in the subscale Coaching are: "Helps my work group see areas in which we need more training" and "Pays attention to my

work group's efforts." The Informing subscale has items such as "Explains company goals" and "Explains his/her decisions to my work group." Examples of items in Showing Concern/Interacting with the Team are "Treats work group members as equals," and "Gets along with my work group members."

### Theoretical Basis

The ELQ is perhaps the most recent scale to emerge in the leadership literature. It reflects the changes that are taking place in organizations in response to increasing globalization and international competition faced in today's marketplace. Traditional roles of directing and monitoring have passed from the hands of individual managers to empowered teams. Whereas the tall organizational structure of traditional firms operated on a model of transactional leadership through several levels of a hierarchy, a need for quick adaptation to a rapidly changing environment has led to a relatively flat organizational structure. The focus in the new organizations is on enhancing employees' feelings of self-efficacy and involvement in decision making, and in general fostering a sense of empowerment in determining the organization's performance (Arnold et al., 2000).

### Test Development

The ELQ was developed by Arnold et al. (2000) as an improvement over the conceptual and methodological foundations of the Self-Management Leadership Questionnaire (SMLQ; Manz & Sims, 1987). Items for the ELQ were developed through in-depth interviews with team leaders and members in three organizations that provided empowering environments. All of the teams interviewed were self-managing work teams, but varied in function, scope, and level of autonomy vested with workers. The interviews were structured, with five open-ended questions about effective and ineffective leadership behaviors in self-managed work teams. The transcribed interviews were content coded by three industrial/organizational (I/O) psychologists to generate lists of behaviors mentioned in the interviews. The final list of behaviors (with redundant ones removed) were sorted into conceptually distinct groups by the three coders. The sorting task resulted in eight categories of leader behaviors in empowered environments, which they labeled respectively as: (1) Leading by Example, (2) Coaching, (3) Encouraging, (4) Participative Decision Making, (5) Informing, (6) Showing Concern, (7) Interacting with the Team, and (8) Group Management.

In order to have data meet the linearity assumption of standard factor analysis models or the multivariate normality assumption of the maximum likelihood estimation models,

Arnold et al. (2000) summed pairs of items within subscales. An item-level factor analysis performed by Arnold et al., however, produced nonconvergent results for eight- as well as seven-factor solutions. Further, Arnold et al. report that the six-factor solution, in which Interacting with the Team and Group Management were merged into one factor, still yielded a high correlation ($r = .97$) between this sixth factor and the fifth factor (Showing Concern). The authors therefore combined the two factors and examined the five-factor model. The authors took the "relatively small difference in chi-square, 9.33, with 5 degrees of freedom" between the six- and five-factor models as support for combining Factors 5 and 6. However, there still were high correlations between Factors 2 and 3 (Coaching and Participative Decision Making: $r = .94$) and between Factors 3 and 5 (Participative Decision Making and Interacting with the Team: $r = .93$). The authors therefore examined 2 four-factor models, combining the relevant pairs of factors in turn. The authors report that the slightly higher ratios of changes in chi-square to changes in degrees of freedom, viewed in light of the sample size of 205 (2.6 and 2.5, respectively, for the two models, compared with 1.87 between the six- and five-factor solutions examined earlier) provide "evidence for the existence of separate factors underlying Participative Decision Making, Showing Concern/Interacting with the Team, and Coaching behaviors" (p. 258). The model fit for the four-factor models was almost as good as for the five-factor model. Lacking an empirical difference, the authors explored a conceptual distinction between these three factors by having 12 I/O psychologists sort the relevant items. On the basis of a theoretical distinction, they adopted the five-factor solution.

### Psychometric Characteristics

Coefficient alphas for all five subscales were above .85 in the initial study and the cross-validation study reported by Arnold et al. (2000). The factor intercorrelations ranged between .60 and .90, with all but two ranging between .70 and .82. Disattenuated correlations (Lord & Novick, 1968) turned out to be lower than the original correlations by an average of .10, leading the authors to conclude that the factor intercorrelations estimated by LISREL VIII were probably inflated. In my opinion, the rationale for applying a disattenuation procedure meant for mental tests to a scale measuring frequency of observed behaviors is not compelling. However, as Arnold et al. noted, even the disattenuated correlations were high, suggesting that the behaviors assessed by these scales are highly correlated.

### Range of Applicability and Limitations

As with many other scales on leadership, the ELQ seeks to provide a description of leaders based on behaviors that organization members in self-managed teams perceive to be effective. The ELQ is presumably an instrument for assessing leader-empowering behaviors, although all of the factors except Participative Decision Making are relevant to any organizational structure, traditional or contemporary.

Three features of this instrument are to be noted. First, the items in the scale express behaviors in very subjective terms. As such, the equivalence of ratings across respondents is suspect. Second, the assessment is not obtained from the leader, but from members of the work group. The authors have not provided a way of profiling the leader based on these scores. Third, the power of the analysis in Arnold et al.'s studies is not as high as the $N$ of 205 would suggest, since the ratings pertain to only a few leaders. Thus, the responses are inherently correlated to the extent that sets of responses within the sample describe the same individual. The subjectivity in the nature of the items serves to further complicate the issue.

This measure in its current form has potential for furthering our understanding of the leadership construct in an academic sense. Its applicability in selection or leader development programs needs further study, however.

### Accommodation for People with Disabilities

This instrument is in paper survey format, and its administration presents no special problems for people with disabilities.

### Cross-Cultural Factors

The ELQ has not been specifically examined in cross-cultural contexts at this time. The items are sufficiently general in the behaviors represented to permit its examination in other cultural settings besides the United States.

### Legal/Ethical Considerations

The scores on ELQ scales were shown to be correlated with LBDQ and MPS scales. The correlations ranged from .54 to .68 with LBDQ and .51 to .69 with MPS. However, the ELQ has not been validated with reference to any criterion of leader effectiveness or team performance. As such, this measure cannot be used for selection of personnel or identification of leadership potential until further research is conducted.

## Computerization and Internet Usage

At this time, the ELQ is not available on the Internet. However, computerization of this measure would not be difficult.

## Current Research Status

The ELQ has been developed recently, and at present there is not much research available.

## Use in Organizational Practice

This scale is very recent, and evidence of its use in organizations is not available, although there are inquiries in Internet discussion and interest groups about the availability of the ELQ.

## Future Developments

The ELQ has much scope for use in organizations, and further testing of the properties of the scale to replicate factor structure is recommended.

# APPENDIX: ADDITIONAL MEASURES OF LEADERSHIP

## Leadership Practices Inventory (LPI)

This scale is based on Kouzes and Posner's five-factor model of leadership and measures a variety of behaviors that address five hypothesized dimensions: Challenging, Inspiring, Enabling, Modelling, and Encouraging. The instrument was based on data collected from organizations in several countries, and both public and private organizations. In an initial study, Posner and Kouzes (1988) found good predictive validity of LPI scores with respect to leader effectiveness and behavior, insignificant differences across national borders, and negligible gender differences. In a subsequent study, Posner and Kouzes (1993) examined data collected from 36,000 managers and their subordinates. The hypothesized five-factor structure of the LPI was supported; however, gender differences were reported. Women evidently enacted modeling and encouraging behaviors more frequently than did men.

## The Decision Process Model

The decision process model (Vroom & Jago, 1988; Vroom & Yetton, 1973) does not refer to a specific scale, but to a theoretical framework that can facilitate a leader's decision-making process. Measures of effective leadership have been constructed using this framework. This prescriptive model is in the form of a decision tree with seven questions forming the nodes. The answer to each question (yes/no) leads to a feasible set of decision processes. The seven questions represent situational variables that would influence the decision. The feasible sets, or problem types, may have between one and five decisions in the set that presumably will be "effective" or acceptable decisions for the follower group. Measures based on this framework have vignettes in which the situation is manipulated in terms of the seven situational variables, and the leader then responds by making a decision. The decision can be scored on the basis of whether or not it falls within the feasible set. The Vroom and Yetton model is a prescriptive instrument that has been tested empirically in parts, although testing the entire model presents a challenge in logistics of research design.

## Managerial Practices Survey (MPS)

This instrument, as the name suggests, is more a measure of managerial behavior than of leadership. It was initially called the Managerial Behavior Survey and originated from a program of research started in 1975 to identify and measure categories of managerial behavior associated with managerial effectiveness (Yukl, Wall, & Lepsinger, 1990). The MPS is based on the resulting taxonomy of managerial behaviors involving 11 categories. The initial version of the MPS (1982) had 115 items in 23 scales; the 1986 version had 110 items in 13 scales, with the wording of items changed to address dyadic relationships and thus reduce ambiguity. The 11 categories addressed are: informing, consulting and delegating, planning and organizing, problem solving, clarifying roles and objectives, monitoring operations and environment, motivating, recognizing and rewarding, supporting and mentoring, managing conflict and team building, and networking. The response choices for each item in these categories of behavior are: 1 ("Never, Not at All"), 2 ("Seldom, To a Limited Extent"), 3 ("Sometimes, To a Moderate Extent"), 4 ("Usually, To a Great Extent"), NA ("Not Applicable"), and ? ("Don't Know"). Internal consistency reliabilities, measured by Cronbach's alpha, ranged from .80 to .93 over four different samples.

## ACUMEN Scales and Life Styles Inventory

Whereas most measures of leadership address behaviors and styles of managing, the ACUMEN scales and the Level 1 Life Styles Inventory address thinking styles in three domains: People/Security Orientation; Satisfaction Orientation;

and Task/Security Orientation (Gratzinger, Warren, & Cooke, 1990). This three-domain model is in contrast to the two-domain framework of the behavioral school (namely, Task Orientation and Relationship Orientation). There are four scales in each of the three domains. The 12 scales have a total of 120 items. All of the scales are reported to distinguish between the top and bottom 10% of managers as assessed through four behavioral outcome measures by coworkers, representing what Gratzinger et al. (1990) portray as four "key areas" of management: on-the-job effectiveness, interest in self-improvement, handling negative feedback, and social relationships.

### Campbell Leadership Potential Index (CLPI)

The CLPI is a 160-adjective checklist that is administered to the target individual while also being completed by three to five other observers. The checklist describes the individual on 33 scales classified into six orientations related to "leadership and creativity" Campbell (1990, p. 249). These orientations are labeled as: Leadership, Creativity, Physical Energy, Productivity, Likeability, and Psychological Comfort.

### Leadership Report

The Leadership Report (Burke, 1988, in Sashkin & Burke, 1990) is an 18-item questionnaire that incorporates a form of forced-choice response. Each item has a beginning of a statement with a choice of two phrases for the ending. The respondent is asked to allocate 5 points in any combination to the two alternatives. The instrument is based on the transformational-transactional leadership dichotomy, and the idea that the way a leader uses power in empowering followers is the key to the distinction between the two styles of leadership. Higher scores on the transformational components of the Leadership Report are associated with executive status (as compared with manager status).

### Leader Behavior Questionnaire (LBQ)

The distinctive feature of the LBQ is its focus on leadership at the top. The LBQ was originally developed as a research and training instrument and is based on the works of Bennis (1984) and Bowers and Seashore (1966). Sashkin and Burke (1990) report that over 20,000 managers in North America were exposed to the LBQ in the late 1980s. However, the LBQ was revised to weed out scales that contributed little to the effectiveness of the instrument as a training tool. The present version of the LBQ contains 50 items, with 5 items for each of 10 scales. Social desirability checks are provided

by phrasing two of the five items negatively. The 10 scales are: Focused Leadership, Communication Leadership, Trust Leadership, Respectful Leadership, Risk Leadership, Bottom-Line Leadership, Empowered Leadership, Long-Term Leadership, Organizational Leadership, and Cultural Leadership.

### Tacit Knowledge Inventory for Managers (TKIM)

The TKIM is based on work by Sternberg and his associates on what they term *practical intelligence* (Sternberg & Wagner, 1988). The instrument seeks to measure tacit knowledge in three areas: managing oneself, managing others, and managing tasks. The test contains a number of vignettes relating to work situations that describe a problem. Each is followed by several alternative solutions. This instrument is posed as a measure of cognitive ability that is distinct from traditional IQ. Some empirical evidence indicates that successful managers and executives score high on all three areas of tacit knowledge, and that scores on tacit knowledge may vary even among executives scoring high on IQ.

### Sociopolitical Intelligence (SPIQ)

Hogan and Hogan (2002) argue that role-taking ability is a characteristic of effective leadership, and they term the generalized form of this ability as sociopolitical intelligence, or SPIQ. Their measure of SPIQ consists of items developed by them as well as items from the California Psychological Inventory (CPI; Gough, 1987). Hogan and Hogan (2002) cite evidence from a number of studies to support the notion that SPIQ may predict the success or failure of managers in organizations.

### Executive Intelligence—An Adult Interpersonal Acumen Scale

In the context of social intelligence, another recent measure of cognitive ability in the realm of interpersonal interaction relevant to leadership is the Adult Interpersonal Acumen Scale (Aditya, 1997; Aditya & Rosnow, 2002). Interpersonal acumen (Rosnow, Skleder, Jaeger, & Rind, 1994) is the ability to read underlying motives in other people's behavior and stems from Gardner's (1983) theory of interpersonal intelligence. Aditya's (1997) Adult Interpersonal Acumen Scale is based on Rosnow et al.'s (1994) framework for the operationalization of the construct in the form of a Guttman scale and consists of a number of scenarios of workplace behaviors. The respondent is required to imagine himself or herself as the target of the actor's behavior in the scenario and choose one of three alternative motives for the act.

The Adult Interpersonal Acumen Scale was originally constructed in an interactive computerized format and is now being tested in a paper-and-pencil form (Aditya & Robinson, 2001). Aditya (1997) demonstrated the ordinal structure of the scale and replicated it in subsequent studies (Aditya, Buboltz, Darkangelo, & Wilkinson, 2000; Aditya, Darkangelo, & Morris, 1999). Preliminary evidence from these studies using inspection-time measurements in the computerized task format support the notion of interpersonal acumen as a cognitive ability (Aditya, 1997; Aditya et al., 1999), distinct from traditional IQ (Aditya, 1997) and from personality measures (Aditya et al., 2000). Further, there is some empirical support for its association with indices of executive and managerial success (Aditya, 1997). This measure has implications for the assessment of leadership in cross-cultural contexts as well (Aditya & House, 2002).

## REFERENCES

Aditya, R.N. (1997). *Toward the better understanding of managerial success: An exploration of interpersonal acumen.* Unpublished doctoral dissertation, Temple University, Philadelphia.

Aditya, R.N., Buboltz, W., Darkangelo, D., & Wilkinson, L. (2000, June). *Discriminant validation of a revised interpersonal acumen scale.* Paper presented at the 12th Annual Convention of the American Psychological Society, Miami, FL.

Aditya, R.N., Darkangelo, D., & Morris, M.L. (1999, June). *The structure of interpersonal acumen in adult interaction.* Paper presented at the 11th Annual Conference of the American Psychological Society, Denver, CO.

Aditya, R.N., & House, R.J. (2002). Interpersonal acumen and leadership across cultures: Pointers from the GLOBE study. In R.E. Riggio & S.E. Murphy (Eds.), *Multiple intelligences and leadership* (pp. 215–240). Mahwah, NJ: Erlbaum.

Aditya, R.N., House, R.J., & Kerr, S. (2000). Theory and practice of leadership: Into the new millennium. In C.L. Cooper & E.A. Locke (Eds.), *Industrial and organizational psychology: Linking theory and practice* (pp. 130–165). New York: Blackwell.

Aditya, R.N., & Robinson, D.T. (2001, August). *Measuring interpersonal acumen in adults: Scale structure and format options.* Poster session presented at the 109th Annual Convention of the American Psychological Association, San Francisco, CA.

Aditya, R.N., & Rosnow, R.L. (2002). Executive intelligence and interpersonal acumen: A conceptual framework, preliminary findings, and implications for the performing organization. In B. Pattanayak & V. Gupta (Eds.), *Creating performing organizations* (pp. 225–246). New Delhi: Sage.

Antonakis, J. (2001). *The validity of the transformational, transactional, and laissez-faire leadership model as measured by the Multifactor Leadership Questionnaire (MLQ-5X) Dissertation Abstracts International, 62*(1-A), 233. (UMI No. 3000380)

Arnold, J.A., Arad, S., Rhoades, J.A., & Drasgow, F. (2000). The empowering leadership questionnaire: The construction and validation of a new scale for measuring leader behaviors. *Journal of Organizational Behavior, 21,* 249–269.

Ashour, A.S. (1973). Further discussion of Fiedler's contingency model of leadership effectiveness: An evaluation. *Organizational Behavior and Human Performance, 9,* 339–355.

Avolio, B.J., & Bass, B.M. (1998). You can drag a horse to water, but you can't make it drink, except when it's thirsty. *Journal of Leadership Studies, 5,* 1–17.

Avolio, B.J., Bass, B.M., & Jung, D.I. (1999). Re-examining the components of transformational and transactional leadership using the Multifactor Leadership Questionnaire. *Journal of Occupational and Organizational Psychology, 72,* 441–462.

Bales, R.F. (1954). In conference. *Harvard Business Review, 32*(2), 44–50.

Barnlund, D.C. (1962). Consistency of emergent leadership in groups with changing tasks and members. *Speech Monographs, 29,* 45–52.

Barrick, M.R., & Mount, M.K. (1993). Autonomy as a moderator of the relationships between the Big Five personality dimensions and job performance. *Journal of Applied Psychology, 78*(1), 111–118.

Bass, B.M. (1985). *Leadership and performance beyond expectations.* New York: Free Press.

Bass, B.M. (1988). The inspirational process of leadership. *Journal of Management Development, 7,* 21–31.

Bass, B.M. (1990). *Handbook of leadership: A survey of theory and research.* New York: Free Press.

Bass, B.M. (1997). Does the transactional-transformational leadership paradigm transcend organizational and national boundaries? *American Psychologist, 52,* 130–139.

Bass, B.M., & Avolio, B.J. (1993). Transformational leadership: A response to critiques. In M.M. Chemers & R. Ayman (Eds.), *Leadership theory and research: Perspectives and directions* (pp. 49–88). San Diego, CA: Academic Press.

Bass, B.M., Burger, P.C., Doktor, R., & Barrett, G.V. (1979). *Assessment of managers: An international comparison.* New York: Free Press.

Bennis, W.G. (1984). The four competencies of leadership. *Training and Development Journal, 38*(8), 15–18.

Bennis, W., & Nanus, B. (1985). *Leaders: The strategies for taking charge.* New York: Harper & Row.

Bowen, D., & Lawler, E. (1992). The empowerment of service workers: What, why, how and when? *Sloan Management Review, 33,* 31–39.

Bowers D.G., & Seashore, S.E. (1966). Predicting organizational effectiveness with a four-factor theory of Leadership. *Administrative Science Quarterly, 11,* 238–263.

Burke, W. (1986). Leadership as the empowerment of others. In S. Srivastra (Ed.), *Executive power* (pp. 51–77). San Francisco: Jossey-Bass.

Burke, W.W. (1988). *Leadership report* (Rev. ed.). Pelham, NY: W. Warner Burke & Associates.

Burns, J.M. (1978). *Leadership.* New York: Harper & Row.

Bycio, P., Hackett, R.D., & Allen, J.S. (1995). Further assessments of Bass' conceptualization of transactional and transformational leadership. *Journal of Applied Psychology, 80,* 468–478.

Campbell, D.P. (1990). The Campbell Work Orientations surveys: Their use to capture the characteristics of leaders. In K.E. Clark & M.B. Clark (Eds.), *Measures of leadership* (pp. 249–274). West Orange, NJ: Leadership Library of America.

Caruso, D.R., Mayer, J.D., & Salovey, P. (2002). Emotional intelligence and emotional leadership. In R.E. Riggio, S.E. Murphy, & F.J. Pirozzolo (Eds.), *Multiple intelligences and leadership* (pp. 55–74). Mahwah, NJ: Erlbaum.

Cassel, R.N., & Stancik, E.J. (1982). *The Leadership Ability Evaluation-Revised: Manual.* Los Angeles: Western Psychological Services.

Clover, W.H. (1990). Transformational leaders: Team performance, leadership ratings, and firsthand impressions. In K.E. Clark & M.B. Clark (Eds.), *Measures of leadership* (pp. 171–184). West Orange, NJ: Leadership Library of America.

Conger, J.A. (1989). Leadership: The art of empowering others. *Academy of Management Executive, 3*(1), 17–24.

Conger, J.A., & Kanungo, R.N. (1987). Towards a behavioral theory of charismatic leadership in organizational settings. *Academy of Management Review, 12,* 637–647.

Conger, J.A., & Kanungo, R.N. (1988). The empowerment process: Integrating theory and practice. *Academy of Management Review, 13*(3), 471–482.

Curphy, G.J. (1990). *An empirical evaluation of Bass' (1985) theory of transformational transactional leadership.* Unpublished doctoral dissertation, University of Minnesota.

Dansereau, F. Jr., Graen, G., & Haga, W.J. (1975). A vertical dyad linkage approach to leadership within formal organizations—a longitudinal investigation of the role making process. *Organizational Behavior and Human Performance, 13,* 46–78.

Davis-Blake, A., & Pfeffer, J. (1988). Just a mirage: The search for dispositional effects in organizational research. *Academy of Management Review, 14*(3), 385–400.

Den Hartog, D.N., Van Muijen, J.J., & Koopman, P.L. (1997). Transactional versus transformational leadership: An analysis of the MLQ. *Journal of Occupational and Organizational Psychology, 70,* 19–34.

Dickson, M.W., Aditya, R.N., & Chhokar, J.S. (2000). Definition and interpretation in cross-cultural organizational culture research: Some pointers from the GLOBE research program. In N.M. Askanasy, C.P.M. Wilderom, & M.F. Peterson (Eds.), *Handbook of organizational culture and climate* (pp. 447–464). Thousand Oaks, CA: Sage.

Dienesch, R.M., & Liden, R.C. (1986). Leader-member exchange model of leadership: A critique and further development. *Academy of Management Review, 11*(3), 618–634.

Duarte, N.T., Goodson, J.R., & Klich, N.R. (1993). How do I like thee? Let me appraise the ways. *Journal of Organizational Behavior, 14,* 239–249.

Esposito, J.L., Agard, E., & Rosnow, R.L. (1984). Can confidentiality of data pay off? *Personality and Individual Differences, 5*(4), 477–480.

Ferris, G.R. (1985). Role of leadership in the employee withdrawal process: A constructive replication. *Journal of Applied Psychology, 70*(4), 777–781.

Fiedler, F.E. (1964). A contingency model of leadership effectiveness. In L. Berkowitz (Ed.), *Advances in experimental social psychology* (Vol. 1, pp. 149–190). New York: Academic Press.

Fiedler, F.E. (1967). *A theory of leadership effectiveness.* New York: McGraw-Hill.

Fiedler, F.E. (1971). Validation and extention of the contingency model of leadership effectiveness: A review of empirical findings. *Psychological Bulletin, 76,* 128–148.

Fiedler, F.E. (1973). The contingency model: A reply to Ashour. *Organizational Performance and Human Behavior, 9,* 356–368.

Fiedler, F.E. (1977). A rejoinder to Schriesheim and Kerr's premature obituary of the Contingency Model. In J.G. Hunt & L.L. Larson (Eds.), *Leadership: The cutting edge* (pp. 45–51). Carbondale: Southern Illinois University Press.

Fiedler, F.E. (1995). Cognitive resources and leadership performance. *Applied Psychology—An International Review, 44,* 5–28.

Fiedler, F.E., & Chemers, M.M. (1984). *Improving leadership effectiveness: The leader match concept* (Rev. ed.). New York: Wiley.

Fiedler, F.E., Chemers, M.M., & Mahar, L (1976). *Improving leadership effectiveness: The leader match concept.* New York: Wiley.

Fiedler, F.E., & Garcia, J.E. (1987). *New approaches to effective leadership: Cognitive resources and organizational performance.* New York: Wiley.

Field, R.H.G. (1982). A test of the Vroom-Yetton normative model of leadership. *Journal of Applied Psychology, 67,* 523–532.

Finkelstein, S., & Hambrick, D. (1996). *Strategic leadership: Top executives and their effects on organizations.* St. Paul, MN: West.

Fleishman, E.A. (1989). *Leadership Opinion Questionnaire: Examiner's manual.* Park Ridge, IL: Science Research Associates.

Gardner, H. (1983). *Frames of mind: The theory of multiple intelligences.* New York: Basic Books.

Georgoudi, M., & Rosnow, R.L. (1985). Notes toward a contextualist understanding of social psychology. *Personality and Social Psychology Bulletin, 11*(1), 5–22.

Gerstner, C.R., & Day, D.V. (1997). Meta-analytic review of leader-member exchange theory: correlates and construct issues. *Journal of Applied Psychology, 82,* 827–844.

Gough, H.G. (1987). *California Psychological Inventory administrator's guide.* Palo Alto, CA: Consulting Psychologists Press.

Graen, G., & Cashman, J.F. (1975). A role-making model of leadership in formal organizations: A developmental approach. In J.G. Hunt & L.L. Larson (Eds.), *Leadership frontiers* (pp. 143–165). Kent, OH: Kent State University Press.

Graen, G., Liden, R., & Hoel, W. (1982). Role of leadership in the employee withdrawal process. *Journal of Applied Psychology, 67*, 868–872.

Graen, G., Novak, M.A., & Sommerkamp, P. (1982). The effects of leader-member exchange and job design on productivity and satisfaction: Testing a dual attachment model. *Organizational Behavior and Human Performance, 30*, 109–131.

Graen, G., Orris, J., & Johnson, T. (1973). Role assimilation in a complex organization. *Journal of Vocational Behavior, 3*, 395–420.

Graen, G., & Schiemann, W. (1978). Leader-member agreement: A vertical dyad linkage approach. *Journal of Applied Psychology, 63*, 206–212.

Graen, G.B., & Uhl-Bien, M. (1995). Relationship-based approach to leadership: Development of leader-member exchange (LMX) theory of leadership over 25 years: Applying a multi-level multi-domain perspective. *Leadership Quarterly, 6*(2), 219–247.

Gratzinger, P.D., Warren, R.A., & Cooke, R.A. (1990). Psychological orientations and leadership: Thinking styles that differentiate between effective and ineffective managers. In K.E. Clark & M.B. Clark (Eds.), *Measures of leadership* (pp. 239–247). West Orange, NJ: Leadership Library of America.

Haga, W.J., Graen, G., & Dansereau, F. (1974). Professionalism and role making within a service organization. *American Sociological Review, 39*, 122–123.

Hall, J., & Williams, M.S. (1986). *Styles of Leadership Survey.* Woodlands, TX: Teleometrics International.

Hanges, P.J., & Dickson, M.W. (in press). The development and validation of scales measuring societal culture and culturally-shared implicit theories of leadership. In R.J. House, P.J. Hanges, M. Javidan, P.W. Dorfman, & V. Gupta (Eds.), *Culture, leadership, and organizations: The GLOBE study of 62 cultures.* Newbury Park, CA: Sage.

Hanges, P.J., Lord, R.G., Day, D.V., Sipe, W.P., Smith, W.C., & Brown, D.J. (1997). Leadership and gender bias: Dynamic measures and nonlinear modeling. In R.G. Lord (Chair), *Dynamic systems, leadership perceptions, and gender effects.* Symposium presented at the 12th Annual Conference of the Society for Industrial and Organizational Psychology.

Hater, J.J., & Bass, B.M. (1988). Supervisor's evaluations and subordinates' perceptions of transformational leadership. *Journal of Applied Psychology, 73*, 695–702.

Hersey, P., & Blanchard, K. (1982). *Management of organizational behavior: Utilizing human resources.* Englewood Cliffs, NJ: Prentice-Hall.

Hofstede, G. (1980). Motivation, leadership and organization: Do American theories apply abroad? *Organizational Dynamics, 8*(3), 42–63.

Hogan, J., & Hogan, R. (2002). Leadership and sociopolitical intelligence. In R.E. Riggio, S.E. Murphy, & F.J. Pirozzolo (Eds.), *Multiple intelligences and leadership* (pp. 75–88). Mahwah, NJ: Erlbaum.

Hollander, E.P. (1978). *Leadership dynamics: A practical guide to effective relationships.* New York: Free Press/Macmillan.

House, R.J. (1971). A path goal theory of leader effectiveness. *Administrative Science Quarterly, 16*, 321–338.

House, R.J. (1977). A 1976 theory of charismatic leadership. In J.G. Hunt & L.L. Larson (Eds.), *Leadership: The cutting edge* (pp. 189–207). Carbondale: Southern Illinois University Press.

House, R.J. (1996). Path-goal theory of leadership: Lessons, legacy and a reformulated theory. *The Leadership Quarterly, 7*(3), 323–352.

House, R.J., & Aditya, R.N. (1997). The social scientific study of leadership: Quo vadis? *Journal of Management, 23*, 409–473.

House, R.J., & Baetz, M.L. (1979) Leadership: Some empirical generalizations and new research directions. *Research In Organizational Behavior, 1*, 341–423.

House, R.J., Delbecq, A.L., & Taris, T. (1997). *Value based leadership: A theory and an empirical test* (Working paper). Reginald H. Jones Center for Strategic Management, Wharton School of Management.

House, R.J., Hanges, P.J., Javidan, M., Dorfman, P.W., & Gupta, V. (Eds.). (in press). *Culture, leadership, and organizations: The GLOBE study of 62 cultures.* Newbury Park, CA: Sage.

House, R.J., Hanges, P.J., Ruiz-Quintanilla, S.A., Dorfman, P.W., Javidan, M., Dickson, M.W., et al. (1999). Cultural influences on leadership and organizations: Project GLOBE. In W.H. Mobley, M.J. Gessner, & V. Arnold. (Eds.), *Advances in global leadership* (pp. 171–233). Stamford, CT: JAI Press.

House, R.J., & Mitchell, T.R. (1974). Path-goal theory of leadership. *Journal of Contemporary Business, 3*, 81–97.

House, R.J., & Podsakoff, P.M. (1994). Leadership effectiveness and future research direction. In G. Greenberg (Ed.), *Organizational behavior: The state of the science* (pp. 45–82). Hillsdale, NJ: Erlbaum.

House, R.J., & Shamir, B. (1993). Towards the integration of transformational, charismatic and visionary theories. In M.M. Chemers, & R. Ayman (Eds.). *Leadership theory and research: Perspectives and directions* (pp. 81–107). San Diego, CA: Academic Press.

House, R.J., Shane, S., & Herold, D. (1996). Rumors of the death of dispositional theory and research in Organizational Behavior are greatly exaggerated. *Academy of Management Review, 21*(1), 203–224.

House, R.J., Spangler, D., & Woycke, J. (1991). Personality and charisma in the U.S. presidency: A psychological theory of leadership effectiveness. *Administrative Science Quarterly, 36*, 364–396.

House, R.J., Wright, N., & Aditya, R.N. (1997). Cross-cultural research on organizational leadership: A critical analysis and a proposed theory. In P.C. Earley & M. Erez (Eds.), *New perspectives on international industrial/organizational psychology* «pp. 535–625). San Francisco: Jossey-Bass.

Howard, A., & Bray, D.W. (1990). Predictions of managerial success over long periods of time: Lessons from the management progress study. In K.E. Clark & M.B. Clark (Eds.), *Measures of leadership* (pp. 113–130). West Orange, NJ: Leadership Library of America.

Howell, J., & Avolio, B.J. (1993). Transformational leadership, transactional leadership, locus of control, and support for innovation: Key predictors of consolidated-business-unit performance. *Journal of Applied Psychology, 78*(4), 891–902.

Howell, J.M., & Frost, P.J. (1989). A laboratory study of charismatic leadership. *Organizational Behavior and Human Decision Processes, 43*(2), 243–269.

Howell, J.M., & Higgins, C. (1990). Champions of technological innovation. *Administrative Science Quarterly, 35,* 317–341.

Howell, J.M., & House, R.J. (1992). *Socialized and personalized charisma: An essay on the bright and dark sides of leadership.* Unpublished manuscript, School of Business Administration, The University of Western Ontario.

Hunter, J.E., & Schmidt, F.L. (1991). Correcting for sources of artificial variation across studies. In H. Cooper & L.V. Hedges (Eds.), *The handbook of research synthesis* (pp. 323–336). New York: Sage.

James, L.R., Demaree, R.G., & Wolf, G. (1984). Estimating within-group interrater reliability with and without response bias. *Journal of Applied Psychology, 69*(1), 85–98.

Kahn, R.L., & Katz, D. (1953). Leadership practices in relation to productivity and morale. In D. Cartwright & A. Zander (Eds.), *Group dynamics.* New York: Harper & Row.

Karnes, F.A., & Chauvin, J.C. (1985). *Leadership Skills Inventory: Administration manual.* East Aurora, NY: D.O.K..

Keller, T., & Danserau, F. (2000). The effects of adding items to scales: An illustrative case of LMX. *Organizational Research Methods, 4*(2), 131–143.

Kenny, D.A., & Hallmark, B.W. (1992). Rotation designs in leadership research. *Leadership Quarterly, 3*(1), 25–41.

Kenny, D.A., & Zaccaro, S.J. (1983). An estimate of the variance due to traits in leadership. *Journal of Applied Psychology, 68,* 678–685.

Kipnis, D. (1976). *The powerholders.* Chicago: University of Chicago Press.

Kipnis, D. (1984). The use of power in organizations and in interpersonal settings. In S. Oskamp (Ed.), *Applied Social Psychology Annual 5* (pp. 172–210). Beverly Hills: Sage.

Koene, H., Pennings, H., & Schreuder, M. (1992). Leadership, organizational cultures, and organizational outcomes. In K.E. Clark, M.B. Clark, & D.P. Campbell (Eds.), *The impact of leadership* (pp. 215–223). Greensboro, NC: The Center for Creative Leadership.

Koh, W.L., Terborg, J.R., & Steers, R.M. (1991, August). *The impact of transformational leadership on organizational commitment: Organizational citizenship behavior teacher satisfaction and student performance in Singapore.* Paper presented at the Academy of Management, Fontainbleu, FL.

Kouzes, J.M., & Posner, B.Z. (1987). *The leadership challenge: How to get extraordinary things done in organizations.* San Francisco: Jossey-Bass.

Lee, C., Asford, S.J., & Bobko, P. (1990). Interactive effects of "type A" behavior and perceived control on worker performance, job satisfaction, and somatic complaints. *Academy of Management Journal, 33,* 870–881.

Liden, R.C., & Arad, S. (1996). A power perspective of empowerment and work groups: Implications for human resources management research. *Research in Personnel and Human Resources Management, 14,* 205–251.

Liden, R.C., & Tewksbury, T.W. (1995). Empowerment and work teams. In G.R. Reffis, S.D. Rosen, & D.T. Barnum (Eds.), *Handbook of human resource management* (pp. 386–403). Cambridge, MA: Blackwell.

Likert, R. (1961). *New patterns of management.* New York: McGraw-Hill.

Lord, R.G., Binning, J.F., Rush, M.C., & Thomas, J.C. (1978). The effects of performance cues and leader behavior on questionnaire ratings of leadership behavior. *Organizational Behavior & Human Performance, 21*(1), 27–39.

Lord, R.G., DeVader, C.L., & Alliger, G.M. (1986). A meta-analysis of the relation between personality traits and leadership perceptions: An application of validity generalizations procedures. *Journal of Applied Psychology, 71*(3), 402–410.

Lord, R.G., Foti, R., & De Vader, C. (1984). A test of leadership categorization theory: Internal structure, information processing, and leadership perceptions. *Organizational Behavior and Human Performance, 34,* 343–378.

Lord, R.G., & Maher, K.J. (1991). *Leadership and information processing: Linking perception and performance.* Boston: Unwin Hyman.

Lord, F.M., & Novick, M.R. (1968). *Statistical theories of mental test scores.* Reading, MA: Addison-Wesley.

Lowe, K.B., Kroeck, K.G., & Sivasubramaniam, N. (1996). Effectiveness correlates of transformational and transactional leadership: A meta-analytic review of the MLQ literature. *Leadership Quarterly, 7*(3), 385–425.

Mann, F.C. (1965). Toward an understanding of the leadership role in formal organization. In R. Dubin, G.C. Homans, F.C. Mann, & D.C. Miller (Eds.), *Leadership and productivity.* San Francisco: Chandler.

Manz, C.C., & Sims, H.P. Jr. (1987). Leading workers to lead themselves: The external leadership of self-managed work teams. *Administrative Science Quarterly, 32,* 106–128.

Margerison, C., & Glube, R. (1979). Leadership decision-making: An empirical test of the Vroom and Yetton model. *Journal of Management Studies, 16,* 45–55.

McClane, W.E. (1991). Implications of member role differentiation: Analysis of a key concept in the LMX model of leadership. *Group and Organization Studies, 16*(1), 102–113.

McClelland, D.C. (1961). *The achieving society.* New York: Van Nostrand Reinhold.

McClelland, D.C. (1975). *Power: The inner experience.* New York: Irvington.

McClelland, D.C. (1985). *Human motivation.* Glenview, IL: Scott, Foresman.

McClelland, D.C., & Boyatzis, R.E. (1982). Leadership motive pattern and long-term success in management. *Journal of Applied Psychology, 67,* 737–743.

Miner, J.B., & Dachler, H.P. (1973). Personnel attitudes and motivations. Annual *Review of Psychology, 24,* 379–402.

Mischel, W. (1973). Toward a cognitive social learning reconceptualization of personality. *Psychological Review, 80,* 252–283.

Monson, T.C., Hesley, J.W., & Chernick, L. (1982). Specifying when personality traits can and cannot predict behavior: An alternative to abandoning the attempt to predict single act criteria. *Journal of Personality and Social Psychology, 3,* 385–499.

Nanus, B. (1992). *Visionary leadership—Creating a compelling sense of direction for your organization.* San Francisco: Jossey-Bass.

Nunnally, J.C. (1978). *Psychometric theory.* New York: McGraw-Hill.

Oakland, T., Falkenberg, B.A., & Oakland, C. (1996). Assessment of leadership in children, youth and adults. *Gifted Children Quarterly, 40*(3), 138–146.

Pascarella, S.V., & Lunenburg, F.C. (1988). A field test of Hersey and Blanchard's situational leadership theory in a school setting. *College Student Journal, 22*(1), 33–37.

Pereira, D. (1987). *Factors associated with transformational leadership in an Indian engineering firm.* Paper presented at Administrative Science Association of Canada, Vancouver.

Peters, L.H., Hartke, D.D., & Pohlman, J.T. (1985). Fiedler's contingency model of leadership: An application of the meta-analysis procedure of Schmidt and Hunter. *Psychological Bulletin, 97,* 274–285.

Pillai, R., & Meindl, J.R. (1991). The effects of a crisis on the emergence of charismatic leadership: A laboratory study. In *Best Paper Proceedings, Annual Meeting of the Academy of Management,* Miami, FL.

Posner, B.Z., & Kouzes, J.M. (1988). Development and validation of the Leadership Practices Inventory. *Educational and Psychological Measurement, 48*(2), 483–496.

Posner, B.Z., & Kouzes, J.M. (1993). Psychometric properties of the Leadership Practices Inventory-updated. *Educational and Psychological Measurement, 53*(1), 191–199.

Riggio, R.E., Murphy, S.E., & Pirozzolo, F.J. (Eds.). (2002). *Multiple intelligences and leadership.* Mahwah, NJ: Erlbaum.

Roberts, N.C. (1985). Transforming leadership: A process of collective action. *Human Relations, 38,* 1023–1046.

Rosenthal, R. (1991). *Meta-analytic procedures for social sciences.* Newbury Park, CA: Sage.

Rosnow, R.L. (1978). The prophetic vision of Giambattista Vico: Implications for the state of social psychological theory. *Journal of Personality and Social Psychology, 36*(11), 1322–1331.

Rosnow, R.L. (1986). Shotter, Vico and fallibilistic indeterminacy. *British Journal of Social Psychology, 25,* 215–216.

Rosnow, R.L., Skleder, A.A., Jaeger, M.E., & Rind, B. (1994). Intelligence and the epistemics of interpersonal acumen: Testing some implications of H. Gardner's theory. *Intelligence, 19,* 93–116.

Rush, M.C., Thomas, J.C., & Lord, R.G. (1977). Implicit leadership theory: A potential threat to leader description questionnaires. *Organizational Behavior and Human Performance, 20,* 93–110.

Sashkin, M. (1988) The visionary leader. In J.A. Conger & R.A. Kanungo (Eds.), *Charismatic leadership: The elusive factor in organizational effectiveness* (pp. 122–160). San Francisco: Jossey-Bass.

Sashkin, M., & Burke, W.W. (1990). Understanding and assessing organizational leadership. In K.E. Clark & M.B. Clark (Eds.), *Measures of leadership* (pp. 297–325). West Orange, NJ: Leadership Library of America.

Scandura, T., & Graen, G. (1984). Moderating effects of initial leader-member exchange status on the effects of a leadership intervention. *Journal of Applied Psychology, 69,* 428–436.

Schneider, B. (1983). Interactional psychology & organizational behavior. In L.L. Cummings & B.M. Staw (Eds.), *Research in organizational behavior* (Vol. 5, pp. 1–31). Greenwich, CT: JAI Press.

Schriesheim, C.A., Castro, S.L., & Cogliser, C.C. (1999). Leader-member exchange (LMX) research: A comprehensive review of theory, measurement and data analytic practices. *Leadership Quarterly, 10*(1), 63–113.

Schriesheim, C.A., & Kerr, S. (1977). Theories and measures of leadership: A critical appraisal of present and future directions. In J.C. Hunt & L.L. Larson (Eds.), *Leadership: The cutting edge* (pp. 9–45). Carbondale: Southern Illinois University Press.

Schriesheim, C.A., Neider, L.L., Scandura, T.A., & Tepper, B.J. (1992). Development and preliminary validation of a new scale (LMX-6) to measure leader-member exchange in organizations. *Educational and Psychological Measurement, 52,* 135–147.

Simon, H.A. (1987). Making management decisions: The role of intuition and emotion, *Academy of Management Executive, 1,* 57–64.

Simonton, D.K. (1987). Presidential inflexibility and veto behavior: Two individual-situational interactions. *Journal of Personality, 55*(1), 1–18.

Sipe, W.P., & Hanges, P.J. (1997). Reframing the glass ceiling: A catastrophe model of changes in the perception of women as leaders. In R.G. Lord (Chair), *Dynamic systems, leadership perceptions, and gender effects.* Symposium presented at the 12th Annual Conference of the Society for Industrial and Organizational Psychology.

Spangler, W.D., & House, R.J. (1991). Presidential effectiveness and the leadership motive profile. *Journal of Personality and Social Psychology, 60*(3), 439–455.

Sparks, C.P. (1990). Testing for management potential. In K.E. Clark & M.B. Clark (Eds.), *Measures of leadership* (pp. 103–111). West Orange, NJ: Leadership Library of America.

Staw, B.M., Sandelands, L.E., & Dutton, J.E. (1981). Threat-rigidity effects in organizational behavior: A multilevel analysis. *Administrative Science Quarterly, 26,* 501–524.

Sternberg, R.J., & Wagner, R.K. (Eds.). (1988). *Practical intelligence: Nature and origins of competence in the everyday world.* New York: Cambridge University Press.

Stogdill, R.M. (1948). Personal factors associated with leadership: A survey of the literature. *Journal of Psychology, 25,* 35–71.

Stogdill, R.M. (1974). *Handbook of leadership: A survey of theory and research.* New York: Free Press.

Stogdill, R.M., & Coons, A.E. (1957). *Leader behavior: Its description and measurement.* Columbus: Ohio State University, Bureau of Business Research.

Strube, M.J., & Garcia, J.E. (1981). A meta-analytical investigation of Fiedler's contingency model of leadership effectiveness. *Psychological Bulletin, 90,* 307–321.

Trice, H.M., & Beyer, J.M. (1986). Charisma and its routinization in two social movement organizations. In B.M. Staw & L.L. Cummings (Eds.), *Research in organizational behavior* (Vol. 8, pp. 113–164). Greenwich, CT: JAI Press.

Vecchio, R.P. (1985). Predicting employee turnover from Leader-Member Exchange: A failure to replicate. *Academy of Management Journal, 28*(2), 478–485.

Vecchio, R.P. (1987). Situational leadership theory: An examination of a prescriptive theory. *Journal of Applied Psychology, 72*(3), 444–451.

Vecchio, R.P., & Gobdel, B.C. (1984). The vertical dyad linkage model of leadership: Problems and prospects. *Organizational Behavior and Human Performance, 34,* 5–20.

Vecchio, R.P., Griffeth, R.W., & Hom, P.W. (1986). The predictive utility of the vertical dyad linkage approach. *Journal of Social Psychology, 126,* 617–625.

Vecchio, R.P., & Norris, W.R. (1996). Predicting employee turnover from performance, satisfaction and leader-member exchange. *Journal of Business and Psychology, 49,* 436–458.

Vroom, V.H., & Jago, A.G. (1988). *The new leadership: Managing participation in organizations.* Upper Saddle River, NJ: Prentice-Hall.

Vroom, V.H., & Yetton, P.W. (1973). *Leadership and decision-making.* Pittsburgh, PA: University of Pittsburgh Press.

Wakabayashi, M., & Graen, G. (1984). The Japanese career progress study: A 7-year follow-up. *Journal of Applied Psychology, 69,* 603–614.

Wakabayashi, M., Graen, G., & Uhl-Bien, M. (1990). Generalizability of the hidden investment hypothesis among line managers in five leading Japanese corporations. *Human Relations, 43,* 1099–1116.

Waldman, D., House, R.J., & Ramirez, G. (1996). *A replication of the effects of U.S. CEO charismatic leadership on firm profitability under conditions of certainty and uncertainty based on Canadian executives.* Unpublished manuscript, the Wharton School, University of Pennsylvania.

Waldman, D., Ramirez, G., House, R.J., & Puranam, P. (1996). *The effects of U.S. CEO leader behavior on firm profits under conditions of environmental certainty and uncertainty: A longitudinal investigation* (Working paper). Reginald Jones Center for Strategic Management, Wharton School of Management.

Weiss, D.J., Dawis, R.V., England, G.W., & Lofquist, L.H. (1967). *Manual for the Minnesota Satisfaction Questionnaire.* Minneapolis, MN: Industrial Relations Center, University of Minnesota.

Winter, D.G. (1973). *The power motive.* New York: Free Press.

Winter, D.G. (1978). *Navy leadership and management competencies: Convergence among tests, interviews, and performance ratings.* Boston: McBer & Company.

Winter, D.G. (1991). A motivational model of leadership: Predicting long-term management success from TAT measures of power motivation and responsibility. *Leadership Quarterly, 2*(2), 67–80.

Wofford, J.C., & Liska, L.Z. (1993). Path-goal theories of leadership: A meta-analysis. *Journal of Management, 19,* 857–876.

Yammarino, F.J., & Bass, B.M. (1990). Transformational leadership and multiple levels of analysis. *Human Relations, 43,* 975–995.

Yukl, G. (1993). A retrospective on Robert House's 1976 theory of charismatic leadership and recent revisions. *Leadership Quarterly, 4*(3/4), 367–373.

Yukl, G.A., Wall, S., & Lepsinger, R. (1990). Preliminary report on validation of the Managerial Practices Survey. In K.E. Clark & M.B. Clark (Eds.), *Measures of leadership* (pp. 223–237). West Orange, NJ: Leadership Library of America.

Zaccaro, S.J. (2002). Organizational leadership and social intelligence. In R.E. Riggio, S.E. Murphy, & F.J. Pirozzolo (Eds.), *Multiple intelligences and leadership* (pp. 29–54). Mahwah, NJ: Erlbaum.

Zaccaro, S.J., Foti, R.J., & Kenny, D.A. (1991). Self-monitoring and trait-based variance is leadership: An investigation of leader flexibility across multiple group situations. *Journal of Applied Psychology, 76,* 308–315.

Zaleznik, A. (1977). Managers and leaders: Are they different? *Harvard Business Review, 55*(3), 67–78.

# BIOGRAPHICAL, EXPERIENCE DATA, AND INTERVIEWS

# CHAPTER 15

# Biodata

GARNETT S. STOKES AND LISA A. COOPER

## BIODATA OVERVIEW

Biodata measures (also known as biographical data, autobiographical information, and life histories) are instruments assessing an individual's previous life experiences, usually with a focus on targeting those previous experiences that predict future behaviors of interest. Past behavior is "hypothesized to capture causal events or correlates of causal events that influence job candidates' future behavior" (Dean, Russell, & Muchinsky, 1999, p. 260). Early uses of biodata included the practice of scoring and weighting application blank information, and although scored essays or resumes continue to be used (Harvey-Cook, 2000), the need to collect and score a wider range of experiences in a more objective and standardized manner has led to a multiple-choice format consisting of questions that require individuals to recall and report typical behaviors in referent situations. Many practitioners and researchers hold different views about the structure, content, and scoring of biodata items, and the lack of a single, widely held definition of biodata has created some confusion among those who might consider using it for selection. What is undisputed is the extent to which biodata forms tend to be multidimensional, capturing behaviors, attitudes, skills, values, and interests that cut across cognitive and "noncognitive" domains. Table 15.1 provides examples of biodata items that could easily be classified within different individual difference domains.

Although widely accepted as a valid predictor with low adverse impact for many jobs and criteria, and described by Fleishman (1988) as being among the most promising avenues for new knowledge generation in personnel selection, biodata measures continue to be underused by businesses (Hammer & Kleiman, 1988; Ryan, McFarland, Baron, &

**TABLE 15.1   Examples of Biodata Items Across Individual Difference Domains**

| Domain | Biodata Items |
| --- | --- |
| Cognitive Ability | What grades did you receive in your high school science classes? |
| | What was your academic rank in your high school graduating class? |
| Personality | How often did you attend social events during your last year of high school? |
| | During high school, how sensitive were you to criticism? |
| Vocational Interests | During college, how often did you read magazines about computer technology? |
| | In high school, how much did you enjoy your classes in mathematics? |
| Values | During high school, how important was it to you to be regarded as successful? |
| | In college, what was the extent of your involvement in national political issues? |

Page, 1999; van Rijn, 1992). In this chapter we address issues and controversies associated with the development and use of biodata, beginning with a discussion of the history of biodata and its utility in selection, including validity evidence, applicability to jobs and criteria, and adverse impact. Next we discuss methodological issues such as item construction, scale construction, and scoring that are relevant for applying biodata methodology. Finally, we introduce areas of special concern in biodata form development and use.

## Brief History and Primary Theorists

The applied use of life histories to distinguish between job applicants evolved primarily in the insurance industry and was first mentioned in 1894 at a meeting of the Chicago Underwriters. Colonel Thomas L. Peters of the Washington Life Insurance Company of Atlanta suggested that the selection of life insurance agents could be improved through asking applicants a series of standard questions about relevant prior experiences in the life insurance industry and elsewhere (Ferguson, 1961). The quantification or "weighting" of responses to questions that distinguished good performers from poor performers soon followed. Goldsmith's (1922) article providing explicit descriptions of analyses and weighting procedures for identifying successful salesmen was followed by a number of articles advancing the empirical methods and expanding the application to a variety of occupations (Kenagy & Yoakum, 1925; Manson, 1925; Viteles, 1932). The multiple-choice format that emerged during World War II advanced the technique to what most researchers commonly refer to today as biodata. In this format, individuals are presented with standardized, multiple-choice questions concerning their past behaviors and experiences. Scores are typically obtained by weighting responses that differentiate good performers from poor performers, a method commonly referred to as empirical keying. In 1947, Guilford and Lacey found that an empirically keyed set of multiple-choice questions predicted success in air force training programs. Numerous studies followed that demonstrated the successful application of biodata in both the military (Levine & Zachert, 1951; Parish & Drucker, 1957; Roy, Brueckel, & Drucker, 1954) and civilian sectors (England, 1961, 1971).

Empirically scored biodata forms were highly successful for many years, yet an increasing focus on theory and content/construct issues led to serious questions about their value. Similar to criticisms made of the Minnesota Multiphasic Personality Inventory (MMPI) and early versions of the Strong Interest Inventory (Rogers, 1995), biodata measures were regarded to be part of a "dustbowl empiricism" that contributed little to theory and understanding in psychology. In response to such criticisms, research on biodata during the last two

decades has become more theory based (Dean et al., 1999; Stokes, Mumford, & Owens, 1994).

William A. Owens conducted the most comprehensive and influential investigations of life history information and its meaning. Considered the "granddaddy" of biodata, Owens's Developmental-Integrative (D-I) model served as a framework for investigating subgroups of individuals with similar adolescent life experiences as college freshmen and following them from college into adulthood. Owens's extensive longitudinal work is best documented in a monograph (Owens & Schoenfeldt, 1979) and a book (Mumford, Stokes, & Owens, 1990). Owens's model was later replaced by the ecology model, developed by one of Owens's students, Michael Mumford, and his colleagues. Shown in Figure 15.1, the ecology model is an interactional model of adult development in which the dynamic interchange between the characteristics of persons and the situations to which individuals are exposed lead ultimately to individual differences in life experiences. The focus of the ecology model is on the motivational influences that provide the pattern of situations selected by individuals. Building on work in developmental psychology, the ecology model "views the individual as an active, purposeful entity, who through learning, cognition, and action seeks to maximize personal adaptation in a world of shifting environmental opportunities" (Mumford & Stokes, 1992, p. 77). The ecology model focuses not only on individual differences but on the processes that influence individuals' choices (Dean et al., 1999). The model has served to provide biodata researchers with a framework for biodata item generation that focuses on individuals' choices, reactions, behaviors, and outcomes related to situations in which job-relevant behaviors are likely to occur.

Although several important studies have been published in the last few years, the *Biodata Handbook,* edited by Stokes et al. (1994), remains the most comprehensive source for information about biodata. Also notable is the research of Fred Mael, who has integrated social identity theory with the ecology model to provide some theoretical basis for biodata's predictive ability (Mael, 1991; Mael & Ashforth, 1995; Mael & Hirsch, 1993). Finally, Craig Russell continues to pursue a theory of biodata in his efforts to create a model of life experience learning (Russell, 1994; Dean et al., 1999).

## Validity

The predictive validity of biodata keys has been established in numerous studies. Reviews by Asher (1972), Ghiselli (1973), Mumford and Owens (1987), Mumford and Stokes (1992), Owens (1976), and Reilly and Chao (1982) have indicated that empirically keyed scales typically yield cross-validities in the .30–.40 range for a variety of criteria. Hunter

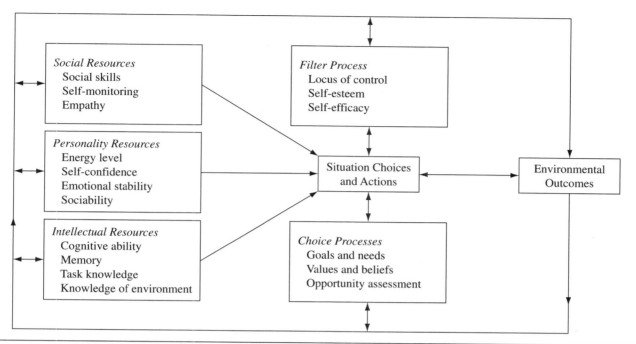

**Figure 15.1**    The ecology model.
*Note.* Adapted from Dean, M.A., Russell, C.J., & Muchinsky, P.M. (1999). Life experiences and performance prediction: Toward a theory of biodata. *Research in Personnel and Human Resources Management, 17,* 245–281.

and Hunter (1984) meta-analyzed cross-validated biodata keys across four criterion variables to determine the average validity coefficients for supervisor ratings ($r = 0.37$), promotions ($r = 0.26$), training success ($r = 0.30$), and tenure ($r = 0.26$). More recently, Bobko, Roth, and Potosky (1999) estimated the uncorrected correlation between biodata and job performance to be .28. Few reviews of rational or factorial scales have been published, but where data are available, most reveal validity coefficients similar to those of empirical keys (Hough & Paullin, 1994; Stokes & Searcy, 1999). Studies that have compared empirical scoring methods to rational scoring methods have found similar coefficients when estimates are cross-validated (Stokes & Searcy, 1999).

Validity estimates established through concurrent study designs have been found to be higher than estimates obtained in predictive study designs (Barge & Hough, 1986; Bliesener, 1996); however, Schmitt, Gooding, Noe, and Kirsch (1984) did not find differences between predictive and concurrent validities in their evaluation of various predictor tests. The conflicting results suggest caution in the validation paradigm pursued for biodata form development, and this issue is addressed later in the chapter.

## Incremental Validity

Although validity is often of primary concern, it is not unusual for biodata forms to be combined with other instruments to make personnel decisions. When this is the case, incremental validity is of greater concern than the validity coefficient alone.

### Cognitive Ability

As measures of typical performance, as opposed to maximum performance, biodata generally have low correlations with traditional tests of abilities and skills and often account for unique variance when combined with traditional measures. Many studies (Allworth & Hesketh, 1999; Dean & Russell, 1998; Karas & West, 1999; Mael & Ashforth, 1995; Mount, Witt, & Barrick, 2000; Stokes, Toth, Searcy, Stroupe, & Carter, 1999) have established that biodata scales, both empirically keyed and rationally keyed, can account for significant incremental variance beyond that captured by general mental ability (GMA) for a variety of criteria. One exception in the literature is the work reported by Schmidt and Hunter (1998), who concluded that biodata measures add only a 2% increase in validity over cognitive ability in the prediction of supervisory ratings of job performance and no increase for overall performance in job training programs. Their study led to the conclusion that biodata measures are among the least optimal alternative predictors to use in conjunction with GMA. However, Schmidt and Hunter's study reported a considerably higher relationship between GMA and biodata than what has been found by other researchers (Bobko et al., 1999;

Gandy, Dye, & MacLane, 1994; Pulakos & Schmitt, 1996; Schmitt, Rogers, Chan, Sheppard, & Jennings, 1997; Stokes et al., 1999), suggesting that Schmidt and Hunter's (1998) results greatly underestimate the incremental validity of biodata measures.

*Personality*

McManus and Kelly (1999) and Mount et al. (2000) demonstrated the incremental validity of biodata over measures of the Big Five dimensions of personality. McManus and Kelly (1999) replicated and extended the work of Mael and Hirsch (1993) by examining the relationship between independent biodata scales and measures of the Big Five. Their biodata instrument included measures of insurance-related experiences, number of contacts in the insurance industry, method of recruiting or knowledge of the position, financial and occupational stability, and commitment to present job situation. Correlations between the biodata instrument and the personality measures were not significant. Hierarchical regression analysis was used to evaluate the incremental validity of biodata scores over the Big Five dimensions. The change in $R^2$ from .16 (for the personality measures alone) to .23 for the combined set of personality and biodata demonstrated that the biodata could account for variance above that accounted for by the personality variables.

Mount et al. (2000) examined whether or not empirically keyed, cross-validated biodata scales would account for incremental variance in four performance criteria above that contributed by measures of the Big Five and GMA. Separate biodata scales were developed for each of four performance dimensions. For both the quantity and quality of work and retention probability criteria, the criterion-specific biodata scales added significant incremental validity over that accounted for by tenure (to control for incumbent experience), GMA, and the personality variables. A biodata problem-solving scale accounted for marginally significant incremental validity over tenure, GMA, and personality for the problem-solving criterion. The amount of incremental variance accounted for by the biodata scales was 5% or more for three of the dependent measures.

*Interviews*

Although the content areas covered in an interview may overlap with that assessed in a typical biodata form (and biodata can assess such content in a more economical fashion), Bobko et al.'s (1999) estimate of the relationship between biodata and interviews was .16, suggesting that the two methods yield independent information. Dalessio and Silverhart (1994) ex-

plored the combined use of a structured interview with a biodata inventory developed and used for selecting insurance agents and found that both the biodata instrument and the structured interview made a significant contribution toward the prediction of the interviewer's final decision to continue the selection process and the prediction of a candidate's 12-month survival.

*Summary*

When combined with measures frequently used in employee selection, biodata clearly can improve the prediction of job performance. It should be stressed, however, that depending on its content, biodata instruments could have substantial correlations with measures of cognitive ability and personality. Consequently, it is essential to understand the constructs assessed by any individual biodata instrument, particularly when it is to be included in a selection battery or in meta-analytic studies.

## Utility

Concern for demonstrating the usefulness of selection methods to personnel managers and decision makers has led to the development of many different ways of conducting utility analyses for demonstrating costs and benefits (see Mitchell, 1994, for an overview). Dalessio and Silverhart (1994) used regression analysis to demonstrate that a one score unit increase on a biodata instrument resulted in an approximate gain of $215 in monthly commissions for insurance salespersons. Conte, Tesluk, and Jacobs (1996) demonstrated the utility of biodata for predicting safety and attendance for bus drivers. Using a .10 selection ratio, attendance of those who would have been selected based on their biodata score (top 10%) was compared with those who would not have been selected (bottom 90%). With the biodata and a .10 selection ratio, a bus property could expect to gain more than 14 days per operator per year. Assuming that each absence costs $140/day/driver, the savings to a medium-size city of 100 drivers hired per year was estimated to be $202,720 in the first year. A similar procedure was followed for demonstrating the utility of the biodata predictor for bus driver safety. Again, based on a .10 selection ratio, there was an estimated reduction of 34 accidents/100 operators/year. Assuming that each accident costs $12,000 (a lower bound estimate), using the safety predictor would result in a savings of $408,000 per year.

As Schmidt and Hunter (1998) noted, the economic gains from improved hiring are generally large and are directly proportional to the size of the increase in validity resulting from the change from the old to the new selection method. As previously discussed, biodata instruments typically have good predictive validity, as well as incremental validity, and are likely to have good utility for organizations that incorporate them into their personnel decision making. In particular, biodata have been found to be valid measures when traditional predictors, such as cognitive ability tests and personality measures, have not (Jacobs & Conte, 1996; Vinchur, Schippmann, Switzer, & Roth, 1998). Biodata may have greater applicability, and hence utility, for jobs that do not typically use extensive selection processes or for criteria in which traditional measures have proven to be unsuccessful.

## Generalizability

Because empirically scored biodata keys are referenced against a specific criterion and reference group, biodata have often been considered situationally specific (Dreher & Sackett, 1983; Hunter & Hunter, 1984; Thayer, 1977). However, several studies (Brown, 1981; Buel, Albright, & Glennon, 1966; Campbell, Dunnette, Lawler, & Weick, 1970) have demonstrated generalizability across different organizations and job functions.

Much of the research investigating the generalizability of biodata has focused on keys specifically developed to be applicable across situations. In 1970, Campbell et al. developed a key for identifying managers in five affiliates of Standard Oil of New Jersey. By focusing on the core functions of the management positions and ignoring unique functions across specialty areas, they were able to develop a biodata key that generalized. Rothstein, Schmidt, Erwin, Owens, and Sparks (1990) developed and validated a biodata key for selecting first-line supervisors in 79 different organizations. Items that were related to the criteria across multiple organizations were retained for the final instrument, referred to as the Supervisory Profile Record (SPR). In a validity generalization study, the mean true validity of the SPR was found to be .36 with a standard deviation of .08 and with a 90% credibility value of .26.

Gandy et al. (1994) developed the Individual Achievement Record (IAR), a biodata form used as a component in the selection of entry-level nonsupervisory positions in over 100 professional and administrative occupations across most federal agencies in the United States. Half of the total sample of 6,300 obtained from 900 servicing personnel offices of 35 agencies was used for developing a scoring key based on the relationship between item responses and a "job-generic" supervisory performance appraisal form. Results of five separate meta-analyses (105 occupations, 6 occupational families, 98 occupations represented in small samples, 7 occupations with large samples, and 28 agencies) supported the general-

izability of a common scoring key. The sample-size-weighted mean validity coefficients across the five different categories ranged from .29 to .31. The 90% credibility values ranged from .19 (for small sample occupations) to .30 (for agencies).

More recently, Carlson, Scullen, Schmidt, Rothstein, and Erwin (1999) demonstrated that the use of multiple organization development and keying is not necessary to obtain generalizability. Items were selected from a preexisting research instrument developed by the Early Identification of Management Potential (EIMP) research program sponsored by Standard Oil of New Jersey. Items were selected by EIMP researchers based on their scoring key weights to two criteria of management performance: success (position and salary) and potential (rankings of highest likely job grade) within a single organization. The final instrument, referred to as the Management Profile Record (MPR), consisted of 196 items that could be grouped into five rational, descriptive (i.e., not scored) scales: Developmental Influences, Academic Achievements, Present Self-Concept, Present Family and Social Orientation, and Present Work Orientation. A meta-analytic study of 24 different organizations in varied industries identified the mean observed validity of the MPR scores for predicting rate of managerial progress to be $r = .48$. The estimated true validity, with corrections for range variation and criterion unreliability, was .53; and the 90% credibility value for true validities was .47.

Carlson et al. (1999) concluded that in addition to ensuring an adequate sample size, three additional factors are important to the development of generalizable biodata inventories. The first is a reasonable expectation that the validity of the instrument will be applicable to other populations and situations. Second, the validity and reliability of the criterion for keying items are important. Carlson et al. (1999) placed considerable emphasis on the development of a criterion measure, level of progression within organization, which they believed would be a more reliable and valid measure of job performance than supervisory ratings. The third factor concerns establishing and retaining only those items that have a demonstrated relationship to the criterion and have a sound rational or behavioral justification for their validity.

Although Rothstein et al. (1990) and Carlson et al. (1999) demonstrated that biodata can be generalizable, it should be kept in mind that the development of biodata instruments is still highly dependent on both the samples and criteria. With measures of ability and aptitude, sufficient research exists to provide evidence that different instruments are indeed measuring the same or highly similar constructs (Schmidt & Rothstein, 1994). However, the same cannot be said about biodata forms, which typically measure vastly different constructs. The generalizability of rationally developed scales in which there is a focus on the constructs measured has received less attention than empirically scored keys (Mumford, 1999). It would be expected that construct-oriented measures would exhibit greater generalizability than empirically scored biodata forms because of their focus on composite factors or dimensions rather than items.

## Biodata's Applicability to Jobs and Functions

Biodata have been found to be valid predictors for a wide variety of jobs, and there is reason to believe that biodata instruments could be developed for virtually any job, provided a sufficient sample can be obtained. Although valid biodata inventories have been found for jobs as diverse as bus drivers and scientists, several literature reviews reveal more studies within sales, clerical, military, and management/ supervision occupations (Barge & Hough, 1986; Mumford & Owens, 1987; Reilly & Chao, 1982). Mumford and Owens (1987) found the average validity coefficients for these occupational areas ranged from .34 to .48. Biodata have also been found to be valid predictors for skilled/unskilled laborers (median $rs$ = .11 and .10, respectively; Barge & Hough, 1986) and factory workers (average $r$ = .46; Mumford & Owens, 1987). Pannone (1994) concluded that biodata are underused and underreported for blue-collar jobs. Blue-collar occupations typically include hourly workers employed in manufacturing, repair, and construction industries, such as carpenters, mechanics, electricians, and machine operators. Although the development and scoring of biodata for blue-collar occupations is not unlike applications to professional occupations, Pannone discussed several issues that deserve special consideration, including face validity, level of education, unionization, criteria, and sample sizes. Blue-collar jobs are frequently performed by small groups organized by specific function areas, which places limitations on the applicability of the various development and scoring methods (described later). However, this is an issue that many organizations encounter, as many jobs, including both professional and nonprofessional, do not have the number of incumbents or applicants that are required to develop and validate a biodata inventory. Consequently, use of consortium data has long been recommended (Gandy et al., 1994).

## Criteria

In addition to being applicable for a wide range of jobs, biodata have also been validated for many performance indicators of interest to organizations. Research by Reilly and Chao (1982), Barge and Hough (1986), Hunter and Hunter (1984), and Schmitt et al. (1984) reveals that biodata are particularly useful for predicting training success ($rs$ ranging from .25 to .39), proficiency ratings ($rs$ ranging from .32 to .37), and wages ($rs$ ranging from .34 to .53). Somewhat lower validity coefficients are found when predicting tenure ($rs$ from .26 to .32) and production data ($rs$ ranging from .21 to .46). Biodata forms have also been useful for a number of adjustment criteria such as substance abuse, delinquency, unfavorable discharge, and promotion and status change ($rs$ ranging from .20 to .27). In a meta-analytic study of predictors of sales performance, Vinchur et al. (1998) found a validity coefficient of .52 for ratings of sales success and .28 for actual sales criterion data—although they caution against overinterpretation of their results due to the small number of studies included in the analysis. Biodata have also been successfully developed and applied to less frequently studied criteria, such as occupational discontinuity, integrity, safety/accidents, job satisfaction, and team performance (Stokes & Cooper, 1994).

## Special Concerns

In evaluating the value of biodata forms for selection, special attention must be given to issues of adverse impact and criterion development.

### Adverse Impact

Biodata measures tend to have low adverse impact and are among the most favorable of assessment techniques for women, minorities, and older applicants (Mitchell, 1994; Reilly & Warech, 1989). Reilly and Chao (1982) summarized the results of 10 studies that reported race and ethnic group differences and concluded that the validity and fairness of biodata can be expected to hold across racial groups, though several researchers have noted differences in empirical validities for men and women (Hogan, 1994). In a recent review of federal court cases regarding selection devices, Terpstra, Mohamed, and Kethley (1999) found no challenges to biographical information blanks in the 158 district and appellate court cases they reviewed. However, information regarding the number of challenges to biodata instruments that may have been filed but did not proceed to federal court was not presented.

Although biodata generally provide unbiased and valid predictions across various racial and ethnic groups, Hogan (1994) and Mumford and Stokes (1992) cautioned that strictly adhering to a "blind" empirical approach can lead to the selection of items that may be correlated with race, ethnicity, and sex. Owens (1976) suggested rationally screening items during the development process to decrease the likelihood of selecting items with subgroup differences. However, because many culturally based response differences may be subtle, advance screening may not remove all potentially problematic items. Schmitt and Pulakos (1998) recently investigated race and ethnic differences in responses to rationally developed biodata scales and individual biodata items. Their subgroup analyses revealed many scales and/or items that had positive and likely useful validities for the White subgroup, yet were zero and sometimes negative for the ethnic-minority subgroups. They caution against the overinterpretation of their findings, but their results do point to the potential for greater racial and ethnic differences than previously thought.

Because biodata forms tend to be multidimensional, it is possible that some measured constructs will exhibit group differences. Certainly, it is important to examine biodata forms for potential adverse impact, and particularly so when the constructs being measured are closely related to constructs in which group differences are common.

### Criterion Development

Because the scoring of an empirically keyed biodata measure is structured by the criterion of interest, extensive evidence for the reliability and validity of the criterion is a necessary component to developing and interpreting biodata. However, criterion development has generally not received sufficient focus, even though many criterion measures may be deficient, contaminated, or biased. Even a well-developed item that reflects an antecedent of some aspect of performance will not be retained in an empirical key if the criterion measure fails to fully capture the performance domain in question, resulting in the exclusion of relevant development influences and misleading inferences concerning individual performance (Mumford & Owens, 1987). Because the scoring of empirical keys is always framed in reference to a particular type of performance within a particular sample, limitations are placed on the interpretability of the key (Mumford, 1999). Of course, the predictive power of *any* instrument will decline with changes in the nature of the criterion. Biodata form development requires a thorough assessment of the criteria of interest, and a study conducted with the U.S. Department of Labor (Stokes et al., 1999) provides a good example of extensive criterion development.

### Overview Summary

Biodata measures have a long history of successfully predicting job performance across a variety of job families, and biodata forms tend to significantly increase the usefulness of many existing selection processes. Recent research supports the possibility of creating biodata forms that can generalize across organizations, jobs, and criteria. Although adverse impact tends to be low for biodata, subjective and statistical analysis to examine group differences is an important step in creating a biodata measure.

## DEVELOPING A BIODATA MEASURE

Developing a biodata form requires dealing with two major methodological issues: (1) the construction and screening of biodata items and (2) biodata key development and validation. Both item construction and validation require reliable and valid job information and criteria. Knowing the specific use of the biodata inventory and the criteria it is designed to predict is an essential first step in the development of any biodata inventory.

### Item Construction and Screening

In 1976, Owens noted that "biodata items are much more likely to validate if they are knowledgeably beamed at a specific target" (p. 614). This suggests that biodata items should be written to have at least a logical, if not theoretical, connection to the criterion of interest. However, researchers and practitioners have few sources for existing items and limited guidelines for generating new biodata items. Mumford and Owens's (1987) review of biodata methodology was the first comprehensive source to provide specific recommendations for developing biodata items. The first step involves providing a definition of both the jobs involved and the criteria of interest. Obtaining an adequate understanding of the jobs and criteria usually requires some type of job analysis.

### Job Analysis and Biodata Form Development

Fine and Cronshaw (1994) discussed the role of job analysis in developing and validating biodata and noted the extent to which formal job analysis information has been underused by biodata practitioners and researchers. The choice of a job analysis strategy is often determined by the following factors: (1) the nature of the job and its requirements; (2) the applicant pool (experienced or inexperienced); (3) the intended development/validation strategy (e.g., empirical keying or construct-oriented); and (4) the criterion of interest (e.g., turnover, accidents, general job performance). Job analysis has typically been used to identify the environment in which performance takes place and to determine the attributes and behaviors that distinguish successful from unsuccessful performers.

Because most biodata validation is accomplished through criterion-related and/or construct-related strategies, there has been little emphasis on how job analysis results can be used to write items with a focus toward content validation. One exception is Fine and Cronshaw's (1994) application of a content-oriented strategy that used Functional Job Analysis (FJA) to develop clearly job-relevant biodata items. Three types of biodata items were developed to assess: (1) specific experiences that closely matched the behaviors required on the job; (2) generalized experiences that corresponded to tasks performed on the job; and (3) adaptive skills required by the job that could have been learned in previous life experiences. Many formal job analysis methods, such as FJA, are developed from theoretical frameworks of the performance domain and as such can lead to the development of life history items that are oriented around the core components of job performance. Fine and Cronshaw suggested that using the adaptive, functional, and specific content skills determined by FJA can be particularly useful for enhancing the theoretical understanding of how people choose particular jobs and why they perform well or poorly in them.

Because job analysis methods provide different types of information about the job, the methods vary in their usefulness for generating biodata items. Ash (1982) classified the major methods of job analyses as task based, attribute based, and behavior based. Although successfully used by Pannone (1984) and Levine and Zachert (1951), a task-based approach may not be as useful as an attribute-based approach for a job in which the specific skills or abilities are acquired on the job. Because the applicant pool may be inexperienced, questions pertaining to prior work experiences will not be as informative as those that assess the prior abilities, skills, and other attributes needed to acquire the job-specific skills.

Fine and Cronshaw (1994) pointed out that many formal job analysis methods fail to provide all the information that may be needed to develop and validate biodata items, which may contribute to its underutilization as a source for generating biodata items. Hough (1984) used the critical incident technique to develop an accomplishment record, and worker-oriented job analysis systems, such as Fleishman's (1972, 1975) Ability Requirements Scales, have successfully been used to generate specific constructs to be measured with biodata items (Mumford, Cooper, & Schemmer, 1983). Using information from multiple job analysis sources in the development of biodata inventories has great potential for identifying life experiences that distinguish successful performers from unsuccessful performers.

## Other Sources of Information for Biodata Form Development

In addition to some use of formal job analysis procedures, practitioners have relied on less formal methods, such as in-

terviews of job incumbents or supervisors, to obtain information about the kinds of life experiences they feel lead to successful job performance. Mumford and Owens (1987) also identified five additional sources of information for constructing biodata items. These include: (1) existing relevant research, particularly in the area of adult development; (2) known life history correlates of various characteristics; (3) typical factor loadings of biodata items: (4) known predictive characteristics of specific biodata items; and (5) general psychological knowledge. Two of these methods require that the researcher or practitioner have access to existing pools of biodata items as well as validity evidence and/or factor structures. Furthermore, relying on general psychological knowledge can be greatly limited by the item developer's experience.

Russell (1994) argued for using interviews and essays to gather facets of life episodes that incumbents believe influence their capacity to perform their jobs. Questions can be structured to address environmental conditions (such as task requirements and resources), cognitions and perceptual processes, attitudes, behaviors, and task outcomes. Content analysis of the responses is used to decompose the described events into a sequence of exposures to different environments and responses to those environments to form hypotheses for generating biodata items. Russell, Mattson, Devlin, and Atwater (1990), Russell and Domm (1990), and Siegel (1956) demonstrated that information obtained from essays can be successfully used to generate criterion-valid items. Russell (1994) also argued for using existing research to link theories of individual differences to the procedures (i.e., interviews and essays) for generating biodata items, and he provided examples of interview and biodata questions derived from personality, expectancy, and leadership theories. A specific hypothesized relationship between the item and criterion is believed to promote greater validity across situations and time (Mumford & Owens, 1987; Owens, 1976) and was recently demonstrated in research conducted by Reiter-Palmon and Connelly (2000), who found that empirical keys developed from pools of theory-based items were more valid than keys developed from a pool of non-theory-based items. Moreover, theory-based keys exhibited less shrinkage in predictive power across samples than non-theory-based keys.

Adequate job and criterion information appears to be critical to the development of good, valid biodata items. Yet other attributes of items are believed to be important in biodata form development.

## Biodata Item Attributes

The most common format for biodata items is multiple choice. Owens, Glennon, and Albright (1962) provided the earliest direction regarding biodata item format. They developed four rules for writing biodata items that would have reliability: (1) Biodata items should be short, with an average stem length of two lines (inconsistent items were 2.5 lines); (2) response options should be in a numerical format whenever possible; (3) the full range of response options should be covered or an escape option should be included; and (4) items should carry a neutral or pleasant connotation for the respondent. In 1976, Owens identified seven common biodata response formats, including: (1) yes-no; (2) single choice from a noncontinuum; (3) single choice from a continuum; (4) multiple selections from a noncontinuum; (5) noncontinuum with an escape option; (6) continuum with an escape option; and (7) a single common item with multiple continuum responses (e.g., "Use the following scale to indicate how well you performed in each of these academic subject areas: a) English, b) math, c) history"). He suggested that the continuous formats were preferable in terms of validation probability and adaptability to subsequent statistical analysis, but researchers who conduct option keying rather than validation at the item level are not usually quite as concerned with the continuum provided by the various options.

More recently, some researchers have questioned the need for all biodata items to be neutral or pleasant. Reiter-Palmon, DeFilippo, and Mumford (1990) found that negative items, or those dealing with negative experiences (such as parental criticisms), were more predictive of neuroticism, whereas positive items were more predictive of high school and college grade point average. Russell et al. (1990) factor analyzed a biodata inventory used to select U.S. Naval Academy midshipmen and found that the initial dominant factor contained unpleasant life events. Dean et al. (1999) discussed the recall of positive and negative life events and concluded that although autobiographical memory may be biased toward positive life events, there is qualitative and quantitative evidence that negative career-related events may be vividly recalled. They further emphasized the developmental role of learning how to respond to negative life events and suggested future research to develop a taxonomy of negative life events and responses to adversity.

Discussions concerning the definition and characteristics of biodata have often been integrally tied to descriptions of appropriate item attributes and content. Mael's (1991) taxonomy of item attributes is the most comprehensive to date and is outlined in Table 15.2. The taxonomy is divided into three categories. The first category is historical, and it is seen as defining the domain of biodata. The premise underlying the use of biodata, that previous behaviors have the potential to shape future behavior, implies that items should pertain solely to historical events, that is, those that have taken place

in the past or continue to take place. Consequently, items that inquire about behavioral intentions or request responses to hypothetical situations would not be considered appropriate content for a biodata item. Because individuals may draw on past behaviors to project their responses to unknown situations, some researchers may consider hypothetical questions appropriate. However, Mael concluded that hypothetical items belong to the realm of temperament or opinion measures and, as such, represent a departure from the conceptual rationale of biodata.

Mael's (1991) second category consists of item attributes that address methodological considerations for ensuring self-report accuracy and includes external, objective, firsthand, discrete, and verifiable attributes. Their value as *defining* attributes of biodata is controversial. In particular, verifiability was once considered to be the distinguishing characteristic of biodata items (Mael, 1991); however, like most of the other item characteristics, researchers disagree about the degree to which verifiability is an essential attribute. Though many insist on verifiable items, others prefer a less stringent standard of "verifiable in principle" (Gandy, Outerbridge, Sharf, & Dye, 1989; Stricker, 1987, 1988), which includes factual, external behaviors performed in the presence of others that could be corroborated, even though verification would be difficult or unlikely. Other researchers accept that nonverifiable items can also have a place in the biodata domain.

The few studies that have been conducted to empirically investigate the relationships between item attributes and reliability and validity have produced inconsistent results. Barge (1987) found that homogeneous items that assess a single disposition or tendency were more predictive of performance criteria than heterogeneous items and that discrete items were more predictive than summary or evaluative items. McManus and Masztal (1999) found stronger validities with items that were historical, external, objective, discrete, and verifiable, but their results were not entirely replicated in studies conducted by Lefkowitz, Gebbia, Balsam, and Dunn (1999) and Stanley et al. (2000). Stanley et al., in particular, examined item attributes across five different samples and found numerous inconsistent results. A somewhat clearer pattern was identified once their criteria were separated into objective and subjective categories. Verifiability appeared to be important for both types of criteria. External and objective items were found to be good predictors of objective criteria, such as turnover and GPA, but results were more mixed for subjective criteria such as supervisory job performance ratings. Although the taxonomy described by Mael (1991) provides a useful framework for describing biodata items, there are some limitations with its applicability to creating rules for writing good items. More research investigating the relative strengths

**TABLE 15.2    Descriptions of Attribute Categories**

| Mael's Categories | Attributes | Definitions |
|---|---|---|
| Domain of Biodata | *Historical/Present/Future* | |
| | Historical | Past behaviors, events, or experiences |
| | Present/Future | Intentions or behaviors in hypothetical situations |
| Accuracy of Response | *External/Internal* | |
| | External | Participation in real events that occur in real-life situations |
| | Internal | Attitudes, thoughts, feelings, or opinions about events |
| | *Objective/Subjective* | |
| | Objective | Requiring only the faculty of recall of specific information |
| | Subjective | Requiring the interpretation of information or events |
| | *First-Hand/Second-Hand* | |
| | First-hand | Information reported by the individual |
| | Second-hand | Information reported by others |
| | *Discrete/Summative* | |
| | Discrete | Simple count of unique events |
| | Summative | Summary of events in past |
| | *Verifiable/Nonverifiable* | |
| | Verifiable | Corroborated by an independent source |
| | Nonverifiable | Cannot be corroborated from independent sources |
| Legal/Moral Concerns | *Controllable/Uncontrollable* | |
| | Controllable | Actions chosen by the individual |
| | Uncontrollable | Actions or situations not chosen by the individual |
| | *Equal-Access/Nonequal-Access* | |
| | Equal-Access | Experiences that all individuals may have had |
| | Nonequal-Access | Experiences limited to certain individuals |
| | *Job-Relevant/Nonjob-Relevant* | |
| | Job-Relevant | Reflecting a sample of work-related behavior |
| | Nonjob Relevant | Reflecting a sign of work-related behavior |
| | *Invasive/Noninvasive* | |
| | Invasive | Invasions of privacy |
| | Noninvasive | Not invading privacy |

and weaknesses of different item characteristics is needed before definitive statements can be made regarding which item attributes contribute to validity, and it is likely premature to conclude that some item types produce greater validity than other item types.

A study by Clifton, Mumford, and Baughman (1999) drew upon cognitive studies of autobiographical memory to identify characteristics of items that may contribute to accurate reporting and recall. They developed items based on findings that autobiographical memory is organized in terms of goal-relevant activities and summaries of events or goal-related actions (Barsolou, 1988; Conway, 1990; Kolodner, 1983a, 1983b; Reiser, Black, & Abelson, 1985). Based on these theories, Clifton et al. proposed that items focusing on behavior occurring in multiple situations and those focusing on outcomes and reactions would result in greater accuracy and consistency of responses. They also expected that recall and accuracy would be better for typical kinds of situations rather than highly specific or unusual situations. The authors con-

cluded "that background data items should be written to capture event summaries which reflect significant goals in people's lives" (p. 69) because items that measured goal-relevant activities that occurred in multiple situations had the best recall consistency of any of the other types of items (e.g., an item asking about an average grade in math would be more accurately recalled than an item asking about a grade on a first algebra test). The authors also found that people tend to accurately recall information about their reactions to situations and to others as well as decision outcomes. Though much of the previous research has supported the greater validity of discrete events, the results of this study suggest that summary events *could* be equally valid, provided that the items inquire about goal-directed behavior. (Unfortunately, Clifton et al. did not obtain any validity evidence for their items.) Their finding that reactions to events and to others were accurately recalled argues against reliance on only external, objective, and verifiable items. Clifton et al.'s study demonstrates that existing research can be used to determine the kinds of experiences that people accurately and consistently recall and provides more specific information about how to frame the context of biodata items, thus extending the recommendations offered by Mael's (1991) taxonomy.

The third category of Mael's item attributes' taxonomy reflects legal or moral concerns with using specific types of items for selection purposes. These attributes include controllability, equal accessibility to experiences, job relevance, and invasions of privacy. We will return to this third category of item attributes in later sections of the chapter.

## Prescreening

Prescreening of biodata items to ensure the appropriateness of item content is an essential step in biodata form development. Rational prescreening of items can produce a biodata form that contains minimal bias and objectionability (Mumford & Owens, 1987). Item content may be reviewed to ensure: (1) the meaning of each item is clear; (2) response alternatives include the entire range of possible responses to the question; and (3) item content is appropriate for the target population.

Some researchers and practitioners may also prescreen their items to mitigate negative applicant reactions. Job-relatedness is a category about which applicants express concerns. Mitchell (1994) observed that there seems to be a growing demand within the profession for items that are face valid. Mitchell objects to prescreening items for job relevance because the nonintuitive nature of biodata prohibits those involved in the screening from accurately predetermining the validity of particular items. Results of studies conducted by Crosby and Mitchell (1988) revealed that job experts' estimations of the validity of biodata items were negatively correlated with the empirical validities for the items. These results demonstrate that prescreening, even by job experts, may eliminate many valid items, which can have a detrimental effect on the development of a valid biodata instrument. However, several studies have also provided evidence that expert judges can determine the relevance of items to job content and underlying constructs (Mumford & Stokes, 1992). Collectively, results suggest that depending on the purpose, prescreening by experts may be more or less beneficial. As many items will be lost during the statistical tryout, reducing the item pool during prescreening may place limitations on identifying valid items. A better strategy may be to combine both expert opinions obtained during prescreening with the results from statistical analysis to determine the impact of rejecting an item.

Another primary focus of prescreening is related to legal or moral concerns about the content of items that are used for selection purposes. Mael (1991) identified three biodata item attributes, controllability, equal accessibility, and invasiveness, which represent item content areas that are frequently of concern to applicants, employers, and test developers. Concerns about litigation and negative reactions by applicants will lead many researchers and practitioners to continue to develop decision rules for eliminating items for a variety of reasons. We will return to these rules when we discuss accommodations for disabilities and legal and ethical concerns later in the chapter.

## Scaling Methods

Many variables, such as purpose, sample size, and criterion type, must be considered in the process of developing and validating biodata, which prohibits a simple summarization in a "how to" or "cookbook" format (Brown, 1994). The numerous methods that exist for scaling biodata items generally fall under externally based methods (such as the empirical approach) and internally based methods (such as rational, theoretical, and construct approaches). Traditionally, various empirical techniques have been the most popular among researchers and practitioners, but recent research efforts have focused on the development of biodata scales from a content and/or construct framework. Research comparing the various techniques has not yet been able to sufficiently identify which approach is best. Brown (1994) offered a framework for suggesting which techniques might best fit various study goals, but this has yet to be empirically tested. The major approaches are discussed here briefly, and the reader is referred to Mumford and Owens (1987), Stokes et al. (1994), and Mumford and Stokes (1992) for more in-depth discussions of scaling methods and issues.

## Empirical Approach

The empirical approach focuses on the prediction of an external criterion and is the most commonly employed method when maximization of prediction is of primary interest (Brown, 1994; Guion, 1965; Hogan, 1994). A composite score is usually computed as a weighted linear combination of a subset of items or item options based on the statistical relationship between the items (or options) and the criterion. A variety of methods exist for identifying and weighting items on the basis of their ability to differentiate good from poor performers. These methods frequently involve statistical techniques for generating differential item or option weights and rely on variance maximizing procedures. As these methods tend to capitalize on chance factors that may be operating within the development sample, the stability of the scoring keys is of great concern, and cross-validation is essential.

Consequently, large samples are required to ensure that criterion group membership is accurately identified based upon nonchance differences in observed performance. To minimize chance influences, one should maximize the ratio of persons to predictors (items or responses) because the opportunities to take advantage of chance are positively related to the number of predictors and negatively related to the number of persons (Hogan, 1994). Conservative estimates of the minimum ratio range from 5:1 to 10:1 (Nunnally, 1978). Because some empirical methods derive weights for each response option to each item and large numbers of items are typically tested in the development of a biodata measure (usually 100 or more), the minimum recommended development sample size can be quite large (500 or more). Furthermore, cross-validation is essential with empirical keys, which further increases the required sample size. It is highly recommended that a second sample of similar size be independently drawn from the same population to cross-validate the scoring key. Frequently, however, a single sample is randomly split into a development sample and a cross-validation or "hold-out" sample. Recommendations for the size of the hold-out sample vary, but many practitioners follow England's (1961) suggestion that the development sample should be 33% larger than the hold-out sample. In addition, whenever cross-validation is accomplished with a hold-out sample, Pedhazur (1982) recommended that the final key be developed using the total sample (development and hold-out) to enhance the stability of the scoring weights (Hogan, 1994). Although popular, the use of formulas to estimate the shrinkage of validity coefficients is inappropriate with empirically keyed biodata as it greatly distorts the amount of shrinkage in prediction (Mitchell & Klimoski, 1986).

The various keying methods differ primarily regarding whether each response option is scored (generally referred to as option keyed) or the item is scored as a whole (e.g., correlational method). The methods also differ regarding how criterion performance is measured (e.g., a dichotomous criterion reflecting group membership or performance ratings or rankings), how item scores are related to criterion scores, and how item weights are statistically derived (Hogan, 1994). One of the more popular of the option-keyed methods is the vertical percent method (also known as the weighted application blank; England, 1971). This method involves weighting response options by determining the differences in the percentage of each criterion group's (e.g., high versus low performers) responses to each alternative for an item and requires criterion groups that are well differentiated, lending itself well to criteria that are truly dichotomous. Dichotomous groups may be formed from continuous data, but care should be exercised to ensure that they are sufficiently large and approximately equal in size (Hogan, 1994). Strong's Tables of Net Weights for Differences in Percents (England, 1971; Stead & Shartle, 1940) are used to assign a net weight to each response option. This method is also capable of identifying nonlinear item-criterion relationships, which can be appropriately weighted based on the identification of differences in response patterns to the items by the contrasting criterion groups.

The correlational and the differential regression methods are most appropriate for items that have continuous underlying response properties. Furthermore, the item-criterion relationships should be approximately linear. Instead of scoring and weighting each response option, these methods score the items as a whole and a single weight is assigned to each item based on the size and direction of the correlation between the item and criterion. In the correlational method, the weight may be the actual correlation coefficient or unit weights based on the presence or absence of statistical significance. The differential regression method uses least squares regression procedures to select and weight items based on the increment in criterion variance an item accounts for over and above those items already in the model (Hogan, 1994).

Although used less frequently, several other methods for developing empirical scales also exist. The horizontal percent method (Stead & Shartle, 1940) is a variant of the weighted application blank. With this method, weights are derived for each alternative from the ratio of the number of upper criterion group members who choose the response option to the total number who responded to the alternative, regardless of group membership (Brown, 1994). Neidt and Malloy (1954) suggested use of the deviant response method for adding items to an existing test battery. This technique uses criterion groups defined by the distance above or below the regression line between the existing predictor and criterion. The difference between actual and predicted criterion scores is used for developing item weights by either correlational or weighted application blank procedures (Brown, 1994). The rare response method is a variation of the deviant response method in which responses are weighted on the basis of infrequent selection of a response option. Item responses chosen by 15% or less receive the highest weights and those chosen by more than 30% are assigned no weight. Used primarily in developing clinical diagnostic instruments, Hogan (1994) reported only on one known study where the technique was applied to biodata and was found to be superior to the percentage methods (Telenson, Alexander, & Barrett, 1983).

The few studies that have compared the various techniques have focused primarily on differences in scale stability as well as the maximization of prediction, yet no clear consensus has emerged. Most empirical methods involve strategies for generating differential weights, but unit weighting may be preferable in many applications (Dawes, 1971) and may be more stable (Owens, 1976). England (1971) suggested that percentage methods should generally yield more stable weights than the alternatives, which was supported by Aamodt and Pierce (1987). However, several studies (Lecznar & Dailey, 1950; Malone, 1978; Pickrel, 1954) have demonstrated that correlational and regression methods show less shrinkage upon cross-validation. Campbell (1974) investigated the effects of validity and sample size in a Monte Carlo study of the multiple regression, unit weighting, and zero-order correlational procedures. Based on his results, multiple regression techniques were not recommended for samples less than 150, and zero-order correlations were recommended as weights when sample sizes are smaller than 250 and validity is less than .50. Recently, Reiter-Palmon and Connelly (2000) investigated the influence of the quality of the item pool on keying strategies. When the keys were developed from the same pool of nontheoretical items, they found that vertical percent empirical keys produced higher validities and less shrinkage for all but one of the three criteria. However, no difference between these approaches was found when a pool of theoretically based items was used for key development. Furthermore, empirical keys generated from theory-based item pools generally demonstrated little shrinkage in cross-validation. This study supports the observation made by Mumford and Owens (1987) and many others that empirical keys are only as good as the items from which the scales are developed. Moreover, the pattern of relationships that emerge may be difficult to interpret, and empirically keyed biodata forms often tend to have low face validity. The need for a greater understanding of the relationships between life experiences and future behaviors has led many researchers to adopt internal rather than external methods of biodata scale development.

### Theoretical Approaches

Researchers and practitioners have used a variety of methods to discover psychologically meaningful life history dimensions. Frequently referred to as rational or theoretical approaches, these are internally based methods in which biodata items are scaled based on their relationships to each other and not to an external criterion. Identification of dimensions are based on a priori hypotheses concerning the content and item groupings generally drawn from the results of job analyses or relevant theories of development and performance (Stokes & Reddy, 1992). Hough and Paullin (1994) distinguished between the "inductive" approach that uses factor analysis to select and weight items and the "deductive" approach that

uses expert opinions based on theory and research to select and weight items. Both methods focus on forming scales that are internally consistent and homogeneous. The primary difference between the two approaches is that the inductive method assumes that some basic structure of individual differences exists that can be discovered in previously constructed items, and the deductive approach identifies and defines the individual difference variables prior to item construction. Mitchell (1994) referred to using factor analysis in a broad, exploratory, post hoc approach to discovering the dimensionality of a given set of biodata items as "more akin to rationalization than to rationality" (p. 486). Both approaches, however, have frequently been referred to under the broad category of "rational keying" to distinguish them from the empirical approach. The distinctions between the approaches are further blurred as practitioners often use both, with inductive methods used to refine scales identified and developed initially with the deductive approach. Both methods lead to the identification of relevant dimensions of life experiences, but the underlying structures obtained from the internal analysis of items keyed against a criterion may differ from those obtained from rationally keyed items (van Rijn, 1992). Recent studies, such as Schmitt, Jennings, and Toney (1999) and Stokes and Searcy (1999), have begun to more clearly differentiate between these types of scales by referring to scales generated by factor analysis as internal or factorial scales and those based on deductive methods as rational or content/construct scales.

### Internal/Factorial Approaches

The use of factor analysis or principal components analysis (PCA) has been a popular strategy for identifying the patterns of correlations between biodata items and criteria (Schoenfeldt & Mendoza, 1994). Although correlations between items and between biodata factors and criteria provide some insight into the structure of life experiences, Hough and Paullin (1994) noted several problems with relying on this approach to identify biodata dimensions. The first is that biodata factor scales typically ignore large amounts of variance. In a review of several studies, the variance accounted for ranged from 19% for a 10-factor solution (Schoenfeldt, 1989) to 49.6% for 15 components (Lautenschlager & Shaffer, 1987). Although biodata's ability to capture unique variance is generally considered one of its strengths, a factor-analytic approach presumes that the common variance among items is more important than unique variance. Some researchers are concerned that the lost information might be important (Hough & Paullin, 1994). This parallels the bandwidth/fidelity issue that has occurred in the field of personality testing. In an investigation of global versus specific biodata scales, Stokes and Searcy (1999) found that specific (20 component solution) scales developed by PCA predicted somewhat better than global (9 component solution) scales, although they were less interpretable. However, scales developed by PCA were not found to be as interpretable or as predictive as specific construct scales developed by a rational approach. Stokes, Searcy, and Toth (1998) found that when PCA was used to identify the subconstructs of global constructs established from rational and empirical methods, the subscales were meaningful, easily interpreted, and stable across five samples. When examined within a construct, the subscales differentially predicted the criteria. These types of differential relationships could also account for the lower validity rates that are sometimes found when factorial scales are compared with empirical scales. Brown (1994) also noted that even when responses lie along a continuum, the relationship of the response alternatives to the criterion is sometimes nonlinear, which can also affect the validity of the factor scale.

Other methodological considerations include differences in item extremeness, which can cause problems that may result in spurious factors or loss of important items (Fruchter, 1954). The method also presumes that item alternatives are ordered along some continuum. This leads to concerns for imposing order among variables that do not fall along a natural continuum (e.g., occupations held) and the factoring of dichotomous items that are frequently included in biodata forms (Brown, 1994).

Although factor analysis does lead to homogeneous scales and can provide a greater understanding about the underlying characteristics being measured, the factors derived are dependent upon the composition of the original item pool. Hough and Paullin (1994) noted that the factor-analytic approach is not likely to lead to an adequate taxonomy of individual difference variables. However, incorporating factor analysis with methods that focus on more theoretical development of items and rational scales may be beneficial. Stokes and Searcy (1999) suggested that PCA might be valuable for evaluating the unidimensionality of global constructs that have been developed by a rational approach. Future research of this nature could lead to the development of hierarchical structures among biodata predictors that could eventually be tested by confirmatory factor analysis.

### Content/Construct Approaches

Traditionally, the rational approach relied primarily on the test developer or a panel of experts to make judgments regarding item inclusion and weighting. The process involves writing items to elicit information regarding the manifesta-tion of the relevant individual difference variables identified by the test developer. Investigators use either a direct approach or an indirect approach in determining the relevant individual characteristics. The direct approach, which is content oriented, uses items written to directly reflect the expression of the performance dimensions in prior behaviors and experiences. The indirect approach is more construct oriented and leads to the development of items that reflect prior behaviors and experiences that are thought to contribute to the development of traits required for performance (Stokes & Reddy, 1992). Although test developers may use the results of a thorough job analysis and/or research literature, the primary determination of whether an item is included in the scale is based on the test developer's judgment. Critics of this approach argue that empirical analyses should not be abandoned in favor of a method that relies heavily on the test developer's insight and knowledge about the relationship between an item and the underlying characteristic that it is intended to measure (Hough & Paullin, 1994).

More recently, researchers (Allworth & Hesketh, 1999; Kilcullen, White, Mumford, & Mack, 1995; Mumford, Costanza, Connelly, & Johnson, 1996; Stokes & Cooper, 2001) have begun to incorporate both content- and criterion-related strategies in order to develop and validate biodata constructs. The goal of a construct approach is to use various strategies in a continual effort to accumulate a pattern of evidence from which the meaning of a scale can be inferred. Mumford (1999) pointed out that although each of the different scaling techniques embodies different assumptions with different objectives, they are not necessarily mutually exclusive and, when combined judiciously, may lead to stronger biodata scales. Some evidence demonstrates that combining rational approaches with empirical approaches may be most useful for maximizing predictability and psychological interpretability (Karas & West, 1999; Mael & Hirsch, 1993; Stokes & Reddy, 1992).

Rational scale development has often focused on maximizing internal consistency without investigating the relationship between the scale and other measures. Though a high degree of internal consistency should be a minimum condition, it is not sufficient for establishing the substantive meaning of a scale. Without evidence of convergent and discriminant validity, it is possible that the items are measuring an irrelevant construct, such as respondents' tendencies to engage in impression management (Kilcullen et al., 1995). Criterion-related strategies, therefore, play a valuable role in establishing whether or not a construct predicts performance in the target situation. In particular, a stronger basis for inferring the meaningfulness of a biodata scale is obtained when it can be shown that it generalizes to other jobs and situations and predicts multiple types of the criterion construct. Additional support is also gained from formulating and testing hypotheses regarding the scale's relationships to other performance and reference measures (Mumford & Stokes, 1992).

In a series of field and laboratory studies, Mumford et al. (1996) demonstrated how a developmental approach to item generation based on an interactional model can be used to write construct-oriented biodata items. The model holds that "underlying psychological constructs, such as intelligence and openness, interact with situational demands to condition the behaviors and experiences that occur in people's lives" (p. 392). Based on this premise, item writers identify situations that would elicit the construct of interest and generate markers of typical expressions of the construct by focusing on individual differences in choices, reactions, behaviors, and outcomes from the situations. Scales developed by this approach were found to be effective predictors of relevant performance criteria with validity coefficients comparable to most other biodata scales. Furthermore, many of the scales predicted multiple criteria and exhibited expected relationships with reference measures.

In a different approach, Kilcullen et al. (1995) developed biodata scales specifically targeted to measure six job-relevant temperament constructs. Adequate discriminant validity was found for four of the biodata scales, and the expected relationships with a previously validated temperament measure were confirmed. They also found that the biodata scales were more subtle and more predictive of job performance than the scales from the temperament measure. Schmitt et al. (1999), however, were somewhat less successful in developing and validating construct-oriented biodata scales. Items were written to assess six dimensions relevant to an investigative officer's job performance. Hypothesized relationships were confirmed for only three of the constructs, and except for one scale, there was almost a complete lack of predictive ability. Although Allworth and Hesketh (1999) also found evidence for the construct validity for a number of the scales they developed to capture adaptive and contextual performance, only one of the eight constructs was significantly related to task and adaptive performance, and none were related to contextual performance.

Methodological and outcome differences among the studies create some uncertainty about why some biodata scales exhibit construct and predictive validity while others fail to do so. Kilcullen et al. (1995) observed that the multidimensional nature of biodata may hinder the development of distinctly different constructs. Because each behavior can have multiple antecedents and consequences, items may represent many underlying constructs simultaneously, which could contribute to a lack of discriminant validity. Furthermore, it is also possible that some constructs may be more easily approximated than others by the behavioral focus of biodata. Although additional research is clearly warranted, a construct-oriented approach to biodata development appears to be a promising method for more fully understanding the relationships between biodata and other measures of individual differences. The results from some studies demonstrate that although biodata constructs may be highly related to measures of personality and cognitive ability, they also exhibit differential relationships to job performance. It is only through the careful development of biodata items and scales and the systematic investigation of the relationships among those measures that a greater level of understanding about the measurement of life experiences can be reached.

## Typical Psychometric Results

Typical validity coefficients for biodata scales were provided in the previous discussion of validity. To briefly summarize, biodata measures tend to have validity coefficients in the .30 to .40 range, though in some cases, useful validity coefficients in the .20s have been identified (e.g., Stokes et al., 1999).

Many studies investigating the reliability of biodata forms have found that test-retest coefficients have generally been quite high, in the .80s and .90s, for extended periods of time (Mumford & Stokes, 1992). At the item level, test-retest reliability coefficients tend to be somewhat lower, particularly for subjective items (Shaffer, Saunders, & Owens, 1986). Factual, objective, and verifiable items, such as final college GPA, are usually recalled with greater reliability.

Due to the heterogeneity of typical biodata items, measures of internal consistency are usually lower than test-retest estimates. Typical internal consistency estimates for construct-oriented biodata scales range from the .60s to the .80s, and in some cases, it can be difficult to construct a scale that meets a minimum cutoff of .70. Mount et al. (2000) reported alphas of .54 to .81 for rationally formed, empirically keyed biodata scales to measure work habits, problem-solving ability, interpersonal-relation skills, and situations perseverance (consisting of 28 to 40 items per scale). Factors derived by Morrison (1977) had coefficient alphas that ranged from .41 to .98. Russell et al. (1990) found coefficient alphas of .62 to .91. Stokes and Cooper (2001) reported alphas of .62 to .83 for scales developed by a content/construct approach with 6 to 12 items per scale. Because empirically derived biodata scales are constructed to predict an external criterion, their heterogeneity makes internal consistency an inappropriate method for estimating scale reliability.

Clause, Mullins, Nee, Pulakos, and Schmidt (1998) successfully applied an "item-cloning" technique to develop parallel biodata forms. The multidimensional nature of biodata items and the use of empirical-keying methods have largely precluded the development of parallel forms through traditional methods of sampling similar test items from general content item pools. The item-cloning technique involved writing one or more items to parallel, in terms of content, grammatical structure, and option structure, each item on an existing inventory. The new items were then reviewed by test developers and by subject matter experts, and evidence of parallelism was obtained not only from content judgment, but also through empirical evidence that panel participants responded similarly to parallel items. The item-cloning technique was found to be better for generating parallel forms than a traditional domain sampling method.

### Accommodation for People With Disabilities

Because biodata forms have usually been paper-and-pencil, untimed measures, there has been infrequent need for accommodation in test administration, except to accommodate those with reading or visual impairments, and there is no published evidence to date that such accommodations represent a significant threat to the validity of biodata forms. It would seem, however, that different forms of administration could influence accuracy of responding. Martin and Nagao (1989) found that the least amount of socially desirable responding occurs in computer interviews and the most in face-to-face interviews, suggesting that changes in mode of biodata form administration could influence response accuracy.

Most concerns regarding individuals with disabilities revolve around the content of the biodata items themselves, and prescreening of items is typically designed to eliminate items that might be problematic. The importance of prescreening has become a more salient issue in light of the Americans with Disabilities Act (ADA), which prohibits prehire medical inquiries. Individuals with disabilities may view biodata questions that inquire about activities from which they may have been precluded as an attempt to identify their physical disabilities. Sharf (1994) pointed out that the ADA categorically prohibits questions about an applicant's physical condition, which would preclude items that were signs that indirectly define a disabled person's physical condition, such as "not having participated in team sports, debating society, or cheerleading, to give but a few examples" (p. 365). Sharf (1994) also noted that should it become necessary for an employer to defend the use of specific biodata items, empirical evidence may not be sufficient for establishing job-relatedness and/or business necessity. Consequently, there are growing concerns that biodata demonstrate face validity or even a point-to-point correspondence between the items and the jobs. As noted previously, prescreening of items by experts has become an important step in developing biodata forms and can be used to ensure compliance with the ADA.

### Cross-Cultural Factors

Few studies have been conducted examining cross-cultural factors and their influence on biodata form development and validation. The prediction of management success using a biodata form was found to be similar in Denmark, the Netherlands, Norway, and the United States, though several items had to be deleted or modified to fit local cultural conditions (Laurent, 1970). Cassens (1966) derived similar biodata factors for individuals completing forms in the United States and Latin America. Most recently, Dalessio, Crosby, and McManus (1996) applied a key developed in the United States for selecting sales representatives in the life insurance industry to a sample of insurance agents in the United Kingdom (UK) and Republic of Ireland (RI). The correlation between the biodata measure and a standardized production measure was not significantly different from that obtained in the U.S. sample, demonstrating that the predictive validity of the key generalized to a comparable sample. Dalessio et al. also examined the stability of the factor structure of the biodata measure across the two samples by conducting a confirmatory factor analysis in the UK/RI sample with factors derived from an exploratory analysis in the U.S. sample. With small modifications, the factor structure derived in the United States was found to fit the UK/RI data. Similar results were also found when internal consistency estimates for the two samples were compared. To the extent that the occupations across cultures demand the same knowledge, skills, abilities, and other characteristics (KSAOs), then one might expect a biodata form developed in the United States to show similar validity elsewhere. However, one must explore cultural differences in each case to ensure comparability.

### Legal and Ethical Considerations

As mentioned earlier in this chapter, Mael's final category of biodata item attributes focuses on issues of legal and moral concern regarding item content. Three of the attributes, controllability, equal access, and invasiveness, have been controversial topics among biodata developers.

The issue of controllability concerns the degree to which respondents have the option to choose to perform or not to perform an action. Consequently, noncontrollable items represent actions that happened to the individual and include many content areas traditionally assessed in biodata instruments, such as demographic variables and information concerning applicants' parents, childhood, or physical characteristics. Some would also include as uncontrollable such things as educational level. As one can readily surmise, the issue of controllability tends to be controversial, with some taking the position that it is not ethical to evaluate people based on things that they could not control (Stricker, 1987, 1988) and others taking the position that even noncontrollable events shape and affect later behavior. Strict adherence to a rule including only "controllable" items would exclude many items that typically have been found on job application blanks and can also place severe limitations on test developers to adequately cover performance domains of interest (Mael, 1991).

Equal accessibility refers to item content regarding skill and experiences that not all applicants will have had the opportunity to acquire. A frequently cited example is an item that asks if the respondent has been the captain of a football team. Many individuals would be precluded from having achieved this position by virtue of their gender, physical ability, and size or by the lack of such recreational activities in their neighborhoods and/or school systems. Mael (1991, 1994) suggested that two different perspectives influence practitioners' positions concerning equal accessibility. If one takes the position that biodata items are indices of previously existing characteristics, then it would be unfair to reject someone who was precluded from acquiring the experiences assessed by an item. For example, if being captain of the football team is indicative of leadership, then this item is unfair to those individuals who could not play football but have had other leadership experiences. Others take the position that biodata measures participation in an activity that is itself a potential indicator of future behavior. That is, by virtue of having participated in a specific activity, the participant begins to identify with that role and gains expertise in filling it. From this perspective, the only thing that matters is that the person had a particular experience and not that some people were unable to obtain it.

Many question whether it is feasible to eliminate all items that preclude equal accessibility and rely instead on an item matching strategy, such as pairing softball for women with football for men. Although this will minimize some effects, there are still limitations with an item matching strategy, as some groups will still be precluded from participation. Without sufficient knowledge regarding why a particular item predicts job performance, it seems reasonable to strive for a balance by attempting to write items that refer to situations or experiences that are accessible to the largest number of people possible.

The final attribute, invasiveness, is regarded as a serious concern with the use of biodata (Dean et al., 1999). Certainly, questions about national origin, religious and political affiliations, sexual behaviors, and financial status may violate federal, state, or local privacy protection laws. Sharf (1994) provided appendixes of many previously predictive biodata items that have been identified as illegal under certain privacy statutes. However, other topics may also be intrusive, resulting not only in legal action, but also leading to a variety of response deviations resulting from omitted items, random responding, or willful faking. Thompson-Feith (2001) found that individuals' willingness to respond to biodata items in a selection context was strongly related to their perceptions of the items' invasiveness.

Even though invasion of privacy is becoming a frequent source for litigation and concern for employers, there has been limited research effort into identifying the invasiveness of item content (Sharf, 1994). In 1996, Mael, Connerley, and Morath investigated perceptions of the invasiveness of biodata item attributes as well as individual difference factors that influence perceptions of invasiveness. Their results reveal the complexity of defining and identifying the attributes associated with perceptions of invasiveness. In general, they found that items that are more verifiable, more transparent in purpose (i.e., more job relevant), and more impersonal were seen as less invasive. Contrary to expectations, however, within a military sample negative items were seen as less invasive than positive items. The authors proposed that their findings could be due to the military personnel's perceptions that the purpose of the questionnaire was an exclusionary screen, and the relevance of excluding someone based on his/her prior positive accomplishments was not apparent. In separate student and subject matter expert samples, negative items were seen as more invasive only after controlling for item transparency. Individuals with more education and those with more positive attitudes toward biodata and organizational selection measures found fewer items invasive.

Based on their findings, Mael et al. (1996) offered tentative suggestions regarding invasion of privacy. They proposed that events that are personal, that is, do not occur in the workplace or some other public arena, should be particularly avoided if their recall could traumatize the applicant or raise concerns about being stigmatized. Items about religion and political affiliations should be avoided, particularly if they inquire about specific denomination or party affiliations. Items related to intimate behaviors and those activities that are likely to involve stigma and shame should also be avoided. Furthermore, because noncontrollable items were not seen as more invasive in general, the authors did not believe such items should be eliminated unless they were invasive for another reason.

Although there are preliminary indications that some individual difference variables are associated with perceptions of invasiveness (e.g., need for privacy, dominance, achievement locus of control; see Thompson-Feith, 2001), the content of the items themselves appears to be the strongest influence on invasiveness perceptions. Thus, it should be possible to avoid writing items in categories perceived as invasive, and prescreening to further ensure that items are not offensive can be very helpful. Baehr, Jones, Baydoun, and Behrens (1994) developed less invasive biodata constructs with content similar to two factors, Financial Responsibility (FR) and General Family Responsibility (GR), that had contained invasive items related to marital and family status and financial practices. The goal was to create new constructs that would be legally compliant, valid measures but that would also be perceived as having face validity. The new constructs assessed interest and success in financial management without quantitative information and comfort and success in assuming responsibility and directing others in a work environment. The new scales were highly correlated with the original scales and were significantly correlated with important criterion variables, demonstrating that comparable measures can be developed that are valid but less invasive.

## Computerization and Internet Usage

The explosion of selection processes administered on computers and, more recently, on the Internet has had its influence on the use of biodata. To our knowledge, there are no published studies examining the impact of technology on biodata selection testing, and to a large extent, the use of technology has been several steps ahead of the research examining its influence. The computer has offered many organizations increased ease and efficiency of administration and scoring, and it has the potential to provide new avenues for monitoring of response accuracy (Gore, 2000). Similarly, Internet testing has also increased, and two firms associated with well-known biodata experts are prominent today in that arena: e-selex.com and ePredix.com. One avenue of research that has generated considerable interest is that of applicant reactions to computer and Internet testing (Sinar & Reynolds, 2001). Crandall and Cunningham (2001) took particular note of the "digital divide"—the fact that access to computers and the Internet may not be the same across socioeconomic and ethnic groups, and they voiced the need for research investigating potential adverse impact associated with instruments administered via the new technological avenues. Certainly, we can expect much

more research on the use of the computer and the Internet with biodata selection devices in the years to come.

## Special Concerns With Biodata Form Development and Validation

There are two areas that should be a focus for organizations planning to implement biodata-based testing systems and represent domains in which future research is needed and likely to occur. They involve issues associated with the validation sample and response distortion.

### Reference Sample

Biodata instruments are most often developed and validated with a concurrent validation strategy because the necessity for large sample sizes generally precludes a predictive validation study. When developing and validating biodata instruments using a sample of current job incumbents, generalization to applicant samples could be a problem. Test developers must determine the similarity of the potential applicant sample to the current job incumbents in order to include situational contexts that both applicants and job incumbents are likely to have experienced. Typically, most think of the differences between the samples in the context of job experience, but if the ages of two samples differ, validities may not be comparable (Stokes & Reddy, 1992). Furthermore, some constructs of interest, such as computer literacy, may only be adequately assessed with an applicant sample, as applicants may be more likely to have a wider range of experiences with computers.

Job experience has often been identified as a potential moderator for biodata validity. Barge and Hough (1986) and Hogan (1988) found that the validities obtained in concurrent studies were higher than those obtained in predictive studies. Additionally, Bliesener (1996) determined that at least 16% of the variance observed in validities could be explained by the validation design variable, predictive or concurrent, with a clear drop in validity with a predictive design. One hypothesis for the higher validities that occur in concurrent studies is that they may stem from the measurement of knowledge acquired from job experience. However, some evidence indicates that job experience may not have a moderating effect on biodata validity. Rothstein et al. (1990) conducted a meta-analysis of the validity of their concurrently developed biodata form and found that mean validities across job experience levels did not decline, which suggests that increasing job experience probably does not produce increases in concurrent validities.

The differences between predictive and concurrent validities could also be due to motivational differences between incumbents and applicants. In particular, applicants may be more motivated to fake or, at the very least, exhibit a higher degree of socially desirable responding. Stokes, Hogan, and Snell (1993) compared an incumbent sample with an applicant sample for sales positions within the same company. They found that when the key developed with a concurrent design was applied to the applicant sample, the accuracy of turnover prediction was not any better than the base rate. Furthermore, a key developed with a predictive design did not share any items in common with the concurrently developed key. The differences could be partially explained by the presence of greater socially desirable responding in the applicant sample.

Researchers and practitioners must pay careful attention to identify situations to which individuals in the target population would most likely have been exposed (Mumford & Stokes, 1992). It is reasonable to expect life experiences to vary with such variables as age, job experience, educational experience, race, sex, and/or other cultural subgroups. An assessment of the range of situations that members of the target group are likely to have encountered will ensure adequate variability in behavior and experiences. For example, items that inquire about college experiences will not elicit the same degree of response variability in a sample of mechanics as they would in a sample of managers.

Mumford and Owens (1987) noted that biodata items are less likely to be predictive and interpretable if the item pool fails to capture significant antecedents, or is contaminated by irrelevant behaviors and experiences, or is biased by a failure to capture differences in the developmental patterns of different subgroups. Failure to adequately define the reference sample may result in one or more of these problems. Research has demonstrated that biodata keys that are developed with a more theoretical rationale generally are more predictive in a wider range of situations, which may also mitigate some problems of generalizing from incumbents to applicants.

### Response Distortion

One reason that the characteristics of biodata items are often emphasized is that many item attributes are valued for setting a higher standard for self-report accuracy. It has long been held that items that are historical, objective, external, discrete, verifiable, and firsthand serve to minimize the amount of response distortion that occurs in self-report measures. Additionally, empirical-keying methods can also identify "subtle" items, or those for which the "correct" answer is not readily apparent to the respondent. These item and method charac-

teristics have often been viewed as an advantage that biodata offers over other noncognitive measures, but the current focus on the creation of more homogeneous scales is also accompanied by an increase in the use of more subjective and nonverifiable items, raising concerns that measurement accuracy is being sacrificed in the attempt to improve our understanding of what biodata measures (Mael, 1991). Consequently, research regarding the relationship between item attributes and response distortion is of great interest to both researchers and practitioners.

Lautenschlager (1994) reviewed 12 studies published from 1950 to 1990 that addressed the topics of response distortion, faking, and accuracy of responses to biodata questions. One of the general findings from this review was that objective items are less susceptible to distortion than subjective items. Becker and Colquitt (1992) examined the fakability of several item attributes from Mael's (1991) taxonomy. Their results corroborated previous findings that objective and verifiable items are less susceptible to faking. They also found that items that are faked more in practice are less historical, discrete, and external and are more job relevant. Results obtained by McManus and Masztal (1999) contradicted previous findings, but their index of response distortion, a social desirability measure, may have been the explanation. In an examination of the relationship between item attributes and various measures of response distortion across five different samples, Stanley et al. (2000) found that items that were internal, subjective, and summative were more related to response distortion indices than were external, objective, and discrete items. Their results were similar to Becker and Colquitt's (1992) findings and consistent with suggestions made by Mael (1991). Overall, studies generally support the view that some types of biodata attributes lead to improved response accuracy.

There is evidence, however, that also suggests that under the proper motivation to fake, all biodata items can be faked. Hough and Paullin (1994) reviewed research on both item subtlety and objectivity and concluded that neither item type was significantly less fakable. Likewise, Lautenschlager (1994) found that when instructed to do so, respondents are capable of distorting their responses to either increase or decrease their scores as directed. Mael (1991) noted that it is important to understand the climate under which the biodata instrument will be administered. Certain considerations about not only the applicant population, but the employer as well, should be addressed. Under different conditions, it is reasonable to expect that some applicants may be highly motivated to fake or that some employers or current employees may coach applicants. Consequently, it is not sufficient to presume that response distortion can be controlled by item type.

Lautenschlager (1994) offered several useful recommendations for ways to minimize response distortion, one of which is strict protection of the scoring key and frequent monitoring of the testing process. In addition, several research studies have demonstrated that including a warning that responses may be verified reduces intentional distortion. Doll (1971) found that warning that a follow-up interview was possible was even more effective in reducing response distortion than a warning that the instrument included a lie detection scale. Trent, Atwater, and Abrahams (1986) found that using a warning statement about the potential verification of responses and the consequence of detected faking, along with items that were verifiable, could reduce faking. However, Lautenschlager noted that care should be taken to ensure that the warning is appropriate and does not lead to unintended consequences. Warnings could easily become ineffective if the applicant has any reason to question that the response verification will occur. Thus, it is important that a biodata instrument includes obviously verifiable items if respondents are warned of such verification. Mael (1991) suggested that nonverifiable items should be combined with verifiable items, with many of the verifiable items loaded at the beginning of the instrument.

Some additional suggestions for dealing with response distortion include using items or scales intended to detect distortion, such as some type of response validity scale and/or the repetition of some items as a form of an accuracy check. One must use caution in "correcting" scores using responses to a validity scale as the research is equivocal regarding the equivalence of such scales and the "faking" that such scales are often used to detect. Mitchell and Stokes (1995) suggested the need to validate one's validity scales with the same care with which one validates one's selection instruments.

Snell, Sydell, and Lueke (1999) discussed potential areas for reducing faking with item content, format, and scoring. Some types of nonsubtle items may be less fakable because it is difficult for applicants to ascertain how the items will be scored. Griffith, Frei, Snell, Hamill, and Wheeler (1997) demonstrated that under fake good conditions, respondents used a "good thing versus a bad thing" strategy, which led to increases in scores on a conscientiousness measure. However, scores on a measure of openness to new experiences remained relatively stable because respondents could not identify the "right" responses to fake for this construct with respect to the target job. Snell et al. (1999) recommended adopting an item writing strategy to confuse the respondents as to which choice on an item represents the "good thing" and which choice represents the "bad thing." An item such as "I frequently help coworkers with their tasks so they can meet their deadlines even when I have not finished my assigned tasks" (p. 225) would inhibit potential fakers' abilities to determine the optimal answer. Snell et al. reported that preliminary work by Bernal (1998) demonstrated that scales that consist of these multidimensional items have lower levels of internal consistency but still maintain respectable correlations to the original constructs. The most positive finding has been that under incentives to fake, individuals identified as trying to provide overly positive responses were less likely to rise to the top of the distribution.

Snell et al. also observed that Likert-type scales easily contribute to the fakability of noncognitive measures. Once a respondent determines whether or not the trait measured by the item is positive or negative, the correct response is clear. There is some evidence that forced-choice formats produce less score inflation than Likert-based scales when honest conditions are compared with fake-good conditions. Forced-choice formats can create measurement issues that must be addressed, however, and many biodata form developers opt to write items that are placed on a continuum as recommended by Owens (1976). Faking is an important issue in the use of biodata and all other noncognitive measures, and Snell et al.'s recommendation of pursuing the development of alternative response formats as a means of reducing item fakability is worthy of exploration.

The keying method may also influence response distortion. Kluger, Reilly, and Russell (1991) studied faking using item-keying and option-keying methods and found that option-keyed responses were less susceptible to inflation in a sample of students applying for a fictitious job. This method serves to reduce the applicant's ability to fake because the scored options are not apparent and are at times counterintuitive. Gore (2000) replicated Kluger et al.'s findings on one biodata form but not another in a sample of job incumbents. Hogan (1994) noted that the advantage of using option keying would hold primarily when item-criterion relationships are significantly nonlinear.

The computer also offers new avenues for detecting and reducing faking, including examining response latencies and tracking the length and number of times applicants view specific items on the measure. Studies by Holden and his colleagues (Holden, 1995; Holden & Kroner, 1992; Holden, Kroner, Fekken, & Popham, 1992) and others (Dwight & Alliger, 1997; Gore, 2000) have produced inconsistent results, and further research is necessary to adequately explore the use of technology for detecting and potentially controlling for faking.

Concerns over how much an applicant may or may not be faking and how this will affect the validity of the biodata instrument is just one among many issues that must be addressed in the biodata form development process. Biodata researchers and practitioners must often attempt to balance many different, and at times, apparently contradictory goals (e.g., job relevant *and* not fakable). However, as Lautenschlager observed in 1994, "to date, we are really not much closer to knowing the absolute truthfulness of the responses given to biographical data items, and it is reasonable to question whether such knowledge is obtainable, or even necessary" (p. 414). Consequently, though it is valuable to consider that some item types and methodology have the potential benefit of improved response accuracy, this should not replace the intended purpose of the instrument as the primary determination of item type, item content, and scoring methodology.

## SUMMARY

Biodata instruments have a long history of successfully predicting criteria of importance to organizations, and they do so with less adverse impact than cognitive ability measures. Organizations attempting to develop and implement biodata measures as part of their selection/promotion processes must have a good understanding of their performance criteria. Several alternative strategies for creating biodata measures exist that are valid, fair, and generalizable, and the strengths and weaknesses of those alternatives must be considered along with the goals of the organization in use of the instrument. Response distortion continues to be an issue of concern, but new avenues for identifying and controlling faking are currently under way. In spite of its underutilization in organizations, biodata measurement remains a valuable alternative selection testing process.

## REFERENCES

Aamodt, M.G., & Pierce, W.L. Jr. (1987). Comparison of the rare response and vertical percent methods for scoring the biographical information blank. *Educational and Psychological Measurement, 47,* 505–511.

Allworth, E., & Hesketh, B. (1999). Construct-oriented biodata: Capturing change-related and contextually relevant future performance. *International Journal of Selection and Assessment, 7,* 97–111.

Ash, R.A. (1982). Job elements for task clusters: Arguments for using multiple methodological approaches to job analysis and demonstration of their ability. *Public Personnel Management Journal, 11,* 80–90.

Asher, J.J. (1972). The biographical item: Can it be improved? *Personnel Psychology, 25,* 251–269.

Baehr, M.E., Jones, J.W., Baydoun, R.B., & Behrens, G.M. (1994). Proactively balancing the validity and legal compliance of personal background measures in personnel management. *Journal of Business and Psychology, 8,* 345–354.

Barge, B.N. (1987, August). *Characteristics of biodata items and their relationship to validity.* Paper presented at the 95th Annual Meeting of the American Psychological Association, New York, NY.

Barge, B.R., & Hough, L.M. (1986). Utility of biographical data for predicting job performance. In L.M. Hough (Ed.), *Utility of temperament, biodata, and interest assessment for predicting job performance: A review of the literature* (ARI Research Note No. 88–02, pp. 91–130). Alexandria, VA: U.S. Army Research Institute.

Barsalou, L.W. (1988). The content and organization of autobiographical memories. In U. Neisser & E. Winograd (Eds.), *Remembering reconsidered: Ecological and traditional approaches to the study of memory* (pp. 193–243). Cambridge: Cambridge University Press.

Becker, T.E., & Colquitt, A.L. (1992). Potential versus actual faking of a biodata form: An analysis along several dimensions of item type. *Personnel Psychology, 45,* 389–406.

Bernal, D. (1998). *Reducing the effects of individual faking on non-cognitive measures: Let's send those fakers to the bottom of the distribution!* Unpublished dissertation proposal, University of Akron, Akron, OH.

Bliesener, T. (1996). Methodological moderators in validating biographical data in personnel selection. *Journal of Occupational and Organizational Psychology, 69,* 107–120.

Bobko, P., Roth, P.L., & Potosky, D. (1999). Derivation and implications of a meta-analytic matrix incorporating cognitive ability, alternative predictors, and job performance. *Personnel Psychology, 52,* 561–589.

Brown, S.H. (1981). Validity generalization and situational moderation in the life insurance industry. *Journal of Applied Psychology, 66,* 664–670.

Brown, S.H. (1994). Validating biodata. In G. Stokes, M. Mumford, & W. Owens (Eds.), *Biodata handbook: Theory, research, and use of biographical information in selection and performance prediction* (pp. 199–236). Palo Alto, CA: Consulting Psychologists Press.

Buel, W.D., Albright, L.E., & Glennon, J.R. (1966). A note on the generality and cross-validity of personal history for identifying creative research scientists. *Journal of Applied Psychology, 50,* 217–219.

Campbell, J.P. (1974). *Psychometric theory in industrial and organizational psychology* (Rep. No. 2001). Arlington, VA: Personnel and Training Research Programs, Office of Naval Research.

Campbell, J.P., Dunnette, M.D., Lawler, E.E., & Weick, K. (1970). *Managerial behavior and performance effectiveness.* New York: McGraw-Hill.

Carlson, K.D., Scullen, S.E., Schmidt, F.L., Rothstein, H., & Erwin, F. (1999). Generalizable biographical data validity can be achieved without multi-organizational development and keying. *Personnel Psychology, 52,* 731–755.

Cassens, F.P. (1966). *Cross-cultural dimensions of executive life history antecedents.* Greensboro, NC: The Creativity Research Institute, The Richardson Foundation.

Clause, C.S., Mullins, M.E., Nee, M.T., Pulakos, E., & Schmitt, N. (1998). Parallel test form development: A procedure for alternate predictors and an example. *Personnel Psychology, 51,* 193–208.

Clifton, T.C., Mumford, M.D., & Baughman, W.A. (1999). Background data and autobiographical memory: Effects of item types and task characteristics. *International Journal of Selection and Assessment, 7,* 57–71.

Conte, J.M., Tesluk, P.E., & Jacobs, R.R. (1996). The utility of biodata measures in the public transit industry. In R.B. Stennett, A. Parisi, & G. Stokes (Eds.), *A compendium: Papers presented at the first biennial biodata conference* (pp. 149–166). Athens: University of Georgia.

Conway, M.A. (1990). Associations between autobiographical memory and concepts. *Journal of Experimental Psychology: Learning, Memory, and Cognition, 16,* 799–812.

Crandall, R.W., & Cunningham, C.A. (2001). Bridging the divide naturally. *Brookings Review, 19,* 38–43.

Crosby, M.M., & Mitchell, T.W. (1988, April). The obscurity of biodata predictor-criterion relationships: A blessing in disguise? In T.W. Mitchell (Chair), *Advancing the theory and method of biodata.* Symposium conducted at the annual meeting of the Society for Industrial and Organizational Psychology, Dallas.

Dalessio, A.T., Crosby, M.M., & McManus, M.A. (1996). Stability of biodata keys and dimensions across English-speaking countries: A test of the cross-situational hypothesis. *Journal of Business and Psychology, 10,* 289–296.

Dalessio, A.T., & Silverhart, T.A. (1994). Combining biodata test and interview information: Predicting decisions and performance criteria. *Personnel Psychology, 47,* 303–315.

Dawes, R. (1971). The robust beauty of improper linear models in decision making. *American Psychologist, 34,* 571–582.

Dean, M.A., & Russell, C.J. (1998, April). *A comparison of g and biodata criterion-related validity in a sample of air traffic controllers.* Paper presented at the 13th Annual Conference of the Society for Industrial and Organizational Psychology, Dallas, TX.

Dean, M.A., Russell, C.J., & Muchinsky, P.M. (1999). Life experiences and performance prediction: Toward a theory of biodata. *Research in Personnel and Human Resources Management, 17,* 245–281.

Doll, R.E. (1971). Item susceptibility to attempted faking as related to item characteristics and adopted faking set. *The Journal of Psychology, 77,* 9–16.

Dreher, G.F., & Sackett, P.R. (1983). *Perspectives on staffing and selection.* Homewood, IL: Irwin.

Dwight, S.A., & Alliger, G.M. (1997, April). *Using response latencies to identify overt integrity test dissimulation.* Paper presented at the annual conference of the Society for Industrial and Organizational Psychology, St. Louis, MO.

England, G.W. (1961). *Development and use of weighted application blanks.* Dubuque, IA: Brown.

England, G.W. (1971). *Development and use of weighted application blanks* (Bulletin No. 55). Minneapolis: Industrial Relations Center, University of Minnesota.

Ferguson, L.W. (1961). The development of industrial psychology. In B.H. Gilmer (Ed.), *Industrial psychology* (pp. 18–37). New York: McGraw-Hill.

Fine, S.A., & Cronshaw, S. (1994). The role of job analysis in establishing the validity of biodata. In G. Stokes, M. Mumford, & W. Owens (Eds.), *Biodata handbook: Theory, research, and use of biographical information in selection and performance prediction* (pp. 39–64). Palo Alto, CA: Consulting Psychologists Press.

Fleishman, E.A. (1972). On the relation between learning, abilities, and human performance. *American Psychologist, 27,* 1017–1032.

Fleishman, E.A. (1975). Toward a taxonomy of human performance. *American Psychologist, 30,* 1127–1149.

Fleishman, E.A. (1988). Some new frontiers in personnel selection research. *Personnel Psychology, 41,* 679–701.

Fruchter, B. (1954). *Introduction to factor analysis.* Princeton, NJ: Van Nostrand.

Gandy, J.A., Dye, D.A., & MacLane, C.N. (1994). Federal government selection: The individual achievement record. In G. Stokes, M. Mumford, & W. Owens (Eds.), *Biodata handbook: Theory, research, and use of biographical information in selection and performance prediction* (pp. 275–310). Palo Alto, CA: Consulting Psychologists Press.

Gandy, J.A., Outerbridge, A.N., Sharf, J.C., & Dye, D.A. (1989). *Development and initial validation of the Individual Achievement Record.* Washington, DC: U.S. Office of Personnel Management.

Ghiselli, E.E. (1973). The validity of aptitude tests in personnel selection. *Personnel Psychology, 26,* 461–477.

Goldsmith, D.B. (1922). The use of a personal history blank as a salesmanship test. *Journal of Applied Psychology, 6,* 149–155.

Gore, B.A. (2000). *Reducing and detecting faking on a computer-administered biodata questionnaire.* Unpublished doctoral dissertation, University of Georgia, Athens, GA.

Griffith, R.L., Frei, R.L., Snell, A.F., Hamill, L.S., & Wheeler, J.K. (1997). *Warning versus no warnings: Differential effect of method bias.* Paper presented at the 12th Annual Meeting of the Society for Industrial and Organizational Psychologists, St. Louis, MO.

Guilford, J.P., & Lacey, J.I. (1947). Printed classification tests. *AAF Aviation Psychology Research Program reports.* Washington, DC: U.S. Government Printing Office.

Guion, R.M. (1965). *Personnel testing.* New York: McGraw-Hill.

Hammer, E.G., & Kleiman, L.S. (1988). Getting to know you. *Personnel Administrator, 33,* 86–92.

Harvey-Cook, J.E. (2000). Biodata in professional entry-level selection: Statistical scoring of common format applications. *Journal of Occupational and Organizational Psychology, 73,* 103–118.

Hogan, J.B. (1988). *The influence of socially desirable responding on biographical data of applicant versus incumbent samples: Implications for predictive and concurrent research designs.* Unpublished doctoral dissertation, University of Georgia, Athens, GA.

Hogan, J.B. (1994). Empirical keying of background data measures. In G. Stokes, M. Mumford, & W. Owens (Eds.), *Biodata handbook: Theory, research, and use of biographical information in selection and performance prediction* (pp. 69–107). Palo Alto, CA: Consulting Psychologists Press.

Holden, R.R. (1985). Response latency detection of fakers on personnel tests. *Canadian Journal of Behavioural Science, 27,* 343–355.

Holden, R.R., & Kroner, D.G. (1992). Relative efficacy of differential response latencies for detecting faking on a self-report measure of psychopathology. *Psychological Assessment, 4,* 170–173.

Holden, R.R., Kroner, D.G., Fekken, G.C., & Popham, S.M. (1992). A model of personality test item dissimulation. *Journal of Personality and Social Psychology, 63,* 272–279.

Hough, L.M. (1984). Development and evaluation of the "accomplishment record" method of selecting and promoting professionals. *Journal of Applied Psychology, 69,* 135–146.

Hough, L.M., & Paullin, C. (1994). Construct-oriented scale construction: The rational approach. In G. Stokes, M. Mumford, & W. Owens (Eds.), *Biodata handbook: Theory, research, and use of biographical information in selection and performance prediction* (pp. 109–145). Palo Alto, CA: Consulting Psychologists Press.

Hunter, J.E., & Hunter, R.F. (1984). Validity and utility of alternative predictors of job performance. *Psychological Bulletin, 96,* 72–98.

Jacobs, R.R., & Conte, J.M. (1996). Why biodata works in forecasting the success of bus operators: Synthesis of results across predictors. In R.B. Stennett, A.G. Parisi, & G.S. Stokes (Eds.), *A compendium: Papers presented at the first biennial biodata conference* (pp. 167–187). Athens: University of Georgia.

Karas, M., & West, J. (1999). Construct-oriented biodata development for selection to a differentiated performance domain. *International Journal of Selection and Assessment, 7,* 86–96.

Kenagy, H.G., & Yoakum, C.S. (1925). *The selection and training of salesmen.* New York: McGraw-Hill.

Kilcullen, R.N., White, L.A., Mumford, M.D., & Mack, H. (1995). Assessing the construct validity of rational biodata scales. *Military Psychology, 7,* 17–28.

Kluger, A., Reilly, R.R., & Russell, C.J. (1991). Faking biodata tests: Are option-keyed instruments more resistant? *Journal of Applied Psychology, 76,* 889–896.

Kolodner, J.L. (1983a). Maintaining organization in dynamic long term memory. *Cognitive Science, 7,* 243–280.

Kolodner, J.L. (1983b). Reconstructive memory: A computer model, *Cognitive Science, 7,* 281–328.

Laurent, H. (1970). Cross-cultural cross-validation of empirically validated tests. *Journal of Applied Psychology, 54,* 417–423.

Lautenschlager, G.J. (1994). Accuracy and faking of background data. In G. Stokes, M. Mumford, & W. Owens (Eds.), *Biodata handbook: Theory, research, and use of biographical information in selection and performance prediction* (pp. 391–419). Palo Alto, CA: Consulting Psychologists Press.

Lautenschlager, G.J., & Shaffer, G.S. (1987). Reexamining the component stability of Owens' biographical questionnaire. *Journal of Applied Psychology, 72,* 149–152.

Lecznar, W.B., & Dailey, J.T. (1950). Keying biographical inventories in classification test batteries. *American Psychologist, 5,* 279.

Lefkowitz, J., Gebbia, M.I., Balsam, T., & Dunn, L. (1999). Dimensions of biodata items and their relationships to item validity. *Journal of Occupational and Organizational Psychology, 72,* 331–350.

Levine, A.S., & Zachert, V. (1951). Use of biographical inventory in the Air Force classification program. *Journal of Applied Psychology, 35,* 241–244.

Mael, F.A. (1991). A conceptual rationale for the domain and attributes of biodata items. *Personnel Psychology, 44,* 763–792.

Mael, F.A. (1994). If past behavior really predicts future, so should biodata's. In M.G. Rumsey, C.B. Walker, & J.H. Harris (Eds.), *Personnel selection and classification* (pp. 273–291). Hillsdale, NJ: Erlbaum.

Mael, F.A., & Ashforth, B.E. (1995). Loyal from day one: Biodata, organizational identification, and turnover among newcomers. *Personnel Psychology, 48,* 309–333.

Mael, F.A., Connerley, M., & Morath, R.A. (1996). None of your business: Parameters of biodata invasiveness. *Personnel Psychology, 49,* 613–650.

Mael, F.A., & Hirsch, A.C. (1993). Rainforest empiricism and quasi-rationality: Two approaches to objective biodata. *Personnel Psychology, 46,* 719–738.

Malone, M.P. (1978). *Predictive efficiency and discriminatory impact of verifiable biographical data as a function of data analysis procedure.* Unpublished doctoral dissertation, University of Minnesota, Minneapolis.

Manson, G.E. (1925). What can the application blank tell? Evaluation of items in personal history records of four thousand life insurance salesmen. *Journal of Personnel Research, 4,* 73–99.

Martin, C.L., & Nagao, D.H. (1989). Some effects of computerized interviewing on job applicant responses. *Journal of Applied Psychology, 74,* 72–80.

McManus, M.A., & Kelly, M.L. (1999). Personality measures and biodata: Evidence regarding their incremental predictive value in the life insurance industry. *Personnel Psychology, 52,* 137–148.

McManus, M.A., & Masztal, J.J. (1999). The impact of biodata item attributes on validity and socially desirable responding, *Journal of Business and Psychology, 13,* 437–446.

Mitchell, T.W. (1994). The utility of biodata. In Stokes, G., Mumford, M., & Owens, W. (Eds.), *Biodata handbook: Theory, research, and use of biographical information in selection and performance prediction* (pp. 485–516). Palo Alto, CA: Consulting Psychologists Press.

Mitchell, T.W., & Stokes, G.S. (1995, April). *The nuts and bolts of biodata.* Workshop presented at the annual meeting of the Society for Industrial and Organizational Psychology, Orlando, FL.

Mitchell, T.W., & Klimoski, R.J. (1986). Estimating the validity of cross-validity estimation. *Journal of Applied Psychology, 71,* 311–317.

Morrison, R.F. (1977). A multivariate model for the occupational placement decision. *Journal of Applied Psychology, 62,* 271–277.

Mount, M.K., Witt, L.A., & Barrick, M.R. (2000). Incremental validity of empirically keyed biodata scales over GMA and the five factor personality constructs. *Personnel Psychology, 53,* 299–323.

Mumford, M.D. (1999). Construct validity and background data: Issues, abuses, and future directions. *Human Resource Management Review, 9,* 117–145.

Mumford, M.D., Cooper, M., & Schemmer, F.M. (1983). *Development of a content valid set of background data measures.* Bethesda, MD: Advanced Research Resources Organization.

Mumford, M.D., Costanza, D.P., Connelly, M.S., & Johnson, J.F. (1996). Item generation procedures and background data scales: Implications for construct and criterion-related validity. *Personnel Psychology, 49,* 361–398.

Mumford, M.D., & Owens, W.A. (1987). Methodology review: Principles, procedures, and findings in the application of background data measures. *Applied Psychological Measurement, 11,* 1–31.

Mumford, M.D., & Stokes, G.S. (1992). Developmental determinants of individual action: Theory and practice in applying background measures. In M.D. Dunnette & L.M. Hough (Eds.), *Handbook of industrial and organizational psychology* (2nd ed., Vol. 3, pp. 61–138). Palo Alto, CA: Consulting Psychologists Press.

Mumford, M.D., Stokes, G.S., & Owens, W.A. (1990). *Patterns of life history: The ecology of human individuality.* Hillsdale, NJ: Erlbaum.

Neidt, C.O., & Malloy, J.P. (1954). A technique for keying items of an inventory to be added to an existing test battery. *Journal of Applied Psychology, 38,* 308–312.

Nunnally, J.C. (1978). *Psychometric theory.* New York: McGraw-Hill.

Owens, W.A. (1976). Background data. In M.D. Dunnette (Ed.), *Handbook of industrial and organizational psychology* (pp. 609–644). Chicago: Rand-McNally.

Owens, W.A., Glennon, J.R., & Albright, L.W. (1962). Retest consistency and the writing of life history items: A first step. *Journal of Applied Psychology, 46,* 329–332.

Owens, W.A., & Schoenfeldt, L.F. (1979). Toward a classification of persons. *Journal of Applied Psychology, 65,* 569–607.

Pannone, R.D. (1984). Predicting test performance: A content validity approach to screening applicants. *Personnel Psychology, 37,* 507–514.

Pannone, R.D. (1994). Blue collar selection. In G. Stokes, M. Mumford, & W. Owens (Eds.), *Biodata handbook: Theory, research, and use of biographical information in selection and performance prediction* (pp. 261–273). Palo Alto, CA: Consulting Psychologists Press.

Parish, J.A., & Drucker, A.J. (1957). *Personnel research for officer candidate school* (Tech. Research Rep. No. 117). USA TAGO Personnel Research Branch.

Pedhazur, E.J. (1982). *Multiple regression in behavioral research.* New York: Holt, Rinehart, & Winston.

Pickrel, E.W. (1954). *The relative predictive efficiency of three methods of utilizing scores from biographical inventories* (USAF Tech. Rep., AFPTRC-TR-54-73, Project 503-001-0015). Personnel Research Division.

Pulakos, E., & Schmitt, N. (1996). An evaluation of two strategies for reducing adverse impact and their effects on criterion-related validity. *Human Performance, 9,* 241–258.

Reilly, R.R., & Chao, G.T. (1982). Validity and fairness of some alternative employee selection procedures. *Personnel Psychology, 35,* 1–63.

Reilly, R.R., & Warech, M.A. (1989). *The validity and fairness of alternative predictors of occupational performance.* Paper invited by the National Commission on Testing and Public Policy, Washington, DC.

Reiser, B.J., Black, J.B., & Abelson, R.P. (1985). Knowledge structures in the organization and retrieval of autobiographical memories. *Cognitive Psychology, 17,* 89–137.

Reiter-Palmon, R., & Connelly, M.S. (2000). Item selection counts: A comparison of empirical key and rational scale validities in theory-based and non-theory-based item pools. *Journal of Applied Psychology, 85,* 143–151.

Reiter-Palmon, R., DeFilippo, B., & Mumford, M.D. (1990). *Differential predictive validity of positive and negative response options to biodata items.* Paper presented at the annual meeting of the Southeastern Psychological Association, Atlanta, GA.

Rogers, T.B. (1995). *The psychological testing enterprise: An introduction.* Pacific Grove, CA: Brooks/Cole.

Rothstein, H.R., Schmidt, F.L., Erwin, F.W., Owens, W.A., & Sparks, C.P. (1990). Biographical data in employment selection: Can validities be made generalizable? *Journal of Applied Psychology, 75,* 175–184.

Roy, H., Brueckel, J., & Drucker, A.J. (1954). Selection of army and air force reserve training corps students. *USA Personnel Research Branch Notes, 28.*

Russell, C.J. (1994). Generation procedures for biodata items: A point of departure. In G. Stokes, M. Mumford, & W. Owens (Eds.), *Biodata handbook: Theory, research, and use of biographical information in selection and performance prediction* (pp. 17–37). Palo Alto, CA: Consulting Psychologists Press.

Russell, C.J., & Domm, D.R. (1990, April). *On the construct validity of biographical information: Evaluation of a theory-based method of item generation.* Paper presented at the annual meeting of the Society for Industrial and Organizational Psychology, Miami.

Russell, C.J., Mattson, J., Devlin, S.E., & Atwater, D. (1990). Predictive validity of biodata items generated from retrospective life experience essays. *Journal of Applied Psychology, 75,* 569–580.

Ryan, A.M., McFarland, L., Baron, H., & Page, R. (1999). An international look at selection practices: Nation and culture as explanations for variability in practice. *Personnel Psychology, 52,* 359–391.

Schmidt, F.L., & Hunter, J.E. (1998). The validity and utility of selection methods in personnel psychology: Practical and theoretical implications of 85 years of research findings. *Psychological Bulletin, 124,* 262–274.

Schmidt, F.L., & Rothstein, H.R. (1994). Application of validity generalization to biodata scales in employment selection. In G. Stokes, M. Mumford, & W. Owens (Eds.), *Biodata handbook: Theory, research, and use of biographical information in selection and performance prediction* (pp. 237–260). Palo Alto, CA: Consulting Psychologists Press.

Schmitt, N., Gooding, R.Z., Noe, R.A., & Kirsch, M. (1984). Meta-analyses of validity studies published between 1964 and 1982 and the investigation of study characteristics. *Personnel Psychology, 37,* 407–422.

Schmitt, N., Jennings, D., & Toney, R. (1999). Can we develop measures of hypothetical constructs? *Human Resource Management Review, 9,* 169–183.

Schmitt, N., & Pulakos, E.D. (1998). Biodata and differential prediction: Some reservations. In M.D. Hakel (Ed.), *Beyond multiple choice: Evaluating alternatives to traditional testing for selection* (pp. 167–182). Hillsdale, NJ: Erlbaum.

Schmitt, N., Rogers, W., Chan, D., Sheppard, L., & Jennings, D. (1997). Adverse impact and predictive efficiency of various predictor combinations. *Journal of Applied Psychology, 82,* 719–730.

Schoenfeldt, L.F. (1989, August). *Biographical data as the new frontier in employee selection research.* Division 5 presidential address at the annual meeting of the American Psychological Association, New Orleans.

Schoenfeldt, L.F., & Mendoza, J.L. (1994). Developing and using factorially derived biographical scales. In G. Stokes, M. Mumford, & W. Owens (Eds.), *Biodata handbook: Theory, research, and use of biographical information in selection and performance prediction* (pp. 147–169). Palo Alto, CA: Consulting Psychologists Press.

Shaffer, G.S., Saunders, V., & Owens, W.A. (1986). Additional evidence for the accuracy of biographical information: Long-term retest and observer ratings. *Personnel Psychology, 39,* 791–809.

Sharf, J.C. (1994). The impact of legal and equal employment opportunity issues on personal history inquiries. In G. Stokes, M. Mumford, & W. Owens (Eds.), *Biodata handbook: Theory, research, and use of biographical information in selection and performance prediction* (pp. 351–390). Palo Alto, CA: Consulting Psychologists Press.

Siegel, L. (1956). A biographical inventory for students: I. Construction and standardization of the instrument. *Journal of Applied Psychology, 40,* 5–10.

Sinar, E.F., & Reynolds, D.H. (2001, April). *Applicant reactions to internet-based selection techniques.* Paper presented at the annual meeting of the Society for Industrial and Organizational Psychology, San Diego, CA.

Snell, A.F., Sydell, E.J., & Lueke, S.B. (1999). Towards a theory of applicant faking: Integrating studies of deception. *Human Resource Management Review, 9,* 219–242.

Stanley, S.A., Hecht, J.E., Montagliani, A., Stokes, G.S., Barroso, C.R., & Hause, O.R. (2000, April). *Biodata item attributes in multiple samples: Validity and response distortion.* Paper presented at the annual meeting of the Society for Industrial and Organizational Psychology, New Orleans, LA.

Stead, N.H., & Shartle, C.L. (1940). *Occupational counseling techniques.* New York: American Book.

Stokes, G.S., & Cooper, L.A. (1994). Selection using biodata: Old notions revisited. In G. Stokes, M. Mumford, & W. Owens (Eds.), *Biodata handbook: Theory, research, and use of biographical information in selection and performance prediction* (pp. 311–350). Palo Alto, CA: Consulting Psychologists Press.

Stokes, G.S., & Cooper, L.A. (2001). Content/construct approaches in life history form development for selection. *International Journal of Selection and Assessment, 9,* 138–151.

Stokes, G.S., Hogan, J.B., & Snell, A.F. (1993). Comparability of incumbent and applicant samples for the development of biodata keys: The influence of social desirability. *Personnel Psychology, 46,* 739–762.

Stokes, G., Mumford, M., & Owens, W. (1994). *Biodata handbook: Theory, research, and use of biographical information in selection and performance prediction.* Palo Alto, CA: Consulting Psychologists Press.

Stokes, G.S., & Reddy, S. (1992). Use of background data in organizational decisions. In C.L. Cooper & I.T. Robertson (Eds.), *International review of industrial and organizational psychology* (pp. 285–322). West Sussex, England: Wiley.

Stokes, G.S., & Searcy, C.A. (1999). Specification of scales in biodata form development: Rational vs. empirical and global vs.

specific. *International Journal of Selection and Assessment, 7,* 72–85.

Stokes, G.S., Searcy, C.A., & Toth, C.S. (1998, April). *Is it rational to be empirical? An indepth look at an unresolved issue.* Paper presented at the 13th Annual Conference of the Society for Industrial and Organizational Psychology, Dallas, TX.

Stokes, G.S., Toth, C.S., Searcy, C.A., Stroupe, J.P., & Carter, G.W. (1999). Construct/rational biodata dimensions to predict salesperson performance: Report on the U.S. Department of Labor sales study. *Human Resources Management Review, 9,* 185–218.

Stricker, L.J. (1987, November). *Developing a biographical measure to assess leadership potential.* Paper presented at the annual meeting of the Military Testing Association, Ottawa, Ontario.

Stricker, L.J. (1988, November). *Assessing leadership potential at the Naval Academy with a biographical measure.* Paper presented at the annual meeting of the Military Testing Association, San Antonio, TX.

Terpstra, D.E., Mohamed, A.A., & Kethley, R.B. (1999). An analysis of federal court cases involving nine selection devices. *International Journal of Selection and Assessment, 7,* 26–34.

Telenson, P.A., Alexander, R.A., & Barrett, G.V. (1983). Scoring the biographical information blank: A comparison of three weighting techniques. *Applied Psychological Measurement, 7,* 73–80.

Thayer, P.W. (1977). Somethings old, somethings new. *Personnel Psychology, 30,* 513–524.

Thompson-Feith, K.E. (2001). *An investigation of item content and individual difference variables influencing perceptions of invasiveness of biodata items.* Unpublished doctoral dissertation, University of Georgia, Athens, GA.

Trent, T.T., Atwater, D.C., & Abrahams, N.M. (1986). Biographical screening of military applicants: Experimental assessment of item response distortion. In G.E. Lee (Ed.), *Proceedings of the Tenth Symposium on Psychology in the Department of Defense* (pp. 96–100). Colorado Springs, CO: U.S. Air Force Academy, Department of Behavioral Sciences and Leadership.

van Rijn, P. (1992). Biodata: Potential and challenges in public sector employee selection. *Personnel Assessment Monograph, 2.* Alexandria, VA: International Personnel Management Association Assessment Council (IPMAAC).

Vinchur, A.J., Schippmann, J.S., Switzer, F.S., & Roth, P.L. (1998). A meta-analytic review of predictors of job performance for salespeople. *Journal of Applied Psychology, 83,* 586–597.

Viteles, M. (1932). *Industrial psychology.* New York: Norton.

# CHAPTER 16

# Judgmental Assessment of Job-Related Experience, Training, and Education for Use in Human Resource Staffing

EDWARD L. LEVINE, RONALD A. ASH, AND JONATHAN D. LEVINE

*Polonius's Advice to Laertes Upon His Departure to France:*

And these few precepts in thy memory
Look thou character. Give thy thoughts no tongue,
Nor any unproportion'd thought his act.
Be thou familiar, but by no means vulgar;
Those friends thou hast, and their adoptions tried,
Grapple them unto thy soul with hoops of steel;
But do not dull thy palm with entertainment
Of each new-hatched, unfledg'd comrade. Beware
Of entrance to a quarrel, but, being in,
Bear 't that th' opposed may beware of thee.
Give every man thy ear, but few thy voice;
Take each man's censure, but reserve thy judgment.
Costly thy habit as thy purse can buy,
But not express'd in fancy; rich not gaudy;
For the apparel oft proclaims the man,
And they in France of the best rank and station
Are of a most select and generous clef in that.
Neither a borrower, nor a lender be;
For loan oft loses both itself and friend.

And borrowing dulleth edge of husbandry.
This above all: to thine own self be true,
And it must follow, as the night the day,
Thou canst not then be false to any man.

> (Shakespeare's *The Tragedy of Hamlet,
> Prince of Denmark,* Act I, Scene 3)

Polonius's advice as a father to his son is a condensation of much of the knowledge and wisdom acquired from his (presumptive) life experiences. There is advice about dress and bearing, forming acquaintances, handling feedback, dealing with cultural differences, managing finances, resolving conflict, and the value of integrity. That the advice rings true today provides ample evidence of the impact of experience on our worldview, our knowledge of how to negotiate the trials and tribulations the world may throw at us, and the manner in which we present ourselves to others. It should be a foregone conclusion that the straightforward use of life experiences, including education and training as attempts to compress and convey life's lessons, in assessing the suitability and competence of future employees will provide infallibly valid information. Unfortunately, the conclusion is overly simple and suffers from the devilishly complex nature of life and work.

The complexity of the construct of work experience is well illustrated by a recent study. Clevenger, Pereira, Wiechmann, Schmitt, and Harvey (2001) studied work experience in three separate samples, along with several other predictors. Among 412 federal investigative officers, experience was measured as number of years in current job. Among 233 customer service representatives in an international transportation company, experience was measured as the sum of years in their jobs and years with the company. Among 126 engineering employees in a large manufacturing organization, experience was measured as the sum of job tenure and years with the company.

In the first sample, experience showed no significant relationship with any of the other predictors, including cognitive ability, situational judgment, job knowledge, or conscientiousness, but it was significantly and positively related to job performance at .13. In the second sample, experience was significantly *negatively* correlated with quantitative reasoning and job knowledge, while there was no significant relationship with job performance. In the third sample, experience was significantly *negatively* correlated with cognitive ability ($-.33$), a job simulation score and job performance, the last correlation reported at $-.31$. Experience was not significantly related to conscientiousness or situational judgment for the engineers. The one consistency observed seems to be that length of work experience is unrelated to conscientiousness—a finding that would have surprised Polonius no doubt. This confusing pattern of results is played out in other research as well. Polonius would have been thoroughly confused at these outcomes, and we too must admit consternation at what the research has revealed about experience, and its partners, education and training. Nevertheless, those in the business of staffing today and in times past rely or have relied heavily on experience, training, and education. They are often the first and sometimes the only basis upon which we base our employment decisions. Thankfully, we have seen a good bit of progress toward elucidating the measurement characteristics and validity of experience in the recent past, and we may soon be in a position to rival Polonius by providing robust advice to those who would use experience, education, and training in assessing candidates for positions in work organizations.

In this chapter, we intend to unravel the mysteries of this construct—experience and the education and training embedded within it—to the extent permitted by our current state of knowledge, and how it may validly be used to assess candidates and applicants for positions in work organizations.

## DEFINITION OF THE ASSESSMENT DOMAIN

Before beginning our exploration let us define our domain. The assessments we deal with here are based solely on information provided by individuals about their past experience, education, and training on job applications, resumes, or supplementary questionnaires. Primarily the information is centered on work history, credentials such as licenses, education and training, and past accomplishments at work or in other settings that bear a relationship to work. An example of the last-mentioned factor might be leadership positions in clubs held while attending school that might be germane when considering someone for a supervisory or managerial role (e.g., Howard, 1986). However, the information may include self-reported competencies based on tasks or knowledge, skills, abilities, or attributes like motivation so long as these self-reports are anchored or "validated" by an explicitly stated link to those specific elements of experience, education, or training where the competency was acquired. One or more members of a hiring organization subject the written information provided by individuals to a judgmental evaluation. If panels or teams are involved, the members' assessments may be rendered independently and averaged, or they may be combined by consensus. Where technology permits, a computer algorithm that automates judgmental criteria may be employed to complete the assessment. The purposes for the assessment might include recruitment, initial screening, selection or deselection (i.e., layoffs and termination), but for this chapter would not deal with compensation, career planning, rehabilitation, performance evaluation, licensing, certification, or compensation (cf. Tesluk & Jacobs, 1998). Judgmental evaluation rules out any empirical keying of personal history as employed in weighted application blanks or extensive biographical information blanks, which are treated in Chapter 15 of this volume.

When assessments of the type to be described here are used for any of the stated purposes, they are subject to the Uniform Guidelines on Employee Selection Procedures (1978) (Equal Employment Opportunity Commission [EEOC], U.S. Civil Service Commission, U.S. Department of Labor, & U.S. Department of Justice, 1978). Section 1607.2B of the Guidelines states: "*Employment decisions.* These guidelines apply to tests and other selection procedures which are used as a basis for any employment decision. Employment decisions include but are not limited to hiring, promotion, demotion, membership (for example, in a labor organization), referral, retention, and licensing and certification . . ." (italics in original).

## CHAPTER ORGANIZATION

The chapter begins with coverage of what we know about the primary elements that form the basis of the assessments—experience, education, and training. Then there is a general overview of the research dealing with how these elements are evaluated to score or rank applicants or to make employment decisions. Their degree of validity and reliability as well as legality is treated as part of this presentation. When application materials are formally scored according to some systematic judgmental process, they are referred to in the public sector as training and experience evaluations (T&Es) or education and experience evaluations (E&Es) (Porter, Levine, & Flory, 1976). They are sometimes called unassembled examinations in the public sector because applicants need not assemble at a given location to provide the information (Maslow, 1968). Another name used in this context is the accomplishment record, where information about an applicant's past achievements is evaluated and scored (Hough, 1984). A variation of this approach has been termed the behavioral consistency method (Schmidt et al., 1979).

Following this we delve more deeply into particular methods of performing the assessments, and the validity and reliability associated with each. The final section covers approaches that are done online or electronically using simple algorithms such as keyword searches or more sophisticated approaches.

## WORK-RELATED EXPERIENCE, EDUCATION, AND TRAINING

It is somewhat artificial to separate education and training from work experience. We are, after all, the product of the sum total of our life experiences. Cooperative programs in secondary and higher education institutions recognize and exploit this linkage (Rowe, 1988). However, the assessments of the type considered here have typically and traditionally treated these as separable components of an evaluation. We will proceed accordingly.

### Experience

Work-related experience has three faces. Two of these are framed from the perspective of the applicant. One represents the *personal attributes* affected by exposure to, and performance in, work-related settings and activities. A second covers the *perceived outcomes of experience*—the meaning that we attach to our experiences, the perceived changes in our attributes we derive from them, and the manner in which we present our experiences to others; for example, in what we choose to include on an application form. The third is framed from the perspective of the evaluator of the experience. It deals with those *aspects of experience judged relevant and important* in assessing qualifications and suitability for recruitment, screening, and selection.

### *Effects on Personal Attributes*

It has long been known that experience, especially, for our purposes, work experience, has substantial effects on knowledge, abilities, skills, values, motivation, and competencies. As just one example almost 50 years ago Tannenbaum (1957) demonstrated that individual personalities will change in the direction of closure with their environment. After a year in an environment designed to produce heightened autonomy, the personality trend toward obeisance to superiors and dependence on superiors to get things done decreased. The reverse tended to occur for those exposed to a hierarchical environment. Rowe (1988) cited evidence that those with previous work experience exhibit greater commitment to work and value jobs more.

Unquestionably the most definitive research on changes wrought by experience was conducted by Douglas Bray and his associates (Bray, Campbell, & Grant, 1974; Howard, 1986; Howard & Bray, 1988). Their work dealt with managers in the Bell System. The research was both longitudinal in nature and included separate cohorts to capture the impact of different cultural epochs. The earlier work revealed increases in cognitive ability after eight years of managerial experience, but, perhaps not surprising in light of our assumption about the complexity of the experience construct, there was no change in administrative skills, and a cohort average *decrease* in interpersonal skills. Overall management ability showed no change. Tracking differences within the cohort revealed that those who advanced but were not assessed as being of high potential showed the greatest gains in interpersonal skills. It was conjectured that advancement may have forced practice of this skill or that advancement increased managers' self-confidence and allowed their latent interpersonal ability to emerge. Personality changes were also observed. Over time, need for advancement, tolerance for uncertainty, and goal flexibility showed decreases, while self-confidence and need for achievement increased. One important cohort effect in comparing the earlier and later samples was an observed decrease in the need for advancement, owing perhaps to cultural changes.

The positive changes produced by experience that underlie their use in screening and selection may be captured in the notion of increases in task specific proficiency for those in routine, repetitive jobs such as sewing machine operators (Gordon & Fitzgibbons, 1982). In the study by Gordon and Fitzgibbons (1982) length of tenure with the company and in the job was positively associated with performance (.23 and .15, respectively). When operators changed jobs, the degree of similarity between the old and new jobs predicted performance on the new job at .20, while company tenure and job seniority did not.

For professional, technical, and managerial jobs we may conceive of a progression from novice to expert, rookie to seasoned professional (Sonnentag, 1998). Russell (2001) reported on the predictive validity of competencies among executives derived by exploring in detail, among many other factors, such aspects of past experience as managing conflicts and overcoming obstacles. Use of the fine-grained analysis of past experience and performance produced an estimated gain of millions of dollars in profit for each candidate selected under the system. The literature in cognitive psychology provides a rich depiction of how novices may be developed into experts (Anderson, 1990), and this knowledge may be exploited by developing such training programs as intelligent tutoring systems to speed the process of transitioning from novice to expert (Quiñones & Ehrenstein, 1997).

For jobs in trades, crafts, sports, and the arts we may conceive of a progression from apprentice to journeyperson to master. This process takes years of experience in jobs like line mechanic or electronics repair technician and may involve cycles of working and on-the-job training alternating with full-time schooling. The model has been extended also to technical jobs in health care (Goldstein & Ford, 2002).

The distinctions among these broad job types may provide us with guidance on the type of experience indicator that may be most effective for screening and selection for varying job types.

### Experience and Job Performance

A key question in this realm is how experience affects performance. This question moves us directly into theoretical efforts linking experience in nomological nets with other constructs in causing performance. Although promising findings have emerged, many questions remain to be answered. Schmidt, Hunter, and Outerbridge (1986) tested a model exploring the relationships among experience (months on present job), job knowledge, task proficiency, general ability, and supervisory ratings of job performance. The model was tested by means of path analysis among a sample of 1,474 soldiers in four different, nonsupervisory, trades occupations. They restricted their job set to those where incumbents had an intermediate level of experience because they conjectured that too little experience would not permit sufficient acquisition of job knowledge or task proficiency, and too much would reduce the relative discriminability of experience. Their findings suggested that experience exerts its impact on performance first through job knowledge and second through task proficiency. However, for raw, ungrouped experience data there was still a residual direct link to performance. Schmidt et al. (1986) offered the possibility that this outcome may have been due to the factors supervisors relied on to rate the more senior performers, or to the role of the most experienced workers in providing training to new workers. The latter would conceivably broaden the role of senior employees and produce higher ratings. Still, the model and the unexpected findings are based exclusively on the link of experience to task performance.

Borman, Hanson, Oppler, Pulakos, and White (1993) also tested a model linking experience to performance. Although still confined to the military, this study dealt with more experienced supervisory personnel, 570 in all, across a more diversified job set, including trades, technical jobs, law enforcement, and health care. Experience was simply defined as the number of months employed as a supervisor. Structural equation modeling using LISREL VI was the analytic mode. Their results suggested a slightly different model from that supported by the data of Schmidt et al. (1986). Experience was more influential in producing its effects on ratings through supervisory task proficiency than job knowledge, but the paths from experience to proficiency and knowledge and the direct impact of these on job performance ratings was similar between the two studies. A key difference in this model was that ability as measured by the Armed Services Vocational Aptitude Battery (ASVAB) seemed to increase the chances that an incumbent would be given more opportunities to acquire supervisory experience. Again, however, only task performance was the focus.

Taking a more detailed look at the constructs involved in the criterion of job performance than the studies by Borman et al. (1993) and Schmidt et al. (1986), Vance, Coovert, MacCallum, and Hedge (1989) studied a sample of 201 U.S. Air Force jet engine mechanics. Their criteria included two measures on a work sample, and task ratings from supervisors, peers, and the mechanics themselves. Experience was measured as number of months working on the current engine assignment and—for two of the three task types, which served as the context for model testing—the frequency of performing eight tasks that were the basis of proficiency ratings. Tests of the models separately in the context of three task types using LISREL VI suggested experience had a positive impact on both tested and rated task proficiency. Once again task performance was the focus of attention.

Given that experience influences a host of personal attributes other than task performance, such as commitment and self-confidence (e.g., Bray et al., 1974; Rowe, 1988; Tannenbaum, 1957), we expect that a more complete exploration of the construct domain surrounding experience should include facets of performance other than task performance. Motowidlo and Van Scotter (1994) added evidence in support of this notion. In their study of U.S. Air Force mechanics they found that experience, which was measured by years of experience grouped into six levels (1 = 1–2 years, 6 = 17–20 years), was significantly correlated with both task (.34) and contextual performance (.16).

Another line of research that bears on the nomological net surrounding the relationship of experience to job performance has dealt with the changing nature of the relationship of abilities to performance with growth in experience. If experience does not alter the relationship between, for example, cognitive ability and job performance, then we may view experience as fostering a steady growth in task performance over time. This would allow a safe assumption that experience will predict task performance in a straightforward manner, and monotonic increases in performance would be expected as people gain in experience. Schmidt, Hunter, Outerbridge, and Goff (1988), using the same sample as the earlier study by Schmidt et al. (1986), found evidence supporting this interpretation at least out to five years of experience.

Farrell and McDaniel (2001) tested this notion again in exploring Ackerman's (1988) model, which suggested systematic changes in the relationship between component abilities and performance over time depending on whether jobs (tasks) are consistent or inconsistent. Their findings are based on meta-analytic aggregations of data over a broad cross section of jobs with over 24,000 incumbents. Experience was measured by years of experience in an occupation with current and prior employers. Results suggested that increasing experience produces modest gains in both consistent and inconsistent jobs out to 8 years of experience (and out to 10 for inconsistent jobs), although most of the productivity gain comes within the first 5 years. For consistent and inconsistent jobs the pattern of correlations followed Ackerman's model to a degree, but for purposes of this chapter the data suggest that the effects of experience on task performance will not be simple and straightforward over time. Taken in conjunction with Schmidt et al.'s (1988) data, the weighting of experience beyond five years seems unlikely to add much predictive

value. Sonnentag's (1998) study of software designers also supports the notion that experience makes a difference only for the early portion of an employee's tenure, since she found that differences among high versus low performers resided not in their years of experience but in their cognitive activities in solving problems. The group of high performers in that study had 6.6 years of experience on average compared with 7.8 years for the lower performing group. Likewise, Maranto and Rodgers (1984) showed that the greatest gains in productivity among wage claims investigators occurred during the first year of employment, and the rate of gain declined in subsequent years.

An even more recent meta-analysis (Keil & Cortina, 2001) used a sample of 49 longitudinal studies with 1,157 predictor-criterion pairs. Results here suggest a highly complex pattern of interrelationships between abilities and performance with increases in experience. Validity of component abilities deteriorates over time in contrast to Schmidt et al.'s (1986) findings. The complexity of the pattern of decline may be a function of the nature of tasks and criteria, which ranged from rudder control test performance to grade point average to salary growth. Again, however, it appears that the manner in which experience affects task performance changes with increases in experience and that the validity of length of experience in predicting task-based aspects of performance will diminish over time. The diminution will occur faster, the data in this and the study by Farrell and McDaniel (2001) suggest, when jobs are routine and repetitive.

The theoretically based empirical work summarized in the preceding is limited in at least two important ways. First there is no attempt to explore the non-task-based elements of performance, including such aspects as contextual performance and turnover. For example, Giniger, Dispenzieri, and Eisenberg (1983) found that greater experience among 667 workers, as measured by length of time in garment industry jobs at one company, was associated with lower turnover and lower absenteeism, in addition to better performance. Second, in all cases the experience construct itself is measured in a primitive fashion. Attempting to remedy these problems Tesluk and Jacobs (1998) formulated the most comprehensive model of work experience extant. They tackled the experience construct itself as a primary focus, and their model shows the deficiencies in how many researchers have measured the variable. They proffer a three-facet framework for experience—quantitative (frequency of task repetition, time on task/job), qualitative (task variety, challenge, complexity), and interaction of these (density or intensity of task performance and proper timing of the task performance during skill or competency acquisition). These are crossed with levels at which these factors may occur—task, job, work group, organization, or occupation. Contextual factors such as availability of training condition the developmental opportunities that may arise for the employee, and individual factors such as self-efficacy influence the degree to which the individual actually learns from experience. Outcomes of experience may affect motivation, knowledge and skills, and work attitudes, and these in turn influence job performance and career development.

Although not a direct test of this model, Russell's (2001) recent study of executive selection provided support for this enriched conceptualization. The intense and expanded review and elaboration of developmental experiences in that study attained a high level of predictive power in a job category where performance is notoriously difficult to capture. One example of corroborating evidence concerns timing. In that study it seems that the more successful general managers followed advice of mentors to seek ways to get a quick score or success in the fiscal domain early on, and to take time to develop relationships. Thus, resource-oriented competencies predicted early performance, whereas interpersonal competencies predicted later performance.

This evidence notwithstanding, we still note some shortcomings in the model. First, the experience concept focuses on "exposures," not the degree of excellence with which people perform a task, which is the basis for some methods of evaluating experience (Schmidt et al., 1979). Second, the study by Russell (2001) suggests that industry (e.g., advertising, agricultural, health care) may be a worthwhile addition to the level component of Tesluk and Jacobs's model. Those broader contexts may add significant grounded learning as experience grows. Additional evidence in support of this notion comes from a study by Solomon (1986), who found important differences among public and private, production and service organizations, in aspects like emphasis on practices that promote efficiency. Third, the constructs dealing with outcomes such as job performance should be elaborated to reflect recent thinking, such as the now common practice of distinguishing between task and contextual performance. Nevertheless, Tesluk and Jacobs (1998) have provided a road map or matrix that should guide future work on the theoretical underpinnings of the experience construct.

### Perceived Outcomes of Experience and Providing Veridical Information

As we gain experience we store lessons learned in memory. How we evaluate our own experiences may lead us to grow in self-efficacy (Bray et al., 1974), which in turn may produce greater levels of mastery and ultimately heightened performance. However, our memories both at the conscious and unconscious levels do not precisely encode and retrieve lessons learned. Pasupathi (2001) pointed out that much of our learning takes place in social contexts, which of course characterize most work activities, and our attempts to extract meaning from the memories of events are shaped by how we recount them to others and how others react. Constructions of past events may affect both what changes actually occur in our attributes and whether we perceive the changes as positive or negative.

Conversational reconstruction according to Pasupathi may produce consistency in what we recall but may not provide a veridical account of what actually transpired. For example, we may recount to a supervisor how we made a serious blunder in hiring someone without verifying past education. Our supervisor could register outrage, belittling us in the process. Or the supervisor might suggest that this represented a good lesson from a mere oversight that will guard against future errors of this kind. As we recount the experience, it may in the former context become consistently more serious and lead us to reset our career aspirations. Or it may be remembered consistently as a minor mistake, which fostered our continued development as a human resources manager.

Meta-memory issues involved in our own assessment of our own state of competence may, according to Bjork (1994), be as critical in determining our level of performance as the actual changes in our attributes. We may be subject to overconfidence about the extent of our comprehension or mastery of a skill due to the operation of such factors as presumed familiarity or hindsight bias. An example of the latter could occur when one observes a model using a practiced approach to a problem with the solution included, and then assumes he or she can easily handle similar problems of that type.

There appear to be stable individual differences in our capacity to learn from our experiences. Spreitzer, McCall, and Mahoney (1997) listed several factors that might provide the basis for a measure: (1) proactively seeking challenge; (2) nondefensiveness in learning from mistakes and criticism; (3) adaptability; and (4) seeking and using feedback. Although their efforts at producing a scale resulted in reliable subscales with internal consistency estimates ranging from .70 to .85, validity of the scale was lacking perhaps because the end-state competencies produced by these differences in learning from experience outweighed the differences themselves in predicting the criteria of interest. Pulakos, Arad, Donovan, and Plamondon (2000) addressed this issue also by focusing on adaptability, which includes such attributes as solving problems creatively and demonstrating interpersonal adaptability in circumstances where, for example, one's team constantly shifts personnel. This capacity may help overcome the tendency of experienced people toward applying their habitual methods of working despite radical changes in circumstances. This factor seems to apply also at the team and organizational levels, where our dynamic, global economy demands a learning organization (Senge, 1990).

Turning now to how we share our experiences in the employment context, we note that impression management comes into play. Our rendering of our past experiences may vary from outright lies, to expected distortions, omissions, or exaggerations that are part of the employment "game," to distortions that come from the biases produced in memory despite our attempts to be truthful, to veridical, verifiable accounts of our past work-related experience. One need not look too hard to find reams of advice on how to prepare a winning resume. One example of an attempt to influence people to provide pertinent, structured information may be found in a reference like Porter and Levine (1974). In a study of 188 managers and professionals, Stone and Stone (1987) found evidence that failing to provide information on an application, rather than protecting privacy, can backfire. Employers may assume that this represents an attempt to suppress unfavorable information and may downgrade their evaluations of applicants accordingly. On the other hand, self-promotion as an impression management strategy does seem to pay off in more favorable interview evaluations, so its use in obtaining a job is reinforced (Nguyen & McDaniel, 2001).

Anderson, Warner, and Spencer (1984) cleverly explored the extent of bias in self-reports of task proficiency. Three hundred fifty-one applicants for 13 different jobs (e.g., mechanics, clerk-typists, groundskeepers) with a state government rated their level of mastery for each task in a task inventory on a scale ranging from 0 ("I Have No Experience Doing This Task") to 4 ("I Have Trained and/or Supervised Others Doing This Task.") Bogus task statements were placed in each inventory. Some of our favorites included: "Subtracting positive statuarials"; "Scheduling ichnite contacts"; "Matrixing solvency files"; and "Filling rhetaguards." Sums of ratings to the bogus items measured the extent of inflation. They called inflation "extensive," based on the fact that 45% of all applicants indicated they had observed or performed at least one of the bogus tasks, and that the inflation score was correlated at .48 on median with scores on the self-report form. Furthermore, the reliability of the inflation scores exhibited substantial reliability at .86 on median. When validity against a criterion of typing test performance was assessed using multiple regression, the inflation score added incrementally, based on its negative relationship with the criterion, to scores on the self-report form. Nguyen and McDaniel (2001) provided meta-analytic evidence supporting these results. Studying the impact of different aspects of impression management, they found that self-promotion, while apparently functional in obtaining favorable ratings in the selection process, is unrelated to job performance, and providing an inflated image of one's capabilities as a hardworking employee apparently leads to lower performance ratings.

These results along with other research indicating that there is a considerable amount of distortion of past experience (Gatewood & Feild, 1998) suggest that steps must be taken to guard against inflation. Verification through reference and background checks, pledges of accuracy of information that an applicant must sign, penalties such as loss of job for falsification, and the use of an inflation correction like the one described by Anderson et al. (1984) must be considered during the assessment process.

### Aspects of Experience Judged Relevant and Important for Prediction

We turn now to a consideration of the experience factors assessors view as relevant and important in establishing the suitability and qualifications of applicants. Two streams of thought provide the basis for the factors: (1) the views of assessors based on their experience, evaluation of research, and concern for the practical issues involved in the measurement process; and (2) the actual usage of measures and factors by those who are actively involved in assessment. One early treatment suggested quantity, recency, quality, and relevancy (Porter et al., 1976). Quantity was viewed as number of months or years of experience, and these authors recommended that length of experience be credited up to five years for highly skilled work experience or no more than three years of experience on routine jobs. Recency of experience was cautiously advocated when it is obvious that major changes in such aspects as work methods, technology, or laws have altered radically the nature of desired performance. An example might be crediting computer experience that has been obtained in the PC era to a much greater extent than experience gained during the days of large mainframes. Interestingly, this scenario was recently reversed during the Y2K crisis, when programmers with old experience in COBOL programming were in high demand. Quality was viewed as difficult to assess because determining performance levels on one's current job is difficult, and this difficulty is multiplied when trying to judge performance on numerous past jobs. Quality viewed in the context of the quality of the organization where one worked was also viewed as an imprecise indicator.

Relevancy, the most preferred factor in the view of those authors, refers to the degree of similarity between the job to be filled and past jobs. This could be gauged in terms of size and kind of organization (e.g., large public vs. small private), variety of tasks performed, the level of authority exercised, and the complexity of problems handled. Support for this factor rests on empirical studies (e.g., Gordon, Cofer, & McCullough, 1986; Gordon & Fitzgibbons, 1982) and on the use of a content-oriented strategy for validating selection procedures. In addition, a substantial body of evidence supports the utility of person-organization fit in predicting performance and other outcomes such as satisfaction and, by extension, turnover (e.g., Caldwell & O'Reilly, 1990). Issues of adverse impact and what kinds of information one can reasonably expect to be provided by applicants quickly and at low cost entered into their recommendations.

Quiñones, Ford, and Teachout (1995), whose framework for evaluating experience served as the basis for Tesluk & Jacobs' (1998) model, suggested that work experience could be assessed using three different measurement modes (amount in terms of frequency or variety, length of time, and complexity or criticality) crossed with level (task, job, organization). For example, we might assess number of times performing a task, length of job tenure or seniority, or the degree of criticality conveyed by the type of organization one works in, such as law enforcement versus night security agencies. Although Tesluk and Jacobs (1998) introduced additional dimensions such as the timing of an experience element, it is unclear that these additional elements can be feasibly collected in application materials. For example, Russell's (2001) study of executive selection relied on extensive, structured series of interviews of applicants and their bosses, 360-degree appraisals, and reviews of biodata to assess applicants on a set of target competencies.

Primoff (1958) in the 1940s introduced a quality rating approach in which experience was used as a basis for rating an applicant on those job elements (knowledge, skills, abilities, and other characteristics) established as important for successful performance and practical to expect among applicants. Tryouts of the approach among drivers and metalsmiths led to the creation of a systematized method and questionnaire for translating background work experience and other biodata into ratings. The method continues to be used (Eyde, 2000).

Schmidt et al. (1979) reviewed much of the work done in the federal service and elsewhere, including Primoff's work, and concluded that the excellence of past performance, not just the reported nature of experience or credentials, was critical. They advocated collecting what in effect are critical incidents of past accomplishments for each dimension of those attributes important for performance as determined by a job analysis. They exhorted applicants to include as many instances as possible but at least two incidents for each dimension. More details on this method are provided in the section where methods are described in detail.

Moving on to assessors' "policies," Brown and Campion (1994) explored recruiters' perceptions and use of biographical information in resume screening. They undertook an extensive effort to derive a comprehensive list of biodata items. In the context of college recruiting for entry-level management hires, they looked at past research, actual resumes, and applications. The result was six categories of experience items—full-time work experience, whether the candidate supervised others, individual job achievement, summer internships, worked during college, and experience as a dorm advisor. A sample of 113 recruiters reported relying on all of these factors in their assessments, with the most importance ascribed to the factors individual job achievement, worked during college, and full-time work experience. Although reactive biases may have been operating due to the study design, this study revealed that recruiters use the experience indicators more for assessing candidates on attributes like motivation than on ability—a finding that underscores the deficiencies in the models tested to date of experience by performance linkages. As we have pointed out, these focused primarily on task performance.

## Education and Training

Education and training are targeted directly at producing changes in personal attributes. In one sense they may be viewed as offering condensations of experiences that should quicken the developmental process as opposed to an accidental learning strategy or trial-and-error exploration. Certainly they provide a safer and less costly road to development than is often the case when we try things out in the "real world." Flying a simulator is much less expensive and safer than learning to fly on a real aircraft. The distinction between them can be fuzzy at the extremes, but we may separate them to a degree by viewing education as providing learning and individual development that is not aimed at improving specific occupational or job performance. Education and training have the same three faces as does experience—their impact on personal attributes, the learner's perceptions of the meaning of the changes and how these are reported to others, and the aspects of education and training judged as important for prediction.

Training enjoys a rich tradition of research and practice. Clearly we have gained considerable knowledge of how to effect changes in knowledge and skills, and how to ensure their transfer from the training to the job setting both at the team and individual level (Bjork, 1994; Goldstein & Ford, 2002; Noe, 2002; Quiñones & Ehrenstein, 1997). It is beyond the scope of this chapter to explore this topic in detail. Moreover, treating training independently of work experience is perhaps both theoretically and practically infeasible. A goodly portion of the work experience construct treated in this chapter incorporates and embeds training and learning. We point to on-the-job training, mentoring, structured feedback, job rotation, cooperative work-study programs, and apprenticeships as examples of how experience is enriched by training during the accomplishment of work. Of course, work experience itself facilitates learning (cf. Maranto & Rodgers, 1984). Developmental assignments challenging and broadening one's abilities have been found to foster career progression for both male and female executives (Lyness & Thompson, 2000).

It is reasonable to assume that the bulk of training occurs as part and parcel of work experience. Thus, we can say with certainty that well-designed and well-administered training produces important changes on job or occupationally relevant personal attributes, affects performance, and alters how we view ourselves—for example, as experts versus novices. As far as what aspects of training are viewed as important and relevant by assessors, we point first and foremost to training sequences that serve as indicators of minimum competency. Law enforcement officers must have completed police academy training. Physicians must have completed medical training at an accredited school. Possession of proper terminal degrees and certification reflecting completion of training is necessary for appointment as a university professor, a dental hygienist, or an elementary school teacher. Truck drivers must be properly licensed. It is less clear that possession of these credentials signifying training guarantees high-level performance, but adequate performance would not generally be possible without it, and often laws require satisfactory completion of a course of training to be allowed to practice. Thus, possession of degrees, certificates, and licenses signifying successful completion of occupational training are relatively easy to incorporate into our screening and selection. Verification is a critical component here.

But what of those training courses that our company has provided, or that we took from an outside provider in the course of our job? Practically speaking, those who have worked for some years are rarely able to recall and may be unwilling to produce each and every formal training intervention to which they have been exposed within the context of their past jobs when they apply for a new job. Nor is it clear how we can assess their impact over and above work experience. The training may not have been completed or taken seriously. Performance in the training may not have been adequate, or even if we shone in training the learning may not have been sufficient to transfer, or may have decayed in part due to insufficient mastery (Bjork, 1994; Driskell, Willis, & Copper, 1992). On the other hand, those methods of assessing training and experience that rely on ratings of job elements like knowledge and skill or past achievements

do permit past training to play a role in the presentation of competencies. Weeklong or monthlong workshops in such skill-based areas as use of software for programmers, or engine analyzers for auto mechanics, also seem worthy of inclusion in our assessments. Indeed, in areas like software design or team performance there may be no alternative to formal training, which should foster systematic practice across a variety of situations to develop needed metacognitive skills for solving software problems and shared mental models to facilitate team processes (Mathieu, Heffner, Goodwin, Salas, & Cannon-Bowers, 2000; Sonnentag, 1998).

Unfortunately there is not much research available on questions like what kinds of past in-house training will offer evidence of applicants' quality and suitability for a job in a different organization. Generally indicators like the sheer number of training courses taken seem impractical to request and would not offer valid evidence if content is ignored or if the courses bear little similarity to the job's needs. Courses of study that are offered by applicants and used in assessment should be described in some detail, including their content beyond a title and their length. There should also be evidence of passing or satisfactory performance of some kind.

In the area of education Brown and Campion (1994) found that the following items, pertinent to education, were used by college recruiters: job-related degree, grades in major, overall grades, whether an applicant earned college expenses, computer experience, foreign language, varsity athletics captain, elected offices, college clubs, social fraternity, Dean's list, scholarships. Of these the ones most important in screening were grades, elected offices, and being named to the Dean's list. Lavigna (1992) surveyed 64 managers in a large public sector agency and found that they viewed grade point average, college quality, and graduate degree as predictive of performance. On the other hand, they viewed the source of the application, that is, whether the applicant was interviewed on campus or applied directly, as unimportant.

There is little if any research, to our knowledge, that develops and evaluates theoretical models of how these factors interact with personal attributes to cause job performance or other work-related criteria. Nor have we found any research dealing with the perceived meaning for the applicant of these factors. There are reports of misrepresentation of educational background. In summarizing available research, Gatewood and Feild (1998) cited studies showing frequent falsification of educational credentials, including falsely stated possession of the MBA degree, and the distortion of academic records by up to one-third of checked applications as reported by a national verification service. These distortions suggest that applicants certainly view their credentials as important for success in the job hunt, and in many cases manipulate them in ways that would present a positive impression.

Howard (1986), reporting on the longitudinal, dual cohort study of managers in the Bell System, provided perhaps the best information about the impact of education on personal attributes. The two cohorts of management staff in the Bell System were augmented in this study by an additional, comparable sample of 766 managers drawn from a diverse set of organizations. A variety of indicators associated with education were explored, among them degrees held, grade point average, extracurricular activities, the number of leadership positions held, major field, and quality of the institution attended. One advantage of the study's design is that gains (or losses) in particular attributes can be attributed more directly to education, especially when education was acquired after employment. Those with a college education were higher in intellectual ability and motivation for advancement. Those with master's degrees in business showed gains in general effectiveness as managerial candidates, and this seemed due to growth in administrative skills over time. Higher grades were associated with higher work standards, more social objectivity, low need for job security, and a broader range of interests. Surprisingly, graduates from more prestigious institutions exhibited a higher level of cynicism, less interest in work, and lower expectations for what a management career can offer. Those with liberal arts and humanities backgrounds apparently benefited by acquiring greater interpersonal skills, decision-making skills, written comprehension skills, and need for advancement as compared with those with math, science, or engineering backgrounds.

To quote Howard (1986, p. 541): "The test scores [on several personality inventories] suggest that the humanities and social science majors had self-concepts that support relating to other people in a self-assured, outgoing, and flexible manner. The engineers were more controlled, orderly, rule-oriented, and reserved with others. . . ." Of course those selecting the different majors may have differed in their level of interpersonal skills or cognitive ability prior to selecting their major also. Thus, college major may both signal attribute differences to start with and may serve to heighten preexisting areas of excellence.

This landmark study provides a number of caveats when education is used for assessment. First, the indicators do not operate independently; multiple regression analyses showed that these factors acted in combination to predict personal attributes and future performance. Second, evidence of grade inflation in the later cohort suggests that the effectiveness of grades as predictors may be attenuated by lowered discriminability. Third, specific contents of the educational background should be more instructive than a mere count of years

of education. In light of this assessors must stay abreast of curriculum changes over time. Fourth, the use of education in a credentialistic fashion, such as awarding jobs and higher rankings to those who have graduated from reputedly more prestigious institutions, can backfire not only because it may not predict performance or advancement but also because it may screen into an organization those with less desirable attributes. In practice, unfortunately, our experience has been that one cannot aspire to many high-profile jobs in the professions, business, and government without the imprimatur of a degree from a prestigious institution. Finally, attempts to validate the use of education indicators will be impaired both by range restriction, since these predictors are so widely used in the selection process, and by criterion contamination, since those who may be called upon to provide performance data will often be aware of the target's educational background.

## RELIABILITY, VALIDITY, AND LEGALITY OF ASSESSMENTS OF EDUCATION, TRAINING, AND EXPERIENCE

A great deal of research has focused on the validity of education, training, and experience in selection, and particular methods of evaluating these factors. However, the research is by no means definitive, both because of serious deficiencies in past studies and because of the psychometric snags associated with the measures used in the assessment process. In the language of the newly issued *Standards for Educational and Psychological Testing* (American Educational Research Association [AERA], American Psychological Association, & National Council on Measurement in Education, 1999), we note that the bulk of the evidence falls into two categories—evidence based on test content, and evidence based on relations to other variables. The *Standards* also remind us that validity inheres in *purposes* served by inferences based on test or assessment scores. It is, as we know, incorrect to speak of the validity of a test without specifying purpose.

In practical applications of education, training, and experience, by far the most reliance has been placed on the former category, where the evidence often rests on the facial similarity between job requirements and background education, training, and experience, or on the judged correspondence between job components or constructs and those presumed to be measured by aspects of education, training, and experience (Arvey & Faley, 1988; Ash, Johnson, Levine, & McDaniel, 1989). Problems such as low hiring rates, point estimation of standing on constructs (e.g., college degree vs. no degree), criterion contamination, insufficient coverage of the full range of jobs, inability to specify the precise number and kind of constructs captured by overly crude and broad measures, and use of the predictors in selection all mitigate against the feasibility of empirical tests.

A particularly vexing aspect in evaluating both kinds of evidence is the imprecise, error-prone setting of passing or cutoff points in this domain. Here the cutoff points are referred to as *minimum qualification requirements (MQs)*. These are often set by convention; labor market or compensation considerations; poorly informed, tip-of-the-tongue estimates; or by an overriding concern for adverse impact and legality without due attention to applicant suitability for a job. MQs set either too low or too high may have a substantial effect on the estimation of validity. Requiring a master's degree instead of a doctoral degree, a high school diploma for routine assembly jobs, or 10 years of experience for relatively unchanging jobs are examples of often unsubstantiated and perhaps overly high or low levels of background factors used in MQs. Despite these rather serious problems, the extant research points to the reliability, validity, and usefulness of these aspects of applicants' backgrounds in the staffing function, although there may be considerable variability in their applicability. An example of the last point is illustrated by reference to entry jobs that do not call for past experience since all those hired will be trained on the job.

## Education and Training

Turning first to education, we found persuasive evidence of validity of grade point average. Roth, BeVier, Schippmann, and Switzer (1996), in a meta-analysis of 71 studies with an aggregated total of 13,984 subjects, estimated empirical validity at .32, which was corrected for range restriction and criterion unreliability. The observed value was .16. Grade point average at the master's level exhibited even higher validity at .23 uncorrected or .46 corrected. Predictors were restricted to grade point average; rank in class was excluded. Criteria included objective indicators of job knowledge, ratings by supervisors, and ratings by subject matter experts. These levels of validity parallel those found by Hunter and Hunter (1984), with advancement and training success serving as criteria. Types of organizations covered by the component studies included business, medical, scientific, education, and military. However, job types were not identified. Validity evidence was not convincing for Ph.D. or M.D. grades. Roth et al. (1996) noted that there is little theory undergirding these relationships, and that the level of validity decreases as the time between schooling and the measurement of performance increases. Validity estimates were higher in educational organizations. Roth et al. (1996) relied on an internal consis-

tency estimate of .84 reported in prior research as the level of reliability for this measure.

Lyons (1989) reported comparable estimates of validity with both job performance and training success as criteria. Upper level grades and grades in the major exhibited higher validity in that review. Clearly the primary job types that may make use of this and any other aspects of college background are professional, technical, and managerial. In a primary study, Lavigna (1992) corroborated the validity of undergraduate grade point average in predicting performance appraisal ratings averaged over several years early in the careers of those hired into a large public agency. The sample size was 564, but job types were not specified. An uncorrected coefficient of .32 was found despite range restriction.

Howard (1986) also provided evidence supporting the validity of grade point average for advancement in management even out to 20 years for the first cohort. For that earlier sample, use of rank in class did not demonstrate superiority over self-reported grades in predicting advancement. In fact the opposite tended to be true—a finding that may be due to the more rigorous grading experienced by the earlier sample. In the later cohort, validity was not found for predicting advancement, perhaps owing to the influence of grade inflation. Rank in class, which was not assessed for the later group, might have resulted in higher validity.

Sheer length of education apparently does not provide valid information. Lyons reports estimates of $-.04$, and .10 (corrected to .13), the latter of which was not generalizable. Hunter and Hunter (1984) reported a similar level of validity (.10 corrected) for entry-level jobs in 425 studies with an aggregated sample size of 32,124 and criteria of supervisory ratings. There can be exceptions, however. Keller and Holland (1978) reported a correlation of .22 between years of education and peer ratings of innovativeness among professional employees in three research and development organizations. This result may be due to the fact that years of education in this study represented differences almost exclusively in years of graduate education beyond the bachelor's degree. Also noteworthy is that years of education did not predict ratings of managerial or administrative communication.

Field of study appears to offer valid information. Lyons (1989) reported an observed coefficient of .24, corrected to .31 for predicting job performance across a sample of seven studies and 737 study participants. The level of validity was similar for predicting training success across 46 studies with an aggregated sample size of 43,724. Howard (1986) likewise found support for the validity of major field of study, with humanities and social science majors outperforming science, math, and engineering majors. The incremental validity of major field held up when it was combined with other variables in a multiple regression analysis.

Among the other possible indicators, participation in extracurricular activities offers promise although evidence in different settings is mixed (Howard, 1986; Lyons, 1989). Possession of a bachelor's degree also offers promise, even in law enforcement where it was correlated with supervisory ratings of job knowledge and dependability at .26 and .24, respectively, and with rank at .40 in a study of 84 police officers in a southern city's police department over a 10-year period (Truxillo, Bennett, & Collins, 1998). Little evidence is available on recency of education, although logically one would expect more recent education to be the antithesis of obsolescence. Indirectly, the moderator—the length of time between measurement of grade point average and performance—found by Roth et al. (1996) supports this factor. The longer the interval, the lower was the validity. Also bearing on the validity of education is a study by Childs and Klimoski (1986). They found an education composite based on educational achievement and extracurricular activities predicted two of three separate self-rated criteria, job effectiveness and career success in terms of earnings and occupational prestige, collected two years later. The composite also showed incremental validity when entered into multiple regression equations.

If sheer number of extracurricular activities are used, or possession of a degree in any field, evidence of correspondence between job and selection procedure will need to be empirically evaluated, because the constructs assessed are not well identified. In addition, the use of high school graduation or GED is viewed unfavorably because it fails to measure applicant attributes with any degree of precision (Arvey & Faley, 1988).

Howard's (1986) advice is most pertinent here. She indicated that type of job should dictate the nature of educational experience to assess. Without question, more research is needed to determine the latent constructs tapped by the measures of education used here.

Training performance has been less studied as a predictor. Clear evidence indicates that training does lead to improved performance in such diverse occupations as managers, correctional officers, and police officers, and it provides an incremental boost over and beyond initial competency (e.g., Burke & Day, 1986; Hanisch & Hulin, 1994; Sistrunk & Smith, 1982). Hunter and Hunter (1984) reported a reanalysis of 51 coefficients in military studies showing an aggregated validity of .27 (corrected for criterion unreliability) for training performance against supervisory ratings of overall performance. Performance in extended training programs such as the training offered in police academies does appear to predict job performance. However, virtually no evidence has been located that deals with length of training or number of training courses taken. Again, validation efforts in practice have relied on evidence based on the correspondence between training and job content (cf. Goldstein & Ford, 2002). For example, Levine and Cannon (1986) used this strategy in evaluating a training program developed in-house for the job of line mechanic in an electric utility. They found almost complete coverage of the attributes needed for job performance in the training program. They also found positive evidence based on the consequences of the training program, which is another of the streams of evidence that may support test validity according to the *Standards* (AERA et al., 1999). Safety and productivity improved after the program was introduced, but these data were viewed as inconclusive because of lack of proper controls. This program included a shorter, two-week evaluation that was used for selecting workers into the apprentice program. Again the evidence based on training content supported the validity of this selection strategy. Numerous utility companies have adopted the training program subsequently.

## Experience

As we have seen, experience has an impact on many personal attributes, including job knowledge and motivation. The research record of its validity has shown increasingly positive evidence of validity in predicting job performance over the past 50 years (Ash et al., 1989; Hunter & Hunter, 1984; Lyons, 1989; McDaniel, Schmidt, & Hunter, 1988a; Schmidt et al., 1986; Quiñones et al., 1995). Perhaps this is due to greater sophistication in measurement both of the experience variable and job performance (cf., for example, Vance et al., 1989). Or perhaps researchers are using more suitable research designs. Hunter and Hunter (1984) reported a corrected validity coefficient of .18 based on 425 coefficients and an aggregated sample size of 32,124 for supervisory ratings. Their studies were restricted to a wide variety of entry-level jobs. Presumably experience would be less instrumental in performance for jobs of that type. Schmidt et al. (1986) found a mean validity corrected for criterion unreliability across four occupations at .33. Here mean length of experience in the samples was purposely held at a so-called intermediate level. McDaniel et al. (1988a) found a validity coefficient corrected for unreliability in the criterion and range restriction of .32 across 83 occupational groups with an aggregate sample size of 16,058 (uncorrected validity .21), and when length of experience was held to three years or less, the coefficient was .49 (uncorrected coefficient .20). The last result was based on 235 coefficients and a sample size of 4,490.

Quiñones et al. (1995) conducted the most recent meta-analysis. Recall that their conceptual framework for experience crossed measurement mode (amount, time, type) with level (task, job, organization). The 23 studies they included were completed during the period from 1968 through 1993; 17 of these were completed in the period from 1980 to 1993. There were a wide variety of criteria including peer and supervisor ratings and objective measures. Job types ranged from mechanics in the military to firefighters to managers. Overall, for a sample size of 25,911 in aggregate, the mean validity coefficient was .22 (uncorrected) and .27 corrected for unreliability in the criteria. This level of validity was expected to generalize, given the small variance in the corrected coefficient. In all the comparisons for the cells within the framework across the various types and measurement modes, generalizable levels of validity were found. Too few studies in some cells of the matrix precluded findings on the interaction of these two factors. Studies using the frequency of performance of tasks exhibited corrected coefficients of .43 (uncorrected .36), and those measuring performance at the task level of specificity exhibited coefficients of .41 (uncorrected .34). Length of experience in jobs and occupations or with the organization produced a coefficient of .27 (uncorrected .22), whereas type of experience in terms of similarity between past experience and the job in question produced a coefficient of .21 (uncorrected .19). The last result and the one for amount were based on only four and five coefficients, respectively, and so are not definitive by any means. Coefficients for task level measures exceeded those for job level and organization level.

There are some problems with this study that preclude a full acceptance of the results. First, a meta-analysis may not capture all the nuances of individual studies. For example, the Gordon and Fitzgibbons (1982) study found that tenure did not predict performance when workers changed jobs, and the coefficients in the meta-analysis do not reflect this. Second, we may question the sample of studies. The study by Ash and Levine (1985) was not included in the database despite the fact that it meets the decision rules for inclusion. That study found validity for a method of measuring experience, which dealt with similarity between past experience and the job's duties, but not for a task-based method. That same study illustrates another problem with the framework for experience that served as the basis for the meta-analysis. The valid method in the Ash and Levine (1985) study actually relied on a combination of type and time to measure experience. Looking more closely at the framework reveals another flaw; namely, that some combinations of measurement mode and level may not be distinguishable from each other.

Time on task may be confounded with frequency of task performance as one example.

Despite some of the problems with the experience construct and the nature of the research designs used to assess validity we can conclude that assessing experience will provide useful information in many situations, but probably not all (cf. Clevenger et al., 2001). Questions remain about whether taking recency into account will make a difference, and about whether we can easily assess some of the additional concepts that Tesluk and Jacobs (1998) introduced in their treatment of experience. A promising example, which speaks to the potential for adding more subtle features, may be found in a study by Vicino and Bass (1978). They assessed a manager's perceived degree of challenge in his or her first job for 140 managers with Exxon using a brief questionnaire. The measure correlated .34 with a composite measure of supervisory success from which had been partialed their predicted standing on the criterion derived from a battery of aptitude and personality tests. Still another issue is whether it would be better to measure excellence of past performance rather than past exposures. The validity of the former will be covered briefly in the next section dealing with the validity of particular methods of assessing education and experience.

## Validity of Methods of Assessing Education, Training, and Experience

In contrast to the use of individual elements of education, training, and experience, assessments will usually rely on an impressionistic or systematically derived judgment about an applicant's suitability based on a combination of any or all of these factors. In some widely used approaches there is often a compensatory use of one factor for another—that is, education is used to substitute for experience or vice versa on a month-for-month or year-for-year basis. To our knowledge the psychometric soundness of this practice has never been evaluated and probably reduces validity of the methods that rely on this practice. The particular methods for assessing experience and education are presented in the next main section. Here we provide a brief summary of available evidence that estimates the reliability and validity of those assessment methods that produce scores, rankings, or quantified ratings of applicants.

The use of MQs in many of these methods to make a first cut in an applicant pool speaks to the importance of establishing their reliability and validity. Levine, Maye, Ulm, and Gordon (1997) presented the first formalized methodology for establishing and validating MQs. The general approach relies on evidence from content of the selection procedure. A domain for establishing the MQs is defined through job

**TABLE 16.1   Comparison of Old and New MQs for Pharmacy Technician**

| Original | New |
|---|---|
| Two years of experience in assisting a registered pharmacist in the compounding and dispensing of prescriptions. | Eighteen months of experience assisting a pharmacist in a nonhospital setting. Such duties must include maintaining patient medication records; setting up, packaging, and labeling medication doses; and maintaining inventories of drugs and supplies.<br><br>OR<br><br>Nine months of experience assisting a pharmacist in a hospital setting. Such duties must include maintaining patient medication records; setting up, packaging, and labeling medication doses; filling routine orders for stock supplies of patient-care areas; and maintaining inventories of drugs and supplies.<br><br>OR<br><br>Completion of a Hospital Pharmacy Technician program accredited by the American Society of Hospital Pharmacists.<br><br>OR<br><br>Completion of a Pharmacy Technician technical school program which provided at least 600 clock hours or 15 weeks of classroom training AND an internship in a pharmacy.<br><br>OR<br><br>Six months of experience as a Licensed Practical Nurse or Advanced Emergency Medical Technician in an inpatient setting and 6 months of experience assisting a pharmacist where duties included maintaining patient records; setting up, packaging, and labeling medication doses; and maintaining inventories of drugs and supplies. Work experience must include some exposure to computers/computer systems.<br><br>OR<br><br>Twelve months as a medication technician (a nonlicensed worker who administers medications) in an inpatient setting plus 6 months of experience assisting a pharmacist where duties included maintaining patient records; setting up, packaging, and labeling medication doses; and maintaining inventories of drugs and supplies. Work experience must include some exposure to computers/computer systems. |

*Note.* Table adapted from Levine et al. (1997, p. 1016) with permission.

analysis in terms of tasks and personal attributes. Profiles of experience and education are formed, which expressly avoid the arithmetic substitution of months of education and experience one for another, and their relevance to the domain as well as their suitability in sorting qualified from unqualified applicants is judged by subject matter experts. Levine et al. (1997) reported that for 14 diverse jobs a valid set of profiles was established. The median interrater reliability found when the profiles are applied independently to actual application blanks by trained judges was .96. Table 16.1 compares the original MQs for the job of pharmacy technician with those developed using the new method. It is readily apparent that the new MQs offer several ways to qualify, and that length of experience required has been reduced in all of the new profiles.

Virtually all of the methods of assessment of education, training, and experience receiving research attention were developed and investigated in the public sector. These methods include the following variations (Ash & Levine, 1985; Ash et al., 1989; Porter et al., 1976; Schmidt et al., 1979):

1. Rating schedules where length of education and experience, weighted by relevance to the target job, are scored by trained analysts. This is often referred to as the traditional point method.

2. Rating schedules where key job elements (knowledge, abilities, skills, and other characteristics) are self-rated for level, and experience or education corroborating these ratings is included.

3. Rating schedules where applicants use a task inventory to check those they have performed in the past and in some instances the level of task mastery. Again, past experience and education where the task was performed must be shown.

4. Rating schedules based on applicant reports of their accomplishments within several dimensions derived from the critical incidents method of job analysis. This is referred to as the behavioral consistency method.

5. Rating schedules describing profiles consisting of amounts and types of education, training, and experience singly or in combination. These profiles are then scaled in nominal categories from most to least suitable for the target job. Applicants are placed into the category or group, which their background most closely resembles. This is referred to as the grouping method.

6. Assessment methods that combine features of those listed above.

Ash et al. (1989) provided a comprehensive summary of reliability and validity evidence. Acceptable and high reliability estimates in the .80s are noted. Most of these approaches are validated using evidence based on the comparison of selection procedure contents with job contents. Job analysis is a sine qua non here (cf., for example, Langdale & Weitz, 1973). Empirical validity estimates are low and are viewed as not generalizable. Only the behavioral consistency and a combination method developed by the State of Illinois yield useful levels of estimated validity that generalize ($r = .25$ observed across 15 studies, .45 corrected for criterion unreliability and range restriction for the behavioral consistency method, and $r = .11$ observed, $r = .20$ corrected for the Illinois method). Unfortunately, serious practical difficulties are noted with these methods. The behavioral consistency method is both expensive and time-consuming to develop, and applicants may not be willing or able to document their accomplishments in writing. The Illinois method is expensive to develop and complex to score. In both cases more primary research is needed. The grouping method has been researched infrequently but shows promise (Ash & Levine, 1985). Perhaps the most robust conclusion from the empirical work is that the point method lacks empirical validity ($r = .06$ observed across 132 studies with 12,048). It should be abandoned for this reason and because of legal considerations. We include it in our coverage of methods for its historical interest, but we recommend strongly against its use.

Given the evidence cited regarding the validity of separate aspects of experience and education and the evidence of validity of the methods of scoring these factors, we view their use in recruitment, screening, and selection as appropriate. Judgmental assessments of these factors will continue to be among the most frequently used screening and selection devices. The task facing researchers in this area is to continue to refine and validate assessment methods, and to establish taxonomies of jobs crossed with methods most suitable and valid for the jobs. At this stage of development, they must undoubtedly be used in combination with other assessment devices since their level of validity is infrequently high enough to base selection decisions on these methods alone. Moreover, their use in applied settings will benefit from standardization of scoring or rating formats, careful training of developers and raters, and standardization of the format with which applicants record their education, training, and experience.

A model of how such methods might be used is exemplified by the work of Baugher, Varanelli, and Hall (1994), who reported on the development of a promotional examining system for budget examiners in the New York State Division of the Budget. Their system was based on a combination of a training and experience evaluation (T&E) and a performance appraisal. The T&E method first derived a set of knowledge, skills, and abilities (KSAs) from job analysis. Candidates must indicate past experience and education relevant to each KSA. They also must supply references who can verify their statements. Spot checks of listed references are made randomly, and more complete checking is done where the random checks are questionable. Candidates also self-rate the extent to which their training and experience is valuable for the target job. These self-ratings act as a check on the subsequent reviews by others and are also included in the scoring. Two trained subject matter experts independently rate the candidate's background blindly. If there are disagreements, discussions are held to resolve the discrepancies. All this information along with a detailed performance appraisal report is presented to a Verification Committee of three experienced budget examiners not employed with the agency. They review information, and they interview candidates as well as others if necessary to clarify the information. They place the candidates into categories or bands ranging from Fail to Highly Qualified. Candidates may receive career counseling based on their scores. A total of 192 candidates for promotion took the exam between the years 1983 and 1992, and 79 took the exam over approximately the same period for a higher level classification. Across both groups the interrater reliability of the T&E scoring process was .73, while uncorrected correlations between the T&Es and the performance appraisals, which might be viewed as a form of concurrent validation, were .18 for the lower level position and .51 for the higher level one.

## Legal Considerations

Assessments of the kind treated in this chapter are subject to the Uniform Guidelines on Employee Selection Procedures (1978) (EEOC et al., 1978). As such, their degree of adverse impact is at issue, and court cases dealing with the legality of assessments of education, training, and experience for recruitment, screening, and selection are relevant. Legal issues also apply to online and Internet-based methods, and these are reviewed in the context of our discussion of those assessment methods in the last portion of this chapter.

A preliminary consideration in this context is how applicants gauge the fairness of these procedures. If the prevailing view is that they are fair, the probability of lawsuits should be low. Steiner and Gilliland (1996) had college students in the United States and France rate the fairness of several selection techniques. Use of resumes was rated as among the fairest techniques in both samples—second to interviews in the United States and second with interviews behind work sample tests in France. In both samples the ratings were supported by the view that employers had a right to such information. In the study by Baugher et al. (1994), attitudes were more favorable toward the new exam with a T&E component compared with the previously used written and oral examinations. They also reported an appeal rate of 3.7% vs. 8.1% for the new as compared with the traditional examining approach.

There are indications of the potential for adverse impact when these methods are employed. For example, Roth and Bobko (2000) reported adverse impact of grade point average. Overall they found a moderate effect size of grade point average between African Americans and Whites, and this difference was greater for senior-level grades. Using various cutoffs in a simulation of a selection process, they found violation of the Guidelines' 80% rule in every case. Ash and Levine (1981) also found evidence of adverse impact with the traditional point method of assessing education, training, and experience against females for two of the three jobs they studied. Should a task-based method be used, the findings of Schmitt and Cohen (1989) suggest that women relative to men may be disadvantaged where jobs call for fiscal and budgetary experience, as well as experience in contacts with external constituencies or professional groups. They found significantly fewer women indicating that they performed these types of tasks as compared with men among 411 middle level, civil service managers in state government. Arvey and Faley (1988) indicated that the use of educational credentials will likely produce adverse impact on minority group members, and experience requirements may disadvantage both females and minority group members. They suggest that these requirements will likely not survive court challenges if adverse impact is demonstrated without countervailing evidence of validity. Anderson et al. (1984) found adverse impact against minorities in the score indexing inflation of experience reports from applicants. Minimum qualification requirements have also been found to produce adverse impact. The court case that led Levine et al. (1997) to develop a new method of establishing and validating MQs found adverse impact of previously used MQs in 36 diverse job classes (*Kennedy v. Crittenden,* Civil Action No. 77-200-MAC-WDO). Application of the new method resulted in a reduction of adverse impact for six jobs but an increase in eight.

Despite these examples, in Gutman's view (2002) evidence of validity will be less rigorously examined in the case of education and work experience relative to cognitive tests. This will be especially likely where the job in question has an impact on public safety. Jobs such as police officer or airline pilot are examples. Generally, for jobs other than the former, high school diplomas are not likely to survive a challenge. Where higher level professional jobs are concerned, use of a master's or doctoral degree is likely to survive a challenge, especially if the user can demonstrate some evidence of validity. With respect to experience, Arvey and Faley (1988) present a summary across 39 court cases. Generally, experience requirements are more likely to be legally sanctioned if the target job is complex or has a potentially high impact on public safety. Experience requirements are not safe if adverse impact occurs and new hires in the target job may perform their work satisfactorily after a brief training period.

The safest posture that may be taken by employers is to ensure that scoring methods for assessing education, training, and experience are established based on a job analysis and validated using one or more streams of evidence endorsed by the *Standards* (AERA et al., 1999). Once established, these scoring methods must be uniformly applied. Since the entire process relies on a written exchange of information, training, use of other means of information exchange such as oral administration to blind applicants as called for by the American with Disabilities Act, and complete instructions should be offered to applicants whose written comprehension and composition skills are suspect. From the perspective of both legality and validity, the amount of experience required to meet MQs or to attain a particular score should usually be limited to no more than five years. Cutoffs on such indicators as grade point average and even inflation scores must be set only after careful analysis of the job's requirements and the potential for adverse impact. Proper feedback to applicants, including counseling as requested, may enhance attitudes about fairness of these assessment methods. We note also that the method for establishing and validating MQs developed by Levine et al. (1997) has been approved by a federal district court.

We turn now to a detailed description of assessment methods.

## FORMAL METHODS OF JUDGMENTALLY ASSESSING EXPERIENCE, EDUCATION, AND TRAINING

As Ash et al. (1989) pointed out, much of the assessment of application materials and resumes, especially in the private sector, proceeds on the basis of intuitive, holistic evaluations to identify suitable applicants. Those identified may be assessed further using written tests, interviews, or other screening methods. The validity of such assessments is both indeterminate and indeterminable because the basis for judgments is not explicitly documented and because lack of documented scores or ratings precludes empirical validation efforts. The methods presented in the following are primarily associated with the public sector, although there is no fundamental reason why the more valid ones cannot be employed in the private sector.

## Traditional Point Method

The traditional point method of T&E evaluation consists of a mechanical formula set out in a formal schedule. Points are credited for the number of months or years of different types of relevant applicant training, education, or work experience. Through some form of job analysis, often a cursory one, types of training or education thought to be relevant to obtaining job-related KSAs are identified. Similarly, types of work experience thought to be relevant to obtaining the job-related human attributes are identified. In more elaborate variations input is solicited from subject matter experts to assign different types of training or work experience differential point values. These presumptive qualitative differences in types of training or work experience often manifest in the form of a matrix containing from one to three or four different point levels for each unit of education (e.g., 30, 60, 90, etc. semester hours), and a similar number of point levels for each unit of work experience (e.g., month, year). These established point values are typically multiplied by the respective number of education units or months or years of experience associated with each applicant's background. The points are then summed to arrive at the applicant's score. Each score derived tends to be unique, and the collection of scores tends to be distributed continuously. In organizations that adopt the traditional civil service convention of a "passing" score equal to 70 points, applicants are assigned a passing score if they meet the minimum qualification requirements, and additional points are added for months or years of specified types of training and experience.

In a meta-analysis including 91 validity studies of the traditional point method, McDaniel et al. (1988b) reported the uncorrected validity estimate of $r = .06$ (estimate corrected for range restriction and unreliability in the criterion yields $r = .11$). The validity value of zero is within the 90% confidence interval. Hence, the validity of the traditional point method is quite low and often not significantly different from zero. Reflecting on these procedures for a moment, one can readily understand why they lack validity. Even in situations in which highly detailed applicant information is available, the effect of different or even identical training and work situations on different individuals cannot be measured with

high accuracy (cf. Ash & Levine, 1985; Porter et al., 1976). Although traditional point methods appear to yield rather precise scores taking into account the types and amounts of applicant training and experience, this precision is certainly more specious than real. Is an applicant who scores 91 more qualified than an applicant who scores 90 or 89? How does one know what, if any, additional KSAs the applicant with the score of 91 gained in the additional month or two of work experience, or the additional semester of education that the applicant with the score of 89 or 88 does not have? It is apparent to any thoughtful teacher or professor that two individuals taking the same course at the same time and earning the same grade may not gain identical amounts of knowledge from the course. Similarly, two individuals working in the same job for the same organization may not gain the same knowledge or skill set by virtue of having this similar experience. This kind of measurement error in point method scores is even more severe when one considers that the quality and content of knowledge gained at different educational institutions and employers can be considerably different.

The presumed simplicity of the method is likewise illusory. In practice, issues crop up that further reduce the reliability and validity of the method. For example, if some applicants list only month and year of employment, does the analyst credit both the first and last month of experience? In jobs for which there are large applicant pools, applicants who list exact dates can be disadvantaged considerably if the less exact information results in a credit for the first and last month.

We present this method here only for the sake of completeness, and because of its historical significance. In the 1980s and earlier, the traditional point method was the most prevalent formal T&E evaluation method used by public sector organizations (Cook, 1980). This method constituted 69% of the T&E evaluation validity studies found by McDaniel et al. (1988b). For nearly two decades the International Personnel Management Association Assessment Council (IPMAAC) has conducted workshops on job applicant training and work experience evaluation in locations all over the United States. Presenters at these workshops have strongly discouraged the use of the traditional point method of T&E evaluation for personnel selection due to the method's dubious measurement practices and its lack of validity. We also enjoin those involved in personnel selection activities to refrain from using this method.

## Knowledge, Skill, and Ability-Based Methods

In knowledge, skill, and ability-based methods of T&E evaluation, applicants are presented with a list of knowledge, skills, abilities, and other characteristics (KSAOs) and are asked to check the ones they have acquired, or to rate their level of possession of the attributes. More specifically, the human attributes important for consideration in selection are identified by means of a job analysis (e.g., Primoff, 1975) and arranged in a format that required the applicant to first indicate the level of each attribute he/she possesses (e.g., on a 5-point scale ranging from "0—I Know Little or Nothing About this" to "4—I Possess This Attribute at a Superior Level and Am Called on to Do Unusually Difficult Jobs Requiring It"). The applicant must also specify the jobs or training courses through which he or she acquired the nonzero level of each attribute. The attributes may be differentially weighted based on importance or criticality information gained from the job analysis. An applicant's score is a weighted function of the self-ratings provided. An alternative way to implement the knowledge, skill, and ability-based method is by use of a simple checklist on which the applicant simply checks whether or not he or she possesses each attribute. Scores can be the simple or weighted sum of attributes checked, or designated critical attributes can be used to eliminate applicants as "not qualified" if they are not checked.

This is a self-rating approach. As such, it requires the job applicants to make judgments or evaluations of their backgrounds in terms of their current possession of job-related human attributes. It can be time-consuming to develop, but only in the sense that it requires a detailed job analysis (e.g., the Primoff [1975] Job Element Method) to generate the human attributes important to consider in selection. The approach is efficient to score in that it can be easily adapted for machine scoring using an optical scanner or through direct entry into the computer by the applicant. One problem with this and other self-rating approaches is that they are highly subject to inflation bias or misrepresentation on the part of the applicants. This problem can be addressed by careful checking of the jobs or training courses listed by the applicant as sources for acquisition of the attributes, especially for the most highly scoring applicants reaching the final stages of the selection process. Another way to address the problem is by incorporating bogus or nonexistent human attributes into the inventory or checklist to be completed by applicants. Applicants who check or indicate high levels of bogus attributes may be eliminated from further consideration. The validity of the knowledge, skill, and ability methods is based primarily on the direct link of the human attributes included in the inventory or checklist and the job analysis results. Criterion-related validity evidence on these methods is scarce. Based on our experience and the literature extant on the knowledge, skills, and abilities-based method of T&E evaluation, it appears that this verbally oriented method may work for entry-level jobs where the KSAs may have been acquired through experiences other than work, for example, in school or in volunteer efforts. This approach may also be useful in jobs requiring a high interpersonal component.

## Task-Based Methods

The task-based approach is based on the premise that adequate validity can be achieved by obtaining detailed information on specific job-related tasks that an applicant has performed in the past, regardless of the job in which the task was performed. Job tasks serve as indicants of past performance that are presumed to predict future performance. In its basic form, the task-based approach is operationalized by means of a supplemental application form consisting of an inventory composed of nontrivial tasks derived through a job analysis of the target job. Applicants are asked to check the tasks they have performed in the past. In more detailed forms of this approach, applicants may be asked to rate the tasks using a more complex scale (e.g., "0—I Have Not Performed This Task"; "1—I Have Performed This Task Under Close Supervision"; "2—I Have Performed This Task Independently, Seeking Advice in Only the Most Difficult Situations"; "3—I Am Considered an Expert in This Task by Others"). An applicant's score is a weighted (based on job analysis information) function of the ratings he or she provides.

Hence, the task-based approach is also a self-rating approach. Applicants should also be asked to specify the setting or job in which they performed each task for verification purposes to reduce the likelihood of inflation bias or misrepresentation. Actual verification for those high-scoring applicants who move to the final stages of selection is recommended. Another approach to dealing with possible inflation bias or misrepresentation is incorporation of bogus tasks into the task listing (cf. Anderson et al., 1984; Farrell, 1979). Applicants who report having performed or being proficient in nonexistent tasks are judged to be falsifying their responses. Like the knowledge, skill, and ability-based methods, the task-based methods are time-consuming to develop, but only in terms of the detailed job analysis needed from which to select the job-related tasks for inclusion in the supplemental application form. This approach, too, is efficient to score in that it can be easily adapted for machine scoring using an optical scanner or through direct entry into the computer by the applicant. The validity of the task-based approaches, in particular, appears to be justifiable on the basis of content similarity between the assessment and the job. There should be a very close match between what candidates are required to do on the job and the tasks the applicants are asked to rate their proficiency on. Similar to the knowledge, skill, and ability-based methods, criterion-related validity evidence for the task-based approach is scarce. Based on our experience with and the literature extant on the task-based method of T&E evaluation, it appears that using a task frequency approach may work best for routine jobs such as assemblers or sewing machine operators. For less routine jobs in the professions, crafts, or trades, without a high interpersonal component, the self-ratings of level of task mastery may work well. As stated previously, Quiñones et al. (1995) found in their meta-analysis that assessments of work experience at the task level of specificity exhibited the highest levels of validity.

## Behavioral Consistency Method

The behavioral consistency method of T&E evaluation is based on the assumption that past behavior, in particular the level of performance indexed by the behavior, is the best predictor of future behavior. The *behavioral consistency* approach (Schmidt et al., 1979) has also been referred to as the *achievement history questionnaire* approach (State of Wisconsin, 1979) and the *accomplishment record* approach (Hough, 1984). There are some subtle differences among these three variations of the method, but the goal of these behaviorally oriented methods is to rank order applicants on the basis of the kind of achievement behaviors that are required for superior performance in the target job.

The first step involves identifying and developing statements describing major achievement dimensions for the job, usually from 5 to 10. In the Schmidt et al. (1979) procedure, these dimensions are derived by combining KSAs generated by subject matter experts. In the accomplishment record approach (Hough, 1984), the dimensions are derived by grouping critical incidents (Flanagan, 1954) generated by subject matter experts. In the second step, for each major achievement dimension applicants are encouraged to describe in detail at least two past achievements that best demonstrate their capabilities. Applicants are asked to include the following information for each achievement: (1) what the problem or objective was; (2) what they actually did and when; (3) what the outcome or result was; (4) the percentage of credit they claim for the outcome; and (5) the name, address, and phone number of someone who can verify the achievement.

After achievements have been collected from an applicant or present employee group, a sample of the achievements is subjected to a scaling process similar to that used in deriving behaviorally anchored rating scales (e.g., Campbell, Dunnette, Arvey, & Hellervik, 1973; Smith & Kendall, 1963). First subject matter experts independently sort the achievements into the achievement dimensions. Only achievements that are assigned consistently to respective dimensions are retained for

further consideration as scale anchors. Then subject matter experts rate the surviving incidents in terms of the level of achievement each represents. Based on these ratings, the scale builder chooses achievements as scale anchors that reliably represent the continuum from high to low accomplishment for each of the respective achievement dimensions. T&E evaluators use these rating scales to score the achievements supplied by each applicant. Typically achievement scores are combined across dimensions to derive a single score for each applicant. In theory, this score indicates the applicant's relative standing in terms of his or her past level of *behavioral achievement* in areas directly related to performance in the target job.

Of all the T&E methods covered in this chapter, the behavioral consistency approach appears to offer the most promise for predicting job performance. McDaniel et al. (1988b) found 15 validity studies in which the behavioral consistency method was used as the predictor and incorporated these into a meta-analysis. They report the mean uncorrected validity of this method as $r = .25$, and the mean corrected (for range restriction and unreliability in the criterion) validity as $r = .45$. The 90% credibility value of .33 supported a conclusion of validity generalization for the behavioral consistency method. In addition, the behavioral emphasis in the job analysis and rating scale development phases works in favor of the content validity of selection decisions based on these methods. Yet the behavioral consistency scores are affected by applicant memory, verbal ability, and writing skill. Therefore, this method is supported by evidence based on assessment contents only when applied to jobs in which these attributes are of nontrivial importance for job performance (Ash, 1983). Another complication involves the fact that applicant completion rates for the application supplements relied on by this method are often substantially lower than those for standard application forms or self-assessment supplements (cf. Ash, 1983, 1986; Schmidt et al., 1979). Thus the method may have a chilling effect on applicants, especially those who are in high demand. Based on our experience with and the literature extant on the behavioral consistency method of T&E evaluation, this method may prove most useful when the job market favors the employer (i.e., relevant unemployment rates are high) and when applicants are expected to be highly verbal (as in the case of lawyers).

## The Grouping Method

In the basic grouping method, applicants are usually divided into a small number of groups on the basis of *simultaneous* consideration of training and experience (Porter et al., 1976). The applicants do not receive points for months of experience or semesters of education as in the traditional point method. Hence the grouping method does not result in applicant score distributions that are continuous in nature (in contrast to the point method). Rather, applicants are divided into a small number of groups, typically two to five or six, depending on the nature and complexity of the grouping called for by the job in question and the training and experience variations represented in the applicant pool. The basic idea of the grouping approach is to identify the well-qualified and well-suited candidates for job openings, and to the extent feasible, allow all of those equally qualified to be screened further or considered directly by the hiring manager.

As an example, consider the following five groups established to differentiate among applicants for the position of automotive equipment repair foreman:

**Score = 95 Group**
Three months of motorized vehicle repair schooling, and five years of experience in equipment repair on all types of systems (transmissions, brakes, etc.), which must have included heavy equipment repair (e.g., draglines, bulldozers, caterpillars) in addition to servicing a variety of motor equipment (cars, trucks, gas and diesel). At least two years of the five must have been in a lead worker or supervisory capacity. This experience must have occurred all within the last 10 years. At some point in the work history there should also be evidence of ordering parts and supplies, writing service orders, and so on, to indicate the capacity to do paperwork.

**Score = 90 Group**
No schooling but experience as in the 95 Group.

**Score = 80 Group**
Four years of experience as in the 95 Group without evidence of recency or lead worker/supervisory experience or paperwork handling.

**Score = 70 Group**
Four years of automotive repair experience that consisted of one make and one type of vehicle or specializing in only one function (e.g., brakes, transmissions).

**Score = Not Qualified Group**
Minimum qualifications not scored. All other applicants should be placed in this category (e.g., automotive serviceman). MQs: Four years of experience as an automotive mechanic.

The development of this scoring guide requires careful job analysis and involvement of subject matter experts at all stages. A T&E evaluator using this guide would examine data from a standard application form or resume, and then would determine which of the five categories described in the guide best matched the background of the applicant. The applicant would then be assigned the score for that group or category.

Unanticipated types of education, training, and experience that arise during the evaluation process are duly noted and the basis for placement into a category is also documented. Note that the minimum qualifications—four years experience as an automotive mechanic—are too general to be treated as a single category. Depending on the specific nature of the experience, four years of automotive mechanic experience may be scored as 70 or 80. Note, too, that applicants receive no credit for experience or education beyond the optimal levels specified in the rating plan. Thus this method escapes several of the "traps" associated with the traditional method. Its level of measurement is appropriately nominal rather than continuous. The scoring process is simplified. And suitable combinations of education, training, and experience are explicitly formulated; there is no assumption of the compensatory value of one component, for example, education, for another, for example, experience.

Grouping applicants seems to make the rating procedure conform better to the actual level of precision attained in T&E evaluation and measurement based on data obtained from traditional application forms and resumes than the specious precision implied by the continuous score distributions resulting from point methods (cf. Ash & Levine, 1985; Porter et al., 1976). However, grouping methods are similar to point methods in that both use credentials—indirect and fallible indicants of applicant competencies. Criterion-related validity evidence on grouping methods is scarce. Ash and Levine (1985) report significant quasi-validity coefficients ($r = .21$ and $r = .30$) for two of three jobs in which the validity of grouping methods was studied. (Note: "quasi-validity" refers to validity studies using as criteria peer nomination scores derived from statements of who would make the best supervisors if promoted.) These results, however, are particularly noteworthy because the study applied several of the methods described here to the same set of employees, and only the grouping approach produced valid coefficients. Based on our experience with and the literature extant on the grouping method of T&E evaluation, this method will be most useful when there is a short time to develop the T&E method, and when other screening methods (e.g., tests, structured interviews) are to be used subsequent to initial screening via the T&E method. The occupational versatility of the method is yet another benefit, since it can be applied to professional, craft, or managerial jobs quite easily. Of course, this approach is not appropriate for true entry jobs where little previous experience or education are called for.

**The Illinois Job Element Method**

In a meta-analysis McDaniel et al. (1988b) reported results from 16 validity studies of a method of T&E evaluation used in the University Civil Service System of Illinois. They named this method the "Illinois job element" approach. In this approach applicants describe their work experience and education and then provide a self-assessment on each of the KSA attributes identified from job analysis as important for successful job performance. A T&E evaluator reviews the job experience description to determine if it supports the self-rating on the respective attributes. If so, the self-rating is the applicant's score on the particular attribute, or "biographic element"; if not, the applicant is given no credit on that attribute. This method combines the use of a T&E evaluator in evaluating the relevance of education and work experience with self-assessment of job-related attributes seen in knowledge, skills, and ability T&E approaches. McDaniel et al. (1988b) reported the mean uncorrected validity of this method as $r = .11$, and the mean corrected (for range restriction and unreliability in the criteria) validity as $r = .20$. The corrected standard deviation of the distribution of validity coefficients was 0, yielding a 90% credibility value $= .20$, indicating that the validity of the Illinois job element method is generalizable across studies.

## ONLINE AND INTERNET-BASED METHODS OF ASSESSING EXPERIENCE, EDUCATION, AND TRAINING

The Internet has become an increasingly popular medium through which information about job seekers and jobs is shared. Over the last few years, many web-based companies have come into being that provide products and services to assist those looking for work and those searching for employees. Job seekers create and post resumes, search for jobs, take online assessments, and in some cases, manage their careers. Employers search resume databases for qualified candidates, post job openings, and use online tools, such as keyword resume searching to sift through large numbers of applicants.

In this section we discuss online resumes, ways in which resumes can be posted using web-based tools, and privacy concerns surrounding resumes posted to the Net. A detailed presentation of current methods of online screening follows. Legal considerations in the context of equal employment opportunity are described, and then newer online screening endeavors and future directions for web-based screening are presented. The section concludes with a brief discussion of the urgent need for empirical research in this area.

### The Online Resume

Resumes are posted online at an increasing rate. For example, Monster.com, a leading career web site, had a database of over 8 million resumes at the time this chapter was prepared and a growth rate of more than 20,000 resumes daily. Employers pay a fee to access and search Monster's resume database in order to find a small, targeted number of candidates possessing the minimum qualifications and experience required to move to the next stage in the hiring process.

Resumes may be placed online in various formats, ranging from free-form text entry to cutting and pasting an already created resume to preformatted resume builders. Preformatted resume builders have set fields, standard check boxes, and drop downs for users to enter and choose information; some fields are optional and some required. Although this method of resume entry may take considerably longer than simply cutting and pasting, it is superior in that it provides standardization. In addition, more targeted searches are possible and large numbers of standardized resumes may be found with greater levels of success.

In some cases, resumes may be posted on the Web as static pictures (e.g., as .gif or .jpeg files). These resumes are not instantly searchable via online means. They must be either printed and reviewed manually or converted to searchable text using optical character recognition (OCR) technology. OCR technology converts a static picture file into text fields. This technology has been available for some years, but initially was not very accurate and formatting would often be lost, resulting in a useless document. In recent years, OCR technology has advanced to the point of easily allowing a user to convert a picture file to searchable text with a high level of accuracy.

Some career web sites provide the option for resumes to be posted confidentially, whereby name, address, phone number, and any other identifying information entered are encrypted and hidden from view. In these cases, candidates passing an initial prescreening may be contacted via an anonymous e-mail address and have the choice to respond to the inquiry or not. Job seekers who do not wish their current employers to know that they are job hunting clearly benefit. Also, certain web-based career companies provide resume writing assistance (often for a fee) and others allow job seekers to enter more than one resume. Different resumes may each be tailored to target specific jobs and employers. Unfortunately, because of the massive quantity of resumes posted to career-related web sites daily, verification of experience, education, and other credentials is often not feasible. Such verification, if done at all, is typically carried out by a third-party organization or by the hiring organization, and at a later stage in the hiring process.

Employers searching large online databases of resumes are, in a sense, taking a leap of faith. Handler (2001a) equates finding the right candidate in an online pool of thousands to finding a needle in a haystack. However, the popularity and continued use of such online services offered by web-based companies is evidence that some level of recruiting and screening success is achievable.

### The Online Resume and Privacy Concerns

According to the Denver Privacy Foundation, over one-third of the online workforce in the United States is being systematically monitored (www.privacyfoundation.org). Another study carried out by the American Management Association (2001) found that 77.7% of U.S. firms "record and review employee communications and activities on the job, including e-mail and Internet transactions and computer files." Employees may want to think twice about posting their resume online and engaging in job search activities while at the office!

Posting resumes online poses other privacy and security problems for individuals. The Privacy Foundation takes an extremist view: ". . . [J]ob seekers who post their resumes online face considerable threats to their privacy. Resumes may be stored by online job sites for many years, and may be misused for data mining and even identity theft" (www .privacyfoundation.org, p. 1). Tracking of online resumes and other personal information may occur at any time by third-party vendors. Sensitive data may be stored and used by job-oriented web sites and advertising networks and without the knowledge of the user. It is the responsibility of such organizations to make known privacy and security statements and practices. For example, many well-known career web sites, such as Careerbuilder.com and Monster.com, provide a clear link on their web sites to their privacy commitment statements. Unfortunately not all sites do. What is often missing from many of these statements is a clear explanation as to what happens to the data once inputted. Stanton cited privacy- and security-oriented legal cases (*Bohach v. City of Reno et al.,* 1996; *State v. Bonnell,* 1993) that taken together convey an important message to job sites: ". . . selection websites should contain disclaimers that explicitly tell applicants what happens to their data, who has [and will have] access to their data, and the degree to which their data and their involvement in the hiring process are kept private and confidential" (1999, p. 15).

### Online Screening

Finding an applicant online who will meet the minimum qualifications of an open position can be extremely difficult. Fortunately, tools are available that allow large numbers of resumes to be searched or prescreened easily based on pre-determined search criteria. These tools also provide more detailed screening that targets specific education, experience, and other required qualifications. It is important to note in view of lack of supportive research that online candidate screening should serve only as an initial step in a multistage recruiting and hiring process.

According to Handler (2001a), online screening is a process that entails, "creating a blueprint of the requirements for success at a given job, gathering information from each applicant in a standardized manner in order to assess how well he or she matches this blueprint, and providing recruiters or hiring managers with a summary of the results of this matching process" (p. 2). Each of these tasks is no different from those carried out during traditional job analyses and administrations of self-assessments. Although there is nothing new here, Handler is simply suggesting that these tasks can now be carried out via the Internet.

Handler (2001a) groups online screening methods into one of two categories, nonscientific and scientific. Nonscientific screening is the most common method currently used and relies on only that basic information the candidate has provided on a resume, such as years of experience, educational level obtained, type of employment desired (full-time, part-time, contract), and willingness to relocate. So-called scientific screening, on the other hand, is more complex in that considerable groundwork, such as a job analysis and standardized candidate data collection, is required. Nonscientific screening is itself functionally separated into two types, simple prescreening and detailed screening. Prescreening (also called simple searching) is a method that allows for a quick reduction of a large set of resumes to a more manageable number. The user is able to select a small number of basic criteria, such as willingness to relocate, degree held, and whether or not a candidate resides in a preferred location, to pinpoint specific resumes instantly and with some degree of accuracy. Simple searching also enables the user to check for currency of resume postings. For example, one can view resumes posted on a given date or all resumes posted during the most recent week.

Conducting a more comprehensive prescreening (or searching) of applicants is possible using widely available detailed search functionality. The comprehensive search differs from simpler prescreening searches only by the number of criteria selected. Users select numerous search criteria to further refine their search. As increasing numbers of criteria are selected at the same time, smaller and more suitable sets of resumes will result. Additional examples of commonly selected criteria are length of current employment and previous work experience, career or educational level, preferred salary, and preferred company and industry. Advanced online search engines are able to instantly and accurately process requests that include an array of selected search criteria. Complex computerized algorithms operate "behind the scenes" to drive search functionality. Unfortunately, specific algorithms employed by various online recruiting organizations are proprietary and unavailable for a full description here.

Another screening tool frequently employed is the web-based, free-text search. The most common and widely used type of free-text search is the keyword search. Keyword searching of text-based resumes and text-based experience fields within an online resume can be easily carried out. A recruiter or hiring manager may use the keyword search to look further into the resume for terms describing relevant experience, education, and specific skills that may meet the predetermined minimum qualifications of an open position. Keyword searching, however, is infamous for often not yielding desired or accurate results. Fortunately, keyword search algorithms however, are continually being refined, updated, and perfected. Keyword algorithms incorporate Boolean logic. Boolean functionality has become commonplace, and its logic is embedded in most search engines that exist today. Boolean search involves using words such as "and" and "or" and characters such as parentheses, all of which can be used to refine a search.

It is important to mention that virtually all types of resume searching can be accomplished more efficiently and accurately when resumes are posted using preformatted text- and numeric-based fields. Monster.com, for example, offers job seekers a Resume Builder that contains one standard format, which includes a specific set of required and optional fields; some are drop-down menus, others radio buttons or check boxes, and many are free-text fields. All such fields are easily queried by search engines (whether prescreening or keyword searching) based on user requests for information contained in those fields.

The screening processes just described include only methods that have not been scrutinized with rigorous research, yet these methods represent the overwhelming majority of tools currently available. Clearly, job analyses, validation research, and verification of the information presented online and the use of the information for assessment purposes are urgently needed. Therefore, these methods should be only a first step in the selection process. Person-to-person contact and other manual screening methods are warranted, at least until scientifically supported online screening methods become available.

## Online Screening and Equal Opportunity Law

Waclawski (2000) provided some interesting statistics, as reported in 1999 from internetstats.com, on Internet and computer usage. For example, only 32% of the United States population is on the Net. Possession of computers is far from universal. However, as the population of those purchasing computers and those signing up for online services continue to increase, it may not be long before most U.S. households are online. The potential for adverse impact will then decline considerably.

Until then as the online recruiting industry grows and as web-based recruiting and screening methods used by employers become commonplace, problems may arise. Qualified members of protected applicant groups without means to access such services may be passed over for employment or be excluded from the screening process. Stanton (1999) stated that it has been difficult to guarantee equal employment opportunity for protected classes of applicants when web-based methods are used. Based on Internet usage survey results, users in the United States are primarily White males younger than age 40. Stanton also asserted that the EEO outlook may continue to worsen, since minorities and women are underrepresented in both the highly technical fields (which makes up the bulk of the online industry) and the overall pool of online job seekers. It appears, based on a perusal of the EEOC's web site (www.eeoc.gov), that specific regulations pertaining to hiring practices based in the World Wide Web have not yet come into being. However, existing EEOC guidelines and applicable federal laws, while established for hiring practices in general, certainly apply to such practices on the Web.

In light of the current state of affairs, employers using online technologies to recruit and select qualified candidates must make every attempt to use valid, accurate, and fair procedures in their assessments. Recent advances in online screening methodologies have the potential to assist the hiring organization in accomplishing this very important mission.

## Recent Advances in Online Screening

Web-based applicant ranking systems, competency profiling, candidate questionnaire approaches, and matching applicant profiles to position MQs are examples of even more recent ways the computer is being used to assist in the online screening process. For example, competency-based job profiles and position-specific questions can be developed online. Applicants interested in a position are directed to the set of targeted questions that tap KSAs and experience (and anything else of interest to the hiring firm). Applicant responses are then scored and compared with position minimum requirements (also developed using online tools), allowing applicants to be prescreened and ranked. A user-friendly, real-time report may be generated and reviewed by the hiring manager. This online approach is advantageous because (1) it can be accomplished in seconds and (2) it minimizes the need for resumes, which may or may not be an accurate representation of a candidate's experience and capabilities. Accuhire.com is a company that offers this competency-based questionnaire and ranking approach to candidate screening. Although these techniques are promising and appear to be modeled on scientifically based approaches, whether these methods attain useful levels of validity awaits rigorous empirical study.

Handler (2001b) provided a detailed prototype for the type of online screening that may serve as a basis for research and development efforts. In his view so-called scientific screening involves three basic steps:

1. *Defining, online, the job to be filled.* Online screening systems "must offer a way to create a blueprint of what is required for success at the job" (p. 3).
2. *Online collecting of data from applicants.* Standardized sets of questions will be asked that measure items defined on the job's blueprint. Predictive validity evidence would drive the choice of questions.
3. *Providing comparative indices and feedback.* Responses to sets of questions can be compared with the previously defined blueprint of the job. Instant feedback is provided that discusses areas of fit, as well as gaps. Any candidates that do not meet a minimum set of qualifications can be removed from further consideration.

Web-based companies currently exist that provide online job analyses, job description writing, and job opening creation tools. In addition, other companies collect experience, education, skills, and other competency-based information from candidates and perform gap analyses based on the self-reported information. Needed is an integration of these online services and well-designed research to produce a comprehensive and valid system for online recruiting and screening needs.

### Research Issues

Empirical research has not yet truly pervaded the Internet. However we have begun to see some progress. One study, for example, carried out by Zickar (1997) suggests that applicants fake responses to computerized assessment tests. Though this study and others like it use the computer as the administration mode, it remains to be seen whether or not results can be generalized to the Web and to education, training, and experience information posted online. Stanton (1998) argues that the Web is an uncontrollable environment, and therefore concern is warranted regarding cheating, test security, and applicant identification (i.e., is the person responding the same person who is applying for the job?).

Because of the uncontrollable nature and newness of the Internet as a medium for recruiting and screening, definitive research may prove elusive. Nevertheless, worthwhile research efforts have begun. Weiss and Barbeite (2001) explored age and gender differences in job seeker preferences for web-based job search functionality. It was found that disparate age groups reported differences in their preference for certain web-site features. In addition, privacy concerns were examined and results revealed that younger participants and men felt more comfortable about providing information online. Burnkrant and Taylor (2001) compared paper/pencil and Internet-based data collection and found scale reliability and latent structure similarities between different respondent groups. They concluded, ". . . data collected over the Internet and in a traditional paper-and pencil setting are largely equivalent [and] no general 'Internet effect' emerged" (p. 5).

Another paper worth noting is that of Stanton and Rogelberg (2001), who looked at online organizational data collection. They stressed the need for a "bill of rights" applicable to online respondents, ensuring the appropriate use of the Web as a medium.

Clearly, the domain of online assessments offers an exciting and timely arena for research by organizational scientists. From the perspective of industrial and organizational psychology, Mondragon (1999) advocated this view in his statement:

> I can't think of a better arena for I-O psychologists to step up to the plate and lead the definition or practice of technology-based solutions for the field. We should be discussing the important needs from the field, designing creative technology-based solutions with multidisciplinary teams, and relentlessly driving the importance of the scientific rigor our field offers in the [technology] development process. (p. 1)

### CONCLUSIONS

Experience, education, and training are widely used for recruitment, screening, and selection. We have detailed much recent progress in fostering a greater understanding of these key contributors to the development of work-related human attributes. We now have a more elaborate conceptual framework of the experience construct, and a body of research that circumscribes its validity for staffing purposes. Although education and training have not enjoyed the same degree of theoretical development as the experience construct, research does support the selective use of various elements in choosing employees. We briefly distill here the key lessons for judgmental assessments of past experience, education, and training as contained in applications, resumes, and supplemental questionnaires. The reader should recall that the assessment methods described in this chapter are subject to equal opportunity laws and associated regulations.

1. Job analysis provides the basis for culling those elements of experience, education and training likely to be valid, and provides a definition of the domain necessary to support the use of these kinds of assessments based on content evidence.

2. Development of suitable minimum qualifications (MQs) is a critical feature of assessments of the type reviewed here. A recently developed method offers a means to increase the likelihood of establishing valid MQs (Levine et al., 1997).

3. Elements of experience likely to be useful include those past accomplishments, jobs held for a sufficient length of time, task proficiency, and experience-based levels of KSAOs directly relevant to a target job, organization, and industry. Length of experience beyond five years is unlikely to offer substantial incremental validity.

4. Elements of education likely to be useful include years of graduate education, possession of a degree, specific courses taken, grade point average, college major, extracurricular activities, and offices held in college clubs where these are directly related to the target job, organization, and industry. Completion of extended, formal training programs, such as apprenticeships, and earning a license or certification are also likely to be useful. Evidence of high school graduation is likely not to be useful.

5. Reported levels of validity suggest strongly that the judgmental assessment of education, training, and experience must be used in combination with other methods of assessment. The level of precision expected indicates that continuous scoring is less desirable than banding applicants into more and less desirable groupings or categories.

6. Whether online or manual screening is employed, the methods of judgmental assessment must be uniformly applied. Standardization of information-gathering tools, methods of scoring, using the scores, and providing feedback to applicants will enhance validity. Training of raters is crucial unless a computer algorithm is employed. Verification of claimed experience, education, and training is essential, especially when online resumes form the basis of an assessment. Placing bogus items in supplemental questionnaires may also help in identifying those who are falsifying credentials.

7. Some of the formal methods that structure the assessment process appear promising, although research is not fully definitive. The grouping method, the task-based method, and the knowledge, skill, and ability-based method where a trained rater is included in the process are worth consideration. When conditions are favorable, the behavioral consistency method offers perhaps the most valid alternative. The traditional point method should not be used.

8. Although a proliferation of assessment methods are available online, rigorous research on validity and potential adverse impact is lacking.

9. Additional avenues of future research include the development of a matrix that pairs job types with assessment methods and elements of experience, education, and training most likely to provide valid information, and the investigation of more subtle factors in assessing these variables as can be captured in applications and resumes. Examples of these factors are the degree of perceived challenge experienced early in one's career, and the timing of particular experiences in a developmental sequence.

# REFERENCES

Ackerman, P.L. (1988). Determinants of individual differences during skill acquisition: Cognitive abilities and information processing. *Journal of Experimental Psychology: General, 117,* 288–313.

American Educational Research Association (AERA), American Psychological Association, & National Council on Measurement in Education. (1999). *Standards for educational and psychological testing.* Washington DC: Author.

American Management Association. (2001). *Workplace monitoring & surveillance: Policies and practices.* New York: Author.

Anderson, C.D., Warner, J.L., & Spencer, C.C. (1984). Inflation bias in self-assessment examinations: Implications for valid employee selection. *Journal of Applied Psychology, 69,* 574–580.

Anderson, J.R. (1990). *Cognitive psychology and its implications.* New York: W.H. Freeman.

Arvey, R.D., & Faley, R.H. (1988). *Fairness in selecting employees* (2nd ed.). Reading, MA: Addison-Wesley.

Ash, R.A. (1983). The behavioral consistency method of training and experience evaluation: Content validity issues and completion rate problems. *Public Personnel Management, 12,* 115–127.

Ash, R.A. (1986). The activity/achievement indicator: A possible alternative to the behavioral consistency method of training and experience evaluation. *Public Personnel Management, 15,* 325–343.

Ash, R.A., Johnson, J.C., Levine, E.L., & McDaniel, M.A. (1989). Job applicant training and work experience evaluation in personnel selection. In G.R. Ferris & K.M. Rowland (Eds.), *Research in personnel and human resources management* (Vol. 7, pp. 183–226). Greenwich, CT: JAI Press.

Ash, R.A., & Levine, E.L. (1981). *An investigation of career service unassembled examinations* (Final report for STAR grant No. 80-011). Tampa, FL: Center for Evaluation Research, University of South Florida.

Ash, R.A., & Levine, E.L. (1985). Job applicant training and work experience evaluation: An empirical comparison of four methods. *Journal of Applied Psychology, 70,* 572–576.

Baugher, D., Varanelli, A. Jr., & Hall, J. (1994). Ten years of experience with a performance-based promotional selection and career development system within state government. *Public Personnel Management, 23,* 551–571.

Bjork, R.A. (1994). Memory and metamemory considerations in the training of human beings. In J. Metcalfe & A. Shimamura (Eds.), *Metacognition: Knowing about knowing* (pp. 185–205). Cambridge MA: MIT Press.

Bohach v. City of Reno, Weston, Gibson, & McDonald. (1996). 932 F. Supp. 1232; 1996 U.S. Dist. LEXIS 10715; 11 BNA IER CAS 1707. July 22, 1996, Decided.

Borman, W.C., Hanson, M.A., Oppler, S.H., Pulakos, E.D., & White, L.A. (1993). Role of early supervisory experience in supervisor performance. *Journal of Applied Psychology, 78,* 443–449:

Bray, D.W., Campbell, R.J., & Grant, D.L. (1974). *Formative years in business: A long-term AT&T study of managerial lives.* New York: Wiley.

Brown, B.K., & Campion, M.A. (1994). Biodata phenomenology: Recruiter's perceptions and use of biographical information in resume screening. *Journal of Applied Psychology, 79,* 897–908.

Burke, M.J., & Day, R.R. (1986). A cumulative study of the effectiveness of managerial training. *Journal of Applied Psychology, 71,* 232–246.

Burnkrant, S.R., & Taylor, C.D. (2001, April). *Equivalence of traditional and internet-based data collection: Three multigroup analyses.* Paper presented at the 16th Annual Conference of the Society for Industrial and Organizational Psychology, San Diego, CA.

Caldwell, D.F., & O'Reilly, C.A. III. (1990). Measuring person-job fit with a profile-comparison process. *Journal of Applied Psychology, 75,* 648–657.

Campbell, J.P., Dunnette, M.D., Arvey, R.D., & Hellervik, L.V. (1973). The development and evaluation of behaviorally based rating scales. *Journal of Applied Psychology, 57,* 15–22.

Childs, A., & Klimoski, R.J. (1986). Successfully predicting career success: An application of the biographical inventory. *Journal of Applied Psychology, 71,* 3–8.

Clevenger, J., Pereira, G.M., Wiechmann, D., Schmitt, N., & Harvey, V.S. (2001). Incremental validity of situational judgment tests. *Journal of Applied Psychology, 86,* 410–417.

Cook, C.L. (July, 1980). *Rating education, training, and experience in the public sector.* Paper presented at the annual conference of the International Personnel Management Association Assessment Council, Boston.

Driskell, J.E., Willis, R.P., & Copper, C. (1992). Effect of overlearning on retention. *Journal of Applied Psychology, 77,* 615–622.

Equal Employment Opportunity Commission (EEOC), U.S. Civil Service Commission, U.S. Department of Labor, & U.S. Department of Justice. (1978). Uniform guidelines on employee selection procedures (1978). *Federal Register, 43,* 38290–38315.

Eyde, L. (2000, December). In-service presentation on job element examining. Washington, DC: U.S. Office of Personnel Management.

Farrell, B.M. (December, 1979). *Task performance self-evaluations: An alternative selection procedure to traditional experience and training ratings.* Minneapolis, MN: State of Minnesota, Department of Personnel, Selection Research Unit.

Farrell, J.N., & McDaniel, M.A. (2001). The stability of validity coefficients over time: Ackerman's (1988) model and the General Aptitude Test Battery. *Journal of Applied Psychology, 86,* 60–79.

Flanagan, J.C. (1954). The critical incident technique. *Psychological Bulletin, 51,* 327–358.

Gatewood, R.D., & Feild, H.S. (1998). *Human resource selection* (4th ed.). Orlando: Dryden.

Giniger, S., Dispenzieri, A., & Eisenberg, J. (1983). Age, experience, and performance on speed and skill jobs in an applied setting. *Journal of Applied Psychology, 68,* 469–475.

Goldstein, I.L., & Ford, J.K. (2002). *Training in organizations* (4th ed.). Belmont, CA: Wadsworth.

Gordon, M.E., Cofer, J.L., & McCullough, P.M. (1986). Relationships among seniority, past performance, interjob similarity, and trainability. *Journal of Applied Psychology, 71,* 518–521.

Gordon, M.E., & Fitzgibbons, W.J. (1982). Empirical test of the validity of seniority as a factor in staffing decisions. *Journal of Applied Psychology, 67,* 311–319.

Gutman, A. (2002). Review of case law and implications for work experience screens. In M.R. Redmond (Chair), *Work experience measures—most used, least validated and often overlooked.* Symposium presented at the Society of Industrial and Organizational Psychology, for its annual conference, Toronto, April.

Handler, C. (2001a, July). Online screening of job applicants: A better tool. (Part 1 in a 3 part series). *The Electronic Recruiting Exchange.* (www.erexchange.com).

Handler, C. (2001b, August). Online screening: Inside scientific screening. (Part 2 in a 3 part series). *The Electronic Recruiting Exchange.* (www.erexchange.com).

Hanisch, K.A., & Hulin, C.L. (1994). Two-stage sequential selection procedures using ability and training performance: Incremental validity of behavioral consistency measures. *Personnel Psychology, 47,* 767–785.

Hough, L.M. (1984). Development and evaluation of the "Accomplishment Record" method of selecting and promoting professionals. *Journal of Applied Psychology, 69,* 135–146.

Howard, A. (1986). College experiences and managerial performance. *Journal of Applied Psychology, 71,* 530–552.

Howard, A., & Bray, D.W. (1988). *Managerial lives in transition: Advancing age and changing times.* New York: Guilford.

Hunter, J.E., & Hunter, R.F. (1984). Validity and utility of alternative predictors of job performance. *Psychological Bulletin, 96,* 72–98.

Keil, C.T., & Cortina, J.M. (2001). Degradation of validity over time: A test and extension of Ackerman's model. *Psychological Bulletin, 127,* 673–697.

Keller, R.T., & Holland, W.E. (1978). Individual characteristics of innovativeness and communication in research and development organizations. *Journal of Applied Psychology, 63,* 759–762.

Langdale, J.A., & Weitz, J. (1973). Estimating the influence of job information on interviewer agreement. *Journal of Applied Psychology, 57,* 23–27.

Lavigna, R.J. (1992). Predicting job performance from background characteristics: More evidence from the public sector. *Public Personnel Management, 21,* 347–361.

Levine, E.L., & Cannon, J.A. (1986). *Evaluation of the transmission and distribution training program.* Tampa FL: Tampa Electric Company. (Unpublished technical report)

Levine, E.L., Maye, D.M., Ulm, R.A., & Gordon, T.R. (1997). A methodology for developing and validating minimum qualifications (MQs). *Personnel Psychology, 50,* 1009–1024.

Lyness, K.S., & Thompson, D.E. (2000). Climbing the corporate ladder: Do female and male executives follow the same route? *Journal of Applied Psychology, 85,* 86–101.

Lyons, T.J. (1989). *Validity of education and experience measures in traditional rating schedule procedures: A review of the literature* (OPRD Report 89-2). Washington, DC: U.S. Office of Personnel Management.

Maranto, C.L., & Rodgers, R.C. (1984). Does work experience increase productivity? A test of the on-the-job training hypothesis. *The Journal of Human Resources, 19,* 3–341–356.

Maslow, A.P. (1968). The unassembled examination. In J.J. Donovan (Ed.), *Recruitment and selection in the public sector* (pp. 239–254). Chicago: Public Personnel Association.

Mathieu, J.E., Heffner, T.S., Goodwin, G.F., Salas, E., & Cannon-Bowers, J.A. (2000). The influence of shared mental models on team process and performance. *Journal of Applied Psychology, 85,* 273–283.

McDaniel, M.A., Schmidt, F.L., & Hunter, J.E. (1988a). Job experience correlates of job performance. *Journal of Applied Psychology, 73,* 327–330.

McDaniel, M.A., Schmidt, F.L., & Hunter, J.E. (1988b). A meta-analysis of the validity of methods for rating training and experience in personnel selection. *Personnel Psychology, 41,* 283–314.

Mondragon, N.J. (1999, July). Should we be driving technology solutions or just be passengers on the wild ride? A positive look at our field and technology. *The Industrial-Organizational Psychologist, 37,* 42–50.

Motowidlo, S.J., & Van Scotter, J.R. (1994). Evidence that task performance should be distinguished from contextual performance. *Journal of Applied Psychology, 79,* 475–480.

Nguyen, N.T., & McDaniel, M.A. (2001). *The influence of impression management on organizational outcomes: A meta-analysis.* Poster session presented at the 16th Annual Conference of the Society for Industrial and Organizational Psychology, San Diego, April.

Noe, R.A. (2002). *Employee training and development* (2nd ed.). Boston: McGraw-Hill.

Pasaputhi, M. (2001). The social construction of the personal past and its implications for adult development. *Psychological Bulletin, 127,* 651–672.

Porter, W.R., & Levine, E.L. (1974). Improving applicants' performance in the completion of applications. *Public Personnel Management, 3,* 314–317.

Porter, W.R., Levine, E.L., & Flory, A. (III) (1976). *Training and experience evaluation: A practical handbook for evaluating job applications, resumes, and other applicant data.* Tempe, AZ: Personnel Services Organization.

Primoff, E.S. (1958). *Report on validation of an examination for electrical repairer, McClellan Field California.* Washington, DC: U.S. Civil Service Commission.

Primoff, E.S. (1975). *How to prepare and conduct job element examinations* (TS-75-1). Washington, DC: U.S. Government Printing Office.

Pulakos, E.D., Arad, S., Donovan, M.A., & Plamondon, K.E. (2000). Adaptability in the workplace: development of a taxonomy of adaptive performance. *Journal of Applied Psychology, 85,* 612–624.

Quiñones, M.A., & Ehrenstein, A. (Eds.) (1997). *Training for a rapidly changing workplace: Applications of psychological research.* Washington, DC: American Psychological Association.

Quiñones, M.A., Ford, J.K., & Teachout, M.S. (1995). The relationship between work experience and job performance: A conceptual and meta-analytic review. *Personnel Psychology, 48,* 887–910.

Rowe, P.M. (1988). The nature of work experience. *Canadian Psychologist, 29,* 109–115.

Roth, P.L., BeVier, C.A., Schippmann, J.S., & Switzer, F.S. III. (1996). Meta-analyzing the relationship between grades and job performance. *Journal of Applied Psychology, 81,* 548–556.

Roth, P.L., & Bobko, P. (2000). College grade point average as a personnel selection device: Ethnic group differences and potential adverse impact. *Journal of Applied Psychology, 85,* 399–406.

Russell, C.J. (2001). A longitudinal study of top-level executive performance. *Journal of Applied Psychology, 86,* 560–574.

Schmidt, F.L., Caplan, J.R., Bemis, S.E., Decuir, R., Dunn, L., & Antone, L. (1979). *The behavioral consistency method of unassembled examining* (Tech. Memorandum 79–21). Washington, DC: U.S. Office of Personnel Management.

Schmidt, F.L., Hunter, J.E., & Outerbridge, A.N. (1986). Impact of job experience and ability on job knowledge, work sample performance, and supervisory ratings of job performance. *Journal of Applied Psychology, 71,* 432–439.

Schmidt, F.L., Hunter, J.E., Outerbridge, A.N., & Goff, S. (1988). Joint relation of experience and ability with job performance:

Test of three hypotheses. *Journal of Applied Psychology, 73,* 46–57.

Schmitt, N., & Cohen, S.A. (1989). Internal analyses of task ratings of job incumbents. *Journal of Applied Psychology, 74,* 96–104.

Senge, P.M. (1990). *The fifth discipline: The art and practice of the learning organization.* Garden City, NY: Doubleday.

Sistrunk, F., & Smith, P.L. (1982). *Review of validity studies of personnel assessment methods in law enforcement and corrections.* Tampa, FL: Center for Evaluation Research.

Smith, P.C., & Kendall, L.M. (1963). Retranslation of expectations: An approach to the construction of unambiguous anchors for rating scales. *Journal of Applied Psychology, 47,* 149–155.

Solomon, E.E. (1986). Private and public sector managers: An empirical investigation of job characteristics and organizational climate. *Journal of Applied Psychology, 71,* 247–259.

Sonnentag, S. (1998). Expertise in professional software design: A process study. *Journal of Applied Psychology, 83,* 703–716.

Spreitzer, G.M., McCall, M.W., & Mahoney, J.D. (1997). Early identification of international executive potential. *Journal of Applied Psychology, 82,* 6–29.

Stanton, J.M. (1999, January). Validity and related issues in web-based hiring. *The Industrial-Organizational Psychologist, 36,* 69–77.

Stanton, J.M. (1998). An empirical assessment of data collection using the Internet. *Personnel Psychology, 51,* 709–725.

Stanton, J.M., & Rogelberg, S.G. (2001). Beyond online surveys: Internet research opportunities for industrial and organizational psychology. In S. Rogelberg (Ed.), *Handbook of research methods in industrial and organizational psychology* (Vol. 4, pp. 199–216). London: Blackwell.

State of Wisconsin, Department of Employment Relations. (April, 1979). *Sample of an actual achievement history questionnaire and cover letter.* Madison, WI: Author.

State v. Bonnell, No. 16031, No. 16032, No. 16033, No. 16034, No. 16035, No. 16036, Supreme Court of HI, 75 Haw. 124; 856 P.2d 1265; (1993). Haw. LEXIS 34; 8 BNA IER CAS 1226, August 17, 1993, Decided.

Stone, D.L., & Stone, E.F. (1987). Effects of missing application-blank information on personnel selection decisions: Do privacy protection strategies bias the outcome? *Journal of Applied Psychology, 72,* 452–456.

Steiner, D.D., & Gilliland, S.W. (1996). Fairness reactions to personnel selection techniques in France and the United States. *Journal of Applied Psychology, 81,* 134–141.

Tannenbaum. A.S. (1957). Personality change as a result of an experimental change of environmental conditions. *Journal of Abnormal and Social Psychology, 55,* 404–406.

Tesluk, P.E., & Jacobs, R.R. (1998). Toward an integrated model of work experience. *Personnel Psychology, 51,* 321–356.

Truxillo, D.M., Bennett, S.R., & Collins, M.L. (1998). College education and police job performance: A ten-year study. *Public Personnel Management, 27,* 269–279.

Vance, R.J., Coovert, M.D., MacCallum, R.C., & Hedge, J.W. (1989). Construct models of job performance. *Journal of Applied Psychology, 74,* 447–455.

Vicino, F.L., & Bass, B.M. (1978). Lifespace variables and managerial success. *Journal of Applied Psychology, 63,* 81–88.

Waclawski, J. (2000, January). The real world: The e-business revolution—Faster than a speeding bullet. *The Industrial-Organizational Psychologist, 37,* 70–80.

Weiss, E.M., & Barbeite, F.G. (2001, April). *Online job search: Group differences in preferences and privacy concerns of job seekers.* Paper presented at the 16th Annual Conference of the Society for Industrial and Organizational Psychology, San Diego, CA.

Zickar, M. (1997, April). Computer simulation of faking on a personality test. In G. Alliger, *Faking matters.* Symposium conducted at the 12th Annual Conference of the Society for Industrial and Organizational Psychology, St. Louis, MO.

## WEB SITE REFERENCES

www.internetstats.com

www.accuhire.com

www.careerbuilder.com

www.eeoc.gov

www.erexchange.com

www.monster.com

www.privacyfoundation.org

CHAPTER 17

# Behavioral and Situational Interviews

ROBERT L. DIPBOYE, KEVIN WOOTEN, AND STEFANIE K. HALVERSON

Decades of research have produced a variety of scored procedures that have been shown to be effective in the selection of employees, including cognitive ability tests, biographical information, personality inventories, work samples, assessment centers, and experience and training evaluations (Schmidt & Hunter, 1998). Despite the evidence, employers have sought alternatives to these scored procedures for several reasons. First, it is becoming increasingly clear that success at work requires attributes that may not be measured by these approaches, including organizational citizenship and the ability to relate effectively with team members and internal and external customers. A second concern is the adverse impact that some of these measures have on the hiring of minorities. This is a particular concern with cognitive ability tests (Bobko, Roth, & Potosky, 1999; D'Souza, 1995; Martocchio & Whitener, 1992; Ryan, Ployhart, & Friedal, 1998). A third problem with both cognitive ability and personality tests is that they may hurt recruiting efforts as the result of evoking negative reactions from applicants (Harland, Rauzi, & Biasotto, 1995; Macan, Avedon, Paese, & Smith, 1994; Rosse, Miller, & Stecher, 1994). Finally, some of these measures may be time-consuming and costly for employers to develop and

use. As noted by Campbell and Kleinke (1997), "Organizations want tests that identify competent people, don't have adverse impacts, don't offend anyone, look like tests should look, don't cost a lot of money, and can be developed quickly" (p. 308).

In the attempt to balance these often-competing demands, the interview has been the method of choice for many employers. Rather than using traditional unstructured interviews to assess global traits, employers have focused in recent years on structuring interviews to assess job-related, behavioral dimensions. These have gone by a variety of labels, including "behavioral," "situational," and "structured" interviews. Structured interviews come in a variety of forms, however, and in this chapter we examine the more common varieties and explore factors that account for their effectiveness. We start by deconstructing the behavioral interview to show the alternative strategies that have been used to avoid the judgmental biases common in traditional trait-based interviews. Next, we discuss several exemplars of behavioral interviews in use today and compare how they have incorporated one or more of these strategies. Finally, we consider some of the issues involved in implementing behavioral interviews in organizations.

## STRATEGIES FOR IMPROVING THE INTERVIEW PROCESS

Interview research has painted a dim picture of the typical unstructured interview and has shown how structuring the selection process should enhance the reliability and validity of interviewer judgments. For more than 70 years, industrial psychologists have been advocating the strategies that are characteristic of behavioral and situational interviewing. Take, for example, the following quote from a classic text in industrial psychology written by Morris Viteles and published in 1933:

> . . . although the interview as ordinarily conducted is unreliable and of low validity, better results can be obtained from the interview by making certain changes in it. . . . Traits to be rated in the course of the interview should be carefully defined and objective methods for expressing judgments on these traits be provided. The traits chosen for rating will naturally be those required on the particular job and will differ from job to job. Such estimates can best be expressed on carefully prepared rating scales. . . . Questions to be asked in the interview must be carefully phrased so as to convey the correct meaning. . . . Interview procedures are in need of standardization. . . . Some have gone as far as to require that all questions be written out and presented on cards so as to avoid the influence of intonation of voice and facial exprssion in questioning. . . . As far as possible the occasion should be provided for objective activities in the course of the interview and for judgments based on the observations of reaction during such performance. (pp. 178–179)

Subsequent qualitative reviews of the interview research provided support for these recommendations (Ulrich & Trumbo, 1965). More important, recent quantitative reviews have concluded that if interviews are designed as suggested by Viteles and others, they can achieve high levels of validity without the adverse impact against minority groups found for cognitive ability tests (Huffcutt & Arthur, 1994; Huffcutt & Roth, 1998; McDaniel, Whetzel, Schmidt, & Maurer, 1994; Wiesner & Cronshaw, 1988;). In a meta-analysis of 31 studies, Huffcutt and Roth (1998) found that Black and Hispanic applicants were rated only about one quarter of a standard deviation lower than White applicants on structured interviews. Huffcutt and Arthur (1994) examined four levels of structure based on standardization of questioning and response scoring and found observed validities of .11, .20, .34, and .34 for Levels 1 (least structure) through 4 (most structure), respectively. Once they were corrected for criterion unreliability and range restriction, these validities were .20, .35, .56, and .57. Generally, the corrected validities for highly structured interviews are surprisingly high and comparable to the validities obtained with cognitive ability tests (Schmidt & Hunter, 1998).

## What Are the Failings of the Unstructured Interview?

In addressing the answer to this question, we should first consider what can go wrong in the typical unstructured interview. These problems include biases that can occur in the gathering and processing of information and the decisions made on the basis of this information.

### Biased and Undifferentiated Theories of the Ideal Applicant

At the root of the problem with unstructured interviews is the absence of guidelines on what constitutes a qualified applicant. Interviewers are often left to their own resources and as a consequence, they rely on ideas about job requirements and applicants that are lacking in specificity and distorted by stereotypes (Anderson & Shackleton, 1990; Hakel & Schuh, 1971; Rowe, 1984).

### Biased Information Gathering

Possibly reflective of their implicit theories of job requirements, interviewers in an unstructured procedure have discretion in what they ask and how they ask it. A perusal of the "how-to" advice will reveal a bewildering assortment of questioning strategies. In one article the advice is to give sales applicants "the brush off" to see if they assertively attempt to get an interview (Rose & Garrett, 1992). If the applicants manage to get an interview, the advice is then to embarrass and insult them in the interview. Another recruiter for managers of Internet start-up companies suggests that interviewers ask candidates to drive them to the cleaners to pick up their clothes (Frase-Blunt, 2001). On the way the interviewer attempts to rattle the candidate by giving confusing directions and asking interview questions at the same time.

These idiosyncratic approaches to gathering data on an applicant may be illegal. They can also bias the conduct of the interview and influence how well applicants perform in presenting their qualifications (Dougherty, Turban, & Callender, 1994). As a consequence, the candidate's performance in the interview may reflect more of the interviewer's conduct of the session than the actual qualifications of the candidate. This seems most likely among candidates who are low in self-esteem and perhaps more vulnerable to external influence (Liden, Martin, & Parsons, 1993).

### Potential Influence of Nonverbal Behavior on Interviewer Judgments

In the unstructured interview, interviewers may pay inordinate attention to applicants' nonverbal and paralinguistic behavior and neglect the substance of what is said (Burnett & Motowidlo, 1998; DeGroot & Motowidlo, 1999; Howard & Ferris, 1996; Motowidlo & Burnett, 1995; Wright & Multon, 1995). Although nonverbal behavior may be indicative of some aspects of qualifications (cf., Motowidlo & Burnett, 1995), an overreliance on nonverbal and paralinguistic cues and interviewers' idiosyncrasies in interpreting these cues pose perhaps the greatest threat to the validity of interviewer judgments.

### Impression Management

Candidates' impression management tactics in interviews are important determinants of interviewer ratings (Kacmar & Carlson, 1999; Stevens & Kristof, 1995; Young & Kacmar, 1998). An explosion of advice to applicants in "how-to-interview" articles, books, tapes, courses, and web sites has raised doubts as to whether interviewers can trust what they see and hear in the interview session. One unsubstantiated claim is that structured interviews reduce impression management and help the interviewer see through a well-prepared candidate's facade (Santo, 2000).

### Categorical and Biased Judgments

Unstructured interviews encourage biased, categorical judgments that can detract from the validity and reliability of interviewer judgments. Ideally, interviewers focus their attention on the knowledge, skills, abilities, and other characteristics (KSAOs) important to the position and then infer from the information they gather the degree to which the applicant possesses each KSAO. Contrary to this ideal, the research suggests that the initial reaction of interviewers is to *categorize* the applicant as qualified or unqualified on the basis of very limited information (Rowe, 1984). A variety of rating biases have been found that possibly reflect the tendency to categorize applicants on the basis of the vague and undifferentiated conceptions of the ideal applicant, including positive and negative halo, overemphasis on negative information, and contrast effects. Rating biases can also occur on the basis of gender, race, appearance, age, and ethnicity of the candidate (cf., Biernat & Kobrynowicz, 1997; Finkelstein, Burke, & Raju, 1996; Lee, Castella, & McCluney, 1997; Marlowe, Schneider, & Nelson, 1996; Moss & Tilly, 1996; Parsons & Liden, 1984; Perry, Kulik, & Bourhis, 1996).

### Biases in Decision Making

Beach (1990) noted that "most decisions are made quickly and simply, on the basis of 'fittingness,' and only in particular circumstances are they made on the basis of anything like the weighing and balancing of gains and losses that is prescribed by classical decision theory. . . ." (p. xiii). Consistent with this conception of the decision process, it has been shown that interviewers make their decision early in the interview (Springbett, 1954; Tschirigi & Hegli, 1979; Tucker & Rowe, 1977; Tullar, Mullins, & Caldwell, 1979). The hallmark of a structured procedure is that each interviewer is held to the same degree of assessment of the applicants so that coherence and consistency can be maintained in evaluating a pool of applicants.

All of these are potential problems that can threaten the validity of an interviewer's judgments of an applicant. What follows is a consideration of alternative strategies of structuring the interview to avoid these problems.

## How Behavioral Interviews Correct These Problems

All of the aforementioned problems with the unstructured interview can threaten the validity of an interviewer's judgments of an applicant. A plausible hypothesis is that behavioral interviews achieve their higher levels of validity and reliability by avoiding or eliminating these problems. The most highly structured behavioral interviews incorporate features that counter most or all of these biases. The procedures for conducting the interview and evaluating applicant answers is based on a common specification of a qualified applicant that is based on a careful analysis of the job requirements. In this way the idiosyncratic and often conflicting opinions of interviewers are replaced with a uniform definition of what constitutes an ideal applicant. Rather than allowing interviewers to follow whatever line of questioning they desire, all interviewers are expected to adhere to the same line of questioning or, in the most structured interviews, the exact same questions. The attention of the interviewer is focused on the content of the applicant's answers to questions in an attempt to minimize the influence of the applicant's nonverbal behavior on the interviewer's impressions. Also, by focusing the interviewer on content of answers and providing standardized guidelines for questioning and evaluation, applicants have less freedom to manage impressions and fool the interviewer. The information gathering and evaluation procedures require interviewers to delay judgment and avoid rush decisions, thus avoiding the categorical, snap judgments so characteristic of unstructured interviews.

All of these are strategies for improving the interview process that are commonly associated with behavior interviews. Previous discussions of interview structure have provided a laundry list of these and other factors (Campion, Palmer, & Campion, 1997; Dipboye & Gaugler, 1993). What has been missing is a model that provides a coherent and more parsimonious conceptual framework for integrating these various strategies. What follows is a consideration of one such model.

## A MODEL OF INTERVIEW STRUCTURE

There have been two comprehensive attempts to define interview structure (Campion et al., 1997; Dipboye & Gaugler, 1993). In this chapter we build on these previous attempts by providing a tighter conceptual framework and to distinguish those components that are integral to a behavior approach from those factors that are more concerned with implementation. Figure 17.1 presents the components of behavioral interviews in terms of the life cycle of an interview. This cycle begins with the development of the interview system. Next, there is the conduct of the interview session. Finally, the data gathered in the interview are used in evaluating applicants and making decisions about them. We suggest that much of the variance in the validities obtained with various forms of structured interviews in the prediction of job performance can be attributed to differences among structured interviews on these dimensions. In the development of the interview we distinguish those high on job-relatedness from those that are low on this dimension. In the conduct of the interview we distinguish those high on standardization of the process from those that that are low on this dimension. In the evaluation of the applicant and decision making after the interview, we distinguish those that are highly structured from the less structured approaches. Highly structured evaluation includes behaviorally based rating scales, statistical methods of combining evaluations, and consistently applied decision rules.

### Job-Relatedness of the Interview

Two components are involved in the job-relatedness dimension. An interview is more job related to the extent that it is based on a systematic analysis of task dimensions in a job and an identification of the KSAOs required for successful performance of the job. The degree of job-relatedness of an interview could be evaluated using content validation procedures (cf., Feild & Gatewood, 1989). Meta-analyses have shown that interviews that are based on job analysis achieve higher levels of predictive validity than those that are less job related (McDaniel, Schmidt, & Hunter, 1988; Wiesner & Cronshaw, 1988). An explanation for this can be found in the behavioral consistency model of Wernimont and Campbell (1968). They argued that, rather than using "signs" of behavior in the form of general constructs such as intelligence, the

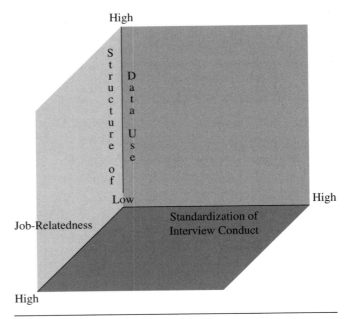

**Figure 17.1** A three-dimensional model of interview structure.

best prediction is achieved when one samples directly from the behavioral domain. Job-relatedness is perhaps the most important and the defining characteristic of behavioral and situational interviews.

### Job Analysis

Whereas the most unstructured approaches tend to pay little attention to the specific tasks and requirements of the position for which the candidate is being considered, structured interviews are anchored in a thorough and systematic analysis of the job for which the candidate is being considered. A job analysis is crucial to the subsequent design of the interview, including the development of questions and rating scales. At relatively low levels of structure, an interview may be based on little more than a qualitative description of tasks in a job. More structured interviews go beyond description of the content of the job and are based on an analysis of the fundamental behavioral dimensions underlying this content. Incumbents and other subject matter experts (SMEs) are typically surveyed to determine the frequency and importance of various tasks they perform. On the basis of an analysis of these data, a determination is made of which incumbents occupy similar positions and the fundamental task dimensions that underlie these tasks. These dimensions could serve as the agenda and protocol for what is discussed in the interview as well as the specific questions that are asked (cf., Holdeman, Aldridge, & Jackson, 1996).

## *Specification of KSAOs*

Another characteristic of highly structured interviews is that they attempt to identify the KSAOs required in the job. One approach would be to have SMEs judge the extent to which various KSAOs are required for successful performance of the job. For instance, the Multiattribute Job Questionnaire of Fleishman and Reilly (1992) could be used for this purpose. A more direct approach is to use a critical incidents methodology (Flanagan, 1954) in which incumbents and supervisors generate specific behavioral examples of successful and unsuccessful performance that they have observed. These behavioral examples are in the form of incidents that describe in detail what happened, why it happened, and the circumstances surrounding the performance. SMEs sort and classify the incidents to determine the fundamental dimensions of performance in the job (e.g., customer service, leadership). A determination is then made of KSAOs crucial to performing well on each dimension. The more important KSAOs and those that are most amenable to evaluation in the interview are chosen as the basis for designing the interview.

## Standardization of the Interview Process

The next dimension in the proposed taxonomy concerns the actual conduct of the interview. Unquestionably, this dimension has been the most influential among those studying structure in the interview process. The key issues here are the focus of the questions that are asked and the flexibility allowed to the interviewer in asking these questions.

## *Question Focus*

The questions in behavioral interviews focus on the specific behaviors of the applicant that are believed relevant to the performance of the job. This can be contrasted with the traditional unstructured trait-based interview in which interviewers ask about general, unspecified dimensions using unfocused questions (e.g., tell me about yourself, why are you applying for this job, etc). Campion et al. (1997) distinguished among four question types. First, there are situational questions where applicants are provided hypothetical situations and asked how they would respond. These types of questions are frequently based on job analyses that have identified critical incidents and how effective and ineffective employees have handled these incidents. Behavior and experience questions have candidates relate how they handled situations in the past that are related to the requirements of the position for which they are being considered. This type of question is particularly useful where the applicant is an entry-level employee with little prior experience in the job.

For instance, the applicant might be asked to relate how he or she dealt with difficult people at school as a way of getting at how well the applicant will handle difficult people in the future on the job. Biographical questions focus on the applicant's background and are most often used to determine whether the individual has been involved in work, school, and leisure activities relevant to the job (Carlson, Thayer, Mayfield, & Peterson, 1971; Roth & Campion, 1992). Finally, there are job knowledge and skill questions. These are used to quiz candidates about specific procedures, tools, concepts, and definitions to determine whether the applicant has the know-how to perform the job (Arvey, Miller, Gould, & Bush, 1983; Walters, Miller, & Ree, 1993). In asking about knowledge, interviewers might ask definitional questions (e.g., "What is a . . ." or "What does . . . refer to or mean?"), causal questions ("What happens when . . ." or "What is the result of . . ."), and explanatory questions (e.g., "Why would you . . ." or "How would you explain . . ."). In assessing skill, interviewers may physically present applicants a simulation of the job and have them act on some aspect of it or may have the applicants role-play how they would handle interpersonal situations.

The research comparing situational and behavioral description questions has yielded mixed results and appears to show that each type of question has advantages and disadvantages (Campion, Campion, & Hudson, 1994; Conway & Peneno, 1999; Pulakos & Schmitt, 1995). The best advice is to use a mix of questions rather than limiting the interview to any one type.

## *Flexibility*

A defining element of structured interviews is that interviewers are constrained to some degree in their phrasing of questions and the use of follow-ups and probes (Huffcutt & Arther, 1994). In the case of highly structured (Campion, Pursell, & Brown, 1988) and situational (Latham, Saari, Pursell, & Campion, 1980) interviews, exactly the same questions are asked in the same order with no follow-ups or probes. Moreover, the interviewers are required to devote approximately the same amount of time to each of the dimensions assessed in the interview. The imposition of such uniformity should help ensure that information gathered in the session reflects the actual qualifications of the applicant rather than biases in the conduct of the session. In contrast to this extreme level of structure, semistructured behavioral interviews present interviewers with a common set of questions but allow them to follow up with their own probes to explore areas not included in the schedule of questions. At even lower levels of structure, interviewers may be constrained to the extent that they must follow the same topical outline, although they may ask whatever questions they wish with regard to each topic. The most unstructured interviews impose no limits on either the topics addressed or the specific questions asked.

Some evidence suggests that interrater agreement is higher when interviewers are not permitted to use follow-up questions (Schwab & Heneman, 1969). However, much of the practical advice assumes that some degree of follow-up is crucial to accurate and valid judgments. For instance, Santo (2000) states that follow-up questions are crucial to detect "interview chameleons," and to see through the act, "interviewers must ask open-ended questions to get the candidate talking and then probe in depth with behavioral event questions" (p. 22). Bell (1999) suggested that the highest level of structure may be appropriate to interviewing for low-level jobs but is inappropriate to interviewing for high-level, professional jobs. The accuracy of these assertions has not been assessed in the research literature.

### Note Taking

Focusing questions on specific behaviors may mean little if interviewers fail to remember this information after the interview. Behavioral and situational interviews often require interviewers to document answers to questions during the actual interview to reduce errors in recall. The most structured interviews not only have note taking but also impose a consistent framework for taking notes. Huffcutt and Woehr (1999) conducted a meta-analysis that found that the effects of note taking on the validity of interviewer judgments in predicting job performance were inconclusive. Nevertheless, some recent research has shown positive effects of note taking when notes are behaviorally based, specific, and voluntary (Burnett, Fan, Motowidlo, & DeGroot, 1998). Biesanz, Neuberg, Judice, and Smith (1999) found that note taking reduces the biasing effects of preinterview expectations.

### Structured Use of Data to Evaluate the Candidate

The third and last dimension in our proposed model is that of using data obtained to evaluate the candidate's responses and to make a decision regarding that candidate. We consider four components of this dimension: (1) the extent to which the scoring system is behaviorally based, (2) the use of ancillary data, (3) the combination of data to form a judgment, and (4) the decision model in actually reaching a decision. The more structured behavioral interviews minimize access to any information other than what is gathered in the interview, employ psychometrically sound rating scales having specific behavioral anchors, statistically combine the inter-

viewer evaluations of applicants, and use consistent decision rules to reach decisions about candidates. In contrast to behavioral interviews, the typical trait-based unstructured interviews typically require holistic ratings of overall qualifications, uses poorly defined graphic scales or qualitative comments, and rely on intuitive strategies of combining data on the applicant. Moreover, no explicit decision-making rule is imposed in deciding hiring, rejection, or further interviewing.

### Behaviorally Based Rating Scales

The first component shown is that of using a structured scale to perform ratings on each answer to the questions posed during the interview. Behaviorally anchored rating scales (BARS) are generally considered preferable to graphic scales in structuring behavioral interviews (Maas, 1965; Vance, Kuhnert, & Farr, 1978). Smith and Kendall (1963) developed the BARS method as a means of clarifying the anchors on rating scales and increasing the reliability of scales. The construction of a BARS begins with the generation of critical incidents that are grouped into dimensions of performance. Employees submit examples of high, moderate, and low levels of each dimension of performance, and these are edited into statements of expectations. These incidents are then sorted into dimensions, and those that cannot be clearly agreed on are discarded. The final product is a vertical scale for each dimension, anchored with expected behaviors.

Bell (1999) provided the following example of a behavioral question in a BARS:

> Question: "When reviewing previous contracts in preparation for a meeting with a client, you come across a reference to 'other considerations' that the client has apparently received in the past. With a little digging, you discover that these considerations involve virtual carte blanche travel at any time to the United States for the client at your company's expense. You know that these considerations no longer accord with company policy, if they ever did. How do you let the client know that he will no longer be receiving these behind the contract benefits?"
>
> 5 (excellent): In a face-to-face meeting, reassure the client that he is highly valued by the company. Explain the corporate rules under which you must do business in the future. Ask for the client's cooperation and understanding in finding contract terms that are mutually acceptable.
> 3 (marginal): Write the client a letter explaining that the travel benefits will be discontinued, with a copy of the pertinent company policies attached.
> 1 (poor): Attempt to "finesse" the matter gracefully by placing the client's expenses under a different budget category where they will be less obvious.

The interviewees are not expected to say the precise words suggested in the anchor responses. Rather, the interviewers simply use these benchmarks to determine the appropriate numeric score for the applicant's actual answer.

### Statistical Combination of Ratings to Form Judgments

In unstructured interviews, interviewers combine their impressions of the applicant subjectively to form an overall judgment. In contrast, in the more structured behavioral interviews, the interviewer not only provides numerical ratings on each of several dimensions, but also the interview is "scored" by statistically combining the interviewer's ratings of the applicant across the separate dimensions (e.g., by averaging or adding the separate ratings).

Previous research has consistently shown that using statistical combinations of data to form judgments yields better results than using clinical combinations of data. In a recent meta-analysis, Grove, Zald, Lebow, Snitz, and Nelson (2000) found that mechanical-prediction techniques were consistently better than clinical prediction techniques, regardless of the judgment task, type of judges, judges' amounts of experience, or the types of data being combined.

### Limited Access to Ancillary Data

The most structured behavioral interviews typically do not make available biographical information, test scores, references, and other ancillary data to the interviewer at the time that the applicant is evaluated and decisions rendered. When such data are made available, specific guidelines are provided on how to evaluate and use this information (Brown & Campion, 1994; Dalessio & Silverhart, 1994). In the typical unstructured procedure, interviewers are given access to other data such as test scores and biographical data, and they are free to use this information as they wish.

One consequence of not providing ancillary information and forcing the interviewer to focus solely on information gathered in the interview session is that evaluations formed from the session may be relatively independent of the information provided in test scores and other ancillary information. Huffcutt, Roth, and McDaniel (1996) found in a meta-analysis of 49 studies that 16% of the variance in interview constructs represented cognitive ability but that correlation of interviewer ratings with cognitive ability declined as structure of the interview increased. The lower the correlation between interviewer judgments and other information provided on the applicant, the more likely the interview will contribute incrementally to the prediction of job performance, above and beyond the level of prediction achieved with ancillary data.

Another consequence of limiting access to ancillary data is to improve the reliability, accuracy, and validity of interviewer judgments. Having access to the application has been shown to lower the reliability and accuracy of assessments as the result of increasing the variability with which the interview is conducted (Dipboye, Fontenelle, & Garner, 1984). Also, previous meta-analyses have shown higher validities when interviewers do not have access to test scores (McDaniel et al., 1994) and do not have access to ancillary data (Searcy, Woods, Gatewood, & Lance, 1993).

### Consistent Use of a Decision Model

So far we have discussed the alternative approaches to forming a judgment of an applicant on the KSAOs considered important to the job. Once all applicants have been judged on these KSAOs, a decision has to be made as to which ones to hire, reject, and subject to further interviewing. The last component of the use of data dimension is one of actually making decisions on the basis of the data. Structured approaches apply an explicit rule in deciding among applicants who have been interviewed (Heneman, Judge, & Heneman, 2000). Different types of decision rules may be used in different behavioral interviews (minimum score, top down, random selection, ranking, grouping) but the rule used in any one system is explicit and consistently applied across applicants. In contrast, unstructured procedures typically have no explicit or consistently applied decision rules.

### Hypothesized Relationship of Interview Structure to Interviewer Validity

There is insufficient research to allow strong statements about the precise nature of the relationship of structure to interviewer validity. In Figure 17.2 we speculate on what seems reasonable on the basis of the research conducted so far. One assumption of this model is that the three components of structure are not equally important. Rather, job-relatedness is hypothesized as the most influential dimension with the largest increases in validity occurring as a consequence of increased job-relatedness. This is based on research and theory showing that criterion-related validity increases to the extent that the selection technique directly samples the criterion (Schmidt & Hunter, 1998; Wernimont & Campbell, 1968). The structure of the interview process is hypothesized as the second most influential dimension with increased standardization of the interviewer's conduct of the session resulting in higher validities. Finally, structure of data use is hypothesized to be the least important of the three dimensions primarily on the basis of findings of limited increases in judgmental

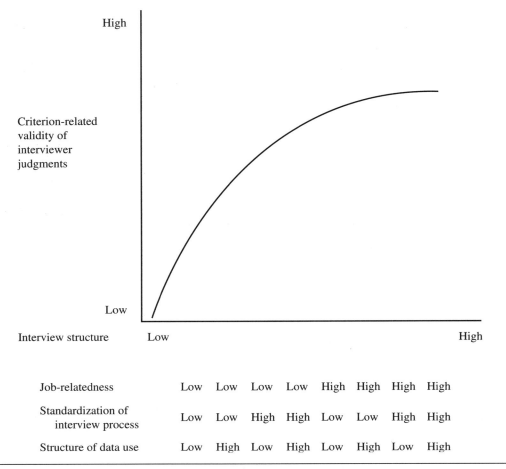

**Figure 17.2** The hypothesized relationship of interview structure to the criterion-related validity of interviewer judgments.

accuracy as the result of rating scale type. The relationship of structure to criterion-related validity is proposed to be curvilinear on the basis of the meta-analysis of Huffcutt and Arthur (1994), such that the rate of the increase in validity as a function of structure declines and levels off at the highest levels of structure.

## EXEMPLARS OF STRUCTURED INTERVIEW PROGRAMS

Thus far we have presented the possible components that might be included in behavioral interviews. The various interview programs that have been actually applied vary in the degree to which each of these components is represented. We review four specific programs: situational interviews, Personnel Decision Incorporated's (PDI's) Behavior Description Interviews (BDIs), the Life Insurance Management Research Association's (LIMRA's) Agent Selection System, and Di-

mension Decision International's (DDI's) Targeted Selection®. We also present two eclectic interviewing procedures: the highly structured interview, and the multimodal interview. All of these programs are highly job related and are standardized in that they require coverage of the same topics. They differ, however, in the extent to which they impose constraints on the process. The situational interview and the highly structured interview allow very little discretion on the part of the interviewer and applicant, whereas the Targeted Selection®, LIMRA's Agent Selection System, the BDI, and the multimodal interview impose common standards but allow some freedom in the conduct of the session.

### Situational Interview

Latham et al., (1980) based their approach on the hypothesis that intentions are among the best predictors of behavior. In the design of a situational interview, a critical incidents job analysis is first conducted to identify the dimensions on which applicants are evaluated. Using the critical incidents technique, SMEs relate incidents they have observed over the last 6 to 12 months of job performance under instructions to describe the circumstances, background, or context; what the person did that was effective or ineffective; and how the incident was an example of effective or ineffective performance. Another group of SMEs then sorts the incidents into categories representing the criteria that can be used in evaluating employees. A third group of SMEs then takes the incidents and the overall job categories and allocates each incident to one category. Those incidents reallocated by a high percentage of this group are retained, thus eliminating ambiguous incidents. Finally, the incidents that are retained and the categories to which they have been assigned are given to other SMEs who rate each incident on the degree to which it reflects the performance dimension. The next step in the development of the situational interview is to have a group of experienced interviewers list answers that they have heard from high-, mediocre-, and low-performing employees. Specifically, a consensus is reached as to the answers to use as benchmarks.

J. Peter Leeds and Wayne Burroughs (1997) described the following situational question used in the selection of security officers and the way that answers were scored (http://www.securitymanagement.com/library/000334.html):

> You are the security officer on duty and you see an elderly man parking in a "Loading Zone Only" area. You remind him of the sign, but he ignores you and walks into the medical facility. . . . What do you do?

In this case an answer typical of the best response would be a flexible one in which the candidate indicates something such as posting a warning, whereas the worst answer would indicate a rigid enforcement of the rules such as forcing the person to repark. Another situational question was:

> You are the security officer on duty. You have a walkie-talkie radio. A person has been assaulted and injured. The assailant is making his getaway on foot. The injuries look bad and an ambulance is on the way. No one has arrived yet. What do you do?

In this case the worst answer was one where the candidate would chase the fleeing suspect without giving attention to the victim, whereas the best answer was one where the candidate first helped the victim and obtained a description of the assailant.

In the conduct of a situational interview, interviewers do not preview the application or other ancillary data on the applicant prior to the interview. Interviewers ask the questions exactly as they are worded in the guide, with no follow-ups or variations allowed. The applicant is then rated on each

of the dimensions using BARS that are anchored with exemplars of good, mediocre, and poor answers. The mean of these ratings forms the final judgment of the applicant. Latham and his colleagues have conducted several studies showing the superiority of situational interviewing over either traditional interviews or other versions of structured interviews (Kataoka, Latham, & Whyte, 1997; Latham et al., 1980; Latham & Saari, 1984; Latham & Skarlicki, 1996; Latham & Sue-Chan, 1996, 1999; Maurer & Lee, 2000). One potential problem with situational interviews is that in asking applicants questions about what they would do in specific job situations, they may run the risk of violating the *Uniform Guidelines on Employee Selection Procedures* as set forth by the Equal Employment Opportunity Commission. Specifically, Part 1607, Section 5F of the *Guidelines* states that "users should avoid making employment decisions on the basis of measures of knowledges, skills, or abilities which are normally learned in a brief orientation period, and which have an adverse impact" (Equal Employment Opportunity Commission, Civil Service Commission, Department of Labor, & Department of Justice, 1978, p. 205).

## Behavior Description Interview

As in the case of the situational interview, the design of a BDI begins with a critical incidents job analysis to determine the dimensions on which applicants are evaluated. Incumbents, supervisors, executives, and customers describe specific situations illustrating effective, average, or ineffective job performances and describing what happened, why, and the results. A minimum of 80 to 100 incidents is gathered. These incidents are then sorted by SMEs into groups to determine the underlying dimensions of performance.

Questions are developed from these incidents that ask about past behaviors that are related to each dimension. Unlike the situational interview, in which the interviewer asks the applicant "what would you do if. . . . ," in the BDI the interviewer asks "what did you do when. . . ." (Janz, Hellervik, & Gilmore, 1986). For example, in the development of an interview to assess applicants for the position of sales representatives, a job analysis revealed that one of the performance dimensions was "establishing new client contacts." One incident from that dimension described a situation in which the salesperson experienced difficulty with a new client contact because the client, a farm implements dealer, was busy at the time. The salesperson persisted, offering to help the dealer load a truck with parts and talking about business when the dealer took a break. This critical incident was turned into a question by asking applicants: "Tell us about the most

difficult new client contact you made in the last six months."
The probes were:

What was the obstacle you faced?

What did you say when you were stumped?

What did you do to overcome the difficulty?

After designing questions for applicants experienced in
the job, question stems and probes are designed for those who
have limited or no direct job experience. Questions can be
organized in two ways. One alternative is to organize them
around the various performance dimensions. Janz et al.
(1986) recommended, however, that the questions be reor-
ganized into major topics from the applicant's experience.
The most common pattern divisions are recent direct work
experiences, job-related work experience, educational experiences, and job-related interpersonal experiences.

Leeds and Burroughs (1997) provided two examples of
BDI questions used in the selection of security officers (http://
www.securitymanagement.com/library/000334.html):

(A) Think about a time when you were on a duty post when
you had to deal with a person who was mentally dis-
turbed. In what context did this event occur? How did
you respond to the emergency? How did you interpret
this person's behavior? What could have been done differently? What were the results of this situation?

(B) Tell me about a time when you had to choose between
making yourself look good or your employer look good.
What were the circumstances? Why did you make that
particular choice? What would have happened if you had
chosen differently? What was the outcome? How did
your employer respond?

In each case the interviewer would probe the candidate's answers. Applicants who provide a poor answer (as determined
by prior evaluations by SMEs) and those who gave inconsistent or no answer receive a low score on the question. Those
who provide examples of how they effectively handled these
events, and can provide supporting detail, receive a higher
score on the question. In this particular case, two behavior
description questions were asked for each of seven dimensions identified with job analysis.

In the actual conduct of a BDI, interviewers are encouraged to take concise notes during the interview and to rate
the applicants on the criterion dimensions as soon after the
interview as possible. Janz et al. (1986) recommended rating
the applicants on a 5-point scale in which the top category
places the applicant in the top 20% of all applicants, a 4 puts
the applicants in the 60–80% range, a 3 is average, a 2 is below
average in the 20–40% range, and a 1 places the applicant

in the bottom 20%. If the dimensions are of equal importance,
all the interviewer has to do is sum the ratings. If importance
differs, then 100 points can be divided among the dimensions,
and each rating is multiplied by the points. The weights can
be determined through participation of interviewers in a workshop. The validation studies conducted on Patterned Behavior
Description Interviewing have yielded positive results (Janz,
1982; Orpen, 1985).

**The LIMRA Agent Selection System**

The Life Insurance Marketing and Research Association
(LIMRA) developed a semistructured interviewing package
for the selection of life insurance agents that has been thoroughly researched over the last three decades. Prior to the
conduct of the interview, the interviewer is given the opportunity to preview the applicant's scored biodata. A structured
guide sets forth questions to ask for each of 11 dimensions
that have been identified through job analysis as important
in the performance of insurance agents (e.g., communication
ability, ability to control situations, interpersonal relations
skills, time management, and administrative ability). Interviewers are allowed to ask follow-up questions and are expected to take notes on the applicant's answers. At the end
of the interview, the interviewer rates the applicant on each
of the 11 qualification dimensions and indicates whether the
applicant should be considered for employment.

LIMRA began conducting programmatic research on selection of sales agents in the mid-1960s, and the first practical
application of these results was in the form of the Agent
Selection Kit (ASK; Carlson, Thayer, Mayfield, & Peterson,
1971). The ASK included a highly structured format for conducting the interview and evaluating the applicant with the
overall interview process broken down into information gathering, evaluation, job behavior prediction, selection decision
making, and follow-up. The interviews were quite laborious
and took over 120 minutes to complete. In the place of ASK,
the Selection Interview Blueprint (SIB) was later introduced,
which included a personal history form and one structured
interview guide that required about 75 minutes to use. A personal history form was developed to assist the interviewer in
the previewing of information about the applicant prior to the
interview. The interview guide contained questions about past
work experiences, educational experiences, activities outside
of work and school, ability to handle finances, past experiences with life insurance and insurance agents, and future
goals. Questions focused on not only specific activities such
as duties in previous jobs but also on more abstract constructs
such as personal relations, motivation, and future goals. Next
to each of the questions, space was provided for taking notes,

and a rating form was constructed to help the interviewer form summary judgments. Research has shown the LIMRA system to be valid when judged on the basis of the productivity and tenure of sales agents (Carrier, Dalessio, & Brown, 1990), although higher validities are typically found for applicants with previous sales experience than for those without such experience (Brown, 1979a, 1979b, 1980).

## DDI Targeted Selection®

Development Dimensions International (DDI) has developed an interviewing system that contains the following practices:

- The use of past behavior to predict future behavior.
- The identification of the critical job requirements (target dimensions) for the position.
- The organization of selection elements into a comprehensive system.
- The application of effective interviewing skills and techniques.
- The involvement of several interviewers in organized data-exchange discussions.
- The augmentation of the interview with observations from behavioral simulations.

A job analysis is conducted to identify specific job dimensions that define the behaviors, knowledge and motivations needed to be successful in a job. Table 17.1 shows one of four dimensions identified in an analysis of the position of customer representative in an organization. The other three dimensions in this case were building customer loyalty, communication, and managing work. For each dimension key actions related to each dimension are listed.

The actual interview session begins with casual chitchat and an overview to build rapport and relax the candidate. The interviewer then proceeds to pose behavioral questions for each of the criterion dimensions identified through the job analysis. In behavioral questions, examples of current and/or past performance are sought as the best predictors of future performance. Each question is phrased in the past or present tense, but not the future tense. For instance, interviewers ask candidates for examples of past or current performance using phrases such as "Tell me about . . . ," "Describe a time. . . . ," and "Give me an example of. . . ." The behavioral questions used to assess the dimension of strategic working relationship were as follows (DDI, 1998b):

1. Others' work principles sometimes conflict with our own. Tell me about a time when this happened to you. What did you do?

**TABLE 17.1   An Example of a Dimension Assessed in a Targeted Selection® Interview Designed to Select Customer Service Representatives (DDI, 1998a)**

**Building Strategic Working Relationships**—Developing and using collaborative relationships to facilitate the accomplishment of work goals.

*Key Actions:*

**Seeks opportunities**
Proactively tries to build effective working relationships with other people.

**Clarifies the current situation**
Probes for and provides information to clarify situations.

**Develops others' and own ideas**
Seeks and expands on original ideas, enhances others' ideas, and contributes own ideas about the issues at hand.

**Subordinates personal goals**
Places higher priority on team or organization goals than on own goals.

**Facilitates agreement**
Gains agreement from partners to support ideas or take partnership-oriented action; uses sound rationale to explain value of actions.

**Uses Key Principles**
Establishes good interpersonal relationships by helping people feel valued, appreciated, and included in discussions (enhances self-esteem, empathizes, involves, discloses, supports).

*Note.* Reprinted with permission from Development Dimensions International, Inc. (1998a). Dimensions for Customer Service Representative Bridgeville, PA: DDI Press.

2. Working with others usually involves some give and take. Describe a time when you worked out an agreement with a peer/team member. What did you do?

3. Have you ever been in a team/group with an unproductive person? What did you do?

The interviewer follows up each question with probes to obtain a complete understanding of a past performance. Questions are asked to obtain information on the problem and the circumstances surrounding the example of the problem situation, the task that needed to be performed to solve the problem, that action that was taken, and the results of the action. This is sometimes called the STAR pattern: Situation, Task, Action, and Result. An example of the question pattern is (DDI, 1995):

Situation: Think about when you _____. (Interviewer describes a specific situation)

Task: What needed to be done about the situation?

Action: What did you do to resolve the situation?

Result: What was the result?

If a candidate does not provide a complete example in response to an effective lead question, the interviewer follows up with probes aimed at gathering more specifics.

After asking behavioral questions for each dimension, the interviewer closes the session by asking if the applicant has additional strengths that he or she would like to mention and if there are any questions. In some targeted selection systems, a simulation is provided so that the applicant has an opportunity to demonstrate specific skills. In closing the interview session, the interviewer provides information to the applicant on the position and the organization or location, checks on whether the applicant correctly understands, explains the next steps of the selection process, and thanks the applicant for a productive session. In the postinterview stage, the interviewer categorizes the behavioral examples given by the candidate under the appropriate target dimensions. The interviewer compares the responses with benchmark responses gathered prior to the interview from individuals already in the position. These benchmarks provide examples of good, average, and bad answers to the situations. A good response is one that matches the response of those who have succeeded in the position. On the basis of matching to benchmarks, the interviewer categorizes STARs into appropriate dimensions and indicates whether the candidate's behavior in each dimension's Key Actions was effective ( + ), neutral (0), or ineffective/absent ( − ). The interviewer considers the weight of each STAR according to the recency, impact, and similarity to the target job, and then rates the candidate on each dimension on a 5-point scale (DDI, 1995):

5–Much More Than Acceptable (Significantly exceeds criteria for successful job performance)

4–More Than Acceptable (Exceeds criteria for successful job performance)

3–Acceptable (Meets criteria for successful job performance)

2–Less Than Acceptable (Generally does not meet criteria for successful job performance)

1–Much Less Than Acceptable (Significantly below criteria for successful job performance)

Finally the interviewer rates the candidate on two global dimensions: communication and impact. Communication refers to the extent that the candidate clearly conveyed information and ideas in a way that helped the audience understand and retain the message. Impact refers to creating a good first impression, commanding attention and respect, and showing an air of confidence.

## Eclectic Techniques

Two other approaches have received much less attention than the ones we have discussed so far and represent eclectic programs that combine a variety of techniques.

### Highly Structured Interview

The highly structured approach combines biographical, situational, patterned behavior description, and knowledge questions and is perhaps the most structured of all the interviewing formats proposed so far in the conduct of the interview and the evaluation of candidates. In this approach, Campion et al. (1988) listed a set of requirements to guide the development of the procedure: (1) a job analysis is conducted to determine the dimensions used to evaluate applicants, and questions are constructed on the basis of this analysis; (2) interviewers ask exactly the same questions with no follow-ups or variations allowed; (3) anchored scales are used to evaluate applicants and to ensure consistency across interviews; (4) note taking is encouraged to avoid memory decay; (5) interviewers do not preview the paper credentials of the applicants prior to the sessions; (6) panels are used in interviewing and rating the applicants; (7) the final judgment is formed by a simple average of the panel members ratings; and (8) the process is administered in exactly the same way for all applicants with no variations.

### Multimodal Employment Interview

Perhaps the least structured approach among the structured interviews is the multimodal employment interview (MEI), which has been used primarily in Germany. As described by Schuler and Funke (1989), the MEI is a semistructured, task-oriented procedure that adapts several different procedures. Highly structured procedures are often inappropriate in Germany because of legal and cultural mandates that selection techniques be acceptable to the applicants and to the unions that represent them. The first step in the development of the interview is to conduct a critical incidents job analysis to determine the dimensions for evaluating applicants. Situational, PBDI, and self-presentation questions are then constructed to gather information on these dimensions. In the actual conduct of a session, interviewers follow the same pattern: (1) an introductory period of small talk; (2) self-presentation questions to assess expression, self-confidence, and liveliness; (3) questions about vocational interests and choices; (4) a period in which interviewers can ask whatever questions they wish; (5) biographical questions (some of which were structured along the lines of the BDI); (6) a realistic job preview;

and (7) a series of situational questions. Finally, applicants are allowed to ask the interviewer questions.

## IMPLEMENTATION ISSUES

Despite the evidence to support the use of a structured interview process, organizations continue to rely primarily on unstructured interviews. For instance, in a survey of U.S. corporations, Terpstra and Rozell (1997) found that only 29% of firms used structured interviews. When structured interviews are used, evidence indicates that there may be slippage and degradation in the process of implementing these procedures (Latham & Saari, 1984; Weekley & Gier, 1987). The small amount of research that exists suggests that careful consideration needs to be given to potential problems in implementation. Among the factors to consider are the impact on the structured interview on recruiting, the personal needs of the decision maker, providing a good fit to the job context, the politics of the organization, and fit to the national culture. Several vehicles for implementing behavioral interviews and dealing with these constraints are considered later, including training and selection of interviewers and computerizing the interview process.

### Barriers to Implementing Structured Interviews

There are several barriers that exist to implementing structured interviews. These include the potential adverse impact on recruiting, resistance due to organizational politics, the incongruence of interview structure with some national and organizational cultures, and the personal needs of the interviewer.

#### Concerns About Recruiting

A structured selection procedure may allow an accurate assessment of candidates but may be ineffective if it harms the ability of the company to recruit applicants. Some characteristics of structured interviews appear to negatively affect applicants' attitudes toward the organization and the job (Bies & Shapiro, 1988; Conway & Peneno, 1999; Dipboye, 1992; Hyde, 1998; Latham & Finnegan, 1993; Rynes, 1993; Schuler, 1993; Tyler & Bies, 1990).

#### Organizational Politics

Unstructured interviews offer several advantages to decision makers seeking power and influence. Ripley and Ripley (1994) described how a large city's selection of firefighters was influenced by politics:

a person's potentials were not considered and there were no measurable criteria as to what a successful. . . . firefighter 'looked like.' . . . Candidates would make certain they got to know particular chiefs and captains and would get recommendations from them. . . . There was a great deal of political jockeying prior to the interview boards. If candidates did not become part of this process, they were at a distinct disadvantage. . . . The previous oral boards were composed of senior firefighter chiefs and union leaders. The board members would discuss their individual opinions and scores regarding a candidate at the end of each interview as a group and then decide what the candidate's score should be. Often the most persuasive or politically positioned chief or union member determined the candidate's final score. (p. 28)

The inherent ambiguity of unstructured interviews can prevent close scrutiny and monitoring of the selection process by outside parties, such as the HRM department or governmental agencies (Daniel, 1986). As the result of politics, structured approaches may be avoided and when implemented may become corrupted.

### Cross-Cultural Concerns in Implementation

A factor that has been relatively ignored in the previous work on the interview is the compatibility of the interview procedure with the national culture. To the extent that a structured interview procedure clashes with the values and norms of a country, one can expect problems in implementation. Spence and Petrick (2000) suggested that two of the value dimensions identified by Hofstede (1991), femininity-masculinity and collectivist-individualistic, are particularly important in determining reactions to recruitment practices. They concluded from their research that "national culture values can supersede and undermine . . . cosmetic attempts to standardise the formal interview questions" (p. 63). Along similar lines, Lee (1998) examined selection practices in Korea, contrasting the traditional Confucian influence of *yon-go,* which means a special social relationship or special connection based on family ties (*hyul-yon*), school ties (*hakyon*), and birthplace (*ii-yon*). Many of the larger Korean corporations have attempted to shift to *gong-chae* systems of recruitment and selection. In these systems, there is an emphasis on behavioral interviews that incorporate simulated exercises and that focus interviewers on answers to problems and interview questions. Typically a "blind interview" is used in which there is no prior access allowed to biographical data, recommendation letters, or test scores. Attempts to implement structured, behavioral interviews in masculine, collectivist cultures are likely to confront more resistance than in feminine, individualistic cultures.

## Fit of Interview to the Organizational Culture

The emphasis in structured interviewing is on providing a good fit to the KSAOs of the job, and yet an increasing number of organizations are moving toward a model of staffing in which persons are selected for *organizational membership* (Bowen, Ledford, & Nathan, 1991). In this emerging model, the ideal candidate becomes the person who not only has KSAOs that fit a job but who also shares the values and goals of the organization and is prosocial, a good team member, and a good organizational citizen. In the attempt to provide a good person-organization (P-O) fit, selection procedures may be emphasized that are unstructured. For instance, Melohn (1994) described the interview process at North American Tool & Die as a "mini-Rorschach." At Euro-Disney, the most important part of the application is the section for extracurricular activities, hobbies, and outside interests (Gooding, 1992). Moreover, few set questions are asked; the interview consists mostly of a casual conversation about topics such as what the applicant likes to do in his or her spare time.

Sunoo (1995) described how Southwest Airlines has attempted to tailor Targeted Selection® to fit its unique corporate culture. But some scholars suggest that structured interviews can be incompatible with attempts to achieve good P-O fit in corporations with strong cultures. Judge and Ferris (1992) argued that "calls for structured interviews as a way to improve the validity of the interview may be misplaced if the true goal, and utility, of the interview lies not in selecting the most technically qualified, but the individual most likely to fit into the organization" (p. 61). Accordingly, some interview procedures have been specifically designed to assess fit of the applicant's values to the core values of the recruiter's organizational culture (Parsons, Cable, & Wilkerson, 1999).

## The Personal Needs of the Interviewer

For structured interview procedures to be successfully implemented, interviewers must want to use the procedures as they were originally intended (Lewis & Seibold, 1993). Failures to implement structured procedures can reflect the interviewers' personal dissatisfaction with these procedures. For interviewers who value the role of interviewing and see it as an important part of their position, a highly structured procedure could be seen as deskilling the task and reducing it to a boring, monotonous exercise, whereas an unstructured interview could offer challenge and autonomy.

## Vehicles for Implementing Structured Interviews

In dealing with the potential barriers to structured interviews, it is important to consider the alternative vehicles by which structured interviews can be implemented in organizations. Training is almost always used as part of structured interviewing, although we do not consider it a defining element of interview structure. Selection of interviewers is a potential vehicle for dealing with resistance to behavioral interviewing, yet it is largely unused and unresearched. An increasingly common vehicle is information technology in the form of computerized and web-based interviews. We next consider each of these as potential ways of dealing with the barriers to implementation.

## Training Interviewers

Training usually accompanies the implementation of structured interviewing and is likely to be crucial in overcoming the barriers associated with interviewer preferences. The types of training that are required depend on where the interview is positioned on the three dimensions stated in Figure 17.1.

An important role of training is to obtain buy-in of interviewers to the interviewing system and ensure that they will follow the prescribed procedures. To the extent that the interview allows discretion in the conduct of the session, it also becomes important to improve the interviewers' skill in asking questions and probing for information. An example of a program that is typical of interviewer training in how to conduct sessions is a five-day workshop described by Fear (1984) in which role playing is used to provide practice and feedback in questioning strategies. There have been surprisingly few evaluations of these programs, but there is some evidence that training can improve the conduct of interview sessions (Motowidlo et al., 1992; Stevens, 1998). Huffcutt and Woehr (1999) conducted meta-analysis in which they found higher validities when training was provided to interviewers.

To the extent that the interview procedures involve observation of interviewee behavior and formal scoring, training is also needed to improve translation of observations into ratings. Smith (1986) concluded from his review that the best way to improve rating accuracy is to use a combination of performance standards and performance dimensions training. "Before raters are asked to observe and evaluate the performance of others, they should be allowed to discuss the performance dimensions on which they will be rating. They should also be given the opportunity to practice rating sample performance. Finally, they should be provided with 'true' or expert ratings to which they can compare their own ratings" (p. 37).

An example of a comprehensive, integrated training program is a two-day workshop used by Development Dimensions International, Inc. in implementing Targeted Selection® that contains instruction in all three of the dimensions depicted in Figure 17.1 (DDI, 1998c). Trainees are first introduced to the techniques and concepts underlying the determination of job requirements and practice how to classify behaviors into dimensions in a "job-specific Behavior Categorization Exercise" (p. 1). They then learn how to conduct the interview, using the Targeted Selection® interview guide and how to ask follow-up questions, take notes, build rapport, and manage the pace and direction of the interview. Finally, trainees learn how to evaluate and integrate the information gathered in the session. The workshop incorporates a variety of training methods, including lecture, videotapes depicting various concepts and techniques, paper-and-pencil exercises, discussion, role playing, and feedback.

### Selection of Interviewers

Evidence of large differences among interviewers in the accuracy, validity, and reliability with which they can assess applicants suggests that this could be a particularly potent ancillary in the implementation of structured interview procedures (Dougherty, Ebert, & Callender, 1986; Dreher, Ash, & Hancock, 1988; Kinicki, Lockwood, Hom, & Griffeth, 1990; Zedeck, Tziner, & Middlestadt, 1983). To the extent that interviewers have individual differences, some consideration needs to be given to assessing the relationship between interviewer attributes and the effectiveness of the interview. Once identified, those attributes found to predict interview effectiveness could be used in assessing, screening, and selecting interviewers. The strongest evidence seems to support selecting intelligent interviewers, although much of this research was conducted with tasks other than interviews (e.g., Borman, 1979; Ickes et al., 2000; Smither & Reilly, 1987). Other promising attributes that deserve attention include accuracy in decoding nonverbal behavior (e.g., the Pons test; Rosenthal, Hall, DiMatteo, Rogers, & Archer, 1979) and self-monitoring (Snyder, 1974).

The most profitable approach to selecting interviewers may not be paper-and-pencil tests of personality and ability constructs, however, but simulations or samples of the interviewing task. Although we are not aware of any work such as this, it would be interesting to design an interviewing simulation in which persons must work their way through three dimensions depicted in Figure 17.1. Thus, prospective interviewers would analyze jobs to determine job specifications, preview applications of interviewees, conduct interviews, and evaluate the applicants. The task could be structured such that accuracy of evaluations and validity of judgments could be assessed. Further, the skill with which the interview is conducted could be rated and used as an additional predictor. The closest approximation to a simulation reported in the

literature is probably Borman's (1982) use of an assessment center to screen military recruiters. In this case, however, the emphasis was on selecting persons who would be effective in recruiting enlistees in the army, not on effective screening and selecting.

### Computerizing the Interview Process

Some of the problems associated with implementation of structured behavioral interviews could possibly be avoided by computerizing the process and taking it out of the hands of the individual interviewer. The use of the Internet can allow a compression of the traditional steps in the employment process. For example, a job can be posted on the Internet along with an online realistic job preview to solicit applicants and provide some self-selection. The application, biodata, and initial screening questions can be compressed into a single web activity designed to minimize the number of individuals requiring an actual interview. Finally, those applicants screened for further interviewing can be given online, behaviorally based questions that can be systematically scored by scanning software. Such computerization of the interview promises to radically change the selection process. These newer technologies are likely to be blended with traditional selection techniques to allow custom fitting to specific needs of organizations (Click, 1997). Meyer (2000) described one computer-based system (SmartHire) that supports the preparation for interviews, as well as the conduct of interview sessions and the evaluation of candidates. At the first step of the hiring process, software is provided to help in defining the KSAOs and competencies required for a given position. Using this software, employers generate examples of individuals who were excellent, average, and poor in their performance and then identifies the abilities, behaviors, technical skills, and traits that most contributed to the level of performance achieved by each exemplar. The program then assists in defining the essential technical skills and competencies an applicant must have and generating questions to allow assessment of the interviewee against the technical criteria. In facilitating an assessment of personal traits, the software allows the development of a profile for the job on conscientiousness, likability, undogmaticness, extroversion, and stress tolerance (CLUES) and questions for assessing the applicant on these traits against the ideal profile. The end result is that the employer can click on an applicant's name to show the degree of match of the applicant's CLUES profile to the requirements of the position.

In addition to the potential for replacing the traditional interviewer-applicant process, the use of information technology may provide the opportunity for optimum customization of criteria, interview documentation, and systematic scoring. Personalized interview guides can be created to depict applicant qualifications, work environment preferences, interview topics, behavioral questions, and rating of such responses. Thus, information technology can be used to produce processes to guide and make systematic those situations where there can be direct interviewer-applicant or even Internet/online exchanges in the traditional sense. The practical implication is that information technology can provide an environment to both make interviews more structured as well as provide a high degree of flexibility and customization (Janz & Mooney, 1999).

Although the use of information technology may clearly help in the implementation of structured procedures, many of the factors found to influence more traditional interviewing are likely to continue to influence the effectiveness of interviewing. One important consideration is the implication of computerized interviewing for accuracy of assessment. Dwight and Feigelson (2000) conducted a meta-analysis in which they found less impression management with computer assessment. However, the strength of the effect of computer administration on impression management appears to have diminished over time such that more recent studies have found small or no effects. These findings suggest that as people become increasingly comfortable and familiar with online interviewing, the computer mystique may diminish and online assessments may become as vulnerable to socially desirable responding as more traditional methods.

## CONCLUSIONS

Despite the increasing sophistication of the selection tools available to employers, interviews provide a convenient means of balancing the often-competing demands of attracting, assessing, and recruiting applicants. For at least 70 years, we have known that structuring the interview can substantially improve the quality of interviewer judgments. In this chapter we propose a model in which the structure of an interview can be located in the three-dimensional space consisting of job-relatedness, standardization of the conduct of the interview, and structure of evaluation and decision making. We also propose that job-relatedness is the most important of these three components, whereas structure of evaluation and decision making is the least important. Finally, we propose that structuring the interview will enhance the validity of interviewer judgments but that the rate of increase substantially decreases at higher levels of structure. The most highly structured interviews not only may provide fewer gains in validity, but also may incur substantial costs such as detracting from

recruitment of applicants and failing to consider fit of the applicant to the organization. There is little research to allow an exact determination of how best to combine the three components of structure and the optimal level of structure. Given the subjective and casual manner in which applicants are typically interviewed, however, we suspect that most employers are far from this optimal level. Consequently, most employers can do much more than they have to increase the job-relatedness of interview content, the standardization of the interview process, and the structure of interviewer evaluation and decision making.

## REFERENCES

Anderson, N.H., & Shackleton, V.J. (1990). Decision making in the graduate selection interview: A field study. *Journal of Occupational Psychology, 63,* 63–76.

Arvey, R.D., Miller, H.E., Gould, R., & Bush, P. (1983). Interview validity for selecting sales clerks. *Personnel Psychology, 40,* 1–12.

Beach, L.R. (1990). *Image theory: Decision making in personal and organizational contexts.* Chichester: Wiley.

Bell, A.H. (September, 1999). Gut feelings be damned. *Across the Board, 36,* 57–62.

Biernat, M., & Kobrynowicz, D. (1997). Gender- and race-based standards of competence: Lower minimum standards but higher ability standards for devalued groups. *Journal of Personality and Social Psychology, 72,* 544–557.

Bies, R.J., & Shapiro, D.L. (1988). Voice and justification: Their influence on procedural fairness judgments. *Academy of Management Journal, 31,* 676–686.

Biesanz, J.C., Neuberg, S.L., Judice, T.N., & Smith, D.M. (1999). When interviewers desire accurate impressions: The effect of notetaking on the influence of expectations. *Journal of Applied Social Psychology, 29,* 2529–2549.

Bobko, P., Roth, P.L., & Potosky, D. (1999). Derivation and implications of a meta-analytic matrix incorporating cognitive ability, alternative predictors, and job performance. *Personnel Psychology, 52,* 561–589.

Borman, W.C. (1979). Format and training effects on rating accuracy and rater errors. *Journal of Applied Psychology, 64,* 410–421.

Borman, W.C. (1982). Validity of behavioral assessment for predicting military recruiter performance. *Journal of Applied Psychology, 67,* 3–9.

Bowen, D.E., Ledford, G.E., & Nathan, B.R. (1991). Hiring for the organization, not the job. *Academy of Management Executive, 5,* 35–51.

Brown, B.K., & Campion, M.A. (1994). Biodata phenomenology: Recruiters' perceptions and use of biographical in resume screening. *Journal of Applied Psychology, 79,* 897–908.

Brown, S.H. (1979a). Validity distortions associated with a test in use. *Journal of Applied Psychology, 64,* 460–462.

Brown, S.H. (1979b, April). *The results of a fifteen year research program investigating the selection interview.* Paper presented at the meeting of the Eastern Psychological Association, Philadelphia, PA.

Brown, S.H. (1980). *The interview—putting research results into practice.* Paper presented at the Conference of Alternatives to Tests as an Employee Selection Procedure, San Francisco, CA.

Burnett, J.R., Fan, C., Motowidlo, S.J., & DeGroot, T. (1998). Interview notes and validity. *Personnel Psychology, 51,* 375–396.

Burnett, J.R., & Motowidlo, S.J. (1998). Relations between different sources of information in the structured selection interview. *Personnel Psychology, 51,* 963–983.

Campbell, W.J., & Kleinke, D.J. (1997). Employment testing in private industry. In R.F. Dillon (Ed.), *Handbook on testing* (pp. 308–331). Westport, CT: Greenwood Press/Greenwood Publishing Group.

Campion, M.A., Campion, J.E., & Hudson, J.P. (1994). Structured interviewing: A note on incremental validity and alternative question types. *Journal of Applied Psychology, 79,* 998–1002.

Campion, M.A., Palmer, D.K., & Campion, J.E. (1997). A review of structure in the selection interview. *Personnel Psychology, 50,* 655–702.

Campion, M.A., Pursell, E.D., & Brown, B.K. (1988). Structured interviewing: Raising the psychometric properties of the employment interview. *Personnel Psychology, 41,* 25–42.

Carlson, R.E., Thayer, P.W., Mayfield, E.C., & Peterson. (1971). Improvements in the selection interview. *Personnel Journal, 50,* 268–275, 317.

Carrier, M.R., Dalessio, A.T., & Brown, S.H. (1990). Correspondence between estimates of content and criterion-related validity values. *Personnel Psychology, 43,* 85–100.

Click, J. (1997). Blend established practices with new technologies. *HR Magazine, 42,* 59–64.

Conway, J.M., & Peneno, G.M. (1999). Comparing structured interview question types: Construct validity and applicant reactions. *Journal of Business & Psychology, 13,* 485–506.

Dalessio, A.T., & Silverhart, T.A. (1994). Combining biodata test and interview information: Predicting decisions and performance criteria. *Personnel Psychology, 47,* 303–315.

Daniel, C. (1986). Science, system, or hunch: Alternative approaches to improving employee selection. *Public Personnel Management, 15,* 1–10.

DeGroot, T., & Motowidlo, S.J. (1999). Why visual and vocal cues can affect interviewers' judgments and predict job performance. *Journal of Applied Psychology, 84,* 986–993.

Development Dimensions International, Inc. (DDI). (1995). *Behavior categorization exercise for customer service representative.* Bridgeville, PA: DDI Press.

Development Dimensions International, Inc. (DDI). (1998a). *Dimensions for customer service representative.* Bridgeville, PA: DDI Press.

Development Dimensions International, Inc. (DDI). (1998b). *Human resource recruiter—Interview guide for the customer service representative* (pp. 1–15). Bridgeville, PA: DDI Press.

Development Dimensions International, Inc. (DDI). (1998c). *Workshop at a glance—Targeted Selection®: Interviewer Training* (Module at a Glance; pp. 1–4). Bridgeville, PA: DDI Press.

Dipboye, R.L. (1992). *Selection interview: Process perspective.* Cincinnati, OH: South-Western.

Dipboye, R.L., Fontenelle, G.A., & Garner, K. (1984). Effects of previewing the application on interview process and outcomes. *Journal of Applied Psychology, 69,* 118–128.

Dipboye, R.L., & Gaugler, B.B. (1993). Cognitive and behavioral processes in the selection interview. In N. Schmidt & W. Borman (Eds.), *Personnel selection in organizations* (pp. 135–170). San Francisco: Jossey-Bass.

Dougherty, T.W., Ebert, R.J., & Callender, J.C. (1986). Policy capturing in the employment interview. *Journal of Applied Psychology, 71,* 9–15.

Dougherty, T.W., Turban, D.B., & Callender, J.C. (1994). Confirming first impressions in the employment interview: A field study of interviewer behavior. *Journal of Applied Psychology, 79,* 659–665.

Dreher, G.F., Ash, R.A., & Hancock, P. (1988). The role of the traditional research design in underestimating the validity of the employment interview. *Personnel Psychology, 41,* 315–327.

D'Souza, D. (1995, October). The testing trap. *Chief Executive, 107,* 50–53.

Dwight, S.A., & Feigelson, M.E. (2000). A quantitative review of the effect of computerized testing on the measurement of social desirability. *Educational & Psychological Measurement, 60,* 340–360.

Equal Employment Opportunity Commission, Civil Service Commission, Department of Labor, & Department of Justice. (1978). Uniform guidelines on employee selection procedures. *Federal Register, 43*(166), 38295–38309.

Fear, R.A. (1984). *The evaluation interview.* New York, McGraw-Hill.

Feild, H.S., & Gatewood, R.D. (1989). Development of a selection interview: A job content strategy. In R.W. Eder & G.R. Ferris (Eds.), *The employment interview: theory, research, and practice* (pp. 145–157). Thousand Oaks, CA: Sage.

Finkelstein, L.M., Burke, M.J., & Raju, N.S. (1996). Age discrimination in simulated employment contexts: An integrative analysis. *Journal of Applied Psychology, 80,* 652–663.

Flanagan, J.C. (1954). The critical incident technique. *Psychological Bulletin, 51,* 327–358.

Fleishman, E.A., & Reilly, M.E. (1992). *Handbook of human abilities: Definitions, measurements, and job task requirements.* Palo Alto, CA: Consulting Psychologists Press.

Frase-Blunt, M. (2001, January). Games interviewers play. *HRMagazine, 46*(1), 106–114.

Gooding, J. (1992). Of mice and men. *Across the Board, 29,* 40–44.

Grove, W.M., Zald, D.H., Lebow, B.S., Snitz, B.E., & Nelson, C. (2000). Clinical versus mechanical prediction: A meta-analysis. *Psychological Assessment, 12,* 19–30.

Hakel, M.D., & Schuh, A.J. (1971). Job applicant attributes judged important across seven diverse occupations. *Personnel Psychology, 24,* 45–52.

Harland, L.K., Rauzi, T., & Biasotto, M.M. (1995, September). Perceived fairness of personality tests and the impact of explanations for their use. *Employee Responsibilities & Rights Journal, 8*(3), 183–192.

Heneman, H.G., Judge, T.A., & Heneman, R.L. (2000). *Staffing organizations.* Boston: Irwin McGraw-Hill.

Hofstede, G. (1991). *Cultures and organisations: Software of the mind.* London: McGraw-Hill.

Holdeman, J.B., Aldridge, J.M., & Jackson, D. (1996). How to hire Ms./Mr. Right. *Journal of Accountancy, 182,* 55–57.

Howard, J.L., & Ferris, G.R. (1996). The employment interview context: Social and situational influences on interviewer decisions. *Journal of Applied Social Psychology, 26,* 112–136.

Huffcutt, A.I., & Arthur, W. (1994). Hunter and Hunter (1984) revisited: Interview validity for entry-level jobs. *Journal of Applied Psychology, 79,* 184–190.

Huffcutt, A.I., & Roth, P.L. (1998). Racial group differences in employment interview evaluations. *Journal of Applied Psychology, 83,* 179–189.

Huffcutt, A.I., & Woehr, D.J. (1999). Further analysis of employment interview validity: A quantitative evaluation of interviewer-related structuring methods. *Journal of Organizational Behavior, 20,* 549–560.

Huffcutt, A.I., Roth, P.L., & McDaniel, M.A. (1996). A meta-analytic investigation of cognitive ability in employment interview evaluations: Moderating characteristics and implications for incremental validity. *Journal of Applied Psychology, 81,* 459–473.

Hyde, B.G. (1998). Applicants' reactions to interview structure. *Dissertation Abstracts International, 59*(5-B).

Ickes, W., Buysse, A., Pham, H., Rivers, K., Erickson, J.R., Hancock, M., Kelleher, J., & Gesn, P.R. (2000). On the difficulty of distinguishing good and poor perceivers: A social relations analysis of empathic accuracy data. *Personal Relationships, 7,* 219–234.

Janz, T. (1982). Initial comparisons of patterned behavior description interviews versus unstructured interviews. *Journal of Applied Psychology, 67,* 577–580.

Janz, T., Hellervik, L., & Gilmore, D.C. (1986). *Behavior description interviewing: new, accurate, cost-effective.* Boston: Allyn & Bacon.

Janz, T., & Mooney, G. (1999, August). *Designing a behavior descriptions interview for the Internet: Options and initial data.*

Paper presented at the annual conference of the Society for Industrial and Organizational Psychology, Atlanta, GA.

Judge, T.A., & Ferris, G.R. (1992). The elusive criterion of fit in human resource staffing decisions. *Human Resource Planning, 15,* 47–67.

Kacmar, K.M., & Carlson, D.S. (1999). Effectiveness of impression management tactics across human resource situations. *Journal of Applied Social Psychology, 29,* 1293–1315.

Kataoka, H.C., Latham, G.P., & Whyte, G. (1997). The relative resistance of the situational, patterned behavior, and conventional structured interviews to anchoring effects. *Human Performance, 10,* 47–63.

Kinicki, A.J., Lockwood, C.A., Hom, P.W., & Griffeth, R.W. (1990). Interviewer predictions of applicant qualifications and interviewer validity: Aggregate and individual analyses. *Journal of Applied Psychology, 75,* 477–486.

Latham, G.P., & Finnegan, B.J. (1993). Perceived practicality of unstructured, patterned, and situational interviews: In H. Schuler, J.L. Farr, & M. Smith (Eds.), *Personnel selection and assessment: individual and organizational perspectives* (pp. 41–55). Hillsdale, NJ: Erlbaum.

Latham, G.P., & Saari, L.M. (1984). Do people do what they say? Further studies on the situational interview. *Journal of Applied Psychology, 69,* 569–574.

Latham, G.P., Saari, L.M., Pursell, E.D., & Campion, M.A. (1980). The situational interview. *Journal of Applied Psychology, 65,* 442–431.

Latham, G.P., & Skarlicki, D.P. (1996). The effectiveness of situational, patterned behaviour, and conventional structured interviews in minimising in-group favouritism of Canadian francophone managers. *Applied Psychology: An International Review, 45,* 177–184.

Latham, G.P., & Sue-Chan, C. (1996). A legally defensible interview for selecting the best. In R.S. Barrett (Ed.), *Fair employment strategies in human resource management* (pp. 134–143). Westport, CT: Quorum Books/Greenwood Publishing Group.

Latham, G.P., & Sue-Chan, C. (1999). A meta-analysis of the situational interview: An enumerative review of reasons for its validity. *Canadian Psychology, 40,* 56–67.

Lee, H. (1998). Transformation of employment practices in Korean businesses. *International Studies of Management & Organization, 28,* 26–39.

Leeds, J.P., & Burroughs, W. (1997). *Finding the right stuff.* Retrieved February 22, 2003, from http://www.securitymanagement .com/library/000334.html.

Lee, J.A., Castella, D.M., & McCluney, M. (1997). Sexual stereotypes and perceptions of competence and qualifications. *Psychological Reports, 80,* 419–428.

Lewis, L.K., & Seibold, D.R. (1993). Innovation modification during intraorganizational adoption. *Academy of Management Review, 18,* 322–354.

Liden, R.C., Martin, C.L., & Parsons, C.K. (1993). Interviewer and applicant behaviors in employment interviews. *Academy of Management Journal, 36,* 372–386.

Maas, J.B. (1965). Patterned scaled expectation interview: Reliability studies on a new technique. *Journal of Applied Psychology, 49,* 431–433.

Macan, T.H., A., Marcia, M.J., Paese, M., & Smith, D.E. (1994). The effects of applicants' reactions to cognitive ability tests and an assessment center. *Personnel Psychology. 47*(4), 715–738.

Marlowe, C.M., Schneider, S.L., & Nelson, C.E. (1996). Gender and attractiveness biases in hiring decisions: Are more experienced managers less biased? *Journal of Applied Psychology, 81,* 11–21.

Martocchio, J.J., & Whitener, E.M. (1992). Fairness in personnel selection: A meta-analysis and policy implications. *Human Relations, 45,* 489–506.

Maurer, S.D., & Lee, T.W. (2000). Accuracy of the situational interview in rating multiple job candidates. *Journal of Business & Psychology, 15,* 73–96.

McDaniel, M.A., Schmidt, F.L., & Hunter, J.E. (1988). A meta-analysis of the validity of methods for rating training experience in personnel selection. *Personnel Psychology, 41,* 283–314.

McDaniel, M.A., Whetzel, D.L., Schmidt, F.C., & Maurer, J.D. (1994). The validity of employment interviews: A comprehensive review and meta-analysis. *Journal of Applied Psychology, 79,* 599–616.

Melohn, T. (1994). Hiring the eagles. *Incentive, 168,* 47–52.

Meyer, G. (2000). Interview tool helps match candidates to jobs. *HR Magazine, 45,* 197–200.

Moss, P., & Tilly, C. (1996). Soft skills and race: An investigation of Black men's employment problems. *Work and Occupations, 23,* 252–276.

Motowidlo, S.J., & Burnett, J.R. (1995). Aural and visual sources of validity in structured employment interviews. *Organizational Behavior and Human Decision Processes, 61,* 239–249.

Motowidlo, S.J., Carter, G.W., Dunnette, M.D., Tippins, N., Werner, S., Burnett, J. R., & Vaughan, M.J. (1992). Studies of the structured behavioral interview. *Journal of Applied Psychology, 77,* 571–587.

Orpen, C. (1985). Patterned behavior description interviews versus unstructured interviews: A comprehensive study. *Journal of Applied Psychology, 70,* 774–776.

Parsons, C.K., & Liden, R.C. (1984). Interviewer perceptions of applicant qualifications: A multivariate field study of demographic characteristics and nonverbal cues. *Journal of Applied Psychology, 69,* 557–568.

Parsons, C.K., Cable, D., & Wilkerson, J.M. (1999). Assessment of applicant work values through interviews: The impact of focus and functional relevance. *Journal of Occupational & Organizational Psychology, 72,* 561–566.

Perry, E.L., Kulik, C.T., & Bourhis, A.C. (1996). Moderating effects of personal and contextual factors in age discrimination. *Journal of Applied Psychology, 81,* 628–647.

Pulakos, E.D., & Schmitt, N. (1995). Experience based and situational interview questions: Studies of validity. *Personnel Psychology, 48,* 289–308.

Ripley, R.E., & Ripley, M.J. (1994). CREAM: Criteria-Related Employability Assessment Method: A systematic model for employee selection. *Management Decision, 32,* 27–36.

Rose, R.C., & Garrett, E.M. (1992, December). Guerrilla interviewing. *Inc., 14,* 145–147.

Rosenthal, R., Hall, J.A., DiMatteo, M.R., Rogers, P.L., & Archer, D. (1979). *Sensitivity to nonverbal communications: The PONS test.* Baltimore, MD: John Hopkins University Press.

Rosse, J.G., Miller, J.L., & Stecher, M.D. (1994). A field study of job applicants' reactions to personality and cognitive ability testing. *Journal of Applied Psychology, 79,* 987–992.

Roth, P.L., & Campion, J.E. (1992). An analysis of the predictive power of the panel interview and pre-employment tests. *Journal of Occupational and Organizational Psychology, 65,* 41–60.

Rowe, P.M. (1984). Decision processes in personnel selection. *Canadian Journal of Behavioral Science, 16,* 326–337.

Ryan, A.M., Ployhart, R.E., & Friedal, L.A. (1998). Using personality testing to reduce adverse impact: A cautionary note. *Journal of Applied Psychology, 83,* 298–307.

Rynes, S.L. (1993). When recruitment fails to attract: Individual expectations meet organizational realities in recruitment. In H. Schuler, J. Farr, & M. Smith (Eds.), *Personnel selection and assessment. Individual and organizational perspectives* (pp. 27–49). Hillsdale, NJ: Erlbaum.

Santo, M. (2000). Interviewing the chameleon. *Agency Sales Magazine, 30,* 22–24.

Schmidt, F.L., & Hunter, J.E. (1998). Validity of personnel assessment methods: 85 years of research findings. The validity and utility of selection methods in personnel psychology: Practical and theoretical implications of 85 years of research findings. *Psychological Bulletin, 124,* 262–274.

Schuler, H. (1993). Social validity of selection situations: A concept and some empirical results. In H. Schuler, J.L. Farr, & M. Smith (Eds.), *Personnel selection and assessment: Individual and organizational perspectives* (pp. 11–26) Hillsdale, NJ: Erlbaum.

Schuler, H., & Funke, U. (1989). The interview as a multimodal procedure. In R.W. Eder & G.R. Ferris (Eds.), *The employment interview: Theory, research, and practice* (pp. 183–189). Newbury Park, CA: Sage.

Schwab, D.P., & Heneman, H.G. (1969). Relationship between interview structure and interviewer reliability in an employment situation. *Journal of Applied Psychology, 53,* 214–217.

Searcy, C.A., Woods, P.N., Gatewood, R., & Lance, C. (1993). *The validity of structured interviews: A meta-analytical search for moderators.* Paper presented at the annual meeting of the Society for Industrial and Organizational Psychology, San Francisco.

Smith, M. (1986). A repertory grid analysis of supervisory jobs. *Applied Psychology: An International Review, 35,* 501–512.

Smith, P.C., & Kendall, L.M. (1963). Retranslation of expectations: An approach to the construction of unambiguous anchors for rating scales. *Journal of Applied Psychology, 47,* 149–155.

Smither, J.W., & Reilly, R.R. (1987). True intercorrelation among job components, time delay in rating, and rater intelligence as determinants of accuracy in performance ratings. *Organizational Behavior and Human Decision Processes, 40,* 369–391.

Snyder, M. (1974). Self-monitoring of expressive behavior. *Journal of Personality and Social Psychology, 30,* 526–537.

Spence, L.J., & Petrick, J.A. (2000). Multinational interview decisions: Integrity capacity and competing values. *Human Resource Management Journal, 10,* 49–67.

Springbett, B.M. (1954). *Series effects in the employment interview.* Unpublished doctoral dissertation, McGill University.

Stevens, C.K. (1998). Antecedents of interview interactions, interviewers' ratings, and applicants' reactions. *Personnel Psychology, 51,* 55–85.

Stevens, C.K., & Kristof, A.L. (1995). Making the right impression: A field study of applicant impression management during job interviews. *Journal of Applied Psychology, 80,* 587–606.

Sunoo, B.P. (1995). How fun flies at Southwest Airlines. *Personnel Journal, 74,* 62–73.

Terpstra, D.E., & Rozell, E.J. (1997). Why some potentially effective staffing practices are seldom used. *Public Personnel Management. 26*(4) Win 1997, 483–495.

Tschirigi, H.D., & Huegli, J.M. (1979). Monitoring the employment interview. *Journal of College Placement, 39,* 37–39.

Tucker, D.H., & Rowe, P.M. (1977). Consulting the application form prior to the interview: An essential step in the selection process. *Journal of Applied Psychology, 62,* 283–288.

Tullar, W.L., Mullins, T.W., & Caldwell, S.A. (1979). Effects of interview length and applicant quality on interview decision time. *Journal of Applied Psychology, 64,* 669–674.

Tyler, T.R., & Bies, R.J. (1990). Beyond formal procedures: The interpersonal context of procedural justice. In J.S. Carroll (Ed.), *Applied social psychology and organizational settings* (pp. 77–98). Hillsdale, NJ: Erlbaum.

Ulrich, L., & Trumbo, D. (1965). The selection interview since 1949. *Psychological Bulletin, 63,* 100–116.

Vance, R.J., Kuhnert, K.W., & Farr, J.L. (1978). Interview judgments: Using external criteria to compose behavioral and graphic ratings. *Organizational Behavior and Human Performance, 22,* 279–294.

Viteles, M.S. (1933). *Industrial psychology.* New York: W.W. Norton.

Walters, L.C., Miller, M.R., & Ree, M.J. (1993). Structured interviews for pilot selection: No incremental validity. *The International Journal of Aviation Psychology, 3,* 25–38.

Weekley, J.A., & Grier, J.A. (1987). Reliability and validity of the situational interview for a sales position. *Journal of Applied Psychology, 77,* 484–487.

Wernimont, P.F., & Campbell, J.P. (1968). Signs, samples, and criteria. *Journal of Applied Psychology, 52,* 372–376.

Wiesner, W.H., & Cronshaw, S.F. (1988). A meta-analytic investigation of the impact of interview format and degree of structure on the validity of the employment interview. *Journal of Occupational Psychology, 61,* 275–290.

Wright, G.E., & Multon, K.D. (1995). Employer's perceptions of nonverbal communication in job interviews for persons with physical disabilities. *Journal of Vocational Behavior, 47,* 214–227.

Young, A.M., & Kacmar, K.M. (1998). ABCs of the interview: The role of affective, behavioral, and cognitive responses by applicants in the employment interview. *International Journal of Selection & Assessment, 6,* 211–221.

Zedeck, S., Tziner, A., & Middlestadt, S.E. (1983). Interviewer validity and reliability: An individual analysis approach. *Personnel Psychology, 36,* 355–370.

# JOB-SPECIFIC KNOWLEDGE AND SKILLS, SIMULATIONS, AND ASSESSMENT CENTERS

CHAPTER 18

# Simulations and Assessment Centers

GEORGE C. THORNTON III AND DEBORAH E. RUPP

## OVERVIEW

Simulations have a long and rich history in the field of industrial and organizational (I/O) psychology assessment. Since the early part of last century I/O psychologists, human resource managers, and other assessment professionals and scientists have used individual simulations or combinations of simulations and other assessment techniques in assessment centers for recruitment, selection, promotion, training, organizational development, and research (Thornton & Byham, 1982; Thornton & Cleveland, 1990). We begin this chapter with definitions of simulations and assessment centers and give short descriptions of their availability, applicability, reliability, and validity. Then we describe examples of simulations and assessment centers used by I/O psychologists and summarize evidence of their effectiveness and limitations. Because few simulation exercises are commercially available, most users construct their own. Thus, we include a brief section on developing simulations. An essential element of simulation methodology is the use of observers to evaluate

performance in the exercises. Therefore, this chapter describes and evaluates the processes of observing, classifying, and evaluating behavior displayed by participants in the exercises, and it draws implications for training assessors. Next, we discuss the current status of research on and application of simulations and assessment centers. Finally, we explore special related issues, including assessing diverse populations and complying with applicable regulations and guidelines for assessment.

### Definitions

*Simulations* are a type of situational test (Anastasi & Urbina, 1997) in which the stimulus material presented to the examinee is moderately similar to actual organizational settings and problems. The situations are very much like realistic situations on the job but may not be exact replicas of any one actual job in a specific organization. Thus, simulations contain more fidelity than a paper-and-pencil test, but less fidelity than a job sample (e.g., a flight simulator) where the situation nearly exactly replicates the job.

Simulations are also a type of performance test in which the examinee is expected to display some complex, overt, and observable behavior. Thus, simulations differ from most paper-and-pencil tests that call for rather simple behavior, such as selecting an alternative answer on a multiple-choice item or indicating agreement or disagreement with a statement on a personality questionnaire. Other examples of performance tests include essay examinations in classrooms, problem-solving tasks in individually administered cognitive ability tests, and projective techniques such as drawing tests. Even though these latter examples of assessment tools call for complex behavioral responses, they are not simulations of realistic job or life situations.

An *assessment center* is a method of evaluating performance in a set of assessment techniques, at least one of which is a simulation. Usually several simulation techniques are used in combination to give multiple measures of the target dimensions that have been established to be related to effectiveness on the job (Byham, 1970). Other essential ingredients of the assessment center method are the use of multiple assessors and some method of integrating behavioral observations of the simulations across simulations and assessors (International Task Force on Assessment Center Guidelines, 2000).

### Availability of Simulations

With few exceptions, there are no standardized, published, commercially available simulation exercises. In most cases, simulations have been developed for specific purposes within specific organizations and thus are usually not available for general application. This situation means that the standard test evaluation sources, such as the *Mental Measurements Yearbook* (e.g., Conoley & Impara, 1995) and *Test Critiques* (e.g., Keyser & Sweetland, 1985), usually do not contain reviews of simulations that are available to would-be users. Therefore, this chapter describes some of the general concepts of simulation methodology, explains how simulations are developed, provides examples of some common "types" of simulations, reviews selected evidence of simulations' reliability and validity, discusses a number of issues related to the development and use of simulations, and identifies research needs for further expansion of this assessment methodology.

Exceptions to the generalization that simulations are developed for specific organizations can be found in the few commercially available in-baskets exercises (Management & Personnel Systems, Inc., n.d.), and in large-scale organizational simulations such as Looking Glass and other simulations developed by the Center for Creative Leadership (McCall & Lombardo, 1978; Center for Creative Leadership, n.d.). In

addition, some consulting firms sell previously built simulation exercises to clients who have completed training programs on the administration and scoring of simulations available from that firm. Finally, a British consulting firm offers several "off the shelf" simulation exercises but provides no evidence of their reliability or validity (www.ADCltd.co.uk).

### Applicability

Simulations have been proven to have adequate reliability and validity for assessment of many managerial and professional skills, as well as other behavioral proficiencies such as selling, providing customer service, and relating to others in team environments (Bray & Grant, 1966; Thornton & Byham, 1982). To achieve these qualities, organizations must build simulations systematically and thoroughly train the assessors. Simulations and assessment centers provide means for assessing individuals on a variety of attributes, which cannot be assessed well by other techniques such as paper-and-pencil tests and questionnaires. As situational exercises, simulations present the examinee with complex, realistic stimuli and the examinee is required to display overt behavior to solve problems, interact with other people, or prepare written and oral presentations. Simulations and assessment centers enable organizations to assess and develop such complex attributes as problem-solving abilities, communication skills, leadership, and other interactional skills.

Simulations are particularly appropriate in promotions when the current job and setting do not provide adequate information about the qualifications of individuals for performance on a new job or situation. For example, the current job may not provide individuals the opportunity to demonstrate the knowledge and skills necessary for the target job. In addition, persons making decisions about candidates may not have the opportunity to consistently observe the performance of various candidates. And, in some situations, information in current performance appraisals may be considered inadequate, incomplete, or unfair for some individuals. Likewise, in certain organizations there may be some lack of trust in supervisors and managers to make relevant and fair judgments about promotability. Simulations, sometimes observed by assessors outside the organization, provide a means of providing consistent, valid, and fair information about job-related skills.

### Conclusions About Reliability and Validity

Standard concepts and evidence of reliability and validity of tests are only partially relevant to simulation techniques. Seldom does the notion of internal consistency apply to simulations, because simulations typically do not have multiple items that can be correlated with one another. Because of their novelty, simulations may not be considered equivalent measures when administered on multiple occasions and therefore not amenable to test-retest evaluations. Thus, the typical way of evaluating reliability of a simulation is to study interrater agreement among observers.

Some forms of evidence of validity can also be difficult to collect. Because simulations are built to represent some aspect of organizational conditions and they elicit overt and complex behaviors similar to behaviors required on the job, they ostensibly appear to represent the situations and behavior of interest in I/O psychology. Thus, the assertion is sometimes made that simulations possess a form of validity called content representativeness (American Educational Research Association, American Psychological Association, & National Council on Measurement in Education, 1999), sometimes called content validity. Simulations typically have a high degree of face validity—they appear to test takers and users to be valid measures of relevant performance domains. Proper substantiation of validity requires more than this appearance of relevance, and thus in this chapter we explore the actual evidence of validity of selected, common simulation exercises. We will see that developers and users must take special precautions to clearly link job requirements to assessment content, and to clearly demonstrate that assessors can accurately observe and evaluate behavior in specified dimensions of performance. Thus, although the predictive validity of simulations in the context of assessment centers has been well established, there is much debate about the actual constructs that are being assessed when assessors evaluate behavior in simulations.

## History

These and other recent controversies in the field of simulation assessment reflect a somewhat muddied, long, rich history of the use of simulation methods in I/O psychology assessment. That is, extensive work on simulations has demonstrated the validity of specific techniques: group discussions assess emergent leadership (Bass, 1950); in-baskets assess administrative skills (Frederikson, Sanders, & Wand, 1957; Hemphill, Griffiths, & Frederikson, 1962), role plays assess interpersonal effectiveness (Goldstein & Sorcher, 1974); large-scale organizational simulations can assess decision-making skills (Streufert & Swezey, 1986). Combined with the substantial research on the use of these techniques in assessment centers over the past 40 years (Thornton & Byham, 1982), these studies show the effectiveness of simulation methodology in the arsenal of I/O assessment techniques. At the same time, this

area has not been without controversy. Recent reviews of the literature in these fields have questioned the actual construct validity of the typical instantiation of simulation methods in actual organizational settings (Klimoski & Brickner, 1987; Schippmann, Prien, & Katz, 1990). These controversies are explored in subsequent sections of this chapter.

### Special Concerns

Along with the many strengths and advantages of simulation methodology in comparison with other forms of assessment, a number of special concerns and potential disadvantages must be considered. These concerns are relevant to individual simulation techniques and may be especially problematic for assessment centers. These concerns include the difficulty of development and implementation of simulations, the important roles of the assessors who observe and evaluate behavior in the simulations, and the importance of standardization of the process.

Because simulations and assessment centers are complex assessment techniques, they are difficult to develop and implement. Commercially available paper-and-pencil tests of aptitudes, abilities, personality characteristics, interests, and values can be purchased and used relatively easily by conscientious human resource managers. By contrast, most users of simulations must develop their own. As discussed later in this chapter, this development process can be quite time-consuming and complex. Implementation can also be difficult because the scheduling of participants, assessors, and sometimes role players is typically a very complex task. In addition, some simulations require several rooms, which may lead to logistical challenges.

Other special concerns are the complex roles that assessors play. They observe, classify, and evaluate behavior to render judgments about qualifications on complex performance dimensions (Lievens & Klimoski, 2001; Thornton, 1992; Zedeck, 1986). If more than one simulation is observed by several assessors, as typically practiced in assessment centers, the team of assessors must meet to integrate observations across assessors and simulations. Thus, competent, well-trained assessors are essential to simulation methodology. A more thorough discussion of assessor judgment processes is presented later in this chapter.

## EXAMPLES OF SIMULATIONS

In this section we discuss four examples of simulation exercises: interaction simulations of one-on-one interaction situations, the in-basket exercise, the leaderless group discussion,

**TABLE 18.1  Examples of Simulation Exercises**

One-on-One Interactions
In-Baskets
Leaderless Group Discussions
  Cooperative
  Competitive
Organizational Games
Case Studies
Presentations
Manufacturing Situations
Fact-Finding Exercises

and complex organizational games. These four simulations are representative of the much wider array of techniques, which have been developed and used in I/O assessment situations. Other types of exercises are briefly described. Table 18.1 lists several simulation exercises that have been used in organizations. For each of the four examples discussed here, we describe the typical form and substance of the exercise, present evidence of its reliability and validity, list the constructs the exercise has been found to measure best, and provide conclusions about its effectiveness and limitations.

**Simulations of One-on-One Interaction Situations**

Sometimes referred to as an interview simulation, the one-on-one interactive simulation refers to a simulation exercise in which an assessee participates in an interaction with a role player about some situation that is common to his or her work environment. Such an exercise can simulate many different types of interactions with a wide variety of people. Often the assessee is asked to assume the position of a manager in the target job. The "role" that is played, typically by a confederate or an assessor, is the simulated individual whom the assessee must interact with. Roles typically played include a problem employee, a client, an external stakeholder, a member of the press, or someone from upper management. Some examples of situations include meeting with a subordinate because of recent performance problems, tardiness, or discrimination complaints; coaching a new salesperson; conducting a selection interview; taking a phone call from an angry customer; and briefing the press about a recent environmental or safety issue (Thornton, 1992; Thornton & Byham, 1982; Thornton & Mueller-Hanson, in press).

This type of assessment exercise was adapted from Fishbein and Aijen's (1975) role-play technique, which was developed as a means to foster attitude change. The role-play technique has been used for a variety of purposes (e.g., promotion, development) and is especially successful for training inexperienced supervisors (Goldstein & Sorcher, 1974; Thornton & Cleveland, 1990). The exercise is normally conducted by first providing the assessee with background information and allowing time to prepare for the interaction (typically 15–20 minutes). Then, for 8 to 10 minutes, the participant interacts with the role player and is assessed on dimensions such as oral communication, persuasiveness, leadership ability, listening skills, sensitivity, problem solving/analysis, empathy, and trust building.

During the simulation, the role player may ask and answer questions, make suggestions, and react to the assessee's suggestions and comments. Thus, an essential aspect of designing this exercise is providing role players with enough background information and thoroughly training them such that the exercise is carried out in a standardized way.

There are added complexities when the assessors simultaneously serve as role players. That is, it has been shown that because of the multiple demands placed on assessors, they often do not make use of all the information available to them when making judgments about participant performance in simulation exercises (Birkeland, Borman, & Brannick, 2001; Neidig, Martin, & Yates, 1978; Sackett & Hakel, 1979). Where research has shown that individuals can attend to multiple sources of information and can carry out multiple tasks simultaneously (Posner, 1982), a concern still exists that the added responsibility of being the role player might limit an assessor's ability to objectively observe important behaviors and make decisions about them.

One-on-one interactive simulations have many advantages. First, this type of exercise portrays a realistic situation common in most organizations. Second, adequate levels of interrater reliability and criterion-related validity have been demonstrated (Russell & Byham, 1980; Thornton & Byham, 1982). Third, participant reactions to this type of exercise have been quite favorable. Fourth, the time it takes to administer this type of exercise is quite short. In fact, because of the ease of facilitation, many organizations use several different interactive simulations together to increase their ability to reliably predict future performance. For example, in one exercise the role player might depict a cooperative employee, coworker, or board member, whereas in second exercise, another role player may depict the antithesis, for example, a hostile customer, coworker, or news reporter.

This type of exercise also has potential disadvantages. First, developing background information and training role players can be difficult. Second, ensuring that the role player acts consistently with different assessees is challenging because the role player must adapt to and react to the actions of individual participants. Third, in most practical situations, more than one role player must be used. Therefore, the training and monitoring required to ensure adequate levels of standardization add to the complexity of using such an exercise.

Fourth, steps may need to be taken to eliminate potential gender bias in ratings of role-play performance. Female assessors have been found to give higher ratings than men to both men and women (Shore, Tashchian, & Adams, 1997) and assessor-assessee gender interactions may occur (Walsh, Weinberg, & Fairfield, 1987).

## In-Basket Exercise

The in-basket is a simulation of the work coming into the office of a job incumbent. This work may come in the form of memos, letters, reports, phone messages, and other material. Traditionally, the exercise has consisted of paperwork that might have accumulated in the in-tray on the worker's desk. Recently, the paperwork has been augmented with electronic input that appears in an e-mail or voice mail in-box. The use of high-technology forms of presenting the stimulus material are discussed in another section of this chapter.

The examinee is also presented with background material to provide a context for responding. The ancillary material typically includes a description of the situation at hand, reasons why the respondent must respond immediately, the job he or she holds, a simple organizational chart, a calendar, information about the company (e.g., products and services), information about the industry, and basic policies and procedures.

The respondent is then asked to respond as he or she sees appropriate. Possible actions the respondent might take include writing memos or letters, giving directions to subordinates or coworkers, delegating to others, passing information to a supervisor or other staff member, scheduling meetings, and requesting information. Typically, the respondent is directed to actually construct the memos and letters, write down what he or she will discuss with others if meetings are scheduled, and refrain from simply saying "I would tell the person such and such."

The in-basket was originally designed to assess administrative skills, and subsequent research has shown that it measures dimensions such as complying with instructions, preparing to take action by soliciting more information, making decisions, and directing others (Frederiksen, 1962; Hemphill et al., 1962). Other early research was equally supportive of the predictive validity of the in-basket for managerial performance and progress (Thornton & Byham, 1982). More recent reviews of the research literature are less supportive. Schippmann et al., (1990) examined studies over the past 30 years and found evidence of low interrater agreement, alternate-form reliability, and split-half reliability. In addition, they concluded that only limited evidence of content, predictive, and construct validity has been marshaled in recent studies. They summa-

rized by saying, "The compiled evidence provides only modest support of the usefulness of the in-basket test as a measurement tool" (p. 837). On a more positive note, the authors also concluded that in-baskets can be scored reliably, and the validity is higher in situations where the in-basket was developed for a defined target job. They observe that the latter practice is seldom followed, but our observation 11 years after the Schippmann et al. review is that few off-the-shelf in-baskets are available, and tailor-made in-baskets for specific organizations are much more common today. Thus, if an organization develops an in-basket following the principles described in the later section of this chapter, it can be more confident that it will provide reliable and valid measures of target dimensions.

This optimism is not to negate the difficulty of building a good in-basket and having it provide valid assessments. Because the in-basket is a written exercise tapping cognitive abilities to read and comprehend complex material, to analyze complex interrelated problems, and to make sound judgments, in-basket performance is probably at least partially related to general mental ability. Goldstein, Yusko, Braverman, Smith, and Chung (1998) found evidence that Whites scored higher than Blacks on the exercise, and these differences were eliminated when scores on a cognitive ability test were statistically controlled. On a more positive note, Rotenberry, Barrett, and Doverspike (1999) found no differences in the factor structure of in-basket ratings for racial groups.

An in-basket exercise is difficult to construct and time-consuming to administer. To construct an effective in-basket, one must make several important strategic decisions. For example, the material must be written so that all candidates can relate to the industry, the organizational setting, the work being done, and the types of problems presented. The level of complexity of the problems must be appropriate for the level of the target job. The supplemental information must provide enough background information to appear realistic to the assessees, yet not be overwhelming or burdensome for the time allowed. The items should include a combination of trivial information (which can and probably should be ignored), highly demanding requests, and others that allow more discretion.

The in-basket can consume up to two hours of each participant's time. The time requirements are even more demanding on the assessor, who must read and score the in-basket and may be asked to interview the participant to obtain explanations of reasons for action. Subsequently, the scoring may need to be adjusted to account for new insights.

## Leaderless Group Discussion

The leaderless group discussion (LGD) is a simulation exercise in which a group of assessees (typically four to eight) discusses one or more topics while being observed by assessors. At the start of the exercise, participants are provided written problems similar to actual problems in the target organization. The group is then given a collective goal that must be met within a specified time limit (typically an hour). Examples of such scenarios include developing a new policy, allocating department funds or office space, devising a new safety procedure, developing a program for visitors, and generating a new market strategy. After discussing the situation and developing a plan of action, participants often have to submit their final decisions in writing, and all group members must sign the submitted plan.

There are two general forms of the LGD: competitive and cooperative. In competitive LGDs, participants are typically assigned different roles of equal status, and the task often involves negotiating how different types of resources will be divided. In cooperative LGDs, roles are typically unassigned, and the task is such that everyone works together to reach a common goal.

In the past, LGDs have been used to assess a wide array of behavioral dimensions. These include emergent leadership, general leadership skill, tolerance for ambiguity, group problem solving, interpersonal communication, tendency to initiate structure, sociability, general effectiveness, motivation, flexibility, initiative, independence, and problem/decision analysis (Bass, 1950, 1954; Bray, 1973; Bray & Grant, 1966; Cronbach, 1970; Thornton, 1992; Thornton & Byham, 1982; Thornton & Cleveland, 1990). Research on LGDs has shown adequate levels of reliability and validity and has shown the exercise to be an appropriate assessment tool for middle and upper management (Bass, 1954; Cascio, 1991; Thornton & Byham, 1982).

Gatewood, Thornton, and Hennessey (1990) assessed three different forms of reliability of LGD exercise ratings. By considering correlations of assessee ratings between assessors with an LGD, they found interrater reliabilities ranging from .66 to .99. By considering the correlation of consensus ratings between assessor groups, they found intergroup reliability coefficients ranging from .66 to .84. By considering the correlations of individual assessors' ratings across different LGD exercises, they found alternate form reliability coefficients ranging from .35 to .62. These authors concluded that where interrater reliability is strong for LGDs, stability in ratings may fluctuate due to differences between LGD exercise content as well as differences between assessee groups.

Watson and Behnke (1990) explored how individual differences in group identification, independence, and self-monitoring characteristics affect dimension ratings within an LGD. They found that ratings on group orientation, leader behavior, and oral communication were high when individuals possessed higher levels of individual worth and lower

levels of acting and group identification. In a similar study, Hills (1985) found that LGD ratings were higher among individuals who (according to a self-report adjective checklist) were assertive, competitive, self-confident, and autonomous. Those reporting high levels of cooperativeness, self-discipline, and tact received lower ratings.

Research has found that LGD validity is enhanced when the scenario is similar to situations that commonly occur in the organization (Thornton & Byham, 1982). Thus, it is important that the exercise is developed to be as realistic as possible. It is also important that the participant group is made up of people with similar levels of experience and ability. All members also need to have adequate verbal skills so that their contributions can be assessed and no one is "shut out" from the discussion because of inability to voice his or her contribution. This also points out the importance of considering language abilities and cultural differences when assessing international participants.

LGDs were among the most popular of organizational simulation exercises until the late 1970s. After that time, concern arose over how such an exercise might affect equal employment opportunities of diverse employees (Thornton & Byham, 1982). Other criticisms of this technique are that standardization is very difficult because the climate and tone of the group is dependent on the individuals making it up. Furthermore, using the LGD to make individual employment decisions about people may be inappropriate because assessors may find it difficult to separate individual and group influences. Thus, LGDs are used less frequently for selection and promotion assessment. This being said, research has shown that this type of exercise can be quite useful for developmental purposes and often leads to heightened self-awareness within participants (Thornton & Cleveland, 1990).

**Large-Scale Organizational Games**

Large-scale organizational games are similar to LGDs in that both are group exercises, but they are different in that games are simulations of broader, more comprehensive situations than the situations depicted in other exercises. Both the stimuli presented and the responses expected are more complex. The stimuli may include extensive information about the organization's products and services; the structure of the organization, including names and positions of managers in numerous subsidiaries; operations manuals covering policies and procedures; financial statements and historical manufacturing and sales records; and personnel information about numerous staff members represented in the game. The expected responses of participants are also more complex. Participants are expected to interact with numerous others in ambiguous situations, identify hidden problems and opportunities, analyze complex sets of information, and make decisions affecting long-range operations and financial stability.

Games can range in complexity from a simulation of one unit of a company (e.g., a manufacturing operation) to an entire set of companies making up an international conglomerate. Participants may be assigned various organizational positions, such as president, vice president, or department manager, and may be asked to make decisions about a range of functions, including operations, marketing, sales, and finance. Games are often designed to assess executive functions, which require awareness of global market forces, strategic planning and decision making, and organizational skills.

Because games can vary greatly in terms of their size and content, it is impossible to make general statements about the reliability and validity of resulting assessments. As with any simulation exercise, reliability is a function of the quality of assessor training and the opportunity for assessors to observe enough relevant behavior. Observation in games is sometimes difficult because participants move around and interact with so many different people. The more well developed complex organizational simulations have well substantiated content validity. For example, the Looking Glass simulation presents many demands of the typical manager in a multi-faceted organization (McCall & Lombardo, 1978, 1982), and Streufert's simulations (Streufert, Pogash, & Piasecki, 1988; Streufert & Swezey, 1986) involve many complex managerial decision-making tasks.

Games differ from LGDs in several ways. First, some participants are assigned leadership positions, and by necessity others do not serve in these roles. In comparison with the typical group discussion of 4 to 6 participants, games typically involve 10 or 12 persons and can have as many as 20 participants. Games usually involve more complex background information so that participants must understand a global business environment. Whereas the LGD lasts 45 to 60 minutes, games usually last 2 or 3 hours, or even an entire 8-hour day. Some decision-making games simulate a series of business cycles over a period of several years. Finally, games often involve physical objects for the participants to deal with. For example, a manufacturing game may call for the participants to assemble products for the organization to sell; managers may buy and sell shares of stock; decision makers may have a physical model of a city to use in planning disaster relief.

Large-scale organizational games provide several advantages over simpler simulations. Content representativeness may be high, and the simulation may have high fidelity to the real-life organizational complexities managers typically face. Games often involve the multilevel hierarchical organizational structures of real organizations. Finally, participants must simultaneously deal with multiple individuals, each representing diverse objectives.

Although games have been used for assessment, development, and research purposes (Thornton & Cleveland, 1990), this chapter deals only with their effectiveness as assessment techniques. As assessment techniques, complex games involve several features, which may reduce their psychometric effectiveness. Because participants are assigned different positions in the simulated organization, the situation is rarely standardized for the participants. Thus, it is difficult to compare the assessments that result for different individuals. Because of the large number of participants, and the fact that they are often moving among physical locations, assessors may have difficulty making thorough, consistent observations. Games are usually quite time-consuming and thus afford only one observational setting. If a participant does poorly in this one exercise, there is little opportunity to redeem one's self in subsequent exercises.

## Other Simulations

In addition to the simulations described in the preceding sections, many other types of simulations have been devised. Case studies require the participant to read and analyze a set of written materials and provide written suggestions for a financial decision, a marketing plan, or an organizational action plan. The presentation exercise calls for the participant to deliver a stand-up speech. Participants may be given time and resources to prepare a relatively formal presentation, or they may be asked to speak extemporaneously. Manufacturing simulations often involve tools, machinery, equipment, and raw materials. For example, a welder may be given metal pieces, a torch, and blueprints and asked to produce a product according to specifications. Customer service applicants may be asked to answer questions about products and services during a telephone call with a simulated client. A teacher seeking certification may be asked to prepare and present a lesson plan. A computer programmer may be asked to write and execute code in a prescribed language. A technician may be asked to troubleshoot and correct malfunctions in a piece of electronics. A graphic designer may be asked to create an advertising layout for the classified section (yellow pages) of a telephone directory. Only the boundaries of the collective creativity of a design team limit the types of simulations that can be created.

## Examples of Assessment Centers

As described previously, organizations often employ the assessment center methodology whereby they combine multiple simulation exercises and other assessments to determine individuals' competence on a select number of dimensions. Assessment centers have been developed for many purposes within a wide variety of organizations (Kudisch et al., 2001; Spychalski, Quiñones, Gaugler, & Pohley, 1997). Thus, a wide variety of configurations of dimensions and simulation exercises have been employed. In this section, we describe four assessment centers that represent this diversity.

AT&T developed what has been recognized as the first full-blown application of the assessment center methodology in American industry in the Management Progress Study (MPS) for studying the development of managerial lives (Bray & Grant, 1966) and later for the early identification of management potential (Campbell & Bray, 1967). The simulation package in the MPS consisted of an in-basket, an LGD, and a manufacturing game, along with a background interview and several paper-and-pencil tests. In the initial research centers, psychologists served as assessors, but later applications used middle-level managers. More than 15 dimensions were evaluated. Follow-up research showed that the assessments predicted management progress over a 15-year period. Subsequently, the assessment center process was implemented extensively throughout the Bell system.

Given the success of the longitudinal research in the MPS, many operating companies in the Bell system initiated assessment centers for promoting staff into managerial positions. Participants came from technical, sales, and supervisory ranks and were assessed for potential to succeed in middle management (Campbell & Bray, 1967). Thornton and Byham (1982) reviewed the evidence demonstrating the validity of these programs. The simulation exercises used in these programs varied somewhat from program to program but typically included an in-basket, one or more LGDs, and a business game, along with paper-and-pencil tests and a background interview.

The Colorado Division of Kodak used variations of assessment centers to identify developmental needs of current middle managers, first-level supervisors, and administrative staff. Each program consisted of specially developed simulation techniques in the following categories: in-basket, group discussion, case study, and one-on-one interaction simulation. Middle managers were trained to serve as assessors and then as "coaches" for the participants. These managers gave initial feedback to the participants and then subsequent feedback to the participants and their immediate supervisors. The assessment results formed the basis of a diagnosis of developmental needs and then development plans for improvement in areas of deficiency.

Wilkerson Manufacturing Company used an assessment center to screen manufacturing employees to work in a new team environment. Dimensions relevant to team effectiveness, such as giving and receiving feedback, and willingness and ability to make suggestions for improved work performance, were assessed by a combination of current team members and human resource managers. The simulations included a manufacturing game, an LGD, and an interaction simulation.

Sun Microsystems developed an assessment center to certify the high-level proficiency of their education consultants. Sun Education Consulting Services (ECS) assists organizations in maximizing the investments made in high-tech employees. ECS consultants must have participated in a number of projects and then passed a series of knowledge tests before participating in the behavioral assessment process. The simulations include a group discussion involving a real-time organizational problem, a simulated interaction with a client, a presentation of one's credentials, and a discussion with assessors about a series of project reports they have previously submitted in a portfolio. If the consultant demonstrates proficiency to a team of assessors consisting of headquarters' staff, field managers, and university assessment experts, he or she is granted the status of certification.

### Range of Applicability

These examples of individual exercises and assessment centers suggest the wide range of applicability of simulation methodology for various jobs and purposes. Simulations have been used to assess all levels of management from team leaders, to first-line supervisors and middle levels of management, to executives. They have been used to screen manufacturing employees in the automobile, electronic, bottling, and ceramic industries. Customer services personnel in the banking, computer, and telecommunications industries have been assessed. In addition, salespeople, teachers, and undergraduate and graduate students have been assessed.

The information from these assessments has been used for diverse purposes. Most commonly, the assessments are used to supplement other information in deciding whom to select for initial hire or for promotion to higher levels of responsibility. The second most common use is for development purposes, including the identification of persons with high-level potential who are put on "fast tracks" to higher management, the diagnosis of training needs leading to developmental planning, or the actual training of performance skills. In other applications, the information is used for diagnosis of organizational needs, organizational development, certification of competence, or to help make layoff decisions.

## DEVELOPING A SIMULATION

The decision that one or more of the several types of simulations is appropriate for a given application is only an initial step. In most cases, the user of simulations will have to construct the specific exercise material. Thus, in this section, we discuss the process of developing simulation exercises.

## Gathering Information to Develop a Simulation

An essential part of the development of simulation exercises is the process of gathering information about tasks, attributes, and the organizational setting of the target job. This information is essential for several steps in developing simulations. The critical questions include: What industry and organization are to be depicted in the simulation? What tasks and problems are to be built into the exercise? What attributes are to be evaluated from observations of behavioral responses to the exercises? What are the desirable responses that assessors are to look for in evaluating performance?

These and many other questions can only be answered in a meaningful way by gathering extensive information through job analysis (Harvey, 1991) and competency modeling (Schippmann et al., 2000) techniques. The specific techniques are beyond the scope of this chapter, but the following information should be gathered. Task analyses should document the duties and responsibilities of incumbents. Attribute analyses should identify the attributes required to complete these tasks, as well as the dimensions to be assessed. This includes dimensions demonstrated by current employees in attaining effective performance and new dimensions representing competencies desired by management and expected for effective performance in the future. Finally, organizational analysis should capture the type of industry and the products and services that are to be depicted in the simulation exercise.

## Steps in Developing a Simulation

Table 18.2 provides a series of steps to follow in developing a simulation technique. These represent a modification of the typical steps in developing any test or measurement device. More details on the process of constructing behavioral simulation exercises can be found in Thornton and Mueller-Hanson (in press).

The first step is to clearly state the purpose of the simulation exercise. Simulations developed for selection of exter-

nal candidates may be quite different from those used for making promotion decisions. At this step, one also needs to know who will be participating in the assessment. A simulation for relatively new, inexperienced examinees may be quite different from one for more experienced examinees. The developer also needs to know who will be administering, observing, and scoring the exercise. The qualifications of the assessment staff will determine the level of sophistication that can be built into the exercises. Other very practical issues include the number of persons to be assessed, how this simulation fits with other assessment techniques being employed, and what policies will be in place for assessment and reassessment.

The second step involves defining the dimensions to be assessed. This information comes directly from the job/competency analysis. For the simulation to be valid and job related, the constructs to be assessed in the simulation must be clearly defined and operationalized in terms of the target job. These constructs may include knowledge, skills, abilities, personality characteristics, values, interests, or any other attributes that can be specified in behavioral terms. Table 18.3 lists several dimensions that have been assessed in past simulations and assessment centers. The process of identifying these attributes often involves reviewing previous job descriptions, observing incumbents performing the target job, exploring extant literature in the organization (e.g., training material) or general profession (e.g., government documents), conducting interviews, administering questionnaires, and holding strategic clarification sessions with key managers.

Next, the format of the simulation should be specified. A variety of different formats might be used. The simulation may be written or oral. Instructions may come from both live and videotaped administrators. Participants may be given the exercise individually or in groups. Assessors may play major, minor, or no role in interacting with the participants. Role players may be utilized to interact with the participants.

All the preceding considerations may have an effect on the assessment materials that are prepared. Various degrees of specificity may be included in the instructions. Because simulation exercises contain some degree of ambiguity (e.g., how the participant should respond, how detailed should the responses be), the instructions should clarify these options for the participant. A variety of support materials also need to be prepared, including information about the position the participant is assuming, information about the organization such as its products or services, and the supplies the participant has available. Most important, the actual stimulus material must be realistic. Problems for the group discussion, letters and memos in the in-basket, information in the case study, and so on, all must be representative and realistic. If role players are to be used (e.g., in simulations of a discussion with a problem employee), their instructions must be written

**TABLE 18.2   Steps in Developing a Simulation Exercise**

State the purpose of testing and resources available.
Define the human attributes or competencies to be assessed.
Specify the format of the assessment procedure.
Prepare the stimulus material.
Try out the preliminary materials with pilot sample.
Establish reliability and validity.
Implement assessment procedures.

**TABLE 18.3** **Examples of Behavioral Dimensions**

| | | |
|---|---|---|
| Selling | Decision Making | Compliance with Instructions |
| Providing Customer Service | Oral Communication | Directing Others |
| Relating to Others on a Team | Written Communication | Tendency to Take Initiative |
| Problem Solving Ability | Persuasiveness | Organizing and Planning |
| Communication Skill | Willingness/Ability to Make | Sociability |
| Leadership | Suggestions | General Effectiveness |
| Emergent Leadership | Giving/Receiving Feedback | Motivation |
| Administrative Skill | Listening Skill | Initiative |
| Interpersonal Effectiveness | Interpersonal Sensitivity | Independence |

to provide adequate and standardized background and guidance for the "set" they are to assume and the type of role they are to portray. If assessors are to interact in any way with the participants, their instructions must be thorough (e.g., can they answer questions by the participant?; what do they do if disruptions occur?).

After the materials are prepared with the guidance of the job analysis results, they should be tried out with a pilot sample. This tryout is designed to give the developers feedback about how a representative sample of potential participants reacts to the simulation materials. This pilot effort gives insights into the clarity of instructions and difficulty of the assignments. Unwanted contaminants such as age, racial, and gender biases may be detected. The input can then be used to prepare the next draft of the exercises.

The reliability and validity of the simulations should also be studied. Although highly desirable, information about test-retest and internal consistency is usually not relevant for simulations. More germane is evidence of interscorer reliability. Part of the test development effort includes specification of behaviors relevant to the dimensions being evaluated. Evaluation of interrater agreement gives feedback on the adequacy of these support materials. At the very least, evidence of content representativeness should be gathered from a sample of subject matter experts not involved in the exercise development.

Systematic judgments of the relevance of simulation tasks to job demands and of the similarity of behavioral responses to job behaviors should be obtained. Further evidence of the relationship between exercise performance and job effectiveness is also important. Ideally, evidence of the psychological constructs measured by the simulation should also be obtained. Developers should also check for bias against racial/ethnic groups, women, older participants, and the disabled, followed by appropriate revisions.

Finally, procedures for implementing the simulation exercise should be prepared. These should be written in clear language so that standardized and secure practices are followed each time the simulation is administered. Written assessment policies should cover who, what, when, where, and why the exercise is to be administered. A manual should be prepared to document all the prior steps. Such documentation is helpful if the procedure is challenged in the future.

Developing the simulations and support materials on one's own or selecting a simulation exercise from a vendor is only one step in the implementation of simulation methodology. Another critical step is preparing assessors to observe and evaluate behavior. In the next section, we discuss the many issues surrounding the observation processes and some methods of training assessors.

## OBSERVATION AND EVALUATION OF PERFORMANCE

To review, we have shown how organizational simulation exercises can be developed to depict situations similar to those encountered in the real work settings and that elicit important work-related behaviors. Someone (preferably multiple someones) must observe, classify, and evaluate this behavior in a consistent and reliable manner that will maximize the validity of the measure. These "someones" are referred to as assessors, and it is to the assessor that we direct our attention in this section. By reviewing the roles, responsibilities, and cognitive processes of assessors, we hope to answer the following questions:

- How do assessors form decisions about performance in a simulation exercise?

- How is behavior observed, classified, integrated, and evaluated?

- What factors facilitate accurate observation, classification, and evaluation?

- What factors limit assessors' ability to make accurate judgments?

- What elements can be incorporated into the design and implementation of organizational simulation exercises that maximize the benefits and minimize the risks of using human judgment to make decisions about employees?

- What is the optimal way to train assessors?

## The Assessment Process

A great deal of evidence shows that when developed and administered appropriately, organizational simulation exercises can be valid predictors of future performance and therefore useful tools for making organizational decisions. What have been given less research attention until recently, however, are the reasons why such exercises predict so well (Klimoski & Brickner, 1987). To understand what it is that makes simulation exercises "work" is to understand the cognitive and behavioral processes carried out by the assessors who are observing participant behavior, classifying this behavior into categories (the dimensions that the exercise is measuring), and evaluating participant performance on these dimensions. In other words, accuracy in prediction must be viewed in terms of *both* the dynamics of the situation and how the assessors process information to reach judgments (Lievens & Klimoski, 2001; Sackett & Dreher, 1982; Zedeck, 1986).

Two cognitive orientations have been proposed to explain how assessors process information (Pulakos, 1986; Thornton, 1992). The first orientation has been termed the behavior-driven or data-driven approach (Abelson, 1981; Borman, 1977, 1978; Fiske & Taylor, 1984; Rumelhart & Ortony, 1977). This orientation assumes that individuals have the ability to accurately observe behavior, classify behaviors into dimensions, and form accurate, objective judgments about participants. This process is "bottom-up" in the sense that specific behavioral observations are the basis of higher order generalizations. The alternative to this view is captured in schema-driven theories of human judgment (Cantor & Mischel, 1977; Fiske & Taylor, 1984; Nisbitt & Ross, 1980; Srull & Wyer, 1989). This orientation suggests that as individuals experience people and events, they develop and hold mental schemas or theories about how things typically are. For example, in the case of organizational simulation exercises, assessors hold "typical managerial performance" schema and then scan the behaviors of participants for actions that are consistent with this schema. As compared to data-driven approaches, schema-driven theory is a "top-down" approach (i.e., it assumes assessors' general mental frameworks influence specific behaviors observed). This type of processing is sometimes considered less objective than behavior-driven processing.

Comparing these two approaches, a data-driven approach would suggest that assessors actively attend to all participant behaviors, whereas a schema-driven approach would suggest that assessors selectively attend only to those behaviors that are consistent with their personal theory of job performance. In terms of encoding and storage, the behavior-driven theory says that specific actions are encoded and stored, whereas schema-driven theories purport that only general impressions are processed and retained in memory. Where behavior-driven theory would argue that these stages and subsequent stages of recall and judgment occur in a strict sequential order, proponents of schema-driven theory instead contend that many of these processes occur simultaneously, in that all observations are framed by the past perceptions, memory, and general impressions held by the assessors.

Given these two alternative models to information processing, the question remains: Which one is predominant in the context of observation of organizational simulation exercises? That is, how do assessors actually process the information they observe, classify, and evaluate? We contend that both types of processing occur within simulation exercises as they have typically been executed. We base this argument on the mixed theory of perceptions and memory of social observation that Ebbesen (1981) proposed. According to this idea, it is accepted that assessors have the ability to observe, encode, and store specific behavioral events. However, mental schemas can also influence how assessors process information. Therefore, organizational simulation exercises stand to be the most effective when assessors are trained in such a way that behavior is observed and recorded systematically, but where collective schemas are developed in assessors that reflect both real indicators of successful performances as well as the norms and values of the organization (Lievens, 2001b). This leads us to our next section, which describes how assessors can be prepared to observe, record, classify, and evaluate performance in simulations.

## Assessor Training

In any organizational assessment incorporating behavior-based exercises, it is critical that assessors are properly instructed in all elements of the exercise, their roles, and the decision-making process in general (International Task Force on Assessment Center Guidelines, 2000). Research has shown that the assessors and their preparedness are a critical factor in the validity of assessments using multiple simulations (Lievens, 2001b). The International Task Force on Assessment Center Guidelines (2000) suggests several elements that should be included in *all* assessor-training programs. Table 18.4 lists the major requirements laid out by the *Guidelines*. These elements can be tied to processing theories of assessor judgment previously discussed. Thus, we discuss important training elements within this framework.

### Training on Dimensions

One way in which an assessment program can take advantage of schema-based processing is to create a collective schema

**TABLE 18.4  Suggestions for Assessor Training as Laid out by the Assessor Center Guidelines**

Ensuring that all assessors have knowledge of the organization, the job the exercise is simulating, the job family to which the job belongs, and general information about the group of individuals to be assessed

Training on the dimensions to be assessed: Ensuring that assessors understand and have a common knowledge of the meaning of the performance dimensions as well as a collective agreement of what inadequate, average, and excellent performance is for each of these dimensions

Practice recording, classifying, and evaluating behaviors relevant to the dimensions to be assessed in the simulation exercises; practice with rating forms or observation tools that are to be used

A review of the evaluation and integration procedures

A review of any organizational policies that impact the assessment program, the assessees, or the assessors

A review of how results will be fed back to participants

Instruction on how to play any roles assessors might take on during the exercise(s)

of managerial performance by thoroughly training assessors on the behavioral dimensions to be assessed by the exercise(s). First, training assessors to organize their observations in terms of dimensions reduces the amount of information that they must process and store and helps facilitate recall at the time of judgment (Zedeck, 1986). This is consistent with cognitive psychological findings that the use of categories simplifies what individuals must know and look for (Cantor & Mischel, 1977).

Extensive training on the meaning of dimensions to be assessed has been termed "frame-of-reference training" in the performance appraisal and assessment center literatures (Bernardin & Buckley, 1981; Schleicher & Day, 1998; Schleicher, Day, Mayes, & Riggio, 2002; Woehr, 1994). Frame-of-reference training instructs assessors to replace their existing schema with an imposed performance schema based on the empirical data from which the dimensions were derived. Because assessors often have different backgrounds and varying amounts of experience (e.g., in management, job, and the organization), the mental schemas they might otherwise activate while assessing might be quite varied. Providing them with a common frame of reference not only puts all assessors on the "same page," but it also serves as a means to allow the organization's norms and values to influence what is considered high-, moderate-, and low-level performance (Lievens, 2001b).

This type of dimension-based training typically begins by informing assessors that accuracy in judgment is best obtained by thoroughly understanding the essence of effective, average, and ineffective behavior with regard to each dimen-

sion. After assessors are provided definitions and multiple behavioral examples at each level of proficiency of each dimension, they are taught to scan observed behaviors using this collective frame of reference as a mental framework. Consistent with the schema-driven approach, this method instructs assessors to observe, classify, and evaluate behaviors simultaneously. Assessors are provided opportunities to practice observing and evaluating behaviors, either by viewing a videotaped exercise, watching practice participants, or playing out the exercises themselves. Research has shown that this method of training not only increases rater accuracy and interrater reliability, but it also enhances construct and criterion-related validity (Schleicher & Day, 1998; Schleicher et al., 2002).

### Process Training

Assessor training also focuses on the process by which assessors observe, classify, and evaluate behavior. The behavior-driven approach contends that assessors are highly capable of these duties, and accuracy is fostered by carrying out the duties sequentially (Lievens, 2001b). Thus, a process component of assessor training instructs assessors to carefully distinguish among and proceed through the stages of observing, recording, classifying, and evaluating behavior. During the training, assessors practice observing exercises, writing behavioral descriptions, classifying behavior into dimensions, and rating participants on dimensions based on the observed behaviors. The majority of organizations using simulations or assessment centers use behavior-oriented training strategies, which include elements of both the behavior-driven and schema-driven approaches (Thornton, 1992).

### Comparing Data-Driven and Schema-Driven Training Strategies

Much of the research in the area of assessment centers has compared process-based and schema-based approaches as two alternative "types" of training. For example, Lievens (2001b) provided three groups of assessors with either schema-driven training, data-driven training, or no training prior to assessing a simulation exercise. Results indicated that although both types of training (as compared with no training) led to superior rating accuracy, interrater reliability, and ability to differentiate among dimensions, the schema-based training group outperformed the data-driven group on all three of these outcomes.

Despite these findings, we do not support the notion that organizations need to choose *either* a data-driven or schema-driven approach to assessor training. Instead, consistent with the mixed theory of social observation (Ebbesen, 1981), we believe that both approaches suggest elements of effective assessor training. From the top-down theories, organizations should capitalize on the importance of carefully defining dimensions and ensuring all assessors have a collective agreement on what excellent, average, and inadequate performance is for each dimension. From the bottom-up theories, organizations should train assessors to take the observation task seriously, to observe and write down behaviors, and to make ratings soon after observation to reduce dependence on long-term memory and long-held, potentially imprecise schemas (Thornton, 1992). In addition, research has shown that making assessors accountable for their ratings (e.g., making them report behaviors to a group), choosing assessors who are familiar with the job being simulated and with no vested interest in the progress of the assessees, and providing instruction in potential rating biases (e.g., halo effect, recency effect, leniency, severity, central tendency, stereotyping) can also be important elements of assessor training (Thornton, 1992). Because all of the training elements we have discussed parallel different components of the assessment center guidelines, organizations should apply the logic of *both* behavior-driven *and* schema-driven theories in assessor training programs.

## Aids for Recording and Rating Behaviors

A great deal of research in the area of organizational assessment has centered around how observation forms and rating scales should be formatted to best facilitate rater accuracy (Baker, 1986; Binning, Hesson-McInnis, DeVille, & Srinivasagam, 1998; Campbell, 1986; Hennessy, Mabey, & Warr, 1998; LeBreton, Gniatczyk, & Migetz, 1999; Reilly, Henry, & Smither, 1990). Traditionally, assessors of behavioral exercises have been instructed to take notes in a narrative form as they observe participant performance in simulation exercises. However, research has revealed that rating systems that simplify the information-processing demands and cognitive load on assessors can increase accuracy in judgment (Baker, 1986; Borman, 1978; Campbell, 1986; Louiselle, 1986). Two well-researched observation and rating formats designed to meet this goal are behavioral checklists and behaviorally anchored rating scales (BARS).

Behavioral checklists provide lists of behaviors that participants may display during the course of the simulation. While observing performance, assessors simply check off the behaviors that they observe. The obvious disadvantage to such a method is that it is very difficult to develop comprehensive lists of all possible behaviors. Furthermore, even if this could be done, searching for items on the list that match observed behaviors could also place heavy cognitive demands

on assessors that might hinder their ability to observe the continuing stream of behavior of participants. The research on the effectiveness of behavioral checklists is mixed. Whereas some studies have found the method to increase construct validity (Binning, Adorno, & Kroeck, 1997; Donahue, Truxillo, Cornwell, & Gerrity, 1997; Reilly et al., 1990) and legal defensibility (Wiersma & Latham, 1986) of simulations used in the context of assessment centers, other research has found the method to show little or no improvement in construct validity (Fritzsche, Brannick, & Hazucha-Fisher, 1994; Schneider & Schmitt, 1992). In addition, LeBreton et al. (1999) have recently found that the predictive validity gained from using checklists was mediated by assessors' judgmental ratings.

Behaviorally anchored rating scales contain behavior examples for numerical values indicating high, moderate, and low performance levels. At each of these levels, BARS provide several examples of specific behaviors that the participant might display. Similar to the research on behavioral checklists, the research on BARS is also mixed. Baker (1986) found behavior checklists to be superior to BARS when used in certain exercises but not others. Campbell (1986) found that the use of BARS provided superior discriminant validity of the assessment center method as compared with the use of behavioral checklists, but neither format proved to be superior in terms of convergent validity.

The research on the effects of rating formats in the area of organizational simulations and assessment centers parallels the rating format research in the area of performance appraisal (Bernardin & Beatty, 1984; Murphy & Cleveland 1991). That is, although it is certainly important to consider processing limitations and to develop rating formats that help to facilitate quick and accurate recording, classification, and evaluation of behaviors, no one method seems to be superior over another. Thus, of greater importance is ensuring that any behavioral examples provided adequately sample relevant behaviors likely to be elicited in the exercise, and that such behaviors are anchored to appropriate levels of performance.

## Other Process Elements

Our last section in this discussion of the assessment process briefly mentions other process issues that have received research attention in the area of organizational simulations and assessment centers. One such factor involves the number of behavioral dimensions to which assessors can attend. Gaugler and Thornton (1989) found that behaviors could be more correctly classified into dimensions when fewer dimensions were present. A smaller number of dimensions were also shown to increase accuracy in rating. Subsequent research has validated this finding, showing that only a small number of dimensions are needed to make accurate performance predictions (LeBreton et al., 1999; Sackett & Hakel, 1979; Shore, Thornton, & Shore, 1990).

In addition, Lievens and Klimoski (2001) have called for research in seven distinct areas within social information processing within the context of assessment centers, including social judgment accuracy, assessor expectancies, the role of cognitive structures (e.g., stereotypes, scripts), the use of controlled versus automatic processing, and the roles of motivated cognition, attributions, and accountability in assessor judgment. Although a discussion of each of these factors is outside the scope of this chapter, it important to note that the process of observation and evaluation of behavior must be considered when designing this type of assessment. Attention must be given to not only the context in which assessors make judgments (e.g., cognitive load, opportunity to observe, etc.), but also the characteristics of the assessors themselves. These include assessor background, experience with the organization, job, and participants, experience in making organizational assessments, and demographic considerations. Although planning for such an assessment process involves consideration of many factors, carefully designing organizational simulations to address the many issues covered here will enhance the assessors' ability to reliably evaluate performance dimensions and to predict future job performance.

## CURRENT STATUS OF SIMULATIONS AND ASSESSMENT CENTERS

Carefully constructed simulation exercises and assessors well trained in observation processes are essential ingredients in an effective simulation methodology. Even with these elements in place, considerable controversy still exists about some aspects of the validity of simulation methods and assessment center judgments. In this section, we examine the evidence of predictive and construct validity of assessor judgments. The largely supportive research partially explains the extensive use of simulations and assessment centers. Results from surveys of usage in the United States and around the world are summarized.

### Current Research Status

Researchers have gathered extensive evidence about the validity of simulations and assessment centers over the past 50 years. In the following sections, we summarize a representative sample of the evidence related to predictive accuracy and construct explication.

### *Predictive Validity Established*

The criterion-related validity of assessment centers using simulations has been well established and few assessment center researchers and practitioners would argue the method's power to predict a wide range of important work outcomes (Howard, 1997). Three meta-analytic studies give evidence to this claim. Hunter and Hunter (1984) found assessment centers ($\bar{r} = .43$) and work sample tests ($\bar{r} = .54$) to have adequate criterion validity for promotion and certification. Gaugler, Rosenthal, Thornton, and Bentson's meta-analysis (1987) found an average corrected validity coefficient of .37, varying from .21 to .53. Schmidt and Hunter (1998) found assessment centers to have substantial criterion validity ($\bar{r} = .37$), but a very small incremental validity when combined with cognitive ability tests. Where some have argued that this should be taken as evidence that the assessment centers may be a relatively inefficient assessment strategy (Schmidt & Hunter, 1998; Scholz & Schuler as cited in Lievens & Klimoski, 2001), others have pointed out that assessment centers provide richer and more varied information, lead to less adverse impact, and allow for the assessment of actual behavior (Howard, 1997). In addition, other research has reported assessment center rating to have substantial incremental validity above that of supervisor ratings (Chan, 1996), personality tests (Goffin, Rothstein, & Johnston, 1996), and cognitive ability tests (Dayan, Kasten, & Fox, 2002) in predicting promotion.

A factor that does *not* seem to affect validities is whether clinical or mechanical rating methods are used to reach the overall assessment rating (McEvoy, Beatty, & Bernardin, 1987; Pynes & Bernardin, 1989). What does seem to have a positive effect on assessment center validities is using multiple exercises, using a variety of exercises, using psychologists as well as managers as assessors, incorporating peer evaluations into the overall assessment rating (Gaugler et al., 1987), and using an appropriate criterion in conducting the validation study (Binning, Adorno, & LeBreton, 1999; McEnvoy & Beatty, 1989; Moser, Schuler, & Funke, 1999).

This latter issue of using an appropriate criterion has been recently receiving a good deal of research attention. This is because validation studies have employed a wide range of criterion measures, including overall performance, career progress, dimensional performance, career potential, training performance, subsequent promotion, and concurrent supervisor ratings. Gaugler et al.'s (1987) meta-analysis found that studies using potential as a criterion produced the highest validity coefficients. Chan (1996) found concurrent supervisory ratings to be substantially less well predicted ($r = .06$) than subsequent promotion ($r = .59$).

At the heart of this matter is that any validation study must consider the appropriateness of both the predictors and criterion used (Murphy & Shiarella, 1997). Just as overall assessment ratings may suffer from subtle criterion contamination because they may not be adequately tied to the dimensions being assessed (Klimoski & Strickland, 1977), the criteria used to evaluate assessment ratings may include variance not attributable to its intended dimensions. For example, McEvoy and Beatty (1989) found that assessment center ratings predicted uncontaminated criteria better than a contaminated criterion.

Moser et al. (1999) further pointed out that one potential contaminant to performance ratings may be unreliability in ratings stemming from inadequate opportunities to observe performance. In an assessment center containing six personality inventories, 10 ability tests, and nine work samples, they found that the criterion validity coefficient ($r = .37$) was moderated by opportunity to observe work performance. For employees being observed less than two years, the validity coefficient was .09, where the validity for employees who had been observed for more than two years was .50.

Another factor affecting criterion contamination is criterion complexity. Binning et al. (1999) found that validity coefficients of overall judgmental ratings in both assessment centers and an inspection simulation exercise were moderated by the number of dimensions the criterion assessed. The overall assessment ratings were more valid when a more complex criterion was employed. Whereas determining and assessing behavioral dimensions is commonplace in the design of an assessment center, considering the dimensions of criteria may be less obvious. Because the use of contaminated criteria may indirectly affect human resource policy decisions and subsequent decisions regarding employees, it is crucial to consider such matters (Binning et al., 1999). As Murphy and Shiarella (1997) point out, it is essential to consider the validity of the entire selection system, not only the validities of individual predictors.

### Construct Validity

Whereas the criterion-related validity evidence for assessment centers is well established, there is substantially less consensus in the literature regarding the method's construct validity. That is, studies of convergent and discriminant validity of ratings provided by individual assessors has not provided strong evidence that the constructs actually measured are the prescribed behavioral dimensions that the assessment center sets out to measure. This has even been found to be the case with developmental centers, where one would expect construct validity since feedback on dimensions is provided to participants (Lievens & Klimoski, 2001). This is not to say that assessment centers lack construct validity. Studies of construct validity of final dimension ratings, representing the aggregation of judgments across various exercises and multiple assessors, have provided considerably more evidence that the assessment center method yields evaluations of prescribed dimensions. In addition, taking a unitarian view of validity (Binning & Barrett, 1989), we know that since both criterion validity (Gaugler et al., 1987) and content validity (Sackett, 1997) evidence has been established, then logically, construct validity is present as well.

Thus, rather than questioning if assessment centers have construct validity, the questions that plague assessment center researchers are: What methods of assessing construct validity are appropriate to evaluate assessment centers? and what constructs are being measured (Lievens & Klimoski, 2001; Sackett & Dreher, 1982; Sackett & Tuzinski, 2001)? We contend that the internal validation method of studying the relationships among within-exercise dimension ratings provided by a single assessor after observing behavior in only one exercise is inappropriate, because it does not capture the essence of the assessment center method, which relies on aggregating observations of behavior by multiple assessors across multiple simulation exercises.

The most debated topic in this area is whether the specified dimensions, some unspecified dimensions, individual exercise performance, or some form of systematic error is being measured. The following sections describe the methods that have been employed to answer these questions and the results associated with each method. As we will show, often very different conclusions are drawn depending on the analytic approach taken. Therefore, we argue that it is necessary to take a broad approach to collecting construct validity evidence in further understanding the underpinnings of assessment centers and the simulations comprising them.

### Internal Approach to Construct Validation

The most commonly used approach to assessment center construct validation is the internal approach. The term *internal* is used because only information internal to the assessment center is used. Correlations among ratings on dimensions within exercises are compared with a single dimension's ratings across exercises. Such an approach utilizes a multitrait-multimethod (MTMM) strategy (Campbell & Fiske, 1959) to study within-exercise ratings. That is, convergent validity is evidenced when the correlation of an individual dimension rating across exercises is high, whereas discriminant validity is evidenced when ratings of different dimensions within (and between) exercises is low (relative to convergent coefficients).

Sackett and Dreher (1982) argued that in order to make the case that behavioral dimensions are central to assessment centers, it must be shown that the ratings on these dimensions can be differentiated from one another and have cross-situational consistency.

A similar internal approach to construct validation uses factor analysis. This method treats within-exercise dimension ratings as individual items. When ratings associated with single dimensions across exercises cluster together, this is considered to be construct validity evidence. If instead, ratings were clustered by exercise, assessor, or some other factor, this would be considered evidence against construct validity of specified dimensions.

The results of studies utilizing the internal approach have produced largely negative findings. That is, studies have consistently found convergent validity coefficients to be modest and discriminant validity coefficients to be quite large (Born, Kolk, & van der Flier, 2000). Likewise, in factor-analytic studies, exercise factors consistently rule over dimension factors (Bycio, Alvares, & Hahn, 1987; Fleenor, 1996; Robertson, Gratton, & Sharpley, 1987; Sackett & Dreher, 1982; Sackett & Harris, 1988). Subsequent studies have attempted to improve on these results by making methodological improvements suggested by past research. These include modifying the scoring procedure (Harris, Becker, & Smith, 1993; Silverman, Dalessio, Woods, & Johnson, 1986), using behavioral checklists (Donahue et al., 1997), making dimensions more transparent (Kolk, Born, & can der Flier, 2000), and using job functions instead of dimensions (Joyce, Thayer, & Pond, 1994). Although some of these studies found small increases in construct validity, overall the effects were negligible. Exercise factors continue to emerge over dimension factors, and discriminant validity evidence continues to be lacking in most studies using an internal approach.

Many authors have argued that the lack of construct validity evidence found in these studies may be more attributable to methodological artifacts than a true lack of construct validity (Howard, 1997; Sackett & Tuzinski, 2001; Shore et al., 1990; Thornton, Tziner, Dahan, Clevenger, & Meir, 1997). That is, to employ the MTMM or factor-analytic approaches, it is necessary to collect within-exercise ratings on each dimension. Such ratings were not part of the original assessment center design, and, as Howard (1997) pointed out, several factors could cause high discriminant and low convergent validity coefficients using this strategy. First, a single exercise may not elicit enough behavior to adequately assess multiple dimensions. Second, often the same behavior may be used to score an individual on multiple dimensions, which would make an exercise effect more likely. Third, because the exercises are not designed to be parallel forms of one

another, they may measure different facets of the same dimension. And last, such validation strategies treat the within-exercise dimension ratings equally across dimensions, whereas in reality, during the integration session, the assessors may come to differentially weight behaviors elicited from different exercises.

An additional problem with the internal method is that assessors are typically nested within exercises. That is, in a typical assessment center, all assessors do not observe all assessees in all exercises. Therefore, it becomes impossible to partition out assessor, exercise, and dimension variance (Howard, 1997). Two studies have explored the possibility that common rater variance within exercises contributes to the lack of construct validity evidence found in assessment center research (Kolk et al., 2000; Robie, Osburn, Morris, Etchegaray, & Adams, 2000). These authors compared internal construct validity evidence when assessors rated all dimensions in a single exercise (a within-exercise rating process) with validity evidence when an assessor would be responsible for a single dimension across exercises (a within-dimension rating process). Kolk et al. (2000), using an MTMM design standardizing rater effects found that within-exercise correlations decreased when a within-dimension approach was used. Using a factor-analytic approach, Robie et al. (2000) found that using a within-exercise rating process led to factors resembling exercises, where a within-dimension rating process lead to factors resembling dimensions. Although having one assessor per dimension may not be practically feasible, these studies show that the lack of construct validity evidence provided in past studies may at least in part be due to how the studies are conducted.

Arthur, Woehr, and Maldegan (2000) used a slightly different approach to show that construct validity evidence can in fact be gleaned from assessment center ratings. Using generalizability analyses, these authors were able to partial out the variance in assessment center ratings due to the person, the dimensions, the exercises, and the rater. They provided evidence of discriminant validity by showing that the person-dimension interaction accounted for a large percentage of the variance in ratings. This evidence was strengthened by the fact that other factors, such as the exercise and rater, accounted for only a small portion of the total variance.

A study by Lievens (2001a), also employing generalizability analysis, found similar results. Lievens had managers and I/O psychology students rate videotaped assessment center exercises where assessees either performed consistently across exercises or exhibited performance fluctuations across dimensions within exercises. By holding "true performance" constant and by utilizing a fully crossed design (all assessors rated all assessees in all exercises), this study was better able to determine assessor ability to distinguish among dimensions and detect performance fluctuations than field studies incorporating the MTMM approach. Lievens's generalizability analyses revealed evidence of both convergent and discriminant validity and showed that assessors are indeed capable of detecting performance differences on dimensions, when such differences truly exist. A follow-up MTMM analysis replicated the results from the generalizability analysis, suggesting that perhaps other factors such as assessment center design, assessor training, using nonmanager assessors, and candidates' performance levels may be contributing to the lower validity coefficients found in past studies of internal relationships.

### External Approaches to Construct Validation

Whereas these modified internal approaches to construct validation have revealed limitations to the traditional construct validation strategies, other authors have called for a completely different approach (Chan, 1996; Howard, 1997; Shore et al., 1990; Thornton et al, 1997). This approach, termed the external or nomological network approach, explores the correlations between overall dimension ratings and external measures of similar and dissimilar constructs. The logic of this method is that dimensions can be clustered into domains that are similar to well-researched constructs such as personality characteristics and cognitive abilities. Because individual exercises may primarily tap into a single dimension (e.g., in-basket primarily assesses administrative skills, coaching exercise primarily assesses interpersonal skills, case analysis primarily assesses cognitive skills), it is no surprise to researchers supporting the external approach that exercise factors emerge when a small number of diverse exercises are used (Howard, 1997). The advantage of the external approach method is that the analyses use final attribute ratings, which represent an aggregation of judgments across multiple raters and multiple exercises. Such an approach overcomes many of the methodological artifacts mentioned earlier that are associated with the internal approach.

Evidence for construct validity using the external approach is mixed but promising. Shore et al. (1990) grouped dimensions into two clusters, performance/administrative and interpersonal. Performance-related dimensions correlated best with external measures of cognitive ability, and interpersonal-related dimensions correlated best with external measures of personality. Chan (1996) used Shore et al.'s same method and was unable to uncover such a pattern.

Although the Chan and Shore et al. studies used the same method of clustering dimensions and correlating them with outside measures of constructs similar and dissimilar to the clusters, the studies did differ in terms of how final dimension ratings were reached. In Chan's study, assessors made within-exercise dimension ratings, and the final dimension ratings were obtained by averaging dimension ratings across exercises and assessors. Shore et al. derived their final attribute ratings using an alternative method: the behavioral reporting method. Such a method does not have assessors make within-exercise dimension ratings. Instead, they take detailed behavioral observation notes and report these to the other assessors during the integration session. Only then are assessees rated on dimensions as part of the consensus process.

It is important that research taking an external approach to construct validation distinguish between these two methods. Because it avoids evaluation at the level of the exercise, only the behavioral reporting method is completely free of the aforementioned confounds associated with internal approaches. Using this method, Thornton et al. (1997) found considerable evidence of construct validity. This study found that ratings of 16 dimensions correlated with external measures of comparable constructs measured by both ability tests and psychological assessments (based on interviews and personality scores).

### Conclusions

Considering all of this research, it becomes apparent that some traditional, internal approaches to collecting construct validity evidence may not be completely appropriate (Howard, 1997; Joyce et al., 1994). It seems necessary to move away from within-exercise dimension ratings and consider both internal and external analyses.

Researchers have made other suggestions for increasing the construct validity of assessment centers as well. For example, Howard (1997) called for dimensions that are more "user friendly." She cited one organization's current approach of using three to eight "key behaviors" to characterize each dimension. She also suggested using fewer, more observable dimensions that can be defined clearly and unambiguously. Other researchers have suggested using tasks in place of dimensions (Russell & Domm, 1995). However, subsequent research has found that tasks can be just as complex as dimensions, are not easily generalized, create an unnatural structure for describing individuals, and do not lead to increased construct or criterion validity (Russell & Domm, 1995; Thornton, 1992; Thornton, Kaman, Layer, & Larsh, 1995).

Last, Sackett and Dreher (1982) suggested using exercises as individual assessments of an individual's competence in a particular role. In this case, exercise factors would be desired in the sense that each exercise would measure performance in a different role. Dimensions may be used as observational aids, but they would not be aggregated across exercises. Future research needs to evaluate these and the many other suggestions provided in the assessment center literature for improving the construct validity of the method (see Lievens, 1998 for additional suggestions). However, such modifications must be tested using the multiple approaches to construct validation reviewed here.

Before concluding this section on the validity of assessment centers and simulation exercise scores, it is important to note that the majority of validity evidence to date has been collected using assessment centers and simulation exercises that have been designed for use in selection, promotion, or diagnostic decisions. What has not been studied nearly as much is the validity associated with using assessment centers and simulation exercises as a developmental process (Carrick & Williams, 1999; Thornton, 2002). Although developmental assessment centers (DACs) have gained popularity in practice, the true ability of DACs to change individuals' thinking and acting has yet to be established (Jones & Whitmore, 1995). Furthermore, many of the behavioral dimensions assessed in traditional ACs (typically abilities and stable traits) may not be trainable or developable in any reasonable period of time, and therefore may be inappropriate for use in DACs. Instead, it may be more appropriate for DACs to focus on knowledge and skills that can be learned in a relatively short period of time. Although this has caused some researchers to argue that DACs may be ineffective because more stable abilities and traits are more predictive of general job performance (Jones & Whitmore, 1995), others have argued that the criteria used to test the predictive validity of traditional ACs are less relevant to the validation of DACs (Carrick & Williams, 1999). That is, the focus of DACs is on individual development on particular dimensions. The focus is also more on the well-being, self-esteem, and growth of individual staff members, and less on overall organizational effectiveness. Therefore, validity would be better established by showing increased skill on particular dimensions over time rather than collecting evidence of correlations of assessment ratings with job performance or other external variables.

## Current Use in Organizational Practice

We now turn our attention to how assessment centers and simulation exercises are actually being used worldwide. Surveys of such practices are important not only to understand the extent to which these methods are being utilized in organizations, but also to identify the areas in which organizations comply and fail to comply with professional guidelines and research-based suggestions. Identifying areas of disconnect

may assist practitioners in maximizing the efficiency, reliability, validity, and legal defensibility of their methods.

### Relative Frequency of Use

Thousands of organizations use simulations for assessing applicants and employees (Ralphs & Stephen, 1986; Thornton & Cleveland, 1990). However, their frequency varies across both industries and countries. For example, in a study on the use of structured assessment in the information technology (IT) workforce, Murphy and Byrne (2000) found that only a marginal percentage of IT organizations are using work simulations or assessment centers to assess entry-level and experienced applicants. Their data also showed that a large majority of IT organizations rarely used scores from any type of structured assessment for making decisions about both types of applicants. In another study, a survey of selection methods by United Kingdom (UK) organizations revealed that 44% used assessment centers when hiring college graduates (Keenan, 1995). However, in almost every one of the UK assessment centers an employment interview (as contrasted with simulation methods) was reported as having the most dominant role in making the hiring decision.

### Purpose and Nature of Assessment

Worldwide surveys show that assessment centers are used most frequently for selection, promotion, professional development, and (to a lesser extent) training (Kudisch et al., 2001; Spychalski et al., 1997). The most current global data available suggest that where management-level assessment centers are used for both decision making and development, executive-level assessment centers are more often used for developmental purposes, and entry-level assessment centers are more often used for decision making.

One surprising disconnect between research and practice in this area is the paucity of research on developmental assessment centers (DACs) relative to their frequent use in organizations. The key difference between assessment centers used for selection, promotions, or diagnosis and assessment centers used for development is that in developmental centers, the simulation exercises not only elicit relevant behaviors that can be observed and evaluated, the exercises themselves provide the opportunity for experiential learning, self-reflection, and performance improvement. In this situation, assessment and development are one and the same—DACs may actually change the behavior of participants rather than simply measuring aspects of managerial performance (Jones & Whitmore, 1995; Klimoski & Brickner, 1987; Klimoski & Strickland, 1977). In fact, it has been suggested that it is this intervention quality of DACs that has led to their continued use in organizations (Hollenbeck, 1990). A survey by Spychalski et al. (1997) revealed that nearly 40 percent of the assessment centers being used in organizations are for the purpose of employee development. Despite the growing reputation of DACs, a paucity of research exists exploring their psychometric characteristics as well as whether the past findings on traditional assessment centers generalize to assessment centers used for development (Carrick & Williams, 1999; Thornton, 2002).

In terms of what types of exercises are used most extensively in organizations using simulations and assessment centers, survey results have indicated that the most popular assessment techniques are (in order of popularity) in-baskets, LGDs, interviews, analysis problems, presentations, fact-finding exercises, and skills and abilities tests (Spychalski et al., 1997).

An interesting finding with regard to *how* exercises and assessment centers are carried out is that the suggestions by researchers encouraging practitioners to take advantage of technology to make assessment more efficient and effective are *not* being carried out in organizations. Kudisch et al.'s (2001) survey asked individuals associated with assessment centers in 14 different countries whether they took advantage of video and computer-aided technology to enhance their assessment processes. These methods include videotaping candidate performance; using computerized checklists, classification, report writers, and exercises; and implementing "disassembled" assessment centers where videotaped exercises are assessed by assessors in remote locations or where assessment is staggered over a number of weeks. Although the advantages to using these methods have been strongly encouraged in the literature (Howard, 1997; Hughes, Deaver, & Winn, 1995; Ryan et al., 1995), the Kudisch et al. survey found that these types of technology are rarely used.

Other findings with regard to how assessment centers are conducted involve the extent to which participants are informed about the assessment purpose and process. Despite the fact that the majority of complaints filed by assessment center participants are with regard to a lack of knowledge about the purpose, intentions, and process of the program, Spychalski et al.'s data showed that the majority of assessment center programs provide participants with limited information about the program. It may be in an organization's best interest to provide assessees with a brief orientation to the program prior to their participation to control for negative reactions and make the experience more worthwhile.

Spychalski et al. (1997) also found that organizations rarely incorporate peer ratings in assessment centers or use them as criteria in their validation efforts. This is in direct contrast with research findings showing increased criterion-related validity when peer ratings are employed (Gaugler et al., 1987). This is an additional area where practitioners might consider altering their methods to improve the quality of their assessment.

### Assessor Training and Program Evaluation

Another area of disconnect between the research/guidelines and what is actually being carried out in organizations is that of assessor training and program evaluation. Survey data indicate that the length of assessor training is relatively short in many organizations (Spychalski et al., 1997). In addition, at the end of assessor training programs, it is rare for programs to verify assessors' skills prior to the assessment event. Furthermore, a majority of the centers surveyed by Spychalski et al. did not have a process for evaluating the reliability and validity of their assessment center. These practices are surprising, given the *Guidelines* explicitly recommend two days of training per day of assessment, assessor certification, and full psychometric evaluation.

### A Positive Note

Although we thought it important to point out areas where practice has not completely complied with recommendations and suggestions stemming from research findings and guidelines in the area of assessment centers, we want to point out the multiple ways in which practitioners are maintaining the professional integrity and psychometric quality of the assessment center method. That is, research has shown that assessment centers and simulation exercises are often developed and administered by qualified professionals. These programs almost always include assessor training that covers the major components set out by the *Guidelines*. These programs contain multiple exercises (at least one that is a simulation), multiple assessors, and formalized data recording and integration procedures. Assessment centers and simulations are used for multiple purposes, including both administrative decisions and professional development, and almost always include formal feedback to participants, in the form of an oral meeting, a written report, or both. It seems that organizations and consultants are certainly in accordance with the professional guidelines in developing, administering, and evaluating assessment centers in many areas, and perhaps the method will be even further advanced by giving special attention to those areas where inconsistencies exist.

## SPECIAL ISSUES

In this section we discuss two special issues related to the use of simulations in assessment. First, we discuss the use of simulations with diverse populations. By diversity we mean individuals of different race, gender, age, and disability status. In addition, the use of simulations across different cultures is discussed. We then discuss compliance with various statutory and professional guidelines and regulations.

## Diversity

With today's changing, heterogeneous, and global workforce, assessment techniques must be free of inadvertent biases and fair to all examinees. In addition, in today's global economy, multinational organizations need to consider whether assessment processes are appropriate for persons in different countries and cultures. Cultural issues can be especially problematic when persons of different cultures are assessed in the same simulation exercise or assessment program. Two approaches have been taken to make simulations fair to diverse examinees. First, steps have been taken to build in fairness in the development and implementation of simulations and assessment centers. Second, studies have been conducted to evaluate the psychometric properties of simulations when they have been used to assess various subgroups.

### Building Fair Simulations

The earlier section of this paper describing the process of developing simulations outlined several steps for ensuring fairness. First, the simulation must be job related; that is, it must include dimensions and content that are representative of the important performance domains. Additional steps can be taken to include issues that are particularly relevant to diverse groups and names that vary in terms of gender, race, and ethnicity. At the very least, women and minorities should not be portrayed in derogatory or unfavorable ways that perpetuate negative stereotypes. For example, problem employees in the scenarios should not always be minorities, and executives should not always be men. One step to avoid gender biases is to use gender-neutral names such as Pat and Chris for various important characters in the simulations, especially the position the assessee is to assume. Equally important, steps should be taken to design the exercises to minimize the effects of differences in behavioral styles that are irrelevant to the dimensions being assessed. For example, in one assessment center where Koreans were mixed with Americans and Europeans, the instructions for the group discussion specified that each discussant would first present his or her ideas before the general discussion. This was intended to minimize the potential problem that, due to cultural differences in interpersonal communication, the Koreans might be somewhat reticent to participate fully with the other participants.

### Diversity Effects

The effects of race, gender, and age on assessment center ratings have been studied. Thornton and Byham (1982), Hoffman and Thornton (1997), Goldstein et al. (1998), and Lievens and Klimoski (2001) summarized the results of early studies and concluded that there may be subgroup differences in level of assessment ratings and sizes of correlations of assessment scores and criterion measures in some instances but not others. When subgroup differences were present, they tended to be rather small and less than the oft-observed one standard deviation difference between Whites and Blacks observed in cognitive ability test scores. More recent studies have begun to clarify the reasons for differences and to identify more precisely where they exist. For example, Goldstein et al. (1998) found that differences between Whites and Blacks varied by the type of simulation exercise. Differences were greatest for a team preparation exercise (i.e., about .40 standard deviation units) and least for the subordinate exercise (i.e., only .03 standard deviation units). White-Black differences tended to be largest for exercises that tapped cognitive abilities. On the basis of these findings, Goldstein et al. recommended minimizing the cognitive loading of exercises designed to measure dimensions like interpersonal relations. Although most studies have found no systematic differences of men and women in levels of performance in assessment centers or in the predictive validity for men and women, women may score higher than men on some dimensions (Schmitt, 1993; Shore, 1992). Extending an early study by Burroughs, Rollins, and Hopkins (1973), Clapham and Fulford (1997) found that age was inversely related to overall assessment center ratings, and persons 40 years of age and older scored lower than persons under the age 40. The authors speculated that the reasons may be either that the exercises are biased, older assessees actually possessed lesser abilities, or the younger assessees had more and different education compared with older assessees.

An area that has, to our knowledge, not been explored is the potential bias of simulations against individuals with disabilities. In the United States, the Americans with Disabilities Act (ADA; 42 U.S.C. 12101) stipulates that individuals with disabilities who are otherwise qualified for a job must not be discriminated against by the use of personnel assessment techniques. Organizations are obligated to make accommodations in the administration of tests for individuals with documented disabilities. An accommodation might include the alteration of time limits in an in-basket for a person with a reading disability, if it could be established that the specified time limits were not essential for performance on the job. We are aware of no instances where accommodations in the administration of simulations have been requested, no challenges to simulation exercises by disabled individuals, and no research on the effects of accommodations on the effectiveness of simulations. These areas are ripe for research.

Cultural differences also need to be considered in the development and use of simulations and assessment centers. Developers and users should consider cultural issues in the design of exercises materials, implementation of the program, the judgment and evaluation of behavior, and feedback to participants (Brisco, 1997). Given the differences in norms of behavior in the areas of leadership, decision making, and interpersonal communication, users of simulations need to be sensitive to cross-cultural differences in the importance of dimensions for organizational effectiveness, the behaviors that are considered relevant to a given dimension, subtle differences in leadership styles and decision making, and the special skills that are needed for effective work in multicultural and multinational organizations. At the design phase, developers need to consider what types of exercises are appropriate, who will participate in exercise design, and who will serve as assessors. At the implementation phase, the mix of assessees and cultural differences in normative behavior need to be considered. Assessors need to be trained to be sensitive to cultural "biases" they may have. Finally, traditional practices of individual feedback may not be valued highly in certain collectivist cultures (Brisco, 1997). With the increased globalization of business and human resource management practices, more research is needed into the influence of cultural factors on simulation methodology before we can be confident that standardized assessments can be accomplished across cultures.

## Guidelines and Standards

Simulations are one form of psychological test and must comply with all professional and legal regulations governing devices that provide information that has some effect on the employment status of workers. *Standards for Educational and Psychological Tests* (American Educational Research Association et al., 1999) prescribes the types of psychometric evaluations that should be conducted in the development and implementation of tests, and the types of information that should be disseminated to support their use. When simulations are used to make personnel selection decisions, *Prin-*

*ciples for the Validation and Use of Personnel Selection Procedures* (Society for Industrial and Organizational Psychology, 1987) provides guidance on validation procedures. If personnel decisions based on assessments resulting from a simulation cause adverse impact against legally protected groups, *Uniform Guidelines on Employee Selection Procedures* (Equal Employment Opportunity Commission, Department of Labor, & Department of Justice, 1978) comes into play. These guidelines specify the types of evidence one needs to present to demonstrate that the simulation is job related and fair.

The document most relevant for evaluating simulations and assessment centers is *Guidelines and Ethical Considerations for Assessment Center Methods* (International Task Force on Assessment Center Guidelines, 2000). It describes the essential elements of the assessment center method and several important considerations for their use in personnel assessment. These guidelines specify that job analysis should be used to identify the dimensions to be assessed, the simulations should be designed to represent important job requirements and should be thoroughly tested before put in use, assessors should be thoroughly trained and evaluated, and information from different simulations should be integrated in some systematic fashion.

## SUMMARY

Simulations provide a highly versatile means of assessing complex behavioral performance of organizational personnel for a wide variety of purposes. In contrast to paper-and-pencil tests, simulations require the examinee to display overt, complex behaviors that provide unique opportunities to assess dimensions such as decision making, leadership, and interaction skills. Simulations can be built for virtually any type or level of job from entry-level manufacturing worker, salesperson, and customer service representative to consultant, middle manager, and executive. Simulations have been used successfully for selection, promotion, diagnosis of developmental needs, and training. They have also been used for basic research on performance skills and adult development.

Because simulations are usually designed for specific organizations and jobs, users of simulations frequently develop their own exercises. When developing simulations, care must be taken to analyze organizational and job requirements, operationally define the dimensions to be assessed, and build the stimulus material to have the appropriate level of fidelity.

Because assessors play such a critical role in observing and evaluating behavior, they must be thoroughly trained. Training is based on an understanding of the processes of social cognition. It seeks to maximize the benefits of assessing complex behavior and minimize the potential hazards of the social perception process. When observations from more than one simulation are to be combined, as is done in the assessment center method, users may choose between alternative methods of integrating the information, including the traditional method of asking assessors to reach consensus or the statistical method of averaging scores across exercises.

When simulations are used to help make decisions affecting the employment status of workers, users must take special steps to avoid bias against legally protected groups and to comply with applicable professional and legal standards. Research suggests that subgroup differences are substantially smaller in assessments conducted with simulations than are typically present in paper-and-pencil cognitive ability tests.

## REFERENCES

Abelson, R.P. (1981). Psychological status of the script concept. *American Psychologist, 36,* 715–729.

American Educational Research Association, American Psychological Association, and National Council of Measurement in Education. (1999). *Standards for educational and psychological tests.* Washington, DC: American Educational Research Association.

Anastasi, A., & Urbina, S. (1997). *Psychological testing* (7th ed.). Upper Saddle River, NJ: Prentice-Hall.

Arthur, W. Jr., Woehr, D.J., & Maldegan, R. (2000). Convergent and discriminant validity of assessment center dimensions: A conceptual and empirical re-examination of the assessment center construct-related validity paradox. *Journal of Management, 26,* 813–835.

Baker, T.A. (1986). *Multitrait-multimethod analysis of performance ratings using behaviorally anchored and behavioral checklist formats.* Unpublished master's thesis, Old Dominion University, Norfolk, VA.

Bass, B.M. (1950). The leaderless group discussion. *Personnel Psychology, 3,* 465–492.

Bass, B.M. (1954). The leaderless group discussion. *Psychological Bulletin, 51,* 465–492.

Bernardin, H.J., & Beatty, R.W. (1984). *Assessing human behavior at work.* Boston: Kent.

Bernardin, H.J., & Buckley, M.R. (1981). Strategies in rater training. *Academy of Management Review, 6,* 205–212.

Binning, J.F., Adorno, A.J., & Kroek, K. JG. (1997, April). *Validity of behavior checklist and assessor judgmental ratings.* Paper presented at the 12th Annual Conference of the Society for Industrial and Organizational Psychology, St. Louis, MO.

Binning, J.F., Adorno, A.J., & LeBreton, J.M. (1999). *"Sociotechnical" moderators of assessment center criterion-related validity.* Paper presented at the 14th Annual Conference of the Society for Industrial and Organizational Psychology Conference, Atlanta, GA.

Binning, J.F., & Barrett, G.V. (1989). Validity of personnel decisions: An examination of the inferential and evidential bases. *Journal of Applied Psychology, 74,* 478–494.

Binning, J.F., Hesson-McInnis, M.S., DeVille, J.O., & Srinivasagam, N.M. (1998). *Effects of checklist design on the behavioral content of assessment center judgments.* Paper presented at the 13th Annual Conference of the Society for Industrial and Organizational Psychology Conference, Dallas, TX.

Birkeland, S.A., Borman, W.C., & Brannick, M.T. (2001). *Using judgment analysis to investigate assessment center ratings.* Poster session presented at the 16th Annual Conference of the Society for Industrial and Organizational Psychology, San Diego, CA.

Borman, W.C. (1977). Consistency of rating accuracy and rating errors in the judgment of human performance. *Organizational Behavior and Human Performance, 20,* 238–252.

Borman, W.C. (1978). Exploring the upper limits of reliability and validity in job performance ratings. *Journal of Applied Psychology, 63,* 135–144.

Born, M.P., Kolk, N.J., & van der Flier, H. (2000). *A meta-analytic study of assessment center construct validity.* Paper presented at the 15th Annual Conference of the Society for Industrial and Organizational Psychology Conference, New Orleans, LA.

Bray, D.W. (1973). New data from the Management Process [*sic*] Study. *Assessment and Development, 1,* 3.

Bray, D.W., & Grant, D.L. (1966). The assessment center in the measurement of potential for business management. *Psychological Monographs, 80* (17, Whole No. 625), pp. 1–27.

Brisco, D.R. (1997). Assessment centers: Cross-cultural and cross-national issues. *Journal of Social Behavior and Personality, 12,* 261–270.

Burroughs, W.A., Rollins, J.B., & Hopkins, J.J. (1973). The effect of age, department experience, and prior rater experience on performance in assessment center exercises. *Academy of Management Journal, 16,* 335–339.

Bycio, P., Alvares, K.M., & Hahn, J. (1987). Situational specificity in assessment center ratings: A confirmatory factor analysis. *Journal of Applied Psychology, 72,* 463–474.

Byham, W.C. (1970). Assessment center for spotting future managers. *Harvard Business Review, 48,* 150–160, plus appendix.

Campbell, W.J. (1986). *Construct validation of role-playing exercises in an assessment center using BARS and behavioral checklist formats.* Unpublished master's thesis, Old Dominion University, Norfolk, VA.

Campbell, R.J., & Bray, D.W. (1967). Assessment centers: An aid in management selection. *Personnel Administration, 30,* 6–13.

Campbell, J.P., & Fiske, D.W. (1959). Convergent and discriminant validation by the multitrait-multimethod matrix. *Psychological Bulletin, 56,* 81–105.

Cantor, N., & Mischel, W. (1977). Traits as prototypes: Effects on recognition memory. *Journal of Personality and Social Psychology, 35,* 38–48.

Carrick, P., & Williams, R. (1999). Development centres—A review of assumptions. *Human Resource Management Journal, 9,* 77–92.

Cascio, W.F. (1991). *Applied psychology in personnel management* (4th ed.) Englewood Cliffs, NJ: Prentice-Hall.

Center for Creative Leadership. (n.d.). *Center for Creative Leadership Online.* Retrieved September 1, 2001, from http://www.org/products/.

Chan, D. (1996). Criterion and construct validation of an assessment centre. *Journal of Occupational and Organizational Psychology, 69,* 167–181.

Clapham, M.M., & Fulford, M.D. (1997). Age bias in assessment center ratings. *Journal of Managerial Issues, 9,* 373–387.

Conoley, J.C., & Impara, J.C. (1995). *The 12th mental measurements yearbook.* Lincoln, NE: The Buros Institute of Mental Measurements.

Cronbach, L.J. (1970). *Essentials of psychological testing.* New York: Harper & Row.

Dayan, K., Kasten, R., & Fox, S. (2002). Entry-level police candidate assessment center: An efficient tool or a hammer to kill a fly? *Personnel Psychology, 55,* 827–849.

Donahue, L.M., Truxillo, D.M., Cornwell, J.M., & Gerrity, M.J. (1997). Assessment center construct validity and behavioral checklists: Some additional findings. *Journal of Social Behavior and Personality, 12,* 85–108.

Ebbesen, E.B. (1981). Cognitive processes in inferences about a person's personality. In T. Higgins, C. Herman, & M. Zanna (Eds.), *Social cognition: The Ontario symposium* (Vol. 1, pp. 247–276). Hillsdale, NJ: Erlbaum.

Equal Employment Opportunity Commission, Department of Labor, & Department of Justice. (1978, August 25). Uniform guidelines on employee selection procedures. *Federal Register, 43*(166), 38290–38309.

Fishbein, M., & Aijen, I. (1975). *Belief, attitude, intention, and behavior: An introduction to theory and research.* Reading, MA: Addison-Wesley.

Fiske, S.T., & Taylor, S.E. (1984). *Social cognition.* Reading, MA: Addison-Wesley.

Fleenor, J.W. (1996). Constructs and developmental assessment centers: Further troubling empirical findings. *Journal of Business and Psychology, 10,* 319–335.

Frederiksen, N. (1962). Factors in in-basket performance. *Psychological Monographs, 76* (Whole No. 541).

Frederiksen, N., Saunders, D.R., & Wand, B. (1957). The in-basket test. *Psychological Monographs, 71* (9, Whole No. 438).

Fritzsche, B.A., Brannick, M.T., & Hazucha-Fisher, J. (1994). The effects of using behavioral checklists on the predictive and construct validity of assessment center ratings. In J.R. Schneider (Chair), *Important, insufficiently answered questions about as-sessment center validity and utility.* Symposium conducted at the 9th Annual Conference of the Society for Industrial and Organizational Psychology, Nashville, TN.

Gaugler, B.B., Rosenthal, D.B., Thornton, G.C. III, & Bentson, C. (1987). Meta-analysis of assessment center validity. *Personnel Psychology, 40,* 243–259.

Gaugler, B.B., & Thornton, G.C. III. (1989). Number of assessment center dimensions as a determinant of assessor accuracy. *Journal of Applied Psychology, 74,* 611–618.

Gatewood, R., Thornton, G.C. III, & Hennessey, H.W. Jr. (1990). Reliability of exercise ratings in the leaderless group discussion. *Journal of Occupational Psychology, 63,* 331–342.

Goffin, R.D., Rothstein, M.G., & Johnston, N.G. (1996). Personality testing and the assessment center: Incremental validity for managerial selection. *Journal of Applied Psychology, 81,* 746–756.

Goldstein, A.P., & Sorcher, M. (1974). *Changing managerial behavior.* New York: Pergamon Press.

Goldstein, H.A., Yusko, K.P., Braverman, E.P., Smith, D.B., & Chung, B. (1998). The role of cognitive ability in the subgroup differences and incremental validity of assessment center exercises. *Personnel Psychology, 51,* 357–374.

Harris, M.M., Becker, A.S., & Smith, D.E. (1993). Does the assessment center scoring method affect the cross-situational consistency of ratings? *Journal of Applied Psychology, 78,* 675–678.

Harvey, R.J. (1991). Job analysis. In M.D. Dunnette & L.M. Hough (Eds.), *Handbook of industrial & organizational psychology* (Vol. 2, pp. 71–164). Palo Alto, CA: Consulting Psychologists Press.

Hemphill, J., Griffiths, D., & Frederiksen, N. (1962). *Administrative performance and personality: A study of the principal in a simulated elementary school.* New York: Teachers College Bureau of Publications, Columbia.

Hennessy, J., Mabey, B., & Warr, P. (1998). Assessment center procedures: An experimental comparison of traditional, checklist, and coding methods. *International Journal of Selection and Assessment, 6,* 222–231.

Hills, D.A. (1985). Prediction of effectiveness in leaderless group discussions with the Adjective Check List. *Journal of Applied Social Psychology, 15,* 443–447.

Hoffman, C.C., & Thornton, G.C. III (1997). Examining selection utility where competing predictors differ in adverse impact. *Personnel Psychology, 50,* 455–470.

Hollenbeck, J. (1990). The past, present, and future of assessment centers. *The Industrial/Organizational Psychologist, 28*(2), 13–17.

Howard, A. (1997). A reassessment of assessment centers: Challenges for the 21st century. *Journal of Social Behavior and Personality, 12,* 13–52.

Hughes, M., Deaver, P., & Winn, P. (1995, May). *Technological alternatives to traditional assessment centers.* Paper presented at the 23rd International Congress on the Assessment Center Method, Kansas City.

Hunter, J.E., & Hunter, R.F. (1984). Validity and utility of alternative predictors of job performance. *Psychological Bulletin, 96* 72–98.

International Task Force on Assessment Center Guidelines. (2000). Guidelines and ethical considerations for assessment center operations. *Public Personnel Management, 29,* 315–331.

Jones, R.G., & Whitmore, M.D. (1995). Evaluating developmental assessment centers as interventions. *Personnel Psychology, 48,* 377–388.

Joyce, L.W., Thayer, P.W., & Pond, S.B. (1994). Managerial functions: An alternative to traditional assessment center dimensions? *Personnel Psychology, 47,* 109–121.

Keenan, T. (1995). Graduate recruitment in Britain: A survey of selection methods used by organizations. *Journal of Organizational Behavior, 16,* 303–317.

Keyser, D.J., & Sweetland, R.C. (1985). *Test critiques,* Kansas City: MO: Test Corporation of America.

Klimoski, R., & Brickner, M. (1987). Why do assessment centers work? The puzzle of assessment center validity. *Personnel Psychology, 40,* 243–260.

Klimoski, R., & Strickland, W.J. (1977). Assessment centers: valid or merely prescient. *Personnel Psychology, 30,* 353–363.

Kolk, N.J., Born, M.P., & van der Flier, H. (2000). *The transparent assessment center: The effects of revealing dimensions to applicants.* Paper presented at the 15th Annual Conference of the Society for Industrial and Organizational Psychology Conference, New Orleans, LA.

Kudisch, J.D., Avis, J.M., Fallon, J.D., Thibodeaux, H.F., Roberts, F.E., Rollier, T.J., & Rotolo, C.T. (2001). *A survey of assessment center practices in organizations worldwide: Maximizing innovation or business as usual?* Paper presented at the 16th Annual Conference of the Society for Industrial and Organizational Psychology, San Diego, CA.

LeBreton, J.M., Gniatczyk, L.A., & Migetz, D.Z. (1999). *The relationship between behavior checklist ratings and judgmental ratings in an operational assessment center: An Application of structural equation modeling.* Paper presented at the 14th Annual Conference of the Society for Industrial and Organizational Psychology, Atlanta, GA.

Lievens, F. (1998). Factors which improve the construct validity of assessment centers: A review. *International Journal of Selection and Assessment, 6,* 141–152.

Lievens, F. (2001a). Assessors and use of assessment center dimensions: A fresh look at a troubling issue. *Journal of Organizational Behavior, 22,* 203–221.

Lievens, F. (2001b). Assessor training strategies and their effects on accuracy, interrater reliability, and discriminant validity. *Journal of Applied Psychology, 86,* 255–264.

Lievens, F., & Klimoski, R.J. (2001). Understanding the assessment centre process: Where are we now? In C.L. Cooper & I.T. Robertson (Eds.) *International review of industrial and organizational psychology* (Vol. 16, pp. 245–286). New York: Wiley.

Louiselle, K.G. (1986). *Confirmatory factor analysis of two assessment center rating procedures.* Paper presented at the Seventh Annual IO/OB Graduate Student Conference, Minneapolis, MN.

Management & Personnel Systems, Inc. (n.d.). The Unique MPS Business Model. Retrieved August 31, 2001, from http://www.mps-corp.com/.

McCall, M.W., & Lombardo, M.M. (1978). *Looking Glass, Inc.: An organizational simulation* (Tech. Rep. No. 12). Greensboro, NC: Center of Creative Leadership.

McCall, M.W., & Lombardo, M.M. (1982). Using simulation for leadership and management research: Through the Looking Glass. *Management Science, 28,* 533–549.

McEvoy, G.M., & Beatty, R.W. (1989). Assessment centres and subordinate appraisals of managers: A seven-year examination of predictive validity. *Personnel Psychology, 42,* 37–52.

McEvoy, G.M., Beatty, R.W., & Bernardin, H.J. (1987). Unanswered questions in assessment center research. *Journal of Business and Psychology, 2,* 97–111.

Moser, K., Schuler, H., & Funke, U. (1999). The moderating effect of raters' opportunities to observe ratees' job performance on the validity of an assessment centre. *International Journal of Selection and Assessment, 7,* 133–141.

Murphy, K.R., & Byrne, Z. (2000). *Application of structured assessment in the IT workforce.* Commissioned by Workforce Needs in Information Technology Committee, National Research Council.

Murphy, K.R., & Cleveland, J.N. (1991). *Performance appraisal: An organizational perspective.* Boston, MA: Allyn & Bacon.

Murphy, K.R., & Shiarella, A.H. (1997). Implications of the multidimensional nature of job performance for the validity of selection test: Multivariate frameworks for studying test validity. *Personnel Psychology, 50,* 823–854.

Neidig, R.D., Martin, J.C., & Yates, R.E. (1978). *The FBI's Management Aptitude Program Assessment Center: Research report no. 1* (YM78–3). Washington, DC: Applied Psychology Section, Personnel Research and Development Center, U.S. Civil Service Commission.

Nisbett, R., & Ross, L. (1980). *Human inference strategies and shortcomings of social judgment.* Englewood Cliffs: NJ: Prentice Hall.

Posner, M.I. (1982). Cumulative development of attentional theory. *American Psychologist, 37,* 168–179.

Pulakos, E.D. (1986). The development of training programs to increase accuracy with different rating tasks. *Organizational Behavior and Human Decision Processes, 38,* 76–91.

Pynes, J.E., & Bernardin, H.J., (1989). Predictive validity of an entry-level police officer assessment center. *Journal of Applied Psychology, 74,* 831–833.

Ralphs, L., & Stephen, E. (1986, October). HRD in the Fortune 500. *Training and Development Journal, 40,* 69–76.

Reilly, R.R., Henry, S., & Smither, J.W. (1990). An examination of the effects of using behavior checklists on the construct validity of assessment center dimensions. *Personnel Psychology, 43,* 71–84.

Robie, C., Osburn, H.G., Morris, M.A., Etchegaray, J.M., & Adams, K.A. (2000). Effects of the rating process on the construct validity of assessment center dimension evaluations. *Human Performance, 13,* 355–370.

Robertson, I.T., Gratton, L., & Sharpley, D. (1987). The psychometric properties and design of managerial assessment centres: Dimensions into exercises won't go. *Journal of Occupational Psychology, 60,* 187–195.

Rotenberry, P.F., Barrett, G.V., & Doverspike, D. (1999, May). *Determination of systematic bias for an objectively scored in-basket assessment.* Paper presented at the 14th Annual Conference of the Society of Industrial and Organizational Psychology, Atlanta, GA.

Rumelhart, D.E., & Ortony, A. (1977). The representation of knowledge in memory. In R.C. Anderson, R.J. Spiro, & W.E. Montague (Eds.), *Schooling and the acquisition of knowledge* (pp. 99–136). Hillsdale, NJ: Erlbaum.

Russell, P., & Byham, W.C. (1980). *Reliability and validity of assessment in a small manufacturing company.* Pittsburgh: Development Dimensions International.

Russell, C.J., & Domm, D.R. (1995). Two field tests of an explanation of assessment centre validity. *Journal of Occupational and Organizational Psychology, 68,* 25–47.

Ryan, A.M., Daum, D., Bauman, T., Grisez, M., Mattimore, K., Nalodka, T., & McCormick, S. (1995). Direct, indirect, and controlled observation and rating accuracy. *Journal of Applied Psychology, 80,* 664–670.

Sackett, P.R. (1997). Assessment centers and content validity: Some neglected issues. *Personnel Psychology, 40,* 13–25.

Sackett, P.R., & Dreher, G.F. (1982). Constructs and assessment center dimensions: Some troubling empirical findings. *Journal of Applied Psychology, 67,* 401–410.

Sackett, P.R., & Hakel, M.D. (1979). Temporal stability and individual differences in using assessment information to form overall ratings. *Organization Behavior and Human Performance, 23,* 123–137.

Sackett, P.R., & Harris, M.M. (1988). A further examination of the constructs underlying assessment center ratings. *Journal of Business and Psychology, 3,* 214–229.

Sackett, P.R., & Tuzinski, K. (2001). *The role of dimensions and exercises in assessment center judgments.* Paper presented at the 16th Annual Conference of the Society for Industrial and Organizational Psychology, San Diego, CA.

Schippmann, J.S., Prien, E.P., & Katz, J.A. (1990). Reliability and validity of in-basket performance measures. *Personnel Psychology, 43,* 837–859.

Schippmann, J.S., Ash, R.A., Battista, M., Carr, L., Eyde, L.D., Hesketh, B., Kehoe, J., Pearman, K., Prien, E.P., & Sanchez, J.I. (2000). The practice of competency modeling. *Personnel Psychology, 53,* 703–740.

Schleicher, D.J., & Day, D.V. (1998). A cognitive evaluation of frame-of-reference rater training: Content and process issues. *Organizational Behavior and Human Decision Processes, 73,* 76–102.

Schleicher, D.J., Day, D.V., Mayes, B.T., & Riggio, R.E. (2002). A new frame of reference training: Enhancing the construct validity of assessment centers. *Journal of Applied Psychology, 87,* 735–746.

Schmidt, F.L., & Hunter, J.E. (1998). The validity and utility of selection methods in personnel psychology: Practical and theoretical implications of 85 years of research findings. *Psychological Bulletin, 124,* 262–274.

Schmitt, N. (1993). Group composition, gender, and race effects on assessment center ratings. In H. Schuler, J.L. Farr, & M. Smith (Eds.), *Personnel selection and assessment* (pp. 315–332). Hillsdale, NJ: Erlbaum.

Schneider, J.R., & Schmitt, N. (1992). An exercise design approach to understanding assessment center dimension and exercise constructs. *Journal of Applied Psychology, 77,* 32–41.

Shore, T.H. (1992). Subtle gender bias in the assessment of managerial potential. *Sex Roles, 27,* 499–515.

Shore, T.H., Tashchian, A., & Adams, J.S. (1997). The role of gender in a developmental assessment center. *Journal of Social Behavior and Personality, 12,* 191–204.

Shore, T.H., Thornton, G.C. III, & Shore, L.M. (1990). Construct validity of two categories of assessment center dimension ratings. *Personnel Psychology, 43,* 101–116.

Silverman, W.H., Dalessio, A., Woods, S.B., & Johnson, R.L. (1986). Influence of assessment center methods on assessor ratings. *Personnel Psychology, 39,* 565–578.

Society for Industrial and Organizational Psychology. (1987). *Principles for the validation and use of personnel selection procedures* (3rd ed). College Park, MD: Author.

Spychalski, A.C., Quiñones, M.A., Gaugler, B.B., and Pohley, K. (1997). A survey of assessment center practices in organizations in the United States. *Personnel Psychology, 50,* 71–90.

Srull, T.K., & Wyer, R.S. (1989). Person memory and judgment. *Psychological Review, 96,* 58–83.

Streufert, S., Pogash, R., & Piasecki, M. (1988). Simulation-based assessment of managerial competence: Reliability and validity. *Personnel Psychology, 41,* 537–557.

Streufert, S., & Swezey, R.W. (1986). *Complexity, managers, and organizations.* New York: Academic Press.

Thornton, G.C. (1992). *Assessment centers in human resource management.* Reading, MA: Addison-Wesley.

Thornton, G.C. III. (2002, April 12–14). *Alternate approaches to examining assessment center construct validity.* Symposium presented at the 14th Annual Meeting of the Society for Industrial and Organizational Psychology, Toronto, Ontario, Canada.

Thornton, G.C. III, & Byham, W.C. (1982). *Assessment centers and managerial performance.* New York: Academic Press.

Thornton, G.C. III, & Cleveland, J.N. (1990). Developing managerial talent through simulation. *American Psychologist, 45,* 190–199.

Thornton, G.C. III, Kaman, V., Layer, S., & Larsh, S. (1995, May). *Effectiveness of two forms of assessment center feedback: Attribute feedback and task feedback.* Paper presented at the 23rd International Congress on the Assessment Center Method, Kansas City.

Thornton, G.C. III, & Mueller-Hanson, R.A. (in press). *Developing simulation exercises.* Mahwah, NJ: Erlbaum.

Thornton, G.C. III, Tziner, A., Dahan, M., Clevenger, J.P, & Meir, E. (1997). Construct validity of assessment center judgments: Analyses of the behavioral reporting method. *Journal of social behavior and personality, 12*(5), 261–270.

Walsh, J.P., Weinberg, R.M., & Fairfield, M.L. (1987). The effects of gender on assessment center evaluations. *Journal of Occupational Psychology, 60,* 305–309.

Watson, W.E., & Behnke, R.R. (1990). Group identification, independence, and self-monitoring characteristics as predictors of leaderless group discussion performance. *Journal of Applied Social Psychology, 51,* 1423–1431.

Wiersma, U., & Latham, G.P. (1986). The practicality of behavioral observation scales, behavioral expectation scales, and trait scales. *Personnel Psychology, 39,* 619–628.

Woehr, D.J. (1994). Understanding frame-of-reference training: The impact of training on the recall of performance information. *Journal of Applied Psychology, 79,* 525–534.

Zedeck, S. (1986). A process analysis of the assessment center method. *Research in Organizational Behavior, 8,* 259–296.

CHAPTER 19

# Work Samples, Performance Tests, and Competency Testing

DONALD M. TRUXILLO, LISA M. DONAHUE, AND DANIEL KUANG

## INTRODUCTION

For years, the holy grail for personnel selection researchers has been a predictor with high validity, low adverse impact, and high face validity to applicants. To a large extent, work sample and performance tests fit this description. Despite their potential drawbacks regarding issues such as development and scoring costs, they hold great potential for many selection contexts.

This chapter explores the issues involved in using work sample tests in the prediction of job performance. First, we begin by defining the range of instruments that can be classified as work samples, performance tests, or competency tests, including a discussion of the theory underlying these tests' validity. Next, we review the validity, adverse impact, and applicant reactions evidence regarding these tests. Fi-

nally, we provide a generic description of the development of work sample tests, including job analysis, item and exercise development, and response format and scoring issues. We also discuss the practical issues associated with the development and use of work samples and performance tests.

## What Is Meant by Work Samples, Performance Tests, and Competency Tests?

A range of tests fall into the category of work samples, performance tests, and competency tests. (See Table 19.1.) The similarity among these predictors stems from the degree to which they directly sample the knowledge, skills, and abilities (KSAs) needed to perform essential job tasks as indicted by a job analysis. This dimension has been referred to as *psychological fidelity* (Binning & Barrett, 1989; Goldstein,

**TABLE 19.1  Overview of Work Sample, Simulation, and Competency Test Formats**

| General Category | Description | Specific Types | Examples in Literature | Stimulus Format | Response Format | Psychometric and Practical | |
|---|---|---|---|---|---|---|---|
| | | | | | | Advantages | Disadvantages |
| **High Fidelity** "Authentic" Performance Assessments | "Tests" that are virtually identical to the job itself | Job tryouts<br><br>Probationary assessment<br><br>Records and portfolios | | Actual job materials and equipment | Work processes or products | Allows for the assessment of more aspects of job than lower-fidelity tests<br><br>Relatively little involved in the construction of test/assessment | Applicant must be hired for an assessment to be made |
| Work Samples and Simulations | Tests that are standardized samples of actual work-related problems that applicants must solve, as if they were on the job | Cockpit simulations<br><br>Performance tests<br><br>Minicourses and trainability tests<br><br>Physical abilities tests<br><br>Assessment center exercises (e.g., leaderless group discussions) | U.S. Army Skill Qualification Tests (Osborn, Campbell, & Ford, 1976)<br><br>AT&T Trainability Tests (Reilly & Israelski, 1988)<br><br>AT&T Management Assessment Center (Bray, Campbell, & Grant, 1974) | Actual job materials and equipment | Work processes or products | Better predictors of job performance than lower-fidelity tests | Expensive to develop and administer<br><br>Gains in validity may not offset costs |
| Low-Fidelity Simulations | Tests that are standardized samples of actual work-related problems that applicants must solve by describing how they would handle them | "Talk through" interviews | Structured Behavioral Interview (Motowidlo et al., 1992) | Interview | Oral<br><br>———<br>Written | Flexible—can be developed for a variety of jobs<br><br>Can assess more complex skills than lower-fidelity tests<br><br>Moderate levels of criterion-related validity<br><br>Response fidelity higher with oral response format<br><br>Scoring less complicated with written response format | Response fidelity lower with written response format<br><br>Scoring more complicated with oral response format |

346

| Fidelity | Description | Examples | Format | Response format | Advantages | Disadvantages |
|---|---|---|---|---|---|---|
| | | Video-based simulation exercises  Video situational judgment tests | Video | Oral | Can assess more complex skills than lower-fidelity tests  Cost-effective administration  Response fidelity higher with oral response format | Less known about psychometric characteristics  More expensive to develop than most higher-fidelity tests  Response fidelity lower with written response format |
| | | Video-based Situational Tests (Weekley & Jones, 1997)  B-PAD (Corey et al., 1995) | | Written (multiple-choice) | Scoring less complicated with written response format | Scoring more complicated with oral response format |
| Low Fidelity | Tests that describe abstracted versions of work-related problems that the applicants must solve by describing how they would deal with them | Situational judgment tests  Computerized Tests  Situational interviews | Written | Written (multiple-choice) | Flexible—can be developed for a variety of jobs  Acceptable levels of criterion-related validity  Cost-effective administration | Response fidelity lower with written response format  Scoring more complicated with oral response format |
| | | Low-Fidelity Simulation (Motowidlo, Dunnette, & Carter, 1990)  Teamwork KSA Test (Stevens & Campion, 1999) | | Oral | Response fidelity higher with oral response format  Scoring less complicated with written response format | |
| | | Situational Interview (Latham, Saari, Pursell, & Campion, 1980) | Oral | Written (multiple-choice) | Less expensive to develop than higher-fidelity simulations  Response fidelity higher with oral response format | |
| | | | | Oral | Scoring less complicated with written response format | |

Zedeck, & Schneider, 1993) and is central to the concept of content validity. Accordingly, most of the tests described in this chapter share a high degree of content validity; that is, they are developed by carefully sampling the job through a job analysis and getting input from subject matter experts (SMEs). By the same token, most tend to have a high degree of face validity.

We argue that where these tests differ, however, is the degree to which they display *physical fidelity,* or the extent to which a test itself involves the actual tasks performed on the job. Clearly, by definition these tests all reflect job tasks, and as we will see later, task information is essential for their development. However, Goldstein et al. (1993) held that physical fidelity is less important to content validity than psychological fidelity. Several authors (e.g., Callinan & Robertson, 2000; Felker & Rose, 1997; Motowidlo, Hanson, & Crafts, 1997) have classified these tests in a similar manner.

The first group of tests is those that are physically just like (or almost like) the job. This would include true job tryouts, such as the working tests and probationary periods frequently used in the public sector (Felker & Rose, 1997; Motowidlo et al., 1997). Such "tests" are just like the job except that applicants have not been given permanent status in the organization (Felker & Rose, 1997). And such a "test" truly samples the job in question, except to the extent that it does not capture the employee's true motivation; that is, employees typically are aware that they are in a probationary period.

The second group of tests includes those that closely sample the tasks performed on the job, such as the physical ability tests often used for selecting into public safety positions (e.g., Hoover, 1992; Hughes, Ratliff, Purswell, & Hadwiger, 1989). From the applicant's perspective, these tests closely resemble what the job entails and would be classified more as true "samples" (rather than as "signs") of job performance (Wernimont & Campbell, 1968). To some degree, assessment center exercises (covered in Chapter 18) also fall into this category.

The third, broad group of tests includes those that closely resemble the job in that they present applicants with a work-related situation, for example, through a video. But rather than applicants showing what they would do, applicants *describe* what they would do in a given situation. Such a description could be open-ended or could involve applicants choosing from among a range of options (e.g., Dalessio, 1994; Smiderle, Perry, & Cronshaw, 1994; Weekley & Jones, 1997). Or applicants could receive a written description of what a job involves, or a job situation could be described to them. They would then describe what they would do in that situation. Certain types of structured interviews fall into this category (Hedge & Teachout, 1992; Motowidlo et al., 1997),

as do tests that are sometimes referred to as "low-fidelity simulations" (e.g., Motowidlo, Dunnette, & Carter, 1990; Motowidlo et al., 1997). In addition, most competency tests typically used for licensure and certification fall into this category.

## What Underlies the Validity of These Tests?

Several suggestions have been made as to why work sample tests are effective predictors of job performance. Perhaps the most simple explanation is that provided by Wernimont and Campbell (1968), such that "samples" rather than "signs" of job performance will be more likely to show the strongest relationship with the criterion space. Asher and Sciarrino (1974) made similar arguments, noting that such tests represent a high degree of point-to-point correspondence between the predictor and the criterion spaces.

Callinan and Robertson (2000) noted that the validity of work samples is not clearly understood. Depending on the type of work sample test in question, cognitive ability appears to underlie the validity of these tests, at least to some extent. However, in their meta-analysis, Schmidt and Hunter (1998) found that work samples exhibit incremental validity over general mental ability. For this reason, Callinan and Robertson (2000) noted that many work samples appear to tap job performance dimensions unrelated to cognitive ability. Accordingly, some researchers (e.g., Callinan & Robertson; McDaniel, Morgeson, Finnegan, Campion, & Braverman, 2001) have also suggested the relationship between tests that simulate the work environment and measures of tacit knowledge, or the know-how that is acquired without explicit instruction or explanation (e.g., Sternberg, Wagner, & Okagaki, 1993). In addition, they have suggested that work samples and simulations can assess the interaction of individual skills and aptitudes in a setting simulating the job, something that is missing when assessing skills individually and later combining them into a statistical composite. Finally, the positive perceptions many applicants have of these tests due to their high face validity could affect test-taking motivation and hence increase validity; this has been suggested by models of applicant reactions (e.g., Gilliland, 1993).

## VALIDITY EVIDENCE

Overall, the validity of both high- and low-fidelity simulations is impressive. Narrative and meta-analytic reviews have consistently identified high-fidelity performance tests as strong predictors of job performance and trainability (e.g., Asher &

Sciarrino, 1974; Cascio & Phillips, 1979; Hunter & Hunter, 1984; Robertson & Downs, 1989; Robertson & Kandola, 1982; Schmitt, Gooding, Noe, & Kirsch, 1984). For example, Schmidt and Hunter (1998) found in their meta-analysis that work sample tests ($\rho = 0.54$) are slightly better predictors of job performance than cognitive ability tests ($\rho = 0.51$). Meta-analysis of work sample tests as predictors of trainability ($\rho = 0.41$; Robertson & Downs, 1989) indicates that it is second only to cognitive ability tests ($\rho = 0.56$; Schmidt & Hunter, 1998). Similarly, job knowledge tests ($\rho = 0.48$) and assessment centers ($\rho = 0.37$) are also valid predictors of job performance (Schmidt & Hunter, 1998). Recently, a meta-analysis of the paper-and-pencil situational judgment test (SJT), a low-fidelity work sample test, by McDaniel et al. (2001) reported a validity of 0.34. This meta-analysis also found higher validity for SJTs that are based on a job analysis ($\rho = .38$) than for those that are not ($\rho = .29$).

Because work sample testing is a measurement *method,* rather than a measure of a specific *construct* (such as the case with cognitive ability tests), it is important to understand the performance of its many variants beyond that of a single validity coefficient as reported in meta-analyses. Specifically, simulation test media vary in (1) the test stimulus and (2) response format—both of which vary in fidelity. The test stimulus may vary from low fidelity (e.g., reading passage of a SJT) to high fidelity (e.g., hands-on work sample problem). Similarly, the response format may vary from low fidelity (e.g., multiple-choice paper-and-pencil response) to high fidelity (e.g., hands-on work sample). Funke and Schuler (1998) varied combinations of test stimulus fidelity and response format fidelity of an SJT and examined the respective effects on test validity. Specifically, the test stimuli were either low fidelity (video) or high fidelity (oral), and the response format was either low fidelity (multiple-choice paper-and-pencil) or high fidelity (open-ended paper-and-pencil). Regardless of the test stimulus's level of fidelity—video or oral—the higher fidelity open-ended response format resulted in higher validity (Funke & Schuler, 1998). It is important to keep differences in test content, stimulus formats, and response formats in mind when interpreting the results reported in this chapter.

There has been a great deal of research on simulations, and Table 19.2 presents a representative, but noncomprehensive summary of published research on work samples and simulations. We describe this research in the following sections.

## High-Fidelity, Hands-On Work Samples

As indicated by review and meta-analysis research (e.g., Hunter & Hunter, 1984; Robertson & Kandola, 1982; Schmitt et al., 1984), high-fidelity work samples exhibit high validity

(e.g., $\rho = 0.54$; Hunter & Hunter, 1984). As a specific example, Mount, Muchinsky, and Hanser (1977) applied a work sample to the prediction of visual-spatial and mechanical ability. Participants were shown a diagram of a model and asked to assemble a replica using parts from an erector set. The hands-on work sample exhibited higher validity ($r = .78$) than the paper-and-pencil tests (Wonderlic Personnel Test or Bennett Test of Mechanical Comprehension; $r = .55$ and .56; Mount et al., 1977).

## Multimedia Simulations

With advances in technology, the movement toward computerized multimedia-based work sample tests is a reality. Born, Van der Maesen de Sombreff, and Van der Zee (2001) developed and validated a computerized multimedia-based SJT of social intelligence. Using conflict resolution as the performance criterion, Olson-Buchanan et al. (1998) developed and validated a computerized multimedia-based SJT. Because of the interactive and branching nature of the multimedia-based SJT, the sequence of test questions is not necessarily the same for all test takers. For this reason, the validity coefficient for overall performance was estimated through several methods ($r = .03$, *ns;* $r = .13–.20$, $p < 0.05$). Schmitt and Mills (2001) applied multimedia technology to simulate the position of service representative. The simulation assessed working with written material, oral communication, solving problems, and writing skills. Overall, the multimedia simulation was found to be a significant predictor ($r = .32$; $r = .36$ corrected for range restriction) of service representative performance.

## Video Simulations

Moving an SJT from a multimedia format into the video-based medium decreases the test's fidelity, but the validity remains comparable. Weekley and Jones (1997) examined a video-based SJT with a paper-and-pencil-based multiple-choice response format for hourly service employees at a discount retailer. The validity was .22–.24 (mid-0.30s when corrected for criterion unreliability). Dalessio (1994) applied a video-based SJT with multiple-choice response format toward the prediction of turnover rates among insurance salespeople. The video-based SJT was significantly associated with turnover ($r = .17$, corrected correlation; Dalessio, 1994). Similarly, a video-based SJT with multiple-choice response format—Metro Seattle Video Test (MSVT)—has been developed for transit operators. Smiderle et al. (1994) examined the validity of the MSVT on a sample of transit employees

TABLE 19.2 A Noncomprehensive List of Work Sample and Simulation Research

| Study | Format | Skills Assessed | Job/Sample | Validity | Adverse Impact |
|---|---|---|---|---|---|
| *High-Fidelity Hands-on Work Samples* | | | | | |
| Arvey et al. (1990) | Work sample | • Job content (reading and referencing tables) | Applicant for a county financial worker position | | • AA < W |
| Cascio & Phillips (1979) | Work sample | • 11 motor skills tests (e.g., water equipment mechanic, carpenter, mason, etc.) • 10 verbal-type test (e.g., library assistant, programmer/analyst, parking meter checker, etc.) | Public sector applicants (e.g., plumbing, library assisting, electrical, masonry, etc.) | | • No adverse impact in any of the 21 performance tests |
| Mount et al. (1977) | Work sample vs. cognitive ability | Assembling models according to diagram (Work Sample) vs. Mechanical Comprehension and Wonderlic (Cognitive) | Students | Concurrent Validity (criteria: more complicated model assembling exercise) • Work Sample ($r = 0.78$) • Mechanical ($r = 0.55$, *ns*) • Cognitive ($r = 0.56$, *ns*) Predictive Validity • Work Sample ($r = 0.67$) • Mechanical ($r = 0.62$) • Cognitive ($r = 0.48$, *ns*) | |
| Robertson & Downs (1989) | Meta-analysis of work sample | Trainability | | Training Performance ($r = 0.41$), ($r = 0.24$; 1 yr. later) Job Performance ($r = 0.24$) | |
| Schmidt et al. (1977) | Work sample vs. paper and pencil | Job content (metal trades skills) vs. Achievement (paper) | Metal trade apprentices | | • Work Sample (*SD* = 0.81) • Achievement (*SD* = 1.44) |
| *Multimedia Simulations* | | | | | |
| Olson-Buchanan et al., (1998) | Interactive multimedia | Conflict resolution | 6 samples of supervisors and managers from: • telecom. co. • university • printing co. • hospital | Supervisor ratings of conflict resolution ability • $r = 0.14$–$0.26$ Supervisor overall rating • $r = 0.03$, ns; and • $r = 0.13$–$0.20$ | No adverse impact—no significant gender or ethnic differences |
| Schmitt & Mills (2001) | Computerized simulation exercise vs. traditional paper-and-pencil-based test battery | Service representative skills (e.g., working with written material, oral communication, interpersonal skills, problem solving, writing skills, etc.) | Job applicants for a service representative position | Observers rated candidates on 8 performance areas, e.g., oral communication, interpersonal skills, problem solving, organizational skills, etc. • Simulation $r = 0.32$ ($0.36^A$) • Traditional paper-and-pencil test battery $r = 0.29$ ($0.46^A$) | • Simulation (*SD* = 0.30) • Traditional (*SD* = 0.61) |

*Video Simulations*

| Study | Instrument | Construct measured | Sample | Criterion-related validity | Subgroup differences / Adverse impact |
|---|---|---|---|---|---|
| Chan & Schmitt (1997) | Video-based SJT vs. Paper-and-pencil SJT | SJT for work habits and interpersonal skills | Student sample | | • Video-based ($SD = 1.19$ corrected for unreliability) • Paper-based ($SD = 0.28$ corrected for unreliability) |
| Dalessio (1994) | Video-based stimulus/ Multiple-choice response | SJT of sales situations | Insurance Sales Agents | • Turnover ($r = 0.17$, corrected correlation) | |
| Funke & Schuler (1998) | Video-based orally presented SJT, and interview | SJT for social competency | • Students | Performance criteria was a participant's score in a high-fidelity role-play situation; Video presentation of stimulus • Multiple-choice response ($r = .17$, *ns*) • Open-ended paper-and-pencil response ($r = 0.36$); Orally presented stimulus • Multiple-choice response ($r = 0.13$, *ns*) • Open-ended paper-and-pencil response ($r = 0.37$) • Open-ended oral response—situational interview ($r = .59$) | |
| Pulakos & Schmitt (1996) | Paper-and-pencil job sample; Video-based job sample; Paper-and-pencil SJT | Paper: reading a job sample and writing persuasive essay; Video: writing reports of video; Paper-SJT: practical intelligence (e.g., problem solving, planning, organizing, adapt, etc.) | Public transit operators | Performance criteria, "Can do" • Video-job sample ($r = 0.29^A$) • Paper-job sample ($r = 0.38^A$) • Paper-situational ($r = 0.38^A$); Motivational Criteria, "Will do" • Video-job sample ($r = 0.04$) • Paper-job sample ($r = 0.05$) • Paper-situational ($r = 0.25^A$) | African American *vs.* White • Video-job sample ($SD = 0.45$) • Paper-job sample ($SD = 0.91$) • Paper-situational ($SD = 0.41$) • Hispanic *vs.* White • Video-job sample ($SD = 0.37$) • Paper-job sample ($SD = .52$) • Paper-situational ($SD = .02$) |
| Smiderle et al. (1994) | Video-based stimulus/ Multiple-choice response | SJT of interpersonal skills | Public transit operators | • Complaints ($r = -0.12$) • Commendations ($r = 0.03$, *ns*) | • No significant (AA & W) and gender differences |
| Weekley & Jones (1997) | Video-based stimulus/ Multiple-choice response | Friendliness, teamwork, diplomacy, etc. | Study 1: hourly service worker at a discount retailer; Study 2: caregiver at a nursing home | Supervisor ratings • $R$ ($0.22–0.33$) | Study 1 • AA: $SD = 0.61$; Study 2 • Race by method interaction in predicting performance not significant |

*(continued)*

**TABLE 19.2** *Continued*

| Study | Format | Skills Assessed | Job/Sample | Validity | Adverse Impact |
|---|---|---|---|---|---|
| *Interview-Based Tests* | | | | | |
| Funke & Schuler (1998) | (see Video Simulations) | | | | |
| Hedge & Teachout (1992) | Interview-based (job content) vs. Work Sample | Air Force related skills (e.g., mechanical, administrative, avionic communication, etc.) | Job incumbents in their first enlistment with the Air Force | Performance criteria (noninterpersonal) were composed of supervisors, peer, and self-ratings <br>• Interview ($r = 0.20$–$0.25$) <br>• Hands-on ($r = 0.25$–$0.31$) <br>Interpersonal criteria <br>• Interview ($r = 0.02$–$0.14$) <br>• Hands-on ($r = 0.03$–$0.14$) | |
| *Paper-and-Pencil Simulations* | | | | | |
| Clevenger et al. (2001) | Paper-and-pencil-based SJT | e.g., ability to plan, prioritize, organize, maintain positive image, evaluate information, etc. | Federal investigative officers, customer service personnel, engineers in manufacturing | • Supervisor ratings ($r = 0.18$–$0.27$) | • AA: $SD = 0.37$ <br>• HS: $SD = 0.01$ |
| Hattrup & Schmitt (1990) | Paper and pencil (job content) vs. Aptitude | Job content (table reading, technical reading, industrial measurement, following instruction, eye-hand coordination) | Journey-level apprentice | • Job content ($r = 0.55^A$) <br>• Aptitude ($r = 0.49$–$0.50^A$) | Predictive Validity <br>• Job content (HS & AA < W, i.e., adverse impact) <br>• Aptitude (HS & AA > W, i.e., no adverse impact) |
| Motowidlo et al. (1997) | Paper and pencil SJT | General management performance (problem solving and interpersonal skills) | Telecom. Employees recently hired and promoted into management and job applicants | Performance Criteria <br>• Interpersonal ($r = 0.35$) <br>• Problem-Solving ($r = 0.28$) <br>• Communication ($r = 0.37$) <br>• Overall Effectiveness ($r = .30$) | • Subgroup differences very small—not significant |
| Pulakos & Schmitt (1996) | (see Video Simulation) | | | | |
| Stevens & Campion (1999) | Paper and pencil SJT | Teamwork situations | Pulp-mill and cardboard-box plant employees | • Teamwork ($r = 0.21$–$0.44$) <br>• Taskwork ($r = 0.25$–$0.56$) <br>• Overall ($r = 0.23$–$0.52$) | |
| Weekley & Jones (1999) | Paper and pencil SJT | Customer service interactions, coworker and loss prevention situations | Retail | Supervisor ratings (e.g., customer service, dependability/punctuality, quality of work) <br>• ($r = 0.16$–$0.23$) | W vs. AA ($ES = 0.52$–$0.85$) <br>W vs. H ($ES = 0.23$–$0.36$) <br>Male vs. Female ($ES = .19$–$.31$) |

*Physical Ability Tests*

| Blakley et al. (1994) | Physical ability | Isometric Strength | Law enforcement | Supervisor performance rating of physical ability | Overall Physical Ability Score |
|---|---|---|---|---|---|
| | | Grip strength | Firefighter | • Grip ($r = 0.17$; $r = 0.20^A$) | • Law Enforcement |
| | | Arm lift | Gas Service | • Arm ($r = 0.27$; $r = 0.32^A$) | No Significant Difference |
| | | Shoulder lift | Pipeline Service | • Shoulder ($r = 0.24$; $r = 0.28^A$) | • Firefighter |
| | | Torso lift | Pipefitter | • Torso ($r = 0.19$; $r = 0.22^A$) | (W & AA > HS) |
| | | | Utility worker | • Composite ($r = 0.28$; | • Gas Service |
| | | | Utility line repair | $r = 0.32^A$) | (Male > Female) |
| | | | | | (W & AA > H) |
| | | | | | • Pipeline Service |
| | | | | | (Male > Female) |
| | | | | | • Pipefitter |
| | | | | | (Age Difference) |
| | | | | | • Utility Worker |
| | | | | | (W > HS, AA, NA) |
| | | | | | (Age Difference) |
| | | | | | • Utility Line Repair |
| | | | | | No Significant Difference |

*Note.* SJT = situational judgment test, W = Whites, HS = Hispanics, AA = African Americans, NA = Native American, *SD* = Standard Deviation difference between subgroups with Whites as the comparison group, [A]Corrected for Range Restriction. All statistics are significant ($p < 0.05$) unless indicated differently, Blank Validity or Adverse Impact cells indicate that the study did not assess it.

353

and found that the measure significantly predicted customer complaints ($r = -.12$), but not commendations. In a meta-analysis of 12 video-based tests, the corrected validity coefficient for video-based SJT was found to be .56 (Salgado & Lado, 2000). Recently, Swander (2001) directly compared the validity of paper-and-pencil-based SJT versus video-based SJT and found that only the video-based SJT was significantly related to performance ($r = .47$); the paper-and-pencil based SJT was not ($r = .18$, ns).

The validity of video-based SJTs may be moderated by the open-endedness of the response format. Funke and Schuler (1998) gave participants the same video SJT stimulus, but one group responded in a multiple-choice format while the other group responded in an open-ended written format. The results suggest that the non-open-ended response format (multiple-choice) showed lower validity ($r = .17$, ns) than the open-ended response format ($r = .36$).

In addition to the SJT paradigm, the video-based medium has been applied to other measurement contexts. Pulakos and Schmitt (1996) presented a three-minute video of activities that employees are required to observe and then report on in writing. Correcting for range restriction, the validity of this video simulation was .29.

### Interview-Based Tests

As discussed earlier, the traditional interview lends itself to the SJT format (Latham & Saari, 1984; Latham, Saari, Pursell, & Campion, 1980). Interview-based SJTs are structured interviews, and meta-analysis has indicated that the validity of structured interviews comes close to that of cognitive ability measures ($\rho = .51$; McDaniel, Whetzel, Schmidt, & Mauer, 1994). Validity coefficients for the situational interview have ranged from $-.02$ to .46 (Latham & Saari, 1984; Latham et al., 1980; Pulakos & Schmitt, 1995). The validity of the interview-based SJT has been found to be moderated by the degree of open-endedness of the response format. Funke and Schuler (1998) orally presented SJT items to participants but varied the degree of open-endedness of the response formats. The results suggest that validity increased as a function of open-endedness: multiple-choice response ($r = .13$, not significant); open-ended written response ($r = .37$); and open-ended oral response ($r = .59$; Funke & Schuler, 1998).

The interview-based medium has also been used to measure job knowledge. Hedge and Teachout (1992) developed a *Walk Through Performance Test* (WTPT) where applicants are required to verbally describe the steps involved in completing a task. The validity of WTPT ($r = .20-.25$) was comparable to the hands-on work sample measure ($r =$ .25–.31) used in the study. Because the interview-based measure is based on an oral-verbal medium, it was a concern that the measure may be tapping too much of the verbal ability construct. As a result, these authors assessed verbal ability, and it was not found to moderate differences between the work sample and the interview-based measure of job knowledge. As a supplement or a stand-alone, the interview-based measure of job knowledge was concluded to add considerable value to the selection system.

### Paper-and-Pencil Simulations

At the lower end of the fidelity continuum is the paper-and-pencil test format where both the stimulus and response formats are paper and pencil based. Hattrup and Schmitt (1990) compared four traditional aptitude measures against five pencil-and-paper-based measures of job content. The paper-and-pencil-based performance measures ($r = .55$, correcting for range restriction) were found to be more valid than the aptitude measures ($r = .49-.50$, correcting for range restriction). Studies of paper-and-pencil-based SJTs with a multiple-choice response format have reported validities of $.18-.38$ (Clevenger, Pereira, Wiechmann, Schmitt, & Harvey, 2001; Motowidlo et al., 1990; Pulakos & Schmitt, 1996; Weekley & Jones, 1999). Specifically, the SJT is significantly related to interpersonal effectiveness, problem solving, and communication effectiveness ($r = .35$; Motowidlo et al., 1990). For example, a paper-and-pencil-based SJT was found to be a significant predictor of customer service, dependability/ punctuality, and quantity and quality of work among retail employees ($r = .16-.23$; Weekley & Jones, 1999). Paper-and-pencil-based SJTs have also been developed to predict teamwork performance ($r = .21-44$), taskwork performance ($r = .25-.56$), and overall performance ($r = .23-.52$; Stevens & Campion, 1999).

### Physical Ability Tests

Physical ability testing, as already reviewed, is employed for physically demanding jobs. In a meta-analysis of physical ability studies across seven different jobs, Blakley, Quiñones, Crawford, and Jago (1994) found that measures of hand grip ($r = .17$), arm lift ($r = .27$), shoulder lift ($r = .24$), and torso lift ($r = .19$) are significant predictors of supervisor ratings of physical abilities. As a composite, the four measures of physical ability have a validity of 0.28. Both content validation (e.g., Hughes et al., 1989) and construct validation (e.g., Arvey, Landon, Nutting, & Maxwell, 1992) approaches to developing physical performance tests have been described in the literature.

# ADVERSE IMPACT, APPLICANT REACTIONS, TEST FAIRNESS, AND LEGAL ISSUES

In addition to validity, key considerations in the choice of a selection method are its adverse impact and applicant perceptions. We discuss these issues in the following sections.

## Adverse Impact

In general, work-sample tests have substantially less adverse impact against minority groups than traditional paper-and-pencil cognitive ability tests. Cascio and Phillips (1979) applied various performance and work-sample tests to the selection of 21 public sector jobs. The overall selection rates among the 21 jobs for African-American, White, and Hispanic applicants were 0.60, 0.64, and 0.57, respectively. Differences in selection rates among the subgroups were not significant (Cascio & Phillips, 1979). Schmitt and Mills (2001) compared test performance between African-American and White job applicants on a call simulation measure of customer service, a computerized simulation of job content (e.g., accessing database, working with written material). The results indicated that subgroup differences in the simulations ($SD = 0.30$) were half those of traditional tests ($SD = 0.61$; Schmitt & Mills, 2001). Studies of paper-and-pencil-based SJTs have reported small standardized mean differences between Whites and African Americans ($SD = 0.37–0.41$) and Whites and Hispanics ($SD = 0.01–0.02$; Clevenger et al., 2001; Pulakos & Schmitt, 1996).

Overall, however, it is not possible to conclude that all simulations will not exhibit adverse impact; the results have been mixed. Weekley and Jones (1997) reported that Whites outperformed African Americans on a video-based SJT. Specifically, performance differences on the video-based SJT ($SD = 0.61$) were similar to those found in the cognitive ability measure ($SD = 0.58$) used in this study. However, Weekley and Jones cautioned that the results might be due to an underrepresentation of minorities in the study sample. Similarly, Hattrup and Schmitt (1990) found that White participants outperformed African-American participants in a paper-and-pencil-based performance test. Arvey, Strickland, Drauden, and Martin (1990) administered three tests (two cognitive ability and one work sample) to applicants for a local county financial worker position. White examinees significantly outscored African Americans on all three measures, and the work-sample test of tools exhibited the greatest subgroup difference. Similarly, a hands-on work sample of machinery exhibited high subgroup differences between African Americans and White apprentices ($SD = 0.81$; Schmidt, Greenthal, Hunter, Berner, & Seaton, 1977).

## Adverse Impact and Test Medium

Test modality (e.g., written, aural) is believed to moderate subgroup differences, that is, adverse impact (Goldstein, Braverman, & Chung, 1992). Specifically, Goldstein et al. (1992) hypothesized that tests requiring writing favored Whites over African Americans, whereas tests that were more interactive, behaviorally oriented, and aurally-orally oriented would result in fewer White/African-American differences. Chan and Schmitt (1997) tested this theory by comparing a paper-and-pencil-based SJT to a video-based SJT. Because paper-and-pencil tests require stronger reading-comprehension skills, but video-based tests do not, it was hypothesized that test performance differences between the two formats are moderated by reading comprehension demands. In support of the hypothesis, the results showed a significant method-by-ethnicity interaction. Differences in mean test performance between African-American and White test takers differed between test methods (video or pencil-and-paper based). Pulakos and Schmitt (1996) reported that subgroup differences in the video-based simulation ($SD = .37–.45$) were half those of a writing-based simulation ($SD = 0.52–0.91$). Similarly, Hattrup and Schmitt (1990) found that a pencil-and-paper-based measure of job criteria exhibited adverse impacts. In contrast, non-paper-and-pencil-based simulation measures generally exhibit no adverse impact, for example, call simulation (Schmitt & Mills, 2001), computer-based multimedia measures of conflict resolution (Olson-Buchanan et al., 1998).

The moderating effects of medium and simulation fidelity on subgroup differences have not been consistent. Paper-and-pencil-based SJTs have been found to exhibit no significant African-American/White differences (Clevenger et al., 2001; Motowidlo et al., 1990) and no Hispanic/White differences (Pulakos & Schmitt, 1996). Additionally, a paper-and-pencil-based SJT had the same degree of African-American/White difference as a video simulation (Pulakos & Schmitt, 1996), and a video-based SJT had the same degree of adverse impact as cognitive ability test (Weekley & Jones, 1997).

Overall, it is difficult to make a general conclusion regarding the adverse impact of simulations. The inconsistency in observed adverse impact results may be attributed to the fact that, as noted earlier, simulation is a method, and such tests vary significantly in terms of content (Hunter & Hunter, 1984); that is, each of these studies is not necessarily measuring with the same method—a function of fidelity—or the same content or construct (e.g., flight skills versus situational judgment). Accordingly, tests that load highly on cognitive ability could be expected to result in greater adverse impact. In light of this, comparisons and interpretations of studies must be made with caution and a keen awareness of these differences. For this reason, current discussions of cross method and context comparisons will reference their associated method and context so the reader may decide for him- or herself the value in these comparisons.

## Applicant Reactions

Selection procedures that reflect the job generally receive more favorable applicant reactions than more abstract measures (Arvey et al., 1990; Chan & Schmitt, 1997; Macan, Avedon, Paese, & Smith, 1994; Richman-Hirsch, Olson-Buchanan, & Drasgow, 2000; Robertson & Kandola, 1982; Schmidt et al., 1977; Smither, Reilly, Millsap, Pearlman, & Stoffey, 1993). Applicants favor procedures that: (1) exhibit strong relationship to job content, (2) appear as both necessary and fair, (3) are administered in non-paper-and-pencil format, and (4) are delivered in a face-valid format (Rynes, 1993). Simulations, in general, meet these criteria. Recently, Richman-Hirsch et al. (2000) examined applicant reactions to different versions of a simulation measure of conflict resolution. The study compared three versions of the Conflict Resolution Skills Assessment (Olson-Buchanan et al., 1998) at varying levels of technological sophistication: (1) paper-and-pencil form, (2) computerized paper-and-pencil form (presents the text of the pencil-and-paper form, through the computer medium), and (3) multimedia form (full-motion audio/video computer medium). Compared with the paper-and-pencil and computerized paper-and-pencil tests, the multimedia assessment was perceived as more face valid, content valid, predictively valid, and satisfying and was viewed as providing more relevant information about the job (Born et al., 2001; Richman-Hirsch et al., 2000). In terms of fairness, the results showed no significant difference between the three media, but the trend supported Richman-Hirsch et al.'s hypothesis that multimedia assessment would be perceived as more fair. Interestingly, simply computerizing a paper-and-pencil test does not necessarily result in enhanced test-taker reactions. Possibly, "simple computerization is too mundane to be noticed by today's computer-savvy workforce" (Richman-Hirsch et al., 2000, p. 884).

### Implications of Applicant Reactions

Clearly, work samples and simulations lead to improved applicant perceptions, and applicant reactions are important for their potential effects on outcomes such as litigation intentions and motivation (e.g., Gilliland, 1993). Applicant reactions to simulations are a concern because reactions are believed to enhance test performance and reduce subgroup differences through their effects on test-taking motivation (see Chapter

27 of this volume). Chan, Schmitt, DeShon, Clause, and Delbridge (1997) found that differences in test performance among subgroups on two formats—simulation versus paper-and-pencil—may stem from differences in test-taking motivation. Specifically, Chan et al. (1997) found some evidence linking the effects of face validity and test performance: "face validity perceptions affect test-taking motivation, which in turn affects cognitive test performance" (p. 308). This would explain some of the reduction in subgroup differences for the simulation medium (more positive applicant reactions) as opposed to the paper-and-pencil format (lower applicant reaction) (Chan et al., 1997; Schmitt & Mills, 2001). African-American/White differences in test performance were found to be partially mediated by differences in face validity perceptions and test-taking motivation (Chan & Schmitt, 1997).

Similarly, Arvey et al. (1990) found that test-taking motivation was significantly related to ethnicity. In their study, White examinees were significantly more motivated to exert effort and to work harder on the preemployment test than African-American examinees. Although the test battery exhibited adverse impact, subgroup differences between African-American and White applicants significantly diminished after controlling for the effects of motivation (Arvey et al., 1990).

## Special Concern—Rating Bias

Performance scores or ratings on a simulation test may be objective, subjective, or somewhere in between. For example, performance in wiring a circuit for a light may be rated objectively (e.g., the light turns on), or subjectively (e.g., observation that proper safety precautions were taken while wiring). Because human judgment is involved in subjective ratings of performance or work samples, rater bias and its associated threats to reliability and validity are unavoidable. Borman and Hallam (1991) examined observation and rating accuracy among work-sample assessors. Accuracy in observation across two rating tasks exhibited low consistency; that is, accurate observations of one task did not necessarily predict accurate observations in another task. However, positive rating bias across rating tasks contributed to a stable response style—ratings were very reliable (Borman & Hallam, 1991). Additionally, characteristics of an accurate observer correlated with analytical ability and general cognitive ability. However, characteristics of an accurate observer do not significantly predict performance evaluation accuracy (Borman & Hallam, 1991). Overall, no definitive conclusions may be drawn, with the exception that subjective performance ratings are susceptible to biases.

Beyond its threat to validity, rater bias has the potential to produce subgroup differences, which raises concerns over adverse impact. Hamner, Kim, Baird, and Bigoness (1974) found that gender and ethnicity influenced work-sample task ratings even when objective measures were defined. Specifically, Hamner et al. (1974) found that African Americans rated African-American ratees higher than White ratees, whereas Whites rated African-American ratees lower than White ratees. Additionally, the spread of ratings for high- and low-performing African-American ratees were confined around the average, while White ratees were rated more accurately—high performers were rated high and low performers were rated low. Brugnoli, Campion, and Basen (1979) examined and addressed some of the concerns raised by Hamner et al. (1974). Because it was hypothesized that rater bias was a function of the rating instrument, a global rating scale was developed to closely mimic the one employed in Hamner et al. (1974). Additionally, a behavioral recording form was developed with the goal of minimizing rater judgment; the rater simply recorded whether a behavior was or was not exhibited. Brugnoli et al. (1979) found that the global rating scale exhibited race-linked bias when participants observed the ratee performing irrelevant job behavior. Race-linked bias was not found on the behavioral recording form or the global rating scale if the raters had completed the behavioral recording form first. Additionally, race-linked bias was not found on either measure when the ratee performed only job-relevant behavior. Similarly, Cascio and Phillips (1979) tested for rating bias among 19 possible comparisons and found none. More recently, Lance, Johnson, Douthitt, Bennett, and Harville (2000) examined task ratings obtained in global rating and behavioral recording forms as described by Smith (1991). The ratings were found to significantly and substantially reflect actual work-sample behavior. Together, gender, race, perception of motivation and other variables were not found to be of any practical consequence.

In sum, bias in ratings may be avoided by "assisting subjects [raters] in focusing on and recording relevant behavior" (Brugnoli et al., 1979). We suggest that raters can be assisted in focusing on such behaviors through the development of behaviorally specific rating scales, and through rater training focused on observation of behaviors to be assessed. Of course, objectivity can also be increased with multiple-choice format, although this may sacrifice some physical and psychological fidelity.

## Special Concern—Physical Abilities

Physical ability tests reliably produce significant gender differences that adversely impact women (e.g., Arvey, Nutting, & Landon, 1992; Bell, 1987; Blakley et al., 1994; Campion, 1983; Hogan, 1991; Hogan & Quigley, 1986; Hoover, 1992).

In a meta-analysis, Blakley et al. (1994) reported that women, in general, possessed 50% to 60% of the upper body strength and 70% to 80% of the lower body strength as men. Controlling for height, weight, and fat composition, however, gender differences diminish and become nonsignificant (Blakley et al., 1994).

There is some limited research comparing ethnic differences on physical ability test performance. Generally, physical ability tests produce no significant subgroup difference among African-American and White test takers. However, both African Americans and Whites tend to score significantly higher than Hispanics and Asians (Arvey, Nutting, & Landon, 1992; Blakley et al., 1994).

## Litigation

The threat of litigation and the likelihood of an unfavorable outcome are two concerns that strongly influence decisions regarding measurement and testing. Positive applicant perceptions of simulations often influence the decision to use them in selection, as such perceptions are assumed to lead to fewer legal challenges (e.g., Gilliland, 1993). As reviewed, some forms of simulations have been found to produce adverse impact. Once a plaintiff establishes a prima facie case of adverse impact, the litigation machinery is set in motion. Terpstra, Mohamed, and Kethley (1999) analyzed federal court cases involving nine selection devices. Work-sample tests and assessment centers elicited a much smaller observed frequency in charges of discrimination than statistically expected—a total of 5%. Physical ability tests, however, had a higher observed frequency in charges of discrimination (14%) than statistically expected (4%).

Terpstra et al. (1999) hypothesized that differences in the rate of litigation among nine selection devices may be due to: (1) applicant reactions to the selection device or (2) the validity evidence supporting the selection device. Specifically, Terpstra et al. proposed that the initial motivation to bring charges may be related to applicant reactions. However, the type of cases that lead to litigation in the federal courts may be a function of lawyers' assessments of the soundness (validity) of specific types of selection devices (Terpstra et al., 1999). The results of their study support the second hypothesis that "the validity evidence associated with different selection devices may be linked to differences in relative litigation rates" (p. 32).

Due to the small number of federal court cases that were reviewed in Terpstra et al. (1999), the reported successful defense rates must be interpreted with caution: assessment centers (100%, 1 of 1 cases), physical ability tests (58%, 11 of 19 cases), and work-sample tests (86%, 6 of 7 cases).

Indeed, Shepherd (1997), as cited in Biddle and Sill (1999), examined court rulings on cases involving police and firefighter physical ability tests; in total, 90% of the rulings were in favor of the plaintiffs.

### Uniform Guidelines

The validity of simulations is often established though a content validation strategy. Because a simulation test measures samples of job content, establishing its link to the job through job analysis is straightforward. Unfortunately, content validation alone is not appropriate for all situations, and the *Uniform Guidelines* (1978) recognizes this limitation. Specifically, when the selection procedure involves KSAs that an employee is expected to learn on the job, content validation alone is not appropriate. Other validation methods, such as criterion-related or construct validity, have to be used. Under such conditions the use of work samples and simulations is also questionable.

## PRACTICALITY

In addition to validity, adverse impact, and legal concerns, application of a simulation-type measure requires a careful consideration of its practicality, that is, advantages and disadvantages.

### Advantages

The major strength of simulation tests (especially high-fidelity simulations) is their high validity and a tendency to exhibit low adverse impact. Because work-sample tests are face valid and elicit favorable applicant reactions, the threat of litigation is low. Even when challenged, the courts have tended to favor its use (Terpstra et al., 1999). This can translate into substantial reduction in litigation risk and costs in the long run.

Despite the disadvantage of their costs (as reviewed in the preceding), simulations are not necessarily expensive and can contribute to reducing organizational costs. For low-fidelity simulations, such as paper-and-pencil-based measures (e.g., SJTs), the cost of development is comparable to typical paper-and-pencil-based tests (Clevenger et al., 2001). Additionally, low-fidelity simulations may be administered economically; video-based and paper-and-pencil-based tests may be efficiently administered to a group. In terms of reducing organizational costs, Cascio and Phillips (1979) found that the implementation of work-sample tests substantially reduced turnover for 21 government jobs, and test complaints to human resources were entirely eliminated. The reduction in turnover is not surprising because the work samples of-fered a unique and truly realistic job preview to job applicants. From the applicants' perspective, work-sample tests may be used to counsel unsuccessful candidates in very specific terms (Cascio & Phillips, 1979).

### Disadvantages

It is generally agreed that work-sample tests are the costliest among available test options (Guion, 1998; Hunter & Hunter, 1984; Schmidt & Hunter, 1998). This is due to the high test development and administration costs. A notable exception has been made by Cascio and Phillips (1979) who found that the performance test was more cost-effective than paper-and-pencil measures.

It is costly to develop and validate a simulation. Because of its specificity, development and validation of a unique simulation may be required for each job/group/family. In developing the video-based SJT, Weekly and Jones (1997) spent $1,500 per finished minute when taking into account the cost of scripting, filming, and editing and the employment of professional actors/actresses. The estimated figure, however, did not take into account the costs associated with administering the test—facilities where a TV and VCR are required. Dalessio (1994) employed a clever cost-saving alternative to the costly development and production of video footages; the researcher borrowed a collection of scenes from existing training videos for his video-based SJT. In general, the equipment and resources that are required for each administration (often on an individual basis) become a great financial concern, especially for high-fidelity simulations. Health and safety concerns for the test taker and/or the equipment used may limit the utility of a simulation. And once a simulation is in place, it must be revalidated after a certain period of time: Predictive validity is found to attenuate over time (Down, 1982, as cited in Robertson & Kandola, 1982; Siegel & Bergman, 1975).

Another disadvantage of simulation tests is the concern over its construct validity. Specifically, the constructs measured in simulations are often not fully understood. Validation strategies—especially among high-fidelity simulations—typically involve establishing content validity. As argued by Hunter and Hunter (1984), this weakness has hindered the research and development of selection measures with lower adverse impact. From a physical ability testing perspective, Arvey, Nutting, and Landon (1992) discussed the perils of using a content validation strategy to establish the link between job performance and physical ability, especially when challenged in court.

Overall, due to a wide range of formats, no specific advantage or disadvantage may be generalized to all simulations. That is, these tests have many variants, and they are capable of measuring a variety of content/constructs. Additionally, differences in stimulus and response format combinations may affect a simulation's validity regardless of the content it is measuring. As a selection strategy for lowering adverse impact, there are no guarantees. However, higher fidelity performance tests tend to exhibit lower subgroup differences. Tests that load more highly on cognitive ability can be expected to have greater adverse impact. In light of these uncertainties, it is recommended that each simulation be examined on a case-by-case basis.

## DEVELOPMENT, ADMINISTRATION, AND SCORING

It is possible to buy a few work samples and simulations "off the shelf." But this is not typically the case, and as already noted, one of the characteristics of these tests is that they typically reflect a specific job or organization. Thus, organizations or their consultants find themselves in the position of needing to develop a work-sample, simulation, or competency test. In this section, we describe the process involved in developing these tests.

As Table 19.1 illustrates, performance tests come in a variety of types and formats. Although each type of performance test has particular features that will dictate the specific steps a test developer follows in its construction, there is considerable similarity among these tests in how they are developed, because a basic content validation approach is employed in their construction. This section presents a generic approach to developing, administering, and scoring performance tests based on the commonality in the features. As mentioned previously, what all performance tests have in common is that they require test takers to respond to a sample of task-related situations that are critical to successful job performance.

Although the approach we describe is generic, we do deviate from it at various points in our discussion to describe the additional steps required in constructing performance tests using different stimulus and response formats. For the reader who is interested in additional guidance on the development of specific types of performance tests, including oral interviews, work-sample tests, and low-fidelity simulations, we recommend Gatewood and Feild (2001), Guion (1998), and Whetzel and Wheaton (1997).

One way in which this section differs from the description of the test development process found in the preceding sources is that we devoted substantial attention at each step to the "real-world" issues and problems based on our own experience. In so doing, we hope to provide some practical guidance to test developers in carrying out the test development process amid such organizational realities as legal requirements, political issues, and resource constraints.

### Preparing for the Test Development Process

Ensuring the fidelity of performance tests requires considerable involvement from subject matter experts (SMEs), from the identification of appropriate test content to the generation of possible responses for test items. For this reason, it is important to view the test development process as nothing less than a human resource intervention. By "intervention" we not only mean that the test development process is a change activity introduced for the purpose of improving the organization, but also that it is an interruption to the work lives of the organizational members involved. More specifically, participating in the test development process may take SMEs away from their jobs for considerable periods of time. Such time demands may result not only in the reluctance of some SMEs to assist in the process, but also in an unwillingness on the part of the organization to allow its top performers to participate. For these reasons, test developers should direct considerable effort at obtaining the organizational support necessary to ensure the involvement of high-quality SMEs in the process. As suggested by Gatewood and Feild (2001) in their recommendations for managing job analysis projects, one way in which this can be done is to hold meetings between top management, prospective participants, and members of the test development staff. The goal of these meetings would be to communicate such information as (1) the purpose of the test for the organization, (2) the steps in the test development process, and (3) the importance of SMEs' involvement that is necessary and the types of information needed from SMEs. Another goal of the meeting would be to establish an open, nonthreatening climate for the process so that effective information exchange can occur between the participants and the test development staff.

In addition to obtaining organizational support through top management and SME "buy in," test developers should prepare for the test development process by gaining a better understanding of the role/placement of the test in the broader organizational context. This requires analyzing the relationship of the test with other human resource functions, understanding the political and legal environment surrounding the test, and determining budget and facility resources. This requires that the test developer analyze the broader organizational environment.

### Practical Issue #1: Selecting the "Right" SMEs to Participate in the Test Development Process

As previously mentioned, the development of valid performance tests requires considerable involvement of SMEs to ensure the relevance of the test to the content of the job. SMEs provide judgments about critical job behaviors, situations that require the performance of these behaviors, and the appropriate responses to these situations. Because they are an integral part of the test development process, it is important to select SMEs who are capable of providing high-quality judgments to guide the test development process.

Although relatively little research exists to direct the selection of SMEs in organizations, we can recommend the use of several criteria based on both the extant research (see Gatewood & Feild, 2001 for a review) and our own experience working with SMEs. First, the SMEs selected should be those who are willing to participate. This is based on the supposition that SMEs who are motivated to participate will provide better quality judgments. Often this motivation stems from an interest in ensuring the validity of the final test product. For this reason, supervisors, training instructors/coordinators, and representatives from important constituent groups (e.g., labor unions, internal customers) often constitute highly motivated and interested SMEs. In the development of a report-writing simulation for police recruit, for example, the second author found district attorneys to be especially willing to participate in the development process: The selection of police recruits with serious report-writing deficiencies had hampered their ability to prosecute crimes/offenses.

Second, the SMEs should have sufficient knowledge of the job in question. Such knowledge is essential in providing complete and accurate job information. Job incumbents and supervisors are examples of SMEs who meet this criterion. One caution against the use of supervisors, however, is that they tend to characterize subordinates' work in terms of what *should* be done rather than what is *actually* done (Gatewood & Feild, 2001). This problem may be mitigated by selecting supervisors who work closely with subordinates with varying degrees of job experience. This helps to ensure that they have exposure to all levels of potential incumbent performance and thus can better judge what is actually done on the job (see Donahue, Truxillo, & Finkelstein, 2001).

A third criterion is that SMEs should possess good written and oral communication skills. As mentioned, SMEs are relied upon to communicate extensive amounts of information about the job in question over the course of the development process. This may be accomplished through either written or verbal descriptions provided to the test developers. The quality of these descriptions will be enhanced if SMEs are effective communicators. Recommendations from superiors and, if available, past performance ratings may be used to identify SMEs who meet this criterion.

Where else might SMEs who meet these criteria be found? Often, test developers need to look no further than their own files. In beginning a test development process, we found old test documents to be especially helpful in providing the names of SMEs who proved to be particularly good sources of job information. Over time, we began developing a list of these individuals to invite to participate in future test development efforts.

## Specifying the Performance Domain

Once SMEs have been selected, the next step is to specify the performance domain and determine which part of it is to be tested. The performance domain consists of all of the tasks performed on a job. It is often not possible—or even desirable—to test the entire performance domain. Instead, a portion of the performance domain is selected depending on the purpose of the test. To ensure the representativeness and generalizability of the test content to the entire performance domain, it is necessary to (1) first specify the complete performance domain and (2) then construct a valid and defensible sampling strategy to select tasks from the domain (Felker & Rose, 1997).

The performance domain is typically specified through a job analysis. Because they sample job content, work samples should be based in task-specific job analysis methods such as task-KSA analysis and the critical incidents approach. The goal of the test developer in employing the job analysis is to derive the dimensions that underlie performance for the job in question and the KSAs needed to perform these. These *performance dimensions* provide structure to the job performance domain and thus assist the test developer in designing a sampling strategy that ensures that the test content is job relevant.

Gatewood and Feild (2001) noted that job analysis methods that give detailed task information are needed for content validation efforts. One of the most commonly used task-oriented job analysis methods is task-KSA analysis. Gatewood and Feild provided substantial detail in the use of this approach. Generally, however, this analysis begins with collecting detailed information about the tasks performed on the job and the KSAs needed to do them through means such as observation, SME interviews, and archival data. The tasks are then combined into a task list and rated in terms of their criticality on criteria such as importance and frequency, usually as part of a survey.

Once the critical tasks have been identified, they can then be grouped together as a means of deriving the performance dimensions needed in constructing job performance tests. This grouping can be performed using either rational or statistical approaches. The first implies the use of SMEs who, independently, identify broad categories and then assign task statements to them. Guion (1998) described a particularly useful rational grouping approach that entails using panels of

SMEs to iteratively sort tasks, starting with the two most clearly different tasks, and then determining if the remaining tasks are like one, like the other, or like neither. This process is repeated until all "like neither" tasks have been sorted. Any tasks not meeting an agreement criterion are either reassigned or discarded. Grouping tasks through statistical approaches involves the application of cluster or factor analysis to identify the underlying factors of job performance, although the appropriateness of factor analysis for this purpose (Cranny & Doherty, 1988) has been questioned.

Finally, a key step to task-KSA analysis involves the linkage of KSAs back to tasks or task clusters by SMEs, typically by means of a survey. This final step is necessary for tests developed using a content validity approach (Gatewood and Feild, 2001; *Uniform Guidelines,* 1978). From this, one can develop a test plan of the KSAs needed to perform the job. The test can then be designed around the KSAs linked to the most critical job tasks.

### Critical Incidents Approach

In addition to the preceding job/task analysis methods, performance dimensions may also be drawn from the critical incidents approach. This approach is designed to generate a list of especially effective and ineffective examples of performance demonstrated by job incumbents. To accomplish this, a panel of SMEs is assembled and asked to describe, either verbally or in writing, the details of situations in which an incumbent performed especially effectively or ineffectively. Anderson and Wilson (1997) offered a thorough description of the various steps involved in this process.

The objective of the critical incidents approach is to gather information regarding observed behaviors, not inferred trait-oriented descriptions of performance (Anderson & Wilson, 1997; Gatewood & Feild, 2001). These behaviors are then grouped into performance dimensions based on their behavioral content. The resulting list of performance dimensions describes the behavioral patterns that differentiate effective and ineffective performers and can be used to guide the construction of prospective test situations for performance tests (Motowidlo et al., 1997).

### Performance Competencies

A particular class of job competencies that has received considerable attention in the personnel selection literature recently is *performance competencies* (see Shippmann et al., 2000). Performance competencies consist of clusters of KSAs demonstrated in a particular performance context (Ulrich,

Brockbank, Yueng, & Lake, 1995). Thus, they describe the demonstrated capabilities that distinguish superior from average performers. By emphasizing the behavioral patterns associated with effective job performance, they bear much in common with the performance dimensions that are specified for constructing performance tests. However, as noted by Schippmann et al. (2000), competency modeling approaches may not provide the detailed information provided through a job analysis. As such, they may not have sufficiently detailed task information that is required for content validation. We thus caution their use in the development of work-sample and competency tests unless detailed task information is also available. More information concerning the development of performance competencies can be found in Shippmann et al. (2000).

### Practical Issue #2: Constructing a Valid and Defensible Test Plan for Constructing Test Situations to Represent the Performance Domain

Once the performance domain has been specified, the test developer must construct a test plan that will ensure that the test content is representative of and generalizable to the entire performance domain. The first step in developing this test plan is to determine the relative importance of the various dimensions comprising the performance domain. SME judgments are often utilized for this purpose. Specifically, the SMEs are asked to review the various performance dimensions and then assign weights to indicate their relative importance to overall job performance. These weights are then averaged to determine the proportion of the total number of test situations that will represent each of these performance dimensions. This total depends on the stimulus and response format of the test, as well as practical considerations, such as the desired administration time and the amount of equipment and materials required. For a one-hour exam, for example, Motowidlo et al. (1997) have recommended that test developers include approximately 40 test situations in their test plan.

Next, the test developer must select the tasks or critical incidents that will be used in constructing test situations. This involves identifying from each performance dimension the tasks or critical incidents that are both critical to successful job performance and that strongly represent their respective dimensions.

In the case of higher fidelity tests, which rely on task information, critical tasks are selected through the use of task ratings gathered in the course of conducting a job analysis. Specifically, tasks associated with each performance dimension are ordered according to their mean importance ratings;

the tasks with the highest importance ratings would then be selected to represent their dimensions. The number of tasks selected would depend on the relative importance of the performance dimension, as assigned by SMEs. Other job analysis information that should also be consulted in selecting the most critical tasks from each performance dimension includes ratings of frequency, level of difficulty, and consequences of error (Gatewood & Feild, 2001). Another approach we have seen is to focus on tasks most closely associated with critical KSAs.

Because critical incidents have an established link with successful job performance, the focus in their selection for lower fidelity tests shifts to ensuring that a representative number are selected from each of the targeted performance dimensions. As described, the number of critical incidents chosen from each dimension would be in proportion to the dimension's overall importance in the performance domain. Once a representative number of critical incidents is selected, they would be provided to SMEs to assist in generating actual test situations. In the next section, we describe in more detail the process to be followed in generating test situations from tasks or critical incidents.

## Developing the Test

The test development process for both higher and lower fidelity performance tests entails generating test situations that represent each of the performance dimensions and developing scoring procedures to evaluate applicant performance. For higher fidelity simulations, in which the respondent is asked to actually perform a task or part of a task, the goal is to generate a number of *task situations*. Scoring procedures for these simulations may focus on evaluating the task process, product, or both. For moderate to lower fidelity tests, in which respondents are asked to describe what they would do in work-related problems and situations, the goal is to generate a number of *problem situations* (i.e., situational incidents). These are typically scored in terms of the effectiveness of the strategy chosen by applicants for handling the situation.

In this section, we describe a general approach for developing lower and higher fidelity performance tests and their related scoring procedures. Because performance tests come in a wide variety of types and formats, test developers should modify the general approach we describe to suit their needs. We follow up this description with recommendations for how to gather the best quality information from SMEs during this very judgment-intensive process.

### High-Fidelity Performance Test Development

High-fidelity performance tests are standardized samples of actual work tasks or subtasks in which applicants are evaluated in terms of the quality of their task process or products. In developing high-fidelity simulations there is an even greater reliance on the task information collected during the job analysis. This information is not only used for constructing the task situations, it is also used in specifying how the tasks are to be performed and describing the level of competency and quality expected (Felker & Rose, 1997).

In the previous section, we discussed the use of task ratings to select the tasks that would serve as the basis for constructing task situations to appear on the test. Although it is important to identify the tasks that have a strong bearing on job performance, this is not the only consideration when selecting tasks for higher-fidelity simulations. As outlined by Gatewood and Feild (2001), for practical reasons other important criteria to be used in selecting tasks to simulate include the following:

1. Tasks in which the total time required for completion is reasonable.
2. Tasks that are representative of the job in terms of difficulty and complexity. Tasks that are too easy or too difficult will not help to distinguish among applicants in terms of proficiency.
3. Tasks that require less expensive materials, equipment, or facilities.
4. Tasks that have standardized operations or products or have easily defined verbal or interaction components. It is easier to both develop and score test situations based on such tasks.

Because high-fidelity performance tests represent abstractions of the actual work performed on the job, decisions need to be made regarding which compromises in psychological fidelity are necessary to accommodate the practical constraints of the test environment (Felker & Rose, 1997). Physical fidelity, for example, must be sacrificed when it is impossible to duplicate the exact working conditions or doing so would prove too costly. Instead, these conditions are simulated, but in such a way as to elicit the same knowledge and skills needed to perform the task (Felker & Rose, 1997). This would thus ensure the test's psychological fidelity.

Even when tasks are simulated, some authenticity may be lost due to practical considerations such as time and equipment/material requirements. Some tasks, for example, may only be tested in part (versus in whole) because they are too long or consist of repetitive or trivial tests. Or, the performance environment may need to be modified because the tasks have idiosyncratic features and can only be done by experienced workers (Gatewood & Feild, 2001). In this case, applicants would be given the information necessary to perform the task (e.g., instructions on how to operate the equipment, background information on company policies, etc.).

The next step in the development of high-fidelity performance tests is to devise procedures for scoring applicant performance. As previously mentioned, applicants may be evaluated in terms of their task process, product, or both. Although objective measures are often available—especially in the case of scoring task products—ratings represent the primary means for scoring high-fidelity performance tests. These ratings can be dichotomous (e.g., satisfactory or unsatisfactory) or a scale point (Guion, 1998).

Because of the problems associated with the accuracy and reliability of subjective ratings, Felker and Rose (1997) and Guion (1998) made several recommendations for the development of scoring procedures based on ratings. The first of these relates to developing a scoring key or protocol that requires scorers to make as few subjective decisions as possible (Felker & Rose, 1997). To accomplish this, test developers should make the performance steps to be scored readily observable or should design the administration protocol to include prompts for applicants to verbalize their cognitive processes (e.g., "checking," "observing," etc.). In addition, the scoring key should specify the performance steps in terms of behavioral units so that scorers can determine when task performance starts and ends. Further, where tasks are to be performed at certain levels of proficiency, the standard of performance should be specified using objective standards whenever possible.

A second recommendation for ensuring accurate and reliable ratings relates to thoroughly training scorers in the use of the scoring key. Training approaches that focus on improving scorers' ability to observe performance-relevant behavior and to make judgments based on these observations (e.g., Hedge & Kavanagh, 1988) should be used in training the raters. Felker and Rose (1997) also recommended that scorers practice performing the tasks they will score, as well as observe others performing these tasks as part of their training.

A final recommendation is to have the same task performance or product evaluated, if possible, by two or more independent scorers. Impermissible differences in the scorers' ratings should also be defined and the procedures for reconciling these differences should be specified (Guion, 1998).

### Low-Fidelity Performance Test Development

As previously mentioned, low-fidelity performance tests present applicants with problem situations that might be encountered on the job and ask them to describe either verbally or in writing how they would respond to the situation. Performance tests that are the most stereotypic of this category include oral interviews and SJTs. More elaborate discussions on the development of these types of performance tests can be found in Whetzel and Wheaton (1997) and Motowidlo et al. (1997).

The low-fidelity test development process begins by generating descriptions of a number of problem situations. The critical incidents generated during job analysis are particularly helpful for this purpose. Specifically, critical incidents representing each of the targeted performance dimensions would be given to a group of SMEs as guidance in generating more specific problem situations. In doing this, the SMEs would be asked to describe—either verbally or in writing—an instance in which a job incumbent encountered a special problem or situation reflective of the critical incident. These descriptions would include the details of the situation, as well as the incumbent's response. This process would be repeated to ensure that several problem situations exist for each performance dimension. A second group of SMEs would then perform a retranslation process in which they categorize the problem situations according to their performance dimensions. The final set of problem situations to appear on the test would then be sampled from those surviving the retranslation process. Specifically, problem situations would be selected to represent each performance dimension consistent with the original test plan. These final problem situations, edited to limit the description to just a few sentences, would provide the basis for questions appearing on such low-fidelity simulations as a situational interview or a SJT. Note that more complex problem situations are often likely to tap more than one performance dimension or KSA.

The next step in the development of low-fidelity tests is to generate response options for each of the problem situations appearing on the test. As discussed by Motowidlo et al. (1997), the goal in developing response options is to ". . . represent classes of broadly different strategies for handling each situation" (p. 256). These strategies would be scaled in terms of their effectiveness for handling the problem situation and used for scoring applicant performance on the test.

Different approaches exist for developing response options for the test problems. A very low-cost approach is to ask the group of SMEs who provided the descriptions of the problem situations to also describe, based on their experience, how outstanding, average, and poor job incumbents would deal with the situation. An alternative to using SMEs to develop responses is to administer the items to less experienced job incumbents, who would be asked to describe how they would respond to the problem (Motowidlo et al., 1997). The response options gathered using either of these different approaches would then be rated by a second group of SMEs in terms of their effectiveness (i.e., from very effective to very ineffective). The SMEs would also be asked to indicate for each problem situation which alternative is the most and least effective. Mean ratings of effectiveness and agreement indices (e.g., proportion of SMEs endorsing alternative as most/least effective, intraclass correlations of the relationship among SME ratings for each set of alternatives) would then be used to scale the various response options.

For written response formats, these options would be translated into multiple-choice alternatives. In selecting from among these alternatives, applicants may be asked to choose the alternatives they would be most and least likely to take in the situation (e.g., Motowidlo et al., 1990), the alternatives they think are the best and worse course of action in the situation (e.g., Weekley & Jones, 1999), or simply, the alternative they think is the best response in the situation (e.g., Stevens & Campion, 1999; Weekley & Jones, 1997). Using this latter approach, the SME ratings discussed in the preceding would be used to identify the most effective response. Applicants correctly choosing this alternative would receive a score of 1 for the item; otherwise they would receive a 0.

SME ratings can also be used in scoring items for which applicants are instructed to select two responses. Motowidlo et al. (1990) described such a scheme in which each of the two alternatives chosen by an applicant are scored either 1, 0, or $-1$, with the final score for an item ranging from $-2$ to 2. A score of $-2$ means that an applicant chose as the most likely (or best) course of action the alternative rated by SMEs as being the least effective and also chose as the least likely (or worse) course of action the alternative rated by SMEs as being the most effective. A score of 2 means that an applicant chose as the most likely (or best) course of action the alternative rated by SME as being most effective and chose as the least likely (or worse) course of action the alternative rated as being least effective. As an alternative to using SME judgments for developing a scoring key, items can be empirically keyed against a performance criterion. Such an approach is described in detail by Weekley and Jones (1999).

In the case of oral response formats, the options scaled from the SME ratings would serve as benchmarks against which applicants' answers are rated somewhat like the de-

velopment of behaviorally anchored rating scales (BARS) (Smith & Kendall, 1963). Training approaches, such as frame-of-reference training (FOR) (Bernardin & Pence, 1980), that focus on increasing rater accuracy would be used in training raters in the use of the rating scales. To further increase the accuracy and reliability of the ratings, two or more raters, if possible, should evaluate applicant performance.

### Practical Issue #3: Collecting the Highest Quality Information from SMEs

Many prescriptions for working with SMEs to generate test situations recommend that SMEs describe situations to test developers individually in writing. Although this is often the most efficient approach for collecting information, it may not always yield the best descriptions of possible test situations. SMEs vary in terms of their ability to observe incumbents perform in different task situations or respond to various problems. In addition, SMEs may not recall all relevant situations they may have observed over a given period of time. For these reasons, groups or panels of SMEs facilitated by a test development staff member may often provide more accurate and detailed information. We have used groups of SMEs at this stage in the development process with great success. Specifically, we have found that groups of SMEs stimulate each other's memories of situations, allowing for a greater number and more detailed descriptions of situations to surface.

The use of groups or panels of SMEs may not be appropriate in every situation. Status differences (e.g., position, authority) among the SMEs, for instance, may lead to decreased participation. This may occur either because of the inclination of lower status members to defer to higher status members or because of the reluctance of higher status members to discuss instances of ineffective performance in the presence of lower status members. If such status differences exist, the test developer should collect the descriptions of test or problem situations from SMEs independently.

### Practical Issue #4: Translating Written Scenarios Into Videos

If one is developing a video-based test, verbal problem situations developed by SMEs must be translated into video format, that is, enacted. Our experience is that this can lead to subtle changes in scenarios that were not originally intended—although these can be more interesting and just as valid. For example, we were once involved in the development of a video scenario that included a conflict between two subordinates. The video was made using one male and one female actor in the roles of the subordinates. Although this was not the original intention, after viewing the completed video, SMEs developing the scoring scales noted the possibility of the conflict being due to gender differences—a distinct possibility in this male-dominated organization. The lesson here is to be sure that a video scenario conveys the information it was intended to convey and to develop final scales based on SMEs' take on the final video, not the just the verbal scenario.

## Administering the Test

Because performance tests are typically more resource-intensive than other types of selection tests, a major consideration in their administration is locating or establishing a test site that can accommodate their equipment and material needs. If the test is to be administered to large groups of applicants over a relatively short period of time, the test site should also be able to handle multiple, simultaneous administrations. Appropriate office space can often be leased by organizations whose facilities do not meet these requirements.

As is the case with other types of tests, efforts are made to standardize the testing conditions to ensure that performance tests are administered consistently across applicants. To standardize these conditions, an administration protocol would be developed that details the procedures for setting up and administering the test, and test administrators would be thoroughly trained to ensure their adherence to this protocol.

In addition to training the test administrators, testing conditions would also be made more uniform by providing orientation to the applicants. Gatewood and Feild (2001), for example, recommend that instructions be developed for the applicants that inform them of the nature of the test, what they will be asked to do, and the material and equipment that will be used.

When performance tests are to be scored at the same time they are administered, there is the added need to ensure the standardization of the scoring procedures. Approaches for devising objective and reliable scoring approaches were described in the preceding section of developing high-fidelity performance tests. In addition to these scoring approaches, standardization depends on thoroughly training the test administrators and raters in observing, recording, and evaluating process-oriented behaviors and/or scoring the quality of resulting task products. As previously mentioned, observation training should be conducted to train the raters in how to observe and score performance-relevant behavior.

### Practical Issue #5: Protecting the Security of the Performance Test's Content

As we have shown here, performance tests are quite costly to develop and administer. For this reason, organizations may be interested in using the test beyond a single administration. Safeguarding the content of the test becomes a serious issue in this case, as knowledge of the test situations would provide an unfair advantage to applicants who were previously exposed—either by participating in earlier administrations or by receiving information from other applicants—to the test situations.

If test security concerns exist because applicants are allowed to retake the test, parallel forms of the test could be developed. If costs prohibit the development of strictly parallel forms, then a subset of the items could be exchanged with parallel items in subsequent administrations. If neither of these approaches is viable, an alternative would be to require "waiting periods" between test administrations. A typical waiting period would require applicants to wait six weeks before being able to retake the test.

Receiving information from other applicants may be a particular threat when the performance test is used for promotional purposes. In their experience administering promotional exams, the first two authors have implemented a number of safeguards to protect the security of the test's content. These have ranged from having applicants sign security agreements, to scheduling groups of applicants at overlapping time periods, to sequestering the applicants until all applicants have completed the test, to reminding applicants that dissemination of test content to coworkers only lessens their own chances for hiring or promotion. In cases where serious concerns over the test's security have existed, we have used all four approaches and have found them to be effective for dealing with these concerns.

## Setting Passing Scores

Setting cutoff scores for personnel selection tests is not always necessary, desirable, or easy. Many researchers (e.g., Schmidt, Mack, & Hunter, 1984) emphasize that top-down approaches to selection enhances selection utility, and the *Principles for the Validation and Use of Personnel Selection Procedures* (Society for Industrial and Organizational Psychology, 1987) notes that with valid predictors, a top-down approach is best from the organization's perspective. If a top-down selection approach is used, it may be unnecessary to determine who actually "passed" the test. Moreover, it is difficult to establish a cutoff for many tests as they are intended to produce a continuum of scores, rather than a dichotomy.

On the other hand, cutoff scores are sometimes necessary. The most obvious example is licensure tests: Having a cutoff score is usually a necessity for certification and licensure tests. In the selection context, personnel rules may require a determination of who "passed" and "failed" a selection process. Also, cutoffs are necessary if the selection method is used as part of a series of hurdles. Under these conditions, cutoffs may be set based on anticipated vacancies or to ensure that the most qualified candidates go through later selection procedures. Finally, cutoff scores are appropriate where the purpose of the test is only to ensure minimum competency, as is often the case with physical ability tests.

If it is necessary to set a passing score for a work sample, particularly one that reflects minimum job performance, we believe the most appropriate method would be one based on expert judgment such as the Angoff method (Angoff, 1971). The Angoff method is typically used for content-validated tests, and it had been used to set passing scores for work-sample (e.g., Truxillo, Donahue, & Sulzer, 1996) and certification (Busch & Jaeger, 1990) tests. For these reasons, we believe that this approach is most applicable to clearly job-related tests such as work samples and job simulations. Note that despite its subjectivity, the Angoff method is commonly used and has withstood legal challenge (e.g., Biddle, 1993). It has also received the greatest attention in the personnel psychology literature (e.g., Hudson & Campion, 1994; Truxillo et al., 1996), largely due to its proven legal defensibility (see Biddle).

In the Angoff method, judges are asked to review each test item and to estimate the percentage of minimally competent persons (MCPs) who could answer the item correctly or the likelihood that an MCP would answer the item correctly. The cutoff is based on the average estimate across items and judges. Detailed recommendations regarding the implementation of this method are given in past reviews (e.g., Biddle; 1993; Biddle & Sill, 1999; Truxillo et al., 1996). These involve including a sufficiently large sample of Angoff judges (7–10), including a group of judges that represents the demographics and organizational units so that the cutoff will seem fair to stakeholders and training judges.

## Application of the Angoff Method to Different Scoring Formats

Research on the Angoff method has focused primarily on tests with multiple-choice formats (e.g., Hudson & Campion, 1994). However, many work-sample types of tests use Likert or checklist scales. The approach to standard setting under these circumstances is similar to the approach used for multiple-choice tests. For example, Schmitt and Klimoski (1991) described an approach to standard setting for an assessment center. And although standard setting for physical ability tests is a difficult area (e.g., Arvey, Landon, Nutting, & Maxwell, 1992; Hogan, 1991), Truxillo et al. (1996) described the development of a cutoff score for a firefighter physical ability test based on the Angoff method.

### Legal Issues and Cutoff Scores

With regard to legal issues and standard setting, Cascio, Alexander, and Barrett (1988) noted that the cutoff score should be based on some combination of criteria, such as the expected number of vacancies, affirmative action goals, and some consideration of minimum competency. Biddle (1993) noted that when using judgmental methods for setting passing scores (e.g., the Angoff method), it is appropriate to modify the score by setting the cutoff one, two, or three standard errors of measurement below the Angoff estimate, depending on the level of confidence desired.

### Practical Issue #6: Reducing the Cognitive Load for Judges Setting Passing Scores

Setting passing scores for tests is a problem in most organizational settings. Entire sessions at the Society for Industrial and Organizational Psychology conference are commonly devoted to this issue (e.g., Grubb et al., 2001). We focus here on the key issue encountered with judgment methods for setting passing scores such as the Angoff method: reducing the cognitive load on judges. Setting cutoffs through judgment methods is an extremely subjective process and one that judges often find uncomfortable. Reducing cognitive load should not only increase judges' confidence with the process but should also lead to more accurate estimates.

Based on past research (e.g., Busch & Jaeger, 1990; Fehrmann, Woehr, & Arthur, 1991; Maurer & Alexander, 1992) and our experience, we recommend three procedures to help judges set passing scores. First, judges should be given a clear definition of an MCP (e.g., it is not an *average* employee) and trained on how the standard-setting process works. Second, if available, normative data about item difficulty should be given to judges to provide some idea of the relative difficulty of items. Finally, judges should discuss their judgments in groups before making a final rating.

## FUTURE DEVELOPMENTS

In the last several years technological advances have greatly changed the field of testing. But the implications for simulations and certification testing are profound. We see technological advances as affecting the issues of both delivery and scoring of these assessments.

## Delivery of Assessments

Technology such as virtual reality is becoming less of a fantasy and more of an actuality, and we believe this technology could have a great impact on the delivery of the sorts of tests discussed in this chapter. Simple videotape technology has already affected the development and delivery of work samples, simulations, and competency testing: It is now commonplace for scenarios to be delivered to assessees in a video format, with respondents either describing how they would handle a situation or choosing from a response set. As technology progresses and becomes more affordable and practical, such procedures should become more commonplace, and there is the potential for increased fidelity.

Technology should also increase the flexibility of such assessments. For example, a very wide range of technology-based scenarios can be developed and pooled by test development companies. Based on a job analysis, scenarios and questions can then be chosen to develop a test for a particular job, allowing the premade scenarios to be tailored into a test. Such is the practice with assessments such as the B-PAD (Corey, MacAlpine, Rand, Rand, & Wolf, 1995), used for the assessment of police officers. Another possibility is the delivery of assessments via the Internet. Although there are security issues still to be resolved with this medium, it could allow for considerable flexibility in the scheduling of assessments. For example, we have seen certification training for university human subjects review boards begin to be delivered via the Internet.

## Scoring

New technology is already leading to more convenient response formats. For example, raters can now give their assessments in an electronic file rather than on paper so that test data can be scored quickly and incorporated into other assessment information. In addition, it seems probable that more sophisticated technology will lead to increased use of scoring formats that better reflect reality and less reliance on multiple-choice.

## Challenges

Technology seems poised to facilitate much of the process of delivery and scoring of these tests. But with increased speed come increased expectations. Because technology should speed up the delivery and scoring of simulations, the development process may become the substantial hindrance to their use. As noted, the development of banks of scenarios may help ease this problem. In addition, newer (and faster) approaches to job analysis such as O*NET may alleviate this problem, although it is unclear whether they provide the detailed task information needed for the development of these sorts of tests. Finally, before Internet delivery of simulations becomes commonplace, managing the security of these tests must be addressed.

## CONCLUSION

Work samples, simulations, and competency tests provide valid prediction and tend to be viewed favorably by applicants and organizational members. In addition, they tend to result in reduced adverse impact compared with other measures, making them attractive to organizations wishing to increase diversity. Despite the challenges involved in their development and delivery, they provide a viable option in many testing contexts.

## REFERENCES

Anderson, L., & Wilson, S. (1997). Critical incident technique. In D.L. Whetzel & G.R. Wheaton (Eds.), *Applied measurement methods in industrial psychology* (pp. 89–112). Palo Alto, CA: Davies-Black.

Angoff, W.H. (1971). Scales, norms, and equivalent scores. In R.L. Thorndike (Ed.), *Educational measurement* (pp. 508–600). Washington, DC: American Council on Education.

Arvey, R.D., Landon, T.E., Nutting, S.M., & Maxwell, S.E. (1992). Development of physical ability tests for police officers: A construct validation approach. *Journal of Applied Psychology, 77,* 996–1009.

Arvey, R.D., Nutting, S.M., & Landon, T.E. (1992). Validation strategies for physical ability testing in police and fire settings. *Public Personnel Management, 21,* 301–312.

Arvey, R.D., Strickland, W., Drauden, G., & Martin, C. (1990). Motivational components of test taking. *Personnel Psychology, 43,* 695–716.

Asher, J.J., & Sciarrino, J.A. (1974). Realistic work sample tests: A review. *Personnel Psychology, 27,* 519–533.

Bell, L. (1987). Where does physical testing leave women? *Management Review, 76,* 47–50.

Bernardin, H.J., & Pence, E.C. (1980). Effects of rater training: Creating new response sets and decreasing accuracy. *Journal of Applied Psychology, 65,* 60–66.

Biddle, R.E. (1993). How to set cutoff scores for knowledge tests used in promotion, training, certification, and licensing. *Public Personnel Management, 22*, 63–79.

Biddle, D., & Sill N.S. (1999). Protective service physical ability tests: Establishing pass/fail, ranking, and banding procedures. *Public Personnel Management, 28*, 217–225.

Binning, J.F., & Barrett, G.V. (1989). Validity of personnel decisions: A conceptual analysis of the inferential and evidential bases. *Journal of Applied Psychology, 74*, 478–494

Blakley, B.R., Quiñones, M.A., Crawford, M.S., & Jago, I.A. (1994). The validity of isometric strength tests. *Personnel Psychology, 47*, 247–274.

Borman, W.C., & Hallam, G.L. (1991). Observation accuracy for assessors of work-sample performance: Consistency across task and individual-differences correlates. *Journal of Applied Psychology, 76*, 11–18.

Born, M. Ph., Van der Maesen de Sombreff, P.E.A.M., & Van der Zee, K. (2001, April). *A multimedia situational judgment test for social intelligence*. Paper presented at the 16th Annual Conference of the Society for Industrial and Organizational Psychology, San Diego, CA.

Bray, D.W., Campbell, R.J., & Grant, D.L. (1974). *Formative years in business: A long-term study of managerial lives*. New York: Wiley.

Brugnoli, G.A., Campion, J.E., & Basen, J.A. (1979). Racial bias in the use of work samples for personnel selection. *Journal of Applied Psychology, 64*, 119–123.

Busch, J.C., & Jaeger, R.M. (1990). Influence of type of judge, normative information, and discussion on standards recommended for the National Teacher Examinations. *Journal of Educational Measurement, 27*, 145–163.

Callinan, M., & Robertson, I.T. (2000). Work sample testing. *International Journal of Selection and Assessment, 8*, 248–260.

Campion, M.A. (1983). Personnel selection for physically demanding jobs: Review and recommendations. *Personnel Psychology, 36*, 527–550.

Cascio, W.F., & Phillips, N.F. (1979). Performance testing: A rose among thorns? *Personnel Psychology, 32*, 751–766.

Cascio, W.F., Alexander, R.A., & Barrett, G.V. (1988). Setting cutoff scores: Legal, psychometric, and professional guidelines. *Personnel Psychology, 41*, 1–24.

Chan, D., & Schmitt, N. (1997). Video-based versus paper-and-pencil method of assessment in situational judgment tests: Subgroup differences in test performance and face validity perceptions. *Journal of Applied Psychology, 82*, 143–159.

Chan, D., Schmitt, N., DeShon, R.P., Clause, C.S., & Delbridge, K. (1997). Reactions to cognitive ability tests: The relationships between race, test performance, face validity perceptions, and test-taking motivation. *Journal of Applied Psychology, 82*, 300–310.

Clevenger, J., Pereira, G.M., Wiechmann, D., Schmitt, N., & Harvey, V.S. (2001). Incremental validity of situational judgment tests. *Journal of Applied Psychology, 86*, 410–417.

Corey, D.M., MacAlpine, D.S., Rand, D.C., Rand, R., & Wolf, G.D. (1995). *B-PAD technical reports* (3rd ed.). Napa, CA: The B-PAD Group.

Cranny, C.J., & Doherty, M.E. (1988). Importance ratings in job analysis: Note on the misinterpretation of factor analyses. *Journal of Applied Psychology, 73*, 320–322.

Dalessio, A.T. (1994). Predicting insurance agent turnover using a video-based situational judgment test. *Journal of Business and Psychology, 9*, 23–32.

Donahue, L.M., Truxillo, D.M., & Finkelstein, L.M. (2001, April). Comparison of three approaches for dealing with aberrant Angoff judges. Poster session presented at the 16th Annual Conference of the Society for Industrial and Organizational Psychology, San Diego, CA.

Fehrmann, M.L., Woehr, D.J., & Arthur, W. (1991). The Angoff cutoff score method: The impact of frame-of-reference rater training. *Educational and Psychological Measurement, 51*, 857–872.

Felker, D.M., & Rose, A.M. (1997). Tests of job performance. In D.L. Whetzel & G.R. Wheaton (Eds.), *Applied measurement methods in industrial psychology* (pp. 319–352). Palo Alto, CA: Davies-Black.

Funke, U., & Schuler, H. (1998). Validity of stimulus and response components in a video test of social competence. *International Journal of Selection and Assessment, 6*, 115–123.

Gatewood, R.D., & Feild, H.S. (2001). *Human resource selection* (5th ed). Fort Worth, TX: Harcourt College Publishers.

Gilliland, S.W. (1993). The perceived fairness of selection systems: An organizational justice perspective. *Academy of Management Review, 18*, 694–734.

Goldstein, H.W., Braverman, E.P., & Chung, B. (1992, May). *Methods versus content: The effects of different testing methodologies on subgroup differences*. Paper presented at the 8th Annual Conference of the Society for Industrial and Organizational Psychology, San Francisco.

Goldstein, I.L., Zedeck, S., & Schneider, B. (1993). An exploration of the job analysis-content validity process. In N. Schmitt, W.C. Borman, & Associates (Eds.), *Personnel selection in organizations* (pp. 3–34), San Francisco: Jossey-Bass.

Grubb, A.D., Baker, K.Q., (Co-Chairs), Baker, T., Truxillo, D.M., McPhail, S.M., & Zimmer, S. (2001). *When your test is not making the cut: Revising test cut scores for organizational purposes*. Panel discussion at the 16th Annual Conference of the Society for Industrial and Organizational Psychology, San Diego, CA.

Guion, R.M. (1998). *Assessment, measurement, and prediction for personnel decisions*. Mahwah, NJ: Erlbaum.

Hamner, W.C., Kim, J.S., Baird, L., & Bigoness, W.J. (1974). Race and sex as determinants of ratings by potential employers in a simulated work-sampling task. *Journal of Applied Psychology, 59*, 705–711.

Hattrup, K., & Schmitt, N. (1990). Prediction of trades apprentices' performance on job sample criteria. *Personnel Psychology, 43,* 453–466.

Hedge, J.W., & Kavanagh, M.J. (1988). Improving the accuracy of performance evaluations: Comparisons of three methods of performance appraiser training. *Journal of Applied Psychology, 73,* 68–73.

Hedge, J.W., & Teachout, M.S. (1992). An interview approach to work sample criterion measurement. *Journal of Applied Psychology, 77,* 453–461.

Hogan, J.C. (1991). Physical abilities. In M.D. Dunnette & L.M. Hough (Eds.), *Handbook of industrial and organizational psychology* (2nd ed., pp. 753–831). Palo Alto, CA: Consulting Psychologists Press.

Hogan, J., & Quigley, A. (1986). Physical standards for employment and the courts. *American Psychologist, 41,* 1193–1217.

Hoover, L.T. (1992). Trends in police physical ability selection testing. *Public Personnel Management, 21,* 29–41.

Hudson, P.J., & Campion, J.E. (1994). Hindsight bias in an application of the Angoff method for setting cutoff scores. *Journal of Applied Psychology, 79,* 860–865.

Hughes, M.A., Ratliff, R.A., Purswell, J.L., & Hadwiger, J. (1989). A content validation methodology for job related physical performance tests. *Public Personnel Management, 18,* 487–504.

Hunter, J.E., & Hunter, R.F. (1984). Validity and utility of alternative predictor of job performance. *Psychological Bulletin, 96,* 72–98.

Lance, C.E., Johnson, C.D., Douthitt, S.S., Bennett W.B., & Harville, D.L. (2000). Good news: Work sample administrators' global performance judgments are (about) as valid as we've suspected. *Human Performance, 13,* 253–277.

Latham, G.P., & Saari, L.M. (1984). Do people do what they say? Further studies on the situational interview. *Journal of Applied Psychology, 69,* 569–573.

Latham, G.P., Saari, L.M., Pursell, E.D., & Campion, M.A. (1980). The situational interview. *Journal of Applied Psychology, 65,* 422–427.

Macan, T.H., Avedon, M.J., Paese, M.S., & Smith, D.E. (1994). The effects of applicants' reactions to cognitive ability tests and an assessment center. *Personnel Psychology, 47,* 715–738.

Maurer, T.J., & Alexander, R.A. (1992). Methods of improving employment test critical scores derived by judging test content: A review and critique. *Personnel Psychology, 45,* 727–762.

McDaniel, M.A., Morgeson, F.P., Finnegan, E.B., Campion, M.A., & Braverman, E.P. (2001). Use of situational judgment tests to predict job performance; A clarification of the literature. *Journal of Applied Psychology, 86,* 730–740.

McDaniel, M.A., Whetzel, D.L., Schmidt, F.L., & Maurer, S.D. (1994). The validity of employment interviews: A comprehensive review and meta-analysis. *Journal of Applied Psychology, 79,* 599–616.

Motowidlo, S.J., Carter, G.W., Dunnette, M.D., Tippins, N., Werner, S., Burnett, J., & Vaughan, M.J. (1992). Studies of the structured behavioral interview. *Journal of Applied Psychology, 77,* 571–587.

Motowidlo, S.J., Dunnette, M.D., & Carter, G.W. (1990). An alternative selection procedure: The low-fidelity simulation. *Journal of Applied Psychology, 75,* 640–647.

Motowidlo, S.J., Hanson, M.A., & Crafts, J.L. (1997). In D.L. Whetzel & G.R. Wheaton (Eds.), *Applied measurement methods in industrial psychology* (pp. 241–260). Palo Alto, CA: Davies-Black.

Mount, M.K., Muchinsky, P.M., & Hanser, L.M. (1977). The predictive validity of a work sample: A laboratory study. *Personnel Psychology, 30,* 637–645.

Olson-Buchanan, J.B., Drasgow, F., Moberg, P.J., Mead, A.D., Keenan, P., & Donovan, M.A. (1998). Interactive video assessment of conflict resolution skills. *Personnel Psychology, 51,* 1–24.

Pulakos, E.D., & Schmitt, N. (1995). Experience-based and situational interview questions: Studies of validity. *Personnel Psychology, 48,* 289–308.

Pulakos, E.D., & Schmitt, N. (1996). An evaluation of two strategies for reducing adverse impact and their effects on criterion-related validity. *Human Performance, 9,* 241–258.

Reilly, R.R., & Israelski, E.W. (1988). Development and validation of minicourses in the telecommunications industry. *Journal of Applied Psychology, 73,* 721–726.

Richman-Hirsch, W.L., Olson-Buchanan, J.B., & Drasgow, F. (2000). Examining the impact of administration medium on examinee perceptions and attitudes. *Journal of Applied Psychology, 85,* 880–887.

Robertson, I.T., & Downs, S. (1989). Work-sample tests of trainability: A meta-analysis. *Journal of Applied Psychology, 74,* 402–410.

Robertson, I.T., & Kandola, R.S. (1982). Work sample tests: Validity, adverse impact and applicant reaction. *Journal of Occupational Psychology, 55,* 171–183.

Rynes, S.L. (1993). Who's selecting whom? Effects of selection practices on applicant attitudes and behavior. In N. Schmitt, W. Borman, & Associates (Eds.), Personnel selection in organizations (pp. 240–274). San Francisco : Jossey-Bass.

Salgado, J.F., & Lado, M. (2000, April). *Validity generalization of video tests for predicting job performance ratings.* Paper presented at the 15th Annual Conference of the Society for Industrial and Organizational Psychology, New Orleans, LA.

Schippmann, J.S., Ash, R.A., Battista, M., Carr L., Eyde, L.D., Hesketh, B., Kehoe, J., Pearlman, K., Prien, E.P., & Sanchez, J.I. (2000). The practice of competency modeling. *Personnel Psychology, 53,* 703–740.

Schmidt, F.L., Greenthal, A.L., Hunter, J.E., Berner, J.G., & Seaton, F.W. (1977). Job sample vs. paper-and-pencil trades and technical tests: Adverse impact and examinee attitudes. *Personnel Psychology, 30,* 187–197.

Schmidt, F.L., & Hunter, J.E. (1998). The validity and utility of selection methods in personnel psychology: Practical and theoretical implications of 85 years of research findings. *Psychological Bulletin, 2,* 262–274.

Schmidt, F.L., Mack, M.J., & Hunter, J.E. (1984). Selection utility in the occupation of U.S. park ranger for three modes of test use. *Journal of Applied Psychology, 69,* 490–497.

Schmitt, N., Gooding, R.Z., Noe, R.A., & Kirsch, M. (1984). Meta-analyses of validity studies published between 1964 and 1982 and the investigation of study characteristics. *Personnel Psychology, 37,* 407–422.

Schmitt, N.W., & Klimoski, R.J. (1991). *Research methods in human resources management.* Cincinnati: South-Western.

Schmitt, N., & Mills, A.E. (2001). Traditional tests and job simulations: Minority and majority performance and test validities. *Journal of Applied Psychology, 86,* 451–458.

Schneider, B., & Schmitt, N. (1986). *Staffing in organizations.* Glenview, IL: Scott, Foresman.

Siegel, A.I., & Bergman, B.A. (1975). A job learning approach to performance prediction. *Personnel Psychology, 28,* 325–339.

Smiderle, D., Perry, B.A., & Cronshaw, S.F. (1994). Evaluation of video-based assessment in transit operator selection. *Journal of Business and Psychology, 9,* 3–22.

Smith, F.D. (1991). Work samples as measures of performance. In A.K. Eigdor & B.F. Green Jr. (Eds.), *Performance assessment for the workplace* (Vol. 2, pp. 27–52). Washington, DC: National Academy Press.

Smith, P.C., & Kendall, L.M. (1963). Retranslation of expectations: An approach to the construction of unambiguous anchors for rating scales. *Journal of Applied Psychology, 47,* 149–155.

Smither, J.W., Reilly, R.R., Millsap, R.E., Pearlman, K., & Stoffey, R.W. (1993). Applicant reactions to selection procedures. *Personnel Psychology, 46,* 49–76.

Society for Industrial and Organizational Psychology, Inc. (1987). *Principles for the validation and use of personnel selection procedures* (3rd ed.). College Park, MD: Author.

Sternberg, R.J., Wagner, R.K., & Okagaski, L. (1993). Practical intelligence: The nature and role of tacit knowledge in work and at school. In J.M. Puckett and H.W. Reese (Eds.), *Mechanisms of everyday cognition* (pp. 205–227). Hillsdale, NJ: Erlbaum.

Stevens, M.J., & Campion, M.A. (1999). Staffing work teams: Developments and validation of a selection test for teamwork settings. *Journal of Management, 25,* 207–228.

Swander, C.J. (2001, April). *Exploring the criterion validity of two alternate forms of situation judgment test.* Paper presented at the 16th annual conference of the Society of Industrial and Organizational Psychology, San Diego, CA.

Terpstra, D.E., Mohamed, A.A., & Kethley, R.B. (1999). An analysis of federal court cases involving nine selection devices. *International Journal of Selection and Assessment, 7,* 26–34.

Truxillo, D.M., Donahue, L.M., & Sulzer, J.L. (1996). Setting cutoff scores for personnel selection tests: Issues, illustrations, and recommendations. *Human Performance, 9,* 275–295.

Ulrich, D., Brockbank, W., Yueng, A.K., & Lake, D.G. (1995). Human resource competencies: An empirical assessment. *Human Resource Management, 34,* 473–495.

*Uniform Guidelines on Employee Selection Procedures.* (1978). *Federal Register, 43,* 38295–38309.

Weekley, J.A., & Jones, C. (1997). Video-based situational testing. *Personnel Psychology, 50,* 25–49.

Weekley, J.A., & Jones, C. (1999). Further studies of situational tests. *Personnel Psychology, 52,* 679–700.

Wernimont, P.F., & Campbell, J.P. (1968). Signs, samples, and criteria. *Journal of Applied Psychology, 52,* 372–376.

Whetzel, D.L., & Wheaton, G.R. (1997). *Applied measurement methods in industrial psychology.* Palo Alto, CA: Davies-Black.

# ASSESSING JOB PERFORMANCE

CHAPTER 20

# Job Performance Ratings

DANIEL A. NEWMAN, TED KINNEY, AND JAMES L. FARR

## OVERVIEW OF CHAPTER

Job performance is a complex, multidimensional construct that can be defined and assessed in varying ways. Job performance can be defined (and assessed) in terms of quantifiable outcomes of work behaviors (e.g., amount of sales measured in dollars, number of academic journal publications, number of lines of computer code written) and in terms of behavioral dimensions (work-related communication, decision making, attention to detail) that are less quantifiable. It can be defined (and assessed) solely in terms of task performance (those activities that support the technical core of the organization and are a formal part of the relevant job description) but can also be defined as contextual performance (those activities that support the social and psychological environment of the organization and its employees; see Borman & Motowidlo, 1993).

Job performance can be assessed in terms of overall effectiveness in the job and in terms of specific components that the job comprises. Performance assessment information can be obtained from one or more individuals who are in one or more role relationships with the target employee (e.g., a supervisor, coworker, or subordinate).

In this chapter we focus on judgments (ratings) of the task performance of a target employee that are obtained from one or more individuals in a single role relationship with the target. Most commonly, the target employee is rated on several behavioral dimensions related to task performance and the source of the ratings is the employee's supervisor. Contextual performance ratings are discussed in Chapter 22 by Kaufman and Borman. Assessments that use ratings from individuals who are in several different role relationships with the target employee (frequently called multisource or 360-degree ratings) are discussed in Chapter 21 by Balzer, Greguras, and Raymark. We use the term *performance ratings* to refer to the judgments of an employee's task performance-related behaviors.

## OVERVIEW OF PERFORMANCE RATINGS: A BRIEF HISTORY

The measurement of job performance is a fundamental assessment procedure in work organizations that serves as the basis for many personnel decisions and as the stimulus for more specific assessments of the individual employee. Job performance ratings have been a primary assessment tool of the industrial-organizational psychologist since the earliest years of the field. Performance ratings were initially developed because of the recognition that judgments about job performance were essential for those job functions for which more objective measures were not available. Such ratings were typically made by the supervisors of the group of employees whose job performance was evaluated.

Bingham and Freyd (1926) included two chapters on performance rating scales in their book, *Procedures in Employment Psychology*. Several rating methods that had previously been described in the research literature were discussed and possible standards for evaluating the quality of the performance ratings obtained by the use of rating scales were also described. Among the possible indicators of rating quality that Bingham and Freyd considered were interrater agreement, the central tendency and dispersion of distributions of ratings, intercorrelations among ratings of various job elements, and correlations between ratings of employees on specific aspects of the job and rankings of the same employees on overall merit or value to the organization. Such indices of the quality of a set of performance ratings would still be reasonable ones today, suggesting the resilience of research and application related to performance ratings in the first part of the twentieth century.

Much of the focus of both research and application from 1925 to 1975 was devoted to a search for superior rating instrument formats that would maximize the *accuracy* of the resulting performance ratings or minimize what came to be known as *traditional rating errors*. These errors included *leniency* and *severity* (mean ratings that tend to be more favorable or more unfavorable, respectively, than warranted by the individuals' job performance), *central tendency* (almost all ratings in the middle of the scale and almost none at the endpoints), and *halo* (tendency of ratings of various dimensions of job performance to be more highly correlated than warranted by individual's job performance).

The basic assumption of the rating error approach was that the measurement of employee job performance could be conceptualized in a manner similar to the way that classical test theory modeled the measurement of human abilities. Thus, rated job performance was viewed as a function of "true job performance," along with systematic and random error. The accuracy of rated job performance would increase as error decreased. Rating instrument format was hypothesized to have an important effect on systematic rating error and received much research attention. However, the results of rating instrument format research were generally disappointing, and Landy and Farr (1980) called for a moratorium on research

on rating format, following their extensive review of the rating research literature.

Landy and Farr (1980) also suggested that research attention be given to the cognitive processes involved in performance rating. Their suggestion was consistent with a theory of rating that Wherry proposed in the early 1950s but that was not well known until its publication both as a journal article (Wherry & Bartlett, 1982) and as an appendix in a performance measurement volume (Wherry, 1983, in Landy & Farr, 1983) about 30 years later. Several other cognitive-based models of the rating process were also suggested in the 1980s, including those of Ilgen and Feldman (1983) and DeNisi, Cafferty, and Meglino (1984). Rating research in the 1980s and 1990s did shift to an examination of cognitive factors affecting the processing of performance information by raters and the resulting ratings of that performance. Cognitive-based theories and research have increased our knowledge about how such processes as attention, categorization of information, encoding and storage, and memory and recall influence the judgments that raters make. However, concern has been expressed that the impact of the cognitive approach on actual ratings of job performance in work organizations has been minimal to date (e.g., Murphy & Cleveland, 1995). One advantage of cognitive research and theory has been its important contribution to the development of effective rater training, a point that is addressed in more detail later.

Murphy and Cleveland (1995) emphasized the role of contextual factors on the rating process, suggesting that a shift was needed from research and theory about performance rating *judgments* to research and theory about performance *appraisal*. They noted that much of the cognitive-based research was concerned with rating judgments that were never conveyed to the ratees. Performance appraisal implies that the raters' judgments are communicated to the ratees as part of a performance feedback process. A number of contextual variables affect performance appraisal, including rater goals, organizational norms, culture, and politics, and purpose of the rating process (Murphy & Cleveland, 1995). An important implication of this perspective is that the effectiveness of a performance rating and appraisal process is also dependent on these contextual factors.

## BASIC CONSIDERATIONS IN THE RATING OF JOB PERFORMANCE

Rating job performance accurately requires that both *job performance* and *rating accuracy* be defined in a manner appropriate to the type of job being rated.

## Definition of Job Performance

Before setting about the task of operationalizing and assessing job performance, it is critical to have an adequate conceptualization of what "performance" is. Without an appropriate specification of what does or does not constitute successful job performance in a given context, the usefulness of performance ratings will be unknown.

Historically, ratings of an individual's job performance have included judgments about such diverse content as job behaviors (e.g., interpersonal interactions with a customer), job outcomes or results (e.g., dollar value of products sold by the employee), and individual traits (e.g., sociability). Although behaviors, outcomes, and traits are all intuitively germane to the performance concept, they are not all equally appropriate as the content of rating judgments, as will be discussed later. Summarily, *behavioral measures* of job performance have been acclaimed both as a more accurate basis than *results measures* for indexing individual job success (see Campbell, Gasser, & Oswald, 1996; Campbell, McCloy, Oppler, & Sager, 1993; Ouchi & Maguire, 1975), and as easier to define and observe than *trait measures* (Wexley & Klimoski, 1984). We echo Campbell et al. (1993) in recommending that job performance ratings be limited to judgments concerning observable employee behaviors.

When studying job behaviors, researchers have classically thought of job performance as a unidimensional construct, citing intercorrelations among various performance measures as their primary evidence (Viswesvaran, 1993). In contrast, recent attempts to specify the types of behaviors that together constitute the job performance domain have produced some overlapping multidimensional conceptualizations of performance, which vary in terms of both content and specificity (e.g., Borman & Brush [1993] review managerial performance; Borman & Motowidlo [1993] review prosocial contextual performance). One of the more influential multifactor models of job performance is one advanced by Campbell et al. (1993), which specifies eight general, interrelated aspects of performance: (1) job-specific task proficiency, (2) non-job-specific task proficiency, (3) written and oral communication task proficiency, (4) demonstration of effort, (5) maintenance of personal discipline, (6) facilitation of peer and team performance, (7) supervision/leadership, and (8) management/administration. Although the importance of these eight aspects of performance will differ across specific jobs, they provide a widely applicable set of job behaviors that constitute a useful starting point for defining job performance.

Although performance ratings are commonly based on the rater's judgment of the target's average or "typical" performance, some performance appraisal scholars have noted that performance can be a dynamic criterion, exhibiting intraindividual variability over time. Kane (1986) has suggested that the ubiquitous use of "typical" performance ratings should be supplemented by raters' assessments of the target employee's entire *performance distribution,* based on the rater's judgments of the *frequencies* of performance behaviors along a continuum from least effective to most effective. Distributional assessment has two proposed advantages: it has the conceptual advantage of incorporating the notion of consistency into the performance criterion, and it has the cognitive advantage of being more resistant to the memory biases and distortions usually found in judgments of typical performance, which require "mental averaging" prior to rating (see Kane, 2000). Building on the notion of distributional assessment, Sackett and colleagues have emphasized the distinction between an individual's *maximum* performance and *typical* performance, demonstrating that maximum and typical measures are only weakly related (Sackett, Zedeck, & Fogli, 1988), with maximum performance showing the closer relation to cognitive ability measures (DuBois, Sackett, Zedeck, & Fogli, 1993). Last, research has demonstrated that there can be reliable individual differences in performance trajectories across time (e.g., Hofmann, Jacobs, & Baratta, 1993; Ployhart & Hakel, 1998).

To summarize, when using job performance ratings as an assessment of an individual employee, more information about that employee is obtained when the rating procedure contains judgments about multiple aspects of job behavior, about the individual's typical and maximum job behavior, and about the frequencies of more and less effective behaviors. The specific format of the final rating instrument does not generally have a major impact on the quality of the ratings that are obtained, given that the behavioral dimensions and scale anchors are developed from a careful analysis of the job and its context.

## Rating Accuracy

Performance ratings obtained for an assessment of an employee may be assumed to be accurate without explicit consideration of the factors that influence rating accuracy. This section discusses what is meant when the term accuracy is used, how accuracy has been measured, and several important conditions that can lead to accurate ratings. Finally, we discuss whether rater accuracy is always the most important goal when developing a performance assessment system.

The term *rating accuracy* has traditionally referred to the degree to which the judgment made by a rater represents the actual performance of the target (i.e., the target's true score). One weakness of such a definition is that the true score of a ratee is an unknown, making it impossible to determine whether the rater is accurately judging performance. In a multiple-rater situation, accuracy is often mistakenly considered to be the extent to which multiple raters' evaluations agree. That is, when there are multiple raters, interrater reliability or consensus is frequently considered a proxy for accuracy. In fact, it is possible for the raters to agree, but for the ratings to not represent the target's true score (Kenny, 1991; Murphy & DeShon, 2000).

When each target performer is rated by only one rater, it is not possible to compute the interrater agreement index. Researchers have developed several other accuracy measures that can be applied in such situations, where there are a number of employees, each of whom has been rated. Different accuracy indices vary in their level of complexity, but each operationalization of accuracy attempts to accomplish the same goal, which is to provide a 'true-score' that approximates the rating given by a hypothetical perfect rater under ideal circumstances (Murphy & Cleveland, 1995).

Typically, accuracy measures fall into two categories: evaluative accuracy and observational accuracy (Cardy & Dobbins, 1994; Cardy & Krzystofiak, 1998). Evaluative accuracy measures indicate the accuracy of the rater's evaluations of performance level. This type of measure is tabulated as the squared difference between the actual rating and a true score. Observational accuracy measures indicate whether or not the rater identified the occurrence of various ratee behaviors (Lord, 1985). These types of measures reflect the accuracy with which the rater recalls or recognizes behaviors that were displayed by the ratee. For details of these measures, see Murphy and Cleveland (1995). It is important to note that the various measures of evaluative accuracy are not highly correlated, so that if a single such measure is used to determine accuracy, only part of the accuracy picture will be uncovered (Cardy & Dobbins, 1986). Generally, multiple measures of accuracy should be used (Murphy & Cleveland, 1995).

Murphy (1991) suggested that no one type of accuracy measure is preferable over another, although some researchers advocate one or the other type (e.g., Padgett & Ilgen, 1989, prefer observational methods). Further, the relative applicability of an accuracy measure may depend on the research question or particular assessment purpose. For example, Lord (1985) suggests that observational accuracy measures are more important when researching rater memory. Additionally, Murphy (1991) suggested that observational accuracy may be better suited when the goal is to provide behavioral feedback or to justify an administrative decision. On the other hand, Murphy (1991) pointed out that if the goal is to understand the quality of the judgments made by a rater, then evaluative indexes of accuracy may be more important. The

bottom line is that there is not one accuracy measure that is always preferred.

Research and practice do suggest that some general conditions can lead to more accurate ratings of job performance, regardless of the accuracy measure chosen. An important condition to ensure accurate ratings is whether the rater has an adequate opportunity to observe the ratee's behavior (Borman, 1978; Kenny, 1991). Kenny (1991) suggested that the more information a rater has about an employee, the more accurate the rater's evaluation will be. The point is that the more opportunities the rater has to observe behavioral samples of the ratee, the more likely the rater will be able to recall and accurately use those behaviors when making judgments. Rothstein (1990) found empirical support for the importance of the rater's observational opportunity for the accuracy of performance ratings in a work setting.

Another necessary condition for accurate ratings concerns the rater's familiarity with the rating format. As discussed in a later section of this chapter, performance rating instruments can take many forms. A rater must be familiar with and have practice using the chosen form. This consideration should not be taken lightly. For example, if a rater is accustomed to making behavioral ratings, then a trait-rating format may be difficult for the rater to understand. Further, to encode the appropriate information, raters should be familiar with the type of information that they will be asked to recall (Murphy & Cleveland, 1995). Cheung (1999) listed this source of inaccuracy as a common source of error variance in performance ratings. To prevent this problem, raters should have adequate opportunities to practice using the rating instrument.

Related to familiarity with the rating format is familiarity with the performance domain. Ratings can only be accurate to the extent that the rater is accustomed to the performance domain. Feldman (1985) suggested that raters should have experience with the rating domain based on performing or supervising in the performance domain, and raters should have training and experience in rating the performance domain. To meet this condition it is crucial that the performance domain be well defined and clearly communicated to the rater. For example, if the rater is under a false impression that a global rating of job performance will be asked for, but the ratings are separated into several dimensions, the rater may have difficulty recalling behaviors unique to each dimension.

Further, the rater must have an in-depth understanding of what types of behaviors make up each of the performance domains. Cheung (1999) suggested that when different raters have different perceptions of the composition of a performance domain, the evaluations the raters make may not be reliable. For example, if a rater is asked to assess a target's communications skills, then the organization must be explicit about what type of communication is relevant. If the organization is interested in both written and verbal communication, but the rater only considers written communication in his or her assessment, accuracy will likely suffer.

Another condition that has received research attention is accountability (see Antonioni, 1994; Klimoski & Inks, 1990). Accountability refers to the organizational or social pressure for a rater to justify his or her ratings (Tetlock, 1992). Although it was initially hypothesized that a rater who is held accountable for ratings will be more likely to provide accurate ratings, a frequent finding is that raters distort ratings in a positive direction if they are accountable (Antonioni, 1994). This finding has led many researchers to consider accountability as a source of bias in ratings (Stone, Rabinowitz, & Spool, 1977). However, more recently Mero and Motowidlo (1995) found that raters who were accountable made more accurate ratings than anonymous raters. Thompson (1995) suggested that holding raters accountable may increase accuracy if the raters do not have a goal to achieve a predetermined conclusion, but that accuracy may suffer when they do. Haeggberg and Chen (1999) found that the effect of accountability depended on the accuracy measure that was used. No unequivocal conclusions can yet be reached about the effect of accountability on rating accuracy. Thus, the question of whether to hold raters accountable for ratings during a specific application should be given careful consideration in each situation.

A final contextual factor relevant to rating accuracy is the motivation of the raters. Although it is frequently assumed that raters will always choose to provide the most accurate ratings possible, this assumption may be untenable (Murphy & Cleveland, 1991, 1995; Tetlock, 1992). Murphy and Cleveland (1991, 1995) have discussed how rater goals influence performance ratings. For example, if a rater decides that an employee deserves to be promoted, the rater may give that employee ratings that will achieve the desired outcome as opposed to giving the most accurate ratings.

To combat a rater's goals to rate in a manner that is not accurate, some researchers have suggested that rewards be offered for accurate ratings (see Mohrman & Lawler, 1983). The problem with this idea is that even if rewards are offered for accurate rating, such accuracy can be difficult to measure and, thus, the link between accurate ratings and subsequent rewards may be weak. If a rater does provide accurate ratings and is not rewarded, the rater may then begin to distrust the performance appraisal system (Murphy & Cleveland, 1995) and start a negative spiral of reduced rating accuracy over time. The negative consequences surrounding the giving of low ratings may also outweigh the rewards. Therefore, rewarding accurate rating does not seem to be an effective

means to boost accuracy in ratings. One way to combat divergent rater motivation is to address and stress the importance of accurate rating in a training program. Although it is doubtful that this solution will remedy the problem entirely, it appears to be one of the more feasible options.

A final point is whether it is appropriate to consider rating accuracy the sole legitimate goal of the users of a performance assessment system. Murphy and Cleveland (1995) argued that accurate ratings are not always a positive outcome for all users. These authors suggested that the various indexes of accuracy are context-free, but performance ratings are not given in a context-free environment. Many organizational forces influence ratings. Murphy and Cleveland (1995) pointed out that ratings are a means of communication by the rater to the organization and its members. It is sometimes possible that the most crucial message is not communicated with strictly accurate ratings. That is, inaccurate ratings may deliver a more meaningful and important message to organizational members than accurate ratings. For example, if a rater inflates the ratings of an employee whom the rater believes should be promoted, then rating inaccurately could lead more efficiently to the appropriate employee promotions than accurate ratings could.

To summarize, while rating accuracy is a somewhat controversial topic, some clear-cut recommendations are possible. First, although existing rating accuracy measures are by no means perfect indicators, they do impart some useful information about the quality of a set of performance ratings. Second, some conditions lead to more accurate ratings. The raters should always have ample opportunities to observe the target's performance. Also, the raters should be intimately familiar with the rating format and the performance domain. Finally, other issues such as accountability and the importance of accurate ratings should be considered.

## Jobs for Which Ratings Are Most Suitable

Performance ratings can be applied to almost any job and its various performance domains. The exceptions would be those relatively rare domains of specific jobs for which an accurate and bias-free objective or countable measure does exist. An assessment should include these results measures only when they are judged by relevant organizational members as providing useful and valid information, given the purpose for which performance information is to be used.

The exact performance domains and the specific form of the rating instrument depend on the information provided from an analysis of the job in question. Details of these procedures are provided next.

## DEVELOPING AN APPLICATION OF PERFORMANCE RATINGS

When developing a performance rating system for use in organizations, five important choices must be made. These choices are illustrated by the following questions:

1. What is the *purpose* of the rating system?
2. What perceptions, behaviors, outcomes, and traits constitute an appropriate *operationalization of performance* for this purpose?
3. What is the appropriate *format* for collecting rating information?
4. *Who* should make the ratings?
5. How should the *raters be trained* prior to making ratings?

All five of the these questions are interdependent, and each of the five choices they represent is indispensable to the overall rating process. Next we offer a brief discussion of alternative answers to the five questions.

### Clarifying the Purpose of the Rating System

In 1989, Cleveland, Murphy, and Williams reported results from a large-scale survey describing the uses to which performance ratings are put. Four general uses of performance appraisal were identified and labeled: (1) between-individuals comparisons (salary administration, promotion, retention and termination, individual recognition, layoffs, identifying poor performers), (2) within-individuals comparisons (identifying individual training needs, performance feedback, determine transfers and assignments, identifying strengths and weaknesses), (3) systems maintenance (personnel planning, determining organizational training needs, evaluating goal achievement, assisting in goal identification, evaluating personnel systems, reinforcing authority structure, identifying organizational development needs), and (4) documentation (documenting personnel decisions, defining criteria for validation research, and meeting legal requirements). Of these four purposes, performance ratings were most often used for between- and within-individuals comparisons. Interestingly, most organizations used performance ratings for multiple purposes simultaneously.

The purposes an organization has for ratings can influence the ratings given. Research has shown that rating behavior varies as a function of the purpose for which the rater believes the ratings will be used (Jawahar & Williams, 1997), with more lenient ratings given when salaries and promotions are on the line, compared with ratings made for individual feedback or research purposes only. Furthermore, organizational purposes are not the only purposes relevant to rating; individual raters can have their own agendas for the ratings, such as protecting a subordinate from disciplinary action or avoiding negative attention that would be brought to a work unit with low-rated individuals (Longenecker, Sims, & Gioia, 1987).

### Operationalizing Performance

Closely related to the choice of purposes for a performance rating system is the decision of what to measure in order to achieve those purposes. Many options are available when attempting to quantify performance, although the multiplicity of options is often blurred by the blanket use of the term *performance* to refer to any and all of them. The basic options for operationalizing performance have been reviewed by many performance rating researchers (Cardy & Dobbins, 1994; Landy & Farr, 1983; Smith, 1976; Wexley & Klimoski, 1984), and they are reviewed again here.

Four common operationalizations of performance are (1) *subjective criteria* (e.g., ratings of overall performance), (2) *outcomes/results/nonjudgmental criteria* (e.g., sales, turnover, product quality, speed), (3) *behavioral criteria* (e.g., duties and tasks), and (4) *trait criteria* (e.g., knowledge, skill, experience, motivation). Each of the operationalizations has strengths and limitations. Subjective criteria suffer from vulnerability to bias and error, can be manipulated for political purposes or to advance an individual rater's personal agendas, and may be perceived by the ratee as invalid or unfair, particularly when negative feedback is given. Results criteria have the disadvantage of not being completely under individual control. Because the quality or amount of product someone makes can depend in large part on the initial material inputs, resources, and opportunities available for obtaining positive results, these criteria are often more indicative of system performance than individual performance. It can be perceived as unfair to discipline or reward individuals on the basis of results "performance" over which they had little personal control (e.g., low total sales of luxury items during an economic recession). Advantages of results criteria are that they are closely linked to financial indexes of organizational productivity/effectiveness and are "objective" in the sense that they are less subject to rating errors. Behavioral criteria provide a partial solution to the problem of person versus situation attributions for performance, since behaviors are more under individual control than results criteria. Behavioral criteria are also a good basis for feedback. Last, trait criteria can suffer from rating bias and error and are only useful when it is possible to move personnel to different positions or teams.

In any attempt to select operational criteria for a performance management system, one should keep in mind that the *intended purpose* of the performance ratings is itself the ultimate criterion. If ratings are being made for the purpose of promotion decisions, then the ultimate criterion is the relative proficiency of those who are promoted over those who are not. If ratings are being made for the purpose of individual development, then personal change is the ultimate criterion. Specifying the criterion for a performance rating system is a problem of measurement validity and therefore merits a careful consideration of criterion contamination and deficiency, as well as convergent, discriminant, and substantive construct validity (Cronbach & Meehl, 1955). Meta-analysis has shown the correlation between objective and subjective performance measures to be low, indicating that these two types of measures are reflections of somewhat distinct concepts (i.e., have low convergent validity) (Bommer, Johnson, Rich, Podsakoff, & Mackenzie, 1995).

The performance construct has two important features that have been frequently overlooked by past research: (1) performance time frame (short- vs. long-term; Rambo, Chomiak, & Rountree, 1987), and (2) unit of analysis (individual performance vs. team performance vs. organizational performance; DeNisi, 2000; Schneider & Klein, 1994). It is expected that future research on the performance construct will elaborate these temporal and multilevel features, particularly in areas where the intended purposes of performance rating emphasize the need for such operationalizations.

## Rating Format

Historically, the choice of rating formats was believed to influence rating accuracy and interrater reliability. The major rating format options have included graphic rating scales (GRS; in which an employee is rated on her exhibition of some trait or behavior using a Likert scale—e.g., from 1 to 5), behaviorally anchored rating scales (BARS; in which behavioral statements are developed to represent typical behavior at various levels of performance along the scale, helping the rater to calibrate the rating given; Smith & Kendall, 1963), behavior observation scales (BOS; in which raters judge the frequency with which each behavior was exhibited by the ratee; Latham & Wexley, 1981), mixed standard scales (MSS; in which behavioral statements are made for good, medium, and poor performance on each performance dimension, then the ratee's behavior is compared with each of the three performance-level statements for each aspect of performance on a three-point scale [i.e., more effective, equally effective, less effective]; Blanz & Ghiselli, 1972), behavioral summary scales (BSS; like BARS, but with more generic behavioral statements; Borman, 1979), performance distribution assessment (which elicits both modal performance and variance in performance over time; Kane, 1986), and computerized adaptive rating scales (CARS; presents pairs of scaled behavioral statements iteratively, adapting presented pairs on the basis of previous responses; Borman et al., 2001). In a comparison of the various rating scales developed up to that point in time (e.g., BARS, GRS, etc.), Landy and Farr (1980) demonstrated that various rating formats were virtually indistinguishable in their effects on rater error, and they concluded that the choice of format matters little as long as ratings are behavior based and job related.

## Selecting a Rating Source: Who Should Make the Ratings?

Performance ratings can be made by several different sources, including supervisors, peers, subordinates, external customers, skip-level supervisors, and even self-ratings. Each of these sources is likely to be privy to unique types of information, to have some degree of shared perspective based on the source's position relative to the rating target, and to have personal agendas for the ratings. For instance, supervisors are likely to be knowledgeable about the target's productivity, peers are likely to be knowledgeable about the opportunities and constraints involved in a particular job, and external customers are likely to be knowledgeable about the quality of the target's work product.

When selecting a rating source, one should think about how the ratings will be used. If the ratings are part of a promotion decision, then asking for ratings from a peer who is in competition for the promotion can produce a conflict of interest. If the purpose of the ratings is to give the ratee developmental feedback but with no consequences for organizational reward or punishment, then there might be advantages to letting ratees select their own raters from among those who are likely to be knowledgeable.

A great deal of recent research and practice has incorporated the idea that multiple sources should be used to rate each target (see Chapter 21 of this volume; Bracken, Timmereck, & Church, 2001). Such multirater systems have special implications for rater training, choice of rating instrument, and rating purpose. With regard to the selection of rating sources for a given application, Farr and Newman (2001) have noted that little empirical research exists to guide source selection. Until such research accumulates, prescriptions for source selection must be based on common sense and the general finding that rating reliability improves as raters have more opportunity to observe ratees (Rothstein, 1990).

## Rater Training

It is important to remember that in the performance rating situation, the raters are the measurement instruments. Because raters are subject to many idiosyncratic social, political, and cognitive sources of variation, it is naive to assume that all raters give equally valid ratings by default. After the rating source is identified, the raters must be trained. Without training, the different measurement instruments (i.e., raters) cannot be expected to make precise assessments. To accomplish this task several types of training programs have been developed and implemented. These training programs include rater error training (RET), frame of reference training (FORT), performance dimension training (PDT), rater variability training (RVT), and behavioral observation training (BOT). Some of these training programs have been around for 30 years (e.g., RET), while others are newer (e.g., FORT), but all of them attempt to improve ratings. Evidence regarding the effectiveness of each of these programs also is discussed.

Rater error training has been used in performance rating situations for several decades. Its general purpose is to improve rater accuracy by minimizing rater errors, discussed earlier in this chapter, such as central tendency, leniency, and halo. This approach is probably still the most common form of rater training. The problem is that RET does not seem to achieve its purpose very well. Several sources have reported that accuracy drops or fails to improve after RET programs have been implemented (Bernardin, Cooke, & Villanova, 2000; Hauenstein, 1998; Woehr & Huffcutt, 1994). The consensus seems to be that RET is not particularly effective but is frequently implemented.

Among rater training researchers, FORT seems to have taken the place of RET as the dominant type of training. The main problem with FORT is that most uses of FORT have been in laboratory settings (Bernardin et al., 2000), with relatively little evidence accumulated for the effectiveness of FORT in applied settings. Keown-Gerrard and Sulsky (2001) stated that FORT focuses on calibrating raters so they agree on the dimensions on which performance is judged and what constitutes different levels of performance. Bernardin and Buckley (1981) noted that FORT emphasizes the multidimensionality of performance, the definition of performance, defining and describing performance examples, and practice and feedback using these established standards.

The steps in developing a FORT program are straightforward but require several judgment calls during the development of the procedure. For example, one of the goals of a FORT program is to help the raters understand the definition of performance within a given setting, which creates the need for training the program developers to make specific decisions about what will and will not be included in the performance

domain. The steps involved in creating a FORT program are as follows (Bernardin et al., 2000; Bernardin & Buckley, 1981):

1. A definition of performance must be generated. This definition must be very precise and should include descriptions of what types of behaviors should and should not be considered a part of the performance domain.

2. The raters must become familiar with performance dimensions and performance levels across dimensions. This task is accomplished by giving the raters the rating materials and meticulously going over every aspect of the rating format and the performance domain with the raters.

3. Presentation and discussion of critical incidents depicting different levels of performance across dimensions should be presented and discussed. This activity helps solidify the different dimensions of performance in the raters' mind. Through this process the rater is exposed to clear examples of poor, average, and favorable behavioral examples of performance on the different performance dimensions.

4. The key step in FORT is to allow the raters to practice rating. The raters should practice rating using the rating instrument until they are entirely comfortable with its use and the performance domain being rated.

5. After the raters have completed assigning practice ratings, detailed quantitative and qualitative feedback sessions should be held with each rater. Through this process, the rater can gain a better understanding of how ratings should be assigned and how he or she can improve. If possible, these sessions should be followed by more practice and feedback.

Several reviews suggest that FORT is effective (Arvey & Murphy, 1998; Bernardin et al., 2000; Woehr & Huffcutt, 1994), using the criterion of rating accuracy. At the present time, FORT is in need of more research in applied settings.

Much less has been written about other types of training, including performance dimension training, rater variability training, and behavioral observation training. That said, Hauenstein (1998) conducted a thorough review of the existing work on these training programs. His conclusion was that these types of training can be effective, but not as effective as FORT. These results must be considered preliminary, however, because very few studies of rater training methods, other than RET and FORT, have been conducted (Bernardin et al., 2000).

Performance dimension training attempts to help the rater become more familiar with the rating system elements. PDT is not necessarily concerned with accuracy; rather, it helps the rater to discriminate between different dimensions of performance. Hauenstein (1998) stated that this training is necessary but not sufficient for establishing rating accuracy. PDT could be thought of as a focus on steps two and three of a FORT program.

Rater variability training is designed to increase variability in ratings to reflect the variability in true performance. Although this practice may seem like a good idea, it may ultimately obtain similar results to those RET has received. The danger of this type of training is that it does not train raters how to rate a target's performance but, rather, teaches raters how their rating distribution should look. This practice could be dangerous if the target group happens to have a true performance distribution other than the one prescribed by the training. Therefore, RVT may lead to rating inflation and deflation for the sake of attaining an attractive distribution.

Behavioral observation training improves detection, perception, observation, and recall of relevant behaviors. BOT methods such as keeping diaries have been shown to be effective.

The bottom line of this discussion is that there are several types of rater training to choose from, and the pros and cons of each type should be weighed when choosing any of them. FORT seems to be the highest regarded type of training in the research literature. PDT, RVT, and BOT seem to work, but not as well as FORT (although not enough research has been conducted on these types of training). RET, while still enjoying popularity, may be the least effective of the various types of training programs.

## VALIDITY AND RELIABILITY OF PERFORMANCE RATINGS

When developing a performance rating application using the five aspects of method just outlined, a key goal is to produce ratings that are valid and reliable representations of an individual's performance. Each of the five aspects of method— purpose, definition of performance, format, source selection, and rater training—has important implications for validity and reliability of the ratings.

### Validity

Rating validity, or the extent to which the ratings measure what they are designed to measure, mandates clear decision making on the part of the rating system designer regarding what "performance" should mean for a particular application. If the purpose of the rating system is to change individuals' performance (through feedback and development), then performance should be operationalized at the individual level in very specific, behavioral, and absolute terms. By contrast, if the purpose of assessing performance is to support decisions

of which individuals should be moved (promotions, transfers, terminations), then performance can be operationalized as both behavioral and results criteria, measured *relative to others* in the work unit. Last, if the purpose of the performance appraisal is to aid in organizational redesign and strategy, then performance measures should include system-level results criteria that are aligned with the competitive strategy of the company (i.e., brokerage firms measure sales, grocery stores measure return customers, factories measure productivity and absences, pharmaceutical companies measure patents, etc.). Failure to align performance measures with the intended purpose of the appraisal system will likely result in construct validity problems, such as *criterion contamination* (measuring something in addition to what was intended) or *criterion deficiency* (not measuring all of what was intended) (Brogden & Taylor, 1950). The concept of measurement validity is inherently value-laden, and hence the goals of the rating system need explicit specification prior to selection of the rating instrument, raters, and rater training. The performance construct should be matched to the purpose for which ratings are used in content, level of specificity, and level of analysis (e.g., task vs. contextual performance, specific task performance vs. overall performance, team facilitation vs. individual performance vs. performance over time, etc.)

On the topic of rater source selection and rating instrument selection, one contemporary method for assessing the construct validity of performance ratings is to use a version of the Multitrait-Multimethod matrix (Campbell & Fiske, 1959). In this approach, ratings of the intended performance construct(s) can be made by multiple rating sources, using multiple instruments. Since each rating source is providing a rating of each performance dimension using each rating instrument, it is possible to statistically model the components of the ratings that are idiosyncratic to a specific rating source or instrument. It is also possible to establish the convergent validity of ratings across sources and instruments, as well as the discriminant validity of various performance criteria that are proposed to be theoretically distinct (for updated statistical techniques, see Conway, 1998; and Bagozzi, Yi, & Phillips, 1991). Conway (1999) provided an example of a multitrait-multisource approach for assessing the construct validity of managerial performance, in which he modeled the relative contributions of various performance facets (e.g., job dedication, interpersonal facilitation, task performance) to overall performance ratings made by both peers and supervisors.

### Reliability

No rating can be valid without being reliable. The reliability, or consistency of measurement, of performance ratings has been assessed in several different ways. Although performance rating reliability has been indexed by both interrater reliability (among several raters) and intrarater reliability (across time or scale items), Schmidt and Hunter (1977) advised that the most appropriate measure of criterion reliability is reliability across two raters who rate the target at distant points in time. Viswesvaran, Ones, and Schmidt (1996) have critiqued the use of intrarater agreement as an index of reliability because it includes transient and idiosyncratic rater errors. These authors interpreted empirical research as favoring the use of interrater reliability and reported a meta-analytic estimate of interrater reliability of .52 for supervisor ratings of overall performance (leading to the conclusion that 25% of the variance in supervisor performance ratings is true score variance). In spite of these unimpressive results regarding the reliability of performance ratings, some researchers believe .52 to still be an overestimate of true reliability. Specifically, the use of interrater reliability has been criticized because it includes systematic rating biases that raters share in common (Murphy & DeShon, 2000; but see Schmidt, Viswesvaran, and Ones [2000] for a critique of Murphy and DeShon's critique, positing that such views of measurement result in nihilism). Scullen, Mount, and Goff (2000) shed some additional light on the subject, using a generalizability theory framework (Cronbach, Gleser, Nanda, & Rajaratnam, 1972; Shavelson & Webb, 1991) to demonstrate that over 50% of the variance in performance ratings is due to idiosyncratic rater effects (halo error), whereas only 25% of rating variance is due to the ratees' actual performance. These results indicate that performance ratings may reveal more about the rater than about the ratee, and they provide a rich area for future research.

### More on Reliability in Performance Ratings

The purpose of performance ratings may influence the ratings' apparent reliability as a result of distributional artifacts associated with rating purpose. Specifically, the finding that ratings made for between-persons decision making (e.g., promotions, terminations) are subject to leniency errors (Jawahar & Williams, 1997) implies that the range of such ratings would be restricted. This restriction of range (e.g., raters only using response options 6 and 7 on a 7-point scale) could result in an artificially inflated estimate of interrater agreement and could also artificially deflate estimates of interrater reliability based on the correlations among multiple raters' ratings. Obtaining estimates of the overall effect of rating purpose on rating reliability is an issue for future research.

The definition of performance also has implications for rating reliability, because some performance constructs (communication and interpersonal competence) are rated less reliably on average than other performance constructs (pro-

ductivity and quality) (interrater reliability; Viswesvaran et al, 1996).

Using the measurement approach of item response theory (IRT; Hambleton, Swaminathan, & Rogers, 1991), Facteau and Craig (2001) have demonstrated that raters from various rating sources (supervisors, peers, self) discriminate ratees equally well across the range of performance. These results imply that reliability of performance ratings may not be greatly influenced by any systematic biases attributable to the rating source.

Last, rater training can be an important part of establishing rating reliability. Previously discussed techniques such as FORT can be implemented to improve the consistency of calibration between raters.

### LIMITATIONS

The use of subjective ratings of individual performance as a basis for personnel decisions and feedback has many limitations. Such limitations are reflected throughout this chapter and pervade most discussions of the science and practice of performance appraisal. In particular, performance ratings are subject to the aforementioned systematic errors (e.g., leniency, halo, recency, contrast), can be manipulated in accord with rater goals (i.e., social and political motives), and depend on the rater's knowledge of and opportunity to observe job behavior. Furthermore, job requirements may vary across occasions and situations, or may be poorly defined, leaving the rater with the complex task of assessing a fuzzy, moving target. Last, performance ratings are rendered meaningless when put to purposes other than those understood by the rater (e.g., using ratings designed for feedback purposes as a basis for deciding whom to terminate). At the extreme, staunch critics have claimed that performance ratings are inherently antithetical to organizational productivity (e.g., see Deming, 1986).

### CROSS-CULTURAL ISSUES IN PERFORMANCE RATINGS

Throughout the past 20 years culture researchers have suggested that culture can influence several human resource functions (cf., Erez, 1997; Hofstede, 1984; Triandis, 1994). Despite these suggestions, performance rating research involving culture has been slow to develop. Although culture has been assumed to affect performance rating, there is not consensus about the nature of culture's influence on rating and little empirical research from which to draw.

Evidence has been mounting that the cultural dimension of individualism-collectivism may be critical in understanding performance rating. According to Bailey, Chen, and Duo (1997), individualism-collectivism refers to "cultural dispositions to understand oneself primarily in terms of either satisfying personal aspirations or attending to group needs." Erez (1997, p. 606) pointed out that individual performance appraisal may not be acceptable in collectivist cultures because collectivists focus on the workgroup rather than the performance of any one person in the group. Oyserman, Coon, and Kemmelmeier (2002) pointed out several potential problems with the measurement of individualism and collectivism but still concluded that these are useful constructs. Space does not permit here a full discussion of the issues raised by Oyserman and colleagues, and the interested reader is referred to their paper.

As Triandis (1994) discussed, performance appraisals often assume that most of the variance in performance can be attributed to individuals (rather than group variance or situational variance). This assumption is based on research that has been conducted on performance appraisal in Western cultures. It is important to understand the effects that such an ethnocentric bias may have as organizations become increasingly more global. Triandis (1994) stated that more than half of the people in the world are socialized in collectivist cultures. If research in individualist cultures regarding performance ratings does not generalize to collectivist cultures, the use and interpretation of performance ratings as conceptualized in Western research traditions will be inappropriate for much of the world's population.

It seems likely that differences in performance rating across the individualist-collectivist cultural dimension could be caused by differences in attribution strategy or by generic beliefs about the causes of behavior. Social psychological literature has discussed the role of attribution differences across this cultural dimension. According to Triandis (1996), understanding what causes things to occur in our world provides perceivers with some capability to make sense of—and to foresee the consequences of—actions and events. Several studies from the last 10 years can be summarized by the general conclusion that, as Triandis (1994) and Triandis and Bhawuk (1997) noted, collectivists attribute success externally (e.g., to luck, circumstance, etc.), whereas individualists attribute success internally (e.g., to effort). These differences in attribution suggest that raters from different cultures will perceive performance from a ratee differently, and thus assign ratings differently. Kitayama, Markus, Matsumot, and Norasakkunkit (1997) analyzed 23 Asian studies and found a robust self-effacing effect. That is, people in Asian cultures tended to attribute their own success externally and attribute their failures to a lack of ability and talent. They also found that Japanese employees accept failure better than they accept success. The authors suggested that the self is made mean-

ingful in individualist cultures by reference to a set of attributes that are internal and bounded to the self, whereas in collectivist cultures, a self-critical view is held, which serves as a symbolic act of affirming one's belongingness to the group. Menon, Morris, Chiu, and Hong (1999) presented similar findings, also concluding that the bias toward attributing success to personal attributes in Western cultures is robust, while the effect is markedly reduced in Asian collectivist societies. Building on attribution theory's position that consistent behavior is attributed to stable causes, they suggested that collectivists attribute behavior to stable characteristics within the situation, whereas individualists attribute behavior to stable characteristics within the person. Morris and Peng (1994) made a similar point, concluding that Americans are person centered and Chinese are situation centered. These authors suggested that Americans view people as individual units: They can leave groups at any time and are socialized to behave according to personal preferences. Conversely, the Chinese view people as group members who cannot leave groups at will and must behave according to group norms, role constraints, and situational scripts. Consistent with this idea, these authors found that individualists are likely to reward short-term individual behaviors, and collectivists are likely to reward long-term group behaviors.

Given that most performance appraisal formats try to evaluate performance at the individual level, asking about specific behaviors, our methods of performance rating may not be appropriate in collectivist cultures. Attributional differences between individualist and collectivist cultures are deeply rooted in their respective dominant social representations (i.e., Judeo-Christian belief in individual soul and free will vs. Confucian primacy of social relationships and virtue of role-appropriate behavior) (Morris & Peng, 1994). For this reason, cultural differences in performance rating should not be expected to disappear through brief, local interventions such as rater training.

Research evidence on attribution styles suggests that it would be naive to expect high levels of agreement across individualist and collectivist raters. This theoretical argument is becoming increasingly more important as organizations move into international markets. As organizations become global, researchers must ask and answer questions designed to understand precisely how performance ratings differ across cultures.

## LEGAL ISSUES IN PERFORMANCE RATINGS

Because performance ratings are used as a subjective basis for making personnel decisions, they are fair game in the legal arena. The performance appraisal process is often challenged in the courts (Malos, 1998). To gain an appreciation of the role of the legal system in performance ratings it is important to understand how the courts tend to decide in performance appraisal cases, as well as the laws regarding performance appraisal.

The most influential law relevant to performance appraisal is Title VII of the Civil Rights Act of 1964. This act made it unlawful to discriminate on the basis of race, color, religion, sex, or national origin when making administrative decisions (Gutman, 1993). Further extending the rules set by Title VII was the 1967 Age Discrimination Act, which prohibits discrimination against those over 40 years of age. Finally, in 1992 the Americans with Disabilities Act was passed, which prohibits discrimination on the basis of a person's disabilities.

Although these laws establish protected classes against whom personnel decisions must not discriminate, the laws do not address the definition of discrimination. In 1978, to help define when unfair discrimination occurs, the Equal Employment Opportunity Commission adopted the *Uniform Guidelines on Employee Selection Procedures.* Murphy and Cleveland (1995, p. 11) cited this as the "single greatest influence on the development and use of performance assessment in the United States." The courts have turned to these guidelines when interpreting the laws discussed previously. The *Uniform Guidelines* specify criteria to be used in determining whether any subgroup has been discriminated against (Ledvinka & Scarpello, 1992).

In addition to the *Guidelines,* there have also been landmark court decisions relevant to the legal interpretation of performance ratings. Precedents set by these decisions must be considered when attempting to predict how judges will interpret ratings cases. For example, in *Watson v. Fort Worth Bank and Trust* (1988), the Supreme Court ruled that if subjective ratings are used for administrative decisions, they must be job related. Further, it was ruled that ratings are subject to the same statistical tests to determine discrimination as objective tests. In *Abermarle Paper Company v. Moody* (1975), the Supreme Court ruled that accuracy and validity of a performance appraisal process could be assessed in a validation study. Further, in *Brito v. Zia* (1973), the courts ruled that performance ratings are tests and must conform to the *Uniform Guidelines* (Cascio & Bernardin, 1981). Bersoff (1988) reiterated the suggestion that subjective ratings be validated in the same manner as objective tests.

In an alternative approach to the *test metaphor,* Folger, Konovsky, and Cropanzano (1992) presented performance appraisal using a *due process metaphor.* These authors suggested that the test metaphor is deficient because it assumes that work situations allow for reliable and valid measurement, which is probably not the case in our rapidly changing work environments. Also, as mentioned earlier, treating performance ratings as a test ignores the cognitive limitations and/or goals adopted by the raters as a source of systematic rating variance. The due process metaphor presented by Folger et al. (1992) suggests that the legality of personnel decisions should be based on how the decisions are implemented (i.e., Did all parties involved have plenty of notice before the decision, voice in the decision, and confidence that the decision was based on evidence?).

Feild and Holley (1982) analyzed influential factors in 66 judicial decisions regarding performance appraisal between 1965 and 1980. These authors identified five important factors: (1) the use of job analysis, (2) the use of behavioral-oriented appraisal (as opposed to trait-based ratings of performance), (3) whether or not the raters were provided with adequate instruction, (4) whether or not the ratings would be reviewed by the ratee, and (5) the type of organization. In sum, these researchers concluded that nonindustrial organizations using behavioral rating scales based on job analyses are the most defensible, especially when raters are given the proper instruction and ratings are shown to the targets.

In a more recent review by Werner and Bolino (1997) both the test metaphor and the due process metaphor were examined regarding court decisions. Similar to the Feild and Holley (1982) study, these authors found that judges favorably considered job analysis, written rater instructions, and ratee review of ratings. Contradictory to Feild and Holley (1982), Werner and Bolino (1997) found that the type of organization and type of appraisal did not make a difference in court decisions. Further, appraisal systems incorporating multiple raters with adequate levels of agreement were preferable to single rater assessments. These researchers also found that the issues described regarding the due process metaphor are important to judges when evaluating appraisal cases. Finally, the authors found that validation concerns in subjective ratings were virtually ignored, which argues against the importance of the test metaphor. In support of this notion, Beck-Dudley and McEvoy (1991) found that the courts have a general hesitation to consider performance appraisal validity evidence.

Beck-Dudley and McEvoy (1991) also concluded that the courts have not clearly expressed to performance-rating consumers what the essential characteristics of appraisal systems are that make them legally defensible. The best available advice is that of Feild and Holley (1982) and Werner and Bolino (1997). For further insights into how to make an appraisal system legally defensible, the interested reader can refer to Ashe and McRae (1985), Barrett and Kernan (1987), Feild and Holley (1982), Malos (1998), Martin and Bartol (1991), Veglahn (1993), and Werner and Bolino (1997).

# FUTURE DEVELOPMENTS

Both empirical research and theoretical development related to performance ratings continue. We have selected for brief discussion a few topics that we believe likely to have an important impact in the near future.

## Rater Goals

Murphy and Cleveland (1991, 1995) suggested that it may be advantageous to think of the performance rating process as a goal-directed communication process. These authors noted that when evaluating performance, raters attempt to use their ratings to communicate information consistent with their personal interests. This idea is important because it implies that raters are not always motivated to provide accurate ratings.

Research on rater goals is in its infancy, and there are still many unanswered questions about what types of goals raters adopt, as well as the effects that those goals exert on ratings. Some progress has been made, however. In a recent study investigating the goals of raters, goals were found to influence performance ratings. Skattebo, Newman, Kinney, and Cleveland (2002) found support for four goals adopted by university students when rating instructors. Raters adopted the goal of identifying strengths in their instructor's performance, identifying weaknesses in the instructor's performance, motivating the instructor, or rating fairly. These goals were related to the ratings assigned by students. Specifically, to the extent that a student endorsed "identify strength" goals, he or she was more likely to assign high performance ratings for the instructor. Also, to the extent that students endorsed "identify weakness" goals, they were likely to assign low ratings. The results of this study suggest that the adoption of different goals by the raters does relate to the level of the performance rating.

The key point in considering the goals adopted by raters is that if raters' goals are not to rate accurately, raters will not rate accurately regardless of the rater training, the rating scale format, the cognitive judgment, and so on. As Bjerke, Cleveland, Morrison, and Wilson (1987) pointed out, the choice of exactly what message the rater communicates with performance ratings depends on the goals being pursued by such rater. If the impact of rater goals on performance ratings is not considered, consumers of performance appraisal information will not gain an accurate understanding of the messages communicated by the performance rating process. Although research has yet to answer a lot of the questions surrounding rater goals, this area does promise to be a hot topic in the future.

## Rater Training and Cognitive Processes

As stated earlier in this chapter, in the 1980s and 1990s much attention was focused on researching the cognitive processes of raters. Through this research, an understanding of how raters observe, encode, and retrieve performance information has been gained. A criticism of this research is that the advances in understanding of rater cognitive processes have not led to improvements in the practice of performance appraisal (Murphy & Cleveland, 1995).

One area where this research could inform practice is the area of rater training. As discussed earlier, several recent advances have occurred in the methods used in training raters. A number of these advances involve training raters on how to process information. For example, FORT and BOT teach raters what behaviors are important to encode, retrieve, and recall. However, at this time not enough research has accumulated about the effectiveness of these "cognitive training" approaches.

FORT has received favorable evaluations (see Arvey & Murphy, 1998; Bernardin et al., 2000; Woehr & Huffcutt, 1994), although Bernardin et al. (2000) noted that most FORT research has been within laboratory settings. Given the distinction between performance judgment and performance appraisal suggested by Murphy and Cleveland (1995) and explained at the beginning of this chapter, the restriction to laboratory settings is an important consideration. Because strict controls can be placed on ratings in the lab, the ratings can exist in an environment less affected by contextual variables. Therefore, ratings made in these settings are a closer reflection of the rater's judgments than could be expected in a context-rich organizational setting.

Given these concerns, two areas for future research can be identified. First, more information is needed to determine the effectiveness of these "cognitively based" training methods in applied settings. Second, if research in this area does show that cognitively-based training methods are not as effective outside the laboratory, a shift in focus of rater training may be in order. Specifically, training could focus on preparing raters to filter away context and make ratings that are consistent with their judgments. Such an intervention would likely address rater goals and organizational goals with the purpose of minimizing the discrepancy between the two.

## Rating Format Research

Recent research has called to question Landy and Farr's (1980) moratorium on rating format research on two grounds: (1) the use of ratings for feedback purposes requires that raters be allowed to communicate global performance information (consistent with memory categorization principles), whereas ratees desire feedback that is specific and behavioral (identifying relative personal strengths and weaknesses) (Jelley & Goffin, 2001), and (2) adaptive formats that are customized to fit the information-processing tendencies of individual raters (CARS) show greater accuracy than BARS or GRS (Borman et al., 2001). Although the contentions introduced by these studies mark the implicit promise of future research on the topic of rating formats, respective effect sizes for differential accuracy of various formats were small (typically less than .10). If future research on rating formats is to ever become justifiable, then it is essential for innovative new formats to be introduced through conscientious application of theories of rater cognition. Whether such custom alignment of rating formats to each rater's cognitive processes will bear fruit remains to be seen.

## Toward a Multilevel Conceptualization of Performance

Ultimately, human resource professionals and managers who use job performance ratings are interested in improving firm-level performance (DeNisi, 2000). Within the paradigm of performance appraisal research, it has often been assumed that individual-level improvements in performance will cumulate to produce firm-level improvement. This is exemplified by utility analysis (Schmidt, Hunter, McKenzie, & Muldrow, 1979). Utility estimates are problematic, however, because they ignore important processes by which individual performance aggregates (e.g., teamwork, information sharing between workgroups) and are thus subject to an *atomistic fallacy* of ignoring the lack of generality from an individual unit of analysis to a group or organizational unit of analysis (House, Rousseau, & Thomas-Hunt, 1995; Kozlowski & Klein, 2000).

On many occasions, strong individual-level performance does not enhance group-level performance, such as when a team is engaged in a sequentially interdependent task, for which group performance is determined by the "weakest link" rather than by the average performance of team members (Tesluk, Mathieu, Zaccaro, & Marks, 1997). Furthermore, performance rating is an inherently multilevel phenomenon when ratings are used to make between-persons comparisons for personnel decisions. When making such decisions as, "Which employee should be promoted?," the basis for each individual decision must incorporate information about the performance of all group members (DeNisi, 2000). Our reason for pointing out the multilevel nature of the performance construct is to make clear that the ultimate imperative of *attaining organization-level objectives* should be recognized as the driving force behind every step in the design of the performance rating system.

## REFERENCES

Antonioni, D. (1994). Improve the performance management process before discontinuing performance appraisals. *Compensation and Benefits Review, 26*(3), 29–37.

Arvey, R.D., & Murphy, K.R. (1998). Performance evaluation in work settings. *Annual Review of Psychology, 49,* 141–168.

Ashe, R.L., & McRae, G.S. (1985). Performance evaluations go to court in the 1980s. *Mercer Law Review, 36,* 887–905.

Bagozzi, R.P., Yi, Y., & Phillips, L.W. (1991). Assessing construct validity in organizational research. *Administrative Science Quarterly, 36*(3), 421–458.

Bailey, J.R., Chen C.C., & Dou, S.G. (1997). Conceptions of self and performance-related feedback in the U.S., Japan and China. *Journal of International Business Studies, 3,* 605–625.

Barrett, G.V., & Kernan, M.C. (1987). Performance appraisal and terminations: A review of court decisions since *Brito v. Zia* with implications for personnel practices. *Personnel Psychology, 40,* 489–503.

Beck-Dudley, C.L., & McEvoy, G.M. (1991). Performance appraisals and discrimination suits: Do courts pay attention to validity? *Employee Responsibilities and Rights Journal, 4,* 149–163.

Bernardin, H.J., & Buckley, M.R. (1981). Strategies in rater training. *Academy of Management Review, 6,* 205–212.

Bernardin, H.J., Cooke, D.K., & Villanova, P. (2000). Conscientiousness and agreeableness as predictors of rating leniency. *Journal of Applied Psychology, 85*(2), 232–234.

Bersoff, D. (1988). Should subjective employment devices be scrutinized? *American Psychologist, 43,* 1016–1018.

Bingham, W.V., & Freyd, M. (1926). Procedures in Employment Psychology. Chicago: A.W. Shaw Company.

Bjerke, D.G., Cleveland, J.N., Morrison, R.F., & Wilson, W.C. (1987). *Officer Fitness Report Evaluation Study* (Navy Personnel Research and Development Center Report, TR 88-4). San Diego: NPRDC.

Blanz, R., & Ghiselli, E.E. (1972). The mixed standard scale: A new rating system. *Personnel Psychology, 25,* 185–200.

Bommer, W.H., Johnson, J., Rich, G.A., Podsakoff, P.M., & Mackenzie, S.B. (1995). On the interchangeability of objective and subjective measures of employee performance: A meta-analysis. *Personnel Psychology, 48*(3), 587–605.

Borman, W.C. (1978). Exploring the upper limits of reliability and validity in job performance ratings. *Journal of Applied Psychology, 63,* 135–144.

Borman, W.C. (1979). Format and training effects on rating accuracy and rater errors. *Journal of Applied Psychology, 64,* 410–421.

Borman, W.C., & Brush, D.H. (1993). More progress toward a taxonomy of managerial performance requirements. *Human Performance, 6*(1), 1–21.

Borman, W.C., Buck, D.E., Hanson, M.A., Motowidlo, S.J., Stark, S., & Drasgow, F. (2001). An examination of the comparative reliability, validity, and accuracy of performance ratings made using computerized adaptive rating scales. *Journal of Applied Psychology, 86*(5), 965–973.

Borman, W.C., & Motowidlo, S.J. (1993). Expanding the criterion domain to include elements of contextual performance. In N. Schmitt & W.C. Borman (Eds.), *Personnel selection in organizations* (pp. 71–98). San Francisco: Jossey-Bass.

Bracken, D.W., Timmereck, C.W., & Church, A.H. (Eds.). (2001). *The handbook of multisource feedback.* San Francisco: Jossey-Bass.

Brogden, H., & Taylor, E.K. (1950). The theory and classification of criterion bias. *Educational and Psychological Measurement, 10,* 159–186.

Campbell, D.T., & Fiske, P.W. (1959). Convergent and discriminant validation by the multitrait-multimethod matrix. *Psychological Bulletin, 56,* 81–105.

Campbell, J.P., Gasser, M.B., & Oswald, F.L. (1996). The substantive nature of job performance variability. In K.R. Murphy (Ed.), *Individual differences and behavior in organizations* (pp. 258–299). San Francisco: Jossey-Bass.

Campbell, J.P., McCloy, R.A., Oppler, S.H., & Sager, C.E. (1993). A theory of job performance. In N. Schmitt & W.C. Borman (Eds.), *Personnel selection in organizations* (pp. 35–70). San Francisco: Jossey-Bass.

Cardy, R.L., & Dobbins, G.H. (1986). Affect and appraisal accuracy: Liking as an integral dimension in evaluating performance. *Journal of Applied Psychology, 71,* 672–678.

Cardy, R.L., & Dobbins, G.H. (1994). *Performance appraisal: Alternative perspectives.* Cincinnati, OH: South-Western.

Cardy, R.L., & Krzystofiak, F.J. (1998). *Observation and Rating Accuracy: WYSIWYG?* Paper presented at the annual convention of the Society for Industrial and Organizational Psychology, Dallas, TX.

Cascio, W.F., & Bernardin, H.J. (1981). Implications for performance appraisal litigation for personnel decisions. *Personnel Psychology, 34,* 211–226.

Cheung, G.W. (1999). Multifaceted conceptions of self-other ratings disagreement. *Personnel Psychology, 52,* 1–36.

Cleveland, J.N., Murphy, K.R., & Williams, R.E. (1989). Multiple uses of performance appraisal: Prevalence and correlates. *Journal of Applied Psychology, 74,* 130–135.

Conway, J.M. (1998). Estimation and uses of the proportion method variance for multitrait-multidimensional data. *Organizational-Research-Methods, 1*(2), 209–222.

Conway, J.M. (1999). Distinguishing contextual performance from task performance for managerial jobs. *Journal of Applied Psychology, 84*(1), 3–13.

Cronbach, L.J., Gleser, G.C., Nanda, H., & Rajaratnam, N. (1972). *The dependability of behavioral measurements: Theory of generalizability for scores and profiles.* New York: Wiley.

Cronbach, L.J., & Meehl, P.E. (1955). Construct validity in psychological tests. *Psychological-Bulletin, 52,* 281–302.

Deming, W.E. (1986). *Out of the crisis.* Cambridge, MA: MIT Institute for Advanced Engineering Study.

DeNisi, A.S. (2000). Performance appraisal and performance management: A multilevel analysis. In K.J. Klein & S.W.J. Kozlowski (Eds.), *Multilevel theory, research, and methods in organizations: Foundations, extensions, and new directions* (pp. 121–156). San Francisco: Jossey-Bass.

DeNisi, A.S., Cafferty, T.P., & Meglino, B.M. (1984). A cognitive model of the performance appraisal process: A model and research propositions. *Organizational Behavior and Human Decision Processes, 33,* 360–396.

DuBois, C.L., Sackett, P.R., Zedeck, S., & Fogli, L. (1993). Further exploration of typical and maximum performance criteria: Definitional issues, prediction, and white-black differences. *Journal of Applied Psychology, 78*(2), 205–211.

Erez, M. (1997). A culture-based model of work motivation. In P.C. Earley & M. Erez (Eds.), *New perspectives on international Industrial/Organizational Psychology* (pp. 193–242). San Francisco: The New Lexington Press.

Facteau, J.D., & Craig, S.B. (2001). Are performance appraisal ratings from different rating sources comparable? *Journal of Applied Psychology, 86*(2), 215–227.

Farr, J.L., & Newman, D.A. (2001). Rater selection: Sources of feedback. In D.W. Bracken, C.W. Timmereck, & A.H. Church (Eds.), *The handbook of multisource feedback* (pp. 96–113). San Francisco: Jossey-Bass.

Feild, H.S., & Holley, W.H. (1982). The relationship of performance appraisal system characteristics to verdicts in selected employment discrimination cases. *Academy of Management Journal, 25,* 392–406.

Feldman, J.M. (1985). Instrumentation and training for performance appraisal: A perceptual-cognitive viewpoint. In K. Rowland & G. Ferris (Eds.), *Research in personnel and human resources management* (Vol. 3, pp. 45–72). Greenwich, CT: JAI Press.

Folger, R., Konovsky, M.A., & Cropanzano, R. (1992). A due process metaphor for performance appraisal. In B. Staw & L. Cummings (Eds.), *Research in organizational behavior* (Vol. 14, pp. 129–177). Greenwich, CT: JAI Press.

Gutman, A. (1993). *EEO law and personnel practices.* Newbury Park, CA: Sage.

Haeggberg, D., & Chen, P.Y. (1999). *Can accountability assure the accuracy of upward appraisals?* Paper presented at the 14th Annual Conference of the Society for Industrial and Organizational Psychology, Atlanta, GA.

Hambleton, R.K., Swaminathan, H., & Rogers, H.J. (1991). *Fundamentals of item response theory.* Thousand Oaks, CA: Sage.

Hauenstein, N.M.A. (1998). Training raters to increase the accuracy of appraisals and the usefulness of feedback. In J. Smither (Ed.), *Performance appraisal: State of the art in practice* (pp. 404–442). San Francisco: Jossey-Bass.

Hofmann, D.A., Jacobs, R., & Baratta, J. (1993). Dynamic criteria and the measurement of change. *Journal of Applied Psychology, 78,* 194–204.

Hofstede, G. (1984). *Culture's consequences: International differences in work-related values* (Abridged ed.). Newbury Park, CA: Sage.

House, R., Rousseau, D.M., & Thomas-Hunt, M. (1995). The meso paradigm: A framework for the integration of micro and macro organizational behavior. In L.L. Cummings & B.M. Staw (Eds.), *Research in organizational behavior* (Vol. 17, pp. 71–114). Greenwich, CT: JAI Press.

Ilgen, D.R., & Feldman, J.M. (1983). Performance appraisal: A process focus. In B.M. Staw & L.L. Cummings (Eds.), *Research in organizational behavior* (Vol. 5, pp. 141–197). Greenwich, CT: JAI Press.

Jawahar, I.M., & Williams, C.R. (1997). Where all the children are above average: The performance appraisal purpose. *Personnel Psychology, 50*(4), 905–925.

Jelley, R.B., & Goffin, R.D. (2001). Can performance-feedback accuracy be improved? Effects of rater priming and rating-scale format on rating accuracy. *Journal of Applied Psychology, 86*(1), 134–144.

Kane, J.S. (1986). Performance distribution assessment. In R. Berk (Ed.), *Performance assessment: Methods and applications* (pp. 237–273). Baltimore: Johns Hopkins University Press.

Kane, J.S. (2000). Accuracy and its determinants in distributional assessment. *Human Performance, 13*(1), 47–84.

Kenny, D.A. (1991). A general model of consensus and accuracy in interpersonal perception. *Psychological Review, 98*(2), 155–163.

Keown-Gerrard, J.L., & Sulsky, L.M. (2001). The effects of task information training and frame of reference training with situational constraints on rating accuracy. *Human Performance, 14,* 305–320.

Kitayama, S., Markus, H.R., Matsumoto, H., and Norasakkunkit, V. (1997). Individual and collective processes in the construction of the self: Self-enhancement in the United States and self-criticism in Japan. *Journal of Personality and Social Psychology, 72*(6), 1245–1267.

Klimoski, R., & Inks, L. (1990). Accountability forces in performance appraisal. *Organizational Behavior and Human Decision Processes, 45,* 194–208.

Kozlowski, S.W.J., & Klein, K.J. (2000). A multilevel approach to theory and research in organizations: Contextual, temporal, and emergent processes. In K.J. Klein & S.W.J. Kozlowski (Eds.), *Multilevel theory, research, and methods in organizations: Foundations, extensions, and new directions* (pp. 3–90). San Francisco: Jossey-Bass.

Landy, F.J., & Farr, J.L. (1980). Performance Rating. *Psychological Bulletin, 87,* 72–107.

Landy, F.J., & Farr, J.L. (1983). *The measurement of work performance: Methods, theory and applications.* New York: Academic Press.

Latham, G.P., & Wexley, K.N. (1981). *Increasing productivity through performance appraisal.* Reading, MA: Addison-Wesley.

Ledvinka, J., & Scarpello, V. (1992). *Federal regulation of personnel and human resource management* (2nd ed.) Boston: Wadsworth.

Longenecker, C.O., Sims, H.P., & Gioia, D.A. (1987). Behind the mask: The politics of employee appraisal. *Academy of Management Executive, 1,* 183–193.

Lord, R.G. (1985). Accuracy in behavioral measurement: An alternative definition based on raters' cognitive schema and signal detection. *Journal of Applied Psychology, 70,* 66–71.

Malos, S.B. (1998). Current legal issues in performance appraisal. In J. Smither (Ed.), *Performance Appraisal: State of the art in practice* (pp. 49–94). San Francisco: Jossey-Bass.

Martin, D.C., & Bartol, K.M. (1991). The legal ramifications of performance appraisal: An update. *Employee Relations Law Journal, 17,* 257–286.

Menon, T., Morris, M.W., Chiu, C., & Hong, Y. (1999). Culture and the construal of agency: Attribution to individual versus group dispositions. *Journal of Personality and Social Psychology, 76*(5), 701–717.

Mero, N.P., & Motowidlo, S.J. (1995). Effects of rater accountability on the accuracy and the favorability of performance ratings. *Journal of Applied Psychology, 80,* 517–524.

Mohrman, A.M., & Lawler, E.E. (1983). Motivation and performance appraisal behavior. In F. Landy, S. Zedeck, & J. Cleveland (Eds.), *Performance measurement and theory* (pp. 173–189). Hillsdale, NJ: Erlbaum.

Morris, M.W., & Peng K. (1994). Culture and cause: American and Chinese attributions for social and physical events. *Journal of Personality and Social Psychology, 67*(6), 949–971.

Murphy, K.R. (1991). Criterion issues in performance appraisal research: Behavioral accuracy versus classification accuracy. *Organizational behavior and human decision processes, 50,* 45–50.

Murphy, K.R., & Cleveland, J.N. (1991). *Performance appraisal: An organizational perspective.* Needham Heights, MA: Allyn & Bacon.

Murphy, K.R., & Cleveland, J.N. (1995). *Understanding performance appraisal: Social, organizational, goal-based perspectives.* Thousand Oaks, CA: Sage.

Murphy, K.R., & DeShon, R. (2000). Interrater correlations do not estimate the reliability of job performance ratings. *Personnel Psychology, 53*(4), 873–900.

Ouchi, W.G., & Maguire, M.A. (1975). Organizational control: Two functions. *Administrative Science Quarterly, 20*(4), 559–569.

Oyserman, D., Coon, H.M., & Kemmelmeier, M. (2002). Rethinking individualism and collectivism: Evaluation of the theoretical assumptions and meta-analyses. *Psychological Bulletin, 128,* 3–72.

Padgett, M.Y., & Ilgen, D.R. (1989). The impact of ratee performance characteristics on rater cognitive processes and alternative measures of rater accuracy. *Organizational Behavior and Human Decision Processes, 44*(2), 232–260.

Ployhart, R.E., & Hakel, M.D. (1998). The substantive nature of performance variability: Predicting interindividual differences in intraindividual performance. *Personnel Psychology, 51*(4), 859–901.

Rambo, W.W., Chomiak, A.M., & Rountree, R.J. (1987). Temporal interval and the estimation of the reliability of work performance data. *Perceptual and Motor Skills, 64*(3), 791–798

Rothstein, H.R. (1990). Interrater reliability of job performance ratings: Growth to asymptote level with increasing opportunity to observe. *Journal of Applied Psychology, 75*(3), 322–327.

Sackett, P.R., Zedeck, S., & Fogli, L. (1988). Relations between measures of typical and maximum performance. *Journal of Applied Psychology, 73,* 482–486.

Schmidt, F.L., & Hunter, J.E. (1977). Development of a general solution to the problem of validity generalization. *Journal of Applied Psychology, 62*(5), 529–540.

Schmidt, F.L., Hunter, J.E., McKenzie, R.C., & Muldrow, T.W. (1979). The impact of valid selection procedures on work-force productivity. *Journal of Applied Psychology, 64,* 609–626.

Schmidt, F.L., Viswesvaran, C., & Ones, D.S. (2000). Reliability is not validity and validity is not reliability. *Personnel-Psychology, 53*(4), 901–912.

Schneider, B., & Klein, K.J. (1994). What is enough? A systems perspective on individual-organizational performance links. In D.H. Harris (Ed.), *Organizational linkages: Understanding the productivity paradox* (pp. 81–104). Washington, DC: National Academy Press.

Scullen, S.E., Mount, M.K., & Goff, M. (2000). Understanding the latent structure of job performance ratings. *Journal of Applied Psychology, 85*(6), 956–970.

Shavelson, R.J., & Webb, N.M. (1991). *Generalizability theory: A primer.* Thousand Oaks, CA: Sage.

Skattebo, A.L., Newman, D.A., Kinney, T.B., & Cleveland, J.N. (2002). Rater goals and unit climate affect rating behavior. Paper presented at the 17th Annual Conference of the *Society for Industrial and Organizational Psychology,* Toronto, Canada.

Smith, P.C. (1976). Behavior, results, and organizational effectiveness: The problem of criteria. In M.D. Dunnette (Ed.), *Handbook of industrial and organizational psychology* (pp. 745–775). Chicago: Rand McNally.

Smith, P.C., & Kendall, L.M. (1963). Retranslation of expectations: An approach to the construction of unambiguous anchors for rating scales. *Journal of Applied Psychology, 47,* 149–155.

Stone, E.F., Rabinowitz, S., & Spool, M.D. (1977). Effect of anonymity on student evaluations of faculty performance. *Journal of Educational Psychology, 69*(3), 274–280.

Tesluk, P., Mathieu, J.E., Zaccaro, S.J., & Marks, M. (1997). Task and aggregation issues in the analysis and assessment of team performance. In M. Brannick, E. Salas, & C. Prince (Eds.), *Team performance, assessment, and measurement: Theory, methods, and applications* (pp. 197–224). Mahwah, NJ: Erlbaum.

Tetlock, P.E. (1992). The impact of accountability on judgment and choice: Toward a social contingency model. In M.P. Zanna (Ed.), *Advances in experimental social psychology* (Vol. 25, pp. 331–376). New York: Academic Press.

Thompson, L. (1995). They saw a negotiation: Partnership and involvement. *Journal of Personality and Social Psychology Bulletin, 68,* 839–853.

Triandis, H.C. (1994). Cross-cultural industrial and organizational psychology. In M.D. Dunnette & L.M. Hough (Eds.), *Handbook of industrial and organizational psychology* (2nd ed., Vol. 4, pp. 102–172). Palo Alto, CA: Consulting Psychologists Press.

Triandis, H.C. (1996). The psychological measurement of cultural syndromes. *American Psychologist, 51*(4), 407–415.

Triandis, H.C., & Bhawuk, D.P.S. (1997). Culture theory and the meaning of relatedness. In P.C. Earley & M. Erez (Eds.), *New perspectives on international industrial/organizational psychology* (pp. 13–52). San Francisco: The New Lexington Press.

Veglahn, P.A. (1993, October). Key issues in performance appraisal challenges: Evidence from court and arbitration decisions. *Labor Law Journal,* pp. 595–606.

Viswesvaran, C. (1993). *Modeling job performance: Is there a general factor?* Unpublished doctoral dissertation, University of Iowa, Iowa City.

Viswesvaran, C., Ones, D.S., & Schmidt, F.L. (1996). Comparative analysis of the reliability of job performance ratings. *Journal of Applied Psychology, 81*(5), 557–574.

Werner, J.M., & Bolino, M.C. (1997). Explaining U.S. courts of appeals decisions involving performance appraisal: Accuracy, fairness, and validation. *Personnel Psychology, 50,* 1–24.

Wexley, K.N., & Klimoski, R. (1984). Performance appraisal: An update. In K.M. Rowland & G.R. Ferris (Eds.), *Research in personnel and human resource management* (Vol. 2, pp. 35–79). Greenwich, CT: JAI Press.

Wherry, R.J., & Bartlett, C.J. (1982). The control of bias in ratings: A theory of rating. *Personnel Psychology, 35,* 521–551.

Woehr, D.J., & Huffcutt, A.I. (1994). Rater training for performance appraisal: A quantitative review. *Journal of Occupational and Organizational Psychology, 67,* 189–205.

# CHAPTER 21

# Multisource Feedback

WILLIAM K. BALZER, GARY J. GREGURAS, AND PATRICK H. RAYMARK

## OVERVIEW OF MULTISOURCE FEEDBACK

Although the conceptualization and first applications of multisource feedback are only three decades old, a significant body of work has already accumulated to guide both researchers and practitioners. In this section, we review the definition, history, and, most appropriate, workplace applications of multisource feedback.

### Conceptual Definition and Model

Multisource feedback (MSF) systems represent processes that gather information about a target employee from two or more sources of information (e.g., peers, subordinates, superiors, self, customers) and then share this feedback with the target employee for one or more purposes (e.g., personal development, performance assessment). MSF systems, sometimes referred to as 360-degree feedback, multirater assessment, and upward feedback, typically are characterized by five distinct steps:

1. Preparation: determining whether the organization is ready for MSF, clarifying the purpose of the MSF process (e.g., developmental or administrative), developing a behavioral model that is tied to the objectives and strategies of the organization, and securing necessary resources.

2. Instrumentation/Design: identifying or developing a specific MSF instrument, determining who will provide the ratings, specifying the frequency of the MSF process, and training the raters and ratees.

3. Data Collection/Analysis: collecting and integrating the vast array of information gathered through the MSF process.

4. Feedback: determining how the information should be reported to users and aligning the feedback with organizational objectives.

5. Evaluation: assessing whether each of the prior steps was conducted appropriately and whether the MSF process achieved its desired results (Bracken, Timmreck, & Church, 2001).

This gathering of information from multiple perspectives and the formal return of feedback to the target differentiates MSF from traditional performance appraisal systems (i.e., systems in which only supervisors provide performance feedback to employees) and employee development programs.

*Acknowledgments:* We would to thank Alan Walker for his careful review of an earlier draft of this chapter. We also thank Kathy DeBouver, Molly Russ, and Denise Rollins for their administrative support.

MSF assumes that a ratee's self-awareness is increased by reviewing self-other rating discrepancies, which, in turn, facilitates performance development and improvement (Tornow, 1993a).

This chapter is organized into several general sections. First, we review the underlying history and logic behind MSF and the evidence supporting its effectiveness. Next, we provide a review of commercially available MSF instruments, primarily drawn from a recently published book from the Center for Creative Leadership (Leslie & Fleenor, 1998). Because each organization often has unique needs due to history and culture, purpose for MSF, sources of ratings, and so forth, we also include a section describing steps for developing a customized MSF system (including instrument). In our final section, we discuss research directions for improving the development and application of MSF systems. Space limitations prohibit an extensive and detailed review of the design, implementation, and evaluation of MFS systems. Fortunately, a number of excellent resources are available (Bracken et al., 2001; Church & Bracken, 1997; Dalessio, 1998; Fletcher & Baldry, 1999; Tornow & London, 1998).

## History and Development of MSF

MSF feedback is a relatively new intervention in the field. Its genesis began in the 1970s with the coalescing of several areas (e.g., multirater measurement, data-based feedback, employee involvement) into the practice of the standardized collection of behavioral feedback for managers (Hedge, Borman, & Birkeland, 2001). The 1993 special issue of *Human Resource Management,* edited by Tornow, is recognized as the formal establishment of a coordinated focus on the merits of MSF (and known more popularly as 360-degree feedback) based on both research and practice. However, the early roots of MSF can be traced back almost 80 years to the reported collection of graphic rating data from both subordinates and customers for the purpose of performance appraisal (Cook & Manson, 1926; Shelton, 1919, as noted in Link, 1920).

World War II and its associated need for assigning military personnel to distinct duties in order to increase the effectiveness of the war effort resulted in a period of unprecedented interest in performance rating research and application (Hedge et al., 2001). Rating research continued after the war, with the expansion of interest of peer ratings in the military (e.g., Hollander, 1954) and subordinate ratings in industry (e.g., Maloney & Hinrichs, 1959). Lawler's (1967) classic article on multitrait-multirater data highlighted the richness of the information that could be obtained by rating systems covering a wide range of performance dimensions and sources of information (i.e., self, peer, supervisor, and subordinate).

Critical during this period was the recognition that the lack of rating agreement among these sources did not necessarily reflect poor quality ratings but, in fact, reflected the unique sources of performance information observed from each of these perspectives (Borman, 1991). Finally, both the growing interests in (1) the use of survey data for personal feedback and development, improved work relations, and enhanced organizational effectiveness (Nadler, 1977) and (2) the investigation of the role of performance feedback on individual and group behavior (Ilgen, Fisher, & Taylor, 1979) provided a strong foundation for the development of MSF as a distinct area of research and practice (Fletcher & Baldry, 1999).

## General Effectiveness of MSF Interventions

One of the reasons why MSF systems have become so commonplace is the assumption that they are an effective developmental method (Edwards & Ewen, 1996). Whether this is an accurate assumption, however, is still a matter of debate. In reviewing the research on the psychometric characteristics of multisource ratings, Murphy, Cleveland, and Mohler (2001) concluded that although ratings from different sources typically show relatively low levels of interrater reliability, they do show some evidence of construct validity. (Incidentally, this pattern of results is exactly what we would expect if MSF ratings are doing what they have been designed to do: specifically, to gather different, yet not necessarily inaccurate, perceptions of the target's performance.) At the same time, however, this characteristic of inconsistent MSF ratings can provide a certain degree of confusion for the target of the feedback, who may be left with the task of trying to integrate contradictory and yet valid feedback.

Besides the confusion that may erupt from contradictory feedback, participants may have other reactions to MSF systems that limit their effectiveness. For example, there are several reasons why supervisors may question the ratings provided by subordinates (e.g., subordinates' inexperience as raters, the tendency to rate demanding managers more harshly; Bernardin, 1986). Evidence also indicates that employees dislike rating one another, and that they view peer ratings as being unduly biased by friendship and the similarity between the rater and ratee (Cederblom & Lounsbury, 1980; Love, 1981). These types of reactions may influence whether or not participants accept the feedback provided by the MSF process, thereby possibly impacting the overall effectiveness of the MSF system.

The preceding research, however, only provides indirect evidence concerning the effectiveness of MSF systems. A more direct evaluation of effectiveness would assess whether the MSF process changes subsequent behavior over and above that of other feedback systems. Despite the importance of this question, surprisingly few empirical studies directly address the effectiveness of MSF systems for changing behavior.

Hazucha, Hezlett, and Schneider (1993) evaluated the effectiveness of an MSF program for middle managers in a utility company in which the feedback consisted of self, subordinate, peer, and supervisor ratings. Although the self-ratings of the managers' skills were significantly higher two years after feedback than at the time of the original ratings, this pattern failed to reach significance for the ratings made by others. Rosti and Shipper (1998) conducted a similar study using middle managers but did not collect self-ratings. Once again, the difference between the prefeedback and postfeedback ratings for subordinates, peers, and bosses failed to reach significance, suggesting limited change due to the MSF intervention. Finally, Siefert, Yukl, and McDonald (2001) reported the results of a field experiment designed to assess the effectiveness of an MSF program for senior and midlevel mangers of a savings bank. Their study included both a feedback "treatment" condition and a "no treatment" control group (but unfortunately did not include a "placebo" control group). Some support for MSF system effectiveness was found in that the ratings provided by the subordinates of the managers in the treatment (i.e., feedback) condition were significantly higher postfeedback, while no difference in ratings over time was found for subordinates of the managers in the control (no feedback) condition. At the same time, however, ratings provided by peers/bosses (combined) actually decreased postfeedback, regardless of whether the focal manager was part of the treatment or control condition. Overall, the limited evidence available provides no clear support for the positive effects of MSF systems on performance change in organizations.

In contrast to the limited findings on the effectiveness of MSF systems, the data are a bit more encouraging concerning the effectiveness of upward feedback systems. Several authors (Atwater, Roush, & Fischthal, 1995; Hegarty, 1974; Johnson & Ferstl, 1999; Reilly, Smither, & Vasilopoulos, 1996; Smither et al., 1995) have reported a significant improvement in performance ratings following the presentation of upward feedback. The study by Hegarty is particularly noteworthy in that it was a field experiment (i.e., it included a control group). The results of this study revealed a positive change in supervisor performance for the experimental group on each of 15 behavioral items three months after receiving upward feedback. In contrast, a field experiment by Atwater, Waldman, Atwater, and Cartier (2000) failed to find a significant improvement in subordinate ratings of supervisor leadership for the experimental (i.e., feedback) group. In addition, Atwater et al. found a significant *decrease* in self-rated leadership for the experimental group, and no such change

was found for the control group. These authors explain this pattern of results as being due to the effects of individual attitudes (e.g., organizational cynicism). In summary, the somewhat inconsistent pattern of results, and the absence of appropriate control groups in many of the studies, makes it difficult to determine the true impact of upward feedback systems. Furthermore, there is little evidence concerning the incremental effects of either upward feedback or MSF relative to the more traditional supervisor feedback systems. This seems to be a critical omission, especially given the amount of time and money that typically goes into the development and implementation of these more complex feedback systems.

Overall, the available research evidence concerning the effectiveness of MSF systems is limited and inconclusive. In addition, two interrelated methodological issues have plagued this line of research. First, there are several problems with the way in which change has been assessed in many of these studies (i.e., comparing ratings at time 1 with ratings at time 2). Specifically, response shift bias, regression to the mean, and ceiling effects all complicate the interpretation of change data collected in this manner (Smither & Walker, 2001). Second, most of the available research has used test-retest designs without control groups (cf. Hegarty, 1974; Siefert et al., 2001). Although there are certainly practical reasons for this omission, the bottom line is that the results of this research do not tell us much about the effectiveness of MSF systems. Thus, an enhanced concern over these methodological issues is clearly needed to support the implicit assumption that MSF systems are an effective developmental or administrative tool.

One final point should be noted. It is important to recognize that the criteria for assessing the effectiveness of MSF systems will depend in part on the purpose or use of the MSF. Thus, effectiveness criteria should be carefully chosen and used to provide an appropriate assessment based on the goals of the MSF system (Balzer & Sulsky, 1990).

## Jobs and Functions for Which MSF Systems Are Most Suitable

In what workplace situations are MSF systems more likely to be effective? The various rater sources that compose an MSF system may not be equally appropriate for different jobs or functions. For example, jobs that are autonomous in nature (e.g., computer programmer) may limit the number of individuals who have direct knowledge of the target individual's performance. Similarly, if a particular rater source is composed of only a few people, the anonymity of that set of ratings may be compromised. Finally, for jobs in which good objective indicators of performance exist (e.g., assembly line operators), there may be no need to incur the resources required to gather information from multiple sources. Thus, one way to assess the suitability of an MSF system is to consider whether sufficient numbers of useful information sources are available.

As mentioned earlier, the implementation of MSF systems can be very costly in terms of both time and money. As such, several large organizations have developed and then abandoned paper-based MSF systems because of their high administrative burden (Ewen & Edwards, 2001). Thus, it may make sense to limit the implementation of MSF systems to where the perceived return on investment will be significant.

## APPLICATIONS IN PRACTICE: COMMERCIALLY AVAILABLE INSTRUMENTS

An Internet search of keywords such as "multisource feedback," "360-degree feedback," and "multirater" provides several thousands of sites, suggesting that the number of commercially available MSF instruments is already quite large. Although Timmreck and Wentworth (2001) have provided some useful suggestions for working with vendors of commercially available MSF instruments, an important task is finding and selecting the most appropriate instrument. Fortunately, a recent book by Leslie and Fleenor (1998) reviewed 24 commercially available instruments. Although the authors acknowledge in the preface to their book that the growing number of MSF instruments will quickly make any catalog of MSF instruments obsolete, they reviewed instruments that they felt were the best available based both on the American Psychological Association's standards of instrument development and "reasoned principles and techniques" for using feedback to improve performance. Their book details each instrument and its development, reports reliability and validity evidence, describes the feedback report, provides an overview of support materials (e.g., videos, workshops), and lists additional information (e.g., cost, vendor contact information). In Table 21.1, we provide a summary of the 24 MSF instruments included in Leslie and Fleenor's (1998) book (we also contacted each vendor to review the accuracy of our summary in the event an instrument had been updated; only a handful responded to our request). Also included in Table 21.1 is an additional instrument not reviewed by Leslie and Fleenor, *e360®*, which we felt represented other commercially available options for MSF systems.

Not shown in Table 21.1 are the common features found in these available instruments. For example, these instruments all have national norms, have been translated into at least one additional language, and provide technical support and manuals. Differences exist, however, in the number of

dimensions measured, the types (and numbers) of each source that can be included in the feedback process, the extent to which the instrument can be customized, and how feedback is presented to the target ratee. Readers interested in choosing from among these MSF instruments should consult Leslie and Fleenor (1998) for a more comprehensive review. Their compilation of detailed information provided by the vendors of these MSF systems is an excellent starting point for conducting a careful review of the appropriateness of using one of these commercially available MSF instruments.

## DEVELOPING AND IMPLEMENTING AN MSF SYSTEM

For a variety of reasons (e.g., the direct expense of purchasing a commercially available MSF instrument, the preference for a customized, proprietary MSF system), organizations may choose to develop their own MSF system. Thus, this section overviews the process of developing and implementing an MSF system (see also Bracken et al., 2001; Dalessio, 1998; Tornow & London, 1998).

### Preliminary Analysis When Developing and Implementing an MSF System

The successful development, implementation, and maintenance of an MSF system requires a careful analysis and consideration of contextual, individual, and instrumentation factors. These factors, both independently and reciprocally, influence the effectiveness of MSF systems as discussed in the following.

#### Contextual Considerations

To develop and implement an effective MSF system, contextual factors must be considered (Bernardin & Beatty, 1984; Landy & Farr, 1980; Murphy & Cleveland, 1995). Contextual factors define the environment in which information from multiple sources will be collected, tabulated, and fed back to the target employee. The consideration of contextual factors is especially important for MSF because such systems violate traditional organizational hierarchies (e.g., upward appraisals) and likely place many of the sources of feedback in new and uncomfortable situations (Funderburg & Levy, 1997). Unfortunately, contextual factors often are given little attention when designing MSF systems (Giles & Mossholder, 1990; Waldman, Atwater, & Antonioni, 1998). Three critical contextual factors that should be considered when developing and implementing an MSF system are the purpose of

**TABLE 21.1  Commercially Available Multisource Feedback Instruments**

**BENCHMARKS®:** Center for Creative Leadership, 336-545-2810.

| | |
|---|---|
| Purpose: | Assesses skills, perspectives, and values that a manager can learn and develop. |
| Target Audience: | Mid- and upper-level managers. |
| Instrumentation: | Contains 164 items covering four sections: Section 1: Managerial Skills and Perspectives; Section 2: Potential Flaws; Section 3: Evaluates how effectively the target would handle 16 job assignments; Section 4: Rater chooses 8 of the 16 managerial skills and perspectives that are most important for managerial success. Approximately 30 minutes are required to complete the instrument. Customization is not available. BENCHMARKS may be administered via the World Wide Web. |

**Campbell Leadership Index®(CLI):** NCS Assessments, 800-627-7271.

| | |
|---|---|
| Purpose: | Assesses leadership characteristics. |
| Target Audience: | All levels. |
| Instrumentation: | Contains 100 adjectives that form 22 scales measuring five orientations: Leadership, Energy, Affability, Dependability, and Resilience. Approximately 20–30 minutes are required to complete the instrument. Customization is not available. CLI is not currently available via the World Wide Web. |

**COMPASS:** The Managerial Practices Survey: Right Manus, 800-455-0942.

| | |
|---|---|
| Purpose: | Assesses current leadership/managerial behaviors. |
| Target Audience: | All levels. |
| Instrumentation: | Contains 70 behavioral items measuring 14 dimensions (e.g., Informing, Clarifying). Of these, 3 of the dimensions are only responded to by direct reports (e.g., Delegating). Raters also indicate whether the target should do more, less, or the same on 14 managerial practices. Approximately 20 to 35 minutes are required to complete the instrument. Customization is available. COMPASS is not currently available via the World Wide Web. |

**Executive Success Profile (ESP):** Personnel Decisions International, 800-633-4410.

| | |
|---|---|
| Purpose: | Assesses executive competencies and behaviors related to effective performance. |
| Target Audience: | Upper-level managers. |
| Instrumentation: | Contains 140 items measuring 22 competencies that are grouped into eight factors (e.g., Thinking, Communication). In addition, executives are evaluated on a 13-item scale labeled Leading Continuous Improvement. Approximately 30 minutes are required to complete this instrument. Customization is available. ESP is not currently available via the World Wide Web. |

**Survey of Executive Leaderships (EXEC):** The Clark Wilson Group, Inc., 800-537-7249.

| | |
|---|---|
| Purpose: | Assesses executive-level leadership competencies. |
| Target Audience: | Upper-level managers. |
| Instrumentation: | Contains 84 items grouped into five phases (i.e., Forward Thrust, Executive Perspective, Executive Implementation, Drive, and Acknowledging Contributions) and an assessment of Outcomes and Power Sources. This instrument also contains three narrative questions. Approximately 25 to 30 minutes are required to complete the instrument. Customization is available. EXEC is not currently available via the World Wide Web. |

**Leader Behavior Analysis II™ (LBAII):** Blanchard Training and Development, 800-728-6000.

| | |
|---|---|
| Purpose: | Assesses a manager's leadership style, the flexibility of one's style, and the match between the leadership style and the needs of the situation. |
| Target Audience: | Mid- and upper-level managers. |
| Instrumentation: | Contains 20 brief descriptions of leadership challenges to which respondents indicate how the target would respond by choosing among four possible actions. The 20 responses form six scales measuring three dimensions: Leadership Style, Leadership-style Flexibility, and Leadership-style Effectiveness. Approximately 20 minutes are required to complete the instrument. Customization currently is not available. LBAII is not currently available via the World Wide Web. |

**The Visionary Leader: Leader Behavior Questionnaire (LBQ):** Human Resource Development Press, 800-822-2801.

| | |
|---|---|
| Purpose: | Assesses one's approach to leadership and its relation to organizational effectiveness. |
| Target Audience: | Mid- and upper-level managers. |
| Instrumentation: | Contains 50 items that form 10 scales that form three dimensions: Visionary Leadership Behavior, Visionary Leadership Characteristics, and Visionary Culture Building. Approximately 10 to 20 minutes are required to complete the instrument. Customization currently is not available. LBQ is not currently available via the World Wide Web. |

**Leadership Effectiveness Analysis (LEA):** Management Research Group®, 207-775-2173.

| | |
|---|---|
| Purpose: | Assesses leadership practices, perspectives, and behaviors. |
| Target Audience: | All levels. |
| Instrumentation: | The LEA contains 22 scales measuring six areas: Creating a Vision, Developing Followership, Implementing the Vision, Following Through, Achieving Results, and Team Playing. Approximately 25–30 minutes are required to complete the instrument. Customization currently is not available. LEA is not currently available via the World Wide Web. |

**TABLE 21.1**    *(Continued)*

**Acumen® Leadership Skills (Leadership Skills):** Acumen International, 415-499-8181.

| | |
|---|---|
| Purpose: | Assesses leadership skills and behaviors. |
| Target Audience: | All levels. |
| Instrumentation: | Contains 116 items that form 16 scales grouped into four dimensions: Task Management, Team Development, Business Values, and Leadership. In addition, the coworker instrument contains six management effectiveness questions. Approximately 20 minutes are required to complete the instrument. Customization is available. Leadership Skills may be administered via the World Wide Web. |

**Leadership/Impact™ (L/I):** Human Synergistics/Center for Applied Research, Inc., 847-590-0995.

| | |
|---|---|
| Purpose: | Assesses a leader's impact on others and the strategies and techniques associated with this impact. |
| Target Audience: | All levels. |
| Instrumentation: | Contains 156 items on the self form and 169 items on the observer form. These items form 35 scales that are organized into three dimensions: Leadership Strategies, Impact on Others, and Effectiveness. Approximately 20–25 minutes are required to complete the instrument. Customization currently is not available. L/I is not currently available via the World Wide Web. |

**Leadership Practices Inventory (LPI):** Jossey-Bass/Pfeiffer, 415-433-1740.

| | |
|---|---|
| Purpose: | Assesses everyday behaviors linked to leader achievements. |
| Target Audience: | All levels. |
| Instrumentation: | Contains 30 statements to which respondents indicate the frequency at which the target uses each behavior. These statements form five scales: Challenging the Process, Inspiring a Shared Vision, Enabling Others to Act, Modeling the Way, and Encouraging the Heart. Approximately 10 minutes are required to complete the instrument. Customization currently is not available. LPI is not currently available via the World Wide Web. |

**Life Styles Inventory® (LSI):** Human Synergistics International, 800-622-7584.

| | |
|---|---|
| Purpose: | Assists individuals in identifying and understanding their thinking patterns and self-concepts. |
| Target Audience: | All levels. |
| Instrumentation: | Contains 240 items that form 12 thinking styles that form three general orientations: Constructive Styles, Passive/Defensive Styles, and Aggressive/Defensive Styles. Approximately 20–30 minutes are required to complete this instrument. Customization is available. LSI is soon to be available via the World Wide Web. |

**Manager View/360™:** Organizational Performance Dimensions, 800-538-7628.

| | |
|---|---|
| Purpose: | Assesses managerial competencies. |
| Target Audience: | All levels. |
| Instrumentation: | Contains 100 items that form 20 scales that are organized into four dimensions: Communication Skills, Task Management Skills, Interpersonal Skills, and Problem-solving Skills. Approximately 20–30 minutes are required to complete the instrument. Customization currently is not available. This instrument is not currently available via the World Wide Web. |

**MATRIX: The Influence Behavior Questionnaire:** Right Manus, 800-445-0942.

| | |
|---|---|
| Purpose: | Assesses one's use of power and influence to understand current and potential behavior. |
| Target Audience: | All levels. |
| Instrumentation: | Contains 53 items that form 11 scales that are grouped into four dimensions: Overview, Core Tactics, Support Tactics, and Last Resort Tactics. Approximately 15–20 minutes are required to complete the instrument. Customization currently is not available. MATRIX is not currently available via the World Wide Web. |

**Management Effectiveness Profile System (MEPS):** Human Synergistics International, 800-622-7584.

| | |
|---|---|
| Purpose: | Assesses managers' on-the-job skills and behaviors. |
| Target Audience: | Mid- and upper-level managers. |
| Instrumentation: | Contains 98 items that form 14 scales that combine into three areas: Task Skills, Interpersonal Skills, and Personal Skills. In addition, 14 items assess overall performance perceptions. Approximately 35 minutes are required to complete the instrument. Customization is available. MEPS is not currently available via the World Wide Web. |

**Multifactor Leadership Questionnaire (MLQ):** Mind Garden, 650-261-3500.

| | |
|---|---|
| Purpose: | Assesses specific behaviors related to transformational, transactional, and nontransactional leadership. |
| Target Audience: | All levels. |
| Instrumentation: | Contains 45 items that measure five Transformational Leadership factors (e.g., Idealized Influence), one Transactional Leadership factor (e.g., Contingent Reward), one Nonleadership factor (i.e., Laissez-faire) and three Outcome factors (e.g., Satisfaction with the Leader). Approximately 15 minutes are required to complete the instrument. Customization currently is available. MLQ may be administered via the World Wide Web. |

*(continued)*

**TABLE 21.1**   *(Continued)*

**The PROFILOR®:** Personnel Decisions International, 800-633-4410.

| | |
|---|---|
| Purpose: | Assess job-specific skills related to effective performance in one's present or future jobs. |
| Target Audience: | Mid-level managers. |
| Instrumentation: | Contains 130 items that form 24 scales (e.g., Analyze Issues, Use Sound Judgment). In addition, five items measure Overall Performance, and a subset of the 130 items form an Empowerment and Career Issues composite scale. Approximately 30 minutes are required to complete the instrument. Customization is available. This instrument may be administered via the World Wide Web. |

**PROSPECTOR™:** Center for Creative Leadership, 336-545-2810.

| | |
|---|---|
| Purpose: | Assesses managerial strengths and developmental needs. |
| Target Audience: | All levels. |
| Instrumentation: | Contains 48 items that form 11 dimensions that are clustered into two categories: Engages in Opportunities to Learn, and Creates a Context for Learning. Approximately 20 minutes are required to complete the instrument. Customization currently is not available. This instrument is not currently available via the World Wide Web. |

**Survey of Leadership Practices (SLP):** The Clark Wilson Group, Inc., 800-537-7249.

| | |
|---|---|
| Purpose: | Assesses managerial skills and attributes associated with effective leaders in changing organizations. |
| Target Audience: | All levels. |
| Instrumentation: | Contains 85 items and three narrative questions. The items form six skill-oriented phases: Entrepreneurial Vision, Leadership for Change, Gaining Commitment, Monitoring Personal Impact, Drive, and Recognizing Performance. In addition, a Residual Impact and a Sources of Power factor are formed from the items. Approximately 25–30 minutes are required to complete the instrument. Customization is available. SLP is not currently available via the World Wide Web. |

**The Survey of Management Practices (SMP):** The Clark Wilson Group, Inc., 800-537-7249.

| | |
|---|---|
| Purpose: | Assesses managerial skills and attributes used in daily operations with a focus on interactions with direct reports. |
| Target Audience: | All levels. |
| Instrumentation: | Contains 145 items that form 23 scales that are grouped into three categories: Management Task•Cycle® Phases, Interpersonal Relations, and Group Motivation and Morale. Approximately 25–30 minutes are required to complete the instrument. Customization is available. SMP is not currently available via the World Wide Web. |

**System for the Multiple Level Observation of groups (SYMLOG®):** SYMLOG Consulting Group, 619-673-2098.

| | |
|---|---|
| Purpose: | Assesses patterns of values and behaviors of individuals, groups, and organizations. |
| Target Audience: | All levels. |
| Instrumentation: | Two forms are available and each contains 26 items that comprise a three-dimensional space. For the Individual and Organizational Values form, the three axes include: Values of Dominance versus Submissiveness; Values of Friendly Behavior versus Unfriendly Behavior; and Values on Acceptance of, versus Opposition to, the Task-orientation of Established Authority. For the Interpersonal Behaviors Form, the three axes include: Dominant versus Submissive Behavior, Friendly versus Unfriendly Behavior, and Controlled versus Expressive Behavior. Approximately 15 minutes are required to complete the instrument. This instrument may be administered via the World Wide Web. |

**Types of Work Index (TWI):** Team Management System, 703-318-7206.

| | |
|---|---|
| Purpose: | Assesses the critical functions of teamwork. |
| Target Audience: | All levels. |
| Instrumentation: | Contains 64 items that form eight work scales (e.g., Advising, Innovating). Approximately 10–15 minutes are required to complete the instrument. Customization currently is not available. TWI is not currently available via the World Wide Web. |

**VOICES®:** Lominger Limited, Inc., 952-345-3600.

| | |
|---|---|
| Purpose: | Assesses managerial competencies. |
| Target Audience: | Mid- and upper-level managers. |
| Instrumentation: | Contains 86 competencies that form 10 scales (e.g., Focus on Future, Flexibility) and 19 stallers/stoppers that form three scales (e.g., Trouble with Others). Approximately 30–45 minutes are required to complete the instrument. Customization is available. This instrument may be administered via the World Wide Web. |

**TABLE 21.1**    *(Continued)*

**Acumen® Leadership Work***Styles*™ (WORKSTYLES): Acumen International, 415-492-9190.

| | |
|---|---|
| Purpose: | Assesses thinking styles and attitudes associated with effective leadership. |
| Target Audience: | All levels. |
| Instrumentation: | Contains 96 items that form 12 thinking styles (e.g., Affiliation, Approval, Conventional). Approximately 15 minutes are required to complete the instrument. Customization is not available. This instrument may be administered via the World Wide Web. |

**e360®:** Performaworks, 919-836-9986.

| | |
|---|---|
| Purpose: | Not determined. |
| Target Audience: | All levels. |
| Instrumentation: | Instrument content based on client's competency model. Complex models can be accommodated (e.g., different competencies/items based on job classification). Web-based administration includes rater nomination, rater list approval, rating, and reporting. Written comments per competency or at end of instrument. Interactive features to discourage common response sets. Numerous features to meet needs of clients conducting large-scale cycles for development-only or administrative purposes. |

MSF, organizational culture and structure, and organizational readiness.

### Purpose of MSF

Perhaps the most important consideration when designing an MSF system is deciding for what purpose or purposes the system will be used (Dalessio, 1998). Potential purposes lie along a continuum with individual feedback and development at one end and administrative decision making (e.g., promotion, wage administration) at the other (Dalessio, 1998). Considerable debate over the appropriate use(s) of MSF systems has emerged (for a discussion, see Bracken, Dalton, Jako, McCauley, & Pollman, 1997). Proponents of using MSF for developmental purposes suggest that MSF systems used for administrative purposes leads to (1) data of lower quality (Dalton, 1997; London & Wohlers, 1991), (2) ratees who may be less accepting of the data (Dalton, 1997), and (3) appraisals that may become more punitive than developmental (Pollman, 1997), and the target employees may react more negatively to less-than-perfect feedback (Timmreck & Bracken, 1997). In contrast, proponents of using MSF for administrative purposes suggest that MSF will improve existing performance management systems (Bracken, 1997), communicate to raters that their viewpoints are important (Dalessio, 1998; Jako, 1997), increase the amount of relevant information available to decision makers (Jako, 1997; Van Velsor, 1998), empower organizational members to make decisions about who gets rewarded (McCauley, 1997), and increase ratee accountability for performance development (Bracken, 1997; Dalessio, 1998).

Historically, most organizations have used MSF for developmental purposes only, but there is an increasing shift toward using such systems for administrative purposes (London & Smither, 1995). Attempting to minimize potential problems associated with using MSF for administrative purposes, organizations may at first implement their system for developmental purposes and then gradually shift to a combination of developmental and administrative purposes once participants become comfortable with, and trust, the system (London, 2001; Van Velsor, 1998; Waldman et al., 1998). Because the processes and conditions needed for MSF effectiveness will vary depending on the particular purpose(s) of the system (Fleenor & Brutus, 2001; McCauley, 1997), the challenge for researchers and practitioners is to identify the purpose(s) of the MSF system so that the processes and conditions needed for successful implementation and maintenance of a particular MSF can be designed (Sulsky & Keown, 1998; Tornow & London, 1998). Although the debate continues regarding whether or not MSF should be used for some purposes and not for others, *all* agree that MSF purpose must be clearly identified, articulated to all constituencies, and aligned with the selected purpose (Antonioni, 1996).

### Organizational Culture and Structure

Organizational culture and structural design issues (e.g., organizational levels and span of control) will influence, and perhaps dictate, the design of MSF systems and their interrelation with other organizational systems (Katz & Kahn, 1978; Mintzberg, 1979). McCauley (1997) pointed out that MSF for feedback purposes will better fit a company culture that values personal development and growth, whereas an MSF program designed for administrative decision making may work best in a culture that supports widespread sharing of information and employee involvement in decision making. If the MSF system is not compatible with the prevailing or newly introduced culture, norms, or other human resource processes, problems are likely to occur, limiting both its short- and long-term effectiveness (Cranshaw, Hartmann, &

Winckler, 2001; Jako, 2001). McCauley and Hughes-James (1994) found that a supportive work environment was a significant factor in increasing and maintaining behavioral change among school superintendents participating in an MSF program (see also Dalton & Hollenbeck, 2001; Jako, 2001).

### Organizational Readiness

Before an organization implements an MSF system, its readiness for such an intervention should be assessed (Bracken, 1996). An organization is considered "ready" for the MSF intervention when organizational norms are compatible with an MSF system and when members of the organization believe that MSF will be useful (Ewen & Edwards, 2001). Members' readiness may be assessed using a variety of methods, including focus groups, surveys, and interviews (Ewen & Edwards, 2001).

Bracken (1996) identified five readiness factors that should be assessed prior to the implementation of an MSF system. The first readiness factor is trust. Among other important individual and organizational variables, trust motivates positive working relationships (Ring & Van de Ven, 1994; Wicks, Berman, & Jones, 1999), facilitates cooperation (Dodgeson, 1993; Zucker, Darby, Brewer, & Peng, 1996), and influences justice perceptions (Brockner, Siegel, Daly, Tyler, & Martin, 1997). Users of the MSF system must believe that the stated principles underlying the intervention (e.g., confidentiality of data, purpose of MSF) will be honored as the system is implemented and continued (Bracken, 1996).

The second readiness factor is management commitment. MSF proponents consistently argue that upper- and midlevel management support can have a significant impact on the acceptance and use of MSF systems (Cranshaw et al., 2001; Dalton & Hollenbeck, 2001; Findley, Giles, & Mossholder, 2000). Dalessio (1998) suggested that phasing in the system with visible top-down communication and involvement will result in more commitment to the intervention from employees at all levels. It also is important that management demonstrates its commitment to MSF by providing the necessary resources to those involved in the MSF process (e.g., company time for raters to provide MSF information, financial support for mentors for the individuals receiving feedback; Bracken, 1996). Management support is especially important to sustain MSF systems over time (Dalessio, 1998).

Stability is the third readiness factor that should be considered. Organizations going through numerous changes may not be ready to implement MSF because of user mistrust about the real purpose of the intervention (Bracken, 1996). Further, organizations concurrently undergoing a significant number of changes may not be able to commit sufficient resources to ensure the success of MSF.

The fourth readiness factor is whether the organization can provide a supportive environment for feedback that is essential for employee development and improved performance (Hazucha et al., 1993). Funderburg and Levy (1997) found that the perceived cost of seeking feedback was significantly related to attitudes toward MSF, with individuals in an environment less favorable toward feedback reporting less interest in using MSF. A work environment that is more supportive of employee development-seeking behaviors has been shown to increase the frequency of individual feedback-seeking behaviors (Bracken, 1996; Fedor, Rensvold, & Adams, 1992).

The fifth readiness factor is long-term focus, where organizations that implement MSF recognize the short- and long-term costs and potential benefits that may accrue from its implementation over time. Organizations hoping for immediate and drastic changes from the introduction of MSF will likely be disappointed, grow impatient, and have greater difficulty maintaining the MSF system over time (Bracken, 1996). To facilitate long-term focus, the MSF should be linked to the organization's strategic plan (Dalessio, 1998).

In addition to Bracken's (1996) list, we add user acceptance as a sixth readiness factor. Users may not accept the stated purpose of the MSF system (e.g., for administrative decisions such as salary increases and promotions) even if they believe what they have been told about it. In other settings, ratees may prefer to limit the performance evaluation system to the immediate supervisor only (Gosselin, Werner, & Halle, 1997). Although rater and ratee reactions are often neglected criteria, they are critical determinants of appraisal effectiveness (Keeping & Levy, 2000; Murphy & Cleveland, 1995). Unless an MSF system is accepted by its users, it cannot be effective (Bernardin, Dahmus, & Redmon, 1993; Bettenhausen & Fedor, 1997; Carroll & Schneier, 1982). Including all constituent groups during the development and implementation stages of MSF systems likely increases user acceptance (Giles & Mossholder, 1990).

## Individual Considerations

After selecting the purpose of the MSF system, ensuring its fit with organizational culture and structure, and confirming the organization's readiness for the intervention, several individual factors that relate to the ratees and raters of the MSF system should be considered.

### Ratee Training

Edwards and Ewen (1996) noted that without rater and ratee training, MSF systems likely will not be successful. Ratee training should contain several components, including providing information regarding: (1) the MSF process, (2) the instrument, (3) self-reflection and self-evaluation, (4) how to interpret the feedback report, and (5) how to use the feedback to develop an action plan. In addition to providing information, ratees should be allowed an opportunity to ask questions and seek clarification regarding any aspect of the MSF system (Edwards & Ewen, 1996). There are a variety of training alternatives ranging from supplying the ratee with a workbook that describes the process and instrument to providing each ratee with a one-on-one coach (Bracken, 1996). Training can increase users' trust in the system and is related to more favorable user reactions (Edwards, Ewen, & Vendantam, 2001).

### Ratee Confidentiality/Accountability

An area of considerable debate is who will have access to the obtained performance information. One perspective is that the information should be completely confidential; that is, only the ratee should have access to it and there is no expectation that it will be shared with others. (Interestingly, London, Smither, and Adsit [1997] noted that although ratees prefer confidentiality of their performance information, they want the raters to be identified.) If ratees do not believe that the information will be confidential, they may provide inaccurate self-assessments or may even refuse to participate in the process (Van Velsor & Leslie, 2001). Of course, complete ratee confidentiality is not possible if the purpose of the MSF system is for administrative purposes. In contrast, advocates of ratee accountability suggest that if ratees are unable to be held accountable for using the feedback, the MSF system likely will have little impact if the data are the sole property of the ratees (London et al., 1997). Ratee accountability also may impact rater participation; if ratees are not held accountable for responding to the feedback, raters may view the system as a waste of their time and may either refuse to participate or provide lower quality data.

### Ratee Reactions

Ratee reactions (e.g., acceptance of feedback, perceptions of fairness) have been identified as important criteria for evaluating performance evaluation systems (e.g., Hedge & Teachout, 2000; Murphy & Cleveland, 1995; Waldman, 1997). Ratees' reactions to feedback are important because they are thought to predict whether ratees accept or reject the feedback (Bernardin et al., 1993; London & Smither, 1995) and their subsequent use of the feedback for performance improvement (Ladner & Greguras, 2001). In addition to predicting how ratees may respond to the feedback, ratee reactions also may highlight those areas where the process or instrument may be improved (Edwards et al., 2001). One critical way to influence ratee reactions is to allow ratees to participate in the development of the system (Mohrman, Resnick-West, & Lawler, 1989).

### Choice of Raters and Rater Sources

The choice of rater sources (e.g., peers, customers), as well as the selection of particular raters within each source, should emphasize the identification of individuals knowledgeable about the performance or skills to be evaluated (Farr & Newman, 2001). With respect to the choice of rater sources, research indicates that ratees react more favorably when a more comprehensive group of rater sources is included (Bernardin et al., 1993). With respect to the selection of individual raters within each rater source, the choice may depend on rating purpose. Van Velsor (1998) suggested that, if the MSF system is designed for employee developmental purposes, ratees should choose their raters, thereby making it less likely that they will discount or reject negative feedback. If the goal of MSF is administrative decision making, rater sources and raters within each source should not be chosen by ratees because ratees might be expected to choose more lenient raters, thereby lowering the credibility of ratings. In practice, ratees often are asked to nominate raters and then a manager chooses the actual raters (Bracken, 1996). To increase perceptions of fairness and acceptance, Farr and Newman (2001) suggested: (1) allowing ratees to have input into the rater selection process, (2) applying the selection procedures consistently, and (3) excluding any rater who may have a conflict of interest with the ratee.

### Number of Raters

The number of raters for any given source depends on several factors, including the number of potential raters who are able to provide valid assessments, time and cost considerations, and psychometric considerations. Estimates suggest that generally one supervisor, three to five peers, and three to five subordinates are included (Chappelow, 1998; London & Smither, 1995). If raters are to be anonymous, at least three raters per source (except for supervisors) are desired before the feedback is returned to the ratee (Timmreck & Bracken, 1995). In cases where fewer than three raters from a given source respond, ratings may be combined across sources (Dalessio, 1998), although this practice obscures the unique and valuable information provided by each rating source. Projected reliability estimates for different rater sources and rating purposes as a function of numbers of raters and items are available in Greguras and Robie (1998) and Greguras, Robie, and Goff (2001). These estimates can help guide practitioners when designing and implementing an MSF system to optimize both reliability and cost effectiveness.

### Rater Training

As with ratee training, rater training is critical to the success of the MSF system. Rater training may be especially important when ratings are used for administrative decision making (Bernardin & Beatty, 1984). Unfortunately, rater training is often neglected (Bracken & Timmreck, 2001). Rater training should include information on the rating purpose, process, and instrument. Including information about the instrument should increase raters' familiarity with the dimensions of performance, which has been shown to improve rater accuracy (Day, 1995). Additionally, Dalessio (1998) recommended training raters on rater errors and behavioral observation.

### Rater Anonymity

Raters prefer to be anonymous (Antonioni, 1994; Edwards et al., 2001; London et al., 1997); whether the MSF system supports their preferences is likely to impact their attitudes and behaviors. Ratings that are anonymous are assumed to be more accurate because of the raters' decreased fears of retribution (Van Velsor, 1998); this has led many to recommend that raters should remain anonymous (e.g., Dalessio, 1998; Edwards & Ewen, 1996). Several studies have reported that when raters are not assured of anonymity, ratings are either more lenient or raters report that they would rate differently if anonymity was not provided (e.g., Antonioni, 1994; Ilgen & Knowlton, 1980; London & Wohlers, 1991). In contrast, others suggest that, unless raters are clearly identified, they may not feel any formal commitment to participate (Westerman & Rosse, 1997) and lack the motivation to take the rating task seriously and provide accurate ratings (London et al., 1997). Some research suggests that raters are more accurate when they are held accountable for their ratings (Mero & Motowidlo, 1995), leading some investigators to conclude that raters involved in MSF systems should be held accountable for the quality of their ratings (Bracken, 1996).

### Instrument Considerations

A well-developed MSF instrument is one that is psychometrically sound, practical to use, consistent with the organization's purpose and mission, and accepted by its users. Often during instrument development, trade-offs must be made about the costs and benefits associated with various aspects of instrumentation (e.g., a longer survey may provide more reliable information but may result in lower response rates; gathering narrative comments increases the amount of information but also requires additional resources to tabulate and integrate). Whether choosing a commercially available instrument or designing one specifically for a job or organization, the following factors should be considered.

### Relevance

Regardless of rating purpose, MSF instruments should be relevant to the important job competencies and/or areas of professional development supported by the MSF process. Identifying relevant competencies and their underlying behaviors is best accomplished by conducting both detailed job and career path analyses. However, because of practical considerations (e.g., time, money) organizations may simply opt to use preestablished commercially available instruments (Antonioni, 1996) or may choose to adopt broader, generic competencies identified outside of the organization (Dalessio, 1998). Several empirically derived taxonomies of managerial performance may help identify relevant company-specific competencies (e.g., Borman & Brush, 1993; Mitchell, 1978; Stewart, 1982; Tornow & Pinto, 1976; Whitely, 1985; Yukl, 1983, 1987). Note, however, that most organizations that use MSF for administrative purposes prefer to customize their instruments to ensure their job relevance and legal defensibility (Bernardin & Tyler, 2001; Bracken, 1996; Timmreck & Bracken, 1995).

### Source Specific Forms

Although the majority of organizations use the same form for all rater sources (London & Smither, 1995), different rater sources may have observed different samples of behavior that only allow them to comment on a subset of areas of a manager's performance (Dalessio, 1998). For example, customers may be unable to evaluate a manager's administrative competencies but would be able to provide unique perspectives on customer service orientation. Similarly, research suggests that supervisors consider subordinates to be a useful source of feedback for some performance dimensions but not others (McEvoy, 1990). By using source-specific forms, the MSF process may be perceived as being more valid, which in turn may increase user acceptance of the feedback. As such, instruments should be customized to reflect these differences (Bracken & Timmreck, 2001; Dalessio, 1998; Murphy & Cleveland, 1995). If a common form is used, a "not applicable" response option should be included for each item so that raters may customize the forms themselves.

### Items

Items should be written to be behaviorally focused, clear, unidimensional, observable, free of unnecessary qualifiers (e.g., extremely), face valid, relevant, acceptable, and actionable (Bracken & Timmreck, 2001; DeNisi & Kluger, 2000; Kluger & DeNisi, 1996; Rogelberg & Waclawski, 2001; Van Velsor, 1998). These item characteristics help to increase the quality of the feedback reports and ratees' motivation to take action. For example, focusing on behaviors rather than traits reduces subjectivity (Bracken, 1996) and facilitates a ratee's acceptability of feedback by directing attention to behaviors rather than to the target him- or herself (Kluger & DeNisi, 1996). Further, well-constructed items that meet the criteria listed (e.g., observable, relevant) improve the legal defensibility of administrative decisions based on MSF ratings (Bernardin & Tyler, 2001).

In terms of numbers of dimensions and items, Bracken (1994) suggested using a total of approximately 40–60 items, although many commercially available instruments contain many more items (see Table 21.1). When deciding on the total number of items to include, there is a trade-off between using too few items per dimension to ensure reliable and valid measurement and using too many items (either because of too many dimensions or because of too many items per dimension), which may decrease response rates and the quality of obtained information.

### Response Scale

Different response scales will likely influence the distribution of responses (Bracken, 1996). Most MSF systems use one of two types of response scales: frequency scales, which indicate how often a behavior occurs (e.g., "Never or One Time" to "More Than 10 times"), or mastery scales, which reflect the extent to which a skill is developed (e.g., "Does Not Meet Expectations" to "Far Exceeds Expectations") (Van Velsor, 1998). The choice of response scale should be consistent with the purpose of the instrument. As Bracken and Timmreck (2001) suggested, if the purpose of appraisal is to distinguish among ratees, then the anchors should reflect these between-person comparisons (e.g., "Bottom 5%" to "Top 5 %"). If the purpose of the ratings is for developmental use, then the response scales should facilitate within-person profiling across items or dimensions (e.g., "No Extent" to "A Great Extent"). A greater number of response options (e.g., 9-point vs. 5-point response scales) may be better suited to detect slight differ-

ences between ratees or within ratees over time, although fewer response options may be easier for raters to use (Van Velsor, 1998).

### Narrative Items

Open-ended items can be a valuable source of information for ratees and help ensure that the entire job or career domain is covered (Van Velsor, 1998). Likewise, narrative comments can be useful for raters to explain their ratings and to comment more specifically on certain behaviors or events. The open-ended items also hold considerable potential to inform ratees what they need to do in order to improve performance (which they may not be able to glean from a completely numerical MSF report). Given these benefits, it is not surprising that ratees want narrative comments and raters generally want to provide them (Antonioni, 1996). Most frequently, these items are at the end of the instrument, although some instruments allow for comments to accompany each item or performance dimension.

There are three concerns related to narrative comments (Dalessio, 1998; Van Velsor, 1998). The first concern is that verbatim narrative comments may compromise the anonymity of the rater. Possible solutions to this potential problem are to edit the comments for personally identifying information or to provide the ratee with more generic statements based on a content coding of all narrative comments (Dalessio, 1998). The second concern with narrative comments is that a ratee may overly weight or fixate on this information, especially negative information, at the expense of attending to other information (Ferstl & Bruskiewicz, 2000). Dalessio suggests that this concern may be reduced if (1) ratees receive training to avoid focusing on any one piece of information, (2) raters are urged to provide both positive and negative comments, and (3) the supervisor or feedback coach helps ratees focus on the gestalt provided by the complete set of feedback (both quantitative and qualitative). The third concern regarding narrative comments is the expense of analyzing and typing the write-in comments, typically one of the most costly parts of data analysis and interpretation (Bracken, 1996).

## Typical Psychometric Analyses/Results and What to Expect

Many criteria can be used to evaluate the effectiveness of MSF systems, including rater and ratee acceptance of the system and cost versus benefit of MSF. Here we examine the psychometric quality of ratings provided by MSF systems.

## Reliability

MSF scale ratings should be reliable; consistency in measurement is a prerequisite for the validity of MSF scale ratings. However, not all approaches to assessing reliability are conceptually appropriate for MSF ratings given that ratings are provided by a number of individuals representing different sources or perspectives on the target ratee's behavior and performance. One method of assessing reliability of ratings is assessing consistency of ratings over time (i.e., test-retest). Because MSF systems are designed to change employee behavior and performance, test-retest correlations between MSF rating across time would seem to be an inappropriate conceptualization of reliability; the MSF intervention is expected to result in changes in ratees' behavior and performance over time.

A second approach to assessing the reliability of ratings is interrater reliability, or the agreement among ratings between or within multiple feedback sources. This raises very fundamental questions for assessing the quality of MSF ratings: should ratings *across* different rating sources (e.g., peers, subordinates, self, supervisor, and customer) be consistent and similar? Should ratings within each rating source (e.g., ratings provided by multiple customers or peers) be consistent and similar? An assumption of MSF is that different rater sources are used to provide unique perspectives (Murphy & Cleveland, 1995; Tornow, 1993b). As such, different rater sources should not be expected to agree; research indicates that different rater sources do have relatively distinct perspectives (e.g., Conway & Huffcutt, 1997; Harris & Schaubroeck, 1988).

In contrast, raters within a single feedback source might be assumed to provide consistent ratings, given their similar types of contact with a target ratee and/or a common expectation based on his or her position in the organization (Murphy & Cleveland, 1995). MSF ratings are typically aggregated within a rater source; by using a large enough number of raters from each rating source, reliability estimates can be increased in a cost-effective manner (Murphy et al., 2001), and the larger group of raters may help increase ratee acceptance of the ratings (Bozeman, 1997). However, research on within-source agreement, which generally has focused on supervisor ratings, suggests that interrater agreement among raters from a common rating source is quite low (e.g., Conway & Huffcutt, 1997; Murphy et al., 2001; Scullen, Mount, & Sytsma, 1996; Viswesvaran, Ones, & Schmidt, 1996). Likewise, the limited research that has investigated peer and subordinate ratings indicates that agreement within each of these sources is low (Conway & Huffcutt, 1997; Greguras & Robie, 1998; Greguras et al., 2001). One interpretation of this pattern of findings is that each *rater* (as opposed to each *source*) provides a unique perspective (Mount, Judge, Scullen, Systma, & Hezlett, 1998); just as different rater sources may have different opportunities to observe behaviors, different expectations, and so forth, so likely do individual raters within a source.

Given the preceding, it seems that internal consistency estimates of scale reliability (i.e., across multiple ratings provided by a single rater) would seem to provide the most conceptually appropriate index of reliability for MSF ratings (Dalessio, 1998). This mandates that the MSF instrument includes multiple items for each area or dimension assessed through the MSF system; coefficient alpha reliability estimates can then be computed for each area or dimension. Assuming reliability estimates at or exceeding the rule-of-thumb level accepted by most researchers (i.e., coefficient alpha reliability estimates of .70 and above), internal consistency reliability estimates can be used to infer that lack of consistency in MSF ratings, from either individuals from the same rating source or individuals from different rating sources, is due to differences in their rating perspectives and not due to the inability of individual raters to rate consistently.

## Validity

Gathering validity evidence of an MSF instrument is a continuous process. Several types of validity evidence may be gathered, including face, content, criterion-related, and construct validity.

Although dismissed at times as a less important type of validity, the face validity of an MSF instrument may be extremely important. As discussed earlier, rater and ratee acceptance of the MSF instrument likely impacts its effectiveness. As Murphy et al. (2001) noted, beyond establishing other types of validity, it is critically important that the users perceive the information to be valid and useful. This may be assessed through questionnaires or interviews with the users.

Content validity refers to the extent to which the instrument represents the domain of interest. Job analyses and subject matter experts (SMEs) may be used to establish the content validity of the MSF instrument. If the instrument is used for identifying future managerial potential, SMEs may be used to identify important managerial competencies. Because the same MSF instrument often is used for a variety of managerial jobs, SMEs may be most useful in identifying generic managerial competencies (Dalessio, 1998).

Criterion-related validity refers to the extent to which the MSF ratings are related to some criterion, that is, effective performance. When choosing a criterion, it is important to choose a criterion that is under the control of the ratee (Van

Velsor, 1998). Criterion-related validity is established by correlating scores from the MSF instrument with those of the criterion. Because one assumption of MSF is that different rater sources provide different information, it is important to note that different source ratings might be expected to correlate with some criteria but not with others (Dalessio, 1998). In fact, if the pattern of relations between different rating sources and external criteria matches a logically determined pattern of relations (identified a priori), that would provide additional evidence of the validity of the MSF ratings. Another method for establishing criterion-related validity is to demonstrate that the instrument differentiates between groups of ratees identified as representing different levels of effectiveness on the selected criterion (Dalessio, 1998).

Finally, construct validity refers to whether or not the instrument assesses what it is intended to measure. Construct validity may be assessed in several ways. Leslie and Fleenor (1998) suggested assessing the construct validity of an MSF instrument by relating scores from one instrument to scores on another instrument with already established psychometric properties; few of these studies have been conducted. They further noted that construct validity may be assessed by analyzing whether certain dimensions from the MSF instrument relate to certain personality traits but not to others. Yet another method for assessing construct validity of an MSF instrument is to analyze whether or not different rater sources use the same behaviors to measure the same construct (i.e., factorial invariance; Dalessio, 1998). However, Dalessio cautioned that if different sources are observed to have different factor structures, it does not necessarily indicate that they do not provide useful or valid information. That is, given the assumption that different sources have different perspectives and opportunities to observe behavior, it might be expected that different rater groups would have different factor structures. Although differences might be expected, several empirical studies have observed the same factor structure across rater groups (see the Measurement Equivalence section).

### Measurement Equivalence

Measurement equivalence indicates that the instrument means and functions the same across rater sources, which is required if meaningful comparisons between rater sources, or within rater sources over time, are to be made (Cheung, 1999; Vandenberg, & Lance, 2000). Cheung discussed two types of equivalence: conceptual equivalence and psychometric equivalence. Conceptual equivalence indicates that different rater sources agree on the item loadings and factor structure of an instrument (i.e., the instrument "means" the same thing to the different rater sources). Psychometric equivalence in-

dicates that the different rater sources respond to the instrument in the same way (i.e., equivalent levels of reliability, variance, range of ratings, mean level of ratings, and intercorrelations among dimensions). Conceptual equivalence is a prerequisite to making meaningful comparisons across rater groups (Cheung & Rensvold, 1998; Reise, Widaman, & Pugh, 1993), whereas psychometric inequivalence may reveal meaningful differences between rater sources. As such, the majority of existing studies focus only on establishing the conceptual equivalence of MSF ratings (e.g., Facteau & Craig, 2001). To assess the measurement equivalence of MSF ratings, Vandenberg and Lance (2000) recommended using confirmatory factor analysis (CFA) procedures in a series of hierarchically nested models. For a detailed discussion on measurement equivalence, see Cheung (1999) or Vandenberg and Lance (2000).

### Cross-Cultural Issues

In an era of business globalization, the number of companies conducting business in different countries and cultures is becoming quite common. Unfortunately, the transferability of an MSF system to other countries and cultures cannot be assumed (Leslie, Gryskiewicz, & Dalton, 1998; Brutus, Leslie, & McDonald-Mann, 2001). Brutus et al. argued that MSF is an "American product" based on the cultural dynamics at work in the United States today: the democratization and delayering of organizations, a heritage of meritocracy based on identifiable individual differences, and technological advances that allow MSF data to be collected, tabulated, and reported easily. Hofstede's (1980) two cultural dimensions, *individualism* (the degree to which individual differences take priority over the collective group) and *power distance* (the degree to which individuals accept power differences among members), suggest that MSF will enjoy support in cultures that are strongly individualistic (i.e., MSF focuses on individual assessment and development) and low on power distance (i.e., feedback from all sources is acceptable). Cultures that are more collectivistic (e.g., Japan, China) or with higher levels of power distance (e.g., Mexico, Philippines) may not provide an appropriate environment for MSF. Brutus et al. reviewed cultural differences in rating tendencies, differences in employment law, and the translation and equivalence of MSF instruments across languages that may limit the effectiveness of a cross-cultural application of MSF.

### Legal Considerations

Few court cases have directly addressed the use of MSF systems, although there is some indirect support for multiple rater systems based on cases involving other types of employment decisions (e.g., the employment interview; Veglahn, 1993; Williamson, Campion, Malos, Roehling, & Campion, 1997). Bernardin and Tyler (2001) reviewed several cases in which the courts were critical of appraisal ratings provided by a single supervisor. They speculated that the courts may view MSF systems as a superior alternative to traditional single-rater systems if one assumes that the averaging of perceptions across multiple raters will increase the validity of the feedback and decrease adverse impact (Bernardin & Tyler, 2001). Nonetheless, an MSF system must follow the general guidelines for a legally defensible appraisal system (e.g., the dimensions of performance that are measured should be based on a formal job analysis, the rating instrument should assess job performance and not personal traits) because it will be held to the same legal standards as a single rater system. MSF systems for administrative decision making can enhance their chances of a favorable legal review by using formal, standardized procedures for gathering MSF data from trained raters and by providing ratees with the opportunity to review and challenge the ratings provided by any of the rating sources participating in the evaluation process (Werner & Bolino, 1997).

MSF systems may face legal challenges on the basis of the appropriateness of the raters. Specifically, several reviews have concluded that raters need to be given formal guidelines and/or training on how to make reliable and unbiased ratings (Feild & Holley, 1982; Werner & Bolino, 1997; Williamson et al., 1997). Although the large number of raters within an MSF system may make the prospect of extensive rater training programs daunting or prohibitively expensive, several companies have opted to provide brief legal tutorials concerning the avoidance of biased ratings in their training of raters for an MSF system (Bernardin & Tyler, 2001). Finally, the courts have consistently ruled that raters must have an adequate opportunity to observe directly the performance of the employee. This prescription for legally defensible appraisals clearly favors MSF systems over single-rater systems. In fact, the court has recommended a MSF system in one case where the single rater (i.e., supervisor) had an inadequate amount of firsthand knowledge about an employee's performance (*Brito v. Zia,* 1973).

Overall, despite the lack of a direct ruling on the acceptability of MSF systems for personnel decisions, both the related court cases and the characteristics of a well-designed MSF system suggest that the courts are likely to view MSF systems in at least as favorable a light as single-rater appraisal systems.

### Technological Issues in MSF

Advances in technology (e.g., the wide availability of personal computers, local networks, the Internet) as well as software to collect, tabulate, and report MSF data have greatly expanded the opportunities for organizations to implement MSF. But technological concerns should be considered. Issues such as privacy (e.g., who will have access to MSF data?), changes in technology (e.g., rapid changes in software and data storage systems may make it difficult to retrieve archival data—just try accessing data stored on computer punch cards or reel-to-reel tapes!), and whether online collection of MSF influences its quality (e.g., are rating tendencies different online versus on paper?) are just some areas that should be considered and researched.

## FUTURE DEVELOPMENTS

Given the relatively short history of MSF systems, there are numerous directions for future research and application. For example, research studies are needed to: (1) provide a rigorous assessment of MSF effectiveness across a broad range of organizational settings, (2) assess the strengths and limitations among the wide variety of MSF instrument design options, (3) determine the psychometric qualities of MSF ratings, (4) identify factors that influence the acceptance of MSF systems, and (5) examine the effect of cross-cultural factors on the effective implementation of MSF systems in multinational organizations (e.g., Church & Bracken, 1997; Dunnette, 1993; Fletcher & Baldry, 1999). Space considerations limit our discussion to two areas that pique our interest: how best to provide feedback, and expanded uses of MSF in organizations. We then conclude with two brief, special concerns for the future development of MSF.

### The Content and Format of Feedback

In general, research on MSF has seemed to focus on the "multisource" component (e.g., instrumentation to gather ratings from the different sources, the quality of the ratings from each different source, the effects of purpose or anonymity on the information provide by the source) rather than the "feedback" component (for a notable exception, see Dalessio, 1998). More work is needed on what type of feedback is provided, how it is presented and returned to targets so that they will understand (and hopefully accept) the feedback, and how the organization can facilitate targets' interpretation and response to the feedback (e.g., Dalessio, 1998; DeNisi & Kluger, 2000; Ghorpade, 2000). Perhaps more important is

**TABLE 21.2   The Effects of Purpose on MSF Systems**

| Decision Points | Feedback Purposes | Administrative Purposes |
| --- | --- | --- |
| Content of instrument | Tied to employee short- and long-term development needs | Tied to position description or established performance goals |
| Frequency of use | As needed | Consistent with performance review timetable |
| Source anonymity | Of less importance | Of critical importance |
| Threat/implications of negative feedback | Low (limited consequences) | High (potentially serious consequences) |
| Data ownership | Individual receiving feedback | Sponsoring organization |
| Adherence to legal guidelines | Of less importance | Of great importance |

the need for research on how the targets of MSF perceive, accept, and act on feedback, which affects their job-related attitudes and behaviors (Fletcher & Baldry, 1999). As one example, London and Smither (1995) developed a model that predicts the effects of feedback from multiple rater sources on target ratees' perceptions of themselves as well as their job-related goals, behaviors, and performance. They also hypothesized how individual differences and the organizational context moderate the relations. This and other frameworks for guiding research on how feedback generated via MSF systems is perceived and used (e.g., Ashford, 1989; Balzer, Doherty, & O'Connor, 1989; Ilgen et al., 1979; Kluger & DeNisi, 1996; London, 1994; London & Smither, 1995) can help stimulate our understanding of the impact of feedback.

## Expanding the Uses of MSF

MSF systems are not limited to individual-level employee development and administrative decision making (e.g., performance ratings). Because of its roots (or at least its common history) in the action research model of organizational surveys and feedback (see Hedge et al., 2001, pp. 24–25), the expansion of the purposes of MSF from individual-level assessment and development to organizational development and integration seems natural and appropriate (Church, Waclawski, & Burke, 2001; Harris & Heft, 2001). Harris and Heft identified and discussed five additional applications of MSF for *organizational* purposes: (1) to clarify and direct an organization's mission and vision, (2) to expand the accountability of target individuals to others beyond their immediate supervisors (e.g., customers), (3) to provide an aggregated measure of important employee skills critical to individual and group success, (4) to change an organization's culture, and (5) to improve communication within an organization. The expansion of MSF to new or multiple purposes in an organization provides both challenges (i.e., conflicting purposes may motivate different MSF behaviors as discussed earlier in this chapter) and opportunities (e.g., the combination of individ-

ual and organizational benefits may more than compensate for the high costs of MSF) for future research and practice.

## Special Concerns

The literature we reviewed while preparing this chapter highlights a number of issues that must be considered or addressed to make MSF effective, ranging from an easily administered system to top-level organizational support for MSF. In this section, we briefly elaborate on three concerns that merit special consideration: the expanding purpose of MSF systems, the absence of common instrumentation, and the psychology of combining feedback from different sources.

### Purpose

The drift (or natural evolution, if you prefer) of the original purpose of MSF from its historical roots as a feedback system to a system that includes administrative purposes has dramatic implications and is a point of considerable discussion and debate (for a review, see London, 2001). There are in fact many additional purposes or goals of an MSF system, including clarification of organizational mission, changing organizational culture, and improving communication (Harris & Heft, 2001) and, questionably, because everyone else is doing it (Waldman et al., 1998). As shown in Table 21.2, decisions about the design and implementation of an MSF system may be quite different for the two most frequently discussed purposes of the system: feedback versus administrative. It is therefore critical to determine carefully the purpose(s) of an MSF system, communicate the purpose(s) to all who will participate in the system, and carefully monitor adherence to the purpose(s) (Antonioni, 1996; Bracken, 1996; Fleenor & Brutus, 2001). Although London (2001) suggested that over time it may be possible to gradually shift from development-only MSF to a system that also is used for administrative decision making, others are less sanguine (Jako, 2001).

## Nonstandardization of MSF Instruments

Advances in technology make it easy to develop customized MSF instruments. From a practice perspective, there are clear benefits when instruments can be tailored to each employee or job: It maintains higher levels of "face validity" and helps to limit the length of the instrument by omitting dimensions or areas that are irrelevant. But science is a cumulative process of building on past research in a systematic way. Unfortunately, it is difficult to cumulate findings and draw conclusions across studies without standardized instruments (e.g., are the differences between studies using different purposes due to this difference, or should the difference be attributed to different instrumentation?). The customization of instrumentation is one of many trade-offs where the goals of practitioners and researchers differ.

## Integrating MSF From Different Sources

We know very little about how recipients of MSF value and use the feedback from the various sources (self, peers, customers, bosses, subordinates). These recipients (or targets) of MSF are expected to integrate the feedback generated from others in the MSF process with their own self-assessment of performance. What is not known is how targets weight the feedback from others relative to their own self-assessment, which could influence their overall view of personal strengths and weaknesses (Fedor, 1991). For example, a person might be inclined to weight his or her own self-evaluation quite heavily because it is personally vivid and easily clearly remembered; on the other hand, feedback from other sources may be "discounted" because of a perceived agenda by the feedback source, low confidence in the quality of the information provided by the source, the lack of concreteness of the feedback provided by the source, and so on. Researchers recently have begun to investigate how these sources of evaluative feedback play a role in the assessment of performance and employee development (e.g., Raymark, Balzer, & DeLaTorre, 1999; Thorsteinson & Balzer, 1999). More work is needed to ensure that very rich and expensive MSF is used to its fullest for employee feedback and development.

## REFERENCES

Antonioni, D. (1994). The effects of feedback accountability on upward appraisal ratings. *Personnel Psychology, 47,* 349–356.

Antonioni, D. (1996). Designing an effective 360-degree appraisal feedback process. *Organizational Dynamics, Autumn,* 24–38.

Ashford, S.J. (1989). Self-assessments in organizations: A literature review and integrative model. *Research in Organizational Behavior, 11,* 133–174.

Atwater, L.E., Roush, P., & Fischtal, A. (1995). The influence of upward feedback on self and follower ratings of leadership. *Personnel Psychology, 48,* 35–59.

Atwater, L.E., Waldman, D.A., Atwater, D., & Cartier, P. (2000). An upward feedback field experiment: Supervisors' cynicism, reactions, and commitment to subordinates. *Personnel Psychology, 53,* 275–297.

Balzer, W.K., Doherty, M.E., & O'Connor, R., Jr. (1989). Effects of cognitive feedback on performance. *Psychological Bulletin, 106,* 410–433.

Balzer, W.K., & Sulsky, L.M. (1990). Performance appraisal effectiveness. In K.R. Murphy & F.E. Saal (Eds.), *Psychology in organizations: Integrating science and practice* (pp. 133–156). Hillsdale, NJ: Erlbaum.

Bernardin, H.J. (1986). Subordinate appraisal: A valuable source of information about managers. *Human Resource Management, 25,* 421–439.

Bernardin, H.J., & Beatty, R.W. (1984). *Performance appraisal: Assessing human behavior at work.* Boston: Kent Publishing.

Bernardin, H.J., Dahmus, S.A., & Redmon, G. (1993). Attitudes of first-line supervisors toward subordinate appraisals. *Human Resource Management, 32,* 315–324.

Bernardin, H.J., & Tyler, C.L. (2001). Legal and ethical issues in multisource feedback. In D.W. Bracken, C.W. Timmreck, & A.H. Church (Eds.), *The handbook of multisource feedback: The comprehensive resource for designing and implementing MSF processes* (pp. 447–462). San Francisco: Jossey-Bass.

Bettenhausen, K.L., & Fedor, D.B. (1997). Peer and upward appraisals: A comparison of their benefits and problems. *Group and Organization Management, 22(2)* 236–263.

Borman, W.C. (1991). Job behavior, performance, and effectiveness. In M.D. Dunnette & L.M. Hough (Eds.), *Handbook of industrial and organizational psychology* (2nd ed., Vol. 2, pp. 271–326). Palo Alto, CA: Consulting Psychologists Press.

Borman, W.C., & Brush, D.H. (1993). More progress toward a taxonomy of managerial performance requirements. *Human Performance, 6,* 1–21.

Bozeman, D.P. (1997). Interrater agreement in multi-source performance appraisal: A commentary. *Journal of Organizational Behavior, 18,* 313–316.

Bracken, D.W. (1994). Straight talk about multirater feedback. *Training and Development, 48,* 44–51.

Bracken, D.W. (1996). Multisource (360-degree) feedback: Surveys for individual and organizational development. In A.I. Kraut (Ed.), *Organizational surveys: Tools for assessment and change* (pp. 117–143). San Francisco: Jossey-Bass.

Bracken, D.W. (1997). Maximizing the uses of multi-rater feedback. In D.W. Bracken, M.A. Dalton, R.A. Jako, C.D. McCauley, & V.A. Pollman (Eds.), *Should 360-degree feedback be used only for developmental purposes?* (pp. 11–17). Greensboro, NC: Center for Creative Leadership.

Bracken, D.W., Dalton, M.A., Jako, R.A., McCauley, C.D., & Pollman, V.A. (1997). *Should 360-degree feedback be used only for developmental purposes?* Greensboro, NC: Center for Creative Leadership.

Bracken, D.W., & Timmreck, C.W. (2001). Success and sustainability: A systems view of multisource feedback. In D.W. Bracken, C.W. Timmreck, & A.H. Church (Eds.), *The handbook of multisource feedback: The comprehensive resource for designing and implementing MSF processes* (pp. 478–494). San Francisco: Jossey-Bass.

Bracken, D.W., Timmreck, C.W., & Church A.H. (Eds.). (2001). *The handbook of multisource feedback: The comprehensive resource for designing and implementing MSF processes.* San Francisco: Jossey-Bass.

Brockner, J., Siegel, P.A., Daly, J.P., Tyler, T., & Martin, C. (1997). When trust matters: The moderating effect of outcome favorability. *Administrative Science Quarterly, 43,* 558–583.

Brutus, S., Leslie, J.B., & McDonald-Mann, D. (2001). Cross-cultural issues in multisource feedback. In D.W. Bracken, C.W. Timmreck, & A.H. Church (Eds.), *The handbook of multisource feedback: The comprehensive resource for designing and implementing MSF processes* (pp. 433–446). San Francisco: Jossey-Bass.

Carroll, S.J., & Schneier, C.E. (1982). *Performance appraisal and review systems: The identification, measurement, and development of performance in organizations.* Glenview, IL: Scott, Foresman.

Cederblom, D., & Lounsbury, J.W. (1980). An investigation of user acceptance of peer evaluations. *Personnel Psychology, 33,* 567–579.

Chappelow, C.T. (1998). 360-degree feedback. In C.D. McCauley, R.S. Moxley, & E. Van Velsor (Eds.), *Center for creative leadership handbook of leadership development* (pp. 29–65). San Francisco: Jossey-Bass.

Cheung, G.W. (1999). Multifaceted conceptions of self-other ratings disagreement. *Personnel Psychology, 52,* 1–36.

Cheung, G.W., & Rensvold, R.B. (1998). Testing factorial invariance across groups: A reconceptualization and proposed new method. *Journal of Management, 25,* 1–27.

Church, A.H., & Bracken, D.W. (1997). Advancing the state of the art of 360-degree feedback: Guest editors' comments on the research and practice of multirater assessment methods. *Group and Organizational Management, 22,* 149–161.

Church, A.H., Waclawski, J., & Burke, W.W. (2001). Multisource feedback for organization development and change. In D.W. Bracken, C.W. Timmreck, & A.H. Church (Eds.), *The handbook of multisource feedback: The comprehensive resource for designing and implementing MSF processes* (pp. 301–317). San Francisco: Jossey-Bass.

Conway, J.M., & Huffcutt, A.I. (1997). Psychometric properties of multisource performance ratings: A meta-analysis of subordinate, supervisor, peer, and self-ratings. *Human Performance, 10,* 331–360.

Cook, H.D., & Manson, G.E. (1926). Abilities necessary in effective retail selling and a method of evaluating them. *Journal of Personnel Research, 5,* 74–82.

Cranshaw, V.B., Hartmann, S.F., & Winckler, A.J. (2001). Introducing and sustaining multisource feedback at Sears. In D.W. Bracken, C.W. Timmreck, & A.H. Church (Eds.), *The handbook of multisource feedback: The comprehensive resource for designing and implementing MSF processes* (pp. 389–402). San Francisco: Jossey-Bass.

Dalessio, A.T. (1998). Using multisource feedback for employee development and personnel decisions. In J.W. Smither (Ed.), *Performance appraisal: State of the art in practice* (pp. 278–330). San Francisco: Jossey-Bass.

Dalton, M.A. (1997). When the purpose of using multi-rater feedback is behavior change. In D.W. Bracken, M.A. Dalton, R.A. Jako, C.D. McCauley, & V.A. Pollman (Eds.), *Should 360-degree feedback be used only for developmental purposes?* (pp. 1–6). Greensboro, NC: Center for Creative Leadership.

Dalton, M.A., & Hollenbeck, G.P. (2001). A model of behavior change. In D.W. Bracken, C.W. Timmreck, & A.H. Church (Eds.), *The handbook of multisource feedback: The comprehensive resource for designing and implementing MSF processes* (pp. 352–367). San Francisco: Jossey-Bass.

Day, N.E. (1995). Can performance raters be more accurate? Investigating the benefits of prior knowledge of performance dimensions. *Journal of Managerial Issues, 7*(3), 323.

DeNisi, A.S, & Kluger, A.N. (2000). Feedback effectiveness: Can 360-degree appraisals be improved? *Academy of Management Executive, 14,* 129–139.

Dodgeson, M. (1993). Learning, trust, and technological collaboration. *Human Relations, 46,* 77–95.

Dunnette, M.D. (1993). My hammer or your hammer? *Human Resource Management, 32,* 373–384.

Edwards, M.R., & Ewen, A.J. (1996). *360-degree feedback: The powerful new model for employee assessment and performance improvement.* New York: American Management Association.

Edwards, M.R., Ewen, A.J., & Vendantam, K. (2001). How do users react to multisource feedback? In D.W. Bracken, C.W. Timmreck, & A.H. Church (Eds.), *The handbook of multisource feedback: The comprehensive resource for designing and implementing MSF processes* (pp. 239–255). San Francisco: Jossey-Bass.

Ewen, A.J., & Edwards, M.R. (2001). Readiness for multisource feedback. In D.W. Bracken, C.W. Timmreck & A.H. Church (Eds.), *The handbook of multisource feedback: The comprehensive resource for designing and implementing MSF processes* (pp. 33–47). San Francisco: Jossey-Bass.

Facteau, J.D., & Craig, S.B. (2001). Are performance appraisal ratings from different rating sources comparable? *Journal of Applied Psychology, 86,* 215–227.

Farr, J.L., & Newman, D.A. (2001). Rater selection: Sources of feedback. In D.W. Bracken, C.W. Timmreck, & A.H. Church (Eds.), *The handbook of multisource feedback: The comprehensive resource for designing and implementing MSF processes* (pp. 96–113). San Francisco: Jossey-Bass.

Fedor, D.B. (1991). Recipient responses to performance feedback: A proposed model and its implications. *Personnel and Human Resources Management, 9,* 73–120.

Fedor, D.B., Rensvold, R.B., & Adams, S.M. (1992). An investigation of factors expected to affect feedback seeking: A longitudinal field study. *Personnel Psychology, 45,* 779–805.

Ferstl, K.L., & Bruskiewicz, K.T. (2000). *Self-other agreement and cognitive reactions to multirater feedback.* In J.W. Johnson & K.L. Ferstl (Chairs), *Cognitive reactions to performance feedback.* Symposium conducted at the 15th Annual Conference of the Society for Industrial and Organizational Psychology, New Orleans, LA.

Feild, H.S., & Holley, W.H. (1982). The relationship of performance appraisal characteristics to verdicts in selected employment discrimination cases. *Academy of Management Journal, 25,* 392–406.

Findley, H.M., Giles, W.F., & Mossholder, K.W. (2000). Performance appraisal process and system facets: Relationships with contextual performance. *Journal of Applied Psychology, 85,* 634–640.

Fleenor, J.W., & Brutus, S. (2001). Multisource feedback for personnel decisions. In D.W. Bracken, C.W. Timmreck, & A.H. Church (Eds.), *The handbook of multisource feedback: The comprehensive resource for designing and implementing MSF processes* (pp. 335–351). San Francisco: Jossey-Bass.

Fletcher, C., & Baldry, C. (1999). Multi-source feedback systems: A research perspective. In C.L. Cooper & I.T. Robertson (Eds.), *International review of industrial and organizational psychology* (Vol. 14, pp. 149–193). Chichester, England: Wiley.

Funderburg, S.A., & Levy, P.E. (1997). The influence of individual and contextual variables on 360-degree feedback system attitudes. *Group and Organization Management, 22,* 210–235.

Ghorpade, J. (2000). Managing five paradoxes of 360-degree feedback. *Academy of Management Executive, 14,* 140–150.

Giles, W.F., & Mossholder, K.W. (1990). Employee reactions to contextual and session components of performance appraisal. *Journal of Applied Psychology, 75,* 371–377.

Gosselin, A., Werner, J.M., & Halle, N. (1997). Ratee preferences concerning performance management and appraisal. *Human Resource Development Quarterly, 8,* 315–333.

Greguras, G.J., & Robie, C. (1998). A new look at within-source interrater reliability of 360-degree feedback ratings. *Journal of Applied Psychology, 83,* 960–968.

Greguras, G.J., Robie, C., & Goff, M. III. (2001, April). Effects of rating purpose on the quality of multi-source ratings. In J.R. Williams (Chair), *Has 360-degree feedback really gone amok? New empirical data.* Symposium conducted at the 16th Annual Conference of the Society for Industrial and Organizational Psychology, San Diego, CA.

Harris, M.M., & Heft, L. (2001). Organizational integration. In D.W. Bracken, C.W. Timmreck, & A.H. Church (Eds.), *The handbook of multisource feedback: The comprehensive resource for designing and implementing MSF processes* (pp. 418–432). San Francisco: Jossey-Bass.

Harris, M.M., & Schaubroeck. J. (1988). A meta-analysis of self-supervisor, self-peer, and peer-supervisor ratings. *Personnel Psychology, 41,* 43–62.

Hazucha, J.F., Hezlett, S.A., & Schneider, R.J. (1993). The impact of 360-degree feedback on management skills development. *Human Resource Management, 32,* 325–351.

Hedge, J.W., Borman, W.C., & Birkeland, S.A. (2001). History and development of multisource feedback as a methodology. In D.W. Bracken, C.W. Timmreck, & A.H. Church (Eds.), *The handbook of multisource feedback: The comprehensive resource for designing and implementing MSF processes* (pp. 15–32). San Francisco: Jossey-Bass.

Hedge, J.W., & Teachout, M.S. (2000). Exploring the concept of acceptability as a criterion for evaluating performance measures. *Group and Organization Management, 25*(1) 22–44.

Hegarty, W.H. (1974). Using subordinate ratings to elicit behavioral changes in supervisors. *Journal of Applied Psychology, 59,* 764–766.

Hofstede, G. (1980). *Culture's consequences: International differences in work-related values.* Thousand Oaks, CA: Sage.

Hollander, E.P. (1954). Buddy ratings: Military research and industrial implications. *Personnel Psychology, 7,* 385–393.

Ilgen, D.R., Fisher, C.D., & Taylor, M.S. (1979). Consequences of individual feedback on behavior in organizations. *Journal of Applied Psychology, 64,* 349–371.

Ilgen, D.R., & Knowlton, W.A. (1980). Performance attribution effects on feedback from supervisors. *Organizational Behavior and Human Performance, 25,* 441–456.

Jako, R.A. (1997). Fitting multi-rater feedback into organizational strategy. In D.W. Bracken, M.A. Dalton, R.A. Jako, C.D. McCauley, & V.A. Pollman (Eds.), *Should 360-degree feedback be used only for developmental purposes?* (pp. 19–22). Greensboro, NC: Center for Creative Leadership.

Jako, R.A. (2001). Evolution of multisource feedback in a dynamic environment. In D.W. Bracken, C.W. Timmreck, & A.H. Church (Eds.), *The handbook of multisource feedback: The comprehensive resource for designing and implementing MSF processes* (pp. 403–417). San Francisco: Jossey-Bass.

Johnson, J.W., & Ferstl, K.L. (1999). The effects of interrater and self-other agreement on performance improvement following upward feedback. *Personnel Psychology, 52,* 271–303.

Katz, D., & Kahn, R.L. (1978). *The social psychology of organizations* (2nd ed.). New York: Wiley.

Keeping, L.M., & Levy, P.E. (2000). Performance appraisal reactions: Measurement, modeling, and method bias. *Journal of Applied Psychology, 85,* 708–723.

Kluger, A.N., & DeNisi, A.D. (1996). Effects of feedback interventions on performance: A historical review, meta-analysis, and a preliminary feedback intervention theory. *Psychological Bulletin, 119,* 254–284.

Ladner, H.S., & Greguras, G.J. (2001, April). Effects of mean rating level, interrater agreement, and self-other agreement on ratee reactions to peer feedback. In J.R. Williams (Chair), *Has 360-degree feedback really gone amok? New empirical data.* Symposium presented at the 16th Annual Conference of the Society for Industrial and Organizational Psychology, San Diego, CA.

Landy, F.J., & Farr, J.L. (1980). Performance rating. *Psychological Bulletin, 87,* 72–107.

Lawler, E.E. III. (1967). The multitrait-multirater approach to measuring managerial job performance. *Journal of Applied Psychology, 51,* 369–381.

Leslie, J.B., & Fleenor, J.W. (1998). *Feedback to managers: A review and comparison of multi-rater instruments for management development.* Greensboro, NC: Center for Creative Leadership.

Leslie, J.B., Gryskiewicz, N.D., & Dalton, M.A. (1998). Understanding cultural influences on the 360-degree feedback process. In W.W. Tornow & M. London (Eds.), *Maximizing the value of 360-degree feedback: A process for individual and organizational development* (pp. 196–216). San Francisco: Jossey-Bass.

Link, H.C. (1920). The application of psychology to industry. *Psychological Bulletin, 17,* 335–346.

London, M. (1994). Interpersonal insight in organizations: Cognitive models for human resource development. *Human Resource Management Review, 4,* 311–332.

London, M. (2001). The great debate: Should multisource feedback be used for administration or development only? In D.W. Bracken, C.W. Timmreck, & A.H. Church (Eds.), *The handbook of multisource feedback: The comprehensive resource for designing and implementing MSF processes* (pp. 368–385). San Francisco: Jossey-Bass.

London, M., & Smither, J.W. (1995). Can multi-source feedback change perceptions of goal accomplishment, self-evaluations and performance related outcomes? Theory-based applications and directions for research. *Personnel Psychology, 44,* 375–390.

London, M., Smither, J.W., & Adsit, D.J. (1997). Accountability: The Achilles' heel of multisource feedback. *Group and Organization Management, 22*(2), 162–184.

London, M., & Wohlers, A.J. (1991). Agreement between subordinate and self-ratings in upward feedback. *Personnel Psychology, 44,* 375–390.

Love, K.G. (1981). Comparison of peer assessment methods: Reliability, validity, friendship bias, and user reaction. *Journal of Applied Psychology, 66,* 451–457.

Maloney, P.W., & Hinrichs, J.R. (1959). A new tool for supervisory self-development. *Personnel, 36,* 46–53.

McCauley, C.D. (1997). On choosing sides: Seeing the good in both. In D.W. Bracken, M.A. Dalton, R.A. Jako, C.D. McCauley, & V.A. Pollman (Eds.), *Should 360-degree feedback be used only for developmental purposes?* (pp. 23–36). Greensboro, NC: Center for Creative Leadership.

McCauley, C.D., & Hughes-James, M. (1994). *An evaluation of outcomes of a leadership development program.* Greensboro, NC: Center for Creative Leadership.

McEvoy, G.M. (1990). Public sector managers' reactions to appraisals by subordinates. *Public Personnel Management, 19,* 201–212.

Mero, N.P., & Motowidlo, S.J. (1995). Effects of rater accountability on the accuracy and the favorability of performance ratings. *Journal of Applied Psychology, 80,* 517–524.

Mintzberg, H. (1979). *The structuring of organizations.* Englewood Cliffs, NJ: Prentice-Hall.

Mitchell, J.L. (1978). *Structured job analysis of professional and managerial positions.* Unpublished doctoral dissertation, Purdue University, West Lafayette, IN.

Mohrman, A.M., Resnick-West, S.M., & Lawler, E.E. III (1989). *Designing performance appraisal systems: Aligning appraisals and organizational realities.* San Francisco: Jossey-Bass.

Mount, M.K., Judge, T.A., Scullen, S.E., Systma, M.R., & Hezlett, S.A. (1998). Trait, rater, and level effects in 360-degree performance ratings. *Personnel Psychology, 51,* 557–576.

Murphy, K.R., & Cleveland, J.N. (1995). *Understanding performance appraisal: Social, organizational, and goal-oriented perspectives.* Thousand Oaks, CA: Sage.

Murphy, K.R., Cleveland, J.N., & Mohler, C.J. (2001). Reliability, validity, and meaningfulness of multisource ratings. In D.W. Bracken, C.W. Timmreck & A.H. Church (Eds.), *The handbook of multisource feedback: The comprehensive resource for designing and implementing MSF processes* (pp. 130–148). San Francisco: Jossey-Bass.

Nadler, D.A. (1977). *Feedback and organization development: Using data-based methods.* Reading, MA: Addison-Wesley.

Pollman, V.A. (1997). Some faulty assumptions that support using multi-rater feedback for performance appraisal. In D.W. Bracken, M.A. Dalton, R.A. Jako, C.D. McCauley, & V.A. Pollman (Eds.), *Should 360-degree feedback be used only for developmental purposes?* (pp. 7–9). Greensboro, NC: Center for Creative Leadership.

Raymark, P.H., Balzer, W.K., & DeLaTorre, F. (1999). A preliminary investigation of the sources of information used by raters when appraising performance. *Journal of Business and Psychology, 14,* 319–339.

Reilly, R.R., Smither, J.W., & Vasilopoulos, N.L. (1996). A longitudinal study of upward feedback. *Personnel Psychology, 49,* 599–612.

Reise, S.P., Widaman, K.F., & Pugh, R.H. (1993). Confirmatory factor analysis and item response theory: Two approaches for exploring measurement invariance. *Psychological Bulletin, 114,* 552–566.

Ring, P.S., & Van de Ven, A. (1994). Developmental processes of cooperative interorganizational relationships. *Academy of Management Review, 19,* 90–118.

Rogelberg, S.G., & Waclawski, J. (2001). Instrumentation design. In D.W. Bracken, C.W. Timmreck, & A.H. Church (Eds.), *The handbook of multisource feedback: The comprehensive resource for designing and implementing MSF processes* (pp. 63–78). San Francisco: Jossey-Bass.

Rosti, R.T., & Shipper, F. (1998). A study of the impact of training in a management development program based on 360-degree feedback. *Journal of Managerial Psychology, 13,* 77–89.

Scullen, S.E., Mount, M.K., & Sytsma, M.R. (1996, April). *Comparisons of self, peer, direct report and boss ratings of managers' performance.* Paper presented at the annual meeting of the Society for Industrial and Organizational Psychology, San Diego, CA.

Siefert, C.F., Yukl, G., & McDonald, R.A. (2001). *A field experiment on the effectiveness of 360 degree feedback and training.* Paper presented at the European Work and Organizational Psychology, Prague, Czech Republic.

Smither, J.W., London, M., Vasilopoulos, N.L., Reilly, R.R., Millsap, R.E., & Salvemini, N. (1995). An examination of the effects of an upward feedback program over time. *Personnel Psychology, 46,* 1–34.

Smither, J.W., & Walker, A.G. (2001). Measuring the impact of multisource feedback. In D.W. Bracken, C.W. Timmreck, & A.H. Church (Eds.), *The handbook of multisource feedback: The comprehensive resource for designing and implementing MSF processes* (pp. 256–271). San Francisco: Jossey-Bass.

Stewart, R. (1982). A model for understanding managerial jobs and behavior. *Academy of Management Review, 7,* 7–13.

Sulsky, L.M., & Keown, L. (1998). Performance appraisal in the changing world of work: Implications for the meaning and measurement of work performance. *Canadian Psychology, 39,* 52–59.

Thorsteinson, T.J., & Balzer, W.K. (1999). Effects of coworker information on perceptions and ratings of performance. *Journal of Organizational Behavior, 20,* 1157–1173.

Timmreck, C.W., & Bracken, D.W. (1995, May). *Upward feedback in the trenches: Challenges and realities.* Paper presented as part of the Upward Feedback symposium at the 10th Annual Conference of the Society for Industrial and Organizational Psychology, Orlando, FL.

Timmreck, C.W., & Bracken, D.W. (1997). Multisource feedback: A study of its use in decision making. *Employment Relations Today, 12,* 86–94.

Timmreck, C.W., & Wentworth, T. (2001). Working with a vendor for a successful project. In D.W. Bracken, C.W. Timmreck, & A.H. Church (Eds.), *The handbook of multisource feedback: The comprehensive resource for designing and implementing MSF processes* (pp. 478–494). San Francisco: Jossey-Bass.

Tornow, W.W. (1993a). Editor's note: Introduction to special issue on 360-degree feedback. *Human Resource Management, 32,* 211–219.

Tornow, W.W. (1993b). Perceptions of reality: Is multi-perspective measurement a means or an end? *Human Resource Management, 32,* 221–229.

Tornow, W., & London, M. (1998). *Maximizing the value of 360-degree feedback: A process for successful individual and organizational development.* San Francisco: Jossey-Bass.

Tornow, W.W., & Pinto, P.R. (1976). The development of a managerial job taxonomy: A system for describing, classifying, and evaluating executive positions. *Journal of Applied Psychology, 61,* 410–418.

Van Velsor, E. (1998). Designing 360-degree feedback to enhance involvement, self-determination, and commitment. In W.W. Tornow & M. London (Eds.), *Maximizing the value of 360-degree feedback: A process for successful individual and organizational development* (pp. 149–195). San Francisco: Jossey-Bass.

Van Velsor, E., & Leslie, J.B. (2001). Selecting a multisource feedback instrument. In D.W. Bracken, C.W. Timmreck, & A.H. Church (Eds.), *The handbook of multisource feedback: The comprehensive resource for designing and implementing MSF processes* (pp. 63–78). San Francisco: Jossey-Bass.

Vandenberg, R.J., & Lance, C.E. (2000). A review and synthesis of the measurement invariance literature: Suggestions, practices, and recommendations for organizational research. *Organizational Research Methods, 3,* 4–69.

Veglahn, P.A. (1993). Key issues in performance appraisal challenges: Evidence from court and arbitration decisions. *Labor Law Journal, 44,* 595–606.

Viswesvaran, C., Ones, D.S., & Schmidt, F.L. (1996). Comparative analysis of the reliability of job performance ratings. *Journal of Applied Psychology, 81,* 557–574.

Waldman, D.A. (1997). Predictors of employee preferences for multirater and group-based performance appraisal. *Group and Organization Management, 22(2),* 264–287.

Waldman, D.A., Atwater, L.E., & Antonioni, D. (1998). Has 360 degree feedback gone amok? *Academy of Management Executive, 12,* 86–94.

Werner, J.M., & Bolino, M.C. (1997). Explaining U.S. Court of Appeals decisions involving performance appraisal: Accuracy, fairness, and validation. *Personnel Psychology, 50,* 1–24.

Westerman, J.W., & Rosse, J.G. (1997). Reducing the threat of rater nonparticipation in 360-degree feedback systems: An exploratory examination of antecedents to participation in upward ratings. *Group and Organization Management, 22*(2), 288–309.

Whitely, W. (1985). Managerial work behavior: An integration of results from two major approaches. *Academy of Management Journal, 28,* 344–362.

Wicks, A.C., Berman, S.L., & Jones, T.M. (1999). The structure of optimal trust: Moral and strategic implications. *Academy of Management Review, 24*(1), 99–116.

Williamson, L.G., Campion, J.E., Malos, S.B., Roehling, M.V., & Campion, M.A. (1997). Employment interview on trial: Linking interview structure with litigation outcomes. *Journal of Applied Psychology, 82,* 900–912.

Yukl, G.A. (1983, October). *Development of a taxonomy of managerial behavior by factor analysis.* Paper presented at the annual meeting of the Society for Organizational Behavior, Minneapolis.

Yukl, G.A. (1987, October). *A new taxonomy for integrating diverse perspectives on managerial behavior.* Paper presented at the annual meeting of the American Psychological Association, New York

Zucker, L.G., Darby, M.R., Brewer, M.B., & Peng, Y. (1996). Collaboration structure and information dilemmas in biotechnology: Organizational boundaries as trust production. In R.M. Kramer & T.R. Tyler (Eds.), *Trust in organizations: Frontiers of theory and research* (pp. 90–113). Thousand Oaks, CA: Sage.

# CHAPTER 22

# Citizenship Performance in Organizations

JENNIFER D. KAUFMAN AND WALTER C. BORMAN

This chapter introduces the topic of citizenship performance as a distinct type of employee work performance. Specifically, we trace the origins of employee citizenship performance beginning several decades ago with the notion of employee discretionary behavior. Next, we draw theoretical comparisons among the several conceptualizations of this form of employee behavior and discuss empirical and measurement issues, including the effects of different rating sources and scales, antecedents of citizenship performance, links with organizational effectiveness, and generalizability issues. First, however, we define what we mean by employee work performance and briefly review a theory of performance.

*Performance* is defined as behavior and includes only those actions that are relevant to the organization's goals and that can be measured in terms of each individual's contribution (Campbell, 1990). Performance is not the consequence or result of action; rather, it is the action itself. It is not unidimensional; instead, for any job, performance is complex and consists of several major performance components. Campbell (1990) suggested that individual differences on any performance component are a function of three major determinants: declarative knowledge, procedural knowledge/skill, and motivation. Declarative knowledge is knowledge about facts and things and represents an understanding of the tasks' requirements. Procedural knowledge/skill is knowing how to accom-

plish tasks. Motivation is a combined effect of three choice behaviors: (1) choice to expend effort; (2) choice of level of effort to expend; and (3) choice to persist in the expenditure of that effort.

Most commonly, job performance definitions and measurement revolve around task performance. For instance, most job analysis research focuses on workers' task activities or behaviors that are formally recognized as part of their jobs. However, these behaviors are not the only behaviors relevant to organizational effectiveness. For example, Barnard (1938), Katz and Kahn (1978), and Smith, Organ, and Near (1983) describe extratechnical proficiency components of behavior that contribute to organizational effectiveness by lubricating organizational processes, thus facilitating task activities and group performance. Individual differences in performance within this general class of behavior are explained more by differences in motivation than by differences in knowledge or skill. Due to the assumed importance of this class of behavior for enhanced organizational functioning, a great deal of recent research attention has been devoted to the explication of the citizenship performance domain. The origins of the citizenship performance construct are provided next followed by antecedents to this domain of behavior and links to organizational effectiveness.

## ORIGINS OF THE CITIZENSHIP PERFORMANCE CONSTRUCT

As early as 1938, Barnard first noted the "informal organization" and the need for organizational members to be willing to cooperate for the good of the organization. More recently, Organ (1977) suggested an expanded domain of performance that he labeled organizational citizenship behavior (OCB). OCB is defined as extrarole, discretionary behavior that helps other organizational members perform their jobs or that demonstrates support for, or conscientiousness toward, the organization (Smith et. al, 1983). The OCB literature supports the idea of two broad dimensions of extrarole behavior. Smith et al. (1983) developed the first measure of OCB to represent two distinct factors: *Altruism* and *Generalized Compliance.* Behaviors that are directly intended to help others (e.g., orienting new employees, assisting a fellow employee with a heavy workload) are referred to as altruism. In contrast, the second dimension pertains to a more impersonal form of conscientiousness whereby the behavior does not provide immediate aid to any one specific person but, rather, is indirectly helpful to others involved in the system (e.g., making suggestions for organizational improvements). This factor is referred to as generalized compliance.

Several elements of OCB are included in the related concept of contextual performance. Borman and Motowidlo (1993) noted that many activities do not fall under the category of task performance but are still important for organizational effectiveness. These latter activities were originally referred to as "contextual" and include behaviors such as: (1) volunteering to carry out task activities that are not formally part of the job; (2) persisting with extra enthusiasm or effort when necessary to complete own task activities successfully; (3) helping and cooperating with others; (4) following organizational rules and procedures even when personally inconvenient; and (5) endorsing, supporting, and defending organizational objectives.

Motowidlo and Van Scotter (1994) empirically tested the conceptual arguments advanced by Borman and Motowidlo (1993), where task and contextual performance were introduced as distinct constructs. Specifically, Motowidlo and Van Scotter (1994) demonstrated support for defining performance multidimensionally, and also for both task and contextual performance contributing independently to overall performance. Later, these researchers sought to refine the contextual performance criterion space by dividing it into two narrower contextual performance constructs: (1) *interpersonal facilitation* that includes cooperative, considerate, and helpful acts that assist coworkers' performance; and (2) *job dedication* that includes self-disciplined, motivated acts such as working

hard, taking initiative, and following rules to support organizational objectives (Van Scotter & Motowidlo, 1996). These narrower constructs are similar to the two dimensions that Smith et al. (1983) proposed for OCB. Van Scotter and Motowidlo (1996) empirically tested this model and demonstrated that task performance, interpersonal facilitation, and job dedication are all important components of work performance.

The overlap both conceptually and empirically between the contextual performance and OCB domains resulted in Organ's (1997) observation that the two terms could be considered as synonymous. Thus, for the remainder of this chapter the term *citizenship performance* is used to discuss behavior that may be classified as OCB or contextual work performance.

### Citizenship Performance Dimensions

The past 15 years have seen a great deal of attention dedicated toward further partitioning of the citizenship performance domain. Although both the contextual performance literature and the early OCB literature generally both support a two-dimensional structure, citizenship performance researchers (Folger & Cropanzano, 1998; MacKenzie, Podsakoff, & Fetter, 1991; Organ 1989; Podsakoff & MacKenzie, 1994; Puffer, 1987) have argued for a further division and refinement of the citizenship performance space. Specifically, some researchers recommended the inclusion of as many as seven citizenship performance factors (Organ, 1989). Other researchers broadened the construct boundaries to include a mix of both productive and counterproductive employee work behaviors (e.g., generic work performance [Hunt, 1996] and prosocial organizational behavior [Brief & Motowidlo, 1986]). Some preferred to focus on exclusively employee counterproductive behaviors (cf. Skarlicki & Folger, 1997). Finally, one of the newer conceptualizations defines citizenship performance in terms of the beneficiary of the behavior (Coleman & Borman, 2000; McNeely & Meglino, 1994; Williams & Anderson, 1991). These major developments are overviewed in the following with an emphasis placed on evidence that supports or weakens the tenability of each perspective.

### Partitioning the OCB Criterion Space

Building on the original citizenship behavior research that focused on two broad dimensions (i.e., altruism and conscientiousness), Organ (1989) suggested the refinement of OCB and the inclusion of five additional dimensions. These dimensions are: (1) peacekeeping (i.e., actions that help prevent, resolve, or mitigate unconstructive interpersonal conflict);

(2) cheerleading (i.e., encouraging and reinforcing accomplishments and professional development); (3) sportsmanship (i.e., willingness to tolerate less than ideal circumstances); (4) courtesy (i.e., acts such as keeping others informed of events that may affect them); and (5) civic virtue (i.e., responsible participation in the political life of the organization such as attending meetings and reading memos).

However, Organ's (1989) proposition that there may be seven, rather than two, broad, distinct OCB dimensions has failed to be confirmed empirically. For example, Podsakoff and colleagues (MacKenzie et al., 1991; Podsakoff & MacKenzie, 1994) showed that raters tended to view altruism, courtesy, cheerleading, and peacekeeping as consisting of a single helping behavior dimension (Podsakoff, Ahearne, & MacKenzie, 1997). This single helping dimension showed a great deal of overlap with the originally proposed altruism dimension by Smith et al. (1983).

Van Dyne, Graham, and Dienesch (1994) used political philosophy as a theoretical framework to derive OCB factors. Van Dyne et al. (1994) found some support for their five factors: (1) Loyalty (i.e., allegiance to and promotion of the organization); (2) Obedience (i.e., respect for rules and policies); (3) Advocacy Participation (i.e., innovation and proactively synergizing others; (4) Functional Participation (i.e., work-oriented effort and self-development); and (5) Social Participation (i.e., engaging in group meetings and activities). Clearly, there is some overlap between this depiction of OCB and the Organ factors, but the Van Dyne et al. effort is notable for the factors that conceptualize participation in organizational affairs from a political activist perspective.

Despite the several OCB and citizenship performance conceptualizations, theoretical bases, proposed factor structures, and operationalizations, consistent among these research streams is the idea that OCB/citizenship performance refers to *positive* employee behaviors that fall outside task performance or the technical proficiency part of the job. Expanding this definition are two related constructs, prosocial organizational behavior and generic work behavior, that also have received attention and overlap considerably with most conceptualizations of citizenship performance. The primary difference between these two constructs and those of citizenship performance is the breadth of the conceptualization. That is, the boundaries of these two latter constructs are broader and include negative as well as positive employee behavior.

### Prosocial Organizational Behavior

Prosocial organizational behaviors (PSOBs) are positive social acts carried out to produce and maintain the well-being of others (Brief & Motowidlo, 1986). Specifically, acts such as helping, sharing, cooperating, and volunteering are forms of prosocial behavior (Brief & Motowidlo, 1986). Citizenship performance and PSOB appear to have much in common. However, the primary difference between PSOB and citizenship performance conceptualizations is in the breadth of the PSOB construct. Simply, PSOB may be organizationally functional or dysfunctional, in-role or extrarole, and directed toward specific individuals with whom organizational members interact, or toward the organization as a whole.

Despite the more general nature of the PSOB construct, many of the specific kinds of behavior identified by Brief and Motowidlo (1986) are very similar to citizenship performance dimensions. For example, the PSOB dimension *assisting co-workers with job-related matters* is defined very similarly to the Altruism OCB factor. Altruism includes behaviors such as helping others who have been absent, and orienting new people even though it is not required. Clearly, these types of OCBs may be classified more generally as the PSOB dimension, *assisting co-workers with job-related matters*. The other PSOB dimensions include: *showing leniency in personal decisions, providing services or products to consumers in organizationally consistent ways, providing services or products to consumers in organizationally inconsistent ways, helping consumers with personal matters unrelated to organizational services or products, complying with organizational values, policies, and regulations, suggesting procedural, administrative or organizational improvements, putting forth extra effort on the job, volunteering for additional assignments, staying with the organization despite temporary hardships, and representing the organization favorably to outsiders.*

### Generic Work Performance

Generic work performance is a broader conceptualization of work performance that includes several elements of citizenship performance. Consistent with Campbell (1990), Hunt (1996) adopted the viewpoint that performance is multidimensional. Furthermore, similar to citizenship performance researchers, Hunt (1996) emphasized not only the multidimensionality of those aspects of performance but also that these dimensions are primarily dependent on differences in motivation as opposed to differences in ability (cf. Borman & Motowidlo, 1993). However, in contrast to most definitions of citizenship performance, Hunt, like Brief and Motowidlo (1986) advocated a much broader conceptualization of employee work behavior. That is, Hunt defined generic work behavior as, "performance including both productive and counterproductive employee behaviors that contribute to or detract from organizational goals, including behaviors that are often considered to be separate from performance, and behaviors that might be considered to be conditions of employment instead of aspects of job performance" (Hunt, 1996 p. 52).

Generic work behaviors are behaviors that influence the performance of virtually any job (Hunt, 1996). Although Hunt's construct includes both in-role as well as extrarole behaviors related to generic job performance, this domain of work behavior shares part of the construct space defined by several other constructs such as employee deviance, OCB, contextual performance, and prosocial behavior. Analysis of data from more than 18,000 employees suggests that most of the behaviors that Hunt identified can be grouped into nine different factors. These factors are: (1) Adherence to Confrontational Rules; (2) Industriousness; (3) Thoroughness; (4) Schedule Flexibility; (5) Attendance; (6) Off-Task Behavior; (7) Unruliness; (8) Theft; and (9) Drug Misuse. Hunt (1996) concluded that these nine factors are indeed generic in that most, if not all of the behaviors associated with each factor influence the performance of virtually any job, although the magnitude, consequences, and interrelationships should likely vary across situations. Also, in the context of this review, virtually all of the factors can be considered to reflect citizenship performance or counterproductive behavior.

Borman, Ackerman, and Kubisiak's (1994) research with the Department of Labor also suggested the existence of several general work behaviors. These researchers asked experienced supervisors involved with a wide variety of jobs and industries to provide their views of the important performance requirements of jobs in the U.S. economy. Supervisors recorded, in their own words, the performance dimensions they believed differentiated effective from ineffective workers in all nonmanagement jobs. These performance dimensions were compiled and industrial/organizational (I/O) psychologists sorted the dimensions into categories based on their content. These sorting solutions were pooled using a statistical procedure (Borman & Brush, 1993) and a factor analysis of the resulting correlation matrix resulted in a 12-factor set of dimensions reflecting these supervisors' view of the important performance requirements across nonmanagement jobs in the U.S. economy. Importantly, this research found that 7 of the 12 summary factors could be classified as citizenship performance categories. This body of research provides corroborating evidence that performance not only is multidimensional, but also that a significant portion of the performance domain consists of citizenship behavior.

Still another stream of research has focused on negative employee behavior (Folger & Baron, 1996; O'Leary-Kelly, Griffin, & Glew, 1996; Robinson & Bennett, 1995). Two of the most researched negative employee behavior constructs

are noncompliant behavior (Puffer, 1987) and organizational retaliatory behavior (Skarlicki & Folger, 1997). Each of these two employee deviant behavior constructs is reviewed next.

### Noncompliant Behavior

Puffer (1987) defines *noncompliant behavior* as behavior that has negative organizational implications. More specifically, noncompliant behavior refers to breaking rules or norms and is essentially the negative side of conscientiousness and related constructs that have been previously incorporated in other conceptualizations of employee work performance. However, Puffer argues that the act of *not* complying with established rules and practices can be more informative about an individual than is compliance with organizational rules and policies. Noncompliant behavior includes actions such as: being late, taking excessive breaks, complaining about the company to coworkers, violating rules, making unrealistic promises to customers, and failing to perform a fair share of the work. Puffer's analyses suggested that individual differences in motivation explain the variance in both prosocial and noncompliant behavior. That is, Puffer's findings suggested that prosocial behavior and noncompliant behavior have a common achievement-motivation base but are influenced by different perceived situational contingencies.

### Organizational Retaliatory Behaviors

Like Puffer (1987), Skarlicki and Folger (1997) focused on negative employee behavior, but under a different label. Skarlicki and Folger (1997) referred to negative employee behavior that is used to punish the organization and its representatives in response to perceived unfairness as organizational retaliatory behavior (ORB). These researchers conceptualized ORB as analogous to OCB: Much as OCBs are described as the little things that can be critical to an organization's survival, Skarlicki and Folger (1997) noted that many ORBs may not appear as dangerous as more overtly aggressive acts (e.g., interpersonal violence), but in the aggregate they may detract from organizational functioning. ORB includes behaviors such as: damaging equipment on purpose, disobeying a supervisor's instructions, spending time on personal matters at work, and gossiping about and talking back to the boss.

Notably, there is considerable overlap between the behaviors associated with ORB and those associated with noncompliant behavior and employee deviance. However, Skarlicki and Folger (1997) made a distinction between their ORB construct and the other noncompliant behavior constructs. Skarlicki and Folger asserted that the commonly used term *deviant behavior* has a more pejorative connotation than does the term *retaliatory behavior* in that deviance presumes wrongful and inherently negative employee conduct. Specifically, they argued that unfair treatment toward employees may make retaliation more legitimate than deviant. That is, just as conflict can be used constructively for change, they argued that legitimate retaliation might provoke needed organizational change and as such may be constructive. Finally, they argued that labeling employee behavior as deviant implies an attribution to the employee's disposition, whereas labeling behavior as retaliatory has its basis more in terms of individual motivation. Despite disagreement over the breadth of the citizenship performance construct, the central theme that weaves through most conceptualizations of the related constructs is that these types of behavior are generally regarded as not related to the technical proficiency aspects of the job, and variance is thought to be primarily a function of individual differences in motivation rather than individual differences in ability or skill.

## Distinguishing Among Different Beneficiaries of Citizenship Performance

Some researchers have suggested a reconstruction of the citizenship performance domain based on behavioral beneficiary. For example, Williams and Anderson (1991) relabeled the original OCB factors, Altruism and Generalized Compliance, Organizational Citizenship Behavior-Individual (OCBI) and Organizational Citizenship Behavior-Organization (OCBO), respectively. OCBI is defined as behavior that immediately benefits specific individuals and indirectly through this means contribute to the organization (e.g., helps others who have been absent). In contrast, OCBO is defined as behavior that benefits the organization in general (e.g., gives advance notice when unable to come to work). In addition, these researchers asserted that the previous labels (i.e., altruism and compliance) implied overly restrictive terms inconsistent with definitions of citizenship performance. That is, altruism implies behavior without any external reward, whereas compliance implies behavior with the expectation of reward or with the avoidance of punishment (Williams & Anderson, 1991).

Consistent with the work of Williams and Anderson, McNeely and Meglino (1994) noted that most citizenship performance studies have not adequately separated behavior on the basis of its beneficiary. However, they also noted that although Williams and Anderson argued for defining citizenship performance factors in terms of the behavioral beneficiary, in operation, this may not have been accomplished. For example, Williams and Anderson used the Smith et al. (1983) Altruism Scale as the basis for creating their OCBI factor.

Unfortunately, the Smith et al. Altruism Scale was problematic with regard to distinguishing between the beneficiaries of citizenship behavior because it combined behaviors that are clearly intended to benefit the organization (e.g., making suggestions to improve the department) with those designed to help specific individuals (e.g., helping others who have heavy workloads; McNeely & Meglino, 1994).

Nevertheless, consistent with the theoretical position taken by Williams and Anderson (1991), McNeely and Meglino (1994) identified a rationale for different psychological processes being responsible for citizenship performance directed at different beneficiaries. These researchers showed evidence of construct validity such that when the beneficiaries are clearly separated, different processes appear to be responsible for citizenship behavior directed toward specific individuals versus the organization. Specifically, social exchange theory (Blau, 1964) suggests that persons will direct their reciprocation efforts to the source of benefits they receive. Thus, when employees feel they have been treated properly by an organization, it is logical that they direct their supportive behaviors toward the organization itself. Also, research on mood and helping (e.g., Eisenberg & Miller, 1987; Isen & Levin, 1972) suggests that dispositional variables (concern for others and empathy) are predictive of OCBI, whereas situational variables (perceptions of fairness) are predictive of OCBO.

McNeely and Megino (1994) suggested that a likely explanation for the equivocality of results found in prior citizenship performance research is probably a consequence of utilizing measures that have not specifically delineated the beneficiaries of the behavior. When these beneficiaries are clearly separated, different processes appear to be responsible for citizenship performance directed toward individuals versus the organization. Taken together, the arguments and empirical evidence offered by both Williams and Anderson (1991) and by McNeely and Megino suggest the importance of conceptualizing and measuring citizenship performance relative to the behavioral beneficiary, rather than in terms of alternative ways of organizing employee citizenship behaviors.

Coleman and Borman (2000) also sought to delineate the conceptual organization of the citizenship performance domain. In doing so, they first reviewed the research on OCB, contextual performance, a model of soldier effectiveness (Borman et al., 1985) and related concepts from earlier literature (e.g., Barnard, 1938; Katz & Kahn, 1978), and more recent related conceptualizations (e.g., Williams & Anderson, 1991). In all, they identified 27 different concepts. Next, the authors had several I/O psychologists familiar with this literature sort the concepts into categories according to their content. These sortings were pooled (similar to Borman et al.'s generic work behavior project described previously) and the resulting summary correlation matrix was analyzed by exploratory factor analysis, multidimensional scaling, and subsequent cluster analysis. The results revealed a hierarchical, integrated model. Specifically, the model represents three broad categories of behavior that vary according to the beneficiary of the behavior (Interpersonal Citizenship Performance—behaviors benefiting organizational members; Organizational Citizenship Performance—behaviors benefiting the organization; and Job/Task Conscientiousness—behaviors benefiting the job/task). It is noteworthy that the Coleman and Borman analysis was entirely inductive in the sense that no a priori restrictions were placed on the input to the analyses. That is, the emergence of a factor structure that conforms to the different-beneficiaries view of citizenship performance is somewhat compelling because of the methodology in this research that took no a priori position on a citizenship performance structure.

The most obvious difference between the Coleman and Borman (2000) model and, for example, the Williams and Anderson (1991) conceptualization is the addition of the Job/Task Citizenship dimension. However, other systems have included a similar concept. These are: (1) the Borman and Motowidlo (1993) model including volunteering and extra effort concepts; (2) Van Scotter and Motowidlo (1996), with the broad job dedication construct; and (3) Van Dyne et al. (1994), with the functional participation dimension that includes elements of self-development and accomplishment of work beyond expectations.

The Interpersonal Citizenship Performance dimension in the Coleman and Borman (2000) integrated model is most similar to the Williams and Anderson (1991) OCBI factor and to the Van Scotter and Motowidlo (1996) Interpersonal Facilitation dimension. The Smith et al. (1983) Altruism factor is similar but the "Keeping Others Informed" element is not reflected in the factor as it is in the Coleman and Borman dimension. Although Organ (1988) and Podsakoff et al. (1990) divide this dimension into Altruism and Courtesy, Podsakoff et al. (1990) found that supervisory ratings of performance on those two factors correlated very highly ($r = .86$). Finally, the Organizational Citizenship Performance dimension in the Coleman and Borman (2000) model is most closely aligned with the Williams and Anderson (1991) OCBO factor, the Smith et al. (1983) Generalized Compliance factor, and the Becker and Vance (1993) Conscientiousness factor.

Despite the breadth and the intuitive appeal of the integrated model presented by Coleman and Borman (2000), and subsequently modified in Borman et al., (2001), they concede that there is probably no "best" configuration for the citizenship performance domain. As with any effort toward evaluating construct validity, it will be important to evaluate the differential correlations between the individual constructs and other variables hypothesized to be related to each construct.

## Summary

The importance of employee citizenship performance for organizational functioning has been acknowledged for more than half a century; however, it has only been in the past 15 years that a concerted empirical effort has been launched toward fully exploring the citizenship performance domain. The several different streams of citizenship performance research that have developed in parallel have created some confusion. However, attempts have been made to clarify these constructs (cf. Organ, 1997; Van Dyne et al., 1994). In addition, despite some substantive differences, these seemingly diverse lines of research share a great deal in common.

Common to citizenship performance research is the assumption that employee work performance is multidimensional. Although researchers continue to debate about the precise number and definitions of performance dimensions, the multidimensionality of work performance and the inclusion of employee performance beyond task performance as central to the performance domain is assumed. Furthermore, common among all these constructs is the recognition that variance in employee citizenship behavior lies more in individual differences in motivation than in differences in knowledge, skill, or ability. Finally, researchers agree that the behaviors composing the citizenship performance domain are behaviors generalizable across many types of work.

## RATING SOURCES AND SCALES FOR CITIZENSHIP PERFORMANCE

In addition to the importance placed on referencing the appropriate beneficiary within citizenship performance dimensions, researchers have also pointed to the effects of different rating sources. That is, it is important not only to recognize the impact of whom the behavior is directed toward (i.e., ratee) but also to acknowledge the role played by differences in the respondent (i.e., rater). Furthermore, the issue of the appropriate measurement scale for evaluating this class of employee behavior has also surfaced.

Performance appraisal can be considered a four-step process. The rater begins with certain beliefs and ideas concerning what the job requires and what needs to be done in order to achieve job goals (i.e., cognitions); these cognitions influence employee behavior on the job, followed by evaluation of the behavior in terms of achieving desired results, and finally the effects of this evaluation on cognitions about the job requirements (Campbell & Lee, 1988). Although this four-step process is generally accepted, it is not clear how the model applies to ratings of citizenship performance.

## Rating Source

In evaluating citizenship performance, we might simply ask individuals questions about how frequently ratees perform each of a number of behaviors that represents the target citizenship performance (Organ, 1988). The argument in favor of this approach is that each person probably knows more about his or her total work behavior than does any other person. In addition, research suggests that the use of self-appraisal for measuring citizenship performance may be appropriate. Investigators have emphasized the appropriateness of self-appraisal when used as a developmental appraisal tool (e.g., Mabe & West, 1982; Wexley & Klimoski, 1984). However, research suggests that self-appraisals may be more lenient and less accurate than other source ratings (Campbell & Lee, 1988). In addition, because citizenship performance is usually measured in surveys and correlated with other self-report measures such as employee perceptions of, or feelings about, the work environment (e.g., job satisfaction, trust), there is a great likelihood for common method variance contamination resulting from the use of multiple self-report measures (Organ, 1988).

In an attempt to address the aforementioned criticisms associated with self-appraisal, many citizenship performance researchers ask employees' immediate supervisors to rate subordinates' citizenship performance. The use of supervisory ratings addresses the potential problem of same-source ratings associated with survey collection efforts and offers a unique and likely more objective perspective on employee behavior. However, the use of supervisor citizenship performance ratings is not a panacea for ensuring accurate citizenship performance ratings. Although supervisors may be in a better position to provide an objective perspective of employee behavior, their limited interaction with each employee may lead to observations that do not reflect employee typical behavior, and as such their evaluations may lack representativeness.

Employing peers to provide ratings of citizenship performance is a way to address the criticisms associated with both self-report and supervisory ratings (cf. Skarlicki & Folger, 1997). The advantage of peer ratings is that peers are likely to interact with employees on a day-to-day basis and are thus in a good position to observe a wide range of employee behavior. In addition, because most employees have multiple peers, the use of several peer ratings should enhance the reliability of the ratings. More than a decade ago, Organ (1988)

noted that future researchers likely will move toward pooling citizenship performance estimates from several rating sources (i.e., self, boss, coworkers, clients). As of yet, no single rating source has been agreed upon as superior. Although both researchers and practitioners continue to employ a variety of ratings sources, very few employ multiple rating sources when obtaining estimates of employee citizenship performance.

## Rating Scales and Formats

For many years I/O psychologists have been interested in rating formats and how manipulations of these formats might reduce rating errors and increase interrater reliability (cf. Taylor & Wherry, 1951). Typically, citizenship performance researchers use a 5- to 7-point Likert-type rating scale to measure employee behavior. Although some studies use a scale anchored with "Agree" and "Disagree" or with "Very True" and "Very Untrue" (e.g., Smith et al., 1983), most use a behavioral frequency scale (e.g., "All of the Time" to "Never"). Because citizenship performance is defined as employee behavior, rather than as a work attitude, frequency scales appear more appropriate than agree-disagree-type scales that are typically used in studies intended to capture employee work attitudes.

More recently, Borman et al. (2001) introduced a new type of rating scale for measuring employee citizenship performance. They developed a paired comparison rating task (computerized adaptive rating scales: CARS) that uses adaptive testing principles to help raters estimate a ratee's performance level through an iterative paired comparison rating process. Basically, the rater is initially presented with two behavioral statements associated with a citizenship performance dimension, one reflecting somewhat below average performance and the other somewhat above average performance. Depending on the statement the rater selects as more descriptive of the ratee, the rating algorithm selects two additional behavioral statements, one with a scaled effectiveness level somewhat above the effectiveness value of the statement first picked as the more descriptive, and a second statement with a scaled effectiveness level somewhat below the effectiveness value of the initially chosen statement. The rater's selection of the more descriptive second paired comparison then revises the estimated ratee effectiveness level, and as before, the algorithm selects two more statements whose effectiveness values bracket the revised estimated performance level. Thus, analogous to adaptive testing, a ratee's effectiveness level is estimated in an item response theory sense by an iterative paired comparison rating task that presents in sequence item pairs that maximize the amount of information about performance derived from each choice of an item.

Borman et al. (2001) compared the reliability, validity, and accuracy of the CARS with that found using graphic rating scales and behaviorally anchored rating scales (BARS). Their results showed a 23–37% lower standard error of measurement for CARS compared with the other two methods. In addition, the CARS data showed significantly higher validity and accuracy.

## The Impact of Ratee Citizenship Performance on Overall Performance Ratings

In addition to rating source and scale issues, a more general, but important, issue is the weight ratees place on citizenship performance relative to ratings of task performance when making overall performance judgments. Several studies have shown that ratee citizenship performance has a meaningful impact on these overall performance ratings. Motowidlo and Van Scotter (1994) gathered three supervisor performance ratings on approximately 300 air force first-termers. One rater made an overall performance rating, a second provided ratings on task performance, and a third rated citizenship performance. The correlation between the task and the overall performance ratings was .43. The correlation between citizenship and overall performance was .41. Thus, Motowidlo and Van Scotter's results support the inference that supervisory ratings are a function of both task and citizenship performance. Several researchers have demonstrated corroborating evidence that supports the relationship between task, citizenship, and overall performance (e.g., Borman, White, & Dorsey, 1995; Ferris, Judge, Rowland, and Fitzgibbons, 1994; Van Scotter & Motowidlo, 1996; Werner, 1994). Thus, published results appear to support the position that global performance ratings are influenced substantially by ratee citizenship performance.

## ANTECEDENTS OF CITIZENSHIP PERFORMANCE

This section reviews research on links between individual differences, predictor constructs, and citizenship performance. From a theoretical perspective, Motowidlo, Borman, and Schmit (1997) developed a model hypothesizing that the most substantial predictor-criterion relationship should be between general cognitive ability and task performance and between personality and citizenship performance.

Empirical tests of this model have shown moderate support. The main support comes from a study conducted by Motowidlo and Van Scotter (1994). They obtained correlations between several personality constructs and both task and contextual performance and found that for four of the constructs, the correlations with contextual performance were

significantly higher than with task performance-Work Orientation (.36 vs. .23), Dependability (.30 vs. .21), Cooperativeness (.20 vs. .04), and Internal Locus of Control (.27 vs. .08). Data from Project A, the large-scale test validation research effort conducted in the U.S. Army (Campbell & Knapp, 2001), also supported the model. Results of a concurrent validation study showed, first, that general cognitive ability correlated substantially higher with a technical proficiency criterion ($r = .33$) than it did with a citizenship criterion ($r = .08$). Second, the three personality factors derived in the study correlated higher with the citizenship criterion, especially the Dependability factor (.30 vs. .11).

Three review articles demonstrated more mixed support for the personality-citizenship performance link. Organ and Ryan (1995) found in a meta-analysis that, among the four personality variables they focused on, only Conscientiousness showed a consistent relationship with two organizational citizenship behavior (OCB) factors, Altruism and Generalized Compliance. Mean corrected correlations for these two OCB components were, respectively, .22 and .30. However, when studies using self-ratings of OCB were not considered (because of possible contamination due to common method variance), the mean correlations were reduced to .04 and .23. In a second meta-analytic review, Hurtz and Donovan (2000) explored correlations between the Big Five personality factors and three criteria, task performance and two citizenship performance factors (Job Dedication and Interpersonal Facilitation). Again, the hypothesis was that personality-citizenship performance relations would be higher than personality-task performance relations. For Agreeableness this was the case, .17 with interpersonal facilitation, compared with .07 with task performance. And for Conscientiousness, Emotional Stability, and Extraversion, the correlations were slightly higher compared with task performance for at least one of the citizenship performance criteria.

Finally, Borman, Penner, Allen, and Motowidlo (2001) identified 20 studies conducted since the Organ and Ryan (1995) review that correlated personality constructs with citizenship performance criteria. These authors found somewhat higher correlations than did Organ and Ryan. Weighted *uncorrected* correlations from the Borman et al. review compared with uncorrected correlations from the Organ and Ryan review (with the two criteria, altruism and generalized compliance) were: .24 versus .16 and .21 for Conscientiousness; .13 versus .10 and .08 for Agreeableness; .18 versus .12 and .06 for Positive Affectivity; and −.14 versus −.05 and −.09 for Negative Affectivity. Borman et al. also found five studies where Conscientiousness or a related personality factor (e.g., Dependability) correlated more highly with a citizenship criterion than a task performance criterion.

On balance, personality appears related to citizenship performance at a somewhat higher level than to task performance or overall job performance. This confirms part of the Motowidlo et al. (1997) model, but admittedly, results do not show large differences in relations with the task and citizenship performance constructs. Perhaps most useful for scientific understanding of personality-job performance linkages will be additional studies that represent citizenship performance as a multidimensional concept, using one or more of the recent conceptualizations (Coleman & Borman, 2000; Organ, 1988; Van Scotter & Motowidlo, 1996; Williams & Anderson, 1991). This approach would be in keeping with the Campbell, Gasser, and Oswald (1996) strategy of attempting to build multidimensional models of job performance and then to learn more about linkages between individual differences and relatively specific criterion constructs.

## LINKS WITH ORGANIZATIONAL EFFECTIVENESS

Most OCB researchers study citizenship performance as a criterion rather than examining the consequences of citizenship performance or its relationship with other organizational criteria. Because citizenship performance is defined as behavior that in the aggregate improves the functioning of organizations, it seems logical to explore the relation between citizenship performance and organizational effectiveness. Podsakoff and MacKenzie (1997) provided theoretical and conceptual reasons why a link may exist between citizenship performance and organizational effectiveness. For example, the expression of citizenship behavior is believed to contribute to a more efficient use of resources, thus allowing supervisors to concentrate their efforts on more productive activities such as planning, scheduling, and problem solving (cf. Smith et al., 1983). In addition, citizenship performance may contribute to the stability of an organization by reducing the variance in work group performance by "bringing along" lower performers. Therefore, it seems reasonable to propose that citizenship behavior may facilitate organizational effectiveness, efficiency, and success (Podsakoff & MacKenzie, 1994). Podsakoff and MacKenzie (1997) reviewed recent research on the link between organizational citizenship and effectiveness and concluded that the correlation between the two is relatively high.

For example, Podsakoff, MacKenzie, and Bommer (1996) demonstrated a substantial relationship between citizenship performance and the quality and quantity of the paper produced by 40 work crews at a paper mill factory. Specifically, they found that citizenship performance was positively related to the quantity of paper produced, and it also reduced the percentage of rejected paper (i.e., quality); citizenship performance accounted for nearly 26% of the variance in production quantity and almost 17% in production quality.

In another study, citizenship performance showed a meaningful association with a variety of performance measures in limited-menu restaurants (Walz & Niehoff, 1996). That is, aggregated citizenship performance among restaurant employees was positively related to overall operating efficiency, customer satisfaction, quality of performance, and a reduction in the amount of food ingredients wasted and customer complaints. On average, Walz and Niehoff (1996) showed that citizenship performance accounted for approximately 29% of the variance in these criteria with the proportion of variance accounted for as high as 37% to 43% for some of the variables.

Taken together, the overall pattern revealed by the four studies and across 10 organizational effectiveness indicators reviewed by Podsakoff and MacKenzie (1997) suggests support for the relation between citizenship performance on the part of organizational members and organizational effectiveness. Across these four diverse samples, citizenship performance accounted for approximately 19% of the variance in performance quantity, more than 18% of the variance in performance quality, 25% of the variance in financial efficiency indicators, and 38% of the variance in customer service indicators (Podsakoff & MacKenzie, 1997). Generally speaking, citizenship performance enhances organizational performance.

Further evidence of the link of citizenship performance and organizational effectiveness is provided by utility research. Utility analysis is a means of capturing the valued contribution of an employee's behavior to an organization's bottom line (i.e., dollar value).

Orr, Sackett, and Mercer (1989) examined this link by employing a policy capturing methodology to examine the extent to which supervisors weight citizenship behavior when making dollar judgments about work performance. Specifically, supervisors were given performance profiles for 50 employees and were asked to assign a dollar value for that level of performance. Using the Schmidt, Hunter, McKenzie, and Muldrow (1979) method, supervisors estimated the dollar value of workers who perform at different levels resulting in a value that represents the difference between the dollar value of an average worker and that of workers performing one standard deviation above and below this mean. The supervisors were provided with the dollar value of average performance; this value was determined by assessing the total yearly cost of the employee's services and included salary and benefits.

Results suggest a significant portion of supervisors take citizenship behavior into account when making these dollar judgments. Thus, the results of the Orr et al. (1989) utility analysis provide further evidence of the relation between citizenship performance and indicators of organizational effectiveness. Taken together, the Podsakoff and MacKenzie (1997) review and the Orr et al. (1989) utility analysis provide strong empirical support for the link between citizenship performance and indicators of organizational effectiveness.

## GENERALIZABILITY ISSUES

To this point, our review of the literature has noted considerable convergence around different theoretical positions and empirical findings in the areas of citizenship performance. The research provides evidence of construct validity of the citizenship performance domain, and the building of a nomological net that supports the idea of multiple citizenship performance dimensions and their antecedents and consequences. However, a critical issue that has not yet been addressed is the generalizability of the citizenship performance construct. The generalizability of a construct dictates its scope and potential usefulness. That is, to accurately predict the potential impact a construct may have, it is important to define the boundary conditions for results surrounding the construct. For example, it is important to determine whether a construct holds the same meaning (i.e., construct equivalence) and predicts relationships in the same way across different types of individuals and different cultures.

Although many individual difference and situational variables may affect the generalizability of the citizenship performance construct, gender and cross-cultural issues are salient aspects to all organizations. The following sections provide a brief overview of the empirical findings related to the generalizability of citizenship performance with respect to differences in gender and in national culture.

### Gender

Chen and Heilman (2001) called upon the gender stereotyping literature as the foundation for exploring different behavioral expectations for men and women regarding work performance. Specifically, they sought to investigate whether gender stereotypes dictate different organizational citizenship expectations for men and women and result in different work-related outcomes. Consistent with the gender stereotyping literature they proposed that because female stereotypes dictate that women *should* perform helping types of citizenship behavior, women who do perform these types of citizenry behaviors may not be considered as positive as when men exhibit these same behaviors. Conversely, women may be considered as poorer performers compared with men when they fail to perform such behaviors.

Chen and Heilman's (2001) results showed that after performing citizenship behavior, men were more favorably evaluated or highly recommended for organizational rewards compared with women exhibiting the same behaviors. Furthermore, men who did not exhibit citizenship performance were rated no differently than men about whom no citizenship information was provided, whereas women who did exhibit citizenship behavior were rated at the same level as women about whom no information about citizenship performance was provided.

Additional evidence is provided by Allen (2000) and by Allen and Rush (2001). Allen (2000) showed that the relationship between OCB and promotion was stronger for males than for females. Consistent with Chen and Heilman's (2000) findings, Allen's results provide further evidence about the effect of gender stereotypes on ratings of citizenship performance across gender. Furthermore, Allen and Rush (2001) found that raters made more accurate behavioral observations when evaluating males who exhibited OCB and females who exhibited no OCB than when evaluating males who did not exhibit OCB and females who did exhibit OCB. The explanation may be that more accurate ratings result when the observed behavior is relatively noteworthy, that is, is inconsistent with the gender stereotype.

Finally, Lovell et al. (1999) sought to determine whether the gender of the persons exhibiting citizenship performance would affect the relationship between citizenship performance and job performance ratings. They found that women received higher peer citizenship performance ratings than men, although they did not differ from men on supervisory performance ratings. Taken together, the work of researchers in the area of gender and citizenship performance supports an argument for the impact of gender stereotypes on performance expectations and ratings. Women are assumed to exhibit more citizenship behavior than men, and, as such, they are not given as much credit for citizenship performance.

### Cross-Cultural Issues

Expectation differences are not uniquely associated with gender stereotypes. Similar to the arguments offered with respect to gender differences, stereotypes are also invoked when dealing with different cultures. Research suggests that meaningful differences with respect to citizenship performance occur across cultures, and these differences are a function of the categorization of citizenship behavior as expected behavior or as extrarole behavior. Turnipseed and Murkison (2000) compared citizenship performance in employees from the

United States and Romania. Factor analyses showed significant differences between these two cultures in terms of both item loadings and emergent citizenship performance factors. Their findings suggest that national and organizational cultures appear to be significant determinants of citizenship performance.

Further evidence is offered by Lam, Hui, and Law (1999), who examined citizenship performance across U.S., Australian, Japanese, and Hong Kong samples. Participants in the Lam et al. study were asked to rate the degree to which behavior described in the Podsakoff et al. (1990) citizenship performance scale was an expected part of a subordinate's job. The scale was found to have conceptual equivalence across all samples, although participants from Hong Kong and Japan were more likely to regard some categories of citizenship performance as an expected part of the job than were participants from the United States or Australia.

## Summary

Taken together, the work of researchers in the area of gender and cross-cultural issues and citizenship performance supports an argument for the impact of both gender and cross-cultural stereotypes on performance expectations and ratings. Compared with task performance, citizenship performance is a broad construct that captures a large number of important employee work behaviors. Nevertheless, demographic (e.g., gender, culture) differences may affect the generalizability of this class of behavior. That is, results suggest that the classification of citizenship behaviors into task or citizenship may differ with respect to gender and cultural stereotypes and expectations.

## REFERENCES

Allen, T.D. (2000, April). *The relationship between organizational citizenship behavior, gender, and organizational rewards.* Paper presented at the 15th Annual Conference of the Society for Industrial and Organizational Psychology, New Orleans, LA.

Allen, T.D., & Rush, M.C. (2001). Stereotypes and the "good soldier": Two experiments examining the influence of ratee sex on perceived frequency, value and behavioral accuracy ratings of organizational citizenship behavior. *Journal of Applied Social Psychology, 31,* 2561–2587.

Barnard, C. (1938). *The functions of the executive.* Cambridge, MA: Harvard University.

Becker, T.E., & Vance, R.J. (1993). Construct validity of three types of organizational citizenship behavior: An illustration of the direct product model with refinements. *Journal of Management, 19,* 663–682.

Blau, P. (1964). *Exchange and power in social life.* New York: Wiley.

Borman, W.C., Ackerman, L.D., & Kubisiak, U.C. (1994). *Development of a performance rating program in support of Department of Labor test validation research* (Contract Nos. 93-2 and 93-3). Sacramento, CA: Cooperative Personnel Services.

Borman, W.C., & Brush, D.H. (1993). Toward a taxonomy of managerial performance requirements. *Human Performance, 6,* 1–21.

Borman, W.C., Buck, D.E., Hanson, M.A., Motowidlo, S.J., Stark, S., & Drasgow, F. (2001). An examination of the comparative reliability, validity, and accuracy of performance ratings made using computerized adaptive ratings scales. *Journal of Applied Psychology, 86,* 965–973.

Borman, W.C., & Motowidlo, S.J. (1993). Expanding the criterion domain to include elements of contextual performance. In N. Schmitt & W.C. Borman (Eds.), *Personnel selection* (pp. 71–98). San Francisco: Jossey-Bass.

Borman, W.C., Motowidlo, S.J., Rose, S.R., & Hanser, L.M. (1985). *Development of a model of soldier effectiveness* (Institute Rep. No. 95). Minneapolis, MN: Personnel Decisions Research Institutes.

Borman, W.C., Penner, L.A., Allen, T.D., & Motowidlo, S.J. (2001). Personality predictors of citizenship performance. *International Journal of Selection and Assessment, 9,* 52–69.

Borman, W.C., White, L.A., & Dorsey, D.D. (1995). Effects of ratee task performance and interpersonal factors on supervisor and peer performance ratings. *Journal of Applied Psychology, 80,* 168–177.

Brief, A.P., & Motowidlo, S.J. (1986). Prosocial organizational behaviors. *Academy of Management Review, 11,* 710–725.

Campbell, J.P. (1990). Modeling the performance prediction in industrial and organizational psychology. In M.D. Dunnette & L.M. Hough (Eds.), *Handbook of industrial and organizational psychology* (2nd ed., Vol. 1, pp. 687–732). Palo Alto: Consulting Psychology Press.

Campbell, J.P., Gasser, M.B., & Oswald, F.L. (1996). The substantive nature of performance variability. In K.R. Murphy (Ed.), *Individual differences and behavior in organizations* (pp. 258–299). San Francisco: Jossey-Bass.

Campbell, J.P., & Knapp, D.J. (Eds.). (2001). *Exploring the limits in personnel selection and classification.* Mahwah, NJ: Erlbaum.

Campbell, D.J., & Lee, C. (1988). Self-appraisal in performance evaluation: Development versus evaluation. *Academy of Management Review, 13,* 302–314.

Chen, J.J., & Heilman, M.E. (2001, April). *Need some help? Gender-specific rewards for organizational citizenship behaviors.* Paper presented at the 16th Annual Conference of the Society for Industrial and Organizational Psychology, San Diego, CA.

Coleman, V.I., & Borman, W.C. (2000). Investigating the underlying structure of the citizenship performance domain. *Human Resource Management Review, 10,* 25–44.

Eisenberg, N., & Miller, P.A. (1987). The relation of empathy to prosocial and related behaviors. *Psychological Bulletin, 101,* 91–119.

Ferris, G.R., Judge, T.A., Rowland, K.M., & Fitzgibbons, D.E. (1994). Subordinate influence and the performance evaluation process: Test of a model. *Organizational Behavior and Human Decision Processes, 58,* 101–136.

Folger, R., & Baron, R.A. (1996). Violence and hostility at work: A model of reactions to perceived injustice. In G.R. VandenBos & E.Q. Bulatao (Eds.), *Violence on the job: Identifying risks and developing solutions* (pp. 51–85). Washington, DC: American Psychological Association.

Folger, R., & Cropanzano, R. (1998). *Organizational justice and human resource management.* Thousand Oaks, CA: Sage.

Hunt, S.J. (1996). Generic work behavior: An investigation into the dimensions of entry level, hourly job performance. *Personnel Psychology, 49,* 51–84.

Hurtz, G.M., & Donovan, J.J. (2000). Personality and job performance: The big five revisited. *Journal of Applied Psychology, 85,* 869–879.

Isen, A.M., & Levin, A.F. (1972). Effect of feeling good on helping: Cookies and kindness. *Journal of Personality and Social Psychology, 21,* 384–388.

Katz, D., & Kahn, R.L. (1978). *The social psychology of organizations.* New York: Wiley.

Lam, S.S., Hui, C., & Law, K. (1999). Organizational citizenship behavior: Comparing perspectives of supervisors and subordinates across four international samples. *Journal of Applied Psychology, 84,* 594–601.

Lovell, S.E., Kahn, A.S., Anton, J., Davidson, A., Dowling, E., Post, D., & Mason, C. (1999). Does gender affect the link between organizational citizenship behavior and performance evaluation? *Sex Roles, 41,* 469–478.

Mabe, P.A., & West, S.G. (1982). Validity of self-evaluation of ability: A review and meta-analysis. *Journal of Applied Psychology, 67,* 280–296.

MacKenzie, S.B., Podsakoff, P.M., & Fetter, R. (1991). Organizational citizenship behavior and objective sales productivity as determinants of managerial evaluations of salespersons' performance. *Organizational Behavior and Human Decision Processes, 50,* 123–150.

McNeely, B.L., & Meglino, B.M. (1994). The role of dispositional and situational antecedents in prosocial organizational behavior: An examination of the intended beneficiaries of prosocial behavior. *Journal of Applied Psychology, 79,* 836–844.

Motowidlo, S.J., Borman, W.C., & Schmit, M.J. (1997). A theory of individual differences in task and contextual performance. *Human Performance, 10,* 71–83.

Motowidlo, S.J., & Van Scotter, J.R. (1994). Evidence that task performance should be distinguished from contextual performance. *Journal of Applied Psychology, 79,* 475–480.

O'Leary-Kelly, A.M., Griffin, R.W., & Glew, D.J. (1996). Organization-motivated aggression: A research framework. *Academy of Management Review, 21,* 225–253.

Organ, D.W. (1977). A reappraisal and reinterpretation of the satisfaction-causes-performance hypothesis. *Academy of Management Review, 2,* 46–53.

Organ, D.W. (1988). *Organizational citizenship behavior: The good soldier syndrome.* Lexington, MA: Lexington Books.

Organ, D.W. (1989). *The motivational basis of organizational citizenship behavior.* Unpublished manuscript.

Organ, D.W. (1997). Organizational citizenship behavior: It's construct clean-up time. *Human Performance, 10,* 85–97.

Organ, D.W., & Ryan, K. (1995). A meta-analytic review of attitudinal and dispositional predictors of organizational citizenship behavior. *Personnel Psychology, 48,* 775–801.

Orr, J.M., Sackett, P.R., & Mercer, M. (1989). The role of prescribed and nonprescribed behaviors in estimating the dollar value of performance. *Journal of Applied Psychology, 72,* 615–621.

Podsakoff, P.M., Ahearne, M., & MacKenzie, S.B. (1997). Organizational citizenship behavior and the quantity and quality of work group performance. *Journal of Applied Psychology, 82,* 262–270.

Podsakoff, P.M., & MacKenzie, S.B. (1994). Organizational citizenship behavior and sales unit effectiveness. *Journal of Marketing Research, 31,* 351–363.

Podsakoff, P.M., & MacKenzie, S.B. (1997). Impact of organizational citizenship behavior on organizational performance: A review and suggestions for future research. *Human Performance, 10,* 133–151.

Podsakoff, P.M., MacKenzie, S.B., & Bommer, W. (1996). Transformational leader behaviors and substitutes for leadership as determinants of employee satisfaction, commitment, trust, and organizational citizenship behaviors. *Journal of Management, 22,* 259–298.

Podsakoff, P.M., MacKenzie, S.B., Moorman, R., & Fetter, R. (1990). Transformational leader behaviors and their effects on followers' trust in leader satisfaction and organizational citizenship behaviors. *Leadership Quarterly, 1,* 107–142.

Puffer, S.M. (1987). Prosocial behavior, noncompliant behavior, and work performance among commission salespeople. *Journal of Applied Psychology, 72,* 615–621.

Robinson, S.L., & Bennett, R.J. (1995). A typology of deviant workplace behaviors: A multidimensional scaling study. *Academy of Management Journal, 38,* 555–572.

Schmidt, F.L., Hunter, J.E., McKenzie, R., & Muldrow, T. (1979). Impact of valid selection procedures on work force productivity. *Journal of Applied Psychology, 64,* 359–372.

Skarlicki, D.P., & Folger, R. (1997). Retaliation in the workplace: the roles of distributive, procedural, and interactional justice. *Journal of Applied Psychology, 82,* 434–443.

Smith, C.A., Organ D.W., & Near, J.P. (1983). Organizational citizenship behavior: Its nature and antecedents. *Journal of Applied Psychology, 68,* 653–663.

Taylor, E.K., & Wherry, R.J. (1951). A study of leniency in two rating systems. *Personnel Psychology, 4,* 245–252.

Turnipseed, D.L., & Murkison, E. (2000). A bi-cultural comparison of organizational citizenship behavior: Does the OCB phenomenon transcend national culture? *International Journal of Organizational Analysis, 8,* 200–222.

Van Dyne, L., Cummings, L.L., & Parks, J.M. (1995). Extra role behaviors: In pursuit of construct and definition clarity (a bridge muddies waters). In L.L. Cummings & B.M. Staw (Eds.), *Research in organizational behavior* (Vol. 17, pp. 215–285). Greenwich, CT: JAI Press.

Van Dyne, L., Graham, J., & Dienesch, R. (1994). Organizational citizenship behavior: Construct redefinition, measurement and validation. *Academy of Management Journal, 37,* 765–802.

Van Scotter, J.R., & Motowidlo, S.J. (1996). Interpersonal facilitation and job dedication as separate facets of contextual performance. *Journal of Applied Psychology, 81,* 525–531.

Walz, S.M., & Niehoff, B.P. (1996). Organizational citizenship behaviors and their effect on organizational effectiveness in limited-menu restaurants. In J.B. Keys & L.N. Dosier (Eds.), *Academy of Management best papers proceedings* (pp. 307–311). Briarcliff Manor, NY: Academy of Management.

Werner, J.M. (1994). Dimensions that make a difference: Examining the impact of in-role and extra-role behaviors on supervisory ratings. *Journal of Applied Psychology, 79,* 98–107.

Wexley, K., & Klimoski, R.J. (1984). Performance appraisal: An update. In K.M. Rowland, & G.D. Ferris (Eds.), *Research in personnel and human resources management* (Vol. 2). Greenwich, CT: JAI Press.

Williams, L.J., & Anderson, S.E. (1991). Job satisfaction and organizational commitment as predictors or organizational citizenship and in-role behavior. *Journal of Management, 17,* 601–617.

# ASSESSING TEAMS AND TEAMWORK

# CHAPTER 23

# On Measuring Teamwork Skills

EDUARDO SALAS, C. SHAWN BURKE, JENNIFER E. FOWLKES, AND HEATHER A. PRIEST

Technological challenges and the changing nature of work have caused the use of teams to become a predominant organizational strategy. More specifically, in a survey of work practices in manufacturing firms, Osterman (1994) found that over half of the companies surveyed used teams. Similarly, others have also reported teams being used as a key organizational strategy (Stewart, Manz, & Sims, 1999). The increased use of teams within organizations is heavily based on the assumption that they are an automatic ticket to increased productivity and/or effectiveness. However, many real-world examples have shown that this is not the case (Hackman, 1990). As such, much research has been conducted over the past 20 years aimed at understanding the factors associated with effective team performance.

Perhaps the most parsimonious finding to come out of these efforts is the fact that well-functioning teams must possess teamwork, as well as taskwork competencies, in order to be effective (McIntyre & Salas, 1995). Teamwork competencies have been described as, "the behavioral interactions and attitudinal responses that team members must develop before they can function effectively as a team" (Salas, Dickinson, Converse, & Tannenbaum, 1992, p. 12). In contrast, taskwork competencies are composed of those skills needed for members to understand and acquire task performance. Although there would not be much argument among researchers that these two tracks of competencies are essential for effective team performance, organizations have few mechanisms in place to systematically diagnose these skills.

The lack of systematic team performance measurement systems within operational settings leaves those in charge

(i.e., managers, leaders, supervisors) having to rely on informal data to determine why teams are ineffective. That is, individuals responsible for creating and maintaining effective teams are asked to assess team performance within complex and dynamic environments, but they are not properly equipped to do so. Quality team performance measurement systems are the only method by which teams can be systematically evaluated to catch problems early before they filter into other areas or before incorrect actions and/or attitudes become ingrained within team member cognition.

The lack of team performance measurement systems within organizations is not due to a lack of knowledge about how to create and implement team performance measurement systems but to a failure to translate this information to those "in the trenches." In this chapter, we attempt to do just that—translate what we know. Although a complete treatment of the topic cannot be accomplished here, some initial "translations" are provided. To accomplish this, we first briefly outline the basic elements that compose a team performance measurement system based on what we know about teamwork. Second, we identify some practical requirements for developing, implementing, and evaluating teamwork skills. We accomplish this by listing six "lessons" that have been learned about teams and team effectiveness. Within each lesson are practical requirement(s) for those responsible for measurement within organizations. Finally, we identify specific examples of tools and methods used to evaluate team skills and how they relate back to measurement requirements. These tools relate to both the evaluation of behavioral skills, as well as attitudinal requirements needed for effective teamwork.

## TEAM PERFORMANCE MEASUREMENT

The first step in developing a team performance measurement system is to understand the key competencies (i.e., knowledge, skills, and attitudes) needed to effectively function as a team. Such understanding is important because it provides information related to the assessment, diagnosis, and remediation of individual and team performance. Therefore, a team performance measurement system can be used for several diverse purposes. For example, it can: (1) gauge the progress of an implemented team training program, (2) diagnose problem areas, (3) indicate a team's strengths and weaknesses, and (4) be used as input for tailoring constructive team-level feedback (Cannon-Bowers & Salas, 1997).

Despite the potential benefits of systematic team performance measurement systems, the development and implementation of such systems is not as easy as one thinks. The creation of measurement systems is labor intensive for several reasons. First, they must be psychometrically sound. That is, they must be: (1) reliable in that they can capture stable characteristics of the team, (2) sensitive in picking up measurable changes, and (3) valid (i.e., capture meaningful aspects of performance). So a great deal of upfront work must be done (e.g., team-based task analysis). Second, as teamwork is multidimensional and dynamic, measurement systems must be able to capture this. Herein lies the complexity and difficulty of the system. Third, measurement systems must be practically useful or they will not be implemented or used by those who need them.

What follows are the lessons learned and corresponding measurement requirements needed for the development and implementation of theoretically based, psychometrically sound measurement systems that are practical to use. These lessons are derived from two decades of research in the area conducted by two of us. We offer these as our "translations" of what we know from the research.

### Designing Theoretically Based Measurement System(s)

Team performance measurement systems must be guided by theory. These systems must be designed based on what we know about teams and their performance. Various models of team performance can assist in this process (see Gladstein, 1984; Hackman & Morris, 1975; Marks, Mathieu, & Zaccaro, 2001; and Tannenbaum, Beard, & Salas, 1992 for external reviews). The models and the underlying theory are essential in terms of team performance measurement for they serve to guide: (1) what constructs should be measured (see Baker & Salas, 1992), (2) how constructs should be measured, and (3) whether measures, as well as the feedback flowing from them, should be administered at the individual or team level

(see Tesluk, Mathieu, Zaccaro & Marks, 1997). Flowing from this are two lessons that create the need for theory-based measurement systems.

### Lesson 1: All Teams Are Not Created, Composed, or Managed Equally

**Measurement Requirement 1a: The nature of each team and its operating circumstances must be understood before measurement systems are designed.**   All teams are not the same. Differences in task interdependence and requirements, distribution of expertise, and structure are only a few ways in which teams differ from one another. For example, Sundstrom (1999) identified six types of work teams, distinguished by the type of work they accomplish: (1) production, (2) service, (3) management, (4) project, (5) action/performing, and (6) parallel teams. Each of these teams differs in terms of at least four factors: (1) level of authority within the organization, (2) time till the team is disbanded, (3) degree of specialization, independence, and autonomy in relation to other work units, and (4) degree of interdependency (both within and between teams). The underlying nature of each of these teams drives the functionality of various teamwork competencies. The functionality of each competency, along with measurement goals, must drive the development of team performance measures.

In addition to differentiating between various types of work teams, researchers have argued that the competencies required of teams vary along two axes. More specifically, Cannon-Bowers, Tannenbaum, Salas, and Volpe (1995) argued that competencies can be generic or specific with regard to both the task and the team. Team generic competencies are those that are held by individual members and can influence performance regardless of the particular team members involved. As these skills are generic they are transportable across teams. Conversely, team specific competencies are held by individual team members but influence performance only with regard to the team that the individual is currently working within. Along with being generic/specific in regard to the team, competencies will also vary along the same dimensions with regard to the task. More specifically, task generic competencies are those that influence team performance across all tasks, whereas task specific competencies are tied to promoting effective performance on a particular task. As teams will vary along both of the aforementioned dimensions, the nature of the competencies required by the team (specific, generic), as well as those required by the task (specific, generic) must be considered when determining the content of team performance measurement systems. Cannon-Bowers et al. (1995) have taken this a step further by using this information to create four broad categories of competencies: context driven (team/task specific), team contingent (team specific/task generic), task contingent (team generic/ task specific), and transportable (team/task generic) and delineating the specific competencies falling into each category. Furthermore, they provide guidance as to how certain team characteristics may drive the functionality of some competencies over others, dependent on circumstances and the nature of the team.

**Measurement Requirement 1b: Measurement systems must capture performance throughout the evolution and maturation process of the team.** This requirement relies on a two-pronged argument, one revolving around the assessment of outcomes and one around process. Regarding outcomes, although it is very tempting to focus merely on short-term outcomes (as they are the easiest to measure), the measurement of long-term outcomes is also important. Due to the dynamic nature of teamwork, a single snapshot of team performance will very likely be insufficient (Morgan, Glickman, Woodard, Blaiwes, & Salas, 1986). Team performance needs to be sampled over a variety of conditions and times to get an accurate picture. Many times the true effect of team performance is not borne out in the short term. For example, many interventions may actually cause things to get worse before they get better as members are learning new competencies. Conversely, teams may perform well initially after an intervention, but after spending time back on the job in a culture that does not reinforce the new competencies, performance may falter. As such, the measurement of both short- and long-term outcomes is needed to assess the true pattern of performance.

The second part of this argument relates to the measurement of team process. Teams are composed of individuals who, when first put together, must go through a process of learning how to work together. As such, teams measured early in their life cycle may look very different from teams measured later on. Kozlowski (1998) argued that interventions may be expected to have a differential impact depending on the stage of team development. If measurement is not taken at multiple points throughout a team's life span, faulty conclusions may be reached. In addition, Kozlowski et al. (1994) argued that competencies may vary in their functionality according to where the team is in its development. As such, similar to outcome measures, team process needs to be measured at multiple points during team performance to get a clear picture of what is happening.

*Lesson 2: Teamwork Is a Complex, Dynamic, and Multidimensional Phenomena*

**Measurement Requirement 2a: Measurement must facilitate capturing the dynamic, multidimensional nature of teamwork.** One of the most difficult things about team performance measurement is trying to capture the multidimensional nature of team performance. Within teams, event flow is often largely determined by the real-time interactions among members. However, assessing team process and performance in order to collect diagnostic information is difficult to do under these circumstances. Thus, to facilitate the collection of data pertinent to team behaviors and variables of interest, measurement needs to control task content. When content is not controlled for measurement purposes, three things happen. First, it becomes more difficult to assess performance because the observer may not be able to determine when the behaviors of interest occur, if they occur. Second, measurement opportunities are left to chance in that team members may or may not have opportunities to demonstrate the targeted competencies (i.e., knowledge, skills, attitudes). For example, perhaps the variable of interest is backup behavior, but nothing ever happens during the team's performance that necessitates someone demonstrating this behavior. This leaves the assessor with the question of how to evaluate a skill that was never presented. Finally, when measurement does not control task content it also makes it difficult to compare observations between teams because there is no common standard.

Researchers within the military have provided a possible solution to this problem: event-based approach to training (EBAT, see Dwyer, Fowlkes, Oser, Salas, & Lane, 1997; Dwyer, Oser, Salas, & Fowlkes, 1999). Essentially EBAT is scenario-based training where scenarios are scripted based on training objectives and required competencies (identified through task analysis techniques). Within each scenario, scripted events are inserted that allow team members to perform targeted skills so that mastery can be assessed. In terms of measurement, performance measures are created based on the scripted events. The information gained from the event sets are then utilized as a basis for assessment and feedback (Salas & Cannon-Bowers, 2000).

**Measurement Requirement 2b: Multilevel measurement is essential.** For measurement systems to be truly diagnostic they have to assess performance at multiple levels to include the performance of teams, subteams, and individuals. Several have argued for the importance of multilevel measurement in that teams operate within an organizational context, and although members are interdependent and many times presumed to act as a unified whole, teams are composed of individual members (Dickinson & McIntyre, 1997; Tesluk et al., 1997).

Multilevel measurement is important for several reasons. First, because teams operate within an organizational context, factors within the higher level context may filter down and impact team functioning—some of which may be out of the team's control. Therefore, it is important to consider the context within which the team is operating. Second, because teams are made up of individuals who each possess knowledge, skills, attitudes, and abilities that combine to contribute to overall team performance, it is important to measure these individual competencies (Salas, Bowers, & Cannon-Bowers, 1995; Stout, Salas, & Carson, 1994). If one only looks at the group's product as a whole, then those doing the evaluating are assuming that everyone contributed equally in both effort and skill; this is not always true. An unidentified deficiency in skill or ability at the individual level may eventually lead to lower team performance. In addition, as teams are increasingly composed of members from different cultures, it becomes important to see how the individual cultural dynamics, attitudes, and beliefs interact to affect team performance.

Through the utilization of multilevel measurement systems that systematically work from the top down, practitioners can gain a more detailed, diagnostic assessment of what really happened as well as the true sources of error/problem. This, in turn, will allow them to more efficiently use their resources to target the true source of the error or difficulty.

## Developing Psychometrically Sound Measurement Systems

The second characteristic of an effective team performance measurement system is that it be psychometrically sound; otherwise, the information it provides will be meaningless and no better than the informal mechanisms often used within organizations today. The following are two lessons that have been learned in regard to teams and the corresponding measurement requirements.

### Lesson 3: There Is No One Best Measurement Technique

**Measurement Requirement 3a: Measurement purposes must be defined up front.**   The appropriateness of a particular measurement technique depends on the goal of performance measurement. Paris, Salas, and Cannon-Bowers (1999) identified three types of performance measures: descriptive, evaluative, and diagnostic. Descriptive measures simply describe what is happening at any given time. As such, the type of information provided by these measures is a log of the crucial points of interaction and the moment-to-moment changes in interaction. However, this information is not evaluative; it just describes the events that have transpired. Conversely, evaluative measures judge performance against a standard. These measures provide an indication of effectiveness. Finally, diagnostic measures (e.g., process measures) seek to identify the cause of behavior. As such, they

primarily focus on how and why things occurred. These measures provide the foundation for constructive feedback that targets areas in need of remediation/training.

**Measurement Requirement 3b: Measurement systems must incorporate multiple methods/approaches to measurement.**   Team performance is a complex, multidimensional phenomenon that requires a multitude of behavioral and attitudinal competencies, as well as certain knowledge about the task at hand and specific aspects of teamwork (see Cannon-Bowers et al., 1995, for more detail). Because teamwork is composed of behaviors, knowledge, and attitudes, measurement needs to capture all of these components to get a true picture of the state of the team's ability to work together as a team. Similarly, Stewart et al. (1999) stated, "a multidimensional perspective indicates that work effectiveness should be measured not only by the products or services a team produces but also by the ability of the team to remain intact and the extent to which the team satisfies the individual needs of each member" (p. 140). As such, team performance measurement systems will likely need to incorporate behavioral and cognitive assessment, organizational variables, and process and outcome measures. Otherwise, practitioners will not obtain a complete picture of team performance, perhaps causing invalid inferences and decisions.

Different aspects of teamwork cannot always be measured using the same method. For example, knowledge is typically measured through use of multiple-choice questions, fill-in-the-blank items, or cognitive maps. Conversely, attitudes are typically measured through the use of a Likert scale in which members rate the degree to which they agree with a particular attitudinal statement. Behaviors, on the other hand, are normally measured using expert raters (observational method) or by gathering members' self-ratings of the team's behavior.

In addition to measurement possessing a multidimensional perspective in terms of assessing several criteria, it should also be multidimensional in utilizing several different methodologies to assess each criterion. Utilizing multiple forms of measurement to assess each criterion makes good measurement sense in general, in that it helps to reduce same-method bias. Same-method bias refers to the fact that artificially high relationships between criteria may seem to exist due to the mere fact that multiple criteria were measured utilizing the same method (e.g., paper-and-pencil, computer-based, multiple-choice). Furthermore, multiple indices of the same construct (e.g., teamwork) utilizing different techniques allow practitioners to assess the convergent and divergent validity of measurement systems (i.e., multimethod, multitrait, Campbell & Fiske, 1959). Specifically, it allows practitioners to determine whether constructs that are expected to be related are (convergent), and those that are not expected to be related are not (divergent). In turn, this helps to provide a deeper understanding of team performance within the domain(s) of interest to practitioners.

### Lesson 4: A Good Outcome Does Not Necessarily Suggest One Has an Effective Team

**Measurement Requirement 4: Measurement must assess the moment-to-moment actions and behaviors as well as the outcomes.** For measurement systems to be valid they must be able to pick up meaningful aspects of performance. When examining team performance, this translates into the need to assess not only outcome measures but also process measures. The predominant way in which many organizations assess team effectiveness is the quality of their outcomes. However, when only outcome measures are collected, the result is an incomplete and sometimes faulty picture of team effectiveness. Although outcome measures are relatively easy to collect, they have a number of drawbacks when they are the only assessment tool used. First, they often contain variance that is not attributable to the team itself and may be beyond its control. Second, though outcome measures will answer the question as to "what happened," they provide little guidance in terms of "why" it happened. Therefore, by themselves outcome measures provide little in terms of diagnosis.

Conversely, process measures provide answers as to the "why" and "how" of performance, permitting diagnostic information to be gathered. Process measures have been defined as gathering information on "a collection of activities, strategies, responses, and behaviors employed in task accomplishment" (Cannon-Bowers & Salas, 1997, p. 51). Whereas outcome measures capture the end product, process measures capture the moment-to-moment behaviors exhibited by teams, thereby allowing the diagnosis of strengths and weaknesses. In essence, process measures provide the information needed for diagnostic feedback that allows teams to decide the exact areas in need of remediation (Cannon-Bowers & Salas, 1997). Recently, several advances have been made in the design of measurement tools used to assess team process. The following are a few of the more common methods: critical events, behavioral observation (quantity, quality), modeling procedures, capturing of data via automated systems, and petri-nets. For more information on the types of tools used to measure team process, see Paris et al. (1999), Weingart (1997), and Brannick, Salas, and Prince (1997).

### Practicality/Implementation

When team performance measurement systems are to be used outside the laboratory, it is not enough that they are theory based and psychometrically sound—they must also be practical to use. The following facts and corresponding guidance relate to the practicality of the measurement tool, both in terms of ease of use and provision of information in a timely manner.

### Lesson 5: Observation Is Unavoidable in Assessing Teams

**Measurement Requirement 5: Measurement must facilitate observation.** It was argued in the last section that in order to assess team performance the collection of both process and outcome measures was a necessity. Although some outcome measures can be collected without actual observation, process measures rely almost exclusively on this technique. As such, some have argued that when assessing team performance, observation is unavoidable (Baker & Salas, 1997). In turn, this drives the requirement for measurement to facilitate observation—this is easier said than done.

Perhaps the largest hurdle in attempting to facilitate observation is the requirement that it often takes a team of observers to assess team performance. Due to the multidimensional nature of teamwork and its complexity, researchers have argued that one person may not be able to capture all the relevant process information. In addition, to collect a complete picture of the team processes occurring, each observer may have a different physical viewpoint, training, and responsibility. Furthermore, an added consideration is how the information from the various observers is combined and weighted to result in an overall assessment of team process and performance.

Although the need for multiple observers poses some challenges, a few things have been learned along the way. First, observation can be facilitated by training those who will be conducting the observation (Dwyer & Salas, 2000). Second, measures should have face validity so that results will be accepted by team members. Third, event-based measurement can aid the observation process and is accepted by subject matter experts. More specifically, Dwyer and Salas (2000) reported that event-based behavioral checklists have met with more acceptance than rating scales.

### Lesson 6: Timely Integration of the Data for Feedback Is Essential Within Complex Environments

**Measurement Requirement 6: Measurement must foster real-time diagnosis.** Teams are increasingly operating in complex and dynamic environments. To remain effective, teams must be able to adapt their behaviors in a timely manner. Real-time assessment can contribute to a team's adaptability by providing teams with the information needed to adapt behaviors in a timely manner. Moreover, the timing of feedback can be influential in creating effective team performance. The sooner the team and its members are able to receive feedback, the sooner they can begin to correct faulty knowledge structures (i.e., mental models) and behavioral patterns. Moreover, the longer that teams persist in incorrect cognitive, behavioral, or attitudinal patterns, the harder it is to change these competencies because they have become ingrained within members' cognitive frameworks.

## CAPTURING TEAMWORK

Now that we have reviewed some of the lessons and resulting guidance for the measurement of teamwork skills, we introduce a few examples of the methods by which teamwork is commonly measured. Perhaps the most common tools used to capture teamwork skills are those that measure teamwork by asking members their impressions of the group, followed by those in which teamwork is observed and rated in terms of quality or frequency (Weingart, 1997). These instruments commonly used to measure teamwork can be broken down into three categories, those that capture: member knowledge (cognition), skill (behavior), and attitudes (affect). Since one of the purposes of this chapter is to provide the reader with practical tools, we have focused our sample of measurement techniques on those that capture behavior and affect, as the remaining category provides a bit more of a challenge within actual organizations. However, measurement of team cognition is an important aspect of teamwork, and the reader is referred to the following articles: Cooke, Salas, Cannon-Bowers, and Stout (2000); Heffner, Mathieu, and Cannon-Bowers (1998); Marks, Zaccaro, and Mathieu (2000); and Burke (1999).

### Behavioral Measurement Techniques

Several tools and approaches can be used to capture the behavioral aspects of teamwork, the most popular of which are briefly mentioned next. Specifically, the following approaches or tools are described: event-based measurement, real-time assessment, classification schemes and coding, and behavioral rating scales.

### *Event-Based Measurement*

One method by which teamwork skills can be captured is through the use of event-based measurement techniques. Event-based measurement techniques create measurement opportunities by systematically identifying and introducing events within training exercises that provide known opportunities to observe behaviors of interest (i.e., those that reflect targeted competencies). These techniques present a useful way to maintain links between training objectives, exercise design, and performance assessment. The behaviors to be evaluated are controlled through the selection of events that will be included in a training exercise. Control over the nature of events is used to enhance the relevance of the resulting scores. Control over the number of events, and behaviors observed, is used to enhance measurement reliability. To ensure that all intended events are presented and to maintain task consistency across teams or individuals, scenario scripts are developed and utilized that detail when events should be introduced. In addition, these scripts include the communications that should come from the other agencies and personnel included in the scenario. In research contexts, the script ensures that task conditions are maintained across teams observed. For training, the script ensures standardization of training and that the instructor is able to evaluate trainees on how they perform the behaviors of interest. Done well, scripts are transparent to responses. Moreover, due to the preceding qualities they may be used to provide highly diagnostic performance assessment. Finally, they are associated with excellent psychometric properties, a characteristic that makes them useful for training effectiveness evaluations.

The event-based approach to measurement has spawned a number of specific measurement tools in the military (e.g., Dwyer et al., 1997; Fowlkes, Lane, Salas, Franz, & Oser, 1994; Johnston, Smith-Jentsch, & Cannon-Bowers, 1997) and elsewhere (Wigdor & Green, 1991) and is beginning to filter its way into team measurement systems within organizations. What follows is a brief description of two measurement tools created using the event-based measurement approach.

**Targeted Acceptable Responses to Generated Events or Tasks (TARGETs).**    Fowlkes et al. (1994) have developed an event-based approach known as TARGETs. To apply the methodology, events in a simulator or other exercise (e.g., role-play exercise) are identified to serve as cues or prompts for team members to exhibit behaviors targeted in the training. Acceptable responses (i.e., the TARGETs) to each event are identified a priori so that, prior to the exercise, the instructor has a checklist of training events in the scenario and the acceptable responses to each event. Acceptable responses are determined based on existing documentation (e.g., published procedures) and subject matter expert input. TARGETs has proven useful in that it, or variations of it, have been used to evaluate the effectiveness of team training for aircrews (Salas, Fowlkes, Stout, Milanovich, & Prince, 1999), and to evaluate distributed army and multiservice teams in a number of contexts (Dwyer et al., 1999; Fowlkes, Dwyer, Milham,

TABLE 23.1    Events and Associated TARGETS for a Short Flight Segment in Which an Aircraft Has Experienced an Engine Shutdown

| Flight Segment | Event | Target | Observed Yes/No |
|---|---|---|---|
| En route | Engine flameout due to icing | Delegate tasks (who flies, communicates) | 1 |
| | | Complete appropriate checklists | 2 |
| | | Diagnose cause of flameout (icing) | 3 |
| | | Identify implications of icing (e.g., get out of icing, consider engine restart when out of icing) | 4 |
| | | Make plan to closest suitable airfield | 5 |
| | | Declare emergency | 6 |

*Note.* Items 1 and 2 address leadership (task delegation); items 3, 4, and 5 address mission analysis; and item 6 addresses communication.

Burns, & Pierce, 1999). See Table 23.1 for an example of the TARGETs measurement tool.

**Team Dimensional Training (TDT).**    Smith-Jentsch, Johnston, Cannon-Bowers, and Salas (1997) incorporated another form of event-based measurement within a team training approach known as Team Dimensional Training (TDT). TDT is built around four teamwork constructs—Information Exchange, Initiative/Leadership, Supporting Behavior, and Communication. The focus of TDT is to build shared mental models among team members of how the team constructs apply to job performance as well as to improve job performance. To apply TDT, a scenario is designed to include events that provide rich opportunities for trainees to demonstrate the competencies. Prior to the scenario, the team is introduced to the teamwork competencies. During the scenario, as trainees respond to the scenario events, instructors record instances of strong and weak execution of the team competencies by using a coding sheet similar to that in Table 23.2. Specifically, event time lines are listed in the left-hand column and observers use the right-hand column to record how the team reacts/performs, if it reacts to each embedded event. Event time lines represent prescribed events inserted in the training scenario and as such reflect ground truth or reality. The events provide focused opportunities for instructors to evaluate the teamwork competencies and provide feedback on them. In the example presented in Table 23.2, observers would respond in terms of the following aspects of communication: phraseology, brevity, completeness, and clarity. Instructors record both positive and negative examples of

TABLE 23.2    Coding Instrument for Use with Event-Based Measurement

| Scripted Event Time Line | Communication ± Phraseology, ± Brevity, ± Completeness, ± Clarity |
|---|---|
| 7:00 | |
| 8:00 | |
| 9:00 Watchstander receives two additional targets to process | Used correct terminology and brevity to ask for assistance |
| 10:00 | |
| 11:00 Four targets enter the immediate threat zone | Used closed loop communication (completeness) to ensure that target one of four is neutral. |
| 12:00 | |
| 13:00 | |
| 14:00 | |

the targeted aspects of communication in the right-hand column next to the scripted event.

### Real-Time Assessment

As environments become more complex and ill-structured, real-time diagnosis of teamwork skills is becoming a high priority. Most often used within scenario-based training environments, real-time performance assessment refers to a general category of tools that provide near real-time data capturing and through which reduction/analysis can be quickly completed and fed back to trainees. Real-time assessment is valuable for many different reasons, a few of which follow. It can be used to support: (1) data quality control, (2) decisions to move from one training phase to the next (Vreuls & Obermayer, 1985), (3) the identification of performance patterns or trends, and (4) timely postexercise feedback.

Real-time performance assessment tools may take many forms. In some cases, systems are developed to augment the human's ability to record data in real time or in near real time. Other systems use real-time performance monitoring and assessment. Examples follow of each of the real-time performance measurement tools mentioned in the preceding.

**Automating Performance Measurement.**    The navy is one organization that has used tools to augment the human's ability to record data in near real time. More specifically, the United States Navy uses a tool, implemented on a handheld computer, to assist the instructor in preparing, conducting, and debriefing an exercise (Pruitt, Burns, Wetteland, & Demestre, 1997). In terms of assisting in real-time measurement, this tool, ShipMATE, alerts the instructor to events that are occurring within a scenario that provide measurement opportunities. It also includes analysis tools so that data may be automatically summarized. Furthermore, this tool assists instructors by permitting them to record time-stamped voice or text notes, and through the use of wireless networks it can be used to capture team communication and workstation displays being used by trainees. These capabilities allow the: (1) collection of relevant data, (2) ability to quickly synthesize information, and (3) provision of a timely debrief. Finally, data can also be integrated with performance outcomes. All of the preceding contribute to the ability of this and similar tools to provide near-real-time measurement so that teams can receive immediate feedback and correct faulty cognition and behavior.

**Automated Performance Monitoring.**   Another method that enables real-time performance measurement is through the use of tools that permit automated performance monitoring and assessment. Tools of this nature automatically capture and analyze the trainees' actions in multiple modalities providing varied feedback (see Zachary, Bilazarian, Burns, & Cannon-Bowers, 1997). More specifically, tools of this nature include the ability to conduct an automated analysis of keystrokes that are then analyzed to represent the operator's functional interactions with the system. In addition, automated performance monitoring tools allow the processing of speech communications related to teamwork and the tracking of eye movements. The data are then fused to represent what the trainee is doing compared with what the trainee should be doing based on an expert model. Such systems can be used to reduce the reliance on instructors, prevent data loss, and handle performance assessment in highly dynamic performance environments. In many cases, trainee performance may be inaccessible to human observers, especially as teams are increasingly becoming distributed, making real-time measurement more difficult without such systems.

### Classification Schemes and the Coding Process

The primary method for examining teamwork behaviors within empirically based studies has been through either an examination of communication transcripts or real-time action recorded via videotape. When teamwork is examined in either manner, a teamwork classification scheme (see Brannick, Prince, Prince, & Salas, 1995; Burke, 1999; Marks et al., 2000) is developed to guide raters in placing communication into the proper teamwork dimensions. Furthermore, when coding teamwork behaviors using this method of measurement, raters typically identify differences based on quality, content/patterns, and frequency of teamwork behaviors as indicated through team communication. As with all methods

that involve the rating of behavior, raters must be properly trained in the rating technique along with being trained in the coding scheme being used (see section on behavioral rating scales for greater detail).

Along with capturing the frequency or quality of teamwork behaviors, the coding process can be tailored further. For example, in addition to capturing the frequency of each type of behavior, communication may be categorized within the classification scheme according to whether each communication instance was a request for information or a provision of information. In determining which of the many classification schemes to use during the coding process, a good sound theory should be the driver. In addition, it is wise to choose the simplest number of behaviors that will adequately capture teamwork processes, because the greater the number of categories, the more difficult it is for raters to capture and correctly record communication instances indicative of teamwork. Another common practice in the coding process is to classify the frequency or quality of behaviors during specific time intervals. For example, communication may be classified in five-minute intervals, allowing one to look at trends across the performance period—rather than one overall measure. Specifically, raters would code all the teamwork behaviors in terms of five-minute blocks. Another process that is commonly used is one in which raters code a random sample of performance periods or teams.

The following is an example of a classification scheme for teamwork behaviors. Classification schemes of this type are frequently used in the coding process to help guide the categorization of observed behaviors and/or communication.

Zaccaro and colleagues (1997) adapted Fleishman and Zaccaro's (1992) taxonomy of team performance functions to categorize behaviors indicative of effective teamwork. The classification scheme consisted of the following 10 categories: member resources and constraints, team mission and task goals, environmental constraints, resource distribution, response coordination, motivation, interpersonal support, activity pacing, monitoring, and nonspecific affect (see Table 23.3 for definitions of each).

Although the coding of teamwork behaviors using the processes (i.e., via video- or audiotaped communication, analysis of communication transcripts) and classification similar to those in the preceding may not be that practical for the measuring of teamwork skills within an organizational setting, due to the amount of resources it requires, it deserves mentioning due to the prominence of this method within empirical settings. Furthermore, although the actual coding of behavior in this manner may be cumbersome within organizational settings, the coding categories are often similar, if not the same, as used in behavioral ratings scales (to be discussed

**TABLE 23.3 Example of Teamwork Classification Scheme**

| Teamwork Category | Definition/Examples |
|---|---|
| Member resources/ constraints | Communication intended to make members aware of each other's resources and capabilities, including information exchanges regarding: (1) team members' knowledge, skills, and abilities; (2) ability/inability to continue in their designated roles; (3) availability for assignment to new tasks; and (4) capabilities as a result of conditions in immediate task environment. |
| Team mission/task goals | Communication intended to clarify the mission and goals of the team and to provide progress reports on team accomplishments. |
| Environmental constraints | Communication intended to provide members with knowledge of situation-specific conditions and factors that could influence how the mission is performed. |
| Resource distribution | Communication focusing on the distribution and use of team member resources to complete the task. Emphasis is often on adjustments in resources in the face of task demands. |
| Response coordination | Communication intended to ensure behavior occurs in the proper sequence and in coordination with other ongoing activities. |
| Motivation | Communication intended to define team objectives and energize the team toward these objectives. The intent is also to encourage team persistence in the face of task difficulty. |
| Interpersonal support | Communication intended to support and reward performance-enhancing activities by team members in the conduct of collective action. |
| Activity pacing | Communication focusing on the organization of team resources and activities to ensure that performance tasks are completed within established temporal boundaries. |
| Monitoring | Reflects the monitoring of behavior to ensure compliance with established performance standards. Also includes communication regarding the discovery and correction of member errors in performance. |
| Nonspecific affect | Reflects nonspecific and nondirected affective responses to team task circumstances and performance. |

*Note.* From Zaccaro et al., 1997, adapted from Fleishman and Zaccaro (1992).

next). As such, it might be possible to use a variation of the coding scheme process within actual organizational settings. This coding scheme represents one in which the frequency of each of the mentioned behaviors is captured by trained raters viewing team performance post hoc via videotapes.

## Behavioral Rating Scales

Perhaps one of the most popular methods by which to measure team skills is through the use of behavioral rating scales. Rating scales are a form of psychometric scaling that uses a method of successive intervals to measure aspects of teamwork, team effectiveness, and team performance. The first step in developing a rating scale for team processes is to compile a description of each relevant behavior or component of team performance, which is referred to in some theories as a continuum (Meister, 1985). Next, a set of key words or expected responses that represent the behavior must be incorporated. These key words are associated with the behavior expected of team members when exhibiting the team process of interest. The key words and description of team processes can be identified through critical incident reports, observation of teamwork, and expert opinion. The description of the expected process and associated key words help researchers to define a set of rules on which to base their rating scales. An example using backup behavior is shown in Table 23.4. From these rules and descriptions, rating scales are constructed.

The scale itself can actually be presented in many ways, but for each a trained rater is required to rate team members' behavior based on the continuum and the set of rules established by experts and critical incident reports. For example, a rater may be presented with a scale and told to rate how much a team member exhibited backup behavior when another team member was in need. The rater would have to rate whether the team member in question "Never" (1), "Seldom" (2), "Sometimes" (3), "Generally" (4), or "Always" (5) exhibited the behavior in question, which represents backup behavior based on the definition and the expected responses of backup behavior determined before the observations.

Although behavioral rating scales are commonly used for a trained observer to rate team members' behavior, they may also be used in a self-report type of situation to gather team

**TABLE 23.4 Decision Rules for Backup Behavior**

Backup Behavior

Definition: "Involves assisting the performance of other team members. This implies that members have an understanding of other members' tasks. It also implies that members are willing and able to provide assistance when needed" (Dickinson & McIntyre, 1997, p. 26).

Key Words: Helping behavior, seeking of assistance, provision of assistance, taking control.

Decision Rules: Backup behavior is present when a team member is unable to perform duties (e.g., member is overburdened, incapable, or made a mistake) and another team member performs the necessary actions to ensure the duties are completed. Backup behavior may be physical or in the form of verbal input. It is distinguished from feedback in that it completes an activity or solves a problem (Dickinson & McIntyre, 1997).

members' perceptions of the team's process. Specifically, team members may be asked to subjectively rate the teamwork behaviors of the team as a whole using the rating scales as a guide. Many times, when members themselves rate the team, there is no specific training on how to use the scales. Although it is a common practice, one takes the risk of encountering rating biases and rating errors.

As with all measurement tools, quality rating scales take some time to develop. For example, experts are required in the development of the continuum, the scales, and the rating itself in order to ensure that the measurements are a true representation of what is being observed, that the methods are not responsible for the results, and that raters are measuring what they are intending to measure. In addition, if raters are not experts, they often have to undergo training in order to protect the accuracy, validity, and reliability of the findings. If the preceding steps are taken in the construction of these scales, they have, in general, been found to offer discrimination between behaviors and high scale reliability. Other potential advantages involve ratings being rooted in and easily referable to observed behavior, and the traits or processes observed are operationally defined and are distinguishable from one another by the raters (Smith & Kendall, 1963).

A discussion follows of a few of the many types of behavioral rating scales currently used within research and organizations.

**Graphic Rating Scales.**   One common type of rating scale is the graphic rating scale (see Figure 23.1). The graphic rating scale is typically represented by a line containing intervals that represent the continuum. Each interval is represented by a label definition and adjectives (Meister, 1985). The number of intervals and lines are determined by the developer of the scale, and the lines can be vertical or horizontal. In most cases a 5-, 7-, or 9-point Likert scale (refer to Figure 23.1) is used to represent intervals of some measure.

**Behaviorally Anchored Rating Scale (BARS).**   Perhaps one of the most often used rating scales is the behaviorally anchored rating scale (see Figure 23.2). Smith and Kendall

Question asked: Did the team member provide assistance to other team members when specifically asked?

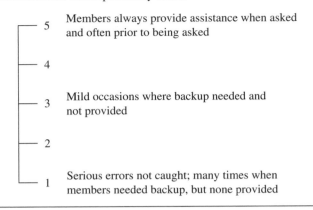

**Figure 23.2**   Example of BARS scale for backup behavior.

(1963) first introduced the BARS, which is similar to a graphic scale. The difference, however, is that BARS includes anchoring illustrations, in addition to the Likert scale. These anchors are concrete and are located at intervals along a vertical scale. The anchors define different levels of the observed team process (e.g., Excellent, Good, or Fair communication), and the rater is given examples of each level. The advantage to the anchors is that they help screen out idiosyncrasies of raters and make ratings more standardized.

**Behavioral Observation Scales (BOS).**   The BOS is another popular rating scale. With BOS, each scale corresponds to one aspect of teamwork and can be used to rate the occurrence of teamwork by a particular team and its members. These scales include a definition of the process being observed and certain items associated with that behavior. The items are rated according to their frequency of occurrence. For example, scores could range from 1 for "Almost Never" to 5 for "Almost Always." Figure 23.3 depicts an example of a BOS scale created using the definition of backup behavior provided by Dickinson and McIntyre (1997).

Tziner, Joanis, and Murphy (2000) provided an in-depth comparison of the three scales addressed here. Additional information on other scales, including mixed standard scales, forced-choice rating scales, and behavioral summary scales, can be found in Meister (1985), Brannick et al. (1997), and Franceschini and Rupil (1999).

### Attitudinal/Affective Measures

The measurement of teamwork behaviors is not the only aspect of teamwork that can be measured. Perhaps even more

Question asked: Did the team member provide assistance to other team members when specifically asked?

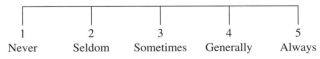

**Figure 23.1**   Graphic rating scale measuring backup behavior.

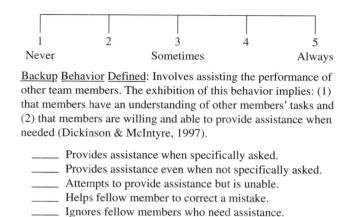

Backup Behavior Defined: Involves assisting the performance of other team members. The exhibition of this behavior implies: (1) that members have an understanding of other members' tasks and (2) that members are willing and able to provide assistance when needed (Dickinson & McIntyre, 1997).

_____ Provides assistance when specifically asked.
_____ Provides assistance even when not specifically asked.
_____ Attempts to provide assistance but is unable.
_____ Helps fellow member to correct a mistake.
_____ Ignores fellow members who need assistance.

**Figure 23.3**   Example of BOS for backup behavior.

common is the measurement of the attitudinal or affective components of teamwork. Attitudes have been defined as "an internal state that influences an individual's choices or decisions to act in a certain way under particular circumstances" (Cannon-Bowers et al., 1995, p. 354). Examples of team attitudes that are commonly measured as important components of teamwork include but are not limited to: group potency, collective efficacy, team cohesion, collective orientation, trust, and member satisfaction with team process.

The attitudinal components of teamwork are more commonly measured as they are easier to capture and require less resources to measure. Although there is no one format regarding measurement of this type, measurement tools typically consist of some type of Likert scale where members are asked to rate their level of agreement with a set of statements. The statements are developed via a combination of the definition of the construct (e.g., cohesion) and input from subject matter experts so that the questions relate to the task or situation at hand. The most common variants of these scales range either from 1 to 5 or from 1 to 7. Several studies have suggested these attitudinal components are associated with team performance (Hackman, 1990; Peterson, Mitchell, Thompson, & Burr, 2000; Shea & Guzzo, 1987). A brief description follows of each of the aforementioned attitudinal components of teamwork and examples of the measurement tools used for each.

### Group Potency

This is a relatively new attitudinal construct that can be defined as a team's collective belief that it can be generally effective (Guzzo, Yost, Campbell, & Shea, 1993). As this is a belief that the team can be generally effective, group potency is relatively stable in the short term and could be argued

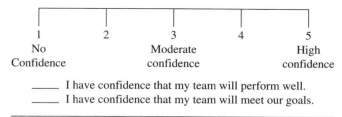

_____ I have confidence that my team will perform well.
_____ I have confidence that my team will meet our goals.

**Figure 23.4**   Group potency scale example.

to be specific to the team one is currently working with, but not specific to the task. However, group potency has been argued to be based on team members believing that the team has the resources needed to succeed (Shea & Guzzo, 1987). Moreover, positive feedback, high levels of task interdependency, and involvement in decision making have been found to be related to high levels of group potency (Shea & Guzzo, 1987). For example, as task interdependency increases members have more opportunity to see and evaluate one another's skills.

Although a relatively new construct, group potency has been found to also be an important factor in team effectiveness (see Hackman, 1990; Shea & Guzzo, 1987; Sosik, Avolio, & Kahai, 1997). Figure 23.4 shows the type of questions that might make up a measure of group potency:

### Collective Efficacy

Collective efficacy is similar to the notion of group potency, but it is task specific. Specifically, as originally conceived, collective efficacy refers to the team members' belief in their ability to perform effectively as a unit, given some set of specific task demands (Bandura, 1986). Others have defined it as: (1) a member's assessment of his or her team's collective ability to perform the task at hand (Riggs, 1989); (2) a shared conviction that a group can execute a specific task (Guzzo et al., 1993); and (3) an individual's belief in his or her group's ability to achieve a desired level of performance (see Greenless, Nunn, Graydon, & Maynard, 1999; Zaccaro, Blair, Peterson, & Zazanis, 1995).

A wealth of conceptual work suggests that collective efficacy is positively related to team performance (Bandura, 1986; Zaccaro et al., 1995). Moreover, empirical work also tends to support this notion (Spink, 1990; Peterson et al., 2000). As such, Figure 23.5 shows questions that may be included in a measure of collective efficacy:

### Team Cohesion

Team cohesion is perhaps one of the most frequently examined of the attitudinal variables (Williams & Widmeyer, 1991).

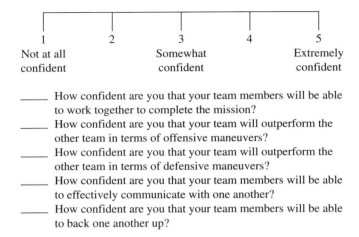

How confident are you that your team members will be able to work together to complete the mission?

How confident are you that your team will outperform the other team in terms of offensive maneuvers?

How confident are you that your team will outperform the other team in terms of defensive maneuvers?

How confident are you that your team members will be able to effectively communicate with one another?

How confident are you that your team members will be able to back one another up?

**Figure 23.5**   Collective efficacy scale example.

It has been defined in several ways, starting with the Festinger, Schachter, and Back (1950) definition of "the total field of forces which act on members to remain in the group" (p. 164). Cohesion has also been defined as the mutual attraction among members of a group and the resulting desire to remain in the group (Eddy, 1985). Recently, many researchers have begun to break down team cohesion into two subcategories—socially based and task based. Socially based cohesion refers to a positive attitude toward developing and maintaining interpersonal relationships within a team. Conversely, task-based cohesion refers to a task-orientated belief about achieving the team's goals through commitment to the team approach (Rainey & Schweickert, 1988).

Although a recent meta-analysis has shown that cohesion has a generally positive effect on team performance (Mullen & Copper, 1994), there are conflicting study results. One reason for this state of affairs is that some studies examine general cohesion, some look at task-based cohesion, and some look at socially based cohesion. A second reason is that the degree to which high levels of cohesion are related to team effectiveness depends on the norms set within the group. For example, a cohesive team can set an internal norm that is counterproductive to performance if the team is not committed to the organization. One example would be a brainstorming group that always leaves at 5:00 no matter if things are flowing well or not.

The following is descriptive of two types of cohesion measures. The first type of cohesion measure is similar to those attitudinal measures reviewed thus far. Specifically, this measurement tool uses a 5- or 7-point Likert scale to assess cohesion. Typical questions might include: (1) to what extent did you feel you belonged to your team; (2) to what extent

would you be willing to work with your team again on another task; and (3) to what extent did you find that your team argued a lot? The second type of cohesion measure is an adjective rating form called the System for Multiple Level Observation of Group (SYMLOG) (Bales & Cohen, 1979). Specifically, Strobel and McIntyre (2001) stated that this measure is designed to measure cohesion based on the following three dimensions: friendly/ unfriendly, task-orientated/ emotional, and dominant/submissive. This rating form is a 26-item self-report measure that uses a 5-point Likert scale.

### Collective Orientation

Collective orientation has been defined as, "the tendency to coordinate, evaluate, and utilize task inputs from other group members in an independent manner in performing a group task" (Driskell & Salas, 1992, p. 278). Cannon-Bowers et al. (1995) argued that it involves the capacity to take others' behavior into account and the belief that the team's goals should have higher priority than the goals of individual members.

Collective orientation is a relatively new construct that is similar to team cohesion. Some would even argue that it is not distinct from cohesion (see Miles, 2000). More specifically, Miles found that for teams solving simple math problems, collective orientation and team cohesion were highly correlated, had similar relationships to team outcomes, and upon conducting factor analysis did not factor into separate dimensions.

As is common, collective orientation is measured using people's responses to statements via a Likert-type scale. The following questions comprise the collective orientation scale constructed by Driskell and Salas (1992) and later used by Miles (2000):

How valuable did you feel your teammate's input was on this task?

How useful was it to work on this task as a team?

As this is a relatively new construct, more research is needed to understand its utility and relation to other constructs.

### Trust

Mutual trust refers to an attitude held by team members regarding the mood of the team's internal environment. More specifically, it refers to an atmosphere within the team where members' opinions are allowed to be brought forth, members are respected for their contributions, and innovative ideas are encouraged (Vaziri, Lee, & Krieger, 1988, as cited in Cannon-

Bowers et al., 1995). Mutual trust is an essential attitudinal component of team effectiveness. Specifically, it is necessary for collaborative work, as well as for the adaptive behavior teams need to exhibit in complex organizational environments.

As with other attitudinal measures, mutual trust is often measured using a Likert scale. The following are indicative of statements reflecting mutual trust:

_____ Members of my team feel free to express their viewpoints.

_____ Members of my team tend to listen to new ideas openly.

_____ Members of my team tend to criticize fellow members for differing viewpoints.

### Member Satisfaction

The last attitudinal measure is a global measure of member satisfaction. Satisfaction can be argued to be an affective reaction reflecting a positive feeling toward team members and team outcomes. Moreover, this attitudinal component may be argued to be specific to the particular team and task that the members are currently working on.

Satisfaction is important, for positive affective reactions tend to increase: (1) motivation, (2) desire to persist on difficult tasks, and (3) a willingness to work with group members in the future. Figure 23.6 is indicative of statements assessing member satisfaction:

### Summary

Several of the most popular attitudinal constructs to be measured in terms of team research were discussed. As stated, there is no one format for any of the attitudinal measures. However, the most common practice is to use a 5- or 7-point Likert scale to gather subjective affective and attitudinal reactions from team members. Although these measures are typically fairly easy to administer, their creation usually involves input from those with subject matter expertise for the task at hand so that questions are relevant. In addition, although normally easy for team members to understand, as with all self-reports there is the possibility of rating bias (behavioral anchors may help with this).

### CONCLUDING REMARKS

While industrial/organizational psychologists know much about the development and implementation of measurement

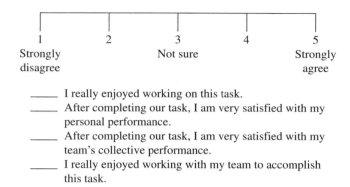

_____ I really enjoyed working on this task.
_____ After completing our task, I am very satisfied with my personal performance.
_____ After completing our task, I am very satisfied with my team's collective performance.
_____ I really enjoyed working with my team to accomplish this task.

**Figure 23.6** Satisfaction scale example.

tools to aid in the diagnostic feedback process, we have not done a good job translating this knowledge to practitioners within organizations. We hope that the lessons learned and measurement requirements that we have offered here will serve as good initial "translations" for those responsible for teamwork measurement within organizations. In addition, perhaps other researchers will be motivated to provide additional translations, since there is no question that more translations are needed.

### REFERENCES

Baker, D.P., & Salas, E. (1992). Principles for measuring teamwork skills. *Human Factors, 34*(4), 469–475.

Baker, D.P., & Salas, E. (1997). Principles for measuring teamwork: A summary and look toward the future. In M.T. Brannick, E. Salas, & C. Prince (Eds.), *Team performance assessment and measurement: Theory, methods, and applications* (pp. 331–356). Mahwah, NJ: Erlbaum.

Bales, R.F., & Cohen, S.P. (1979). SYMLOG: *A system for multiple level observation of groups.* New York: Free Press.

Bandura, A. (1986). *Social foundations of action and thought: A social cognitive view.* Englewood Cliffs, NJ: Prentice-Hall.

Brannick, M.T., Prince, A., Prince, C., Salas, E. (1995). The measurement of team process. *Human Factors, 37*(3), 641–651.

Brannick, M.T., Salas, E., & Prince, C. (1997). *Team performance assessment and measurement: Theory, methods, and applications.* Mahwah, NJ: Erlbaum.

Burke, C.S. (1999). *Examination of the cognitive mechanisms through which team leaders promote effective team processes and adaptive team performance.* Unpublished doctoral dissertation, George Mason University, Fairfax, Virginia.

Campbell, D.T., & Fiske, D.W. (1959). Convergent and discriminant validation by the multitrait-multimethod matrix. *Psychological Bulletin, 56,* 81–105.

Cannon-Bowers, J.A., & Salas, E. (1997). A framework for developing team performance measures in training. In M.T. Brannick, E. Salas, & C. Prince (Eds.), *Team performance assessment and measurement: Theory, methods, and applications* (pp. 45–62). Mahwah, NJ: Erlbaum.

Cannon-Bowers, J.A., Tannenbaum, S.I., Salas, E., & Volpe, C.E. (1995). Defining team competencies and establishing team training requirements. In R. Guzzo, E. Salas, & Associates (Eds.), *Team effectiveness and decision making in organizations* (pp. 333–380). San Francisco: Jossey-Bass.

Cooke, N.J., Salas, E., Cannon-Bowers, J.A., & Stout, R.J. (2000). Measuring team knowledge. *Human Factors, 42*(1), 151–173.

Dickinson, T.L., & McIntyre, R.M. (1997). A conceptual framework for teamwork measurement. In M.T. Brannick, E. Salas, and C. Prince (Eds.), *Team performance assessment and measurement: Theory, methods, and applications* (pp. 19–43). Mahwah, NJ: Erlbaum.

Driskell, J.E., & Salas, E. (1992). Collective behavior and team performance. *Human Factors, 34*(3), 277–288.

Dwyer, D.J., Fowlkes, J.E., Oser, R.L., Salas, E., & Lane, N.E. (1997). Team performance measurement in distributed environments: The TARGET's methodology. In M.T. Brannick, E. Salas, & C. Prince (Eds.), *Team performance assessment and measurement: Theory, methods, and applications* (pp. 137–154). Mahwah, NJ: Erlbaum.

Dwyer, D.J., Oser, R.L., Salas, E., & Fowlkes, J.E. (1999). Performance measurement in distributed environments: Initial results and implications for training. *Military Psychology, 11*(2), 189–215.

Dwyer, D.J., & Salas, E. (2000). Principles of performance measurement for ensuring aircrew training effectiveness. In H.F. O'Neil Jr., & D.H. Andrews (Eds.), *Aircrew training and assessment* (pp. 223–244). Mahwah, NJ: Erlbaum.

Eddy, W.B. (1985). *The manager and the working group.* New York: Praeger.

Festinger, L., Schachter, S., & Back, K. (1950). *Social pressures in informal groups: A study of human factors in housing.* New York: HarperCollins.

Fleishman, E.A., & Zaccaro, S.J. (1992). Towards a taxonomy of team performance functions. In R.W. Swezey & E. Salas (Eds.), *Teams: Their training and performance* (pp. 31–56). Stanford, CT: Ablex.

Fowlkes, J.E., Dwyer, D.J., Milham, L.M., Burns, J.J., & Pierce, L.G. (1999). Team skills assessment: A test and evaluation component for emerging weapon systems. *Proceedings of the 1999 Interservice/Industry Training, Simulation, and Education Conference* (pp. 994–1004). Arlington, VA: National Training Systems Association.

Fowlkes, J.E., Lane, N.E., Salas, E., Franz, T., & Oser, R. (1994). Improving the measurement of team performance: The TARGETs methodology. *Military Psychology, 6,* 47–61.

Franceschini, F., & Rupil, A. (1999). Rating scales and prioritization in QFD. *International Journal of Quality & Reliability Management, 16,* 85–97.

Gladstein, D. (1984). Groups in context: A model of task group effectiveness. *Administrative Science Quarterly, 29,* 499–517.

Greenless, I.A., Nunn, R.L., Graydon, J.K., & Maynard, I.W. (1999). The relationship between collective efficacy and precompetitive affect in rugby players: Testing Bandura's model of collective efficacy. *Perceptual and Motor Skills, 89,* 431–440.

Guzzo, R., Yost, P., Campbell, R., & Shea, G. (1993). Potency in groups: Articulating a construct. *British Journal of Social Psychology, 32,* 87–106.

Hackman, J.R. (1990). *Groups that work (and those that don't).* San Francisco: Jossey-Bass.

Hackman, J.R., & Morris, C.G. (1975). Group tasks, group interaction processes, and group performance effectiveness: A review and proposed integration. In L. Berkowitz (Ed.), *Advances in experimental social psychology* (Vol. 8, pp. 45–99). New York: Academic Press.

Heffner, T.S., Mathieu, J.E., & Cannon-Bowers, J.A. (1998). *The impact of shared mental models on team performance: Sharedness, quality, or both?* Poster presented at the 13th Annual Conference of the Society for Industrial and Organizational Psychology, Dallas, TX.

Johnston, J.H., Smith-Jentsch, K.A., & Cannon-Bowers, J.A. (1997). Performance measurement tools for enhancing team decision-making training. In M.T. Brannick, E. Salas, & C. Prince (Eds.), *Team performance assessment and measurement: Theory, methods, and applications* (pp. 311–327). Hillsdale, NJ: Erlbaum.

Kozlowski, S.W.J. (1998). Training and developing adaptive teams: Theory, principles, and research. In J.A. Cannon-Bowers & E. Salas (Eds.), *Making decisions under stress: Implications for individual and team training* (pp. 115–153). Washington, DC: APA Press.

Koslowksi, S.W.J., Gully, S.M., Nason, E.R., Ford, J.K., Smith, E.M., Smith, M.R., & Futch, C.J. (1994). A composition theory of team development, levels, content, process, and learning outcomes. In J. Mathieu (Chair), *Developmental views of team process and performance.* Symposium conducted at the Ninth Annual Meeting of the Society for Industrial and Organizational Psychology, Nashville, TN.

Marks, M.A., Mathieu, J.E., & Zaccaro, S.J. (2001). A temporally based framework and taxonomy of team process. *Academy of Management Review, 26*(3), 356–376.

Marks, M.A., Zaccaro, S.J., & Mathieu, J.E. (2000). Performance implications of leader briefings and team interaction training for team adaptation to novel environments. *Journal of Applied Psychology, 85*(6), 971–986.

McIntyre, R.M., & Salas, E. (1995). Measuring and managing for team performance: Emerging principles from complex environments. In R. Guzzo & E. Salas (Eds.), *Team effectiveness and decision making in organizations* (pp. 149–203). San Francisco: Jossey-Bass.

Meister, D. (1985). *Behavioral analysis and measurement methods.* Canada: Wiley.

Miles, J.A. (2000). Relationships of collective orientation and cohesion to team outcomes. *Psychological Reports, 86,* 435–444.

Morgan, B.B., Jr., Glickman, A.S., Woodard, E.A., Blaiwes, A.S., & Salas, E. (1986). *Measurement of team behaviors in a Navy environment* (Tech. Rep. No. 86–014). Orlando, FL: Naval Training Systems Center.

Mullen, B., & Copper, C. (1994). The relation between group cohesiveness and performance: An integration. *Psychological Bulletin, 115*(2), 210–227.

Osterman, P. (1994). How common is workplace transformation and who adopts it? *Industrial and Labor Relations Review, 47,* 172–188.

Paris, C.R., Salas, E., & Cannon-Bowers, J.A. (1999). Human performance in multi-operator systems. In P.A. Hancock (Ed.), *Human performance and ergonomics* (pp. 329–386). San Diego: Academic Press.

Peterson, E., Mitchell, T.R., Thompson, L., & Burr, R. (2000). Collective efficacy and aspects of shared mental models as predictors of performance over time in work groups. *Group Processes and Intergroup Relations, 3*(3), 296–316.

Pruitt, J.S., Burns, J.J., Wetteland, C.R., & Demestre, T.L. (1997). Shipboard mobile aid for training and evaluation. *Proceedings of the 41st Annual Meeting of the Human Factors Society* (pp. 1113–1117). Santa Monica, CA: Human Factors and Ergonomic Society.

Rainey, D.W., & Schweickert, G.J. (1988). An exploratory study of team cohesion before and after a spring trip. *Sport Psychologist, 2*(4), 314–317.

Riggs, M.L. (1989). *The development of self-efficacy and outcome scales for general applications.* Paper presented at the annual meeting of the Society for Industrial and Organizational Psychology, Boston, MA.

Salas, E., Bowers, C.A., & Cannon-Bowers, J.A. (1995). Military team research: Ten years of progress. *Military Psychology, 7,* 55–75.

Salas, E., & Cannon-Bowers, J.A. (2000). Designing training systems systematically. In E.A. Locke (Ed.), *The Blackwell handbook of principles of organizational behavior* (pp. 43–59). Malden, MA: Blackwell.

Salas, E., Dickinson, T.L., Converse, S.A., & Tannenbaum, S.I. (1992). Toward an understanding of team performance and training. In R.J. Swezey & E. Salas (Eds.), *Teams: Their training and performance* (pp. 3–29). Norwood, NJ: Ablex.

Salas, E., Fowlkes, J.E., Stout, R.J., Milanovich, D.M., & Prince, C. (1999). Does CRM training improve teamwork skills in the cockpit?: Two evaluation studies. *Human Factors, 41*(2), 326–343.

Shea, G.P., & Guzzo, R.A. (1987). Group effectiveness: What really matters? *Sloan Management Review, 28,* 25–31.

Smith, P.C., & Kendall, L.M. (1963). Retranslations or expectations: An approach to the construction of unambiguous anchors for rating scales. *Journal of Applied Psychology, 47,* 149–155.

Smith-Jentsch, K.A., Johnston, J.H., Cannon-Bowers, J.A., & Salas, E. (1997, December). Team dimensional training: A methodology for enhanced shipboard training. *Proceedings of the 19th Annual Interservice/Industry Training Systems and Education Conference* (pp. 164–173). Washington, DC: National Defense Industrial Association.

Sosik, J.J., Avolio, B.J., & Kahai, S.S. (1997). Effects of leadership style and anonymity on group potency and effectiveness in a group decision support system environment. *Journal of Applied Psychology, 82*(1), 89–103.

Spink, K.S. (1990). Collective efficacy in the sport setting. *International Journal of Sport Psychology, 21,* 380–395.

Stewart, G.L., Manz, C.C., & Sims, H.P. Jr. (1999). *Team work and group dynamics.* New York: Wiley.

Strobel, K.R., & McIntyre, R.M. (2001). *Creating cohesive teams: The effects of teamwork skills training.* Paper presented at the 16th Annual Meeting of the Society for Industrial and Organizational Psychologists, San Diego, CA.

Stout, R.J., Salas, E., & Carson, R. (1994). Individual task proficiency and team process: What's important for team functioning. *Military Psychology, 6,* 177–192.

Sundstrom, E. (1999). The challenges of supporting work team effectiveness. In E. Sundstrom & Associates (Eds.), *Supporting work team effectiveness* (pp. 3–23). San Francisco: Jossey-Bass.

Tannenbaum, S.I., Beard, R.L., & Salas, E. (1992). Team building and its influence on team effectiveness: An examination of conceptual and empirical developments. In K. Kelley (Ed.), *Issue, theory, and research in industrial/organizational psychology* (pp. 117–153). Amsterdam: Elsevier.

Tesluk, P., Mathieu, J.E., Zaccaro, S.J., & Marks, M. (1997). Task and aggregation issues in the analysis and assessment of team performance. In M.T. Brannick, E. Salas & C. Prince (Eds.), *Team performance assessment and measurement: Theory, methods, and applications* (pp. 197–224). Mahwah, NJ: Erlbaum.

Tziner, A., Joanis, C., & Murphy, K.R. (2000). A comparison of three methods of performance appraisal with regard to goal properties, goal perceptions, and ratee satisfaction. *Group & Organization Management, 25,* 175–190.

Vreuls, D., & Obermayer, R.W. (1985). Human-systems performance measurement in training simulators. *Human Factors, 27,* 241–250.

Weingart, L.R. (1997). How did they do that? The ways and means of studying group process. *Research in Organizational Behavior, 19,* 189–239.

Wigdor, A.K., & Green, B.F. Jr. (1991). *Performance assessment for the workplace.* Washington, DC: National Academy Press.

Williams, J.M., & Widmeyer, W.N. (1991). The cohesion-performance outcome relationship in a coaching sport. *Journal of Sport and Exercise Psychology, 13,* 364–371.

Zaccaro, S.J., Blair, V., Peterson, C., & Zazanis, M. (1995). Collective efficacy. In J. E. Maddux (Ed.), *Self-efficacy, adaptation, and adjustment: Theory, research, and application* (pp. 305–328). New York: Plenum Press.

Zaccaro, S.J., Parker, C.W., Marks, M.A., Burke, C.S., Higgins, J.M., & Perez, R. (1997, April). *Team efficacy, communication, and performance: Implications for collective regulatory processes.* Paper presented as part of symposium, at the 12th Annual Meeting of the Society for Industrial and Organizational Psychology, St. Louis.

Zachary, W., Bilazarian, P., Burns, J., & Cannon-Bowers, J.A. (1997). Advance embedded training concepts for shipboard systems [CD-ROM]. *Proceedings of the 1997 Interservice/Industry Training, Simulation, and Education Conference* (pp. 670–679). Arlington, VA: National Training Systems Association.

# CHAPTER 24

# A Theory-Based Approach to Team Performance Assessment

ROBERT M. MCINTYRE AND LARA TEDROW

Our goal in this chapter is to provide guidance for assessing team performance. Therefore, this chapter deals with something larger than *teamwork* assessment or *teamwork skills assessment*. Chapter 23 in this volume by Salas, Burke, Fowlkes, and Priest focuses largely on teamwork skills assessment per se. Our focus is different. We hold that *team performance* subsumes *teamwork skills* (sometimes simply referred to as teamwork). This distinction implies that assessing teamwork is not synonymous with assessing team performance. Teamwork assessment pertains to process. Team performance assessment pertains to process plus outcome.

It is tempting to view the problem of team performance assessment (TPA) as an extension of the individual performance assessment problem. From this view, we might recommend simple extrapolations of standard performance appraisal methods designed for individual performance assessment. We believe the direct application of individual performance assessment methods is inadequate for assessing team performance given the increasing complexity and variability of teams' roles in the modern workplace. Kozlowski, Gully, Nason, and Smith (1999) presented a theory of team performance that takes into account the complexity and variability of team performance. It will be clear to the reader of this chapter that Kozlowski et al. provided the basis of many

of the ideas presented here. We extend their theory to provide practical recommendations for team performance assessment. Before describing this theory and our prescriptions, we provide a short review of recent approaches to TPA. In providing this review, we intend to give the reader an overview of the range of approaches and targeted performance components that have evolved in the past decade or so. With this review, we believe that our recommendations, whose foundation is the Kozlowski et al. theory, can best be appreciated.

## A REVIEW OF TRADITIONAL PERSPECTIVES ON WHAT AND HOW TO MEASURE TEAM PERFORMANCE

Reilly and McGourty (1998) described four necessary components for the creation of a TPA system. The first is a clear definition of the team's key tasks and teamwork behaviors. The second is a "mapping" of the teamwork behaviors to team performance. The third component is an accurate and fair measurement process, including the identification of the person or persons responsible for rating the performance. The fourth component is a mechanism for communicating relevant information about the TPA system to all team members, such as purposes, descriptions, and confidentiality issues.

Zigon (1998) also proposed a seven-step process for creating a performance appraisal system for teams:

1. Review existing organizational measures.
2. Define what is going to be measured.
3. Identify individual team member accomplishments that support the team.
4. Weight the accomplishments.
5. Develop team and individual performance measures.
6. Develop team and individual performance standards.
7. Decide how to track performance.

As can be seen, Zigon's method provided several specific recommendations focusing on accomplishments and results. Alternatively, McIntyre and Salas (1995) and Dickinson and McIntyre (1997) recommended that a TPA system should be based on a theoretical model and should be behaviorally oriented in content. However, the primary issue that Dickinson and McIntyre dealt with was *team process* issues; hence, their recommendation for a theory of *teamwork* process as the basis of teamwork assessment.

Morgan, Salas, and Glickman (1993) theorized that teams develop over time on two different levels. Taskwork is the first and refers to specific content of the team assignment. Teamwork is the second and again involves the more generic teamwork skills necessary for quality interactions among team members. Morgan et al. (1993) indicated that there is a need to measure proficiency in both tracks. The Morgan et al. measurement system appears to be the basis of the Kozlowski et al. approach discussed later in this chapter.

According to Cannon-Bowers and Salas (1997), team performance can be measured on two main dimensions. The first dimension pertains to the *level* at which performance is measured. Although teams are composed of individuals, team performance may be measured at the *individual* or the *team* level. The second dimension concerns the degree to which the appraisal system is process oriented or results oriented. A process-oriented approach focuses on behaviors and the manner in which the work was completed. A results-oriented approach is concerned with the specific outcomes or work produced. These distinctions are not strict—process and result may overlap. Similarly, there may be times when behaviors are not distinctly individual or team. Combining these two dimensions leads to a simple model (Figure 24.1) to guide the performance evaluator.

A process-oriented approach at the individual level would assess how well an individual works with other team mem-

| Process-oriented approach at the individual level | Results-oriented approach at the individual level |
|---|---|
| Process-oriented approach at the team level | Results-oriented approach at the team level |

**Figure 24.1** Basic dimensions for assessing team performance (Cannon-Bowers and Salas (1997).

bers. Measures might include the degree of participation in team meetings that an individual displays, other members' perceptions of that individual, and the quality of communication with other members. This approach promotes a team orientation while maintaining individual accountability. A disadvantage to this approach is the difficulty encountered in trying to isolate an individual's contribution to interactions with other members.

A results-oriented approach at the individual level would focus on specific work products that a member contributes. For example, error rates, timeliness of the product, quality of written reports, or professional recommendations submitted could be measured. Some advantages to this approach include the encouragement of individual productivity, its similarity to most typical performance appraisal systems, and its legal defensibility (United States Office of Personnel Management, 1998). Problems with this approach include the difficulty associated with assessing an individual's specific contributions to a team product and the fact that individual team member focus leads to counterproductive competition among members.

A process-oriented approach at the team level would assess the quality of teamwork displayed or how well the team members work together as a group. The section on components of teamwork offers ideas about specific teamwork behaviors to measure if this approach is being used. The assumption that these kinds of teamwork skills are unimportant in appraising team performance is erroneous and dangerous. In extreme situations, the inability of team members to successfully work together can have life-threatening consequences. For example, breakdowns of team processes have played a significant role in aircraft accidents (Foushee, 1984).

Finally, a results-oriented approach at the team level would measure the products or outcomes of the team's efforts. Number of cases correctly completed, total cost of team project, number of customer complaints, and overall quality of the product are examples of results-oriented, team-level measures. Schuster and Zingheim (1992) highlighted the importance of assessing group outputs by suggesting that group goals are more likely than individual goals to be in alignment with the global goals held by the organization.

A balanced approach that considers team and individual levels and process as well as results seems to be an ideal approach to a comprehensive TPA system. Assessing at the individual level is important because good teams may have one or two incompetent individuals but still get acceptable ratings if measurement only occurs at the team level. However, assessment at the individual level only removes the focus from the team, which may be counterproductive. A results-only approach may be problematic, because teams can produce a quality product but may have such poor teamwork skills that in the long run members' dissatisfaction and faulty team processes may compromise the team's performance. Measurement of teamwork may reveal areas of weakness that can be remedied through training. Alternatively, a team may have excellent teamwork skills but still produce an inferior product or outcome making results-oriented assessment necessary. A TPA system that utilizes all four approaches *may* ensure a complete picture of the static aspects of the team's performance.

## A SYNTHESIS OF SIX PERFORMANCE MODELS

Militello, Kyne, Klein, Getchell, and Thordsen (1999) examined six models of teamwork and team performance and created what they refer to as a "synthesized model of Team Performance." The goal of this scholarly work "was to create a comprehensive picture of the components that underlie the behaviors or processes that are contained in various team assessment tools" (Militello et al., 1999, p. 156). The Militello et al. research team evaluated the following six models of team performance:

- Morgan, Glickman, Woodard, Blaiwes, and Salas (1986): The TEAM model
- McIntyre and Dickinson (1992): The Teamwork model
- Fleishman and Zaccaro (1992): Team Performance model
- Olmstead (1992): Model of Organizational Competence
- Helmreich and Foushee (1993): Crew Resource Management
- Zsambok, Klein, Kyne, and Klinger (1992): Advanced Team Decision Making

The researchers determined that these models converged on a common set of four components of team performance: team competencies, team identity, team planning and decision making, and team self-management. Based on these components, the authors developed a comprehensive list of performance dimensions.

*Team competencies* reflect the proficiency of team members and the procedures used by the team. This component includes two dimensions: member-leadership competence and shared practices. *Member-leadership competence* refers not only to the ability of members to perform their specific jobs but also refers to the leader's competence in leading the team. The *shared practices* component (also called *SOP proficiency*) reflects the team's learned proficiency at handling both routine and nonroutine tasks effectively.

The *team identity component* reflects the degree to which team members treat the team as an interdependent unit and take their membership in that team seriously. It includes four dimensions: defining roles, functions, and resources; engaging all members; compensating and coaching; and interpersonal aspects. *Defining roles, functions, and resources* involves understanding each member's responsibilities, expertise, and roles, as well as any resources needed for task completion. The *engaging all members* dimension refers to team members' levels of participation and how much responsibility they display in helping the team reach its goals. The *compensating and coaching* dimension reflects the team's redistribution of resources in helping team members cover their roles and responsibilities. The dimension of *interpersonal aspects* refers to whether team members' styles mesh harmoniously or whether they conflict.

The *team planning and decision making* component reflects the degree to which the team as a unit effectively formulates plans and makes decisions concerning the completion of the task. There are five dimensions to this component. *Envisioning goals* reflects identification of team goals and members' shared mental models of those goals. *Maintaining dynamic focus* is the team's ability to limit its planning to an appropriate amount of time and breadth. *Situation assessment* reflects how closely and accurately a team member's understanding of the situation is to that of other team members and reality. *Articulating expectations* is defined as the team's ability to verbalize expectations about movement toward the goal. Finally, the *envisioning and evaluating courses of action* dimension reflects the team members' ability to coordinate and synchronize their plan of action.

The final component is *team self-management* and consists of four dimensions: monitoring, adjusting, detecting gaps and inconsistencies, and time management. *Monitoring* refers to how well the team watches for effective and ineffective teamwork behaviors. *Adjusting* is the team's skill in modifying its strategy as circumstances dictate. *Detecting gaps and inconsistencies* refers to the team's ability to examine the team's information base for gaps and to note inconsistencies

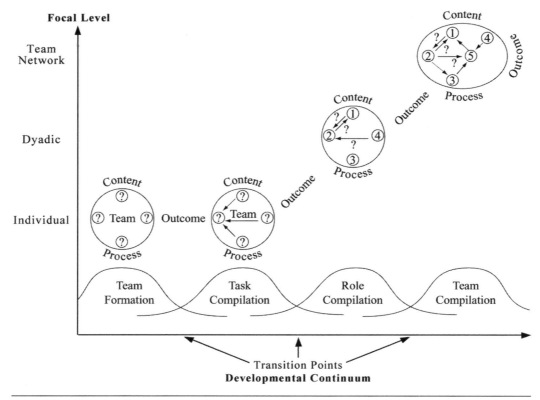

**Figure 24.2** Team compilation: Development, performance, and effectiveness across levels and time.
Copyright © S.W.J. Kozlowski. All rights reserved. Used with permission.

and contradictions. *Time management* is the team's aptitude in meeting goals on time.

As can be seen, the Militello et al. work points to a comprehensive set of processes and characteristics that compose team performance, all of which might be targeted in TPA. Of the models covered so far, the Militello et al. work provides the most guidance with regard to team processes. However, what the Militello et al. work does not fully address is the dynamic nature of team performance. The next theory meets this goal.

## ADAPTIVE TEAM PERFORMANCE THEORY

The title of the article in which the Kozlowski et al. (1999) theory is presented is "Developing Adaptive Teams: A Theory of Compilation and Performance Across Levels and Time." We therefore dub the theory adaptive team performance theory (ATPT). As mentioned early in the chapter, our recommendations for TPA rest on ATPT, a synopsis of which follows.

Figure 24.2 is a graphical depiction of ATPT. Overall, the theory states that team performance occurs in a sequence of phases through time. Each phase involves the group's compiling of content, process, and outcomes required in the team

task. Each phase focuses on one of three levels (individual team member, dyads of team members, and team as a whole). There have been other phase theories of team performance in the past. ATPT differs from these in that it is holistic in perspective. It combines task and process; personal characteristics; team learning of individual, dyadic, and team tasks; and the interpersonal styles of the team members. In other words, ATPT treats as performance not only the intermediate and final *outcomes* of the team but also the key independent variables that lead to these outcomes. The advantage of this approach is explained next.

The initial phase is referred to as team formation. Because individuals are just entering into the team context, they are not yet a team but a collection of individuals. In this phase, these individuals begin to reduce their feelings of ambiguity about team membership by learning about the basic nature of the team, its purpose, and their roles within it. They accumulate what Kozlowski et al. (1999) described as an interpersonal foundation. In phase two, the task compilation phase, each team member primarily engages in individual task learning. However, having made headway with regard to the ambiguity of the interpersonal relationships within the social environment, team members begin to demonstrate their task competency and begin to learn what they need from their fellow team members.

In phase three—the role compilation phase—team members begin to become proficient in the task-interactive aspects of the team. Team members engage in role compilation by probing their dyadic relationships, which the theory holds is the most fundamental task-interactive event in team performance. Kozlowski et al. (1999) asserted that in the role compilation phase, team members "enact horizontal role linkages that are necessary to accomplish particular team tasks" (p. 258). This is really the first step toward full team coordination, which occurs in phase four. Phase four is referred to as the team compilation phase. Team members are moving into the full coordination phase of their development. They "begin to attend to the network of role linkages that connect individuals to the team" (p. 258).

## ASSESSING TEAM PERFORMANCE THROUGH THE ATPT LENS

ATPT points to three dimensions that must be addressed to assess team performance properly. The first is the fact that teams evolve over time through a developmental process. The authors of the theory suggest that there are "soft" transition points at which a team moves from phase one to phase two to phase three and so on. Reflecting back to the classic dynamic criterion concept (Ghiselli, 1956), authors of ATPT implied that the "right thing to assess in teams" depends on "where the team members are" in the developmental process. Although other team performance researchers have made this recommendation (e.g., Morgan et al., 1986), the range of the evaluation "targets" (i.e., what is to be evaluated) is much wider in ATPT. The second fact is that TPA encompasses individual performance, performance by dyads of team members, and coordinated performance of the entire team. This implies that to assess at one extreme or the other (e.g., only the individual or only the team) is to ignore important aspects of team performance. The third fact is that the "stuff of performance" includes development as well as outcome. Therefore, through the perspective of ATPT, an either-or type of decision with regard to whether content or process should be evaluated is nonsensical. Both are important. Which receives emphasis depends on the phase within which a team finds itself. The following four paragraphs describe the central ideas in Table 8.3 of the chapter written by Kozlowski et al. (1999, p. 257).

In phase one, individual team members are focal. They acquire social knowledge, and engage in group socialization. This means, they become aware of the skills and abilities,

personalities, and attitudes and values of other group members. They develop some level of personal commitment to the team's goals, and share their perceptions of the climate of the team. They become aware of the norms of the team members, all of whom are in this formation stage.

In phase two, individual team members remain the focus. However, their task knowledge, skill acquisition, task competence, performance strategies, and decision-making skills are focal. They learn to monitor performance, set goals, acquire self-efficacy, and develop resilience to experienced failure. They also engage in social learning through social experimentation and practice, providing information about themselves, and modeling and persuasion.

In phase three, dyads of team members become the focus. In effect, Kozlowski et al. assert that the process of moving from an individual team member focus to a full team focus involves the intermediate step of team members' pairing off and "learning to master the ropes." The theory states that dyads—through an iterative process of role episodes—develop understanding of their roles in the team, which is refined cyclically through "horizontal negotiation" and repeated dyadic interactions. They acquire an understanding of the following: their own role sets and those of team members; the pacing of activities; how individual team performance is to be coordinated with others'; and the boundaries and limits of their individual responsibility. In this phase, the communication becomes streamlined; individual team members acquire "implicit coordination" skills. There are reduced role conflicts and more personalized interactions.

In phase four, the team becomes focal as a networked system. A repertoire of network options develops such that alternative transactions are explored. Diagnosis and evaluation of the team's coordination in the network are carried out. Network modifications are implemented based on the evaluation. Mutual performance monitoring takes place in which team members are aware of the load of their teammates, backing each other up when necessary, and looking for errors in the team tasks. Team members are adaptive to environmental conditions and internal changes, developing methods of networking where necessary. Coordination among team members is maintained.

We believe that the elements that constitute the four phases of ATPT provide a rich basis for evaluating team performance. In contrast to other approaches to TPA in which bits and pieces of the team performance domain are covered, ATPT provides a comprehensive map for assessing performance that can be used for administrative and developmental purposes. Not only is the theory comprehensive; it is also dynamic in its depiction of the team. Teams as social entities are ever developing and ever changing. This is what ATPT captures. This is what it points to with regard to TPA.

To implement ATPT as a basis for assessment, there are several obvious points to note. First, because team performance is not simple, neither is assessing team performance. This fact must be accepted, we believe, if the organizational researcher intends to do a credible job of assessing team performance. This is not to say that all aspects of ATPT must be used in TPA. It may be appropriate to assess only certain aspects of the team performance domain as outlined in ATPT. The theory provides the basis for selecting options that suit the needs of the research. For example, if an organizational researcher's purpose is to evaluate how new team members are being socialized, he or she may use ATPT to identify the kinds of target performance elements (like information seeking, self-disclosure, personalities, attitudes and values, etc.) that are critical for entry-level teams. Second, assessing team performance requires commitment on the part of the client organization. It requires even more commitment than individual performance assessment. The organizational researcher or consultant must be aware of the commitment required and explain this at the outset. Third, assessing team performance requires a team of evaluators. It takes a team to evaluate a team. This slogan is more than that—it is a principle that must be followed to create valid and reliable team assessment. (Perhaps one exception to this principle is the team comprising two collocated members performing a simple task.) Fourth, assessing team performance evolves into an organizational development intervention. Because of its systems focus, ATPT-based TPA will identify role conflicts, interpersonal difficulties, role unclarity, and skill deficiencies that require some type of "fix."

## OVERVIEW OF THE RECOMMENDED TPA METHOD

The assessment center method provides an ideal system for implementing the implicit guidelines of ATPT for assessing team performance. Essentially, the assessment center method is a behaviorally based method employing trained assessors to observe an individual (or group) over time. It requires that behaviors are recorded and later compiled by the assessor team to form summary evaluations on the key performance dimensions. It depends on the assessors' consensus meeting in which assessors share their individual evaluations and their behavioral rationales for their judgment. The assessment center method requires consensus evaluations, which ensures a reasonable degree of psychometric reliability. Importantly, based on content validity evidence reasoning as well as the predictive validity paradigm, the method is known to be a psychometrically valid means of assessing performance and related skills.

## STEPS IN ASSESSMENT

In applying ATPT to TPA, we envision eight steps.

### Team "Job" Analysis

The first step in applying the assessment center method in the context of ATPT-based TPA is to analyze the team "job." Preliminarily, this requires that the organizational researcher identify the team goal(s), the number of team players, the roles of the team players, the basic knowledge skills, abilities, and other characteristics required of the team members. The researcher should at this early stage in the analysis develop an understanding of the embedding organization, and the key cultural and climate issues pertaining to the team. The latter two areas are recommended to understand the social place that the team holds in the embedding organization.

Following the preliminary analyses, the deeper ATPT analysis begins. Subject matter experts (SMEs) highly familiar with the team should be interviewed to get a complete understanding of the characteristics embodied in ATPT. Although we do not provide a format for this interview, we recommend that Table 8.3 presented by Kozlowski et al. (1999, p. 257) serve as the template for the interview. As an example of the kinds of information one should solicit in this interview, recall that in phase two, team members begin to learn to monitor performance. The interview should include questions that are designed to elicit information about the types of behaviors team members should exhibit that would show they are monitoring other members' performance. In phase three, communication becomes streamlined. SMEs should identify the types and frequency of communication appropriate for the team that would reflect their interactions becoming more efficient (i.e., teams at this point should not be constantly checking with each other before completing routine tasks). The nature of the SMEs' answers should differ depending on the type of team and their task. Most important is to gather information about the target characteristics, qualities, behaviors, and processes that are common to teams of the sort under analysis. Characteristics that are by definition linked to specific individuals (such as personalities, attitudes, values) should not be completely ignored, however. In other words, SMEs may provide examples of the "kinds" of individuals (i.e., the personality types of individuals or the range of values of individuals) who have been team members. Of particular importance in this interview is to identify specific identifiers or markers for each of the target elements so that each is clearly understood. This will lead to a vivid description of the team performance domain.

The final part of the ATPT-based "job" analysis interviews requires that the organizational researcher at least preliminarily identify the transition points for each of the phases. Once again with multiple SMEs interviewed, a picture should emerge depicting what happens within and across the team to effect a transition. The job analysis is complete when the team of organizational researchers synthesizes all interview data and summarizes them in clear language for the next phase.

### Development of Observation Tools

A set of paper-and-pencil checklists should be developed to serve the team performance appraiser. These checklists are the basis for an observation coding system for identifying target elements for evaluation. Recognize that the checklist may contain references to processes (such as role episodes—interactions between two organization members whereby an individual learns about his or her role expectations) as well as content such as levels of success in certain team tasks.

### Design the Process for Team Assessment

Due to the varying nature of teams, it is not reasonable to present a general team assessment process. Therefore, general guidelines are listed here. The first guideline is to decide on the purpose of the team performance evaluation. If it is for developmental purposes, make sure that all constituents clearly understand this. Important outcomes will result from this choice. The next guideline is to decide on the level of disruption allowable in the circumstance. Here, "disruption" refers to whether it is practical to evaluate the team offline in high-fidelity simulations or in vivo as it performs its tasks on a regular basis. The criticality of the team's role and the limits of practicality are the primary considerations here. Offline, high-fidelity simulations provide the basis for in-depth, intensive assessment. The question is whether it is practicable. In vivo observation by a team of assessors is a good alternative and may address practicality issues quite readily.

The next guideline is to identify "where the team resides" in its development. The use of the data from the "job analysis" will be helpful here, particularly data pertaining to the transitions from one phase to the next. For example, teams who are unable to clearly identify the team's mission, articulate their goals, and accurately describe each member's roles would likely be in phase one.

The next guideline is to identify either an offline exercise or an in-vivo work sample in which the team of assessors have access to observe and interview the team. Interviews may be extremely important for the assessors to understand what they observe. Interviews would "bring to the surface" covert aspects of performance. The final guideline is to trial-test the process with a team to ensure that all "wrinkles" are ironed out.

### Assessor Training

After the plan for assessment has been devised, assessors need to be trained in the following areas: (1) the basic tenets of the ATPT model; (2) a review of the team job description (based on the job analysis results); (3) an overview of the assessment process, including the purpose; (4) a review of observation skills, exercise details if relevant, interview skills, assessment tools (paper-and-pencil checklists); and (5) a review of the behaviorally based consensus meeting. If teams are to receive feedback on their performance assessment, then feedback training should be developed and administered as well. The length of the training will be determined by the experience of the assessors and the complexity of the team.

### Approaching the Assessment Task

The organizational researcher involved in the TPA should approach the team members to explain that their team is to be evaluated and the time frame for the evaluation. The purpose of the evaluation must be explained clearly and convincingly, which is to say that the organizational researcher must be skilled in building trust. It may be important for supervision to officially recognize the importance of team evaluation.

### Carrying Out the Assessment

It goes without saying that the duration of the assessment must match the level of complexity and difficulty of the team performance task. This having been said, assessors must strictly follow the procedures that they described to the team members. Assessors should never openly discuss what they have observed with other assessors. Data are to be kept confidential. Assessors should be careful *not* to prematurely evaluate; instead, they should withhold judgment until the other assessors meet with them during the consensus meeting.

### Consensus Meeting

The consensus meeting is similar in format to the consensus meeting in individually based assessment centers. Some basic points can be made. The consensus meeting should take place in a professional environment. Assessors will have been trained in the process. However, in spite of this, the administrator should review the principles for conducting high-quality consensus meetings. Most important, during the discussion, assessors summarize their observations for each of the components constituting the different phases. Each member of the team summarizes observations vis-à-vis the portion of the team for which he or she is responsible. After all assessors have presented their behavioral observations on the different elements of the phases, final evaluations should be formulated. If the purpose of the team assessment is team development, the assessor team should invest time in developing behaviorally specific examples of the positive and negative evaluations.

## Feedback Meeting

After the evaluative data have been organized into a report, the assessors should present them to the team. Irrespective of the purpose of the assessment, the atmosphere of the meeting should be one of openness and clarity. Team members should be given specific feedback. Because the ATPT model is the framework of the assessment, it will be important to explain the model (if they have not received it in team training). This will make the feedback much more useful for the team. Finally, specific recommendations should be made with regard to future team improvements and growth.

## CONTRASTING THE ATPT-BASED APPROACH WITH TRADITIONAL APPROACHES

Most theories of team performance identify the key behavioral processes in which a team engages. The processes may be task focused or process focused. A good example of this is the synthesized model identified by Militello et al. (1999). The latter points to four general components that are usually assessed. These components could very well be the basis of a set of behaviorally based scales. After observation and evaluation training, observers might use these scales to provide summary evaluations of team performance. The other theories described can be used in similar ways.

ATPT goes beyond this. True, as with other team performance theories, ATPT identifies components that should be assessed. More important, it states that TPA requires that the developmental activities in which a team engages are important targets of evaluation. ATPT also views the process through which a team engages to adapt to the demands of the environment as important targets for assessment. Finally, the the-

ory requires the team performance evaluator to consider the stage of the team's development before developing the evaluation plan. In these important ways, the theory on which our suggested TPA approach rests points to the importance of considering the dynamic nature of team performance. ATPT is not only dynamic with regard to time, but also with regard to the levels of analysis and the targets of evaluation. This means both the individual team member's performance and the team-level outcome are important to assess. ATPT provides guidance as to which of the two levels to emphasize by requiring the evaluator to identify first the stage of the team's development. Aggregation issues (that is, issues pertaining to individual team member outcomes, team member processes, or team outcomes) become less confusing because ATPT points to dealing with individual member issues when necessary, to dyadic member issues when necessary, and to team coordination issues when appropriate.

Teamwork process is often the target of team performance assessment. Influenced by ATPT, we believe that team process is an important part of team performance. However, ATPT takes a slightly different perspective on what "process" is. For example, the theory considers not only intrapersonal and interpersonal issues as process but also role episodes, and individual and group learning.

The ATPT-based approach therefore actually combines an evaluation of process, content, and *development/learning*. The latter is rarely mentioned in the literature on assessing team performance. When one evaluates the performance of a team from the perspective of ATPT, the question is asked "What are the team members doing to improve or develop themselves given the phase in which they find themselves?" This provides the evaluator the wherewithal to provide feedback on how they are doing with regard to certain constructs, and why they might be where they are. It provides guidance with regard to how the team might improve in the future as well.

What are the drawbacks of the ATPT-based TPA? Simply put, the system is labor-intensive. The "labor" begins with the organizational researcher or consultant who must lead the way in analyzing the nature of the team in its richest sense (what the team does, who the team members are, at what stage of maturity is the team, etc.). Thereafter, the researcher/consultant must design a practicable assessment system, tailored to the needs of the team. Although the use of the assessment center method as a model implies that reliability and validity issues are dealt with, the time demands may be considered quite high. If high-quality team performance assessment is the desired goal, substantial investment is required. There are ways of reducing the practical costs, but there is no way of completely avoiding them.

## CONCLUSION

We have attempted to describe a state-of-the-art method for assessing team performance that is based on a rich and comprehensive theory of team performance. The mechanics of the method derive from the assessment center method. The assessment center method is well known for its reliability and validity. This means that the approach we espouse deals with one of the critical requirements of TPA. Our recommended approach addresses the problem of what to evaluate by relying on a comprehensive theory developed by Kozlowski et al. (1999). We believe that ATPT provides an understanding of team performance that applies to virtually all teams. Our recommended method—because of its reliance on ATPT—will provide valuable data for feedback as well as for administrative decision making. However, we fully realize that there is a significant investment in implementing our suggestions. Assessment centers (at least the traditional ones) are known to be time- and labor-intensive. The organizational researcher/consultant faced with the challenge to evaluate team performance must be ready to educate the client organization on the value of this theory-based approach. If the team to be evaluated is crucial to the success of the organization, then the researcher/consultant has a relatively easy task ahead. The cost of assessment is notable. The payoff is notable as well.

## REFERENCES

Cannon-Bowers, J.A., & Salas, E. (1997). A framework for developing team performance measures in training. In M.T. Brannick, E. Salas, & C. Prince (Eds.), *Team performance assessment and measurement: Theory, methods, and applications* (pp. 45–62). Mahwah, NJ: Erlbaum.

Cannon-Bowers, J.A., Salas, E., & Converse, S.A. (1993). Shared mental models in expert team decision making. In N.J. Castellan Jr. (Ed.), *Current issues in individual and group decision making* (pp. 221–246). Hillsdale, NJ: Erlbaum.

Davis, L.T., Gaddy, C.D., & Turney, J.R. (1985). *An approach to team skills training of nuclear power plant control room crews* (NUREG/CR-4255GP-R-123022). Columbia, MD: General Physics Corp.

Dickinson, T.L., & McIntyre, R.M. (1997). A conceptual framework for team measurement. In M.T. Brannick, E. Salas, & C. Prince (Eds.), *Team performance assessment and measurement: Theory, methods, and applications* (pp. 19–43). Mahwah, NJ: Erlbaum.

Fleishman, E.A., & Zaccaro, S.J. (1992). Toward a taxonomy of team performance functions. In R.W. Swezey & E. Salas (Eds.), *Teams: Their training and performance* (pp. 31–56). Norwood, NJ: Ablex.

Foushee, H.C. (1984). Dyads and triads at 35000 feet: Factors affecting group process and aircrew performance. *American Psychologist, 39*(8), 885–893.

Ghiselli, E.E. (1956). Dimensional problems of criteria. *Journal of Applied Psychology, 40,* 1–4.

Helmreich, R.L., & Foushee H.C. (1993). Why crew resource management? Empirical and theoretical bases of human factors training in aviation. In E.L. Wiener, B.G. Kanki, & R.L. Helmreich (Eds.), *Cockpit resource management.* (pp. 3–45). New York: Academic.

Kozlowski, S.W.J., Gully, S.M., Nason, E.R., & Smith, E.M. (1999). Developing adaptive teams: A theory of compilation and performance across levels and time. In D.R. Ilgen & E.D. Pulakos (Eds.), *The changing nature of performance: Implications for staffing, motivation, and development* (pp. 240–292). San Francisco: Jossey-Bass.

Lewis, C.M., Hritz, R.J., & Roth, J.T. (1983). *Understanding and improving teamwork: Identifying training requirements* (Report 4). Valencia, PA: Applied Science Associates.

Mathieu, J.E., Heffner, T.S., Goodwin, G.F., Salas, E., & Cannon-Bowers, J. (2000). The influences of shared mental models on team process and performance. *Journal of Applied Psychology, 85*(2), 273–283.

McIntyre, R.M., & Dickinson, T.L. (1992). *Systemic assessment of teamwork processes in tactical environments* (Report submitted to Naval Training Systems Center under Contract No. N61339-91-C-0145). Norfolk, VA: Old Dominion University.

McIntyre, R.M., & Salas, E. (1995). Measuring and managing for team performance: Emerging principles from complex environments. In R.A. Guzzo & E. Salas (Eds.), *Team effectiveness and decision-making in organizations* (pp. 9–45). San Francisco: Jossey-Bass.

Militello, L.G., Kyne, M.M., Klein, G., Getchell, K., & Thordsen, M. (1999). A synthesized model of team performance. *International Journal of Cognitive Ergonomics, 3*(2), 131–158.

Morgan, B.B., Salas, E., & Glickman, A.S. (1993). An analysis of team evolution and maturation. *Journal of General Psychology, 120*(3), 277–291.

Morgan, B.W., Glickman, A.S., Woddard, E.A., Blaiwes, A.S., & Salas, E. (1986). *Measurement of team behaviors in a Navy environment* (Tech. Rep. No. NTSA TR-86-014). Norfolk, VA: Old Dominion University, Center for Applied Psychological Studies.

Olmstead, J.A. (1992). *Battle staff integration* (IDA Paper P-2560). Alexandria, VA: Institute for Defense Analysis.

Prince, C., Chidester, T.R., Bowers, C.A., & Cannon-Bowers, J.A. (1992). Aircrew coordination: Achieving teamwork in the cockpit. In R.W. Swezey & E. Salas (Eds.), *Teams: Their training and performance* (pp. 329–353). Norwood, NJ: Ablex.

Reilly, R.R., & McGourty, J.W. (1998). Performance appraisal in team settings. In J.W. Smither (Ed.), *Performance appraisal: State of the art in practice* (pp. 244–277) San Francisco: Jossey-Bass.

Schuster, J.R., & Zingheim, P.K. (1992). *The new pay: Linking employee and organizational performance.* New York: Lexington Books.

United States Office of Personnel Management: Workforce Compensation and Performance Service. (1998). *Performance appraisal for teams: An overview. Performance Management Practitioner Series* (PMD-14). Retrieved October 13, 2000, from http://apps.opm.gov/publications/pages/default.htm.

Zigon, J. (1998). *How to measure the performance of work teams.* Philadelphia, PA: Zigon Performance Group.

Zsambok, C.E., Klein, G., Kyne, M., & Klinger, D.W. (1992). How teams excel: A model of advanced team decision making. In *Performance Technology—1993: Selected Proceedings of the 31st NSPI Conference* (pp. 19–27). Chicago, IL: National Society for Performance and Instruction.

# EMPLOYEE REACTIONS TO THE WORKPLACE

# CHAPTER 25

# Job Stress Assessment Methods

PATRICK CONNELL, VALENTINA BRUK LEE, AND PAUL E. SPECTOR

The job stress domain is concerned with the health and well-being of people in the workplace. Researchers in this area have focused most of their attention on two classes of variables—job stressors and job strains. *Stressors* are environmental variables (either objective or perceived) that have physical and/or psychological effects on people that have implications for health and well-being. *Strains* represent those effects and can be divided into the categories of behavioral, physical, and psychological (Jex & Beehr, 1991). Behavioral strains include various actions people take in response to stressors, such as drinking alcohol or taking a day off of work. Physical strains can be short term (e.g., rise in blood pressure) or long term (e.g., heart disease). Psychological strains include attitudinal reactions (e.g., job dissatisfaction) and emotions (e.g., anger or anxiety). Additional variables are often used in job stress studies, such as coping styles, social support, and personality, and many of the assessment techniques discussed throughout this volume and the others in this series have been used.

This chapter begins with discussion of the major assessment methods that are used in the job stress domain. The vast majority of studies use incumbent self-report questionnaires, and we discuss both the ubiquitous closed-ended, summated rating scale technique and the open-ended technique. In addition we discuss the use of other, less frequently used methods, including physiological measures and the use of alternative (to the participant) judges/raters such as observers, peers, and supervisors. The second section provides brief summaries of instruments designed to assess individual job stressors or strains, a combination of job stressors and/or strains, or bat-

teries that assess a variety of variables not limited to job stressors and strains. This chapter covers some of the more popular as well as easily available scales that can be found in the literature. Job stress researchers also make use of a variety of more general instruments that are not limited to the occupational domain, but coverage of these is beyond the scope of this chapter.

## ASSESSMENT APPROACHES IN THE JOB STRESS DOMAIN

A variety of approaches have been used in the assessment of occupational stress. These methods have traditionally included incumbent self-reports; however, alternative forms of data have also been obtained from open-ended, physiological, and objective measures.

### Incumbent Self-Reports

The incumbent self-report methodology has been the predominant assessment technique in the job stress area. Most studies utilize cross-sectional designs with participants providing the only source of data. Advantages that have led to the popularity of this approach are appropriateness and efficiency. Many of the variables of interest in the job stress domain concern internal psychological states, such as attitudes, behaviors that might be performed in private, emotions, and perceptions of job conditions/situations. The incumbent might be the only appropriate and available source from which to gather such information (Perrewé & Zellars, 1999). Furthermore, the collection of all data in a single questionnaire is highly efficient, often allowing for the collection of hundreds or thousands of cases within days. Such questionnaires can be placed, for example, on an organization's intranet, which allows for very rapid data collection. Self-reports can also allow for anonymity of response, because it is not necessary to identify participants if their questionnaire responses don't have to be matched to other sources of data. This provides protection to participants in studies that may provide information that might put the participants or others in an unfavorable light, and, thus, self-reports would be expected to increase accuracy of responses as well as participation rates.

However, this approach may have significant disadvantages as well, mainly concerning limits to the kinds of conclusions that can be drawn. One particular limitation inherent in the use of self-reports is their subjectivity. Whereas the self-report can provide information about how a person perceives a situation, such perceptions can be highly idiosyncratic, especially when the underlying construct is complex and abstract, which is true of many of the variables assessed in this area. This makes it difficult to apply conclusions to the objective environment, which is often the goal of a research study (Frese & Zapf, 1999; Schaubroeck, 1999). Another limitation is inherent in the typical cross-sectional design rather than the self-report itself, and that concerns the inability to draw firm causal conclusions (Spector, 1994). Longitudinal designs (Zapf, Dormann, & Frese, 1996) and experimental studies are needed to draw these sorts of conclusions either with or without incumbent self-reports.

### Open-Ended Reports: The Stress Incident Record

The Stress Incident Record was devised by Newton and Keenan (1985; see also Keenan & Newton, 1985) to provide open-ended responses concerning specific stressful incidents at work. Respondents are given a written form that asks for a description of a stressful event at work that occurred in the prior month. Additional questions can be added concerning what led to the event, how the person felt at the time, his or her reactions, and the effects on others, depending on the focus of the study. The open-ended materials are content analyzed, preferably with multiple raters to ensure interrater agreement/consistency. The incidents can be sorted into categories based on the researcher's interests and the specific questions asked, for example, by stressor or by strain reaction. An advantage to using this open-ended approach is that the participant is free to determine what are the most significant job stressors and strains without the constraints imposed by closed-ended rating scales that presuppose what the important dimensions/variables might be.

### Reports by Alternative Data Sources

Many job stress studies utilize sources other than incumbents for information about the incumbent's job stressors. Peers, supervisors, subordinates, and trained observers/judges can be used. In most cases these alternative sources are asked to complete the same job stressor scales as the incumbents. It is also possible to use alternative sources to provide information about job strains, but this procedure has not been popular because many strains are internal states not easily observed. Some studies have found an impressive level of convergence between incumbent reports and alternative source reports for the strain of job dissatisfaction (often used as a job strain), including observers and incumbents (Glick, Jenkins, & Gupta, 1986), supervisors and their subordinates (Spector, Dwyer, & Jex, 1988), and even children and their parents (Trice & Tillapaugh, 1991).

The main advantage of using alternative sources is that they introduce a level of objectivity not possible with a single data source. Although the alternative sources provide ratings based on subjective opinion, they are objective in the sense of being independent of the incumbent (Frese & Zapf, 1988). This allows for more confident conclusions that relations between stressors and strains reflect the potential impact of the objective world and don't just indicate relations among different subjective states within the individual. However, convergence between sources has been quite variable among different stressors, with more concrete constructs, such as workload, having higher correlations between sources than more abstract constructs, such as role ambiguity (Spector, in press). Frese and Zapf (1988) argued that the relatively modest convergence is due in large part to inaccuracy in the alternative sources, which leads to underestimates of relations with other variables. Furthermore, Glick et al. (1986) found that incumbents showed better discriminability (lower correlations) among stressor subscales than alternative sources, suggesting these alternative sources might not be able to provide accurate distinctions among different dimensions along which they are asked to make judgments.

### Job-Focused Versus Incumbent-Focused Methods

So far we have discussed methods for assessing constructs targeting the individual job incumbent. Methods have been used to assess characteristics of jobs rather than incumbents; that is, the unit of analysis is the job. Often such methods are subsumed under job analysis, whereby trained analysts might rate jobs after reviewing descriptions or other materials (e.g.,

Spector & Jex, 1991). In other cases, target jobs are matched to jobs in a job analysis database that contains relevant variables. Examples include Adelmann (1987), who used data from the Dictionary of Occupational Titles (DOT, U.S. Department of Labor, 1977); Shaw and Riskind (1983), who used data from the Position Analysis Questionnaire (McCormick, Jeanneret, & Mecham, 1972); and Liu, Spector, and Jex (2001), who used data from the Occupational Information Network, O*NET (U.S. Department of Labor, 1998), which is an online database replacement to the DOT, available to the general public.

## Physiological Measures

Though a significant amount of the research involving work stress has focused on psychological and behavioral symptoms, other studies have shown that work stress is often associated with a number of physiological symptoms as well (Cox, 1978; Eliot, 1979; Frankenhaeuser, 1975; Fried, Rowland, & Ferris, 1984; McQuade & Aikman, 1974; Morse & Furst, 1979; Weiner, 1979). In general, research investigating the physiological measurement of stress has focused on three main areas: (1) cardiovascular symptoms (e.g., heart rate and blood pressure), (2) biochemical symptoms (e.g., levels of uric acid, blood sugar, steroid hormones, cholesterol, and catecholamines), and (3) gastrointestinal symptoms (e.g., peptic ulcers) (Fried et al., 1984).

Although some researchers consider physiological measures of stress to be a more objective approach to assessing work stress, Fried et al. (1984) noted that this form of measurement is also vulnerable to a number of confounds. They identified three categories of factors that could affect the validity of the findings done in this area: stable or permanent factors (e.g., familial or genetic tendency, race, age, sex, and diet), transitory factors (e.g., time of day, room temperature, room humidity, postural position of subject, physical exertion, consumption of caffeine and nicotine before or during the time of measurement), and procedural factors (e.g., the number of times physiological measurements are made, or the amount of time between measurements). Solutions include the taking of multiple measures over time, control over transitory factors both within and across participants (e.g., being sure participants do not smoke immediately prior to assessment), and adopting a within-subject approach by comparing physiological measures at base rate in a relaxed situation versus at work.

## SELF-REPORT ASSESSMENT INSTRUMENTS

Self-report instruments have been developed to assess a wide variety of job stressors, strains, and other variables of interest

to job stress researchers. Most scales utilize a summated rating scale format with multiple items to assess each construct. In many published studies, one or more instruments were ad hoc, developed specifically for the particular study. However, a variety of scales are available that have seen sufficient use to provide at least some evidence of psychometric soundness. Some of these scales are published by commercial testing companies that charge for their use. Others are provided by researchers free of charge for noncommercial research uses. We provide here a brief description of a number of measures that have been used in job stress research. For a more in-depth discussion of many of these instruments, consult Rick, Briner, Daniels, Perryman, and Guppy (2001).

## Batteries and General Stress Instruments

Several job stress batteries are available that assess a variety of job stressors, job strains, and other variables of interest to job stress researchers (e.g., coping styles, social support, and personality). Although some of these instruments can be used free of charge for noncommercial research purposes, others are copyrighted scales distributed by major testing companies that charge for their use. This has led to perhaps more popularity of the commercial scales among consultants who provide services relevant to employee health and well-being, such as organizational development or stress management. Other instruments, such as the Job Stress Survey, assess a variety of stressful job conditions or sources of job stress rather than individual job stressor variables.

### Advanced Manufacturing Technology Job Characteristics Scales

Jackson, Wall, Martin, and Davids (1993) developed a battery of five scales designed specifically to assess relevant job characteristics for individuals engaged in Advanced Manufacturing Technology (AMT) jobs. These are jobs in highly mechanized factories that use robotic assembly procedures that can result in jobs that are very different from the more traditional factory. The battery consists of 22 items that assess timing control (control over pacing of work), method control (control over how work is done), monitoring demand (extent to which passive monitoring is required), problem-solving demand (requirement for active problem solving), and production responsibility (extent to which employee errors would be costly). Jackson et al. (1993) reported coefficient alphas from .67 to .86 and 1-year test-retest reliabilities ranging from .42 to .57.

## Job Content Questionnaire

The Job Content Questionnaire (JCQ) is made up of five scales (Decision Latitude, Psychological Demand, Social Support, Physical Demands, Job Security) that measure characteristics of work (Karasek et al., 1998), based on Karasek's (1979) demand/control model of job stress. As seen in Table 25.1, each of the five scales is broken down into subscales that can be self-administered in 15 minutes, require minimal guidance, and are each rated on a 4-point scale (Karasek et al., 1998). The JCQ is an expansion of the 27-item scale used in the University of Michigan Survey Research Center Quality of Employment Survey in 1969, 1972, and 1977. Karasek et al. (1998) reported coefficient alphas for the scales ranging from .70 to .84 for males and .64 to .84 for females.

## Job Stress Survey

The Job Stress Survey (JSS; Vagg & Spielberger, 1998), a commercial scale published by Psychological Assessment Resources (PAR), is designed to measure generic sources of job stress that will fit a wide variety of occupations and set-

tings. Each of the 30 JSS items describes an event or situation that often results in psychological strain (e.g., working overtime, making critical on-the-spot-decisions, performing tasks not in the job description). For each item the examinee rates severity and frequency. Severity is on a scale ranging from 1 ("Least Stressful") to 9 ("Most Stressful"). This rating is done in comparison with an average stressor (i.e., assignment of disagreeable duties), which serves as the rating scale's midpoint of 5. A respondent's severity rating for an item reflects whether or not that particular event is perceived as more stressful than average (i.e., greater than 5) or less stressful than average (i.e., less than 5) by the respondent. Frequency is indicated on a 9-point scale, ranging from 0 days to 9 or more days in the past 6 months.

On the basis of factor analysis Spielberger and Reheiser (1994) divided the scale into separate Job Pressure and Organizational Support subscales. Scores can be computed for the overall scale, or the two subscales for frequency, severity, or the combination. Vagg and Spielberger (1998) reported coefficient alphas for the various subscales ranging from .75 to .80.

## Leiden Quality of Work Questionnaire

Development and design of the Leiden Quality of Work Questionnaire was based on two principal models in occupational stress research, the Job Demand-Control-Support model (Johnson, 1989; Johnson & Hall, 1988; Karasek & Theorell, 1990) and the Michigan model (Caplan, Cobb, French, van Harrison, & Pinneau, 1975). The instrument consists of 59 items or statements (e.g., "My job requires me to be creative," "I have a lot to say about what happens on my job," "I am not asked to do an excessive amount of work") to which the respondent must choose from one of four answer categories ("Disagree Completely," "Disagree," "Agree," and "Agree Completely"). Factor analysis and cross-validation of the measure conducted by van der Doef and Maes (1999) indicated that the questionnaire consists of 11 work characteristics (job stressors and social support) and one outcome variable. Each of these 12 factors as well as their internal reliability estimates are listed in Table 25.2.

## Occupational Stress Inventory

The Occupational Stress Inventory (OSI; Osipow, 1998) consists of three sets of scales: The Occupational Roles Questionnaire (ORQ), the Personal Strain Questionnaire (PSQ), and the Personal Resources Questionnaire (PSQ). The ORQ assesses six areas of role stressors: overload, insufficiency, boundary, ambiguity, responsibility for people, and physical

**TABLE 25.1 Job Content Questionnaire Scales and Recommended Number of Items**

| Scale | Recommended Number of Items |
|---|---|
| Decision latitude | |
| 1. Skill discretion | 6 |
| 2. Decision authority | 3 |
| 3. Skills underutilization | 2 |
| 4. Work group decision authority | 3 |
| 5. Formal authority | 2 |
| 6. Union/representative influence | 3 |
| Psychological demands and mental workload | |
| 7. General psychological demands | 5 |
| 8. Role ambiguity | 1 |
| 9. Concentration | 1 |
| 10. Mental work disruption | 2 |
| Social Support | |
| 11. Socioemotional—coworker | 2 |
| 12. Instrumental—coworker | 2 |
| 13. Socioemotional—supervisor | 2 |
| 14. Instrumental—supervisor | 3 |
| 15. Hostility—coworker | 1 |
| 16. Hostility—supervisor | 1 |
| Physical Demands | |
| 17. General physical loading | 1 |
| 18. Isometric load | 2 |
| 19. Aerobic load | 2 |
| Job Insecurity | |
| 20. General job insecurity | 4 |
| 21. Skill obsolescence | 2 |

**TABLE 25.2 Scales and Internal Reliability (Cronbach Alpha) of the Leiden Quality of Work Questionnaire**

| Scale (item) | Number of Items | Cronbach Alpha Rating |
|---|---|---|
| Skill Discretion | 8 | .76 |
| Decision Authority | 4 | .74 |
| Task Control | 4 | .73 |
| Work and Time Pressure | 3 | .73 |
| Role Ambiguity | 6 | .75 |
| Physical Exertion | 3 | .84 |
| Hazardous Exposure | 8 | .93 |
| Job Insecurity | 3 | .75 |
| Lack of Meaningfulness | 3 | .87 |
| Social Support Supervisor | 5 | .89 |
| Social Support Coworkers | 6 | .82 |
| Job Satisfaction | 6 | .84 |

*Note.* Taken from van der Doef and Maes (1999).

environment. The PSQ covers four areas of strain: vocational, psychological, personal and physical. The PRQ contains four subscales to assess recreation, self-care, social support, and rational/cognitive coping. This measure is based on a comprehensive model put forth by Osipow and Spokane (1983), which assumes a causal relationship between types of occupational role stressors and strains as moderated by coping strategies. Coefficient alphas for the subscales ranged from .71 to .94 (Osipow, 1998). This is a commercial instrument published by PAR.

### Pressure Management Inventory

The Pressure Management Inventory (PMI; Resource Systems, 2001; Williams & Cooper, 1998) is a revision of the Occupational Stress Indicator (OSI; Cooper, Sloan, & Williams, 1988) designed to be a more comprehensive and reliable measure of occupational stress. It is based on a transactional model of the stressor-strain relationship that identifies three components of stress, including the sources of pressure, its effects, and individual differences that may serve as moderators of the stressor-strain relation (Williams & Cooper, 1998). It is a 112-item self-report questionnaire that is divided into 24 scales (see Table 25.3) measuring job satisfaction, mental and physical health, sources of pressure, Type A behavior, locus of control, coping, and social support. Respondents rate the items on a 6-point summated rating scale. Williams and Cooper (1998) reported internal consistency reliabilities of greater than .70 for all of the subscales except for the Daily Hassles subscale (see Table 25.3). Williams and Cooper (1998) reported criterion-related validation evidence for the PMI subscales.

The PMI is a copyrighted instrument available for both noncommercial research and organizational use in over 20 languages. It may be used for blue- and white-collar popu-

lations and is appropriate for use in a diverse number of organizations. The PMI can be used to identify stressors, to inform individuals about their stress management skills, and to detect employees who are suffering from work-related stress. It is available in several formats, including paper, e-mail, intranet, and computer disk. In addition, a PMI Personal Profile, an individualized 12-page computer-generated report, is presented to participating employees (Williams & Cooper, 1998).

### University of Michigan Job Stress Questionnaire

One of the first comprehensive studies of job stress was carried out by Caplan et al. (1975) utilizing a battery that was based on a number of existing scales. Job stressors included quantitative workload, responsibility for people, job complexity, role conflict, role ambiguity, underutilization of abilities, pay inequity, and participation in decision making. Strains included job dissatisfaction, boredom, physical health symptoms, depression, anxiety, and irritation. They also included questions concerning health-related habits, such as smoking, and coffee consumption, as well as questions about obesity, doctor visits, and specific illnesses. Finally, scales were included to assess social support and personality. Internal consistencies were reported for most scales from .70 to .89.

### Job Stressors

#### Autonomy/Control

Worker *control* refers to an individual's ability to influence the environment in an effort to reduce threats and increase rewards (Ganster, 1989a). *Autonomy* is a subset of control and is conventionally defined as the degree of employee discretion and latitude in defining work schedules and methods. Its importance in organizational research and applied settings is displayed by its relationship to physical strain, job satisfaction, and absenteeism (Spector, 1986). Autonomy has been studied from a variety of organizational perspectives, including research in the areas of leadership (Yukl, 1981) and organizational climate (Schnake, 1983); however, both control and autonomy are prominent in models of job stress (e.g., Karasek's Demands-Control; Karasek, 1979). Autonomy and control have traditionally been measured using self-report scales, such as the Job Diagnostic Survey (JDS; Hackman & Oldham, 1975), the Global Work Autonomy Scale (Breaugh, 1998), or the Work Control Scale (Dwyer & Ganster, 1991). The more recent Factual Autonomy Scale (FAS; Fox, Spector, & Van Katwyk, 1997) has attempted to reduce subjective bias by using more objective questions in the measurement of employee autonomy.

**TABLE 25.3   Pressure Management Indicator Scale Structure**

| Scale Domain | Number of Items | High Score | Low Score | Coefficient Alpha |
|---|---|---|---|---|
| Job satisfaction | | | | |
| 1. Job satisfaction | 6 | Lots of satisfaction | Little satisfaction | .89 |
| 2. Organization satisfaction | 6 | Lots of satisfaction | Little satisfaction | .83 |
| 3. Organizational security | 5 | Very secure | Very insecure | .77 |
| 4. Organizational commitment | 5 | Very committed | Not committed | .75 |
| Mental and physical health | | | | |
| 5. State of mind | 5 | Feels content | Feels anxious | .82 |
| 6. Resilience | 4 | Good resilience | Poor resilience | .70 |
| 7. Confidence level | 3 | Feels settled | Feels worried | .70 |
| 8. Physical symptoms | 3 | Feels calms | Feels physical discomfort | .72 |
| 9. Energy levels | 4 | More energy/less tired | Less energy/more tired | .79 |
| Sources of pressure | | | | |
| 10. Workload | 6 | More pressure | Less pressure | .84 |
| 11. Relationships | 8 | More pressure | Less pressure | .88 |
| 12. Recognition | 4 | More pressure | Less pressure | .85 |
| 13. Organization climate | 4 | More pressure | Less pressure | .78 |
| 14. Personal responsibility | 4 | More pressure | Less pressure | .79 |
| 15. Managerial role | 4 | More pressure | Less pressure | .73 |
| 16. Home-work balance | 6 | More pressure | Less pressure | .83 |
| 17. Daily hassles | 4 | More pressure | Less pressure | .64 |
| Type A behavior | | | | |
| 18. Type A drive | 5 | More drive | Less drive | .72 |
| 19. Patience-impatience | 5 | More impatient | More patient | .80 |
| Locus of control | | | | |
| 20. Control | 5 | More influence/control | Less influence/control | .72 |
| 21. Personal influence | 3 | More influence/discretion | Less influence/discretion | .71 |
| Coping | | | | |
| 22. Problem focus | 6 | More problem-focusing | Less problem-focusing | .80 |
| 23. Life-work balance | 4 | More life-work balance | Less life-work balance | .73 |
| Social support | | | | |
| 24. Social support | 3 | More social support | Less social support | .80 |

**Job Diagnostic Survey: Autonomy Subscale.** Hackman and Oldham (1975) created the Job Diagnostic Survey (JDS) to measure core characteristics of a job based on their job characteristic theory. The Autonomy subscale has been the most widely used measure of autonomy (Spector, 1986) and can be found used with the entire JDS or alone. This subscale measures general freedom, independence, and discretion the employee perceives in doing the job. The original Autonomy subscale was composed of three negatively and positively worded items written in two different formats. However, most researchers currently use the Idaszak and Drasgow (1987) modification in which all items share the same format. Spector, Dwyer, and Jex (1988) reported a coefficient alpha for the scale of .70 for job incumbents and .75 for supervisors rating their subordinates' jobs, as well as convergent validity of .45 between incumbent and supervisor reports of the incumbent's autonomy. This scale is in the public domain.

**Global Work Autonomy Scale.** The Global Work Autonomy Scale is a multidimensional scale that assesses three aspects of autonomy: method, scheduling, and criteria autonomy (Breaugh, 1985). Specifically, *work method autonomy* refers to how much discretion an individual has in the procedures for accomplishing the job (e.g., "I am free to choose the method(s) to use in carrying out my work"). *Scheduling autonomy* pertains to the control individuals have in timing the activities required by their work (e.g., "I have control over the scheduling of my work"). *Criteria autonomy* relates to an individual's "ability to modify or choose the criteria used for evaluating their performance" (Breaugh, 1985, p. 556). Each facet is measured using three positively worded items that are rated on a 7-point scale ranging from "Strongly Disagree" to "Strongly Agree"), but all 9 items can be combined for a total autonomy score. Breaugh (1998) reported coefficient alphas ranging from .79 to .90 for the Global Work Autonomy Scale total score across three different studies, as well as a 1- to 2-week test-retest reliability of .83. Coefficient alphas for the Method, Scheduling, and Criteria autonomy subscales were .91, .85, and .78, respectively (Breaugh, 1989). Convergence between incumbents' ratings and supervisors was $r = .37$

and between incumbents and coworker was $r = .54$. Breaugh (1998) found a correlation of .54 between the Global Work Autonomy Scale total score and the Autonomy subscale of the JDS.

**Control Scale.**    Dwyer and Ganster (1991) created a 22-item multifaceted self-report Work Control Scale composed of 17 general control items and 5 predictability of work activities items that are summed into a total control score. It includes all of the predictability items and a subset of the general control items in Ganster's (1989b) original scale. The scale assesses control over work procedures and policies, variety of tasks, scheduling of breaks, order of task performance, and physical arrangement of the work environment (Ganster, 1989b). Respondents are asked to rate how accurately the 22 items describe their job on a 5-point summated-rating-type scale ranging from "Very Little" to "Very Much" (e.g., "How much control do you have over the scheduling and duration of your rest breaks?"), and an average is calculated as an index of experienced worker control (Dwyer & Ganster, 1991).

Dwyer and Ganster (1991) reported an internal consistency reliability of .87 for their worker control scale. It showed a significant correlation with work satisfaction ($r = .25$) and significant interactions with a measure of workload in predicting absence and tardiness (Dwyer & Ganster, 1991). In addition, Smith, Tisak, Hahn, and Schmieder (1997) found a two-factor solution for the work Control Scale, which included a General Control factor and a Predictability factor across three samples. However, Smith et al. (1997) reported that some of the General Control items did not load on the hypothesized dimension. Further, they found a high correlation ($r = .85$) between Ganster and Dwyer's (1991) General Control factor and Karasek's (1985) Decision Authority factor, suggesting that both measure a similar construct.

**Factual Autonomy Scale.**    The FAS is a 9-item self-report scale that asks fact-based questions regarding worker autonomy in an attempt to reduce the degree of subjectivity (Fox, Spector, & Van Katwyk, 1997). Six of the items begin in a "Do you have to ask permission to" format and target autonomy in regard to scheduling of activities (e.g., "Do you have to ask permission to take time off?"). The remaining three items are in a "Does someone tell you" format and refer to the process for getting the work done (e.g., "Does someone tell you when you are to do your work?"). Respondents are asked to rate each item on a scale containing five choices ranging from "Never" to "Extremely Often or Always." Research showed that the internal consistency reliability for the FAS was .81 when completed by the incumbent and .82 when completed by the supervisor in regard to the incumbent's job

(Spector, Fox, & Van Katwyk, 2000). Convergent validity for the FAS is indicated by a correlation of .53 between incumbents' and supervisors' ratings.

### Role Ambiguity/Conflict

An individual's role in an organization is defined by a set of behaviors that when communicated unclearly or in a conflicting manner result in role ambiguity or role conflict (Kahn, Wolf, Quinn, Snoek, & Rosenthal, 1964). Both of these role stressors are associated with affective and psychological outcomes and have been key variables in the job stress literature (Jex & Beehr, 1991). Role conflict and role ambiguity are typically measured using a self-report measure such as the Role Ambiguity Scale by Beehr, Walsh, and Taber (1976) or the Role Conflict and Role Ambiguity Scales by Rizzo, House, and Lirtzman (1970).

**Role Ambiguity Scale.**    Beehr, Walsh, and Taber (1976) created a four-item Role Ambiguity Scale intended to measure the clarity with which a supervisor has defined the goals and standards of an employee. It is rated on a 7-point scale ranging from "Strongly Disagree" to "Strongly Agree," and three of the four items are reverse scored (e.g., "My supervisor makes it clear how I should do my work"). An index of role ambiguity is calculated by taking an average of the scores (Beehr et al., 1976). Beehr et al. (1976) reported an internal consistency reliability of .71 for the scale.

**Role Conflict/Role Ambiguity Scales.**    Rizzo et al. (1970) developed a scale to measure both role conflict (eight items) and role ambiguity (six items). Role conflict was measured in terms of job requirement compatibility (e.g., "I receive an assignment without the manpower to complete it"). Role ambiguity was measured in terms of the clarity or existence of guides and requirements, and the predictability of outcomes to the respondent's behavior (e.g., "I know what my responsibilities are"). Respondents rate items on a 7-point scale ranging from "Very False" to "Very True." Rizzo et al. (1970) reported internal consistency reliabilities for role conflict and ambiguity averaging .82 and .80, respectively. across two samples. There has been some criticism of the scale due to confounding of wording direction; the role ambiguity items are worded positively, whereas the role conflict items are worded negatively (see Smith, Tisak, & Schmieder, 1993 for a summary), but it remains one of the most popular measures in job stress research.

### Employee Mistreatment and Interpersonal Conflict

There are several constructs that concern the conflict and mistreatment of employees by one another or managers at work.

Bullying (Hoel, Rayner, & Cooper, 1999) and mobbing (Zapf, Knorz, & Kulla, 1996) refer to the harassment of an employee by others at work. Incivility (Andersson & Pearson, 1999) concerns rude behavior that a person is exposed to at work. Interpersonal conflict (Spector & Jex, 1998) refers to the extent to which an employee experiences conflicts with other people at work, focused mainly on verbal arguments and disagreements. Although each of these constructs is conceptually different, scales to assess each share many of the same items.

**Interpersonal Conflict at Work Scale (ICAWS).** The ICAWS is a four-item, summated rating scale that is intended to assess how well the respondent gets along with others at work (Spector & Jex, 1998). The items ask about getting into arguments with others and about how often others act nasty. A sample item is "How often do you get into arguments with others at work?" Respondents are asked to indicate how often each item occurs at work. Five response choices are given, ranging from 1 ("Less Than Once per Month or Never") to 5 ("Several Times per Day"). High scores on the measure represent frequent conflict with others. Spector and Jex (1998) reported a mean coefficient alpha of .74 across 13 samples. Convergent validity evidence was provided by a correlation of .30 between the ICAWS completed by incumbents versus their supervisors, suggesting at least some objectivity to this self-report measure (Spector et al., 1988).

**Leymann Inventory of Psychological Terrorization.** The Leymann Inventory of Psychological Terrorization (LIPT; Leymann, 1990) is a 45-item scale that contains items concerning mobbing/bullying at work to be completed by the victim. An English slight modification of the original Swedish scale is available in Zapf, Knorz, and Kulla (1996). Respondents indicate how often they experience each item at work using either a 3- ("Never" to "Often") or 5-point ("Never" to "Daily") scale. A sample item is "People treat you like you aren't there." A total mobbing score can be computed, although Zapf, Knorz, and Kull (1996) used factor analysis to create seven subscale scores.

**Workplace Incivility Scale.** The Workplace Incivility Scale (WIS; Cortina, Magley, Williams, & Langhout, 2001) is a behavior checklist respondents can use to indicate their experiences at work. Each of the 7 items is a statement of a behavior that may have been exhibited toward the person in the past 5 years (although time frame can be modified). A sample item is "Put you down or was condescending to you." Cortina et al. (2001) reported a coefficient alpha for the scale of .89.

### Organizational Constraints

Organizational constraints represent conditions or events at work that prevent employees from performing as well as they could on the job (Peters & O'Connor, 1980). Some common constraints within organizations may include faulty equipment, incomplete or poor information, or interruption by others. At least three constraints scales have been developed based on the Peters and O'Connor (1980) analysis of widespread constraint areas within organizations. They defined 11 specific areas in which constraints occur.

**Mathieu et al. Organizational Constraints Measure.** Mathieu, Tannenbaum, and Salas (1992) developed a measure to assess constraints that consists of 14 items. Few details were available other than the internal consistency estimate, which was .85.

**Klein and Kim Organizational Constraints Measure.** Klein and Kim (1998) devised a measure customized for sales personnel to assess constraints. Their scale contains 10 items in a 5-point agree-disagree format. A sample item is "Amount of time I spend correcting mistakes of others makes it difficult for me to perform the job well." Klein and Kim (1998) reported a coefficient alpha of .64 and also reported that their constraints measure correlated with sales performance.

**Organizational Constraints Scale (OCS).** The OCS contains 11 items, each assessing 1 of the 11 Peters and O'Connor (1980) constraints areas. A total constraint score is computed as the sum of these items. For each item, the respondent is asked to indicate how often it is difficult or impossible to do his or her job as a result of that particular constraint. Response choices range from 1 ("Less Than Once per Month or Never") to 5 ("Several Times per Day"). High scores represent high levels of constraints. Spector and Jex (1998) reported a mean coefficient alpha of .85 across eight samples, and mean convergence ($r = .26$ across five samples) was also noted between the OCS completed by incumbents versus other sources.

### Workload

Workload can be described in very general terms as the amount of work required of an employee. Its underlying complexity, however, lies in the fact that it can be measured in a variety of ways. For example, workload can be measured in terms of number of hours worked, level of production, or even the mental demands of the work being performed. Quantitative (amount of work) has been distinguished from qualitative (difficulty of work) workload.

**Van Veldhoven and Meijman Demands Scale.** Van Veldhoven and Meijman (1994) developed a Dutch language 11-item scale that assesses quantitative workload. An English translation can be found in Van Yperen and Snijders (2000). Items ask about the pace and amount of work and are rated using a 4-point scale from "Never" to "Always." Van Yperen and Snijders (2000) reported a coefficient alpha of .86.

**Quantitative Workload Inventory (QWI).** The QWI consists of five items that assess quantitative workload. Each item is a statement about amount of work, and respondents indicate how often each occurs, from 1 ("Less Than Once per Month or Never") to 5 ("Several Times per Day"). A sample item is "How often does your job require you to work very fast?" High scores represent a high level of workload. Spector and Jex (1998) reported a mean coefficient alpha of .82 across 15 studies for the measure. Mean convergence between incumbents and other sources was .35 across five samples.

## Job Strains

Self-report measures exist to assess many behavioral, physical, and psychological strains. However, most strain measures were designed for general use and not specifically for the job stress domain. Since treatment of general measures is beyond our scope, we do little more here than mention the measures most commonly used. The major focus of this section is on those strain measures that were developed for organizational use.

### General Strain Measures

Many measures are available to assess potential reactions to stressors in life that can be used or adapted for use in the workplace. Some assess emotional reactions such as anger, anxiety, or depression. Others assess more general psychological health or well-being. Still others focus on physical symptoms that have been associated with stress. We note those most commonly used in workplace studies.

To assess emotional states, several scales are available. The State Trait Personality Inventory (STPI) is an instrument that contains subscales to assess both anger and anxiety states (Spielberger, 1979). A more in-depth assessment of anger can be conducted with the State-Trait Anger Expression Inventory-2 (Spielberger, 1999). It consists of subscales to measure feeling angry, feeling like expressing anger verbally,

and feeling like expressing anger physically. Two frequently used measures of depression are the Beck Depression Inventory (BDI; Beck, Ward, Mendelson, Mock, & Erbaugh, 1961), and the Center for Epidemiologic Studies Depression Scale (CES-D; Radloff, 1977). The Positive and Negative Affect Schedule (PANAS; Watson, Clark, & Tellegen, 1988) has two subscales, one to assess general positive emotion and one to assess general negative emotion. With appropriate instructions the scale can assess emotional states. Fatigue can be assessed with the Checklist Individual Strength (CIS; Bültmann et al., 2000), a 20-item measure that has been used in work studies.

Scales have been developed to assess more general psychopathology and well-being. Items for these scales often measure both emotional states and other psychological symptoms associated with psychopathology. The Hopkins Symptom Checklist (HSCL; Derogatis, Lipman, Rickels, Uhlenhuth, & Covi, 1974) has been quite popular. The Mental Health Index (MHI; Veit, & Ware, 1983) and the Index of Psychological Well-Being (Berkman, 1971) are other options.

Finally, several scales exist that ask participants to indicate which physical health symptoms (e.g., headache or stomach distress) they have experienced during a specified time period (e.g., past 30 days). Such scales are checklists, with scores often being the number of symptoms indicated. Perhaps the most popular is the General Health Questionnaire (GHQ; Goldberg & Williams, 1988; NFER-Nelson, 2001) that comes in four versions from 12 to 60 items. Other scales include the Health Conditions Index (HCI; Probst, 2000), and the Physical Symptoms Inventory (PSI; Spector & Jex, 1998).

### Boredom/Monotony

Melamed, Ben-Avi, Luz, and Green (1995) devised an adjective checklist to measure subjective monotony in the workplace based on employee descriptions of their work. This particular scale lists four adjectives/phrases (routine, boring, monotonous, and not varied enough). Respondents are asked to indicate how well each adjective describes their work by answering either yes (3), unsure (1), or no (0). A total score for the measure is calculated by summing the scores for each item. Melamed et al. (1995) reported a Cronbach's alpha coefficient of .76. In addition, scores on this scale were shown to be moderately related to objective monotony (rated by experienced observers) in both males and females, respectively (average $r = .28$ and .25).

### Counterproductive Work Behavior Scales

Several distinct constructs concerning behavior that is harmful to organizations have been developed, including counterproductive behavior, deviance, organizational aggression, retaliation, and revenge. They have been operationalized with overlapping checklists of specific behaviors for which incumbents or others indicate how often the target person has done each, including behaviors that might harm organizations (e.g., destroying property) or other employees (spreading a harmful rumor about someone). Most researchers have developed their own behavior scales rather than relying on standardized instruments. Examples can be found in Fox and Spector (1999), Greenberg and Barling (1999), and Skarlicki and Folger (1997).

**Bennett and Robinson Workplace Deviance Scales.** Bennett and Robinson (2000) developed a measure of workplace deviance that contains two subscales. The first of these is a 12-item Organizational Deviance scale (deviant behaviors directly harmful to the organization, e.g., taking property from work without permission, spending too much time fantasizing or daydreaming instead of working). The second subscale, Interpersonal Deviance, consists of seven items designed to assess behaviors directly harmful to other individuals within the organization (e.g., making fun of someone at work, saying something hurtful to someone at work). For both scales respondents must indicate on a scale ranging from 1 ("Never") to 7 ("Daily") how often they have engaged in each of these behaviors over the last year. Total scores for each of the two measures are obtained by summing the responses for the items on each scale. Preliminary psychometric evidence provided by Bennett and Robinson (2000) revealed a coefficient alpha of .81 for the Organizational Deviance scale, and .78 for the Interpersonal Deviance scale. In addition, confirmatory factor analysis lends support for the suggested two-factor structure of workplace deviance.

### Job-Related Affective Well-Being Scale

The Job-Related Affective Well-Being Scale (JAWS) was created to assess a broad range of positive (e.g., content) and negative (e.g., annoyed) emotional reactions to work (Van Katwyk, Fox, Spector, & Kelloway, 2000). Respondents rate the amount to which their job has made them feel a particular emotion in the past 30 days on a 5-point scale ranging from "Never" to "Extremely Often or Always." An overall score and four subscales scores can be calculated. The overall score is derived from the sum of all items with the displeasureable reverse coded, and high scores indicate high levels of job-related affective well-being. The four additional subscales are High Pleasure High Arousal (HPHA), High Pleasure Low Arousal (HPLA), Low Pleasure High Arousal (LPHA), and Low Pleasure Low Arousal (LPLA). Each subscale includes the five most extreme items appropriate for each category, and, for each, high scores represent high levels of that state. The internal consistency reliabilities for the overall JAWS and the HPHA, HPLA, LPHA, and LPLA subscales are .95, .90, .81, .80, and .80, respectively (Van Katwyk et al., 2000).

### Job (Dis)Satisfaction

Job (dis)satisfaction is often assessed as a psychological strain, usually by using either self-report questionnaires or by interviewing employees (Spector, 2000). Numerous scales have been developed to measure job satisfaction. The Job Descriptive Index is one of the most widely used scales, which measures five facets of job satisfaction: work, pay, supervision, coworkers, and promotion opportunities (JDI; Smith, Kendall, & Hulin, 1969). The Minnesota Satisfaction Questionnaire is another popular scale of job satisfaction, which measures 20 facets and can be administered in a long or short form (MSQ; Weiss, Dawis, Lofquist, & England, 1966). Last, the Job in General Scale is a newer scale that assesses job satisfaction in general (Ironson, Smith, Brannick, Gibson, & Paul, 1989). For a more in-depth discussion of job satisfaction scales, see Chapter 26.

### (Lack of) Organizational Commitment

The two most popular organizational commitment scales are the Organizational Commitment Questionnaire (OCQ; Mowday, Steers, & Porter, 1979) that assesses overall commitment and the Meyer, Allen, and Smith (1993) scale that assesses three facets of commitment: affective (emotional attachment to the organization), continuance (investments in the current job and organization), and normative (felt obligations to the organization). For a more in-depth discussion see Chapter 28.

### Organizational Frustration Scale

Research investigating the impact of situational constraints on affective reactions led Peters, O'Connor, and Rudolf (1980) to develop a 3-item Frustration Scale. The items measure the amount of frustration experienced on a job and are rated on a 7-point summated rating scale (e.g., "Trying to get this job done was a frustrating experience"). A total frustration score is calculated by reverse scoring one of the items ("Overall, I experienced very little frustration on this 'job'") and summing the responses, such that a high score indicates high levels of experienced frustration (Peters et al., 1980). Peters et al. (1980) reported an internal consistency reliability of .76.

### *State-Trait Personality Inventory State Anxiety Subscale (Modified)*

The State Trait Personality Inventory (STPI) is a measure of state and trait anger, curiosity, and anxiety (Spielberger, 1979). Particularly important in the assessment of occupational stress is the State Anxiety subscale. It has been modified by Spector et al. (1988) for use in the workplace by asking respondents "how they generally felt at work in the past 30 days" (p. 13). The scale consists of 10 items that ask how the respondent feels at the present moment and are rated on a 4-point scale ranging from "Not at All" to "Very Much So." An example item is "I am tense." A total score is calculated by summing the 10 items after 4 are reversed. Spector et al. (1988) reported a coefficient alpha of .90 for the modified anxiety scale.

### *Tension Index*

Lyons (1971) created a nine-item Tension Index that assesses the tension caused by work-related factors in his study of the effects of role ambiguity. The nine Tension Index items were selected from a longer list of items previously used by Kahn, Wolfe, Quinn, Snoek, and Rosenthal (1964). Respondents rate how often they feel bothered by the nine items on a 5-point scale ranging from "Never" to "Nearly All the Time" (e.g., "How often do you feel bothered by the fact that you can't get information needed to carry out your job?"; "How often do you feel bothered by not knowing what opportunities for advancement or promotion exist for you?"). A final tension score is calculated by summing up the responses to the nine items. Lyons (1971) reported an estimated split-half reliability of .70 for the Tension Index. All the items were positively intercorrelated with a median intercorrelation of .36 and a median item-index correlation of .59 (Lyons, 1971).

### *Withdrawal*

Worker withdrawal involves employees not being at work when either scheduled or needed. This type of behavior can either be temporary, as in tardiness or absence, or permanent as in turnover. In most studies absence is assessed from either employee records or self-report. Indices of time absent are a count of the number of separate incidents of absence regardless of length. Time lost absence is a measure of the number of days or hours the person has missed. Turnover is most frequently assessed by checking organizational records to see which employees have terminated their employment. Reasons for termination can be considered most frequently by dividing turnover into voluntary (person resigned on their own) and involuntary (person was fired or asked to resign).

An instrument designed to assess withdrawal behaviors is the Employee Absenteeism Scale, which evaluates both the frequency and type of worker absence (Paget, Lang, & Shultz, 1998). This scale contains 12 items with each item representing a possible cause of absence (e.g., disagreement with coworkers, feeling depressed, minor domestic problems). The respondent must indicate on a scale ranging from 1 ("Certain to Be Absent") to 5 ("Certain to Go to Work") the likelihood of being absent from work for each item. Another measure of absence is the Employee Reliability Inventory, which consists of 81 true-false items. Included in this measure are seven separate scales designed to evaluate respondents on seven different factors of reliable and productive work behavior (e.g., Freedom from Disruptive Alcohol and Substance Use, Courteous Job Performance, Emotional Maturity) (Borofsky, 2000). Separate scores are reported for each scale and provide an estimate of worker reliability and productivity (Borofsky, 2000).

## CONCLUSIONS

Job stress researchers have used a variety of instruments and methods to assess the variables of interest. Many of those variables concern internal states that can only be determined through some form of self-report. This has in part led to an overreliance on single-source questionnaire studies, and the closed-ended summated rating scale has been the dominant assessment tool. The typical job stress study utilizes a collection of such scales to assess a range of variables, all contained in a single questionnaire administered once. This cross-sectional questionnaire design has allowed for study of relations among variables of interest, but it has limited confident tests of causal hypotheses, as well as tests of relations with the objective work environment. As discussed in the first part of this chapter, methods exist to go beyond the single-source, cross-sectional survey. Many researchers have supplemented self-report surveys with more objective measures that include reports by others (coworkers, observers, or supervisors) or the taking of physiological measures. Although such approaches have been useful in providing additional objectivity, they are not without problems of accuracy and reliability. Nevertheless, the use of alternative data sources can enhance the field.

A potential source of valuable data that has been underutilized is the open-ended self-report, either done with interviews or questionnaires. A problem with the usual closed-ended (e.g., summated rating scale) approach is that the researcher defines what the important variables might be. The open-ended approach allows not only for a richer view of the phenomenon of interest, but also for the participant to define what is important. This can be particularly valuable as a first step in developing new constructs, based not on the researcher's hunches about what might be an important variable, but on the participants who are the target of study. Closed-ended measures can be developed based on the results of preliminary open-ended studies.

Another issue that is in need of attention concerns the distinction between the objective work environment and people's subjective perceptions of it. Job stress models and theories have not always clearly distinguished the objective from the subjective, and interpretations of what self-report measures are presumed to assess have sometimes been unclear. Many of the instruments discussed in this chapter assess rather abstract psychosocial features of the work environment that can be difficult to objectively define. It should come as no surprise that convergent validities between sources for many stressor measures are rather poor. For example, Spector et al. (1988) found convergent validities for seven job stressors ranging from a nonsignificant $-.08$ for role ambiguity to a .83 for hours worked per week. Greater attention to writing concrete and factual items for job stressors might well produce instruments that yield better correspondence between objective work features and subjective perceptions, thus potentially better illuminating the effects that jobs themselves have on employee health and well-being.

The job stress area has been rapidly expanding over the past decade or so and is becoming one of the major areas of study within industrial/organizational psychology. There is perhaps too much reliance on ad hoc measures in cases where preexisting instruments are easily available. This chapter provides information about many such instruments, but it is certainly not an exhaustive list. Furthermore, as a fairly new field of study, job stress is at a stage where construct and instrument development are quite important. Additional instruments and methods will certainly continue to be devised.

# REFERENCES

Adelmann, P.K. (1987). Occupational complexity, control, and personal income: Their relation to psychological well-being in men and women. *Journal of Applied Psychology, 72,* 529–537.

Andersson, L.M., & Pearson, C.M. (1999). Tit for tat? The spiraling effect of incivility in the workplace. *Academy of Management Review, 24,* 452–471.

Beck, A.T., Ward, C.H., Mendelson, M., Mock, J., & Erbaugh, J. (1961). An inventory for measuring depression. *Archives of General Psychiatry, 4,* 561–571.

Beehr, T.A., Walsh, J.T., & Taber, T.D. (1976). Relationship of stress to individually and organizationally valued states: Higher order needs as a moderator. *Journal of Applied Psychology, 61,* 41–47.

Bennett, R.J., & Robinson, S.L. (2000). Development of a measure of workplace deviance. *Journal of Applied Psychology, 85,* 349–360.

Berkman, P.L. (1971). Measurement of mental health in a general population survey. *American Journal of Epidemiology, 94,* 105–111.

Borofsky, G.L. (2000). Predicting involuntary dismissal for unauthorized absence, lateness, and poor performance in the selection of unskilled and semiskilled British contract factory operatives: The contribution of the Employee Reliability Inventory. *Psychological Reports, 87,* 95–104.

Breaugh, J.A. (1985). The measurement of work autonomy. *Human Relations, 38,* 551–570.

Breaugh, J.A. (1989). The work autonomy scales: Additional validity evidence. *Human Relations, 42,* 1033–1056.

Breaugh, J.A (1998). The development of a new measure of global work autonomy. *Educational and Psychological Measurement, 58,* 119–128.

Bültmann, T., de Vries, M., Beurskens, A.J.H.M., Bleijenberg, G., Vercoulen, J.H.M.M., & Kant, I. (2000). Measurement of prolonged fatigue in the working population: Determination of a cutoff point for the checklist individual strength. *Journal of Occupational Health Psychology, 5,* 411–416.

Caplan, R.D., Cobb, S., French, J.R.P., van Harrison, R., & Pinneau, S.R. (1975). *Job demands and worker health: Main effects and occupational differences.* Washington, DC: National Institute for Occupational Safety and Health.

Cooper, C.L., Sloan, S.J., & Williams, S. (1988). *Occupational Stress Indicator.* Windsor, England: NFER-Nelson.

Cox, T. (1978). *Stress.* Baltimore: University Park Press.

Cortina, L.M., Magley, V.J., Williams, J.H., & Langhout, R.D. (2001). Incivility in the workplace: Incidence and impact. *Journal of Occupational Health Psychology, 6,* 64–80.

Derogatis, L.R., Lipman, R.S., Rickels, K., Uhlenhuth, E.H., & Covi, L. (1974). The Hopkins Symptom Checklist (HSCL): A self-report symptom inventory. *Behavioral Science, 19,* 1–15.

Dwyer, D.J., & Ganster, D.C. (1991). The effects of job demands and control on employee attendance and satisfaction. *Journal of Organizational Behavior, 12,* 595–608.

Eliot, R.S. (1979). *Stress and the major cardiovascular disorders.* New York: Futura Publishing.

Fox, S., & Spector, P.E. (1999). A model of work frustration—aggression. *Journal of Organizational Behavior, 20,* 915–931.

Fox, S., Spector, P.E., & Van Katwyk, P.T. (1997, April 11–13). *The structure and dimensions of perceived control.* Paper presented at the annual meeting of the Society for Industrial and Organizational Psychology, St. Louis, MO.

Frankenhaeuser, M. (1975). Experimental approach to the study of catecholamines and emotion. In L. Levi (Ed.), *Emotions, their parameters and measurement* (pp. 209–234). New York: Raven Press.

Frese, M., & Zapf, D. (1988). Methodological issues in the study of work stress: Objective vs. subjective measurement of work stress and the question of longitudinal studies. In C.L. Cooper & R. Payne (Eds.), *Causes, coping and consequences of stress at work* (pp. 375–410). Chichester, England: Wiley.

Frese, M., & Zapf, D. (1999). On the importance of the objective environment in stress and attribution theory. Counterpoint to Perrewé and Zellars. *Journal of Organizational Behavior, 20,* 761–765.

Fried, Y., Rowland, K.M., & Ferris, G.R. (1984). The physiological measurement of work stress: A critique. *Personnel Psychology, 37,* 583–615.

Ganster, D.C. (1989a). Worker control and well-being; A review of research in the workplace. In S. Sauter, J. Hurrell, & C. Cooper (Eds.), *Job control and worker health* (pp. 3–24). Chichester, England: Wiley.

Ganster, D.C. (1989b). *Measurement and worker control.* Final Report to the National Institute for Occupational Safety and Health, Contract No. 88–79187.

Glick, W.H., Jenkins, G.D. Jr., & Gupta, N. (1986). Method versus substance: How strong are underlying relationships between job characteristics and attitudinal outcomes? *Academy of Management Journal, 29,* 441–464.

Goldberg, D.P., & Williams, P. (1988). *A user's guide to the General Health Questionnaire.* Windsor, England: NFER-Nelson.

Greenberg, L., & Barling, J. (1999). Predicting employee aggression against coworkers, subordinates and supervisors: The roles of person behaviors and perceived workplace factors. *Journal of Organizational Behavior, 20,* 897–913.

Hackman, J.R., & Oldham, G.R (1975). Development of the Job Diagnostic Survey. *Journal of Applied Psychology, 60,* 159–170.

Hoel, H., Rayner, C., & Cooper, C.L. (1999). Workplace bullying. In C.L. Cooper & I.T. Robertson (Eds.), *International review of industrial and organizational psychology 1999* (Vol. 14, pp. 195–230). Chichester, England: Wiley.

Idaszak, J.R., & Drasgow, F. (1987). A revision of the Jog Diagnostic Survey: Elimination of a measurement artifact. *Journal of Applied Psychology, 72,* 69–74.

Ironson, G.H., Smith, P.C., Brannick, M.T., Gibson, W.M., & Paul, K.B. (1989). Constitution of a Job in General scale: A comparison of global, composite, and specific measures. *Journal of Applied Psychology, 74,* 193–200.

Jackson, P.R., Wall, T.D., Martin, R., & Davids, K. (1993). New measures of job control, cognitive demand, and production responsibility. *Journal of Applied Psychology, 78,* 753–762.

Jex, S.M., & Beehr, T.A. (1991). Emerging theoretical and methodological issues in the study of work-related stress. *Research in Personnel and Human Resources Management, 9,* 311–365.

Johnson, J.V. (1989). Control, collectivity and the psychosocial work environment. In S.L. Sauter, J.J. Hurrell, & C.L. Cooper (Eds.), *Job control and worker health* (pp. 55–74). Chichester, England: Wiley.

Johnson, J.V., & Hall, E.M. (1988). Job strain, work place social support, and cardiovascular disease: a cross-sectional study of a random sample of the Swedish working population. *American Journal of Public Health, 78,* 1336–1342.

Kahn, R., Wolfe, D., Quinn, R., Snoek, J.D., & Rosenthal, R. (1964). *Organizational stress: Studies in role conflict and ambiguity.* New York: Wiley.

Karasek, R.A. (1979). Job demands, job decision latitude, and mental strain: Implications for job redesign. *Administrative Science Quarterly, 24,* 285–308.

Karasek, R.A., (1985). *Job Content Instrument: questionnaire and user's guide.* Los Angeles: University of Southern California.

Karasek, R.A., Brisson, C., Kawakami, N., Houtman, I., Bongers, P., & Amick, B. (1998). The Job Content Questionnaire (JCQ): An instrument for internationally comparative assessments of psychosocial job characteristics. *Journal of Occupational Health Psychology, 3,* 322–355.

Karasek, R.A., & Theorell, T. (1990). *Healthy work: stress, productivity, and the reconstruction of working life.* New York: Basic Books.

Keenan, A., & Newton, T.J. (1985). Stressful events, stressors, and psychological strains in young professional engineers. *Journal of Occupational Behavior, 6,* 151–156.

Klein, H.J., & Kim, J.S. (1998). A field study of the influence of situational constraints, leader-member exchange, and goal commitment on performance. *Academy of Management Journal, 41,* 88–95.

Leymann, H. (1990). *Presentation av LIPT Formuläret: Konstruktion, validering, utfall* (Presentation of the LIPT Questionnaire: Construction, Validation and Outcome). Violen inom Praktikertjanst, Stockholm.

Liu, C., Spector, P.E., & Jex, S.M. (2001). *The relation of job control and complexity with job strains: A comparison of multiple data sources.* Unpublished paper, University of South Florida, Tampa.

Lyons, T.F. (1971). Role clarity, need for clarity, satisfaction, tension, and withdrawal. *Organizational Behavior and Human Performance, 6,* 99–110.

Mathieu, J.E., Tannenbaum, S.I., & Salas, E. (1992). Influences of individual and situational characteristics on measures of training effectiveness. *Academy of Management Journal, 35,* 828–847.

McCormick, E.J., Jeanneret, P.R., & Mecham, R.C. (1972). A study of job characteristics and job dimensions as based on the Position Analysis Questionnaire (PAQ). *Journal of Applied Psychology, 56,* 347–368.

McQuade, W., & Aikman, A. (1974). *Stress, what it is, what it can do to your health, how to fight back.* New York: Bantam Book.

Melamed, S., Ben-Avi, I., Luz, J., & Green, M.S. (1995). Objective and subjective work monotony: Effects on job satisfaction, psychological distress, and absenteeism in blue-collar workers. *Journal of Applied Psychology, 80,* 29–42.

Meyer, J.P., Allen, N.J., & Smith, C.A. (1993). Commitment to organizations and occupations: Extension and test of a three-component conceptualization. *Journal of Applied Psychology, 78,* 538–551.

Morse, D.R., & Furst, M.L. (1979). *Stress for success: A holistic approach to stress and its management.* New York: Van Nostrand Reinhold.

Mowday, R.T., Steers, R.M., & Porter, L.W. (1979). The measurement of organizational commitment. *Journal of Vocational Behavior, 14,* 224–247.

Newton, T.J., & Keenan, A. (1985). Coping with work-related stress. *Human Relations, 2,* 107–126.

NFER-Nelson. (2001). *General Health Questionnaire* [Online]. Retrieved August 3, 2001, from http://www.nfer-nelson.co.uk/ghq/index.htm.

Osipow, S.H. (1998). *Occupational Stress Inventory-Revised (OSI-R).* Odessa, FL: Psychological Assessment Resources.

Osipow, S.H., & Spokane, A.R. (1983). *Manual for measures of occupational stress, strain, and coping (Form E-2).* Columbus, OH: Marathon Consulting Press.

Paget, K.J., Lang, D.L., & Shultz, K.S. (1998). Development and validation of an employee absenteeism scale. *Psychological Reports, 82,* 1144–1146.

Perrewé, P.L., & Zellars, K.L. (1999). An examination of attributions and emotions in the transactional approach to the organizational stress process. *Journal of Organizational Behavior, 20,* 739–752.

Peters, L.H., & O'Connor, E.J. (1980). Situational constraints and work outcomes: The influences of a frequently overlooked construct. *Academy of Management Review, 5,* 391–397.

Peters, L.H., O'Connor, E.J., & Rudolf, C.J. (1980). The behavioral and affective consequences of performance-relevant situational variables. *Organizational Behavior and Human Performance, 25,* 79–96.

Probst, T.M. (2000). Wedded to the job: Moderating effects of job involvement on the consequences of job insecurity. *Journal of Occupational Health Psychology, 5,* 63–73.

Radloff, L. (1977). The CES-D scale for research in the general population. *Applied Psychological Measurement, 1,* 385–401.

Resource Systems. (2001). *The Pressure Management Indicator* [Online]. Retrieved July 20, 2001, from http://www.stressweb.com/pmi.htm.

Rick, J., Briner, R.B., Daniels, K., Perryman, S., & Guppy, A. (2001). *A critical review of psychosocial hazard measures.* Contract Research Report 356/2001. Brighton, England: Institute for Employment Studies for the Health and Safety Executive, University of Sussex.

Rizzo, J.R., House R.J., & Lirtzman, S.I. (1970). Role conflict and ambiguity in complex organizations. *Administrative Science Quarterly, 15,* 150–163.

Schaubroeck, J. (1999). Should the subjective be the objective? On studying mental processes, coping behavior, and actual exposures in organizational stress research. *Journal of Organizational Behavior, 20,* 753–760.

Schnake, M.E. (1983). An empirical assessment of the effects of affective response in the measurement of organizational climate. *Personnel Psychology, 36,* 791–807.

Shaw, J.B., & Riskind, J.H. (1983). Predicting job stress using data from the Position Analysis Questionnaire. *Journal of Applied Psychology, 68,* 253–261.

Skarlicki, D.P., & Folger, R. (1997). Retaliation in the workplace: The roles of distributive, procedural, and interactional justice. *Journal of Applied Psychology, 82,* 434–443.

Smith, C.S., Tisak, J., Hahn, S.E., & Schmieder, R.A. (1997). The measurement of job control. *Journal of Organizational Behavior, 18,* 225–237.

Smith, C.S., Tisak, J., & Schmieder, R.A. (1993). The measurement properties of the role conflict and role ambiguity scales: A review and extension of the empirical research. *Journal of Organizational Behavior, 14,* 37–48.

Smith, P.C., Kendall, L.M., & Hulin, C.L. (1969). *Measurement of satisfaction in work and retirement.* Chicago: Rand McNally.

Spector, P.E. (1986). Perceived control by employees: A meta-analysis of studies concerning autonomy and participation at work. *Human Relations, 39,* 1005–1016.

Spector, P.E. (1994). Using self-report questionnaires in OB research: A comment on the use of a controversial method. *Journal of Organizational Behavior, 15,* 385–392.

Spector, P.E. (2000). *Industrial and organizational psychology: Research and practice* (2nd ed.). New York: Wiley.

Spector, P.E. (in press). Individual differences in health and well-being in organizations. In D.A. Hofmann & L.E. Tetrick (Eds.). *Individual and organizational health.* San Francisco: Jossey-Bass.

Spector, P.E., Dwyer, D.J., & Jex, S.M. (1988). The relationship of job stressors to affective, health, and performance outcomes: A comparison of multiple data sources. *Journal of Applied Psychology, 73,* 11–19.

Spector, P.E., Fox, S., & Van Katwyk, P.T. (2000). Development of the Factual Autonomy Scale, FAS. Unpublished manuscript, University of South Florida, Tampa.

Spector, P.E., & Jex, S.M. (1991). Relations of job characteristics from multiple data sources with employee affect, absence, turnover intentions and health. *Journal of Applied Psychology, 76,* 46–53.

Spector, P.E., & Jex, S.M. (1998). Development of four self-report measures of job stressors and strain: Interpersonal Conflict at Work Scale, Organizational Constraints Scale, Quantitative Workload Inventory, and Physical Symptoms Inventory. *Journal of Occupational Health Psychology, 3*(4), 356–367.

Spielberger, C.D. (1979). *Preliminary manual for the State-Trait Personality Inventory (STPI).* Unpublished manuscript. University of South Florida, Tampa.

Spielberger, C.D. (1999). *STAXI-2 State-Trait Anger Expression Inventory-2 professional manual*. Odessa, FL: Psychological Assessment Resources.

Spielberger, C.D., & Reheiser, E.C. (1994). Job stress in university, corporate, and military personnel. *International Journal of Stress Management, 1,* 19–31.

Trice, A.D., & Tillapaugh, P. (1991). Children's estimates of their parents' job satisfaction. *Psychological Reports, 69,* 63–66.

U.S. Department of Labor. (1977). *Dictionary of occupational titles* (4th ed.). Washington, DC: U.S. Government Printing Office.

U.S. Department of Labor (1998). *Occupational Information Network, O\*NET* [Online]. Retrieved June 23, 1998, from http://www.doleta.gov/prgrams/onet.

Vagg, P.R., & Spielberger, C.D. (1998). Occupational stress: Measuring job pressure and organizational support in the workplace. *Journal of Occupational Health Psychology, 3*(4), 294–305.

Van der Doef, M., & Maes, S. (1999). The Leiden Quality of Work Questionnaire: Its construction, factor structure, and psychometric qualities. *Psychological Reports, 85,* 954–962.

Van Katwyk, P.T., Fox, S., Spector, P.E., & Kelloway, E.K. (2000). Using the Job-Related Affective Well-Being Scale (JAWS) to investigate affective responses to work stressors. *Journal of Occupational Health Psychology, 5,* 219–230.

Van Veldhoven, M., & Meijman, T. (1994). *Het meten van Psychosociale arbeidsbelasting.* [The measurement of psychosocial job demands]. Amsterdam: Nederlands Instituut voor Arbeidsomstandigheden.

Van Yperen, N.W., & Snijders, T.A.B. (2000). A multilevel analysis of the demands-control model: Is stress at work determined by factors at the group level or the individual level? *Journal of Occupational Health Psychology, 5,* 182–190.

Veit, C.T., & Ware, J.E. Jr. (1983). The structure of psychological distress and well-being in general populations. *Journal of Counseling and Clinical Psychology, 51,* 730–742.

Watson, D., Clark, L.A., & Tellegen, A. (1988). Development and validation of brief measures of positive and negative affect: The PANAS scales. *Journal of Personality and Social Psychology, 54,* 1063–1070.

Weiner, H. (1979). *Psychobiology of essential hypertension.* New York: Elsevier.

Weiss, D.J., Dawis, R., Lofquist, L.H., & England, G.W. (1966). *Instrumentation for the theory of work adjustment.* (Minnesota Studies in Vocational Rehabilitation: XXI). University of Minnesota, Minneapolis.

Williams, S., & Cooper, C.L. (1998). Measuring occupational stress: Development of the Pressure Management Indicator. *Journal of Occupational Health Psychology, 3,* 306–321.

Yukl, G.A. (1981). *Leadership in organizations.* Englewood Cliffs, NJ: Prentice Hall.

Zapf, D., Dormann, C., & Frese, M. (1996). Longitudinal studies in organizational stress research: A review of the literature with reference to methodological issues. *Journal of Occupational Health Psychology, 1,* 145–169.

Zapf, D., Knorz, C., & Kulla, M. (1996). On the relationship between mobbing factors, and job content, social work environment, and health outcomes. *European Journal of Work and Organizational Psychology, 5,* 215–237.

# CHAPTER 26

# Job Satisfaction

RENE V. DAWIS

## SATISFACTION

The English word *satisfaction* comes from the Latin *satis* ("enough") and *facere* ("to make"), hence the dictionary definitions: (1) to fulfill the needs, expectations, wishes, or desires of; (2) to meet or answer the requirements of. There are, then, two basic definitions of satisfaction: satisfaction as fulfillment versus satisfaction as evaluation. In the first definition, a deficit of some sort exists, and its being filled is satisfaction. In the second definition, rather than deficits, criteria (requirements) must be met, and their being met is satisfaction.

Psychologists' usual understanding of the term embraces both dictionary definitions. However, to psychologists, it is the *affect* experienced when one's needs, expectations, wishes, desires, or requirements are perceived as being fulfilled or met that is termed satisfaction. Locke (1976), for example, defines job satisfaction as "a pleasurable or positive emotional state resulting from the appraisal of one's (job) experiences" (p. 1300). Thus, at a minimum, the psychological construct satisfaction has two components: a cognitive component (the perception that one's needs, etc. are fulfilled), and an affective component (the feeling that accompanies the cognition).

## SATISFACTION IN PSYCHOLOGICAL THEORY

Satisfaction was first used as a construct in psychological theory by the pioneering psychologist, E.L. Thorndike, who formulated the famous law of effect (Thorndike, 1911). According to this law, when several responses are made to the same situation, those that are accompanied or closely followed by satisfaction will be more firmly connected with the situation, such that when the situation recurs, those responses will be more likely to recur. Conversely, those responses that are accompanied or closely followed by dissatisfaction will have their connections with that situation weakened, such that when the situation recurs, those responses will be less likely to occur. And the greater the satisfaction or dissatisfaction, the greater will be the strengthening or weakening of this stimulus-response (S-R) bond. Satisfaction or its negative, dissatisfaction, is the "effect" that is responsible for the strengthening or weakening of the S-R bond.

Although the law of effect had a great impact on the science and stimulated much research and theory, the construct satisfaction ran into problems with the positivistic stance of the times. Thorndike (and others who followed him) failed to produce a satisfactory operational definition of satisfaction. There seemed to be no adequate way to measure satisfaction

470

objectively; in particular, responding to a questionnaire was not deemed objective enough to be acceptable to the behaviorists. Hence, satisfaction was thought to be too problematic a theoretical construct for a field that was struggling to gain acceptability as an objective science. As a solution, behavior theorists dropped the construct altogether, in favor of attributing the strengthening or weakening of the S-R bond either to the observable antecedents and/or consequences of the response.

Fortunately, with the reemergence of cognitive theory in the 1950s, the way was paved for the reintroduction of the construct into psychological theorizing. Ironically, satisfaction reappeared in the theorizing not of basic psychology but of applied psychology.

## SATISFACTION IN APPLIED PSYCHOLOGY: JOB SATISFACTION

Although it was banished from the laboratory and from behavior theory, satisfaction continued to be used in applied psychology. To applied psychologists, satisfaction, in particular, job satisfaction, was not just an existent part of reality; it was an *important* aspect of reality that had to be dealt with. Applied psychologists were not as concerned about the theoretical status of job satisfaction as they were about its operational definition, that is, its measurement. If the only way to measure job satisfaction were through questionnaire responses, so be it—such measurement would suffice for the purposes of applied psychology, provided it met the psychometric requirements of reliability and validity. As it turned out, such questionnaire-response measures of job satisfaction proved to be more than merely adequate for the purposes of applied psychology. As Roznowski and Hulin (1992) put it, "the usefulness of measures of g prior to organizational entry is paralleled by the usefulness of measures of job satisfaction after organizational entry" (p. 125).

Studies of job satisfaction by applied psychologists appeared as early as the 1910s (e.g., Munsterberg [1913] found that, contrary to conventional wisdom, not all workers were dissatisfied with monotonous, repetitive jobs!). The first comprehensive treatment of the topic was given by Hoppock (1935) in his book, *Job Satisfaction.* In a series of studies using his now classic questionnaire measure of job satisfaction, Hoppock found that, even in the middle of the Great Depression, more people were satisfied with their jobs than he expected—at least two thirds of those he surveyed. He also reported on the correlates of job satisfaction, such as sex, age, and occupational level.

At about the same time Hoppock was doing his studies, Elton Mayo and his associates were conducting a series of groundbreaking social experiments now known as the Hawthorne Studies (Roethlisberger & Dickson, 1939). These studies probed into the causes of job dissatisfaction, finding these in the human interrelationships and interactions at work, and pointing out the fact that the motivation to work was not wholly economic, even in the unusual period of the Depression. An important offshoot of the Hawthorne Studies was the human relations movement in industry.

Hoppock's work inspired a large number of job satisfaction studies, typically with job satisfaction as the dependent variable studied as a function of demographic variables. The number of such studies grew to such an extent that they became the subject of annual reviews (e.g., Hoppock & Robinson, 1949; Robinson, 1953). In the 1950s, national polling organizations such as Gallup and the National Opinion Research Center began including job satisfaction questions in their surveys of social indicators.

All this time, researchers never questioned the assumption that job satisfaction was related to the motivation to work. The big question of the day was whether job satisfaction was to be measured as global—as an indivisible whole (Hoppock's position)—or whether its correct measurement required the use and summation of specific satisfactions, satisfaction with the various aspects or facets of work.

In the mid-1950s, a study appeared that would startle applied psychologists and especially job satisfaction researchers. Brayfield and Crockett's (1955) survey of the literature found little evidence that would link job attitudes (in particular, job satisfaction) with job performance. They estimated that, across the available cross-sectional studies, the average correlation of job satisfaction and job performance was low, not much higher than .10. This went counter to conventional wisdom.

At about the same time, Herzberg, Mausner, Petersen, and Capwell (1957) undertook a comprehensive survey of the job satisfaction literature and wound up proposing a controversial theory. (Up to this time, applied psychologists had been empirical pragmatists with little interest in theory.) Herzberg proposed that the causes of job satisfaction and job dissatisfaction differed, the former being influenced by job content ("motivator") factors and the latter by job context ("hygiene") factors (Herzberg, Mausner, & Snyderman, 1959). The Herzberg theory spawned literally hundreds of research studies—searching for hygiene factors (also called dissatisfiers) and motivators (satisfiers) and confirming, refuting, modifying, or reformulating the original Herzberg theory.

A decade after Herzberg, another controversial theory appeared: Vroom's (1964) valence-instrumentality-expectancy (VIE) theory of work motivation, in which was nested a theory of job satisfaction. In VIE theory, job satisfaction (more precisely, "anticipated job satisfaction") is the "valence" (importance) of the job, which in turn is a function of the valences of other outcomes (e.g., lifestyle) and the "instrumentality" of the job in attaining these outcomes. In effect, Vroom asserted that it was the expectation of what was to come that determined job satisfaction. As with Herzberg, many studies were conducted to confirm, refute, modify, or reformulate Vroom's controversial theory.

Following Vroom, applied psychologists began exploring work motivation in more detail. Job satisfaction theory became enmeshed with work motivation theory. Besides expectancy theory, there appeared need-fulfillment theory, equity theory, goal-setting theory, intrinsic motivation theory, even behavioral theory. Researchers also became interested in constructs collateral with job satisfaction, such as job involvement and organizational commitment. Before Herzberg and Vroom, applied psychologists were mainly interested in establishing empirical facts based on painstakingly accumulated data. After Herzberg and Vroom, the interest shifted to proposing carefully conceived theories and testing them rigorously, that is, with data.

Even as Herzberg and Vroom ushered in an era of theory building and theory testing, applied psychologists did not altogether neglect the study of job satisfaction itself and its practical consequences. Job satisfaction was studied as a function of demographic variables, performance, comparison level, need fulfillment, and person-environment fit, to name the more popular foci. Its relation to job performance remained a vital topic. Its consequences for work (such as for adjustment, withdrawal, aggression, relations with supervisor and coworkers) and consequences for life (personal adjustment, family life) became important areas of research. There was even spirited debate over whether or not job dissatisfaction was increasing because of the "dehumanization of work" (U.S. Department of Labor, 1974). Consequently, the number of job satisfaction studies escalated from the mere hundreds to the thousands.

In 1987, a conference of leading job satisfaction researchers took place at Bowling Green State University to survey what was then known about job satisfaction, to evaluate this literature, and to propose new directions for job satisfaction research. The papers read at this conference were compiled into a landmark book by Cranny, Smith, and Stone (1992). This book should be a "must" starting point for all researchers who want to study the subject.

## THEORIES OF JOB SATISFACTION

One lesson learned from the various controversies in job satisfaction research is that the research findings are very much contingent on the measures used. But there is a circularity about all this, because we find that the measures that have been developed depend, in turn, on the theory of job satisfaction espoused by the researcher. In fact, many measures of job satisfaction were "tailored" to meet the theoretical requirements of the researcher. Thus, before the measurement of job satisfaction can be discussed, it is important that we first survey the range of theory in job satisfaction, because in this field, theory directs measurement.

### Job Satisfaction as Global Versus Specific

Hoppock's (1935) main thesis was that job satisfaction could only be studied as an indivisible whole, in global form, so to speak. Hoppock would concede that many components—or a few, or even only one component—may go into job satisfaction, but the number of components would differ from person to person, and the weight assigned to any particular component would also differ from person to person. Therefore, Hoppock believed, it would be futile to ascertain these varying and differently weighted components for different individuals, and consequently, that only the level of job satisfaction can be ascertained across persons.

Although Hoppock was highly regarded by all, several job satisfaction researchers broke ranks with him, taking a more analytic view of the phenomenon. These researchers (who do not gainsay the usefulness of global job satisfaction) believed that identifying and measuring specific facets of job satisfaction promised to provide even more potential in the study of work motivation. Both the Cornell group (Smith, Kendall, & Hulin, 1969) and the Minnesota group (Weiss, Dawis, England, & Lofquist, 1967) opted for the specific-facet approach in developing their well-known instruments, the Job Descriptive Index (JDI) by the former, and the Minnesota Satisfaction Questionnaire (MSQ) by the latter.

### Job Satisfaction as Separate from Job Dissatisfaction

Most people would assume that job dissatisfaction is the opposite of job satisfaction, that both lie on the same dimension with the latter on the positive end and the former on the negative end. This is why Herzberg's thesis that job satisfaction and job dissatisfaction are two separate phenomena was met with huge controversy. Herzberg drew from Maslow's (1954) theory of motivation, which stipulated a hierarchy of needs and the principle of prepotency (the lower order need is prepotent to the higher order need). Maslow's hierarchy of needs consists of (from the bottom up): physiological needs, safety (security) needs, belongingness and love needs, esteem needs (including need for mastery/achievement and need for recognition/approval), and the need for self-actualization.

As Herzberg (and Maslow) pointed out, the filling of lower order needs results not so much in satisfaction, but rather, in deferring dissatisfaction. Because a lower order need does not stay filled, the recurring need will bring back dissatisfaction until the need is filled again. Thus, fulfillment of lower order needs does not result in true satisfaction. Only the fulfillment of higher order needs, especially the self-actualization need, will bring about true satisfaction.

Using the "critical incidents" technique (remindful of today's focus group method), Herzberg, Mausner, and Snyderman (1959) identified the following job factors as implicated in job dissatisfaction: salary, interpersonal relations with superiors, interpersonal relations with coworkers, technical aspects of supervision, company policy and administration, and working conditions. The following factors were associated with job satisfaction: achievement, recognition, the work itself, responsibility, and advancement. Clearly, the former factors pertain to job context, whereas the latter pertain to job content. The former appear to be factors extrinsic to the job, and the latter, intrinsic to the job.

Perhaps the main question of the controversy that swirled around Herzberg's theory was which factors were satisfiers and which were dissatisfiers. When methods other than the critical incidents technique were used, conflicting results were obtained. The burden of later and more carefully designed studies (e.g., correcting for the "social desirability" response tendency; Dunnette, Campbell, & Hakel, 1967) was that *both* intrinsic and extrinsic factors appeared to be associated with *both* job satisfaction and job dissatisfaction, depending on what was important to the individual.

The negative results that researchers obtained on Herzberg's theory notwithstanding, an important application of the theory was the approach called "job enrichment." This approach gave rise to several then-innovative but now commonplace techniques such as: increasing worker responsibility and autonomy, providing recognition for job accomplishment, developing work modules (vs. the assembly-line technique of breaking up the overarching work task into minute, repetitive parts), and increasing worker participation in decision making.

A development that was favorable for Herzberg's theory was research in the personality area that supported a two-factor model of emotionality or affectivity. For example, Tellegen (1985) showed in a series of careful studies that

Positive Emotionality is separate from Negative Emotionality. Two of the Big Five factors of personality structure (Digman, 1990) parallel Tellegen's findings: Extraversion/Introversion is equivalent to Positive Emotionality, and Neuroticism versus Emotional Stability is equivalent to Negative Emotionality. It seemed commonsensical that job satisfaction would be associated with positive emotions and job dissatisfaction with negative emotions.

## Job Satisfaction as Need Fulfillment

Another commonsense notion is that satisfaction and need are linked concepts, that "need" implies something to be "satisfied," that there is no "satisfaction" unless there were a prior "need." Several theories of job satisfaction have been based on psychological theories that revolve around the construct of needs. For example, Schaffer (1953), borrowing from Murray (1938), proposed a theory of job satisfaction in terms of need satisfaction. Herzberg (Herzberg et al., 1959) based his two-factor theory of job satisfaction on Maslow's need theory of motivation. The Minnesota group (Weiss, et al., 1967) used Schaffer's study as the starting point in their development of the MSQ; for them, as with Schaffer, job satisfaction consisted of the satisfaction of various work needs.

Ever since Murray (1938), the concept of need has had a checkered history in psychology, alternately falling in and out of favor. Part of the problem has been the definition of need. The concept of psychological need was patterned after that of biological need, which has a solid standing in science. But unlike its older exemplar, which can be defined with sufficient precision, psychological needs defy easy definition. This definitional problem has led some (e.g., Salancik & Pfeffer, 1977) to question the usefulness of need-fulfillment theories of job satisfaction (but see Stone's [1992] defense of the construct).

The Minnesota group resolved the definitional problem by defining needs straightforwardly as workers' reinforcer requirements, where "reinforcer" refers to any well-defined condition that will help maintain or increase work behavior. To identify reinforcers, the Minnesota group asked workers what conditions were important for them to have in their jobs (for which purpose the Minnesota group developed the *Minnesota Importance Questionnaire* [MIQ; Rounds, Henly, Dawis, Lofquist, & Weiss, 1981], which became their measure of needs).

However defined, a need will have varying strengths for different persons, and different needs will have varying strengths for the same person. Hence, two needs may be equally fulfilled, yet one may be more important to the person than the other. The person's job satisfaction will depend more on the fulfillment of the first need than the second need. Conversely, when there is equal lack of fulfillment, job dissatisfaction will be greater for the first need than the second. The strength of the need is therefore an important datum. How to measure need strength, however, is a problem.

Need fulfillment can also be construed from the viewpoint of person-environment-fit theory (Dawis, 1992). In this view, needs are person variables, and reinforcers are environment variables. Commensurate measurement enables the direct assessment of "P-E fit." This assessment then becomes the principal variable that is used to account for job satisfaction.

## Job Satisfaction as Value Fulfillment

This is a variant of job satisfaction as need fulfillment. Locke (1976), for one, viewed job satisfaction as resulting from the perception that the job fulfills, or will allow the fulfillment of, the worker's values, providing that such values are consistent with the worker's needs. Locke distinguished between needs—what one requires for survival and well-being—and values—what one consciously or subconsciously desires, wants, or seeks to attain. Needs are objective and innate, whereas values are subjective and learned (acquired). In Locke's view, the ultimate adaptive function of values is to direct a person's actions and choices so as to satisfy the person's needs; that is, value fulfillment functions in the service of need fulfillment.

Katzell (1964) similarly construed job satisfaction as a function of value fulfillment. Dissatisfaction is the result of the discrepancy between the amount of the stimulus experienced and the amount it is valued. Katzell differed from Locke by adopting an objective definition of value. To Katzell, value is the magnitude of the stimulus that evokes the most pleasurable affect.

The Minnesota group likewise construed job satisfaction as resulting from value fulfillment. In their theory of work adjustment (Dawis & Lofquist, 1984), value is defined as a second-order need or higher order need, both need and value being measured with the same instrument, the MIQ. Drawing a parallel from the relation of skill and ability (where ability is a factor in the factor analysis of skills), the Minnesota group construed value as a factor derived from the factor analysis of needs. They found that a six-factor structure fitted the data well and identified these values on the basis of need scale factor loadings as: Achievement, Altruism, Autonomy, Comfort, Safety, and Status. Multidimensional scaling of the six values yielded the following contrasts: Achievement versus Comfort, Status versus Altruism, and Safety versus Autonomy. Six reinforcer factors on the environment side corre-

sponded to the six values on the person side, thus enabling the evaluation of P-E fit for value fulfillment. Like need fulfillment, value fulfillment is seen as a major predictor of job satisfaction.

## Job Satisfaction as Expectation

In a manner of speaking, need theories of job satisfaction view present status as the result of what has happened in the past. By contrast, expectancy theories of job satisfaction view present status in terms of what is expected to happen in the future. Thus, for Vroom (1964), job satisfaction is based on the expectation of the job's effectiveness (instrumentality) in helping the worker attain desired outcomes such as a certain lifestyle. Vroom's VIE theory introduced three variables that have become important to consider in any psychology of work (or work behavior or work motivation). These are: (1) valence, or the importance to the person of varying outcomes, of which there are two kinds: first-level outcomes such as task completion or getting the job done, and second-level outcomes such as status or lifestyle; (2) instrumentality, or the effectiveness of means, such as the instrumentality of work performance in attaining first-level outcomes or the instrumentality of the job in attaining second-level outcomes; and (3) expectancy, or subjective probability, such as the expectancy of achieving first-level outcomes if one were to expend a certain amount of energy in performing the job. Thus, job satisfaction according to Vroom's model is the valence of the job, which in turn depends on the valences of various second-level outcomes multiplied by the instrumentality of the job in attaining these second-level outcomes. Although it is used, the term *anticipated job satisfaction* is not as correct as *job satisfaction based on anticipation,* that is, expectation.

Porter (1962, 1963) viewed job satisfaction as perceived need fulfillment. To operationalize his view, Porter developed a instrument with items based on Maslow's five needs and measured perceived need fulfillment as discrepancies in achieved versus expected levels of need fulfillment. This was accomplished through ratings on a 7-point scale in response to three questions asked of every item: "How much is there now?," "How much should there be?," and "How important is this to me?" The discrepancy score between the ratings for the first and second questions reflected the person's job satisfaction. Nowhere in the instrument is the respondent asked directly about job satisfaction. Porter believed that his indirect method avoided the problems of response tendencies. The data for the third question were used to rank-order the need categories, which in turn were used in testing Maslow's prepotency principle.

Schneider, Gunnarson, and Wheeler (1992) proposed a different expectancy variable: opportunity. In their view, job satisfaction is a function not only of what one has but also of what one has the opportunity to have. The mere perception that an opportunity is available can be satisfying.

### Job Satisfaction as Perception of Equity

Social comparison theory has been used to explain job satisfaction. In Adams's (1965) equity theory, a worker's ratio of outcomes to inputs is compared (by the respondent) with another person's outcome-to-input ratio. The other person is the respondent's "reference other," who could be a fellow worker, a neighbor, a relative, a friend, and so on—whomever the respondent would wish to be compared with. If the ratios are equal, the result is job satisfaction; otherwise, job dissatisfaction results, although with different consequences for positive and negative inequities. In a sense, the worker expects equity, and when this is not attained, the result is job dissatisfaction.

Smith, Kendall, and Hulin (1969) advanced a theory that incorporated equity, expectancy, and instrumentality. Job satisfaction, in their view, is the result of the perception of a difference between what is expected or aspired to and what is experienced. Key to their formulation was their notion of "frames of reference." These are internal standards that a person uses when evaluating the difference between expected and experienced. Frames of reference develop out of prior experience, conditioned by response set expectations and thresholds for change and anchored by a general adaptation level.

### Job Satisfaction Causes Job Performance

The human relations position of Elton Mayo and his associates was that job satisfaction was important, if not essential, to job performance and work productivity. Actually, in human relations theory, job satisfaction functions as a variable mediating between social relations (with supervisor, coworkers, management) on the one hand and performance and productivity on the other hand. This can be called the "satisfaction-causes-performance" hypothesis: that job performance depends on the worker's being satisfied; and conversely, that job performance will suffer if the worker is dissatisfied.

### Job Satisfaction Is Caused by Job Performance

This seemingly counterintuitive theory was proposed by Lawler and Porter (1967), who argued that job satisfaction was brought about by rewards, and rewards were produced by job performance. Therefore, it was job performance that caused job satisfaction, albeit indirectly, and not the other way around. Lawler and Porter added one more wrinkle to their theory: that the relation between rewards and satisfaction was moderated by the expectation of equitable rewards. That is, it was not rewards per se that caused job satisfaction, but rather the perception that the rewards were equitable. (See also Porter's perceived need-fulfillment theory discussed earlier. For a somewhat different model of the job-performance-to-job satisfaction relation, see Mahoney, 1981).

The seeming contradiction between the positions of Lawler-Porter and the human relations movement are the result of the scientific model that requires one dependent variable and one or more independent variables. If a systems model were used, both positions would be partly correct: The relation between the two constructs would be reciprocal; that is, job satisfaction causes job performance, which (through perceived equitable rewards) causes job satisfaction, which causes (motivates) job performance, and so on. Actually, this "contradiction" is just a variant of the old problem, "which causes which, attitude or behavior?"

Furthermore, there is a third view, which is that job satisfaction and job performance are not directly related at all but only indirectly, through the aegis of intervening variables. Katzell, Thompson, and Guzzo (1992) espoused this view.

### Job Satisfaction as Social Information Processing

Having rejected the need-fulfillment theory of job satisfaction, Salancik and Pfeffer (1978) proposed in its stead a social-information-processing theory that explains job satisfaction and dissatisfaction as the result of comparing oneself with others. They argued that job facets are not as important as the perceptions about how one is doing in relation to the other workers. Being pleased or displeased with job facets are attributions that have to be socially constructed. Thus, a worker on a new job cannot have any real basis for feeling satisfied or dissatisfied until the worker has observed similar individuals who are satisfied or dissatisfied.

### Job Satisfaction as Trigger for Work Adjustment

The Minnesota group had one more wrinkle to add to job satisfaction theory. They proposed a systems model of work adjustment in which job satisfaction/dissatisfaction serves like a thermostat that controls work behavior (Dawis & Lofquist, 1984). Job satisfaction results in the maintenance of work behavior. Job dissatisfaction is tolerated until a threshold is exceeded, which then triggers work adjustment behavior.

Work adjustment can be active (acting on the environment) or reactive (acting on self) to fill the unfilled needs and restore the state of job satisfaction or even just tolerable job dissatisfaction.

## Comment on the Theories

Applied psychology has had a strong tradition of empiricism, emphasizing the primacy of data. No theory would be entertained in applied psychology unless it was supported with data, and unless it could be subjected to empirical test by others. However, as an unintended consequence, this empirical tradition has led to the formulation of predominantly content theories of job satisfaction, because such theories are more amenable to testing by the cross-sectional, data-collection-at-one-time-point type of study that is familiar to applied psychologists. The overwhelming number of studies in the job satisfaction literature are of this type. Longitudinal studies are few and typically only of the two-time-points variety. Few attempts have been made to instrument temporal variables. When processes are incorporated in theories, they are represented by proxy status variables so they might be amenable to conventional data collection methodologies. Thus, a theory such as that advanced by Landy (1978) on an opponent process in job satisfaction, while interesting and stimulating, must be passed over because we cannot collect data on it. We may have theories that include process, but because we do not know how to collect data on process, we are reduced to observing the change in job satisfaction at two widely separated time points. Thus are our theories contingent on, and constrained by, our methodologies.

## THE MEASUREMENT OF JOB SATISFACTION

Job satisfaction can be measured in several ways. Measurement can be *direct* or *indirect*. Indirect measurement of job satisfaction takes the form of inference from the antecedents or the consequences of job satisfaction. Use of antecedents would require the controlled situation of the laboratory, and for that reason, no one has attempted to measure job satisfaction by using antecedent conditions. The use of consequences is more feasible. Job satisfaction (and dissatisfaction) has behavioral consequences such as smiling and being nice (for job satisfaction) or complaining and being hostile (for job dissatisfaction). Job satisfaction can be inferred from such consequences. However, applied psychologists have preferred to study the consequences of job satisfaction for their own sake (as consequences), and no one has used consequences to develop a measure of job satisfaction. Even if this were

done, an inferential measure of job satisfaction will still suffer from the logical onus of *modus tollens* ("p implies q" does not mean that "q implies p"). Thus, the indirect measurement of job satisfaction does not appear to hold much promise.

Direct measurement of job satisfaction can take two forms, *observed* and *expressed*. Measurement by observation can be done either physiologically or behaviorally. If job satisfaction is an affect, physiological measures of affect could conceivably be used to measure job satisfaction, but this possibility is easily ruled out as impractical. Behavioral observation is more practical but would require highly trained observers and psychometrically well-developed observational rating scales. Although feasible, this avenue of measurement has not been explored much.

This leaves us with measurement via expressions of job satisfaction. Expressed job satisfaction can occur in two forms: *emitted* or *elicited*. Emitted expressions of job satisfaction are unsolicited and spontaneous and may occur in the context of some verbal interchange, say, an interview. Because of their sporadic nature, emitted expressions are not good material for job satisfaction measures. All of the preceding contingencies explain why *all* published job satisfaction measures, current and past, are of the elicited, expressed, direct variety.

## Elicited Expressed Measures

Before discussing the different methods of constructing measures of elicited expressed job satisfaction, it is important to point out that all such measures depend on *self-disclosure* on the part of the respondent (Jourard, 1971). Self-disclosure is affected by two main factors: (1) the respondent's *ability* to self-disclose (the eliciting questions may not be understood by the respondent, i.e., worded beyond the comprehension of the respondent or in a language foreign to the respondent), and (2) the respondent's *motivation* to self-disclose (hence, the respondent should be encouraged, and conversely, should not be threatened). There is no foolproof way of verifying the veridicality of self-disclosure. We have no direct access to the consciousness of the respondent. The best we can do is (1) to ascertain the *self-consistency* of the respondent, hence the use of multiple items in measurement, and (2) to evaluate the *logical consistency* of job-satisfaction-measure scores with scores on other variables. The first process is the psychometric determination of *reliability*, and the second process, of *validity*.

Measures of elicited expressed job satisfaction are of two kinds, depending on the criterion used to select items for the measure: whether item selection is based on an *external criterion* (external to the items) or on an *internal criterion* (the items themselves provide the criterion).

An example of a job satisfaction measure constructed by using the external criterion method is the JDI (Smith et al., 1969). The external criterion for this measure was achieved by administering the initial pool of items under two experimental conditions: responding with respect to the best job one could think of, versus responding with respect to the worst job one could think of. Items were selected that discriminated between the two conditions. One could have accomplished the same objective by using a group of obviously satisfied workers in lieu of the "best job" condition, and a demographically comparable group of obviously dissatisfied workers for the "worst job" condition. Because the items are selected on the basis of demonstrated experience with the items, the external criterion method is also known as the *empirical* method. One virtue claimed for this method of selecting items is that the produced instrument is less obvious, that is, less susceptible to faking, hence more likely to be more valid.

Most other measures of elicited expressed job satisfaction are constructed with the use of an internal criterion, and these are of two kinds: those measures in which the items themselves are used as anchors for scale points (*scaled items*), and those in which the items are rated using a numerical scale (*rated items*). An example of a scaled-items measure is the Hoppock Job Satisfaction Blank (JSB; Hoppock, 1935). The JSB is composed of "items" (statements) in response to four questions (e.g., "How well do you like your job?"). Seven graded response statements make up the scale for each question. Hoppock assumed that these statements constituted rank-ordered steps on a continuum. However, there are scaling methods available to check out the assumption of unidimensionality and to select the items (statements) that conform to such a scale. The two best-known are the Thurstone method of scaling (Thurstone, 1928) and the Guttman method (Guttman, 1944).

The Thurstone method consists of having judges rate the position of items (statements) on an 11-point scale representing the attitudinal dimension of concern (e.g., job satisfaction). Items are selected on the basis of their average positional rating ("scale value") and the variability of ratings (the less variable, the better). Two items are selected to represent each of the 11 points on the scale (thus a Thurstone scale is recognizable by its comprising 22 items). Respondents are asked to check the item or items that most accurately reflect their current state. The score is the average scale value of the items chosen. Uhrbrock (1961) provided a useful list of scale values for 2,000 items.

The Guttman method requires the use of a "scalogram" in which the respondents are represented as rows and the items as columns (items are scored 0,1). A perfectly unidimensional scale is demonstrated by a scalogram in which, when items and respondents are arranged in order according to, respectively, item score (number of endorsements) and respondent score (number of items endorsed), a stepwise arrangement of both items and respondents results. In this "reproducible" scalogram, the items endorsed by a respondent can be predicted from the respondent's total score, and the respondents who endorse an item can be predicted from the item's endorsement score. Because this rarely happens, if ever, the quality of the item pool is indicated by a reproducibility coefficient that quantitatively indicates how well the item pool's scalogram reproduces the perfect scalogram. The obtained scalogram will allow the scale constructor to eliminate bad items, those that do not conform to the unidimensional pattern. Thus, the remaining items will constitute a near-unidimensional scale. In such a scale, each item carries a scale value, and items are rank-ordered in scale value. Respondents are asked to check all items they endorse, and the score is the highest scale value of the items endorsed. Also, the self-consistency of the respondent can be checked by examining the scale values of the items endorsed.

Although the mathematical treatment of both the Thurstone and Guttman methods of scale construction has reached a high level of sophistication, the use of these methods in scale construction practice has not been widespread for whatever reason. Perhaps it is difficult to obtain items that meet the rigorous psychometric criteria of these two methods. Discounting the JSB (which, although manifesting the characteristics of a Guttman scale, was not constructed by the Guttman method), I know of only one job satisfaction measure that has been constructed by the "scaled-items" methods. This is Brayfield and Rothe's (1951) Job Satisfaction Index, consisting of 18 items selected by the Thurstone method but presented in Likert format and scored accordingly (see the following section).

By far the most preferred type of measure of elicited, expressed job satisfaction is the rated-items measure, and to develop such measures, most researchers have turned to the Likert method. Likert (1932) discovered that highly reliable scales could be constructed by using "summated ratings" as an internal criterion for item selection. By using a 5-point scale and asking each respondent to rate each item (statement) on this scale, the item ratings could then be summed to constitute a total scale score, and this score could in turn be used to select the best items for the scale. Likert tried two methods: one, using groups that scored high on total score versus low on total score as criterion groups and calculating the mean item-score difference between the groups for each item (the larger the difference, the better the item); and the other, correlating item scores with total score (the higher the correlation, the better the item). Both methods produced similar results. The preferred method today is the second, using item-total-score correlation as the criterion for selecting the items.

Another procedure used nowadays is to factor-analyze the item pool and select items according to size of factor loading. The factor-analytic method is especially useful for those studying job satisfaction in its specific facets. Factor analysis can be used to validate the facets the researcher posits. Whether the item-total-score correlation method or the factor-analytic method is used, the results tend to be similar. It also turns out that total score (Likert's "summated ratings") is a good approximation of the first principal component of an item pool.

## Some Comments on Various Matters

Scale constructors invariably find that the first principal component in self-report item pools (such as job satisfaction items) is a general component, usually interpreted as a general response tendency. It has sometimes been labeled a "social desirability" tendency because most people tend to "lean" toward the socially desirable direction when making elicited responses. A more parsimonious explanation is that it is an idiosyncratic general rating tendency. Some people tend to be more lenient raters, others more strict, still others more evenhanded—regardless of the content being rated. This general rating tendency is easily seen in the mean rating across all items. Of course, the mean rating correlates perfectly with total score because the mean is total score divided by a constant ($n$ items) across all respondents. Thus, the dilemma is that although total score does represent the overall level of job satisfaction of the individual, it also contains in it a generalized rating tendency. This tendency might be associated with genetically based tendencies toward optimism (satisfaction) and pessimism (dissatisfaction), as seems to be indicated by the significant heritability of job satisfaction scores (Arvey, Bouchard, Segal, & Abraham, 1989).

One of the questions asked of rated-item scales is, How should the facet scores be weighted according to the importance of the facet, or should they? For example, Wanous and Lawler (1972) outlined nine different ways of combining the facets of job satisfaction culled from their survey of the literature. They found that these different ways of combining and weighting facet scores were, in essence, different ways of defining job satisfaction that led to different results. Yet each definition was valid in its own way because each reflected a different way by which people prefer to evaluate their jobs, leaving no basis for recommending a preferred way. In a way, this finding lends strong support to Hoppock's view, that each person has a different way of weighting facets,

so that the only comparable datum across persons would be overall level of job satisfaction, that is, global job satisfaction.

There is also a mathematical aspect to weighting that is not widely known. For one thing, the intended weights may not be the effective weights. If everyone weighted a particular facet the same or approximately so, it would be equivalent to multiplying the facet score by a constant, which then can be eliminated arithmetically by dividing by the same constant across all individuals. In effect, the weight, no matter how high, if constant across individuals, will have no effect at all on the outcome. What produces the effect of weights and weighting? It turns out to be the variability (e.g., standard deviation) of the weights across individuals—the larger the standard deviation, the more effective the weight is in contributing to the outcome. And the maximum variability index possible is a function of the number of points on the rating scale. For example, a 5-point scale scored 1,2,3,4,5 (the most popular scale) would have a maximum possible standard deviation of 2.0 (when only 1s and 5s are used). Furthermore, weights are most effective when there are only a few components that go into the combination—the more components, the less effective the weights, so much so that beyond 10 components it is not practical to use weights. Thus, for example, with the 20-facet MSQ, any weighting system would produce practically the same results as an unweighted combination. (A similar phenomenon occurs in multiple regression.)

The most difficult problem in the measurement of job satisfaction is quantifying the affect component of job satisfaction. The use of verbal anchors for the rating points on the rating scale (e.g., "Neutral," "Satisfied," "Strongly Satisfied") is assumed to reflect the intensity of affect. But this *is* an assumption, and to my knowledge, has never been tested empirically. Another assumption is that the same score on a multi-item (e.g., facet) scale stands for the same level of affect. But as is well known, the same sum in a combination of scores can be arrived at by different patterns of scores. Again, it is assumed that these patterns make little difference, but there is no research that I know of to back this assumption.

It would seem, from a perusal of the several measures of job satisfaction, that researchers have done a fairly decent job in representing the cognitive content of job satisfaction, but they have rested on assumptions in their representation of the affective component of job satisfaction. So we do have a ways to go in the measurement of job satisfaction.

## Specific Measures

Three measures of job satisfaction have survived the "theory wars" and are currently the most used in job satisfaction studies:

1. The Hoppock Job Satisfaction Blank (JBS; Hoppock, 1935). This is the earliest and probably the most used measure in job satisfaction surveys because it is brief, easy to understand, and easy to administer. Hoppock believed that only level of job satisfaction could be measured, that each individual had her or his idiosyncratic way of determining what job facets to consider and how to weight these facets. Therefore, only general (unspecific) questions were useful in determining level of job satisfaction.

Hoppock originally tried several questions but ended up using these four: "(1) Choose the ONE of the following statements which best tells how well you like your job, (2) Check one of the following to show HOW MUCH OF THE TIME you feel satisfied with your job, (3) Check the ONE of the following which best tells how you feel about changing your job, and (4) Check one of the following to show how you think you compare with other people" (Hoppock, 1935).

Hoppock used the "scaled-items" method for his measure. A set of seven items is presented as answers to each of the four questions. The seven items in each set are graded, such that they can be scored from 1 (representing the "most dissatisfied" answer) to 7 (the "most satisfied" answer). For example, for the first question, the items (answers) are: (1) "I hate it," (2) "I dislike it," (3) "I don't like it," (4) "I am indifferent to it," (5) "I like it," (6) "I am enthusiastic about it," and (7) "I love it." A total score is computed by adding the scores for the four questions.

Hoppock reported a split-half reliability coefficient of 0.93 for questions (1) and (3) versus questions (2) and (4). Other users have reported reliabilities in the high .80s and low .90s. There is little doubt about the internal consistency of the JSB. There is also no question about its face validity or its construct validity. As an elicited, expressed measure, the JSB's validity depends on the motivation of the respondents to fill in the questionnaire truthfully. This, in turn, depends on the conditions under which the JSB is administered.

Hoppock reported on a number of correlates of the JSB. He found that JSB scores were related to sex (males had higher means), occupational level (the higher the job level, the higher the mean), and age (the older the respondent, the higher the mean). Higher JSB scores were related to better mental health, better human relationships, more favorable family social status, having religious beliefs, having feelings of success, and working in a larger community. Eventually, Hoppock's conclusions were challenged, for example, that the differences between the sexes were not so much in their means as in their variabilities (with the men being the more variable), that the higher satisfaction levels for higher level occupational groups masked deeper, more extreme levels of dissatisfaction, and that the age-level differences were not

linear but curvilinear (or inverted U-shaped). Subsequently, the conflicting findings turned out upon analysis to be mainly a function of sampling differences and particular time periods and economic circumstances.

The JSB's main advantage is its brevity—it takes literally seconds to complete and thus can easily be included in longer survey questionnaires. Furthermore, its language is at a level that is very easy to understand. Its main disadvantage is that only the level of satisfaction or dissatisfaction is obtained, not the source(s) of satisfaction or dissatisfaction.

2. The Job Descriptive Index (JDI; Smith et al., 1969). The JDI is the job satisfaction measure most frequently preferred by researchers. It is a measure of facet satisfaction that gets at job satisfaction indirectly by asking the respondents to describe their jobs, rather than by asking them directly how satisfied or dissatisfied they are. The JDI measures satisfaction with five facets of work: the work itself, supervision, coworkers (originally "people"), pay, and opportunities for promotion. There are 72 items: 18 each for work, supervision, and coworkers, and 9 each for pay and promotion. The items consist of adjectives or descriptive phrases that describe each job facet. For example, for the Work facet scale: "Fascinating," "Routine"; for the Supervision facet scale: "Asks my advice," "Hard to please." Respondents are asked to put a Y (for yes) for each item that describes their job, an N (no) for those that do not describe their job, and ? for those items on which they cannot make up their minds.

These 72 items were selected from a larger experimental pool administered to the same respondents under three conditions. First, respondents were asked to respond with respect to their own jobs; then, with respect to the best job they could think of; and finally, with respect to the worst job they could think of. Only items that discriminated between "best job" and "worst job" conditions were retained. Also, half of the items were chosen to be keyed in the Y or "satisfied" direction, and half in the N or "dissatisfied" direction. A scoring system gives weight to responses in the keyed direction and none to wrongly keyed responses. Reliabilities reported for each facet scale are usually in the .80s, and there is a substantial literature that provides validity evidence. The items having been selected by the external criterion (or empirical) method, it is believed that the JDI is less susceptible to faking because its items are less obvious as to measurement intent. The use of indirection—describing the job versus expressing job satisfaction feelings outright—is also thought to contribute to the validity of the instrument. Its widespread use among researchers is testimony to the instrument's high psychometric quality.

More recently, a Job in General scale has been constructed as a global measure to accompany the JDI (Ironson, Smith, Brannick, Gibson, & Paul, 1989).

3. The Minnesota Satisfaction Questionnaire (MSQ; Weiss et al., 1967). The MSQ is a measure of facet satisfaction developed by the internal criterion Likert method. Twenty facets of work are each described by five items selected by the item-total score method (each facet scale was done separately). The 20 facet scales are: Ability Utilization, Achievement, Activity, Advancement, Authority, Company Policies and Practices, Compensation, Coworkers, Creativity, Independence, Moral Values, Recognition, Responsibility, Security, Social Service, Social Status, Supervision—Human Relations, Supervision—Technical, Variety, and Working Conditions. Each item is rated on a 5-point scale, which has verbal anchors ranging from "Very Dissatisfied" to "Very Satisfied." (Another form of the MSQ uses anchors ranging from "Not Satisfied at All" to "Extremely Satisfied.") The notion of expectation is incorporated in the definitions of the verbal anchors as given in the directions (e.g., ". . . if you feel that your job gives you *more than you expected,* check the box under "Very Sat" [Very Satisfied]," bold in the original). Each facet scale score is the sum of the five constituent item scores (ratings). Coefficient alpha reliabilities for the facet scale scores are reported to be mostly in the .80s, with an occasional high .70.

The MSQ is also scored on two second-order scales: intrinsic job satisfaction and extrinsic job satisfaction. The extrinsic job satisfaction score is the sum of facet scale scores for the following: Advancement, Company Policies and Practices, Compensation, Coworkers, Recognition, Security, Supervision—Human Relations, Supervision—Technical, and Working Conditions. The intrinsic job satisfaction score is the sum of the remaining 11 facet scale scores. A general job satisfaction score is also obtained by summing up all 100 item scores.

Finally, there is a short form of the MSQ, consisting of 20 items, one from each facet scale. The item included in this short form is the item that correlated the highest with the facet scale score. The short form MSQ can also be scored for intrinsic, extrinsic, and general job satisfaction.

## FINAL COMMENTS

A few conclusions may be drawn from this discussion:

1. We can measure job satisfaction, but there are many ways by which it can be measured. One research need is to calibrate these different ways of measuring the construct.

2. We do pretty well in measuring the cognitive component, that is, the semantic content, of job satisfaction. Different theories propose different contents, but they seem to reduce to two: need fulfillment and expectation (including equity, social comparison, and opportunity). However, we have not progressed much in measuring the affect component of job satisfaction.

3. We often forget that job satisfaction is a *state* variable, not a trait variable; that it can change with time and circumstance; that in fact its most promising use is in monitoring the effects of organizational change—and personal change as well.

4. We also tend to forget individual differences, that people differ in what is most important to them, and that this may even change for the same person. Consequently, readings on job satisfaction cannot be limited to only a few facets and only one reading.

5. Finally, even though job satisfaction is an old variable and may have lost its luster and attractiveness as a field of study, it remains one of the most important variables in the study of work, either as dependent or independent variable. In the end, as the law of effect would have it, it is satisfaction that rides herd on human choice and action.

## REFERENCES

Adams, J.S. (1965). Toward an understanding of inequity. *Journal of Abnormal and Social Psychology, 67,* 422–436.

Arvey, R.O., Bouchard, T.J., Segal, N.L., & Abraham, L.M. (1989). Job satisfaction: Environmental and genetic components. *Journal of Applied Psychology, 74,* 187–192.

Brayfield, A.H., & Crockett, W.H. (1955). Employee attitudes and employee performance. *Psychological Bulletin, 52,* 396–424.

Brayfield, A.H., & Rothe, H.F. (1951). An index of job satisfaction. *Journal of Applied Psychology, 35,* 307–311.

Cranny, C.J., Smith, P.C., & Stone, E.F. (1992). *Job satisfaction.* New York: Lexington Books.

Dawis, R.V. (1992). Person-environment fit and job satisfaction. In C.J. Cranny, P.C. Smith, & E.F. Stone, *Job satisfaction* (pp. 69–88). New York: Lexington Books.

Dawis, R.V., & Lofquist, L.H. (1984). *A psychological theory of work adjustment.* Minneapolis: University of Minnesota Press.

Digman, J.M. (1990). Personality structure: Emergence of the five-factor model. *Annual Review of Psychology, 41,* 417–440.

Dunnette, M.D., Campbell, J.P., & Hakel, M.D. (1967). Factors contributing to job satisfaction and job dissatisfaction in six occupational groups. *Organizational Behavior and Human Performance, 2,* 143–174.

Guttman, L. (1944). A basis for scaling qualitative data. *American Sociological Review, 9,* 139–150.

Herzberg, F., Mausner, B., Peterson, R.O., & Capwell, D.F. (1957). *Job attitudes: Review of research and opinion.* Pittsburgh, PA: Psychological Services of Pittsburgh.

Herzberg, F., Mausner, B., & Snyderman, B. (1959). *The motivation to work.* New York: Wiley.

Hoppock, R. (1935). *Job satisfaction.* New York: Harper.

Hoppock, R., & Robinson, H.A. (1949). Job satisfaction researches of 1948. *Occupations, 28,* 153–161.

Ironson, G.H., Smith, P.C., Brannick, M.T., Gibson, W.M., & Paul, K.B. (1989). Construction of a Job in General scale: A comparison of global, composite, and specific measures. *Journal of Applied Psychology, 74,* 193–200.

Jourard, S. (1971). *Self-disclosure.* New York: Wiley Interscience.

Katzell, R.A. (1964). Personal values, job satisfaction, and job performance. In H. Borow (Ed.), *Man in a world at work* (pp. 341–363). Boston: Houghton Mifflin.

Katzell, R.A., Thompson, D.E., & Guzzo, R.A. (1992). How job satisfaction and job performance are and are not linked. In C.J. Cranny, P.C. Smith, & E.F. Stone, *Job satisfaction* (pp. 195–217). New York: Lexington Books.

Landy, F.J. (1978). An opponent process theory of job satisfaction. *Journal of Applied Psychology, 63,* 533–547.

Lawler, E.E., & Porter, L.W. (1967). The effect of performance on job satisfaction. *Industrial Relations, 7,* 20–28.

Likert, R. (1932). A technique for the measurement of attitudes. *Archives of Psychology,* No. 140.

Locke, E.A. (1976). The nature and causes of job satisfaction. In M.D. Dunnette (Ed.), *Handbook of industrial and organizational psychology* (pp. 1297–1349). Chicago: Rand McNally.

Mahoney, T.A. (1981). An integrative model of job satisfaction and performance. In G.W. England, A.R. Negandhi, & B. Wilpert (Eds.), *The functioning of complex organizations* (pp. 51–73). Cambridge, MA: Oelgeschlager, Gunn & Hain.

Maslow, A.H. (1954). *Motivation and personality.* New York: Harper & Row.

Munsterberg, H. (1913). *Psychology and industrial efficiency.* Boston: Houghton Mifflin.

Murray, H.A. (1938). *Explorations in personality.* New York: Oxford.

Porter, L.W. (1962). Job attitudes in management: Part I. *Journal of Applied Psychology, 46,* 375–384.

Porter, L.W. (1963). Job attitudes in management: Parts II, III, IV. *Journal of Applied Psychology, 47,* 141–148, 267–275, 386–397.

Robinson, H.A. (1953). Job satisfaction researches of 1952. *Personnel and Guidance Journal, 32,* 22–25.

Roethlisberger, E.A., & Dickson, W.J. (1939). *Management and the worker.* Cambridge, MA: Harvard University Press.

Rounds, J.B. Jr., Henly, G.A., Dawis, R.V., Lofquist, L.H., & Weiss, D.J. (1981). *Manual for the Minnesota Importance Questionnaire.* Minneapolis: Department of Psychology, University of Minnesota.

Roznowski, M., & Hulin, C. (1992). The scientific merit of valid measures of general constructs with special reference to job satisfaction and job withdrawal. In C.J. Cranny, P.C. Smith, & E.F. Stone, *Job satisfaction* (pp. 123–163). New York: Lexington Books.

Salancik, G.R., & Pfeffer, J. (1977). An examination of need-satisfaction models of job attitudes. *Administrative Science Quarterly, 22,* 427–456.

Salancik, G.R., & Pfeffer, J. (1978). A social information processing approach to job attitudes and task design. *Administrative Science Quarterly, 23,* 224–253.

Schaffer, R.H. (1953). Job satisfaction as related to need satisfaction in work. *Psychological Monographs, 67* (Whole No. 364).

Schneider, B., Gunnarson, S.K., & Wheeler, J.K. (1992). The role of opportunity in the conceptualization and measurement of job satisfaction. In C.J. Cranny, P.C. Smith, & E.F. Stone, *Job satisfaction* (pp. 53–68). New York: Lexington Books.

Smith, P.C., Kendall, L.M., & Hulin, C.L. (1969). *The measurement of satisfaction in work and retirement.* Chicago: Rand McNally.

Stone, E.F. (1992). A critical analysis of social information processing models of job perceptions and job attitudes. In C.J. Cranny, P.C. Smith, & E.F. Stone, *Job satisfaction* (pp. 21–44). New York: Lexington Books.

Tellegen, A. (1985). Structures of mood and personality and their relevance to assessing anxiety with an emphasis on self-report. In A. Tuma & J. Maser (Eds.), *Anxiety and anxiety disorders* (pp. 681–706). Hillsdale, NJ: Erlbaum.

Thorndike, E.L. (1911). *Animal intelligence.* New York: Macmillan.

Thurstone, L.L. (1928). Attitudes can be measured. *American Journal of Sociology, 33,* 529–554.

Uhrbrock, R.S. (1961). 2000 scaled items. *Personnel Psychology, 14,* 375–420.

U.S. Department of Labor (1974). *Job satisfaction: Is there a trend?* Manpower Research Monograph No. 30. Washington, DC: U.S. Government Printing Office.

Vroom, V.H. (1964). *Work and motivation.* New York: Wiley.

Wanous, J.P., & Lawler, E.E. (1972). Measurement and meaning of job satisfaction. *Journal of Applied Psychology, 56,* 95–105.

Weiss, D.J., Dawis, R.V., England, G.W., & Lofquist, L.H. (1967). *Manual for the Minnesota Satisfaction Questionnaire* (Minnesota Studies in Vocational Rehabilitation: XXII). Minneapolis: Department of Psychology, University of Minnesota.

# CHAPTER 27

# The Measurement of Applicant Reactions to Selection

TALYA N. BAUER, DONALD M. TRUXILLO, AND MATTHEW E. PARONTO

Research on job applicant perceptions of selection justice has been a rapidly growing area of study in recent years. One of the reasons for its popularity is the usefulness of considering selection from multiple perspectives. In the past, organizations and personnel specialists were interested in maximizing test validity and selection ratios. More recently, the attitudes of applicants have also been considered by organizations and organizational researchers.

The research in this area has primarily been based on the organizational justice literature (e.g., Greenberg & Cropanzano, 2001). Procedural justice refers to the perceived fairness of the methods used to make organizational decisions (Folger & Greenberg, 1985). In addition, distributive justice refers to the perceived fairness of outcomes of decisions (Bauer, Maertz, Dolen, & Campion, 1998). Such justice perceptions are in turn related to attitudes toward organizations (Gilliland, 1993; Lind & Tyler, 1988). The underlying logic is that applicants perceive a hiring process as more fair to the extent that the selection procedures seem fair. Organizations may have the ability to positively influence procedural justice through such means as giving information or explaining testing procedures in greater detail. These changes cost little and may make a large difference in outcomes such as job offer acceptance and organizational commitment. Thus, procedural justice is an important aspect of reactions that applicants have to selection systems/processes.

Research on applicant reactions to selection systems has been largely driven by Gilliland's (1993) theoretical model. His model includes 10 procedural justice rules that fall under three broad categories. The formal characteristics category includes job-relatedness, chance to perform, reconsideration opportunity, and consistency. Under the explanation grouping is feedback, information known, and openness. The last category, interpersonal treatment, includes treatment at the test site, two-way communication, and propriety of questions. These rules are theorized to influence perceptions of overall fairness of a given selection process and other outcomes. Potential outcomes noted by Gilliland include reactions during hiring such as organizational attractiveness, job acceptance, and test-taking motivation; reactions after hiring such as legal actions, on-the-job performance and attitudes, and reapplication intentions; and self-perceptions such as self-esteem and test-taking self-efficacy.

Studies of applicant reactions and associated outcomes have tended to support Gilliland's (1993) model. For example, applicant reactions relate to outcomes such as applicants' intentions to pursue employment with an organization, recommendations to others to apply at the organization, perceived organizational attractiveness, and turnover intentions (e.g., Bauer et al., 1998; Cropanzano & Konovsky, 1995; Macan, Avedon, Paese, & Smith, 1994; Smither, Reilly, Millsap, Pearlman, & Stoffey, 1993; Truxillo & Bauer, 1999).

In addition, it has also been shown that applicants tend to favor procedures that are seen as job related (e.g., Ployhart & Ryan, 1997; Rynes, 1993; Rynes & Connerley, 1993; Smither et al., 1993; Steiner & Gilliland, 1996).

With the advent of research on applicant attitudes, reactions, and predispositions, empirical research has focused on test-taker perceptions such as test-taking motivation (Arvey, Strickland, Drauden, & Martin, 1990; Chan, Schmitt, DeShon, Clause, & Delbridge, 1997; Sanchez, Truxillo, & Bauer, 2000), test-taking self-efficacy (Bauer et al., 1998), and the perceived fairness of selection procedures (e.g., Bauer et al., 1998; Bauer et al., 2001; Gilliland, 1993; Horvath, Ryan, & Stierwalt, 2000; Macan et al., 1994; Ployhart & Ryan, 1997; Smither et al., 1993; Truxillo & Bauer, 1999). This interest has grown because of the potential effects these factors may have on important outcomes such as test validity (e.g., Schmit & Ryan, 1992), organizational attractiveness (e.g., Bauer et al., 1998; Macan et al., 1994; Truxillo & Bauer, 1999), and legal action on the part of applicants (e.g., Gilliland, 1993; Seymour, 1988). Indeed, a host of outcomes have been cited that can be affected by applicant reactions to selection procedures, including job acceptance intentions, job performance, and organizational climate (Gilliland, 1993).

One of the central issues that has plagued this line of research is the availability of validated measures of the key variables (Truxillo, Steiner, & Gilliland, 2001). For example, although models of applicant reactions have existed for several years (e.g., Arvey & Sackett, 1993; Gilliland, 1993), carefully developed measures of process fairness and outcomes have not appeared to fully test these models. Rather, researchers have tended to use ad hoc measures to assess key variables. Heneman (1985) argued that the use of ad hoc measures can fragment research in a given area. But Ryan and Ployhart (2000) suggested that construct definitions need to be clarified before real progress can be made in the development of measures. Further, Bauer et al. (2001) noted that using common scales for procedural justice rules and associated outcomes and using those specifically constructed and geared to the selection process is important for three reasons. First, reactions to an employee selection process involve complex sets of perceptions. Valid and reliable measurement of the different procedural justice constructs can assist practitioners and researchers in more fully understanding the role that fairness plays among applicants in different selection situations. Second, the measurement of variables such as procedural justice factors is an important component to being able to systematically test theoretical models such as Gilliland's (1993) model of applicant reactions to selection as well as being able to improve understanding of this model (Ryan & Ployhart, 2000). Third, as noted by Greenberg (1990), with-

out the use of established scales, it is difficult to compare results across studies.

This chapter focuses on the measures that are currently available to researchers and practitioners who are interested in exploring applicant reactions (e.g., fairness perceptions, outcomes such as organizational attractiveness) and predispositions (e.g. test-taking motivation, test-taking self-efficacy). We have divided the narrative portion of the chapter into two sections. First, we begin by reviewing two strands of research, applicant reactions (including fairness) and applicant predispositions. Second, we review several measures that have been used in published studies but that have not been systematically validated, as well as validated measures of applicant perceptions that have been published in the literature.

## TWO STRANDS OF APPLICANT PERCEPTIONS: REACTIONS AND DISPOSITIONS

The earliest applicant perceptions research that explored this issue was not based in a particular applicant reactions model. In some of the earliest published applicant reactions research, Schmidt, Greenthal, Hunter, Berner, and Seaton (1977) compared reactions to a work sample test and a content valid written test. Their results indicated that applicants perceived the job sample test as more fair, clearer, and more appropriate in difficulty level than a written test. Cascio and Phillips (1979) logged complaints against selection methods from applicants, noting that there was a drop in employee complaints after the introduction of performance tests.

Later research focused on direct comparisons between selection methods and generally supported the conclusion that applicants view face-valid methods such as simulations and work sample tests more positively than multiple-choice, paper-and-pencil tests. For example Smither et al. (1993) found that managers judged simulations to be more face valid than personality, biodata, and abstract cognitive ability tests. Rynes and Connerley (1993) found that tests with high face validity (e.g., simulations, tests with business-related content) were preferred to less face valid approaches. And Macan et al. (1994) found that applicants preferred an assessment center to a cognitive ability test.

### Applicant Reactions

Research into applicant reactions was greatly enhanced by the introduction of applicant reactions models in the early 1990s. Arvey and Sackett's (1993) model of applicant reactions specified a wide range of issues that could be of interest to an applicant, such as job-relatedness of selection methods and consistency of treatment of applicants during selection. The model that has generally driven the applicant reactions research, however, is Gilliland's (1993) fairness-based model of applicant reactions. Based in organizational justice theory (e.g., Lind & Tyler, 1988), this model specifies 10 procedural and 3 distributive justice rules or facets. According to the model, violation or compliance with these fairness rules affects applicants' perceptions of fairness, which in turn affect important outcomes such as job acceptance decisions, job satisfaction if hired, and self-efficacy.

As a result of the dominance of Gilliland's (1993) model, the majority of subsequent applicant reactions studies have been grounded in organizational justice theory. Research has generally supported this model (e.g., Bauer et al., 1998; Gilliland, 1994). The issues explored have included a wide range of selection issues, such as providing information to applicants (e.g., Horvath et al., 2000; Ployhart, Ryan, & Bennett, 1999), the importance of job-related tests (e.g., Gilliland, 1994), and test score banding (e.g., Truxillo & Bauer, 1999). Research has also begun to explore newer selection methods such as video-based tests (e.g., Chan & Schmitt, 1997; Truxillo, Bauer, & Sanchez, 2001; Weekley & Jones, 1997) and telephone and Internet screening (e.g., Fallon & Kudisch, 2001; Klein & Russell, 2001). An excellent summary of the applicant reactions literature as well as current issues in the area was recently published by Ryan and Ployhart (2000).

## Applicant Dispositions

A second line of research into applicant perceptions has involved applicant dispositions (sometimes referred to as "predispositions"). Research has explored these dispositions both in terms of outcomes of the testing process (e.g., Sanchez et al., 2000) and as preexisting attitudes that affect later applicant behavior (e.g., Schmit & Ryan, 1992). The focus on predispositions appears to have been driven primarily by two critical issues for personnel selection researchers: test validity (e.g., Schmit & Ryan, 1992) and ethnic differences in test performance (e.g., Arvey et al., 1990; Chan et al., 1997; Sanchez et al., 2000; Steele & Aronson, 1995).

One disposition that has received considerable attention as both a precursor and outcome of the testing process is test-taking motivation (e.g., Arvey et al., 1990; Chan & Schmitt, 1997; Chan et al., 1997; Sanchez et al., 2000; Schmit & Ryan, 1992). Other key dispositions include test-taking self-efficacy (e.g., Bauer et al., 1998; Gilliland, 1993; Truxillo, Bauer, & Sanchez, 2001) and stereotype threat (Steele & Aronson, 1995). Interestingly, there is also a tie-in between the applicant reactions research and dispositions, as test-taking

motivation has been theorized to relate to perceptions of organizational justice (e.g., Gilliland, 1993).

## Test-Taking Motivation

One of the most researched areas of applicant or test-taker dispositions is in the area of test-taking motivation (e.g., Arvey et al., 1990; Chan et al., 1997; Sanchez et al., 2000; Schmit & Ryan, 1992). Arvey et al.'s Test Attitude Scale (TAS), a measure of test-taking attitudes, included a motivation subset of items (TAS-M). Arvey et al. proposed that African American/White differences on tests may be partly due to differences between the two groups in terms of test-taking motivation. The TAS formed the basis for much of the subsequent research on test-taking motivation. For example, Schmit and Ryan (1992) found that the complete TAS moderated the validity of a cognitive ability and a personality test, such that the validity of the cognitive ability test was higher for those who scored high on the TAS, but lower for those who scored low on the TAS. The opposite was found for the personality test. Later, Chan et al. (1997) used a TAS-M subscale to demonstrate that test-taking motivation was related to test performance after controlling for ethnicity and previous test performance. Schmit and Ryan (1997) found small differences between African Americans and Whites on test-taking motivation as measured by the TAS-M among a field sample of applicants.

The promise of this research in test-taking motivation has generated interest in measures of the construct that are more grounded in motivation theory. Recently, Sanchez et al. (2000) developed the Valence, Instrumentality, and Expectancy Motivation Scale (VIEMS). Based in expectancy theory (e.g., Vroom, 1964), this measure includes Valence, Instrumentality, and Expectancy subscales. Using a sample of police applicants, Sanchez et al. found that the VIEMS explained variance in test score beyond that measured by the TAS-M, and that the Expectancy subscale was related to actual test performance.

## Test-Taking Self-Efficacy

Gilliland (1993) proposed self-efficacy as a potential outcome of fairness reactions to selection methods, suggesting that process and outcome fairness interact to affect applicants' self-efficacy. Specifically, he proposed that outcome fairness will affect self-efficacy only when process fairness rules are fulfilled. This proposition is based in attribution theory (Weiner, 1985). Research has generally supported this proposition (Bauer et al., 1998; Gilliland, 1994; Truxillo, Bauer, & Sanchez, 2001), and research into self-efficacy both as a precursor of test behavior and as an outcome of the testing process, having ramifications for applicants and organizations, is likely to continue. In addition, Gilliland (1994) suggests that self-efficacy is important to applicant motivation and future job search activities.

### Stereotype Threat

A topic related to the concept of test-taking self-efficacy that is gaining attention in the industrial psychology literature is stereotype threat. This research has its origins in the social psychology literature, and much of the work in this area is associated with Claude Steele and his colleagues (e.g., Steele & Aronson, 1995). In a typical stereotype threat study, research participants are given information about a test to affect their test performance, for example, that people with their gender or ethnic background do poorly on the test. Under such conditions, these participants score lower on the test than other participants. Recently the concept of stereotype threat has been explored in the selection context (e.g., Bergeron, Echtenkamp, & Block, 2001; Brown & Jacobson, 2001), and it appears to be a focus of research in the coming years on explaining ethnic and gender differences on selection tests.

## MEASURES OF APPLICANT FAIRNESS REACTIONS

The most fundamental of the reactions applicants can have toward selection deal with procedural fairness, face validity, predictive validity, and outcome fairness. Tables 27.1–27.4 summarize the scales and items associated with the measures in the literature that tap these constructs to date. Each table presents the name of the scale, the authors, the date the scale was presented or published, the number of items, a listing of the actual items, and the reliabilities of the scales. We only included scales where authors presented at least one sample item. Scales are listed from earliest to latest within each table.

### Procedural Justice

Procedural justice refers to the perceived fairness of the methods used to make organizational decisions (Folger & Greenberg, 1985). Such justice perceptions are in turn related to attitudes toward organizations (Lind & Tyler, 1988).

Ryan and Sackett (1987) developed the Attitude Scale to tap the reactions of individuals regarding honesty tests. Their sample was a group of 148 college students who were asked to pretend they were applicants to a job and they were given the honesty test. This reactions scale appears to tap proce-

dural justice factors such as propriety of questions as defined by Gilliland (1993). Some items, such as "If I had two comparable job offers, I'd reject the company that used such a test," may be tapping other factors such as job choice intentions. This scale seems useful to practitioners or researchers interested in tapping general perceptions of procedural fairness reactions, and it showed acceptable internal consistency ($\alpha = .84$).

In 1993, Kluger and Rothstein presented scales of Perceived Fairness, Test Fairness, and Intrusion that tapped applicant reactions. They asked students to pretend they were applying for a job, and they were asked to take one of four randomly assigned selection devices. The investigators then asked all students to respond to questions assessing their reactions to the selection devices. They found that the type of device affected reactions. Thus, it was established that different devices are seen as more or less attractive by applicants. The four-item Test Fairness Scale seems like a reasonable "barometer" to assess applicants' general reactions to selection devices.

Rynes and Connerley (1993) used three 1-item measures of appropriateness of selection instrument, ability to perform, and feelings of trust to tap applicant perceptions comparing 13 selection devices. Again, they asked students ($N = 390$) to pretend they were applying for a job using selection scenarios. Although these items were useful in comparing these devices, it seems undesirable for future research to rely on such single-item measures.

Schmitt, Gilliland, Landis, and Devine (1993) developed a computer-based testing procedure designed to select secretaries. One of the factors they considered was procedural fairness. They developed a 16-item scale to tap dimensions such as job-relatedness and clarity of instructions, and they asked several current employees to compare the old and new selection procedures. Overall, reactions were more favorable to the new test, adding to their confidence that the test was valid.

Smither et al. (1993) surveyed actual employees and applicants in terms of perceptions of fairness. They developed two 2-item measures of perceived fairness of the selection procedure and perceived job-relatedness. Their Overall Fairness Scale has an alpha of .82 and seems like a good general measure of fairness to use. Because the Job-Relatedness measure has an alpha of only .66, we are cautious about recommending its use.

Gilliland (1994) also studied college students in a hiring scenario although he did actually select and "pay" them for work. He created two scales, Procedural Justice and Distributive Justice. Although both had reasonable alphas (in the .80s), they were also highly correlated ($r = .72$). Thus it is

**TABLE 27.1   Measures of Procedural Fairness**

| Name of Scale | Authors | Year | Number of Items | Items | Reliability ($\alpha$) |
|---|---|---|---|---|---|
| *Construct: Procedural Fairness* | | | | | |
| Reactions | Ryan & Sackett | 1987 | 10 | 1. It is perfectly appropriate for an employer to administer such a test.<br>2. I would refuse to take such a test, even if it meant losing a chance at the job.<br>3. I would enjoy being asked to take such a test.<br>4. This test is an invasion of privacy.<br>5. If I had two comparable job offers, I'd reject the company that used such a test.<br>6. I would resent being asked to take such a test.<br>7. A test such as this is sometimes an appropriate selection procedure.<br>8. Administering a test such as this reflects negatively on the organization.<br>9. Being asked to take such a test would not affect my view of the organization.<br>10. Tests like this are routinely used in the industry today. | .84 |
| Intrusion | Kluger & Rothstein | 1993 | 1 | 1. The test intruded on my privacy. | N/A |
| Test Fairness | Kluger & Rothstein | 1993 | 4 | 1. I think this test is fair.<br>2. Most people would say that this test is fair.<br>3. I believe that this test can predict whether I will be a successful employee.<br>4. I can see the connection between this test and performance of the job. | .81 |
| Ability to Perform | Rynes & Connerley | 1993 | 1 | 1. I feel I would do very well on this procedure. | N/A |
| Appropriateness of Selection Instrument/ Process | Rynes & Connerley | 1993 | 1 | 1. A company needs this kind of information to select the right employees. | N/A |
| Feelings of Trust | Rynes & Connerley | 1993 | 1 | 1. I would have great faith in the company's capacity to evaluate me accurately through this procedure. | N/A |
| Procedural Fairness[1] | Schmitt, Gilliland, Landis, & Devine | 1993 | 16 | 1. The tasks required in the test seem appropriate for the position I am trying to obtain (Relevance).<br>2. Overall, I thought this test was a fair way of assessing secretarial potential (Ability).<br>3. I feel my abilities were truly assessed by my performance on this test (Performance). | .87 |
| Perceived Job-relatedness | Smither, Reilly, Millsap, Pearlman, & Stoffey | 1993 | 2 | 1. Applicants who perform well on the company's selection procedure are more likely to perform well in management jobs than applicants who perform poorly on the company's selection procedure.<br>2. The actual content of the selection procedure is clearly related to management jobs. | .82 |
| Procedural Justice | Smither et al. | 1993 | 2 | 1. Overall, I believe that the examination was fair.<br>2. I felt good about the way the examination was conducted and administered. | .68 |
| Overall Procedural Fairness | Gilliland | 1994 | 4 | 1. Whether or not I get the job, I feel the selection *process* was fair. | .85 |

**TABLE 27.1** *(Continued)*

| Name of Scale | Authors | Year | Number of Items | Items | Reliability (α) |
|---|---|---|---|---|---|
| Selection Fairness Scale | Gilliland & Honig | 1994 | 36 | *Consistency Bias* <br> 1. Personal motives or biases appeared to influence the selection process. <br> 2. I think that my hiring decision was affected by special treatment offered to some people. | .74 |
| | | | | *Ease of Faking* <br> 3. I think some people would distort their responses during the selection process to try to make themselves look better. <br> 4. It would be easy for people to be dishonest when answering questions and make themselves look good. <br> 5. I thought you could beat the tests if you were smart and gave the answers they were looking for. <br> 6. It was obvious how you should respond to some of the questions if you wanted the job. | .65 |
| | | | | *Feedback* <br> 7. I am satisfied with how I was informed of the hiring decision. <br> 8. It took a long time to hear back from the company. <br> 9. I received information on the hiring decision in a timely manner. | .77 |
| | | | | *Honesty* <br> 10. I feel the company lied about the selection process and the way they chose people for the job. <br> 11. The company should have been more honest when telling me about the position and my chances of being hired. <br> 12. I was treated honestly and openly during the selection process. <br> 13. People were candid and frank with me during the selection process. <br> 14. They were straightforward and sincere about the job and what it entailed. | .83 |
| | | | | *Interpersonal Treatment* <br> 15. I was treated with warmth, sincerity, and thoughtfulness during the selection process. <br> 16. During the selection process, I feel I was treated more like a number than a human being. <br> 17. The selection process was like an interrogation—the people were cold and rigid. | .70 |
| | | | | *Job-relatedness* <br> 18. The type of questions asked during the selection process were directly related to the job. <br> 19. The selection process was directly relevant to the job because it involved the same things that are required on the job. <br> 20. The questions asked of me during the selection process were neither relevant nor important for the job. <br> 21. The selection process got right down to what I could and could not do. | .68 |
| | | | | *Opportunity to Perform* <br> 22. I was given adequate opportunity to demonstrate my skills and abilities. <br> 23. I had control over the factors that influenced my performance during the selection process. <br> 24. During the selection process, I never got the chance to prove myself. <br> 25. I *don't* think that the selection procedures used can predict whether or not I will be successful on the job. <br> 26. I can see a connection between the selection procedures and performance on the job. | .78 |

*(continued)*

**TABLE 27.1**   (*Continued*)

| Name of Scale | Authors | Year | Number of Items | Items | Reliability ($\alpha$) |
|---|---|---|---|---|---|
| | | | | *Question Propriety* | .69 |
| | | | | 27. Some of the questions asked during the selection process were intrusive of my privacy. | |
| | | | | 28. I was asked questions that I feel were inappropriate or discriminatory. | |
| | | | | *Selection Information* | .70 |
| | | | | 29. I was offered an explanation of the types of factors that affected the hiring decision. | |
| | | | | 30. I received an adequate explanation of how the selection tests would be scored. | |
| | | | | 31. I was told how selection test scores would be used to make a hiring decision. | |
| | | | | 32. I was given a reasonable explanation for why the specific selection procedures were used to hire people. | |
| | | | | *Two-way Communication* | .73 |
| | | | | 33. Lack of interactive or two-way communication was a problem during the selection process. | |
| | | | | 34. I am satisfied with the communication that occurred during the selection process. | |
| | | | | 35. I was not offered sufficient opportunity to ask questions. | |
| | | | | 36. In a way I was able to conduct my own interview, asking questions about the job and company. | |
| Perceived Fairness of Human Resource Practices | Smither, Millsap, Stoffey, Reilly, & Pearlman | 1996 | 3 | 1. Based on the material I read, I would expect this company's personnel practices (e.g., performance appraisals, salary adjustments, grievance/dispute resolution, promotions) to be fair. | .75 |
| | | | | 2. This company is concerned about its employees. | |
| | | | | 3. This company is likely to treat its employees in a fair way. | |
| Perceived Fairness of the Selection Procedure | Smither et al. | 1996 | 2 | 1. The procedures used by this company to evaluate the qualifications of applicants for management jobs are fair. | .82 |
| | | | | 2. Overall, I believe that the selection process in this company is fair. | |
| Perceived Job-relatedness | Smither et al. | 1996 | 2 | 1. Applicants who perform well on the company's selection procedure are more likely to perform well in management jobs than applicants who perform poorly on the company's selection procedure. | .66 |
| | | | | 2. The actual content of the selection procedure is clearly related to management jobs. | |
| Procedural Justice | Steiner & Gilliland | 1996 | 7 | 1. [This] method is based on solid, scientific research. | N/A |
| | | | | 2. [This] approach is a logical one for identifying qualified candidates for the job in question (face validity). | |
| | | | | 3. [This] method will detect the individuals' important qualities differentiating them from others (opportunity to perform). | |
| | | | | 4. [This] selection instrument is impersonal or cold. | |
| | | | | 5. Employers have the right to obtain information from applicants using this method. | |
| | | | | 6. [This] method invades personal privacy. | |
| | | | | 7. [This] method is appropriate because it is widely used. | |
| Process Favorability | Steiner & Gilliland | 1996 | 1 | 1. How would you rate the effectiveness of this method for identifying qualified people for the job you indicated above? | N/A |
| Test Fairness Perceptions | Chan, Schmitt, Jennings, Clause, & Delbridge | 1997 | 3 | 1. I feel that using this test to select applicants for the State Troopers job is fair. | .77 |
| Fairness | Greguras & Ryan | 1997 | 3 | 1. I think it is fair for organizations to use [name of specific test] | .76–.84 |
| Process Fairness[2] | Ployhart & Ryan | 1997 | 3 | 1. Whether or not I get accepted to the University, I feel the admissions process is fair. | .86 |

**TABLE 27.1**    *(Continued)*

| Name of Scale | Authors | Year | Number of Items | Items | Reliability (α) |
|---|---|---|---|---|---|
| Perceptions of Fairness of Tests[3] | Thorsteinson & Ryan | 1997 | 4 | 1. Whether or not I get the job, I feel the [selection test] was fair. | .90 |
| Perceptions of Procedural Fairness[4] | Thorsteinson & Ryan | 1997 | 4 | 1. Whether or not I got the job, I feel the selection *process* was fair. | .92 |
| Chance to Perform | Bauer et al. | 1998 | 4 | 1. I think that this test gave me a chance to prove myself. <br> 2. I felt like I could really show my skills and abilities on this test. <br> 3. I felt like I could influence my scores on this test. <br> 4. I can see a connection between this test and performance on the job. | .77 |
| Consistency of Test Administration | Bauer et al. | 1998 | 3 | 1. All applicants were treated the same during the testing. <br> 2. Everyone was given the same opportunity to perform during testing. <br> 3. Personal biases appeared to influence the selection process. | .88 |
| Information Known | Bauer et al. | 1998 | 4 | 1. I understood why this test was given to applicants. <br> 2. I understood how this test would affect hiring. <br> 3. I know how this test was developed. <br> 4. I feel this company is honest about the selection process and the way they choose people for the job. | .73 |
| Job-relatedness | Bauer et al. | 1998 | 4 | 1. The questions on this test are directly related to the job. <br> 2. This test fairly reflects my ability to do the job. <br> 3. Low scores on these tests means that you can't do the job. <br> 4. I could *not* see a relationship between this test and what is required on the job. | .76 |
| Treatment at the Test Site | Bauer et al. | 1998 | 3 | 1. I was treated politely during the testing. <br> 2. I felt I could easily ask questions about this test. <br> 3. I was comfortable when I took this test. | .58 |
| Fairness Perceptions | Chan, Schmitt, Sacco, & DeShon | 1998 | 3 | 1. I feel that using the test to select applicants for the job is fair. <br> 2. The use of the test would allow screening every applicant fairly and giving them the same opportunity to compete for the job. <br> 3. Using the test would cut down on favoritism that can sometimes be a problem when applicants are selected for jobs. | .74 |
| Process Fairness[5] | Truxillo & Bauer (Study 1) | 1999 | 2 | 1. Overall, I believe that banding is fair. <br> 2. I feel good about the way banding works. | .88 |
| Process Fairness[6] | Truxillo & Bauer (Study 2) | 1999 | 3 | 1. Overall, I believe that the banding process is fair. <br> 2. I feel good about the way the banding process works. <br> 3. The banding process is fair to job applicants. | .96 |
| Selection Procedural Justice Scale (SPJS) | Bauer, Truxillo, Sanchez, Craig, Ferrara, & Campion | 2001 | 39 | *Structure Fairness Factor* <br> <u>Job-relatedness—Predictive</u> <br> 1. Doing well on this test means a person can do the [*insert job title*] job well. <br> 2. A person who scored well on this test will be a good [*insert job title*]. <br> <u>Information Known</u> <br> 3. I understood in advance what the testing processes would be like. <br> 4. I knew what to expect on the test. <br> 5. I had ample information about what the format of the test would be. <br> <u>Chance to Perform</u> <br> 6. I could really show my skills and abilities through this test. <br> 7. This test allowed me to show what my job skills are. <br> 8. This test gives applicants the opportunity to show what they can really do. <br> 9. I was able to show what I can do on this test. | .88 |

*(continued)*

**TABLE 27.1**   *(Continued)*

| Name of Scale | Authors | Year | Number of Items | Items | Reliability (α) |
|---|---|---|---|---|---|
| | | | | Reconsideration Opportunity<br>10. I was given ample opportunity to have my test results rechecked, if necessary.<br>11. There was a chance to discuss my test results with someone.<br>12. I feel satisfied with the process for reviewing my test results.<br>13. Applicants were able to have their test results reviewed if they wanted.<br>14. The opportunities for reviewing my test results were adequate.<br>Feedback<br>15. I had a clear understanding of when I would get my test results.<br>16. I knew that I would receive feedback about my test results.<br>17. I was satisfied with the amount of time it took to get feedback on my test results. | |
| | | | | *Social Fairness Factor*<br>Consistency<br>18. The test was administered to all applicants in the same way.<br>19. There were no differences in the way the test was administered to different applicants.<br>20. Test administrators made no distinction in how they treated applicants.<br>Openness<br>21. I was treated honestly and openly during the testing process.<br>22. Test administrators were candid when answering questions during the tests.<br>23. Test administrators answered procedural questions in a straightforward and sincere manner.<br>24. Test administrators did not try to hide anything from me during the testing process.<br>Treatment<br>25. I was treated politely during the testing process.<br>26. The test administrators were considerate during the test.<br>27. The test administrators treated applicants with respect during today's testing process.<br>28. The testing staff put me at ease when I took the test.<br>29. I was satisfied with my treatment at the test site.<br>Two-way Communication<br>30. There was enough communication during the testing process.<br>31. I was able to ask questions about the test.<br>32. I am satisfied with the communication that occurred during the testing process.<br>33. I would have felt comfortable asking questions about the test if I had any.<br>34. I was comfortable with the idea of expressing my concerns at the test site.<br>Propriety of Questions<br>35. The content of the test did not appear to be prejudiced.<br>36. The test itself did not seem too personal or private.<br>37. The content of the test seemed appropriate. | .93 |
| | | | | *Job-relatedness Content Factor*<br>Job-relatedness—Content<br>38. It would be clear to anyone that this test is related to the [*insert job title*] job.<br>39. The content of the test was clearly related to the [*insert job title*] job. | .88 |
| Procedural Justice[7] | Bauer et al. | 2001 | 3 | 1. I think that the testing process is a fair way to select people for the job of court officer.<br>2. I think that the tests themselves were fair.<br>3. Overall, the method of testing used was fair. | .89 |

**TABLE 27.1**    *(Continued)*

| Name of Scale | Authors | Year | Number of Items | Items | Reliability ($\alpha$) |
|---|---|---|---|---|---|
| Informational Justice[8] | Colquitt | 2001 | 5 | The following items refer to (the authority figure who enacted the procedure). To what extent: 1. Has (he/she) been candid in (his/her) communications with you? 2. Has (he/she) explained the procedures thoroughly? 3. Were (his/her) explanations regarding the procedures reasonable? 4. Has (he/she) communicated details in a timely manner? 5. Has (he/she) seemed to tailor (his/her) communications to individuals' specific needs? | .85 |
| Interpersonal Justice[9] | Colquitt | 2001 | 4 | The following items refer to (the authority figure who enacted the procedure). To what extent: 1. Has (he/she) treated you in a polite manner? 2. Has (he/she) treated you with dignity? 3. Has (he/she) treated you with respect? 4. Has (he/she) refrained from improper remarks or comments? | .86 |
| Procedural Justice[10] | Colquitt | 2001 | 7 | The following items refer to the procedures used to arrive at your (outcome). To what extent: 1. Have you been able to express your views and feelings during those procedures? 2. Have you had influence over the (outcome) arrived at by those procedures? 3. Have those procedures been applied consistently? 4. Have those procedures been free of bias? 5. Have those procedures been based on accurate information? 6. Have you been able to appeal the (outcome) arrived at by those procedures? 7. Have those procedures upheld ethical and moral standards? | .86 |

[1]This overall scale had four subscales. An overall $\alpha$ value for the 16-item measure was reported by the authors and is presented here.
[2]Fairness measures in this study were taken from Gilliland (1994) and Gilliland and Honig (1994).
[3]Modified from Gilliland's (1994) Procedural Justice measure.
[4]From Gilliland (1994).
[5]Adapted from Smither et al. (1993).
[6]Adapted from Smither et al. (1993).
[7]Adapted from Macan et al. (1994) and Smither et al. (1993).
[8]Based on Bies and Moag (1986) and Shapiro, Buttner, and Barry (1994).
[9]Based on Bies and Moag (1986).
[10]Based on Thibault and Walker (1975) and Leventhal (1980).

unclear whether any discriminant validity exists for these fairness measures, although a factor analysis did find two factors. Subsequent studies (Horvath et al., 2000; Ployhart & Maynard, 1999; Ployhart & Ryan, 1998; Ployhart et al., 1999) have used adaptations of Gilliland's (1994) procedural fairness measure (e.g., "Whether or not I was hired, I feel the selection process is fair") with reasonable alpha levels and found relationships with key study variables.

In a conference paper presented at the Society for Industrial and Organizational Psychology in 1994, Gilliland and Honig presented results of their validation work of the Selection Fairness Survey (SFS). The SFS consists of 40 items that tap the dimensions of Job-Relatedness, Opportunity to Perform, Feedback, Selection Information, Honesty, Interpersonal Treatment, Two-Way Communication, Question Pro-

priety, Consistency Bias, Ease of Faking, and Equity. These 11 dimensions are consistent with Gilliland (1993) in terms of content but are not mapped to the model completely. The scale was validated using two samples. The first sample consisted of 333 recent graduates who completed surveys about recent job search experiences and then responded to 56 items from the first version of the SFS. The second sample was that used by Gilliland (1994): 270 undergraduates who applied for short-term paid employment with him. All participants were also given Arvey et al.'s (1990) Test Attitude Survey (TAS). The SFS was found to be reasonably independent of the TAS, but the main shortcoming of this scale concerns internal consistency. The alphas for these subscales range from .65 to .85 with 9 of the 11 factors falling below the .80 level. Thus, it is not recommended that these scales

**TABLE 27.2   Measures of Face Validity**

| Name of Scale | Authors | Year | Number of Items | Items | Reliability ($\alpha$) |
|---|---|---|---|---|---|
| *Construct: Face Validity* | | | | | |
| Face Validity | Smither, Reilly, Millsap, Pearlman, & Stoffey | 1993 | 5 | 1. I did not understand what the examination had to do with the job. <br> 2. I could not see any relationship between the examination and what is required on the job. <br> 3. It would be obvious to anyone that the examination is related to the job. <br> 4. The actual content of the examination was clearly related to the job. <br> 5. There was no real connection between the examination that I went through and the job. | .86 |
| Face Validity | Macan, Avedon, Paese, & Smith | 1994 | N/A | 1. The actual content of the test is clearly related to the job. | .73 |
| Face Validity Perceptions[1] | Chan, Schmitt, DeShon, Clause, & Delbridge | 1997 | 4 | 1. The actual content of these tests was clearly similar to the job tasks listed above. | .74 |
| Job Relevance Perceptions[2] | Chan, Schmitt, Jennings, Clause, & Delbridge | 1998 | 6 | 1. I can see a clear connection between the test and what I think is required by the State Troopers job. | .80 |
| Face Validity | Chan, Schmitt, Sacco, & DeShon | 1998 | 3 | 1. I can see a clear connection between the test and what I think is required by the job. <br> 2. The actual content of the test is related to the job tasks. <br> 3. I do *not* understand what the test had to do with the job. | .70 |
| Face Validity[3] | Horvath, Ryan, & Stierwalt | 2000 | 5 | 1. I do not understand what the examination has to do with this job. | .88 |

[1]Adapted from Smither et al. (1993).
[2]Adapted from Gilliland (1994) and Smither et al. (1993).
[3]From Smither et al. (1993).

**TABLE 27.3   Measures of Predictive Validity**

| Name of Scale | Authors | Year | Number of Items | Items | Reliability ($\alpha$) |
|---|---|---|---|---|---|
| *Construct: Predictive Validity* | | | | | |
| Perceived Predictive Validity | Smither, Reilly, Millsap, Pearlman, & Stoffey | 1993 | 5 | 1. Failing to pass the examination clearly indicates that you can't do the job. <br> 2. I am confident that the examination can predict how well an applicant will perform on the job. <br> 3. My performance on the examination was a good indicator of my ability to do the job. <br> 4. Applicants who perform well on this type of examination are more likely to perform well. <br> 5. The employer can tell a lot about the applicant's ability to do the job from the results of the examination. | .83 |
| Predictive Validity Perceptions | Chan, Schmitt, Sacco, & DeShon | 1998 | 3 | 1. I am confident that the test can predict how well an applicant will perform on the job. <br> 2. The employer can tell a lot about the applicant's ability to do the job based on the results of the test. <br> 3. Failing to perform well on the test indicates that the applicant cannot perform well on the job. | .76 |
| Predictive Validity[1] | Horvath, Ryan, & Stierwalt | 2000 | 5 | 1. Failing to pass the examination clearly indicates that you can't do the job. | .88 |

[1]From Smither et al. (1993).

**TABLE 27.4    Measures of Outcome Fairness**

| Name of Scale | Authors | Year | Number of Items | Items | Reliability ($\alpha$) |
|---|---|---|---|---|---|
| *Construct: Outcome Fairness* | | | | | |
| Distributive Justice | Smither, Reilly, Millsap, Pearlman, & Stoffey | 1993 | 3 | 1. The test results accurately reflected how well I performed on the examination.<br>2. I deserved the test results that I received on the examination.<br>3. The test fairly reflected my ability to do the job. | .86 |
| Overall Distributive Fairness | Gilliland | 1994 | 4 | 1. I feel the hiring decision (accept/reject) was fair. | .86 |
| Equity | Gilliland & Honig | 1994 | 4 | 1. Given my ability and experience, I was *not* evaluated correctly by this selection process.<br>2. Given my past experience looking for a job, I feel I received an appropriate evaluation.<br>3. The outcome of the selection process was *not* a good reflection of my job capabilities.<br>4. The results of the selection process were consistent with how I view myself. | .85 |
| Distributive Justice | Gilliland & Beckstein | 1996 | 9 | 1. The results of the editorial process were consistent with how I view my paper. | .91 |
| Outcome Fairness | Ployhart & Ryan | 1997 | 4 | 1. Overall, I feel the results of the University's admissions process were unfair. | .89 |
| Perceptions of Distributive Fairness[1] | Thorsteinson & Ryan | 1997 | 4 | 1. I feel the hiring decision was fair. | .79 |
| Equity[2] | Ployhart & Ryan | 1998 | 4 | 1. Given my ability and experience, I was not evaluated correctly by this selection decision.<br>2. The outcome of the selection process was not a good reflection of my capabilities. | .84 |
| Outcome Fairness[3] | Ployhart & Maynard | 1999 | 4 | 1. Overall, I feel the results of the organization's selection process were unfair. | .89 |
| Outcome Fairness[4] | Ployhart, Ryan, & Bennett | 1999 | 4 | 1. I feel the organization's selection decision is fair. | N/A |
| Outcome Fairness | Truxillo & Bauer | 1999 | 3 | 1. Banding will reflect how well a person performed on the test.<br>2. Banding fairly reflects an applicant's ability to do the job.<br>3. Banding will produce a fair outcome. | .81 |
| Outcome Fairness | Truxillo & Bauer | 1999 | 3 | 1. Banding will produce an outcome that fairly reflects an applicant's ability to do the job.<br>2. Banding will produce an outcome that fairly reflects how well an applicant performed on the test.<br>3. Banding will produce a fair result. | .87 |
| Equity[5] | Horvath et al. | 2000 | 4 | 1. Given my ability and experience, I was not evaluated correctly by this test. | .85 |
| Outcome Fairness[6] | Horvath et al. | 2000 | 3 | 1. Overall, I feel the results of the test were fair. | .83 |
| Distributive Justice[7] | Bauer, Truxillo, Sanchez, Craig, Ferrara, & Campion | 2001 | 2 | 1. I think that my being hired is a fair outcome.<br>2. The people who were hired deserved to be. | .78 |
| Distributive Justice | Colquitt | 2001 | 4 | The following items refer to your (outcome). To what extent:<br>1. Does your (outcome) reflect the effort you have put into your work?<br>2. Is your (outcome) appropriate for the work you have completed?<br>3. Does your (outcome) reflect what you have contributed to the organization?<br>4. Is your (outcome) justified, given your performance? | .93 |

[1]From Gilliland (1994); [2]From Gilliland and Honig (1994); [3]Adapted from Gilliland (1994); [4]From Gilliland (1994); [5]From Gilliland & Honig (1994); [6]Adapted from Gilliland (1994); [7]Adapted from Macan et al. (1994) and Smither et al. (1993).

be used unless some pilot work is done to modify the items to enhance internal consistency. It should be noted that Gilliland and Beckstein (1996) modified and used items from the SFS, and the alphas for their scales ranged from .75 to .90 with none in the .60s.

Smither, Millsap, Stoffey, Reilly, and Pearlman (1996) asked college seniors and juniors to review a 12-page college recruiting brochure. They created a 2 × 3 experimental design in which either compensation or selection practices were manipulated. This study was one of the first to find that different selection devices with similar validities do differ in terms of candidates' reactions to the company as well as other outcomes such as job search intentions. Smither et al. created several ad hoc measures of fairness to assess this. Although Smither et al. (1996) included several scales in their paper, for this part of the review, there are two 2-item scales tapping Perceived Fairness that had an internal reliability of .75 and .82 and a Perceived Job-Relatedness Scale that only has an alpha of .66. Based on the ad hoc development and low alpha associated with the second scale, we do not recommend its use in its current form. However, in terms of validity, the Perceived Job-Relatedness Scale was correlated with selection method, such that job simulation was considered more job-related than a bio inventory or cognitive test ($r = .31$). Smither et al.'s (1996) Selection Fairness Scale was also predictive of attitudes about the organization ($r = .28$) and job pursuit intentions ($r = .19$). Finally, their HR Fairness Scale was even more predictive of attitudes about the organization ($r = .52$) and job pursuit intentions ($r = .49$). Therefore, while the job-relatedness measure had a low reliability, it was nevertheless predictive of important organizational outcomes.

Steiner and Gilliland (1996) studied fairness reactions to selection techniques in both the United States and France. They developed a seven-item measure of procedural justice that tapped several different factors. They also created a one-item measure that tapped process favorability. They called their two-item measure Process Favorability, but one item ("If you did not get the job based on this selection method, what would you think of the fairness of this procedure?") seems to tap distributive justice. This probably explains why the two-item measure they presented had weak internal reliability.

Chan, Schmitt, Jennings, Clause, and Delbridge's (1998) ad hoc measure consists of three items and has an alpha of .77. In addition Greguras and Ryan (1997) and Ployhart and Ryan (1997) also created three-item measures of outcome fairness and process fairness. All had reasonable alphas and could be useful for tapping general fairness perceptions.

In addition, Thorsteinson and Ryan (1997) created two 4-item measures of fairness of tests and perceptions of pro-

cedural fairness. These scales had excellent reliability and seem well suited for use in future research. A sample item is "Whether or not I get the job, I feel the selection process was fair." This item does tap distributive justice as well as procedural justice, so individuals should be aware of this and use it appropriately.

Bauer et al. (1998) designed measures to tap 4 of Gilliland's 10 procedural justice factors (Chance to Perform, Consistency of Administration, Information Known, and Job-Relatedness) using three- and four-item measures. They asked actual applicants to respond to surveys tapping fairness perceptions both before and after hiring decisions were made. Three of the four measures had weak internal consistencies and would need additional psychometric work before they could be used. Bauer et al. (2001) created new measures that tapped all of Gilliland's facets and were more psychometrically sound.

Chan, Schmitt, Sacco, and DeShon (1998) asked 197 undergraduate students to respond to fairness perceptions regarding cognitive ability and personality tests. They developed a three-item measure to tap perceptions that has an alpha of .74. As measures with stronger internal validities and similar numbers of items exist, we do not recommend that this scale be used unless further psychometric work is completed to ensure sound properties.

Truxillo and Bauer (1999) conducted a series of three field studies to investigate applicant reactions to test score banding in three police selection contexts. They created two scales to tap process fairness. Both their two-item and three-item scales had solid alphas and factored appropriately. Therefore, we recommend the use of these scales, which include items such as "Overall, I believe that banding is fair" and "I feel good about the way banding works."

Bauer et al. (2001) is one of the few studies reviewed here that set out to systematically develop a psychometrically sound measure of applicant fairness reactions to selection (for an exception see Gilliland & Honig, 1994). Their study consisted of five phases of scale development and validation. They followed Hinkin's (1998) recommendations for scale development. Based on exploratory and confirmatory factor analyses as well as item deletion procedures, they determined that 39 items tapped Gilliland's (1993) procedural justice dimensions. They named this scale the Selection Procedural Justice Scale (SPJS). Further, they found that two dimensions of job-relatedness emerged: job-relatedness-content and job-relatedness-predictive. They also found two higher order factors, which they called Structure and Social Fairness, which are consistent with Greenberg's (1993) conceptualization of fairness. Based on the systematic nature of the development of this scale and the higher internal reliabilities, we recommend this scale for use in understanding Gilliland's specific procedural justice factors as well as procedural justice in general using the higher order factors.

Also in 2001, Colquitt published a measure of general fairness. Although he validated his scale using a performance appraisal context, the items seem general enough to be used in the selection context as well. His 16-item scale consists of three factors: Informational Justice, Interpersonal Justice, and Procedural Justice. Each scale has an alpha in the mid-.80s and was validated systematically. Therefore, we also recommend the use of this scale for researchers interested in tapping these three overarching fairness dimensions rather than the specific selection-related facets as in Bauer et al. (2001) and other measures reviewed earlier.

## Face Validity

Table 27.2 contains measures of face validity, which "concerns the *appearance* of whether a measure is measuring what is intended" (Gatewood & Feild, 1998, p. 167, italics in original). Although face validity is usually considered a component of procedural justice (e.g., Bauer et al., 2001; Gilliland, 1993), we discuss face validity as a separate component because it has been explored separately in numerous studies (e.g., Smither et al., 1993).

The most commonly used scale for assessing face validity has been the one developed by Smither et al. (1993). This five-item measure contains items such as "It would be obvious to anyone that the examination is related to the job." These items could also be construed as a type of job-relatedness. Smither et al.'s factor-analyzed scale has a reliability of .86 and was subsequently used successfully by Chan and Schmitt (1997), Chan et al. (1997), Chan, Schmitt, Jennings, et al. (1998), as well as by Horvath et al. (2000) with similar reliabilities. For example, Chan and Schmitt (1997) found that for their sample the method used (video versus paper-and-pencil) was predictive of face validity perceptions. The video test had more face validity. Therefore, this scale seems well suited for use in future studies where researchers want to assess face validity rather than separate facets of justice.

In terms of the face validity measure, Smither et al. (1993) found that it correlated with Process Fairness ($r = .16$), Outcome Fairness ($r = .09$), and important organizational outcomes such as Attractiveness ($r = .48$) and Recommendation Intentions ($r = .14$). In Chan and Schmitt's (1997) study, face validity was correlated with the type of selection method used. In regression analysis, selection method was predictive of face validity perceptions, such that a video situational judgment test (SJT) was considered more face valid than a paper-and-pencil SJT. Chan et al. (1997) found that the face

validity measure was related to test-taking motivation ($r = .38$). Finally, Horvath et al. (2000) found further support for its validity, as face validity perceptions assessed at Time 1 in their longitudinal study were related to procedural justice perceptions at Time 2 ($r = .28$), outcome fairness ($r = .15$), and self-efficacy ($r = .15$).

## Predictive Validity

Table 27.3 contains information on measures of predictive validity. Predictive, or internal validity, is defined as "the approximate validity with which we infer that a relationship between two variables is causal or that the absence of a relationship implies the absence of cause" (Cook & Campbell, 1979, p. 37). Although predictive validity is usually considered a component of procedural justice (e.g., Bauer et al., 2001; Gilliland, 1993), we discuss it separately because it has been explored separately in numerous studies (e.g., Smither et al., 1993).

Again, Smither et al. (1993) developed a five-item factor-analyzed measure that taps perceived predictive validity with items such as "I am confident that the examination can predict how well an applicant will perform on the job." This scale has an alpha of .83 and was successfully used by Horvath et al. (2000) with an alpha of .88.

In addition, Macan et al. (1994) and Chan, Schmitt, Sacco, and DeShon (1998) each developed shorter measures of predictive validity. However, these subsequent scales did not show better reliabilities. Therefore, we recommend the use of the Smither et al. (1993) scale.

## Outcome Fairness

Table 27.4 contains information on the measures that have been developed to tap distributive justice or outcome fairness. Seven truly new scales are presented in Table 27.4 as well as several scales that were modified from previous measures.

Smither et al. (1993) developed the earliest measure. The scale contains three items and has a reliability of .86. In 1994 Gilliland developed a four-item scale with an alpha of .86 in his study of student workers. Gilliland and Honig (1994) also had a four-item scale with items such as "The outcome of the selection process was not a good reflection of my job capabilities." This scale has an alpha of .85. Due to their reliability and relationships with key study variables, all of these scales seem reasonable to use for future studies of applicants' outcome fairness perceptions.

Gilliland and Beckstein (1996) developed a specific scale tapping fairness perceptions of the editorial process at research journals. This nine-item measure has an alpha of .91.

Ployhart and Ryan (1997) developed a four-item measure about a university's admission process, which has an alpha of .89. And finally, Truxillo and Bauer (1999) developed a three-item measure of banding fairness with an alpha of .81. For all three of these final studies, the created items may not generalize to other contexts easily, as they were developed for very specific uses.

### General Attitudes Toward Testing

We differentiate these measures about belief in tests from other test reactions measures, in that the measures described in this section focus on applicants' perceptions of tests in general rather than their perceptions of one particular test. Table 27.5 contains information about measures tapping beliefs in tests. The first scale was developed by Lounsbury, Bobrow, and Jensen (1989) and tapped general evaluative attitudes toward employment testing. Their 17-item scale included such items as "Testing is a good way to find out if a person is really suited for a job." The reliability of their scale was .87, although increasing the number of items in a scale can dramatically enhance its internal consistency (Cortina, 1993). These researchers found that applicants who failed tests and who subsequently did not receive job offers had more negative attitudes than those selected.

Arvey et al. (1990) also developed a scale to tap general attitudes toward testing as part of their validation of the TAS. Unfortunately, their four-item measure has an alpha of .71. This may be due, in part, to the possibility that one of the items ("This test or tests was a good reflection of what a person could do on the job") is really a job-relatedness item rather than a testing attitudes item, as were the other three items of Lounsbury et al.'s (1989) scale.

Kluger and Rothstein (1993) took a different tack and developed a measure of improvement beliefs. Their four-item scale has an alpha of .81. As mentioned earlier, this study examined a comparison of "failers" to a simulated selection situation where individuals took either a biographical inventory, a cognitive ability test, a trainability test, or a work sample test. They found that individuals who failed the biographical inventory had lower improvement beliefs than those who took other types of tests, though they perceived the tests as less difficult.

Finally, Bauer et al. (1998) developed a scale to tap applicants' general attitudes toward employment testing. This four-item measure has an alpha of .82. Their scale was tested among a group of actual job applicants for the job of entry-level accountant at a school district.

We recommend either the Lounsbury et al. (1989) or Bauer et al. (1998) scale for those interested in understanding general attitudes toward testing. The Lounsbury et al. scale is longer by 13 items, but that might prove advantageous in some instances where more detailed information is needed. For individuals interested in tapping improvement beliefs, the Kluger and Rothstein (1993) scale seems useful and was subsequently used by Greguras and Ryan (1997) with reasonable internal reliabilities.

### MEASURES OF OUTCOMES OF FAIRNESS PERCEPTIONS

Applicant reactions models emphasize the importance of fairness perceptions, as such perceptions are hypothesized to affect variables such as organizational attractiveness, reapplication intentions, and intentions to pursue legal action (Gilliland, 1993). As a result, much of the empirical work in this area has explored the relationship between fairness and these outcomes (e.g., Bauer et al., 1998; Gilliland, 1994). Numerous, mostly ad hoc measures have been thus developed to assess these outcomes. We discuss these measures in this section of the chapter.

### Satisfaction With the Selection Process

Two scales have addressed the issue of satisfaction with the selection process, and these are described in Table 27.6. Macan et al. (1994) developed a two-item measure that included items such as "In general, I am satisfied with the selection process." This scale has an alpha of .84. Truxillo, Bauer, and Sanchez (2001) assessed overall selection system fairness after candidates had received their results using a five-item measure with procedural and distributive justice components ($\alpha = .94$).

### Perceptions of the Hiring Organization

Table 27.7 describes the activity surrounding measurement of perceptions of the organization. These perceptions are important as they have been related to intentions to pursue employment with a given company and job choice (Aiman-Smith, Bauer, & Cable, 2001; Cable & Graham, 2000; Highhouse, Zickar, Thorsteinson, Stierwalt, & Slaughter, 1999; Turban & Keon, 1993; Williams & Bauer, 1991). As this sampling of research indicates, a great deal has been learned about the types of factors that influence job-seeker perceptions.

Kluger and Rothstein (1993) developed a five-item measure that has an alpha of .73. They called their measure "company image," but it appears to be tapping several dimensions at once. For example, of the four items, one appears to tap

**TABLE 27.5  Measures of Belief in Tests**

| Name of Scale | Authors | Year | Number of Items | Items | Reliability ($\alpha$) |
|---|---|---|---|---|---|
| *Construct: Belief in Tests* | | | | | |
| General Evaluative Attitude toward Employment Testing | Lounsbury, Bobrow, & Jensen | 1989 | 17 | 1. Testing is a good way to find out if a person is really suited for a job.<br>2. Tests give everybody a fair chance to get a job.<br>3. Employment tests give a person a good chance to show how capable they are of doing the job.<br>4. I don't think tests really can tell who will do well on the job and who won't.<br>5. Tests are artificial. They do not measure what a person really does on the job.<br>6. Testing is the best way to find the best person for the job.<br>7. Companies that use tests to decide who gets a job usually treat workers more like numbers than human beings.<br>8. Employment tests do not really measure a person's true abilities for a job.<br>9. Tests can measure important abilities that cannot be determined in an interview.<br>10. Testing gives some people a chance to get a job who would not otherwise have an opportunity to get the job.<br>11. Using tests helps cut down on favoritism in selecting people for jobs.<br>12. Using tests to select people for jobs forces workers to compete against each other too much.<br>13. Tests are often used as a way to discriminate against minority group members (like females and Blacks).<br>14. A person's previous job experience should be more important than his/her test scores in choosing someone for a job.<br>15. I think employment testing is an invasion of privacy.<br>16. A person's desire to do a good job can't be measured by employment tests.<br>17. People with equal abilities have the same chance for success on the job. | .87 |
| Belief In Tests[1] | Arvey, Strickland, Drauden, & Martin | 1990 | 4 | 1. This test or tests was a good reflection of what a person could do in the job.<br>2. Tests are a good way of selecting people into jobs.<br>3. This kind of test or tests should be eliminated.<br>4. I don't believe that tests are valid. | .71 |
| Improvement Beliefs | Kluger & Rothstein | 1993 | 4 | 1. A job applicant could improve his/her score by taking the test again.<br>2. With training, a job applicant could improve his/her score on this test.<br>3. With more experience a job applicant could improve his/her score on this test.<br>4. Receiving feedback on test performance would enable a job applicant to improve his/her score on a similar test. | .81 |
| General Attitude Toward Employment Testing | Bauer, Maertz, Dolen, & Campion | 1998 | 4 | 1. I think that testing people is a fair way to determine their abilities.<br>2. I think that written tests are a fair way to hire people for jobs.<br>3. I believe companies that use written tests are fair to applicants.<br>4. There are much fairer ways of selecting employees than written tests. | .82 |
| General Belief in Employment Tests[2] | Chan, Schmitt, Sacco, & DeShon | 1998 | 1 | 1. Employment selection tests are a good way of selecting people into jobs. | N/A |

[1]Subscale of Arvey et al.'s (1990) Test Attitude Survey (TAS); [2]From Arvey et al. (1990).

**TABLE 27.6    Measures of Satisfaction with the Selection Process**

| Name of Scale | Authors | Year | Number of Items | Items | Reliability ($\alpha$) |
|---|---|---|---|---|---|
| *Construct: Satisfaction with the Selection Process* | | | | | |
| | Macan, Avedon, Paese, & Smith | 1994 | 2 | 1. In general, I am satisfied with the application process. <br> 2. So far, participation in the application process has been a positive experience. | .84 |
| | Truxillo, Bauer, & Sanchez | in press | 5 | 1. I think that this testing process is a fair way to select people for the job of police officer. <br> 2. I think that the written and video tests themselves were fair. <br> 3. Overall, the method of written and video testing used was fair. <br> 4. I think that I got a fair outcome as a result of this testing process. <br> 5. I think that others got a fair outcome as a result of this testing process. | .94 |

potential toward discrimination, another attraction, another recommendation intentions, and the final item appears to tap purchase intentions. Thus, the low alpha may be due to the potpourri of concepts included in the single scale.

Rynes and Connerley (1993) developed a two-item measure that clearly taps attitudes and job pursuit intentions. This scale has an alpha of .87 and would be useful for researchers looking to tap attractiveness with a limited number of items.

Smither et al. (1993) developed a three-item measure with an alpha of .80. Smither et al. (1996) developed a five-item measure with an alpha of .87. Bauer et al. (1998) modified items from Smither et al. (1993) and Macan et al. (1994) and obtained an alpha of .83 with their four-item scale. Any of these scales seem reasonable to use for future studies.

More recently, Ployhart and colleagues (Ployhart & Maynard, 1999; Ployhart et al., 1999) have developed several scales with alphas above .90. Unfortunately, they did not present all their items. Truxillo and Bauer (1999) explored applicant reactions in entry-level and promotional samples of police applicants. They created two different organizational attractiveness scales. Each had three items but the alpha for the second scale was much higher (.92 versus .77). Again, the attraction scales appear to merge the concepts of recommendation intentions ("All other things being equal, I would encourage others to apply for a job with an organization that uses banding") and attraction ("All other things being equal, I would prefer to work for an organization that uses banding"). Bauer et al. (2001) also developed a five-item measure of organizational attractiveness that has an alpha of .90. Clearly there are many reasonable choices for individuals wanting to measure perceptions of organizations in the context of fairness perceptions.

## Miscellaneous Organizational Perceptions

Researchers have explored a range of other perceptions of the organization that are pertinent to the selection context. In

our review of the literature, we found eight types of these perceptions. These are summarized in Table 27.8.

### Customer Purchase Intentions

Macan et al. (1994) conducted their study in an actual selection context in a manufacturing environment. The organization was concerned about how their selection process might impact consumers and thus a one-item measure was created to tap customer purchase intentions ("How often would you buy this company's products in comparison to how often you bought them in the past?").

### Perceived Employee Relations

Truxillo and Bauer (1999) were conducting their studies in a police officer context and thus they were concerned about employee relations based on experiences with the selection context. They created a three-item measure that has an alpha of .88 and includes such items as "There would probably be good relations between workers and management in organizations that use banding."

### Job Pursuit Intentions

Job acceptance intentions have been measured in a variety of contexts. For example, Smither et al. (1996) measured it using a four-item scale with an alpha of .90. The scale appears to have face validity as the items include "I would seriously consider this company as a possible employer." Ployhart and Ryan (1997) studied acceptance intentions in the context of graduate school enrollments. Their two-item scale appears to tap acceptance intentions as well as intentions to continue in the selection process and has an extremely high alpha of .98. Ployhart and Ryan (1998) used a one-item measure to tap job acceptance intentions. Therefore, we do not recommend

**TABLE 27.7   Measures of Perceptions of the Organization**

| Name of Scale | Authors | Year | Number of Items | Items | Reliability ($\alpha$) |
|---|---|---|---|---|---|
| *Construct: Organizational Attractiveness* | | | | | |
| Company Image | Kluger & Rothstein | 1993 | 4 | 1. A company that employs this test probably discriminates against minority and female applicants. <br> 2. I would be willing to work for a company that uses a test like this. <br> 3. I would refer my friends to a company that uses a test like this. <br> 4. I would buy products manufactured by a company that uses a test like this. | .73 |
| Attitudes Toward the Company | Rynes & Connerley | 1993 | 2 | 1. After this experience, my attitude toward the company would be much more favorable. <br> 2. After this experience, I would be very motivated to further pursue this company. | .87 |
| Organizational Attractiveness | Smither, Reilly, Millsap, Pearlman, & Stoffey | 1993 | 3 | 1. Civil service is one of the best employers to work for. <br> 2. In general, the pay is good in civil service. <br> 3. There are good chances for advancement in civil service. | .80 |
| Attitudes about the Organization | Smither, Millsap, Stoffey, Reilly, & Pearlman | 1996 | 5 | Ratings made on the following five dimensions: <br> 1. unfavorable—favorable <br> 2. unattractive—attractive <br> 3. undesirable—desirable <br> 4. negative—positive <br> 5. boring—challenging | .87 |
| Organizational Attractiveness[1] | Bauer, Maertz, Dolen, & Campion | 1998 | 4 | 1. This organization is one of the best places to work. <br> 2. In general, the pay is good at this company. <br> 3. There are good chances for advancement at this company. <br> 4. If hired for this job, I think I would like the work I would do. | .83 |
| Attitudes Toward the Organization[2] | Ployhart & Maynard | 1999 | 4 | For each selection scenario: <br> 1. good—bad <br> 2. unfavorable—favorable <br> 3. attractive—unattractive <br> 4. unappealing—appealing | .95 |
| Job Attractiveness | Ployhart & Maynard | 1999 | 2 | 1. I found this job very desirable. | .92 |
| Organizational Perceptions | Ployhart, Ryan, & Bennett | 1999 | 4 | If I received this letter, my attitude toward the organization would be: <br> 1. bad—good <br> 2. unfavorable—favorable <br> 3. unattractive—attractive <br> 4. negative—positive | .97 |
| Organizational Attractiveness[3] | Truxillo & Bauer (Study 2) | 1999 | 3 | 1. I would encourage others to apply for a job with the City of _____. <br> 2. I would like to work for the City of _____. <br> 3. In general, the City of _____ would be a good place to work. | .77 |
| Organizational Attractiveness[4] | Truxillo & Bauer (Study 3) | 1999 | 3 | 1. All other things being equal, I would encourage others to apply for a job with an organization that uses banding. <br> 2. All other things being equal, I would prefer to work for an organization that uses banding. <br> 3. In general, organizations that use banding would be good places to work. | .92 |
| Organizational Attractiveness | Bauer, Truxillo, Sanchez, Craig, Ferrara, & Campion | 2001 | 5 | 1. This organization is one of the best places to work. <br> 2. This organization treats people better than anywhere else. <br> 3. In general, the pay is good at this company. <br> 4. There are good chances for advancement at this company. <br> 5. If hired for this job, I think I would like the work I would do. | .90 |

[1]From Macan et al. (1994) and Smither et al. (1993); [2]Similar to Smither et al. (1996); [3]Adapted from Smither et al. (1993); [4]Adapted from Smither et al. (1993).

**TABLE 27.8   Measures of Intentions Toward the Organization**

| Name of Scale | Authors | Year | Number of Items | Items | Reliability (α) |
|---|---|---|---|---|---|
| *Construct: Customer Purchase Intentions* | | | | | |
| Customer Purchase Intentions | Macan, Avedon, Paese, & Smith | 1994 | 1 | 1. How often would you buy this company's products in comparison to how often you bought them in the past? | N/A |
| *Construct: Employee Relations* | | | | | |
| Employee Relations | Truxillo & Bauer | 1999 | 3 | 1. There would probably be good relations between workers and management in organizations that use banding.<br>2. In general, organizations that use banding would have fewer employee complaints.<br>3. In general, there should be fewer formal employee grievances in organizations that use banding. | .88 |
| *Construct: Job Pursuit Intentions* | | | | | |
| Job Pursuit Intentions | Smither, Millsap, Stoffey, Reilly, & Pearlman | 1996 | 4 | 1. I would seriously consider this company as a possible employer.<br>2. I would request additional information about this company.<br>3. I would sign up for an interview with this company.<br>4. If you were offered a job by this company, how likely is it that you would accept it? | .90 |
| Acceptance Intentions | Ployhart & Ryan | 1997 | 2[1] | 1. If accepted, I intend to attend graduate school at the University.<br>2. I will attend graduate school at the University in the Fall. | .98 |
| Job Acceptance Intentions | Ployhart & Ryan | 1998 | 1 | 1. Even if I was now offered the job, I would not accept it (Rejected applicants). | N/A |
| *Construct: Litigation Intentions* | | | | | |
| Litigation Likelihood[2] | Bauer, Truxillo, Sanchez, Craig, Ferrara, & Campion | 2001 | 4 | 1. An organization that uses a video-based test like this would likely be sued by applicants.<br>2. I think applicants might sue a company that used a test like this.<br>3. If video-based tests become more widely used with job applicants, there will be an increase in the number of lawsuits against employers.<br>4. I would be more likely to sue an organization that used video-based tests than one that did not. | .91 |
| *Construct: Reapplication Intentions* | | | | | |
| Journal Submission Intentions | Gilliland & Beckstein | 1996 | 4 | 1. I will certainly continue to send future manuscripts to be reviewed for publication in this journal.<br>2. I will recommend that others submit their work for possible publication in this journal.<br>3. When an equally desirable outlet is available, I will submit my future work to other journals.<br>4. I will wait to submit future papers to *JAP* until a new person assumes the editorship. | .86 |
| Reapplication Intentions | Ployhart & Ryan | 1997 | 1 | 1. I would apply to the University's graduate psychology program again. | N/A |
| *Construct: Recommendation Intentions* | | | | | |
| Recommendation Intentions | Smither, Reilly, Millsap, Pearlman, & Stoffey | 1993 | 1 | 1. Based on my experience with the examination I would encourage others to apply for employment with the state civil service. | N/A |
| Recommendation Intentions | Gilliland | 1994 | 4 | 1. If I hear about other projects like this, I would be interested in applying for them. | .83 |
| Recommendation Intentions | Ployhart & Ryan | 1997 | 1 | 1. I intend to recommend the University's graduate psychology program to others. | N/A |

**TABLE 27.8**  *(Continued)*

| Name of Scale | Authors | Year | Number of Items | Items | Reliability ($\alpha$) |
|---|---|---|---|---|---|
| Intentions Toward the Organization | Bauer, Maertz, Dolen, & Campion | 1998 | 3 | 1. I intend to encourage others to apply for a job with this company.<br>2. I intend to tell others that this is a good company to apply for a job.<br>3. I intend to apply for a new job here again if I am not offered a job. | .85 |
| Recommendation Intentions | Bauer, Truxillo, Sanchez, Craig, Ferrara, & Campion | 2001 | 3 | 1. I intend to encourage others to apply for a job with this company.<br>2. I intend to tell others that this is a good company to apply for a job.<br>3. I intend to apply for a job here again if I am not offered a job today. | .95 |
| Leader Evaluation | Colquitt | 2001 | 3 | 1. I would probably recommend my instructor to my friends.<br>2. I thought my instructor was a good one.<br>3. I really liked my instructor. | .88 |

[1]One item was used preapplication, and two items postapplication.
[2]From Seitz, Truxillo, and Bauer (2001).

the use of this measure when other, more psychometrically sound measures are available such as Smither et al. (1996) and Ployhart and Ryan's (1997) scale.

### Litigation Intentions

The likelihood of applicants taking legal action is cited as one of the most important outcomes in much of the applicant reactions research (e.g., Gilliland, 1993; Truxillo & Bauer, 1999). Furthermore, legal defensibility is a key factor in test development and may be the primary reason that organizations care about applicant perceptions. However, only one published study has explored this outcome, perhaps because of the reluctance of most organizations to suggest legal action to applicants. Bauer et al. (2001) used a four-item measure of this variable and found that test fairness was negatively correlated with litigation intentions, with items such as "An organization that uses a test like this would likely be sued by applicants." The alpha of this scale was .91.

### Reapplication Intentions

Reapplication intentions are also important, as not everyone is hired or selected each time they take a test or apply, but they may still be viable candidates in the future. For example, in the context of Gilliland and Beckstein's (1996) study of perceptions of journal submission fairness, it is extremely important that authors continue to consider a journal as a viable submission alternative even if one particular manuscript is rejected. Therefore, Gilliland and Beckstein created a four-item measure that has an alpha of .86 and includes items

such as "I will certainly continue to send future manuscripts to be reviewed for publication in this journal." Ployhart and Ryan (1997) used a one-item measure to tap reapplication intentions for graduate school. Both of these measures are specific to the contexts studied and may not generalize to other contexts such as employment testing. Their use should be tempered with this in mind.

### Recommendation Intentions

Recommendation intentions are also important to organizations as this can be a good way to recruit viable candidates. It is also a matter of reputation. If individuals "talk down" an organization, the organization can suffer image problems and dilute its ability to recruit effectively.

Smither et al. (1993) used a one-item measure to tap intentions: "Based on my examination I would encourage others to apply for employment with the state civil service." Ployhart and Ryan (1997) also have a one-item measure of this. However, other multi-item measures exist as well. For example, Gilliland's (1994) four-item measure taps intentions for his context with such items as "If I hear about other projects like this, I would be interested in applying for them." His scale has an alpha of .83 but would probably need to be modified for use in regular selection contexts. Bauer et al. (1998) developed a three-item scale that has an alpha of .85. A sample item is "I intend to encourage others to apply for a job with this company." Further, Bauer et al. (2001) developed a three-item measure that has an attractive alpha of .95. A sample item is "I intend to encourage others to apply for a job here." And finally, Colquitt (2001) also developed a three-item scale tapping recommendation intentions for students regarding instructors rather than a selection context. His scale has an alpha of .88, and a sample item is "I would probably recommend my instructor to my friends."

Overall, we recommend the use of one of the Bauer et al. scales as they are multi-item measures, have high internal consistency, and were developed in actual selection/hiring contexts. The other scales may be appropriate in this context as well but may need some modification. We do not recommend the use of either of the one-item scales unless survey length is a major concern and adding two additional items would pose a serious problem.

## MEASURES OF TEST-TAKING DISPOSITIONS

Applicant perceptions research has delved into what is referred to as applicant "dispositions" or "predispositions." Research has explored these variables both in terms of outcomes of the testing process (e.g., Sanchez et al., 2000) and as preexisting attitudes that affect later applicant test performance (e.g., Sanchez et al., 2000; Schmit & Ryan, 1992). The dispositions that have been measured in the published literature include test-taking self-efficacy and test-taking motivation.

### Test-Taking Self-Efficacy

Test-taking self-efficacy is a variable of interest to organizations. However, it is of particular interest to applicants and society at large due to its hypothesized relationship with test performance and test-taking motivation. Moreover, its relationship with test fairness presents organizations with a paradoxical situation: Greater test fairness increases the self-efficacy of successful applicants, but it actually lowers the self-efficacy of unsuccessful applicants (Bauer et al., 1998; Truxillo et al., 2001).

A total of seven studies have included measures of test-taking self-efficacy. Unfortunately, four of these did not present any items (e.g., Gilliland, 1994; Ployhart & Ryan, 1998; Ployhart et al., 1999; Rynes & Connerley, 1993). For the measures that were presented, Bauer et al. (1998) developed a four-item scale with an alpha of .87. A sample item is "I am confident in my test-taking abilities." Horvath et al. (2000) also developed a two-item scale with an alpha of .72. A sample item is "I believe I will perform well on this test." Finally, Truxillo, Bauer, and Sanchez (2001) utilized a measure of test-taking self-efficacy, based on Bauer et al. (1998) and the description given in Gilliland (1994). Mean alphas for this scale ranged from .83 to .85. See Table 27.9.

### Test-Taking Motivation

Test-taking motivation has received considerable attention as both a precursor and outcome of the testing experience (e.g., Arvey et al., 1990; Chan & Schmitt, 1997; Chan et al., 1997; Sanchez et al., 2000; Schmit & Ryan, 1992). In addition, test-taking motivation is theorized to relate to applicant fairness perceptions (e.g., Gilliland, 1993). However, it is also thought to relate to two critical issues for personnel selection researchers: test validity (e.g., Schmit & Ryan, 1992) and ethnic differences in test performance (e.g., Arvey et al., 1990; Chan et al., 1997; Sanchez et al., 2000).

For those interested in assessing test-taking motivation, two scales exist that were exclusively developed to tap this dimension. Table 27.10 describes these measures. By far the most commonly used scale to date has been the Test Attitude Scale (TAS) by Arvey et al. (1990), which was carefully developed and validated across different applicant samples. Although the TAS measures a range of perceptions besides motivation, the TAS has a 10-item motivation subscale that has an alpha of .85. The TAS Motivation scale has been successfully used in several published studies in explaining test validity and explaining ethnic differences in test performance (e.g., Chan et al., 1997; Schmit & Ryan, 1992, 1997).

However, one criticism of the TAS Motivation scale is that it has no clear basis in a particular motivation theory. To address this issue, Sanchez et al. (2000) developed a 10-item Motivation scale based in expectancy theory called the Valence, Instrumentality, Expectancy Scale, or VIEMS. The VIEMS was developed using a systematic process of item generation and exploratory and confirmatory factor analysis across three samples. As the name suggests, the VIEMS has three subscales: Valence (alpha = .94), Instrumentality (alpha = .86), and Expectancy (alpha = .89). The combined VIEMS (alpha = .80) explained variance in test performance beyond the TAS (Arvey et al., 1990).

## CONCLUSION

Although dozens of measures have been presented in this review of the applicant reactions to selection literature, only seven of them (Arvey et al., 1990; Bauer et al., 2001; Colquitt, 2001; Gilliland & Honig, 1994; Lounsbury et al., 1989; Sanchez et al., 2000; Truxillo & Bauer, 1999) are systematically validated measures. The other measures are all ad hoc and did not go through the rigorous process of item development, revision, and validation. Thus, use of these ad hoc measures should proceed with caution as they may not show clear divergent validity in future studies.

**TABLE 27.9    Measures of Self-efficacy**

| Name of Scale | Authors | Year | Number of Items | Items | Reliability ($\alpha$) |
|---|---|---|---|---|---|
| *Construct: Self-efficacy* | | | | | |
| Test-taking Self-efficacy | Bauer, Maertz, Dolen, & Campion | 1998 | 4 | 1. I am confident in my test-taking abilities.<br>2. I think my chances of being hired as a result of the test I took today are high.<br>3. I expect that I did well on the test I have taken today.<br>4. I know that when it comes to taking written tests, I do well. | .87 |
| Self-perceptions | Ployhart, Ryan, & Bennett | 1999 | 4 | If I received this letter, my opinion of myself would be:<br>1. bad—good<br>2. unfavorable—favorable<br>3. disapproving—approving<br>4. negative—positive | .97 |
| Self-efficacy | Horvath, Ryan, & Stierwalt | 2000 | 2 | 1. I believe I will perform well on this test.<br>2. I am not good at performing well at procedures like this test. | .72 |
| | Truxillo, Bauer, & Sanchez | in press | 3 | 1. I am confident in my ability to do well on video tests.<br>2. When it comes to taking video tests, I generally do well.<br>3. I tend to do better on video tests than most people. | .80[1] |

[1]Average reliability of the scale for pretest and posttest.

**TABLE 27.10    Measures of Test-taking Motivation**

| Name of Scale | Authors | Year | Number of Items | Items | Reliability ($\alpha$) |
|---|---|---|---|---|---|
| *Construct: Test-taking Motivation* | | | | | |
| Test Attitude Scale (TAS) | Arvey, Strickland, Drauden, & Martin | 1990 | 10 | 1. Doing well on this test (or these tests) is important to me.<br>2. I wanted to do well on this test or tests.<br>3. I tried my best on this test or tests.<br>4. I tried to do the very best I could do on this test or tests.<br>5. While taking this test or tests, I concentrated and tried to do well.<br>6. I want to be among the top scorers on this test (or these tests).<br>7. I pushed myself to work hard on this test or these tests.<br>8. I was extremely motivated to do well on this test or tests.<br>9. I just didn't care how I did on this test or tests.<br>10. I didn't put much effort into this test or tests. | .85 |
| Valence, Instrumentality, and Expectancy Motivation Scale (VIEMS) | Sanchez, Truxillo, & Bauer | 2000 | 10 | 1. I would like to be hired for this job (V).<br>2. It would be good to have a job with the police department (V).<br>3. I want to get a job with the police department (V).<br>4. If you do well on this test, you have a good chance of being hired (I).<br>5. I think you will be hired if you get a high test score (I).<br>6. How well you do on this test will affect whether you are hired (I).<br>7. The higher your test score, the better your chances of getting hired (I).<br>8. If you try to do your best on this test, you can get a high score (E).<br>9. If you concentrate and try hard you can get a high test score (E).<br>10. You can get a good score on this test if you put some effort into it (I). | .80[1] |

[1]Composite VIEMS score.

In terms of what is needed at this point, we suggest that researchers focus on developing sound measures of the outcomes that are of greatest interest to organizations, such as organizational attractiveness and litigation intentions. Clearly the association between justice and individual and organizational outcomes exists, but better measures will allow us to further understand how much.

For practitioners who engage in selection activities, the literature on applicant reactions to selection systems seems clear: It is possible to help or hinder your chances of job offer acceptances and job pursuit intentions. We recommend that practitioners focus on ways that their own selection systems can be improved based on applicant reactions using some of the scales described in this chapter.

## REFERENCES

Aiman-Smith, L.A., Bauer, T.N., & Cable, D. (2001). Are you attracted? Do you intend to pursue? A recruiting policy-capturing study. *Journal of Business and Psychology, 16,* 219–237.

Arvey, R.D., & Sackett, P.R. (1993). Fairness in selection: Current developments and perspectives. In N. Schmitt & W.C. Borman (Eds.), *Personnel selection in organizations* (pp. 171–202). San Francisco: Jossey-Bass.

Arvey, R.D., Strickland, W., Drauden, G., & Martin, C. (1990). Motivational components of test taking. *Personnel Psychology, 43,* 695–716.

Bauer, T.N., Maertz, C.P. Jr., Dolen, M.R., & Campion, M.A. (1998). Longitudinal assessment of applicant reactions to employment testing and test outcome feedback. *Journal of Applied Psychology, 83,* 892–903.

Bauer, T.N., Truxillo, D.M., Sanchez, R.J., Craig, J., Ferrara, P., & Campion, M.A. (2001). Applicant reactions to selection: Development of the selection procedural justice scale (SPJS). *Personnel Psychology, 54,* 387–419.

Bergeron, D., Echtenkamp, B.A., & Block, C.J. (2001, April). *Disabling the able: Stereotype threat and women's workplace performance.* Paper presented at the 16th Annual Conference of the Society for Industrial and Organizational Psychology, San Diego, CA.

Bies, R.J., & Moag, J.F. (1986). Interactional justice: Communication criteria of fairness. In R.J. Lewicki, B.H. Sheppard, & M.H. Brazerman (Eds.), *Research on negotiations in organizations* (Vol. 1, pp. 43–55). Greenwich, CT: JAI Press.

Brown, R.P., & Jacobson, K. (2001, April). What's in a name? Test labels can produce stereotype threat for academically stigmatized minorities. In S.R. Klein & J.B. Fallon (Chairs), *User reactions and stereotype threat in online and traditional assessments.* Symposium presented at the 16th Annual Conference of the Society for Industrial and Organizational Psychology, San Diego, CA.

Cable, D.M., & Graham, M.E. (2000). The determinants of job seekers' reputation perceptions. *Organizational Behavior and Human Decision Processes, 21,* 929–947.

Cascio, W.F., & Phillips, N.F. (1979). Performance testing: A rose among thorns? *Personnel Psychology, 32,* 751–766.

Chan, D., & Schmitt, N. (1997). Video-based versus paper-and-pencil method of assessment in situational judgment tests: Subgroup differences in test performance and face validity perceptions. *Journal of Applied Psychology, 82,* 143–159.

Chan, D., Schmitt, N., DeShon, R.P., Clause, C.S., & Delbridge, K. (1997). Reactions to cognitive ability tests: The relationships between race, test performance, face validity perceptions, and test-taking motivation. *Journal of Applied Psychology, 82,* 300–310.

Chan, D., Schmitt, N., Jennings, D., Clause, C.S., & Delbridge K. (1998). Perceptions of test fairness: Integrating justice and self-serving bias perspectives. Paper presented at the 13th Annual Conference of the Society for Industrial and Organizational Psychology, Dallas, TX.

Chan, D., Schmitt, N., Sacco, J.M., & DeShon, R.P. (1998). Understanding pretest and posttest reactions to cognitive ability and personality tests. *Journal of Applied Psychology, 83,* 471–485.

Colquitt, J.A. (2001). On the dimensionality of organizational justice: A construct validation of a measure. *Journal of Applied Psychology, 86,* 386–400.

Cook, T.D., & Campbell, D.T. (1979). *Quasi-experimentation: Design and analysis issues for field settings.* Boston: Houghton Mifflin.

Cortina, J.M. (1993). What is coefficient alpha? An examination of theory and applications. *Journal of Applied Psychology, 78,* 453–464.

Cropanzano, R., & Konovsky, M.A. (1995). Resolving the justice dilemma by improving the outcomes: The case of employee drug screening. *Journal of Business and Psychology, 10,* 221–243.

Fallon, J.B., & Kudisch, J.D. (2001). The impact of assessing demographic data on applicant reactions to online selection procedures. In S.R. Klein (Chair), *User reactions and stereotype threat in online and traditional assessments.* Symposium presented at the 16th Annual Conference of the Society for Industrial and Organizational Psychology, San Diego, CA.

Folger, R., & Greenberg, J. (1985). Procedural justice: An interpretive analysis of personnel systems. *Research in Personnel and Human Resources Management, 3,* 141–183.

Gatewood, R.D., & Feild, H.S. (1998). *Human resource selection* (4th ed.). San Diego, CA: Dreyden Press.

Gilliland, S.W. (1993). The perceived fairness of selection systems: An organizational justice perspective. *Academy of Management Journal, 18,* 694–734.

Gilliland, S.W. (1994). Effects of procedural and distributive justice on reactions to a selection system. *Journal of Applied Psychology, 79,* 691–701.

Gilliland, S.W., & Beckstein, B.A. (1996). Procedural and distributive justice in the editorial review process. *Personnel Psychology, 49,* 669–691.

Gilliland, S.W., & Honig, H. (1994). *Development of the selection fairness survey.* Paper presented at the 9th Annual Conference of the Society for Industrial and Organizational Psychology, Nashville, TN.

Greenberg, J. (1990). Organizational justice: Yesterday, today, and tomorrow. *Journal of Management, 16,* 399–432.

Greenberg, J. (1993). The social side of fairness: Interpersonal and informational classes of organizational justice. In R. Cropanzano (Ed.), *Justice in the workplace* (pp. 79–106). Hillsdale, NJ: Erlbaum.

Greenberg, J., & Cropanzano, R. (2001). *Advances in organizational justice.* Stanford, CA: Stanford University Press.

Greguras, G.J., & Ryan, A.M. (1997). *Test taker reactions, negative affectivity, and test performance.* Paper presented at the 12th Annual Conference of the Society for Industrial and Organizational Psychology, St. Louis, MO.

Heneman, H.G. III. (1985). Pay satisfaction. *Research in Personnel and Human Resources Management, 3,* 115–139.

Highhouse, S., Zickar, M.J., Thorsteinson, T.J., Stierwalt, S.L., & Slaughter, J.E. (1999). Assessing company employment image: An example in the fast food industry. *Personnel Psychology, 52,* 151–172.

Hinkin, T.R. (1998). A brief tutorial on the development of measures for use in survey questionnaires. *Organizational Research Methods, 1,* 104–121.

Horvath, M., Ryan, A.M., & Stierwalt, S.L. (2000). The influence of explanations for selection test use, outcome favorability, and self-efficacy on test-taker perceptions. *Organizational Behavior and Human Decision Processes, 83,* 310–330.

Klein, S.R., & Russell, C.J. (2001). Applicant reactions to selection assessments: Do online and paper-pencil administration evoke similar levels of stereotype threat? In S.R. Klein (Chair), *User reactions and stereotype threat in online and traditional assessments.* Symposium presented at the 16th Annual Conference of the Society for Industrial and Organizational Psychology, San Diego, CA.

Kluger, A.N., & Rothstein, H.R. (1993). The influence of selection test type on applicant reactions to employment testing. *Journal of Business and Psychology, 8,* 3–25.

Kohn, L.S., & Dipboye, R.L. (1998). The effects of interview structure on recruiting outcomes. *Journal of Applied Social Psychology, 28,* 821–843.

Leventhal, G.S. (1980). What should be done with equity theory? In K.J. Gergen, M.S. Greenberg, & R.H. Willis (Eds.), *Social exchange: Advances in theory and research* (pp. 27–55). New York: Plenum Press.

Lind, E.A., & Tyler, T.R. (1988). *The social psychology of procedural justice.* New York: Plenum Press.

Lounsbury, J.W., Bobrow, W., & Jensen, J.B. (1989). Attitudes toward employment testing: Scale development, correlates, and "known-group" validation. *Professional Psychology: Research and Practice, 20,* 340–349.

Macan, T.H., Avedon, M.J., Paese, M., & Smith, D.E. (1994). The effects of applicants' reactions to cognitive ability tests and an assessment center. *Personnel Psychology, 47,* 715–738.

Ployhart, R.E., & Maynard, D.C. (1999). *Broadening the scope of applicant reactions research: An exploratory investigation of the effects of job characteristics and level of competition.* Paper presented at the 14th Annual Conference of the Society for Industrial and Organizational Psychology, Atlanta, GA.

Ployhart, R.E., & Ryan, A.M. (1997). Toward an explanation of applicant reactions: An examination of organizational justice and attribution frameworks. *Organizational Behavior and Human Decision Processes, 72,* 308–335.

Ployhart, R.E., & Ryan, A.M. (1998). Applicants' reactions to the fairness of selection procedures: The effects of positive rule violations and time of measurement. *Journal of Applied Psychology, 83,* 3–16.

Ployhart, R.E., Ryan, A.M., & Bennett, M. (1999). Explanations for selection decisions: Applicants' reactions to informational and sensitivity features of explanations. *Journal of Applied Psychology, 84,* 87–106.

Ryan, A.M., & Ployhart, R.E. (2000). Applicants' perceptions of selection procedures and decisions: A critical review and agenda for the future. *Journal of Management, 26,* 565–606.

Ryan, A.M., & Sackett, P.R. (1987). Pre-employment honesty testing: Fakability, reactions of test takers, and company image. *Journal of Business and Psychology, 1,* 248–256.

Rynes, S.L. (1993). Who's selecting whom? Effects of selection practices on applicant attitudes and behavior. In N. Schmitt, W.C. Borman, & Associates (Eds.), *Personnel selection in organizations* (pp. 240–274). San Francisco: Jossey-Bass.

Rynes, S.L., & Connerley, M.L. (1993). Applicant reactions to alternative selection procedures. *Journal of Business and Psychology, 7,* 261–277.

Sanchez, R.J., Truxillo, D.M., & Bauer, T.N. (2000). Development and examination of an expectancy-based measure of test-taking motivation. *Journal of Applied Psychology, 85,* 739–750.

Schmidt, F.L., Greenthal, A.L., Hunter, J.E., Berner, J.G., & Seaton, F.W. (1977). Job sample vs. paper-and-pencil trades and technical tests: Adverse impact and examinee attitudes. *Personnel Psychology, 30,* 187–197.

Schmit, M.J., & Ryan A.M. (1992). Test-taking dispositions: A missing link? *Journal of Applied Psychology, 77,* 629–637.

Schmit, M.J., & Ryan, A.M. (1997). Applicant withdrawal: The role of test-taking attitudes and racial differences. *Personnel Psychology, 50,* 855–876.

Schmitt, N., Gilliland, S.W., Landis, R.S., & Devine, D. (1993). Computer-based testing applied to selection of secretarial applicants. *Personnel Psychology, 46,* 149–165.

Seitz, R., Truxillo, D.M., & Bauer, T.N. (2001). *Test familiarization: Effects on reactions to written and video tests.* Paper presented at the 16th Annual Conference of the Society for Industrial and Organizational Psychology, San Diego, CA.

Seymour, R.T. (1988). Why plaintiffs' counsel challenge tests, and how they can successfully challenge the theory of "validity generalization." *Journal of Vocational Behavior, 33,* 331–364.

Shapiro, D.L., Buttner, E.H., & Barry, B. (1994). Explanations: What factors enhance their perceived adequacy? *Organizational Behavior and Human Decision Processes, 58,* 346–368.

Smither, J.W., Millsap, R.E., Stoffey, R.W., Reilly, R.R., & Pearlman, K. (1996). An experimental test of the influence of selection procedures on fairness perceptions, attitudes about the organization, and job pursuit intentions. *Journal of Business and Psychology, 10,* 297–318.

Smither, J.W., Reilly, R.R., Millsap, R.E., Pearlman, K., & Stoffey, R.W. (1993). Applicant reactions to selection procedures. *Personnel Psychology, 46,* 49–77.

Steele, C.M., & Aronson, J. (1995). Stereotype threat and the intellectual test performance of African-Americans. *Journal of Personality and Social Psychology, 69,* 797–811.

Steiner, D.D., & Gilliland, S.W. (1996). Fairness reactions to personnel selection techniques in France and the United States. *Journal of Applied Psychology, 81,* 134–141.

Thibault, J., & Walker, L. (1975). *Procedural justice: A psychological analysis.* Hillsdale, NJ: Erlbaum.

Thorsteinson, T.J., & Ryan, A.M. (1997). The effect of selection ratio on perceptions of the fairness of a selection test battery. *International Journal of Selection and Assessment, 5,* 159–168.

Truxillo, D.M., & Bauer, T.N. (1999). Applicant reactions to test score banding in entry-level and promotional contexts. *Journal of Applied Psychology, 84,* 322–339.

Truxillo, D.M., Bauer, T.N., & Sanchez, R.J. (2001). Multiple dimensions of procedural justice: Longitudinal effects on selection system fairness and test-taking self-efficacy. *International Journal of Selection and Assessment, 9,* 336–349.

Truxillo, D.M., Steiner, D.D., & Gilliland, S.W. (2001). *A critical examination of selection justice: Does it really matter?* Paper presented at the Second International Organizational Justice Roundtable, Vancouver, CA.

Turban, D.B., & Keon, T.L. (1993). Organizational attractiveness: An interactionist perspective. *Journal of Applied Psychology, 78,* 184–193.

Vroom, V.H. (1964). *Work and motivation.* New York: Wiley.

Weekley, J.A., & Jones, C. (1997). Video-based situational testing. *Personnel Psychology, 50,* 25–49.

Weiner, B. (1985). An attributional theory of achievement, motivation, and emotion. *Psychological Review, 92,* 548–573.

Williams, M.L., & Bauer, T.N. (1991). The effect of a managing diversity policy on organizational attractiveness. *Group and Organizational Management, 19,* 295–308.

# CHAPTER 28

# Organizational Culture and Organizational Climate Measures: An Integrative Review

DANIEL J. SVYANTEK AND JENNIFER P. BOTT

The explanation of complex human behavior requires the consideration of person, contextual, and behavioral variables (Funder, 2001). The context in which an individual resides, as well as individual differences, is related to the production of behavior. The behaviors exhibited in a situation have an adaptive function (Morris, 1988). This degree to which behavior is adaptive, however, is defined relative to the situation. Therefore, understanding how contexts affect the production of behavior is a critical requirement for understanding how individuals act when in groups and organizations.

Namenwirth and Weber (1987) proposed that culture serves four purposes for any social group. These purposes are to determine: (1) what it means to be a member of the group, (2) how social and economic justice are reflected within the group, (3) how the elements of the group are organized to produce a socially "good" group, and (4) how the group makes the materials or services it was formed to produce.

Within organizations, organizational culture and organizational climate provide this information. A major reason for the formation of organizational culture is the creation of so-

cial order (Trice & Beyer, 1993). Organizational culture allows recurrent behavior patterns among people to develop within organizations. These patterns form the basis of predictable interactions within an organization.

Organizational culture and organizational climate influence behaviors within an organization by defining a *strong situation* (Mischel, 1977) for individuals residing within it. A strong situation provides people with generally accepted rules and guidelines for appropriate behavior. The rules that are present in strong situations constrain people from acting in a manner inconsistent with accepted conduct and behavior. Organizations develop values and norms to set parameters on the behaviors exhibited within an organization. Organizational culture and organizational climate act to provide employees with information about what (1) behavioral styles and (2) specific behaviors that the organization in which they reside values.

For example, organizations possess norms and values regarding proper decision-making practices (Ott, 1989). These have been shown to affect the choice of decision-making strategies through the creation of organizational decision-making styles (Svyantek, Jones, & Rozelle, 1991; Svyantek & Kolz, 1996). Such a collection of norms and values can be labeled an organizational decision climate. The policies and practices of an organization supporting such styles are hypothesized to create a specific decision-making climate for that organization.

The effects of organizational climate are particularly strong when the individual is motivated to adapt (Showers & Cantor, 1985). The ability to recognize and correctly adapt to the reality of organizational life is a critical component of career success (Sathe, 1985) in which managers are very motivated to understand the behaviors supported in their environment (Hannaway, 1989). Managers rely heavily on the information they receive from their social structure to infer appropriate behaviors and use this information to balance organizational goals and their personal career interests when making a decision (Hannaway, 1989; Svyantek et al., 1991; Svyantek & Kolz, 1996). They must, in effect, analyze and interpret their organization's decision-making climate and use these interpretations to guide their decision-making behavior. This maximizes individual rewards and minimizes individual punishments for the decision maker. Thus, the appropriateness of a decision will be contingent upon the organizational culture within which the decision maker operates.

The constraints on the accepted range of behaviors within an organization create multiple organizational climates supporting responses for organizational criteria (e.g., customer service or decision making). These constraints are created by, and reflect, the values and assumptions that compose an organizational culture and/or organizational climate.

## ORGANIZATIONAL CULTURE VERSUS ORGANIZATIONAL CLIMATE

Organizational culture and climate are similar concepts. Indeed, they are so similar that a debate has raged over whether they are actually the same or different constructs.

### The Debate

Schein (1990) suggested that organizational climate is what we perceive when we observe the way a company functions, whereas organizational culture relates to the causes of an organization's operating style. However, this distinction often blurs in practice.

Goodman and Svyantek (1999), for example, used the Litwin and Stringer (1968) Organizational Climate Questionnaire (OCQ) to operationally define dimensions of or-

ganizational culture. Although operationalizing culture with a "climate" questionnaire seems illogical, Goodman and Svyantek concluded that a close examination of the constructs supports the operationalization. This was based on a review of the original Litwin and Stringer (1968) description of the variables measured in the OCQ. The OCQ, according to Litwin and Stringer, assessed the shared beliefs and values of organizational members that constitute the perceived work environment, which is consistent with the definition of organizational culture. Therefore, the original conception of organizational climate is consistent with the constructs that quantitative measures of organizational culture assess.

Organizational culture and organizational climate are closely related constructs that are linked both conceptually and practically (Schneider, 2000). The value of organizational culture and organizational climate is in explaining behaviors and relationships among people who share some sort of common experience or situation (Payne, 2000).

Two closely related distinctions between the two constructs have been defined in the literature. The first distinction is related to the definition of organizational culture and organizational climate. Organizational culture research is believed to occur at a deeper level (e.g., underlying values held by the group) than is organizational climate research (e.g., the observed behaviors of members of a group) (Schein, 2000). For example, Schein's (1985) model of the three levels of organizational culture is a multidimensional, multilevel definition of culture. The first level, which is the most superficial or visible level of culture, is artifacts and creations: These represent the physical and social environment of the situation. It is at this level that climate research is conducted. The second level of culture is values, norms, and attitudes, or a sense of what "ought to be." Finally, at the deepest level lie the unconscious assumptions uniformly held by all members of the culture. These unconscious assumptions make up the true culture of an organization.

The second distinction between culture and climate is a methodological one. Typically, individuals studying organizational culture have emphasized the use of qualitative research methods while individuals studying organizational climate have conducted their research primarily with quantitative research tools (Payne, 2000; Schneider, 2000). This distinction, however, becomes blurred in practice because of two related research issues.

First, measurement of organizational properties may be conducted using either objective or subjective (perceptual) measurement approaches (Hellriegel & Slocum, 1974; Payne & Pugh, 1976). Objective measurement implies a direct assessment of organizational properties without any conceptual transformation occurring (Payne & Pugh, 1976). Subjective measurement implies indirect assessment of organizational properties by instruments measuring individual or group perceptions. From a research methodology perspective, both quantitative and qualitative research approaches share a common problem: They are both examples of subjective measurement approaches. Therefore, neither methodology is inherently superior for gathering data about an organization. Rather, the *purpose* for which the data are being gathered may be more important in the selection of a quantitative or qualitative approach. This is illustrated by the trend in organizational culture research described in the next section.

Research methods used to explore organizational culture have begun to emphasize quantitative measurement of the construct in recent studies. Xenikou and Furnham (1996), for example, stated that the distinction between organizational culture and organizational climate was traditionally defined as the methods used to analyze the constructs. Climate research has tended to be nomothetic, using quantitative methods to make comparisons among organizations. Culture, however, has tended to be idiographic in approach, using qualitative methods to intensively explore the effects of organizational culture on one organization. However, to make comparisons across organizations, culture researchers must use quantitative methods. Xenikou and Furnham (1996) conducted a study comparing four quantitative measures of culture in terms of the instruments' psychometric properties. Their analyses found adequate psychometric properties (e.g., coefficient alphas, factor structure, and convergent validity) for four different organizational culture measures with up to 12 measured dimensions. This study, then, provides evidence that quantitative measures of organizational culture are assessing what they intend to measure.

Thus, the distinction between organizational climate and organizational culture on methodological grounds may no longer be as pertinent as once thought. The descriptions of the dimensions assessed in organizational culture inventories investigated by Xenikou and Furnham (1996) are very similar to the dimensions that Litwin and Stringer (1968) originally proposed.

## A Rapprochement

Schneider (2000) provided a framework for reconciling organizational culture and organizational climate. Organizational climate, according to Schneider, represents the descriptions of the things that happen to employees in an organization. Organizational climate is behaviorally oriented in that climates for safety or service, for example, may be found in the workplace. These climates represent the patterns of interactions and behaviors that support safety or service in the or-

ganization. Organizational climate, therefore, is a description of what occurs within the organization. However, when employees are questioned on why these patterns exist, deeper levels of insight are found. The question of why is answered with stories and myths that describe life in the organization, which defines organizational culture. Organizational culture, therefore, is an antecedent of constructs such as organizational climate and organizational design (Cooke & Szumal, 2000). This framework serves as the basis for our definition of organizational culture and organizational climate and the relationship between the two constructs.

We propose that the following definitions provide a possible rapprochement for the debate on the differences between organizational culture and organizational climate. *Organizational culture* is defined by a set of shared values and norms held by employees that guides employees' interactions with peers, management, and clients/customers (Morgan, 1998). *Organizational climate* is more behaviorally oriented in that climates for creativity, innovation, safety, or service, for example, may be found in the workplace (Schneider, 2000). These climates represent the specific patterns of interactions and behaviors that support safety or service in the organization.

Organizational culture is proposed as the antecedent, causal element for organizational climate. Organizational culture provides the context in which different patterns of interactions and behaviors develop in multiple organizations. It has been proposed that when considering organizational culture as a context for employee behavior, the important cultural values are those related to how employees are treated in the workplace (Svyantek, 1997; Svyantek & Brown, 2000). The management of an organization translates these cultural values into observable practices (e.g., organizational climates or organizational structure), defining important behaviors and creating a vision of the social order in the organization (Trice and Beyer, 1993). However, a reciprocal relationship exists between organizational climate and organizational culture. Therefore, while organizational culture may cause organizational climate, changes in organizational climate level variables are required to cause changes in organizational culture (Schneider, 2000).

## Summary

This chapter describes some quantitative measures of organizational culture and organizational climate. Therefore, the distinction that will be made is not on what type of research method (quantitative versus qualitative) is used to understand one of the two constructs. Rather, we make a distinction between general and specific measures of the organizational context.

The names of the construct being measured, organizational culture or climate, is also not the distinction being made here. The distinction involves the degree to which the instrument is related to a specific organizational behavior. Measures that assess the shared beliefs and values of organizational members that constitute the perceived work environment, which are not linked to a specific behavior, are treated as general measures in this review. Measures that assess the organizational practices related to the performance of a specific organizational behavior are treated as specific measures in this review. This distinction is used in the next two sections.

## GENERAL MEASURES

We review five general measures of the organizational context that use surveys that require quantitative responses by employees of an organization. These measures are (1) The Organizational Climate Questionnaire (OCQ) (Litwin & Stringer, 1968); (2) The Organizational Culture Assessment Instrument (OCAI) (Cameron & Quinn, 1999); (3) The Organizational Culture Inventory (OCI) (Cooke & Rousseau, 1988); (4) The Organizational Culture Profile (OCP-1) (O'Reilly, Chatman, & Caldwell, 1991); and (5) The Organizational Culture Profile (OCP-2) (Ashkanasy, Broadfoot, & Falkus, 2000). These instruments illustrate several things about scales measuring the organizational context. First, the descriptions OCQ versus the OCI and OCP-2 scales show the similarity of dimensions and items for general measures whether organizational climate (OCQ) or organizational culture (OCI and OCP-2) is used to name the construct. Second, the OCP-1 is an instrument assessing person-culture fit. This construct, person-culture fit, represents an important development that is related to the assessment of organizational culture and organizational climate (cf., Goodman & Svyantek, 1999; Kristof, 1996). Finally, the OCAI describes a more practitioner-oriented instrument.

## The Organizational Climate Questionnaire (OCQ)

### Rationale

One of the most popular general measures of organizational climate is the OCQ developed by Litwin and Stringer (1968). Litwin and Stringer's measure assesses the shared beliefs and values of organizational members that constitute the perceived work environment.

### The Instrument

In its original form, the OCQ asks respondents to rate the extent to which they agree/disagree with each item, using a 4-point Likert scale. Later research has used the more typical 5-point Likert scale to assess subject responses (e.g., Goodman & Svyantek, 1999). The questionnaire is one of the better known surveys of its kind (Payne & Pugh, 1976). It consists of 50 items that assess nine dimensions of climate. Table 28.1 describes the OCQ in greater detail. Litwin and Stringer concluded that seven of the nine scales showed good internal consistency.

### Validation

Many studies have assessed the degree to which this instrument is effective in assessing the organizational context. These studies have investigated the characteristics of the OCQ (e.g., factor structure) and the relationship of the OCQ to other organizational behavior constructs.

**TABLE 28.1  Litwin and Stringer's Organizational Climate Questionnaire (OCQ) Scale Descriptions**

| Scale | Description |
| --- | --- |
| Structure | The feeling that employees have about the constraints in the group, how many rules, regulations, procedures there are; is there an emphasis on "red tape" and going through channels, or is there a loose and informal atmosphere? |
| Responsibility | The feeling of being your own boss; not having to double-check all your decisions; when you have a job to do, knowing that it is your job. |
| Reward | The feeling of being rewarded for a job well done; emphasizing positive rewards rather than punishment; the perceived fairness of the pay and promotion policies. |
| Risk | The sense of riskiness and challenge in the job and in the organization; is there an emphasis on taking calculated risks, or is playing it safe the best way to operate? |
| Warmth | The feeling of general good fellowship that prevails in the work group atmosphere; the emphasis of being well liked; the prevalence of friendly and informal social groups. |
| Support | The perceived helpfulness of the managers and other employees in the group; emphasis on mutual support from above and below. |
| Standards | The perceived importance of implicit and explicit goals and performance standards; the emphasis on doing a good job; the challenge presented in personal and group goals. |
| Conflict | The feeling that managers and other workers want to hear different opinions; the emphasis placed on getting problems out in the open rather than smoothing them over or ignoring them. |
| Identity | The feeling that you belong to a company and you are a valuable member of a working team; the importance placed on this kind of spirit. |

Sims and LaFollette (1975) conducted a study to examine the validity and reliability of the OCQ. Their study used a sample of 997 questionnaires from workers at a midwestern medical complex. Factor analysis revealed the items on the nine dimensions of the OCQ loaded on six factors. Split-half reliabilities for the nine dimensions ranged from adequate to inadequate. The split-half reliabilities for the nine scales were (1) Structure (.79); (2) Responsibility (.34); (3) Reward (.67); (4) Risk (.12); (5) Warmth (.76); (6) Support (.69); (7) Standards (.37); (8) Conflict (.21); and (9) Identity (.79).

Muchinsky (1976) replicated Sims and LaFollette's (1975) study. This study used a sample of 695 employees at a large public utility. Factor analysis revealed the items on the nine dimensions of the OCQ loaded on six factors once again. Muchinsky reported alpha coefficients for the nine scales as follows: Structure (.77), Responsibility (.46), Reward (.81), Risk (.77), Warmth (.81), Support (.77), Standards (.49), Conflict (.01), and Identity (.81). These reliabilities were generally higher than the split-half reliabilities reported in Sims and LaFollette (1975). The observed differences between this study's results and the results of the Sims and LaFollette (1975) study were interpreted as potentially due to differences in the samples (e.g., work practices, procedures, goals). Muchinsky concludes that the Litwin and Stringer scales are decent (with the exception of the Conflict scale). Muchinsky notes, however, that it may be difficult to use a standardized climate measure in every organization equally well, and it may make more sense to develop a questionnaire around the four organizational climate factors identified by Campbell, Dunnette, Lawler, and Weick (1970). These factors were Individual Autonomy, Degree of Structure Imposed upon the Position, Reward Orientation, and Consideration.

Rogers, Miles, and Biggs (1980) found similar results in their analysis of the OCQ. The OCQ was given to a sample of 540 managers and nonmanagers at a water and sewage department. These employees were grouped into three categories: (1) Sewage ($n = 253$), (2) Accounting ($n = 80$), and (3) Water ($n = 148$). Factor analysis did not replicate the nine-factor structure of the OCQ proposed by Litwin and Stringer (1968). The authors concluded, after reviewing several studies, in which most found six factors, there is virtually no agreement among researchers regarding which items load best on the different factors. It appears that factor-analytic structure depends greatly on the organization studied (there is little to no interorganizational stability within the measure). They also concluded that the OCQ lacks validity and is not a consistent measurement device.

Studies have been conducted to assess the relationship between the organizational context and job satisfaction. Downey, Hellriegel, Phelps, and Slocum (1974) conducted a study to determine if job satisfaction and climate are in fact the same construct, after controlling for other variables (here the influence of organizational level and job performance). Their study used a sample of 104 responses from a steel corporation's management group. The managers were administered the Job Descriptive Index and the OCQ. Factor analysis revealed six orthogonal factors; two of which (Warmth and Rewards) were highly correlated with job satisfaction scales. The authors also concluded that organization level has a powerful effect on the relationship between job satisfaction and climate and that climate scales are related to job satisfaction scales. Putti and Kheun (1986) investigated the relationship between the OCQ and Job Descriptive Index as well. They also concluded that job satisfaction is highly correlated with organizational climate.

Schnake (1983), however, addressed the question of whether *perceptual* measures of organizational climate are redundant with measures of job satisfaction. It was hypothesized that removing affect (by removing effects of job satisfaction) would improve the discriminant validity of climate measures. The sample was 8,938 nonsupervisory employees from a large utility company. The OCQ and measures of three factors of job satisfaction (Intrinsic Satisfaction, Extrinsic Satisfaction, and Social Satisfaction) were used. The effects of the three types of satisfaction were partialed out of the intercorrelations of the climate instrument items. The general conclusions were that, based on a comparison of the explained variance between satisfaction and climate items, it appears that satisfaction does not explain all of the variance in climate perceptions and that removing the affective response (job satisfaction) does improve the dimensionality of the climate measure.

The OCQ, moreover, is related to important performance behaviors in organizations. Goodman and Svyantek (1999), for example, assessed the relationship between person-organization fit and both job performance and organizational citizenship behaviors of organizational members. Employees rated each item twice (as in O'Reilly et al., 1991). They first used the OCQ to rate the extent to which each item represents the way things are done within their organization (i.e., perceived culture). Second, employees were asked to rate the extent to which each item represents their "ideal" organization's culture. It was found that the Warmth scale was a predictor of employee job performance and employee propensity to perform organizational citizenship behaviors.

## The Organizational Culture Assessment Instrument (OCAI)

### Rationale

The OCAI (Cameron & Quinn, 1999) was developed to identify both current and ideal culture. It allows for the identification of the type of organizational culture that exists in the organization and may be used to assess subcultures as well. This instrument is intended to provide insight into areas of organizational culture that may require change.

### The Instrument

The OCAI assesses six key dimensions of culture. Each dimension is assessed with one question. When answering these questions, respondents are asked to focus on the cultural unit that is under investigation for change. This means that the instrument may be used at levels of analysis other than the organization. The dimensions are: (1) Dominant Characteristics; (2) Organizational Leadership; (3) Management of Employees; (4) Organizational Glue; (5) Strategic Emphases; and (6) Criteria of Success.

### Validation

This instrument may be found in a book by the authors. Little conventional validation information is presented. The results of the survey are graphically plotted using actual (Now) and preferred/ideal culture responses. Scores correspond to a specific type of culture, based on standing in four categories: (1) flexibility and discretion, (2) external focus and differentiation, (3) stability and control, and (4) internal focus and integration. Four general types of cultures are identified: clan, adhocracy, hierarchy, and market cultures. The *clan* culture is described as a friendly place to work, where leaders are mentors, and loyalty holds the organization together. Employee commitment is high. Success is characterized by long-term development of employees, with morale and cohesion important. The *adhocracy* culture is described as dynamic, entrepreneurial, and creative. Taking risks is common and leaders are innovative. Commitment to experimentation and innovation binds the organization together. Being on the leading edge is the emphasis, with success determined by the creation of new products. The *hierarchy* culture is described as structured and formalized, where strict procedures determine what is done. Leaders are efficient and coordinate activities, with an emphasis on smooth operations and stability. Success is determined by smooth delivery, efficiency, and scheduling. Finally, the *market* culture is described as results oriented, with competitive and goal-oriented workers. Leaders in this organization are drivers and producers, who are tough and demanding to subordinates. An emphasis on winning binds the organization together. Success is determined by market share, and the long-term goal is on achievement of measurable goals and targets.

## The Organizational Culture Inventory (OCI)

### Rationale

The OCI was developed to assess organizational culture, which is defined by the authors as: "the ways of thinking, behaving and believing that all members of a social unit have in common" (Cooke & Rousseau, 1988, p. 248). Two main attributes of culture are described: direction and intensity. Direction refers to the content of the culture, as seen through values, behavioral norms, and thinking styles emphasized in the organization. Intensity refers to the strength of these values: It can be thought of as the degree of consensus among organizational members on these values. The OCI was designed to measure intraorganizational, as well as interorganizational, culture and to assess the ways that organizational members are expected to think and their behavior in relation to their tasks and peers/coworkers.

### The Instrument

The OCI has 12 scales. It is made up of 120 items, 10 items per scale. Each item describes a behavior that might be expected of an employee of an organization. The 12 scales are (1) Humanistic-Helpful ($\alpha = .90$) (the degree that employees are managed in a participative, person-centered way); (2) Affiliative ($\alpha = .92$) (the degree that high priority on developing constructive interpersonal relationships is supported); (3) Approval ($\alpha = .81$) (the degree that conflicts are avoided and interpersonal relationships are at least superficially pleasant); (4) Conventional ($\alpha = .87$) (the degree that the organization is conservative and bureaucratically controlled); (5) Dependent ($\alpha = .75$) (the degree that the organization is hierarchically controlled and nonparticipative); (6) Avoidance ($\alpha = .85$) (the degree to which the organization fails to reward success and punishes mistakes); (7) Oppositional ($\alpha = .67$) (the degree that confrontation and negativism are common); (8) Power ($\alpha = .80$) (the degree that behavior is nonparticipative and related to power within individual positions); (9) Competitive ($\alpha = .82$) (the degree that winning is important and members are rewarded for outperforming one another); (10) Competence/Perfectionistic ($\alpha = .77$) (the degree to which perfectionism, persistence, and hard work are valued); (11) Achievement ($\alpha = .85$) (the degree to which the organization values members that set their own goals); and (12) Self-actualizing ($\alpha = .82$) (the degree to which the organization values creativity over quantity and members' individual growth along with task accomplishment).

### Validation

Survey data were gathered from 661 individuals from 18 organizations and an executive development program/graduate business program. Factor analysis revealed three primary factors (total variance predicted is 65%) assessed by the 12 scales of the OCI. These were (1) People/Security Culture (21.3% of the variance); (2) Satisfaction Culture (24.8% of the variance); and (3) Task/security Culture (18.9% of the variance). Eta-squared values indicated there was consistency among units within the organizations regarding norms and expectations. The OCI was also shown to be able to differentiate between organizations and their behavioral norms, as well as between different levels within the organization.

## The Organizational Culture Profile (OCP-1)

### Rationale

Culture is believed to be "a set of cognitions shared by members of a social unit" (O'Reilly et al., 1991, p. 491). This usually involves investigating the values and assumptions within an organization. It may be that a set of shared values helps to shape social expectations or norms, leading to the creation of a social identity for organization members. The authors believe that culture appears to be important when predicting employee fit within an organization. The authors assert that congruency between an individual's values and those of the organization may indicate person-culture fit. They take an explicit profile-matching approach to study this person-culture fit and to determine the influence that person-culture fit exerts on individual commitment, satisfaction, and longevity with an organization.

### The Instrument

The authors developed a Q-sort to assess person-culture fit using profiles and matching techniques known as template matching (e.g., Bem & Funder, 1978). The measure contains 54 values statements that are sorted into nine categories twice. First, the items are sorted on their desirability to the individual conducting the sort. Next, individuals sort items based on how characteristic the values are of the organization to which they belong. The 54 statements assess eight factors of organizational culture. These are: (1) Innovation and Risk-Taking; (2) Attention to detail; (3) Orientation toward outcomes/ results; (4) Aggressiveness and competitiveness; (5) Supportiveness; (6) Emphasis on growth and rewards; (7) Collaboration and team orientation; and (8) Decisiveness.

### Validation

The authors conducted a series of studies investigating the validity of this instrument and the Q-sort technique. The general assumption of this method is that person-culture fit can be determined by correlating the two profile sorts. Results

indicated that the profiles are stable across time. MBA students were asked to do the two sortings twice, 12 months apart. Preferences were highly stable (average $r = .73$). Second, a study was conducted to assess the relationship between person-culture fit, organizational commitment, job satisfaction, intent to leave, turnover, and control variables (i.e., tenure at the firm, age, gender). Five samples of individuals participated in this experiment: (1) 131 first-year MBA students, (2) 93 MBA students at a different university, (3) 171 first-year accountants at eight different firms and 128 senior accountants at the eight different firms, (4) 96 CPAs in six offices of major accounting firms and (5) 730 middle managers at a government agency. High person-culture fit was associated with high positive affect and low intent to leave a year later. Survival analysis also indicated that person-organization fit predicted whether individuals would leave the firm two years later. These results were interpreted as showing that person-job fit and person-culture fit are separate constructs. This method is seen as assessing measure organizational culture and person-culture fit reasonably well.

## The Organizational Culture Profile (OCP-2)

### Rationale

Ashkanasy, Broadfoot, and Falkus (2000) developed the OCP-2 after examining previous literature. It was established to measure behavioral norms and patterns in organizations.

### The Instrument

From a review of other organizational surveys, the authors determined there were 15 underlying themes, which they pared down to 10 summary dimensions. Forty-one items were selected from existing surveys in order to measure these dimensions. The authors wrote nine of their own questions, filling in areas that were weak. Therefore, there are 5 questions for each of the 10 subscales: (1) Leadership; (2) Planning; (3) Communication; (4) Humanistic Workplace; (5) Environment; (6) Job Performance; (7) Development of the Individual; (8) Structure; (9) Innovation; and (10) Socialization on Entry.

### Validation

An initial validation was conducted with a sample of 151 Australian health care workers (Ashkanasy et al., 2000). The authors uncovered mixed reliability evidence. The reliability of the scales fell into three categories. First, there were reliable scales ($\alpha > .80$). These were the Leadership, Planning, Communication, and Humanistic Workplace scales. Second, there were adequately reliable scales ($\alpha > .70$). These were the Environment, Job Performance, and Development of the Individual scales. Finally, some scales were to be used with caution ($\alpha < .70$). These were the Structure, Innovation, and Socialization on Entry scales. Factor analysis indicated that three general factors emerged. Two had acceptable psychometric properties. These were labeled Innovative Leadership ($\alpha > .91$) and Rules Orientation ($\alpha > .69$). A second validation study was then performed with a sample of 297 individuals in 14 Australian organizations. An exploratory factor analysis yielded a two-factor solution: Instrumental ($\alpha > .82$) and Expressive ($\alpha > .87$). There was significant within-organization agreement (as indexed by $r_{wg}$ and between group differences). All scales but Structure were in the hypothesized direction with outcome variables of satisfaction, commitment, and performance. There was considerable overlap between scales; however, the Instrumental and Expressive factors were independently predictive of organizational effectiveness, satisfaction, and commitment. The authors concluded there is more support for a two-factor model, but that this should be accepted cautiously. The 10-factor model may be less parsimonious but may be more useful and descriptive of organizational culture.

## SPECIFIC MEASURES

This section highlights some instruments developed to assess organizational practices related to the performance of a specific organizational behavior. These measures include instruments that assess organizational practices related to (1) creativity, (2) ethical behavior, (3) industrial relations, (4) safety, (5) service, and (6) teams.

### Creativity Climate-The Situational Outlook Questionnaire (SOQ)

#### Rationale

Isaksen, Lauer, and Ekvall (1999) developed the SOQ to assess the climate of creativity and change in organizations. It is a translation of the Creative Climate Questionnaire (a questionnaire developed in Sweden). The instrument is intended to measure characteristics of the climate that influence creativity and change at the individual, group, and organization levels. Isaksen, Lauer, Ekvall, and Britz (2000–2001) defined the climate for creativity as "that which promotes the generation, consideration, and use of new products, services and ways of working. This climate supports the development, assimilation, and utilization of new and different approaches and concepts" (p. 172). The authors view organizational climate as an intervening variable in the relationship between

the external environment and organizational practices (inputs) that influence the organizational and psychological processes (outputs).

### The Instrument

The instrument consists of 50 items. The instrument uses a 4-point scale on which the respondent indicates the degree to which each item is indicative of his or her organization. The scale anchors are 0 ("Not at All Applicable"), 1 ("Applicable to Some Extent"), 2 ("Fairly Applicable"), and 3 ("Applicable to a High Extent"). Nine factors are measured: (1) Challenge/Involvement (the emotional involvement, commitment, motivation in operations and goals of the organization); (2) Freedom (the level of autonomy, discretion, initiative in behavior exerted by individuals in order to make decisions and acquire information); (3) Trust/Openness (the emotional safety and openness found in relationships); (4) Idea Time (the time spent to elaborate new ideas); (5) Playfulness/Humor (the degree to which spontaneity, ease, good-natured joking, and laughing are displayed); (6) Conflict (the personal tensions or hostilities seen); (7) Idea Support (the manner in which new ideas and suggestions are attended to and treated in a kindly manner); (8) Debate (the amount of expression, and consideration of, many different ideas and viewpoints); and (9) Risk-taking (the amount of tolerance of ambiguity and uncertainty exhibited).

### Validation

Isaksen et al. (1999) collected responses from 1,111 individuals and conducted factor analyses and found the nine factors described previously. The reliabilities for the nine factors were (1) Challenge/Involvement ($\alpha = .84$); (2) Freedom ($\alpha = .94$); (3) Trust/Openness ($\alpha = .64$); (4) Idea Time ($\alpha = .88$); (5) Playfulness/Humor ($\alpha = .89$); (6) Conflict ($\alpha = .86$); (7) Idea Support ($\alpha = .90$); (8) Debate ($\alpha = .88$); and (9) Risk-taking ($\alpha = .62$). The low reliabilities for the Risk-taking and Trust/Openness factors were hypothesized to be related to the small number of items.

This instrument was subsequently used in later studies of creative climate. For example, Isaksen et al., (2000–2001) attempted to establish the criterion-related validity of the SOQ. The SOQ was used to differentiate between individual's perceptions of best- and worst-case scenarios when considering creative, innovative organizational environments. Two studies were conducted. For study one, 22 managers (14 men, 8 women) and 24 graduate students (11 men, 13 women) completed the SOQ in reference to their best-/worse-case scenarios (procedure was completed twice; once for each scenario). A significant amount of overlap occurred between both samples' (managers and graduate students) perceptions of best- and worst-case scenarios. The authors concluded the SOQ appears to differentiate between climates for creativity, thus supporting its criterion-related validity.

## Ethical Climate Questionnaire (ECQ)

### Rationale

Corporate ethics represent a set of standards that guide the organization when conflicting values arise (Victor & Cullen, 1987, 1988). The ethical climate within an organization can determine: (1) what members consider ethically important, and (2) what criteria they use to resolve ethically important issues. The ECQ was designed because it is believed that companies (or subunits, departments) have their own moral character, that group members know what this character is, and that members can tell outsiders about this character in an objective way.

### The Instrument

Victor and Cullen (1987, 1988) developed the original instrument. The instrument is used to characterize organizations as (1) Instrumental (egoistic), (2) Caring (benevolence), or (3) Principled (Cullen, Victor, & Bronson, 1993). These three types of ethical standards can be applied to three loci of analysis: the individual, local, and cosmopolitan. This results in nine possible ethical climates that are identifiable with the ECQ. These are as follows: (1) Self-interest (egoism, individual); (2) Friendship (benevolence, individual); (3) Personal morality (principle, individual); (4) Company profit (egoism, local); (5) Team interest (benevolence, local); (6) Rules, standard operating procedures (principle, local); (7) Efficiency (egoism, cosmopolitan); (8) Social responsibility (benevolence, cosmopolitan); and (9) Laws, professional codes (principle, cosmopolitan). The ECQ is used to assess how individuals perceive members of the organization making decisions concerning events, practices, and procedures requiring ethical criteria. The original version contained 26 items (Victor & Cullen, 1987, 1988); The updated version reprinted in Cullen et al. (1993) includes 36 items. Four 5-point Likert scale items are used to assess the nine ethical climates.

### Validation

This study reported validation studies on four accounting firms. Seven types of ethical climates were identified in this sample. The study reported reliabilities for the possible eth-

ical climates: (1) Self-interest ($\alpha$ = .80); (2) Efficiency ($\alpha$ = .69); (3) Friendship/Team interest ($\alpha$ = .85); (4) Social responsibility ($\alpha$ = .85); (5) Personal morality ($\alpha$ = .77); (6) Rules, standard operating procedure ($\alpha$ = .76); (7) Laws, professional codes ($\alpha$ = .76). All items loaded on the appropriate factors, except for items relating to friendship and team interest. These loaded on a single factor and were combined.

## Industrial Relations Climate Questionnaire (IRCQ)

### Rationale

Dastmalchian, Adamson, & Blyton, (1986) proposed that organizations have industrial relations climates that describe an atmosphere that influences the relationship between employees, their representatives, and the management of an organization. The objective was to develop a measure that assesses the various factors within an organization that create the industrial relations climate.

### The Instrument

Dastmalchian et al. (1986) identified a number of important factors affecting industrial relations climate after reviewing the literature on management/union relationships. These factors included Union-Management Cooperation, Aggression, Apathy, Hostility, Union Support, Joint Participation, Trust, Goal Identification, Fairness, and Power Balance in the organization. The instrument is a 40-item survey measuring these factors on a 5-point Likert scale with anchors ranging from "Strongly Disagree" to "Strongly Agree."

### Validation

Dastmalchian et al. (1986) gathered data from managers, union representatives, and arbitrators to assess the validity of their instrument. The first step was to use frequency analyses to determine which areas were most important. Results indicated that union-management cooperation, trust and joint problem solving were considered most important for understanding the industrial relations climate within an organization by this sample. Further analyses showed that six factors were important for assessing industrial relations climate: (1) Union-Management Cooperation ($\alpha$ = .77); (2) Mutual Regard ($\alpha$ = .81); (3) Apathy/Quiescence ($\alpha$ = .72); (4) Joint Participation ($\alpha$ = .87); (5) Trust/Fairness ($\alpha$ = .81); and (6) Hostility/Aggression ($\alpha$ = .86). This measure was also able to distinguish between groups of individuals in organizations. Differences were found between the opinions of management and unions on the scales of the questionnaire.

This instrument was subsequently used in later studies of industrial relations climate. Dastmalchian, Blyton, and Adamson (1989), for example, used a 26-item version of their original IRCQ using a 5-point Likert scale to assess employee responses in two organizations. Here five factors were found: (1) Harmony (Organization A $\alpha = .85$, Organization B $\alpha = .92$); (2) Openness (Organization A $\alpha = .65$, Organization B $\alpha = .75$); (3) Hostility (Organization A $\alpha = .77$, Organization B $\alpha = .81$); (4) Apathy (Organization A $\alpha = .66$, Organization B $\alpha = .80$); and (5) Promptness (Organization A $\alpha = .68$, Organization B $\alpha = .74$). Interclass correlation analyses indicated significant within-organization agreement. These scales also differentiate between organizations, indicating the ability of the measure to discriminate (with the exception of Apathy). Within-group agreement is highest when comparing union with nonunion employees (across organizations). This revised measure is interpreted as accurately profiling the qualities of the organizations in the study. The authors concluded that this instrument can be used in a diagnostic or predictive sense by organizations seeking to assess their industrial relations climate.

## Safety Climate Questionnaire (SCQ)

### Rationale

Zohar (1980) proposed that a number of different climates exist within organizations. Therefore, it is necessary to specify which climate is being investigated in a study. In his studies, the variable of interest was safety climate, which evaluates employee perceptions of management attitudes and organizational policies related to safety in an organization.

### The Instrument

Zohar's instrument is a 40-item questionnaire measuring eight factors relevant for assessing safety climate using a 5-point scale. The factors the SCQ measures are: (1) Perceived Importance of Safety Training Programs; (2) Perceived Management Attitudes Toward Safety; (3) Perceived Effects of Safe Conduct on Promotion; (4) Perceived Level of Risk in the Workplace; (5) Perceived Effects of Required Workplace Practices on Safety; (6) Perceived Status of Safety Officer; (7) Perceived Effects of Safe Conduct on Social Status in the Workplace; and (8) Perceived Status of the Safety Committee.

### Validation

Zohar (1980) collected data from 20 workers in plants from four different industries (metal fabrication, food processing,

chemical industry, and textile industry). The SCQ was able to show differences on safety climates between types of plants in the study (e.g., between chemical and food processing plants). Zohar was unable to validate the SCQ by correlating safety climate scores with a criterion, accident frequency rate in the plants, because the criterion was not a reliable measure. He, therefore, used four experienced safety inspectors to rate the safety practices of and accident prevention programs in the four factories. Results indicated that there was high agreement between safety inspectors' rankings of the four plants and their safety climate scores. This is interpreted as support for the validity of the questionnaire. A stepwise discriminant analysis indicated that perceived importance of safety training and perceived effects of required work pace on safety were most influential in determining safety climate differences between factories.

This instrument was subsequently used in later studies of safety climate. Brown and Holmes (1986), for example, attempted to validate Zohar's (1980) Safety Climate measure for a U.S. sample of workers and to establish the instrument's predictive validity with respect to posttraumatic and pretraumatic events in workers. They used Zohar's 40-item measure. The sample consisted of 425 workers at state-run (Wisconsin and Illinois) manufacturing and produce companies. In the sample, 200 workers had experienced an accident in the past year (posttraumatic), and 225 workers had not experienced an accident in the past year (pretraumatic). Confirmatory factor analysis failed to support Zohar's seven-factor model. A more restrictive three-factor solution was found: (1) Employee Perception of How Concerned Management Was with Their Well-being; (2) Employee Perception of How Active Management Was in Responding to This Concern; and (3) Employee Physical Risk Perception. This factor structure was the same for two groups designated pre- and posttraumatic. It was found that safety climate differentiated the two groups (post- and pretraumatic). In addition, results indicated that, for the level of risk perception and the perception of management concern and action, the posttraumatic group had lower perceptions of the safety climate than the pretraumatic group.

## Service Climate Measure

### Rationale

Schneider, White, and Paul (1998) proposed that service climate focused employee efforts on delivering quality customer service, which is related to positive customer experiences and perceptions of service quality. Service climate perceptions include "practices, procedures and behaviors that get rewarded, supported and expected with regard to customer service and customer service quality" (Schneider et al., 1998, p. 151).

Service climate was hypothesized to be based on contextual factors that serve to create and sustain work behaviors. Two such factors are Work Facilitation and Interdepartment Service. These factors may be an antecedent to service climate, but an alternative causal chain indicates that customer perceptions of climate may contribute to the service climate. These relationships may also be reciprocal.

### The Instrument

Schneider et al. (1998) administered three types of measures. Two measures were administered to employees: (1) measures of work facilitation (leadership, participation, computer support and training) and interdepartment service and (2) measures of the climate for service in the organization. The measures of service climate included items measuring the following scales: (a) the Global Service Climate scale in the organization (7 items: Average $\alpha$ in 1990 = .91; average $\alpha$ in 1992 = .88); (b) the Customer Orientation scale (8 items: Average $\alpha$ in 1990 = .90; average $\alpha$ in 1992 = .89); (c) the Managerial Practices scale (4 items: Average $\alpha$ in 1990 = .91; average $\alpha$ in 1992 = .86); and (d) the Customer Feedback scale (3 items: Average $\alpha$ in 1990 = .90; average $\alpha$ in 1992 = .82).

### Validation

Employee perceptions of service climate were validated against customer measures of service quality (Schneider et al., 1998). These measures included scales describing customer perceptions of the following: (1) overall customer service; (2) the efficiency of customer service; (3) the security of transactions; (4) the competency of employees; and (5) relationships between employees and customers. Data were collected over a three-year period from 134 bank branch employees and customers. In 1990, 2,134 employees and 3,100 customers completed questionnaires. In 1992, 2,505 employees and 2,266 customers participated. In 1993, 1,900 customers participated. These data were aggregated to the unit/organization level. Interclass correlations and $r_{wg}$ statistics indicated these data were appropriate for aggregation. It was found that the Global Service Climate scale (measured in 1990) is related to overall customer perceptions (measured in 1993; $r = .26$).

Global service climate was regressed on the three climate facets managing management practices related to service climate. The relationships between global service climate and customer orientation, managerial practices, and customer feedback were all significant. Cross-lag panel analysis (CLPA) also revealed that customer perceptions of service quality and service climate do impact each other over time (same sign and magnitude). Therefore, this supports reciprocal causality between service climate and customer perceptions.

### Team Climate Inventory (TCI)

#### Rationale

The TCI was developed to assess the climate of the proximal work group (Anderson & West, 1998). The proximal work group is defined as the permanent or semipermanent team in which an individual interacts with others. For individuals to be considered a team, they must (1) interact, at least infrequently; (2) have a common goal; and (3) be interdependent. In particular, this measure may be used to assess innovation within the team.

#### The Instrument

Anderson and West's (1994, 1998) instrument consists of 61 items. The authors proposed four factors can be identified a priori within work groups that influence innovation: (1) Vision (the degree to which the team is guided by a higher goal or motivating force; (2) Participative Safety (the degree to which the team is involved in group interactions that are nonthreatening interpersonally in nature); (3) Task Orientation (the degree to which there is both individual and team accountability, methods for evaluating performance, and clear outcome criteria); and (4) Support for Innovation (the degree to which the team experiences active support for innovative behavior from the organization).

#### Validation

Anderson and West (1998) surveyed 243 individual subjects, composing 27 teams from senior management teams in major hospitals in the United Kingdom. Surveys were returned from 155 respondents in this sample. An exploratory factor analysis showed that five factors could be identified: (1) Vision ($\alpha = .94$); (2) Participative Safety ($\alpha = .89$); (3) Support for Innovation ($\alpha = .92$); (4) Task Orientation ($\alpha = .92$); and (5) Interaction Frequency (a new factor that assesses the frequency of formal and informal interactions between team members) ($\alpha = .84$). The TCI was also used to predict innovation by the team. Reports of innovations were gathered and judged by expert and naïve raters on overall innovativeness, number of innovations, radicalness, magnitude, novelty, and administrative effectiveness.

Support for Innovation was the only predictor of overall innovativeness. Participative Safety predicted number of innovations and team self-reports of innovativeness. Task Orientation predicted administrative effectiveness. Confirmatory factor analysis was also conducted on a 38-item short form of the TCI. Three different groups of teams were used in this analysis (121 teams, 971 individuals). Results indicated the five-factor model has the most parsimonious fit, accounting for 96% of the variance. Interclass correlations and $r_{wg}$ analyses were conducted to determine agreement within teams. Results indicated the TCI was measuring shared climate perceptions. One-way ANOVAs were also conducted to determine if the TCI differentiated between teams. Results indicated that in 22 out of 25 cases, there were significant differences between teams, thus establishing discriminant validity. Anderson and West (1998) concluded that focusing on a single aspect of climate increases predictive accuracy.

This instrument was subsequently used in later studies of team climate. Agrell and Gustafson (1994), for example, have used the short form (38 items) of the TCI on a sample of Swedish work groups. They investigated 17 teams from 13 organizations in which team members had been working together for at least the previous year. The teams were responsible for either administrative (management) or production-type tasks. The reliabilities for the scales were good (Participation: $\alpha = .91$; Support: $\alpha = .86$; Group Goals: $\alpha = .88$; Task Orientation: $\alpha = .86$). The TCI scores were correlated with scores from the Team Production Questionnaire (experts observed and rated teams on this questionnaire) to validate the construct of the TCI. The authors asserted that the pattern of correlations found support for the construct validity of the TCI. In addition, analyses of homogeneity of interrater reliability were very high, indicating that the TCI taps shared perceptions of the climate for innovativeness in work groups.

## QUESTIONS FOR FUTURE RESEARCH ON THE ORGANIZATIONAL CONTEXT

After reviewing the literature and measures of organizational culture and climate, we have identified several questions that we think should guide future research. Three of these questions are concerned with the nature of the constructs themselves: (1) differentiating between organizational culture and organizational climate; (2) describing how the two constructs act on organizational behaviors of importance; and (3) deciding if there are common dimensions of organizations that should be consistently assessed in organizational research.

The final question is concerned with the actual measurement strategy used when assessing the two constructs. Each of these questions is discussed in the remainder of the chapter.

## What Is the Difference Between Organizational Culture and Organizational Climate?

When research is conducted with quantitative, general measures, there does not appear to be much difference between the dimensions and items used to evaluate organizational culture and organizational climate. Therefore, the difference between the two constructs is not what is measured. Rather, as noted earlier, the easiest way to differentiate between the two constructs may be by the degree of specificity and linkage to a specific behavior of the instrument being used.

Organizational culture is measured at a more general level. This construct represents the long-term norms and values that have developed during the organization's history. Organizational climate represents more specific management practices that are linked to specific behaviors deemed important by specific organizations.

Therefore, we propose another distinction between organizational culture and organizational climate: This distinction is concerned with the linkage of the organizational value and/or practices to internally or externally oriented goals. As mentioned at the start of the chapter, Namenwirth and Weber (1987) described four purposes for the development of culture in a system. The first three purposes are closely linked to how a social group integrates individual members in the social system. These three purposes provide group members with information on what the valued behaviors are within a social situation. This is the integrative function of organizational culture (Svyantek, 1997; Svyantek & Brown, 2000). The last purpose of the cultural system is concerned with adaptation of the social group to its external environment. This is the adaptive function of organizational culture (Svyantek, 1997; Svyantek & Brown, 2000).

Organizational culture may be more rightly considered to be concerned with the integrative function. Organizational climate, by its linkage to a specific behavior, is more important in the adaptive function. This has implications for our third question. The development of a common taxonomy of dimensions to consistently measure (the "Big Five" for organizational study) would probably be most fruitful for understanding the integrative function and differences in internal human relations practices across organizations. It is here that the most generalizability of results across organizations may be expected. Organizational climate instruments, on the other hand, will tend to always be more context-specific, and their relationships with other organizational variables may be less generalizable.

## How Do Organizational Culture and Organizational Climate Interact?

An enduring issue in organizational culture and organizational climate research is the degree to which cultural practices of organizations may be linked to organizational performance. There is no clear understanding of this linkage (cf., Barney, 1986). Barney (1986) has noted that for organizational culture to be linked to superior performance, the organizational culture practice must be imperfectly imitable by other organizations. However, imitation is often seen in organizations.

This problem may be better understood given our distinction between organizational culture and organizational climate. Organizational culture represents the enduring patterns of behaviors used to define membership within an organization. Organizational climate links more specific practices to behaviors, and these practices are not imperfectly imitable. They are imitated by other organizations.

Therefore, organizational culture research should not expect to find strong performance-culture linkages. This research has typically tried to link general measures of organizational culture to performance variables. This linkage will always be affected by the specific practices related to the variable in the organization. And these practices may be imitated by other organizations.

In effect, perceptions of organizational culture (general measures) may serve as the defining characteristics of the general state of the organization for employees. Employee perceptions of this general state provide the background for their perceptions of more specific cultural dimensions. These more specific cultural dimensions then differentially affect various measures of organizational performance variables. This implies that both organizational culture and organizational climate measures are required to understand the link between the organizational context and performance. Finally, based on the work of Barney (1986), an important implication is that the same organizational climate (e.g., practices linked to behavior) will *not* necessarily lead to the same results in organizations having two differing organizational cultures.

## Is There a "Big Five" for Organizational Culture and Organizational Climate Research?

After attempting to assess the reliability and validity of Litwin and Stringer's (1968) OCQ instrument, Muchinsky noted that it might be difficult to use a standardized climate measure with many dimensions (e.g., nine in the OCQ) across organizations equally well.

Muchinsky (1976) proposed that it might make more sense to develop a more general questionnaire based on the four organizational climate factors identified by Campbell et al. (1970).

Campbell et al. (1970) synthesized results from a number of surveys of organizational climate (including Litwin & Stringer, 1968). Based on this synthesis, they proposed that four common factors are associated with organizational climate consistent across organizations. The first factor is Individual Autonomy. This factor assesses an individual's ability to oversee his or her own activities and have some decision-making power. The second factor is Degree of Structure, which measures the degree to which objectives and methods for job are established and communicated by supervisors to the individual. The third factor is Reward Orientation. This evaluates organizational reward and promotion practices (and may include a general satisfaction with the organization component). The final factor is Consideration, Warmth, and Support. This factor is concerned with the human relations practices of the organization as they relate to the warm, nurturing practices of the organization and managerial support of employees.

One of the problems with organizational culture and organizational climate measures is that there are approximately as many measures of the constructs as there are researchers conducting research on the construct. This has led to a state of definitional confusion in the field. This has led to a state where, although there is at least a 35-year history of climate research, no common taxonomy of important climate dimensions have been developed that may be used across studies. There is no "Big Five" of organizational culture and climate dimensions as there is for personality. A return to Campbell et al.'s (1970) four factors, however, may be a good starting place for the development of the "Big Five" of organizational culture and climate. This is particularly true for measures fitting within our definition of general measures of organizational culture.

We conducted an analysis of the dimension definitions for the general instruments discussed in this chapter (plus a few more) using Campbell et al.'s (1970) four factors of organizational climate as a framework. This analysis is presented in Table 28.2, which shows that many of the dimensions on these general measures may be assigned to one of these four factors.

Future research and analysis should deal with the dimensions from these scales at the item level to assess the degree

**TABLE 28.2   Comparison of Organizational Climate and Culture Inventories to Campbell et al.'s (1970) Classification System**

| | Campbell, et al. (1970) Classifications | | | | |
|---|---|---|---|---|---|
| | Individual Autonomy | Degree of Structure | Reward Orientation | Consideration, Warmth, Support | Others (Not classified) |
| *Organizational Climate* | | | | | |
| Litwin & Stringer (1968): Organizational Climate Questionnaire | Responsibility | Structure | Rewards; Standards | Warmth; Support; Identity | Conflict; Risk |
| Schneider & Bartlett (1968): Agency Climate Questionnaire | Agent Independence | Managerial Structure | General Satisfaction | Managerial Support; New Employee Concern | Intra-agency Conflict |
| Likert (1976): Profile of Organizational Characteristics | Interaction-Influence; Decision-Making; Control; Goal-Setting | Communication | Motivation | Leadership | |
| Bowers & Franklin (1977): System 4 | Decision-Making Practices; Lower-level Influence | Communication Flow | Motivational Conditions | Human Resources Primacy | Technological Readiness |
| Prakasam (1986): Organizational Climate in Banks | Sharing in Decision Making; Responsibility | Conformity; Supervision in Decision Making; Standards | Non-Financial Rewards; Promotion | Supervision: People Orientation; Supervision: Bureaucratic Orientation; Team Spirit | |
| Agrell & Gustafson (1994): Team Climate Inventory | Participation | Task Orientation | | Support for Innovation | Group Goals |
| Ekvall (1996): Situational Outlook Questionnaire | Freedom | | | Idea Support; Trust/ Openness; Playfulness/Humor; Conflict | Risk-Taking; Challenge/ Involvement; Idea Time; Debate |
| *Organizational Culture* | | | | | |
| Kilman & Saxton (1983): Culture Gap Survey | Personal Freedom | Task Support | | Social Relations | Task Innovation |
| Sashkin (1984): Organizational Beliefs Questionnaire | | Hands-on Management; Communicating to Get the Job Done | Growth/Profit/ Indicators of Success; Being the Best | Worth & Value of People; Importance of Shared Philosophy; Work Should be Fun | Innovation; Attention to Detail; Quality |
| Cooke & Lafferty (1989): Organizational Culture Inventory | Dependence | Conventionality | Achievement | Humanistic/Helpful; Self-Actualization; Affiliation; Approval | Avoidance; Oppositional; Power; Competitive; Perfectionism |
| Zeitz et al. (1997): Total Quality Management and Culture Survey | Employee Empowerment | Communication Between Top Management and Employees; Clarity of Role Expectations | Rewards | Trust; Social Cohesion | Innovation; Effective Conflict Resolution; Organizational Commitment; Job Challenge |
| Ashkanasy et al. (2000): Organizational Culture Profile | | Communication; Structure; Planning | Job Performance | Humanistic Workplace; Development of the Individual; Socialization on Entry | Leadership; Environment; Innovation |

of overlap among items. In this way, it may be possible to develop a "Big Five" for the study of organizations.

### Should We Measure Organizational Culture and Organizational Climate or Measure Person-Organization Fit?

Person-organization fit has been shown to be related to a number of organizational variables including: (1) job choice decisions by organizational applicants (Cable & Judge, 1996); (2) organizational attraction of applicants (Judge & Cable, 1997); (3) selection decisions made by recruitment interviewers (Cable & Judge, 1997); (4) employee job satisfaction, job tenure, and career success (Bretz & Judge, 1994); and (5) employee's level of task and organizational citizenship performance (Goodman & Svyantek, 1999). Person-organization (or person-culture) fit has been defined as "the congruence between patterns of organizational values and patterns of individual values, defined here as what an individual values in an organization, such as being team-oriented or innovative" (Chatman, 1991, p. 459). The emphasis here is on the match of an individual's values, when considered along with the value system in a specific organizational context, and the potential effects that match (or lack of match) has on that individual's subsequent behavior and attitudes. Two issues arise in attempting to answer this question.

First, what is the relative importance of the perceptions of organizational culture and organizational climate versus the match between individuals' perceptions of the current and ideal states of these two constructs in predicting organizational behavior? At this point, the answer to this question is still unknown. It has been hypothesized that actual measures of organizational climate and culture may be more predictive of performance measures than are perceived fit measures (Kristof, 1996). Empirical research, to date, provides mixed results. Goodman and Svyantek (1999), for example, found that actual measures of organizational climate (e.g., the Warmth dimension of the OCQ instrument) were the strongest predictors of task performance and organizational citizenship behaviors. Ratings of preferred, ideal climates, however, added incremental variance and were significant predictors of the same dependent variables. Therefore, this issue is unresolved.

The second issue is related to the first. Researchers must decide how to measure person-organization fit. There are two related methods of doing this. Person-organization fit assessment involves collapsing two constructs into one measure as a predictor of some outcome. The vast majority of person-organization fit studies have operationalized congruency by collapsing two or more measures into a single index. These profile similarity indices (PSIs) combine two sets of measures, or profiles, from corresponding entities (e.g., the ideal state and organization) into a single score intended to represent overall congruence (Cronbach & Glesser, 1953). Examples of this include the use of discrepancy scores and the use of correlations between observed culture and personal values (cf. O'Reilly et al., 1991).

Edwards (1993, 1994, 1995), however, suggested that PSIs should no longer be used in congruence research, such as person-organization fit. Instead, researchers should use polynomial equations containing measures of both entities (here the actual and ideal culture measurements) that typically are collapsed in PSIs (cf. Edwards, 1993, 1994; Edwards & Cooper, 1990; Edwards & Harrison, 1993; Edwards & Parry, 1993). The general approach suggested by Edwards (1993; 1994) offers several advantages over congruence indices currently in use. First, polynomial regression maintains the interpretability of the original component measures. Second, polynomial regression yields separate estimates of the relationships between component measures and the outcome. Third, polynomial regression provides a complete test of models underlying congruence indices, focusing not only on the overall magnitude of the relationship, but also on the significance of individual effects, the validity of implied constraints, and the significance of higher order terms. Finally, the approach proposed by Edwards (1993, 1994) may yield considerable increases in explained variance.

Goodman and Svyantek's (1999) findings were based on the use of Edwards's (1993, 1994) approach. The use of this method allowed interpretable patterns of results to be found for both actual and ideal measures of organizational climate. Therefore, we recommend that Edwards's approach be used when addressing issues of person-organization fit when using quantitative surveys of organizational culture and organizational climate as described in this chapter.

### SUMMARY

Understanding how employees behave within organizations requires that three components be analyzed: (1) the context in which the behavior occurs; (2) the individual difference variables on which employees differ; and (3) the nature of the behavior being performed (Funder, 2001). We believe that understanding how contexts affect the production of behavior is critical. The two primary constructs of interest in defining organizational contexts are organizational culture and organizational climate. We have reviewed general and specific measures of these constructs. In addition, several questions for the researcher interested in contextual effects have been provided. This information and these questions provide researchers with some new directions that may provide insight for understanding how individuals act when in groups and organizations.

## REFERENCES

Agrell, A., & Gustafson, R. (1994). The Team Climate Inventory (TCI) and group innovation: A psychometric test on a Swedish sample of work groups. *Journal of Occupational and Organizational Psychology, 67,* 143–151.

Anderson, N.R., & West, M.A. (1994). *The Team Climate Inventory. Manual and users' guide.* Windsor, England: Assessment Services for Employment, NFER-Nelson.

Anderson, N.R., & West, M.A. (1998). Measuring climate for work group innovation: Development and validation of the Team Climate Inventory. *Journal of Organizational Behavior, 19,* 235–258.

Ashkanasy, N.M., Broadfoot, L.E., & Falkus, S. (2000). Questionnaire measures of organizational culture. In N.M. Ashkanasy, C.P.M. Widerom, & M.F. Peterson (Eds.), *Handbook of organizational culture and climate* (pp. 131–162). Thousand Oaks, CA: Sage.

Barney, J.B. (1986). Organizational culture: Can it be a source of sustained competitive advantage? *Academy of Management Review, 11,* 656–665.

Bem, D., & Funder, D. (1978). Predicting more of the people more of the time: Assessing the personality of situations. *Psychological Review, 85,* 485–501.

Bowers, D.G., & Franklin, J.L. (1977). *Survey guided development I: Data-based organizational change.* La Jolla, CA: University Associates.

Bretz, R.D., & Judge, T.A. (1994). Person-organization fit and the theory of work adjustment-Implications for satisfaction, tenure, and career success. *Journal of Vocational Behavior, 44,* 32–54.

Brown, R.L., & Holmes, H. (1986). The use of a factor-analytic procedure for assessing the validity of an employee safety climate model. *Accident Analysis and Prevention, 18*(6), 455–470.

Cable, D.M., & Judge, T.A. (1996). Person-organization fit, job choice decisions, and organizational entry. *Organizational Behavior and Human Decision Processes, 67,* 294–311.

Cable, D.M., & Judge, T.A. (1997). Interviewer's perceptions of person-organization fit and organizational selection decisions. *Journal of Applied Psychology, 82,* 546–561.

Cameron, K.S., & Quinn, R.E. (1999). *Diagnosing and changing organizational culture.* New York: Addison-Wesley.

Campbell, J.P., Dunnette, M.D., Lawler, E.E. III, & Weick, K.E. Jr. (1970). *Managerial behavior, performance and effectiveness.* New York: McGraw-Hill.

Chatman, J.A. (1991). Matching people and organizations: Selection and socialization in public accounting firms. *Administrative Science Quarterly, 36*(3), 459–484.

Cooke, R.A., & Lafferty, J.C. (1989). *Organizational Culture Inventory.* Plymouth, MI: Human Synergistics.

Cooke, R.A., & Rousseau, D.M. (1988). Behavioral norms and expectations: A quantitative approach to the assessment of organizational culture. *Group and Organization Studies, 13*(3), 245–273.

Cooke, R.A., & Szumal, J.L. (2000). Using the Organizational Culture Inventory to understand the operating cultures of organizations. In N.M. Ashkanasy, C.P.M. Wilderon, & M.F. Peterson (Eds.), *Handbook of organizational culture and climate* (pp. 147–162). Thousand Oaks, CA: Sage.

Cronbach, L.J., & Glesser, G.C. (1953). Assessing the similarity between profiles. *Psychological Bulletin, 50,* 456–473.

Cullen, J.B., Victor, B., & Bronson, J.W. (1993). The Ethical Climate Questionnaire: An assessment of its development and validity. *Psychological Reports, 73,* 667–674.

Dastmalchian, A., Adamson, R., & Blyton, P. (1986). Developing a measure of industrial relations climate. *Relations Industrielles, 41*(4), 851–859.

Dastmalchian, A., Blyton, P., & Adamson, R. (1989). Industrial relations climate: Testing a construct. *Journal of Occupational Psychology, 62,* 21–32.

Downey, H.K., & Hellriegel, D., Phelps, M., & Slocum, J.W. Jr. (1974). Organizational climate and job satisfaction: A comparative analysis. *Journal of Business Research, 2*(3), 233–248.

Edwards, J.R. (1993). Problems with the use of profile similarity indices in the study of congruence in organizational research. *Personnel Psychology, 46,* 641–665.

Edwards, J.R. (1994). The study of congruence in organizational research: Critique and a proposed alternative. *Organizational Behavior and Human Decision Processes, 58,* 51–100.

Edwards, J.R. (1995). Alternatives to difference scores as dependent variables in the study of congruence in organizational research. *Organizational Behavior and Human Decision Processes, 64,* 307–324.

Edwards, J.R., & Cooper, C.L. (1990). The person-environment fit approach to stress: Recurring problems and some suggested solutions. *Journal of Organizational Behavior, 11,* 293–300.

Edwards, J.R., & Harrison, R.V. (1993). Job demands and worker health: Three-Dimensional reexamination of the relationship between person-environment fit and strain. *Journal of Applied Psychology, 78,* 628–648.

Edwards, J.R., & Parry, M.E. (1993). On the use of polynomial regression equations as alternatives to difference scores in organizational research. *Academy of Management Journal, 36,* 1577–1613.

Ekvall, G. (1996). Organizational climate for creativity and innovation. *European Journal of Work and Organizational Psychology, 5*(1), 105–123.

Funder, D.C. (2001). Accuracy in personality judgment: Research and theory concerning an obvious question. In B.W. Roberts & R.

Hogan (Eds.), *Personality psychology in the workplace* (pp. 121–140). Washington, DC: American Psychological Association.

Goodman, S.A., & Svyantek, D.J. (1999). Person-organization fit and contextual performance: Do shared values matter? *Journal of Vocational Behavior, 55,* 254–275.

Hannaway, J. (1989). *Managers managing: The workings of an administrative system.* New York: Oxford Press.

Hellriegel, D., & Slocum, J.W. Jr. (1974). Organizational climate: Measures, research and contingencies. *Academy of Management Journal, 17*(2), 255–280.

Isaksen, S.G., Lauer, K.J., & Ekvall, G. (1999). Situational Outlook Questionnaire: A measure of the climate for creativity and change. *Psychological Reports, 85,* 665–674.

Isaksen, S.G., Lauer, K.J., Ekvall, G., & Britz, A. (2000–2001). Perceptions of the best and worst climates for creativity: Preliminary validation evidence for the Situational Outlook Questionnaire. *Creativity Research Journal, 13*(2), 171–184.

Judge, T.A., & Cable, D.M. (1997). Applicant personality, organizational culture and organizational attraction. *Personnel Psychology, 50,* 359–394.

Kilman, R.H., & Saxton, M.J. (1983). *The Kilman-Saxton Culture Gap Survey.* Pittsburgh, PA: Organizational Design Consultants.

Kristof, A.L. (1996). Person-organization fit: An integrative review of its conceptualization, measurement, and implications. *Personnel Psychology, 49,* 1–49.

Likert, R. (1976). *Human organization: Its management and value.* New York: McGraw-Hill.

Litwin, G.H., & Stringer, R.A. (1968). *Motivation and organizational climate.* Boston: Harvard University Press.

Mischel, W. (1977). The interaction of person and situation. In D. Magnusson & N.S. Endler (Eds.), *Personality at the crossroads: Current issues in interactional psychology* (pp. 333–352). Hillsdale, NJ: Erlbaum.

Morgan, G.R. (1998). *Organizational theory* (2nd ed.). Reading, MA: Addison-Wesley.

Morris, E.K. (1988). Contextualism: The world view of behavior analysis. *Journal of Experimental Child Psychology, 46,* 289–323.

Muchinsky, P.M. (1976). An assessment of the Litwin and Stringer Organization Climate Questionnaire: An empirical and theoretical extension of the Sims and LaFollette Study. *Personnel Psychology, 29,* 371–392.

Namenwirth, J.Z., & Weber, R.P. (1987). *Dynamics of culture.* Boston: Allen & Irwin.

O'Reilly, C.A. III, Chatman, J., & Caldwell, D.F. (1991). People and organizational culture: A profile comparison approach to assessing person-organization fit. *Academy of Management Journal, 34*(3), 487–516.

Ott, J.S. (1989). *The organizational culture perspective.* Pacific Grove, CA: Brooks/Cole.

Payne, R.L. (2000). Climate and culture: How close can they get? In N.M. Ashkanasy, C.P.M. Wilderon, & M.F. Peterson (Eds.), *Handbook of organizational culture and climate* (pp. 163–176). Thousand Oaks, CA: Sage.

Payne, P., & Pugh, D.S. (1976). Organizational structure and climate. In M. Dunnette (Ed.), *Handbook of industrial and organizational psychology* (pp. 1125–1173). Chicago: Rand McNally.

Putti, J.M., & Kheun, L.S. (1986). Organizational climate—job satisfaction relationship in a public sector organization. *International Journal of Public Administration, 8*(3), 337–344.

Prakasam, R. (1986). Organisational climate: Development of a questionnaire measure. *Psychological Studies, 31*(1), 51–55.

Rogers, E.D., Miles, Jr., W.G., & Biggs, W.D. (1980). The factor replicability of the Litwin and Stringer Organizational Climate Questionnaire: An inter- and intra-organizational assessment. *Journal of Management, 6*(1), 65–78.

Sashkin, M. (1984). *Pillars of excellence: Organizational Beliefs Questionnaire.* Bryn Mawr, PA: Organizational Design and Development.

Sathe, V. (1985). *Culture and related corporate realities.* Homewood, IL: R.D. Irwin.

Schein, E.H. (1985). *Organizational culture and leadership.* San Francisco: Jossey-Bass.

Schein, E.H. (1990). Organizational culture. *American Psychologist, 45,* 109–119.

Schein, E.H. (2000). Response to Manfred Kets de Vries' Commentary. *Academy of Management Review, 14*(1), 48.

Schnake, M.E. (1983). An empirical assessment of the effects of affective response in the measurement of organizational climate. *Personnel Psychology, 36,* 791–807.

Schneider, B. (2000). The psychological life of organizations. In N.M. Ashkanasy, C.P.M. Wilderon, & M.F. Peterson (Eds.), *Handbook of organizational culture and climate* (pp. xvii–xxi. Thousand Oaks, CA: Sage.

Schneider, B., & Bartlett, C.J. (1968). Individual differences and organizational climate: I. The research plan and questionnaire development. *Personnel Psychology, 21,* 323–333.

Schneider, B., White, S.S., & Paul, M.C. (1998). Linking service climate and customer perceptions of service quality: Test of a causal model. *Journal of Applied Psychology, 83*(2), 150–163.

Showers, C., & Cantor, N. (1985). Social cognitions: A look at motivated strategies. *Annual Review of Psychology, 36,* 275–305.

Sims, H.P. Jr., & LaFollette, W. (1975). An assessment of the Litwin and Stringer Organizational Climate Questionnaire. *Personnel Psychology, 28,* 19–38.

Svyantek, D.J. (1997). Order out of chaos: Non-linear systems and organizational change. *Current Topics in Management, 2,* 167–188.

Svyantek, D.J., & Brown, L.L. (2000). A complex systems approach to organizations. *Current Directions in Psychological Science, 9*(2), 69–74.

Svyantek, D.J., Jones A.P., & Rozelle, R. (1991). The relative influence of organizational decision frames on decision making. *Advances in Information Processing in Organizations, 4,* 127–145.

Svyantek, D.J., & Kolz, A.R. (1996). The effects of organizational frames and problem ambiguity on decision-making. *Journal of Business and Psychology, 11*(2), 131–150.

Trice, H.M., & Beyer, J.M. (1993). *The cultures of organizations.* Englewood Cliffs, NJ: Prentice-Hall.

Victor, B., & Cullen, J.B. (1987). A theory and measure of ethical climates in organizations. *Research in Corporate Social Performance and Policy, 60,* 318–328.

Victor, B., & Cullen, J.B. (1988). The organizational basis of ethical work climates. *Administrative Science Quarterly, 33,* 101–125.

Xenikou, A., & Furnham, A. (1996). A correlational and factor analytic study of four questionnaire measures of organizational climate. *Human Relations, 49*(3), 349–371.

Zeitz, G., Johannesson, R., & Ritchie, J.E. Jr. (1997). An employee survey measuring total quality management practices and culture. *Group & Organization Management, 22*(4), 414–444.

Zohar, D. (1980). Safety climate in industrial organizations: Theoretical and applied implications. *Journal of Applied Psychology, 65*(1), 96–102.

# Author Index

# Subject Index